Foreign Relations of the
United States, 1969–1976

Volume XVIII

China
1973–1976

Editor   David P. Nickles

General Editor   Edward C. Keefer

United States Government Printing Office
Washington
2007

DEPARTMENT OF STATE PUBLICATION 11442

Office of the Historian

Bureau of Public Affairs

For sale by the Superintendent of Documents, U.S. Government Printing Office
Internet: bookstore.gpo.gov   Phone: toll free (866) 512-1800;   DC area (202) 512-1800
Fax: (202) 512-2104 Mail: Stop IDCC, Washington, DC 20402-0001

ISBN 978-0-16-077110-1

Preface

The *Foreign Relations of the United States* series presents the official documentary historical record of major foreign policy decisions and significant diplomatic activity of the United States Government. The Historian of the Department of State is charged with the responsibility for the preparation of the *Foreign Relations* series. The staff of the Office of the Historian, Bureau of Public Affairs, under the direction of the General Editor of the *Foreign Relations* series, plans, researches, compiles, and edits the volumes in the series. Secretary of State Frank B. Kellogg first promulgated official regulations codifying specific standards for the selection and editing of documents for the series on March 26, 1925. These regulations, with minor modifications, guided the series through 1991.

Public Law 102–138, the Foreign Relations Authorization Act, established a new statutory charter for the preparation of the series which was signed by President George Bush on October 28, 1991. Section 198 of P.L. 102–138 added a new Title IV to the Department of State's Basic Authorities Act of 1956 (22 USC 4351, et seq.).

The statute requires that the *Foreign Relations* series be a thorough, accurate, and reliable record of major United States foreign policy decisions and significant United States diplomatic activity. The volumes of the series should include all records needed to provide comprehensive documentation of major foreign policy decisions and actions of the United States Government. The statute also confirms the editing principles established by Secretary Kellogg: the *Foreign Relations* series is guided by the principles of historical objectivity and accuracy; records should not be altered or deletions made without indicating in the published text that a deletion has been made; the published record should omit no facts that were of major importance in reaching a decision; and nothing should be omitted for the purposes of concealing a defect in policy. The statute also requires that the *Foreign Relations* series be published not more than 30 years after the events recorded. The editors are convinced that this volume meets all regulatory, statutory, and scholarly standards of selection and editing.

Structure and Scope of the Foreign Relations *Series*

This volume is part of a subseries of volumes of the *Foreign Relations* series that documents the most important issues in the foreign policy of Presidents Richard M. Nixon and Gerald R. Ford. The subseries presents in multiple volumes a comprehensive documentary record of major foreign policy decisions and actions of both administrations. This specific volume documents the U.S. policy towards

China, 1973–1976. Although this volume is meant to stand on its own, it is best read in conjunction with three other volumes: *Foreign Relations, 1969–1976*, Vol. XV, Soviet Union, 1972–1974; Vol. XVI, Soviet Union, 1974–1976; and Vol. E–12, East Asia, 1973–1976.

Focus of Research and Principles of Selection for Foreign Relations, *1969–1976, Volume XVIII*

This volume is organized chronologically. As such it conveys the shift in control over U.S. China policy from the White House to the Department of State as a result of the Watergate crisis, the appointment of Henry Kissinger as Secretary of State, the resignation of Richard Nixon as President, and Gerald Ford's request that Kissinger relinquish his position as Advisor to the President for National Security Affairs. The chapters integrate documents about U.S. relations with the People's Republic of China (PRC) and Taiwan, reflecting the fact that the former government received much more attention from high-level American policymakers than did the latter. The central theme of the volume is the effort to strengthen and formalize the PRC–US relationship, which had been established during 1971 and 1972 after decades of bitter estrangement, and the concurrent disestablishment of formal diplomatic relations with Taiwan, a task that remained unfinished at the end of the Ford Administration. The primary means used to improve relations during these years were long conversations between U.S. and PRC leaders, which were supposed to initiate—but generally substituted for—a more developed and institutionalized relationship.

The first chapter, January through May 1973, documents the establishment of unofficial liaison offices in Washington and Beijing, the most concrete achievement of the 1973–1976 period. Both sides expressed their desire to fully normalize relations by 1976. In retrospect, however, Kissinger's February 1973 visit to the People's Republic of China would prove to be the acme of Sino-American relations during this period. Although the United States and China agreed to finesse the Taiwan dispute and formed a tacit anti-Soviet alliance, the two countries did not agree on the war in Cambodia or on the wisdom of détente.

The second chapter, June 1973 through August 1974, demonstrates how domestic politics in both countries threatened the still-fragile Sino-American relationship. In China, aftershocks from the Cultural Revolution and the death of Lin Biao, as well as the aging of China's leadership, raised doubts about the stability of Chinese foreign policy. This chapter also reveals American efforts to reassure Chinese leaders baffled by Watergate and fearful that American policy would become erratic. China was also dissatisfied with the pace of U.S. disengagement from formal diplomatic relations with Taiwan. At the same time in the

United States, escalating economic competition produces fear in U.S. textile manufacturers that they would be hurt by increased American trade with China.

The third chapter, September 1974 through July 1975, covers the Sino-American effort to reestablish a momentum toward normalization. Along these lines, the United States attempted to reconcile the normalization of Sino-American relations with the preservation of Taiwanese security through such policies as a careful diminution of U.S.-Taiwanese military links. Nonetheless, the United States and China continued to bicker over détente and Cambodia.

The fourth chapter, August through December 1975, covers the planning and realization of President Ford's trip to Beijing. China experts within the U.S. Government asserted that the President should attempt to quickly normalize relations, but Secretary of State Kissinger believed that such a policy would produce a right-wing backlash against Ford that would endanger the administration's effectiveness and reelection. The Chinese Government agreed to host Ford without a prior agreement for rapid normalization. The visit maintained existing friendly relations, while breaking little new ground.

The final chapter, January 1976 through January 1977, documents how domestic political developments in both countries distracted policymakers from the Sino-American relationship. During these years, relations between the United States and China were conducted at the highest political level, which meant that incapacitation of the top leadership tended to bring progress to a standstill. More than most volumes in the *Foreign Relations* series, this one documents the influence of domestic politics on foreign policy. However, despite numerous obstacles and failures, each country's troubled relationship with the Soviet Union produced a continual impetus to improve the Sino-American relationship.

Like all recent *Foreign Relations* volumes in the Nixon-Ford subseries, the emphasis of this volume is on policy formulation, rather than the implementation of policy or day-to-day diplomacy. Influence on U.S. policy was mainly restricted to a small circle, including the President and some influential officials trusted by Henry Kissinger.

Editorial Methodology

The documents are presented chronologically according to Washington time. Memoranda of conversation are placed according to the time and date of the conversation, rather than the date the memorandum was drafted.

Editorial treatment of the documents published in the *Foreign Relations* series follows Office style guidelines, supplemented by guidance from the General Editor. The documents are reproduced as exactly as possible, including marginalia or other notations, which are described in the footnotes. Texts are transcribed and printed according to accepted conventions for the publication of historical documents within the limitations of modern typography. A heading has been supplied by the editors for each document included in the volume. Spelling, capitalization, and punctuation are retained as found in the original text, except that obvious typographical errors are silently corrected. Other mistakes and omissions in the documents are corrected by bracketed insertions: a correction is set in italic type; an addition in roman type. Words repeated in telegrams to avoid garbling or provide emphasis are silently corrected. Words or phrases underlined in the original document are printed in italics. Abbreviations and contractions are preserved as found in the original text, and a list of abbreviations is included in the front matter of each volume.

Bracketed insertions are also used to indicate omitted text that deals with an unrelated subject (in roman type) or that remains classified after declassification review (in italic type). The amount and, where possible, the nature of the material not declassified has been noted by indicating the number of lines or pages of text that were omitted. Entire documents withheld for declassification purposes have been accounted for and are listed with headings, source notes, and number of pages not declassified in their chronological place. All brackets that appear in the original text are so identified in footnotes and all ellipses, unless otherwise noted, are in the original documents.

The first footnote to each document indicates the source of the document, original classification, distribution, and drafting information. This note also provides the background of important documents and policies and indicates whether the President or his major policy advisers read the document.

Editorial notes and additional annotation summarize pertinent material not printed in the volume, indicate the location of additional documentary sources, provide references to important related documents printed in other volumes, describe key events, and provide summaries of and citations to public statements that supplement and elucidate the printed documents. Information derived from memoirs and other first-hand accounts has been used when appropriate to supplement or explicate the official record.

The numbers in the index refer to document numbers rather than to page numbers.

Advisory Committee on Historical Diplomatic Documentation

The Advisory Committee on Historical Diplomatic Documentation, established under the *Foreign Relations* statute, reviews records, advises, and makes recommendations concerning the *Foreign Relations* series. The Advisory Committee monitors the overall compilation and editorial process of the series and advises on all aspects of the preparation and declassification of the series. The Advisory Committee does not necessarily review the contents of individual volumes in the series, but it makes recommendations on issues that come to its attention and reviews volumes, as it deems necessary to fulfill its advisory and statutory obligations.

Presidential Recordings and Materials Preservation Act Review

Under the terms of the Presidential Recordings and Materials Preservation Act (PRMPA) of 1974 (44 USC 2111 note), the National Archives and Records Administration (NARA) has custody of the Nixon Presidential historical materials. The requirements of the PRMPA and implementing regulations govern access to the Nixon Presidential historical materials. The PRMPA and implementing public access regulations require NARA to review for additional restrictions in order to ensure the protection of the privacy rights of former Nixon White House officials, since these officials were not given the opportunity to separate their personal materials from public papers. Thus, the PRMPA and implementing public access regulations require NARA formally to notify the Nixon Estate and former Nixon White House staff members that the agency is scheduling for public release Nixon White House historical materials. The Nixon Estate and former White House staff members have 30 days to contest the release of Nixon historical materials in which they were a participant or are mentioned. Further, the PRMPA and implementing regulations require NARA to segregate and return to the creator of files private and personal materials. All *Foreign Relations* volumes that include materials from NARA's Nixon Presidential Materials Staff are processed and released in accordance with the PRMPA.

Declassification Review

The Office of Information Programs and Services, Bureau of Administration, conducted the declassification review for the Department of State of the documents published in this volume. The review was conducted in accordance with the standards set forth in Executive Order 12958, as amended, on Classified National Security Information and applicable laws.

The principle guiding declassification review is to release all information, subject only to the current requirements of national security as embodied in law and regulation. Declassification decisions entailed concurrence of the appropriate geographic and functional bureaus in the Department of State, other concerned agencies of the U.S. Government, and the appropriate foreign governments regarding specific documents of those governments. The declassification review of this volume, which began in August 2005 and was completed in 2007, resulted in the decision to withhold no documents in full, excise a paragraph or more in 3 documents, and make minor excisions of less than a paragraph in 13 documents.

The Office of the Historian is confident, on the basis of the research conducted in preparing this volume and as a result of the declassification review process described above, that the record presented in this volume presented here provides an accurate and comprehensive account of the U.S. foreign policy towards China.

Acknowledgments

The editors wish to acknowledge the assistance of officials at the Nixon Presidential Materials Project of the National Archives and Records Administration (Archives II), at College Park, Maryland. The editors wish to acknowledge the Richard Nixon Estate for allowing access to the Nixon presidential recordings and the Richard Nixon Library & Birthplace for facilitating that access. Thanks are due to the Historical Staff of the Central Intelligence Agency, who were helpful in arranging full access to the files of the Central Intelligence Agency. John Haynes of the Library of Congress was responsible for expediting access to the Kissinger Papers. The editors were able to use the Kissinger Papers, including the transcripts of telephone conversations, with the kind permission of Henry Kissinger. The editors would like to also thank Sandy Meagher for her valuable assistance in expediting the use of files of the Department of Defense.

David Nickles collected the documentation for this volume, made the initial selections, and annotated the documents he chose. The volume was completed under the supervision of Erin Mahan, Chief of the Asia, Africa, and Arms Control Division, and Edward C. Keefer, General Editor of the series. Chris Tudda coordinated the declassification review, under the supervision of Susan C. Weetman, Chief of the Declassification and Publishing Division. Keri E. Lewis and Aaron W. Marrs did the copy and technical editing. Do Mi Stauber prepared the index.

Bureau of Public Affairs   **Marc J. Susser**
December 2007   *The Historian*

Contents

Sources

Sources for the Foreign Relations *Series*

The *Foreign Relations* statute requires that the published record in the *Foreign Relations* series include all records needed to provide comprehensive documentation of major U.S. foreign policy decisions and significant U.S. diplomatic activity. It further requires that government agencies, departments, and other entities of the U.S. Government engaged in foreign policy formulation, execution, or support cooperate with the Department of State historians by providing full and complete access to records pertinent to foreign policy decisions and actions and by providing copies of selected records. Most of the sources consulted in the preparation of this volume have been declassified and are available for review at the National Archives and Records Administration.

The editors of the *Foreign Relations* series have complete access to all the retired records and papers of the Department of State: the central files of the Department; the special decentralized files ("lot files") of the Department at the bureau, office, and division levels; the files of the Department's Executive Secretariat, which contain the records of international conferences and high-level official visits, correspondence with foreign leaders by the President and Secretary of State, and memoranda of conversations between the President and Secretary of State and foreign officials; and the files of overseas diplomatic posts. The Department's indexed central files through December 1975 have been permanently transferred to the National Archives and Records Administration at College Park, Maryland (Archives II). Most of the Department's decentralized office (or "lot") files covering the 1969–1976 period, which the National Archives deems worthy of permanent retention, have been transferred or are in the process of being transferred from the Department's custody to Archives II.

The editors of the *Foreign Relations* series also have full access to the papers of Presidents Nixon and Ford, and other White House foreign policy records. Presidential papers maintained and preserved at the Presidential libraries and the Nixon Presidential Materials Project at Archives II include some of the most significant foreign affairs-related documentation from the Department of State and other Federal agencies including the National Security Council, the Central Intelligence Agency, the Department of Defense, and the Joint Chiefs of Staff. Dr. Henry Kissinger has approved access to his papers at the Library of Congress. These papers are an important source for the Nixon-Ford sub-series of *Foreign Relations*.

Research for this volume involved special access to restricted documents at the Nixon Presidential Materials Project, the Ford Library, the Library of Congress, and other agencies. While all the material printed in this volume has been declassified, some of it is extracted from still classified documents. The staffs of the Nixon Presidential Materials Project and the Ford Library are processing and declassifying many of the documents examined for this volume, but they may not be available in their entirety at the time of publication.

The presidential papers of the Nixon and Ford administrations are the best source of high-level decision making documentation for China during the 1973–1976 period. At the Nixon Presidential Materials Project, located at the National Archives and Records Administration II, in College Park, Maryland, several collections from the National Security Council Files are relevant to research on Sino-American relations. Among these, the Country Files are particularly helpful because they provide the NSC staff's perspective on the day-to-day ebb and flow of the relationship. The Files for the President are intermittently useful. More significant for Sino-American relations are the Henry A. Kissinger Office Files, which were Kissinger's working files. The Institutional Files (H-Files) contain records on high-level meetings, requests for studies, and presidential decisions. The Presidential/HAK Memcons files, also part of the NSC collection, consist of memoranda of conversation between foreign officials and Nixon or Kissinger. The Subject Files are divided into categories, many of them dealing with economic issues. Overall, these NSC files are extremely valuable for assessing NSC staff recommendations and presidential policy towards China. Also useful for tracking the President's daily schedule is the President's Daily Diary from the White House Central Files. The Subject Files of the White House Special Files, the White House Tapes (which ended in July 1973), and the Henry Kissinger Telephone Conversations have scattered valuable material. Some additional useful documents are contained in the Unfiled Material of the NSC Files, a chronological file of documents that was still being processed when President Nixon left office in August 1974. High-level correspondence between President Nixon and foreign heads of state are contained in the Presidential Correspondence files.

Material at the Ford Library is organized into categories similar to those at the Nixon Presidential Materials Project. The National Security Adviser file contains a number of sub-files that are useful when considering U.S. relations with China and Taiwan: the Kissinger Reports, Kissinger-Scowcroft West Wing Office Files, Memoranda of Conversations, National Security Adviser Memcons, National Security Decision Memoranda and Study Memoranda, NSC Staff for East Asia and Pacific Affairs, Presidential Correspondence with Foreign Leaders, Presidential Country Files, Trip Briefing books and Cables for President Ford. The President's Daily Diary is an invaluable resource for following the President's daily work schedule. The Ford Library has separate NSC Institutional (H-Files), which are not part of the National Security Adviser collection. They contain the same system of minutes and related documents for NSC and Senior Review Group meetings as is found in the Nixon Presidential Materials. Also found in the NSC Institutional Files are the valuable Policy Paper files containing National Security Study Memoranda (NSSMs), National Security Decision Memoranda (NSDMs), and related documents.

The Kissinger Papers at the Library of Congress are valuable, although the preponderance consists of duplicate material found also in the Nixon Presidential Materials Project and the Ford Library. The best documents for Sino-American relations in the Kissinger Papers can be found in the Memoranda of Conversation, Chronological Files, Presidential Files, and Geopolitical Files.

After September 1973, Henry Kissinger became Secretary of State and the records of the Department of State take on a new prominence in the making of China policy. The same year, the Department began using the electronic State Archiving System (SAS). Historical documents from this system have been transferred to the National Archives and are part of the on-line Access to Archival Database (AAD). Some of the most tightly held telegrams are not on the electronic system, but rather on microfilm reels. Because the SAS system was in its initial stages in 1973, it is incomplete. Therefore, despite the creation of the SAS, the subject-numeric central files contain useful material for 1973. The records of the U.S. Liaison Office in Beijing (Lot 80F64) partially compensate for this gap in the SAS. A number of Department of State lot files are also of special value: the records of Henry Kissinger (E5403), containing many of his memoranda of conversation; the Transcripts of Henry Kissinger's Staff Meetings with his principal officers at the Department of State (E5177); the files of Winston Lord, the Director of the Policy Planning Staff (E5027, Lot 77D114); the papers of William H. Gleysteen (Lot 89D436); Secretary of State Henry Kissinger's Telephone Conversation (Department of State, Electronic Reading Room, Transcripts of Kissinger Telephone Conversations); and lot files covering relations with the Republic of China (E5412, Lots 76D441 and 77D255).

Some final collections of special note in documenting U.S. relations with China from 1973 until 1976 are the files of the Central Intelligence Agency and the Department of Defense. Of particular interest in the former are the Executive Registry Files, the official files of the Director of Central Intelligence. In the latter, valuable documents are found in the country files (separate files for the People's Republic of China and the Republic of China) of Record Group 330, Records of the Office of the Secretary of Defense and his Assistants, and among the Records of the Assistant Secretary of Defense for International Security Affairs, described in the list below.

Unpublished Sources

Department of State

Central Files. See National Archives and Records Administration below.

Secretary of State Henry Kissinger Telephone Conversations (Telcons), Electronic Reading Room, Kissinger telephone conversations

Lot Files. For other lot files already transferred to the National Archives and Records Administration at College Park, Maryland, Record Group 59, see National Archives and Records Administration below.

EAP Files: Lot 89D436, China Files/Papers of William H. Gleysteen

INR/IL Files

Post Files: Lot 80F64, American Embassy (Beijing) Files

National Archives and Records Administration, College Park, Maryland

Record Group 59, Records of the Department of State

Top Secret Subject-Number Indexed Central Files [25 boxes]

Central Files, 1970–1973

AID (US) CHINAT, ROC, U.S. economic aid to the ROC
DEF CHICOM, military affairs, PRC
DEF CHINAT, military affairs, ROC
DEF 1 CHINAT, defense policy, plans, readiness, ROC
DEF 1 CHINAT–US, defense policy, plans, readiness, ROC–U.S.
DEF 6 CHINAT, armed forces, ROC
DEF 15 CHINAT, bases and installations, ROC
DEF 15 CHINAT–US, bases and installations, ROC–U.S.
DEF 15–3 CHINAT–US, status of forces, ROC–U.S.
DEF 19 US–CHINAT, U.S. military assistance to the ROC
DEF 19–8 US–CHINAT, U.S. provision of military equipment and supplies to the ROC
E CHICOM general economic affairs, PRC
E CHINAT, general economic affairs, ROC
FN CHICOM financial affairs, PRC
FN CHINAT, financial affairs, ROC
FT CHICOM–US, question of trade with the PRC
FT CHICOM–1 US, general policy on the question of trade with the PRC
INCO TEXTILES CHINAT, industries and commodities, textiles, ROC
POL CHICOM, political developments, PRC
POL 1 CHICOM, U.S. general policy toward the PRC
POL CHINAT, political developments, ROC
POL 2 CHINAT, general reports and statistics, ROC
POL CHINAT–US, political affairs and relations, ROC and the United States
POL 1 CHINAT–US, U.S. general policy toward the ROC
POL 17 US–CHICOM, U.S. diplomatic and consular representation in the PRC

Central Foreign Policy Files, 1973–1976

Part of the on-line Access to Archive Databases (http://aad.archives.gov): Electronic Telegrams, P-Reel Index, P-Reel microfilm

Lot Files

Policy Planning Staff (S/P), Director's Files (Winston Lord) 1969–1977, E5027
[formerly Lot 77D114]

Transcripts of Secretary of State Kissinger's Staff Meetings, E5177 [formerly Lot
78D433]

E5412, (Lot 76D441)
Files on East Asia/Republic of China

Subject Files of the Office of ROC Affairs, 1951–75, E5412 [formerly Lots 76D441 and
77D255]

Nixon Presidential Materials Project

National Security Council Files
Country Files
Files for the President
Henry A. Kissinger Office Files
Presidential/HAK Memoranda of conversation
Subject Files
Unfiled Materials

NSC Institutional Files (H-Files)
Policy Papers: National Security Decision Memoranda (NSDMs), National Security
Study Memoranda (NSSMs)

White House Central Files
President's Daily Diary

White House Special Files
Subject Files

White House Tapes

Henry Kissinger Telephone Conversations, January to September 1973

Gerald Ford Library, Ann Arbor, Michigan

National Security Adviser
Kissinger Reports
Kissinger-Scowcroft West Wing Office Files
Memoranda of Conversations
National Security Adviser Memcons
NSC Institutional Files (H-Files)
NSC Staff for East Asia and Pacific Affairs
Policy Papers: National Security Decision Memoranda (NSDMs), National Security
Study Memoranda (NSSMs)
Presidential Correspondence with Foreign Leaders
Presidential Country Files
Trip Briefing Books and Cables for President Ford

President's Daily Diary

Central Intelligence Agency

Executive Registry: Executive Files of the Director of Central Intelligence
  Job 80M01048A
  Job 79M00467A

Washington National Records Center, Suitland, Maryland

Record Group 330, Records of the Office of the Secretary of Defense

OASD/ISA Files: FRC 330–76–117

  Secret Records of the Assistant Secretary of Defense for International Security Affairs, 1973

OASD/ISA Files: FRC 330–77–0063

  Top Secret Records of the Assistant Secretary of Defense for International Security Affairs, 1974

OSD Files: FRC 330–78–0001

  Secret Records of the Secretary of Defense, the Deputy Secretary of Defense, and the Special Assistant to the Secretary and Deputy Secretary of Defense, 1973

OSD Files: FRC 330–78–0010

  Top Secret Records of the Secretary of Defense, the Deputy Secretary of Defense, and the Special Assistant to the Secretary and Deputy Secretary of Defense, 1974

OSD Files: FRC 330–78–0059

  Top Secret Records of the Secretary of Defense, the Deputy Secretary of Defense, and the Special Assistant to the Secretary and Deputy Secretary of Defense, 1975

OSD Files: FRC 330–79–0049

  Secret Records of the Secretary of Defense, the Deputy Secretary of Defense, and the Special Assistant to the Secretary and Deputy Secretary of Defense, 1976

Library of Congress, Washington, DC

  Manuscript Division Kissinger Papers

Published Sources

  Burr, Bill, ed., *The Kissinger Transcripts: The Top-Secret Talks with Beijing & Moscow* (New York: The New Press, 1999)
  Haldeman, H.R., *The Haldeman Diaries: Inside the White House* (New York: G.P. Putnam Sons, 1994)
  ——— *The Haldeman Diaries: Inside the Nixon White House, the Complete Multimedia Edition* (Santa Monica, CA: Sony Electronic Publishing, 1994)
  Kissinger, Henry, *Years of Upheaval* (Boston: Little, Brown and Company, 1982)
  ——— *Years of Renewal* (New York: Simon & Schuster, 1999)
  Lilley, James with Jeffrey Lilley, *China Hands: Nine Decades of Adventure, Espionage, and Diplomacy in Asia* (New York: Public Affairs, 2004)

National Intelligence Council, *Tracking the Dragon: National Intelligence Estimates on China During the Era of Mao,* 1948–1976 (National Intelligence Council, October 2004)

Nixon, Richard M., *RN: The Memoirs of Richard Nixon* (New York: Grosset & Dunlap, 1978)

U.S. Department of State. *Bulletin,* 1973–1976.

U.S. National Archives and Records Administration, *Public Papers of the Presidents, Richard Nixon, 1969–1974* (Washington D.C.: Government Printing Office, 1970–1975)

U.S. National Archives and Records Administration, *Public Papers of the Presidents, Gerald R. Ford, 1974–1977* (Washington D.C.: Government Printing Office, 1975–1978)

Abbreviations and Terms

ACDA, Arms Control and Disarmament Agency
AC&W, aircraft control and warning
ADB, Asian Development Bank
AEC, Atomic Energy Commission
AID, Agency for International Development
AMB, ambassador
AP, Associated Press
AR, Albanian Resolution (UN)
ASEAN, Association of Southeast Asian Nations
ASW, anti-submarine warfare (DOD)

BOP, balance of payments

CCK, Chiang Ching-kuo
CHICOM, Chinese Communist
CIA, Central Intelligence Agency
CIEP, Council on International Economic Policy (U.S.)
CINCPAC, Commander in Chief, Pacific
CNO, Chief of Naval Operations (DOD)
COMNAVFORJAPAN, Commander, Naval Forces, Japan
COMSEVENTHFLT, Commander, Seventh Fleet
COMUSJ, Commander U.S. Forces, Japan
CONGEN, Consulate General
CONUS, Continental United States

DCI, Director of Central Intelligence (CIA)
DCM, Deputy Chief of Mission, United States Embassy
DEPTEL, Department of State telegram
DIA, Defense Intelligence Agency
DIS or DISS., dissemination
DOD, Department of Defense
DOD/ISA, Department of Defense, Office of the Assistant Secretary of Defense for International Security Affairs
DOS, Department of State
DR, Dual Representation (UN)
DRV, Democratic Republic of Vietnam (North Vietnam)
DSP, Democratic Socialist Party (Japan)

E, Bureau of Economic Affairs, Department of State
EA, Bureau of East Asian and Pacific Affairs, Department of State
EA/J, Officer in Charge of Japanese Affairs, Bureau of East Asian and Pacific Affairs, Department of State
EAP, Bureau of East Asian and Pacific Affairs, Department of State
ECM, electronic countermeasures
EDA, excess defense articles
EMBTEL, embassy telegram
ESC, European Security Conference
EXDIS, exclusive distribution (indicates extremely limited dissemination)

FAC, foreign assets control
FBI, Federal Bureau of Investigation
FBIS, Foreign Broadcast Information Service
FCN, Friendship, Commerce, and Navigation (Treaty)
FMS, foreign military sales
FNLA, National Liberation Front of Angola (Frente Nacional de Libertacao de Angola)
FONMIN, foreign minister
FRC, Federal Records Center (U.S.)
FRD, formerly restricted data
FSO, Foreign Service officer
FT, foreign trade
FY, fiscal year
FYI, for your information

GA, General Assembly (UN)
GATT, General Agreement on Tariffs and Trade
GIMO, Generalissimo Chiang Kai-shek (Jiang Jieshi)
GNP, gross national product
GOJ, Government of Japan
GOVT, Government
GPO, Government Printing Office (U.S.)
GRC, Government of the Republic of China on Taiwan
GRUNK, Gouvernement Royal d'Union Nationale du Kampuchéa (Cambodia)
GVN, Government of Vietnam (South)

HAK, Henry A. Kissinger
HK, Hong Kong, also initials for Henry Kissinger
HQ, headquarters

IAEA, International Atomic Energy Agency
IBRD, International Bank for Reconstruction and Development (World Bank)
ICC, International Control Commission
ICCS, International Commission of Control and Supervision
IG, Interdepartmental Group
IMF, International Monetary Fund
INFO, information
INR, Bureau of Intelligence and Research, Department of State
INR/EAP, Bureau of Intelligence and Research, East Asia and the Pacific, Department of State
INTEL, intelligence
IO, Bureau of International Organization Affairs, Department of State
IO/UNP, Bureau of International Organization Affairs, Office of United Nations Political Affairs
IQ, important question (UN)
IRBM, intermediate range ballistic missile
ISA, Bureau of International Security Affairs, Department of Defense
ITAC, Interagency Textile Administrative Committee

J, Under Secretary for Political Affairs, Department of State
JAEC, Japanese Atomic Energy Commission
JCRR, Joint Commission on Rural Reconstruction (ROC)
JCS, Joint Chiefs of Staff
JCSM, Joint Chiefs of Staff memorandum
JDA, Japanese Defense Agency

JGLO, Japanese Government Liaison Office, Ryukyu Islands
JHH, John Herbert Holdridge
JSDF, Japanese Self-Defense Forces
JSP, Japanese Socialist Party

KMT, Kuomintang (Nationalist Party, ROC), also called the Guomindang (GMD)

L, Office of the Legal Adviser, Department of State
LDP, Liberal Democratic Party (Japan)
LIMDIS, limited distribution (see also EXDIS)
LO, liaison office
LTA, The Long Term Arrangement/Agreement on Cotton Textiles

M, Deputy Under Secretary of State for Management
MAAG, Military Assistance Advisory Group
MAP, Military Assistance/Aid Program
MBFR, Mutual and Balanced Force Reductions
MFA, Multifiber Agreement
MFN, Most Favored Nation
MIA, missing in action
MITI, Ministry of International Trade and Industry (Japan)
MOD, minister of defense
MPLA, Popular Movement for the Liberation of Angola (Movimento Popular de Libertacao de Angola)
MST, Mutual Security Treaty

NATO, North Atlantic Treaty Organization
NIE, National Intelligence Estimate
NLF, National Liberation Front
NODIS, no distribution (other than to persons indicated)
NOFORN, no foreign dissemination
NOTAL, not to all
NPT, Nonproliferation Treaty
NSA, National Security Agency
NSC, National Security Council
NSDM, National Security Decision Memorandum
NSSM, National Security Study Memorandum

OASD/ISA, Office of the Assistant Secretary of Defense for International Security Affairs
OBE, overtaken by events
OCI, Office of Current Intelligence (CIA)
OECD, Organization for Economic Cooperation and Development
OMB, Office of Management and Budget
O&M, operation and maintenance (DOD)
ONE, Office of National Estimates (CIA)
OPIC, Overseas Private Investment Corporation
OSD, Office of the Secretary of Defense
OUSD, Office of the Under Secretary of Defense

PACAF, Pacific Air Force (U.S.)
PACOM, Pacific Command (U.S.)
PARA, paragraph
PFIAB, President's Foreign Intelligence Advisory Board
PLA, People's Liberation Army (PRC)

PM, Bureau of Politico-Military Affairs, Department of State; also Prime Minister
POL, political
PRC, People's Republic of China
PRCLO, People's Republic of China Liaison Office (Washington)
PRES, the President
PRG, Provisional Revolutionary Government
PriMin, Prime Minister

QR, Quota Restriction
QTE, quote

REFTEL, reference telegram
REP, representative
RES, resolution (UN)
RET'D, returned (indicates when the President finished reading a document)
RG, record group (National Archives and Records Administration)
RN, Richard Nixon
RNC, Republican National Committee
ROC, Republic of China on Taiwan (see also GRC)
ROCAF, Republic of China Air Force
ROK, Republic of Korea (South Korea)
RPT, repeat
RVN, Republic of Vietnam (South Vietnam)

S, Office of the Secretary of State
SALT, Strategic Arms Limitation Talks
SC, Security Council (UN)
SCA, Bureau of Security and Consular Affairs, Department of State
SCI, Bureau of International Scientific and Technological Affairs, Department of State;
    also sensitive compartmentalized information
SEA, Southeast Asia
SEATO, Southeast Asia Treaty Organization
SECDEF, Secretary of Defense
SECTO, from the Secretary of State (used for telegrams from the Secretary or his party
    while he is on travel)
SECY, Secretary of State
SECY GEN, Secretary General (UN)
SEPTEL, separate telegram
SIG, Senior Interdepartmental Group (NSC)
SNIE, Special National Intelligence Estimate
SOF(A), Status of Forces (Agreement)
S/P, Policy Planning Staff, Department of State
SRG, Senior Review Group (NSC)
S/S, Executive Secretariat, Department of State
SUBPAC, Submarine Force, United States Pacific Fleet
SVN, South Vietnam

TDY, Temporary Duty
TOSEC, to the Secretary of State (used for telegrams to the Secretary while he is on
    travel)
TOSIT, to the White House Situation Room
TS, Top Secret
TV, television

U, Office of the Under Secretary of State
UK, United Kingdom
UN, United Nations
UNC, United Nations Command (Korea)
UNCTAD, United Nations Conference on Trade and Development
UNCURK, United Nations Commission for the Unification and Rehabilitation of Korea
UNESCO, United Nations Educational, Scientific and Cultural Organization
UNGA, United Nations General Assembly
UNITA, National Union for Total Independence of Angola (Uniao Nacional para a Independencia Total de Angola)
UNQTE, unquote
UPI, United Press International
USA, United States Army
USAF, United States Air Force
USFY, United States fiscal year
USG, United States Government
USIA, United States Information Agency
USIB, United States Intelligence Board
USIS, United States Information Service
U–S/M, Under Secretaries' memorandum
USN, United States Navy
USSR, Union of Soviet Socialist Republics
USUN, United States Mission to the United Nations

VN, Vietnam
VOA, Voice of America
VP, Vice President

WESTPAC, Western Pacific
WH, White House
WNRC, Washington National Records Center

Z, Zulu time (Greenwich Mean Time)

Persons

Armstrong, Oscar Vance, Political Advisor to CINPAC until July 1973; Director of People's Republic of China and Mongolian Affairs from July 1973; Deputy Assistant Secretary for East Asian and Pacific Affairs from August 1976

Armstrong, Willis C., Assistant Secretary of State for Economic Affairs until April 16, 1974

Atherton, Alfred L., Jr., Deputy Assistant Secretary of State for Near Eastern and South Asian Affairs until April 1974

Barnes, Thomas J., senior member of the NSC staff from August 1975 until September 1976

Bhutto, Begum Nusrat, wife of Zulfikar Ali Bhutto, mother of Benazir Bhutto

Bhutto, Zulfikar Ali, President of Pakistan until August 14, 1973, then Prime Minister

Brandt, Willy, Chancellor of the FRG (West Germany) until May 6, 1974

Brezhnev, Leonid, First Secretary of the Communist Party of the Soviet Union

Bruce, David K.E., Head of the U.S. Liaison Office in Beijing from May 14, 1973 until September 25, 1974; Ambassador to the North Atlantic Treaty Organization from October 17, 1974 until February 12, 1976

Burger, Warren E., Chief Justice of the Supreme Court

Burns, Dr. Arthur F., Chairman, Federal Reserve System Board of Governors

Bush, George H.W., Representative to the United Nations from February 16, 1971 until January 18, 1973; Head of the U.S. Liaison Office in Beijing from October 21, 1974 until December 7, 1975; Director of Central Intelligence from January 30, 1976

Butz, Earl L., Secretary of Agriculture until 1976

Cai Weiping (Tsai Wei-ping), ROC Vice Minister of Foreign Affairs

Ceausescu, Nicolae, First Secretary of the Romanian Communist Party; President of Romania

Chang Chun-chiao, see Zhang Chunqiao

Chang Wen-chin, see Zhang Wenjin

Chi P'eng-fei, see Ji Pengfei

Chiang Ching, see Jiang Qing

Chiang Ching-kuo, see Jiang Jingguo

Chiang Kai-shek, see Jiang Jieshi

Chiang Kai-shek, Madame, see Jiang Jieshi, Madame

Chiao Kuan-hua, see Qiao Guanhua

Chien Fu (Fredrick F.), Director-General of the ROC Government Information Office from 1972

Chou En-lai, see Zhou Enlai

Chow Shu-kai, see Zhou Shukai

Chu Te, see Zhu De

Colby, William E., Director of Central Intelligence from September 4, 1973 until January 30, 1976

Davis, Jeanne W., Staff Secretary, NSC Staff Secretariat after 1971

De Gaulle, Charles, President of France from January 8, 1959 until April 28, 1969

Deng Xiaoping (Teng Hsiao-p'ing), Vice Premier of State Council after 1973

Dent, Frederick B., Secretary of Commerce until April 1975

Dobrynin, Anatoly Fedorovich, Soviet Ambassador to the United States

Douglas-Home, Sir Alexander Frederick, British Foreign Secretary until March 4, 1974

Dulles, John Foster, Secretary of State from January 21, 1953 until April 22, 1959

Eagleburger, Lawrence S., member of NSC staff from June 1973; Executive Assistant to the Secretary of State from October 1973; Acting Deputy Under Secretary for Management from February 1975 until May 1975; Under Secretary of Management for Management from May 1975

Ehrlichman, John D., Assistant to the President for Domestic Affairs until May 1973

Eliot, Theodore L., Jr., Special Assistant to the Secretary and Executive Secretary of the Department of State until September 26, 1973

Flanigan, Peter, Assistant to the President for International Economic Affairs and Executive Director of the Council on International Economic Policy, Executive Office of the President

Ford, Gerald R., Republican Congressman from Michigan until 1973; House Minority Leader until 1973; Vice President from October 13, 1973 until August 8, 1974; President from August 8, 1974 until January 20, 1977

Franco, Francisco, Spanish head of state until 1975

Freeman, Charles W., Jr., Asian Communist Affairs, Bureau of East Asian and Pacific Affairs until July 1973

Froebe, John A., Jr., assigned to the Australia, New Zealand and Pacific Island Desk, Bureau of East Asian Affairs, Department of State, but actually on the NSC staff beginning in 1971; formally detailed to the NSC in January 1974; left NSC staff in August 1975

Fulbright, J. William, Democratic Senator from Arkansas until 1974; Chairman of the Senate Foreign Relations Committee until 1974

Gandhi, Indira, Prime Minister of India

Gates, Thomas S., Chief of the U.S. Liaison Office in Peking with a personal rank as Ambassador from April 14, 1976

Gleysteen, William H., Jr., Deputy Chief of Mission, Taipei, until 1974; Deputy Assistant Secretary for East Asian and Pacific Affairs from September 1974; Deputy Assistant Secretary for Japan-Korea-Republic of China-People Republic of China from October 1975; NSC Staff from August 1976

Granger, Clinton E., Member of the NSC staff from August 1974 until September 1976

Green, Marshall, Assistant Secretary of State for East Asian and Pacific Affairs until May 10, 1973

Gromyko, Andrei A., Foreign Minister of the Soviet Union

Habib, Philip C., Ambassador to Korea until August 19, 1974; Assistant Secretary of State for East Asian and Pacific Affairs from September 27, 1974 until June 30, 1976; Under Secretary of State for Political Affairs from July 1, 1976

Haig, General Alexander M., Jr., Army Vice Chief of Staff from January to August 1973; Assistant to the President and Chief of Staff from August 1973 to August 1974

Han Hsu, see Han Xu

Han Xu (Han Hsu), Deputy Head of the PRC Liaison Office in the United States from 1973

Heath, Edward, British Prime Minister until March 4, 1974

Helms, Richard M., Director of Central Intelligence until February 2, 1973; U.S. Ambassador to Iran, 1973–1976

Hill, Robert C., Assistant Secretary of Defense for International Security Affairs from 1973 until 1974; Ambassador to Argentina from 1974

Ho Chi Minh, leader of the Vietnamese Workers Party (later the Vietnamese Communist Party)

Holdridge, John Herbert, member of the NSC Operations Staff/East Asia until April 1973; Co-Deputy Chief of Mission in Beijing from 1973 to 1975; Ambassador to Singapore from August 1975

Hormats, Robert, member of the NSC Operations Staff/International Economic Affairs from 1970 until 1973

Howe, Lt. Cmdr. Jonathan, member of the NSC staff from 1970 to 1973

Hua Guofeng (Hua Kuo-feng), Member of Politburo from 1973; Premier of PRC from 1976; Chairman of Chinese Communist Party from 1976

Hua Kuo-feng, see Hua Guofeng

Huang Chen, see Huang Zhen

Huang Hua, Chief Delegate to the Security Council and PRC Ambassador to the United Nations until October 1976

Huang Zhen (Huang Chen), PRC Ambassador to France until March 1973; Chief of the PRC Liaison Office in the United States from March 1973

Hummel, Arthur W., Jr., Deputy Assistant Secretary of State for East Asian and Pacific Affairs until 1975; Ambassador to Ethiopia from February 20, 1975 until July 6, 1976; Assistant Secretary of State for East Asian and Pacific Affairs from July 12, 1976 until March 14, 1977

Hyland, William G., member of the NSC Operations Staff/Europe until 1974; Director of INR from January 1974 until November 1975; Deputy Assistant to the President from November 1975 until April 1976

Ingersoll, Robert Stephen, Ambassador to Japan until November 8, 1973; Assistant Secretary for East Asian and Pacific Affairs from January 8, 1974 until July 9, 1974; Deputy Secretary of State from July 10, 1974 until March 31, 1976

Jackson, Henry M. ("Scoop"), Democratic Senator from Washington State

Jenkins, Alfred le Sesne, Director, Office of Asian Communist Affairs, Bureau of East Asian and Pacific Affairs, Department of State, until February 1973, co-Deputy Chief of Mission in Beijing from early 1973 until May 1974

Ji Pengfei (Chi P'eng-fei), PRC Vice Minister of Foreign Affairs until April 1971; Acting Foreign Minister until February 1972; Foreign Minister from February 1972 to November 1974

Jiang Jieshi (Chiang Kai-shek), President of the ROC until April 5, 1975; Chairman, ROC National Security Council until 1975; Director-General, Kuomintang, until 1975

Jiang Jieshi, Madame (Madame Chiang Kai-shek), wife of Jiang Jieshi; born Song Meiling (Soong Mayling)

Jiang Jingguo (Chiang Ching-kuo), son of Jiang Jieshi; ROC Premier

Jiang Qing (Chiang Ching), wife of Mao Zedong; member of the CCP Politburo until October 1976

Johnson, Lyndon B., President of the United States from November 22, 1963 until January 20, 1969

Johnson, U. Alexis, Under Secretary of State for Political Affairs until February 1, 1973

Kennedy, Col. Richard T., Deputy Assistant to the President for NSC planning from 1973 until 1975

Khan, Agha Muhammad Yahya, President of Pakistan until December 20, 1971

Kim Il-sung (Kim Il Sung), President (Chairman of the Presidium of the Supreme People's Assembly) of the DPRK and General Secretary of the Central Committee of the Workers' Party of Korea

Kissinger, Henry A., Assistant to the President for National Security Affairs until November 3, 1975; Secretary of State from September 21, 1973 to January 20, 1977

Kosygin, Alexei N., Chairman of the Council of Ministers (Premier) of the Soviet Union

Kubisch, Jack B., Deputy Chief of Mission in Paris until May 1973
Kuznetsov, Vasily V., Soviet First Deputy Foreign Minister

Lai Mingtang (Lai Ming-tong), ROC Chief of the General Staff, MND, from 1970
Lai Ming-tong, see Lai Mingtang
Laird, Melvin R., Secretary of Defense until January 29, 1973
Le Duan, General Secretary of the Vietnamese Workers' Party (later the Vietnamese Com-
munist Party)
Le Duc Tho, member of the Politburo of the DRV (North Vietnam) and leader of the
DRV negotiating team in Paris until 1973
Lee Kuan Yew, Prime Minister of Singapore
Li Hsien-nien, see Li Xiannian
Li Xiannian (Li Hsien-nien), Vice Premier of the PRC State Council until 1975
Lincoln, George, Director, Office of Emergency Preparedness until 1974
Lin Biao (Lin Piao), PRC Minister of Defense from 1959 until September 1971; Vice Chair-
man of the CCP Central Committee (Politburo) until September 1971
Lin Piao, see Lin Biao
Lon Nol, President of the Khmer Republic until 1975
Lord, Winston, member of the NSC staff until 1973; Director of the Policy Planning Staff
at the Department of State from October 1973

Malik, Adam, Indonesian Foreign Minister
Malik, Yakov Alexandrovich, Permanent Representative of the Soviet Union to the
United Nations until 1976
Magnuson, Warren, Democratic Senator from Washington State
Mansfield, Michael, Democratic Senator from Montana until 1976, Senate Majority
Leader until 1976
Mao Tse-tung, see Mao Zedong
Mao Zedong (Mao Tse-Tung), Chairman of the Central Committee of the Chinese Com-
munist Party
Marchais, Georges, head of the French Communist Party
McConaughy, Walter P., Jr., Ambassador to the ROC until April 4, 1974
McCloskey, Robert J., Deputy Assistant Secretary of State for Press Relations, and Spe-
cial Assistant to the Secretary, until May 1973; Ambassador to Cyprus in 1973 and
1974; Ambassador at Large and Assistant Secretary of State for Congressional Rela-
tions, 1975–1976
McFarlane, Robert C. ("Bud"), Military Assistant to the National Security Adviser from
1973 until 1977 (promoted to Special Assistant to the President in 1976)
McGovern, George, Democratic Senator from South Dakota
Mitterand, Francois, French Socialist politician
Moorer, Adm. Thomas H., USN, Chairman of the Joint Chiefs of Staff until July 1, 1974
Moynihan, Daniel P., Ambassador to India until 1975; U.S. Permanent Representative
to the UN from 1975 until 1976

Nehru, Jawaharlal, Leader of India's Congress Party and Prime Minister from 1947 to
1964
Nessen, Ron, Press Secretary to President Gerald Ford
Nguyen Van Thieu, President of the Republic of Vietnam (South Vietnam) until April
21, 1975
Nguyen Co Thach, Vice-Foreign Minister of the Democratic Republic of Vietnam
Nixon, Richard M., President of the United States from January 20, 1969, to August 9,
1974

Ohira, Masayoshi, Japanese Foreign Minister until July 12, 1974

Park Chung Hee (Pak Chong-hui), President of the ROK (South Korea)

Pauls, Rolf, West German Ambassador to the United States until May 1973

Phouma, Souvanna, Prime Minister of the Kingdom of Laos until 1975

Pickering, Thomas R., Executive Secretary of State and Special Assistant to the Secretary of State from August 1973

Platt, Nicholas, Deputy Director, and then Director, of the Secretariat Staff, Department of State, until May 1973; political officer in USLO from May 1973 until January 1974; stationed in Japan from July 1974

Podgorny, Nikolai V., President of the Presidium of the Supreme Soviet of the USSR

Pompidou, Georges, President of France until April 3, 1974

Qiao Guanhua (Chiao Kuan-hua), Deputy [Vice] Foreign Minister of the PRC until November 1974; Foreign Minister from November 1974 until December 1976

Rahman, Mujibur, Prime Minister of Bangladesh until 1975

Richardson, Elliot L., Secretary of Health, Education, and Welfare until January 1973; Secretary of Defense from January 30 to May 24, 1973; Attorney General from May to October 1973; Ambassador to Great Britain from 1975 until 1976

Rockefeller, Nelson A., Governor of New York until 1973; Vice-President of the United States from December 19, 1974 until January 20, 1977

Rodman, Peter W., member of the NSC staff

Rogers, William P., Secretary of State until September 3, 1973

Rumsfeld, Donald, Counselor to the President until January 1973; Ambassador to NATO from 1973 until 1974; Secretary of Defense from November 20, 1975

Rush, Kenneth, Deputy Secretary of Defense until January 29, 1973; Deputy Secretary of State from February 2, 1973 until May 29, 1974

Sadat, Anwar, President of Egypt

Sato, Eisaku, Prime Minister of Japan until July 6, 1972

Scali, John, Special Consultant to the President until 1973, U.S. Representative to the United Nations from 1973 to 1975

Scheel, Walter, West German Vice Chancellor and Foreign Minister until May 6, 1974

Schlesinger, James R., Chairman of the Atomic Energy Commission until February 1973; Director of Central Intelligence from February 2 until July 2, 1973; Secretary of Defense from July 2, 1973 until November 19, 1975

Schmidt, Helmut, West German Minister of Finance until May 6, 1974; Chancellor from 1974

Schumann, Maurice, French Foreign Minister until March 28, 1973

Scott, Hugh, Republican Senator from Pennsylvania, Minority Leader

Scowcroft, Brent, Military Assistant to the President until 1973, Deputy Assistant to the President for National Security Affairs from August 1973 until 1975, Assistant to the President for National Security Affairs from November 3, 1975 until January 20, 1977

Shen, James C. H., ROC Ambassador to the United States

Shultz, George P., Secretary of the Treasury until April 17, 1974

Sihanouk, Prince Norodom, Cambodian leader of a government-in-exile in Beijing until 1975

Sirik Matak (Sisowath Sirik Matak, sometimes spelled Sivik), Prince and cousin of Norodom Sihanouk; ally of Lon Nol; Deputy Prime Minister, then member of the High Political Council, from 1970 to 1974

Sisco, Joseph J., Assistant Secretary of State for Near Eastern and South Asian Affairs until February 18, 1974; Under Secretary of State for Political Affairs from February 19, 1974 until June 30, 1976

Smyser, W. Richard, senior staff member of the NSC from 1973 until 1975

Sneider, Richard L., Deputy Assistant Secretary of State for East Asian and Pacific Affairs until September 1974; Ambassador to Korea from September 1974
Solomon, Richard H., senior staff member of the NSC until 1976
Song Zhangzhi (Soong Chang-chih), ROC Commander-in-Chief
Sonnenfeldt, Helmut, member of the NSC Operations Staff/Europe until January 1974; Counselor to the State Department, 1974–1977
Springsteen, George S., Jr., Acting Assistant Secretary of State until August 1973; Deputy Assistant Secretary of State for European Affairs from August 1973 until January 1974; Special Assistant to the Secretary of State and Executive Secretary of the Department from January 1974 until July 1976; Director of the Foreign Service Institute from July 1976
Stein, Herbert, Chairman of the Council of Economic Advisors until July 1974
Stoessel, Walter J., Deputy Assistant Secretary of State for European Affairs until January 7, 1974
Suharto, Mohammed, President of Indonesia
Sullivan, William H., Deputy Assistant Secretary of State for East Asian and Pacific Affairs until July 1973; Ambassador to the Philippines from July 1973 until 1977
Sun Yunxuan (Sun Yun-suan), ROC Minister of Economic Affairs
Symington, Stuart, Democratic Senator from Missouri

Tanaka, Kakuei, Prime Minister of Japan until December 9, 1974
Teng Hsiao-p'ing, see Deng Xiaoping
Thayer, Harry E. T., Member of the US Delegation to the UN General Assembly in 1973 and 1974; Posted in Peking in May 1975; Deputy Director of the Office of PRC and Mongolian Affairs from August 1976
Tito, Josip Broz, President of Yugoslavia
Tsai Wei-ping, see Cai Weiping

Unger, Leonard, Ambassador to Thailand until November 19, 1973; Ambassador to ROC from May 25, 1974

Waldheim, Kurt, Secretary-General of the United Nations
Weinberger, Caspar W., Director of OMB, 1972; Secretary of Health Education and Welfare from 1973 until 1975
Whitlam, Gough, Prime Minister of Australia until November 11, 1975

Xuan Thuy, Foreign Minister of the DRV (North Vietnam) from 1963 to 1965, Chief Delegate to Paris Peace talks from 1968 to 1970

Yan Jiagan (Yen Chia-kan), Vice President of the ROC
Yang Hsi-kun, see Yang Xikun
Yang Xikun (Yang Hsi-kun), ROC Vice Minister of Foreign Affairs
Ye Jianying (Yeh Chien-ying), Marshall, member of the Central Committee and Politburo; Defense Minister from 1975
Yen Chia-kan, see Yan Jiagan
Yeh Chien-ying, see Ye Jianying

Zhang Chunqiao (Chang Chun-chiao), Politburo member until 1976, Vice Premier from January 1975 until October 1976
Zhang Wenjin (Chang Wen-chin), Assistant to the PRC Foreign Minister until September 1973

Zhou Enlai (Chou En-lai), Premier of the PRC until January 8, 1976; member, Standing Committee of the Chinese Communist Party's Political Bureau until 1976

Zhou Shukai (Chow Shu-kai), ROC Minister without Portfolio

Zhu De (Chu Teh), Chairman of the Standing Committee of the National Peoples Congress until 1976

Ziegler, Ronald, White House Press Secretary until 1974

China, 1973–1976

Kissinger's Visits to Beijing and the Establishment of the Liaison Offices, January 1973–May 1973

1.　Memorandum of Conversation[1]

New York City, January 3, 1973, 10:15–11:00 p.m.

PARTICIPANTS

> Dr. Henry A. Kissinger, Assistant to the President for National Security Affairs
> Winston Lord, NSC Staff
>
> Huang Hua, PRC Ambassador to the United Nations
> Mr. Kuo, Notetaker
> Mrs. Shih Yen-hua, Interpreter

Ambassador Huang: Happy New Year.

Dr. Kissinger: I have been calling on your Ambassador in Paris. I don't know whether he sends you reports.

Ambassador Huang: Yes, I understood that.

Dr. Kissinger: I never know how much he understands because we have to communicate with a combination of French and English. (Ambassador Huang laughs) His French interpreter is very good, but mine isn't.

Ambassador Huang: I don't believe it.

Dr. Kissinger: It's true.

You probably realize this, but you have completely seduced Joseph Alsop. He has written articles like Harrison Salisbury did from the Soviet Union. I don't know whether you have read his articles. They have been very fair.

Ambassador Huang: Yes, I have read part of them, particularly his articles on his visit to Yunnan Province. That was a renewed visit of his; he had been there once before to the Province.

---

[1] Source: National Archives, Nixon Presidential Materials, NSC Files, Kissinger Office Files, Box 94, Country Files, Far East, China Exchanges, January 1–April 14, 1973. Top Secret; Sensitive; Exclusively Eyes Only.

1

Dr. Kissinger: He told me when he came back that this was the greatest experience in his 41 years of professional journalism.

I wanted to see you principally to hand you personally a letter from the President to Premier Chou En-lai which he wanted to give you since it was not possible for me to be in China at this time. There is very little about Vietnam in it so that is not its principal . . . (Dr. Kissinger hands over the letter at Tab A and Ambassador Huang scans it.)

Ambassador Huang: It's quite a long letter. It is three pages single-spaced.

Dr. Kissinger: It attempts to summarize our view on our relationships.

Ambassador Huang: We will promptly convey this.

Dr. Kissinger: I wanted actually only to discuss two other matters with you. One, there is a great deal of speculation because of the appointment of Mr. Moynihan as Ambassador to India and also because of some of the overtures India has made to the United States. We want you to know, first of all, that until January 20th it is difficult for us to control everything that is being said by the State Department. But there will be no significant change in our policy toward the Subcontinent without prior discussion with you, and the essential elements of policy which we discussed with the Prime Minister still remain. In the next weeks we will make some shipments of arms to Pakistan, and after our new Ambassador comes to Iran we will do it on a more systematic scale. We simply wanted you to know this.

The only other subject . . . two other subjects. First, as the President says in his letter to the Prime Minister, if the Prime Minister is still interested, the President is still prepared to send me to China after the Vietnam negotiations are concluded, for a general review of the international situation before we are too far along in the second term. If the Chinese side wants to make a specific proposal, we would make every effort to make it possible, maybe toward the end of February or early March.

Now the last subject I wanted to mention to you is the Vietnam negotiation which I will start again next week. Now we have an understanding for your difficulties in this matter, but it is also a matter of extreme difficulty for us. It is simply not true that we are looking for a pretext not to sign the agreement. We feel quite frankly that your allies have courage, but they lack wisdom.

Our basic problem is that as a great power we cannot simply betray an ally, but we are prepared to make an agreement, even if our ally disagrees, which meets certain absolutely minimal conditions for us. You remember when we had dinner with the Vice Minister I told him that we thought we would sign on December 8 or 9. When we met your Ambassador in Paris we told him we wanted to sign by December 22.[2] So it really is not true that we are holding up the agreement. The Vietnamese side has invented obstacles faster than we can remove them.

For example, let me cite one minor problem, and I don't ask you to judge its merits. (To Lord) Did you mention the question of the word "destroyed" in your presentation?

Mr. Lord: No, I did not, although I mentioned that they raised several new issues on the last day.

Dr. Kissinger: For example, with regard to military equipment, there is a provision that says that destroyed, damaged, worn-out or used-up equipment can be replaced. It has always been in there. On the last day of the last negotiations, when things were already not going well, the Vietnamese said that the word "destroyed" had to be taken out. When I asked why, they said you can't destroy something without damaging it. We had already given this language to Saigon as well as to our colleagues in Washington. I wouldn't care about the sentence if it hadn't already been in there. But for me to say that we spent the last day discussing whether one can destroy something without its being damaged won't make a good impression. It does not give an impression of seriousness.

I don't want you to get involved in the drafting details of this nature. (Ambassador Huang smiles.) I use it only as an example. The reason I am talking to you is that I read some speeches made last week in Peking, and I understand your necessities.

Mrs. Shih: Understand . . . ?

Dr. Kissinger: That you have certain necessities as well. Because I pay special attention to my old host Marshal Yeh Chen-ying. (Ambassador Huang smiles.) But that is not the issue.

We have offered the North Vietnamese to sign the agreement as it stood on November 23 with one additional modification. These are all things that had already been accepted. We are not asking for anything new, and if this is done then we have the moral basis to take very strong measures against Saigon, including cutting off aid if they don't agree. (Ambassador Huang nods slightly.)

---

[2] At a dinner on November 13, 1972, Kissinger told Qiao Guanhua, PRC Vice Minister of Foreign Affairs, that he sought to complete the Vietnam negotiations by December 8 or 9. See *Foreign Relations, 1969–1976*, vol. E–13, Document 166. During a late night meeting on December 7, 1972, Kissinger told Huang Zhen, then PRC Ambassador to France, that the United States had proposed a schedule that would allow the signing of a Vietnam treaty on December 22. See ibid., vol. XVII, Document 269.

But if the negotiations fail next week, I cannot possibly commit myself to be kept in Paris another two weeks and dealt with as frivolously as last time. We sent to you the transcripts of some of these meetings so you must have your own judgment, which I may say is more than we have done for our colleagues in the Foreign Ministry. So I hope you won't publish these some day.

If the negotiations now fail, we will abandon the October Agreement completely. We will not then continue to negotiate on the basis of the October Agreement. We may seek another basis of a more bilateral nature, but it will certainly not be the one we now have.

Now the consequences of this . . . we cannot believe, if we look ahead to the next four years . . . it is our conviction, as I told you before, that by 1973 when the new rocket program of your northern ally is completed, we assume certain consequences could follow, we don't know in which direction. Certainly we don't believe these weapons are being built in order to make your friends easier to deal with. What we would like to do—if it were not for the war in Vietnam—what we would like to do is to accelerate the normalization of our relationship with you and accelerate our relationships with Western Europe, and I believe for the same reasons you are accelerating your relationships with Western Europe. You have been long enough in the U.S., and you will have some judgment as to which people in the U.S. hold these convictions, and they are not very many. Therefore, the obvious consequences of discrediting the authority of the White House will go far beyond Vietnam, and conversely to get it finished would accelerate and enable us to concentrate on matters we consider to be of real priority.

We have no interest in a permanent presence in Indochina. Why should we? The decisive events in Asia will occur far north of there, and the hegemonial aspirations will not come from Washington in that area. But it is important that the American people not be so disillusioned by any events in Asia that we will be paralyzed with respect to what are the crucial events.

So if these negotiations fail, our attention will continue to focus on Indochina. We will not accept these pressures either domestically or internationally, and it will be over issues that are not essential for the major developments of the future. Conversely, if we can coexist with Peking we can certainly coexist with Hanoi. Our major concern in Indochina, which is not a central feature of our policy anyway, would be to cooperate with those who want to prevent other hegemonies from being established there.

This is simply our philosophy. I wanted the Prime Minister to know. The next two weeks will be very important. I took the liberty of asking to see you today because I am leaving Sunday and I will not be available the next few days. I also thought it might be important for the Prime Minister to have our thinking.

These are the major things I wanted to mention to you. I don't think you have instructions to give a long reply. (Ambassador Huang laughs.)

Ambassador Huang: We will report what you said to Prime Minister Chou En-lai.

Dr. Kissinger: I also have a very selfish reason—if you can convince your allies to settle by the 10th, then we can still see one of the performances of the acrobats on the 11th. (Ambassador Huang laughs.)

Ambassador Huang: They won't leave until the 13th.

Dr. Kissinger: From Washington? I thought they would be there three days. (There was then some discussion on when the acrobats would be in Washington. It has become clear subsequently that Ambassador Huang meant they would be physically in Washington through the 13th; as the U.S. side thought, they would perform only on the 9th through the 11th.) If they are still there on the 13th I will certainly see them. But in any event I want you to know that they will be given a very warm welcome, and my office will contact them when they get there to see if there is anything to be done which will make them more comfortable.

Ambassador Huang: First, about the visit of our acrobatic troupe to the U.S. We appreciate the meticulous arrangements made by the National Committee for US-China Relations and the New York City Center as its host organization. New York is the third city the acrobats have been visiting, and we have been very satisfied with the results of the visit.

Dr. Kissinger: They are a spectacular success everywhere.

Ambassador Huang: They have been given a very warm welcome for the performances, and the acrobats have been encouraged because they feel that they have done their share and made their contribution to promoting understanding and friendship between the American and Chinese peoples. We believe that they will leave the United States with satisfaction for Latin America. And in this respect we also appreciate Dr. Kissinger's consideration, attention.

Dr. Kissinger: There are two other matters I might mention to you. We have a memorial service for President Truman in Washington.[3] There is a certain category of visitors that the President sees—everyone who is President or Vice President of a country primarily. We have

---

[3] Harry S. Truman died on December 26, 1972. Foreign dignitaries attended a memorial service for him that was held at the Washington National Cathedral on January 5, 1973.

just been informed that Taiwan is sending its Vice President, so the President may see him for 15 minutes. So this has no significance. This is a protocol matter. Everyone of a certain rank is received as a courtesy by the President, only 15 minutes each.

Secondly, I wanted you to know for your own information that the Soviet Union has proposed June for the return visit of Brezhnev to the United States. We have not yet given a definite reply. We said that we will discuss it in February, but we will let you know when anything definite is arranged.

Ambassador Huang: About the Paris talks, I would like to convey a very serious piece of news. If the U.S. side truly wishes a settlement in the forthcoming private sessions, this opportunity should not be missed. It is hoped that serious reciprocal negotiations will be conducted and then fruitful results can be expected.

Dr. Kissinger: If there is a serious attitude on the other side, we will make every effort to settle it. We would like to end the war for the reasons which I have explained to you, and we will make a major effort to do so.

Is this news based on the visit of Le Duc Tho to Peking?

Ambassador Huang: I can't explain it. The last sentence of the message wishes Dr. Kissinger a happy New Year.

Dr. Kissinger: Thank you very much. I appreciate it. When I come to Peking, or through some other formula, we will be prepared to discuss Cambodia with you as I pointed out to the Prime Minister.

It is always a pleasure to see you, Mr. Ambassador, though it is not frequent enough. (Ambassador Huang smiles.)

Ambassador Huang: This evening our acrobatic troupe performed in New York City.

Dr. Kissinger: I didn't think carefully enough—maybe I should have arranged to see them here.

Ambassador Huang: We are very sorry we were late because many representatives to the United Nations were present, and also some American friends.

Dr. Kissinger: I understood that you were the host and couldn't leave. Anyway, it's such an unusual event for me to be here first.

(The Chinese then got up to leave and there was brief small talk about Mr. Alsop's enthusiasm concerning China before the Chinese left to take their own car back to their Mission.)

Tab A

Letter From President Nixon to Chinese Premier Zhou Enlai[4]

Washington, January 3, 1973.

Dear Mr. Prime Minister:

As my second term in office begins, I would like to review with you some of the major questions that affect our two countries. I am writing this letter in lieu of Dr. Kissinger's meetings with you which I had hoped would be taking place during this period but which have had to be postponed due to Vietnam developments.

In looking back over the past four years no international development carries more significance than the reestablishment of communications and the launching of a new relationship between the People's Republic of China and the United States. It is with great personal warmth as well as historical sense that I recall my visit to your country and my frank exchanges with Chairman Mao and yourself. Let me take this occasion to reiterate that the further improvement of relations between our two countries remains one of the cardinal principles of American foreign policy.

I believe we can take satisfaction in bilateral developments since February. A good beginning has been made in people-to-people contacts and exchanges in various fields. We should expand and accelerate these efforts which are already making important contributions to mutual understanding and friendship between the Chinese and American peoples. In addition, we should continue to build on the first foundations which have been laid for meaningful Sino-American trade.

On the governmental level, I believe the candid dialogue between Dr. Kissinger and Ambassador Huang in New York has served well to set forth our respective positions on major issues. In my coming term I propose we maintain this productive channel as the channel for all matters except technical issues which would continue to be discussed in Paris. These exchanges, I believe, should be supplemented by occasional personal visits which allow a more thorough and direct exposition of our policies. To this end I am prepared to accept your kind invitation and to send Dr. Kissinger to Peking as soon as the war in Vietnam has been ended through a negotiated settlement for a full review of Sino-American relations and world developments.

As you know, we have consistently fulfilled our undertaking to keep you apprised of U.S. attitudes and policies on all issues of major concern to the People's Republic of China. I intend to continue this practice

---

[4] No classification marking.

which I consider to be in our mutual interest. For example, you have been aware that the United States places no obstacles in the way of improved Sino-Japanese relations which we believe will contribute to peace in the Asian and Pacific region. We in turn have noted the restraint with which you have conducted your policy toward Japan. Elsewhere in the Far East, we favor the first steps toward more communication and less tension in the Korean peninsula. While this process should be left to the two Korean parties, it can only benefit all those who seek greater stability in the region. Our two governments have been in close contact with respect to South Asia, and we will continue to share with you our policy intentions toward the Subcontinent. In particular I want to assure you that any change in well-established U.S. policy toward the Subcontinent will be first discussed with the People's Republic of China. In our discussions with our allies in Western Europe we have made clear our positive attitude toward their increased communication with you.

As far as direct U.S.-Chinese dealings are concerned, I would like to reaffirm our intention to move energetically in my second Administration toward the normalization of our relations. Everything that has been previously said on this subject is hereby reaffirmed. Dr. Kissinger will be prepared to discuss this fully when he visits Peking.

We remain firmly committed to the principles of the Shanghai Communiqué,[5] including those that deal with aspirations for hegemony and spheres of influence. We believe that a vital and strong China is in the interest of world peace.

In short, a promising framework has been established in the past couple of years. But it is clear that the war in Indochina impedes the kind of further progress that so surely would benefit both our countries. We have kept you fully informed of developments in Paris in recent months, and as Dr. Kissinger will speak to this subject at some length with Ambassador Huang, I will not dwell on it in this letter. No one familiar with the recent record can in good conscience dispute the fact that the United States has made maximum efforts to restore peace in Indochina. We hope at long last to achieve that goal, but this will require from Hanoi a seriousness that was as absent in December as it was evident in October. The central question remains whether it is not in the interest of us all to bring this war to a rapid conclusion and thus remove the major obstacle to many constructive developments in international relations. This is the U.S. attitude. It will shape our approach to the negotiations which resume next week.

---

[5] The Shangai Communiqué, issued on February 27, 1972, is printed in *Public Papers: Nixon, 1972*, pp. 376–379. See also *Foreign Relations*, 1969–1976, vol. XVII, Document 203.

Mrs. Nixon joins me in personal greetings to you and Madame Chou and wishes for a healthy and prospering 1973.

Sincerely,

Richard Nixon

---

2.   Memorandum of Conversation[1]

Washington, January 5, 1973, 4:00–4:15 p.m.

PARTICIPANTS

Vice President Yen Chia-ken, Republic of China
Ambassador James Shen
Vice Minister of Foreign Affairs, Tsai Wei-ping

President Nixon
Richard T. Kennedy, Deputy to the Assistant to the President for National
   Security Affairs

Yen Chia-kan: Let me present you with this. It is a book of pictures of events since 1967.

President: I appreciate the long journey you have made to honor President Truman. It's also an opportunity for me to welcome you here.[2] I remember our meeting two years ago and my many visits to your country. I hope President Chiang is feeling better.

Yen Chia-kan: He is much better, thank you. His doctors advised him against travel. I do much of the protocol work, along with Premier Chiang Ching-kuo.

---

[1] Source: National Archives, Nixon Presidential Materials, NSC Files, Box 1026, Presidential/HAK Memcons, Jan.–Mar. 1973. Secret; Nodis. The meeting was held in the Oval Office. In addition to the participants listed in the memorandum of conversation, the President's Daily Diary indicates that a military aide, Lieutenant Colonel William L. Golden, also attended. (Ibid., White House Central Files) A tape of this conversation is ibid., White House Tapes, Conversation, No. 834–16.

[2] Kissinger initially expressed reservations about advising Nixon to meet Yan Jiagan. (Memorandum from Kennedy to Kissinger, January 4; ibid., NSC Files, Box 523, Country Files, Far East, China, Vol. 11, Aug 1972–Oct 24, 1973) Kissinger modified his position after receiving a letter from Department of State Executive Secretary Theodore Eliot on January 3, which argued that it was important for the President to meet Yan since he was acting as Chief of State in place of the ailing Jiang Jieshi. (Ibid., White House Special Files, Subject Files, Confidential Files, 1969–1974, [CF] CO 34–1, ROC) On January 4, Kissinger sent the President talking points for this meeting. (Ibid., NSC Files, Box 1026, Presidential/HAK MemCons, Jan.–Mar. 1973)

President: I know you have had problems continuing your diplomatic ties with many countries but you still have great economic strength. It comes from hard work.

Yen Chia-kan: Yes, and we will even work harder. The important part of our international relations is trade. We have a great expansion. It has increased from $4.2 billion to $5.9 billion in just two years, and it's going up. What you have done for us is bearing fruit. Our production is up per capita.

We know we will continue to work hard and face our future and keep the support of our friends. We have had an election of our legislative bodies. We are drawing more and more local people into politics, more younger people. Education is moving rapidly. We are also emphasizing citizenship and vocational education.

President: That's an excellent move.

Yen Chia-kan: You have been kind to send us scientists for technical exchange. We hope we can increase this and intensify it.

President: We will do all we can.

Yen Chia-kan: A word about our military situation. We have made the transfer of aircraft to South Vietnam as you wished.

President: The purpose was to strengthen the GVN and our common interest. We hope to break the deadlock soon. They [the North Vietnamese][3] had agreed before our election, then they back off, that's why we resumed the May 8 policy.[4] Now they are willing to start the talks again. We want to settle it—it will include a cease-fire and the return of prisoners. On the political side, there is no coalition. We want to end it, but we must end it the right way. A bug-out would hurt us everywhere in the world. The Congress is giving us a tough time.

Yen Chia-kan: We will do everything possible to coordinate our policy with yours.

On the military side, we are giving gradually more and more attention to our Air Force and Navy. We have to do everything to prevent our isolation. We will appreciate your help to keep us in international organizations. We need your help and support. We will do everything to merit your support.

You know, there is possibly oil near Taiwan. We are cooperating with U.S. oil companies on this. It's in the exploratory stage.

---

[3] All brackets are in the original.

[4] On May 8, 1972, Nixon addressed the nation on the situation in Southeast Asia during which he announced the use of increased military measures against North Vietnam and the presentation of a new peace proposal. See *Public Papers: Nixon, 1972*, pp. 583–587.

President: I hope it is there. If you had the oil Saudi Arabia had, you'd be the strongest nation in the world. You've done remarkably with your resources. It comes from hard work and organization.

Yen Chia-kan: We are helping others in land reforms. Our success in land reform is the result of many factors. We are doing multi-cropping now—with up to four crops a year. We are now producing more industrially than agriculturally. Our industrial growth is greater than our agriculture now. Your help has been very important. Ford's decision to come to Taiwan is very helpful.

President: How is Madame Chiang?

Yen Chia-kan: Fine.

President: She is strong and highly intelligent. We'll keep in close touch. If there is any change in our Ambassadors, we will let you know.

[The President gave him a Presidential ash tray and pin and escorted him to his car].

---

3.   Letter From Chinese Premier Zhou Enlai to President Nixon[1]

Beijing, January 6, 1973.

Mr. President,

I have received your letter of January 3, 1973.[2]

Chairman Mao has read the letter and also takes satisfaction in bilateral developments since last February.

We appreciate Mr. President's wish for continued improvement in Sino-U.S. relations as was expressed in the letter. The Chinese side believes that the normalization of relations between China and the United States step by step in accordance with the principles of the Shanghai Communiqué[3] is not only in the interest of the Chinese and American peoples, but will also contribute to the easing of tension in Asia and the world. However, Mr. President, we would not be frank if we did not point out at the same time that the continuation of the Viet Nam

---

[1] Source: National Archives, Nixon Presidential Materials, NSC Files, Kissinger Office Files, Box 94, Country Files, Far East, China Exchanges, January 1–April 14, 1973. Top Secret; Exclusively Eyes Only. This letter was sent to Nixon under a covering letter, January 8, from Richard T. Kennedy. (Ibid.) A handwritten note on Kennedy's cover letter states, "The President has seen per RTK 1/8/73."

[2] Tab A, Document 1.

[3] See footnote 5, Document 1.

war, particularly such bombings as recently carried out by the United States against the Democratic Republic of Viet Nam, are bound to affect the progress of Sino-U.S. relations. We believe, as Mr. President correctly mentioned in the letter, it is in the interest of us all to bring the Viet Nam war to a rapid conclusion and thus remove the major obstacle to many constructive developments in international relations. As the Chinese saying goes, one should not lose the major for the sake of the minor, and I think it would be of significance to reflect upon these words again at this important juncture. We hope in this round of private meetings between Viet Nam and the United States, interferences can be overcome and an agreement to end the Viet Nam war finally concluded through serious reciprocal negotiations and joint efforts.

It is understandable that Dr. Kissinger's planned visit to Peking cannot materialize as originally envisaged. You are welcome to send Dr. Kissinger to Peking for a meeting at an appropriate time after the negotiated settlement of the Viet Nam war.

With regard to the series of international issues and questions concerning the development of Sino-U.S. bilateral relations as referred to in the letter, we prepare to have a direct and thorough exchange of views with Dr. Kissinger during his visit to Peking.

My wife and I thank you and Mrs. Nixon for your good wishes and extend our regards to you.

Chou En-Lai[4]

---

[4] The letter bears Zhou Enlai's typed signature.

---

4.   **Memorandum From John H. Holdridge of the National Security Council Staff to the President's Assistant for National Security Affairs (Kissinger)**[1]

Washington, January 18, 1973.

SUBJECT

Current State of Sino-American Relations, and Possibilities for the Immediate Future

---

[1] Source: National Archives, Nixon Presidential Materials, NSC Files, Box 526, Country Files, Far East, People's Republic of China, Vol. 6, Jan–Apr 1973. Secret; Sensitive; Eyes Only. Sent for information. Kissinger initialed the memorandum and Richard Solomon initialed it on behalf of Holdridge.

Since your last trip to Peking in June of 1972 there has been substantial movement in non-governmental contacts between the U.S. and
the People's Republic of China, but largely inaction at the governmental
level (in the sense of lack of PRC response to several authoritative proposals that we have made to them for negotiations or contacts of a more
formal nature).

In the cultural exchange area, the Chinese sent to this country in
the second half of 1972 delegations of scientists and physicians on exploratory "friendship-building" missions. In both cases, the groups
were hosted by the Committee on Scholarly Communication with the
PRC, a "facilitating organization" that we had recommended to Peking
in June. In addition, an acrobatic troupe made a highly successful tour
of the U.S. in December and January, again under the sponsorship of
a non-governmental organization that we had recommended to them—
the National Committee on U.S.-China Relations.

In contrast, there has been minimal American "traffic" to China
over the past six months. The National Committee was invited to send
a 15 man delegation in December, and the top leadership of this group
has now completed a successful visit to the PRC that included discussions with Vice Foreign Minister Ch'iao Kuan-hua and top commercial
officials on exchange and trade issues. A number of American journalists visited the PRC for month-long tours in the fall; and U.S. businessmen were given increased access to the Canton Trade Fair in October and November. At the same time, the PRC has accelerated its
effort to develop good relations with Chinese-Americans, in what is
evidently an effort to erode a major constituency of the Republic of
China on Taiwan. About 60% of all Americans traveling to China in
the past year have been of Chinese ancestry; and in recent months
Peking has made special efforts to bring groups of Taiwanese resident
in the U.S. to the PRC for "friendship" tours.

In contrast to the above areas of activity, the PRC has not given
positive responses to a number of official communications addressed
to them via the Paris channel. A series of proposals presented in early
November for sports and artistic exchanges, and a visitation by a group
of state governors, has not been answered.[2] In late July we proposed
to the PRC that we begin negotiations on the issue of private U.S. claims
against the PRC, but as noted in a memorandum to you of January 3
(at Tab A),[3] their response has been an ambiguous one of expressing
the intent to give our proposal "positive consideration," while in fact
focussing attention on the details of individual cases and putting off

---

[2] In telegram 204265 to Paris, November 9, 1972, the Department requested that
the Embassy solicit Chinese reaction to possible visits to the PRC by several American
groups involved in sports or music. (Ibid.)

[3] Attached but not printed.

efforts to establish a general framework for the resolution of this impediment to the expansion of economic relations.

In political matters, the PRC has taken a low-key and two-sided approach to the Vietnam situation, at once expressing verbal support for their Indochina allies, but keeping the tone of their rhetoric against the USG quite cool. On December 22, Peking made an oral protest via the Paris channel in response to the damaging of one of their ships in Haiphong Harbor during a U.S. bombing raid. Throughout the past three months, PRC public statements have continued to call for a peaceful resolution of the Vietnam war, and they have avoided attacking the President by name. More recently they have asserted, however, that the U.S. "went back on its word" in not signing the October draft agreement to end the war; [*less than 1 line not declassified*] Chinese diplomats in Europe have begun to express doubts about the "sincerity" of the U.S. in ending the war. At the same time, the PRC leadership responded to the President's New Year's greeting cards by sending a standard card of their own to the President via Paris, and in late December Foreign Minister Chi P'eng-fei sent a cordial letter to Secretary Rogers thanking him for the exchange of language teaching materials and requesting that such exchanges continue.

Regarding the Taiwan situation, the Chinese have begun to suggest to foreign diplomats—as Mao did last July to French Foreign Minister Schumann—that Taiwan is not really an obstacle to the normalization of Sino-American relations. In addition, Peking's media, as well as their "people-to-people" contacts with Overseas Chinese, have begun efforts to shape opinion among relevant groups of Chinese in the U.S., Japan, and Taiwan for "liberation" of the island.

Areas for Further Progress

Chinese authorities have indicated to several recent visitors that once the Vietnam war is concluded there will be an acceleration in the expansion of Sino-American relations. How far and how fast they might be prepared to move in governmental contacts remains to be seen. Following is a series of suggested bilateral actions which might be taken in the next six months or so which would visibly improve Sino-American relations and build the groundwork for more fundamental steps in the normalization process—particularly the eventual establishment of diplomatic relations. This set of issues would remove important obstacles to progress, yet each can be handled in such a way as to sustain both ambiguity and flexibility about the pace of progress in the normalization process.

Release of U.S. Prisoners

At present the PRC is detaining three American citizens. Two military officers, Major Philip Smith and Lt. Commander Robert Flynn, have been held since 1968 when their aircraft—involved in hostilities related to the Vietnam War—were shot down over Chinese territory. We assume that the PRC will be unwilling to release these men in advance of a prisoner release by Hanoi; but should progress on a peace agreement in the next month or two reach the stage of a return of American prisoners from Vietnam, it would create the context for the PRC to release these two men. Indeed, our expectation is that the Chinese are likely to release these men without our raising the issue with them as a gesture of good will in the context of an ending of hostilities in Vietnam, and as a demonstration of their desire for further progress in Sino-American relations.

A somewhat more complex case is that of John Downey, a USG employee held prisoner since Korean War days. Downey's original life sentence was commuted by the Chinese in late 1971 to five additional years. In October of that year, and again in June of 1972, the Chinese indicated to us that prisoners might obtain early release on the basis of good behavior. Otherwise, they were non-committal when you raised the Downey case with them. We have had reports over the past two months that Downey's elderly mother is in increasingly poor health. Thus, you may wish to raise again with the PRC the matter of Downey's release as a humanitarian action which would give visible reinforcement to our mutual efforts to further normalize relations. We would not be surprised, however, if the Chinese took their own initiative in this case as well as with the release of Flynn and Smith.

Economic and Trade Matters

American trade with the PRC increased significantly during 1972, totalling over $170 million with the balance strongly in our favor. Interest in the China market among U.S. businessmen has expanded along with the increase in trade, and to cope with this we have taken steps, with your approval, to form the *National Council for Sino-American Trade*. We notified the PRC of the formation of this private group via the Paris channel in late December, and now are working with State, CIEP, and Commerce to bring this council into active being.

There remain several major outstanding economic issues in Sino-American relations which impede the development of trade. In July of 1972 we proposed to the Chinese that we begin negotiations on the question of *private American claims against the PRC*. The Chinese, as noted earlier, gave an ambiguous reply to our proposal, requesting additional information on specific cases. On January 3 we sent you a memorandum,[4] on which you have not yet acted, recommending that:

—We supply the PRC with a summary of the Foreign Claims Settlement Commission decisions on private U.S. claims against them.

---

[4] Attached but not printed.

—We provide them as well with a recently completed Treasury census of PRC assets blocked by the USG.

—At some appropriate time you raise with PRC authorities the desirability of moving on the claims negotiations in order to further progress in the normalization process.

We have, in addition, learned that the PRC is very much interested in securing *Most Favored Nation* tariff treatment. At a time when we are planning to request MFN authority from the Congress for the Soviet Union, the PRC will undoubtedly feel discriminated against if we do not accord them equal status.

The PRC is also very interested in having a *trade exhibition* in the U.S., apparently because of their growing trade imbalance with us. PRC officials raised this matter with officials of the National Committee on U.S.-China Relations during their recent visit to Peking, and suggested that the National Committee draw up a proposal for such an exhibition.

Two additional problems relate to *textile exports* and provision of *end use information for products under U.S. Export Control*. Chinese cotton textiles are entering the U.S. at an increasingly rapid rate. We have prevented Commerce from becoming too excited about this, but if imports continue, there will be complaints from the domestic producers and foreign countries whose access to the U.S. textile market is limited by negotiated quotas. With regard to end use information, the Chinese have not seen fit to provide such data. Unless they do so it will be very difficult to extend export licenses on a large number of products requiring that the purchaser provide assurance of peaceful end use. David Packard's company is one of many producers now facing this problem.

It would be very useful to discuss with PRC officials these various economic issues. Moreover, most are interrelated, or can be utilized in an integrated scenario to achieve our objective of removing impediments to the smooth development of Sino-U.S. trade. The Chinese interest in a trade exhibition and MFN might be wrapped up in a negotiating package whereby we secure payment of private claims and unpaid bonds held by American citizens. This would remove the possibility of attachment of PRC products exhibited here (although this problem could be avoided by other temporary measures) or the impounding of any of their ships or aircraft which might call at U.S. ports. Solution of the claims and blocked assets issues would be a visible step which would improve the economic climate, thus making it easier for the President to request from Congress authorization to negotiate with the PRC an MFN agreement. In addition, we could explain to the Chinese the need for end use information and the type of data required, thus facilitating their purchases of U.S. products. The textile problem presumably can be worked out amicably if we go to them with a reasonable limiting figure, ask them to confine their exports to it, and negotiate on any differences.

Permanent U.S. Representation in Peking

While PRC authorities were unresponsive to our low-key suggestion of October 1971 that we establish some form of permanent U.S. presence in Peking, progress on Vietnam and the concomitant prospect of a reduction in the U.S. military role on Taiwan may make the Chinese more inclined to accept some form of American representation in their capital. This might take a number of forms: a non-governmental "liaison office" for the purposes of coordinating trade and cultural exchange activities; a semi-official office for the same purposes, but staffed in part by USG employees who could perform communication and representational functions; or by an official presence of low visibility, such as a special interests section in the embassy of a friendly country already accredited to the PRC (presumably the British).

From the U.S. perspective a special interests section would be the preferred choice as this would give us maximum control over the selection of personnel and the conduct of affairs. However, it is our sense that at present the PRC is most likely to respond favorably to the notion of a "liaison office" related to trade and cultural coordination. Chinese trade officials, at their own initiative, mentioned to the National Committee delegation which visited Peking in December the past PRC practise of establishing unofficial trade offices with countries with which they do not have formal diplomatic relations. (This·was the case with Japan and Italy before they established diplomatic relations with Peking, their trade offices then being converted to commercial sections of their embassies.) It is unclear whether this was a signal of Chinese intent. A good case can be made, however, that at this point in time interests on both sides would be served by some more formal point of contact in Peking (or offices established on a reciprocal basis in an American city as well) which would be less cumbersome than the indirect Paris channel.

Cultural and scientific exchanges are likely to expand significantly over the coming year, and the rather ad hoc planning and management arrangements which have been effective thus far will almost certainly have to be regularized. In addition, the development of Sino-U.S. trade would make reciprocal trade offices to facilitate exchange of information a logical development of value to both sides. A liaison office in Peking might be staffed by State Department specialists in cultural and economic affairs on "temporary leave," and by representatives of the National Committee, the Committee on Scholarly Communication, and the National Council on Sino-American Trade in order to give the office a semi-official status. The Chinese might wish to establish a similar type of office in the United States, probably in New York City rather than Washington given the GRC Embassy in the latter location, as well as the proximity a New York office would have to their U.N. mission and to cultural and trading centers.

5.   Conversation Between President Nixon and his Assistant for National Security Affairs (Kissinger)[1]

Washington, February 1, 1973.

Nixon: I also think when you're in Peking you should explore the possibility of my taking another trip there. I don't know whether we should or not, but let me say—of course, if I go we have to put Japan on.

Kissinger: But that might not be bad.

Nixon: Japan is always a problem because of the radicals. But at the present time, I saw something—a Japanese poll indicating that 60% thought that the Emperor should visit us, and 78% wanted the President to go to Japan. So we have a lot of friends in Japan, you know. The Japanese are not all that dumb.

Kissinger: But if you want that option we have to invite the [unclear] Emperor over here.

Nixon: Have the Emperor first?

Kissinger: Yeah.

Nixon: I don't mind having the Emperor.

Kissinger: I mean, if we could put him on the schedule—

Nixon: That .will be the only other visit this year, Henry. It can't be the Zulus or anything else.

Kissinger: But if you have him here then after that you have the option of going there.

Nixon: I would like to go to China, you see, at a time, again, a better time of year, when it's more pleasant. We might get a better reception too with the Chinese at that time.

Kissinger: Oh, no question.

Nixon: And I just don't see him again, you know what I mean? Chou En-lai?

Kissinger: Oh, you certainly would get a popular reception next time.

Nixon: Yeah. And that could be helpful.

Kissinger: Yeah.

Nixon: See?

Kissinger: I'll get this [unclear] set with Chou.

---

[1] Source: National Archives, Nixon Presidential Materials, White House Tapes, Oval Office, Conversation No. 846–2. No classification marking. The editor transcribed the portions of the tape recording printed here specifically for this volume. The President's Daily Diary indicates that this discussion occurred as part of a longer conversation between 9:45 and 10:03 a.m. (Ibid., White House Central Files, President's Daily Diary)

Nixon: Well, just tell him I'd like to do it. There are great important things that I feel that I have to turn this country around. You can
tell him things like that. But I did not want to do it, but tell him that
we have to meet with the Russians. But I want to keep talking to them.

Kissinger: Well, then I'll tell him that—

Nixon: That I would like to do it.

Kissinger: Well, also that we expect if the Russians attack them it's
very useful to have [unclear].

Nixon: Yeah. Yeah. Another point we have to have in mind is what
the hell we do on Taiwan? Now, as you know, I think they might call
in our chip on that. You think they will?

Kissinger: They will, yes. Well what I thought—

Nixon: Our chip there is not too much anyway. All we promised
is that—

Kissinger: We'd pull out our forces.

Nixon: Cut down our sources—forces, right? Vietnam related
forces come out anyway.

Kissinger: The Vietnam related forces come out immediately. And
the other ones would be reduced gradually.

Nixon: So do it.

Kissinger: I thought I should preempt it by telling them when I
get there that we will pull out the Vietnam related forces and give them
a schedule.

Nixon: Right.

Kissinger: That way they can't raise the other forces.

Nixon: Yeah. But you see, what the Chinese have done to work
out, Henry, is this. And I don't know whether this is in their—I mean,
it wouldn't be possible with the jackasses from North Vietnam. The
Chinese may be subtle enough to understand. Taiwan is such a
bustling, productive, et cetera community, they ought to work out some
kind of federation, you know what I mean?

Kissinger: I think they're willing to do that.

Nixon: What I call—like basically, Puerto Rico. And I mean let both
flowers bloom. See my point?

Kissinger: What I think they will come to, what they will gradually accept—

Nixon: Otherwise it's war. You know what I mean?

Kissinger: No, they won't use force. That you can count on.

Nixon: Well, not with us. But how else are they going to get the Taiwanese, for example? [unclear] But I don't see—the Taiwanese are doing
so well economically, Henry, they're never going to let, never going to
say, "All right, we're now going to become part of the PRC." Never.

Kissinger: No, it's not going to happen that way. I think what they will want from us—well first, that we pull out some of our forces. That will get us through this year.

Nixon: Yeah.

Kissinger: For the time being, what they really want from us is protection against Russia. Taiwan is subsidiary. Eventually, we may have to come to a position similar to Japan's, which is that we maintain consular relations in Taiwan and diplomatic relations in Peking, in return for a promise by them they wouldn't use force against Taiwan, but we hope that Chiang Kai-shek will have died before then.

Nixon: Japan has consular relations with Taiwan?

Kissinger: Yeah.

Nixon: It'd be a bitch for us.

Kissinger: It'd be a bastard.

Nixon: Well, the thing to do is to have it build up—

Kissinger: But this wouldn't be, I don't see that—

Nixon: The thing to do is have it build up in American public opinion before then. We just got to do it.

Kissinger: It can't happen much before '75.

Nixon: The later the better. I still think Chou En-lai should consider—reconsider—not Washington, but San Clemente. You see my point?

Kissinger: Let me talk to him about it.

Nixon: You see my point?

Kissinger: What he could do is go to the UN.

Nixon: He could go to the UN; we've talked about that. And then we'd meet up there, you mean?

Kissinger: No. In connection to that, stop in San Clemente.

Nixon: Oh, I see. I will not in 4 years go to the UN. I'm never going there again.

Kissinger: But of course, it hurts you. If he goes to the UN, he's going to give a tough—

Nixon: Sure.

Kissinger: Now the disadvantage of having Brezhnev in October is that he'll certainly go to the UN.

Nixon: Oh, well, Henry that's part of it. What the hell do we care.

Kissinger: We shouldn't care.

Nixon: Look, we always worry about them huffing and puffing. There are worse things.

Kissinger: I think, Mr. President, from our point of view, assuming—we could find a formulation on that nuclear treaty that doesn't drive the Chinese up the wall. The Russians are sufficiently eager to have it, so if we could keep it out there in front of them until October it would buy us good Russian behavior for the rest of [unclear].

[Omitted here is discussion of Kissinger's schedule.]

---

6.   **National Security Decision Memorandum 204**[1]

Washington, February 6, 1973.

TO

> The Secretary of State
> The Secretary of Defense
> The Secretary of Commerce

SUBJECT

> Sale of Inertial Navigation Systems to the People's Republic of China

The President has considered your memoranda on this subject[2] and has decided that the United States should approve the export of eight inertial navigational systems to be included on four Boeing 707 aircraft, as well as that number of INS required for the three Concordes sold to the People's Republic of China. He has disapproved transferring inertial guidance systems from the U.S. Munitions Control List.

---

[1] Source: National Archives, Nixon Presidential Materials, NSC Files, NSC Institutional Files (H–Files), Box H–238, National Security Decision Memoranda, NSDM 204. Secret. Robert Hormats, with the concurrence of Executive Director of the Council for International Economic Policy Peter Flanigan, sent a January 22 memorandum to Kissinger recommending approval of the sale and disapproval of the transfer of civil inertial navigational systems to the Commodity Control List. (Ibid.) On January 30, Hormats sent Kissinger a memorandum recommending the approval of the draft NSDM which Kissinger initialed and forwarded to the President, who also approved it. (Ibid.)

[2] Acting Secretary of State U. Alexis Johnson sent Nixon a November 24, 1972, memorandum supporting the sale of inertial navigation systems to China and advocating the transfer of civil INS from the U.S. Munitions List, overseen by the Department of State, to the Commodity Control List, administered by the Department of Commerce. Johnson noted, "the Departments of Commerce and State and the Federal Aviation Administration are satisfied that separate definitions can be found to distinguish civil from military INS equipment for purposes of export control safeguards." (Ibid.) On January 4, 1973, Laird sent the President a memorandum opposing both the sale of INS to China and the proposed transfer of INS to the Commodity Control List. (Washington National Records Center, RG 330, OSD Files: FRC 330–78–0001, Box 66, China Reds, 452, 1973)

Approval of the sale of INS in this specific case is subject to the following conditions:

—The manufacturer shall retain control by means of serial numbers and shall report annually to the Department of Commerce on maintenance and supply of spares for each unit.
—The equipment should be of the technology level of the Delco Carousel IV or the Litton LTN–51.
—Maintenance and repair standards should be of a Delco "level 0."
—The Boeing sale shall provide only eight extra INS units.

Future export of INS shall continue to be decided on the merits of each case.

Henry A. Kissinger

---

7.   **Memorandum From the President's Assistant for National Security Affairs (Kissinger) to President Nixon**[1]

Washington, February 7, 1973.

SUBJECT

Grant Military Assistance for Taiwan

Defense, State, and we had agreed that because military equipment grants to Taiwan were so small they are not important to ROC security.[2] We also agreed that defense of our entire Security Assistance Program on the Hill would be greatly eased if we could eliminate the small matériel portion of the FY '74 Taiwan program. Accordingly, we substantially increased the Foreign Military Sales credit requested for

---

[1] Source: National Archives, Nixon Presidential Materials, NSC Files, Box 523, Country Files, Far East, China, Vol. XI, Aug 1972–Oct 24, 1973. Secret. Sent for action. A stamped notation on the memorandum reads: "The President has seen." At the bottom of the memorandum is a typed note: "Flanigan concurs." With Holdridge's concurrence, Richard Kennedy sent this memorandum to Kissinger under cover of a January 17 memorandum, recommending he transmit it to the President. (Ibid.)

[2] According to Kennedy's January 17 covering memorandum to Kissinger, the NSC staff in cooperation with the Departments of Defense and State decided to eliminate the military assistance programs to Taiwan and Greece in anticipation of the Congressional discussion of military aid for the 1974 fiscal year. Kennedy noted that the small amount of aid, when combined with the size and growth of Taiwan's economy, made feasible a shift from grant matériel programs to arms sales backed by more generous U.S. Foreign Military Sales credits.

Taiwan and dropped $4 million for grant matériel. ($6 million of grants for training and supply operations would be retained.)

The Secretary of Defense now has urged that we continue a $10 million grant program.[3] This would actually have the effect of merely reinstating the $4 million in matériel grants.

Given the major increase in military sales credits being made available to Taiwan and continuance of our grant training program, I do not believe this is essential. Moreover, I believe we will get more Congressional support for our total program request if we eliminate this very small matériel request from the list.

The Chinese will understand and have for some time been counting on the sales program to satisfy their military hardware needs.

Secretary Rogers continues to believe that it is not necessary to provide the $4 million in matériel grants. Cap Weinberger agrees.

If you approve, I will so advise Secretary Richardson.[4]

---

[3] Laird defended the continuation of the program by citing Taiwan's assistance to the U.S. war effort in Indochina and warned about the uncertainties of the Congressional authorizations that would be used to reimburse Taiwan. (Memorandum from Laird to Nixon, January 13; Washington National Records Center, RG 330, OSD Files: FRC 330–78–0001, China Nats, 091.3, 1973)

[4] Nixon signed the Approve option. On February 14, Scowcroft informed Laird of the decision to eliminate the Military Assistance matériel grants to Taiwan. (Memorandum from Scowcroft to Laird, February 14; ibid.)

---

8.   Memorandum of Conversation[1]

Beijing, February 15, 1973, 5:57–9:30 p.m.

PARTICIPANTS

Chou En-lai, Premier of the State Council
Chi Peng-fei, Minister of Foreign Affairs
Ch'iao Kuan-hua, Vice Minister of Foreign Affairs
Chang Wen-chin, Assistant Foreign Minister

---

[1] Source: National Archives, Nixon Presidential Materials, NSC Files, Kissinger Office Files, Box 98, Country Files, Far East, HAK China Trip, Memcons & Reports (originals), February 1973. Top Secret; Sensitive; Exclusively Eyes Only. The meeting was held in the Great Hall of the People. Kissinger visited Beijing as part of an 11-day trip to East Asia that included stops at Bangkok, Vientiane, Hanoi, and Tokyo.

Wang Hai-jung, Assistant Foreign Minister
Ting Yuan-hung, Staff
T'ang Wen-sheng, Staff (interpreter)
Shen Jo-yun, Staff (interpreter)
Ma Chieh-hsien, Staff
Lien Cheng-pao, Staff

Henry A. Kissinger, Assistant to the President for National Security Affairs
Mr. Alfred LeS. Jenkins, Department of State
Mr. John H. Holdridge, NSC Staff
Colonel Richard T. Kennedy, NSC Staff
Mr. Winston Lord, NSC Staff
Mrs. Bonnie Andrews, Notetaker

(The Premier greeted Dr. Kissinger and his party and led them to the table where the meeting was held. The meeting was preceded by conversation regarding members of Dr. Kissinger's staff who were visiting the People's Republic of China for the first time.)

Prime Minister Chou: (Referring to Mr. Kennedy.) Is he part of the Kennedy family?

Dr. Kissinger: He is a partial replacement for General Haig. He is a financial expert.

P.M. Chou: You mean you want to talk finances.

Dr. Kissinger: He isn't really.

P.M. Chou: And this is the first time for Mrs. Andrews. Welcome.

Dr. Kissinger: The only time I ever exchanged economic views was in the Azores and I was extremely successful because I did not know what I was doing. I had to stick to what I had written down. I couldn't yield. Like your Vice Minister at the UN.

P.M. Chou: This time you also fought another war?

Dr. Kissinger: Yes. That was a very long and difficult negotiation. Perhaps they will continue.

I don't think your southern friends survived for 2,000 years by being easy to get along with.

P.M. Chou: Not necessarily. It is indeed a very precious thing for a country to have such an independent spirit.

Dr. Kissinger: We will have to continue talking with them. I think we have made a reasonable beginning and I think that we are now on a positive course.

P.M. Chou: First of all in welcoming you here we want to congratulate you on the successful negotiation in Paris.[2] So today we meet

---

[2] On January 27, the Foreign Ministers of the United States, South Vietnam, North Vietnam, and the South Vietnamese Provisional Revolutionary Government (PRG) signed a peace agreement in Paris.

here to welcome you and to hear what you envision. You may begin. And you can say anything you want.

Dr. Kissinger: Mr. Prime Minister, on behalf of my colleagues I want to thank you for the warmth with which we have been received. It is always an honor to be here.

P.M. Chou: That is what we are supposed to do.

Dr. Kissinger: You are supposed to carry out foreign policy on the basis of interests, but there is also a strong feeling of warmth. But Mr. Prime Minister I thought I would depart from my past custom of reading a long statement to you. I have this whole book here.[3] I thought I would talk to you in a general way of why we think this meeting is important and why this is an opportune time for the U.S. and the PRC to exchange views on the future direction of our relations. When I came here first in July 1971, we made an important decision to begin normalization of our relations and to set a definite direction of improving relations between our two countries. And we more or less fulfilled the general direction which we had established. Now we are again at a point where we can make important decisions. You have always been very frank in telling us that the war in Vietnam was a major obstacle to improving our relations. Now the war has a negotiated conclusion. Of course, history will not stop in Southeast Asia and, of course, difficulties will remain. But we now have an opportunity, given the nature of the complexities of our task, to put Southeast Asia into the context of our larger relationship. Let me, therefore, review what I think it might be worthwhile discussing on this occasion.

—We should make a general appreciation of the state of our relationship.

—We should talk about the specific problems connected with the normalization of relations:

• The problems of Taiwan. The Taiwan problems and the specific steps we intend to take regarding it and over what period of time.
• The relationship that the PRC and the U.S. can have in the interval.

—We are prepared to discuss also our assessment of the international situation in general. In this connection two problems are of paramount importance:

• Our assessments and our intention with respect to our relations with the Soviet Union.
• The relationships and the future evolution of Southeast Asia.

---

[3] Winston Lord oversaw the creation of Kissinger's briefing book for his trip to China. (Ibid., Visit to the PRC, Briefing Book, February 1973)

We are also prepared to discuss with the Prime Minister our assessment of the evolution in Korea and Japan, and to have an exchange of views on South Asia.

P.M. Chou: South Asia?

Dr. Kissinger: Yes. India and Pakistan. And also to discuss with the Prime Minister what is likely to happen in European politics this year. We have followed with great interest the visits of various European leaders to China and we believe that their experience here has been very good for what we detect as our common objectives. I remember my conversation with the Prime Minister last summer. I believe that the impact of China on the general situation is in the direction which we have discussed. While I have been here I have already mentioned to the Assistant Minister some of the special problems which I am prepared to discuss when we are in smaller groups and I think we might have a review of the general problems that are being discussed in the Paris channel. These are the major topics which I propose, but, before we turn to them specifically perhaps the Prime Minister will permit me to make some general observations.

First, I think that the Prime Minister notices that I am especially inhibited in his presence right now.

P.M. Chou: Why?

Dr. Kissinger: Because I read his remark to the press that I am the only man who can talk to him for a half hour without saying anything.

P.M. Chou: I think I said one hour and a half.

Dr. Kissinger: This is true. But it destroys my professional secret. The only thing that reassured me was that the Assistant Minister told me on the plane that the Kuomintang knew your strategy but couldn't do anything about it.

Now on the general observations that I wanted to make. We find our relationship to have developed in an usually profitable direction and not by accident, because between China and the United States there are no basic differences except those which have been produced by historical accident. When I came here the first time the Prime Minister mentioned to me that various countries were combining to bring pressure to bear on China, but as far as the U.S. is concerned now and in the future, a strong, self-reliant, independent China exercising control over its own destiny is in our own interest and a force for peace in Asia. So our relationship is not an accident of personalities but based on very fundamental calculations. We both are opposed to hegemonial aspirations, not because we want to do each other a favor, but because a drive toward hegemony in one direction must inevitably seek hegemony in another direction. So we believe that our assessment of the situation is very comparable.

Now let me speak first about our special problem, the problem of Taiwan. The Prime Minister is aware of a number of understandings we have with respect to Taiwan. I think it is important that at the beginning of a second term and at the end of the Vietnam war that we reaffirm those in a very formal way. We have said to the Chinese side, and we have had publicly stated in the Shanghai Communiqué, that we acknowledge that all sides recognize there is only one China. We reaffirm that.

P.M. Chou: That was a famous quotation of yours—all Chinese on all sides of the Taiwan Strait agree there is only one China. I have heard that there is a tendency to copy that phrase in other places.

Dr. Kissinger: It was reported to you, but then I thought we had a monopoly on it.

Mr. Jenkins: It is patented.

P.M. Chou: Pardon?

Dr. Kissinger: He speaks with a southern accent some of the time. Secondly, we have affirmed, and reaffirmed, that we will not support an independence movement on Taiwan or encourage it. Thirdly, we will use our influence to discourage any other countries from moving into Taiwan or supporting Taiwan independence. Fourth, we will support any peaceful resolution of the Taiwan issue and we will give no support whatsoever to an attack from Taiwan against the China mainland, and we will of course work, as I have said before, toward seeking a normalization of our relations. I am reaffirming this only because we had an election and because the war is over in Vietnam, and want no misunderstanding that this was for tactical reasons or because of the election in the U.S. This is the considered policy of our Government. Also, we told you, both I and the President, that upon the conclusion of the Vietnam war we would reduce our forces on Taiwan. During this visit I will give you a precise schedule of our reduction during this year, and it will be substantial. This is being done on a confidential basis because we cannot start until our withdrawal from Vietnam is completed in April. But I will give you a precise schedule.

P.M. Chou: They are saying that you are going to build or assist Chiang Kai-shek to build fighters on Taiwan.

Dr. Kissinger: There are two problems—two separate propositions. One is to give Chiang Kai-shek the Phantom fighter plane. This we have refused. We have not yet made the official notification but I tell you it has been refused and he will be notified during the next week.

The second is not the production but the assembly from U.S. parts of some shorter range fighter planes to replace fighter planes that we borrowed for some other purpose. These planes cannot reach the mainland.

P.M. Chou: They might be able to come but they won't be able to go back.

Dr. Kissinger: No, they don't have the reach to come.

P.M. Chou: If they don't want to go back they can come here!

Dr. Kissinger: But that might be true of the F–4s too. But this . . . we are aware of our understanding in this respect of not augmenting their capability. Our intention in some of these measures is to make it easier for us to disengage from the direct military supply relationship, and we will be prepared to discuss with the Prime Minister future steps that can be taken after this year. At any rate I want to repeat what was discussed when the President was here, and in addition to the steps that I mentioned to the Prime Minister, we will complete the steps that we envisioned while the President was here during the present term of the President. Part of these will occur before our election in 1974, and the remainder after the election.

Translator: You mean the mid-term election?

Dr. Kissinger: Yes. In the meantime we are prepared to proceed as rapidly with the specific steps toward normalization as the PRC may be prepared to take. I would like to explain to the Prime Minister our reasoning. We believe that in assessing military developments, certain proposals which have been made to us, and about which we have informed you, have been submitted against other nations, from which it is not inconceivable that in the next three years some other country may want to develop at least the opportunity for realizing hegemonial aspirations toward one side or the other. I do not predict what will happen, but I am saying that there is a better than even chance it will happen during the term of our President. And when we discuss some of the special problems we can explain to you why. We consider it important.

P.M. Chou: This other country that you mention is seeking hegemonial aspirations. So you mean that they seek hegemonial aspirations toward Taiwan in particular or toward the whole Asian-Pacific region?

Dr. Kissinger: The whole Asian-Pacific region. They may develop some moves toward Taiwan, but basically with respect to the whole Asian-Pacific region.

P.M. Chou: It may also get its satellite countries to cooperate. You probably got some information in Hong Kong.

Dr. Kissinger: Yes, but also in some of the conversations which we and you might be familiar with here. It is very noticeable that they have had some conversations with satellite countries, and for that matter with some Western European countries.

Now with respect to the Soviet Union, we are pursuing a very complicated policy which I will explain to you, and when we discuss it, will be discussed in more detail. At this point I want to concentrate on the basic objectives. We want to bring about a situation in which it becomes clear to our people that an attempt to bring about hegemony in the Asian-Pacific region is not only contrary to the Joint Communiqué, but to point out to our people that the Joint Communiqué represents a basic U.S. interest and is not just polite words issued at the conclusion of the visit. So when we speak about speeding up the process of normalization and make it more visible, it is frankly not because we consider the existing channels inadequate. Almost always they work extremely well. But, because it is important, we believe, in the 2–3 years we have had available, to stress to some extent the symbolic nature of this relationship. Frankly, this is our attitude toward trade, exchanges, and those other matters. To us, it is not a commercial problem, and in this respect our attitude is quite different from the Japanese attitude.

P.M. Chou: But our approach is even far away from the Japanese approach. Has your Department of Commerce given you statistical information?

Dr. Kissinger: Actually, our commercial relationship has developed extremely well.

P.M. Chou: But the situation about Sino-American trade is quite the opposite than to Sino-Japanese trade because your imports of Chinese commodities are much less than our imports of American commodities and much less than the rate of imports from Japan. I can give you examples. And, actually some of the trade between China and the U.S. last year has been indirect although it need not be indirect. It was because of some statement by the press last year that compared our agricultural situation with the Soviet Union's and the fact that the harvest last year was less than the year before, that made us call off the trade.

Dr. Kissinger: Yes, I now about that, and it's also the total inability of some of the departments to keep quiet. We have finally taught a few persons in the State Department, such as Mr. Jenkins, he is one of them. He is here on probation. (laughter)

P.M. Chou: I think we should also put in a good word for Mr. Rogers. On many occasions he says the same things as you. So, it is good for him to come with you? Also, Mr. Jenkins.

Dr. Kissinger: Yes, because if so we have some continuity in our policy.

P.M. Chou: And we think that is one of the good things about your President's serving a second term.

Dr. Kissinger: Exactly. You can be sure that his policies will be such as not to be affected by any changes. So that is why we think that this exchange at the very beginning of the new Administration can be very significant. This is our general approach, and it is in this spirit that I am planning to conduct our discussions. And now I would be happy to speak about any subject more thoroughly—I know I need not tell the Prime Minister this.

P.M. Chou: I would like to thank you first of all for your initial assessment and explanation. And since you have mentioned the international situation I would like to ask you what are the views of the Nixon Government in its second term regarding the over-all situation? Do you think we are moving toward a kind of relaxation, or toward a more intense competition, including a military competition?

Dr. Kissinger: Well, Mr. Prime Minister, we speak a great deal about an era of peace, and there are certain factors which point in that direction. I think, for example, that if certain leading countries show restraint in Southeast Asia, that that area can be tranquil over the next four years. But when we speak in longer term trends I must give the Prime Minister our honest opinion that there are countervailing factors as well. First, there is the factor of the intensive Soviet military preparation which occurred really in all directions simultaneously. Now, I may have a too skeptical assessment of human nature, but I cannot believe that these preparations are being made so that the Soviet leaders can be more pleasant toward us. And, indeed, for the Prime Minister's information I have just ordered a study by our intelligence department of what rationale such leaders might have in their minds when they push for an increase of both strategic and tactical weapons in this particular time frame. We know the facts, but we need the motivation.

The second factor in the situation is the intellectual confusion in Western Europe. The Prime Minister and the Foreign Minister have had occasion to meet with many of the leaders of Western Europe. I don't know if you agree with my judgment, that this is not a period in which leadership in Europe is accomplished via precision of thought. So one problem is that you have here, in effect, local party chieftains who are conducting foreign policy from domestic considerations and who seek to avoid difficulties and complications over what might happen. The result is that one of the richest areas in the world is not playing this role to which its history and resources entitle it and, therefore, it is not acting as a counterweight to the extent it should. We will, if you are interested, discuss this more in relation to the European Security Conference and the MBFR Conference. A third problem area is Japan.

P.M. Chou: Before you go into that I would like to interrupt. Do you know a bit about Chairman Mao's conversation with Mr. Schumann?

Dr. Kissinger: I know Mr. Schumann's version, which improves with each month.

P.M. Chou: But I believe he transmitted the Chairman's words to Pompidou.

Dr. Kissinger: I only know what he told us.

P.M. Chou: One of the things that the Chairman told Mr. Schumann was that if a great war broke out in Europe, including a large-scale nuclear war, France would still have to rely on the U.S. This maybe shook them a bit.

Dr. Kissinger: Yes, it did. Since this is not necessarily the policy of the French Government he didn't tell us quite that much, only about one half of it. But I have enough experience now with the Chinese way of presenting issues to know that if you present anything at all, you do it completely. So I assumed somewhat more was said than what we were told.

P.M. Chou: Sir Alec Douglas-Home seemed to have more understanding.

Dr. Kissinger: Yes, yes.

P.M. Chou: And the results of the West German elections is that the two original parties are still in power. But it was the foreign spokesman of the minority party who came to China.

Dr. Kissinger: Yes.

P.M. Chou: But, they also have to admit that after their Ostpolitik has been put into effect, changes have now begun to appear.

Dr. Kissinger: The Germans believe that if there is a choice between two policies, the best thing is to carry them out simultaneously. (laughter)

P.M. Chou: Maybe that is why their original Ambassador to the U.S. has now been sent to our country—because he supported Adenauer. And, therefore, it might be more suitable to accredit him to China than to your country.

Dr. Kissinger: We would be prepared to support Adenauer's party but it can't seem to win an election.

P.M. Chou: But Mr. Schroeder came first to China, and his work was done not too badly.

Dr. Kissinger: Yes, his work was done well.

P.M. Chou: The question in Europe is not entirely one of ideological confusion, but because there are peaceful illusions which were created by those now in power, and the people might have been taken in. The Soviet Union has made great use of that. I believe you said that we represented Western Europe in meetings with Western European Foreign Ministers, and indeed, I said to each foreign minister from Western Europe that I didn't believe peaceful illusions should be maintained. It seemed that Mr. Schroeder has a clear idea of that.

Dr. Kissinger: Yes, he had. The election was lost by stupidity. But, I agree with the Prime Minister on two counts. First, with respect to Germany, within two years they will face a serious dilemma between Ostpolitik and the requirements of maintaining their western orientation. They will find this course did not advance their national aspirations and will lead to great domestic confusion.

P.M. Chou: But they seem to have treated you rather well in the recent battle to support the U.S. dollar.

Dr. Kissinger: Yes, they are not anti-American. And they do not intend to move toward the Soviet Union, at least not at the present time.

P.M. Chou: That can generate quite large-scale illusions.

Dr. Kissinger: Exactly. The danger is not what they intend but the process they can start. They have reached about the limit of their present course, and then they will have to decide whether to make endless concessions or go back closer to the Adenauer line. Many European leaders as individuals know what is necessary, but don't dare carry it out for domestic reasons.

P.M. Chou: This is one of the results created since the end of the Second World War.

Dr. Kissinger: This is true.

P.M. Chou: Perhaps they want to push the ill waters of the Soviet Union in another direction—eastward.

Dr. Kissinger: They don't think in such long-range terms, but perhaps they may bring that about too.

P.M. Chou: Not necessarily, but we can discuss it at a later time. Is that what you are thinking about?

Dr. Kissinger: Whether the Soviet Union attacks eastward or westward is equally dangerous for the U.S. The U.S. gains no advantage if the Soviet Union attacks eastward. In fact, if the Soviet Union attacks it is more convenient if it attacks westward because we have more public support for resistance.

P.M. Chou: Yes, therefore, we believe that the Western European aspiration to push the Soviet Union eastward is also an illusion.

Dr. Kissinger: I don't think that they want to push the Soviet Union eastwards. They believe that the Soviets don't have any aggressive intentions anyway.

P.M. Chou: Do you believe that?

Dr. Kissinger: No. It is inconsistent with their military preparations. Every time we analyze the Soviet military preparations—and I am not talking about Siberia, but the strategic forces pointed toward the U.S., there is an intense effort of major military proportions going forward which cannot be accounted for unless one assumes that the option of use is being prepared. So, to get back to the original point, we have to prevent the Soviet Union from breaking out in one direction or another in the next four years. Resisting in the East is politically and psychologically more difficult for us. The West is easier, and we have no interest in pushing them to the East. But the consequences to us of not preventing their pushing to the East is equally dangerous for us. This is our assessment.

P.M. Chou: Therefore, we have to prepare for their coming.

Dr. Kissinger: That is correct.

P.M. Chou: But it seems that Western Europe is not in this respect so fully prepared.

Dr. Kissinger: For an attack on the West or East?

P.M. Chou: For an attack on them. At least they do not realize the menace it presents.

Dr. Kissinger: The Europeans do things which pass comprehension, and can only be done by irresponsible leadership. For example, I have one personal obsession with respect to NATO. NATO military dispositions are supposed to be on the basis of supplies for 90 days, but they have done it on an average basis so that in some categories there are 120 days and in others, 35 days, as if a war can be run on anything but a minimum basis. So they don't do you any good if sometimes you run out of the goods. (laughter) This is the bureaucrats' conception of strategy. Then they have not standardized among each other the rate of gasoline, etc. So we do not even know what it means. I don't want to bore you with these details, Mr. Prime Minister, but this is something that I will settle within the next two years because I won't stop until it is settled. This is too stupid not to be solved.

P.M. Chou: Yes, and this is something that the Soviet Union can use both militarily and politically to break down the Western European countries one by one.

Dr. Kissinger: Yes, especially politically because I believe it is too dangerous for the Soviet Union to attack Western Europe. We have 7,000 nuclear weapons in Western Europe and many other weapons, and they can never be confident enough that we won't use them. You know the Soviet leaders. I made a comment about their bureaucracy which they did not like. They do not like to take excessive risks.

P.M. Chou: What I meant by military and political aspects was that they would use this military threat to overcome the Western European countries politically one by one.

Dr. Kissinger: I believe that they will first create such an atmosphere of peace that they can thereby free themselves to move East or South.

P.M. Chou: We think that first of all they want to achieve a certain success in dividing the Western Europe nations politically. So in this aspect you should forgive President Pompidou because if you don't help him in the election and it falls to the Communists or Socialists, the situation will be greatly different.

Dr. Kissinger: We strongly favor Pompidou.

P.M. Chou: You must forgive other points. It isn't easy for him to turn around that corner.

Dr. Kissinger: We forgive. We have shown considerable restraint. We didn't respond to him as we did to his colleague in Sweden.

P.M. Chou: The comparison is favorable to the Swedes in that they stayed the same, while you faced Madame Gandhi, an Asian, down. This does not add much luster to Asia. As soon as the Secretary of State opened his mouth she softened.

Dr. Kissinger: I liked the fact that she said she wasn't talking especially about the U.S. I have been looking for a country that she might have been talking about.

P.M. Chou: And Mr. Heath probably also had some complaints to present in the White House although he is one of your friends.

Dr. Kissinger: In the relations among friends there are always some problems but he didn't have any significant complaints. He would agree with what you and I are saying. We have a problem, I say this confidentially, about the British nuclear program which is becoming obsolete because of advances in the Soviet Union's program. And we, again this is very confidential, we are working on ways to keep them in the nuclear business because we don't want them to leave it. We are in the process of determining what of our advanced technology we can give them. And we will solve this problem. But it was a very amicable discussion. There were no disagreements.

P.M. Chou: But in the economic field there is always trouble.

Dr. Kissinger: Yes, but between Britain and us there are less than between Western Europe and us.

P.M. Chou: But, of course, Britain is also part of Western Europe.

Dr. Kissinger: Yes, but it can be a positive influence in this respect and in retrospect we probably made a mistake in the 1950's—several mistakes by Mr. Dulles—we discouraged them from integrating in defense in favor of economic union. We should have done both.

P.M. Chou: So that resulted in the military and economic fields developing in an unbalanced way.

Dr. Kissinger: Exactly, they are very strong economically, and weak militarily.

P.M. Chou: But, of course, the Soviet Union has its own weak points. They are just the opposite.

Dr. Kissinger: Exactly, but this may create an incentive at some point to use the military machine while it is still so strong.

P.M. Chou: But once they begin that action there will be no end. This will be a mess for them.

Dr. Kissinger: That is true. And, of course, they must decide if they do it, which direction they want to go.

P.M. Chou: We would welcome it. Would you like to talk about Japan?

Dr. Kissinger: So, if you want we can go on to Japan.

P.M. Chou: Do you want to take a five minute break?

Dr. Kissinger: Yes.

(The meeting adjourned at 7:35 p.m. It resumed again at 7:47 p.m.)

Dr. Kissinger: (Speaking of comedians) There are some American comedians who want to come to China and they are driving me crazy. There is one who . . . You probably don't know about it . . . Bob Hope is a very famous comedian who wanted to do a show in China. He wanted to film his own show in China and he kept plaguing me and I . . . So he submitted a letter to Ottawa and you wrote back, I mean your Government wrote back, saying he had addressed it to the Republic of China. (laughter) So you wrote back that since he addressed it to the wrong country that you couldn't accept it now. I think in any event that your Embassy in Ottawa must operate very efficiently. I know one man who sent a request for a visa. He was told the time was not appropriate. He said, could he leave an application? He was told no, applications were accepted only from those who were given visas. (laughter)

P.M. Chou: So, should we go on to Japan.

Dr. Kissinger: With respect to Japan I am still advocating the negative aspects of its involvement in the world. We think that the normalization of relations between Japan and the PRC is a good thing.[4] It is in our interests. And, as the Prime Minister knows, we not only did not place obstacles in the way, we encouraged it.

P.M. Chou: Yes, because you know that it is our policy to do things step by step and you know also that we do not exclude their contacts with others, and, therefore, it has never touched upon your relations. We only borrowed one sentence from the Shanghai Communiqué. A statement which you signed and which they accepted. A common statement that neither side would seek hegemony. It was copied word for word.

Dr. Kissinger: That is a good stance to generalize.

P.M. Chou: We did it to realize a strategic part of our requirement, and as soon as we did it, a fourth country became nervous and unhappy. A fourth country because three others have already given their views on this.

---

[4] The People's Republic of China and Japan signed a joint statement on September 29, 1972, that established diplomatic relations between the two countries.

Dr. Kissinger: They also pointed that out to us.

P.M. Chou: In your Moscow Communiqué,[5] you changed that sentence to a different version. Perhaps that was the result of a controversy.

Dr. Kissinger: What did it say?

P.M. Chou: I don't have it with me.

Dr. Kissinger: I think it said that we "would not seek" hegemony rather than that we "would oppose" it.

P.M. Chou: Perhaps. But in our Communiqué we said that neither should seek hegemony and that we opposed other countries from seeking that hegemony.

Dr. Kissinger: In any declaration we make with the Soviets, our problem is not to provide anything that will bring an action by them against other countries. Oh, it is related in the Soviet-U.S. Communiqué to the UN Security Council. There is no specific sentence about hegemony. (Dr. Kissinger reads the text.)

P.M. Chou: I think it was something about security interest on a reciprocal basis. It was in the Twelve Principles.[6]

Dr. Kissinger: (Mr. Kissinger reads a section of the Communiqué.) Yes. "They will always exercise restraint in their mutual relations, and will be prepared to negotiate and settle differences by peaceful means." But it makes no specific reference to hegemony. It says "they will do their utmost to avoid military confrontations and to prevent the outbreak of nuclear war . . ." "Discussions and negotiations will be conducted in a spirit of reciprocity, mutual accommodation and mutual benefit."

P.M. Chou: Perhaps it was.

Dr. Kissinger: Yes. To go back to Japan, we value your relations positively because we think it is important that Japan be anchored with as many countries as possible that have peaceful intentions. The danger in Japan is what we already discussed, that the very aggressive economic nationalism which now exists could in time become political nationalism and perhaps even military nationalism.

P.M. Chou: That is what we had previously discussed—that economic expansion would lead into military expansion.

Dr. Kissinger: And certain tendencies indicate at least—our experience is (I don't know what yours has been) that the individual Japan-

---

[5] The text of the agreements signed in Moscow during President Nixon's visit in May 1972 are printed in Department of State *Bulletin*, June 26, 1972, pp. 918–927. The text of the Joint Communiqué is ibid., pp. 899–902.

[6] The text that Nixon and Brezhnev signed on May 29, 1972, laying out the twelve basic principles for U.S.-Soviet relations, is ibid., pp. 898–899.

ese leaders are not particularly impressive but the over-all Japanese performance is extremely impressive. And there is also a danger that if the Japanese pursue this economic policy so aggressively they could get sucked into arrangements with other people with less peaceful intentions in Siberia, the Middle East and Southeast Asia, which could affect their interests. But I only mention this on a balance sheet of positive and negative factors. On the whole, developments have been positive. And then, of course, among the several areas which could lead to difficulties is the Middle East. If the Prime Minister asks me, as I look ahead, do we foresee a period of quiet, I would have to say that the majority of the American people and perhaps a majority of our Government *do* foresee a period of quiet. But, the President, who demonstrated his ability to make the decisions, holds the assessment that I have given. Therefore, you shouldn't be misled by even official statements unless they come from the White House if they deal with the strategic situation.

P.M. Chou: Can you say something about the Middle East?

Dr. Kissinger: In the Middle East, right now the situation is that no conceivable solution will leave the Israelis in as strong a position as they are in now, so therefore they are now not willing for a solution. But any solution which the Israelis are likely to accept will be unlikely to be acceptable to the Arabs. Nor am I sure that the Soviet Union really wants a settlement in the Middle East.

P.M. Chou: In my opinion, that is not true either. I think you are wrong.

Dr. Kissinger: You don't agree with me? How?

P.M. Chou: No, it is that our views approach yours. If the Soviet Union feels that a certain kind of settlement would be in their interest, they would be willing to accept it step by step.

Dr. Kissinger: But they now maneuver in such a way that it is difficult to settle step by step, because they always get enough ahead of the Arabs to prevent them from getting a step by step settlement but don't give them enough military equipment to allow them to reach a military solution.

P.M. Chou: And they not only want to maintain their position in the Middle East but also to use it to expand their influence westward in the Mediterranean Ocean and into the Indian Ocean in the East. They actually have made advances in there and also in the Persian Gulf.

Dr. Kissinger: Yes.

P.M. Chou: And recently there has been a most ugly incident. Three hundred machine guns were found in Pakistan in the Iraqi Embassy, with Soviet markings. That was only the portion that was discovered, and there are more in the hands of the Baluchistanis.

Dr. Kissinger: I can tell you that this was one reason why we sent Mr. Helms to Iran[7]—because he understands these special problems and he will have more authority than our normal Ambassador does.

P.M. Chou: In this aspect, your steps have been taken too slowly and prudently but the Soviet Union has not ceased its activities in the Subcontinent and in the Middle East. And, as soon as the Egyptians chased out their foreign advisers, they immediately settled upon the Iraqis. As soon as the British recognized Iranian sovereignty over the three islands (the Tunbs) the Soviet Union took the opposite course and supported Iraq in breaking relations with Iran. And, when Pakistan has been having some internal disruption, then the Soviet Union has never ceased to support nationalistic ambitions in northwest Pakistan and to send them arms. Therefore, you can see they want to link up the issues of the Middle East with those of the Subcontinent, and one must have sufficient assessment of the new Czars in comparison with the old. The new ones are extremely sly. You must not think that they are overly honest, because the Brezhnev doctrine[8] on the one hand has timid aspects and they talk about reducing nuclear weapons with you, but in another aspect they are not timid at all. They are extremely aggressive. They can disregard all diplomatic promises or courtesies, not to mention that they can consider a document like that as waste paper and abolish it at any time. And, as soon as you slack your steps in that area, they will step in.

Dr. Kissinger: Mr. Helms will be given special authority for the Persian Gulf, and also for getting arms to Pakistan through Iran.

P.M. Chou: But they can't be weapons like you gave them last time from Jordan.

Dr. Kissinger: The weapons were all right, but their training was not. There were only 21 planes.

P.M. Chou: You can't fight with some of them like that.

P.M. Chou: But you gave Thieu quite a lot very quickly, including over 30 aircraft from Taiwan. You think we are easy to talk to. You want to reach out to the Soviet Union by standing on Chinese shoulders.

Dr. Kissinger: No.

P.M. Chou: I am speaking now because you know we wouldn't care about this sort of thing because we look at things from the strategic point of view. The more you do this, the more naughty the Soviet Union becomes. That is why I spell out everything.

---

[7] Richard Helms was appointed Ambassador to Iran on February 8 and presented his credentials in Tehran on April 5.

[8] The Brezhnev Doctrine asserted the right of the Soviet Union to intervene in any socialist state in which the leading role of the Communist party was threatened.

Dr. Kissinger: We try to look at things from the strategic point of view as well. By standing on Chinese shoulders, what can we gain?

P.M. Chou: That is what I want to prove to you. And you moved a lot of military equipment into South Vietnam.

Dr. Kissinger: South Vietnam was a special case. We had to see if we could overcome obstacles to the negotiations, but we had accepted restrictions on arms supplies and needed to give as much as possible in advance of a settlement. There were no restrictions on arms supplies to the other side. It had nothing to do with the Soviet Union.

P.M. Chou: You mean that it had something to do with China?

Dr. Kissinger: No. It had something to do with North Vietnam and I wanted to explain why we sent these supplies to South Vietnam. It had to do with the fact that there is no restriction on the importation of weapons into North Vietnam, and that is why I am explaining to the Prime Minister why this situation is not comparable to the Pakistan situation. I'm being very honest. If we want to make a deal with the Soviet Union, we don't need China for that. And it would be equally dangerous for both of us if either tried to use the other now to move against the Soviet Union.

P.M. Chou: Neither would it be favorable to the world.

Dr. Kissinger: If the assessment which we have discussed here of the possible Soviet motivation is correct, then we would be working with the threat against the potential victims and that makes no sense.

I will discuss with the Prime Minister our precise strategy toward the Soviet Union. I believe, Mr. Prime Minister, that you're extremely dangerous if one should attack your basic interests, so I don't assume that China is not going to react if one attacks your basic concerns. We have, I think . . . the reason we talk so frankly here is because confidence in our intentions has to be the key element in our relations, and we have worked very hard on this. Little tricks are very stupid in this connection. Let me say one more thing about the Middle East. First, with respect to such things as Baluchistan and other areas, if you ever have information which suggests we could do something useful, I would appreciate it if you would let us know and we would be very grateful.

P.M. Chou: Madame Bhutto will be here around the 17th and wishes to meet you.

Dr. Kissinger: I would be delighted.

P.M. Chou: And she will tell you much more about South Asia and the Subcontinent.

Dr. Kissinger: Will it be announced?

P.M. Chou: It is not necessary. She will be living in the same compound.

Dr. Kissinger: I wouldn't mind seeing her and having it announced after I return to Washington. It would be difficult to have it announced while I am here.

P.M. Chou: And President Bhutto's search of the Iraq Embassy also is a courageous act because it was very clear that the Soviet Union was behind it all. And then the Soviet Union had already had its hands in the middle of the affairs of the Pakistanis.

Dr. Kissinger: I had already planned to suggest to you that I pay a courtesy call on Madame Bhutto.

P.M. Chou: This would be very useful because now is a time when the Soviet Union is advancing full speed in that area. It is true that the oil interests in the Middle East and the Subcontinent are something that cannot be ignored, and because you have slackened, they have taken the initiative. It is a weak spot.

Dr. Kissinger: As I have pointed out to the Prime Minister, I think the Marxist theory is wrong in one aspect. (The Prime Minister sits up sharply.) Marxist theory holds that most capitalists understand what their own interests are, but in my experience, most capitalists are idiots. What we are doing now . . . (Mr. Kissinger does not finish.)

P.M. Chou: But you must know that Marx and Lenin said also that monopolistic capitalism does not always regard the nationalistic interests. They are not patriotic. You also must admit the American monopolists were this way in regard to Europe, Japan and have caused the present situation.

Dr. Kissinger: But mostly through stupidity and not design.

P.M. Chou: You can put it that way but it was because they have short-sighted interests.

Dr. Kissinger: Yes. But I understand you have some capitalists on that PIA flight.

P.M. Chou: Some from your good country.

Dr. Kissinger: Yes. Is it true that Mr. Kendall is also coming?[9]

P.M. Chou: I don't know the name. I am not very familiar with that name.

Dr. Kissinger: We are staggered by the thought of selling Pepsi-cola to 800,000,000 Chinese. (laughter)

P.M. Chou: They are also bringing a Rockefeller from the Morgan group.

Dr. Kissinger: I will tell you who they are bringing to you when I see the list. But I must say that the thought of 800,000,000 Chinese drinking Pepsi-cola boggles my mind. (laughter)

---

[9] Donald Kendall was Chief Executive Officer of Pepsi-Cola and a friend of Richard Nixon.

Dr. Kissinger: Actually, perhaps you don't know, but the eventuality you just mentioned may not be an immediate reality. However, a Canadian was knighted and went to the *London Times*.[10]

P.M. Chou: He came last year?

Dr. Kissinger: Was he prepared to serve you, Mr. Prime Minister? He does not have a low opinion of you.

P.M. Chou: He invested in Hong Kong. He said he could make money that way. At that time he was impressed that he was talking with Chinese Communists. He told me the various ways of making money. But one thing he told me was quite good. He told me, for instance, how he bought the *London Times* from someone else. And he said he wanted to keep a newspaper with the prestige of the *London Times* as a famous newspaper that did objective reporting. And he said as for all the other newspapers in his chain, he did not care about them. He would let them follow whatever made money and according to whatever region they were in. So that they would have opposite views.

Dr. Kissinger: That is true. He wants them to buy both papers.

P.M. Chou: And he told me how to make money. And his managing editor was sitting at his side, and he said that was the only paper he had that he would let lose money. And I gave him a book by Mr. Maxwell about the Sino-Indian war.[11]

Dr. Kissinger: You gave that to Alec Home, too. You are a great agent for that book. I read it after we met in July 1971 and actually they used the same tactics against you that they had used in Pakistan. The same diplomacy. The only difference was that your army was more efficient. Was it true that you repaired all the captured weapons and returned them?

P.M. Chou: Yes. And they took them. They signed a receipt. (laughter)

Dr. Kissinger: Now the second point about the Middle East is that we believe many mistakes have been made. We believe too much of the diplomacy has been public and therefore both sides have taken positions which make negotiations very difficult. Both sides have also used the opportunity to put forward positions which the other side finds impossible to accept. So what we are now attempting to do, and this is again not known by anybody, not even by Mr. Jenkins' colleagues, we have been working with my opposite number on Sadat's staff for six months and we have just now arranged to bring him to America for an official

---

[10] The Canadian media magnate Roy Thomson had bought *The Times* of London in 1966.

[11] Neville Maxwell's book, *India's China War* (London: Cape, 1970), contended that India was largely to blame for the 1962 Sino-Indian conflict.

visit of just one day. That means nothing, it's just for show. But when he comes to New York we will arrange for him to disappear for two days, and I will spend that time with him in order to see if it is possible to get a solution based on Arab interests and not on the interests of an outside power, and bring about a rapid solution.

P.M. Chou: Like you disappeared to Peking?

Dr. Kissinger: Yes. And no other country knows about this yet, and we may have side by side, public talks which will be a facade for the really important private talks. If you want, we will keep you informed and if you agree with what we are doing, perhaps if you want you might use your own influence. There is a chance of getting a peace settlement in the Middle East but, of course, you will judge this after you know what the positions are. With respect to the oil problem, we have created a committee in the White House composed of Secretary Shultz, Mr. Ehrlichman and myself to create a new policy toward energy, and particularly oil. We are trying to . . . (Mr. Kissinger does not finish.) At this moment all oil producers treat all the oil companies equally, with the result that the Western oil interests are financing Iraq. We want to find a policy where we can shift funds, for example from Iraq to Iran. That will be in train within the next four months. It is also for the Prime Minister's personal information—for his ears only.

P.M. Chou: And what about South Asia and the Subcontinent?

Dr. Kissinger: We are now facing a very difficult Congressional situation, not just with respect to South Asia, but generally.

P.M. Chou: You mean the pro-Indian influence is strong?

Dr. Kissinger: Yes, extremely strong. And the pressures to avoid getting militarily involved are also very strong.

P.M. Chou: Perhaps it must be easy for you to do some work in Bangladesh.

Dr. Kissinger: On the military side, we will release all the military equipment for Pakistan which we have blocked, including 300 armoured personnel carriers. This will evoke violent opposition including from our own bureaucracy.

P.M. Chou: Such a tiny bit?

Dr. Kissinger: Yes. I am just telling you the facts.

P.M. Chou: Is it because of the large investments in India?

Dr. Kissinger: It is not an economic problem, it is essentially because of our intellectuals, newspapermen, and I must say our bureaucracy are basically pro-Indian. In the whole post-war era they have looked on India as our greatest Asian friend. Secondly, when Helms gets to Iran . . . (Mr. Kissinger does not finish.)

P.M. Chou: You mean after Chang Kai-shek got to Taiwan. Of course, otherwise Chiang Kai-shek would be number one.

Dr. Kissinger: Yes. Secondly, after Helms gets to Iran we will work out a means whereby we can shift some equipment from Iran to Pakistan and we will make a maximum effort in the economic field to aid Pakistan. In Bangladesh, we can be quite helpful. But we would frankly appreciate any ideas you have as to how we might be helpful.

P.M. Chou: You seem to have a large part in the UN relief.

Dr. Kissinger: Yes, that is very easy.

P.M. Chou: But can you do anything to make the Indians let go of the Pakistan POW's?

Dr. Kissinger: Well, it is a great injustice and we have not been successful. We have raised it with the Indians on a number of occasions.

P.M. Chou: Both Madame Gandhi and Mujibur Rahman are both finding that Soviet pressure is becoming unbearable.

Dr. Kissinger: Both are making a major effort to move in our direction.

P.M. Chou: We can't have more contacts with them than we have at the present, because that would embarrass Pakistan too much. Madame Gandhi has made at least ten approaches, and wants to improve relations with China. And Mujibur Rahman has also tried through private channels to improve relations. It is all to get our vote in the UN—our vote which is now opposed to the unjust action to dismember Pakistan with Soviet support. The recent UN General Assembly came to a comparatively good result on that, which you had a hand in.

Dr. Kissinger: Oh, yes.

P.M. Chou: And, finally, Yugoslavia came to feel that their dealings (with the Soviets) are too outrageous.

Dr. Kissinger: They have urged me to visit India for a discussion, but I will not do it.

P.M. Chou: We must stand up for the truth. But this is an issue we don't want to get our hands into. We want to express our attitude, which represents justice, but we feel if we enter in a situation . . . Anyhow, in the UN we will stand perhaps to the final one (to vote for the entry of Bangladesh). The only thing we are going to do is to raise our Chargé d'Affaires in India from a First Secretary to a Counselor. It is probably the only one and we . . . not included them any embassy where we have a chargé d'affaires. [*sic*]

Dr. Kissinger: We have sent an ambassador to India who talks a great deal and who is very exuberant. I cannot always guarantee what he is going to say. They are sending us a new ambassador who is very pro-Soviet. Mr. T.K. Kaul, who formerly was Permanent Under Secretary of Foreign Affairs. (laughter) And, he does not inspire overwhelming confidence. So there will be some slow improvements in our relations. We don't have your subtlety. We have not figured out how to raise a First Secretary to a Counselor. But with our cruder mentality, it is the same intention.

P.M. Chou: It is difficult to deal with that problem.

Dr. Kissinger: Yes. If they (Mr. Kissinger does not finish.)

P.M. Chou: Because quite often what they say doesn't count.

Dr. Kissinger: We want them to move from the Soviet Union, but to do so genuinely and not pretend.

P.M. Chou: We will have to wait and see.

Dr. Kissinger: That is exactly our attitude.

P.M. Chou: But you could probably do more with Bangladesh.

Dr. Kissinger: What does the Prime Minister have in mind?

P.M. Chou: They need economic assistance.

Dr. Kissinger: You want us to give more economic assistance?

P.M. Chou: The best thing to assist them with would be food, grains and those things which are most close to the people's needs, and not large construction projects. Giving them what the Soviets can't give.

Dr. Kissinger: We have a proposal of 30 million dollars for food which I have held pending discussions with you. I wanted to ask you your judgment if you thought it was better to give aid or wait for a bit.

P.M. Chou: So long as your relations with them are normal we think it would be good to do some things that are in the interest of the people of Bangladesh because India doesn't give help, and the Soviets are only interested in their own interests.

Dr. Kissinger: We'll release the $30 million next.

P.M. Chou: Does the Soviet Union have some naval ships or boats (in Bangladesh)?

Dr. Kissinger: Yes. They had mine sweepers in Chittagong, but I understand they did a bad job.

P.M. Chou: Do you think they might have deliberately done a bad job in order to prolong the time? They always want to gain privileges.

Dr. Kissinger: I do not think that they have other than mine sweepers.

P.M. Chou: But they will find other ships to replace them and they will expand in that area. Then, their mine sweepers will break down and they will want to repair them. Then they will set up docks to repair various other ships. And then other naval installations can come.

Dr. Kissinger: There is no question but that they want to establish a naval presence in the Indian Ocean.

P.M. Chou: And Chittagong is one of their targets.

Dr. Kissinger: I wouldn't be surprised.

P.M. Chou: Whether or not Mujibur Rahman will accept this depends on the international arena, of course . . . and in this respect the British have not done a good job. They have not been helpful.

Dr. Kissinger: They are blind.

P.M. Chou: I told the British what you said—I didn't say it was from you—that during the war the British actions there were not very glorious. That was what you wanted me to say.

Dr. Kissinger: Yes. Home said you were as bad as he was. But it was still very accurate because after you told him he took it seriously. And I think he understood it.

P.M. Chou: I didn't understand what you said just now about Southeast Asia, but many of those issues are left over from Dulles. And rather than saying that your policies in Europe were influenced by Dulles, I would rather say your policies in Asia were influenced by Dulles and the time you are taking to change them is much longer than elsewhere.

Dr. Kissinger: No. We have made very dramatic changes in our relations with you.

P.M. Chou: That is true.

Dr. Kissinger: And also ending the Vietnam war was a very difficult matter.

P.M. Chou: Yes, it took four years of your President's term to do that. But the result is that perhaps the war will stop in Vietnam but the fighting in Laos and Cambodia might possibly continue for some time. But the manpower and matériel you poured in is too much.

Dr. Kissinger: Yes, but that is a separate problem from where we are today. We still have to deal with the situation as it exists after the settlement.

P.M. Chou: And do you think it would be so easy for the Soviet Union to reach out into Southeast Asia than to reach out in the Middle East and the South Asian Subcontinent?

Dr. Kissinger: I don't think it would be so easy but I think it is their intention.

P.M. Chou: Their intentions are everywhere. Wherever you have gone they want to go.

P.M. Chou: Unless there is a vacuum. Then the people will take their place. Take, for instance, Cambodia. If you hadn't opposed Sihanouk, then the Soviets wouldn't have stepped in. If you dealt with Sihanouk, do you think it would help?

Dr. Kissinger: I wanted to talk about Southeast Asia. Do you, Mr. Prime Minister, want to do it now?

P.M. Chou: It will be all right to do it tomorrow.

Dr. Kissinger: I am very anxious to talk to the Prime Minister about Cambodia and Laos and what we envision about Southeast Asia and when we understand that we can talk about the concrete problems of the situation.

P.M. Chou: And we can also exchange views on the Soviet issue. I hear you also wanted to have Mr. Jenkins exchange views with our Foreign Minister.

Dr. Kissinger: Yes, in the bilateral . . . We are prepared to go at whatever rate you want to go . . . depending on the obstacles. Mr. Jenkins can at least explain where we want to go. Also, we should discuss the developments in Paris. Because otherwise we will keep your Foreign Minister there for months and he can never visit San Marino. (laughter)

P.M. Chou: You said you had an initial draft you were bringing with you?

Dr. Kissinger: (to Mr. Lord) Have we got it here? I will give it to the protocol person in the Guest House.

P.M. Chou: And you had an exchange with your Vietnamese friends.

Dr. Kissinger: Yes. And they will make some counterproposals which we will have tomorrow or the day after. We have agreed that we would try to avoid controversy at the Conference, as much as possible. So we approach it in a very constructive manner. And we are trying to normalize our relations with the DRV. One of the worst problems we have, they created. They proposed the participation of the Secretary General of the United Nations.[12] (laughter) And we accepted it. We never understood why they proposed it.

P.M. Chou: When you gave them a list of the proposed participants it included Japan and Thailand. It may have included the Secretary General.

Dr. Kissinger: Absolutely not.

P.M. Chou: But you mentioned Thailand and Japan?

Dr. Kissinger: We mentioned Japan. I don't know about Thailand. In fact, we were astonished when they proposed the Secretary General and some of Mr. Jenkins' colleagues wrote papers on it. It was quite new to me. Marshall Green was practically in tears.

Dr. Kissinger: But now . . .

P.M. Chou: I would also like to make it clear that there is some ground for your work. During August, you proposed the Secretary General and the North Vietnamese didn't agree.

---

[12] Kurt Waldheim.

Dr. Kissinger: Maybe. If so, we didn't mean it seriously.

P.M. Chou: At that time they wouldn't agree to Thailand and Japan, and did not mention the Secretary General, and they did not ask our opinion. And later on in relation to the guarantee we had a brief notification. All we saw was the October 26 version.

Dr. Kissinger: That was only a summary.

P.M. Chou: But you confirmed that honestly.

Dr. Kissinger: We had two choices—we could scrap it or confirm it. We had to keep Saigon from digging in too firmly and we had to tell Hanoi we would settle.

P.M. Chou: And you gave a very speedy reply too. Because you underestimated Nguyen Van Thieu. He surprised you.

Dr. Kissinger: Yes, but if we had not done it we would have been in a lengthy discussion with Hanoi. We thought it better to risk a fast answer rather than to get the whole situation confused. Were you surprised at the speed of the reply?

P.M. Chou: No. I appreciated it very much. In numerous documents we have also confirmed the record that you had trouble with Thieu. We saw the mischief that Thieu was bringing and we told our Vietnamese friends about it. We also told them that their attitude was not very friendly.

Dr. Kissinger: They both attacked me.

P.M. Chou: It was an attack from two sides?

Dr. Kissinger: That is right.

P.M. Chou: And it was only after the initialing of the Agreement, on his way back, that Tho told us about that, and he also told us about the issue of the Secretary General, and we thought that they hadn't thought it through.

Dr. Kissinger: Yes, that is right. They admit now they didn't know what they had in mind.

P.M. Chou: I put some questions to him and found the answers unclear. We asked you for clarification. You don't find it easy to clarify either.

Dr. Kissinger: It was not our idea. In our view there are only two possibilities. One is that he would be a participant which is ridiculous because he will talk all the time, which is a bad role for the Secretary General. The other is that he be given some administrative position. And I think if he were made Executive Secretary to the Chairman of the Conference he couldn't act without his approval. And as moderator he couldn't take a position. We think this would be the best role for him consistent with his international status. Your colleagues are thinking it over, and we told them we would discuss it with you. I frankly think they are better at revolutionary warfare than at the diplomatic negotiating table. (laughter)

(The Prime Minister exits the room momentarily.)

V.M. Chiao: On today's meeting we were thinking of issuing an item with the title "Chou En-lai, Premier of the State Council and Chi Peng-fei, Minister of Foreign Affairs, held a meeting with Dr. Kissinger. The Premier of the State Council, Chou En-lai, the Minister of Foreign Affairs, Chi Peng-fei, and Vice Minister of Foreign Affairs, Chiao Kuan-hua, held talks this evening with Dr. Kissinger, Assistant to the President for National Security Affairs. Taking part in the talks on the U.S. side were Mr. Alfred Jenkins, Mr. John Holdridge, Colonel Richard Kennedy, Mr. Winston Lord and Mrs. Bonnie Andrews. Participating on the Chinese side were Chang Wen-chin, Wang Hai-jung, Ting Yuan-hung, Tang Wen-sheng, Shen Jo-yun, Ma Chieh-hsien and Lien Cheng-pao."

Dr. Kissinger: At what time will you release it? What time is it now in America? 8:30 a.m.? So we can say the same thing. And we will do it at noon our time. You can do it whenever you wish, if that is agreeable.

(The Prime Minister returns to the room.)

P.M. Chou: Without all your staff, how could you manage all your work?

Dr. Kissinger: I would do it in one half the time. (laughter)

P.M. Chou: No, really, they are very dedicated people. So, anyway, we won't meet tomorrow morning. So if you want to go visiting in the morning, we can arrange for something. We will discuss that later.

---

9.   Memorandum of Conversation[1]

Beijing, February 16, 1973, 2:15–6:00 p.m.

PARTICIPANTS

Chou En-lai, Premier, State Council
Chi P'eng-fei, Minister of Foreign Affairs
Ch'iao Kuan-hua, Vice Minister of Foreign Affairs
Wang Hai-jung, Assistant Foreign Minister

---

[1] Source: National Archives, Nixon Presidential Materials, NSC Files, Kissinger Office Files, Box 98, Country Files, Far East, HAK China Trip, Memcons & Reports (originals), February 1973. Top Secret; Sensitive; Exclusively Eyes Only. The meeting was held at Villa 3. All brackets are in the original.

T'ang Wen-sheng, Interpreter
Shen Jo-yun, Interpreter
Two Notetakers

Dr. Henry A. Kissinger, Assistant to the President for National Security Affairs
Richard T. Kennedy, NSC Staff
Winston Lord, NSC Staff
Jonathan T. Howe, NSC Staff
Miss Irene G. Derus, Notetaker

PM Chou: Mr. Kennedy has a sprained waist. How is it now?

Mr. Kennedy: Much better through the help of your doctors.

Dr. Kissinger: He hasn't had so much attention since he joined my staff. You're spoiling him.

PM Chou: I have read your draft. I received your draft of the Act of Paris. We haven't received the views of our Vietnamese friends yet.

Dr. Kissinger: We haven't either. They were going to give them to us either today or tomorrow.

PM Chou: Yes.

Dr. Kissinger: We just had a general discussion.

PM Chou: Yes. Let us continue with the topics we discussed yesterday according to your order, but I would like to take up the topic of the Soviet Union first. It is just a restricted meeting.

Dr. Kissinger: Yes, I wanted to do two things with the approval of the Prime Minister. One, I wanted to make a comment about a press conference which our Secretary of State gave yesterday.[2]

PM Chou: [laughs] I have read it today, but I have not paid any attention to it because that is for just dealing with those journalists.

Dr. Kissinger: Exactly. And I also wanted to talk about Soviet policy to the Prime Minister also in the context of his remarks of yesterday that we are "standing on your shoulders."[3] [Chou laughs] All I want to say about the press conference remark about Formosa is to tell you what we actually intend to do. We will withdraw five squadrons of airplanes, of C–130 airplanes, this year. They are transport planes. And the total number of men that this will involve is at least 4,500. This will cut the formal strength on Formosa by over half. We will reduce next year by at least two squadrons of F–4s.

PM Chou: That is the planes you sent in last time.

Dr. Kissinger: That is right. They will be withdrawn next year, and they will not be turned over to the Taiwanese.

---

[2] The text of Secretary Rogers' news conference of February 15 is printed in Department of State *Bulletin,* March 5, 1973, pp. 249–260.

[3] See Document 8.

PM Chou: Yes, you mentioned it last time, and its nickname is "Phantom." Actually it is called F–4.

Dr. Kissinger: That's right—F–4 is the right name. "Phantom" is its nickname.

PM Chou: Why it is called "Phantom?"

Dr. Kissinger: I have no idea. I think because of its speed.

PM Chou: And the shape, too, perhaps.

Mr. Kennedy [to Mr. Kissinger]: It gets in before it can be heard.

Mr. Kissinger: Like a phantom, yes. But we will also reduce in addition to these two squadrons other units next year, but we will not know—we are studying this. We will let you know during this year what they will be. So regardless of what official statements may say, this is our firm intention and will be carried out.

PM Chou: It doesn't matter whether you carry this out sooner or later because we have already fixed our principles during our discussion.

Dr. Kissinger: That is right.

PM Chou: It is all right what the State Department would like to say in order to deal with those journalists.

Dr. Kissinger: Well, this is—however, we have told the Prime Minister on previous visits that after the end of the Vietnam War we would take specific measures on reduction of forces. And we want him to know that these are our intentions. [Chou discusses with his interpreter.]

Interpreter: The Prime Minister was reminding us that after you mentioned the component parts to be assembled by Chiang Kai-shek, this was translated into spare parts, so the Premier said how could the spare parts be put together into a single plane.

Dr. Kissinger: Oh, they transferred some. Now, but I also—I am going to look into this problem when I return to the U.S. We have no intention of augmenting the military strength of Taiwan. What we want to do is to reduce our direct relationship of supplying military equipment. And I will have to—this is a matter that was decided at a period when we were all very occupied with the Vietnam war. But we want to solve the issue during this term of the President.

So now does the Prime Minister wish to discuss Soviet matters, or . . . ?

PM Chou: Yes.

Dr. Kissinger: Do you want me to talk or does the Prime Minister have something to say?

PM Chou: Shall we say a few more words on the Taiwan issue? Do you envisage that there will be a definite time limit for your aid to Taiwan, military aid? Is there going to be another contract after this contract? I don't mean that if you do this for their armed forces that it will mean a great deal. I just want to know something about it so we can coordinate our action during our work. I can assure you that we don't mean that we are going to liberate it by the armed forces. We have no such plan at the moment.

Dr. Kissinger: But what I envisage for this and I must—he [referring to Mr. Kennedy] pointed out to me the technical ways by which we are giving aid but that is not the concern. [Dr. Kissinger and Mr. Kennedy confer.] Mr. Kennedy pointed out that we are not giving military equipment. We are selling it or giving it on some credit.

PM Chou: Yes, we imagined this.

Dr. Kissinger: But that does not change the Prime Minister's basic concern. He doesn't care about . . . I will talk frankly how we envisage the evolution. We think that over the next two years we will have a very substantial reduction of our military forces. We are even now going very slow about giving new military equipment. We do this through administrative means, not as policy measures. For example, as I told the Prime Minister yesterday we have refused the sale of two squadrons of F–4s. During that period we are prepared, depending on what the Prime Minister's preference is, to establish some more visible forms of contact between the PRC and the U.S., a Liaison Office or some trade office. We have to discuss the method. This is for two reasons. For the Taiwan reason and for the Soviet reason which we will discuss later this afternoon. In the next two years we would be prepared to move to something like the Japanese solution but we have not worked this out.

PM Chou: What is the time limit?

Dr. Kissinger: The first two years is the reduction of our forces. Then after 1974 we want to work toward full normalization and full diplomatic relations with the People's Republic of China before the middle of 1976.

Now we would like to keep some form of representation on Taiwan, but we haven't figured out a formula that will be mutually acceptable. And we would like to discuss with you, in the spirit of what you have always discussed with us, some understanding that the final solution will be a peaceful one. In that context we will exercise great restraint in our military supply policy. It is our intention, but I will review . . . I frankly [to Kennedy: Can we find out what contracts we have with them?] I will find out while I am here what contracts we have for the supply of military equipment and which are contemplated and then I can be absolutely—then you will know exactly. But this is the direction in which we are determined to move, and these other details are not really decisive.

PM Chou: Just now you mentioned in passing that aside from the Taiwan question you also mentioned the question of relations between our countries.

Dr. Kissinger: Yes.

PM Chou: So you still envisage there is going to be a Trade Office or a Liaison Office?

Dr. Kissinger: Yes. We would prefer a Liaison Office because we could send better personnel for that.

PM Chou: Does it mean that it will cover a wider range?

Dr. Kissinger: Yes, the Liaison Office could handle the things that are now being discussed in Paris plus a few political things. We believe that the very sensitive matters between us, about which no one outside the White House knows, should continue to be handled in the channel of Huang Hua and me. But if we establish a Liaison Office we would put Mr. Jenkins and Mr. Holdridge into it, and they are two friends who have worked with me and whom we trust.

PM Chou: Do you envisage that this is going to be two-way traffic, that is both sides will establish offices?

Dr. Kissinger: We would be prepared to let you establish a Liaison Office in the U.S.

PM Chou: It is easier for you to establish an office here because in name maybe it is an unofficial one, but actually it may be an official one. But our office in Washington needs to be a nonofficial one which will enjoy various diplomatic immunities. And they wouldn't be able to take part in any diplomatic activities because it would be difficult for them to do so.

Dr. Kissinger: Well, you can set up any office that you think is appropriate in Washington. We would see to it that they would enjoy diplomatic immunities. They perhaps couldn't engage in formal diplomatic activities, but they could be a convenient channel of communication to the White House.

PM Chou: So your Liaison Office would cover a wider range than trade?

Dr. Kissinger: That would be our preference, but we could also have a trade office and in fact give it liaison functions. But I think it would be more appropriate to have a Liaison Office.

PM Chou: We have envisaged both. Since Doctor has mentioned it, it can be discussed after we have reported to Chairman Mao.

Dr. Kissinger: We are prepared to do it either or both together— we are prepared to have a PRC office in the U.S., and you could give it officially a non-official character but it will have diplomatic immunities and will be treated on a diplomatic level, and we will continue whatever business you wish through that office. You could call it a trade office or a new agency, whichever you wish. But if you have other ideas, we will follow your suggestions.

PM Chou: So much for this question.

Dr. Kissinger: All right.

PM Chou: Speaking of the Soviet Union question, last time you told us something about the nuclear treaty. How is the situation now?

Dr. Kissinger: The Soviet Union . . . we thought that if we delayed long enough the treaty would just go away. It is a heroic posture . . . [laughter] but sometimes a necessary one.[4]

But since the end of the Vietnam war they have raised it again. You remember we put a series of questions to the Soviet Union of hypothetical cases. And I asked one hypothetical question: whether, if this treaty were signed and if the U.S. would then attack India, some third country like India which would affect the balance, whether then nuclear weapons could be used. And the Soviet Union gave us a written reply which was cautious. The first situation was what happens in case there is a war in Europe. I asked a series of hypothetical questions. I said, "What happens in case there is a war in Europe, can nuclear weapons be used?" The answer was, "Yes, but not against the territory of the Soviet Union and the United States. Only on the territory of each other's allies." But they said . . . do you want me to read what they said with respect to that situation?

PM Chou: Yes, to add to our interest.

Dr. Kissinger: Their English is not as clear as their intention. So they said "we would like to emphasize that the idea of the Treaty would be served by such a mode of actions in that presumed situation when both the USSR and the U.S. firmly proceed from the necessity to localize the use of nuclear weapons and undertake nothing that could increase the danger of our two countries mutually becoming objects of the use of nuclear weapons." In other words they should be—it is almost incomprehensible in English. It is not the fault of your interpreter. You see, in Article 3 of the treaty it says nuclear weapons can be used in defense of allies. So we asked what happens in case of an attack in Europe, of a war in Europe? Now I will read the sentence again. "We would like to emphasize that the idea of the Treaty would be served by such a mode of actions in that presumed situation"—namely a war in Europe—"when both the USSR and the U.S. firmly proceed from the necessity to localize the use of nuclear weapons and undertake nothing that could increase the danger of our two countries mutually becoming objects of the use of nuclear weapons." It is perfectly clear.

---

[4] In his memoirs, Kissinger describes the diplomacy leading to the Agreement on the Prevention of Nuclear War. He states that Brezhnev first proposed a U.S.-Soviet treaty to renounce the use of nuclear weapons during Kissinger's trip to Moscow in April 1972, to which the U.S. Government responded with stalling tactics that continued into 1973. (*Years of Upheaval*, pp. 274–286)

And then they say in the next paragraph that if such a treaty is signed a war in Europe becomes much less likely. When I asked the question "what happens to allies?", to that they gave this answer.

Then I said, second, "What happens to friends who are not allies who are being attacked?" And to that they said in the same bad English: "If to assume that the USSR or the U.S. might use nuclear weapons (Middle East was mentioned as an example) also to assist states with regard to which neither the USSR nor the U.S. have direct treaty obligations, this would devalue our Treaty."

PM Chou: Does that mean that they wouldn't use . . .

Dr. Kissinger: It means nuclear weapons would not be used. Then I said the third question is: "What happens in situations where a country who is neither ally nor a friend is attacked, but whose weight would affect the balance of power in the world such as, for example, India? Can nuclear weapons then be used?" To that they said the following: "These same views and arguments of ours may be fully applied as well to a third situation, which the American side termed as seriously upsetting the global balance and to illustrate which a most hypothetical example of introduction of Soviet or U.S. troops into India was used."

I will read it again, section by section: "These same views and arguments of ours"—namely the ones applied to other areas where friends are involved—"may be fully applied as well to a third situation, which the American side termed as seriously upsetting the global balance and to illustrate which a most hypothetical example of introduction of Soviet or U.S. troops into India was used. Thus the Soviet side believes that the Treaty should exclude a possibility of using nuclear weapons by the Soviet Union and the U.S. against each other in the two situations outlined above." Colonel Kennedy is new to my diplomatic methods. He has not seen me do these things before.

PM Chou: We have got to know each other very well since we have met each other five times.

Dr. Kissinger: That is right. We have met with each other openly and honestly.

PM Chou: Not only openly but also highly confidential.

Dr. Kissinger: Exactly.

PM Chou: And we mean what we have said.

Dr. Kissinger: Your word has counted, and I think so has ours and since so much . . .

PM Chou: You mean President Nixon and you yourself.

Dr. Kissinger: Our word has counted and so has your word. We have been able to count on what you have said. What I meant to say is we have had a relationship of confidence in each other.

In an attack on a friend who is not an ally, or an attack on a country who is not an ally nor a friend, but whose attack would create a change in the balance, nuclear weapons would be excluded. In other words in the case of the Middle East and the case of India, nuclear weapons could not be used under this Treaty.

PM Chou: Do you mean that you wouldn't use nuclear weapons against each other in such two cases?

Dr. Kissinger: I asked three questions: If the treaty is signed, can nuclear weapons be used in these three cases. Attack against allies. Yes, they can be used but not against the territories of the U.S. and USSR. The second case is against a friend who is not an ally, such as the Middle East. There they say they cannot be used. The third case against a country which is neither an ally nor necessarily a friend, but whose fate could affect the world balance of power, and I gave the theoretical example of India. And they said in that case nuclear weapons cannot be used. Then they asked us a question which we have never answered—we have never answered this communiqué. They have asked us what we would do if another country, for example, a U.S. ally or friend would attack an ally of the Soviet Union? They said in that case they would certainly react, but they asked us what we would do in such a case if they would react. I will read you the sentence if you are interested.

PM Chou: Yes.

Dr. Kissinger: "The kind of reaction of the USSR with regard to the state that made such an attack is not to be questioned—it will be determined by the allied duty of the USSR. But a question suggests itself—how in that situation matters would stand directly between the USSR and the U.S., having in mind that the Treaty on the non-use of nuclear weapons would be in effect between them?" We have never answered this.

PM Chou: Is the word from Mr. Gromyko? Perhaps the thought belongs to Brezhnev.

Dr. Kissinger: This was given to us as a communication from Brezhnev, but we cannot tell. It was unsigned, but we were told it was for the President from Brezhnev. And the treaty was first presented to me by Brezhnev.

Now, in our government, Mr. Prime Minister, nobody knows about this except the President, myself and my staff, and this should never be discussed in any other forum.

Now the present situation is that they have again proposed this treaty and they have again—they have said they would like to sign it when Brezhnev visits the United States. And I have told them we would consider it and let them know.

Now it is perfectly clear that we cannot accept this intention and this policy, so there is no possibility whatever that we will agree to a treaty that contains an obligation not to use nuclear weapons. The only question is a tactical question for us—whether we should reject it completely or whether we should reject it evasively. For example, as we have told Ambassador Huang Hua, we were considering last fall the possibility of a draft in which we would agree to create conditions in which nuclear weapons would not be used and then to define these conditions in such a way that they would amount to the renunciation of force altogether, or to create a commission to study when these conditions will be realized. This is what we are now considering, but to assess that I would be very anxious to have your views. But to make a final judgment one must I think assess the basic strategy towards the Soviet Union because only then can the judgment be made.

So I don't know whether the Prime Minister would like to talk about this immediately or whether we should discuss the basic strategy and then come back to this, or whether he would like to express a preliminary view and then go back to it.

PM Chou: Let us continue our discussion on the strategy.

Dr. Kissinger: Should I? [Chou indicates to go ahead.]

Let me make a few observations which were suggested to me by a half-facetious question of the Prime Minister about whether we intend to stand on the shoulders of China to come closer to the Soviet Union. But since I have learned in five meetings that the Prime Minister never says anything without an intention and perhaps it is a good question, I would like to discuss it while we are discussing strategy.

It just occurred to me. We have had a very unequal relationship in one respect in that your interpreters have had to carry the entire load at every meeting. We are very grateful. [Chou laughs]

Now on the strategy with the Soviet Union—and I think we might begin with your question. There is no doubt that our relations with the Soviet Union accelerated after my visit to Peking in 1971. We expected the opposite actually. So our judgment was wrong. And therefore obviously there is merit in the fact, in the Prime Minister's suggestion that our relations with the PRC have given the Soviet Union an incentive to improve their relations with us. This is not our purpose but this has been a result. But then that in itself is irrelevant because the question is why? What are they trying to accomplish?

Now there are two theoretical possibilities. One is they generally want to bring about a relaxation of tensions in the world. If that is true, it is in our common interest and it will not be against the interests of either—I don't believe it is their intention but if they really want to bring about a relaxation of tension in the world, we would welcome it.

The second possibility is, and the evidence seems to point more in that direction, that the Soviet Union has decided that it should pursue a more flexible strategy for the following objectives: To demoralize Western Europe by creating the illusion of peace; to use American technology to overcome the imbalance between its military and economic capability; to make it more difficult for the U.S. to maintain its military capability by creating an atmosphere of détente and isolate those adversaries who are not fooled by this relaxation policy.

PM Chou: Such as China.

Dr. Kissinger: I was trying to be delicate. [Laughter] Five, to gain time to accelerate its own military preparations.

If all of this succeeds, then eventually the U.S. will be totally isolated. If they can demoralize Europe, improve their military situation, neutralize those countries which are politically opposed but are militarily too weak, then sooner or later the U.S. will be completely isolated and become the ultimate victim.

Now what is our strategy? Because I think that is important for the Prime Minister to understand so that he can separate appearance and reality. He can do it anyway, but so that he understands it more fully.

We believe that the second interpretation of Soviet intentions is by far the most probable one. Now first, very candidly, as you must know from your own reports, we have had a very difficult period domestically as a result of the war in Vietnam. So on many occasions we have had to maneuver rather than to have a frontal confrontation. But now the war in Vietnam has ended, especially if the settlement does not turn into a constant source of conflict for the U.S., we can return to the fundamental problems of our foreign policy. Even during this period, which the Prime Minister must have noticed, we have always reacted with extreme violence to direct challenges by the Soviet Union. I don't know whether the Prime Minister followed in 1970—that was before our meetings—the attempt by the Soviet Union to establish a submarine base in Cuba, and we reacted very strongly; less theatrically than President Kennedy, but very strongly, and that submarine base has never been completed. And in September 1970 during the Jordanian crisis we also reacted very sharply. And during the crisis on Berlin. I am just giving them as an example of our basic method. Our experience has been that the Soviet Union has always shied away from a military confrontation with the U.S.

But then what is our strategy? First we had to rally our own people by some conspicuous successes in foreign policy, to establish a reputation for thoughtful action. Secondly, we had to end the Vietnam war under conditions that were not considered an American disgrace. Thirdly, we want to modernize our military establishment, particularly in the strategic forces. We will talk more about this if you want to in a separate meeting. Ultimately we want to maneuver the Soviet Union into a position where it clearly is the provocateur. Fifthly, we have to get our people used to some propositions that are entirely new to them.

Now in Europe right now there is a paradox. In Europe the psychological situation is very poor, but the moral basis as far as U.S. action is concerned is very good.

In Asia the psychological situation is very strong. I speak frankly. In China there is no problem about the willingness of defense. But for Americans to understand that maneuvers such as Czechoslovakia and China, leaving aside the much greater strength of China, affects America directly is a new idea and requires time for preparation. You haven't asked us for any of this. This is our own judgment of the situation. Our interests are determined by our own necessities.

Therefore we have to some extent cooperated in these Soviet maneuvers. But up to now we have made only two kinds of agreements with them, or three kinds: One, those that we thought were on balance unilaterally to our advantage, such as Berlin—we paid nothing for that. So, of course, we did make that agreement.[5]

PM Chou: We don't quite understand that.

Dr. Kissinger: The Berlin Agreement improved the situation for us, and it cost us nothing and those are the best agreements to make. [laughter] No one ever gets them from your Vice Minister. [laughter] Second—but that was really—they did not make that for us—that agreement was made to keep Brandt in office. The Soviet Union made this agreement for Berlin's domestic policies. It is not an international agreement.

The second type of agreement we would be prepared to make . . .

PM Chou: [Interrupting] But it can also be said that this is consistent with the Soviet policy which is meant to lull, to demoralize Western Europe.

Dr. Kissinger: It is consistent. It is very consistent.

The second kind of agreement we would make, of which there is perhaps only one, is an agreement that would be in the interest of all countries such as the limitation on strategic arms. The difficulty with that agreement is that it establishes quantitative limitations at a time when the real dangers come from qualitative improvements.

PM Chou: That is why when you were signing the agreement in Moscow where Mr. Laird said quite a lot in Washington, that is why I

---

[5] The text of the Quadripartite Agreement on Berlin, signed September 3, 1971, are printed in Department of State *Bulletin*, September 27, 1971, pp. 318–325.

was very interested in him. You said that he had talked too much, but I think there is a good point in doing it.

Dr. Kissinger: He talked too much. That doesn't mean there wasn't a good point in it.

PM Chou: This is a good point because it shows that on this point an American must speak from trust.

Dr. Kissinger: We have accelerated it. In fact, Laird said it all. We have, since the Agreement, greatly accelerated the qualitative improvements of our strategic forces.

PM Chou: On this one he has also spoken out.

Dr. Kissinger: Who has?

PM Chou: Mr. Laird. Although the Soviet Union didn't say anything about that, but Mr. Suslov as the Chairman of the Foreign Affairs Committee of the Supreme Soviet of the USSR, he said something about it.

Dr. Kissinger: About Laird?

PM Chou: No, about the position of strength to increase the military budget. Of course, the figure of the budget is furnished, but what he said, those words are true.

Dr. Kissinger: We don't pay any attention to the budget because we have very good photography of the Soviet Union.

PM Chou: But Suslov's words are true by saying they depart from the position of strength.

Dr. Kissinger: They depart?

PM Chou: They proceed.

Dr. Kissinger: They are making very major efforts in every military category. Actually the Prime Minister—one amusing anecdote on a personal basis. When we were in the Soviet Union we were discussing the problem of putting—we were putting limitations on the holes in the silos. And I also pointed to Mr. Brezhnev that even with limitations on the holes of the silos it was possible to put larger missiles into the existing holes, and Mr. Brezhnev said it was totally untrue and started drawing diagrams. He said that there were three ways of doing it, all of which are entirely impossible. In fact there are four ways of doing it, and they are using the fourth, and they are putting larger missiles into the holes. [Chou laughs]

So in almost every significant military category there are major preparations going on. I am not saying for what, but that is a fact. But we learned many things during these negotiations also because in the process of preparing for them we had to study many things in particular detail, and they're being implemented now in our new preparations.

The third type of agreement we are making is on matters that are generally useful but of no major political significance, such as environment, scientific exchange, trade within certain limitations. I admit both sides are gambling on certain trends. The Soviet Union believes that it can demoralize Western Europe and paralyze us. We believe as far as Western Europe is concerned that as long as we are present there is a wide fluctuation possible in their actual attitudes without enabling the Soviet Union to bring military pressure. And we believe that through this policy we are gaining the freedom of maneuver we need to resist in those places which are the most likely points of attack or pressure. And our judgment of the Soviet leaders is that they are brutal, but not necessarily farsighted.

Now to apply this to the nuclear treaty—our tendency therefore is not to have a direct confrontation, but to play for time. But not to give away anything of substance while we are playing for time.

Now this is our general assessment, and that is our general strategy and therefore it is in this context that we have to understand whether we are standing on your shoulders. It would be suicidal for us to participate in a policy whose ultimate objective is to isolate us. We will use certain tendencies or fears as they develop, but that will be for the objections that I have described to the Prime Minister or the goals that I have described to the Prime Minister.

Now I have given you a more candid exposition of our views than we ever have to any foreign leader or for that matter to any of our own people.

PM Chou: The European Security Conference and Mutual Balanced Force Reduction Conference moved toward this direction too.

Dr. Kissinger: Could we have a five-minute break? I want to talk to you about this because here we have a problem with the short-sightedness of our European allies. I want to discuss with you our strategy.

[The group broke briefly at 3:45 p.m., and the meeting resumed at 3:53 p.m.]

Dr. Kissinger: Now about the European Security Conference and the Mutual Balanced Force Reduction. First a few words about the history.

You have to remember that the European leaders have dealt with both of these conferences entirely from the point of view of their domestic politics. When the Soviet Union first proposed the European Security Conference many years ago, the Europeans said that they were more for it than the U.S. so that they could blame us for its not coming into being vis-à-vis their own domestic opposition. So that the principle of it became established. Then when there were some pressures in the American Congress, Senator Mansfield, who incidentally wants to come back here—we will be glad . . .

PM Chou: [Interrupting] And during the conclusion of the general elections you said he would like to come the day after the votes were cast.

Dr. Kissinger: We will be glad to send him if you promise to keep him. [Laughter] No, but it is up to you. It may be a good idea. But that is a different question.

But when Senator Mansfield proposed the reduction of American forces then the Europeans developed the thought of a force reduction conference in order to prevent us from withdrawing forces unilaterally. When we then accepted this proposition they became nervous. [Chou laughs] Then they started pushing the European Security Conference in order to kill the Mutual Balanced Force Reduction Conference, and then we decided that we were getting into a never-never-land of demoralization, confusion and maneuvering and that we should tackle it head on and bring it to some concrete conclusion because it was more demoralizing to talk about it than to deal with it. It is perfectly clear what the Soviet Union wants with the European Security Conference. They want to create an impression that there is no longer any danger in Europe, and therefore they want to create an atmosphere in which the military relationships are replaced by some general European security order. Therefore, it is in our interest, one, that the Conference is as short as possible and as meaningless as possible so that nobody can claim a tremendous result was achieved. It is in the Soviet interest to give the impression that it is a great historic event. It is in our interest to have a meeting that affirms some generally desirable objectives like free travel and cultural exchange, but that cannot be used as a basis for historic transformation.

With Mutual Balanced Force Reductions the problem is exactly the opposite. If one analyses the problem of force reduction seriously one has to study the actual relationship of forces. Now any study of the actual relationship of forces seriously conducted must lead the Europeans to the realization of the extent of their danger. We are in the strange situation where if we discuss military defense with the Europeans directly they will always reject the reality of the danger and our conclusions, because they are afraid we will ask them for more money. But when we discuss force reductions they are so afraid that we will reduce our forces that they have an interest to study the danger. [Chou laughs]

When I was in Moscow last September I made a condition with Brezhnev that we would attend the European Security Conference only if they would attend the Conference on Force Reduction. And therefore whatever marginal benefit they can gain from European Security Conference we can substitute by the kind of investigation that will be produced by the Force Reduction Conference.

Now let me say a word about the actual state of these negotiations. Our biggest problem right now, to be very honest with you, is not the Soviet Union but the Europeans. What we want is a brief description of the agenda items, the European Security Conference to be as meaningless as possible, a short Conference and an exalted but meaningless conclusion. The Europeans ... every European Foreign Minister is already rehearsing the speech he is going to give at that Conference. Every European Foreign Office has submitted an endless agenda for each session. And so that produces a certain confusion, but we can manage that.

Now with respect to the force reductions, we will work very seriously with our European allies and the real problem for that is the temptation to have some general conclusion quickly. The reality is that we must have a very careful study of the actual balance of forces so that we do not make the situation worse as a result. If we do not make this study the Soviet Union someday is going to make a very plausible sounding proposal which for whatever reason everyone will want to accept. But if we have a study of the actual balance of forces we can resist on the grounds of this. This is how we handled the SALT negotiations. If we use these negotiations intelligently, we can use them to strengthen the defense of the West rather than to weaken it. In any event any foreseeable reductions will not exceed 10 to 15 percent and will not occur before 1975. They will be marginal to the global geopolitical balance. They will be on the Soviet side—two divisions maybe [Chou laughs] and they have now ...

PM Chou: [Interrupting] They even want to leave out the two words "mutual balanced."

Dr. Kissinger: They want to leave out the word "mutual."

PM Chou: No, they want to leave out the word "balanced."

Dr. Kissinger: Yes, "balanced," they want to leave out the word "balanced."

PM Chou: They want to leave these words out from the name of the Conference.

Dr. Kissinger: Yes, because they have larger numbers so that if you have equal reductions the relative importance of the gap becomes greater. They also want to leave out Czechoslovakia now. They have already said they want to leave out Hungary, but we also got information they also want to leave out Czechoslovakia. [Laughter]

PM Chou: And to start with, Belgium and Rumania will not come to the ...

Dr. Kissinger: [Interrupting] But there are no Soviet troops in Rumania. So this is our general approach to those two conferences. And we will keep you informed. If we have some easier means of communication, if for example, you do get some sort of office in Washington, we can let you see our study. But we can also do it via New York and while we are here we have some material here which, if your technical experts are interested, we could discuss with you on mutual force reductions. Just to give you a feeling of how we approach it.

PM Chou: What is the possibility for the Western European countries to strengthen their own military capabilities?

Dr. Kissinger: This is not the heroic period of European leadership. We are working with the British right now to improve their nuclear capability. And there may be some possibility of the Germans improving their capability, their conventional not nuclear, and actually the German army is now certainly the largest in Europe, conventional army in Western Europe. In France, a great deal depends on the outcome of the election.

PM Chou: Has Mr. Schumann told you that Chairman Mao advised him to dig tunnels?

Dr. Kissinger: No.

PM Chou: Perhaps he doesn't believe it altogether.

Dr. Kissinger: This is too epic for him. [Chou laughs]

PM Chou: Perhaps the Maginot Line wouldn't work so they think it wasn't good for him to do so. Because they don't understand that during the time when Hitler attacked the Soviet Union the underground did play a part.

Dr. Kissinger: The French are making an effort in the nuclear field, and they have actually modernized their army fairly well. What the Europeans lack is political vision and conviction that what they do makes a difference. So they pursue very cautious policies.

PM Chou: They are nearsighted.

Dr. Kissinger: Very.

PM Chou: Let us come back to the East. Not long ago you mentioned that it would take a long time to settle the questions in Indochina and Southeast Asia. Don't you waste your energies in this region?

Dr. Kissinger: No, I think it is important, however, that the transition between the present and what will work in Southeast Asia occur gradually.

PM Chou: And the same applies to Indochina—that is a gradual . . .

Dr. Kissinger: I am talking about Indochina. When the Prime Minister talked about Southeast Asia what did he mean?

PM Chou: Including Indochina. Because when we refer to Southeast Asia we speak about it in the context of Dulles' policy, because your commitments came from his policies.

Dr. Kissinger: Our objectives in Southeast Asia are quite different from the Dulles objective. Our policy in Southeast Asia is not directed against the PRC obviously.

PM Chou: Then you will have to change the atmosphere in Southeast Asia.

Dr. Kissinger: What concretely does the Prime Minister mean so that I can respond intelligently?

PM Chou: Because SEATO still exists.

Dr. Kissinger: Yes, but as I said at a briefing of Senators, it is not the most vital institution which is now known to the political life of the world. The major problem in Southeast Asia now is the transition in Indochina from a war situation to a peace situation—to do it in such a way that it does not lead to the intrusion of other countries. I was interested to see, for example, that there was an article in *Izvestia* in recent days warning against economic assistance to North Vietnam. It was sent to me from Washington.

PM Chou: Thank you for your information because I hadn't noticed it.

Dr. Kissinger: It was sent to me from Washington this morning. I think it was February 6.

But with respect to Southeast Asia it is our intention to reduce our involvement gradually. But in terms of the strategy which I have outlined, it is important to remember that all the political forces in America who are opposing the philosophy which I have described, including one of your future guests, Miss McLaine, would like nothing more than a total collapse of the settlement that we negotiated. [Chou laughs]

PM Chou: I know nothing about Miss McLaine and thank you for your information.

Dr. Kissinger: I have no objection to her coming. It will be very good for her.

PM Chou: This is a matter concerning our Foreign Ministry, I know nothing about this. I had some contacts with Mrs. Jarvis from NBC.

Dr. Kissinger: Oh, Mrs. Jarvis. She did a very good film. She was very active. She did a very good job. I don't know whether you were pleased with the result, but it really made a very good impression in America.

PM Chou: Yes, I was told by comments from the Foreign Ministry it is not bad.

Dr. Kissinger: It is good.

PM Chou: And the Ministry helped her find a family of three generations—that is what she said in her article. She didn't put it in that speech made to me. She knew very much how to seat herself when she met a Premier in a television interview but which was not included in the film.

Dr. Kissinger: They want to do it separately, I am sure.

PM Chou: She made a very long interview which was not included in the film. Perhaps she was excluded.

Dr. Kissinger: That is her great opportunity to become famous.

So Southeast Asia—our Southeast Asian policies will be put on a new basis, and we will try to avoid a situation where it absorbs all of our energies. On the other hand, if we should be challenged very rapidly then in order to protect the possibility of conducting a strong foreign policy, we will have to react very strongly. So if there can be a gradual evolution, as we have discussed on Taiwan, then many things are possible and we will not be actively involved. But we should have, any time the Prime Minister wishes, a longer talk on Southeast Asia.

PM Chou: Let us touch upon those major questions in Southeast Asia. As for the ending of the war in Vietnam, so far as we know both North and South Vietnam are willing to implement it. As you know the war has been going on for more than ten years and if the time period for the war against Japanese invasion is counted in, then it is a country which has carried on a war for thirty years, so they don't refrain from having the desire to realize peace. And secondly, since we have had contact with the Vietnamese friends for quite a long time, you know they have a strong character of independence. And although the country is not very large, with not a large population, they necessarily have a strong sense of self-dignity—it is a small country with a small population because compared with us their population is not very big.

Dr. Kissinger: Compared with you no population is very big.

PM Chou: But if you count in terms of 100 million then it can't be said it is a big country.

Dr. Kissinger: I agree with the Prime Minister.

PM Chou: And thirdly, they have a very strong inclination towards unity, and the first Geneva Conference bears witness to this point. And the Paris Agreement has covered all the three points. And as far as Thieu is concerned, he has a greedy personal ambition and is bound to fail. Of course, as you said, if the political evolution comes to that point you can do nothing about it, and, of course, if you talk about this to him he will be enraged, but the fact is like that. And just as if you said to the dying Chiang Kai-shek that he no longer hopes to go back to the Mainland any longer, he will also be angry. There is no way to deal with such an ally.

We can leave Chiang Kai-shek as what he is at the moment because this question is bound to be settled finally, because in principle we know each other well. So we won't be very put out about whether you withdraw your troops early or later in that place. But as far as Vietnam is concerned, the fact is that sooner or later the aid you provide will be lost eventually. It is not so easy for our Vietnamese friends to come to see immediately that Thieu will lose all the assistance he has been given, but as long as your country and Vietnam will be able to control the situation then the war in Vietnam will be able to stop. So we think this is the best for your country and Vietnam to be the Chairman of the Conference. This is the best way because if the other side is in charge of the Conference they will not be able to bring the situation under control.

Dr. Kissinger: Which others?

PM Chou: The U.S. and DRV.

Dr. Kissinger: Yes, but which others cannot control?

PM Chou: For instance, if you get into the five major countries in the UN then they will get into a quarrel.

Dr. Kissinger: Particularly if your Vice Minister and Malik are there.

PM Chou: But if Mr. Gromyko goes then Minister Chi P'eng-fei will be able to deal with him.

Dr. Kissinger: I have no question.

PM Chou: And then if this question is left to the four supervisory countries it will be again a difficult question to them because they will lead again to bickering. But sometimes when it is necessary to get into some quarrel they don't do so because so long as the Soviet Union points its finger then Poland will change its position, although Poland does not listen to it completely. So the development of the world situation is changing.

And you see for the ICC in Korea it is—during the Korean War one of the members of the supervisory control on behalf of the U.S. was Sweden. This indicates how quick the psychological situation changes. But in Korea as the result of Dulles' policy there was only an armistice agreement without a peace agreement. But since both North and South Korea don't intend to engage in a fight, and since we don't intend to fight, there isn't anything happening there for the last 10 years. Of course, it is a different situation there from South Vietnam.

In South Vietnam it is the situation in which the two sides are engaged in sort of jigsaw pattern, but only the DRV and the U.S. can talk over this question. So this is the Vietnam question. If you shoulder the responsibility then the ceasefire can be realized. Of course, there are bound to be constant small conflicts. I am not very clear about the situation in Laos. Perhaps the Soviet Union has had a hand in it to a certain extent. We don't know what you learn about this. Can there be any ceasefire there in Laos?

Dr. Kissinger: We have had an understanding with Hanoi that there would be a ceasefire by the 12th—February 12th. That did not happen. Then when I was in Hanoi we made a firm understanding that there would be a ceasefire on the 15th. That apparently has not happened, and we find that very difficult to understand.

PM Chou: Your Ambassador is very active there.

Dr. Kissinger: In Laos he is very active. We had reached a clear understanding with the Democratic Republic on Laos and obviously having reached that understanding our Ambassador would not get in the way of it. That understanding was that both sides would avoid clauses in the agreement that would be humiliating and the terms would be phrased in general language, and the DRV and we agreed on it. We even prepared joint instructions to our Ambassador and their Ambassador. Now the Pathet Lao keep calling the U.S. an aggressor and maybe it is the Soviet Union who has interfered. I can't believe your friends in North Vietnam would make an agreement with me on Monday and then break it on Thursday.

PM Chou: I am not very clear about the reasons.

Dr. Kissinger: I will make an inquiry tonight. Insofar as I know the only obstacle now is that the Pathet Lao now say the U.S. must stop the bombing, and Souvanna Phouma says it should be expressed that all bombing should stop, and we had an understanding on this in Hanoi. They did the same thing about the withdrawal of foreign forces. We want to say all foreign forces should withdraw; they want to name the U.S. separately and Thailand separately.

PM Chou: And what is the opinion of the Vietnamese side?

Dr. Kissinger: The Vietnamese side, when I was in Hanoi, agreed with us. We had no disagreement with them on these points, and therefore I am puzzled why it has not happened.

PM Chou: Yes, we also don't know very well what happened. We only know that the Soviet Ambassador is carrying on certain activities. And the Soviet Ambassador to Phnom Penh has gone back to Phnom Penh.

Dr. Kissinger: As Ambassador?

PM Chou: The Soviet Ambassador.

Dr. Kissinger: They have had a Chargé there.

PM Chou: Recently there was a Chargé there, and according to information they are going to send an Ambassador there.

Dr. Kissinger: I didn't know that.

PM Chou: That is recent information. As for the Cambodian country, why can't you accept to have negotiations with Norodom Sihanouk as head of state?

Dr. Kissinger: I don't know him as well as the Prime Minister. I understand it is a nervewracking experience. [Chou laughs]

PM Chou: Did Senator Mansfield say any words or discuss with you?

Dr. Kissinger: Oh, yes, Senator Mansfield is prepared to conduct negotiations with Sihanouk.

PM Chou: But unfortunately Prince Sihanouk wasn't in Peking. He was elsewhere. So your people say that after the President was elected for a second term, then Senator Mansfield would come again to China.

Dr. Kissinger: Yes, but he is not qualified to discuss that for us, and he would only confuse the situation. He is too emotional about this. This is not an emotional problem. I will—is the Prime Minister finished with his observation?

PM Chou: I have just raised this question and see what you have.

Dr. Kissinger: Can I make comments about Indochina in general, including Cambodia, or would you prefer that I talk about Cambodia first?

PM Chou: Either way will do.

Dr. Kissinger: I would prefer to do the general thing first. The basic problem for us is that the Agreement is kept and that the Agreement does not collapse, or if it collapses that it does not collapse quickly. This will affect our ability to conduct any effective foreign policy, and it is therefore of world interest. And therefore, we will have to defend the Agreement if it is fundamentally challenged. You have seen often enough that no matter what our press says, no matter what our Congress says, when we determine that something is vitally important, we do it.

But conversely if despite our efforts it should happen it would lead to consequences that would make it very difficult for the U.S. to be very active internationally and this may be one reason why I think the Soviet Union is now moving into a position of now undermining the Agreement. Another is to establish its position in Hanoi.

We have no direct interest in Indochina. If we can co-exist with Peking, we can certainly co-exist with Hanoi. Hanoi can never be a threat to the U.S., and we are prepared to deal with Hanoi as openly and honestly as we have dealt with you. And we have made a good beginning on my visit.

Now here is how we understand the Agreement with respect to Vietnam. Our understanding is that it should stop the military conflict, and that it should start a political process, and we will accept the political outcome, especially if it goes on over a reasonable period of time.

So it is possible for us—it seems to us also that the DRV has two choices. It can either use the Agreement as an offensive weapon in the short term and constantly use it to undermine the existing structure, or it can use it in the long term, the way we have handled our relationship, in which we both understand what will happen but in which the situation is tranquil for a period. If they do the second, we will co-operate with them. If they do the first, we will resist them. So they have to be patient. They have to be somewhat patient.

PM Chou: And your analysis is correct, but you should take into account another element. Thieu is more afraid of the occurrence of the second situation you referred to. So Thieu is devoting all efforts to engage in all kinds of unreasonable conspiracy in violation of the Agreement, and we think you should pay attention to it.

Dr. Kissinger: We are paying attention to it. I have told the DRV that we would investigate all violations of the Agreement, and I have sent Ambassador Sullivan to look into the matter in South Vietnam.

PM Chou: And the Two-Party Joint Military Commission hasn't yet been established.

Dr. Kissinger: Yes, we are going to use our maximum influence to bring it about.

PM Chou: And perhaps you have had very clear contacts with both Thieu and his special representative, Duc, his Special Adviser.

Dr. Kissinger: My secret dream is to see Duc and Xuan Thuy in a negotiation. I know him. He has the worst qualities of Harvard University and Hanoi University. On the other hand, Hanoi also has made very many, very serious violations of the Agreement. We know that they are sending in 300 tanks into South Vietnam right now.

PM Chou: Not that many. How can there be so many?

Dr. Kissinger: I assure you. We know it from our sources, not from the Vietnamese.

PM Chou: How can there be 300? It is true that they have buried some in South Vietnam.

Dr. Kissinger: No, they are moving them; that is a different matter. They are moving them from North Vietnam to South Vietnam which is illegal. Now how can we refuse under those conditions when they violate the Agreement? We have not done anything, but if this keeps up we will be forced to send tanks in. On one road, along Route 1068 in the western part of the DMZ, they have sent in 175 tanks which is totally prohibited by the Agreement. I have said this to them also.

PM Chou: But the number of weapons you sent to Thieu during the 100 days after October is also very great.

Dr. Kissinger: But that is a different problem; that was legal.

PM Chou: And this made Vietnam the country with the fourth largest air force.

Dr. Kissinger: Yes, but the Agreement prohibits the introduction of military supplies in South Vietnam. We have not sent anything else in since January 27th.

PM Chou: And how do you carry out the replacement in the future?

Dr. Kissinger: That is another problem. According to the Agreement the two sides were to agree on six points of entry for the replacement.

PM Chou: This is set down in the protocols.

Dr. Kissinger: In the protocols, but they were not mentioned. They were supposed to agree within 15 days.

PM Chou: You have read the protocol many times, whereas I have seen it once.

Dr. Kissinger: I think 15 is right, but I cannot face the humiliation when the Prime Minister is correct.

PM Chou: They have not mentioned the points of entry yet.

Dr. Kissinger: We have named three; they have not named any.

PM Chou: As to 15 days, then the date is already over. (Chinese side member confirms it is 15.)

Dr. Kissinger: 15, I know it was 15. So the 15 days is already over.

PM Chou: Because when you were in Hanoi, it was already 15 days.

Dr. Kissinger: That is right. So they say until these points are mentioned, they can bring in equipment any place, which is an interesting theory. [Chou laughs]

PM Chou: This is a new point in the protocol.

Dr. Kissinger: And we didn't bring any in. I knew what would happen.

PM Chou: But would that be that after your departure in Vietnam you leave the weapons to Vietnam? This is possible and also some military installations there. It is possible because we have been engaged in wars before so we know about it. Especially we have had dealings with Chiang Kai-shek.

Dr. Kissinger: Technically anything we leave we have turned over before January 27.

PM Chou: But it is still possible that in the documents it was signed as January 27, but actually you did it much later; that is February 10th.

Dr. Kissinger: Mr. Prime Minister, there is no sense in making—there is no doubt that for an interim period after an armistice both sides are going to engage in shady maneuvers.

PM Chou: Yes, you are fair in saying that.

Dr. Kissinger: And therefore for an interim period we can be understanding, and I talked openly with your friends in Hanoi on this subject. But if it continues, then it becomes serious.

PM Chou: Then it would be necessary to send the people from the ICCC earlier from the different places and fix the ports of entry.

Dr. Kissinger: The ports of entry must be fixed very soon. This is essential, and we will use our influence, and if anybody else can use their influence it would be very helpful. That is a very important question.

Now with respect to Vietnam our intention is to have a constructive relationship with Hanoi and to move rapidly towards normalization. And our intention is to extend economic aid without any political condition.

PM Chou: Since the Economic Joint Commission has already been announced the Soviet Union is not very satisfied with it.

Dr. Kissinger: I have been told that [pointing to a paper being held by the Chinese side]. Is this the article? I haven't read the text. I just read a summary. Actually the Prime Minister, Pham Van Dong, was astonished when we said that once we give them money for certain categories they can use it for anything within that category. He apparently wasn't used to treatment like that from other countries. [Chou laughs]

But it is important for us to be able to do this. We want the countries of Indochina to be independent. We have no other interest in that area. We don't need any bases in Indochina. But for us to be able to establish this relationship, the DRV must cooperate to some extent. If there is no ceasefire in Laos and no withdrawal of forces, how can we ask our Congress to give money? It is psychologically impossible. Article 20(b) of the Agreement says foreign forces must be withdrawn from Laos and Cambodia without any condition. And we are prepared to withdraw our forces, and we have talked to Thailand, and it will withdraw its forces. So the DRV must live up to this obligation. Now they are very close to a ceasefire in Laos, and I frankly do not understand what is delaying it. Perhaps they will conclude it today.

PM Chou: We will be able to get information every day from official sources as to whether or not it has been signed.

Dr. Kissinger: Well, I will find out when I get back.

Now about Cambodia. It is obviously a very complex situation, and we have no particular interest in any one party.

PM Chou: From the very beginning you would not admit that. I refer to the coup d'etat. It was not done by the CIA. So after you examine your work, you will find how it was not done by them.

Dr. Kissinger: It was not done by them.

PM Chou: Like the situation in Laos.

Dr. Kissinger: It is a different situation.

PM Chou: Then who did it?

Dr. Kissinger: I have told the Prime Minister once before when I first learned of the coup d'etat I thought Sihanouk had done it, that he would come back after three or four days. I thought he had done it so he could show Hanoi that his troops there made the population very unhappy. That was my honest opinion.

PM Chou: Yes, you have told me about it.

Dr. Kissinger: That was my sincere conviction.

PM Chou: But I was quite skeptical about the CIA so I asked you to make a study of it.

Dr. Kissinger: I did make a study of it. Why should I lie to you today? It makes no difference today. The CIA did not do it.

PM Chou: So it was done by France?

Dr. Kissinger: It could have been done by France. It could have been done by other interests. It could even perhaps have been done independently by Saigon. But it was not done by America nor did we know about it. At that time our policy was to attempt to normalize our relations with Sihanouk, and you will remember that the Prime Minister and I exchanged some letters at that time. We have always been opposed to the presence of North Vietnamese troops in Cambodia. We are opposed to that today. We think the North Vietnamese should withdraw their troops into Vietnam. We did not think they had the right to maintain troops on foreign territory.

Now we believe that there should be a political negotiation in Cambodia, and we think that all the political forces should be represented there. And that does not mean that the existing government must emerge as the dominant force, but how can we, when we recognize one government, engage in a direct negotiation with Sihanouk? This is out of the question. But if there were a ceasefire and if North Vietnamese forces were withdrawn we would encourage a political solution in which Sihanouk would play a very important role. We don't want necessarily Hanoi to dominate Laos and Cambodia, but we will not support in either of these countries, and certainly not in Cambodia, one political force against the others.

But if the war continues—first of all, if the North Vietnamese—they are violating Article 20(b) of the Agreement. Secondly, it will be almost impossible for us to go to our Congress and ask for economic support for a country that has its troops on foreign territory. It is difficult enough as long as they have troops in the South, but that we can treat as a special case. We believe a solution consistent with the dignity of Sihanouk is possible, and we have so far refused overtures from other countries that have different views. But there has to be some interruption in military activity because otherwise our Air Force will continue to be active on one side, and there is no end to it. My difficulty in meeting with Prince Sihanouk is no reflection on Prince Sihanouk. It has to do with the situation there.

PM Chou: France has maintained relationships with both sides. And the same is true of the Soviet Union, so things have been so complicated.

Dr. Kissinger: France wants to pick up what is left over without any risk and without any investment. [Laughter]

PM Chou: Three years ago during the time of the occurrence of the Cambodian incident, the French had sent Prince Sihanouk to the Soviet Union so Lon Nol at the time took a further step to announce the overthrow of the Cambodian monarchy and to abolish the royal system. So as a result Kosygin sent Sihanouk to Peking. So in standing on the just side we should give them support. Further, Lon Nol at the time counted on us to maintain the original relationship, and Lon Nol even said that it was permissable to use Sihanouk Harbor to transport weapons to South Vietnam as was done by Sihanouk before. And prior to that Sihanouk also asked Lon Nol to be in charge of this matter—that is to transport weapons to South Vietnam, and he gained money out of that. So Lon Nol was most familiar with this matter. And now after engaging in subversive activities he wanted to directly collect the taxes so that was too unreasonable and unjust so we rejected him. During that month—more than one month, they continued their initiative—our Ambassador proved that. At the beginning he refused to let our Ambassador leave Cambodia.

Dr. Kissinger: Well, I have always believed that if Sihanouk had returned to Phnom Penh rather than Moscow, he would still be King or Prime Minister.

PM Chou: And he might be arrested.

Dr. Kissinger: Yes, possibly.

PM Chou: Because Lon Nol would do anything he wished to.

Dr. Kissinger: Well, we will never know this, but in any event . . .

PM Chou: Do you know Lon Nol very well?

Dr. Kissinger: Once. I didn't think he is an extremely energetic man.

PM Chou: He is half paralyzed.

Dr. Kissinger: He is actually very anxious still to establish relations with you.

PM Chou: No, we wouldn't do that with such a person. You should also not deal with such a man who carries on subversive activities against the King. It is just for you not to support India in dismantling Pakistan. On that one we stood together because you supported justice. But we think it is not very—it is not fair for you to admit Lon Nol.

Dr. Kissinger: But I think it might be possible to find an interim solution that is acceptable to both sides and I think, for example, that the Lon Nol people would be willing to negotiate with the Chief Minister of Sihanouk here. [To Mr. Lord: What is his name again?] Penn Nouth. And that might lead to an interim government which could then decide who should be Chef d'etat. This possibility has also occurred to us.

PM Chou: Would that do if you go without Lon Nol?

Dr. Kissinger: The end result could well be without Lon Nol.

PM Chou: Not only the Prime Minister of Sihanouk wouldn't engage in such a negotiation, but there is the Khmer resistance in the interior area in Cambodia.

Dr. Kissinger: What would not be acceptable?

PM Chou: To take Lon Nol . . .

Dr. Kissinger: Well, it doesn't have to be Lon Nol himself. It could be somebody from that government.

PM Chou: Have you had any contact with the Soviet Union and French on this point, or would they go to you for that?

Dr. Kissinger: No we have not talked to France at all. The Soviet Union had very vague conversations, their Ambassador with me. But I thought they were leaning more towards Lon Nol than the other side. They were certainly not leaning towards Sihanouk.

PM Chou: Because he is not so fond of Sihanouk at all.

Dr. Kissinger: But they made no concrete—because I said to the Vice Minister when he was in New York, "I want to talk to the Prime Minister." I have talked to Le Duc Tho about it, and he said he is in favor of negotiation. He said they wouldn't make the final decision in Hanoi, but, of course, you will be in direct contact with them.

PM Chou: And he told me that you said that you would go to me and talk.

Dr. Kissinger: That is right. He said to me first, that it would be best if I talked to you, and then I said I would be glad to. Le Duc Tho always has a slight problem with his time sequence.

PM Chou: So this question is quite similar to the question of the Secretary General. [Laughter] Of course, since Sihanouk is in China we cannot but tell him your opinion in our wording, but of course, we have our own position on this question.

Dr. Kissinger: We would appreciate it if he would not repeat it in newspapers and interviews. His self-discipline isn't up to Chinese standards.

PM Chou: It is impossible. He often told others what I had told him, and also some times when I hadn't told him. [Laughter] So the word wouldn't be very clear what the Premier had actually told him. So after learning about your ideas and what we learned about it, we wouldn't tell him all about it. Perhaps he would broadcast it and it would be carried in Chinese newspapers, and it wouldn't be all right for us not to carry it in our newspapers. The freedom our *People's Daily* has given to Sihanouk is much greater than any freedom granted to any Heads of State by any country at all. General De Gaulle didn't get freedom like that when he was in Britain. He would be sure to include it in his message if he was told something.

We support his Five Point Declaration of March 23, 1970. That time you were not involved. And we also supported the declaration issued jointly by the Head of State, the Prime Minister and the Deputy Prime Minister of Cambodia which was issued on January 26. And later the three other Ministers in the interior area of Cambodia also supported this declaration. This is still our position. Do you know the Five Point Declaration of March 23, 1970?[6]

Dr. Kissinger: No.

PM Chou: At that time you were not involved with it.

Dr. Kissinger: This is an extremely unusual event. None of my colleagues have ever heard me admit I didn't know something, but I will know it as soon as I can get a copy. Have you English or French copies?

PM Chou: Both.

Dr. Kissinger: Either one I can read. I have not studied it, but the major problem, frankly, is not the formal position but what evolution we foresee. And from our side we are prepared to cooperate with you, if we can find a way with him to come up with a solution consistent with his dignity.

PM Chou: You have told us your ideas, and we have learned about it, but at the moment perhaps this is not possible. We will consider it again, and next time I will tell you our ideas.

Dr. Kissinger: All right.

PM Chou: The French and the Soviet Union are indeed engaged in activities there. What about the question of the neutralization among those five countries; Thailand, Malaysia, Singapore, Indonesia, and the Philippines? If this is going to be a very long discussion perhaps we should leave it until tomorrow.

Dr. Kissinger: I think we should leave it until tomorrow but I have one brief point about Indochina. When I talked to the Prime Minister

---

[6] After this sentence, a notation in unknown handwriting reads: "[Attached]". Both declarations are attached but not printed.

last June about the war in Vietnam, he said after the war in Vietnam ended it would help China to send its MIG–19's to Pakistan instead of Vietnam, and we hope that this will now happen.

PM Chou: We have given some to Pakistan, but we haven't given the number of the planes they want. We gave some to them last year, and we will continue to give them some this year.

Dr. Kissinger: The major concern we have is to see that there is some restraint about the importation of arms by all countries into Indochina.

PM Chou: But here there is a question, that is, Thieu is in possession of large numbers of military equipment although he may not be able to use them.

Dr. Kissinger: But we are not going to send in any additional . . .

PM Chou: But according to the Agreement the DRV will not supply any more weapons to South Vietnam, and you will not supply any more military arms to Thieu. That was laid down in the Agreement and is a joint agreement. You can only replace them piece by piece.

Dr. Kissinger: That is correct, but if there is a large influx of military equipment into the North and the overall balance changes, it will be very dangerous. It has nothing to do with the Agreement.

PM Chou: You mean supply of weapons to North Vietnam?

Dr. Kissinger: Yes.

PM Chou: But the point is the one who helped Thieu is the powerful U.S. You can supply the weapons to the South not only through points of entry, but also through air and sea and by land.

Dr. Kissinger: Not legally.

PM Chou: So legally you can supply weapons through the points of entry.

Dr. Kissinger: Yes.

PM Chou: But is it North Vietnam who supports the PRG in South Vietnam, so they can only do so through North Vietnam and only through points of entry.

Dr. Kissinger: No, we are not saying that there should be no armaments sent into North Vietnam. We recognize that some will be, but now that the war is over we believe that some restraint in the sending of armaments would contribute to the tranquilizing of the situation.

PM Chou: Tranquility is necessary. But logically how is it possible for the DRV to be in possession of such massive arms as the U.S. has, and they don't have the strongest means of transportation. They depended on those trails to transport those supplies previously. And, for instance, in the 100 days from October to January you had very intensive transportation of supplies sent into South Vietnam, and the Pentagon has always been very active.

Dr. Kissinger: That was your friend Secretary Laird.

PM Chou: That is why, although I have never met Mr. Laird but I say I appreciate him, because he has always been very outspoken. As to our supplies to Vietnam, as you know, it is very limited so how can it be compared to those given to Thieu? So we are not clear about this.

Dr. Kissinger: Yes, I understand. I am not criticizing the past. We are talking about the future, and we think that all countries, including the U.S., should contribute to the tranquility. We will be very careful in how we define replacement, and what we replace if other countries act the same way.

PM Chou: According to the Agreement it would be legal to supply arms only through the points of entry. This is the legal way of doing things.

Dr. Kissinger: That is to the South. We are talking of the North.

PM Chou: We support this Agreement, but it is quite another matter for North Vietnam because when they need weapons the emphasis is not here in China. You know this very clearly.

Dr. Kissinger: Yes, but our point is they should need less weapons now than they did when a war was going on.

PM Chou: It depends how you put it. Because for ordinary weapons, they were easily worn out, but as for those sophisticated weapons, we don't have them. So this is again a matter that concerns replacement. If they really want to establish their own system they will have to engage in producing themselves, and this takes time for them.

Dr. Kissinger: I am not talking about the Agreement. I'm talking about acts of restraint and there is no formal agreement on that. I think the Prime Minister understands our general intention, and this is all I want to get across.

PM Chou: It seems that you have put these ideas—you have included this idea in the Act of Paris—your draft.

Dr. Kissinger: Yes, yes.

PM Chou: I have read it. So much for today. I will continue this tomorrow.

Dr. Kissinger: The Prime Minister never wastes an idea.

PM Chou: This evening there will be a banquet and you have to rest now.

[The meeting ended at 6:00 p.m.]

10.   Memorandum of Conversation[1]

Beijing, February 17, 1973, 2:20–6:25 p.m.

PARTICIPANTS

    Chou En-lai, Premier, State Council
    Chi P'eng-fei, Minister of Foreign Affairs
    Ch'iao Kuan-hua, Vice Minister of Foreign Affairs
    T'ang Wen-sheng, Interpreter
    Shen Jo-yun, Interpreter

    Dr. Henry A. Kissinger, Assistant to the President for National Security Affairs
    John H. Holdridge, NSC Senior Staff
    Winston Lord, NSC Staff
    Cdr. Jonathan T. Howe, NSC Staff
    Peter W. Rodman, NSC Staff
    Mary Stifflemire, Notetaker

Dr. Kissinger: We had a very interesting morning at the Imperial City.

Chou En-lai: You have seen it before.

Dr. Kissinger: Yes, but I find it so fascinating I'd like to come back.

Chou En-lai: Last night I heard there was going to be a great wind, but when I got up this morning I saw it wasn't so windy.

Dr. Kissinger: It was a great morning, very clear.

Chou En-lai: But the ground is not so very even.

Dr. Kissinger: No, that is true.

Chou En-lai: But you know it is very strong. It is very durable.

Dr. Kissinger: Yes.

Chou En-lai: Perhaps it might be stronger. The tunnels are built underneath that ground.

Dr. Kissinger: Tunnels are built?

Chou En-lai: There is one in one place under the Forbidden City, but not the place where you were. When we tore down the city wall around Peking we hadn't thought of it, but now as an afterthought if we had let it stay there it would be a very good defense work. It could also stop the radiation of atomic weapons because it has a very deep

---

[1] Source: National Archives, Nixon Presidential Materials, NSC Files, Kissinger Office Files, Box 98, Country Files, Far East, HAK China Trip, Memcons & Reports (originals), February 1973. Top Secret; Sensitive; Exclusively Eyes Only. The meeting was held in the Great Hall of the People. All brackets are in the original.

base and also is very strong. You have been to the Great Wall so you know how the bricks are.

Dr. Kissinger: In World War II it turned out some of the old fortifications withstood bombardment more than the modern ones. In Germany, Nuremberg, the city was surrounded by a wall and the whole city was leveled, but the wall remained. That was from the Medieval period.

Chou En-lai: Yes. [Pointing to Mr. Rodman.] He is new.

Dr. Kissinger: Yes, this is his first visit. He was a student of mine at Harvard University.

The Prime Minister yesterday, when we discussed that nuclear treaty, did not express his own opinion about the strategy that I outlined to him.[2]

[The Premier speaks to the young girl serving tea.]

Miss T'ang: She just went home to get married. The Premier was asking her. He is noting she is back and asking her why isn't she speaking English. You noticed her. She has always worked here. She is the tallest one. [Chou En-lai points to her.] She is slightly embarrassed. She had a very nice honeymoon, from Harbin to Shanghai. Her mother in Harbin. Her father in Shanghai.

Dr. Kissinger: Oh, her father in Shanghai, so she visited them both.

Chou En-lai: This is equality.

Because this question, it seems to me, is that the Soviet Union wants to draw up something that would not be entirely public, or not made to be published. On the one hand it seems they want to have a bit of it published, but on the other hand they don't want some parts of it made public. So it seems to my mind they want to make parts of it public and parts kept secret. I don't think you will agree to that.

Dr. Kissinger: That we will not agree to.

Chou En-lai: And the part that will be made public would serve to deceive the people of the world, including the people of your two respective countries. The part that was kept secret would also be a means to continue the competition with you and to threaten those areas they wish to threaten. And also they could use the three clauses you mentioned yesterday alternately.

Dr. Kissinger: There are a number of things I can say. One, under no circumstances will we make any secret arrangements with the Soviet Union and you will be kept informed of anything that is done, and all of it will be published. Secondly, we will not accept the version that they have given us, which lends itself to the interpretation we discussed

---

[2] See Document 9.

with you yesterday. And thirdly, we will not accept an obligation not to use nuclear weapons.

Chou En-lai: You would undertake the obligations, but actually when they found it necessary they would disregard all the obligations.

Dr. Kissinger: We won't accept an obligation.

Chou En-lai: None of the treaties that China concluded with them are effective. Take for instance the Sino-Soviet Alliance of Friendship and Cooperation of February 14, 1950. Recently Czechoslovakia has written an article about attacking our meeting and they said that we had precisely selected the date of the conclusion of that treaty to hold a meeting between our two sides! Actually their sources of information are quite inaccurate, because on that day you were still in Hong Kong and not in Peking. Of course, probably neither you nor we had thought we were trying to select exactly that date to meet at Peking.

Dr. Kissinger: It didn't occur to me.

Chou En-lai: We didn't either, because they got the date wrong and took the 15th for the 14th. Secondly, although we have a treaty with the Soviet Union and it hasn't expired, it is equal to nonexistent. It is for 30 years. But it is the same as if it did not exist. And our Vice Foreign Minister can also bear witness to the fact that they are very eager to enter into an agreement with us on mutual non-aggression. We think this is very absurd, because since we are allies how can we want to conclude a treaty of mutual non-aggression? It seems they have forgotten we are allies! They want to conclude a treaty on mutual non-use of armed forces including nuclear weapons and rocket units. We said that is not sincere and don't think there is any necessity. It is only for the purpose of propaganda. If they truly indeed want to end the armed conflicts along the border and really enter into negotiations about the border, the first thing would be to clarify the preliminary agreement on the border situation, but they won't agree to do that. So you can see the only motive on their side is to try to hoodwink the world. Brezhnev himself.

Dr. Kissinger: On our part we will pursue the strategy I outlined yesterday. What we may do with respect to the nuclear treaty is . . . we do not accept the treaty they have proposed to us. What we are considering now is to say that we are prepared to discuss conditions under which such a treaty would be meaningful, and we would list a whole number of conditions which would then have to be studied. We do this in part, first, to give us time for repositioning our policy, and, secondly, because some of Soviet policy has been so clumsy that if they get frustrated completely they may do something dramatic.

We have discussed this problem with only one other country, namely the British. And their analysis is the same as yours and ours, as you know. But we will never accept, first, that in the case of a Soviet attack on Europe, Soviet territory will be immune; second, that in case of a war in the Middle East nuclear weapons cannot be used; or third, that it is possible to threaten the international balance without the risk of nuclear war.

We will keep you precisely informed through Ambassador Huang Hua. We promise that . . .

Chou En-lai: Yes, and I would like to add one word. That is, to-morrow evening Minister Chi P'eng-fei will be holding an informal dinner for you, which Ambassador Huang Hua will attend.

Dr. Kissinger: Oh, that will be very nice. And we have promised them an answer during March to their new proposal. But you can be sure now that the answer will be negative. The only question we have yet to decide is whether to pursue it in a dilatory manner by making a counter-proposal which is quite different from their proposal, or whether we should reject it altogether. The practical result will be the same.

Also I have communicated to the President about our discussions with respect to bilateral relations. And he is prepared—he confirms what I already told you informally yesterday—for the establishment of an unofficial office of the PRC in Washington or any other place where you might wish to do so, and that we would give it diplomatic immunity.[3]

Chou En-lai: And I also reported to Chairman Mao about all we discussed yesterday about Taiwan and Sino-American relations. You mentioned two stages yesterday. That is, during the first stage the two sides would each establish a liaison office in the capital of the other country. And it would not be an official diplomatic organ and also would not take part in official collective diplomatic activities, but it would enjoy diplomatic immunities and it could be used to contact the other side for various business excepting those which would be trans-acted through the non-public channel of Ambassador Huang Hua. All other matters could be conducted through this channel. And it is our understanding that all the steps in the two stages shall be concluded within the second term of your President.

Dr. Kissinger: That is our intention.

---

[3] At the bottom of a memorandum describing Kissinger's meeting with Zhou, Stephen Bull wrote, "Discussed with the President personally at 6:25 EST. President said 'OK—yes' to the portion relating to establishment of a trade office or some other PRC presence in the U.S. as is indicated on this page." (Memorandum from Kissinger to Nixon, February 16; National Archives, Nixon Presidential Materials, NSC Files, Kissinger Office Files, Box 29, HAK Trip Files, Bangkok, Vientiane, Hanoi, Hong Kong, Peking, Tokyo Trip, Itinerary Como Info, Memos to Pres., February 7–20, 1973)

Chou En-lai: Of course, we can also consult each other as to the specific timing of the realization of this process—whether it could be fulfilled earlier or later.

Dr. Kissinger: Of course. It depends somewhat on developments. And we have no motive for delaying it unnecessarily.

Chou En-lai: Right. I forgot to report to the Chairman what you told me last night at the dinner—that the Japanese had suggested that they take care of Peking and you take care of Taiwan. That would be a division of work! [Laughter]

Dr. Kissinger: But they said they would use all their good influence in Peking on our behalf. [Laughter]

Chou En-lai: Foreign Minister Chi can also bear with me that I forgot to report that item last night.

Dr. Kissinger: Well, on the question of the liaison office, is it your intention, Mr. Prime Minister, to call your office a liaison office or to give it some other name?

Chou En-lai: I think that would be the best—"liaison office". Because the functions of that office could be wider or narrower as necessary.

Dr. Kissinger: I am sure that would be all right with us. I had understood you to say yesterday that you were thinking of calling yours a trade office, but I am sure our intention in pursuing liaison was also the one you had given.

Chou En-lai: It would be more flexible.

Dr. Kissinger: Yes.

Chou En-lai: Because in the past in our relations with other countries we first established trade offices and then went on to normalization. Of course Japan would be a typical example. But China and the U.S. can invent another new style and form.

Dr. Kissinger: That we have already done in the China Communiqué.[4]

Chou En-lai: Yes, otherwise Tanaka would be claiming you had copied him.

Dr. Kissinger: I will have a very serious problem in Japan, how to tell something about my visit without having it in the Japanese newspapers before I report to the President. I will speak for an hour and a half without saying anything. [Laughter]

Chou En-lai: So you will know by the time you leave Peking that I will be able to give you something that you can say.

---

[4] Kissinger is referring to the Shanghai Communiqué; see footnote 5, Document 1.

Dr. Kissinger: Well, we should agree what I will say, and I will tell you before I leave what I will say. Would it be the Prime Minister's idea afterwards we would be prepared to express this intention in a communiqué concluding my visit?

Chou En-lai: Yes. I think it should be put into that.

Dr. Kissinger: I agree.

Chou En-lai: You can draft it. [Laughter]

Dr. Kissinger: But I have the uneasy feeling that I will run across the Vice Minister before it is concluded.

Chou En-lai: It doesn't matter because you are a specialist in that.

Dr. Kissinger: That is right. We will draft it tonight and perhaps show it to you, discuss it tomorrow. I think it will be very appropriate. Our proposal would be then to release the communiqué on the 22nd, if that is agreeable to the Prime Minister. Our time. Because I return to Washington only on the 20th, around Noon. We need a day to make preparations, and also on the 21st the Secretary of State is testifying before the Senate Foreign Relations Committee on Vietnam and we should not have this in the simultaneous announcement because it would be brought into the wrong context. Therefore if you agree I would propose the morning of the 22nd of February, our time.

Chou En-lai: We agree.

Dr. Kissinger: And then would it be the Prime Minister's idea that after these offices are established the Paris channel should be abolished?

Chou En-lai: Generally speaking it can be dis-used, but if we have some public business we want to contact each other it can also be used.

Dr. Kissinger: Of course. For public diplomatic communications we should continue to use Paris.

Chou En-lai: But the liaison office can issue visas, can't they?

Dr. Kissinger: Oh, certainly.

Chou En-lai: Okay. That would save trouble, instead of going to Paris. And it is not so convenient for someone who wants to make a journey to go through Paris and then come to China.

Dr. Kissinger: We will make very flexible arrangements. Whoever you send will be a very popular person in Washington.

Chou En-lai: [Laughs] We haven't prepared the person yet, because this is your suggestion; so we haven't yet thought up a person to send there.

Dr. Kissinger: When would you in practice establish this office?

Chou En-lai: If there is time enough, perhaps in May. Do you agree?

Dr. Kissinger: Yes, and we will be helpful in an informal way if you need any assistance in finding a property or any other assistance we can give you.

Chou En-lai: That will be the same on our side. And also security, we can guarantee security.

Dr. Kissinger: Any requests you make also of my colleagues and me on a personal basis will not be treated on an official basis but we will deal with this on a basis of personal friendship—to make the life of your people easier.

Chou En-lai: And on our side we shall also do the same.

Dr. Kissinger: On the legal technicalities of how these missions would operate, I will have to consult our people when I return, but we will interpret the regulations in the most flexible way and if necessary make some new ones.

Chou En-lai: And we will wait for your notification. And we think it will be best for you to first give your ideas.

Dr. Kissinger: All right.

Chou En-lai: You have too many legalities on your side. And also including communications, the means of communications, wireless and all that.

Dr. Kissinger: That is not a problem. We will give you within two weeks. The means of communications in New York are satisfactory, are they not?

Chou En-lai: Yes.

Dr. Kissinger: I am certain the same thing can be done in Washington.

Chou En-lai: There are no restrictions?

Dr. Kissinger: I am speaking really without knowledge, but if there are restrictions we will abolish them.

Mr. Holdridge: Not to my knowledge.

Dr. Kissinger: We will just assure it. There are certain frequencies—we have to agree on the frequencies which you will use, but that is a technical matter. And our intention is to facilitate communication and to use these offices for many of our exchanges. [Chou nods] And we will send you what we think is needed and ideas of how many people we propose. Have you any ideas how many people you would propose to send to Washington?

Chou En-lai: None at all. Because this matter has only been discussed between my two assistants and myself with Chairman Mao and at the Central Committee Political Bureau, but in principle. There have been no details.

Dr. Kissinger: This will all be solved very easily. None of this will be a problem. We will probably send Mr. Holdridge and Mr. Jenkins among the group, because they have been participating in our discussions and they know our intentions.

Chou En-lai: So you have better conditions: on the one hand old Chinese hands and also new Chinese hands!

Dr. Kissinger: They are new friends.

Chou En-lai: Yes, new friends.

Dr. Kissinger: Then the channels we will use—simply so that we understand each other—will be as follows: for formal diplomatic exchanges we continue to use Paris.

Chou En-lai: And what you mean by formal diplomatic exchange we do not think would be very numerous.

Dr. Kissinger: Very rare if you want it to. You have on occasion made formal public protests, for which the occasion no longer exists. [Laughter] Or if there is some multilateral international event which involves us all, like sending you an invitation to this Conference, this should probably go through Paris.

Chou En-lai: For instance also, if you wanted to send us some bulky material like the ones you sent us on the private assets which would not be very conveniently immediately transferred to Peking, you could hand them over in Paris.

Dr. Kissinger: All right. Then most of what was discussed in Paris, all the matters now being discussed by Mr. Jenkins and Minister Chang, that will be handled by the liaison office.

Chou En-lai: Yes.

Dr. Kissinger: The communications between the White House will continue to go through Huang Hua, or should I give that also to the liaison office?

Chou En-lai: As you deem the nature of that communication to be. Take for instance the nuclear treaty matter you just now mentioned, perhaps it would be better to have it go through the White House to Huang Hua. It would be easier to keep it secret.

Dr. Kissinger: All right.

Chou En-lai: We would envisage that the liaison office would take care of a rather large wide range of affairs. Of course it would include some confidential matters, but the majority would be public matters. And the channel between the White House and Ambassador Huang Hua would be limited to extremely confidential matters.

Dr. Kissinger: It would help us if the head of your liaison office, when confidential matters are to be discussed, would check with me first, so that I could tell him whether to put it into our official channels or whether we want to keep it in the White House. I will make arrangements for him so that he can reach me immediately. In this manner you can be certain even if it is an official channel that the White House will pay personal attention to whatever matters you send to us.

Chou En-lai: All right.

Dr. Kissinger: And that will be then a very efficient way of proceeding. This is all that I really have on the liaison office. We may consider overnight if any other technical problems occur to us that can be solved here.

Chou En-lai: Yes.

Dr. Kissinger: Also, as you know, we have a more complex system of government than you. When our liaison office is established here I will make certain that it is headed by somebody who has a direct relationship to the White House. Then when your side wishes to communicate something to us through our office rather than through yours, you have to tell them whether it should be sent directly to the White House or not. And we will set up communications for them for either possibility.

Chou En-lai: I understand. Since we have had a year and a half experience.

Dr. Kissinger: Yes, but it is a new arrangement. This is the only reason I mention it. I think this is a very significant step forward.

Chou En-lai: And our Foreign Minister was saying that officially your office would probably still have to be connected some way with our Foreign Ministry and your State Department officially. Do you think that is necessary?

Dr. Kissinger: [To Holdridge] What do you think?

Mr. Holdridge: Yes.

Dr. Kissinger: In fact this will certainly be the case. I think in the initial period we should keep this vague and we should simply call them liaison offices for the whole range of our contacts. When we announce the people who are going it will be clear that many of them are diplomats.

Chou En-lai: That is, what we mean is that not only the personnel but also, besides the non-official contacts with the White House or non-public contacts with the White House, it also should have a certain organ in Peking to contact—the Foreign Ministry, also the Ministry of Foreign Trade—as well as scientific and cultural organizations.

Dr. Kissinger: It certainly should have the right to contact the State Department.

Chou En-lai: It must have some place to go to as the first step for arrangements.

Dr. Kissinger: The State Department. None else can do that.

Mr. Holdridge: That is, next it would have to go through communications with the State Department.

Dr. Kissinger: But we should also maintain the fiction that it is also dealing with the Commerce Department and with cultural groups. But certainly we would envision that the chief of your liaison office would have the right to contact the State Department, and that this would be his normal contact for routine business.

Chou En-lai: That is true.

Dr. Kissinger: And I will act as the traffic manager. [Laughter] But publicly he will be dealing principally with the State Department. And I assume that you would want our liaison man to deal with your Foreign Office.

Chou En-lai: [Nods] Yes, because it would be more convenient to have the channels concentrated. But of course through the Foreign Ministry we will arrange for your liaison office to have communications with the Foreign Trade Ministry, cultural organizations and also people's organizations—organizations similar to what you have as the National Committee on Chinese-U.S. Relations and the scientific organizations.

Dr. Kissinger: Is that what the Foreign Minister had in mind by "related to the Foreign Ministry?"

Chou En-lai: Yes.

Dr. Kissinger: We will send you within two weeks more details of how we envision it. But since this is also a new experience for us you should feel free to correct it or comment on it. We will send it to you of course through Ambassador Huang Hua so it is easy for you to modify it without it becoming publicly known that you have different views. But we will make complete proposals about number of personnel, communications offices, and so forth, and legal status, and then we can easily come to an agreement. We will certainly easily agree.

I know one thing. That the Ambassador of your ally has gone home on vacation on February 8. I think he will return very quickly after February 22. [Laughter][5]

Chou En-lai: And he will have more to ask you after the communiqué.

Dr. Kissinger: Oh, yes.

Chou En-lai: And from the beginning of your first day in Peking, their Embassy here has sent cars to patrol around the Great Hall of the People. We stopped their cars. We said, you don't have the right to patrol our Great Hall. We said it is not a race course. Small tricks and maneuvers. Quite absurd.

Dr. Kissinger: Since they have an embassy in Washington they can have no basis for an objection to a liaison office by you.

Chou En-lai: They probably will try various means and ways to do some tricks or maneuvering.

Dr. Kissinger: I have noticed the press is very critical of my visit.

Chou En-lai: You don't have to mind that. Your press also does something perhaps sometimes also a bit irritating. For instance, immediately your economic mission with North Vietnam has just been

---

[5] Kissinger is referring to Soviet Ambassador Anatoly Dobrynin.

set up—the Soviet *Izvestia* wrote about it beforehand on the 6th of February—while the U.S. newspapers mentioned that you wanted to turn Vietnam into a Yugoslavia. Don't you think that would be irritating to Vietnam?

Dr. Kissinger: Yes, it is irritating to Vietnam, and extremely stupid.

Chou En-lai: Very stupid, I agree.

Dr. Kissinger: First of all, Yugoslavia made its decisions before we gave it any economic aid. [Laughter]

Chou En-lai: So it shows that some of those reporters don't study history. They just write as they wish.

Dr. Kissinger: Our best policy towards Vietnam, in our view, Mr. Prime Minister, is to be the only superpower that has no interested motives in Indochina. If we begin to attempt to maneuver in a shortsighted way with men who have fought for independence and have made revolutions all their lives it will be totally self-defeating.

Chou En-lai: Yes, you mentioned that yesterday.

Dr. Kissinger: So that will be our policy. It is the only possible policy for us.

Chou En-lai: But as soon as those opinions were expressed the dispute broke out in your Congress on whether economic aid should be given. So it is troublemaking.

Dr. Kissinger: We will have a very difficult time in our country. What is most interesting is that our opponents during the Vietnam war, the McGovern people and the liberal community, are most opposed to economic aid now.

Chou En-lai: Indeed.

Dr. Kissinger: Because they are quite cynical. It is not very popular in America to give economic aid to a country with which we have been at war and which is still holding some of our prisoners. That is not very popular. But we will succeed in obtaining it provided that North Vietnam cooperates with us by carrying out the agreement and especially by withdrawing its troops from Laos as it has promised.

Chou En-lai: Oh, yes, there is some matter I would like to tell before I forget it. That is about the two American pilots here.[6] That is, it has been decided that since the Paris Agreement has been signed we would release those two pilots during the period of the release of prisoners from Vietnam.

Dr. Kissinger: Will that be announced publicly?

Chou En-lai: You can use it when you go back and meet the press.

Dr. Kissinger: Can I say it?

---

[6] Major Philip Smith and Lieutenant Commander Robert Flynn; see Document 4.

Chou En-lai: And there is still one more—that is Downey. His attitude has been the best among the three because he probably knows he now has a chance to get out. But in accordance with our legal procedures, although his term has been shortened, he will have to wait until the latter part of this year. You can tell his mother he is in excellent health.

Dr. Kissinger: His mother has been quite ill. May I tell this to his mother, that he may be released in the latter part of this year?

Chou En-lai: Yes. If her situation becomes critical, you can tell us through your liaison officer, Ambassador Huang Hua. His behavior has been very good. It seems to be too good.

Dr. Kissinger: We have no means of communicating with him so we can't tell him to become a little worse.

Chou En-lai: [Laughs] But perhaps when he goes back he won't behave exactly the same as he does. It won't be too much in his interest to do so.

Dr. Kissinger: But these are gestures that are very important to the American public and will be very greatly appreciated. As I said before, Mr. Prime Minister, we recognize that Downey is in prison for reasons that are part of your legal system, and that he was correctly charged. And the President has said so publicly. So we consider this an act of compassion. With respect to the two pilots we have received many questions about them, and we will appreciate it to be able to say they will be released during the period of the release of American prisoners in Vietnam.

I told the Prime Minister two days ago that I would look into the question of military contracts for Taiwan. I would prefer to do this after I return to the U.S., because if I do it from here it is difficult to control what form the investigation takes. But I will communicate with Ambassador Huang Hua within two weeks or so after we return with regard to this.

With respect to Laos, our information is that obviously the cease-fire has still not been concluded.

Chou En-lai: So.

Dr. Kissinger: And partly because the understanding we had in Hanoi that the military arrangements should be made first and the political arrangements should follow does not seem to have been carried out by both parties. And they are now trying to negotiate a total agreement. One of the difficulties is the one I mentioned to the Prime Minister yesterday, the insistence of the Pathet Lao of singling out the U.S. and Thailand. Our position is that we should say "all bombing should stop", rather than "the U.S. and Thailand and other countries should stop".

And apparently also France is playing an excessive role, or at least an active role. [Chou nods] So we are not exactly clear, though we still think an arrangement will be made in the next few days.

Chou En-lai: We have an embassy in Vientiane but the information they give us is very various, sometimes contradictory.

Dr. Kissinger: We have the same problem.

Chou En-lai: We have the Ambassador from Phouma here. Phouma has an ambassador in Peking. The Pathet Lao don't have an ambassador. This ambassador doesn't give us much information either.

Dr. Kissinger: Phouma has told me he is very anxious to have closer relations with the PRC and we have encouraged him to do so.

Chou En-lai: We are waiting until they have settled their problem, because a premature action would not be wise. Their King is not bad either.

Dr. Kissinger: He is a very wise man.

Chou En-lai: He is patriotic and honest. Have you met him?

Dr. Kissinger: I have not met him. But I have been impressed by what I have seen him do. He only intervenes at critical moments but always in an intelligent manner.

Chou En-lai: He is the man of the type of the East. They say you stayed a bit, sat down for a while, in the Imperial Garden this morning.

Dr. Kissinger: Yes.

Chou En-lai: He liked that garden very much, the King of Laos. When he came it was also winter and I accompanied him to the Garden and he did not want to leave.

Dr. Kissinger: May I ask the Prime Minister what the Chinese intentions are with respect to the road-building program after the settlement is achieved?

Chou En-lai: After we finish the road the project will be finished and then we will leave. And we will explain that to the Laotian Government. It was Phouma who asked us to build the road. The King wasn't opposed either. Especially the road from Phong Saly to Samneua. That is a very difficult stretch, because we have to build over the mountains.

Dr. Kissinger: The Thais are very nervous as they see these roads approaching them.

Chou En-lai: But our roads would only reach the Mekong River, and that is still a portion of Laos to that river, and it is a very long distance to Thailand. What is there to be feared? And the most difficult part actually is in the western part, south from Phong Saly east to Samneua and that is the part that Laos wants us to help them.

The main problem of Laos is the lack of the population, the lack of numbers for the population.

Dr. Kissinger: That is true, and the large size of all their neighbors.

Chou En-lai: Yes, indeed, but just to say something offhand, perhaps it would be best for Thailand to send back the part of the population that is of Laotian nationality to Laos, to help them build the road. They speak the same language.

But it was only after the Indochina issue came to our notice that we really came to know about Laos. Before that, when we were making our revolution, we did not know about that country. Although there have been many writings in our historical books about the country called the Land of Vientiane, which is literally in Chinese "the land of 10,000 elephants". And the same with Cambodia. We had very ancient contacts with Cambodia, and many Chinese emigrated there. But still, even at the end of the 40's when we are in power we didn't even know that there was Cambodia. But at that time we had known there was the United States in the world and also Mexico. We did not know there were two countries called Cambodia and Laos at that time. So you can see our knowledge was very limited, so we are not very familiar about surrounding countries.

Dr. Kissinger: Well, we are not so disturbed by the Chinese troops in northern Laos as we would be by others that we could imagine there.

Chou En-lai: And after the ceasefire the Chinese troops in that area will have no role to play, so the anti-aircraft troops will be withdrawn. Otherwise they will be useless there.

Dr. Kissinger: The fear of the Thais is that once the roads are built guerrillas will start traveling them.

Chou En-lai: But the debt that the Thais owe us is that the Chiang Kai-shek troops that retreated out of Yunnan 24 years ago have settled down—the original general who commanded those Chiang Kai-shek troops for 20 years was General _____ who retreated from _____[7] to outside Chinese borders—and since then they have stayed in Burma, Laos and Thailand in the border regions. Their main route of transportation is out of Bangkok to Taiwan. They have settled down there and acquired arms and engaged in smuggling and all other activities. They very often come back to Yunnan. And almost all the special agents we have detected in that area came in from Thailand.

Dr. Kissinger: May I mention that to them?

Chou En-lai: You can.

Dr. Kissinger: Because I have the impression that Thailand is in principle willing to improve its relationship with you, and we have no objection.

---

[7] Omissions are in the original.

Chou En-lai: The greatest fear they have is the large number of overseas Chinese in their country.

Dr. Kissinger: Yes.

Chou En-lai: And as I have mentioned before, the tradition of the Chinese abroad is to be very conservative. They always speak Chinese and even maybe now they don't speak the local language very well, and so when they meet each other they flock together. And besides, those who are laborers for instance in the rubber plantations, a lot of them do a lot of business and quite well, and also some who grow rice and grow vegetables in the outskirts of the cities. Besides those laborers a number engage in small business and thrive, and also restaurants and laundries. Very prosperously. Perhaps the laundries are getting less. Before in the U.S. they opened a number of laundries; perhaps they are nonexistent now.

Dr. Kissinger: I don't know many revolutions that were made by heads of laundries. [Laughter]

Chou En-lai: That is why! But they are very afraid of these things perhaps because of the numbers of Chinese. And so one of the first things we did to solve that issue was during the Bandung Conference[8] we proclaimed we were not in favor of dual nationality, dual citizenship. We would rather they would select one. We think it would be better for them to be citizens of the local country they have settled down in, and not that we, China, would have to tend them. And if they maintain their status as overseas Chinese, then they would have to abide by the laws and regulations of the country in which they resided. Because they have continued to speak Chinese they would also know Chinese writing, and therefore their younger generations would want to read newspapers and pamphlets from China. That would be what your President mentioned in his inaugural speech about ideological influence. But as to how many of the Maoists are really true Maoists, I really do not dare say. I told you about Mr. Reston's son, pistol in hand, claiming he was a Maoist.

Dr. Kissinger: No.

Chou En-lai: Maybe you forgot. I believe I told you something about that.

Dr. Kissinger: Well, there are many self-proclaimed Maoists in the U.S.

Chou En-lai: With arms too, because it is very easy to obtain weapons in your country.

---

[8] The Bandung Conference was a meeting of Asian and African leaders held at Bandung, Indonesia, in 1955.

Dr. Kissinger: The Prime Minister asked yesterday about the neutralization of Southeast Asia.

Chou En-lai: Yes.

Dr. Kissinger: I think we should separate the long-term evolution and the middle-term evolution from the immediate future. It is clear that the assumptions on which American policy was based in the 1950's of creating a bloc of nations to contain the monolithic Communist world, or even to contain the PRC, are no longer valid. And consequently many of the institutions that were created then, such as SEATO, have lost their vitality and much of their meaning.

Chou En-lai: And for this purpose it might be said that the institutions for that purpose in Southeast Asia are more numerous than in any other area in the world. Even you, who are a student of Southeast Asian affairs, perhaps might not be able to remember all the names they have taken. Of course, the most well-known is SEATO. But there was something typical about SEATO: Very few countries that are situated in Southeast Asia have joined it.

Dr. Kissinger: Yes, a very curious phenomenon.

Chou En-lai: At that time Nehru had a famous saying. He said none of the Southeast Asian countries had joined the Southeast Asian Treaty Organization.

Dr. Kissinger: Yes, but I think it is also true that now India is stretching out its hands in that direction, and therefore to create a vacuum in that direction is not necessarily desirable. I think the two countries that now want to create blocs in Southeast Asia are India and the Soviet Union.

Chou En-lai: They probably first want to have neutralization in this area and then go on to create a market for what they want, the Asian security system. And what can you do about them when they still maintain that India is a nonaligned country?

Dr. Kissinger: They want an alliance of the nonaligned.

Chou En-lai: It is a very curious thing, yes, some small alliance among the smaller nonaligned countries and then a large alliance with other large aligned countries. China is the opposite—it is a nonaligned aligned country. [Laughter] So these are two typical cases, India and China, one is the aligned nonaligned country, the other is the nonaligned aligned country. Isn't that correct?

Dr. Kissinger: I agree. But therefore, for two reasons, precipitate American withdrawal from Southeast Asia would be a disaster. It would be very popular in America. One is the point I made to the Prime Minister yesterday: The most difficult task which President Nixon has in his second term is to maintain an American responsibility for the world balance of power, or for an anti-hegemonial policy by the United States. Therefore it is not desirable for the United States to be conducting policies which will support the isolationist element in America. This is our problem. But then I'll come to the second point. The second problem is that we believe that the combination of the Soviet Union and India might want to unify Indochina under one country and then create an Asian security system extending from Burma through Indonesia.

They have proposed it to Indonesia also. You know that India has proposed the same treaty with Indonesia that it has with the Soviet Union. [Chou nods yes] So then they link these two together.

Chou En-lai: The Soviet Union has also directly approached Burma about that. Slightly before General Ne Win paid a non-official visit to Hungary the Soviet Union approached him.

Dr. Kissinger: I didn't know that.

Chou En-lai: He rejected it. That is why he did not go to the Soviet Union. He was planning to go both to Hungary and the Soviet Union, and because of this he rejected the visit to the Soviet Union. And they also probably approached Razak of Malaysia too, when he was visiting Moscow. They probably also approached Lee Kuan Yew who also went to Moscow.

Dr. Kissinger: I will see Lee Kuan Yew very soon. He is very intelligent. Singapore is too small for his talents.

Chou En-lai: It is the problem created by Chinese blood. [Laughter] It is because the percentage of those of Chinese blood in Singapore are too numerous that makes Malaysia and Razak fear him.

Dr. Kissinger: That is why they rejected him.

Chou En-lai: Then they built Malaysia over him and around him and isolated him in the center.

Dr. Kissinger: But still he has the most dynamic state in the area.

Chou En-lai: But his production cannot support him. Their domestic production cannot support them. They rely on trade going through their country. They rely on transit trade and now they can only just lease some of their small islands around them to other countries. We have heard that the Soviet Union . . .

Dr. Kissinger: The Soviet Union wanted to establish a naval facility there.

Chou En-lai: Yes, because a barren island can be used to first build a factory, an oil refinery, and then used to build a dock and then used to repair boats and so on gradually developing into a naval facility.

Dr. Kissinger: Our information was they wanted to use some of the existing facilities. They wanted to lease some of the dry dock facilities. On a regular basis.

Chou En-lai: That would be the first step.

Dr. Kissinger: We prevented that.

Chou En-lai: They have already done that in Hong Kong. Hong Kong has agreed to their repairing ordinary boats but not naval vessels. But it takes them three months to repair one boat, so they maintain all around the year at least one or two naval vessels there that have their intelligence facilities on those boats. Well, now every day they can stroll around in the streets of Hong Kong. And they can also invite guests onto their ships. And they use those methods to serve their intelligence work. These are new activities on the seas which were recently invented since the Second World War.

Dr. Kissinger: Yes.

Chou En-lai: They also use these opportunities, use the fact that Hong Kong is a free port, to buy a lot of daily necessities, especially food, and take it back with them. And they would like to take Singapore the same and make it play a greater role than Hong Kong and gradually project it into a naval base. Britain would probably know about that. They will tell you about it.

Dr. Kissinger: We know about it. Because we in cooperation stopped such an attempt about a year ago. But now that Australia has such a government of limited vision the pressures on Singapore will increase even more.

Chou En-lai: After the Conservative Party in Britain came to power they established the five-power defense arrangement, which played a role in a certain way in checking those activities. Is it now that some cracks might be opening in that arrangement?

Dr. Kissinger: The Australians are in the process of withdrawing their ground forces. But they still maintain the defense arrangements.

Chou En-lai: Yes. New Zealand is more active toward the defense arrangements.

Dr. Kissinger: The Australians may be under the illusion that you will like what they are doing.

Chou En-lai: Perhaps they may have the illusion but we haven't discussed it with them.

Dr. Kissinger: I know that.

Chou En-lai: Because when I met Mr. Whitlam more than a year ago we did not discuss it at all.

Dr. Kissinger: For all these reasons we believe it would be premature for the U.S. to withdraw, because this would only open the field for others. We have no intention of staying there, but we think it would be useful if the situation could first be stabilized. We will gradually withdraw our forces from Thailand, but we think there should not be any sudden changes because any sudden change would accelerate the impact of those countries that are now trying to create their own blocs there. But the long-term trend is clear.

Chou En-lai: It seems that the countries in Southeast Asia have not entirely decided in which direction they are going to move. They have held a lot of meetings and established a lot of organizations. And recently during your visit to Hanoi they held a ministerial conference in ASEAN, Association of Southeast Asian Nations. They held a ministerial conference consisting of Thailand, Philippines, Singapore, Malaysia and Indonesia, and they decided to send an observer group to the Paris Conference. Do you know about that?

Dr. Kissinger: Yes, but I don't think they are really going to do it. I think Thailand may send an observer group.

Chou En-lai: But if they conduct their activities outside the conference you can't very well obstruct them from doing so.

Dr. Kissinger: Oh, no, we are not trying to stop them, and if they want to come in Paris we will certainly talk to them.

Chou En-lai: Who is taking the lead there—Indonesia or Thailand? Both?

Dr. Kissinger: We think both. Maybe Indonesia somewhat more. Foreign Minister Malik. Though Suharto is the more substantial man. Malik is more like my colleagues at Harvard. [Laughter]

Chou En-lai: Was he at Harvard?

Dr. Kissinger: No, but he is better at theory than execution.

Chou En-lai: Yes, he used to preach theory. He also had a slight Trotskyite phase.

Dr. Kissinger: Yes, he had that too.

Chou En-lai: He must be in his 50's. How are the relations between the two Maliks—Soviet and Indonesian?

Dr. Kissinger: I think the relations between the Soviet Malik and the Indonesian Malik are better than the relations between Brezhnev and Suharto. I think the Indonesian Malik is quite adaptable. But I think Suharto understands the problem we have been discussing very well. When we visited Jakarta in July 1969, before we had any contact with you and we still thought of you as the greatest danger in the world, we asked Suharto what the three greatest threats to Indonesia were. He said by far the greatest is the Soviet Union, then Japan, and only in third place China, and only because of the Chinese population in Indonesia. And we were absolutely astonished at that time.

Chou En-lai: And that is why when they were suppressing the people in Indonesia they massacred quite a lot of Indonesians of Chinese origin. And therefore now when they express the desire to restore diplomatic relations with us it is going to be a very difficult step for us. They had first agreed to let us send boats to take back some Chinese from Indonesia—Chinese citizens in Indonesia—but then they stopped the shipping and sent the boats back.

Dr. Kissinger: No, they were very brutal. But now in Southeast Asia they are playing a constructive role.

Chou En-lai: Perhaps. But there are also some of their methods that others might want to ape, that is their succeeding with a military dictatorship and in brutal suppression by armed force. Thailand has been learning from that example, and the Philippines is moving toward it. Perhaps it is difficult only for Singapore not to take such a role. I believe there is still some normal activities in Singapore, parliamentary activities and so on, aren't there?

Dr. Kissinger: Yes.

Chou En-lai: Malaysia is more of a tribal nation. And that is one of the reasons why they fear those of Chinese origin because that is one factor that can unite a portion of the people.

Dr. Kissinger: Well, it really became a state only because those nine kingdoms were all ruled by Britain. [Chou laughs] They needed a common enemy to get a sense of nationhood. They even rotate their King among the nine sultans. There is no national tradition.

Chou En-lai: So British policies in these regions very often lead to unfortunate consequences.

Dr. Kissinger: Past British policies.

Chou En-lai: Now when they want to change those policies it won't be so easy. The South Asian subcontinent is a case in point.

Dr. Kissinger: But there you have an English romantic tradition towards India. They find it very difficult to look at India as a state; they look at it more as an emotional experience. Generations of Englishmen went out to India and this affects their attitude towards India very much. During the India–Pakistan war even Alec Home, who is very intelligent, was extremely emotional and very much against us and, of course, you.

Chou En-lai: And Mountbatten, who was the final one to recognize division between Pakistan and India, also had a pro-India temperament.[9] They deliberately left the issue of Jammu and Kashmir open. You say it's emotional; it is also political. Because they left some remnants and some remaining issues to facilitate in the future the furthering of the division and the furthering of their political interest.

Dr. Kissinger: But even if this is true they are no longer strong enough to carry it out, and it is of benefit to other countries, not to Britain. Britain cannot take advantage of its own legacy.

Chou En-lai: Other people are reaping in the harvesting and gaining benefits from that. The same in the Persian Gulf.

---

[9] Louis Mountbatten, First Earl Mountbatten of Burma, was the Supreme Allied Commander South East Asia Theatre and, later, Viceroy of India immediately before India and Pakistan became independent.

Dr. Kissinger: We will be more active in the Persian Gulf from now on.

Chou En-lai: Yes, and as we mentioned yesterday we believe you are not paying enough attention to the area from the Persian Gulf to the South Asian Subcontinent. Perhaps also affected by your domestic public opinion.

Dr. Kissinger: Well, domestic public opinion with respect to India is very complex, as the Vice Minister remembers from when he was there.

Chou En-lai: Then do you have some kind of British romanticism in your country too? [Laughter]

Dr. Kissinger: It is very difficult to develop romantic feelings towards Mrs. Gandhi. [Laughter] The romantic feeling in our country is different. With the British it was imperial romanticism. Ours is a narcissistic intellectual feeling among academics who believe what Indians say about their superior mentality and who thought that India would execute their favorite economic recipes. In America the attraction of India is largely in the universities. The average American cannot stand the Indians.

But we will work with the Shah to be more active in the Persian Gulf, and we are studying the problem of naval deployment in that area, together with Britain.

Chou En-lai: Begum Bhutto is arriving this afternoon. If you have a free moment would you like to meet her tomorrow morning?

Dr. Kissinger: I will be prepared to pay a courtesy call. If we could avoid having pictures.

Chou En-lai: You can meet just inside the Guest House, the compound Guest House.

Dr. Kissinger: On a personal basis. I don't mind it being announced after she returned that I paid a courtesy call on her. When is she returning?

Chou En-lai: She will leave Shanghai on the 21st.

Dr. Kissinger: Well, after I return or after she returns, whichever you prefer.

Chou En-lai: That would be good, and we can also arrange first of all that it would not be made public.

Dr. Kissinger: So on the 20th you can say I paid a courtesy call. Say the 21st, you can say I paid a courtesy call.

Chou En-lai: That can be done.

Dr. Kissinger: That's all right. We have high regard for Pakistan. We have given in the last year over $200 million of economic assistance. We will continue and even increase this.

Chou En-lai: And this time they also took very courageous steps against Soviet subversion recently. Of course, they will also meet probably with some trouble in the two minority regions, one is Baluchistan and the other is the northwest.

Dr. Kissinger: Yes, Pushtunistan. When Mrs. Gandhi was in America before the Bangladesh war she also pointed out those two areas as areas that did not really belong to Pakistan. [Laughter]

Chou En-lai: So she wants to complete the dismemberment of Pakistan.

Dr. Kissinger: I think that would certainly be her objective. I don't know whether she would start a war but she would certainly encourage movements of breaking away. The Shah is very worried about it. I don't know whether the Prime Minister has ever had the opportunity to exchange views with the Shah.

Chou En-lai: We only met the Shah by note, and the Prime Minister. We had a preliminary exchange of views. And recently our relations with Iran have been pretty good. But they cannot go too far in fear of their northern neighbor.

Dr. Kissinger: Yes, they have a problem. But they understand the dangers.

Chou En-lai: So when the Empress came here the Shah went to Moscow.

Dr. Kissinger: Yes, but he has no illusions. We know him very well. He is a very farsighted man.

Chou En-lai: And in Southeast Asia, which do you think is taking the lead? You just mentioned Indonesia or Thailand. What do you think of the roles of Malaysia and the Philippines?

Dr. Kissinger: I think they are both domestically too weak to play a leading role. The Philippines theoretically should be able to do it but it cannot do it because of its domestic difficulties.

Chou En-lai: And except for Indonesia we only have some trade relations with those countries. And we are not in a hurry to establish diplomatic relations with them. And as you just now mentioned we would wish to see a natural development in the situation. As for the revolutionary movements in those areas, there are bound to be some, but they will not probably be maturing very quickly. That is our opinion. And in Indonesia, the situation was created by mistakes on both sides, both Sukarno and the Communist Party. That was not revolution; that was intrigue, and that inevitably led to defeat.

Dr. Kissinger: It had no objective basis.

Chou En-lai: There was no reliance on the masses.

Dr. Kissinger: It was really a sort of coup.

Chou En-lai: Actually it was a palace coup d'etat, and it was a very particular one too. Because in appearance it was a coup to depose Sukarno. Actually he was the one who instigated it. It was a very curious coup d'etat that has been seen in the world. Because we have had contacts and experiences both with the Indonesian Communist Party and Sukarno. He was one of our good friends, Bung Karno. We called him Bung Karno, which is "friend Sukarno." And the result of the event made it seem as if we were involved. Actually it was done by themselves. They had a very large delegation in Peking at the time of the coup. They were Sukarno's people, and we advised them not to return. But they insisted, and upon return they were all thrown into jail. And you can see from this that all movements that do not rely on the masses are bound to fail.

Dr. Kissinger: The thought at that time that was expressed was that the Communist Party of Indonesia thought Sukarno would not live long and that they had to seize power while he was still alive.

Chou En-lai: That was not entirely so. The situation was very complicated and up to the present time we have still not completely unraveled the inner stories of that coup d'etat. What Sukarno wanted to do was to arrest all the various generals that he was dissatisfied with.

Dr. Kissinger: That is a temptation that one often has.

Chou En-lai: [Shaking finger] One of the generals that was most vehemently opposed to Sukarno was Nasution. But Sukarno did not know he had an underground tunnel beneath his house. Sukarno sent his troops to surround Nasution's house, but then he left through the tunnel.

Dr. Kissinger: They killed Nasution's son-in-law.

Chou En-lai: When he surrounded the house. But the main thing was that he let Nasution flee. And the second point was that the one he placed the most faith in was Suharto. So these palace coups don't work. If it succeeded it would be the same as Khrushchev, who was finally deposed by the one he placed the most faith in, namely Brezhnev.

Any movement that does not rely upon the masses is no revolution. And although at that time in Indonesia there existed a large-scale mass movement, yet they did not employ that mass movement, and the masses were placed in a position in which they could only wait mutely for what was awaiting them. And the result was that the very vigorous and large-scale movement met with major defeat and a large number of the masses were massacred. And as the result Suharto learned a lesson: He wouldn't allow Nasution to grasp power, although they were the two who collaborated in the massacring and operation. Is he still alive, Nasution?

Dr. Kissinger: I think so. I think he is in retirement.

Could we take a five-minute break? And then perhaps I would like to talk briefly to the Prime Minister about Cambodia and the Paris Conference?

Chou En-lai: Fine.

[There was a brief break from 4:40–4:50 p.m.]

Dr. Kissinger: It will be a new experience to have an unofficial official non-diplomatic diplomatic office.

Mr. Holdridge: Until 1959 the British had a "negotiating representative."

Chou En-lai: Until 1954. Until the Geneva Agreement. According to the agreements we reached at Geneva, because I had a direct conversation with Sir Alec Douglas-Home about it and at that time we agreed that we can raise the level to carry the work, but the host will still be the "negotiating representative."

Dr. Kissinger: First, about Cambodia. I cannot add much to what I said yesterday. But we would be in principle prepared—after you have had an opportunity to consult with Sihanouk—to discuss with you who might be acceptable negotiators on both sides and acceptable principals in an interim government. And I repeat, we would make an effort to find a solution which is consistent with the dignity of all sides. We also believe that an interruption in military activities after the withdrawal of North Vietnamese forces . . .

Chou En-lai: As for this question, as I said yesterday it is still under consideration, so I wouldn't reply today. Perhaps tomorrow I will be able to do so.

Dr. Kissinger: I understand. On the Conference, we haven't heard what the Soviet view is. A second secretary of the Soviet Embassy in London who claimed he was a Southeast Asian expert called on our Embassy in London and proposed that the Secretary General should be made the Chairman. This is a very curious means of communication to us and we don't know whether to pay any attention to it. I don't understand it, because normally when the Soviet Union wants to communicate something important they communicate it directly to me. So I don't know whether this was a personal idiosyncrasy. But except for that we have heard nothing from them about the Conference.

Chou En-lai: Does that second secretary have a relationship or friendship with the Ambassador in London?

Dr. Kissinger: No. Our Ambassador in London is not one of the more intellectual members of our diplomatic corps. And he does not deal with Soviet Ambassadors; he prefers to deal with lords. Not these Lords—not this Lord [meaning Winston Lord]. [Laughter] As far as I understand, this second secretary took the initiative and claimed to be a Southeast Asian expert. But never has the Soviet Union communicated any proposals to us in this way and normally we would pay no attention to it at all. Before the Soviet Ambassador left for vacation I told him our ideas about the Conference but they have never replied.

Our view would be to agree on as many matters as we can before the Conference, to avoid as much controversy as we can during the Conference. Therefore, I wondered to what extent we can discuss this Act we gave you. We still have not yet heard from the North Vietnamese.

Chou En-lai: The diplomatic contact you mentioned just now—of course the form was quite curious. But this matter itself isn't anything unexpected to us.

Dr. Kissinger: Oh, really?

Chou En-lai: Because as you have mentioned several times, that is, perhaps in August it was you who accidentally raised the question of the joining of the Secretary General to this Conference and later it was the Vietnamese friends who proposed that the Secretary General should participate in this guarantee conference. But now none of the sides know how to deal with him [laughter], so the inevitable result must be that it must be the Soviet Union who initiated it.

Dr. Kissinger: In Hanoi you say?

Chou En-lai: The idea probably primarily was referring to the ideas coming from the Soviet Union. Because neither of us know how to deal with this question and Premier Pham Van Dong said he did not know how to deal with him.

Dr. Kissinger: Yes. I proposed that because they had agreed on a round table perhaps we should put the Secretary General in the middle. [Laughter]

Chou En-lai: And this proves that you did not know how to make use of his function before.

Dr. Kissinger: I must tell you honestly, Mr. Prime Minister, in August it was my judgment that the North Vietnamese had no intention of settling at that time.

Chou En-lai: Yes.

Dr. Kissinger: So we may have submitted a lot of papers whose only purpose was to show that we were reasonable but where we had no expectation that an agreement would happen. It seemed pointless to speak about an international conference when we had not yet agreed to one line of the agreement. Your ally, as I told you last night at dinner, Mr. Prime Minister, has many historic qualities but a very novel negotiating procedure. For example, at a time when literally we had not agreed on one word of anything, in August and then in September, they would demand that we agree to settle by October 31. And it was in the period when nothing very serious seemed to be going on that it was possible—I have to check when I come home—that we may have put the Secretary General into some document. It is possible.

Chou En-lai: So that has provided them an opportunity. So I have this impression.

Dr. Kissinger: Yes, I understand.

Chou En-lai: So finally the Vietnamese comrades raised this point. Because when Tho said to me on that point there indeed were two possibilities, that you had this idea or they proposed it. But as to who would decide it—the Soviet Union. That is my arbitrary judgment.

Dr. Kissinger: I understand.

Chou En-lai: I could not arrive at any conclusion because both of your sides were unprepared.

Dr. Kissinger: If they had never mentioned it in the serious negotiations we would never have mentioned it. But once they mentioned it—not being in the United Nations—how could we, as a founding member of the UN, reject it?

Chou En-lai: That is why you failed to arrive at any conclusion on that point. That is why I sent you a message asking you to clarify this point, as to what capacity the Secretary General would participate, and perhaps because you were going to meet me that is why you did not give me any reply.

Dr. Kissinger: I think we sent you a reply.

Chou En-lai: But not on this point, that is, what role would the Secretary General play.

Dr. Kissinger: I sent you a reply.

Chou En-lai: And you proposed that there were to be two possibilities.

Dr. Kissinger: We said there would be two possibilities.

Chou En-lai: We gave you two messages, the first asking for clarification, and then when there was no reply we suggested that the two countries rotate. Then you replied.

Dr. Kissinger: Well, it was probably due to the fact that we had not made up our mind.

Chou En-lai: If they are aware of this, the two sides, the RVN and your side, would be able to oppose it and as a result the Soviet Union would oppose it and that would not be very good.

Dr. Kissinger: The Soviet Union does not know of your proposal from us.

Chou En-lai: Well, the Vietnamese friends may tell them about it.

Dr. Kissinger: We have not told them.

Chou En-lai: Therefore they might work out a new method, that is, to ask the Secretary General to be the Chairman. Because France has spread the word. France could have been the Chairman of the Conference in the capacity of the host country, but since Thieu is opposed to them, that is perhaps why the Soviet Union wanted to bypass this point. Perhaps they wanted to support France to start with and they thought that wouldn't be so good and they wanted to ask your approval of it.

Dr. Kissinger: The DRV?

Chou En-lai: The Soviet Union.

Dr. Kissinger: They never discussed France with us.

Chou En-lai: It is only our idea that as the host country France may be Chairman of the Conference.

Dr. Kissinger: But if France is Chairman what happens to the Secretary General?

Chou En-lai: [Laughs] So therein lies the complexity of the problem!

Dr. Kissinger: From many points of view if would not be, except for the fact that the French have an unusual ability to irritate Americans. And especially the Foreign Minister.

Chou En-lai: Yes. I am not very clear about this.

Dr. Kissinger: Well, it is a question of personality, not substance. Because we agree with the Prime Minister about Pompidou. We would like to support him. And we did not react publicly when he attacked us. But France has certain possibilities. It is not acceptable to Thieu, which perhaps could be managed, but it still leaves the question of the Secretary General. The other possibility is your proposal that the U.S. and the DRV are co-chairmen. This has the difficulty that it discriminates against the two South Vietnamese parties. And unless you make the Secretary General the executive secretary of the Conference this is awkward because it is not consistent with his role to be a participant at a conference. The third possibility is to ask the four members of the Central Commission to be rotating chairmen of the Conference, and with the Secretary General as executive secretary.

Chou En-lai: It is true that Vietnam has agreed to the fact that both the DRV and the USA would be the co-chairmen of the Conference but they wouldn't agree to the Secretary General to be acting as either the executive chairman or the executive secretary.

Dr. Kissinger: They have not thought it through. They have not understood the problem and they said they would have to study it. They were also afraid that you would oppose the Secretary General in any role and they wouldn't want to do anything to offend you.

Chou En-lai: And perhaps just because of this they find it a bit difficult for them. And to start with they told both you and us that if there is any new situation they would tell you through their embassy here in Peking.

Dr. Kissinger: They told you that?

Chou En-lai: Yes, and they have told us more than what they told you. They even said they would send people here.

Dr. Kissinger: They did not tell me that.

Chou En-lai: But up to now they haven't sent any people here yet. And their Vice Foreign Minister is coming tomorrow afternoon.[10]

Dr. Kissinger: Thach?

Chou En-lai: Yes.

Dr. Kissinger: Does he want to talk to me?

Chou En-lai: They did not mention that. They just mentioned that Thach would be coming. Up to now we haven't been informed if there are any new views yet, about the arrangement for the Secretary General or about the draft of the Act.

Dr. Kissinger: But maybe, if you agree, it would be useful if I could talk to him while he was here. Because it might avoid a great deal of confusion.

Chou En-lai: That is true. If he comes tomorrow.

Dr. Kissinger: If he comes tomorrow I will see him, because if we exchange messages it will get too confusing, and we have great confidence in him. He is a very good man.

Chou En-lai: He worked with Mr. Sullivan.

Dr. Kissinger: Yes, but he also always sat in with Le Duc Tho. So then perhaps we cannot really discuss it until you have had a chance to talk to Thach.

Chou En-lai: One thing is the draft of the Act. Another thing is about the arrangement for the Secretary General. As for the rest, we can talk.

Dr. Kissinger: We cannot talk about the Act or the arrangement until Thach is here.

Chou En-lai: Because we don't even know what is the view of the hosts here as one of the hosts. That is the DRV. This is the problem. So we can discuss how long will the conference last, and how to host this conference, and also the question of guarantees, how it will be operated.

Dr. Kissinger: First, may I ask the Prime Minister does he mind if we send a message to the North Vietnamese saying we would be prepared to see Mr. Thach here? Or would you prefer to handle this?

Chou En-lai: No, we don't mind. Because we have told you that during your stay in Peking you can consult with them, with their Ambassador. Perhaps their Ambassador hasn't received any instructions from their country.

---

[10] Nguyen Co Thach.

Dr. Kissinger: We usually contact them through Paris.

Chou En-lai: But when you first came here you also mentioned that they can also contact you here in Peking.

Dr. Kissinger: We told them they can contact us through Paris or we would be prepared to have them contact us through Peking—in which case they should put their message into English because we would have no interpreters here.

Chou En-lai: What was their reply?

Dr. Kissinger: Their reply was they might do either.

Chou En-lai: But they did not mention that after Thach came here they might contact you, so it might be a prudent way if after he has arrived here we will tell them your idea.

Dr. Kissinger: Good. So why don't you do it?

Chou En-lai: How do you envision the Paris Conference? What is your assessment?

Dr. Kissinger: We think that if there is no prior understanding on some of these issues there will be an unbelievable confusion.

Chou En-lai: Do you think it is possible that the Soviet Union might formally propose that the Secretary General would act as the Chairman of the Conference?

Dr. Kissinger: I wouldn't have thought so but the only . . . if you had asked me a week ago I would have said no. But on the evidence we have, it is now conceivable to me. But I don't see why they should do it because I don't believe that your Vietnamese friends would want that.

Chou En-lai: Because Tho has told me they have never envisioned that the Secretary General would be the Chairman of the Conference. After we have found this out, after the arrival of Thach, now we can discuss it with him.

Dr. Kissinger: He is arriving tomorrow afternoon.

Chou En-lai: The plane will be taking off at 2:00 in the afternoon so we can talk in the evening.

Dr. Kissinger: Oh, they take off from Hanoi at 2:00. So they get here about 6:00.

Chou En-lai: Yes.

Dr. Kissinger: I will be prepared to discuss it in the evening, and if we can come to an understanding between the PRC, the DRV and the U.S., we will then maintain that position at the Conference. [Chou nods] Our idea is that the conference should be fairly short.

Chou En-lai: From three to four days?

Dr. Kissinger: Four to five days.

Chou En-lai: At most, five?

Dr. Kissinger: Something like that. We think it should have some final declaration similar to what we have proposed to you. We think that the guarantee cannot be expressed in any other way except that the participants indicate some responsibility for restraint in the area and to exercise their influence in that direction. But we also think that the International Control Commission must report to somebody other than the parties. Otherwise the reports are sent to the culprits. So we thought that they could be sent to the Secretary General, for example, for distribution to the members of the Security Council or to some other forum.

Chou En-lai: If the guarantee would be offered by all the participating countries of the Conference plus the Secretary General, then if there should be any especially major issues cropping up then that means that it would only be set up through the holding of the Conference itself. Another Conference.

Dr. Kissinger: That is a possibility, that the Secretary General could reconvene the Conference.

Chou En-lai: Another possibility is to refer the matter to the UN Security Council. We have never thought of that. Because in that way the question would be turned to the UN and this we have never envisioned, and perhaps the Vietnamese friends would not agree to that either.

Dr. Kissinger: We would be prepared to do this, but my judgment would be that your Vietnamese friends would be more willing to have the Conference reconvened than to have the question go to the UN Security Council. But we would accept either one, whichever they prefer.

Chou En-lai: So this is the question concerning guarantee. So the purpose of your recommending the Secretary General as being the Chairman is that no matter whether the two co-chairmen would be agreeable or not, he has the right to reconvene the Conference. Then in that way he would actually act as executive chairman of the Conference.

Dr. Kissinger: That would be one possibility. Another possibility is that he could be the executive secretary of the conference and he could reconvene it only with the agreement of the two co-chairmen.

Chou En-lai: Then it is not so easy to find another secretary? [Laughter]

Dr. Kissinger: I think he is the most logical Secretary.

Chou En-lai: It sounds very ridiculous to us.

Dr. Kissinger: We honestly think that we should not be in this position. But we are in this position, and we believe that to have the Secretary General as one participant is the worst possible solution.

Chou En-lai: [Laughs] And still worse I think, if he participates in the Conference as a member.

Dr. Kissinger: That is what I meant.

Chou En-lai: Because he would represent the UN and would have the greater power.

Dr. Kissinger: That is why we want to get him some administrative function. My associate Lord is an expert on the United Nations and he shivers every time I speak.

Chou En-lai: And the question now is that the Secretary General is very happy at the moment, and he goes to many places to carry out his function.

Dr. Kissinger: If he had only kept his mouth shut he would have been all right. He is very actively travelling around calling attention to himself. He wants to run the economic aid program for Indochina.

Chou En-lai: And will everyone be willing to make contributions? Japan is also very actively interested in his activities. And he has also gathered many assistants and the UN Secretariat to discuss this question.

Dr. Kissinger: I heard there may be a conference in Japan on this. But I don't think your Vietnamese friends will want that. That was my impression.

Chou En-lai: I also think so. It is not a good way of doing things. Could it be that the Soviet Union is in favor of this way of doing things?

Dr. Kissinger: I could not have imagined it. It is inconsistent with the position they have always taken about the Secretary General.

Chou En-lai: That is true.

Dr. Kissinger: So I can't believe it.

Chou En-lai: But there is one reason perhaps that you should consider. That it is directed against China. Whenever they find it is necessary to isolate China then they will get together with the other members of the Security Council. But if the association is just the opposite then they will explain that they don't care for it at all.

Dr. Kissinger: That is why we will be prepared to act together with you and the DRV if it is at all possible.

Chou En-lai: It is better we must have consultation beforehand.

Dr. Kissinger: Yes.

Chou En-lai: That is better. If it is referred to the Paris Conference then there will be no end of it.

Dr. Kissinger: There will be no end, and if you are right about the Soviet position they can drive the DRV into an extreme position, because the DRV cannot be less nationalistic than the Soviet Union. So we will never end it in five days if there is not some prior agreement. We won't even agree on a Chairman in five days. [Laughter]

Chou En-lai: What you said is correct.

Dr. Kissinger: The Foreign Minister had better be prepared for a long stay in Paris.

Chou En-lai: In that case we will have to send the Vice Foreign Minister to take his place.

Dr. Kissinger: That is our intention. If the Conference lasts beyond a week we will leave Mr. Sullivan there.

Chi P'eng-fei: We have our Ambassador in Paris, Huang Chen, and can have him stay.

Dr. Kissinger: I like him.

Chou En-lai: And then we issue an order to designate him as being Vice Foreign Minister. So this is easy to deal with.

Dr. Kissinger: If I am any judge of your Ambassador in Paris, he will get very impatient if there are too many words used. He liked to get to the point.

Chou En-lai: [Nods yes] You have an idea of establishing an organ. Now, how to establish such an organ?

Dr. Kissinger: We believe there should be some device, somebody, either the Secretary General or maybe the permanent members of the Security Council, that can receive the reports from the International Control Commission. We do not believe there should be a permanent organ that maintains a secretariat. Secondly, we are prepared to have some multilateral discussions about the reconstruction of Indochina, but we are not sure that your friends are interested in that.

Chou En-lai: Have you discussed it with the Vietnamese?

Dr. Kissinger: Yes, but they have not stated an opinion. They did not reject it. The way it was left was that they would do a draft of this Act and that we would then compare them.

Chou En-lai: Have they given their drafts yet?

Dr. Kissinger: No. They said Friday or Saturday. But maybe Thach is bringing it with him tomorrow.

Chou En-lai: Yes, perhaps. They told us they had reached an agreement with you on those technical issues, for instance the Conference shouldn't be lasting too long and the form of the Conference should be a round table conference.

Dr. Kissinger: Yes.

Chou En-lai: And as for the arrangement of the participants around the table it should not be strictly in alphabetic order.

Dr. Kissinger: Yes. It is so complicated. I had learned it once but I have forgotten it again.

Chou En-lai: They state also that the two parties of South Vietnam should not sit shoulder to shoulder, side by side.

Dr. Kissinger: That is true. Mr. Prime Minister, we had proposed a Pentagon table, but they rejected it. [Laughter]

Chou En-lai: Perhaps there will be again some problems for signature, for signing the document.

Dr. Kissinger: Yes, there will certainly be.

Chou En-lai: There will be two ways on signing it.

Dr. Kissinger: Maybe we should sign on 13 different pages. [Laughter]

Chou En-lai: Perhaps two of them will be taken away between Tran Van Lam.

Dr. Kissinger: I know the order, but by what principle it was established I have now forgotten. But it occupied some great minds for a long time. We have also agreed that three people can sit at the table and seven can sit behind them for each delegation. And on languages— the technical things are essentially agreed to.

Chou En-lai: The French must be very satisfied with the fact that the Conference is going to be held in Paris.

Dr. Kissinger: We agreed to that, Mr. Prime Minister, to help Pompidou. We had decided not to agree to Paris.

Chou En-lai: There isn't much to be discussed about the Paris Conference. What is the number of people in each delegation?

Dr. Kissinger: Ten—three at the table and seven behind.

Chou En-lai: That is the maximum number, so it will be all right if they don't present too many people.

Dr. Kissinger: But if you have any extra places we will be glad to fill them. [Laughter] We have many bureaucrats. There are three at the table and seven behind.

Chou En-lai: So it is in the shape of radiation. [Laughter]

Dr. Kissinger: It is three, three, and four.

Chou En-lai: Then it is not very easy to deal with this because then people will have to sit shoulder to shoulder, elbow to elbow.

Dr. Kissinger: But we have solved all the difficult problems, so there isn't much left for the Conference to do: the seating arrangement, the shape of the table.

Chou En-lai: That is not important.

Dr. Kissinger: I know, but . . . so we would be prepared, as I said, to meet with Vice Minister Thach.

Chou En-lai: Yes.

Dr. Kissinger: And we think it is very useful to have a settlement of as many issues as possible. And I repeat, we would be prepared to act in concert with you and your North Vietnamese friends if it is at all possible, in order to avoid any attempts to isolate you. We will in no case participate in any attempt to isolate you.

Chou En-lai: And the main purpose is to let the Vietnam Agreement to take effect.

Dr. Kissinger: Exactly.

Chou En-lai: This is most important. It is all right if there is any difference of opinion on one or two small minor issues.

Dr. Kissinger: Oh, of course, that cannot be avoided. It is inevitable. It may even be desirable.

Chou En-lai: And there are bound to be differences.

Dr. Kissinger: Inevitably, and that is to be understood. But if a meeting can be arranged with Minister Thach I can then also give him a message about the general situation in Indochina before I go back to America.

Chou En-lai: That is good. And after I meet him tomorrow I will tell him that. So today, Mr. Jenkins and our Assistant Minister are also having a meeting in the afternoon?

Dr. Kissinger: Yes. They are making good progress.[11]

Chou En-lai: We would like to fix this point, that is that the office should be dealt with on a package basis so that it must not be made too complicated. There shouldn't be too many legalities concerned. In this way this question can be quickly settled.

Dr. Kissinger: Yes. But how should we do it? Should we send the delegation here, or should it be done in Paris?

Chou En-lai: It is better to have it settled in Paris. Since the two Foreign Ministers are going to meet in Paris.

Dr. Kissinger: They can settle it there.

Chou En-lai: They can meet and then this issue can be left to the two Ambassadors to settle there. It seems Mr. Rogers is going to meet Minister Chi P'eng-fei there, and this is chance for them to deal with it.

Dr. Kissinger: Good.

Chou En-lai: After you have the approval of your President.

Dr. Kissinger: I will formally check it with him but I know his views and he will almost certainly agree to it. We have discussed this often.

---

[11] A memorandum of conversation of the February 17, 2:30–4:15 p.m. meeting between Zhang Wenjin and Alfred Le S. Jenkins is in National Archives, Nixon Presidential Materials, NSC Files, Kissinger Office Files, Box 87, Country Files, Far East, PRC Counterpart Talks, 1971–1973.

Chou En-lai: Because this is the simplest and the quickest way of dealing with this issue and it is the easiest accounting for it to your people.

There is one point perhaps they haven't mentioned and I would like to add here, that is, about the blocked assets. After we have announced this perhaps there would be more people who would make claims against China, because at the moment your list is longer than ours.

Dr. Kissinger: Our list is longer than yours? Oh, what we have blocked.

Chou En-lai: You have blocked our banking deposits in your banks. And your list is longer than your deposits in our banks. Because there are people who wouldn't dare to mention it but perhaps now will dare to raise this point. So anyway we will settle this question by ourselves.

Dr. Kissinger: I understand. Our intention is to deal with this comprehensively and politically, and not commercially, and only to create the basis for making progress in the field of trade and other fields. If in the negotiations there should be any extreme technical difficulties, then perhaps you will approach me through our confidential channel and I will do my best to remove them.

Chou En-lai: I guess that once the principles are laid down it wouldn't be very difficult.

Dr. Kissinger: No, but sometimes our negotiators, who don't know the spirit of our negotiations or our total approach, may want to make themselves look good by taking an intransigent position on this or that item. If you then let me know, we can certainly deal with it.

Chou En-lai: So, Mr. Jenkins will not attend the Paris Conference?

Dr. Kissinger: No, but he could come over for the meetings between the Foreign Ministers. But we will make sure that the Secretary of State knows that if there should be any difficulties they will be removed. You can count on what we have told you. It may be done in a complicated form, but it will certainly be done and be done quickly. [Chou nods]

Can I raise two other things in that connection or in connection of the subject matter of exchanges. One has to do with politicians who want to come here. Your policy of insisting that the delegation always have members of both parties is a very wise one, and we think it would be constructive to maintain it.

Chou En-lai: The last time you said it would be desirable for Mr. Mansfield to come alone.

Dr. Kissinger: You are quite right. He is very insistent on coming, and we thought we could get around the problem by sending him on some governmental mission, so it is not your invitation but our proposal—our sending him. But we don't insist on that. We are prepared to tell him that he must find a companion from the other Party. That may be the easiest.

Chou En-lai: But he is quite good at keeping faith, that is he will say what he should say and not say what he should not say.

Dr. Kissinger: That is true. Except where Sihanouk is concerned. He is a little bit emotional on that subject.

Chou En-lai: And he talks a little bit excessively so that is why Sihanouk is already not too happy about it. He said Samdech Norodom Sihanouk should act as provisional head of state. But Sihanouk says he is already head of state. He did it out of good intentions but on the contrary it has led to the unhappiness on the part of Sihanouk. Senator Mansfield looks very earnest but perhaps he is not very mature politically.

Dr. Kissinger: Yes, I agree, and we don't want him involved in political negotiations. He can study humanitarian problems and exchanges and contacts. But he has no standing with us on political problems.

Chou En-lai: Is he still the chairman, the leader of the Democratic Party in the Senate?

Dr. Kissinger: Yes, majority leader in the Senate. So it is worthwhile to keep friendly relations with him. But he is a decent man.

Chou En-lai: And Senator Scott is also not bad. He did not say much when he got back to the States. But not that other Congressman.[12]

Dr. Kissinger: Congressmen are hard to control.

Chou En-lai: Ford said I was most in favor of the Japan-U.S. Security Treaty and was very much in favor of having American troops stay in the Far East.

Dr. Kissinger: I know, it was not very intelligent.

Chou En-lai: And these two Congressmen are quite similar. They talked a lot.

Dr. Kissinger: Yes, well, that is the risk with Congressmen. If you want to, after you have your liaison office, or even before, we will be glad to advise you, but it is of course your judgment as to whom is discussed. Somebody who wants to come and who would be very useful is Senator Jackson. He is a Democrat and he is one of the few Democrats who has a clear understanding of the Soviet problem.

Chou En-lai: Jackson. From which State is he?

Dr. Kissinger: Washington. He would be prepared to come with a Republican Senator so he would not insist on coming alone. But he is very helpful to us in getting our defense budget approved. And he has

---

[12] After this sentence, a note in unknown handwriting reads: "(Jerry Ford!)"

the Prime Minister's view about the agreement to limit strategic arms. He is one of the very few Democratic Senators with a very realistic view of the world.

Chou En-lai: Among the Republican Senators, which of them are similar to him?

Dr. Kissinger: Republican Senators? Buckley of New York, the brother of the one who was here last year.[13] Goldwater, but he is not intelligent, so he is not worthwhile to have here. I will think of some by tomorrow. One other question I wanted to raise with the Prime Minister, because he raised it when we discussed the prisoners. There is one of our Navy pilots who was shot down and fell in the water near Hainan Island in 1968. His name is Lt. Dunn. We only wondered whether you had any information about him. We looked for him for two days. We wonder whether perhaps Chinese authorities looked for him or found his body or found some information about him.

Chou En-lai: On which date?

Dr. Kissinger: February 14, 1968.

Chou En-lai: That was the day of the signing of the treaty between China and the Soviet Union. [Laughter]

Dr. Kissinger: It was a deliberate provocation!

Chou En-lai: We will check it.

Dr. Kissinger: Good.

Chou En-lai: You tell us more clearly about the name of that person. Is he from the aircraft carrier?

Dr. Kissinger: No, he was flying from the Philippines and he was shot down.

Chou En-lai: What type of airplane?

Dr. Kissinger: We will get you the information.

Chou En-lai: And who shot down that plane?

Dr. Kissinger: The Chinese. Here, I give you my information. [Hands over biographical data on Lt. Dunn, Tab A][14] This is all the information I have. But I can get you the information. We will find out the type of plane overnight.

Chou En-lai: So the plane was shot down in air space on Hainan Island.

Mr. Holdridge: It was over your territorial waters, within the 12-mile limit. It wasn't over Hainan itself but over the waters adjacent to Hainan.

---

[13] James L. Buckley, Conservative Party Senator from New York and brother of conservative pundit William F. Buckley.

[14] Attached but not printed.

Dr. Kissinger: We don't contest your actions.

[Miss T'ang reads paper to Chou En-lai.]

Chou En-lai: So according to this paper, the *Peking Review* carried that, so this can be checked up.

Dr. Kissinger: Yes, we just wondered what information you had about the pilot. We are not questioning your actions.

Chou En-lai: Since the *Peking Review* has carried an article about it, then we are sure that we can check it and find out information about it.

Dr. Kissinger: We would be very grateful.

Chou En-lai: And at 7:30 this evening there is going to be a sort of concert. It will last about 1½ hours, and the Foreign Minister will be accompanying you. It is a sort of concert, and they said our orchestra is going to play . . .

Miss T'ang: Try to play . . . [Laughter]

Chou En-lai: A symphony or part of a symphony from Beethoven, Number 6.

Dr. Kissinger: The Pastoral.

Chou En-lai: It is just a Chinese saying, "trying to wield an axe before Lin Pan's door".

Miss T'ang: It means an amateur trying to perform before an expert.

Dr. Kissinger: Are there any experts here? Maybe Mrs. Stifflemire?

Chou En-lai: But in order to save time, this evening I would like to have another meeting with you to talk about our assessment on the Soviet Union. Because you asked me this question and I haven't given you the reply yet. And since you have asked quite a few questions I would also like to answer this.

Dr. Kissinger: After the concert?

Chou En-lai: When are you having your dinner, before the concert or after the concert?

Dr. Kissinger: Probably before, because my colleagues are going to go shopping.

Chou En-lai: Then that is better. Then we will have the meeting after the concert at a guest house, that building where we had a meeting yesterday. And after you get back you will be able to have a rest, about a half hour, and we will check the time. We don't know whether the concert will be prolonged or not [laughter], because I know nothing about symphony.

Dr. Kissinger: I think you are carrying hospitality to extremes on this occasion, and I want to apologize to the Chinese audience who will have to suffer through an hour and a half of Western music. Not to speak of the Foreign Minister who will have to look interested. [Laughter] But he is a great diplomat.

Chou En-lai: Our Vice Foreign Minister knows something about music.

Dr. Kissinger: Really?

Chou En-lai: Our Assistant Minister understands music pretty well. He studied it. And he can speak German. Has he ever tried to speak German with you?

Dr. Kissinger: No.

Chou En-lai: Perhaps it is because you did not speak German to him.

Dr. Kissinger: No, he doesn't like my accent. Does the audience tonight know what it is coming for?

Chou En-lai: They know. There are quite a few number of people in the Foreign Ministry who know.

Dr. Kissinger: Well, we appreciate it very much.

[The meeting then adjourned.]

---

11.   Memorandum of Conversation[1]

Beijing, February 17, 1973, 10:22–11:10 p.m.

PARTICIPANTS

    Chou En-lai, Premier, State Council
    Chi P'eng-fei, Minister of Foreign Affairs
    Ch'iao Kuan-hua, Vice Minister of Foreign Affairs
    Chang Wen-chin, Assistant Foreign Minister, Acting Director of American Pacific
        Affairs Department
    Ting Yuan-hung
    T'ang Wen-sheng, Interpreter
    Shen Jo-yen, Interpreter
    Ma Chieh-hsien, Notetaker
    Lien Cheng-pao, Notetaker

    Dr. Henry A. Kissinger, Assistant to the President for National Security Affairs
    Alfred Le S. Jenkins, Department of State

---

[1] Source: National Archives, Nixon Presidential Materials, NSC Files, Kissinger Office Files, Box 98, Country Files, Far East, HAK China Trip, Memcons & Reports (originals), February 1973. Top Secret; Sensitive; Exclusively Eyes Only. The meeting was held in Villa 3. All brackets are in the original.

Richard T. Kennedy, NSC Staff
Winston Lord, NSC Staff
Mrs. Bonnie Andrews, Notetaker

Dr. Kissinger: We enjoyed the concert very much. [Light discussion about the concert.] It is much more tender when you play the music.

PM Chou: Well, Madame Bhutto has arrived here this afternoon. So we have told her that you would be ready to meet her tomorrow morning. You will go to her place. As for the others they might go to the Summer Palace. Only the Ambassador will remain there [for the Mrs. Bhutto meeting].

Dr. Kissinger: Yes, his brother was there when we visited. And his sister was a student of mine. She arrived in America in 1950 or '51, and she believed strongly in the independence of women, which she couldn't always realize in Pakistan. So we picked her up at the ship and took her to an amusement park called Coney Island and she went on something, I don't know if this exists here, a roller coaster, ten times in a row. Then she was sick for two days. After that we became good friends.

PM Chou: So she would have some courage.

Dr. Kissinger: Great courage.

PM Chou: So we have had a talk for three times already, including the day before yesterday, yesterday and today. We have touched upon some strategic issues. Why was it that we mentioned to the Doctor that the Europeans want to push the evil waters of the Soviet Union eastward?[2]

Because there have been historical examples. That was what happened during the two World Wars. During World War I King William fought in the West and was also in the East. The Czar at the beginning didn't intend to get into the fight. And as a result of the battle the main force and the thrust went East.

Dr. Kissinger: In World War I or II?

PM Chou: In World War I. As a result of that the revolution of 1917 occurred. Hindenburg put his forces in the East and then someone said that if he wouldn't put his main force in the East but in the West instead he would be successful. But this might not be true since later the U.S. entered the war.

And during World War II the Western world also wanted to push Hitler toward the Soviet Union and this also was a failure because he

---

[2] On February 15, Zhou told Kissinger, "Perhaps they [Western European leaders] want to push the ill waters of the Soviet Union in another direction—eastward." See Document 8.

put his forces in the West. This was also dangerous. But as a result the Soviet Union had an easier time. And since Hitler advanced Eastward the war had provided you an opportunity.

So the idea of going Eastward is a traditional one and now it is time for the Soviet Union to do so. Just as you said the other day, that if there was a feeling of peace in the West then the Soviet Union could use more forces in the South and in the East. But as a matter of fact the main forces are still in the East. Do you think so?

Dr. Kissinger: No. According to our calculations . . . in Europe now they have twice as many divisions in Europe as they have on your border, if you count Western Russia. If you count the divisions west of the Urals and east of the Urals it is 50–50. But there are more air forces in the West.

PM Chou: But in the West there are also the satellite countries.

Dr. Kissinger: Yes. We are only counting Soviet divisions. But satellite divisions need Soviet divisions to watch them. [Laughter]

PM Chou: That is quite another matter. If the force of the satellite countries are included then it is quite a bit more.

Dr. Kissinger: Yes. If you count them, then they are larger.

PM Chou: But for the forces in Western Europe, if your forces are not included then the forces are very small. So the increasing illusion of peace is something very deceptive and also very dangerous. So on this point perhaps we have shared the same view.

Dr. Kissinger: Exactly.

PM Chou: But there is a difference. We have made this point publicly. It was made at Comrade Ch'iao's speech in the UN last year.

Dr. Kissinger: Yes.

PM Chou: Although the two superpowers are contending for hegemony in the world, their deception is greater and the danger is greater.

Dr. Kissinger: But do you really think we are contending for hegemony right now?

PM Chou: Because it was brought out by the objective situation, and your country which has deployed in such a situation after World War II.

Dr. Kissinger: Yes, but now . . .

PM Chou: And this is the reason why we praised the speech made by President Nixon on July 6, 1972 in Kansas City.[3]

---

[3] Nixon's speech was actually on July 6, 1971. In it, he declared that "there are five great power centers in the world today," and that "Mainland China" was one of these centers. (*Public Papers: Nixon, 1971*, pp. 802–813)

Dr. Kissinger: I heard about the speech from the Prime Minister. I first saw the text when the Prime Minister sent it to me.

PM Chou: And during the annual convention of the Conservative Party in Britain Heath also expressed the same view in his concluding speech.

Dr. Kissinger: That was another speech to which the Prime Minister called my attention.

PM Chou: So this is the situation that was brought about by the U.S., and now it is a question of whether you drop it or not. If you drop it then the Soviet Union will come and problems will arise. And there still exist such questions but because we have differences, our views are different from yours. And we say that there is the possibility, but first one must call upon the people to awake and prevent this from happening. Otherwise how can you carry out defense? So on this issue, as you have mentioned recently, there have been two possibilities but there is only one possibility we think. As we have said in the UN, their so-called détente is false. They are talking about détente but actually they are engaged in expansion. Of course, some people might say that the period of Cold War has come again. But I don't think that will come true. Although the Soviet Union is engaged in expansion, it is afraid of fighting a nuclear war. And they are even worried that fighting with conventional weapons might lead to a nuclear war. That is why they have silly ideas like a nuclear treaty. That is why during the exchange of views the past three days here too we have the same view. So we can make some assessments on the various issues in the international arena.

That is the first point. I think that the central point is that the Soviet Union is afraid of fighting a war and it thinks it is better that you fight in some remote areas. And this has been borne out by the situation in the last few years. And in approaching the Middle East they will try their best to suppress them and not let them take action.

Dr. Kissinger: They specialize in using their armies against their allies.

PM Chou: And as you admit there do exist two blocs. As Chairman Mao says, one is firing empty guns. They introduced so many weapons and yet they can't use them.

Dr. Kissinger: In what areas?

PM Chou: Egypt. They have always said that they give the weapons to the Egyptians but that they don't know how to fight with them. Kosygin said that at the airport in 1969. And then they were fighting a war concerning the Suez Canal in 1956 against France and Britain.

Dr. Kissinger: Egypt?

PM Chou: So how can you say they can't fight a war? Because they . . . It is as if only the Vietnamese could fight a war. Of course, the Vietnamese should be respected but one can't say that only the people in one region can fight a war while people in another region can't.

So this is an essential point with regard to the Soviet Union. And it was principally because of this that their rhetoric about the situation will easily be accepted by others and deceives people. So I agree with your assessment about the second possibility. They seem that they are going toward that direction. And they have reaped some results to some extent. They worked out a communiqué on relaxation and you weren't able to object to it. And again in the UN Gromyko worked out a proposal on the non-use of force and permanent non-use of nuclear weapons. We opposed it, but the U.S. only abstained. And if you rejected it then you would have shown that you resort to force. So there were a great number of countries that voted abstention and there were only four countries left. Two on the left and two on the right. Our friend was only Albania, and South Africa and Portugal were on the right. And then the Soviet Czars talked about the left faction and the right faction.

Dr. Kissinger: We always play the bull to the Prime Minister who makes us come charging predictably. He comes to every meeting with a firm intention.

PM Chou: What does this indicate? It indicates that the deceptive nature has its market. So this is a fact. So we could not but expose them. Without that what would the situation be like? Otherwise only Portugal and South Africa would oppose them. Then what would it be like in the international arena? This indicates that to expose the deceptive nature of the Soviet Union is a very complicated struggle. And possibly that resolution was adopted and more than seventy countries were for it.

So on this point it is very important to expose the true features of the Soviet Union as being engaged in false relaxation of tension and engaged in expansion. So the first point is about their deceptive nature. And this is why in Europe there have been illusions of peace. So we say that the European Security Conference is not really a security conference but really an insecurity conference. This was spoken by Ch'iao, and is the words of Chairman Mao. And now it can be proved. What is coming out of that conference?

Dr. Kissinger: Nothing.

PM Chou: It seems the same is true of the Mutual Balanced Force Reduction Conference.

Dr. Kissinger: Not exactly. We discussed this.

PM Chou: That is a strong point, that it will expose them and their advances. But the conclusion must be made very clear. Otherwise the world will be deceived continually. And then, as a result, they will sign a treaty with you and import some goods and you wouldn't be able to reject it. And, as you said, in order to strengthen their arms preparation they will import arms technique. You said they were going to use technology in the U.S. to lessen the gap.

Dr. Kissinger: No. I will answer this in a minute. They want to use our technology to improve their economic position, not their military position. I agree with the Prime Minister that they want to improve their military position also.

PM Chou: The inevitable result would be that by improving their economic strength it would serve also to add to their military power and this would serve as a backing for their military strength. That is all that they have thought about, but how to realize that is another matter.

And the fourth point you have said is that they want to isolate China, claiming that China is war-like, and saying that China is against relaxation. And the result will be that they will surpass you. But we think that it is not easy for them to attain that goal. If they reach out their hands to the whole world then it will be in the same position as the U.S. was in before. You will be in a passive position. But the overall situation will be depending on the larger aspect of things.

So, we have covered the issues in Europe, the Middle East, the Mediterranean, the Indian Ocean, Indochina, the Subcontinent, and also Southeast Asia and Japan. And they want to get an upper hand in all respects, but actually that is impossible for them.

So we must realize that it is important to expose them. That is, the strategic principle should be to expose them that they are for general expansion and for false relaxation. And for the past years we have never ceased in exposing the Soviet Union's expansionism and their false relaxation. We have done this since the Chen Pao incident in 1969.[4] And in the meeting at the Peking airport we agreed to have discussions with them to test them. But after these negotiations, after they got back, what they promised would not be realized because their leadership would not endorse it. And, what Kosygin said didn't count. Actually it was he who asked me to set forward a plan, and later he was opposed to it. They even went so far as to suggest last year that we could have a mutual non-aggression treaty with them.

Dr. Kissinger: Among Allies? [Laughter]

PM Chou: But they did not agree. They would not agree that there do exist disputed areas. In the 19th century there was a treaty that was

---

[4] Chen Pao (Damansky Island) was the site of a clash during Sino-Soviet fighting at the Ussuri River in 1969.

unequal, and yet we took that treaty for the disputed areas. There do exist disputes about the areas, both in the east and the west. But they don't accept these to be disputed areas, because if they accepted, that would bring about a chain reaction.

They are so neurotic. Ch'iao was locked in a quarrel with Kuznetzov and then Minister Han Nien-long took his place and then Vice Minister Fu Haol (?)[5] took Mr. Han's place. And the negotiations have been going on for three years. Kuznetzov has been conducting another negotiation since. He does administrative work now. He is taking care of the administrative work. So the Soviet Union is so neurotic about everything. So there is a strategic consideration for these questions.

This is what I have to say.

I would like to let you know a new piece of news. Chairman Mao has invited you to a meeting. You can go with your colleague, Mr. Lord.

Dr. Kissinger: With Mr. Lord.

PM Chou: And I will go with you.

Dr. Kissinger: Now?

PM Chou: We are supposed to arrive there at 11:30. Would you like to take a rest?

Dr. Kissinger: I will leave that up to you.

PM Chou: So much for today. Now we can continue our talks tomorrow.

Dr. Kissinger: And I will make some comments tomorrow because you raised some very important questions.

PM Chou: Will you be able to give us a copy of the draft communiqué? Whenever you have finished it, you can give it to us.

Dr. Kissinger: We haven't finished it. Either tonight or tomorrow.

PM Chou: Tomorrow.

Dr. Kissinger: Fine. Should I meet you here, Mr. Prime Minister?

PM Chou: I will go to your place.

Dr. Kissinger: This is a great honor.

PM Chou: Tomorrow we can talk more deeply.

---

[5] No Chinese official with the name "Fu Haol" has been identified.

12.   Memorandum of Conversation[1]

Beijing, February 17–18, 1973, 11:30 p.m.–1:20 a.m.

PARTICIPANTS

Mao Tsetung, Chairman, Politburo, Chinese Communist Party
Chou En-lai, Premier of the State Council
Wang Hai-jung, Assistant Minister of Foreign Affairs
Tang Wen-sheng, Interpreter
Shen Jo-yun, Interpreter

Dr. Henry A. Kissinger, Assistant to the President for National Security Affairs
Winston Lord, NSC Staff

(At 11:00 p.m. February 17, 1973 at a meeting in a villa near the Guest House where Dr. Kissinger and his party were staying, Prime Minister Chou En-lai informed Dr. Kissinger that he and Winston Lord were invited to meet with Chairman Mao Tsetung at 11:30 p.m. that evening. He told Dr. Kissinger that he would come to the Guest House shortly to escort him to the Chairman's residence.

Dr. Kissinger and his delegation members at the meeting went back to the Guest House. Prime Minister Chou En-lai came to the Guest House at 11:20 p.m. and rode with Dr. Kissinger to Chungnahai. Mr. Chu, Deputy Director of Protocol, accompanied Mr. Lord. Prime Minister Chou En-lai escorted Dr. Kissinger into the outer room of the Guest House and then through another room to Chairman Mao's sitting room.

The Chairman was helped up from his chair by his young female attendant and came forward to greet Dr. Kissinger. Photographers took pictures. He welcomed Dr. Kissinger and Dr. Kissinger pointed out that it was almostly exactly a year ago that he had first met the Chairman. The Chairman then greeted Mr. Lord and commented that he was so young, younger than the interpreters. Mr. Lord replied that he was in any event older than the interpreters. The Chairman then motioned to the large easy chairs and the parties sat down. The photographers continued to take pictures.)

Chairman Mao (As he headed toward his chair): I don't look bad, but God has sent me an invitation.

---

[1] Source: National Archives, Nixon Presidential Materials, NSC Files, Kissinger Office Files, Box 98, Country Files, Far East, HAK China Trip, Memcons & Reports (originals), February 1973. Top Secret; Sensitive; Exclusively Eyes Only. The meeting was held in Mao's residence at Chungnahai. All brackets are in the original. A February 17 memorandum from Kissinger, sent telegraphically through Scowcroft, to Nixon recounted that the meeting with Mao "was extremely frank and cordial, but the substance is of such sensitivity that I should report it to you in person." (Ibid., HAK Trip Files, Box 29, Bangkok, Vientiane, Hanoi, Hong Kong, Peking, Tokyo Trip, Itinerary Como Info, Memos to Pres., February 7–20, 1973)

(To Mr. Lord) You are a young man.

Mr. Lord: I am getting older.

Chairman Mao: I am the oldest among those seated here.

Prime Minister Chou: I am the second oldest.

Chairman Mao: There was someone in the British Army who was opposed to the independence of your country. Field Marshal Montgomery was one of those to oppose your policy.

Dr. Kissinger: Yes.

Chairman Mao: He opposed the Dulles policy.[2] He probably doesn't oppose you anymore. At that time, you also opposed us. We also opposed you. So we are two enemies (Laughter).

Dr. Kissinger: Two former enemies.

Chairman Mao: Now we call the relationship between ourselves a friendship.

Dr. Kissinger: That's our sentiment.

Chairman Mao: That's what I am saying.

Dr. Kissinger: I have told the Prime Minister that we speak to no other country as frankly and as openly as we do to you.

Chairman Mao (To the photographers): That's all for you.

[The photographers leave.]

But let us not speak false words or engage in trickery. We don't steal your documents. You can deliberately leave them somewhere and try us out. Nor do we engage in eavesdropping and bugging. There is no use in those small tricks. And some of the big maneuvering, there is no use to them too. I said that to your correspondent, Mr. Edgar Snow.[3] I said that your CIA is no good for major events.

Dr. Kissinger: That's absolutely true. That's been our experience.

Chairman Mao: Because when you issue an order, for example, when your President issues an order, and you want information on a certain question, then the intelligence reports come as so many snowflakes. We also have our intelligence service and it is the same with them. They do not work well (Prime Minister Chou laughs). For

---

[2] This memorandum of conversation is also printed in *The Kissinger Transcripts*, edited by William Burr (pp. 86–101). In explaining Mao's comment about Field Marshal Montgomery, Burr notes that the British war hero visited China in 1960 and 1961. On that trip he met with Mao and Zhou and condemned the American policy associated with former Secretary of State John Foster Dulles of opposing recognition of Communist China.

[3] The journalist Edgar Snow wrote the book, *Red Star Over China,* that introduced Mao to an American audience during the 1930s.

instance, they didn't know about Lin Piao.[4] (Prime Minister Chou laughs) Then again they didn't know you wanted to come.

I read two articles in 1969. One of your Directors of your China desk in the State Department wrote an article later published in a Japanese newspaper.

Dr. Kissinger: I don't think I read that.

Prime Minister Chou: I hadn't mentioned it to you before.

Dr. Kissinger: No.

Chairman Mao: Your business was done well. You've been flying everywhere. Are you a swallow or a pigeon? (Laughter) And the Vietnamese issue can be counted as basically settled.

Dr. Kissinger: That is our feeling. We must now have a transitional period toward tranquility.

Chairman Mao: Yes, that's right.

Dr. Kissinger: The basic issues are settled.

Chairman Mao: We also say in the same situation (gesturing with his hand) that's what your President said when he was sitting here, that each side has its own means and acted out of its own necessity. That resulted in the two countries acting hand-in-hand.

Dr. Kissinger: Yes, we both face the same danger. We may have to use different methods sometimes but for the same objectives.

Chairman Mao: That would be good. So long as the objectives are the same, we would not harm you nor would you harm us. And we can work together to commonly deal with a bastard. (Laughter)

Actually it would be that sometime we want to criticize you for a while and you want to criticize us for a while. That, your President said, is the ideological influence. You say, away with you Communists. We say, away with you imperialists. Sometimes we say things like that. It would not do not to do that.

Dr. Kissinger: I think both of us must be true to our principles. And in fact it would confuse the situation if we spoke the same language. I have told the Prime Minister that in Europe you, because of your principles, can speak more firmly than we can, strangely enough.

Chairman Mao: As for you, in Europe and Japan, we hope that you will cooperate with each other. As for some things it is alright to quarrel and bicker about, but fundamental cooperation is needed.

Dr. Kissinger: As between you and us, even if we sometimes criticize each other, we will coordinate our actions with you, and we would

---

[4] Lin Biao, PRC Minister of Defense from 1959 to September 1971, allegedly plotted to assassinate Mao.

never participate in a policy to isolate you. As for Japan and Europe, we agree that we should cooperate on all essential matters with them. Europe has very weak leadership right now.

Chairman Mao: They don't unite with each other.

Dr. Kissinger: They don't unite, and they don't take farsighted views. When they are confronted with a danger they hope it will go away without effort.

Prime Minister Chou: I told Dr. Kissinger you [the U.S.] should still help Pompidou.[5]

Chairman Mao: Yes indeed.

Dr. Kissinger: We are doing our utmost, and we will do more.

Chairman Mao: (Gesturing with his hands) Now Mr. Pompidou is being threatened. It is the Socialist Party and the Communist Party putting their strength against him.

Dr. Kissinger: Yes, and they have united.

Chairman Mao: (Pointing at Dr. Kissinger) They are uniting and the Soviet Union wants the Communist Party to get into office. I don't like their Communist party, just like I don't like your Communist party. I like you, but not your Communist party. (Laughter)

In the West you always historically had a policy, for example, in both World Wars you always began by pushing Germany to fight against Russia.

Dr. Kissinger: But it is not our policy to push Russia to fight against China, because the danger to us of a war in China is as great as a war in Europe.

Chairman Mao: (Before Dr. Kissinger's remarks are translated, he makes remarks in Chinese and counts on his fingers. Miss Tang then translates Dr. Kissinger's remarks and after that Chairman Mao's remarks.)

What I wanted to say is whether or not you are now pushing West Germany to make peace with Russia and then push Russia eastward. I suspect the whole of the West has such an idea, that is to push Russia eastward, mainly against us and also Japan. Also probably towards you, in the Pacific Ocean and the Indian Ocean.

Dr. Kissinger: We did not favor this policy. We preferred the German opposition party which did not pursue this policy. (Chairman Mao, smoking a cigar, offers cigars to Dr. Kissinger and Mr. Lord who decline.)

---

[5] France held a general election on March 4 and 11. The coalition associated with French President Georges Pompidou maintained a majority in the National Assembly.

Chairman Mao: Yes, that's our feeling. We are also in favor of the opposition party in Germany.

Dr. Kissinger: They conducted themselves very stupidly.

Chairman Mao: Yes, they were defeated. The whole of Europe is thinking only of peace.

Prime Minister Chou: The illusions of peace created by their leaders.

Dr. Kissinger: Yes, but we will do our best to strengthen European defenses and keep our armies in Europe.

Chairman Mao: That would be very good.

Dr. Kissinger: We have no plan for any large reduction of our forces in Europe for the next four years (Chairman Mao turns to Prime Minister Chou).

Prime Minister Chou: In talking about reducing your troops, you mean only at the most 10 to 15 percent.

Dr. Kissinger: That is exactly correct.

Chairman Mao: What is the number of American troops in Europe? They are probably mostly rocket units.

Prime Minister Chou: There are between 300–350,000 including the Mediterranean.

Chairman Mao: That probably does not include the Navy.

Dr. Kissinger: It does not include the Navy. There are about 275,000 in Central Europe. That does not include the Sixth Fleet in the Mediterranean.

Chairman Mao: And your troop deployment to Asia and the Pacific Ocean is too scattered. You have them in Korea. I heard the number is about 300,000.

Dr. Kissinger: About 40,000.

Chairman Mao: And from 8 to 9,000 with Chiang Kai-shek.

Prime Minister Chou: In Taiwan.

Chairman Mao: Then it is said that there are two groups in Japan, 40,000 in Okinawa and 20 to 30,000 in Japan proper. I don't know how many there are in the Philippines. Now you have remaining in Vietnam a bit over 10,000.

Dr. Kissinger: But they will all be withdrawn.

Chairman Mao: Yes, and I heard that you have 40,000 in Thailand.

Dr. Kissinger: That is correct. But all the units the Chairman mentioned are mostly air force units and therefore they probably cannot be measured by the number of personnel.

Chairman Mao: You also have ground forces, for instance, in South Korea.

Dr. Kissinger: In South Korea we have ground forces.

Chairman Mao: That was all begun by Truman and Acheson. So this time you held a memorial service for Truman and we didn't go. (Laughter)

Dr. Kissinger: When you have a liaison office in Washington it will be more possible in the future.

Prime Minister Chou: You've held all these memorial services, both for Truman and Johnson (Chairman Mao and Prime Minister Chou laugh).

It seems to me that your voice is hoarse today. You should have a day's rest tomorrow. Why do you want to continue to talk so much?

Dr. Kissinger: Because it is very important that you and we understand what we are going to do and to coordinate our actions, and therefore we always tell the Prime Minister what our plans are in various areas of the world so that you can understand the individual moves when they are made.

Chairman Mao: Yes. When you pass through Japan, you should perhaps talk a bit more with them. You only talked with them for one day and that isn't very good for their face.

Dr. Kissinger: Mr. Chairman, we wanted this trip's emphasis to be on the talks in Peking, and I will take a separate trip to Tokyo.

Chairman Mao: Good. And also make clear to them.

You know the Japanese feelings towards the Soviet Union are not so very good.

Dr. Kissinger: They are very ambivalent.

Chairman Mao: (Gesturing with his hand) In a word, during the Second World War, Prime Minister Tanaka told our Premier, what the Soviet Union did was that upon seeing a person about to hang himself, they immediately took the chair from under his feet.

Dr. Kissinger: Yes.

Chairman Mao: It could be said that they didn't fire a single shot and yet they were able to grab so many places (Prime Minister Chou chuckles). They grabbed the People's Republic of Mongolia. They grabbed half of Sinkiang. It was called a sphere of influence. And Manchukuo, on the northeast, was also called their sphere of influence.

Dr. Kissinger: And they took all the industry out of it.

Chairman Mao: Yes. And they grabbed also the islands of Sakhalin and the Kuriles Island. (Chairman Mao and Prime Minister Chou discuss among themselves.) Sakhalin is the southern part of the Kuriles Island. I will look it up in the dictionary to see what its Chinese translation is.

Dr. Kissinger: The Japanese are tempted by the economic possibilities in Russia.

Chairman Mao: (Nodding yes) They want to grab something there.

Dr. Kissinger: But we will encourage closer ties between Japan and ourselves, and also we welcome their relationship with the People's Republic.

Chairman Mao: We also believe that rather than Japan having closer relations with the Soviet Union, we would rather that they would better their relations with you. That would be better.

Dr. Kissinger: It would be very dangerous if Japan and the Soviet Union formed closer political relations.

Chairman Mao: That doesn't seem likely.

Prime Minister Chou: The prospects are not too good.

Chairman Mao: We can also do some work there.

Dr. Kissinger: The Soviet Union has made overtures but the Japanese have not responded. They have invited Ohira to go to Moscow.

Prime Minister Chou: Yes, this year, the second half.

Dr. Kissinger: This year.

Prime Minister Chou: And it seems on this question that Ohira has a clearer idea of the Soviet Union than others. But there are some not so clear in their understanding as their Foreign Minister.

Dr. Kissinger: That is correct.

Prime Minister Chou: That is also the bureaucracy as you term it.

Dr. Kissinger: We are prepared to exchange information with you on these matters.

Prime Minister Chou: (To Chairman Mao) We have decided besides establishing a liaison office in each capital to maintain the contact between Huang Hua and the White House.

Chairman Mao: (To Prime Minister Chou) Where is the stress?

Prime Minister Chou: The liaison office will handle the general public exchanges. For confidential and urgent matters not covered by the liaison office we will use the channel of Ambassador Huang Hua.

Chairman Mao: Huang Hua has met an ill fate (Prime Minister Chou laughs). He was doing very well in your place and immediately upon his return to Shanghai, he twisted his back.

Dr. Kissinger: We will find a doctor for him when he returns.

Chairman Mao: Yes. (Prime Minister Chou laughs). He seemed more safe in your place. Immediately upon his return to Shanghai he collapsed.

From the atmosphere with which your President received our acrobatic troupe, I thought that the Vietnamese issue was going to be settled.

There were some rumors that said that you were about to collapse (laughter). And the women folk seated here were all dissatisfied with that (laughter, especially pronounced among the women). They said if the Doctor is going to collapse, we would be out of work.

Dr. Kissinger: Not only in China.

Chairman Mao: Yes, and the whole line would collapse like dominos.

Dr. Kissinger: Those were just journalists' speculation.

Chairman Mao: Only speculation?

Dr. Kissinger: Only speculation.

Chairman Mao: No ground whatsoever?

Dr. Kissinger: No ground whatsoever. In fact the opposite was true. We have now been able to place our men into all key positions.

Chairman Mao: (Nodding yes) Your President is now saying that you are proposing something as if you were moving the Great Wall from China to the United States, that is, trade barriers.

Dr. Kissinger: What we want to do is lower barriers.

Chairman Mao: To lower them? Then you were doing that just to frighten people. You are saying that you are going to raise tariffs and non-tariff barriers and maybe you do that to intimidate Europe and Japan.

Dr. Kissinger: Partly. We are proposing a trade bill which gives both the power to raise and lower barriers, in order to get it passed through Congress. We must create the impression that we might increase barriers. We want executive authority to do it without Congressional approval, but if we ask Congress to reduce barriers they would refuse. (Prime Minister Chou laughs.) And this is why we are asking for executive authority to move in either direction.

Chairman Mao: What if they don't give it to you?

Dr. Kissinger: We think they will give it to us. It will be a difficult battle, but we are quite certain we will win. We are proposing it also in such general language that we can remove discrimination that still exists towards the People's Republic.

Chairman Mao: The trade between our two countries at present is very pitiful. It is gradually increasing. You know China is a very poor country. We don't have much. What we have in excess is women. (Laughter)

Dr. Kissinger: There are no quotas for those or tariffs.

Chairman Mao: So if you want them we can give a few of those to you, some tens of thousands. (Laughter)

Prime Minister Chou: Of course, on a voluntary basis.

Chairmain Mao: Let them go to your place. They will create disasters. That way you can lessen our burdens. (Laughter)

Dr. Kissinger: Our interest in trade with China is not commercial. It is to establish a relationship that is necessary for the political relations we both have.

Chairman Mao: Yes.

Dr. Kissinger: That is the spirit with which we are conducting our discussions.

Chairman Mao: I once had a discussion with a foreign friend. (The interpreters hold a discussion with Chairman Mao.) I said that we should draw a horizontal line—the U.S.-Japan–Pakistan–Iran (Chairman Mao coughs badly.)–Turkey and Europe.

Dr. Kissinger: We have a very similar conception. You may have read in a newspaper that Mr. Helms has been moved to Iran, and there was a great deal of speculation how this affected my position. In fact we sent Helms to Iran to take care of Turkey, Iran, Pakistan and the Persian Gulf, because of his experience in his previous position and we needed a reliable man in that spot who understands the more complex matters that are needed to be done. (Chairman Mao lights his cigar again.) We will give him authority to deal with all of these countries, although this will not be publicly announced.

Chairman Mao: As for such matters we do not understand very much your affairs in the United States. There are a lot of things we don't know very well. For example, your domestic affairs, we don't understand them. There are also many things about foreign policy that we don't understand either. Perhaps in your future four years we might be able to learn a bit.

Dr. Kissinger: I told the Prime Minister that you have a more direct, maybe a more heroic mode of action than we do. We have to use sometimes more complicated methods because of our domestic situation. (Chairman Mao queries about the translation and Miss Tang repeats "mode of action.") But on our fundamental objectives we will act very decisively and without regard to public opinion. So if a real danger develops or hegemonial intentions become active, we will certainly resist them wherever they appear. And as the President said to the Chairman, in our own interests, not as a kindness to anyone else.

Chairman Mao: (Laughing) Those are honest words.

Dr. Kissinger: This is our position.

Chairman Mao: Do you want our Chinese women? We can give you ten million. (Laughter, particularly among the women.)

Dr. Kissinger: The Chairman is improving his offer.

Chairman Mao: By doing so we can let them flood your country with disaster and therefore impair your interests. In our country we have too many women, and they have a way of doing things. They give birth to children and our children are too many. (Laughter)

Dr. Kissinger: It is such a novel proposition, we will have to study it.

Chairman Mao: You can set up a committee to study the issue. That is how your visit to China is settling the population question. (Laughter)

Dr. Kissinger: We will study utilization and allocation.

Chairman Mao: If we ask them to go I think they would be willing.

Prime Minister Chou: Not necessarily.

Chairman Mao: That's because of their feudal ideas, big nation chauvinism.

Dr. Kissinger: We are certainly willing to receive them.

Chairman Mao: The Chinese are very alien-excluding.

For instance, in your country you can let in so many nationalities, yet in China how many foreigners do you see?

Prime Minister Chou: Very few.

Dr. Kissinger: Very few.

Chairman Mao: You have about 600,000 Chinese in the United States. We probably don't even have 60 Americans here. I would like to study the problem. I don't know the reason.

Miss Tang: Mr. Lord's wife is Chinese.

Chairman Mao: Oh?

Mr. Lord: Yes.

Chairman Mao: I studied the problem. I don't know why the Chinese never like foreigners. There are no Indians perhaps. As for the Japanese, they are not very numerous either; compared to others there are quite a few and some are married and settled down.

Dr. Kissinger: Of course, your experience with foreigners has not been all that fortunate.

Chairman Mao: Yes, perhaps that is some reason for that.

Yes, in the past hundred years, mainly the eight powers, and later it was Japan during the Boxer Revolution. For thirteen years Japan occupied China, they occupied the major part of China; and in the past the allied forces, the invading foreigners, not only occupied Chinese territory, they also asked China for indemnity.

Dr. Kissinger: Yes, and extraterritorial rights.

Chairman Mao: Now in our relations with Japan, we haven't asked them for indemnity and that would add to the burden of the people. It would be difficult to calculate all the indemnity. No accountant would be able to do it.

And only in this way can we move from hostility to relaxation in relations between peoples. And it will be more difficult to settle relations of hostility between the Japanese and Chinese peoples than between us and you.

Dr. Kissinger: Yes. There is no feeling of hostility of American people at all toward the Chinese people. On the contrary. Between us right now there is only essentially a juridical problem. (Chairman Mao nods agreement.) Which we will solve in the next years. But there is a strong community of interest which is operating immediately.

Chairman Mao: Is that so?

Dr. Kissinger: Between China and the U.S.

Chairman Mao: What do you mean by community of interest? On Taiwan?

Dr. Kissinger: In relation to other countries that may have intentions.

Prime Minister Chou: You mean the Soviet Union?

Dr. Kissinger: I mean the Soviet Union.

Prime Minister Chou: Miss Shen understood you.

Chairman Mao: (Looking toward Miss Shen.) The Chinese have a good command of English. (To Prime Minister Chou.) Who is she?

Prime Minister Chou: Miss Shen Jo-yun.

Chairman Mao: Girls. (Prime Minister Chou laughs.) Today I have been uttering some nonsense for which I will have to beg the pardon of the women of China.

Dr. Kissinger: It sounded very attractive to the Americans present. (Chairman Mao and the girls laugh.)

Chairman Mao: If we are going to establish a liaison office in your country do you want Miss Shen or Miss Tang?

Dr. Kissinger: We will deal with that through the channel of Huang Hua. (Laughter)

Chairman Mao: Our interpreters are truly too few.

Dr. Kissinger: But they have done a remarkable job, the interpreters we have met.

Chairman Mao: The interpreters you have met and our present interpreters who are doing most of the work are now in their twenties and thirties. If they grow too old they don't do interpretation so well.

Prime Minister Chou: We should send some abroad.

Chairman Mao: We will send children at such a height (indicating with his hands), not too old.

Dr. Kissinger: We will be prepared to establish exchange programs where you can send students to America.

Chairman Mao: And if among a hundred persons there are ten who are successful learning the language well, then that would be a remarkable success. And if among them a few dozens don't want to come back, for example, some girls who want to stay in the United States, no matter. Because you do not exclude foreigners like Chinese. In the past the Chinese went abroad and they didn't want to learn the local language. (Looking toward Miss Tang) Her grandparents refused to learn English.[6] They are so obstinate. You know Chinese are very obstinate and conservative. Many of the older generation overseas Chinese don't speak the local language. But they are getting better, the younger generation.

Dr. Kissinger: In America, all, or the vast majority, speak English.

Prime Minister Chou: That is the younger people. The first generation ones don't learn the local language. There was an old overseas Chinese who came back to China after living abroad. She was old and died in Peking in the 1950s when she was in her nineties. She was a member of our People's Government. She didn't speak a word of English. She was Cantonese, extremely conservative.

Dr. Kissinger: Chinese culture is so particular that it is difficult to assimilate other cultures.

Chairman Mao: Chinese language is not bad, but the Chinese characters are not good.

Prime Minister Chou: They are very difficult to learn.

Chairman Mao: And there are many contradictions between the oral and written language because the oral language is monosyllabic while the written language develops from symbols. We do not use the alphabet.

Dr. Kissinger: There are some attempts to use an alphabet I am told.

Prime Minister Chou: First we must standardize the oral language.

Chairman Mao: (Gestures with his hand and points to his books.) But if the Soviet Union would throw its bombs and kill all those over 30 who are Chinese, that would solve the problem for us. Because the old people like me can't learn Chinese. We read Chinese. The majority of my books are Chinese. There are very few dictionaries over there. All the other books are in Chinese.

Dr. Kissinger: Is the Chairman learning English now?

Chairman Mao: I have heard that I am studying it. Those are rumors on the outside. I don't heed them. They are false. I know a few English letters. I don't know the grammar.

Miss Tang: The Chairman invented an English word.

---

[6] Tang Wen-sheng (Nancy Tang) was born in the United States.

Chairman Mao: Yes, I invented the English term "paper tiger."

Dr. Kissinger: "Paper tiger." Yes, that was all about us. (Laughter)

Chairman Mao: But you are a German from Germany. But your Germany now has met with an ill fate, because in two wars it has been defeated.

Dr. Kissinger: It attempted too much, beyond its abilities and resources.

Chairman Mao: Yes, and it also scattered its forces in war. For example, in its attack against the Soviet Union. If it is going to attack, it should attack in one place, but they separated their troops into three routes. It began in June but then by the winter they couldn't stand it because it was too cold. What is the reason for the Europeans fear of the cold?

Dr. Kissinger: The Germans were not prepared for a long war. Actually they did not mobilize their whole forces until 1943. I agree with the Chairman that if they had concentrated on one front they would almost certainly have won. They were only ten kilometers from Moscow even by dispersing their forces. (Chairman Mao relights his cigar.)

Chairman Mao: They shouldn't have attacked Moscow or Kiev. They should have taken Leningrad as a first step. Another error in policy was they didn't cross the sea after Dunkirk.

Dr. Kissinger: After Dunkirk.

Chairman Mao: They were entirely unprepared.

Dr. Kissinger: And Hitler was a romantic. He had a strange liking for England.

Chairman Mao: Oh? Then why didn't they go there? Because the British at that time were completely without troops.

Dr. Kissinger: If they were able to cross the channel into Britain . . . I think they had only one division in all of England.

Prime Minister Chou: Is that so?

Dr. Kissinger: Yes.

Prime Minister Chou: Also Sir Anthony Eden told us in Germany at that time that a Minister in the Army of Churchill's Government said at that time if Hitler had crossed the channel they would have had no forces. They had withdrawn all their forces back. When they were preparing for the German crossing, Churchill had no arms. He could only organize police to defend the coast. If they crossed they would not be able to defend.

Dr. Kissinger: It also shows what a courageous man can do because Churchill created by his personality much more strength than they possessed.

Chairman Mao: Actually by that time they couldn't hold.

Prime Minister Chou: So Hitler carried some romantic feelings about Britain?

Dr. Kissinger: I think he was a maniac, but he did have some feelings about Britain.

Chairman Mao: I believe Hitler was from the Rhine area?

Dr. Kissinger: Austria.

Prime Minister Chou: He was a soldier in the First World War.

Dr. Kissinger: He was in the German Army, but he was a native of Austria.

Prime Minister Chou: From the Danube.

Dr. Kissinger: He conducted strategy artistically rather than strategically. He did it by intuition. He had no overall plan.

Chairman Mao: Then why did the German troops heed him so much?

Dr. Kissinger: Probably because the Germans are somewhat romantic people and because he must have had a very strong personality.

Chairman Mao: Mainly because during the First World War the German nation was humiliated.

Dr. Kissinger: Yes, that was a very important factor.

Chairman Mao: If there are Russians going to attack China, I can tell you today that our way of conducting a war will be guerrilla war and protracted war. We will let them go wherever they want. (Prime Minister Chou laughs.) They want to come to the Yellow River tributaries. That would be good, very good. (Laughter) And if they go further to the Yangtse River tributaries, that would not be bad either.

Dr. Kissinger: But if they use bombs and do not send armies? (Laughter)

Chairman Mao: What should we do? Perhaps you can organize a committee to study the problem. We'll let them beat us up and they will lose any resources. They say they are socialists. We are also socialists and that will be socialists attacking socialists.

Dr. Kissinger: If they attack China, we would certainly oppose them for our own reasons.

Chairman Mao: But your people are not awakened, and Europe and you would think that it would be a fine thing if it were that the ill water would flow toward China.

Dr. Kissinger: What Europe thinks I am not able to judge. They cannot do anything anyway. They are basically irrelevant. (In the midst of this Chairman Mao toasts Dr. Kissinger and Mr. Lord with tea.) What we think is that if the Soviet Union overruns China, this would dislocate the security of all other countries and will lead to our own isolation.

Chairman Mao: (Laughing) How will that happen? How would that be?

Because since in being bogged down in Vietnam you met so many difficulties, do you think they would feel good if they were bogged down in China?

Dr. Kissinger: The Soviet Union?

Miss Tang: The Soviet Union.

Chairman Mao: And then you can let them get bogged down in China, for half a year, or one, or two, or three, or four years. And then you can poke your finger at the Soviet back. And your slogan then will be for peace, that is you must bring down Socialist imperialism for the sake of peace. And perhaps you can begin to help them in doing business, saying whatever you need we will help against China.

Dr. Kissinger: Mr. Chairman, it is really very important that we understand each other's motives. We will never knowingly cooperate in an attack on China.

Chairman Mao: (Interrupting) No, that's not so. Your aim in doing that would be to bring the Soviet Union down.

Dr. Kissinger: That's a very dangerous thing. (Laughter)

Chairman Mao: (Using both hands for gestures) The goal of the Soviet Union is to occupy both Europe and Asia, the two continents.

Dr. Kissinger: We want to discourage a Soviet attack, not defeat it. We want to prevent it. (Prime Minister Chou looks at his watch.)

Chairman Mao: As for things, matters, in the world, it is hard to say. We would rather think about things this way. We think this way the world would be better.

Dr. Kissinger: Which way?

Chairman Mao: That is that they would attack China and be defeated. We must think of the worst eventuality.

Dr. Kissinger: That is your necessity. (Prime Minister Chou laughs.)

Chairman Mao: We have so many women in our country that don't know how to fight.

Miss Tang: Not necessarily. There are women's detachments.

Chairman Mao: They are only on stage. In reality if there is a fight you would flee very quickly and run into underground shelters.

Miss Wang: If the minutes of this talk were made public, it would incur the public wrath on behalf of half the population.

Chairman Mao: That is half of the population of China.

Prime Minister Chou: First of all, it wouldn't pass the Foreign Ministry.

Chairman Mao: We can call this a secret meeting. (Chinese laughter) Should our meeting today be public, or kept secret?

Dr. Kissinger: It's up to you. I am prepared to make it public if you wish.

Chairman Mao: What is your idea? Is it better to have it public or secret?

Dr. Kissinger: I think it is probably better to make it public.

Chairman Mao: Then the words we say about women today shall be made nonexistent. (Laughter)

Dr. Kissinger: We will remove them from the record. (Laughter) We will start studying this proposal when I get back.

Chairman Mao: You know, the Chinese have a scheme to harm the United States, that is, to send ten million women to the United States and impair its interests by increasing its population.

Dr. Kissinger: The Chairman has fixed the idea so much in my mind that I'll certainly use it at my next press conference. (Laughter)

Chairman Mao: That would be all right with me. I'm not afraid of anything. Anyway, God has sent me an invitation.

Dr. Kissinger: I really find the Chairman in better health this year than last year.

Chairman Mao: Yes, I am better than last year.

[The photographers entered the room.]

They are attacking us. (The Chairman then gets up without assistance to say goodbye to the Americans.)

Please give my warm regards to President Nixon. Also to Mrs. Nixon. I was not able to meet her and Secretary Rogers. I must apologize.

Dr. Kissinger: I will certainly do that.

Prime Minister Chou: We will send you a press release in one hour.

(Chairman Mao escorts Dr. Kissinger into the outer room where he says goodbye to Dr. Kissinger and Mr. Lord. Prime Minister Chou then escorts Dr. Kissinger to his waiting car.)

13.   Memorandum of Conversation[1]

Beijing, February 18, 1973, 2:43–7:15 p.m.

PARTICIPANTS

Chou En-lai, Premier, State Council
Chi P'eng-fei, Minister of Foreign Affairs
Ch'iao Kuan-hua, Vice Minister of Foreign Affairs
Chang Wen-chin, Assistant Foreign Minister, Acting Director of American Pacific
    Affairs Department
Wang Hai-jung, Assistant Foreign Minister
T'ang Wen-sheng, interpreter
Shen Jo-yun, interpreter
Two Chinese notetakers

Dr. Henry A. Kissinger, Assistant to the President for National Security Affairs
Richard T. Kennedy, NSC Staff
Alfred Le S. Jenkins, Department of State
Winston Lord, NSC Staff
Peter W. Rodman, NSC Staff
Miss Irene G. Derus, Notetaker

The group was greeted by the Prime Minister and proceeded to the room where the meeting was held.

PM Chou: We were just now counting the years, and I find when I was your age we were just liberating Peking. I was saying that you have very high spirits, full of energy, while I am on the decline.

Dr. Kissinger: I understand that means now you only work 18 hours a day.

PM Chou: It might not be entirely 18 hours. When I was your age that was more or less the case. So you now probably want to exceed me and work 20 hours a day.

Mr. Jenkins: He uses his staff for that. [laughter]

Dr. Kissinger: I said, Mr. Prime Minister, you instill a revolutionary spirit in my staff. They are dissatisfied with their condition. Colonel Kennedy and Mr. Rodman have never had so much attention since they joined my staff since they fell ill here.

PM Chou: But you have been very fair in bringing three secretaries this time so they can take it, at least. After you gain experience you are able to improve your work; that is the same with anyone. So would you like to begin first?

---

[1] Source: National Archives, Nixon Presidential Materials, NSC Files, Kissinger Office Files, Box 98, Country Files, Far East, HAK China Trip, Memcons & Reports (originals), February 1973. Top Secret; Sensitive; Exclusively Eyes Only. The meeting took place in the Great Hall of the People. All brackets are in the original.

Dr. Kissinger: I have a number of items. But first a technical one, and then I want to make a few comments on what the Prime Minister said last evening.

First, the practical question about the Liaison Office: Our intention would be to staff it with people who have worked with us on these trips so that they understand the basic approach that we are following. Like for example Mr. Jenkins and Mr. Holdridge. Now, we don't know what your intention was as to the kind of person you wanted to send to Washington, but we can adjust the rank of our people by giving them a higher rank for the purpose of their being here if this makes it possible for you to send somebody more experienced, if that is what your desire is.

PM Chou: I agree with your opinion that those who would be working in the Liaison Office should be more or less familiar with the exchanges we have had over the year and a half. Otherwise they wouldn't be able to pick up the thread.

Dr. Kissinger: That is our thinking. So if we don't send a well-known personality, that is not a reflection on the importance we attach to it, but rather the opposite.

PM Chou: We would fully understand that. It is no question.

Dr. Kissinger: But if for some reason you have a preference in that direction, it would be helpful to hear it so we can take it into account.

PM Chou: No, we are fully in agreement of sending the two colleagues you just now mentioned, Mr. Jenkins and Mr. Holdridge. But we have difficulty on our side because it is very difficult for us to find any "old Washington hands." We don't have any. [laughter] We could find the oldest one, that would be Dr. Wellington Koo. Do you know him?[2]

Dr. Kissinger: I don't know him. I know who he is. We must arrange a secret trip for some Chinese delegation so they can get experience in Washington.

PM Chou: If necessary.

Dr. Kissinger: Well, after I have discussed it with the President, in a very few weeks we will make some suggestion.

PM Chou: I would like to turn to another piece of news. That is, Vice Minister Thach will be arriving in Peking rather late. He won't be here before 7 o'clock this evening. I will be meeting with him, with the Vietnamese Vice Foreign Minister, when you are having dinner with our Foreign Minister, and after that meeting I will contact you.

---

[2] Wellington Koo (1887–1985) was a diplomat for the Republic of China who served as a delegate to the 1919 Paris Peace Conference and to the 1946 conference that founded the United Nations, and as an Ambassador to France, Great Britain, and the United States.

Dr. Kissinger: Yes, I will be prepared to meet him.

PM Chou: You must be prepared to meet rather late into the morning.

Dr. Kissinger: That is the usual—that has happened to me once before when I came here!

PM Chou: That was October.

Dr. Kissinger: October, 1971. No, I will be prepared to do that and I think it would be useful if we could meet. Our basic intention, as I told you, Mr. Prime Minister, towards North Vietnam—though conditions are different—is to move towards normalization with the same sincerity as we did after July 1971 towards the People's Republic.

PM Chou: Yes, you have mentioned that twice here.

Dr. Kissinger: Now perhaps I could make a few comments about the observations of the Prime Minister last night.

PM Chou: I was preparing originally to elaborate more on the issue last night, but as the Chairman asked to see you, I cut myself short. And anyhow I knew the Chairman would explain it in clearer terms. But anyway I will be prepared to hear you.

Dr. Kissinger: Would the Prime Minister like to say more?

PM Chou: No, I stop myself last night.

Dr. Kissinger: I understand very well what the Prime Minister was saying, and I of course paid great attention to what the Chairman was saying in elaboration. They are the important issues of our period. Because if we understand each other's purposes with respect to this issue then we can settle the practical questions. But if we doubt each other's motives, then it will be difficult to settle these issues, and then there will also be the danger that each of us, in order to anticipate the other, takes steps to the disadvantage of everyone. [Chou nods yes.]

So let me first make a comment about the historical facts which the Prime Minister mentioned at the beginning. And I make it not for academic reasons but to draw a different lesson from the Prime Minister. Actually in World War I—it is a problem that had always fascinated me so I have studied it in great detail—in the first months of World War I the vast bulk of the German Army was in the West and not in the East.

PM Chou: For the first months.

Dr. Kissinger: For the first two months. Hindenburg defeated the Russians with 200,000 troops because the Russians were stupid. Which was not the only time in their history!

PM Chou: Yes, but Hindenburg became famous due to that.

Dr. Kissinger: That is true. Later on, the balance changed. In World War II what happened was that Stalin pushed the Germans toward the West.

PM Chou: Originally Western Europe had hoped that Germany would go eastwards.

Dr. Kissinger: Western Europe.

PM Chou: At Munich.

Dr. Kissinger: Yes, at Munich. Western Europe had very superficial leaders. They didn't have the courage to pursue any policy towards a conclusion. Once they had done Munich it made no sense to fight for Poland. But that is a different issue. And I don't blame Stalin, because from his point of view he gained himself the essential time.

PM Chou: But there was one weak point, that they were not sufficiently prepared.

Dr. Kissinger: That is right.

PM Chou: They did make preparations but they were not entirely sufficient. And in Zhukov's memoirs he also touched upon this. Have you read this?

Dr. Kissinger: Yes. And they deployed their forces too far forward.

PM Chou: Also scattered in three directions.

Dr. Kissinger: So, but the basic point that I want to make is not to debate history but to say the lessons of both wars are that once a big war starts its consequences are unpredictable, and a country which encourages a big war in the hope that it can calculate its consequences is likely to produce a disaster for itself. The Germans had made very careful plans in World War I, and they had exercised them for 30 years, but when the war . . .

PM Chou: You mean after the Pact of Berlin?

Dr. Kissinger: World War I—1914—the Schlieffen Plan.

PM Chou: You mean after the Treaty of Berlin.

Dr. Kissinger: Oh, after 1878, yes, that's right. But they had exercised the Schlieffen Plan every year after 1893, for 21 years, and they had calculated everything except the psychological strain on a commander under battle conditions. So they thought they were starting a 6-months war and they wound up with a 4-year war. Not one European leader in 1914, if he had known what the world would look like in 1918, would have gone to war. And nor would Hitler in 1939.

Let us apply it to the current situation, these observations. If one analyzes the problem of pushing the Soviet Union toward the East, or maybe you trying to push it towards the West . . .

PM Chou: [laughing] We wouldn't have the strength to push them to the West! We can only make preparations for their coming into China.

Dr. Kissinger: There are three motives, or three causes, that could produce this. One is that we want the Soviet Union to defeat China. The second, much more subtle one, is the one the Chairman mentioned last night, that we don't want the Soviet Union to defeat China but we want China to exhaust the Soviet Union and have a stalemate. And the third possibility, which the Prime Minister delicately alluded to, is that we could produce this result through incompetence, not through intention. So that the objective result despite our intentions or policies might so demoralize the West and other countries that the Soviet Union feels free to attack somebody else even though we don't want this.

Now let me deal with each of these points.

The first possibility, that we want the Soviet Union to defeat China. If this were to happen, I am assuming from history that Japan would end up on the side that looks stronger to Japan. That has always been the case. If China were to be defeated, Japan would join the Soviet Union. Europe would become like Finland, and the United States would be completely isolated. So whether the Soviet Union defeats China first or Europe first, the consequences for us will be the same. So this can never be our policy.

Now let us take the second case, that the Soviet Union attacks China and we do not discourage this because we think China cannot be defeated and then perhaps both communist countries will exhaust each other. I believe, and the President believes, that, first of all, the chance of a war between the Soviet Union and China would have cataclysmic effects in the world regardless of the outcome. With very unpredictable consequences. But if the Soviet Union should succeed in gaining even the kind of control Japan acquired in the '30s and '40s, many of the same consequences that I described earlier would also happen. India would certainly not be idle. We do not know what temptations Japan would encounter in this new circumstance. And the U.S. would be forced either into a position of demonstrated impotence and irrelevance to the rest of the world or into a series of delicate and extremely complex decisions.

I am speaking very honestly with you, Mr. Prime Minister.

But if a situation would arise in which the Soviet military move would be exhausted or stalemated, and if the Soviet Union encounters some of the difficulties you mentioned we encountered in Vietnam, then given the nature of the Soviet system, the consequences could be very unpredictable. And they might then break out of their dilemma in some other direction. And we might then have the situation of World War I or World War II, on a greater scale, with the Soviet Union in the position of Germany. So if a war occurs between the Soviet Union and China as a result of our action, it will be the result of misjudgment by us, not the result of a deliberate policy.

Now this is a point that the Prime Minister has made and that I take very seriously because there is a great deal of merit in this. There is a danger that the Soviet Union might succeed in creating such a false atmosphere of relaxation that it feels free to turn all its energies in one direction, and that the West and the U.S. disarm themselves morally and psychologically, and this despite our intention. This is a real danger. [Chou nods.]

While this is theoretically correct, let us analyze it by region, and let me explain to you what we think we are doing and why we are doing it.

We do not believe that we are likely to disarm China psychologically, so let me talk about Western Europe, where the principal difficulty occurs. Even before my trip to Peking, and even before the Soviet Union began its present relaxation policy, our West European allies made very little effort in defense. On the contrary. Indeed, under the pressure of their Communist parties, and even worse, of those intellectuals who listened to the communists without having their discipline, they adopted the view that every crisis was the result of America's policy and the only danger of war was American intransigence, not Soviet. So every European leader was in the happy position that when he needed some cheap popularity he could come to Washington and recommend détente, secure in the knowledge that we would refuse him. [laughter] In the spring of 1971 a European leader came to Washington to lecture us again about our intransigent policy and I said to him, "You had better enjoy this trip, because very soon you will be in a position where you will have to be very careful what you recommend because we might accept it." [laughter]

So if you compare the defense efforts of the Europeans before 1971 with after 1971, it is actually higher today. Now, how is this paradox to be explained? Until 1971 the Europeans wanted to make sure that if there was a war—they had exactly the opposite view of Brezhnev in his communication to us—they wanted to make sure it would devastate the U.S. but not devastate Europe. So they made just enough of an effort to induce us to keep our forces there but never enough of an effort so that we could actually defend Europe in Europe.

Now why have we acted as we have since 1971? Partly because of Vietnam. I will be very honest with you; we couldn't have two crises simultaneously. But even if it had not been for Vietnam we would have acted the same way for a while.

PM Chou: I don't quite understand.

Dr. Kissinger: That is what I want to explain. We wanted to give those forces in Europe that were in favor of defense a greater freedom of maneuver, and for that reason we had to dissociate ourselves somewhat from Europe, strangely enough. Because as long as we were overwhelmingly dominant in Europe, there was no incentive for the Europeans to do anything for themselves. So we have always respected President de Gaulle, for example, and we now respect President Pompidou; they are more difficult than some other governments but they encourage national pride and therefore national willingness to defend themselves.

Now, our policy of relaxation with the Soviet Union has forced the Europeans to examine the requirements of their own situation. Whenever we have asked the Europeans to spend more money for defense, they told us there was no danger. Now that we are discussing the reduction of forces in Europe they are telling us the danger is so great that our forces cannot be moved.

PM Chou: Even Switzerland.

Dr. Kissinger: Even Switzerland, but the Swiss at least defend themselves.

PM Chou: Although they are a neutral country they also admit there is danger.

Dr. Kissinger: That's right.

PM Chou: Yes, and when I spoke to a Swiss they also admit the fact that the Soviet Union was the danger to Europe, and that if a nuclear war would break out that war would not know any boundaries and it would not distinguish between the front and the rear and it would abolish the difference between a neutral and allied country.

Dr. Kissinger: No question. And the Austrian government, which is also neutral technically, has all its military dispositions facing the east. They are not very much, but still whatever they have is facing the east. I had a long discussion with a member of the Austrian General Staff a few years ago, just before taking this office. They have no plan at all for defense against the West.

So our purpose with the Mutual Force Reduction Conference is twofold: One, pedagogical toward the Europeans, to force them to examine their military problem, in a framework in which they cannot avoid it, rather than in a budgetary framework where they will never face it. And secondly, to prevent our Congress, particularly Senator Mansfield, from cutting our forces unilaterally by claiming first that while negotiations are going on there can be no cuts.

So we have the paradox that our policy, in my view, actually strengthens the West.

Now I agree with you on the European Security Conference. I have nothing good to say about that. That was imposed on us by our allies and the only thing to do with it is to finish it quickly with a minimum of rhetoric.

But let me say we greatly welcome what you have been saying to European leaders. You cannot say it strongly enough for our taste, and we will never contradict you. We think it is a very positive contribution. Now the major . . .

PM Chou: And perhaps precisely because of that, the West German Foreign Minister Mr. Scheel sent their original Ambassador in your country to our country because he followed the Adenauer line, but that line might not be exactly his.

Dr. Kissinger: I know Pauls very well. He is a good man.

PM Chou: We have agreed.

Dr. Kissinger: He is the best man they could have sent. And he will be emotionally on your side. Scheel is not the strongest foreign minister of which history informs us.

PM Chou: Yes.

Dr. Kissinger: Now I want to tell the Prime Minister that the President and, therefore I, shall now pay very personal attention to European policy.

PM Chou: Yes, it was proclaimed by your President that this year would be the year of Europe.

Dr. Kissinger: We will attempt to develop in the next six months a common economic and military policy and then to have a summit meeting between the President and the major European leaders to develop a kind of Charter for our relationship. And we will ask Japan to participate in the economic aspects of this. So, we hope that we can counteract some of the dangers that you have described. But we will, as I have told you, make some maneuvers with the Soviet Union, in the interest of gaining time. But that will be in the direction of what I have described, and there will not be any secret understandings or discussions. Well, there will be secret discussions but no secret understandings.

Now let me turn to the Southern area. This has two parts, the Middle East and the area described yesterday evening—Turkey, Iran, Pakistan, and through Southeast Asia. They are connected but not identical.

In the Middle East the problem is this: that the Soviet Union has attempted to perform mischief but has not been willing to run any risks. So it has tried to maximize its influence but without any constructive outcome. Now you and we have, I believe, a difference on the Middle East because we stand for the preservation of Israel. But let us leave this aside for the time being. Because we want a settlement. Now I want to inform the Prime Minister, I have already tried . . .

PM Chou: And in your basic policy what do you envisage about Palestine, the Palestinian people?

Dr. Kissinger: The future of the Palestinian people will have to be part of a general settlement.

PM Chou: But now the Jewish people are increasing. The inflow of the Jewish people is increasing into that area.

Dr. Kissinger: Many from the Soviet Union.

PM Chou: That is what I meant. In particular the Soviet Union. It is quite unreasonable, including those from the Soviet Union who have gone to Israel to assist Israel. Among them are some of the Jewish nationality who have been to Egypt to assist in the construction of the Aswan Dam and also especially those who have experience in constructing military installations, they have also gone into Israel.

Dr. Kissinger: I didn't know that.

PM Chou: Soviet authorities say in regard to that that it is the freedom of the people. And for a Socialist country to say that. And if Egypt agrees, we would like to make this public. It is terrible.

Dr. Kissinger: On the future of the Palestinian people ... Incidentally, Mr. Prime Minister, if Mr. Jenkins reports this conversation to his colleagues, Harvard University will soon have a new professor. [Chou laughs.]

Mr. Jenkins: It's very possible.

Dr. Kissinger: No, I have Mr. Jenkins here because I have confidence in him. I want him to hear what our policy is since we don't tell him unless he is here with you.

Our view on the Palestinian refugees is that the practical solution is to establish the principle that they can return, but to have an understanding that in fact only a certain small percentage of them will return, but that the Israeli Government will make a contribution to resettling them in other parts including in that part of Palestine which remains Arab.

PM Chou: Do you think you can help me investigate on the information I just now gave you?

Dr. Kissinger: Yes. I have never heard it.

PM Chou: It is very terrible to hear.

Dr. Kissinger: I don't know whether it is true. I have never heard it, but that doesn't prove anything.

PM Chou: Of course it is also a public matter that they have trade relations with Israel—the Soviet Union.

Dr. Kissinger: Yes.

PM Chou: They said that is the normal state of affairs.

Dr. Kissinger: I said what I did because I do not want any misapprehension on the part of the Prime Minister. We cannot join you in any policy that would have to do with the dismemberment of Israel, but we can join you on any policy that would reduce Soviet influence and help establish a stable peace. And perhaps if you know what we are doing you can perhaps encourage it.

PM Chou: How can Israel be destroyed? It is impossible. But anyway it must be said that the establishment of such a country in such a manner is a very curious and peculiar phenomenon to be witnessed since the First and Second World War.

Dr. Kissinger: That is a different question.

PM Chou: To which the Soviet Union also gave its full favor. At that time the Soviet Union was against the Arabs.

Dr. Kissinger: Most of the arms came at that time from Czechoslovakia.

PM Chou: And the Soviets just can't stand any mention of the matter. Even in their movies they gave a very bad . . .

Dr. Kissinger: In their?

PM Chou: In their movies they gave a very bad display. Even in the Soviet films of the Arab world they show the Arabs very badly. But at the same time the Soviet Union treats very badly the Jews in their country.

Dr. Kissinger: Very badly.

PM Chou: So what they want to do is establish a state and then push the Jews out of their own country. That is what they are continuing to do.

Dr. Kissinger: Whatever the motives, it is conceivable that their purpose is to create a situation of turmoil so they can then create bases, as in Iraq and Syria.

Now, I want to give the Prime Minister some information which we have not given to our own government and also therefore not to any foreign government. I mentioned it briefly the other day. We have been in contact with—that is the White House has been in contact with Egypt for the last five months, of the sort of exchange that you and we had prior to my first trip here. Very careful. And we have now used a pretext to invite the person who has the same position . . .

PM Chou: But on the very day you told me of that, I think on the 15th, we saw in the Lebanon newspapers approximately the same story saying that the United States had contacts with Ismail.[3]

Dr. Kissinger: Particularly because the Arabs can't keep any secrets. But there are so many rumors that no one believes it any more.

PM Chou: We hope it will be that way.

Dr. Kissinger: For this reason, what we have done—we first wanted to bring Ismail secretly to the U.S. We thought this would never work, so we are bringing him for official meetings with Mr. Jenkins' colleagues for one day. And then we will make him disappear and I will have two days of secret meetings with him. Is that what was in the Lebanon newspaper?

---

[3] Ismail Fahmi was the Egyptian Minister for Foreign Affairs from 1973 until 1977.

PM Chou: Not so detailed. They only said you had contacts with Ismail.

Dr. Kissinger: I personally?

PM Chou: They said that you were going to hold secret talks with Mr. Ismail in Paris.

Dr. Kissinger: That is certainly nonsense. They have been saying I will have secret talks with Heykal and with Zayyat. I am now having so many secret talks with Arabs that I can now have secret talks and no one will believe it. But what is important is not whether the talks can be kept secret—but I frankly believe we have to announce it after the event, since they aren't emotionally capable of keeping a secret. What is more important is the attitude in which they will be conducted. And what we have said to them is that we will talk to Egypt as long as it speaks for itself and not for some other country, and that afterwards it should follow its own national purposes. And they have now given us a very long reply, of which the key point is—I will just read the key paragraph: "If Egypt thinks that there is a good solution that meets at least the minimum requirements of its people and the people of the area, it will go ahead with it and will not allow it to be vetoed by anybody. Only in this way can the problem be settled so that both we and you are helped." And then they say they look forward to the discussions. These conversations begin next Sunday and Monday. Just as your Foreign Minister gives his opening remarks in Paris. [laughter]

PM Chou: We hope it will also be the final statement! [laughter]

Dr. Kissinger: We will keep you informed. And we are also talking to Jordan. But we think Egypt should settle first because if Jordan settles first I think your Vice Foreign Minister will agree it will create more turmoil in that area.

PM Chou: Indeed and they are those with the least secrecy.

Dr. Kissinger: Jordanians?

PM Chou: Yes.

Dr. Kissinger: It is hard to choose among Arabs. Now the third area—Turkey, Iran and then through Southeast Asia—that is the most difficult part. But I agree with what was said last evening and we will address this problem very seriously. I had a serious talk with Begum Bhutto this morning, and I spoke to her in the sense I have spoken to you.

So all of this long explanation is to make clear: Yes, we will pursue a policy of relaxation, but we will not pay a real price in weakening the possibility of resistance, at least not consciously, and we believe not in reality. I have spoken at such length only so that the Prime Minister genuinely understands how we see the international environment and also so that he sees what our major intentions are.

In fact, I think the greatest danger is that the Soviet Union will become so frustrated that it will do something rash. When I notice how nervous they are about my visit here, it indicates that they do not feel that they are gaining ground. They should not think that moving in any direction, south or east, will leave the United States disinterested. And for that we need some time to prepare the ground.

But this is our genuine strategy.

PM Chou: Your general relations with Turkey are all right.

Dr. Kissinger: Yes, they are good. Turkey has a difficult domestic situation but that does not affect us.

PM Chou: The Soviet Union will also try to make use of that.

Dr. Kissinger: Yes.

PM Chou: But anyway you have military strength there and they are part of NATO.

Dr. Kissinger: Yes, we have some air force there. And the Turks are fairly immune to the Soviet Union because they have had historical experience with both Russia and the Soviet Union.

PM Chou: The same with Iran.

Dr. Kissinger: That is right. Turkey and Iran, especially Iran, are in good condition now, and that is why when Mr. Helms gets in Iran we can take a more general view of the situation.

PM Chou: Besides bases in Japan, does your 7th Fleet also have any other bases in the Indian Ocean?

Dr. Kissinger: We have, of course, a base in the Philippines, Subic Bay. And we are developing a small station on Diego Garcia.

PM Chou: In the previous British area.

Dr. Kissinger: And we have a station in Bahrein. And we will review the whole question of deployments in the Indian Ocean. But with nuclear carriers the bases are not that important.

PM Chou: The Soviet Union doesn't pay attention to that. They just nose in everywhere. They also have developed quite a fishing industry in the Indian Ocean. [laughter]

Dr. Kissinger: And they help their fishermen by equipping their trawlers with the best electronic equipment.

PM Chou: That is also a kind of fishing but a different kind of fish. [laughter]

Dr. Kissinger: But our naval strength, Mr. Prime Minister, is far superior to that of the Soviet Union, even though the Soviet Union is gaining. There is no relation between the two strengths. In every analysis we have made, in the Mediterranean, for example, we have always assumed that the 6th Fleet could wipe out the Soviet fleet in the Mediterranean completely. And in September of 1970 when we moved our aircraft carriers into the Eastern Mediterranean—they are usually in the Western Mediterranean; we moved two carriers into the Eastern Mediterranean during the Syrian-Jordanian crisis and doubled them—the Soviet fleet headed for the ports. But the Soviet navy is effective to threaten other countries that do not have large navies, and in the Indian Ocean and Africa and in the Middle East where we are not present, they can be very effective.

PM Chou: That is where the problem lies.

Dr. Kissinger: Exactly. So I recognize the problem you mentioned. The Shah, for example, has exactly the same feeling that the Prime Minister has. And he is also concerned with the Indian Navy, the Shah.

PM Chou: Navy?

Dr. Kissinger: Navy.

PM Chou: Is the Indian navy equipped with Soviet equipment?

Dr. Kissinger: Largely. They have some . . .

PM Chou: They have already replaced the British equipment then.

Dr. Kissinger: Well, they have an old British aircraft carrier but all of their new equipment comes from the Soviet Union. They are getting four Soviet submarines and five patrol destroyers this year from the Soviet Union. All their new equipment is either Soviet or built in India.

PM Chou: And about those assembled in India, are they done by Soviet technique or by technique left over from the British?

Dr. Kissinger: No, Soviet models.

PM Chou: So that is one of the reasons why Pakistan is complaining to you—because the Soviet Union is supplying the Indians so quickly and so amply.

Dr. Kissinger: They are right. We have a very difficult Congressional situation.

PM Chou: You well know that the equipment we give to Pakistan is ordinary army equipment and mainly light weapons.

Dr. Kissinger: Yes.

PM Chou: Secondly, we gave them some air force equipment, for instance a kind of MIG–19 that we have made ourselves, that was slightly improved on the basis of Soviet kind. Those are some of the fighters we have given them, and the total number was slightly better than 130. We don't have the capability now to provide them with naval equipment. So if you could give them besides army equipment, also naval equipment, and besides giving them some assistance on the ground and in the air, if you could give them some assistance on the seas it would also be of good use. And the fighting ability of the MIG–21s are not so very great. MIG–23s are better.

Dr. Kissinger: Yes, that was the experience in the India/Pakistan War. Actually your MIG–19s are better.

On the military side, Mr. Prime Minister, we face bureaucratic problems and Congressional problems. And the two are related, because every time we give an order to the bureaucracy they leak it to the Congress. There are some things we can do from the White House, but a military supply program cannot be done on a personal scale.

PM Chou: Can the Pentagon also—does the Pentagon also leak secrets?

Dr. Kissinger: Oh yes. When your Liaison Office is established we will give them a little education. This is why we are so concerned with keeping our contacts in the White House. We never leak.

PM Chou: Yes, and that is why Chairman Mao mentioned yesterday that we have too little knowledge about your country. Perhaps with a four-year study we might be able to learn it.

Dr. Kissinger: He also made some other promises of which I will remind him. [laughter]

PM Chou: But we are not planning to put that into effect.

Dr. Kissinger: You don't have to start with a maximum program. You can have a pilot program.

PM Chou: But it must be on a voluntary basis. No one will respond. Perhaps very few. Madam Shen [Jo-yun] said to you last night there would be none but I think that is not very satisfactory, so I will say only a very few. I believe the intellectual overseas Chinese family in the U.S. would be only now in the tens of thousands, and to my knowledge many children of those families, no matter whether sons or daughters, have married Americans. And therefore they have already become American citizens, which enables them to be more qualified to run for the President than you.

Dr. Kissinger: So is Miss T'ang.

PM Chou: So this is one of the difficulties we are facing, that is that you cannot keep your military assistance entirely secret.

Dr. Kissinger: We cannot keep military assistance secret at all, because it has to have Congressional approval. During the war we did some illegal things by transferring equipment from a few countries to Pakistan.

PM Chou: But too few in number, and very painstakingly.

Dr. Kissinger: I agree, and at enormous personal risk.

PM Chou: And then finally the records of certain meetings that you held were also made public. Those are some of the difficulties you come up with.

Dr. Kissinger: There are some embassies in Africa that are now staffed with new personnel since those leaks. But that is quite true.

That was a very difficult period. But we cannot give military assistance secretly; it will inevitably become public.

So what we have to do is reestablish some categories. We will reestablish sending spare parts for existing equipment. We will release equipment that has already been contracted for. We will do that in the next four to six weeks. And we will make a major effort to see what can be done through third countries.

PM Chou: You have a very peculiar Congress, that can at once propose to withdraw your troops from Indochina immediately and unconditionally, but yet on the contrary in the 100 days since October last year they also did their utmost to mobilize all forces to give military assistance to Nguyen Van Thieu from countries that did not need keeping them.

Dr. Kissinger: That was something else. That was not Congress.

PM Chou: Then why was that made possible?

Dr. Kissinger: That was made possible because there existed authorization from Congress already to do this over a two-year period, and we simply delivered two years of equipment in a three months period. That had already been approved by Congress. But it is true Congress did approve this. It is peculiar.

PM Chou: It is also what the Pentagon is in favor of.

Dr. Kissinger: It depends on the area. There is no main policy.

PM Chou: So if you deal with them area by area as you mentioned in the beginning, as you dealt with the discussion today from an area to area basis, then that would be holding up time.

Dr. Kissinger: We will, particularly in the light of my discussion last night, I will review this whole problem with the President and we will see what can be done in this axis which was discussed yesterday.

Mr. Jenkins: May I have one brief word? To borrow a Shakespearean phrase, I would like to make insurance doubly sure on one point. I didn't hear Miss T'ang translate when Mr. Kissinger said he had confidence in me. I want that in the record. I am looking forward to a possibility which will become a reality.

PM Chou: She translated that. And I can also assure you that Dr. Kissinger's confidence in you has left a very deep impression on me. Of course the main confidence is from your President too.

Dr. Kissinger: I think the Prime Minister uses an interpreter only to gain time to think out his answers even better. He understands English very well. [laughter]

PM Chou: No, no, no, I don't understand all of it, but I understand most of the parts that I pay attention to.

[The meeting broke briefly, from 4:18 to 4:40 p.m.]

PM Chou: I would first of all like to thank you for what you said just now about strategy, because I believe that this is relevant not just to the present day but also to future developments. I think that the three different kinds of analyses you gave us actually are one. Why is that? Because I think that if in the first case it was thought that China would be easily attacked and would collapse the moment it was attacked, then there would have been no reason in favor of the improvement of relations between China and the United States.

Dr. Kissinger: Exactly.

PM Chou: Because we would be equal to Czechoslovakia, and it would not be worth it for you to spend so much time and energy in this. And the second and third points are two sides of one thing, because you know you stress on the prevention of certain events and therefore you stress the third danger, and therefore you attach importance to the danger I described yesterday; that is, you attach importance to lessening and even finally eliminating that danger. But neither do you exclude that some day the Soviet Union might embark on an adventure because of their unlimited ambition and imprudently launch a nuclear war. That is why we must be prepared for the worst. That was the portent that Chairman Mao mentioned to you; that is, to make—to timely envision that the Soviet Union might one day go mad, and not to consider that inconceivable, and therefore we must be prepared for the worst.

And I mentioned yesterday the proof of that, that we have concretized our principle of being prepared against war, and against natural disasters. The people have a phrase, "to dig tunnels deep, to store grain everywhere, and never seek hegemony." The interpreter didn't remember the third phrase correctly, which shows her tendency to big-nation chauvinism. [laughter] We are educating the people along these lines, "to dig tunnels deep, store grain everywhere, and never seek hegemony." But the interpreter just now made it into a long sentence, which shows big-nation chauvinism, which must be criticized!

The first sentence shows a means of preparedness against war. Of course it is a defensive preparedness, but this prevention must be implemented in all the major and small cities of the country. Because the experience of the Second World War, and also the experience of the Vietnam war, have proved that the underground works have proven that they have been useful in preserving effectives and that they can be linked together and coordinated in battle and that they can withstand bombing. As for storing grain everywhere, that principle—as you just now mentioned, the digging of tunnels is sometimes not quite conceivable to some in Western Europe—that is the same case with to store grain everywhere. Many countries don't find it conceivable to do that. And the natural disasters in the Soviet Union last year proved that after 50 years of construction their agriculture did not pass the test and as a result the First Vice Premier of the Council of Ministers was sacrificed—Polyansky. He was one whom Khrushchev appreciated and Brezhnev especially praised, and his division with Kosygin was that he was in charge of agriculture. One year of natural disasters had reduced the Soviet Union to such a state, so what would they do if the natural disasters would continue for a few more years? And that also was a great lesson to Japan.

Because if there truly is going to be a big war and any country is going to enter into that great war, then if they have no food then how are they going to fight? Our natural disasters last year also put a test to us, but it proved that our grain reserves were much better than before. But we still have to make efforts. The 1972 harvest was 4% less than the 1971 harvest. That was 10 million tons less of grain; 4% of our harvest was 10 million tons. And the year before, 1971, our grain output was 250 million tons. Last year we imported about 5 million tons of grain but we also exported around 3 million. Our imports include some through your country through third countries. Actually we didn't mean to cancel the first purchase of grain—I think there was a one-million-ton purchase. The first one we cancelled but because of the propaganda in the press which compared us and put us on the same par as the Soviet Union; we felt we had to cancel that.

Dr. Kissinger: What was that?

PM Chou: The first deal was through the French businesses. The second time they kept quiet but it was still through a third country. I think in the future there will be no need to go through a third country. We can do it directly. So I think . . . But in importing grain we have two main purposes. One is to adjust the various varieties, and the second is to get more grain reserves. Because many of the countries that need our supply of grain eat rice—Vietnam, Korea, Ceylon, Cuba and African countries. But now, because of Soviet purchases, the price of wheat is going up. It is not like in the old days when we could exchange one ton of rice for two tons of wheat.

No matter what, we have to have such preparations. If not, how could we be prepared against a war?

Dr. Kissinger: The Soviet crop is likely to be very bad again this year. They had very little snow.

PM Chou: So it seems that perhaps Polyansky will perhaps lose his status in the Politburo and as a Minister too.

Dr. Kissinger: They have already dismissed Matskevich and . . .

PM Chou: And put Polyansky in.[4]

Dr. Kissinger: Yes.

---

[4] Dmitry Stepanovich Polyansky replaced Vladimir Matskevich as Soviet Minister of Agriculture in 1973.

PM Chou: He will probably have to go, too. But with material preparations alone, if the mental preparations are not sufficient, then one can still not be fully prepared against war. With only material preparations and the wrong mental preparations, then the preparations will be incorrect. Therefore we have to stress "never to seek hegemony". We not only put that into our joint communiqué, and also the joint statement issued with Japan, but we are also educating our people at home that they should stress the fact that we should never seek hegemony. Because the good point of the aggression likely to come from the north to China is that this can enhance our national self-confidence. And the half century of Japanese aggression in the past also has educated the Chinese people and awakened their confidence.

But another side of the picture is that the objective fact of the largeness of the Chinese nation and Chinese area easily create a tendency to nationalistic sentiments and big-nation chauvinism. Because if there are too strong nationalist feelings, then one will cease to learn from others; one will seal oneself in and believe one is the best or will cease to learn from the strong points of others. For instance, one will cease to speak or to learn the language of others. Because there are so many people who can speak Chinese and speak it among themselves, they find it very easy to live and don't have to learn foreign languages. For instance, in your country you have Chinatowns.

Dr. Kissinger: Still? Yes.

PM Chou: They are very conservative. They stick together.

Dr. Kissinger: New York and San Francisco.

PM Chou: Other countries don't seem to have that happen—they stick together.

Dr. Kissinger: They are the most law abiding parts of the cities, too.

PM Chou: Not necessarily.

Dr. Kissinger: Seriously, the crime statistics are less in the Chinese areas than anywhere else. I am serious. It is true. I am not being polite.

PM Chou: We have heard from other people in the United States that since 1965 when you lifted the quota for immigrants from Hong Kong, since then the crime rate has gone up because they have begun street fighting.

Dr. Kissinger: I don't know.

Mr. Jenkins: More recently, but for a long time it was traditional that the Chinese community was the most peaceful.

PM Chou: [To Winston Lord] Is your wife Cantonese?

Mr. Lord: From Shanghai.

Dr. Kissinger: A very strong lady.

PM Chou: Strong lady. With a vast population it is easy to project big-nation chauvinism feeling especially toward smaller bordering countries. So on the one hand we must develop the spirit of resisting the tide, resisting erroneous things, no matter how strong they may be. One must not fear them at all. On the other hand we must be modest and prudent and to treat the people of all countries no matter big or small, equally and the same. Because others always have strong points and one must learn from the strong points of others to correct our own shortcomings. But in what way can one create such a spirit and temper the people in such a matter? That would be through exchanges. Through exchanges the people will temper themselves.

Take, for instance, the relations between our two countries since the ping-pong teams—only less than two years, and still through the increasing exchanges we have learned more of each other and begun to understand each other's strong points and weak points. And in this way one can give play to one's good habits and lessen the bad habits. That is the same with Japan. Since Liberation we have never ceased exchanges between the Chinese and Japanese people, and therefore with regard to the aspects that we have had contact with, we have been able to increase understanding. As to those aspects which we do not have contact with, there is still quite a large amount of prejudice.

Therefore, we must, in our preparation against war, we must be prepared against surprise attacks. Although at the beginning—it might not be very probable at the very beginning that there shall be major attacks, but there always is this possibility. A good thing to us, a relatively good phenomenon recently in the recent two years is that there has been an increasing number of foreign friends to visit China. And generally speaking they all understand that China is not a country that wants to commit aggression abroad. China is opposed to aggression. The impression they have got is that China is not a warlike or aggressive nation. But at the same time we must maintain constant preparations against all eventualities, because we must always be prepared against some surprise incident in case something happens. In Chinese, "We must be prepared against one case in ten thousand." It is, as you have said, that other countries might not be prepared for such sudden incidents, might not have envisaged such a possibility. Of course, with more contacts and exchanges, gradually this matter will become understood.

But what if the attack comes early? That is why Chairman Mao said that we can fight for one year, or two years, and gradually the world will come to understand and the voices of reproach against the Soviet Union will be raised higher. But we must be prepared to withstand that attack; we must be prepared to make it so that they will be able to come in but not go out. One case might be as you envisage, that they will not send their forces in but will just throw bombs; that is, to wage an undeclared war. We must be prepared to withstand that; that is, we must be prepared to resist after the bombing. So that is why the Chairman said we must be able to stand for one year, two years, three years, four years or five years—to withstand the attack until that time so that the people in the world will come to understand the situation. That is why Chairman Mao said that you might make some moves at that time from their back—you might poke them in the back. Of course that is the worst eventuality.

Dr. Kissinger: That is very probable, that we would do that.

PM Chou: And it can be only in this way that we will be able to maintain our self-confidence and also gain the mutual assistance of others. With regard to the world there are bound to be some twists and turns, and some events that we are not prepared for, and there also might be a few countries who would like to fish in troubled waters. I discussed with you the possibility that there might be some come from the east or from the southwest. But we must be prepared—even in that eventuality, we must be able to resist and to wipe them out. Because then if they do not come into our territory and just continue the bombing, then by that time the whole world would be against them and we could not maintain the position of only defending our own land and not attack. Of course Chairman Mao put it in a more subtle way. He asked you to organize a committee to study that problem.

So with regard to this problem you have said that you think it is best to prevent the event before it happens. Of course that would be good if it can be done. And that will call for joint efforts, that is, to envisage all aspects. But if we ourselves did not make own preparations ourselves, that would not be right. Of course there is the possibility that if we are prepared they would not dare to come, or anyway they will have to think a bit.

Therefore in the future four years which you mentioned, it is most essential to do more work.

Our views on Western Europe are almost the same. Even the Nordic countries, although they might have said some things about you in the Scandinavian countries, they still are vigilant against the Soviet Union.

Dr. Kissinger: Even Sweden.

PM Chou: Even Finland.

Dr. Kissinger: Even more Finland.

PM Chou: They are the victim.

Dr. Kissinger: Finland is morally the strongest of the Scandinavian countries.

PM Chou: They resist. They wouldn't agree to submit. Don't you remember the battle of 1939? Tammersing lost very badly in the battle there. He broke his leg and lost his arm. And the Soviets would find themselves in an even colder place there; they would have dropped into an ice hole. That was the result of being too proud and arrogant.

They thought that they could take Finland by moving only a finger. That is one of the greatest lessons of arrogance and pride.

At that time, exactly that time, I was in the Soviet Union treating my elbow. I didn't get my elbow fixed but I learned quite a lesson about that. At the beginning the Soviet Union was extremely arrogant. Kuusinen had already become an "excellency" [laughter] and he was preparing to go to Finland to become its Chairman. So after its major defeat he came back and became "Comrade Kuusinen." You could see the change in the newspapers. It seemed to be a joke on him. But finally a part of it was carved out—Karelia—and then he went there to become the "Chairman". He was a good man but he was incapable.

So it still seems possible to gradually rid the European people of their illusions about peace, but that will take some time. So we think it is all right to hold some security conferences and mutual force reduction meetings in Europe, because it will serve to educate them. Because some truth will be told to them at those conferences. We will not play that role. The Soviet Union is saying that we are now the most warlike because we are even opposed to a security conference. Actually we are saying you can hold it if you want but it won't be of any consequence.

Take for instance the Geneva Disarmament Conference: It has also been going on endlessly and the more they disarm the more the armaments increase! So we have been outside, but coordinating with those inside. Britain seems to understand that point now. They now said that they understand our not taking part. Before they wanted everyone to enter the Conference and fight inside, but to go inside and quarrel sometimes is not necessary. The British now agree that we can remain outside. But sometimes you have to go inside and fight. For instance, the United Nations.

Dr. Kissinger: Mr. Prime Minister, many delegations of professors from the U.S. might urge you to join these things. But we understand your point of view. They are not being sent by us. [laughter]

PM Chou: It doesn't matter. As soon as they open that subject we can take the opportunity to make propaganda against them. I have already taken the lead in doing that, and now the Foreign Minister can do the rest of the work. I won't spend my time doing that. But there are some American friends to whom it is easy to convey the notion; there are some who are more naive.

The second is Japan, because we have already discussed France. We don't have to say any more about that.

Dr. Kissinger: We are in complete agreement with you.

PM Chou: As for Japan, we have, and still hold, the view that Japan is at a crossroads. From the point of security they cannot leave you now. Although generally speaking in our propaganda we are not, and we truly are not, in favor of a transition from Dulles' Japan-U.S. Security Treaty. We are not in favor of that. But proceeding from the present situation, out of consideration of the present situation, we have not touched on that matter when we established relations with Japan.

Dr. Kissinger: We are well aware of that.

PM Chou: So when certain correspondents clamor that I am in support of the U.S.-Japanese Security Treaty I just ignore that. Let them go on. The Soviet Vice Foreign Minister approached our Vice Foreign Minister and asked for clarifications on that point, but we paid no attention to him. We said, "You have been cursing us enough."

But Japan, due to its economic development, will inevitably also bring with it an ideology of military expansion that is objective. And about this point I believe I mentioned at the very beginning of our discussions that it is you who have fattened up the Japanese. Of course in the beginning perhaps you did that in order to prevent what you thought to be the expansion of communism.

Dr. Kissinger: And China.

PM Chou: Not only China but in Dulles' time he viewed both China and the Soviet Union as a monolith. But if that was truly so, then you should have not let Japan expand economically so unrestrictedly. But that is an objective development that does not heed the will of man. That is, there are sudden expansions of such. The foundation was laid after the Second World War. There was the fact also that you had thrown atom bombs on Japan and therefore you wanted to create a better impression on the Japanese people and did not ask indemnities. And I believe the expenses of your occupation troops in Japan were mainly provided by yourself, and you also encouraged the support of your investments and techniques to Japan.

Dr. Kissinger: And we gave aid. I forget what the amount was but it was very substantial, several billion.

PM Chou: At the same time as the Marshall Plan.

Dr. Kissinger: Japan wasn't part of the Marshall Plan. Japan received a separate program.

PM Chou: At the same time?

Dr. Kissinger: It started a little later but it overlapped in the '50s.

PM Chou: In addition they gained a lot, and you should say they made money, out of the wars in the East. They profited out of the Chinese Civil War because of the transportation of your assistance to Chiang Kai-shek, which had to go through them. Then the Korean War, three years, then the Indochina War. You fattened them up. [laughter] How could you have foreseen that? Of course, in our point of view that is a matter of system. But we don't have to answer about that philosophical problem now. We can concentrate on matters of practical interest to the people.

What Japan now has is only an attempt, an ambition, but they want to gain more independence out of this development. Like when a young man grows up he wants more freedom. But if it has restraint of its spirit, that is different, if it has a spirit of restraint it would be better. But its economic base doesn't allow it to restrain itself; it will compel it to develop. But it is true indeed that the various countries in Asia and the Pacific Ocean have learned their lesson about the economic development abroad of Japan, and therefore their great fear of it. That is why Suharto said to you he thought the second major threat was Japan. That was due to the lessons of the Pacific. Japan itself cannot be said to be completely ignorant of that. They have enough of the spirit of self-criticism to see that if they do not obey a spirit of restraint in their economic development they will become "economic animals." I heard those very words from monopoly capitalists. Was that a term that was given to them by the people in Asia or is it their own coin?

Dr. Kissinger: I think it is their own coinage.

PM Chou: It is in this very room that I met them and I heard from their own mouths these words.

Dr. Kissinger: Have you ever seen them put the principle in practice?

PM Chou: No.

Dr. Kissinger: They're like my colleagues, good in theory but not in practice.

PM Chou: Including your student [Nakasone]?[5]

Dr. Kissinger: Yes, especially my student.

PM Chou: So where do you think a way out lies? There is a way out but they refuse to take it. So that is why they now are trying to find ways out for the expansion of their investments abroad, and that is why Siberia holds such an attraction for them—natural gas, oil, timber—because in this way they can develop their war supply material in case of danger. Can't you cooperate with them in that?

Dr. Kissinger: We can cooperate with them. Especially in the gas project.

PM Chou: I believe they also want to develop the oil fields. The Tyumen oil project.

Dr. Kissinger: Yes, that is the one where they want us to participate 50 percent.

---

[5] Kissinger taught Japanese Minister of International Trade and Industry Yasuhiro Nakasone during a summer school program at Harvard.

PM Chou: A good thing that would come out of that would be mutual restraint on each other. They were afraid that we would oppose it. We said we didn't care. We said that was something for you to decide. Of course the way they have done things is due to ambivalence.

Dr. Kissinger: Everything you tell them they will tell the next party.

PM Chou: It doesn't matter. You see we are very large-minded. We don't care. We let them say what they want. Even if they made it public it wouldn't be of much use to others. But we think you should give consideration to trying to win over Japan. But your student also said something that is in accordance with reality. Before we established diplomatic relations we had relations with him. Our correspondent had a meeting with him and he also mentioned the five powers that your President mentioned. But when we mentioned that your President had mentioned the five powers, Mr. Nakasone said that the strength of Japan was an imaginary strength, because they relied on foreign countries for their raw materials and their markets. We can accept that sentence, but the question was about the conclusion he drew . . . The facts he mentioned were correct, but we don't know what way out he imagined. And he came for his visit recently and when we talked to him about it, it seems he still is not quite decided about that. Perhaps it is unfair to blame him for that because they are in such a situation.

Because the Soviet Union is quite attractive to them, especially because of the three things I mentioned just now—oil, gas and timber—and it is perhaps not good to oppose them. It might on the contrary have bad results. Because you are qualified to cooperate in that.

Of course we will also say other things to them too. For instance, the words of Tanaka that the Chairman told you yesterday about the Soviet Union: When someone is about to hang himself, they will bring a chair. Various leaders of Japan have said similar things. For instance, we support their recovery of their northern islands. But the Soviet Union puts up a ferocious front.

It is difficult to blame them because they have to rely on foreign countries for both their raw materials and their markets. And therefore their economic basis is not complete. And their present capability of self-defense is also limited, and if they are going to develop their capability of self-defense, internationally it probably would not be allowed, and domestically they would probably meet with great opposition. And that brings us back to what we discussed one-and-a-half years ago about the danger of the resurgence of Japanese militarism. I think now you would agree to that. But if they insist on embarking on that road, then what could we do about that? We should try to harness the trend and try to administer them into the best channels. The slogan of the Socialist Party is "No armed forces."

Dr. Kissinger: Yes.

PM Chou: I asked the Chairman of the Socialist Party, "Do you think you would be able to gain many votes from people by such a slogan?" It wouldn't be possible to rule with such a slogan either, but they don't change it. So Japan's politics is very complex, but it is due to their environment. But we believe no matter what, work should be done with Japan to prevent Japan's being won over by the Soviet Union and to be used to threaten the world.

And now to come back to the Middle East. We oppose the situation in the Middle East. We are not simply opposed to Israel, or singly. The existence of Israel is now a fact. But before they give up the territory they have come by by aggression, we cannot establish diplomatic relations with them. That is a principle. But the present situation there is one of no war, no peace.

Dr. Kissinger: That's Trotsky at Brest-Litovsk! [laughter]

PM Chou: But it is also a situation in turmoil which is more favorable towards the Soviet Union. It is also a turbulent situation. Take for instance the Arabs—they also claim socialism. There are a lot of socialisms. Now especially Mr. Qaddafi claims to be a socialist. You know he doesn't have relations with us?

Dr. Kissinger: No.

PM Chou: He has relations with Chiang Kai-shek.

Dr. Kissinger: I didn't know that. He wants to buy Malta. [laughter]

PM Chou: Yes, we know. [laughter] He is another expansionist. He says, "I have money in my pocket," and the Soviet Union is making use of that money. They are reaching into his pockets through Egypt and Syria and they are raising the price of their arms. The Soviet diplomats openly say to the Egyptians, "You have money, because Qaddafi will give you the money." You probably also buy Libyan oil, don't you?

Dr. Kissinger: Yes, it is one of the things we have to change.

PM Chou: So the Middle East issue.

Dr. Kissinger: Yes. He is buying Malta with our money. [laughter] And Iraq is using our money to make revolution.

PM Chou: They are not only buying Malta, they are sending your money to the Soviet Union.

Dr. Kissinger: Indirectly we did.

PM Chou: The issue of the Middle East is complex indeed. I acquired all this knowledge from Mr. Mintoff. He is the one who enlightened us in the beginning, but of course now we are getting it from other sources. You just now mentioned that Iraq was using your money to make revolution. In the final analysis they will use it to revolutionize themselves. You know the Socialist ruling party in Syria. What are they called?

Dr. Kissinger: Ba'ath.

PM Chou: Yes, Ba'ath. You know, the Ba'ath party in Iraq when they came into power they massacred a large number of followers of Kassem.

Dr. Kissinger: Including him.

PM Chou: So their present maneuvers there will not be able to be prolonged. Things will change. Of course there are quite a number of Soviet officers that are going to Iraq and Syria now, but those two countries are not very harmonious either.

And therefore with regard to the Middle East issue, our principle is to settle the issue in a manner that will be in the interests of all the Arab people including the Palestinian people. If you wish to inform us in the future of future developments it is all right with us, but I must say beforehand that we do not have the capability of doing anything here. The only thing we can do is give expressions to our opinion.

Dr. Kissinger: We will just inform you for your own information. We do not expect you to do anything.

PM Chou: And we have also openly told our Arab friends that since the Soviet Union is dominating that area it would do no good for us to go into that area. It would only increase the trouble in that area, and their burden.

The Soviet Union is making use of the Middle East issue to expand into the Subcontinent and the Indian Ocean. How are your relations with Sri Lanka?

Dr. Kissinger: Quiet.

PM Chou: Better now?

Dr. Kissinger: Yes, a little better, and we are prepared to improve them further. Mrs. Bandaranaike has some domestic trouble, and India keeps bringing pressure on her. But in principle we are prepared to improve our relations and go as far as she is willing to go. I will make sure she understands this. But if you talk to her people we have no objection if you say this is your impression.

PM Chou: So there are two—one to the north and another to the south of India—that dare to stand up and resist India. In the north and in the south. Do you have diplomatic relations with Bhutan?

Dr. Kissinger: No.

PM Chou: Is it because India doesn't allow that?

Dr. Kissinger: India won't permit anyone to have diplomatic relations with Bhutan. India controls the foreign relations of Bhutan.

PM Chou: Maybe like Ukraine.

Dr. Kissinger: Like Ukraine. They want Bhutan in the UN but they don't want anyone to have diplomatic relations.

PM Chou: They also have their Byelorussia—Sikkim.

Dr. Kissinger: Yes.

PM Chou: Since the Soviet Union and India are now allied to each other they copy each other.

Dr. Kissinger: Also, there is an American girl who is Queen of Sikkim.

PM Chou: We saw her.

Dr. Kissinger: Here?

PM Chou: No, when we went to visit Nehru. Is it the original one that married the King in the 50s?

Dr. Kissinger: That is right. She keeps using her prayer beads and sifting her beads all the time. She has become more Buddhist than the population. She makes me so nervous I always avoid seeing her.

PM Chou: In 1956 there was a very interesting incident when I was in India. Mr. Nehru invited me to a kind of fashion show dinner party and he had a lot of ladies there in various costumes, and among the guests he invited was the King of Sikkim and his American queen. The portrait of her was like you just now described. It makes others easily nervous. But in 1957 on my way back to China from the Soviet Union and Poland I also stopped in India. The scene then was different—another story. Nehru invited me to a tea party in his garden and among the guests were people in costume. There were two Tibetan lamas, and there suddenly appeared a female lama. Do you know who she was?

Dr. Kissinger: Madame Binh?

PM Chou: Madame Gandhi. [laughter] She was dressed up entirely in Tibetan costume. That was something that Nehru was capable of doing. I am not among those that go in for memoir-writing.

Dr. Kissinger: It is a pity.

PM Chou: So perhaps we can ask you to write it in your memoirs since you have it now in your minutes. [laughter] I was speechless confronted with such a situation. It was impossible for me to say anything.

But because Nehru insistently wanted to seize hold of Kashmir and Jammu, during the interval of the first Geneva Conference, 1954, I went to visit India. It was my first visit, and in that visit Nehru kept on asking me if I knew where he came from. Then he told me he was from Kashmir, which therefore proved Kashmir was Indian territory!

And he insisted on getting me to visit Kashmir, and I resisted him. But Khrushchev was very obedient and he visited that territory; it was also during his first visit to India, in 1955.

So that is what is called politics. But in our view it is only intrigue, small tricks. It is not open and above-board political activity. India cannot be considered a small country but still stoops to such tricks. A small country could perhaps win at doing such things, though perhaps some small nations would have more backbone than that. You are not so familiar with Nehru?

Dr. Kissinger: I met him once.

PM Chou: Only once.

Dr. Kissinger: But I must say that until well into the 1960's I had always accepted the view that in the Sino-Indian War you had attacked. It was not until I visit India in 1962 and talked to Khrishna Menon that I suddenly realized they had been bringing pressure on you. I have never been an admirer of Indian policy.

PM Chou: So you hold a minority opinion among the upper strata of the U.S.

Dr. Kissinger: Yes.

PM Chou: Now there are two other matters I would like to discuss with you. One is Cambodia. Because it seems this time during this visit it will be difficult to make further progress. We know your documents in English and French. We gave you already the 5-point statement of March 23, 1970, and also the January 26, 1973,[6] but we should further give you the January 23 one of the three Vice Ministers of the Royal Government of National Union in the interior part of Cambodia. And we are in agreement with Vietnam in respecting the position of the Front of National Union of Cambodia and also the Royal Government of National Union of Cambodia. Our tendency would be that you should cease your involvement in that area. Of course you would say in reply that other parties should also stop their involvement.

Dr. Kissinger: That is right.

PM Chou: If it was purely a civil war the matter would be relatively more simple. Of course it wouldn't be easy to immediately confine it to a civil war. The situation would be like China in the past. Of course it is not possible to hope for Cambodia entirely copying the previous China situation. But one thing can be done, that is, we can talk in various ways to make your intention known to the various responsible sides in the National United Front of Cambodia. Because the National United Front of Cambodia is not composed of only one party; it also is composed of the left, the middle and the right. Of course, Samdech Norodom Sihanouk wishes to be in a central position, as is the King of Laos and Prime Minister Phouma. They actually now have two leading persons; one is the head of state, the other is the Prime

---

[6] The Chinese Government gave these documents to the United States at a meeting two days earlier. See footnote 6, Document 9.

Minister, Penn Nouth. Of course in the interior the strength of the left is larger. And we also believe that differences will also occur in the Lon Nol clique.

France is also active, and so is the Soviet Union. The Soviet Union is also attempting to fabricate their own Red Khmer but they can't find many people. But it might in the future appear. So, in the future, if there is some information you would like to give us in this respect, we can also give you some too. But it would only be information. It would not be—we have not yet reached the stage where we could provide any views or suggestions.

Dr. Kissinger: I understand.

PM Chou: And we would like to take very prudent steps, because we wish to see the final goal of Cambodia realized; that is, its peace, independence, unity, sovereignty and territorial integrity.

Dr. Kissinger: We completely agree with these objectives.

PM Chou: But we will still have to wait and see in which way these objectives can be realized. And you know, and Samdech Norodom Sihanouk also knows, that we would never want to turn Samdech Norodom Sihanouk into someone who would heed to our beck and call. If we did that, that would be like hegemony. Many of the views he expresses in our *People's Daily* are not necessarily our views, but we give him complete freedom. Although he has written songs about nostalgia about China—in Peking he wrote a very good poem about China being his second motherland—and although he is writing such poems we do not cherish illusions. I was going to try to persuade him not to try and publish the second song. I advised him to use "homeland" because "motherland" was too excessive. He insisted on "motherland." We must be prepared for the day when he says it doesn't count! Anyway it was all written by him; it has nothing to do with us. Of course he is now saying I am one of his best friends, that I am one of his best friends, "as Mr. Mansfield is." It doesn't matter. That is only personal relations. He is still the Head of State of the Buddhist State of Cambodia. So we still have to wait and see the developments of that issue.

So if we wish to see Southeast Asia develop along the lines of peace and neutrality and not enter a Soviet Asian security system, then Cambodia would be an exemplar country.

Dr. Kissinger: We are in complete agreement with that objective. And we have the same difficulty determining in exactly which direction to put our influence.

PM Chou: We still have to study that problem.

Dr. Kissinger: We are prepared to exchange information. It would be kept in strictest confidence. And we also believe . . .

PM Chou: Anyway I believe you to a certain degree answered me, when I said about the fact that Lon Nol will not do. I do not mean that the forces that he represents do not count.

Dr. Kissinger: I understand that. But before one can act on that, one has to have some idea of the alternative. I also agree that if it can become a Cambodian civil war rather than a foreign war, that would be the first step toward realizing these objectives.

PM Chou: We understand the directions. We understand our respective orientations. Because it is impossible for Cambodia to become completely red now. If that were attempted, it would result in even greater problems. It should be settled by the United Front, on the basis of the policy I just now mentioned; that is, independence, peace, neutrality, unity and territorial integrity.

Dr. Kissinger: Those principles we agree with, and we now have to find some framework for achieving them in a way that takes account of all the real forces.

PM Chou: So, one we agree.

Dr. Kissinger: The Prime Minister had a second issue.

PM Chou: So I would like to stop here about this issue and go on. That is the Korean issue.

Dr. Kissinger: I was hoping the Prime Minister might forget about it. I nearly got out of here all right. [laughter] I have already crossed it out of my book. [laughter]

PM Chou: No, it won't be crossed out. You know it hasn't been easy for that area to have remained without any major incident during these 20 years. You know there is only an armistice there. Dulles broke up the 1954 Geneva Conference discussion about Korea. It seems in retrospect that was very good. That was the only time that we looked into each other's eyes. We were seated opposite each other at a round table in a room that was about one-quarter of this one. That was the only time he stared at me and I stared at him. That was when he made the decision that the Korean question was not to be discussed, and that was the final time, and after that he left Geneva and left it to his assistant Mr. Smith to deal with us. It seems in retrospect there were good points in that. That means we are not fettered, and the result has been that the two sides have maintained the desire to maintain a status of peace there.

It has been 15 years since our volunteers withdrew from Korea; your troops have remained there until the present day. Now there are these few issues that need to be solved. Because in principle there will be a day when your troops will be totally withdrawn and therefore it is not incorrect for the DPRK to put forward that principle. Because we have indeed left Korea 15 years ago, and the Korean army has neither

Chinese nor Soviet military advisers. The Soviet Union is now trying to exert pressure on them but the Koreans resist them. Of course, it has to have some relations and exchanges with the Soviet Union. It was, I believe, precisely yesterday that they were celebrating the 70th birthday of Brezhnev and sent him telegrams of congratulations. Both our Vietnamese friends and Kim Il-sung sent a greeting to Brezhnev yesterday. But that was the very day that Chairman Mao Tse-tung sent his regards to President Nixon. So the Soviet Union probably will be making great fuss about that. [laughter] It is entirely coincidental.

Dr. Kissinger: A coincidence.

PM Chou: And it was only this morning when I read the news that I saw this happened. We hadn't calculated it before. We gave the news at 4 o'clock in the morning then it was released. How could I know he turned 70 yesterday? And Chairman Mao has still less regard for such matters; he is highly opposed to birthday celebrating. You probably didn't premeditate that.

Dr. Kissinger: No, I didn't know I was meeting Chairman Mao.

PM Chou: Perhaps your President will have to telegram something.

Dr. Kissinger: Actually Brezhnev sent birthday greetings to President Nixon. I have just made a note to see if we sent any. Normally I am told.

PM Chou: We couldn't care less if you sent him a telegram out of courtesy.

Dr. Kissinger: I don't know whether we did or not. I doubt that we did.

PM Chou: It doesn't matter.

Dr. Kissinger: But I am not sure. I will have to check.

PM Chou: Because we couldn't care less about such matters.

As for the Korean issue, you said the year before last and last year that probably this year you would abolish UNCURK. How do you envisage this?

Dr. Kissinger: We envisage that we can get UNCURK abolished probably in the second half of this year. We will talk first to the South Koreans to see whether they are willing to propose it. If not, we will talk to some of the other members.

PM Chou: Yes, it would be best if they did it.

Dr. Kissinger: That is what we will try to bring about.

PM Chou: So if you can give us that promise then, we will do our best to avoid the issue becoming acute.

Dr. Kissinger: I am almost certain. Let me confirm it within the next few weeks. It has that much time.

Miss T'ang: What has that much time?

Dr. Kissinger: I mean it has that much time to let you know definitely. I am almost certain we can do it. I want to check to see if there are any complications I cannot predict, but I am almost certain. Say, by the middle of March we will confirm it. I know the President agrees with it. I have to study the mechanics of how to do it.

PM Chou: Yes.

Dr. Kissinger: I am almost certain we can do it.

PM Chou: That is one thing. The second point is the gradual troop withdrawal. We believe that is a reasonable request on the part of Korea. We know that you are anyway going to gradually withdraw your troops from Korea, and during that period you want to increase the self-confidence of the South Koreans to make sure they are going to be able to defend themselves.

Dr. Kissinger: That is correct.

PM Chou: Anyway, there is no one who is going to commit aggression against them. But one thing that must be guarded against is that the Japanese should not be able to force themselves on them.

Dr. Kissinger: Yes, we have an understanding on that. And that understanding is maintained. That makes it important that the withdrawal be gradual and not sudden.

PM Chou: The principle that you should withdraw your troops is a principle that neither the Korean people nor the Democratic People's Republic of Korea can change. But the fact that the troop withdrawal will be gradual and Japan should not be allowed to enter into that area is something that we have also told our Korean friends and that is something that they must understand.

Dr. Kissinger: On the principle of withdrawal we have an understanding, and the principle that Japanese forces will not enter the territory of South Korea we maintain. On withdrawal we will be able to give better understanding of the direction in which we are moving within the next year.

Miss T'ang: You mean in 1973, 12 months?

Dr. Kissinger: By this time next year.

PM Chou: Next year? When I talked with Nakasone I asked him whether it was true or not that when he was in charge of defense he had sent military men in civilian costume into South Korea, and he denied it. I didn't tell him you had admitted it was true.

Dr. Kissinger: We gave you that information.

PM Chou: You proved it. I said the Koreans don't have a good impression of the Japanese. He said, that's true. Many Koreans are pro-Japanese, and were trained by the Japanese.

Dr. Kissinger: Their President was trained by the Japanese.

PM Chou: And the third point is that you are giving the South Koreans some military equipment and changing some of it too. As for the 40,000 American troops which will be withdrawn, will they also go back into Korea with modern weapons—the troops from South Vietnam?

Dr. Kissinger: Oh, the troops from South Vietnam. The Prime Minister has too much experience with ceasefires. And I don't want to be in the position of Nakasone. About half will go back to the U.S. and about half will leave their weapons there and receive new weapons in Korea. The Prime Minister knows it already. [laughter] But the equipment was transferred legally before January 27. [laughter]

PM Chou: I don't care much for that deadline, January 27th.

Dr. Kissinger: This is why I do not express as much moral outrage now as I will in two months about their tanks moving South.

PM Chou: It would be impossible two months hence. The important thing now is for the Commission of Control and Supervision to go as quickly as possible to their posts.

Dr. Kissinger: I agree.

PM Chou: It is also ridiculous that the Two-Party Commission should continue to hold its meetings in Paris and not be able to go to their own country, to Saigon.

Dr. Kissinger: What is the matter is that Chapter VI is so complicated that it can be understood only by the one or two people who have drafted it. I am sure Minister Thach probably understands it. The people who met in Paris is not the Two-Party Commission, but the political discussions. The Two-Party Commission has not yet been formed, but that is no great tragedy because it will automatically appear when the Four-Party Commission is disbanded, then the Two-Party Commission will remain.

PM Chou: There are also protocols to the Agreement.

Dr. Kissinger: Oh, for the Two-Party Commission, yes, that is true. The Four-Party Commission protocol exists.

PM Chou: Both exist?

Dr. Kissinger: No, the Four-Party one. After it ceases then the two parties will agree on their own protocol. But we will strongly support the Two-Party Commission. On the other hand, the PRG has refused to name points of entry, and as I told the Prime Minister they take the astounding view that in the absence of points of entry the frontiers are open. I would have thought they are closed. That we cannot accept for a long time.

PM Chou: The complexities, it is really something to have to go through all your documents. [laughter] But this time it is somewhat better. As Chairman Mao said after, it is not bad to have reached a basic settlement, because it doesn't seem that Nguyen Van Thieu is likely to act like Chiang Kai-shek in disrupting the Agreement entirely in half a year.

Dr. Kissinger: We would strongly oppose it.

PM Chou: Because then, with Chiang Kai-shek, the U.S. was in a position of a mediator; it was the chairman of the three-man committee, but also had a veto. I heard that the veto was an invention of Marshall when the allies got together in the Second World War. On military actions between the Soviet Union, Britain and the U.S. That was when Marshall invented it. Is that so?

Dr. Kissinger: I don't think so.

PM Chou: Of course, later on it was used in negotiation.

Dr. Kissinger: I don't think we ever tried to veto military action. I will look it up.

PM Chou: Have you studied to do some research on it? Then it showed up in the UN. That is what Marshall told me, and he prided himself very much in that. That was when Mr. Chang Wen-chin was the interpreter when I met Marshall in Chungking.[7]

Dr. Kissinger: That might have been the problem, the interpretation. [laughter]

PM Chou: That was what he said during the first encounter with me. Of course, that might not have been merely the allied armed forces but the allied powers in Tehran. Maybe it came from Tehran.

Dr. Kissinger: That is possible. But we never knew about Soviet actions until they started them. The Soviet Union never told us ahead of time what they planned to do.

PM Chou: You mean military action.

Dr. Kissinger: Military action.

PM Chou: But the military orders issued on the Western front were indeed very long.

Dr. Kissinger: Yes, very bureaucratic.

PM Chou: The ones about the landing, Marshall told me, were hundreds of thousands and maybe millions of words long. And I asked him, "How did you read it, Mr. Chief of Staff?" He said, "I read only the outline." So sometimes one must be practical and use the bureaucracy.

Dr. Kissinger: One must shortcut the bureaucracy.

PM Chou: And another thing in South Korea, what they are doing now—they are doing their utmost to establish a dictatorship and suppress the people and leave them with no freedom at all. They orig-

---

[7] President Truman sent General George C. Marshall to China in 1945 to negotiate a coalition government between the Communists and the Nationalists. Marshall returned to the United States in 1947.

inally had a constitution, now they suppress it. Actually the present dialogue is only an initial contact between the two sides, and how is it possible to fundamentally change a system by initial contact? And even if a confederation was established between two states of different social systems it would only be outward appearance, and it would not be possible to immediately obliterate the differences. The only thing that could be done is to give the people the kind of hope that in the future unity would be achieved, and it would add to the atmosphere of national harmony. But they are greatly afraid of that.

Dr. Kissinger: The South Koreans?

PM Chou: Pak Chung Hee. Because they lack self-confidence. We don't know how strong your influence is there.

Dr. Kissinger: We support these negotiations and at every opportunity exert our influence. But is it your impression that South Korea is the principal obstacle now?

PM Chou: Yes, they do in several instances create a bit of trouble. For instance, they might suddenly arrest a group of people. And they are deeply afraid there might be some inner turmoil, because in the lower strata of their country, in the lower ranks of the political parties, there is a desire to achieve more democracy, which they have done away with. They have abolished the Parliament and they proclaim a new constitution in which the President would be for life. It shows a lack of self-confidence. In our view it will be impossible to completely change a system in one stroke.

I might tell you an interesting matter. That is, the written language of North and South Korea are different.

Dr. Kissinger: I think you are thinking of Vietnam.

PM Chou: It is a very curious situation.

Dr. Kissinger: The written language is different?

PM Chou: In North Korea they implemented a reform of the written language. Because before, the Korean written language used square characters, like Chinese. But now North Korea has made a reform of their written language. They are now using symbols. It has not been completely Latinized, but they are using different symbols for the sounds.

Each symbol is the sound for a square and then the various squares are put together to produce the sound. In North Korea there is not a single Chinese character in their language. But South Korea uses Chinese characters the same as we do, but it is classical Chinese. It is likely your highly refined gentleman from your State Department.

Dr. Kissinger: Mr. Freeman.

PM Chou: Who is quite literary in his spoken Chinese. So you see in that same land even the written language is different. And therefore the present matter of conducting affairs in South Korea is to rely on foreign forces. So if you don't pay too much attention they will allow the Japanese economic forces to enter that area. Although indeed the relations between Japan and Korea are deeper than ours, because they have been for 50 years a colony of Japan.

Dr. Kissinger: Yes. When the Prime Minister said that if UNCURK was abolished this year we could avoid difficulties, did he mean we could avoid a debate in the UN?

PM Chou: Yes.

Dr. Kissinger: On that basis I think we can do it.

PM Chou: And South Korea should be made to understand that the abolishment of UNCURK should not impair their self-confidence, that is, if they are able to manage their part of the country well. There is only one aspect in which the two Koreas are united, and that is in sports. They are quite strong in sports. In the Olympics they sent a joint team. They are very strong in some matters. So that shows that the people desire unity.

Dr. Kissinger: Football. On the political talks, Mr. Prime Minister, we strongly encourage them. We are told by the South Koreans that the North Koreans are the obstacle; you tell us the South Koreans are the obstacle. Perhaps we should exchange some information. If you tell us the concrete issues that are creating difficulty we will know where to use our influence.

PM Chou: There is another area, that is the Military Armistice Commission that is standing in between them.

Dr. Kissinger: In Panmunjom.

PM Chou: I think they call it now the Ceasefire Committee. On the South Korean side you are the main participant and they are the deputy.

Dr. Kissinger: The Prime Minister taught me that in October, 1971. I hadn't done my homework. [laughter]

PM Chou: On our side the main representative is that of the armed forces of the Democratic People's Republic of Korea and the representative of the Chinese People's Volunteers is only the deputy. And the supervisors on behalf of your side are Switzerland and Sweden, and on our side Poland and Czechoslovakia.

Dr. Kissinger: Do you want to trade Sweden for Czechoslovakia? [laughter]

PM Chou: We have no interest at all in that committee, but we often play host to them because the four members of the committee often like to pay a tourist visit to Peking.

Dr. Kissinger: That I can understand.

PM Chou: Because they have nothing to do there and they are stationed on either side, and every two years they have to change their personnel. It has been going on for 20 years now.

Dr. Kissinger: Oh, and then each group comes to Peking.

Chi P'eng-fei: I don't know the details, but the Premier was saying they all come to Peking and spend their vacation here.

Dr. Kissinger: They work too hard.

PM Chou: Not hard at all. They didn't work hard. They are overtired.

So there are two more points. One is the communiqué. You have given us a draft. We have just glanced over it and we believe it generally acceptable. Of course we have to report to our Political Bureau and to the Chairman, so I will contact you later in the night. And the second point is that after I meet Minister Thach about the Paris Conference I will contact you.

Dr. Kissinger: Yes. I will be available and it makes no difference how late it is.

PM Chou: So it is easy for you. Now you can have your supper. I still have a lot of work. I have to meet Madame Bhutto, Mr. Thach, and then you.

Dr. Kissinger: May I ask what time should we release the communiqué?

PM Chou: You said the morning of the 22nd.

Dr. Kissinger: What time? 10:00 or 11:00—do you have a preference?

PM Chou: It makes no difference.

Dr. Kissinger: I think we prefer 11:00.

PM Chou: That would be our midnight. It doesn't mater. It is the same to us. It will be in the next day's newspaper.

Dr. Kissinger: May I ask the Prime Minister what I can tell the Japanese? [laughter]

PM Chou: You can tell them what is in the communiqué.

Dr. Kissinger: That is the absolute maximum I would tell them. [laughter] There is no possibility that I will tell them more. I am trying to figure out a way to tell them less.

PM Chou: You can say for instance that both our sides expressed appreciation about the establishment of diplomatic relations between China and Japan and that we believed this was in the interests of peoples of the three countries and the other people in Asia and the Pacific Ocean.

Dr. Kissinger: I will certainly say that. Let me suggest this about the Liaison Office. I will say only that we agreed to establish some form of contact and we will still exchange messages about what it is. But then you should not tell them any more.

PM Chou: We won't say anything.

Dr. Kissinger: Our view about Japan is—I didn't tell the Prime Minister—we agree with his analysis, and the dangers. Why we didn't foresee the consequence of its industrial growth is an interesting historical question, which we should discuss sometime. But I believe the biggest danger is that if the Japanese are torn between too many conflicting pressures from too many sides they will become more and more nationalistic. Therefore on our side we will not encourage them into an anti-Chinese direction. We are trying to influence them to develop relations, and if you on your side encourage them in the direction you expressed, I think this is the best thing we can jointly do at this point.

PM Chou: Yes.

Dr. Kissinger: One other general point, and then I would like to make one very minor suggestion about the communiqué. I agreed with the Prime Minister's initial statement about the necessity of being prepared for the worst, and I wanted to say that if despite our intentions the situation which Chairman Mao described yesterday should come to pass, it would be the aim of this Administration to develop our policy in such a way that we can take the measures which Chairman Mao foresaw.[8] [Chou nods.]

Thirdly, in the communiqué, I have noticed we said we "agreed on a program for expanded scientific, educational and cultural exchanges." We don't mention trade. I think we should mention trade. We should say "of expanding trade as well as scientific, cultural and other exchanges."

PM Chou: "They agreed on a concrete program for expanding scientific, cultural, trade or other exchanges."

Dr. Kissinger: Right, and "details will be announced as they are settled," or we can just leave that sentence out. Let us just drop the whole sentence. [Chou nods yes.]

Ch'iao Kuan-hua: I thought you had made a decision not to mention trade!

Dr. Kissinger: When foreigners try to analyze another's foreign policy they never leave room for incompetence. They always think it is by design.

I don't know whether I told the Prime Minister: we analyzed after the Shanghai Communiqué was published your Chinese version, and we found that in every ambiguous case you resolved the issue slightly in our favor. It was a very gentlemanly procedure.

If you can let us have the Chinese text when we have agreed on it, to take back with us. You will let us know tonight?

---

[8] Mao raised the possibility of a Soviet attack on China. See Document 12.

PM Chou: We don't want you to have to leave too late tomorrow. That will make your arrival in Tokyo even later, which will not be in accordance with the suggestions of the Chairman.

Dr. Kissinger: I have extended my stay in Tokyo even longer after the suggestions of the Chairman. I am staying until after lunch.

PM Chou: Are you going to the teahouses?

Dr. Kissinger: They are giving a dinner for me tomorrow night, and then the next day where I have lunch I don't know yet.

PM Chou: You probably appreciate the Japanese teahouses.

Dr. Kissinger: I prefer Chinese food. I like Japanese food. My difficulty is sitting on the floor. I suffer so much sitting on the floor that I forget what I am being fed. I once stayed in a Japanese hotel where I was the only Western guest, and no matter what I said they took my pants and pressed them. They pressed my pants 10 times a day. [laughter]

---

14.   Memorandum of Conversation[1]

Beijing, February 19, 1973, 12:35–2:20 a.m.

PARTICIPANTS

Chou En-lai, Premier, State Council
Chi P'eng-fei, Minister of Foreign Affairs
Ch'iao Kuan-hua, Vice Minister of Foreign Affairs
Chang Wen-chin, Assistant Minister of Foreign Affairs
Wang Hai-jung, Assistant to Minister of Foreign Affairs
T'ang Wen-sheng, Interpreter
Shen Jo-yun, Interpreter

Dr. Henry A. Kissinger, Assistant to the President for National Security Affairs
Winston Lord, NSC Staff
Commander Jonathan T. Howe, NSC Staff
Peter W. Rodman, NSC Staff
Mary Stifflemire, Notetaker

PM Chou: First of all, a final question. Would that be all right?

Dr. Kissinger: Please.

---

[1] Source: National Archives, Nixon Presidential Materials, NSC Files, Kissinger Office Files, Box 98, Country Files, Far East, HAK China Trip, Memcons & Reports (originals), February 1973. Top Secret; Sensitive; Exclusively Eyes Only. The meeting took place in Guest House #3. All brackets are in the original.

PM Chou: That is the communiqué.[2] We have only two points of revision. Are you ready?

Dr. Kissinger: Yes.

PM Chou: The first point is in the first paragraph, before the word "President," we have added the word, "U.S." [See U.S. draft in Tab A.]

Dr. Kissinger: Oh, yes. I might want to leave some ambiguity. To give the President an ecumenical role. [Laughter]

PM Chou: Then paragraph 3, the last sentence. I have changed the sentence, "They hoped that the progress that has been made during this period will be beneficial to the people of their two countries."

Dr. Kissinger: How about, "they expressed confidence"? "Hope" makes it look as if there is some doubt about it.

PM Chou: "They held."

Dr. Kissinger: Oh, "they held." That is fine. Can you give this to us?

Miss Shen: "They held that the progress that has been made during this period will be beneficial to the people of their two countries." We can give you a copy.

Dr. Kissinger: Then we will take the copy. Oh, you have underlined it.

PM Chou: Yes. And I underlined another sentence which is at paragraph 6. [Hands over Chinese draft at Tab B.][3]

Dr. Kissinger: You want to substitute "relaxation of tensions" for "peace"?

PM Chou: Yes.

Dr. Kissinger: Fine.

PM Chou: Only three points then.

Dr. Kissinger: I have a change, which I think isn't important. In the second—oh, are you finished?

PM Chou: Yes.

Dr. Kissinger: In the second paragraph, where it says "they held extensive conversations" I like the word "wide-ranging" in your announcement yesterday. "Wide-ranging" has a fuller meaning.

PM Chou: It is the same as "extensive." So you want "wide-ranging." The Chinese word is the same.

Dr. Kissinger: Which do you think is better? Then we say "wide-ranging."

---

[2] Attached but not printed at Tab A is the draft communiqué. For the published communiqué, see Department of State *Bulletin*, March 19, 1973, p. 313.

[3] Attached but not printed.

PM Chou: Fine. We don't have to change our Chinese version.

Minister Chang: Just like the Vietnamese. [Laughter]

PM Chou: As the Doctor has said this afternoon, our changes are all in your favor. That is, he referred to the communiqué, the Shanghai Communiqué; when they were ambiguous they were all slightly in your favor.

Dr. Kissinger: In Chinese, we found that whenever you had two [possible] words, you always picked the one we would have slightly preferred had we been given the choice. We really were very impressed with that, and I always looked for an opportunity to tell you. They changed no substance but . . .

PM Chou: No substance. We have already got a Chinese copy of the communiqué. The Chinese version. I will read to you the original text. The draft communiqué sent to us from the U.S. side at 8:00 in the morning on February 18 was revised and adopted by our Political Bureau on the evening of the 18th. And we hadn't had the last sentence. Just now the Chairman phoned us and said that he agrees to it. So our formalities are finished.

The date is not there. We need a date. The 22nd.

Dr. Kissinger: Oh, the date. The 22nd, Washington time. It will be 23rd for you in the morning.

PM Chou: No, midnight. So it should be at 24 hours.

Dr. Kissinger: We will do it at 11:00 a.m.

PM Chou: It should still be counted as the 22nd.

Dr. Kissinger: The 22nd is fine.

PM Chou: It seems too difficult to put the place here, so we will just leave the place out. Without Peking. Just February 22, 1973. Without the place.

Dr. Kissinger: Oh, fine. [Chou hands over Chinese text, Tab C.][4]

PM Chou: So we have finished this piece of our work. So I have completed my work very quick. Now let us discuss the Paris Conference.

Dr. Kissinger: May I go through a few very quick items?

PM Chou: Yes.

Dr. Kissinger: I would like to let Mr. Ziegler say tomorrow that I made a courtesy call on Mrs. Bhutto. [Chou nods] Because if we wait three days it sounds very mysterious.

PM Chou: That is good.

Dr. Kissinger: And he will just say I made a courtesy call.

---

[4] Attached but not printed.

PM Chou: She told me so and she is satisfied with it.

Dr. Kissinger: Oh, she told you. But I told her we would say it on the 21st, but on reconsideration it is better to do it tomorrow, the 19th, our time.

PM Chou: That is the morning of your time?

Dr. Kissinger: Yes. He won't write it. He will just, at his morning press conference, confirm our meetings and he will say, "In addition Mr. Kissinger paid a courtesy call on Mrs. Bhutto."

According to our records, the type of airplane that was shot down near Hainan with Lt. Dunn was an A–1.

PM Chou: According to our records, it was an A–1H.

Dr. Kissinger: Yes, A–1H.

PM Chou: But for our information it was an A–1H. Perhaps we haven't made it clear.

Dr. Kissinger: That is correct. It is a special type.

PM Chou: It took place on the 14th of February, and we searched for it for three or four days by naval ships but nothing has been found. There were no remains or no bodies found. We think that anyway the plane was shot down and he was also shot down. To make it more specific, it is something like this: "Concerning the U.S. search for the U.S. pilot Lt. Dunn."

Dr. Kissinger: This is an official report.

PM Chou: "Point one: On the morning of February 14, 1968, at 10:41, fighters under the Air Force of our South Sea Fleet downed and damaged two U.S. aircraft. And the type of the planes were A–1H." We are not sure whether it is "1" or "I."

Dr. Kissinger: A–1H.

PM Chou: "After intruding into our air space, one of the planes dropped into the sea about 20 kilometers away from Lohui, Wan-ning County, Hainan Island. Our South Sea fleet sent escort boats for searching which lasted three or four days, but they did not find anything. A U.S. destroyer ship has also carried out search operations on the above-mentioned sea area." The aforementioned material was provided by our General Office of the Chief of Staff.

There is another material here: "On February 15, 1968, the U.S. Defense Department issued an announcement saying that the U.S. aircraft inadvertently intruded five kilometers over Hainan Island. One of them was downed by a Communist MIG plane. On the 5th of March of the same year, in the Sino-U.S. Ambassadorial talks, we set forth to the U.S. side saying that two A–1H type attackers of the Navy of the United States intruded into the air space over our Hainan Island, and one of them was downed and one of which was damaged. And we also served serious warning for this." That is the records we had during the Warsaw Talks. And later on March 6 and June 15 of the same year the U.S. side had on many occasions inquired about the whereabouts of Lt. Dunn. Then on November 15 we formally replied to the U.S. side, saying that there was no result after searching. This is the material provided by the Foreign Ministry.

These two materials provided similar information as you mentioned, Doctor. Do you want any written information from us?

Dr. Kissinger: Not for our reasons, perhaps for the families concerned. We are satisfied with your oral explanation.

PM Chou: Well, so then we will work out a document to be sent to you, to facilitate your work. It is a kind of memorandum so that you can account for it to the families. [Aide-mémoire later given to U.S. side, Tab D][5]

Dr. Kissinger: We will give it to the family and we will confirm to the family that this coincides exactly with our own information and that we consider this a satisfactory explanation. And of course we recognize that our plane had no right to be over Hainan Island to begin with.

PM Chou: And you also mentioned that the plane inadvertently flew into our territory.

Dr. Kissinger: Yes.

PM Chou: According to your information it was just because of the climate that the machine had broken down.

Dr. Kissinger: We will confirm all of this to the family. So there will be no public discussion.

PM Chou: And another point related to that. There was a fishing boat of ours that was sunk last year. Many were killed and 12 were missing. Some of the fishermen were retrieved and after that an American naval ship signaled to our boats that they had personnel to hand over.

Dr. Kissinger: That we had prisoners?

PM Chou: That you had wounded personnel you wanted to hand over to us. At that time our ships did not dare to reply, so it went without response. This occurred twice.

Dr. Kissinger: Can you give me the date and the location?

PM Chou: Yes. Would you help us to investigate?

Dr. Kissinger: Of course. We will send you a written report within a week.

---

[5] Attached but not printed.

Minister Chang: We will give you a written report and then you can check the question. We will give you a document, a memo; we will give you some material.

Dr. Kissinger: Of course. If you can give us the date and the location and what you know about the type of the American ship, we will take immediate action.

PM Chou: Thank you.

Dr. Kissinger: One other final thing. I will probably have a press conference when we present this communiqué. I will not add much to the communiqué but I will do it in conciliatory language. Most questions will concern the liaison office. I will say it has no diplomatic status, and it will handle . . . But we will arrange immunities as a courtesy for both sides. They will ask me about the title of the head of it. We will just say we will call him Chief of the Liaison Office. Or Chief of the Liaison Mission.

PM Chou: Just now you said "Mission."

Dr. Kissinger: Yes, it will be "Office." Chief of the Liaison Office.

PM Chou: Chief of the Liaison Office.

Dr. Kissinger: Right.

PM Chou: Chief, and the others will be members who . . .

Dr. Kissinger: And the others will be "members."

I will certainly be asked many questions about Chairman Mao. I think it might be helpful if you permitted me to say that I thought he was in very good health. They will ask me. I won't volunteer it. Otherwise I will make no comment beyond what is in your announcement.

PM Chou: [Nods] We will give you both the television and also the movie film.

Dr. Kissinger: That will be very nice. And we are free to release that?

PM Chou: Yes.

Dr. Kissinger: We will release that tomorrow or the day after. If I am asked about Taiwan, about the forces on Taiwan, I will say we will study this problem in terms of the tensions in the area and when we have anything to do we will say it. We have no immediate decision. Because our plan is to start the movement I mentioned to you in July. But that will be done. I just wanted you to know what I would say, and if you have any objections I will modify it. May we tell the groups to which you agreed such as the Philadelphia Orchestra, that in principle it is agreed?

PM Chou: Yes.

Dr. Kissinger: And I may mention that at the press conference, as an example? I may mention the two prisoners that you will release.

[Chou nods] And I will say that will be within the time period of the other releases. [Chou nods] And if I am asked about Downey I will say we discussed this in terms of an act of compassion by your government and you said you would take it under consideration. Or can I say more?

PM Chou: If you want to say more about it then you can say that in the latter half of this year we will consider this question.

Dr. Kissinger: That you will review it in the second half of this year.

PM Chou: That will be understood.

Dr. Kissinger: Those are the items that I have for the press conference. I will not tell the Japanese about the liaison office or about the specifics of the program. I will say we decided to establish some contacts and we will still exchange some messages. [Chou nods] That way it will not become public.

So now, if the Prime Minister wants to discuss the Paris Conference . . .

PM Chou: You are finished?

Dr. Kissinger: Yes.

PM Chou: About the Paris Conference. Vice Minister Thach has come to exchange views with us. Since he has not permission to meet Dr. Kissinger, so he will not meet you.

Dr. Kissinger: I understand.

PM Chou: And the second point is about the Paris Conference. You have already reached some agreements on certain points and this is just the same as we have agreed on.

Dr. Kissinger: Yes.

PM Chou: This is just the same as we have agreed on. That is, 12 countries will be the official members of the Conference, that is, they will sign. And the Secretary General of the United Nations will not sign the document. Then it is up to you to carry out consultations. How did you put it?

Dr. Kissinger: I was not clear that this had been agreed upon, but there could have been some exchanges during the week. It would be amazing. Did Thach think it was agreed upon in Hanoi?

PM Chou: He said that the Secretary General will not sign the document but he can make speeches, send messages of congratulations, and so on.

Dr. Kissinger: Yes, you are right. I don't think this was agreed upon about the Secretary General not signing. We do not think this was agreed upon. This is Hanoi's proposal.

PM Chou: So it is not yet decided?

Dr. Kissinger: No, it depends partly on the status of the Secretary General at the Conference. [Chou laughs] If he is executive secretary or something like that, it would be easy. If he is a participant it would be more difficult. [Chou laughs]

PM Chou: It is a matter that concerns your two sides. Because you have sent out the same invitation letters.

Dr. Kissinger: We avoided the answer to this question.

PM Chou: But in the letter there is the name of the Secretary General. His name is mentioned. Is that right?

Dr. Kissinger: That is right, but that is because he is invited by his position, not because of his personality. [Laughter] Or he would never get there.

PM Chou: That is why we have always asked you to clarify his position. That is why you mentioned that it would be better if he would be given sort of a function.

Dr. Kissinger: I would too think that. What do your Vietnamese friends think now?

PM Chou: I won't be able to make him appear about this time. I haven't met him yet.

Dr. Kissinger: Oh, Thach.

PM Chou: Because he arrived very late and they haven't worked out their document yet. So only after I have studied the document can I meet him. That is why we had a meeting among ourselves to talk about our own affairs.

Dr. Kissinger: Can you express a view on your own?

PM Chou: If you ask my opinion.

Dr. Kissinger: Yes, personally.

PM Chou: That is the opinion of the China side, we especially are not in favor of it.

Dr. Kissinger: Of what?

PM Chou: The participation by the Secretary General in the Conference. [Laughter] If we are asked to vote, since we can't vote against it we cannot but abstain. If we are asked to vote, since we cannot use the veto, so we cannot but abstain. But the difficult part . . .

Dr. Kissinger: But what are you thinking of vetoing now? I am not absolutely sure, Mr. Prime Minister, what you would veto if you had the chance. [Laughter]

PM Chou: Since you two host countries have invited him and he is included in the list, so how can we veto it? So you have to put us in a very embarrassing position. [Laughter]

Dr. Kissinger: He is still travelling around the world planning his participation.

PM Chou: And he has got a very extensive plan.

Dr. Kissinger: Yes, he is in charge of economic rehabilitation and peacekeeping. [Laughter]

PM Chou: Yes.

Dr. Kissinger: The concrete issue is, since he has been invited, would you oppose his being given an administrative function in the Conference which would remove him as a participant?

PM Chou: We can make our decision only after you two host countries have consulted among yourselves.

Dr. Kissinger: But your allies have apparently still not clarified their minds.

PM Chou: That is true.

Dr. Kissinger: We are waiting for them. You can tell them that we would like to have some understanding with them before the Conference. We really don't want a public controversy with them or you.

PM Chou: But there is one point which is definite. That is, he cannot act as the Chairman, the single Chairman of the Conference.

Dr. Kissinger: I understand that. Now I don't believe it can happen but if the Soviet Union should propose this, which I do not believe, it would put us into a very difficult position. I don't think they will do it but we have absolutely no information about Soviet intentions.

PM Chou: Well, there is one secretary who has gone to your Ambassador in London.

Dr. Kissinger: Yes, but that is incomprehensible. Normally they send their ambassador in Washington, who is on vacation—but after yesterday I think he will be coming back soon. Normally they send him in with their considerations, at least to the White House.

PM Chou: And after you get back if you meet him and you know about their views, then if you find it is necessary to let us know, we can be informed of it.

Dr. Kissinger: Yes. We will send a message tonight to their Chargé. Or we will send it tomorrow, after we have left here, because it will be better to send it from Tokyo. So that they can have an answer for me when I get back. And we will let you know in any event what the answer is. But unless the Soviet Union proposes it we will try to come to an understanding this week with the DRV to an alternative. If we come to an understanding this week with the DRV we will maintain it at the Conference no matter what is proposed by the others. I think then you will not accept the chairmanship but you might accept the Secretary General as the executive secretary of the Conference under the chairmanship of some other group. Provided the Democratic Republic of Vietnam agrees?

PM Chou: That means both the U.S. and the DRV agree.

Dr. Kissinger: Both sides agree.

PM Chou: If both of your two sides agree to it then we will abstain.

Dr. Kissinger: [Laughs] I understand.

PM Chou: Because we are simply opposed to that man taking part in the Conference. When I reported this to the Political Bureau at a meeting, they all laughed. They said, "what is the use of asking him to participate in the Conference?" [Laughter]

Dr. Kissinger: That is a great mystery.

PM Chou: I said that you were going to cut a hole in the middle of the table and place him there. Finally you were going to find out how it came that he was participating in the Conference.

Dr. Kissinger: I think it is as I said when the Prime Minister and I discussed this: We may well have put him into some document in August when we weren't paying attention and did not think it was a serious negotiation. Then the other side put him into a document and we had no basis for opposing it. So we had always believed that they made the first proposal but I must check it. It is possible that in August we gave them some document in which we mentioned that.

PM Chou: The second point is you have given us a draft, and after their draft has arrived then we will compare this to our draft and make a study. Then only can we let you know our opinion. They have never given us their draft. I am sure we will get it soon. Only after we have studied it can we raise our view.

Dr. Kissinger: I understand.

PM Chou: We believe it would not be very easy to include in this document the word "restraint," because it is very difficult to put it in a very appropriate way because the conditions for all the 12 countries are different. The situations are different. And it would be better if we say we "firmly guarantee" that the Paris Agreement will be implemented. If there should be any serious problems arising then we would look into the problems. This is our common commitment. I have just told you our idea. As to how to put it into wording, that is another matter.

Dr. Kissinger: We will definitely let you have our reaction before the end of the week. Maybe by Wednesday American time. I will work with Ambassador Sullivan on the plane home.

PM Chou: Today is Sunday.

Dr. Kissinger: Yes.

PM Chou: That means the 21st.

Dr. Kissinger: I hope to be able to get a cable off to you by Tuesday night Washington time. Your thought, if I understand it clearly, is that rather than "restraint" it should say all parties will do their utmost to bring about implementation of the Agreement, and will do what if it isn't being implemented? What was the Prime Minister's phrase—"make arrangements," or "discuss," "look into it"? Can you give me the text? "Look into it if there are any serious problems"? [Chou nods] Let me see whether we can phrase something that expresses that thought.

PM Chou: But there might be various forms to say exchange of views or exchange messages by correspondence. But the biggest problem is to reconvene the Conference. Unless the situation is very serious.

Dr. Kissinger: Can we say "create conditions to further the implementation of the Agreement"?

PM Chou: Too general.

Dr. Kissinger: What is more specific then?

PM Chou: "Make effort."

Dr. Kissinger: All right. The Prime Minister was speaking of reconvening the Conference.

PM Chou: That is when there is any very serious problem arising. We won't do it if this is not mentioned at all.

Dr. Kissinger: It should be mentioned that it can be reconvened. But who can reconvene it?

PM Chou: If you ask my view, then I would say that the two chairmen, that is the United States and the DRV. And of course you might ask what would happen if there is no result coming out of it, that is, if you can't come to an agreement. I just speak in physical terms: on this side there will be six votes, and the other side six. So if 1 to 1 there is no settlement, and 6 to 6 there still will be no settlement.

Dr. Kissinger: No it will be 5½ to 6½ because France will be on both sides. [Laughter]

PM Chou: If that is the case it will be easier. Otherwise the Secretary General will appear again and strike the gavel!

Dr. Kissinger: But we of course propose that the Secretary General should have the right to reconvene the Conference.

PM Chou: That will indicate that the UN will be in charge of it then. That would be the problem. And you wouldn't surely agree to that.

Dr. Kissinger: I think we could be persuaded.

PM Chou: But we would not agree to that.

Dr. Kissinger: It is not to us a question of principle.

PM Chou: Yes. If this is referred to the United Nations, the five big countries would then again be involved.

Dr. Kissinger: But we are there already anyway.

PM Chou: Then the situation will appear that there will be 12 countries plus one person. [Laughter] So we always find that this matter is very curious.

Dr. Kissinger: The other problem is, to whom the International Commission reports.

PM Chou: They can report to the two chairmen.

Dr. Kissinger: Yes, but the two chairmen are parties that are being investigated. The International Commission will report to the culprits. There are two possibilities that have occurred to me. No, three. One is, it could report to the Secretary General. If the U.S. and the DRV are co-chairmen it could conceivably report to them. You understand we have not yet agreed to the co-chairmen idea. We are considering it very seriously. The third possibility is that the Commission reports to the permanent members of the Security Council.

PM Chou: That means the five big countries. Then you have returned to this point.

Dr. Kissinger: These would be three theoretical possibilities. It would not be possible to keep Canada part of the Commission if the Commission reports only to itself.

PM Chou: Yes, they have expressed this view. We have read their public statement.

Dr. Kissinger: And it is also possible that the Commission reports to every member of the Conference. That means everyone except itself because four of the members of the Conference are the Commission. It would be the Security Council plus the three Vietnamese parties really. Plus the Secretary General. [Laughter]

PM Chou: And he would appear again.

Dr. Kissinger: That we are doomed to have happen one way or another. Mr. Lord's mother has been very active in the United Nations. We will hide these discussions from her. He joined my staff as the expert on the UN. He handled the UN. He says he is not an expert but he handled it. [Laughter] Does the Chinese side have any preferences on this subject?

PM Chou: Our preference is that this matter should not be referred to the UN, because from the very beginning the UN has never been in charge of this matter. Since you have signed a peace agreement, why should it be referred to the UN again? And besides, you ought to hope that the ceasefire agreement will be genuinely implemented. If it can be genuinely implemented, then the United States will not be involved again in the armed conflict in Vietnam, and the South Vietnamese people will be left to settle their own problems themselves. Of course, the time may not be as short as was laid down in the Agreement. It might be longer. That is to say, the ICC has another responsibility, that is to supervise the election. This is a very important point and this has been laid down. And this is confined to South Vietnam; it does not mean the unification of Vietnam. Because unification of Vietnam will take an even longer time. So there is going to be three steps: For the first stage, the troops will be withdrawn and the war will be ended and the prisoners will be returned. And at the second stage both sides will work out a plan for general elections. And for the final stage reunification will be realized. So since the Agreement has been signed it is hoped that it will be implemented, and it would not be good for the UN to intervene.

Take for instance the Middle East question. Although there was a resolution adopted in the UN, it could never be implemented, and among the five permanent members of the Security Council there would always be one that would express their disagreement. If you two countries, that is the U.S. and Vietnam, that is the DRV, would be able to create a situation in which you maintain a normal relationship, that is something that is most worthwhile to support.

Dr. Kissinger: That will be our effort. But it means also they have to cooperate.

PM Chou: Yes. If things are moving towards this direction, that is more hopeful. It would be not beneficial if the quarrel will be going on endlessly. Any more points?

Dr. Kissinger: I think the next step should be that we consider the remarks the Prime Minister has made and we will send him a reply by Wednesday. Some methods of dealing with them, some suggestions. We will also ask the Soviet side what their ideas are, and as soon as we have received an answer—if we receive an answer—we will let you know.

PM Chou: Good.

Dr. Kissinger: One other thing. At the Conference—it is difficult for us to run all the details of the Conference from Washington. If at the Conference something happens that raises concern, if you communicate with me directly I will do my best to attend to it. Because our discussions will not be known in detail to the participants. [Chou nods yes] So that will not mean we are going back on any word we have given. I can't foresee any concrete case now, but it could happen.

PM Chou: Yes. Since our Foreign Minister is going, perhaps he will meet with some new problems. And if there is any we will let you know.

Dr. Kissinger: Yes, if they develop. It is hard for me to control the relationship with the Soviet Union and all the other nations at the Conference. But if you get in touch with us, we will give the necessary instructions if it should arise. But I will speak to Ambassador Sullivan before, and we will probably be able to avoid it.

PM Chou: [Laughs] There are complexities in it. Because the four parties directly concerned are already very complicated, and on top of that there will be another four and then another four. And then you have found another one. [Laughter]

Dr. Kissinger: I took forward to the meetings between the Foreign Minister and the Secretary General.

PM Chou: Their meetings will be very easy for them to discuss because we have already built foundations for them. The problem doesn't lie between the U.S. and China but at the Conference.

Dr. Kissinger: No, you mean between the Secretary of State and the Foreign Minister. Yes, that will be easy. I meant the Secretary General.

Minister Chi P'eng-fei: Oh, yes. I have met him before.

Dr. Kissinger: No one has yet broken the news to the Secretary General.

PM Chou: He is quite different from Hammarskjold.[6] You knew him?

Dr. Kissinger: I did not know him.

PM Chou: He died quite early. He was quite capable.

Dr. Kissinger: Yes. I know Waldheim.

PM Chou: He was picked quite accidentally because it was difficult to find anyone.

Dr. Kissinger: And not because he was thought to be a very far-sighted personality.

PM Chou: He was elected just because people were in a helpless state.

Dr. Kissinger: Yes.

PM Chou: But anyway at a certain time the forum in the UN is still necessary. But it would be very dangerous if you would use it constantly.

Dr. Kissinger: Yes.

PM Chou: Are there are other points? You said that you would like to talk about your problems in your own country. Your domestic problems.

Dr. Kissinger: I have substantially explained the situation to the Prime Minister indirectly. We have reorganized the State Department by putting our own men into the number 2, 3 and 4 positions. Deputy Secretary Rush, and Porter the Under Secretary for Political Affairs, and Casey the Under Secretary for Economic Affairs. So some of the

---

[6] Dag Hammarskjöld was Secretary-General of the United Nations from 1953 to 1961.

difficulties we encountered in previous years can now be avoided. And we will give them some greater responsibility for our affairs. We still envision a transition later on.

So as I pointed out to the Prime Minister when we discussed the operation of the liaison office, it would be best if they would check with us to determine in which channel they should go. I will set up, when your chief arrives, a relationship between him and Deputy Secretary of State Rush. And then we can tell you in which channel to put it. And once your liaison office exists then this will operate very smoothly. Either Rush or Porter, I haven't decided yet. But either one you can then count on, once I have talked to the chief of your office. And if you can instruct him in that sense, that would be helpful.

PM Chou: After we have picked the chief of our office we will let you know in advance.

Dr. Kissinger: That was the major thing, and since it is the beginning of an Administration other political considerations are just newspaper speculations at this point.

PM Chou: There are too many comments and discussions in the U.S. press.

Dr. Kissinger: Yes.

PM Chou: Of course Japan ranks first, and the second place should be given to the United States.

Dr. Kissinger: Yes, it is terrible, and then they report each other's stories. You remember when we were here with the President last year, they all reported that at the second banquet there was great tension between you and the President and a terrible deadlock in the drafting of the communiqué. [Laughter] It was all total nonsense. And then they interpreted the communiqué in terms of their previous reporting. [Laughter]

PM Chou: It is hard to blame them, since there are so many people who have to work and there are so many papers that have to be published.

Dr. Kissinger: But they don't make any analysis; they only look for some immediately sensational news.

PM Chou: Perhaps this phenomenon can also be found in Europe, but we haven't paid attention to that area. In France there is also similar phenomena.

Dr. Kissinger: In France, somewhat, but not as intense as in the U.S. You see, in Washington there is only one industry, that is government, and indeed social life consists of government officials and journalists. And the journalists go to the dinner parties to watch what is happening among the officials. [Chou laughs] It is not like London or Paris where there are other occupations. So it has a very curious atmosphere, as the chief of your mission will discover. As I told the Chairman yesterday, during the transition from after the election there was much speculation that friends of mine were being removed from the government. It was all nonsense. I have explained to you why Helms was moved, and that was done by us, and the other case that was mentioned had a personality problem with the President; he just did not get along with him. No change was made that did not go through normal procedures, but the press kept speculating about a purge and we could not stop them.

PM Chou: Yes. Even when you did not meet the President but phoned him, there would be some kind of speculation about that. [Laughter]

Dr. Kissinger: Since we have a confidential relationship, I want to tell the Prime Minister what really happened on that day. The President was in Camp David.

PM Chou: Yes.

Dr. Kissinger: And I had gone to see him and we had completed our discussion on Friday. That is very confidential. So on Saturday he was all alone in Camp David and he got bored and a little lonely. So he came back to Washington. So Ziegler, in order to have some explanation for his returning to Washington which was on a weekend, said he came back to consult with me—which was total nonsense. [Chou laughs] And actually he and I did talk on the telephone several times that day on social things, but personal matters, not about business. So Ziegler stupidly said the President and Dr. Kissinger spoke on the phone to each other. [Laughter] But that was the true story of why the President came back and why there was no formal meeting. There was nothing to talk about! I had been in Camp David the day before and it was all settled and he came back on the spur of the moment. [Chou laughs] So these speculations were totally ridiculous at the time.

PM Chou: They have nothing to do.

Dr. Kissinger: They have nothing to do.

PM Chou: And since they have nothing to do they want to write a news report for the issue.

Dr. Kissinger: And sometimes quite frankly it is our fault, because the President is very reluctant ever to give the impression that he is doing nothing. So if he is in Florida or resting, they will say he has talked to me. [Chou laughs] Then if there is somebody who is not very quick they will say he talked to me on the telephone. So then the press says, "Aha, he talked on the telephone. There must be some trouble!" So this is really—it was total nonsense at that time.

PM Chou: I would like to put a new question to you. Did you mention that the Governor of your New York State is coming for a visit—wishes to go?

Dr. Kissinger: No, but I think he would like to come, yes. The Vice Foreign Minister has met him. If I can speak candidly to the Prime Minister, David Rockefeller is of course the man who is most active in the economic field, but the Rockefeller family usually does things as a unit, and of the Rockefellers Nelson is the one with the greatest imagination.

PM Chou: That is the Governor of the State.

Dr. Kissinger: But they are both very worthwhile people. And I think they would both like to come.

PM Chou: In that case it is not necessary for them to come on a bipartisan basis because as a Governor of the State he is independent. It is different from the Senators or Congressmen. If there are people from the Congress of course this is different, but the Governor is different from Congress.

Dr. Kissinger: Jackson would like to come with Buckley. Buckley's brother was here and he wrote very unfavorable articles. But I think you will find that Senator Buckley's interpretation of the nature of the international danger is almost identical to yours.

PM Chou: So he is different from his brother?

Dr. Kissinger: He is less artistic. His brother is a bit more emotional.

PM Chou: Is it because that during his stay here we did not give him a very good reception? That is why he did not have a very good impression of us?

Dr. Kissinger: No. He did not understand the nature of what we were doing, both of us. His mind was still in the Dulles era.

PM Chou: So he is very fond of art?

Dr. Kissinger: No, he is a mind that operates more emotionally. As a psychological type.

PM Chou: Is he a columnist?

Dr. Kissinger: William Buckley is a columnist, yes.

PM Chou: He wrote a lot after he got back?

Dr. Kissinger: What he wrote was more critical of President Nixon than of China. We have since calmed him down. He hasn't said anything in the last year. He objected to the President quoting from Chairman Mao on American television. He was not so critical of China.

PM Chou: [Laughs] So he joined us while we visited at some cities.

Dr. Kissinger: Yes. He was in Hangchow I think.

PM Chou: But that time when we were in Shanghai and Hang-chow you were kept busy with the documents. Perhaps you did not meet him then.

Dr. Kissinger: I did not meet any of the press while I was here.

PM Chou: At the press conference in China you did meet them.

Dr. Kissinger: Yes, but I am at my most effective when I can supplement my press conference with individual tutorials.

PM Chou: Tutorials?

Dr. Kissinger: Tutorials means seminars.

PM Chou: [Laughs] Oh.

Dr. Kissinger: When I say nothing to them individually they think they are getting exclusive information.

PM Chou: [Laughs] So your secret is no longer a secret. [Laughter]

Dr. Kissinger: Yes, but the Assistant Minister pointed out today your secret wasn't secret either, but your opponents never could do anything about it.

PM Chou: He just said it off-handedly. You can't say it that way. Anything else?

Dr. Kissinger: May we thank your interpreters for their excellent and devoted performance? We would like to thank you, Mr. Prime Minister, and your colleagues for the reception we received and for what we believe was very important work.

PM Chou: This time we have very extensive and deep-going talks. And we look forward—we will have to assess all possibilities—but we consider the orientation clear.

Dr. Kissinger: We considered the orientation settled.

PM Chou: That is true. We will have to anticipate all kinds of possibilities. In that way we won't be blinded. Otherwise we will be caught unaware if there should be anything arising unexpectedly.

Dr. Kissinger: Yes. And this is why we should regularly exchange information and ideas. We will certainly do it on our side.

PM Chou: That is why the Chairman asked you whether you will be coming again this year, and you said it is probable you will come by the end of this year.

Dr. Kissinger: I think it might be appropriate if we do it.

PM Chou: According to need.

Dr. Kissinger: Yes, I agree. The latter part.

PM Chou: Your colleagues also kept us company. We thank them for that. These two are new friends?

Dr. Kissinger: Mr. Rodman is a new friend.

PM Chou: I am told he is your student.

Dr. Kissinger: Yes, I made him rewrite his thesis 15 times.

PM Chou: He is the youngest in your group?

Dr. Kissinger: Yes.

PM Chou: How old are you?

Mr. Rodman: 29.

[The meeting then ended. The Premier and his colleagues joined Dr. Kissinger's party in walking most of the way back to the Guest House at which the American delegation resided.]

---

15.   Conversation Between President Nixon and his Assistant for National Security Affairs (Kissinger)[1]

Washington, February 21, 1973.

Nixon: Let me ask you one other thing about the China position. I like the two names you suggest, but here is something if you well realize, where we have Bruce—

Kissinger: Yeah.

Nixon: I wonder if we couldn't offer it to Bruce.

Kissinger: I'll have to check it with the Chinese whether they want someone quite that visible. But I—

Nixon: See my point?

Kissinger: But our minds have really been working very similarly.

[Omitted here is discussion of a congressional reception.]

Kissinger: Our minds have been working exactly the same wavelength. I was thinking after I left China why not let in Bruce, and—

Nixon: Well I think we do want to [unclear]. And maybe they may not like that.

Kissinger: And we could still have Holdridge—

Nixon: Holdridge—look, Holdridge [unclear] it will work, but Bruce has such class. And he would know, and he has such judgment. And it would be a hell of a bipartisan stroke.

---

[1] Source: National Archives, Nixon Presidential Materials, White House Tapes, Conversation No. 859–32. No classification marking. The editor transcribed the portions of the tape recording printed here specifically for this volume. According to the President's Daily Diary, Nixon met with Kissinger in the Oval Office between 11:33 a.m. and 12:04 p.m. (Ibid., White House Central Files)

Kissinger: And, of course, they love old men.

Nixon: Well, listen. You understand another thing, it's a bipartisan stroke; he's a Democrat. You know? He's the only establishment Democrat I know that supported us. Do you know any other?

Kissinger: No. And we could have the two others. If we had Bruce, Jenkins and Holdridge we would have one powerhouse team.

Nixon: Yeah.

Kissinger: I'd like Holdridge because I'd like to get rid of him. That's no reflection on him. He'd be good there but I need a somewhat more intellectual type here now.

Nixon: But you see, we want to keep it—Bruce will play our game; he'll keep it out of the State Department channels. Everybody of course would want to go. But we must not let this go to a career man. We must not.

Kissinger: Mr. President, if you send a career man there, you might as well—you're better off not having it.

Nixon: But they won't understand the game.

[Omitted here is discussion of Cyrus Vance and Clark Clifford.]

Nixon: I think the program of working with the Chinese can have great possibilities.

Kissinger: But that really has to be done by you and me.

Nixon: Alone!

Kissinger: Alone.

Nixon: Alone. Alone.

Kissinger: This is too dangerous.

Nixon: You know I was thinking that—

Kissinger: But you know, it's amazing, I thought exactly the same thing about David Bruce as you did.

[Omitted here is discussion of the timing of President Nixon's call to William Downey.][2]

---

[2] Nixon was preparing to call William Downey, the brother of John Downey, with the news that John would probably be released soon.

16.   Memorandum of Conversation[1]

Washington, February 21, 1973, 6 p.m.

PARTICIPANTS

  James C. H. Shen, Ambassador, Embassy of the Republic of China
  Mr. Hengli Chen, Counselor, Embassy of the Republic of China
  Dr. Henry A. Kissinger, Assistant to the President for National Security Affairs
  John H. Holdridge, Senior Staff Member, NSC

SUBJECT

  Mr. Kissinger's Remarks to Ambassador Shen Concerning U.S. Relations with
  the PRC and the ROC

After a few preliminary remarks between Ambassador Shen and Mr. Kissinger concerning the tiring nature of Mr. Kissinger's recent trip, Mr. Kissinger said that, first, he wanted to show the Ambassador the Joint U.S.–PRC Communiqué which was to be issued the following day.[2] He assumed, of course, that the Ambassador would keep the Communiqué confidential. After Ambassador Shen had read it, he, Mr. Kissinger, could then answer any questions about our general policy.

Ambassador Shen quickly scanned the text of the Joint Communiqué, and then asked what the diplomatic level of the liaison offices would be. Mr. Kissinger explained that the liaison offices would be non-diplomatic, and that there would therefore be no diplomatic level. The senior man's title would be chief of the liaison office, and he would not be at the ambassadorial level. For several reasons we had not wanted to call the offices "trade offices." What we had done was to more or less abolish the Paris channel; however, if we had a diplomatic note to present, for example, a protest, this couldn't be handled by the liaison office. The liaison office would handle exchange and trade matters, and other things of a non-diplomatic nature.

Mr. Kissinger wanted to emphasize two things: first, the liaison offices would not have any effect on our recognition of Taiwan, and secondly, he wanted to make it absolutely clear that he didn't anticipate any other steps in this direction for the foreseeable future.

---

[1] Source: National Archives, Nixon Presidential Materials, NSC Files, Box 523, Country Files, Far East, China, Vol. XI, Aug 1972–Oct 24, 1973. Secret; Sensitive. The meeting was held in Kissinger's office from 6:05 until 6:25 p.m. (Library of Congress, Manuscript Division, Kissinger Papers, Box 438, Miscellany, 1968–1976, Record of Schedule) Holdridge sent this memorandum of conversation to Kissinger under a March 1 covering letter. (National Archives, Nixon Presidential Materials, NSC Files, Box 523, Country Files, Far East, China, Vol. XI, Aug 1972–Oct 24, 1973) On February 20, Froebe sent Kissinger talking points for this meeting. (Ibid.)

[2] See footnote 2, Document 14.

Ambassador Shen wanted to know how this matter had come up—was it at the initiative of the U.S. Government? Mr. Kissinger recalled that when the President had been in Peking he had said we were willing to do this, but they wouldn't agree so long as an ROC Embassy was in Washington and we maintained diplomatic relations with Taiwan. Now, however, they had withdrawn this objection. When asked by Ambassador Shen why they had done so, Mr. Kissinger conjectured that it was due to fear of Russia. This was only conjecture, though.

Mr. Kissinger went on to say that the chief of the PRC liaison office in Washington would not be part of the diplomatic corps—there would be no presentation of credentials, and the office could not fly the flag. "But, could he conduct business with the Government through the State Department?" Ambassador Shen asked. Mr. Kissinger replied that we hadn't worked out the details yet, but obviously the PRC representatives could conduct business with Government agencies. It was interesting that the PRC was willing to go this far while the U.S. was still maintaining diplomatic relations with the ROC.

Ambassador Shen raised the question of the size of the liaison offices. Mr. Kissinger indicated that this had to be worked out, but that a staff of between five and ten might be envisaged. We might send around four people plus a supporting staff. When asked by Ambassador Shen how soon this might be, Mr. Kissinger expressed the view that it would not be too soon, but probably would take place in three or four months. Ambassador Shen wondered what the position of the liaison office might be comparable to—minister, consul general, or chargé? Mr. Kissinger indicated that the liaison officer would not be put on the diplomatic list, and so he didn't see how this individual would be comparable to anything at all. If, for example, the President gave a reception for the diplomatic corps, the liaison officer wouldn't be invited, because he had no diplomatic status. But, Ambassador Shen pressed, would he have diplomatic immunities and privileges? Mr. Kissinger replied, yes, very probably. Ambassador Shen asked if he would be able to use codes, and Mr. Kissinger answered affirmatively. Ambassador Shen then remarked that this would be an embassy without the name of it. Mr. Kissinger demurred saying that he did not think so.

Ambassador Shen commented that the Joint Communiqué impressed him as being strikingly brief and touched upon just this one point of the liaison offices. Was there anything else which Mr. Kissinger cared to tell him? Mr. Kissinger declared that there was nothing else to say. Some more exchanges had been agreed upon—we would send the Philadelphia Orchestra to Peking and they would send some physicists here, etc. There was literally nothing more, and this had exhausted the discussions.

Mr. Kissinger added that he had read in the newspapers that we were going to reduce our forces on Taiwan, but this was ridiculous. The subject had come up more in the way that they had to state for the record rather than as a part of the negotiations, and not as a part of the regular discussions. As to what we would do with our forces on Taiwan, we wouldn't even look at the problem until after our withdrawal from Vietnam, and then only in connection with our forces supporting Vietnam. We did not expect to remove any combat forces.

When Ambassador Shen stated that there were no U.S. combat forces on Taiwan as such, Mr. Kissinger responded by citing Air Force units. Of course, there were also intelligence units on Taiwan. In any event, we would work within the framework of the forces moved in since March 30 of last year.

Mr. Kissinger said it was his personal view that what we were doing had to be looked at in historical perspective, because what happened on the Mainland after the departure of Mao Tse-tung and Chou En-lai was hard to foresee. At this, Ambassador Shen remarked that Mr. Kissinger had spent some time with Mao Tse-tung—how had he seemed? Had his physical condition changed? Mr. Kissinger replied that while Mao had seemed all right, the Chinese were smart, but not that smart.

Continuing, Ambassador Shen asked Mr. Kissinger if he had been able to get any feeling for the situation on the Mainland. Mr. Kissinger then spoke of the great Chinese culture and of the magnificant quality of the Chinese to make one feel at ease. The situation in China was much different from that in Russia, and the Chinese atmosphere did not seem to be a Communist atmosphere. What the real internal situation was, he didn't know, but for the last two years he had always dealt with the same people: Chou En-lai and others around him.

Ambassador Shen wondered if Mr. Kissinger had seen Yeh Chien-ying, to which Mr. Kissinger responded affirmatively. When asked by the Ambassador if Yeh was in control of the PRC armed forces, Mr. Kissinger said that according to our information, the answer was to some extent yes and to some extent no. Our information was not obtained from our impressions of Peking, which on the surface looked very good. However, information from the provinces suggested that many of them were not under firm government control. The situation was very complicated for the Chinese leaders, and he personally did not know how they proposed to handle the succession problem.

Ambassador Shen commented that he had thought the Chinese had everything worked out in connection with the succession. What about Yao Wen-wuan, who had been mentioned by Chou En-lai? To this, Mr. Kissinger remarked that no person designated as a successor to Mao had ever survived.

Changing the subject, Ambassador Shen asked if there had been any discussion in Peking of an increase in trade. Mr. Kissinger indicated that there had been such a discussion in the context of what had been said in the Shanghai Joint Communiqué. The discussion had been in general terms only, and the Chinese had said that they didn't want credit loans, but wanted to pay for what they ordered in hard currency. Ambassador Shen speculated on the size of the PRC's specie reserve, and then raised the question of Most Favored Nation treatment for the PRC. Had they asked for MFN treatment? Mr. Kissinger replied that they were not eligible for MFN right now, but they had said that they did want it. Ambassador Shen asked, was this within the President's power to grant, or was Congressional approval required? Mr. Kissinger explained that MFN could not be granted without Congressional approval, although it would not be needed if the future new trade bill passed. Congressional approval was not needed by the President to grant credit loans.

Ambassador Shen turned the conversation to the question of Sino-Soviet relations, and wondered if the PRC fear of the Soviets was genuine. Was the situation serious, and if so, how serious? To a statement from Mr. Kissinger that he thought the Chinese fear of the Soviets was genuine, Ambassador Shen raised the possibility that it might be overblown. Mr. Kissinger reiterated that, while he didn't know for sure, the people in Peking felt that the threat was serious enough. He did not believe that they were doing what they were with respect to the U.S. because they liked him personally. Ambassador Shen expressed some doubts, but noted that of course he had not been there. It was at least possible, though, that they were simply going through the motions of showing great admiration—everything they did was for a purpose. Mr. Kissinger agreed, but added that we did everything we had done, at least for the time being, for mutual self-interest.

Ambassador Shen wanted to know if any other matters had been discussed in Peking. What about the 12-nation conference? Mr. Kissinger agreed that there had, in fact, been some discussions on this question. Ambassador Shen wondered whether there had been any reservations expressed with respect to the position of the U.N. Secretary General, to which Mr. Kissinger indicated that there indeed had been some reservations but did not elaborate further.

Ambassador Shen then asked how Mr. Kissinger's talks in Japan had gone. Mr. Kissinger said that after their (the Japanese) "very generous behavior" toward Taiwan, they had become very solicitous of Taiwan's position in relation to the PRC. He had told them that we had not been the ones to betray Taiwan, they had—we were not breaking diplomatic relations.

Mr. Kissinger observed that the Japanese Government was in trouble. Ambassador Shen expressed the view that the Japanese Government was not in trouble which would cost it too much. Mr. Kissinger said that he didn't know about this. Most of the people with whom he had talked felt that Tanaka would not serve out his full three years. At any rate, the Japanese now showed great interest in Taiwan's future. Ambassador Shen was surprised at this, and felt that any such attitude on the part of the Japanese must have been an after-thought. According to Mr. Kissinger, the Japanese liked to play the game with Taiwan's chips because this didn't cost them anything.

Ambassador Shen questioned Mr. Kissinger as to the latter's next visit to Peking, and Mr. Kissinger declared that he had no present plans for another visit. To a question as to whether we had picked the staff yet for the U.S. liaison office in Peking, Mr. Kissinger indicated that we had not really made a judgment on this matter.

At this point Ambassador Shen produced some pictures of himself standing next to Mr. Kissinger, and asked Mr. Kissinger to sign one for him. Ambassador Shen jokingly said that he would include this picture in his book if he were to write one.

Ambassador Shen called attention to the fact that Mr. Kissinger had spent 20 hours talking to the people in Peking. What had gone on in all this time? Mr. Kissinger explained that most of the conversation had consisted of a review of the world and of the individual exchange programs we had with the PRC. Strangely enough, there had been no more than one-half hour on Taiwan. They had said that they could not accept our presence, and we had stayed within the confines of what we had said in the Shanghai Communiqué.

Ambassador Shen asked what they (the PRC) wanted the ROC to do. Mr. Kissinger's response was: "negotiate." When Ambassador Shen asked if they were serious, Mr. Kissinger said that they were indeed serious. At social events they had said that they didn't want to change the social system on Taiwan, they just wanted to maintain the principle that it was part of China. The question of Taiwan's social system was separate from that of maintaining the integrity of China. They had repeatedly said that they wouldn't use force against Taiwan and therefore the question of U.S. troops defending Taiwan would not arise because there would be no use of force. Nevertheless, we had no illusions, and remembered what they had said about us four years ago. They could change again. But we believed that they wanted talks they always said that they admired and respected Chiang Kai-shek for one thing: he had always wanted to maintain the unity of China.

Ambassador Shen asked if the PRC has asked the President to mediate or to play any other role. Mr. Kissinger said no, but he was sure that if we were asked we would be willing to listen; we weren't asked, though, and would not take the initiative in any future which he, Mr. Kissinger, could see. At this, Ambassador Shen asked how far in the future Mr. Kissinger could see. Mr. Kissinger remarked that he had told the Ambassador last year that nothing would happen until now. Looking forward the same would be the case until 1974, which was all which he could foresee at this time. Nothing would happen in this period.

Ambassador Shen queried Mr. Kissinger as to whether he had any opinion of the way that the Chinese on Taiwan had been conducting themselves. Mr. Kissinger replied that he had a very high opinion of them on this score. They had behaved with great dignity and skill. We had no complaints. Ambassador Shen agreed that Taiwan had not caused the U.S. any difficulties. Mr. Kissinger declared that if personal feelings had entered in, the talks would have been different. Ambassador Shen's people had behaved with nobility, and we had no complaints.

Ambassador Shen stated that the ROC was gratified over the agreement on co-production of F–5s, which had now been signed. There were now just a couple of other small matters about which he would like to ask. The first was the situation of three over-aged destroyers which were to be transferred to the ROC—he had heard that this matter was in the hands of the White House. Mr. Kissinger noted that he had not heard of this but would look into it.[3]

Continuing, Ambassador Shen referred to another co-production product, that of fast PT boats. He understood that there was some hitch in obtaining agreement on this. Mr. Kissinger again indicated that he had not seen anything of this matter.[4] He emphasized that our general trend was to maintain all of our relationships with Taiwan, and to be helpful where we could.

Ambassador Shen expressed some misgivings to Mr. Kissinger as to what would happen when he, Ambassador Shen, faced a representative from Peking. Mr. Kissinger said that this would not happen for several months yet and referred earlier to what he had said about the non-diplomatic status of Peking's liaison office. Ambassador Shen nevertheless felt that Taipei would look upon it as an embassy without a name. Mr. Kissinger disagreed, saying that it could not do everything while the ROC had an embassy here. This certainly proved that Japan had paid too hard a price in return for its normalization of relations with Peking. He had said this to Tanaka, and to Sato as well. Sato had agreed.

---

[3] The request for the destroyer transfer was then working its way through the Department of Defense and had not yet reached the White House. (Memorandum from Holdridge to Kissinger, March 1; National Archives, Nixon Presidential Materials, NSC Files, Box 523, Country Files, Far East, China, Vol. XI, Aug 1972–Oct 24, 1973) Kissinger approved the destroyer transfer on March 27. (Memorandum from Kissinger to Laird; ibid.)

[4] At the time of this conversation, the Department of State was in the process of responding to a request from the Office of Management and Budget to finance patrol boat co-production. (Ibid.)

17.   Memorandum From the President's Assistant for National
Security Affairs (Kissinger) to President Nixon[1]

Washington, February 27, 1973.

SUBJECT

My Asian Trip

My trip to Bangkok, Vientiane, Hanoi, Peking, and Tokyo was
timely.

We have just concluded a Vietnam settlement: I was able to tell
ally and adversary alike that you will insist on strict implementation
of the Agreement, maintain forces in the region to deter violation, and
key economic aid to compliance.

The war continued in Laos and Cambodia: I stressed the need for
early ceasefires and North Vietnamese withdrawals. The conversations
on Laos served to hasten the ceasefire; the ones on Cambodia may lead
to a negotiating process, but the many forces at play make this problem especially difficult.

This is the start of your second term: I expressed your determination to maintain a strong world leadership role the next four years. This
message not only reassured our friends but also remains the key element in our developing relations with Peking. With the Chinese we are
now entering into a positive new relationship of greatly expanded bilateral contacts and tacit cooperation in our global approach. With the
North Vietnamese we may have laid the foundation for better relations;
we have at least made clear that they must choose between restraint,
reconciliation and reconstruction on the one hand and cheating and
confrontation on the other.

Following are the highlights of each of my stops.

[Omitted here is discussion unrelated to China that was excised
by the NSC staff.]

China

I had twenty hours of talks with Chou and almost two with Mao
in addition to several informal hours with Chou and other Chinese
leaders. Following within the framework which your trip clearly
established, these talks were exceedingly frank and cordial. With the

---

[1] Source: National Archives, Nixon Presidential Materials, NSC Files, Kissinger Office Files, Country Files, Far East, Box 98, HAK China Trip, Memcons & Reports (originals), February 1973. Top Secret; Sensitive; Exclusively Eyes Only. Sent for information.
There are no markings on the memorandum indicating that Nixon saw it.

Vietnam settlement behind us, the reception was the warmest and easiest ever. The conversations made clear that the Chinese are bent on accelerating our relationship. This was reflected outwardly as well in innumerable ways. My meeting with Mao was splashed across the top half of the *People's Daily* and a film on our trip ran for twelve minutes on national television. Guards saluted us for the first time as we entered the Great Hall and our Guest House. Our plane taxied right up to the terminal, etc., etc.

I will send you separate memoranda on the atmospherics and substantive discussions in Peking.[2] Following are the main conclusions.

We are now in the extraordinary situation that, with the exception of the United Kingdom, *the PRC might well be closest to us in its global perceptions*. No other world leaders have the sweep and imagination of Mao and Chou nor the capacity and will to pursue a long range policy. Our ideologies and views of history clash, but objective factors induce tacit cooperation for at least several years. If the Soviet danger fades and/or China becomes stronger over a period of time, the Chinese could follow an antagonistic policy with the same single-mindedness. For now, however, they need us, and their course is set.

Peking has chosen normalization because of our strength. It is precisely your assertion of a responsible American world role and taking strong measures when necessary that has convinced the PRC that the U.S. is a useful counterweight to the Soviet menace. Indeed, we have come full circle since July 1971. In my first trip to Peking I was treated to dissertations by Chou on our "stretching out our hands" around the world like the Soviet Union. It is true that Chinese perceptions had already evolved to the point that American imperialism was largely in the past while the Soviet variety was in full bloom. But the Chinese emphasis was nevertheless on American withdrawals from Asia; the Japan-U.S. military ties were at a minimum unhelpful; we were told to get out of Korea; there was considerable attention to Taiwan; there was almost no interest in Europe; and the U.S. might be capable of colluding with the USSR, Japan and India to carve up China.

We have come a very long way. The watershed clearly was your discussions with Mao and Chou when you stamped your personal imprint on our course. Substantial manifestation of our shared world view

---

[2] See Document 18. On March 2, Kissinger also sent Nixon a memorandum on the "Atmospherics of My Trip to Peking." (National Archives, Nixon Presidential Materials, NSC Files, Kissinger Office Files, Box 98, Country Files, Far East, HAK China Trip, Memcons & Reports (originals), February 1973) Kissinger's report on his meeting with Mao, February 24, is also ibid.

showed up in my subsequent June visit, as you will recall, but the Vietnam war still inhibited Chinese moves. On this trip the floodgates opened. Mao and Chou were obsessed by Moscow's intentions. With Vietnam out of the way as an obstacle and age closing in, they spoke with complete candor and an extreme cordiality which was reflected in every facet of our reception.

The contrast of their views with July 1971 was remarkable. Rather than being scolded for our *global presence* we were scolded for not doing enough to counter Soviet pressures. Mao said our forces were spread too thin. Chou complained that we were too slow and too slack in such areas as the Persian Gulf, South Asia and the Indian Ocean. For example, he urged us to give military aid to Pakistan, grant economic aid to Bangladesh, improve relations with Sri Lanka (Ceylon) and Nepal, etc. in order to oppose Moscow and its agent, New Delhi. I assured the Chinese of your determination to maintain a strong foreign policy and our willingness to undertake some of the specific steps he recommended.

Mao and Chou also urged us in work more closely with *Japan*. Our view that the U.S.-Japanese Security Treaty serves to brake Japanese militarism has now been accepted. I was told that I should be spending more than one day consulting with Japanese leaders. I responded that we intended to continue our close relationship with Tokyo and favored improvement of Chinese-Japanese relations.

Even on *Indochina,* where our formal positions inevitably differ, we share a common interest in independent states rather than dominance by Hanoi as an agent of the Soviet Union. I stressed this general theme and the need for restraint by all parties. We were prepared to normalize relations with Hanoi but only if it honored its obligations and was prepared to pursue its objectives through political evolution. I think Chou clearly understands our requirements in this regard, and Peking can have no interest in Hanoi's risking renewed confrontation with us. As for the need for Chinese restraint in military shipments, Chou pointed to the much more dominant Soviet aid role, but I think we can expect some Chinese moderation.

I also emphasized the need for an early ceasefire in Laos and direct negotiations among the Cambodians. The Chinese approach remained essentially hands-off. However, Chou clearly favored an early end to hostilities in Laos, and promised them to pull out Chinese anti-aircraft and withdraw their road-building teams when the road is completed. On Cambodia, he introduced some cynical remarks about Sihanouk. There is a definite cooling off in their relationship though Chou made a pro forma pitch for me to talk to Sihanouk which I rejected. He agreed to study my suggestion that Lon Nol's government talk directly to Sihanouk's representatives, and we agreed to keep each other informed on Cambodia through our New York channel.

Our talks on the International Conference were inconclusive and not very encouraging. The PRC will follow Hanoi's lead which means they will favor a brief, anodyne Conference which would do little concrete to guarantee the Vietnam settlement and would avoid Laos and Cambodia.

Chou expressed their desire for a stable *Southeast Asian region* in general made up of independent countries. It was up to the people of those countries to bring about revolution. Not even lip service was paid to PRC support of such efforts. Here—as elsewhere around the globe—Peking finds it more important to counter Soviet and Indian designs.

Chou didn't mention *Korea* until the very end of our discussions. He made only a pro forma pitch for gradual U.S. withdrawal. There was virtually no discussion of *Taiwan* and only then at my initiative. When I outlined your intentions on troop withdrawals, Chou shrugged this off, saying the timing was a matter of indifference to them.

Europe is now a major concern to Peking. A series of European leaders have visited China and the PRC Foreign Minister is undertaking a tour there. The Chinese are worried that Europe is being beguiled by the Soviet-sponsored illusions of peace and will thus cease to be a factor in the global balance. Chou contrasted Europe's growing economic strength with its military weakness. In short, the Chinese see a false détente in the region freeing the Russians' Western flank and "pushing the ill waters of the Soviet Union eastward."

I emphasized that we had no illusions about Soviet motives in Europe. We would try to keep the European Security Conference brief and meaningless. We would use MBFR to educate our allies about the military threat and need for vigilance, as well as to fend off Congressional pressures for unilateral American withdrawals. Any MBFR reductions would not be before 1975 and not exceed 10–15%. We would encourage European political and security unity. And we welcomed Chinese education of Europe's short-sighted leadership.

Finally, Mao and Chou, though they sounded warnings about our dealings with the Soviet Union, clearly dismissed any American designs on China and urged closer *U.S.-PRC relations*. Thus, in addition to encouraging a vigorous U.S. international presence, they were anxious to step up our bilateral relationship in every field. They not only accepted our proposal for an American liaison office in Peking, they proposed one of their own in Washington. These non-diplomatic offices will be established by May. Mao and Chou urged greater trade between us. They agreed to a large, specific, and two-way program of exchanges in the scientific, cultural and other fields. They pointed up the need for increased travel and the learning of English. These positive steps were reflected in our Joint Communiqué.[3] Typically, they accepted our draft almost verbatim; with most countries there would have been at least some haggling, even if the document was generally acceptable. In addition, Chou informed me that the two American pilots captured while on Vietnam-related missions will be released within the 60-day period of the Vietnam Agreement; and Downey, the CIA agent, will be set free the latter part of this year.

Against this background, the following elements are essential in our policy toward the PRC:

—*We must continue being meticulous in our bilateral dealings.* Our practice of keeping Peking informed of major policy developments has clearly paid off. We have shown a consistent willingness to take PRC views into account and act in parallel where possible. This approach has helped to gain Peking's confidence and to slacken it now would erode this precious commodity.

—*We need to institutionalize our relationship.* As explained above, this trip produced significant advances in this respect. The liaison offices and accelerated trade and exchanges will provide visible evidence of our growing ties which others will have to take into account. They also serve to accustom our two peoples to full-scale relations and lay a foundation that should survive the departure of China's aging leadership and a new American Administration four years hence.

—*We must continue to play a strong world role, especially in Asia.* A weak or passive America is of no use to the PRC. Mao and Chou have clearly been impressed with your strong policies and willingness to take tough decisions despite domestic pressures. If the Chinese see us turn inward or lose our will, they will cast about for other ways to deal with the threat of the "new czars." In that case they might as well emphasize ideology.

—*We need to be very careful in our policies toward Moscow and New Delhi.* These are now the two principal threats for Peking; faced with almost total isolation a couple of years ago, the PRC has opted for normalization with us and Tokyo. Mao and Chou both voiced suspicion that, whether or not by design, we could contribute to pressures on China. Therefore while we should not be paralyzed in our Soviet and India policies—and indeed with Moscow we have very important business—we will need to be deliberate and keep the PRC informed.

Our reception and conversations on this trip convince me that *the PRC has firmly set its course:* explicitly toward normalization and tacitly as ally. They are ready to move quickly—with the Soviet threat

---

[3] See footnote 2, Document 14.

growing, the Vietnam war over, and age crowding the Chinese leadership. If we proceed carefully and observe elements such as those listed above, we are now launched on a totally new relationship that should last through your second Administration.

18.   Memorandum From the President's Assistant for National Security Affairs (Kissinger) to President Nixon[1]

Washington, March 2, 1973.

SUBJECT

My Trip to China

Overview

Separate reports have given you the substantive highlights and atmosphere of my visit to the People's Republic of China, plus a complete rundown of my conversation with Chairman Mao.[2] This will give you a more detailed account of my talks with the Chinese and place them in the context of our developing relationship.

I spent twenty hours in formal meetings with Chou, almost two hours with Mao, and several more hours with Chou and other Chinese officials at banquets and on sightseeing tours.[3] This included talks with Vice Chairman Yeh Chien-ying, Foreign Minister Chi Peng-fei, and Vice Foreign Minister Ch'iao Kuan-hua. These talks were the freest and most candid, and our reception the most cordial and public-oriented, of any of my visits. This was due to a combination of factors:

—The Vietnam settlement;

—our meticulous handling of the Chinese and fulfillment of our undertakings since July 1971;

—the growing Chinese preoccupation with the Soviet threat;

---

[1] Source: National Archives, Nixon Presidential Materials, NSC Files, Kissinger Office Files, Box 98, Country Files, Far East, HAK China Trip, Memcons & Reports (originals), February 1973. Top Secret; Sensitive; Exclusively Eyes Only. There are no markings on the memorandum indicating that Nixon saw it.

[2] See footnote 3, Document 17.

[3] See Documents 8–14. All memoranda of conversation of Kissinger's meetings of February 15–19 are in National Archives, Nixon Presidential Materials, NSC Files, Kissinger Office Files, Box 98, Country Files, Far East, HAK China Trip, Memcons & Reports (originals), February 1973.

—the shadow of advancing age of the PRC leaders;

—the consequent urge to accelerate the normalization and institutionalization of our bilateral relationship; and

—the fact that we are now familiar interlocutors after five trips and literally hundreds of hours of talks in Peking and New York.

Evolution of Our Relationship

The progression of our relationship in the past twenty months is remarkable. I believe it is one of your most striking successes in foreign policy. If we continue to handle it carefully, it should continue to pay dividends—in relaxing tensions in Asia, in furthering relations with Moscow, and generally in building a structure of peace.

When you sent me to China in July 1971 we had almost no idea what to expect as we penetrated twenty years of accumulated isolation, distrust and enmity. Since then we have progressed faster and further than anyone would have predicted, or the rest of the world realizes. *For in plain terms we have now become tacit allies.* The evolution has gone as follows:

—*When you took office* there was total lack of diplomatic communication between our two governments, no personal or commercial interchange between our two peoples, mutual public recrimination, and clashing world views.

—*In the first two and a half years of your Administration,* we put out private feelers through third countries, took unilateral public steps in such fields as trade and passports in order to send signals, and pointed our rhetoric toward a new relationship. This resulted in agreement in principle that you would meet the Chinese leaders and my secret exploratory trip of July 1971.

—*My July 1971 trip* reestablished direct communications, confirmed your trip to Peking and suggested that the PRC was ready to move toward normalization. On the other hand, Chou presented his quota of rhetoric and our policies clashed on most major issues.

—*In October 1971* we established the framework for your trip, including the outlines of the joint communiqué. The Taiwan issue remained hanging in the communiqué, however, and our policies continued to conflict in many areas.

—*Your February 1972 visit* was the watershed. It stamped your and Mao's personal imprints on the move toward normalization. The Shanghai Communiqué contained joint principles in international affairs, finessed the Taiwan problem through mutual and ambiguous compromise, set in motion bilateral trade and exchanges, established the public Paris channel, and accelerated the private New York channel. However, as the communiqué publicly, and your conversations privately demonstrated, we were improving our relations *despite* different world outlooks.

—*My June 1972 trip* marked substantial evolution toward our views in the Chinese private positions on international issues. But the Vietnam war continued to inhibit the Chinese, and publicly all we could register was a modest increase in exchanges and trade.

—*On this trip in February 1973*, the flood gates opened privately and publicly for the reasons stated. The Chinese leaders are among the very few in the world with a global and longer term perspective—and it now parallels ours in many important respects. In such areas as the Soviet Union, Europe, South Asia and even Japan we have similar outlooks. In others, like Indochina and Korea, we each back our allies but share an interest in independent states and relaxed tensions. And on Taiwan we have reached a clear modus vivendi—on our part, continued, concrete evolution toward full relations with all its implications; and on their part, patience and a pragmatism reflected most vividly in the coming side-by-side presence of a GRC Embassy and a PRC Liaison Office. On the bilateral plane, it is full speed ahead on trade and exchanges. As for public relations, the Chinese have long since singled out the USSR for attack and have shown increasing cordiality in their public contacts with us.

Following are the main points of my talks with the Chinese, topic by topic.

Soviet Union

The Soviet Union dominated our conversations. In 1971 there were somewhat guarded references by the Chinese to Soviet designs, but they ritualistically linked the U.S. and the USSR as the two superpowers seeking hegemony. By the time of your visit the Chinese leaders were quite candid about the Soviet menace but stayed away from extended discussion. By last June the Soviet Union had become one of the two major topics in my conversations, the other one being Indochina. On this trip it was the centerpiece and completely permeated our talks. The Chinese views generally surfaced in the regional discussion and are detailed later in this report. Following are the more general observations.

Chou raised the USSR in our first meeting and kept coming back to it. He called a special meeting the night of February 17 to discuss this subject and at the end of his presentation he announced my meeting with Mao, where again it was a major topic. We discussed it at length the next day as well. In literally every region of the world the Chinese see the Soviet hand at play. As you will see in the area discussions below, Mao and Chou urged us to counter the Russians everywhere—to work closely with our allies in Europe and Japan, and to take more positive action to prevent the Soviets filling vacuums or spreading their influence in areas like the Middle East, Persian Gulf, Near East, South Asia and Indian Ocean.

In our first meeting, after my opening statement, Chou asked me in effect whether we thought the world was moving toward peace or war. I said that there were some positive developments, but we were not naive about potential dangers, such as the intensive Soviet military buildup. I made clear that we had major business to do with Moscow, but we were under no illusions about its possible motivations. We would continue our policy of keeping the Chinese fully informed and not concluding any agreements that could be directed against Peking.

Chou pointed to developments in Europe and said perhaps we sought to "push the ill waters of the Soviet Union eastward." He also cited our diversion of fighters from Taiwan to South Vietnam last fall in Enhance Plus[4] as an example of our taking advantage of Peking; somewhat out of context, he said that this showed that we might be standing on Chinese shoulders to reach out toward the Soviet Union.

The next day I purposely detailed our proposed force reductions on Taiwan and then made a more sweeping analysis of our policy toward the Soviet Union. I said that the nature of our relationship meant that we had to pursue a more complicated policy than the PRC which could oppose the Soviet Union outright on issues. We were making several agreements with Moscow, but we would not let these constrain us in the event that our interests were jeopardized. I pointed out that the USSR could follow one of two courses. If they truly wanted peace, we would welcome that course, and the agreements we were making might contribute to that end. If, however, as seemed more likely, they were bent on a more threatening road, we had shown in the past that we would react strongly if our interests were jeopardized. In any event, I emphasized, we would maintain strong defenses and improve our strategic forces so long as the Soviet buildup continued. And on issues of direct concern to Peking we would take Chinese interests into account, such as on the Soviet initiative on a nuclear understanding, where we have been fighting a delaying action ever since last spring.

Chou and then Mao, however, both replayed the theme that we might be helping the Soviet Union, whether or not purposely. Whereas we saw two possibilities, i.e. that the Soviet Union would either pursue a peaceful or a menacing course, the Chinese saw only the latter. They were spreading their influence everywhere with the help of their satellites, like India, and were out to isolate the Chinese. The "new czars" were neurotic and omnipresent. It was the Chinese duty to try and expose their designs wherever possible, however lonely their efforts in a world enamored with false détente.

---

[4] "Enhance Plus" was an effort by the United States to expand and improve the armed forces of the Republic of Vietnam before the peace agreement came into effect. It lasted from October 23 to December 12, 1972. See also footnote 3, Document 73.

Mao even went so far as to suggest that we might like to see the Russians bogged down in an attack on China; after wearing themselves out for a couple of years, we would then "poke a finger" in Moscow's back. I rejoined that we believe that a war between the two Communist giants was likely to be uncontrollable and have unfortunate consequences for everyone. We therefore wished to prevent such a conflict, not take advantage of it.

Given Mao's and Chou's skeptical comments on this issue, I treated it at considerable length the day after my meeting with the Chairman. I said there were three hypothetical U.S. motives in a policy that contributed to pressures on the PRC from the USSR. First, we might want the Soviet Union to defeat China. I stressed emphatically that whether Moscow defeated China or Europe first, the consequences for us would be the same; we would be isolated and the ultimate target. Thus this could never be our policy.

The second possible motive was the one Mao mentioned—our wish for a stalemated Moscow attack on Peking, so as to exhaust the Soviet Union. I pointed out that even partial Soviet dominance of China could have many of the consequences of the first option. In any event, such a major conflict would have unpredictable consequences. The Soviet Union might take rash actions if they were stymied as the Chairman claimed we had been in Vietnam. And we would be forced either to demonstrate our impotence and irrelevance, or make a series of extremely complex decisions.

The third possibility was that we might contribute to a war between China and the Soviet Union through misjudgment rather than policy. This I recognized as a danger despite our intentions. I then analyzed at length our policy around the world, with emphasis on Europe, to demonstrate that we plan to maintain our defense, continue a responsible international role, and work closely with our allies. In short, while seeking relaxation with Moscow, we would also ensure that if it did not choose a peaceful course we and our friends would be in a position to resist and defend our national interests. And I made it evident that we would consider aggression against China as involving our own national security.

It is not at all clear that we have fully allayed Chinese suspicions. While they have nowhere else to go in the short term, they will certainly watch our Soviet moves with wariness, and take out insurance with Japan and Europe.

Europe

Europe is now a major preoccupation of the Chinese leaders. Since my June trip there has been a series of high-level visitors from European capitals to Peking. The Chinese believe that Europe is becoming demoralized and sapped of its strength through the illusions of peace fostered by the Soviet Union. Such a fake détente, most evident in Ost-politik but also spreading elsewhere, is not only deceptive but danger-ous in the Chinese view. They see these European developments as adding to the Soviet pressures against China. The atmospherics of events like the European Security Conference and the possible concrete results of events like the MBFR negotiations free the Soviet western flank so that Moscow can concentrate on its Chinese flank. Both Mao and Chou suggested that we were cooperating in this enterprise and thus, whether or not inadvertently, contributing to the pressures on them.

The Chinese have contempt for the Communist parties of Europe, which are generally Moscow-dominated, and favor the Conservatives over the Socialist and Labor parties. This is most evident in France where the Mitterand challenge to Pompidou causes Peking great con-cern. Mao told Pompidou to maintain strong ties with the U.S. The Chi-nese are also worried about German weakness and were anxious to hear why the Christian Democrats had lost the election there. The British seem the most level-headed to them.

In general, Chou pointed out, Europe has grown strong econom-ically but weak militarily, in direct contrast to the Soviet Union whose military strength continues to increase but whose mismanagement has caused serious economic problems. The latter, however, can be eased by U.S. and European trade and credits.

Mao and Chou both stressed the need for us to maintain close ties with Europe. As in the case of Japan, we should not let trade barriers and other frictions disrupt our political bonds. Mao included Europe in the anti-Soviet axis that he urged across the world, together with Japan, the U.S., Iran, Pakistan and Turkey.

In response I emphasized the top priority that we give to our Eu-ropean allies. You plan to concentrate greatly during the coming months on our political, economic and security relations with Europe with a view toward a high-level conference once we had coordinated a general strategy. We had no illusions about Soviet intentions in Eu-rope, and we would conduct our policy so as not to render allied de-fense vulnerable. The European Security Conference had been foisted upon us by our allies, and we were forced to go through with it. Our only choice was to make it as brief and as meaningless as possible. On the other hand, I said that the MBFR talks were useful, not only to de-ter Congressional pressures for unilateral American troop reductions in Europe but also to educate our European allies about the military threat posed by Soviet forces. I assured Chou that there would be no reductions before 1975 and these in any event would not exceed 10 to 15%. We would encourage European political and security unit, and we welcome Chinese education of Europe's shortsighted leadership.

South Asia

Mao and Chou made clear that in addition to the Soviet Union's Eastward pressures, the other major threat was hegemonial drives toward the South. In their view Soviet designs include a variety of maneuvers directed along the whole axis running from the Middle East through the Near East, South Asia and the Indian Ocean.

In South Asia, the Chinese believe India remains Moscow's principal agent; their distrust of New Delhi remains as potent as ever. When we first began talking directly to the Chinese twenty months ago Chou cited four potential enemies—the Soviet Union, the United States, Japan, and India. The PRC has now decided to improve relations with us and Japan, reassured that we are not colluding with the Soviet Union. This leaves two enemies in its pantheon, Moscow and New Delhi.

Chou displayed a particular contempt for the Indians and a personal dislike for Indian leaders. He related several cynical and disdainful anecdotes about Prime Ministers Nehru and Gandhi. The Indians have been pressing Peking for improved relations, and the reestablishment of embassies in both capitals. Chou related that Peking had responded with a typical Chinese ploy—they raised their chargé d'affaires in New Delhi from first secretary to counsellor!

As evidence of the Moscow–New Delhi alliance Chou pointed to those two countries' attempt to dismember Pakistan by encouraging dissident movements in Baluchistan and Pushtunistan and the fact that most of the Indian Navy is becoming Russian-built. He did not demur when I suggested that New Delhi was seeking to expand its influence in Indochina as well.

As in other areas of the world the Chinese urged an active U.S. foreign policy to counter their enemies' designs. Chou suggested the following:

—I should see Mrs. Bhutto while I was in Peking.

—We should increase our military aid to Pakistan. China had given it some assistance, but it was up to us to take the lead for Peking's capability was limited.

—We should better our relations not only with Sri Lanka (Ceylon) and Nepal but also with the Indian protectorates of Bhutan and Sikkim.

—We should provide Bangladesh with humanitarian assistance and establish some influence there to counter New Delhi. Peking would be willing to do so as well at some point, but couldn't move so long as the emotional issue of Pakistani prisoners held by Bangladesh was not resolved.

—He asked about our bases in the Indian Ocean.

In response I stated that our policies toward South Asia were still in parallel. We would go slow in any improvement of relations with

New Delhi and would keep the PRC informed. With regard to Pakistan, I assured Chou that we would resume our pre-war policy of providing spare parts for equipment it already possessed; that we would release military equipment that Pakistan had already contracted for, including 300 APC's; and that we would work vigorously with third countries like Iran and Turkey to encourage them to provide military assistance to Pakistan which was awkward for us because of our Congressional problems. We would also maintain, perhaps increase, our $200 million in economic aid. As you know, I paid a courtesy call on Mrs. Bhutto while I was in Peking, during which I stressed our continued support and friendship for Pakistan.

On Bangladesh, I informed Chou that we had been holding up $30 million in food assistance until we had elicited Chinese views, but that we would now move immediately to release this. On Sri Lanka, we were prepared to improve our relations at whatever pace Madame Bandaranaike desired. As for the Indian Ocean, we would review our naval deployments in that region, suggesting that we would maintain a meaningful presence. I emphasized that in any event our naval strength was far superior to that of the Soviet Union.

The Near and Middle East

In past trips, the Chinese leaders have shown only passing interest in this region. Now it is an area of great concern, subject to Soviet southward pressures. As in South Asia, Chou claimed that here too we were too slack in our efforts and should do more to counter Soviet designs. Mao explicitly included Iran and Turkey as well as Pakistan in the friendly axis that he suggested we shape; Chou urged us to be more active in the Persian Gulf and queried me on Iran and Turkey specifically.

I replied that the Shah of Iran was a very farsighted leader, and that we considered him a pivotal ally. For this reason we were sending Helms to be Ambassador, not only to step up our efforts with Iran but to organize a more active and cooperative American role with other friendly countries in the Near East and Persian Gulf regions. I reassured Chou that our relations remain good with Turkey, but pointed out that it had domestic problems. Chou commented that the Soviet Union was trying to take advantage of these.

Chou also showed significant interest in the Middle East for the first time, again because of Soviet efforts which he cited in such places as Egypt, Syria, Iraq and Libya. He cited the discovery of Soviet arms in the Iraqi Embassy in Pakistan as evidence of the interlocking web of Soviet designs throughout the entire axis. He made clear that China fully supported the Arabs in their efforts to regain all lost territories and solve the plight of the Palestinian refugees. When I forcefully pointed out that we were committed to the survival of Israel, he acknowledged that Israel could not be destroyed and that its existence was now a fact. He said that PRC relations with Israel were not possible until it gave up its territorial aggression.

Despite our opposing views he clearly looked with favor on our continuing presence in the Middle East to counter the Soviets. The Chinese, he said, were unable to do much in that area except to try to expose Soviet designs. I filled him in on my upcoming talks with Ismail and said that we were prepared to deal with the Arab countries on the basis of their own interests, so long as these were distinct from Moscow's. He agreed with us that we should try to reach a settlement with Egypt before Jordan. He welcomed my suggestion that we keep him posted on any significant developments in our negotiations on the Middle East.

Indochina and Southeast Asia

The Chinese held up agreeing to my visit until the Vietnam settlement was completed. In turn the ceasefire in Vietnam paved the way for the success of my trip to the PRC. Mao and Chou welcomed the settlement, with the Chairman pointing out that we had done "good work" and getting my confirmation that the basic issues were settled.

I said that we would, of course, strictly implement the Agreement but I emphasized that we expected Hanoi to do the same. I described my trip to Hanoi and underlined the two choices for Hanoi which we saw. The first was to use the Agreement as an offensive weapon, pressuring us and the GVN and seeking their Indochina objectives through violations. I made clear that this would mean confrontation with us and obviously no possibility of economic assistance. Hanoi's other choice was to use the Agreement as an instrument of conciliation as we wish to do. This would allow us to move towards normalization of relations and economic reconstruction which we considered in our own interests.

I also stressed the need for restraint in Indochina, not only by the DRV but also by major outside powers. When I specifically mentioned limits on military assistance, Chou was ambiguous, saying that the Soviet Union was the dominant supplier and China only supplied small arms. I believe, however, that we can expect some moderation on the Chinese part.

My corollary emphasis was on the need for a gradual evolution in Indochina and a period of tranquility. Mao and Chou seemed to recognize this, although their basic posture is that Indochina problems are up to the individual countries themselves. We agreed that we shared an interest in there being independent states in the region, to alleviate the threat of a Soviet and Indian-dominated Indochina.

While I was in Peking, the Laos ceasefire was still not pinned down. I pointed out the urgent need to cease hostilities there and begin North Vietnamese withdrawals. Chou indicated that they would welcome a settlement in Laos, although he maintained a hands-off attitude on the pending issues. He assured me that as soon as there was a ceasefire their anti-aircraft units would withdraw from Laos and that once the Chinese road was completed they would withdraw their engineer teams as well. I indicated that Souvanna Phouma, who had requested me to raise the issue of the Chinese road, was prepared for better relations with Peking. Chou seemed receptive, and noted his respect for the King of Laos.

We both agreed that Cambodia presented a more complex problem because of the many factions involved. I rejected Chou's rather pro forma request that I talk to Sihanouk. I stated that Lon Nol's government was a major factor and that Sihanouk's representatives should speak to him. As in Laos I emphasized the importance of the withdrawal of North Vietnamese troops as stipulated in the Vietnam Agreement. I said that our objectives were to bring about a ceasefire and North Vietnamese withdrawal and direct contacts between the various factions. Chou agreed that the situation would be more manageable if the conflict became a purely civil war. He made some cynical remarks about Sihanouk; I believe their alliance has cooled somewhat. He said he would think over my proposal that representatives of Lon Nol and Sihanouk get together, and he agreed that we should exchange views on Cambodia on a continuing basis.

At Bangkok's request I brought up the subject of Chinese support of the insurgency in Thailand. Chou denied PRC involvement, saying that revolutions were the responsibility of the indigenous peoples. He pointed out that some Chinese Nationalist troops were still left in Thailand and often crossed over into Chinese territory. When I noted Thai nervousness about the Chinese road in Laos, he assured me that the road would stop at the Mekong Valley, way short of Thai territory, so there was no cause for Bangkok concern.

Chou also indicated an interest in other countries in Southeast Asia, and we briefly touched on them. He gave only lip service to revolutionary movements—the peoples themselves must accomplish this task, and it seemed that revolutionary movements were not maturing quickly in the region. He echoed his approach of June when he called for a neutral and stable region; clearly he is concerned here as elsewhere about Moscow and New Delhi influence. I made clear that if there were sudden changes in the situation in the region we might have to react, but otherwise we were prepared for a gradual evolution and genuine independence and neutrality for the countries of the region over the longer term.

We also discussed the International Conference. The basic Chinese position was to back whatever the DRV wanted; they clearly were reluctant to get out in front. Thus they were for a short conference which was free of recrimination and endorsed the Vietnam Agreement, but treated Laos and Cambodia only in the context of the Agreement. Chou would not be drawn out on other issues, such as continuing authority for ceasefire reports and chairmanship of the Conference, leaving that up to Hanoi. We continued to keep in touch with Peking in the period before the Conference and during the Conference itself.

Japan

The Chinese have done a major turnabout in their attitude toward Japan and the U.S. in the last 20 months. Chou's approach this time continued the marked evolution which I noticed last June. From Peking's perspective in 1971 Japan was one of the potential large powers that might help to carve up China. It had been fattened economically by the U.S. and was now threatening to expand its militarism throughout the region, in such areas as Taiwan and Korea. Both publicly and privately China used to oppose the U.S.-Japan Security Treaty.

Although Chou still urged us to keep Japan out of Taiwan and Korea and noted the continuing threat of Japanese militarism, the Chinese now clearly consider Japan as an incipient ally along with ourselves to counter Soviet and Indian designs. Publicly this has been reflected in Tanaka's visit to the Mainland, PRC-Japan establishment of diplomatic relations, and (since my visit) Chou's expressed desire to visit Japan.

Privately, the change in their attitude is even more marked. Chou stated that Japan is at a crossroads; having grown up it wants its freedom. He now acknowledges that our Security Treaty is a brake on Japanese expansionism and militarism; he pointed out that Peking had not attacked the Treaty in any way in recent months in their dealings with Japan, despite its original opposition to it. Since we had fattened Japan and still had great influence with Tokyo, he suggested that we had a great responsibility to restrain it. He urged the closest U.S.-Japanese cooperation generally and mentioned development of Siberian resources specifically. He said that work should be done with Japan to win it over and prevent the situation where the Soviet Union became its ally instead of the U.S., for this would be a threat to the world.

Mao said that it was a mistake for me to spend only one day in Tokyo on my way home and that I should take more time with our ally. He wanted to make sure that trade and other frictions with Tokyo (as well as with Europe) would not mar our fundamental cooperation. He cited the U.S. and Japan, together with Europe and the friendly Near East countries, as the axis to be formed to oppose the Soviet Union.

In response I noted our similarity of approach and stressed the restraining factor of our Security Treaty. I assured both Mao and Chou that you put the highest value on our relations with Japan, as well as with our European allies, and we would be working hard to foster this relationship. I acknowledged Chinese restraint in dealing with the Japanese and cautioned that any attempt to compete for Tokyo's allegiance could end up encouraging resurgent Japanese nationalism through conflicting pressures. Accordingly, we favored improvement in PRC-Japanese relations and expected reciprocal treatment from Peking.

Korea

While this had been a significant area of interest in our past conversations and there had been much speculation that Chou would raise Korea this time as a prime topic, it did not come up until the very end of my trip. In his final tour d'horizon Chou repeated, with somewhat less emphasis, past Chinese views on the Korean Peninsula. He called for the abolition of both UNCURK and the United Nations Command, said that our forces should be withdrawn, and favored relaxation of tensions and reunification between the two Koreas. At the same time he made it clear that the Chinese were prepared for a gradual evolution in the situation. He informed me that they had been telling Pyongyang in effect to be patient with gradual U.S. withdrawals and re-unification, and that the North Koreans were beginning to understand. He stressed that we should make sure that as we left Korea, Japan did not send its own forces to replace us.

I said that we were prepared to consider abolishing UNCURK—we would check with our South Korean allies and let Peking know in a few weeks—in exchange for his pledge that Peking would defuse the Korean issue, specifically in the next UN General Assembly debate. I indicated that we would entertain a gradual withdrawal of troops over time but made clear that this was in the context of the Nixon Doctrine[5] and a strengthening of South Korean defenses. Chou did not demur. In fact, given gradual withdrawal and gradual reunification and the keeping out of Japan, he was quite sure that "no one will commit aggression" in the Korean Peninsula.

Taiwan

Purposely I brought up the issue of Taiwan at the very outset of our conversations. I reaffirmed the principles that you had outlined to Chou concerning our formula on China and Taiwan in the Shanghai Communiqué; our disassociation from any Taiwan independence movement; our discouragement of the Japanese moving into Taiwan;

---

[5] According to the Nixon Doctrine, the origin of which can be traced to a July 25, 1969, informal background briefing on Guam that Nixon gave to reporters, the United States would stand by its commitments but encourage Asian nations to take responsibility for their own security. See *Foreign Relations*, 1969–1976, vol. I, Document 29.

our support for any peaceful resolution of the Taiwan issue; and our intention to seek normalization of relations with Peking. I also promised to give Chou a specific schedule of the reduction of some of our forces on Taiwan now that the Vietnam war was over.

Chou was more concerned about our military assistance to Taiwan, which he said should be phased out over time, and our providing Taiwan with the ability to produce its own F–5 airplanes. As noted above, he also complained that in diverting F–4's from Taiwan to South Vietnam during Enhance Plus last fall, we were taking advantage of China, and this was an example of standing on China's shoulders to reach out toward the Soviet Union.

In our second meeting, before giving Chou a long analysis of our policy toward the Soviet Union in reaction to his comment, I gave him a specific schedule for the reduction of our Taiwan forces. I told him that we would withdraw five air force squadrons, or about half of our 9,000 military personnel on Taiwan, during the coming year. I also said that we would withdraw at least two squadrons of F–4's during the following year and would look at other military units carefully.[6] Chou professed disinterest in a specific timetable for withdrawal, saying that the important thing was the principle had already been established. He returned to our military aid policy which I said we would review. He assured me that Peking had no intention to liberate Taiwan by armed force.[7]

In response to this latter comment I reaffirmed our intention to move toward normalization of relations. This set up the eventual deal for an exchange of liaison offices in each other's capital. I also told Chou that we would be prepared to move after the 1974 elections toward something like the Japanese solution with regard to diplomatic relations and before mid-1976, we were prepared to establish full diplomatic relations. I added that we would want to keep some form of representation on Taiwan but I was sure that we could find some mutually acceptable formula. He agreed with this approach.

Bilateral Relations

The public manifestations of the discussions with the Chinese are reflected in the substantial progress in our bilateral relations. The factors I have cited impelled the Chinese to move forward faster than we

---

[6] The figures cited by Kissinger were most likely based on those he received in a February 6 memorandum from Secretary of Defense Elliot Richardson. (National Archives, Nixon Presidential Materials, NSC Files, Kissinger Office Files, Box 98, Country Files, Far East, HAK China Trip, Memcons & Reports (originals), February 1973)

[7] After this sentence, a notation in unknown handwriting reads: "not so clear cut." Zhou remarked on February 16, "I can assure you that we don't mean that we are going to liberate it [Taiwan] by the armed forces. We have no such plan at the moment." See Document 9.

anticipated. The most dramatic development was the establishment of liaison offices in each other's capitals. We had expected them to agree to a trade, or perhaps liaison, office in Peking, but Chou quickly raised the question of their having an office in the United States. This contrasts their consistent policy of not having a significant mission in the same capital as an Ambassador from the Republic of China. And these offices, which as you know may well be at Ambassadorial rank, and will enjoy diplomatic immunity and privileges, will be closely equivalent to Embassies in everything but name. Yet Chou never mentioned the GRC Embassy or our diplomatic relations. This is the best proof of Chinese eagerness to institutionalize our relationship. It reflects our approach, which I reiterated at the very first meeting, that we need greatly to increase our contacts and to get our peoples used to U.S.-Chinese exchanges and cooperation.

The counterpart meetings we held on exchanges and trade went very smoothly.[8] The Chinese were prepared with a whole series of specific programs which they were ready to approve in various scientific, cultural and other fields. In contrast to the past, they put as much emphasis on our groups going to China as on their groups coming here. They are ready to invite more Senators and Congressmen. They also expressed interest in increased bilateral trade and readily agreed to our approach of a political package deal of a lump sum exchange between private claims against them and blocked PRC assets. Since then Secretary Rogers and Foreign Minister Chi Peng-fei have launched this negotiation in Paris.[9]

Both Mao and Chou went to considerable length to show their interest in trade, exchanges, and the liaison offices. They supplemented this with a desire to increase the knowledge of English in their country and the number of Americans residing in China. They agreed to the release of the two captured American pilots within the same time period as the release of other prisoners under the Vietnam Agreement, and Chou clearly indicated that Downey's case would be reviewed favorably in the second half of this year. They also cooperated in providing information on Lieutenant Dunn, a pilot who has been missing in action since 1968 near Hainan Island. Unfortunately no new facts turned up in this case, and his death now seems confirmed. We have provided this information to Mrs. Dunn.

---

[8] Memoranda of conversation of these talks are at National Archives, Nixon Presidential Materials, NSC Files, Kissinger Office Files, Box 87, Country Files, Far East, PRC Counterpart Talks, 1971–1973.

[9] In a memorandum to Kissinger, March 9, 1973, Theodore Eliot reported that the PRC "has agreed to settle U.S. private claims through an assignment of blocked Chinese assets to the U.S. Government for use in compensating American claimants." (Ibid., Box 527, Country Files, Far East, People's Republic of China, Vol. 7, May, 1973–Jul 9, 1973)

All these steps were taken against the background of your approach to the PRC which I emphasized. We see a strong and independent China as being clearly in our interest and the interest of world peace. We would consider an attack on China as an ultimate threat to our own national security. We therefore would not encourage nor try to take advantage of any attack on China from other countries. Indeed we would develop our global policies in the way that Chairman Mao had indicated would be needed to counter possible hegemonial designs.

Problems

The current trend therefore is positive, but there are no grounds for complacency. There are at least two areas which have substantial potential for trouble in our relationship:

—*Our dealings with the Soviet Union.* To date the Soviet factor has been the main leverage in our dealings with the PRC. At the same time—and contrary to the predictions of almost all Soviet experts—our opening to Peking has paid us substantial dividends with Moscow as well. With conscientious attention to both capitals we should be able to continue to have our mao tai and drink our vodka too. Peking, after all, assuming continued hostility with the USSR, has no real alternative to us as a counterweight (despite its recent reaching out to Japan and Western Europe as insurance). And Moscow needs us in such areas as Europe and economics.

But this is nevertheless a difficult balancing act that will increasingly face us with hard choices. Mao and Chou both suggested that, inadvertently or not, our Soviet policies could increase the pressures on China. It was even intimated that we might favor a Sino-Soviet conflict, so as to bog down the Soviet Union and weaken it for our own attack. A cutting edge is the Soviet initiative on a nuclear understanding. One of Moscow's motives is certainly to embarrass us in our relations with Peking, since they know their initiative is anathema to Peking. We have fought a delaying action on this issue for almost a year now, but Brezhnev is apt to push it to a head in conjunction with his visit here. To satisfy him and not dissatisfy Chou at the same time will be a challenge. Other concrete awkward areas in our triangular relationship include European security policies and the granting of credits to Moscow.

—*The coming change in Chinese leadership.* Mao is in his 80s and has received an "invitation" from "God." Chou is 75 and has just publicly noted the need for new leadership soon in his country. They obviously control PRC policy now, but it is not at all clear that they can assure continuity in their policy lines. The Lin Piao affair was obviously a major challenge and may have been a close thing. They have not managed to fill many key party and military posts since then. Mao constantly referred to the difficulties posed by women in China, undoubtedly a reference to his wife who represents the challenge from the left. All of this is reflected in Chinese eagerness to institutionalize our relationship, even if it means bending the sacred "one China" policy to do it.

We know little about power relationships in the PRC and even less about the succession problem. We can only assume—both from the above indices and because of the objective choices facing China—that substantial opposition to present policies exist and that this includes foreign policy. There are undoubtedly those who favor accommodation with Moscow over Washington for example. Thus, before the present dynasty passes from the scene, we must strengthen bilateral ties, get our two peoples used to a closer relationship, and reach out to more layers of Chinese leadership so as to strengthen the advocates of an opening to America.

There are two other potential problems, but these would seem to be more manageable and under our control:

—*The need for a strong American world role.* We are useless to Peking as a counterweight to Moscow if we withdraw from the world, lower our defenses, or play a passive international game. Mao and Chou urged a more aggressive American presence—countering Soviet designs in various areas, keeping close ties with our allies, maintaining our defense posture. If the Chinese became convinced that we were heeding the inward impulses of voluble sectors of Congress, the public and the press, we would undoubtedly witness a sharp turn in Peking's attitude. You and I have, of course, assured the PRC leaders privately, as well as proclaiming publicly, our intentions to maintain a responsible international role. So long as you are President, Peking should certainly be convinced that we will be a crucial factor in the world balance.

—*The issue of Taiwan.* The Chinese have been farsighted and patient on this question. Their willingness to ease our predicament is now most dramatically shown in their setting up a liaison office in Washington while we maintain diplomatic relations with the GRC. On the other hand, we have largely bought their public reasonableness with your own private assurances—to normalize fully our relations by 1976 and to withdraw our forces from Taiwan now that the Vietnam War is over. Taiwan is a problem we should be able to control, both internationally and domestically, as we continue to add to the handwriting on the wall and condition our audiences. However, we should be under no illusions that our final step will be anything but painful—there are few friends as decent as our allies on Taiwan.

19.   **Memorandum From John H. Holdridge and Mark Linton of the National Security Council Staff to the President's Assistant for National Security Affairs (Kissinger)**[1]

Washington, March 8, 1973.

SUBJECT

Message to the PRC Regarding Textile Export Restraints

In August, 1972, we provided the People's Republic of China with an explanation of the Long-Term Textile Agreement (LTA) and informed PRC authorities via the Paris channel that the U.S. may find it necessary to request that they restrain exports of certain categories of cotton textiles to the U.S. (See this message at Tab B).[2] PRC exports of textiles to the U.S. have not reached a level sufficient to warrant such a request. The Department of State has prepared a memorandum for transmission through the Paris channel to inform the PRC that we will in the near future request that exports of four categories of textiles be restrained.[3]

Article 4 of the LTA provides for the negotiation of bilateral agreements regulating trade in cotton textiles, and the U.S. currently has 31 such agreements. Articles 3 and 6(c) permit the U.S. to act unilaterally to restrain textile imports. PRC exports of cotton textiles to the U.S. in the 12 months ending January 31, 1973 grew to an equivalent of more than 16 million square yards. These exports are in several categories well over the levels at which we have initiated restraint agreements with other countries. Considerations of equity for traditional suppliers as well as the need to avoid disruption of our domestic markets make it necessary to take steps to regulate our textile imports from the PRC. Since PRC textile exports are continuing to grow rapidly, we should transmit the State memorandum to the PRC soon. All concerned agencies have cleared this memorandum. CIEP concurs.[4]

Recommendation: That you approve the transmittal to the PRC representatives in Paris of the memorandum at Tab A.[5]

---

[1] Source: National Archives, Nixon Presidential Materials, NSC Files, Box 526, Country Files, Far East, People's Republic of China, Vol. 6, Jan–Apr 1973. Secret. Sent for action.

[2] Attached but not printed. The Long Term Agreement on Cotton Textiles, established in 1962, set guidelines for negotiated quotas between cotton importers and exporters.

[3] On February 8, Edward R. Cheney of the Fibers and Textiles Division in the Bureau of Economic and Business Affairs sent this memorandum to Hormats. It is attached at Tab A but not printed.

[4] Cheney noted that his draft was "cleared by the Departments of State, Commerce, Labor and the Treasury."

[5] Kissinger initialed the Approve option.

20.   **Conversation Between President Nixon and his Assistant for National Security Affairs (Kissinger)**[1]

Washington, March 12, 1973.

Kissinger: The Chinese have agreed that you can announce—[2]

Nixon: Thursday?

Kissinger: Thursday. Now that we've told them that you're going to do it, they've sort of [unclear]—

Nixon: Oh, sure. Well, I [unclear]—

Kissinger: I don't think—if you don't have a press conference it would make it too high if you just step out—we should tell them ahead of time—as long—

Nixon: Yeah.

Kissinger: I did tell them that you would make the announcement.

Nixon: [unclear] Sure. We'll work it out. They won't notice the difference.

Kissinger: We've got a good play out of this Downey thing.[3]

Nixon: Yeah.

[Omitted here is a discussion of the Vietnamese ceasefire.]

Kissinger: My view is we have to make the Japanese inability to choose work for us. We should suck them into Siberia, we should suck them into Southeast Asia for the reason that the more they frighten others, the better it is for us vis-à-vis China.

Nixon: That's right.

Kissinger: Again, I wouldn't say this publicly, but we must prevent the Japanese from tying up with any one other country. The great danger is that they'll choose China, and that their resources and Chinese intelligence are going to do to us in Asia what the Common Market may do to us in Europe. That's why it—one reason we must lean a little bit towards China wherever we can. On the other hand, we should tie the Japanese to us where we can, but one good guarantee—

---

[1] Source: National Archives, Nixon Presidential Materials, White House Tapes, Conversation No. 876–4. No classification marking. The editor transcribed the portions of the conversation printed here specifically for this volume. According to the President's Daily Diary, Nixon met with Kissinger in the Oval Office between 9:30 and 10:29 a.m. (Ibid., White House Central Files)

[2] Kissinger is most likely referring to China's approval of the announcement that David Bruce would head the U.S. Liaison Office in Beijing. On March 15, President Nixon announced Bruce's appointment as Chief of the U.S. Liaison Office. For text of the news conference, see *Public Papers: Nixon, 1974*, pp. 202–213.

[3] On March 12, China released John Downey. See footnote 2, Document 15.

that's why I am not against having the Japanese active in North Vietnam. If they're active in North Vietnam, the Chinese get worried. If they're active in Siberia, the Chinese get worried. If they're active in China, the Russians get worried. It is in our interests to have the Japanese 10% overextended.

Nixon: That's right.

Kissinger: I know that's a cynical approach but that way they are always a little bit off-balance. And since it is impossible to make conceptual deals with the Japanese. Now I think the deal we made with Mao and Chou is going to last for 3–5 years. We don't have to maneuver the Chinese through every little device because they understand that. I don't know whether you've signed these letters—[4]

Nixon: No. I want to put some writing on it. I'll have them by [unclear].

[Omitted here is a brief discussion of the Soviet Union and North Vietnam.]

Nixon: China is bigger than ending the war. Russia [unclear] is bigger than ending the war. The war was going to end. It's a question of how, and the war [unclear]. Now the China and Russia angle—even as big as those things are, we don't look at those as ends in themselves, which many of the jackasses in the press think. They think it's great we've gone to China, we've shaken hands and everything is going to be hunky-dory. It's not going to be hunky-dory; it's going to be tough titties. So now, now that we have come this far, the real game is how do you build on these great initiatives.

[Omitted here is a discussion of Nixon's view of revolutionaries.]

Kissinger: I think, incidentally, Mr. President, that after the Russians are here I ought to go for two days to Peking to brief them.

Nixon: Oh, of course.

Kissinger: And on that occasion—

Nixon: I understand—

Kissinger: Tell Chou En-lai he should come here, and that then you come back.

Nixon: Where would he go? The UN?

Kissinger: He can come for the UN and then he comes and visits his liaison mission here.

Nixon: Will we give a dinner?

---

[4] On March 8, Kissinger gave Nixon draft letters to Mao and Zhou, which Nixon had not yet approved or signed. The letters are printed as Documents 21 and 22.

Kissinger: Oh, yeah. I'm sure that's what's going to happen.

Nixon: Yeah, I think you should tell him that.

[Omitted here is a discussion of the timing of the upcoming Soviet summit.]

---

21.   Letter From President Nixon to Chinese Chairman Mao Zedong[1]

Washington, March 16, 1973.

Dear Mr. Chairman:

Dr. Kissinger has reported to me fully on his most recent visit to the People's Republic of China and especially his conversation with you.

Let me first express my appreciation for your gracious gesture of receiving Dr. Kissinger. This was evidence to the world of the major progress we have made in our relations and underscored our joint determination to continue on the path toward full normalization. I am grateful for your kind message to me which was also specified in the announcement of the meeting.

Your frank and wide-ranging discussion with Dr. Kissinger was a very positive elaboration of our own talks a year ago which I recall with great warmth. I wish to reaffirm all the basic principles that Dr. Kissinger expressed to you on my behalf. The integrity of China is a fundamental element in American foreign policy. We believe that the viability and independence of your country is in the U.S. national interest and the interest of world peace. Our international approach will reflect this view.

While our two countries will continue to have differences, it is clear from Dr. Kissinger's talks with you and Prime Minister Chou En-lai that we increasingly share common views about the world situation. We take great satisfaction in the progress of our dialogue and the specific steps that are now being taken to accelerate the normalization of our relations.

---

[1] Source: National Archives, Nixon Presidential Materials, NSC Files, Kissinger Office Files, Box 94, Country Files, Far East, China Exchanges, January 1–April 14, 1973. No classification marking. The President received this letter for his approval and signature under a March 8 covering memorandum from Kissinger. (Ibid.) Lord gave it to Chuang Yen, Deputy PRC Representative to the United Nations, on March 17, during a meeting at the PRC Mission to the United Nations. (Ibid.)

I think we can look back on this recent period with a genuine sense of accomplishment. Our joint task now is to continue advancing on the course we have well established. This will be the firm policy of the United States.

Sincerely,

Richard Nixon[2]

---

[2] Nixon added the following handwritten postscript: "Our common dangers and our common interests have drawn our two nations together at this critical juncture in history. I intend to do everything I can to see that nothing drives us apart during my service as President. RN"

---

22.   Letter From President Nixon to Chinese Premier Zhou Enlai[1]

Washington, March 16, 1973.

Dear Mr. Prime Minister:

You have my gratitude for once again receiving Dr. Kissinger and his party with extreme courtesy, thoughtfulness, and cordiality. In listening to the personal accounts of his visit to the People's Republic of China, I recalled with warm pleasure my own journey there a year ago. Let me also take this occasion to thank you for the exquisite vase that was presented to me.

I have heard and read Dr. Kissinger's detailed accounts of his discussions with Chairman Mao and yourself with great interest and satisfaction. It was clear to me last year during my own talks that, differences notwithstanding, our two governments have parallel views on important aspects of the international situation. These most recent conversations demonstrate that we have continued to make substantial progress. It is inevitable—even useful—that our approaches to world problems will not be identical; each country must adhere to its principles. But it is also evident that we have reached mutual understanding in many areas and that we share many principles as well. The latter, of course, found expression in the Shanghai Communiqué which was so forcefully reaffirmed in the joint announcement after Dr. Kissinger's trip.

---

[1] Source: National Archives, Nixon Presidential Materials, NSC Files, Kissinger Office Files, Box 94, Country Files, Far East, China Exchanges, January 1–April 14, 1973. No classification marking. The President received this letter for his approval and signature under a March 8 covering letter from Kissinger. (Ibid.) Lord gave it to Chuang Yen, Deputy PRC Representative to the United Nations during a March 17 meeting at the PRC Mission to the United Nations. (Ibid.)

The advancement in our dialogue has been accompanied by concrete progress in our bilateral relations. In my January 3 letter to you[2] I noted the headway that had already been made. With the achievement of a Vietnam settlement and as a result of Dr. Kissinger's trip, there will now be substantial acceleration in the fields of trade and exchanges. This will serve further to enrich understanding between our peoples and bring tangible benefits to both countries. We are especially pleased that Liaison Offices will be established in our two capitals. This step will not only facilitate our bilateral programs and communication but also holds important symbolic value.

The normalization of relations with the People's Republic of China remains basic to our policy. We will pursue it with as much dedication in my second term as we did in my first. I wish to reaffirm all the undertakings that Dr. Kissinger conveyed to you, and I am writing separately to Chairman Mao in the same vein.

With my best personal wishes.

Sincerely,

Richard Nixon[3]

---

[2] Tab A, Document 1.

[3] Nixon added the following handwritten postscript: "I am convinced that our new relationship has contributed enormously to the cause of security for our two nations and to peace in the world. I look forward to working with you over the next four years toward further guaranteeing these objectives. RN"

---

23.   Memorandum From the President's Assistant for National Security Affairs (Kissinger) to President Nixon[1]

Washington, March 16, 1973.

SUBJECT

Department of State Analysis of China's Troubled Domestic Political Situation

---

[1] Source: National Archives, Nixon Presidential Materials, NSC Files, Box 526, Country Files, Far East, People's Republic of China, Vol. 6, Jan–Apr 1973. Secret; Noforn Attachment. Sent for information. Holdridge sent this memorandum to Kissinger on January 29; Kissinger initialed it and passed it on to Nixon. (Ibid.) According to the attached correspondence profile, Nixon saw it on March 29.

At Tab A is an analysis of current political conditions in the People's Republic of China prepared by the Department of State, which Secretary Rogers has sent to you.[2] This analysis seems to embody the view most prevalent in the government that there is a continuing and tenuous political balance between Communist Party and military officials in the wake of the Lin Piao affair of September 1971. The State paper emphasizes the following points:

—There is a continuing effort by Party leaders to downgrade the power of the military in political affairs. This power was built up by Lin Piao and his followers during the Cultural Revolution. The civilian leaders now find the military reluctant to relinquish their authority, even in the wake of Lin's death while fleeing toward the Soviet Union.

—The central leadership in Peking is finding it difficult to recentralize power. There is considerable instability in personnel assignments in the provinces, suggesting continuing efforts to remove local and provincial leaders not responsive to Peking.

—The national leadership remains in a state of precarious balance, with continuing inability to reach consensus on new personnel assignments. There is still no Defense Minister; less than half of the state ministries have appointed ministers in command; and only 12 of the 25 Party politburo members are active.

—China gives all appearances of a country in an unresolved succession crisis. While officials stress that there is "collective leadership," it is anticipated that the death of Mao Tse-tung and/or Chou En-lai could lead to considerable instability as political institutions are still fragile four years after the conclusion of the Cultural Revolution.[3]

---

[2] Dated January 8, attached but not printed.

[3] The President underlined "death of Mao Tse-tung and/or Chou En-lai" and wrote, "K—what is your analysis as to what we can expect in the event?—What should our contingency be?" On March 29, Scowcroft asked Holdridge to prepare a response to the President. (National Archives, Nixon Presidential Materials, NSC Files, Box 526, Country Files, Far East, People's Republic of China, Vol. 6, Jan–Apr 1973) According to the White House correspondence profile attached to Rogers' memorandum, this request was instead fulfilled by other analyses of the Chinese political situation that reached the NSC.

24.   Memorandum of Conversation[1]

Washington, March 29, 1973, 11:05 a.m.–noon.

PARTICIPANTS

Ambassador David Bruce, Chief-designate of US Liaison Office in Peking
Dr. Henry A. Kissinger, Assistant to the President
Alfred leS. Jenkins, Deputy-designate of US Liaison Office
John H. Holdridge, Deputy-designate of US Liaison Office
Peter W. Rodman, NSC Staff

Dr. Kissinger: David, I thought we could just review what the group is going to do there and what our concept is in setting this thing up.

Basically, the idea of the Liaison Office escalated. As you know, Al and John, between them, were with me on every trip, and between them they have sat in on every conversation of major substance on every trip. The Liaison Office started really as something primarily for conducting the business of the Paris Embassy, with political things conducted by me and Ambassador Huang Hua in New York. Now with the level of representation on both sides it is something different.

Incidentally, Al, your colleagues don't know this yet, but the Chinese are sending Huang Chen, their Ambassador to France and also a member of their Central Committee. They are also sending the chief of their protocol department, Han Hsu. There will be an announcement tomorrow. So at this point I see no point on continuing our contact in New York. You should confirm, Al, when you are there [with the advance party], that we can do this. You should repeat that Ambassador Bruce knows everything, and has the President's full confidence, and that I can talk to the Ambassador here.

Will you get to see the Prime Minister? You should try to see him, or at least Ch'iao Kuan-hua. Don't do it at a level lower than Ch'iao. I think you should have one substantive talk with a restricted group—in fact, just you. Can you manage that?

Mr. Jenkins: Yes. That will be no problem, especially with the group I have with me on this trip.

---

[1] Source: National Archives, Nixon Presidential Materials, NSC Files, Kissinger Office Files, Box 94, Country Files, East Asia, China Exchange January 1–April 14, 1973. Top Secret; Sensitive; Exclusively Eyes Only. The meeting took place in Kissinger's office in the White House. All brackets are in the original. On March 26, Kissinger received talking points for this meeting from Holdridge. (Ibid., Box 526, Country Files, Far East, People's Republic of China, Vol. VI, Jan–Apr 1973)

Dr. Kissinger: Tell them: one, that you have been asked by me on behalf of the President to reaffirm everything I said to the Prime Minister. Needless to say, in preparation for the Soviet Summit there will be more intensive consultations with the Soviet Union, but they will be kept fully informed. There will be no surprises, and everything will be fully consistent with the strategy the Prime Minister and I agreed upon.

Ambassador Bruce: When is the Soviet Summit?

Dr. Kissinger: June 18. This is known only in the White House.

Tell them that we will let them know about the details, but our strategy is to gain the time without making substantive concessions—to gain the time we need to prepare our public opinion for closer relations with the People's Republic, to lay the basis for other measures if they become essential. Say that nothing new has happened since Mr. Lord dealt with their Ambassador on my behalf, but that we will give them the details as they develop and we will keep them fully informed on anything that should develop before doing anything.

On Vietnam, we realize that history will not stop in Vietnam, but it is also impossible for the United States to tolerate flagrant violations of the Agreement that we signed. The violations have been flagrant and the justifications have been insulting. We know all the equipment they are sending; to say that they are civilian goods is insulting to our intelligence. Tell them that there is a time for everything.

Secondly, we never asked them to slow down their military supply while the war was on, because we realize they have their principles. But to keep pouring in military supplies at a time when there is supposed to be peace cannot be considered a friendly act. You can assure them that we are strictly sticking to the replacement provisions, and if there are any questions about it we would be glad to give them a list of what we are sending into South Vietnam on a monthly basis, for their private information. In fact, we will do this.

Ambassador Bruce: Are they pouring equipment into North Vietnam, or are the North Vietnamese bringing down equipment they have already accumulated?

Mr. Kissinger: We don't really know. If it is only what they have already accumulated, then we are in good shape, because they will not launch an offensive unless there is a pipeline. We have good assurances from the Soviets that they are sending no more military equipment. But we won't tell the Chinese, at least at this level. Ambassador Bruce can do this.

We will start withdrawing the squadrons from Formosa in July as we have told them.[2]

---

[2] See footnote 6, Document 18.

Tell them also that we will be seeing Brandt, Pompidou and Andreotti this spring, and we will inform them about these meetings. These meetings will be in the interest of the strategy of Western cohesion that we talked about.

Tell them also that I will be taking Ambassador Bruce with me to New York to meet Ambassador Huang Hua, for a general discussion. [To Ambassador Bruce] I will take you in early April when we get back.

Al, make sure that I have a back channel to Ambassador Bruce. Do you have a CIA man on the trip?

Mr. Jenkins: No, we don't.

Mr. Holdridge: You saw the memo we did and sent over last night.[3] The CIA is being squeezed out. There is no CIA man in the Liaison Office.

Dr. Kissinger: That is impossible. There must be one Agency representative and one communicator. I will take care of it with the Chinese. David can raise it with the Chinese and explain the reason for it. They will welcome it. We will deal with them completely openly.

Mr. Jenkins: On reporting this meeting I have . . .

Dr. Kissinger: Don't report it. Or report it just to me.

Mr. Jenkins: We won't have a channel yet. I will be busy with so many things, I don't know if I can come back.

Dr. Kissinger: We have got to know what happened before the Ambassador goes. David?

Ambassador Bruce: Yes.

Dr. Kissinger: Why don't you plan on coming back.

Mr. Jenkins: All right.

Dr. Kissinger: We need a channel. I have got to be able to report to you out there on my conversation with Huang Chen. Or else you will be in an impossible position. You will end up like the Paris channel.

Mr. Jenkins: You will tell them that there will be dual communications?

Dr. Kissinger: Yes, I will tell them there will be dual communications. They will welcome that. We will tell them that there will be one intelligence man in the Embassy and that he won't do anything that David won't discuss with them. He can't do anything they won't know about anyway. If they want him walled up in the Liaison Office, that's okay. But there has to be an Agency man so there can be an Agency communicator.

---

[3] Memorandum from Holdridge to Kissinger, March 28. (National Archives, Nixon Presidential Materials, NSC Files, Box 526, Country Files, Far East, People's Republic of China, Vol. 6, Jan–Apr 1973)

[At this point Dr. Kissinger telephoned James Schlesinger[4] to say that we wanted an Agency man in the Liaison Office and that he would be there on condition that he did literally nothing that was not cleared by both Ambassador Bruce and Dr. Kissinger. If the CIA would abide by these rules, we would tell the Chinese who the man was and what his job was. This was an unusual procedure, but we had always found with the Chinese that total honesty was the best policy. Dr. Kissinger explained that he would handle the bureaucratics of it.]

We have just got to have all the communicators CIA people, or at least a dual system. How do we do this?

Mr. Jenkins: Porter is handling this at the Department. You will handle it?

Dr. Kissinger: I will take care of it with Porter before you leave. Do you agree with this, David?

Ambassador Bruce: Absolutely. Now the other messages, routine messages on the administrative details, will be coming out through Hong Kong?

Mr. Jenkins: Yes, that is our understanding. These can go through State channels, can't they?

Dr. Kissinger: Yes, Al, you know the fraternity over there. Your effectiveness with the Chinese depends totally on your being a White House man. I know the bureaucracy will want to assert its own interest. Anything you can tactfully suggest to your colleagues as your own idea will make it much easier.

Mr. Jenkins: Should I tell Chiao that we are having a special channel?

Dr. Kissinger: Yes, he will welcome it.

Mr. Jenkins: Should I mention this only if they raise it, or should I volunteer it?

Dr. Kissinger: You should raise it. They should understand from the beginning that Ambassador Bruce is the President's man.

Ambassador Bruce: If you have only CIA communicators, there will be a lot of traffic to State.

Mr. Holdridge: That's no problem. The communicators can send stuff to State with a different code. They just send it with a different addressee.

Dr. Kissinger: Alternatively, if they want State communicators we would have to set up special facilities.

---

[4] A transcript of the March 29 telephone conversation between Kissinger and Schlesinger, 11:35 a.m. is ibid., Kissinger Transcripts, Telcons, closed, National Security, Box 2, 1973, 28–31 March.

Ambassador Bruce: The other would be much simpler.

Dr. Kissinger: Yes.

Mr. Jenkins: A couple of things I want to mention. Privileges and immunities. Am I to nail this down while I am there?

Dr. Kissinger: Yes, if you can.

Mr. Jenkins: Travel restrictions. They normally restrict diplomats to within 12 miles of Peking, except for the Ming Tombs. Occasionally they allow visits to other cities like Canton, Shanghai and Tientsin. What should we do?

Dr. Kissinger: Tell them that we have to put on them the same restrictions we put on the Soviets, but you can tell them that we won't enforce them. And ask them what they will do for you. We will just give them blanket exceptions.

Mr. Jenkins: We will tell them we plan not to enforce the restrictions.

Dr. Kissinger: Yes, just tell them what we propose to do. I am sure they will be forthcoming if we don't press them.

Mr. Jenkins: Some people in my shop have the idea that the Ambassador should present a Moon Rock when he goes over there. I think it's a silly idea this late.

Dr. Kissinger: It's already been done! We did it in July 1971.

Mr. Jenkins: That takes care of that.

Dr. Kissinger: Don't tell them it's already been done, just tell them we won't do it.

Mr. Jenkins: Right.

Dr. Kissinger: On personnel, the Ambassador wants Nick Platt as his assistant. We favor that. My requirement is—of course anything that Ambassador Bruce wants, he can do—but to have it as disciplined an organization as possible. We can't have people running around trying to improve the world, or writing private letters.

Mr. Jenkins: It's a well-disciplined group. There should be no problem.

Mr. Holdridge: It's my old Hong Kong Consulate General staff reconstituted. They all used to work for me.

Mr. Jenkins: Because of the servant problem there, the Ambassador will need an Aide to handle these things, a young man. We have a boy named McKinley whom Graham Martin recommended. Martin wanted to take him to Saigon, but China was the boy's area, so he suggested that Ambassador Bruce should have him.

Dr. Kissinger: That's all right. Incidentally, I see a lot of mention in the traffic about putting us in the diplomatic enclave. I think, one, that they might want to do better by us, and two, they can use the fact of the Liaison Office as an excuse to do something better for us. So there is no reason for us to propose the diplomatic enclave.

Mr. Jenkins: No. In fact, they might even give us our old compound back.

Dr. Kissinger: It is inconceivable that they would accept someone of the distinction of Ambassador Bruce and not treat us better. They had a chance to turn down this level of representation. When we suggested Ambassador Bruce, we also asked if they would not prefer a lesser level of representation. They had two weeks to mull it over.

Ambassador Bruce: As to my personal requirements, I can say for myself and Evangeline that we don't care at all what the living conditions are. Don't let them tell you that because I am an old man I need a soft bed and special conditions.

[At this point, Mr. Kissinger took a call on the secure line from Mr. Schlesinger.][5]

Dr. Kissinger: Schlesinger says the problem is that if there are both State and CIA communicators there, the State communicators will know the volume of the traffic through the other channel. And the volume will be greater in the special channel than in the State channel. Therefore, we will need CIA communicators—if you agree.

Ambassador Bruce: I agree, yes. It's easier.

Dr. Kissinger: We will just insist on it.

Ambassador Bruce: What is the time difference with Peking?

Mr. Jenkins: 13 hours.

Dr. Kissinger: Except in the summer, when it is 12. It works very well.

We can send you messages in the evening our time; you will receive them in the morning and then reply to us in time for morning here.

They may or may not want us in the diplomatic compound. I would leave it to them. They have never failed us on technical arrangements.

Mr. Holdridge: If we don't ask them, they will have more leeway.

Dr. Kissinger: Al, on their visit here, tell them that anything we can do for their advance party to make it more comfortable for them we will do. As I already told the Prime Minister, they can make requests in two categories—one, to the US Government, and two, to their old friends on a personal basis. Both will be dealt with as a matter of priority.

---

[5] No record of the call has been found.

We have already told them that they can send people down from New York in advance of the advance party, if they wish. Can we pay their expenses?

Mr. Jenkins: We've never done this.

Dr. Kissinger: Will they make you pay your expenses?

Mr. Jenkins: I don't know. They may put me up in the Peking Hotel.

Dr. Kissinger: Let us know. If they make you pay, then we will make the Chinese pay. If not, we will know what to do. We will just get the money, maybe from the Agency.

Mr. Jenkins: I will just mention it parenthetically, in a regular cable. I will just say that they have asked me to stay as their guest. If I don't mention anything like this, you will know that I paid my expenses.

Dr. Kissinger: When their advance party comes, can your colleagues avoid it becoming a circus?

Mr. Jenkins: I won't be here!

Mr. Holdridge: I can handle that.

Dr. Kissinger: Han Hsu is heading their advance team.

Okay. [To Mr. Rodman] Make sure we send a message to them to tell them that we will be setting up a direct White House channel, and that I have asked Mr. Jenkins to bring one substantive message.

[At that point the meeting ended. Ambassador Bruce departed. Dr. Kissinger then brought Mr. Jenkins and Mr. Holdridge back into his office and repeated to them that the effectiveness of the Liaison Office depended on its being a reliable channel for the White House. If Mr. Jenkins had any problem setting up a secure channel, the White House would just have to bypass the Peking Liaison Office. It would be easier bureaucratically if Mr. Jenkins could get this done by making his own suggestions rather than having it be the result of White House suggestions.]

25.   Memorandum From Richard H. Solomon of the National Security Council Staff to the President's Assistant for National Security Affairs (Kissinger)[1]

Washington, April 2, 1973.

SUBJECT

Peking's Current Campaign to Recover Taiwan, and Options for the U.S.

In view of the now heightened pace of U.S.–PRC normalization, I have undertaken an analysis of recent developments which indicate Peking's desire to rapidly open negotiations with Taipei. The analysis, at Tab A,[2] reaches the following conclusions:

—The PRC is increasing its pressures on the Nationalist government to come to a negotiated solution regarding the future status of the island. Peking is proceeding at four levels of activity;

—Sustaining efforts to isolate Taiwan internationally.
—Heightening the visibility of its media appeals for reunification.
—Actively cultivating overseas Chinese, who will stimulate opinion trends on the island for reunification.
—Moving rapidly toward normalization with the U.S. in order to "elbow aside" Washington's relationship with Taipei.

—On Taiwan, the Nationalist leadership appears to have made a smooth transition from Chiang Kai-shek's leadership to that of his son Chiang Ching-kuo. However, there is increasing uncertainty about what policy the ROC should adopt toward Peking and the U.S. Individuals in the leadership have begun making informal appeals for greater candor on the part of the White House about its intentions regarding the PRC and ROC. There appears to be a growing public mood of fatalism on Taiwan about the likely prospect of some form of reconciliation between Taipei and Peking.

—In these circumstances, the U.S. has essentially three options regarding the uncertain prospect of negotiations between the two Chinese capitals: do nothing; attempt to stimulate talks; or play a more subtle catalyzing role without directly intermediating in negotiations. The virtues of the latter posture are explored in the analysis.

—The study concludes by noting that in the period ahead it would be useful to have more systematic periodic assessments of public opin-

---

[1] Source: National Archives, Nixon Presidential Materials, NSC Files, Box 526, Country Files, Far East, People's Republic of China, Vol. 6, Jan–Apr 1973. Secret; Sensitive. Sent for action.

[2] Undated, attached but not printed.

ion and leadership trends on Taiwan regarding the future status of the island. Because of the sensitivity of this issue, however, you may wish to do nothing out of the ordinary in this regard.

Recommendation:

That you authorize more systematic and periodic assessments of public opinion and leadership trends on Taiwan regarding the island's future status.

—Do nothing at this time.

—Request CIA to undertake such an effort.[3]

—Request that we prepare for you other "outside the system" alternatives to such an effort.

---

[3] Kissinger initialed the Approve option.

---

26. Memorandum From Richard T. Kennedy of the National Security Council Staff to the President's Assistant for National Security Affairs (Kissinger)[1]

Washington, April 7, 1973.

SUBJECT

Security Assistance, Taiwan

Our security assistance program for Taiwan has changed during the last few years as grant MAP decreased and FMS credits assumed more importance. At the end of FY 73, grants for MAP *equipment* will end, though we will continue to pay for training and supply operations costs on prior year MAP programs. In addition, in FY 73–74, there are sizable special grants resulting from our commitment to F–5E coassembly on Taiwan deriving from the GRC's help during Enhance Plus. The table below reflects the changing nature of these programs and itemizes the major military credit sales programs.

---

[1] Source: National Archives, Nixon Presidential Materials, NSC Files, Kissinger Office Files, Box 94, Country Files, Far East, China Exchanges, May 16–June 13, 1973. Secret. Sent for information.

	Fiscal Years ($ million)				
	72	73	74	75	76
Enhance Plus grant	—	18	28	—	—
MAP	11	10	5.8**	5.8**	.5
FMS Credit	45	44	65	135	124
—F–5E coassembly	—	(5)	(23)	(69)	(61)
—Helo coproduction	(9)	(7)	(7)	(11)*	(10)*
—Trucks	(12)	(3)	(6)*	(5)*	(5)*
—Patrol Boats	—	(4)*	(8)*	(6)*	(12)*
—Hawk bns.	—	—	—	(17)*	(14)*
Total Grants and FMS	56	72	99	141	125

* Not yet approved.

** 5.3 for supply operations, .5 for grant training.

You will note that though matériel grants are phasing out, total assistance has increased through FMS credits. This is consistent with Taiwan's continually improving economy, our commitment to the GRC, and the self-sufficiency aspects of the Nixon Doctrine.

	Fiscal Years ($ million)				
	72	73	74	75	76
Grant Matériel	3	1.5	0	0	0
Credit Sales	45	44	65	135	124
Cash Sales	46	49	*	*	*
Total	94	94.5	65*	135*	124*

* Cash sales unknown for FY 74–76

27. **Memorandum From Winston Lord of the National Security Council Staff to the President's Military Assistant (Scowcroft)**[1]

Washington, April 16, 1973.

SUBJECT

Brief Highlights of New York Meeting

Our Liaison Office

HAK introduced Bruce, said he had complete trust of the President. [2½ *lines not declassified*] When HAK asked Huang if they agree that the New York channel will dissolve and we will use the Liaison Offices, Huang said Peking was still studying this. HAK said that we had heard that Jenkins was pressing for American newsmen to be admitted to Peking for the opening of the office; he assured Huang we had no special interest in this and that it was entirely up to the Chinese.

Chinese Liaison Office

Huang read out their understandings on their office and HAK confirmed that all were okay. They will hoist national flag and put out emblem; they won't join the Diplomatic Corps or participate in any functions which involve the Chinese Nationalists; they will maintain contact with countries with whom they have diplomatic relations; while technically they will be under the same travel restrictions as the Soviets, in practice they will be free to go where they want.

HAK told Huang that Solomon was our man to greet their advance party and would respond to all requests. While technical arrangements would be up to the State Department, substantive matters should be discussed first at the White House. HAK wants to see Han Hsu Wednesday morning; invites the top three guys to lunch Friday; and Bruce will give a dinner for entire delegation Friday night. We will be in daily touch with the advance party and in addition, the New York Mission can send people down here if they wish.

Indochina

HAK was very starchy on North Vietnamese violations and handed over all messages on this subject to and from the North

---

[1] Source: National Archives, Nixon Presidential Materials, NSC Files, Kissinger Office Files, Box 94, Country Files, Far East, China Exchanges, April 15–May 15, 1973. Top Secret; Sensitive; Exclusively Eyes Only. A memorandum of conversation of the meeting, which took place at China's UN Mission, is ibid.

Vietnamese since the ones I gave the Chinese in my meeting.[2] He also explained our position on Cambodia. Huang responded quite moderately and claimed he was speaking personally. HAK at one point indicated that discussions would be acceptable with Sihanouk's representative—the way he put it suggested that it might be the United States talking to them rather than the Cambodian Government but he was fuzzy on this and earlier said that negotiations had to be among the Cambodians. Huang particularly directed our attention to the various public statements made by Sihanouk recently. [*Comment:* I will round these up and we will have a closer look at them though I doubt they hold anything promising.][3]

Soviet Union

HAK gave the standard line on ESC, MBFR, SALT and bilateral matters. On MBFR, he reaffirmed that cuts would be no more than 10% and that we would make some suggestions to our allies, but not to the Soviets before this fall. He promised the Chinese a look at our proposals when they are firmer.

On SALT, he mentioned the recent comprehensive Soviet proposal and promised to send a summary tomorrow (Tuesday). [*Comment:* I will follow up with Sonnenfeldt–Hyland and get a summary by midday.] He also promised to send them a copy of our counterproposal on SALT which he said should be completed in about 10 days.

On the Nuclear Treaty,[4] he gave the usual line about watering this down and said that we were awaiting a Soviet proposal following up our rejection of the last draft we gave the Chinese. He said that we don't make proposals but rather get them from the Soviet Union. He promised to give the Chinese a copy of the next Soviet proposal (by messenger because of sensitivity).[5] [*Comment:* In short, he is keeping the Chinese about two or three laps behind.] He indicated we might reach an agreement at the summit but not without prior consultations with the Chinese. He reaffirmed that we would never incur an obligation not to use nuclear weapons nor aim at third countries.

---

[2] Lord complained to the Chinese Government about North Vietnamese violations during a March 17 meeting with Chuang Yen, Deputy PRC UN Representative. (Memorandum of conversation, March 17; ibid., January 1–April 14, 1973)

[3] These and all subsequent brackets are in the original.

[4] The "Agreement Between The United States of America and The Union of Soviet Socialist Republics on the Prevention of Nuclear War," signed on June 22, committed both countries to consult with the other in order to avoid the risk of a nuclear war.

[5] On April 24, an American messenger gave the new Soviet draft to Chinese officials in New York. (Memorandum for the record by McManis, April 25; National Archives, Nixon Presidential Materials, NSC Files, Kissinger Office Files, Box 94, Country Files, Far East, China Exchanges, April 15–May 15, 1973)

Korea–UNCURK

HAK said that we could agree to a two-step process of first adjourning sine die and then having the UN abolish the organization. In return we would expect delineation of the entire Korean item from the Assembly debate.[6] Huang indicated their unhappiness over our alleged backsliding, both because of our two-stage approach (even though it would be this year presumably) and because we want to postpone the entire Korean debate item.

Miscellaneous

In response to their number two guy's inquiry to me, HAK said that we had authorized American firms to investigate the possibilities to develop oil in Siberia with Japan but had given no financial guarantees as yet.

HAK filled Huang in on the various foreign visitors coming to Washington. On behalf of the President, he said that if Prime Minister Chou En-lai were to visit the UN this fall, he would be welcome in Washington. He didn't have to go to the UN, HAK added, but this might be a convenient method.

HAK asked the Chinese to get Eugene Ormandy off his back.[7]

Huang asked what the implication was in the President's recent letter to Chairman Mao about our interest in Chinese viability and independence.[8] HAK replied we consider this in our own interest and did not ask reciprocity.

Huang offered to give Bruce a farewell dinner, but Bruce graciously declined because of a full schedule until his departure on about May 1. Huang then offered to host a dinner the first time Bruce comes back for consultations.

---

[6] During an April 9 telephone conversation at 5:58 p.m., Rush advised Kissinger to make this offer to the PRC Government. (National Archives, Nixon Presidential Materials, Kissinger Telcons, Box 19–2 [March–April 1973])

[7] In September 1973, the Philadelphia Orchestra, conducted by Eugene Ormandy, visited the People's Republic of China.

[8] See Document 21.

28.   Memorandum of Conversation[1]

I–22420/73   Washington, April 17, 1973, 3:30–4:10 p.m.

SUBJECT

　　Courtesy Call by Ambassador David K. E. Bruce, Chief of the Liaison Office
　　in Peking

PARTICIPANTS

　　Acting Assistant Secretary of Defense (ISA)—Lawrence S. Eagleburger
　　Department of State, Chief Peking Liaison Office—David K. E. Bruce
　　Deputy Assistant Secretary of Defense (ISA/EAPA)—Dennis J. Doolin
　　Director, East Asia & Pacific Region (ISA)—RADM Thomas J. Bigley
　　Department of State, Acting Director, People's Republic of China and Mongolian
　　　　Affairs—Roger W. Sullivan
　　Assistant for People's Republic of China (ISA)—Robert L. Vandegrift

Ambassador Bruce said he and Mr. Holdridge would leave for
Peking about 1 May and that he hoped to get settled early since the
Chinese were cooperating very well with Mr. Jenkins in the prelimi-
nary arrangements for quarters and other housekeeping chores.

Mr. Eagleburger explained that DOD had a much stricter interpretation of the Shanghai Communiqué and harder view of the Taiwan
situation than State and that it would probably be a long time before
all U.S. forces were withdrawn from Taiwan. Mr. Doolin stated that
most of the personnel stationed there were assigned to regionally oriented security assignments not connected with the defense of Taiwan.
RADM Bigley explained that the men attached to the C–130 units on
Taiwan were related in part to Southeast Asian commitments and could
gradually be transferred elsewhere as tensions in Indochina diminished. Mr. Sullivan stated that State and DOD views on the issue of
U.S. forces on Taiwan were now much closer since the establishment
of the Liaison Offices had made it clear that this issue was no longer
an obstacle to PRC normalization moves with the U.S.

In regard to Chinese language fluency, Ambassador Bruce stated
he possessed no ability whatsoever but that everyone on his staff was
competent. After a general discussion of the great differences between
Chinese dialects and the great difficulty the Chinese themselves had
in understanding the local dialects of their leaders, Mr. Sullivan said

---

[1] Source: Washington National Records Center, RG 330, OASD/ISA Files: FRC
330–76–117, China, 333, April 23, 1973. Secret. The memorandum of conversation was prepared by Robert L. Vandegrift and approved by Dennis Doolin. The meeting was held in
Lawrence Eagleburger's office.

the State Department has no one who can understand the Hunan dialect spoken by Mao. Even the discussions President Nixon had with Mao, not to mention the other U.S. officials, were completely incomprehensible to the Americans. Translations were made by Chou En-lai or a Chinese interpreter and it was not possible to verify the accuracy of the translation even to subject, let alone inflections and nuances. As a result, no one at State really is certain what Mao said or whether he was coherent. Mr. Doolin and the Ambassador then discussed the realities of one's interpreter taking liberties with both what and how he translates without the principal even being aware of the change.

Mr. Eagleburger assured Ambassador Bruce that DOD had no plans to complicate his mission by pushing for a Defense Attaché Office in Peking. Mr. Doolin pointed out there was no advantage to have a DAO while current PRC surveillance and travel restrictions remained in force, but that the PRC might at some point make some initiatives along this time.

Ambassador Bruce then asked for and received the latest DOD analysis of the Chinese military capabilities, their science and technology efforts, and their present relations with the USSR from Mr. Doolin and RADM Bigley. Ambassador Bruce also raised questions on Soviet naval capabilities which RADM Bigley answered.

The meeting concluded with a general discussion which included Chinese archives and libraries, a book the Ambassador had written on President Lincoln, stories concerning prominent personalities he had known, and some of his personal experiences in the Foreign Service.

29.   **Memorandum From the President's Assistant for National Security Affairs (Kissinger) to Secretary of State Rogers, Secretary of Defense Richardson, Secretary of the Treasury Shultz, Secretary of Agriculture Butz, and Secretary of Commerce Dent**[1]

Washington, April 24, 1973.

SUBJECT

Coordinating USG Contacts with the Liaison Office of the People's Republic of China

The People's Republic of China is now in the process of establishing a Liaison Office in Washington which will open for business some time in early May. This will provide all agencies of the U.S. Government a more ready contact point with Chinese authorities as the process of normalization of Sino-American relations proceeds.

Given the still sensitive stage of our relations with the People's Republic, however, the President has requested that all contacts with the PRC's Washington Liaison Office be coordinated with the National Security Council and the Department of State.

Henry A. Kissinger

---

[1] Source: National Archives, Nixon Presidential Materials, NSC Files, Box 526, Country Files, Far East, People's Republic of China, Vol. 6, Jan–Apr 1973. Secret. A copy of this memorandum was sent to the Assistant to the President for International Economic Affairs, Peter Flanigan. Kissinger approved the memorandum after receiving it under an April 16 covering memorandum from Holdridge. (Ibid.) On May 16, Kissinger sent it to all department and agency heads. (Ibid., Box 527, Country Files, Far East, People's Republic of China, Vol. 7, May, 1973–Jul 9, 1973)

30.   Conversation Between President Nixon and the Chief-Designate of the Liaison Office in China (Bruce)[1]

Washington, May 3, 1973.

[Omitted here is Nixon and Bruce's meeting with reporters.]

Nixon: Well, the great thing for you, as you know, substantively, probably not a great deal will happen for a while.

Bruce: Yes.

Nixon: But the most important thing about this is the symbolism. I mean, symbolism sometimes is not important, but now it is enormously important.

Bruce: The fact that—

Nixon: The fact that you are there. Let me tell you one thing that I particularly would like to see. I know that the social world is a total pain in the [neck], but to the extent that you can, if you could get around, and have your colleagues get around and give us an evaluation of the people on the way up who are there now.

Bruce: Yes. Yes.

Nixon: You've got to understand, Mao will soon be leaving; Chou En-lai is in his 70s but he's as vigorous as can be—terrific. You're going to really like him, you'll like them both. Chou En-lai is an amazing man. But on the other hand, except for some men in their 30s—late 30s and 40s—I don't see much coming up. And I think, you know, you can do that. Look around, see who the power is. That's one thing that would be very important for us to know. Isn't it?

Bruce: Well, I think it is, yes. Because if they have sort of a collegial [unclear]—

Nixon: The Russians have quite a few in their shop that you know might come along.

Bruce: Yes.

Nixon: And you know, an interesting thing, the Russians too [unclear], so pretty soon we know in four or five years there's going to be change there. But there will be a change in China. And the world changes. Well, there's that. Then, of course, the just, you know, your sense of the country, its people. I mean, I'm really, really more interested in that than

---

[1] Source: National Archives, Nixon Presidential Materials, White House Tapes, Conversation No. 911–9. No classification marking. The editor transcribed the portions of the conversation printed here specifically for this volume. According to the President's Daily Diary, Nixon spoke with Bruce in the Oval Office from 9:48 until 10:12 a.m. (Ibid., White House Central Files)

I am in the routine cables, "Well, today we did this, or that, or the other thing. We signed an agreement." You know, this is how we grow figs.

Bruce: Exactly.

Nixon: Huh?

Bruce: Yes.

Nixon: Don't you agree?

Bruce: I do agree.

Nixon: We're trying to see what this great—I mean, we've got to get along with this one-fourth of all people in the world. The ablest people in the world in my opinion—potentially. We've got to get along with them. It's no problem for the next 5 years, the next 20 years, but it's the critical problem of our age.

Bruce: Yes, I think it is.

Nixon: The other thing is, if you could, constantly of course, whenever you're talking, they've very subtle—and they're not like the Russians, who, of course slobber at flattery and all that sort of thing. But you should let them know how—two things: one, from a personal standpoint how much I appreciated the welcome while we were there. Second, we look forward to some time returning. Third, I would very much hope that Chou En-lai will see his way clear to come here to the UN.

Bruce: Yes.

Nixon: Or something. I'd like to take him here, and it can be worked out in a proper way. And fourth, and I think this is the most important, that I look upon the Chinese-American relationship as really the key to peace in the world. Always have in the back of your mind without playing it too obviously, the fact that the only thing that makes the Russian game go is the Chinese game. Always have in the back of your mind that if you say anything pro-Russian, [unclear]. Always have in the back of your mind that the Russians are their deadly enemies. And they know it, and we know it. And that we will stand by them.

Bruce: Yes.

Nixon: And that's the commitment that I have made. I have.

Bruce: Yes.

Nixon: How we do it, I don't know. But that's what keeps. Because David, what is probably in our time maybe that big collision could occur, and collisions even between enemies these days will involve all nations of the world, they're that big. So we want to avoid that too. But my point is the Chinese must be reassured they have one heck of a friend here. They hate the Indians, as you know.

Bruce: Yes.

Nixon: Well, they don't hate them as much as they have contempt for them. They think that India is becoming a, you know, a sort of satellite of Russia. And of course the Japanese, they have a fear and respect for them as well. So with the Japanese, sort of say the right thing in terms of we want to get along with Japan and the rest. And it's very important that we have our, that we maintain our, in other words the shield there, because otherwise Japan goes into business for itself and that's not in our interest. And the other point that they're fairly interested in, looking at the world scene, another point, apart from the fact they'll go through the usual jazz [unclear] keeping revolutions in mind. That's fine. What they do in Africa I don't care anymore. But Europe. They don't want us to get out of Europe. Because they realize as long as the Russians have a tie down in Europe, that—you see what I mean?

Bruce: Oh, I do.

Nixon: So some of our well-intentioned Congressmen go over there and reassure them, "Oh, look, we're going to get out of Asia. We're going to get out of Japan, we're trying to reduce our forces in Europe." Well, that for the Chinese scares them to death.

Bruce: Well, I was struck by the conversations that you've had, and how they came back to the necessity about preserving forces in Europe. They were very pro-NATO for their own reasons. It was interesting.

Nixon: Absolutely.

Bruce: Well, I've got all those points in mind. Those conversations that you had there I've read. I must say they really are quite [unclear] fascinating to read.

Nixon: Yeah. You're one of the few in the country who's read them.

Bruce: I'd forgotten—but I do think they're absolutely fascinating.

Nixon: Yeah. A lot of history was made there.

Bruce: It was indeed. I think probably the most significant history, diplomatic history, of our time. No question about it. And I don't see anything, which could really ruin it in the time being. Without any hesitation I can tell you I always thought the preservation of good relations should have sort of ordinary courtesies and what not in the beginning, it'll probably be all business, but you try and get to know as many people as possible. [unclear]

Nixon: Let them think that we are strong, respected, and we're not going to be pushed around by the Russians or anybody else. Middle East—we have no answer there, as you know.

Bruce: I know.

Nixon: They haven't either. But I think the great irony is that today the United States of all nations is China's most important friend. [laughter] Romania? Tanzania? Albania?

[unclear exchange]

Bruce: That's pretty good stuff.

Nixon: My point is, with that in mind—would you like a little coffee?

Bruce: No, I wouldn't like some. I just had some.

Nixon: Oh, fine. I'll have a little, just a cup.

Bruce: But this is a most fascinating development, I think.

Nixon: It sure is.

Bruce: We must replace the policies that have become so embedded almost in the American consciousness that nobody in particular complained about it, and nobody intended [unclear].

Nixon: Look, for 20 years, do you know, we were sort of—now look, I'm supposed to be the number one Red-baiter in the country. I have earned that reputation for what you know very well. Had we just continued the policy of just a silent confrontation and almost noncommunication with the PRC—

Bruce: Yes.

Nixon: In the end we would reap a nuclear war. No question.

Bruce: Yes. Yes.

Nixon: We just had to breakthrough.

Bruce: Yeah.

Nixon: Also, as I said, it was so important to the Russian game.

Bruce: Terribly important.

Nixon: Yeah.

Bruce: Terribly important.

Nixon: Yeah.

Bruce: It must have [unclear]. How about does one explain to the Chinese that we want to preserve a relationship that has great importance to us, a meaningful relationship with Russia? The Chinese are undoubtedly our favorites between the two. But—

Nixon: The Russians are saying: Now look, this is very important. That Nixon is having another meeting with Brezhnev. There's going to be a lot of reasons for having that meeting. The important thing there to remember is that Russia and the United States are superpowers. That our interests do rub together in the Mideast and in Europe, particularly. That their rubbing together is a danger that is almost unbelievably great, and that under these circumstances we feel what we have to do is try to limit that danger as much as we can through communication. But, on the other hand, we do not consider putting it quite bluntly as between the two. We consider the Soviet, because of its power and of its long history of expansionism, we consider it more of a danger that we have to deal with than we do China, which has a longer history of, frankly, defense. Now, I think a little of that is well worth saying. In other words—and also I'd be very blunt about it. Just say you've had a long talk with the President and there's no illusions—our systems are different. They're better Communists than the Russians are today. But we want to get back to our national interest. And the President considers—he's a man of the Pacific. He considers that China and America have a hell of a lot more in common than Russia and America, and that is the God's truth.

Bruce: Yes, that's true.

Nixon: And that therefore, looking at the historical process, I want to work toward that direction. And I think that's what we have to do. But the Chinese-American relationship can be the great lynchpin of peace in the world.

Bruce: Well, I'll tell you that after you've talked to Brezhnev, the Chinese will be filled in rather completely.

Nixon: Totally. I've instructed, I'll have, of course we'll be in touch with you, but we'll probably have Kissinger go over again. Incidentally, I want to tell you one thing. Normally on these visits when he goes, this is very important, he has sometimes met alone. So far. But in this instance, I want you to feel, David, that you are basically, not the State Department's ambassador, you are the President's, and I want you to be in on everything. You see what I mean? You've got to remember that we cannot—there's parts of these games that we don't want to go to the bureaucracy. It's no lack of confidence in Bill or any of the others. But you know how it is. So will you have this in mind, please?

Bruce: I will, Mr. President. I certainly will. Because the security of the State Department is, in my mind, non-existent.

Nixon: It's non-existent.

Bruce: [unclear]

Nixon: That's right.

Bruce: No, I think that I understand that part of the [unclear]. And I think the back channel can be used [unclear]

Nixon: Well, I want to use the backchannel. And also, when Henry gets over there to do the briefings. I think it's very important that you be with him.

Bruce: Well, I would like that.

Nixon: So that you can, you know, get the feel of the thing too.

Bruce: Yes, I think it would be on that occasion, good. They offered when they came to Paris in connection with the Vietnam peace talks taking me to secret meetings. And I was very indisposed to do it. I think it would have been a great mistake. I never would have been able to—

Nixon: Oh, yes. When you were there?

Bruce: Yes. But I think with China it's probably a different thing.

Nixon: Well, in China [unclear]. I'll see that it's done.

Bruce: All right, sir. I've only got one other thing, which I have not [unclear]—because they are behind the times with what's going on. This Cambodia thing, I wonder if it's possible to settle.

Nixon: I wish it were. We're willing to settle; China can have it. Whether they can still get that [unclear] Sihanouk back in I don't know. We don't care. The Cambodians don't want it at the moment. What ideas did you have? I mean, anything we can do—God, Cambodia is a terrible, terrible place.

[Omitted here is further discussion of Cambodia and South Vietnam.]

---

31.   Memorandum From Robert D. Hormats and Richard H. Solomon of the National Security Council Staff to the President's Assistant for National Security Affairs (Kissinger)[1]

Washington, May 3, 1973.

SUBJECT

Textiles and PRC

As you know, the Chinese recently responded to our March 22 memorandum on cotton textiles by indicating that it was unreasonable for us to ask them to restrain textile exports when such products were at a low level of importation and represented China's most important export to the U.S.[2] We responded (see the cable at Tab A) by indicating that the U.S. has no intention of discriminating against the PRC, but it does have equity obligations to other trading partners.[3] We said that our memorandum was intended to identify a problem which is developing—not to ask for PRC to take any action at this time—and that questions involved should be discussed in Washington after the PRC liaison office is established.

The *Chinese position* on this is understandable in light of the fact that PRC textile exports to the U.S. are in fact at a relatively low level—

---

[1] Source: National Archives, Nixon Presidential Materials, NSC Files, Box 527, Country Files, Far East, People's Republic of China, Vol. 7, May–Jul 9, 1973. Secret. Sent for action.

[2] Regarding the March 22 memorandum, see Document 19. Telegram 10468 from Paris, April 14, conveyed the Chinese response. (National Archives, RG 59, Central Foreign Policy Files, 1973)

[3] Tab A, telegram 75300 to Paris, April 21, is attached but not printed.

16 million square yards—compared with much higher levels of Japan, Hong Kong, Korea, and Thailand, etc. Moreover, China has purchased substantial amounts of U.S. products—about $90 million worth in 1972—while only exporting about half as much to the U.S. Thus, if the PRC is to move toward a trade balance, it believes increases in textile exports to the U.S. are necessary and should be permitted.

From *our point of view*, however, we have restrained cotton textile imports from other nations (many of whom are close to us politically). Some of these nations have already inquired as to why we have not restrained textiles from the PRC. Moreover, domestic textile producers have expressed concern to us that the U.S. Government's attempt to improve relations with the PRC will be at the expense of their interests. Thus, we continue to feel that it is necessary to work out some arrangement with the PRC which would limit imports to a reasonable level.

The *amount* at which we limit imports is a tricky issue. Under the Long-Term Arrangement on Cotton Textiles (LTA)—an agreement to which we and most textile exporting nations subscribe—there is a set formula which would determine this number based on how much was exported by the PRC in the period before restraints were imposed. If utilized *now* that formula would lead to a restraint level unacceptably low to the Chinese. If we were to waive the formula and agree to imports at a level substantially higher than that permitted under it, all other members of the agreement would complain.

The best way to handle this problem would be to discuss quietly with PRC representatives the issues we face but to delay on *formally* notifying them that we want them to restrain their textile imports until a sufficient base has been established so that the LTA formula would give them a high restraint level. In this way, although we would be neglecting our other trading partners by permitting the Chinese to import unreasonably large amounts of cotton textiles without applying the LTA, we could, once we do apply the LTA, adhere to its formula. From the PRC point of view, their exports next year would then be limited at a level sufficiently higher than they would be if we applied the formula today, and in subsequent years their textile exports could grow by a certain percentage about the 1974 base number.

Recommendation:

That we hold off on making any representations to the PRC on textiles until their mission in Washington is fully established and PRC textile exports have reached a substantially higher level.[4]

---

[4] Kissinger initialed the Approve option. According to an attached correspondence file, he approved the recommendation on May 25.

32.   Memorandum of Conversation[1]

Washington, May 15, 1973, 10:20–11:00 a.m.

PARTICIPANTS

Dr. Henry A. Kissinger, Assistant to the President for National Security Affairs
Winston Lord, NSC Staff
Han Hsu, Deputy Chief of the PRC Liaison Office
Chien Ta-yung, Official of the PRC Liaison Office
Chi Chiao Chu, Official of the PRC Liaison Office
Mr. Kuo, Official of the PRC Mission to the United Nations

[Before Dr. Kissinger arrived, Mr. Lord and the Chinese held informal conversation. Mr. Lord asked them if everything was going well and said that he had heard they had narrowed down their choices for a residence for their Liaison Office to a couple of places. The Chinese responded that things were going smoothly and confirmed that they had narrowed down their choices. Mr. Lord hoped they had some chance for sightseeing and relaxation, and Ambassador Han replied that they had not had to work too hard. They had been sightseeing on two occasions. Mr. Lord welcomed Mr. Kuo from New York and asked him if it was his first time to Washington. Mr. Kuo said that it was and that he had come on short notice just for a couple of days.

Mr. Kuo said that he had heard about Mr. Lord's departure from the staff from the newspapers. Mr. Lord confirmed this, and he noted that he had talked to Mrs. Shih about this and earlier to members of the Liaison Office. Mr. Lord reviewed the reasons for his leaving, namely, rest, reflection, recharge his batteries, and see more of his family. He reiterated that he would stay in the Washington area and hoped to see the Chinese on a personal basis. He said that he might be back in government some day, perhaps working for Dr. Kissinger, but that he needed to take a break at this point. If he did come back, he would then be all the more efficient. The Chinese repeated their regrets that Mr. Lord was leaving and their hope to see him on a private basis and inquired about his replacement. Mr. Lord responded that the staff was being somewhat reorganized and Dr. Kissinger was bringing in some good new people, but that in any event there would be continuity. He cited Messrs. Howe (temporarily), Rodman, and Solomon.

After ten minutes Dr. Kissinger arrived and the meeting began.]

---

[1] Source: National Archives, Nixon Presidential Materials, NSC Files, Kissinger Office Files, Box 94, Country Files, Far East, China Exchanges, April 15–May 15, 1973. Top Secret; Sensitive; Exclusively Eyes Only. The meeting took place in the Map Room of the White House. All brackets are in the original.

Dr. Kissinger: I'm sorry I'm late. I was with the President, and I could not get away. How is your search for housing progressing?

Ambassador Han: There's been some slight progress. The Skyline place has been ruled out.

Dr. Kissinger: You mean the one in Southwest?

Ambassador Han: Yes. The Ramada Inn is not bad.

Dr. Kissinger: Where is that?

Mr. Chi and Mr. Lord: Thomas Circle, on 14th Street.

Dr. Kissinger: Does it have some grounds?

Ambassador Han: There's a larger area than in the Embassy Row Apartments. There's a big swimming pool.

Dr. Kissinger: I will come for a swim. Has there been any progress in finding a residence?

Ambassador Han: No.

Dr. Kissinger: First, you are concentrating on finding an office and then the residence. I'm eager for your cook to arrive. (Laughter)

Ambassador Han: We are also hoping for an early arrival.

Dr. Kissinger: I am sure of that.

I appreciate your agreeing to see me here, Mr. Ambassador. It is very difficult for me to go to New York since I'm leaving tomorrow for Paris. I wanted the Prime Minister to have an account of our meeting. (Mr. Lord indicated to Dr. Kissinger while this was being translated that the Chinese wished to keep the meeting secret. They had told Mr. Lord this as they were walking from their car to the Map Room.) We can keep this meeting secret very easily. The entrance at this point of the White House is not known to the press. If you are seen, we will say that it concerned preparations for housing and technical things. But there is no possibility that it will be seen.

Ambassador Han: Our hope is that this meeting will be, as previous meetings, kept secret.

Dr. Kissinger: You can be sure that from our side there will be no discussion of it. Just on the one chance in a thousand that someone sees you drive out—this has never happened before—we will just say this is a routine visit connected with technical arrangements for housing. There's no possibility. I'm just protecting against the possible chance. I use this room for meetings when I do not want them to become known.

Let me talk about my visit to Moscow and my general impressions.[2] I spent four days in Zavidovo, which is the hunting lodge of

---

[2] Kissinger visited the Soviet Union May 4–9.

the Politburo. Most of my time was in conversations with General Secretary Brezhnev. First I'll talk to you about matters that concern the United States and the Soviet Union. Then let me talk about what we said concerning China. And then let me tell you what our policy is, because it is important that Peking and Washington understand each other completely.

First let me talk to you about the various drafts of the nuclear proposals that the Soviet Union has made to us. (He pulls out his folder.) We've given you every previous draft, and I have attached the last draft that the Soviet Union gave us, and where it stands now after discussion there. (Dr. Kissinger writes an addition on one of the attachments that he is about to hand over.)

Let me explain what we are trying to do. If we want to establish a condominium with the Soviet Union, we don't need a treaty. We've had many offers to that effect. If we want to gang up with China against the Soviet Union we don't need to make any arrangements, as I will explain to you later. What we are trying to do first of all is to gain some time. Secondly, to establish a legal obligation as between us and the Soviet Union that requires the Soviet Union to consult with us before taking any military acts, so if they do take any military actions without consulting us, they will have taken unilateral acts which gives us the basis for common action, which we do not now possess with regard to third countries. So what we have done in our discussions, which are not yet finally completed, is first of all to insist that any obligation that applies between us and the Soviet Union applies also between the Soviet Union and third countries. Secondly, that the objective of not using nuclear weapons can be realized only if there's a renunciation of the use of any force. Thirdly, any consultations that occur between us and the Soviet Union are confined to those cases where the two countries might go to war against each other or they might threaten a war against a third country. Thirdly (*sic*) where it says in the draft that nothing should impair existing agreements, etc., the Soviet Union wanted only to say when there are treaties and formal agreements, and we insisted that it should include "other appropriate instruments" such as letters and communiqués.

Ambassador Han: That's the fourth point.

Dr. Kissinger: Yes.

Ambassador Han: Nothing should impair . . . ?

Dr. Kissinger: (reading from the draft treaty) "Nothing in this agreement shall affect or impair the obligations undertaken by the United States and the Soviet Union toward their allies or other countries in treaties, agreements, and other appropriate instruments."

We have prepared a document on where this now stands with our explanation of what it means, for whatever views you want to express.

There are three basic objectives. First, to gain time. Secondly, to force the Soviet Union if it engages in military actions to do so out of a posture of peace rather than an atmosphere of tension. Thirdly, it gives us legal obligations for our position in case of countries where we don't have formal arrangements. (He hands over the annotated current draft and the previous version that the Chinese had seen, attached at Tab A).[3]

Mr. Chi: The second principle concerned . . . could you kindly repeat this?

Dr. Kissinger: We want to make sure that when the Soviet Union attacks it will be from a posture of relaxation of tension immediately to war, rather than from a prolonged period of tension which confuses the issue.

Of course, no one knows we are giving you this. The single-spaced part is our comment.

While talking on this subject, let me mention a discussion with Mr. Brezhnev that concerned China. Brezhnev took me hunting one day, which is a sport I have never engaged in (the Chinese smile). In fact he went hunting, and I just walked along. In the Soviet Union one hunts from the stand in the trees with the animals below, so it is not excessively dangerous. After the shooting was over Brezhnev had a picnic lunch brought in, and it was just he and I and one interpreter. In this conversation he expressed his extremely limited admiration of China. (Laughter from the Chinese.) And he is a somewhat less disciplined and controlled leader than your Prime Minister. That is not new. That has been done before.

But then he said the Soviet Union and the United States had a joint obligation to prevent China from becoming a big nuclear power. And he said, "do you consider China an ally?" I said, "no, we don't consider it an ally—we consider it a friend." He said, "well you can have any friends you want, but you and we should be partners"— he meant Moscow and Washington. He repeated again that we have a joint responsibility to prevent China from becoming a nuclear power. And I said we recognize no such joint responsibility. That was it, in effect. The rest was simply tirades about China which there is no sense in repeating—things like big power chauvinism, and as soon as you are strong enough you will also turn on us. That sort of thing, immaterial.

Then on the last day, I flew from that lodge to Moscow just to stop at our Embassy for 15 minutes, and I was accompanied by Dobrynin, their Ambassador here. He said that Brezhnev had asked him to make

---

[3] Attached but not printed.

sure that I understood that the conversation at the hunting stand was meant to be serious and not a social conversation. He said he wanted to know whether there existed a formal agreement between the People's Republic and the United States. I said there didn't exist any agreement, but there existed appropriate instruments which we took from this draft, and that in any event we will be guided by our national interest—which we had expressed in the President's Annual Report.[4]

These were all the conversations which concerned China . . . except every time we mentioned third countries here, Gromyko would say that we were acting as the lawyer for China. Our views remain exactly as expressed by me to the Chairman and the Prime Minister, and by the President in his letters to the Chairman and the Prime Minister.[5] We continue to believe that it should be the objectives of both our governments to continue to accelerate normalization to the point where it becomes clear that we have a stake in the strength and independence of the People's Republic.

I would be prepared, if the Prime Minister wanted, to come to Peking in August after the summit here in order to make a visit. It wouldn't have to be as long as previous visits because we've had basic talks. Maybe two days, or two or three days. If the Prime Minister—we mentioned this in New York once—were considering a visit to the United Nations, we would, of course, give him a very warm reception here in Washington, or if he would come only to Washington. Then we could announce that in the summer. But we could think of other measures to symbolize this.

I have a self-interest in this anyway because if those two things happen, Winston Lord would certainly come back from vacation. So you should also consider it from this wide perspective.

This is the general perspective. I also want to tell you that even though there are many changes in the staff, such as the departure of Winston Lord, there are also some compensations like the return of General Haig to the White House. And you can count on the continuity of our policy that we have been pursuing.

Those are the most important things from Moscow. Now I want to tell you a few minor things.

With respect to SALT, we do not foresee an agreement this year on anything except general principles. (To Lord) Did we give them our latest proposal?

---

[4] Nixon submitted the Fourth Annual Report on U.S. Foreign Policy to Congress on May 3. For text, see *Public Papers: Nixon, 1973*, pp. 348–518.

[5] See Documents 21 and 22.

Mr. Lord (to Kissinger): We gave them the Soviet proposal.

Dr. Kissinger: By the end of this week we will give you our proposal, so you know what is being discussed in Geneva.[6] We are working on this proposal this week. From my conversations in Moscow it's quite clear that there will be no concrete agreement except on general principles, and those principles are not yet worked out. When they are, we will show them to you. They will not be distinguished by excessive precision.

On MBFR there was practically no discussion except for the timing of negotiations later this year. We will also give you a summary of the position we are discussing with our allies. We have not yet discussed it with the Soviet Union. We will do that next week.

We are also preparing for the Summit a number of bilateral agreements of the same sort as last year—agricultural research, oceanography, cultural exchange, civil aviation.

On the economic side, it was simply another reiteration by the Soviet leaders of their need for long term credits.

Again, we want to repeat that anything we are prepared to do with the Soviet Union we are prepared to do with the People's Republic. And conversely, we may be prepared to do things with the People's Republic that we are not prepared to do with the Soviet Union.

Those are the major things I discussed in the Soviet Union.

As to the visit of Brezhnev, he will be here eight days.[7] He will spend five probably in Washington and two in Los Angeles or San Clemente. We haven't decided yet on some place in between, it may be Key Biscayne, it may be Detroit—he is crazy about automobiles.

You know I'm going to Paris on Thursday[8] to meet with—I can't call him Special Advisor anymore, he's the Deputy Prime Minister now (Laughter). Again I want to repeat what I've said to Ambassador Huang Hua and the Prime Minister, that it is really in the interest of all countries to bring about an observance of the ceasefire.

Let me say one thing about all the domestic excitement you find in the United States at this point. Once you are here for some time you will see that there are always fits of hysteria descending on Washington in which people talk about nothing else. And six months later it's

---

[6] On May 17, Lord reported, "The summary of our SALT proposal is going to the Chinese today." (Memorandum from Lord to Scowcroft; National Archives, Nixon Presidential Materials, NSC Files, Kissinger Office Files, Box 94, Country Files, Far East, China Exchanges, May 16–June 13, 1973)

[7] Leonid Brezhnev visited the United States June 16–25.

[8] May 17.

difficult to remember exactly all the details of the controversy. The conduct of foreign policy is unaffected, and may in fact be even slightly strengthened in some fields, because many of our opponents may even want to show how responsible they are. It will become clear within the next two months that control of foreign policy in the government is being strengthened.

So the lines laid down in the conversations in February in Peking were fixed and will be pursued with vigor, and I would not let the noise here in Washington be too distracting.

On Korea we would like to give you an answer in two weeks. Frankly I have not had time to prepare an adequate answer.[9]

Cotton textiles. You sent us a note. We've asked the agencies not to pursue this subject until your Ambassador comes here.[10] We have certain legal obligations imposed on us by the Congress. I can tell you now that if our relations are ever impaired it will not be because of cotton textiles. [laughter] This is an issue that will be easily settled.

I don't know whether the Ambassador has anything. [The Chinese discuss among themselves.]

Ambassador Han: I have two things I would like to take up with Dr. Kissinger. The first thing is that the day before yesterday, on the 13th, there was a demonstration here against us in which, according to reports, they burned the national flag.

Dr. Kissinger: We regret this deeply. It is inexcusable. We will do the maximum permitted under law to prevent this. We cannot prevent demonstrations in authorized places. We will do our best to minimize these incidents. And when we can physically stop them, we will, of course, stop them. I know I express the view of the President and the whole U.S. Government when I speak of our regret over this incident.

Ambassador Han: Another thing—this is a minor matter. The American columnist, Mr. Marquis W. Childs, he is in Peking now, and he told our people that Dr. Kissinger suggested that he call on the Premier.

Dr. Kissinger: I'm a great admirer of the Premier and therefore I always think it is of benefit for someone to see him. I think Marquis Childs is basically so well disposed toward China and so eager to be helpful that it might be in your interest if the Prime Minister saw him. He will certainly write very favorably, and is socially well-connected

---

[9] According to Kissinger's briefing to the President of this meeting with Chinese diplomats, "just before you left for Moscow, the Chinese asked us for our scenario on abolishing UNCURK in two steps during the latter half of this year, and we said that we would respond to their inquiry later." (National Archives, Nixon Presidential Materials, NSC Files, Kissinger Office Files, Box 94, Country Files, Far East, China Exchanges, April 15–May 15, 1973)

[10] See Document 31.

so that what he brings back will be very positive. But except for this I have no personal interest. If the Prime Minister is too busy it would not be considered a personal affront to me. (There is discussion among the Chinese.)

Ambassador Han: About keeping this meeti ıg secret from the press. If in the one of a dozen possibilities we were seen as you mentioned . . .

Dr. Kissinger: I won't say anything. I will deny that I saw you.

Ambassador Han: . . . We will say that it was an ordinary call and in addition to an ordinary call we will say that we expressed our regret over the incident on the 13th.

Dr. Kissinger: That is fine. That is all right. We should not look for an opportunity to say anything. (laughter) There is practically no chance of your being seen. (To Mr. Lord) Correct?

Mr. Lord: That's right.

Dr. Kissinger: I'm glad to see my old friend (Mr. Kuo). I hope the Ambassador will come here.

Mr. Kuo: I came on very short notice.

Dr. Kissinger: I know about the system—we will work it out.

Mr. Chi: Mr. Solomon and Mr. Romberg are working this out.

[There was some more light talk during which Dr. Kissinger said that U.S. policy wouldn't change with Mr. Lord's absence although it would be less efficient. He was counting on Mr. Lord's getting bored on the outside and also on the good sense of his Chinese wife.]

Dr. Kissinger: I saw that Ambassador Bruce arrived yesterday. We need to expand our office since 10,000 Americans want to work there. [laughter]

You still don't know when your Ambassador arrives?

Ambassador Han: There is still no news. As soon as we do know, we will let you know. Mr. Solomon asked Mr. Chi whether the Ambassador might come while you are in Paris. [Dr. Kissinger indicates puzzlement.]

Ambassador Han: We have no news. He was just wondering if the Ambassador might come while you were away.

Dr. Kissinger: Whenever he does come he will be highly welcomed. Of course, the President will see him very soon after his arrival.

Ambassador Han: We are looking forward to that.

Dr. Kissinger: It is always a pleasure to see our friends. I will leave first and separately so that you can leave more discreetly.

[There were then cordial farewells. Mr. Lord checked to make sure that there were no people around to notice the Chinese departure. There was a brief discussion in which Mr. Lord told the Chinese that they should contact Mr. Lord the next day or two, and after that, Mr. Howe. Mr. Lord again indicated he was looking forward to seeing the Chinese on a personal basis. He asked Mr. Kuo to give his warm regards to Ambassador Huang Hua and Mrs. Shih in New York. There were then very warm farewells as Mr. Lord escorted the Chinese to their limousine waiting at the diplomatic entrance.]

---

33.   Memorandum of Conversation[1]

Beijing, May 18, 1973.

PARTICIPANTS

Chou En-lai, Premier of the State Council
Ch'iao Kuan-hua, Vice Foreign Minister
Huang Chen, Chief, PRCLO
Chu Ch'uan-hsien, Acting Director, Ministry of Foreign Affairs' Department of Protocol
Lin P'ing, Director of the Department of American and Oceanian Affairs, MFA
T'ang Wen-sheng, MFA Interpreter
Shen Jo-yun, Notetaker
Lien Cheng-pao, Notetaker

David K. E. Bruce, Chief, U.S. Liaison Office
Alfred le S. Jenkins, Deputy Chief, U.S. Liaison Office
John H. Holdridge, Deputy Chief, U.S. Liaison Office
Nicholas Platt, Chief, Political Section, U.S. Liaison Office

Introduction

Premier Chou began the conversation by asking whether Ambassador Bruce had met Ambassador Huang Chen prior to coming to China. Ambassador Bruce replied that he had not had the opportunity. Although Ambassador Huang had been in Paris while he was there, his own work had been concentrated on the negotiations with the North Vietnamese.

Ambassador Bruce told Premier Chou what a great pleasure it was to meet him, and assured the Premier that he, Chou, had a great num-

---

[1] Source: National Archives, Nixon Presidential Materials, NSC Files, Box 527, Country Files, Far East, People's Republic of China, Vol. 7, May, 1973–Jul 9, 1973. Secret; Nodis. The meeting took place in the Great Hall of People. The USLO sent this memorandum of conversation as an attachment to airgram 9 from Beijing, May 21. The USLO also sent a cable reporting the substance of this conversation. (Telegram 121 from Beijing, May 19, 0500Z; ibid.)

ber of admirers in the United States. Premier Chou asked after President Nixon's health, and Ambassador Bruce replied that the President was in excellent health, unaffected by certain domestic difficulties. Chou replied that such domestic difficulties frequently arise in the course of American political life.

Sino-U.S. Negotiations

Premier Chou then asked after Dr. Kissinger, commenting that he was a very busy man and remembering with a smile that he had once been able to disappear for a few days on a mission of which even the CIA was unaware. Ambassador Bruce answered that Kissinger's first trip to Peking was one of the best kept secrets in the history of international relations, as was the decision to establish Liaison Offices in the two capitals. The negotiations, he continued, were carried on in the grand manner, quietly, in a way quite different from any other negotiations.

Premier Chou replied with satisfaction that outside observers could not believe the fact of the Sino-U.S. negotiations because, prisoners of old attitudes and behavior patterns, they could not imagine relations between the two countries could develop so quickly. He believed that the secrecy was essential, because major policy changes require careful preparations and prior consideration. Ambassador Bruce replied that in the United States there was a tendency and an ambition in the press and the media to attempt to formulate foreign policy. The Premier agreed, adding that Congress was also influenced by the media at times. Sometimes unwisely, Ambassador Bruce interjected.

Premier Chou said that the Chinese Government paid great attention to the world press, particularly in the United States and Japan. The two internal reference digests published and circulated each day within the Chinese Government stressed articles from the U.S. press first, Japanese materials next, and then articles from Europe. Soviet press materials received the least attention because they were so repetitious and abusive.

Columnists

Premier Chou said that the journalist Marquis Childs had requested an interview, and asked Ambassador Bruce's advice. Marquis Childs had been a friend for 25 years, the Ambassador replied, which prejudiced his view, but he knew Childs to be trustworthy and intelligent.[2] Premier Chou said that he had heard some of Childs' views were the same as those of columnist Joseph Alsop. Ambassador Bruce replied

---

[2] Marquis Childs visited China later in the month and wrote two columns about his conversations with Zhou. ("A Conversation With Chou En-lai," *The Washington Post*, May 25, p. A31; "Talking With Chou En-lai," ibid., May 26, p. A19)

that there were marked differences between the two writers. Premier Chou then said the PRC had invited Walter Lippmann to visit but had heard that his health was poor and that he used a pacemaker for his heart. Ambassador Bruce said that a visit to China would be a very happy thing for Lippmann at his age and at the end of a distinguished writing career. Lippmann was an exceptionally intelligent observer, an old friend in every sense and perhaps the most admired columnist in America in a profession noted for jealousy. Lippmann has strong personal convictions and has been wrong from time to time, but this was a fault we all shared, the Ambassador concluded. Strong convictions were a good thing, Chou replied. Ambassador Bruce ventured that it would be rather difficult to converse with Mr. Lippmann because he was very deaf. Chou replied that the interpreter would simply have to shout. Ambassador Bruce replied that if Lippmann had a pacemaker for his heart, he could probably install a hearing aid for his ear. On balance, however, Chou said, he thought it would be difficult for Lippmann to make the trip, and doubtful that he would come.

"Your ears are very keen, Mr. Ambassador," Chou said. "They hear what they want to hear, sir," Ambassador Bruce replied. There followed a brief discussion on accents around the room involving the other members of the two delegations.

The Shanghai Communiqué

Premier Chou then asked Ambassador Bruce his plans for mission activities. Ambassador Bruce replied that he was prepared to discuss any substantive questions of mutual interest. Chou replied that if Ambassador Bruce had any ideas or views to put forward he should contact Vice Minister Ch'iao Kuan-hua. It was Ch'iao who had finalized the Shanghai Communiqué. Ambassador Bruce said he understood it had taken a long time to finish the Communiqué. Chou replied that though agreement in principle had been reached during Kissinger's trip in October 1971, differences over wording continued to exist until February of 1972 in Shanghai. Since the Communiqué had been formulated in such a careful and painstaking way, we should exert vigorous efforts to implement it. Ambassador Bruce agreed that the Communiqué was a document of great importance.

Premier Chou said that the Communiqué represented a new style for such documents in that it stated the different positions of both sides, then listed areas of agreement. Ambassador Bruce replied that this was an excellent innovation. He had grown weary of reading empty communiqués which simply said that talks between the two sides had been carried on in a friendly atmosphere and then ended. At international conferences he had attended during his younger days, he had found it ridiculous that the final communiqués had been drafted and approved before the meetings began. Chou replied that the standard communiqués were empty documents not designed for implementation, but that we had done it differently and very earnestly. It was important and necessary, he continued, that the common points agreed on in the Shanghai Communiqué be carried out speedily.

Indochina

Chou then spoke of Indochina, hoping Dr. Kissinger would succeed in his negotiations with Le Duc Tho at Paris. Ambassador Bruce assured Chou that no one desired success in this endeavor more than the President. Chou observed that "to drag out" the negotiations would have a bad effect on the general situation and on mutual progress on other issues. Ambassador Bruce agreed that the issues must be settled so that the Governments concerned could move to other problems. Chou mentioned the problem Viet-Nam had already posed for satisfactory PRC–U.S. relations, a matter which he had frequently called to Dr. Kissinger's attention.

He then asked Ambassador Bruce to tell the President that "the Democratic Republic of Viet-Nam and the Provisional Revolutionary Government of South Viet-Nam ardently wish to comply with all the clauses of the Agreement. It is necessary for the situation in the South to stabilize before the political negotiations can proceed. The North must also have time to recover."

Cambodia

Shifting the conversation to Cambodia, Chou said that the only way to find a solution was for the parties concerned to implement fully all the subsidiary clauses of Article 20.[3] Ambassador Bruce replied that the United States Government is thoroughly in accord and feels an overwhelming necessity to bring the issue to a close. He knew personally that the President is devoted to this purpose. Chou hoped that Dr. Kissinger's talks in Paris would find a way to settle the Cambodian problem. If this was not possible then "we should discuss the issue later." Although our stands are different, he continued, we share the hope for a peaceful, independent and neutral Cambodia. Ambassador Bruce replied that all countries involved share this goal. "More peaceful, neutral and independent than ever before," the Premier added. Though some countries may say they support this goal, they do not always act this way, he continued.

Chou expressed concern that the Cambodian issue might be submerged due to President Nixon's concentration on summit meetings with Pompidou and Brezhnev during June. Ambassador Bruce assured

---

[3] Article 20 of the Paris Peace Accords, signed on January 27, addressed military activities in Cambodia and Laos.

the Premier that the June meetings would not detract from the primacy that the President ascribed to the achievement of a settlement in Indochina. Chou then noted that Ambassador Huang would leave Peking May 25 and arrive in Washington by June 1. He invited the Ambassador to pass to Ch'iao Kuan-hua ideas the U.S. might wish to convey before then. Any further Chinese ideas would be passed by Huang Chen in Washington.

The Premier then asked whether Ambassador Bruce had ever met Prince Sihanouk. Ambassador Bruce replied that he had not. Chou said that he had considered Sihanouk's visit to Angkor a courageous and marvelous act. He went with his wife only and had no forces to protect him. Premier Chou was convinced that Sihanouk was the only person who could unify Cambodia and cited in support of this position the views of Senator Mansfield, and the Sirik Matak *New York Times* interview predicting that Sihanouk would win over Lon Nol in a referendum.[4] In an aside, Chou complained that the *New York Times* had recently carried an advertisement favoring the Chiang Government in Taiwan[5] which the PRC had formally protested. The reply which the PRC had received was that the *New York Times* printed "everything". Ambassador Bruce reminded Premier Chou that the *Times'* motto was "all the news that's fit to print", but they sometimes exercised bad judgment in the interpretation of the motto.

Chou told Ambassador Bruce that he had received the mistaken impression that Senator Mansfield was being designated by the U.S. Administration to mediate the Cambodia issue last year. Ambassador Bruce replied that under the American system members of Congress could not mediate on behalf of the Executive Branch. Private citizens were sometimes given special appointments to handle international problems, but never members of the Legislature. Members of the Congress have the freedom to express themselves "at any length", to block the Executive by refusing to appropriate funds, and to appeal to the public. But the primacy of the Executive Branch in foreign policy is guaranteed by the Constitution. The President can veto legislation but the Senate can override his veto with a two-thirds majority. Conflicts between the Executive and Legislative branches on foreign policy matters, Ambassador Bruce continued, have led in the past to some tragic mistakes. He cited Woodrow Wilson's experience with the Senate over the Fourteen Points as evidence. Chou En-lai noted that both he and Ambassador Bruce were in middle school when that happened.

---

[4] See "Ousted Cambodian Premier Speaks Out," *The New York Times*, March 24.

[5] See the advertisement "Foreign Trade of the Republic of China Surpasses That of Chinese Mainland," ibid., January 21.

Ambassador Bruce asked the Premier whether Prince Sihanouk had reported any damage to the temples of Angkor Wat. While there had been some minor damage, Chou replied, the temples were largely intact. The films and movies Prince Sihanouk had brought back proved this. Prince Sihanouk, he continued, is an artist at heart. He had shown Chou some beautiful shots that the Prince had taken at dawn in Angkor with his wife in the foreground.

The conversation ended with further expressions of welcome on Chou's part, a brief discussion of the weather, and a final invitation for Ambassador Bruce to contact Vice Foreign Minister Ch'iao Kuan-hua on any questions.

34.   Memorandum for the President's File by the President's Assistant for National Security Affairs (Kissinger)[1]

Washington, May 30, 1973, 9:15–9:30 a.m.

SUBJECT

The President's Meeting with Ambassador Huang Chen, Chief of PRC Liaison Office in Washington

PARTICIPANTS

The President
Ambassador Huang Chen
Dr. Henry A. Kissinger

The President greeted Ambassador Huang Chen. The Ambassador said he wanted to thank the President for the friendly reception. He brought with him best wishes from Mr. and Mrs. Mao, and Mr. and Mrs. Chou En-lai. The President thanked him, and said he wanted the Ambassador to convey his personal messages to Chairman Mao and to Premier Chou En-lai.

Dr. Kissinger had had sensitive talks with the Chairman and the Premier, the President noted, especially as the Brezhnev talks might

---

[1] Source: National Archives, Nixon Presidential Materials, NSC Files, Kissinger Office Files, Box 94, Country Files, Far East, China Exchanges, May 16–June 13, 1973. Top Secret; Sensitive; Exclusively Eyes Only. A tape of this conversation, which took place in the Oval Office, is ibid., White House Tapes, Conversation No. 930–7. Nixon saw talking points prepared on May 29 by Kissinger prior to the meeting. (Ibid., NSC Files, Kissinger Office Files, Box 94, Country Files, Far East, China Exchanges, May 16–June 13, 1973)

affect third parties. Dr. Kissinger had told Huang Chen we were prepared to reach an understanding about consultations. His statements reflected U.S. policy. If the Premier and Chairman Mao approved, we were prepared to make a more formal understanding on these points.[2]

Our commitment to better relations with the PRC was made, the President stressed. People who knew the President well knew that his commitment, when made, was solid. Good relations with the People's Republic of China were in the self-interest of the United States. Our self-interest required an independent and strong China. It was a cornerstone of U.S. policy to see that action was taken for the strength of China. A meeting was coming up with Brezhnev; the important thing was that there would be eight days of conversations.[3] But nothing would be agreed to that in any way would be detrimental to the People's Republic of China. The President had talked to Dr. Kissinger and instructed him to keep the Ambassador fully informed.

The other point the President wished to make to the Ambassador concerned the Southeast Asian situation. The Vietnam peace agreement removed a major irritant in our relations. But there was one outstanding problem, that is Cambodia. He could not emphasize too much the importance of reaching a settlement in Cambodia similar to that in Laos. Now China played a very important role. It would be a tragedy if we allowed Cambodia to flare up and reopen the conflict all over Indochina. The President wanted to emphasize that the United States was not committed to any one man. But there could not be peace at the point of a gun—on either side. We wanted a settlement that let the warring elements live together. Over a period of time the Cambodian people could determine which is better for their future. The highest priority, the President reiterated, was to work out some sort of peace agreement in Cambodia.[4]

---

[2] On May 27, Huang Hua gave Kissinger a note that asserted that the latest Soviet draft of the "Agreement on the Prevention of Nuclear War" was unacceptable because it "still aims at the establishment of U.S.-Soviet nuclear hegemony over the world." (Ibid.) Two days later, during a meeting that began at 6 p.m., Kissinger told Huang Zhen, "We would be prepared to consider some joint declaration that neither of us will engage in any negotiation against the other or that neither of us will join in any agreement without consultation with the other." (Ibid.)

[3] Brezhnev arrived in the United States on June 16 and the summit began on June 18.

[4] During their meeting on May 27, Kissinger told Huang Hua of the U.S. determination to stabilize the situation in Cambodia. (Memorandum of conversation, May 27, 10:00–11:15 a.m.; National Archives, Nixon Presidential Materials, NSC Files, Kissinger Office Files, Box 94, Country Files, Far East, China Exchanges, May 16–June 13, 1973)

Political Turmoil in the United States, June 1973–September 1974

35. Conversation Between President Nixon and his Assistant for National Security Affairs (Kissinger)[1]

Washington, June 4, 1973.

Nixon: With regard to Mao, you know, that is quite significant, don't you think?[2]

Kissinger: Oh, I think that's of enormous significance, Mr. President.

Nixon: The other thing I was going to say, though, that—

Kissinger: Because it means that they think that they are going to deal with you for the foreseeable future.

Nixon: Right. The other thing is do you think that we should get in—well we can't do it before you leave—but if you could get a message to the Ambassador here that we think it's very important for Chou En-lai to come to the UN. Or do you want to wait till August to do that?

Kissinger: I've already done that, Mr. President.

Nixon: You have?

Kissinger: I did that—

Nixon: You see—

Kissinger: I took the liberty of doing that in response—[3]

Nixon: You see, it's going to look rather strange if I go running to China if he doesn't come here.

Kissinger: No, I've already done that.

Nixon: How'd you do it?

Kissinger: I had already extended an invitation at your suggestion a few months ago.

---

[1] Source: National Archives, Nixon Presidential Materials, White House Tapes, Conversation No. 39–87. No classification marking. The editor transcribed the portions of the conversation printed here specifically for this volume. According to the President's Daily Diary, Nixon met with Kissinger from 11:16 until 11:22 p.m. (Ibid., White House Central Files)

[2] Nixon is referring to a statement that Huang Zhen gave Kissinger that afternoon, indicating "Chairman Mao welcomes President Nixon to visit China at an appropriate time." (Memorandum of conversation, June 4, 3–3:30 p.m.; ibid., NSC Files, Kissinger Office Files, Box 94, Country Files, Far East, China Exchanges, May 16–June 13, 1973)

[3] Kissinger told Huang Zhen that Zhou "has a standing invitation from the President and we would be pleased to welcome him, either on a visit to Washington or in combination with a visit he may take to New York." (Ibid.)

Nixon: Yeah, I know, but recently?

Kissinger: I repeated it and I said we can do it in one of two ways: either to go to the UN, or better yet just come to Washington on a personal visit.

Nixon: No, what he should do is come to the UN and then drop down here and we'll give him a nice dinner, you know, without the head of state thing, but it will be everything except the drill.

Kissinger: Right. Well, I told him we could handle it either way. And—

Nixon: And he's going to forward that to them, huh?

Kissinger: And he said—well, he didn't turn it down. You know, in the past they said they could never do it as long as the ROC was—

Nixon: Yeah, I know. I know. Yeah.

Kissinger: He said, well he's very busy and he'll look at his calendar.

Nixon: Well in view of the Mao thing, you see, the Mao thing has to be significant, because if it came from Chou En-lai that would be one thing, but coming from Mao—

Kissinger: It came from both. It was a joint invitation.

Nixon: Right.

Kissinger: And I don't know whether you noticed, Mr. President, when he came that he said to you, "Mr. and Mrs. Mao."

Nixon: Yeah! Yeah, I know.

Kissinger: Well, that was very significant considering her role in the Cultural Revolution.

Nixon: Yeah, and as a member of the Central Committee.

Kissinger: Yes, and of the Politburo.

Nixon: Politburo, I meant. Yeah. Yeah.

Kissinger: So I thought it was an extremely significant event.

Nixon: Yeah.

Kissinger: And also that they answered you within three days. I mean, you only saw him last Wednesday.[4]

Nixon: Right. Right.

Kissinger: And they also gave us a rather good message on Cambodia.[5]

---

[4] See Document 34.

[5] The message about Cambodia that Huang read to Kissinger earlier that day is in National Archives, Nixon Presidential Materials, NSC Files, Kissinger Office Files, Box 94, Country Files, Far East, China Exchanges, May 16–June 13, 1973.

Nixon: Oh, did they?

Kissinger: Yes, but we mustn't refer to that it in any sense.

Nixon: Oh, no, no, no. Because they can't get caught at it, I know.

[Omitted here is discussion unrelated to China.]

---

36.   Editorial Note

On June 13, 1973, Henry Kissinger, the President's Assistant for National Security Affairs, visited Ji Pengfei, the Chinese Minister of Foreign Affairs, at the residence of the Chinese Ambassador in Paris. Kissinger requested that the Chinese Government assist American efforts to stabilize the situation in Cambodia, but Ji replied that he could do little until Prince Norodom Sihanouk, head of the Cambodian Government in exile, returned to Beijing. A memorandum of conversation of the meeting is in National Archives, Nixon Presidential Materials, NSC Files, Kissinger Office Files, Box 94, Country Files, Far East, China Exchanges, May 16–June 13, 1973.

The following day, June 14, Kissinger met in his White House office with Huang Zhen, Chief of the PRC Liaison Office in the United States. Kissinger gave Huang a memorandum that explained U.S. support for the dissolution of the United Nations Commission for the Unification and Rehabilitation of Korea (UNCURK) and the decision to postpone discussion of the future of the United Nations Command. (Memorandum from Kennedy to Kissinger, June 14; ibid., Box 99, Country Files, Far East, PRC–UNCURK/UNC)

On the subject of Southeast Asia, Kissinger remarked, "We can't reiterate enough that the key element in Indochina is now Cambodia, and everything else will be easy once that is settled." Kissinger also described the agenda for the upcoming summit with Brezhnev, which was to begin on June 18. Concerning the Strategic Arms Limitation Talks, Kissinger stated that there would be an "agreement on the principles," but no "concrete agreement." Kissinger also addressed the Chinese Government's displeasure with U.S.-Soviet plans for an "Agreement on the Prevention of Nuclear War." Two weeks earlier, the Chinese Government had decried this agreement as an attempt to establish a "U.S.-Soviet nuclear hegemony." (See footnote 2, Document 34.) Kissinger noted, "We have decided to proceed [with the agreement] even though we take your views extremely seriously. It is important for you to understand our position. If we want to establish hegemony with the Soviet Union, we don't need an agreement. We have many offers without an agreement." (Memorandum of conversation; National Archives, Nixon Presidential Materials, NSC Files, Kissinger Office Files, Box 95, Country Files, Far East, China Exchanges, June 14–July 9, 1973)

In response to Kissinger's position, Huang produced a note from the Chinese Government rejecting the proposed U.S.–PRC accord requiring the two countries to consult each other before engaging in negotiations that could affect the other nation. Kissinger and Nixon had suggested such an accord in order to alleviate Chinese concern over U.S.-Soviet cooperation in the prevention of nuclear war. (See footnote 2, Document 34.) The Chinese note stated, "the joint declaration proposed by Dr. Kissinger on May 29 does not go beyond the scopes [sic] of the Shanghai Communiqué in principle, but on the contrary would, in effect, provide the Soviet Union with a pretext to peddle its bilateral agreements and Asian security system." (National Archives, Nixon Presidential Materials, NSC Files, Kissinger Office Files, Box 95, Country Files, Far East, China Exchanges, June 14–July 9, 1973)

---

37.   Memorandum of Conversation[1]

Washington, June 19, 1973, 10–10:50 a.m.

PARTICIPANTS

> Ambassador Huang Chen, Chief, PRC Liaison Office, Washington
> Han Hsu, Deputy Chief, PRC Liaison Office
> Chi Chiao-chu, Interpreter
>
> Dr. Henry A. Kissinger, Assistant to the President for National Security Affairs
> Lawrence S. Eagleburger, Deputy Assistant to the President for National Security Operations
> Peter W. Rodman, NSC Staff

Huang Chen: You are very busy.

Dr. Kissinger: With your allies here! We took out three paragraphs of a speech he wanted to make last night. I will show them to you.

---

[1] Source: National Archives, Nixon Presidential Materials, NSC Files, Kissinger Office Files, Box 95, Country Files, Far East, China Exchanges, June 14–July 9, 1973. Top Secret; Sensitive; Exclusively Eyes Only. The meeting was held in Kissinger's office at the White House. All brackets are in the original.

[These were later delivered to the Ambassador. Tab A][2] He wanted to attack countries who were opposed to the improvement of US-Soviet relations, because it showed warlike intentions. We told him he couldn't criticize third countries in the White House.

[Dr. Kissinger then hands over an autographed picture of the President and Huang Chen, signed by the President.]

Huang Chen: Thank you.

Dr. Kissinger: We have yesterday asked Ambassador Bruce to request an appointment with the Prime Minister, and we have asked him to deliver a letter to the Prime Minister, which we telegraphed to him. And I wanted to give you the original of the letter. Why don't you read it? And if you have any questions, I can explain it to you. [He hands over the letter at Tab B.[3] The Ambassador examines it.]

I knew the Ambassador was learning English!

Huang Chen: It is progressing slowly.

Dr. Kissinger: Oh, really. How is your search for a house coming?

Huang Chen: Han Hsu can tell you.

Han Hsu: We have been looking at a large building and apartment house north of 16th Street.

Dr. Kissinger: Near the Soviet Embassy!

Han Hsu: No, much further north. Past the bridge.

[Chi then translates the letter for the Ambassador.]

Dr. Kissinger: Notice I am on a one-man campaign to change the Premier's title [to Prime Minister]. It is because I can't pronounce Premier. It is the Assistant Minister's fault; he gave him the title in Yenan. [Chi translates the letter.] And we have asked Ambassador Bruce to hand the telegraphic copy to the Prime Minister. We sent it last night. In case he has any questions.

But I think we have stated our policy here quite clearly.

Huang Chen: It is very clear.

Dr. Kissinger: And we consider that an obligation.

Huang Chen: And I believe Ambassador Bruce will see the Premier today.

Dr. Kissinger: I am amazed by your communications. I cannot find out what Eagleburger does in 24 hours.

---

[2] Attached but not printed. Tab A is a copy of Brezhnev's speech on the evening of June 18. The three paragraphs, which criticized those who cast aspersions on U.S.-Soviet cooperation, were delivered with a covering letter from Scowcroft to the PRCLO on June 19. (Ibid.)

[3] Document 38.

Huang Chen: Your communications are very rapid.

Dr. Kissinger: Yours seems to be extremely efficient. Another thing that impresses me in China is that one is in a continuous conversation. Anything one says—first of all, the Prime Minister knows about it, and second, it is likely to be answered by another Chinese. [Laughter]

Huang Chen: We have the practice of what you call briefing. Don't you have this, this briefing of correspondents?

Dr. Kissinger: Yes, but we don't do it so elegantly. Once, when I first took Jenkins there, the Prime Minister came to visit the Guest House within one-half hour of our arrival, and he already knew about the house Jenkins had stayed in twenty years ago and whether it was still standing.

When I write my biography, I will ask for the Chinese file on me. It is probably better than my own.

Huang Chen: If Dr. Kissinger agrees, I would like to give you a message from our Government. [Tab C][4]

Dr. Kissinger: If I don't like it I won't give you this one! [referring to UNCURK note in his hand]

[The Ambassador hands over the note at Tab C, and Dr. Kissinger reads it.]

Dr. Kissinger: They are doing to you what they are trying to do to us.

We appreciate the communication. And it is within the spirit of our mutual consultation. And I will keep you fully informed about our discussions here, and I will talk to you in a minute about them.

I have a paper on the Korean situation. [He hands over note on UNCURK/UNC at Tab D.][5] Let me fix one word. [He takes it back, crosses out phrase in fourth paragraph.] It is not "at least."

[Chi translates the note for the Ambassador.]

Specifically, Mr. Ambassador, to make it slightly more concrete, we are prepared to bring about the termination of UNCURK during the 1973 UN General Assembly and the United Nations Command by the session of the 1974 General Assembly.

Han Hsu: You handed me another note on the 14th.[6] This one is more specific.

---

[4] Attached but not printed. Tab C is a message from the Chinese Government about the Soviet Union's proposed "Treaty of Non-Aggression Between the Union of the Soviet Socialist Republics and the People's Republic of China."

[5] Attached but not printed.

[6] See Document 36.

Dr. Kissinger: Yes. This is an elaboration of the other one. The other one was more preliminary.

Also, we have reason to believe the Seoul Government would be prepared to establish some contacts with your government, and if we can be helpful in this respect we are willing to do this. At the same time, to the extent that you have contacts with Seoul, we are prepared to have this with Pyongyang.

Huang Chen: We will report this to our Government.

What you said about the termination of UNCURK this year and of the UNC next year, it is not in here [in the note].

Dr. Kissinger: It is an elaboration. And we will encourage the Government of South Korea to make some of these proposals publicly, in the near future. Not about the United Nations Command.

One other matter, about Senator Mansfield's visit to the People's Republic. Everything being equal, we would prefer it if he came after I have been to Peking.

Huang Chen: That is up to you, to your convenience.

Dr. Kissinger: It is up to your skill in managing. You can do it more tactfully than I can!

Huang Chen: Last Thursday, when Senators Mansfield and Scott invited me to lunch, they said they had invited Dr. Kissinger but Dr. Kissinger had not been able to attend.

Dr. Kissinger: I had just returned from Paris.

Huang Chen: Senator Mansfield mentioned this. He said there were various factors involved.

Dr. Kissinger: We are in favor of his going.

Huang Chen: Didn't you speak with him?

Dr. Kissinger: He mentioned last night that he was thinking of August. Why don't you just schedule it after mine?

Huang Chen: Have you preliminarily decided on the date of your visit?

Dr. Kissinger: Would you like a proposal? We will do it soon. I will make a proposal within a week. Maybe when you come to San Clemente. [Laughter]

I want to tell your Prime Minister that if by the time I get to Peking a ceasefire exists in Cambodia, I would be prepared to meet Prince Sihanouk to have political discussions. But it should not be announced in advance.

Huang Chen: I will convey this view of yours to the Prime Minister. In talking about the visit of Senator Mansfield, you mentioned the interest of Senator Jackson. We welcome him to go but we would welcome him to go with the present Congressional delegation.

Dr. Kissinger: I think the Prime Minister and Senator Jackson will get along very well. Another person who would like to go, whom the Prime Minister and I discussed, is Govenor Rockefeller of New York.

Chi Chiao-chu: Nelson Rockefeller.

Dr. Kissinger: Yes. David you know.

Huang Chen: I invited his brother to lunch.

Dr. Kissinger: He may be an important factor in 1976.

Huang Chen: David Rockefeller, at a luncheon with me, said his house in Maine is near Ambassador Watson's house.

Dr. Kissinger: That is right.

Huang Chen: Ambassador Watson has invited me to visit Maine. So Mr. David Rockefeller invited me to visit him in Maine if I come to visit Watson in August. I don't know whether I can visit Maine in August because I don't know whether our housing situation will be solved by then.

On this subject, I would like to come to your suggestion. We have so far called upon various people in Washington, according to a list provided by the State Department. We called upon Senators Mansfield and Scott, the Vice President, and we will call on the Secretaries of Finance and Agriculture. So far there are many other friends who would like to contact us, but we have had to say we are busy. We would like to ask your advice of which friends we should visit.

Dr. Kissinger: Do you have a list? We can give you our suggestions. Or we can give you our recommendations. In 48 hours.

Huang Chen: There is no need for such a hurry.

Dr. Kissinger: We will do it. But you are of course free to see anybody you like.

When you speak of friends, do you mean private people or people in government?

Huang Chen: In government, or members of Congress or the Senate, or well-known personages.

Dr. Kissinger: We will make a list of recommendations for you.

Huang Chen: As for the list provided by the State Department, we told it to General Scowcroft over the phone.

Then about the call on the Vice President. I would like to tell you that the Vice President gave us a very friendly reception but didn't mention his wish to visit China as had been indicated by General Dunn.

Dr. Kissinger: We would like to defer that until we have settled the time of the visit by the President—and of the visit of the Prime Minister to America. [Laughter]

Huang Chen: These are all questions we should discuss in August.

Dr. Kissinger: Maybe he should come on a secret visit. [Laughter]

Huang Chen: As I told Dr. Kissinger some time ago, as of my departure from Peking the Prime Minister had no plans to go abroad.

Dr. Kissinger: I understand. Have you any decision on whether you can visit us in San Clemente?

Huang Chen: Personally speaking, of course I would be happy to have the chance to visit you. But there still is some time.

Dr. Kissinger: Of course. You can let us know. It would be better for us, actually, the week after next.

Huang Chen: The week after next. The beginning or the middle?

Dr. Kissinger: It is up to you. Next week the French Foreign Minister will visit me in San Clemente.

Huang Chen: Jobert.

Dr. Kissinger: Jobert. You know him! Very cynical and very intelligent. We are counting on the Prime Minister to help us with the European program when Pompidou comes [to Peking] in September.

Huang Chen: Mr. Pompidou is coming here? Or to China?

Dr. Kissinger: China.

Huang Chen: Many questions will be discussed.

Dr. Kissinger: On the meeting with Brezhnev, I don't know whether you know him, but he doesn't have the same precision of mind as your Prime Minister. So the President asked him yesterday if he wanted to make any opening remarks. He started, and 2½ hours later he said he would make a brief conclusion, and then ½ hour later he finished his opening remarks. [Laughter] And they were very emotional and very general. And really less precise than what I had already told you from Zavidovo.

His basic strategy is to attempt to prove there are no differences left between the United States and the Soviet Union and that there is total solidarity on a global basis.

Huang Chen: So he thinks there is a relationship of partnership, as he said.

Dr. Kissinger: That is the impression he is trying to create. But that is not our policy. On very practical grounds it makes no sense to support the stronger against the weaker. And we will not do anything practical to support that policy.

Huang Chen: I don't know this man personally. I only know Gromyko.

Dr. Kissinger: Gromyko is very precise. But Brezhnev is very emotional. And very brutal. I will give you a full report as the discussions develop.

Huang Chen: You mentioned there are three paragraphs you wanted him to delete.

Dr. Kissinger: I will send them to you this afternoon. They don't mention China but it is obvious. They sent us over a text, and we said it was inappropriate to deliver at the White House. It is not exactly according to protocol, Mr. Minister. [Laughter]

I will in any event try to see you before we leave, but if you come to San Clemente we can have a long talk. And we will arrange housing for you when you are there.

Huang Chen: How many hours will it take?

Dr. Kissinger: If you wanted to, you could use one of our planes. But about 4½ hours. You are welcome to stay as long as you can. It can be done in two days. It can be done in one day but it is very exhausting. You should stay one night. If you think it is appropriate, I could invite some California friends for a dinner with you.

Huang Chen: Certainly if I go I would be happy to have dinner with you. And I thank you in advance for arranging if I go.

You are very busy, so I won't keep you.

[The meeting then ended.]

---

38.   Letter From President Nixon to Chinese Premier Zhou En-lai[1]

Washington, June 19, 1973.

Dear Mr. Prime Minister:

I have been following the discussions between Dr. Kissinger and Ambassador Huang Chen with great attention and I have also studied the notes that have been sent to us by the Chinese Government with respect to the proposed draft agreement. As you know, we differ in our assessment of the consequences of the agreement, though not in the purposes it is supposed to serve. It remains our view that this agreement confers no special rights on the U.S. or the U.S.S.R.—and we would oppose any such claim. On the other hand, there is no way re-

---

[1] Source: National Archives, Nixon Presidential Materials, NSC Files, Kissinger Office Files, Box 95, Country Files, Far East, China Exchanges, June 14–July 9, 1973. No classification marking. According to a handwritten notation, Kissinger handed the letter to Huang Zhen during their June 19 meeting. (See Document 37) On June 20, Bruce delivered the contents of the letter to Qiao Guanhua. (Telegram 3 from Beijing, June 20; National Archives, Nixon Presidential Materials, NSC Files, Kissinger Office Files, Box 95, Country Files, Far East, China Exchanges, June 14–July 9, 1973)

course to force can be initiated by the U.S.S.R. without violating this agreement and thus creating a legal basis for resistance. As we have told your representatives and also other governments we intend to use this agreement to obtain greater scope for actions in areas not now covered by formal obligations.

Whatever our disagreement as to tactics, I want to use this occasion to tell you formally that the U.S. will oppose a policy that aims at hegemony or seeks to bring about the isolation of the People's Republic of China. For this reason Dr. Kissinger has assured Ambassador Huang Chen on my behalf that the U.S. will not change its vote at the United Nations on the issue of the prohibition of nuclear weapons.

I understand the hesitation of the Chinese side to sign a formal declaration along the lines proposed by Dr. Kissinger on May 29.[2] Let me, therefore, state our policy unilaterally: The U.S. will not engage in consultations that could affect the interests of the People's Republic of China without a full prior discussion with the Chinese Government. Specifically, any consultation under Article 4 of the agreement will be fully discussed with the Chinese Government before it is initiated and will not be concluded before the Chinese Government has an opportunity to express its view. In no case will the U.S. participate in a joint move together with the Soviet Union under this agreement with respect to conflicts or disputes where the People's Republic of China is a party.

Dr. Kissinger will be prepared to repeat our opposition to hegemony and our readiness for full consultation publicly on the occasion of his visit in August if the Chinese Government should consider it appropriate.

I recognize that the Chinese Government will reserve the right to express its views on this agreement. I hope, however, that it will do so in a manner that will not complicate the fixed course of the U.S. policy which is to oppose hegemonial aspirations no matter what their pretext.

Sincerely,

Richard Nixon

---

[2] See footnote 2, Document 34.

39.   Backchannel Message From the Head of the Liaison Office in China (Bruce) to the President's Assistant for National Security Affairs (Kissinger)[1]

Beijing, June 26, 1973.

5. Subject: Meeting with Chou En-lai.

1. I was called with no prior notice on June 25 at 5 pm and told Prime Minister Chou wanted to see me. I met him at Great Hall of the People at 5:45 pm, accompanied by Jenkins and Holdridge. On Chinese side were Chou, Ch'iao Kuan-hua, Chang Wen-chin, Lin P'ing (Head American/Oceanian Department, MFA), Ting Yung-hung (Deputy Head, American/Oceanian Department EARAN), Nancy T'ang, Shen Jo-yun, and two others.

2. Chou began with polite chit-chat about weather, and then worked the conversation around to modern science—"It can't be said that there is no progress, but there are many unknowns." We talked about archeology, elimination of disease in China, and cancer research. (*Comment:* I recall from record of your conversation with Chou that cancer research was often mentioned, and wonder if this subject might have a special interest for Chou.)

3. We then got on to topic of way that scientists today keep in touch with one another in various parts of the world. Noted that this included nuclear scientists, who often felt an obligation to share their discoveries with fellow scientists in other countries regardless of security considerations. Chou picked this up, saying it was not possible for nuclear secrets to be spread throughout the world because their purpose was not to cure disease but to cause harm. He then referred to an article he had read in a Japanese newspaper about the USSR having stolen secret plans, weapons and equipment from NATO since World War II, which had given it much military knowledge. There had been more than ten major cases of this.

4. I told Chou I accepted the dissemination of nuclear science secrets as an exceedingly dangerous thing. I considered that any nation would be foolish to let other nations know about its technical developments in this field, regardless of whether these nations were friendly or not.

---

[1] Source: National Archives, Nixon Presidential Materials, NSC Files, Kissinger Office Files, Box 95, Country Files, Far East, China Exchanges, June 14–July 9, 1973. Top Secret; Sensitive; Exclusively Eyes Only.

5. Chou promptly agreed. "No matter how friendly people are to each other around the Western White House swimming pool, it is impermissible to make an exhibition of their nuclear secrets." There was a political question here, and in spite of the fact that so many agreements had been signed, people still viewed them with suspicion.

6. Chou emphasized that this was his own view even after receiving the President's letter.[2] He thanked the President for writing, but the Chinese would maintain the position set forth in the U.S.–PRC Joint Communiqué of February 1972. This position has been conveyed to you through Ambassador Huang Hua and Huang Chen, and so no further renunciation necessary. Similar reactions among others in the world would become evident in a short period of time.

7. Chou indicated the Chinese had been notified through "friends in the White House" that they would be informed about the Brezhnev talks. Ambassador Huang Chen was to be invited to the Western White House on July 5. Colonel Kennedy had also informed them in a letter that Brezhnev would make public the non-aggression agreement. (Chou referred in this context to four articles.) Brezhnev had told the President he would do so.

8. Chou declared that the Chinese had expected something like this ever since they had seen the draft agreement two days before Brezhnev's departure for the U.S. They had said so to the President through you, and had also forwarded their conclusions. They were quite familiar with Soviet tricks, and could imagine what kind of show the Soviets would put up both before and afterwards.

9. I said I thought that the Chinese position was perfectly well known in the U.S., and was indeed indicated by the President's letter. It was quite unique that in the course of all our negotiations with the USSR, the President had instructed you to keep Prime Minister Chou informed before, during, and after, about what had gone on. I deduced from this that there was a certain amount of suspicion also in the U.S. regarding the USSR.

10. I remarked it seemed to me that it had been a Soviet tactic for a considerable length of time to try to divide the U.S. and China. They must have been surprised at the turn taken in U.S.–PRC relations, and in fact had given every indication of it. If PM Chou recalled the original draft agreement submitted to you by the Soviets, it was evident this was an attempt on their part to arrive at a bilateral agreement with the U.S. in which the interests of third parties were not taken into account. As I understood the present agreement, the U.S.

---

[2] Document 38.

has undertaken with the Soviets to renounce the aggressive use of nuclear weapons, and not only by one power against the other but against a third power. This raised an interesting question—if two parties entered into an agreement not to take certain action, could one nation trust the other not to violate this agreement if it was not a treaty but an executive agreement?

11. Chou said the agreement was a mere statement about which we could not be sure. World opinion also had doubts. "When a nation has very adequate weapons, do you think it would renounce them?" Besides, even treaties had not been honored by the Soviets in the past. The Sino-Soviet Friendship Treaty had been signed to last for a thirty-year period and still had seven years to run, so why was it necessary to propose another non-aggression? (*sic*) To conclude a new treaty would show that the old one did not exist; hence, the (old) treaty was not reliable. If there was good faith, then a tacit understanding or a simple statement would be useful, but without good faith nothing was useful. Even a treaty would be useless.

12. Chou raised another point: Since only the two major powers were engaged in this agreement, there were grave doubts among other states as to whether these two powers wanted to dominate the world. The U.S.–PRC Joint Communiqué stated that neither party should seek hegemony, and it was also mentioned in the President's letter that you would mention this when you came. But from the speeches and statements of the Soviet leaders, it could be seen they were seeking out-and-out domination by the two world powers.

13. I said I sincerely believed that the U.S. was not out to dominate the world even if it could. It had had enough difficulties in its worldwide endeavors, even in the recent past. However, I frankly could not say I had the same judgement or opinions about the Soviet Union. In my opinion, the agreement would be inoperable in case of aggression as far as its practical effects were concerned because its status would not affect any existing treaties, alliances, or rights involving third parties. Therefore, the U.S. was in exactly the same position as before—if there were an attack on a NATO country, or more dangerously, on Berlin, we had an obligation under existing agreements to come to their assistance. Such undertakings could not be breached now or in any other way.

14. Chou observed that in this case, we would give the world the impression it was possible to have a relaxation of tension. There would be a false sense of security.

15. I said that might be. I referred to the dangerous situation which already had been created for us in Europe by the measures advocated by some members of our Congress. They wanted to withdraw troops from NATO and rely entirely on nuclear power for defense. I did not

know what the consequences would be if our people were lulled into a false sense of security regarding the USSR.

16. Chou injected at this point that we would have to wait and see. It did not yet matter, because there was still time.

17. Continuing, I explained their attitude as being one of trying to make arrangements of one kind or another via trade, aid, etc. to get as many guarantees as possible no matter whether these were later violated or not. Knowing of the President's and your own communications and talks with PM Chou, I realized the Chinese attitude regarding this operation was different from ours. Nevertheless, we were informing them of what we had in mind every step of the way. In my opinion, this was a very unique situation.

18. Chou remarked there had been direct Chinese contact with the U.S. for less than two years, and so there were various speculations as far as the world was concerned. He noted that although I had just arrived, I had read the records of previous conversations. He wanted to repeat what Chairman Mao had said to you last February:[3] The U.S. wanted to step on the Chinese shoulders to reach the USSR. He, Chou, repeated this to indicate that such things could happen. Chairman Mao extended this philosophy to visualize what might happen if a war broke out between China and the USSR. In the beginning, the U.S. would maintain a position of non-involvement, but give military supplies to the USSR. Then, after waiting until China had dragged out the USSR for a period of time, the U.S. would strike the Soviets from behind. Chou reiterated that he was only repeating what the Chairman had said; however, the Chinese had made material preparations.

19. I said that I could see from this why they had such strong reservations about the agreement. Chou asked me if I had read the passage from the record, and I said I had.

Comment: I in fact do not recall Mao having spoken in such terms, though Chou himself did speak elsewhere of the U.S. standing on China's shoulders to reach the USSR.

I added that I thought that estimate was highly pessimistic.

20. Chou declared that as he had told you, they had all along calculated on fighting on two fronts. They were digging tunnels and storing grain, and hence did not fear isolation. You had said they were approaching this question from the standpoint of revolutionaries, and they agreed. This was right—from the beginning they were revolutionaries, they had made revolution, they would never abandon their revolutionary principles. Chou said he wanted to tell me this frankly

---

[3] See Document 12.

so that I could understand their general picture. They were not pessimistic but had to be realistic. This was why they went overseas to seek friends everywhere, and opposed hegemony.

21. I said I hoped and believed our people understood. Every country had to consult its own self-interest and prepare for the worst. It should not be optimistic; that would be foolish.

22. Chou stated that there were many people in the world however not aware of this. They wanted to rely on other kinds of forces rather than on their own people themselves. I observed that it would be a terrible mistake for a great nation not to be self-sufficient, and to rely largely on other nations.

23. I went on to say that I had been refreshed and invigorated (by) the Shanghai Joint Communiqué because it contained statements which outlined the differences between us—e.g., our political and social systems. However, there were also areas of agreement, and we could reach more agreement if we proceeded carefully and frankly. All too often people talked together and ignored their differences, and left them still in existence. In our case, I did not see the differences between our two countries as irreconcilable over the long run if we proceeded with patience.

24. Chou paused for a long moment without comment, and then asked me how long my diplomatic experience had been—forty or fifty years? I replied, not that long, about twenty to twenty-five years. He referred to my previous statement as having been made on the basis of practical experience, and then said in effect that if things become too complicated and too many empty words are said, matters turn out superficially. It would be far better to work out one thing effectively and keep one's promises.

25. I said the U.S. would never want, nor could it achieve hegemony over China, over the USSR, or indeed over any peoples in the world, because hegemony in the old imperialistic sense is gone. Nationalism is dominant. People may make a mess of their internal affairs, but it is their mess. This is the great change which has come about in my life time. Chou added, especially after World War Two.

26. I continued that the real point of possible difference between our two countries might arise from each of us acting on our own vis-à-vis the USSR. If we acted independently in this regard, it could cause great international difficulty. The situation in Western Europe also figures in the equation. The emergence of WE economically has been startling and beneficial. But if it could also develop political cohesion, this would be beneficial to you and to us—but not to the Soviet Union. Chou interjected that the Soviets have tried different tricks to divide us. I said the Soviets since 1947 had tried to destroy Western Europe or to dominate it. I was skeptical that they would surrender that am-

bition. Chou said emphatically, "they haven't." I said if WE could form its own political apparatus (economic cohesion was comparatively easy), it would be at least as strong as the U.S., and stronger than the USSR. I did not know whether this could be achieved. Some progress had been made, but they had been talking unification for thirty years.

27. Chou said Soviets were not applying pressure on Japan. He asked whether it would be possible to improve our relations with Japan now, or whether this possibility had become more doubtful. I said I would like to answer by asking the Premier a question: Can any nation as economically prosperous as Japan, which has had a past history of imperialism and expansionism, ever renounce it? Chou said the Chinese at many times expressed to us the conviction that economic expansionism would bring about military expansionism. They also said this to their Japanese friends. It is necessary for us to work together with respect to Japan, for it is still at the crossroads. Chou said he had discussed this with you several times, emphasizing that we must work to keep Japan on the right course. Japan still speaks of its alliance with the U.S. now. It was important that Japan not be left in a position where it felt there was no way out. Japan should not listen to Soviet recommendations. For a time it might be possible for Japan to derive advantage (*note*: "win more rights") but this could not be relied upon.

28. I said it was essential that Japan not fall under Soviet influence. China and the U.S., for different reasons, should take the position of keeping Japan from engaging in some mad adventure, e.g. allying themselves with a great power in a way which would put them under its control.

29. Chou observed that Japan has its own self-dignity, but economically its development was lop-sided. With such a large population in a small area it was dependent on foreign markets. To export, it had to import large quantities of raw materials. It might be beneficial to export Japanese capital to certain places, such as Siberia. The USSR has left the door wide open. Chou said China would not mind if the U.S. and Japan made investment there if we thought there was profit in it. We will feel more reassured if you are in it with Japan. If you are both in it together, you will not be so easily taken advantage of.

30. At this point the conversation had lasted over an hour and a half. Chou's colleagues were consulting their watches; they probably had dinner engagements. The PM said when he left: "I've enjoyed this talk; I wish it could have continued."

31. *Comment:* Perhaps because of U.S.-Soviet summit, most Chinese officials present appeared unusually serious at first, but warmed during hour and half meeting. Chou was relaxed and friendly throughout, although deputies thought he too was more serious than usual. In sorrow but not in anger he dismissed U.S.-Soviet agreement as a fait

accompli, but several times referred to Soviet unreliability and duplicity. Neither Indo-China nor Taiwan was mentioned.

32. Chou appeared to be in excellent health and spirits. Would appreciate if you would have check made as to textual accuracy of Chou's reference to Chairman Mao's statement (twice emphasized by Chou) of possibility of Soviets attacking China, and then in turn being attacked by the U.S.[4] *End of comment.*

33. Warm regards.

---

[4] In backchannel message 23 to Beijing, June 28, Kissinger suggested that Chou was referring to an exchange with Kissinger (see Document 12) that began with a statement from Mao: "And then you can let them get bogged down in China, for half a year, or one, two, or three, or four years. And then you can poke your finger at the Soviet back." (National Archives, Nixon Presidential Materials, NSC Files, Kissinger Office Files, Box 95, Country Files, Far East, China Exchanges, June 14–July 9, 1973)

---

40. Memorandum From the President's Assistant for National Security Affairs (Kissinger) to President Nixon[1]

Washington, July 5, 1973.

SUBJECT

Butz' Meeting with Huang Chen

On June 21 Secretary Butz (memo at Tab A)[2] met with PRC Liaison Office Chief Huang Chen. Butz was told by Huang of his deep respect for American agriculture. Huang asked whether the U.S. would welcome a visit by PRC agricultural specialists. Butz responded that we would and would also like to send similar groups to the PRC. Huang said that his country would probably be buying grain and soybeans from us for a number of years, and that in the near future it would be appropriate to have discussions regarding PRC longer-term needs.

---

[1] Source: National Archives, Nixon Presidential Materials, NSC Files, Box 527, Country Files, Far East, People's Republic of China, Vol. 7, May 1973–Jul 19, 1973. Official Use Only. Sent for information. The attached correspondence profile indicates that the President noted this memorandum on July 9.

[2] Attached but not printed at Tab A is a June 22 memorandum from Butz to Nixon. During a telephone conversation with Kissinger on June 24, Butz described his meeting with Huang Zhen. (Ibid., Kissinger Telcons, Box 20–3 [June–July 1973])

With respect to the present PRC crop outlook, Huang indicated that prospects were generally favorable but the weather was somewhat of a problem. It is too early to make a judgment on the wheat problem. The PRC has bought heavily from the U.S. in the first half of this year, and might need even more in the last half. Butz indicated that it would be helpful in our planning to have PRC estimates of their requirements for the entire 1973–1974 crop. Huang said he would ask Peking for the information.

Huang showed interest in the possibility of export controls. Butz indicated that he hoped we would not have to impose such controls; however, if they became necessary we would do our best to deal with customers on an equitable basis.

Huang took great pleasure in comparing our response and attitude to trade with that of France. The PRC had spent months negotiating an airplane purchase with the French, but had managed to buy the ten U.S. Boeings after only a short negotiation.

My View: This rather open discussion by Huang points up the importance the PRC attaches to agricultural purchases in the U.S. That they are interested in discussions regarding longer-term needs raises the possibility that they may be contemplating an agreement similar to that which we signed last year with the Soviets.

---

41.   Memorandum of Conversation[1]

San Clemente, California, July 6, 1973, 10 a.m.

PARTICIPANTS

USA
Henry A. Kissinger
    Assistant to the President for National Security Affairs
Brent Scowcroft
    Deputy Assistant to the President for National Security Affairs
Lawrence S. Eagleburger
    Deputy Assistant to the President for National Security Council Operations

---

[1] Source: National Archives, Nixon Presidential Materials, NSC Files, Kissinger Office Files, Box 95, Country Files, Far East, China Exchanges, June 14–July 9, 1973. Top Secret; Sensitive; Exclusively Eyes Only. The meeting was held in Kissinger's office at the Western White House. Eagleburger prepared Kissinger's talking points prior to the meeting and drafted the memorandum of conversation after the meeting. (Memorandum from Eagleburger to Kissinger, July 2; ibid.)

PRC
Ambassador Huang Chen
Mr. Chi (interpreter)

[Omitted here is discussion of American entertainer Danny Kaye, the date of Kissinger's next visit to China, and Scowcroft's promotion to general.]

Ambassador Huang: While we are on the subject of speculation, let me discuss the visit of Prime Minister Chou En-lai to the U.S. There has been a great deal of speculation in the press, including one report on June 27 from San Clemente that the Prime Minister might consider a visit to the Western White House since it would not be so detrimental to our "principled stand."

Dr. Kissinger: You must understand that we had nothing to do with those stories.

Ambassador Huang: The U.S. side must understand that it still has relations with the Chiang group. Last year a message of congratulations was sent to Chiang from President Nixon, and the Chiang group still has an embassy in Washington. Under these conditions, how would it be possible for our Prime Minister to visit the U.S.? A visit to San Clemente would only be using the side door or the back door. I should also tell you that the Prime Minister has no plans to visit the UN.

Dr. Kissinger: The stories did not come from us. We have always officially denied them.

Ambassador Huang: My personal recommendation is that it is beneficial when Ziegler says there are no grounds for such speculation, as he recently did.

Dr. Kissinger: That's our position. As the President has said, he is willing to visit China again. But it would be difficult for us when there is no intermediate meeting in Washington. It would have eased matters if something took place between the first Presidential visit to Peking and the next Presidential visit, which we are prepared to do in 1974.

Ambassador Huang: This can be discussed in Peking.

Dr. Kissinger: Yes; we will stop all speculation in the meantime. How should we proceed? We have a number of concrete problems to discuss. I want to review the Brezhnev visit and one particular matter arising from it. Further, there are Cambodia, Korea, and a number of minor things.

Ambassador Huang: I'll finish up and then listen to you. The other thing I want to discuss is Cambodia. I have a paper here to give you. (Hands over paper, text of which follows.)

"The Chinese side informed the U.S. side earlier that as Samdech Norodom Sihanouk was visiting in Africa and Europe, it was yet infeasible for the Chinese side to communicate to him U.S. tentative thinking on a settlement of the Cambodian question. Although the Chinese side had informed the U.S. side that negotiations between Samdech Sihanouk and the Phnom Penh traitorous clique would be impossible, the U.S. side nevertheless openly refused to negotiate with Samdech Sihanouk, which enraged him all the more. However, according to news reports, U.S. government officials have recently made some disclosures on this question, which have given rise to various speculations. At the same time, it is learned that the Lon Nol clique has gone to the length of spreading the rumour that the Phnom Penh authorities will enter into official negotiations with the National United Front of Cambodia very soon, with the United States and the Chinese Communists serving as go-betweens. In spreading such utterly groundless assertions, the Lon Nol clique harbours ulterior motives, widely attempting to confuse public opinion and forestall the settlement of the Cambodian question. The Chinese side is of the view that such a turn of events is extremely disadvantageous to seeking a settlement of the Cambodian question and will even cause trouble. The Chinese side cannot but bring this to the serious attention of the U.S. side."

Ambassador Huang: This message was received before Prince Sihanouk returned to Peking.

Dr. Kissinger: (reading paper) He is certainly enraged.

Ambassador Huang: Since you always indicated in the past that you didn't want to talk to him, he is angry.

Dr. Kissinger: Yes, but you have received several communications from us. These were before his return to Peking.

Ambassador Huang: Now that Sihanouk has returned to Peking, we will hand over your thinking to him.

Dr. Kissinger: I gather he had not received this by the time of his arrival.

Ambassador Huang: By the looks of it, no.

Dr. Kissinger: I did not know that the Prime Minister could speak French.

Ambassador Huang: He was in France.

Dr. Kissinger: I had forgotten. He made some comments in French about us.

Let me give you our view on Cambodia. First, we cannot control what the Lon Nol people are saying. But they do not know what we have said to you; the proposals we have made to you. It is just speculation on their side.

I want to speak frankly. What we have proposed to you—a cease-fire if necessary for only 90 days, we believe takes care of the situation. We have no interests in Cambodia other than what the Prime Minister said to Ambassador Bruce the first time he saw him.[2] This is our objective. We have no objection—in fact, we would welcome it—if the Government in Phnom Penh is on very friendly terms with Peking and would refuse to participate in great power hegemonial activities in Southeast Asia.

As I have expressed before, it is a delicate problem for us as to how to manage the transition. If we are pushed into an undignified position, it will only strengthen the forces in this country who will oppose other things we may judge it necessary to do over the next three or four years. So we think it important that the matter in Cambodia be ended in a way not necessarily wounding for the U.S. We take great care not to embarrass you publicly. We really think it is not in our interest to create a situation which is unnecessarily difficult for either side.

Ambassador Huang: I will report this to my Government. Our attitude has already been made clear by the Prime Minister to Ambassador Bruce. As the Prime Minister said, all sides should respect Cambodia's sovereignty. We cannot negotiate about Cambodia. That must be between you, those now in power in Phnom Penh, and Sihanouk.

Dr. Kissinger: We're not asking to negotiate with you, but we have made suggestions as the basis for a solution. If the Prince proposes a ceasefire before my arrival we could stop bombing, and then reach a solution satisfactory to everyone's needs.

Ambassador Huang: It is up to the Prince. It is not for us to predict.

Dr. Kissinger: No, but our thinking could be mentioned to him.

Ambassador Huang: I can only report. It depends thereafter on my Government.

Dr. Kissinger: Of course.

Ambassador Huang: The Prince said a great deal at the airport.

Dr. Kissinger: I know. The guns have been going off all over Peking these days. The Prime Minister, for example, made some remarks to our Congressional delegation the other day.[3]

Ambassador Huang: I have not seen this.

Dr. Kissinger: I'm not criticizing. He bracketed us, but he hasn't hit us yet.

Ambassador Huang: We haven't heard anything of this.

---

[2] See Document 33.

[3] Zhou Enlai's comments about Cambodia to a Congressional delegation led by Senator Warren Magnuson (D–Washington) were reported in telegram 493 from Beijing, July 6. (National Archives, RG 59, Central Foreign Policy Files)

Dr. Kissinger: No? What he said was in the spirit of what you said before. It was new to the Congressmen, but not to us.

Let me say a few words about Brezhnev. I take it rather seriously. I want to tell it to you as it happened. I want first to discuss our conversations about China. Brezhnev sought for a week to see the President without me.

Ambassador Huang: You are a dangerous man.

Dr. Kissinger: Brezhnev is persistent but not subtle. He did see the President for about 30 minutes alone at Camp David. His comments about China were not favorable, but you may know that. But on the last day—on Saturday—Brezhnev had three hours with the President at which I was present.[4] We talked about China at great length. It was his initiative. During the first part of the meeting he violently attacked the Chinese leadership and gave us his explanation of the Lin Piao affair. I won't discuss that unless you want me to.

Ambassador Huang: It's up to you.

Dr. Kissinger: It was in that context that he told us about the non-aggression treaty about which you had already informed us. He said he would publish it at a suitable interval after his return as an example of the bellicosity of the PRC.

On Lin Piao, the only thing that may be of interest is that he said he would be prepared to let us see their investigation report. We said we were not interested.

He then discussed a number of things. He said it would be intolerable to imagine a Chinese nuclear capability in 15 years equal to what the Soviets have today. This, he said, would be intolerable and unacceptable to the USSR. He suggested we cooperate on this problem, as he had hinted at Zavidovo. Now he was making a formal and more explicit proposal.

He proposed as well that the U.S. and USSR begin exchanging information on your nuclear program. We said we would not exchange military information and were not interested. Brezhnev then asked if we are prepared to exchange other information on China. We said we could not make one country the subject of regular exchanges. They could always tell us what they had on their minds, but we would make no such undertaking. Brezhnev then said he expected our relations with you to improve, and that they could not object to this. But if military arrangements were made between the U.S. and the PRC, this would have the most serious consequences and would lead the Soviets to take drastic measures. Those were the key points.

---

[4] June 23.

They asked if we were planning any military arrangements. We replied three times that we have made no military arrangements, but we said nothing about the future. We do this as a question of principle. Neither of us has any plans along these lines, but we don't believe the Soviets can tell us with whom we can have arrangements.

The meeting was between Brezhnev, the President, myself, and the Soviet interpreter. We have told no one in our Government of this conversation. It must be kept totally secret. We have not told Ambassador Bruce, but I would have no objection if, when you return, you talk to Ambassador Bruce about it. But no one else should be present.

Ambassador Huang: I won't say anything to Bruce. You discuss it when you are there. As for us, as the President said to me last time, the Chinese side is very careful.

Dr. Kissinger: Brezhnev told us that only those in the room would hear of this conversation. But that evening, Gromyko asked to see me and asked what I thought of the Brezhnev conversation. (laughter)

He asked if I understood Brezhnev's proposal about China. I said that I understood it to have something to do with military arrangements between us. Gromyko then said I had misunderstood. Brezhnev not only meant military arrangements, but also political arrangements directed against the USSR. I asked what was meant by political arrangements, and who determined whether they were directed against the USSR. Gromyko was very evasive. I then called his attention to the Shanghai Communiqué and told him that we had an understanding not to make agreements directed at other parties.

It is my impression that the Soviet Union was quite serious about some of the matters we discussed previously. They were more openly brazen and brutal than I would have thought possible.

Under these conditions we think it is very important that we understand each other and what our intentions are. Your Prime Minister mentioned to Ambassador Bruce that you think in the event of a Sino-Soviet war we would give arms and supplies to the Soviet Union. That is absurd. We have no interest in supporting the stronger against the weaker.

Ambassador Huang: The Prime Minister said that?

Dr. Kissinger: (Reading from Ambassador Bruce's cable of June 26)[5] "In the beginning, the U.S. would maintain a position of non-involvement, but give military supplies to the USSR. Then, after waiting until China had dragged out the USSR for a period of time, the U.S. would strike the Soviets from behind."

---

[5] Document 39.

If China was attacked by the USSR, we would certainly cut off all credits to the Soviets. The second part of the Prime Minister's remarks might be true, but certainly not the first part. Under no circumstances would we give military or other supplies to the Soviets if they attacked the PRC. We would certainly cut off all economic ties, but we don't know whether that would be enough.

We must do the maximum we can to deter an attack on China. I used the Nuclear Agreement in a press conference to say that no attack on China would be conceivable that would not threaten peace and security. There would have been an unbelievable uproar in the Congress without the Agreement. So don't attack the Agreement too much. Give us a chance to use it in the one way we want. I think we have out-maneuvered your allies on this one.

I have set up a very secret group of four or five of the best officers I can find to see what the U.S. could do if such an event occurred. This will never be publicly known. I tell it to you in the strictest confidence. The group is only being formed this week. I talked to the Chairman of the JCS about it when he was here this week. I am prepared to exchange views on this subject if it can be done in secret.

Further, I have talked to the French Foreign Minister about our interest in strengthening the PRC. We will do what we can to encourage our allies to speed up requests they receive from you on items for Chinese defense.

In particular, you have asked for some Rolls Royce technology. Under existing regulations we have to oppose this, but we have worked out a procedure with the British where they will go ahead anyway.[6] We will take a formal position in opposition, but only that. Don't be confused by what we do publicly. In the future, now that we have our military establishment understanding the problem, we can handle these problems in a different way.

When I come to Peking I think we should discuss this complex of issues rather seriously. That is, how we can do the maximum to deter an attack without providing an excuse to undertake it.

You above all should understand what our policy is. If we wanted to cooperate with the USSR, then we would not have to be so complicated. We are trying to gain time and be in a position for maximum resistance should it happen. This is our position. I must say that we considered our discussions with the Soviets quite ominous.

---

[6] Rolls Royce sought to sell Spey jet aircraft engines to the PRC. (Memorandum from Sonnenfeldt to Kissinger, July 12; National Archives, Nixon Presidential Materials, NSC Files, Box 527, Country Files, Far East, People's Republic of China, Vol. 8, July 10, 1973–December 31, 1973)

Ambassador Huang: I will report to my Government. As to the U.S.-Soviet Nuclear Agreement, I have already told you our position.

Dr. Kissinger: I know. It does not give us any great pain. It would be worse if you supported the Agreement. I just want you to understand our position. But don't tell our Congressmen that it is just a scrap of paper. We want to use it. You can criticize it in other ways.[7]

Ambassador Huang: Our Prime Minister said that?

Dr. Kissinger: Our newspapers so report. As I have said, we don't object to criticism. The Soviets would think something was wrong otherwise.

Ambassador Huang: Our experience has been that if means nothing to the Soviets when they sign a paper.

Dr. Kissinger: I understand. Its purpose is in terms of our own problems; it has no impact on the Russians. But if I had said an attack on China threatened the U.S., there would have been a major uproar in the absence of the Agreement. But with the Agreement it was possible to say this relatively quietly.

I have to talk to the press now. What should I say about our meeting? That we had a review of the situation, and that we had a friendly talk? Nothing more specific? Do they know you are returning to China?

Ambassador Huang: Not yet.

Dr. Kissinger: The press will now say I have upset you so much you are returning to China.

Ambassador Huang: Others will say that I am so happy that I am returning to report.

(Break for meeting with the press and the President.)

Dr. Kissinger: I have just had a report from Ambassador Bruce about the Prime Minister's meeting with the Congressmen. He did say what I reported, but he was provoked by our side. He did not volunteer his comments, they insisted on raising it. We understand that he has no choice but to express his view when asked. Then the Senators repeated it to the newsmen.

Our Congressmen do not have a capacity for keeping confidential information, and Senator Magnuson knows nothing about foreign policy, which makes it worse. We will have a chance to deal with it in our channels.

We have told you our views on Korea. I suppose that the Prime Minister will discuss it with me when I get there.

---

[7] On July 7, the *Washington Post* reported, "Chou told the Congressmen that he thought the recent Nixon–Brezhnev agreement aimed at preventing nuclear war was unreliable and 'only a piece of paper.'" ("Chou Condemns Bombing by U.S.," p. A10)

Ambassador Huang: Did Dr. Kissinger see what our Prime Minister said about Korea at the Mali reception? He supported Kim Il Sung's 5 points.

Dr. Kissinger: Yes, but that was a general statement. Now, however, we have to decide how we will deal with specifics—UNCURK and the UNC—over the coming years.

Ambassador Huang: You can discuss this in Peking.

Dr. Kissinger: You mentioned in an earlier conversation the possibility of an exchange of chancery sites. It is complicated legally, but we would be prepared to facilitate an exchange when you are ready.

Ambassador Huang: I am grateful for your concern. I wanted to discuss the general problem at a convenient time anyway. An exchange of property for a chancery is not an immediate problem, but I do need to ask your help now in obtaining an office building.

We have located 4 houses near each other—near S Street and Massachusetts Avenue. We have looked over hotels but find that they will not work. Now we have learned that office work is not possible in the area where the 4 houses are located because of zoning restrictions. So we have 2 requests.

First, can you help us find an office building near the 4 houses? We would then use the 4 houses as residences. The houses are located at 1) 2230 S Street (to be used as the Ambassador's Residence); 2) 2200 S Street; 3) 2301 S Street; 4) 2339 S Street.

Second, can we get permission to use these houses for offices? We had been dealing with the Ramada Inn but when they heard we were interested they raised their price and are now asking far too much. So, can we find a small hotel or apartment (50 rooms or so) for our office work and for some of our staff to live in?

Dr. Kissinger: We will try two things: First, to get the zoning regulations removed from one of the buildings you have already found. Second, if that is not possible, we will see if we can find some small office building for your use.

Ambassador Huang: But we would still like, if possible, your help in finding a small building of 50 rooms or so.

Dr. Kissinger: We will do what we can. We are not well equipped for efforts of this sort, but we will do what we can.

Ambassador Huang: If any of the Rockefellers have real estate nearby, we would appreciate their help.

Dr. Kissinger: I was thinking precisely along those lines.

About my trip. I had thought of going to Hong Kong to get used to the time change, and then coming in from Hong Kong. Does this cause any problems?

Ambassador Huang: I am sure not. Ambassador Bruce stayed there several days. You should, too. Stay as long as you like. If you want to contact any of our people in Hong Kong, feel free to do so.

Dr. Kissinger: I know about your conversation with Secretary Butz.[8] We will cooperate as much as we can on your purchase of agricultural products. You should know that Brezhnev proposed a five year agreement of 5 million tons of grain per year for five years. We agreed in principle, but went no further.

Ambassador Huang: Yes, I had a good discussion with Secretaries Butz and Dent. Both took a very positive attitude toward the development of relations.

Dr. Kissinger: If you ever encounter bureaucratic problems, let my office know. You will get sympathetic treatment from us.

Ambassador Huang: Secretary Butz mentioned the possibility of having officers in charge of agriculture in each Liaison Office. I have put this proposal to my Government. Personally, it looks sensible to me.

---

[8] See Document 40.

---

42.   Memorandum for the President's File by the President's Assistant for National Security Affairs (Kissinger)[1]

San Clemente, California, July 6, 1973, 11:30 a.m.

SUBJECT

Meeting with Ambassador Huang Chen, Head of the PRC Liaison Office in Washington, Friday, July 6, 1973, 11:30 a.m.

PARTICIPANTS

The President
Ambassador Huang Chen
Dr. Henry A. Kissinger, Assistant to the President for National Security Affairs
Chi Ch'ao-chu (Interpreter)

---

[1] Source: National Archives, Nixon Presidential Materials, NSC Files, Kissinger Office Files, Box 95, Country Files, Far East, China Exchanges, June 14–Jul 9, 1973. Top Secret; Sensitive; Exclusively Eyes Only. The meeting was held in the President's office at the Western White House. Kissinger provided Nixon with talking points prior to the meeting. (Briefing paper from Kissinger, July 6; ibid.) Brackets are in the original.

The President welcomed Ambassador Huang to the Western White House. He told the Ambassador that he expected the sun to be returning in the afternoon. Ambassador Huang Chen thanked the President and expressed his happiness to be in the Western White House to pay his respects. The President told the Ambassador that he would drive the Ambassador over there to see the President's house. The Ambassador noted that looking across the Pacific, we realize China is just on the other side.

The President pointed out that it was from here in July 1971 that he had announced his visit to China.

The President then said that he wanted to reaffirm the matters that Dr. Kissinger had discussed with the Ambassador. These assurances all had the President's complete support. Sometimes one may wonder which assistants speak for the President. But Dr. Kissinger never spoke for himself alone. He always reflected the President's own views.

[At this point in the conversation there was a break for picture-taking.]

The President continued by saying that he wanted to re-emphasize the point made in his letter to Premier Chou En-lai regarding the President's meetings with Brezhnev.[2] The Ambassador and the Premier would recall the President's first meeting with Huang Chen in Washington when the President said that nothing would be done with Brezhnev in derogation of our relations with the PRC.[3] We had kept both the letter and the spirit of this commitment, the President stressed. Any interpretation that this nuclear agreement set up a condominium or inhibited the United States from doing what it required if there was an attack, nuclear or otherwise, on third countries was inaccurate. When Dr. Kissinger had had his press briefing on the nuclear agreement, the President had asked him to say that an attack on the PRC would endanger international peace and security.[4] This President wanted this point made, not because we feared an attack or because we have good relations with the PRC, but because we had determined on the basis of the security interests of the United States that the PRC should be free, independent, and secure. One could have tried to put

---

[2] Document 38.

[3] See Document 34.

[4] A transcript of Kissinger's press conference of June 25, in which he discussed China, international peace and security, as well as the nuclear agreement, is in Ford Library, National Security Adviser, Kissinger–Scowcroft West Wing Office Files, 1974–1977, China Exchanges, Box 4. When asked whether the United States was signaling "the Russians that they have a free hand where China is concerned," Kissinger replied, "it is difficult to conceive a military attack by anybody on the People's Republic of China that would not endanger international peace and security and, therefore, it would be thought to be, from whatever direction it came, not consistent with our view of this treaty."

it on the basis of a personal relationship, but this was a lasting national interest. Each country had an interest in the survival of the other. We could sign a piece of paper with great fanfare and clinking of glasses. But we knew from history that every war has started with the breaking of a treaty.

Our interests today coincided and would continue to coincide for many years to come, the President continued. These personal discussions with the Ambassador, while not reduced to a formal agreement, represented the policy of the United States, which would be implemented without question in the years to come. We did not say things privately to the PRC and another thing publicly to the Russians. Our interests required us to meet with the Soviet leaders and find ways to agree. But we totally rejected a condominium of the two superpowers. And we totally rejected the idea of giving the Soviets a free hand to move against their neighbors. So the United States would work hard for continuing to develop its relations with the PRC, having in mind the personal warmth which characterized this relationship but also that our interests required that we be inseparable on security matters.

Ambassador Huang wanted again to express his happiness to come to the Western White House. He would surely report to Chairman Mao and Premier Chou En-lai what the President had said. He would be returning to China but he will see Dr. Kissinger again in August in Peking. The President pointed out the importance we attached to taking care of our confidential channel. The Ambassador repeated that he would report all this to Premier Chou En-lai.

The President then turned to Cambodia. At the present time it was our judgment, he said, that the Chinese Government held the key, through the influence it may exert on Sihanouk. The situation was urgent, because if it continued to deteriorate, the possibility of the conflict spreading was real. The war in South Vietnam was over, and in Laos. They were continuing to negotiate in typically Laotian fashion. But in Cambodia the war was going on, and the President felt very strongly that it did not serve our mutual interest to be dragged into differences and even a confrontation about Cambodia. The United States had no desire to retain a special position of influence or to retain any military forces there. Our desire was to have a government in Phnom Penh to bring peace. If our two countries could work together it would have a good effect not only in the relations of our two countries but also on world opinion. There were many danger spots, like the Middle East. The small country of Cambodia was the only one where a war was going on. We therefore felt a way must be found to settle it. The United States had no unilateral solution, but rather it took the influence of all interested parties.

The President then said he was not asking for an immediate comment from the Ambassador. But the President hoped the Ambassador would convey these ideas to Premier Chou En-lai so that the US and PRC could discuss it if it was not settled by the time Dr. Kissinger got to Peking. Ambassador Huang responded that he would carefully convey the President's words to the Premier. He added that China, too, wished for an early end to the war.

43. Memorandum of Conversation[1]

Washington, July 19, 1973, 11:00–11:46 a.m.

PARTICIPANTS

Henry A. Kissinger
General Brent Scowcroft
Lawrence Eagleburger
Winston Lord
Jonathan T. Howe
Richard Solomon
Peter W. Rodman

Mr. Kissinger convened the meeting in order to discuss the note received from the PRC the previous evening (Tab A)[2]—its implications with respect to Cambodia, his prospective trip to Peking, and the course of Sino-U.S. relations; and how the U.S. should respond.

Mr. Kissinger began by pointing out that the note had to be read against the background of the course of the U.S.-Chinese relationship over the past several months. This note was clearly intended as a cancellation or postponement of the Kissinger trip and an opting-out by the Chinese of any involvement in negotiations for a Cambodian settlement. This was a complete reversal of the Chinese position on both counts.

---

[1] Source: National Archives, Nixon Presidential Materials, NSC Files, Kissinger Office Files, Box 95, Country Files, Far East, China Exchanges, July 10–Oct. 31, 1973. Top Secret; Sensitive; Exclusively Eyes Only. The meeting took place in Kissinger's office at the White House.

[2] Attached but not printed is a note that Han Xu handed to Scowcroft on July 18 at 6:30 p.m. In the note, the Chinese Government expressed support for Sihanouk's demand that the United States end its military involvement in Cambodia and declared its unwillingness to communicate the U.S. point of view to Sihanouk under present circumstances. The Chinese blamed the inability to settle the Cambodia question on the U.S. Government's unwillingness to accept Sihanouk's "reasonable demands," and asserted, "It is up to the doer to undo the knot. The key to the settlement of the question is held by the United States, and not by others."

On each and every previous Kissinger trip to China the Chinese had proposed that he meet with Sihanouk. Sihanouk has now said, in a speech on July 10,[3] that we should negotiate with the Khmer Rouge and not with him, Mr. Solomon interjected. That is true, Mr. Kissinger replied. But on each previous trip, especially in February 1973, Cambodia had been discussed extensively. At the end of May we had made a proposal and the Chinese had said they would convey it to Sihanouk once he returned from his travels.[4] Their message of June 4 went to the extraordinary length of reciting our proposal back to us to make sure they understood it correctly—something they had never done on any other subject.[5] Therefore this note represented a reneging on a clear assurance.

What had happened in the interim? Mr. Kissinger asked. The Congressional vote to cut off the bombing had destroyed the balance in Cambodia. It was clear the Chinese couldn't deliver.

The bombing cut-off had fundamentally changed the situation in Cambodia. Formerly, Sihanouk's utility to the Khmer Rouge had been that he gave them legitimacy which they had not had. Now they didn't need legitimacy; they saw they could win. Sihanouk's utility to the Chinese had been that he gave them influence over the Khmer Rouge and could resist other outside influences. The utility of the Chinese to us was that they had some control over Sihanouk. Sihanouk's utility to us was that, once he returned to Cambodia, he might be able to keep things balanced. Ironically the Chinese needed the Lon Nol group—this was a restraint on Sihanouk and on the Khmer Rouge. The Congressmen had totally misjudged the situation. Now this was all lost. Sihanouk couldn't deliver the Khmer Rouge and the Chinese couldn't deliver Sihanouk.

With respect to the trip, the Chinese had virtually agreed in June that it would take place in early August. They had invited us to choose any date we wanted. We had then proposed August 6. They had spread

---

[3] See "Sihanouk Tells U.S. To Negotiate With the Cambodia Communists," *The New York Times,* July 12, 1973, p. 3.

[4] On May 27, Kissinger told Huang Hua, "We are prepared to stop our bombing in Cambodia, and we are prepared to withdraw the very small advisory group we have there. And we are prepared to arrange for Lon Nol to leave for medical treatment in the United States. In return we would like a ceasefire—if necessary, say for ninety days—a negotiation between the Sihanouk group and the remainder of the Lon Nol group; and while this negotiation is going on in Cambodia, we would authorize some discussions between the staff of Ambassador Bruce and Prince Sihanouk in Peking." (Memorandum of conversation; National Archives, Nixon Presidential Materials, NSC Files, Kissinger Office Files, Box 94, Country Files, Far East, China Exchanges, May 16–June 13, 1973) Kissinger reiterated this proposal in a meeting with Huang Chen on May 29. (Memorandum of conversation; ibid.)

[5] Huang Zhen read the U.S. proposal on Cambodia during a June 4 meeting with Kissinger, lasting from 3 to 3:30 p.m. (Ibid.)

the word around that it would be early August and had even leaked the date of August 6th to the press in Peking. But then Huang Chen was called back the beginning of this month and we received the note that they couldn't reply on a date until he got to Peking. We had yet to receive a reply to our proposed dates for the trip and for the announcement. We had first proposed July 16th for the announcement. But July 16th had come and gone. The Chinese had to know that this delay in replying, and the turn-around on Cambodia, meant a postponement.

This was a conscious decision, Mr. Kissinger concluded. The question was whether it reflected only the Cambodian issue or something more fundamental that was happening to the relationship. Brent had told Han Hsu that Dr. Kissinger's authority would be undermined if he came back empty-handed on Cambodia and that he and the President were the key men who embodied American support for China for the right reasons. All this talk about 25 years of mutual estrangement was crap. What the Chinese wanted was support in a military contingency. We might not be able to pull it off, but at least he and the President understood this. Alex Eckstein[6] and other chowder-headed liberals loved China but if you asked them about military actions in a contingency they'd have 600 heart attacks. Liberals kept talking about how isolation was so psychologically disturbing to the Chinese. It might have been psychologically disturbing to us, but it wasn't to the Chinese. For 3,000 years it didn't bother them to be isolated. They've been self-contained more than they've been in contact with the rest of the world, and they have the self-assurance to handle it quite well.

To cancel a Kissinger trip was a major international event. It had to be a major decision for them. To assess this question—this was the real reason Mr. Kissinger had called together this group.

Mr. Solomon pointed out the disastrous Magnuson conversation with Chou En-lai.[7] Chou had been visibly angered by Magnuson's attempt to engage him with the Congress against the President. Mag-

---

[6] Alexander Eckstein, an authority on the Chinese economy at the University of Michigan, led a delegation to China that aimed to promote Chinese-American cultural exchanges during a month-long trip. See "U.S. Scholars End a Visit to China," *The New York Times*, January 7, 1973, p. 9.

[7] Solomon, who accompanied the Magnuson delegation, reported that "the Magnuson delegation almost certainly made a *negative impact on the Chinese* regarding its general intellectual level." Solomon continued, "Magnuson's repeated assertions of the independence of Congress and the obvious interest of many Senators and Representatives in using trips to the PRC for their own domestic political purposes, very likely has left PRC leaders with a contemptuous feeling toward our governmental system, and a belief that they could use these men against an Administration position which they did not like." (Memorandum from Solomon to Kissinger, July 18; National Archives, Nixon Presidential Materials, NSC Files, Kissinger Office Files, Box 95, Country Files, Far East, China Exchanges, July 10–Oct. 31, 1973)

nuson had talked for 45 minutes about Cambodia in spite of everyone else's efforts to get off the subject. While Chou attacked the U.S.-Soviet nuclear agreement, and uttered some harsh words about the Cambodian bombing,[8] Magnuson stressed the role of Congress in cutting off the bombing and repeatedly urged Chou to "Be patient. It'll be over soon." Jenkins and Holdridge, Mr. Solomon noted, thought that the tone of the note may have reflected their irritation at Magnuson's performance. Mr. Kissinger said he had thought that was a stupid point. There was something more fundamental underlying this. He suggested that from a coldly calculated Chinese point of view they now saw a paralyzed President unable to provide firm support in matters affecting their security. This may have made them now question the value of our relationship. General Scowcroft emphasized that the Chinese wanted firm action from the U.S.

Mr. Solomon turned again to the Cambodian aspect. Sihanouk had displayed his own powerlessness and admitted he could be only a figurehead in asserting that we should now talk to the Khmer Rouge. This was probably true. In addition, the Chinese might not want him to expose his weakness in negotiations with us, as they probably hoped to use him as a point of influence in Cambodia in the future. Nor would the Chinese leadership want to expose themselves to criticism from domestic or foreign sources for pressuring an evidently successful "people's war" into compromising negotiations on the eve of an apparent victory. Certainly not before a Party Congress.

Mr. Eagleburger suggested that the unfortunate juxtaposition of press leaks here about the "delicate negotiations in progress" and the Kissinger trip to Peking may have provoked a change in the Chinese attitude. He asked if some members of the Chinese leadership might not be saying that China had, wittingly or unwittingly, been used by the Americans to obtain a 45-day extension of the bombing.

Mr. Kissinger responded that the bombing cutoff was the decisive thing, not the bombing extension. We had been bombing the bejesus out of them since May. There had in fact been no intensification of the bombing since the Congressional vote. General Scowcroft confirmed this. Next to us, Mr. Kissinger continued, the ones most hurt by the bombing cutoff were the Chinese. Before, our bombing gave them and Sihanouk something they could deliver to the Khmer Rouge, namely a bombing halt worked out with us. Now if the Chinese try to exert their influence for a settlement it comes across as a brute big-power play between us and them.

---

[8] See footnote 3, Document 41.

Mr. Lord commented that to him the language in the note didn't seem especially harsh. Mr. Rodman mentioned that the language was their standard line on Cambodia, which was not new. They had always been relatively abusive to us on Cambodia in their public statements. Mr. Kissinger said he was sure the Chinese didn't like the bombing. But this was nevertheless in marked contrast to all their previous exchanges with us on the subject and with the experience we had had with them on Vietnam. On Vietnam when they had harsh things to say in a message, they would always have other things to say, or would make clear in other ways that this did not hurt our relationship. This time, the failure to reiterate the invitation, and indeed the failure to reply at all to our date proposal, was a major step, and very puzzling.

Commander Howe noted that we had established a clear link between movement on Cambodia and the trip. They were on the spot and couldn't deliver. By commenting only on Cambodia they may have been trying to make a clean break and separate the two issues. They wanted to make a "principled stand."

Mr. Lord asked what the tone of the previous few months had been. Mr. Kissinger reiterated that it had been totally positive and that this note was something new. Mr. Lord asked how they had taken the Brezhnev visit. They had taken it all in stride, Mr. Kissinger replied. They didn't like the nuclear agreement but had said so in very restrained fashion. General Scowcroft pointed out how extensively we had consulted with them on that.

Mr. Solomon stated that there was no other evidence of a basic shift in the line toward the U.S. On the contrary, three days before, Mao himself had taken the unusual step of receiving a Chinese-American nuclear physicist, and then Chou had had a banquet for him. This was an unmistakable signal to the Chinese people and overseas Chinese that the Sino-U.S. relationship was still on. And Madame Mao's appearance with Ambassador Bruce at the basketball game a few weeks before showed that the very people who might have been challenging the rapprochement with the U.S. were now solidly lined up with it.[9]

Mr. Kissinger commented that this was all people-to-people stuff and did not exclude a shift in the political line.

Mr. Kissinger returned to the issue of the Chinese seeing a paralyzed President. They might want to provide themselves with a little more flexibility, particularly with respect to the Russians. There was no

---

[9] In mid-July 1973, Mao met with Chinese-American physicist Yang Chen-ning. (See "Meeting with Mao," *The Washington Post*, July 19, 1973, p. C–17) Jiang Qing attended a Sino-American basketball game on June 19. (Telegram 349 from Beijing, June 20; National Archives, Nixon Presidential Materials, NSC Files, Kissinger Office Files, Box 95, Country Files, Far East, China Exchanges, June 14–July 9, 1973)

question about the significance of turning off a Kissinger trip, particularly after the Brezhnev summit. Mr. Rodman pointed out that the Chinese message was a response to a question we had put, namely, what could we expect on Cambodia? They were giving us an honest answer. We had linked the trip with Cambodia. It was now being left to us how to respond. Mr. Kissinger reiterated that the Chinese response was unmistakably a postponement of the trip. They could have done any one of a number of things to take the edge off the Cambodian note. Responding in any way to our proposed date would have done this. They could have said, "We can't do anything for you on Cambodia but we are glad to have you on August 6—or some other date." Mr. Rodman suggested that they might not want to propose August 6 knowing it was now impossible for us to come. General Scowcroft stated that there were a hundred other ways they could have played it.

Mr. Eagleburger concluded that we were simply not going to be able to answer Mr. Kissinger's question as to why the Chinese had behaved in this way.

The discussion then turned to how to respond. It was agreed that we should answer the Cambodian note in strong terms and also postpone the trip. Mr. Kissinger said that we should have Bruce deliver a tough note on Cambodia which would express regret that for the first time in our relationship the Chinese word had not counted. We should just list all the things they had said before—their assurances that they would convey our proposal to Sihanouk. There had been no change in the situation. The idea that we had to communicate with Sihanouk through Mauritania was absurd. Sihanouk was in Peking. And the Chinese themselves had said they couldn't contact Sihanouk when he was abroad because it wasn't secure.

We should try to find out what their message means about our relationship. We should have Bruce go in and sound out Ch'iao Kuan-hua about the status of our relations generally. We should say we are asking Bruce to have a general review of Sino-American relations. If they answer, we'll find out. Even if they give us no answers, that in itself is an answer. Either way, we learn something. We should have Bruce deliver a stern message on Cambodia and then raise the other questions orally. We should do that next week, on the 24th or 25th.[10]

It was agreed that we had no choice but to postpone the trip with a cool note. On the 21st we should give a note to Han Hsu here doing this, Mr. Kissinger said. There was some discussion about whether we should propose a date after September 1st, or propose "some time in the fall," or ask them to propose a time period. The note should be "ice

---

[10] See footnote 4, Document 44.

cold." The second question was whether we should propose the text of a joint announcement or ask them for their proposal on an announcement. This would put them on the spot. A formal announcement would have a heavy impact. But we had to have some announcement, Mr. Kissinger said, or at least some answer to give to press queries, because as August went by there would surely be a flood of press questions. We could just say that because of scheduling difficulties the two sides agreed to postpone until September.

Postscript: At 5:00 p.m. on July 19, Han Hsu delivered a second Chinese note (Tab B)[11] proposing that Mr. Kissinger come on August 16. By the end of the day it was tentatively decided to respond to the two Chinese notes in sequence, as they had done—replying to Cambodia on one day and proposing a September trip on the second day. It would be done here, on paper, with Han Hsu. There was now no need for Bruce to raise "fundamental questions" with Ch'iao.

---

[11] Attached but not printed.

---

44. Note From the Government of the United States to the Government of the People's Republic of China[1]

Washington, July 24, 1973.

The US side has consistently sought a ceasefire and political settlement in Cambodia since the January 27 Paris Agreement. The other side has continually refused to end the war in Cambodia and responded to the unilateral ceasefire proclaimed by the Phnom Penh government and the cessation of US air actions in Cambodia in February with an intensified military offensive.

---

[1] Source: National Archives, Nixon Presidential Materials, NSC Files, Kissinger Office Files, Box 95, Country Files, Far East, China Exchanges, July 10–October 31 1973 [2 of 2]. No classification marking. According to a handwritten notation, Scowcroft passed the note to Han Xu during a July 24 meeting, which took place in the Map Room at the White House at 6 p.m. (Memorandum of conversation, July 24; ibid., Box 1027, Presidential/HAK MemCons, MemCons-HAK & Presidential, April–November 1973 [3 of 5]) Scowcroft also communicated an oral message: "My Government notes, with regret, that this is the first time in the development of our new relationship that the Chinese word has not counted." (Ford Library, National Security Adviser, Kissinger–Scowcroft West Wing Office Files, 1969–1977, Box 4, China Exchanges) On July 25, Scowcroft informed Han that Kissinger could not arrive in China on August 16 and proposed instead that Kissinger visit September 13–16 or September 6–9. (Ibid.)

The Chinese side declared to the US side in its message of June 4 that it would communicate the US peace proposal of May 27 to Prince Sihanouk.[2] This proposal accepted a long-standing Chinese suggestion for direct talks with Prince Sihanouk made during every visit by Dr. Kissinger to Peking. The contents of the June 4 message were reiterated on June 13 by Foreign Minister Chi P'eng-fei and again in the Chinese message of July 6, that this awaited only the return of Prince Sihanouk from his travels. On July 6, Ambassador Huang Chen declared that the Chinese side would convey the US proposal to Prince Sihanouk now that he had returned to Peking.[3]

The Chinese message of July 18 has therefore been noted with astonishment.[4] There has been no change in US policy and no increase in US activities. In light of these earlier assurances, and the principles and spirit of the Shanghai Communiqué, it is difficult to understand why the Chinese side is unable to communicate an American peace proposal to a leader located in Peking. It is utterly unreasonable that this leader should publicly demand that communications to him go through Mauritania to which the Chinese side would not entrust the original US communication of May 27. This raises special difficulties because in reliance on the June 4 note and subsequent assurances, the US had not engaged in any other negotiations or responded to any other channels.

As to the substance of the Chinese note of July 18, the Chinese side will not be surprised that the US side rejects a "solution" so arbitrarily weighted against it. This is inconsistent with the requirements of reciprocity and equality. It is beyond the bounds of logic to be asked to negotiate on an issue when the other side, clearly and from the outset, leaves no room for negotiations. In such circumstances the US side will leave negotiations to the Cambodian parties.

---

[2] See footnotes 4 and 5, Document 43.

[3] For additional information concerning Kissinger's June 13 meeting with Ji Pengfei, see Document 36. For the July 6 note and meeting between Kissinger and Huang, see Document 41.

[4] See footnote 2, Document 43. Backchannel message 19 to Beijing, July 18, referred to the Chinese note as relatively "brutal," asked the advice of the USLO, and proposed that "On Monday or Tuesday [July 23 or 24] Ambassador Bruce would pass a harsh response to their Cambodia note, express his astonishment and offer a fundamental discussion of the full range of US/Chinese relations." (National Archives, Nixon Presidential Materials, NSC Files, Kissinger Office Files, Box 95, Country Files, Far East, China Exchanges, July 10–Oct. 31, 1973 [2 of 2]) In backchannel message 21 to Beijing, July 19, Jenkins and Holdridge responded: "We do not read this as a brutal message, but rather a restatement of a firm Chinese position." They questioned whether a Party Congress might be about to occur and also noted, "Chinese calculate we are in weak position in Cambodia. They unquestionably angered by our last spurt of intensified bombing, not to mention Chou's anger produced by Magnuson's counseling 'patience' while that was going on." (Ibid.)

**45.   Memorandum From Richard H. Solomon of the National
        Security Council Staff to the President's Assistant for
        National Security Affairs (Kissinger)[1]**

Washington, July 30, 1973.

SUBJECT

U.S.–PRC Exchanges May be Adding to Chou En-lai's Problems

Over the weekend additional corroborative evidence has become available which strengthens the interpretation that Chou En-lai is under some pressure from radical elements in the PRC who object to his relatively pragmatic policies toward the intellectual community and related efforts to depoliticize both university entrance requirements and scientific research. The available material is pieced together in a fine bit of analysis from the Hong Kong Consulate at Tab A.[2]

Of particular interest is the evidence (in paragraphs 2 and 3) that two PRC scientific groups which visited the U.S. last year[3] drew criticism from radicals around Mao's wife who found their attitudes toward America too favorable. If accurate, these reports suggest that U.S.–PRC exchanges, particularly those which involve China's scientific and academic communities, may be adding to Premier Chou's political vulnerability. The Hong Kong analysis adds, however, that Chairman Mao's July 17 public meeting with Chinese-American scientist Yang Chen-ning may have represented Mao siding with Chou in this dispute.[4]

You should know that this evidence of political resistance in China to U.S.–PRC exchanges comes at a time when American academics involved in facilitating such exchanges—particularly those in the scientific community—are miffed at Chinese authorities for apparently calling all the shots on exchange programs and for not being responsive to the particular interests of American scientists. These same people feel that the U.S. Government has not pressed Peking sufficiently in

---

[1] Source: National Archives, Nixon Presidential Materials, NSC Files, Box 527, Country Files, Far East, People's Republic of China, Vol. 8, Jul 10–Dec 31, 1973. Secret. Urgent; sent for information. A notation on the memorandum indicates Kissinger saw it.

[2] Attached but not printed is telegram 7602 from Hong Kong, July 30.

[3] Eleven Chinese medical specialists visited the United States in October 1972. A delegation of nonmedical scientists from China visited the United States in November–December 1972.

[4] See footnote 9, Document 43.

terms of American interests in these exchanges. Department of State officers concerned with exchanges will be meeting with representatives of the Committee on Scholarly Communication and National Committee on U.S.-China Relations next week to discuss differences. I will attend the meeting in an effort to keep the participants sensitized to the larger interest that is being served by exchange programs, and to discourage any uncoordinated approaches to the PRC Liaison Office on exchange matters that might compound the above-mentioned situation.

---

46.   Memorandum of Conversation[1]

Washington, August 6, 1973, noon.

PARTICIPANTS

> James C. H. Shen, Republic of China Ambassador to the United States
> Henry Chen, Political Counselor, Embassy of the Republic of China
>
> Henry A. Kissinger, Assistant to the President for National Security Affairs
> John A. Froebe, Jr., Staff Member, NSC

SUBJECT

> Rumored changes in ROC foreign policy, Dr. Kissinger's planned Peking trip, possible high-level exchange of visits with ROC, current conditions in PRC, possible U.S. recognition of PRC

Ambassador Shen: It's been five and one-half months since I've seen you.

Mr. Kissinger: That shows how good our relations are.

Ambassador Shen: I was in Taipei in March. Premier Chiang asked to be remembered to you. When I returned I saw Under Secretary Porter to assure him that there was absolutely no truth to the rumors making the rounds at that point—that we were in contact with the Soviets, and that we were undertaking discussions with the PRC.

Mr. Kissinger: What about the rumor that the Soviets were interested in establishing a naval base in the Pescadores Islands?

---

[1] Source: National Archives, Nixon Presidential Materials, NSC Files, Box 523, Country Files, Far East, China, Vol. XI, Aug 1972–Oct 24, 1973. Secret; Sensitive. The meeting took place at the White House. All brackets are in the original. On August 18, Scowcroft approved this memorandum of conversation. (Memorandum from Froebe to Kissinger, August 18; ibid.) In response to a Department of State request for a copy, Kissinger wrote, "Don't send anything." (Note from Scowcroft to Kissinger, undated; ibid.)

Ambassador Shen: This rumor is merely the latest. It is true that the Pescadores have deep water and are suitable for subs, but the ROC will never permit a Soviet naval base there.

Mr. Kissinger: I've never been to Taipei.

Ambassador Shen: Then how about visiting there in the near future?

Mr. Kissinger: We'll have to see later this year.

Ambassador Shen: When are you going to Peiping?

Mr. Kissinger: I've not set a date. I didn't want to be there at the time of the Cambodian bombing halt. I didn't want to give them the satisfaction of my being in Peking at the time of the bombing halt.

Ambassador Shen: How are your relations with Peiping?

Mr. Kissinger: We don't plan any major new initiatives in the near future. Our deputy in the Liaison Office there is returning soon.

Ambassador Shen: But if you are going to Peiping in the near future, isn't it unusual that the deputy would be returning?

Mr. Kissinger: Not necessarily.

Ambassador Shen: How do you see the state of U.S.–ROC relations?

Mr. Kissinger: I think they are cordial, don't you?

Ambassador Shen: In general I agree, but people have been talking because of the amount of attention that you have been showering on Huang Chen and his Liaison Office. You even look him out to San Clemente on a special jet.

Mr. Kissinger: That was to counterbalance the Russians. As to the flight, Huang took a regular courier flight, not a special flight.

Ambassador Shen: My understanding was that this was a special jet.

Mr. Kissinger: No, this was a regular courier flight; it goes out three times a week. We have taken others on this flight as well.

Ambassador Shen: But when Huang Chen was out there he was introduced to the movie stars. You haven't done this for me.

Mr. Kissinger: That is true. You have a point there. But do we have any problems in our bilateral relations?

Ambassador Shen: People notice a cooling in the relationship. There is much pessimism in Taipei. People there fear that the U.S. and Peiping will recognize each other.

Mr. Kissinger: We have no plans to that effect. Didn't I tell you a year ago that we would not be moving on recognition soon? I can assure you that it won't come in the immediate future.

Ambassador Shen: The people noticed that when Secretary Rogers went to Japan and South Korea, he skipped Taipei. This causes the people to wonder. They are disturbed by the fact that no ranking U.S. officials have visited Taiwan in some time. It is as if there were a deliberate attempt to downgrade U.S.–ROC relations.

Mr. Kissinger: There is no deliberate attempt to downgrade our relationship. As to Secretary Rogers, I don't control his travel.

Ambassador Shen: How about our Foreign Minister visiting the United States?

Mr. Kissinger: Let me consider this.

Ambassador Shen: The Premier has not visited the U.S. since he was shot at [in May 1970].

Mr. Kissinger: I will look into it. I see no basic obstacle in the Foreign Minister's coming here. In the case of the Premier, however, I would have to consult the President's schedule.

Ambassador Shen: The Premier would be able to sit down with you and the President for some basic discussions.

Mr. Kissinger: I will check.

Ambassador Shen: People on Taiwan are working hard to get ahead.

Mr. Kissinger: Everyone who has visited there is impressed.

Ambassador Shen: Premier Chiang is also seeing that more Taiwanese are taken into government ranks.

Mr. Kissinger: You have no contacts with Peking? I noticed that Singapore Prime Minister Lee Kuan Yew visited Taipei recently.

Ambassador Shen: Yes, Lee visited Taiwan about two months ago, but he is not acting as an intermediary.

Mr. Kissinger: Prime Minister Lee told me he would not go to Peking.

Ambassador Shen: My government has relations with Singapore. This was Lee's first visit to Taiwan.

Mr. Kissinger: What are your impressions of the current conditions on the Mainland?

Ambassador Shen: I think in general they are quiet for now. The regime may hold the National People's Congress in late September. The Party Congress, which is the important one of the two, would come earlier. What is your estimate on the timing?

Mr. Kissinger: Our intelligence had been saying that the Party Congress would be held in early August. This has obviously been overtaken. Now our intelligence is saying that the Party Congress will be held in late September. This just shows you how little they know.

Ambassador Shen: How is your Liaison Office in Peiping getting along?

Mr. Kissinger: There is not much going on. The PRC is watching the United States. Possibly they are wondering whether the U.S. will have a cultural revolution.

Ambassador Shen: Will Chou En-lai come to New York for this fall's General Assembly? He told Senator Magnuson recently that he would not come to Washington as long as the ROC's Ambassador is here. But this does not exclude the possibility of New York.

Mr. Kissinger: I don't think he will come.

Ambassador Shen: Chou's picture now seems to appear alongside of Mao's in public.

Mr. Kissinger: We've noticed that they have dropped the "Great Leader" caption from Mao's picture.

Ambassador Shen: But why should they change this now? I would think they would continue to call him the "Great Leader" until he is dead.

Mr. Kissinger: Someone just sent me a copy of the *I-Ching*.

Ambassador Shen: This is the right kind of book for you. This is one of our most valued classics.

What should Taiwan do now?

Mr. Kissinger: Anything that will symbolize your permanence. You are behaving very ably and skillfully.

Ambassador Shen: But we are just a little boat.

Mr. Kissinger: The U.S. won't tolerate a military invasion of Taiwan. Besides, the PRC does not have the capability to pull off such an invasion.

Ambassador Shen: But what if the U.S. recognizes Peiping as the sole legitimate government of all China?

Mr. Kissinger: This will not happen unless Peking recognizes your separate existence. But the U.S. has no plans for recognizing Peking.

Ambassador Shen: Does U.S. recognition of Peiping mean automatic de-recognition of Taipei?

Mr. Kissinger: My trip to Peking will not result in U.S. recognition of the PRC.

Ambassador Shen: There is speculation that your trip to Peiping will achieve some settlement on the Cambodian situation. Your strong interest in a settlement there would appear to give Chou En-lai some leverage over you.

Mr. Kissinger: But Chou can't wind up Cambodian hostilities.

Ambassador Shen: What will happen in Cambodia?

Mr. Kissinger: The Communists will probably win.

Ambassador Shen: How will this affect the settlement in Vietnam?

Mr. Kissinger: Unfavorably.

Are you taking a vacation this summer?

Ambassador Shen: As I was just telling Jack [Froebe], when others leave town I have to stay on. I did, however, just get away this past week for a couple of days at St. Marys. You have taken no vacation?

Mr. Kissinger: I have no chance to at this point. I usually take some time off in the spring and go to Acapulco.

You can be sure that nothing startling will happen during my trip to Peking—and certainly nothing as regards Taiwan.

Ambassador Shen: We appreciate that very much. We believe we should begin trying to look down the road a distance.

Mr. Kissinger: You ought to consider the possibility that the PRC might decide to give in to dual recognition. After all, they have done some unusual things before.

Ambassador Shen: This is possible in the case of the U.S. in light of the clout which you have with Peiping. The Japanese were miffed at the exceptions Peiping made for you.

Mr. Kissinger: The Japanese behave treacherously towards you.

I can assure you, Mr. Ambassador, that it won't take five and one-half months the next time.

---

47.   Memorandum of Conversation[1]

I–24725/73   Washington, August 7, 1973, 2:10–2:50 p.m.

SUBJECT

   Secretary of Defense Schlesinger's Visit With General Lai Ming-tang, Chief of the
   General Staff, Ministry of National Defense, Republic of China

PARTICIPANTS

   United States
   Secretary of Defense—James R. Schlesinger
   Deputy Secretary of Defense—William P. Clements

---

[1] Source: Washington National Records Center, RG 330, OASD/ISA Files: FRC 330–76–117, China, Republic of, 333, 16 August 1973. Secret. The meeting took place in Schlesinger's office at the Pentagon. Drafted by Doolin on August 16 and approved by Hill. Brigadier General Taylor also approved the memorandum.

Assistant Secretary of Defense (ISA)—Robert C. Hill
Director, Defense Security Assistance Agency—VADM Ray Peet
Deputy Assistant Secretary of Defense (ISA)—Dennis J. Doolin
Military Assistant to the Secretary of Defense—BGEN Robert C. Taylor

Republic of China
Republic of China Ambassador to the U.S.—James C. H. Shen
Chief of the General Staff, MND, ROC—General Lai Ming-tang
Deputy Chief of the General Staff/Plans, MND, ROC—VADM Chih Ming-ping

Opening Remarks. General Lai expressed his gratitude for the call and his government's thanks for our continued assistance. He said that he first came to Washington in 1943 after finishing school at Leavenworth. Mr. Clements said that Admiral Moorer told him that he had known General Lai for some thirty years.

U.S.–ROC Relations. Secretary Schlesinger said that there have been some adaptations in our international relations, but told General Lai that the loss of rigidity in U.S.–PRC relations will not affect our alliance with the Republic of China. Mr. Clements added that this requires understanding on both sides. General Lai agreed with the foregoing and said that that is the value of visits such as this. He then tendered an invitation to Secretary Schlesinger to visit Taiwan. The Secretary said that he would accept when his schedule permits.

The Situation in Taiwan and U.S. Aid to the ROC. General Lai said that his government is doing everything it can to strengthen internal political stability, as economic development cannot proceed in the absence of stability. The General said that the ROC faces a great threat from the mainland and must maintain a strong military deterrent. Secretary Schlesinger said that we have taken note of Taiwan's fabulous economic development and added that we envy Taiwan its growth rate and its BOP position. The Secretary pointed out that our world-wide grant MAP is now in real terms about 25% of what it was a decade ago. He complimented General Lai on Taiwan's economic development which has enabled the GRC to increase its own military expenditures. General Lai then made a strong representation for more excess defense articles (EDA). Admiral Peet said that the EDA pool is drying up. General Lai then asked whether additional EDA would be available when U.S. force levels in Europe are reduced. The Secretary replied that this ran counter to his instincts as we must remain strong in NATO. General Lai then said that the basic national policy of his government would never change. The GRC will stick to a democratic system, will never undertake peace talks with the PRC, and will endeavor to strengthen ties with the U.S. He said again that any assistance to Taiwan will pay high dividends as it is in our mutual defense. In response to a question from Mr. Clements, General Lai said that the size of the ROC Army is 600,000 but added quickly that it has to be substantial because the threat is substantial. General Lai said that 10% of Taiwan's

GNP goes to defense. A discussion of military personnel costs followed, with Secretary Schlesinger noting that the all-volunteer force has increased U.S. defense spending from 5% to 6.2% of GNP. General Lai then commented on the increasing capability of the PRC armed forces, including indigenous production of advanced jets and TU–16 bombers. Secretary Schlesinger responded that the F5E is better than anything the PRC has. This seemed to unsettle General Lai a bit, but he did allow that Nationalist Chinese pilots were much better than their mainland counterparts and cited by way of example the fact that in the 1958 Strait crisis the Communists lost thirty-one aircraft as compared with only one by Taiwan and, finally, General Lai allowed, quality not quantity is the most important. General Lai then commented in passing on the two submarines that we are providing to the Nationalist navy, and said that they will be quite expensive to maintain (see Addendum). Secretary Schlesinger replied that we must not provide items with high O&M costs as such items are not really assistance; we're really creating problems both for the recipients of such items and for ourselves. Finally, General Lai passed around some pictures of mainland Chinese fishermen that were captured and taken to Quemoy. They were all in rags. General Lai added that he was struck by the fact that none of them had any schooling. Mr. Clements asked General Lai how good the ROC intelligence capability is concerning the PRC. General Lai said that they would like to know more about mainland events, especially with regard to how the Communist regime maintains control. The Deputy Secretary then expressed his admiration for Taiwan's adjustment and accommodation to international developments in light of the new U.S.–PRC relationship. The Deputy Secretary said that he considered this adjustment to be remarkable and evidence of a great deal of grace on the part of Taiwan. General Lai was clearly quite pleased.

Addendum. With regard to General Lai's professed astonishment at the O&M cost for submarines, this was pointed out on numerous occasions to Nationalist Chinese officials (including Chiang Ching-kuo and Admiral Ko) before the agreement was concluded. Over two years ago, Mr. Doolin told Admiral Ko that the cost of operating a submarine could run as high as $10,000 per day. The Chinese CNO dismissed these figures and indicated that his navy could do this for one-tenth the cost. Admiral Ko was told that experience would prove him wrong. At the time the Chinese were pressing hard to secure these submarines, they told us over and over again that they required these submarines solely for ASW training for their surface units inasmuch as SubPac assets were not always available at the time the Chinese navy wished to conduct the exercise. At a meeting with Secretary Laird in 1971 prior to the conclusion of the submarine agreement, Chiang Ching-kuo said in Chinese that the reason his government required these two boats would be to maintain naval superiority in the Taiwan Strait. His astute interpreter did not translate this sentence. Mr. Doolin, who attended the meeting, speaks Chinese. He noted the omission; informed the Secretary of the omission after the meeting; and described the incident in the Memorandum of Conversation of that meeting.

---

48.   National Security Decision Memorandum 230[1]

Washington, August 9, 1973.

TO

    The Secretary of State
    The Secretary of Defense

SUBJECT

    U.S. Strategy and Forces for Asia

Based on a review of the NSSM 171 study,[2] the President has decided that the following guidance should govern our future military planning for Asia.

Strategic Planning

The basic strategic guidance for Asia as originally defined by NSDM 27[3] shall remain in force. U.S. forces should be planned so that U.S. and Allied forces would be capable of conducting a combined conventional defense against a joint PRC/Communist ally attack in either Northeast or Southeast Asia as well as a non-PRC attack in the other

---

[1] Source: National Archives, Nixon Presidential Materials, NSC Files, Box 364, Subject Files, National Security Decision Memoranda Nos. 145–264. Top Secret. Copies were sent to the Director of ACDA, the Director of Central Intelligence, the Chairman of the JCS, and the Director of OMB.

[2] NSSM 171, February 13, "directed that in the aftermath of the Vietnamese conflict, current U.S. strategy for Asia should be reviewed" with particular emphasis on proper force levels and requirements, basing postures, security assistance programs, and the diplomatic ramifications of changes in these areas. (Ibid., NSC Files, Subject Files, Box 365, National Security Study Memoranda, Nos. 104–206) A committee chaired by a representative of the Department of Defense and composed of representatives from the Departments of Defense and State, the CIA, and ACDA performed the review requested in NSSM 171 and produced a paper which is ibid., NSC Institutional Files (H-Files), Box H–196, National Security Study Memoranda, NSSM 171 [1 of 2]. NSSM 171 and the response study are scheduled for publication in *Foreign Relations, 1969–1976*, vol. E–12.

[3] Scheduled for publication ibid., vol. XXXIV.

Asian theater. The U.S. should continue to plan for an adequate capability to reinforce our Allies in support of this strategy, including the full range of land, naval, and tactical air forces.

Tactical nuclear forces should be planned in Asia as a hedge against the failure of a conventional defense. [1½ lines not declassified]

Security Assistance planning will continue to focus on assisting our Allies to meet indigenous and non-PRC communist nation threats. Planning will not be based on building Allied self-sufficiency in meeting major threats from the PRC. However, improvements in Allied capabilities to enhance a joint U.S./Allied defense will be planned as a lower priority goal.

U.S. Deployments

U.S. planning for the next five years should include Asian baseline deployments at essentially current levels in Korea, Japan/Okinawa, and the Philippines. Normal minor adjustments in manning and support forces would be made, but any proposed changes in combat force levels or major changes in manpower levels should be submitted to the President for approval. Deployments on Taiwan and in Thailand will be kept under continuous review. There will be no increases in forces or manpower on Taiwan without prior Presidential approval.

The Department of State should develop a scenario for informing the governments of Korea, Philippines, and Japan and other governments they believe appropriate of our deployment plans for FY 74. This scenario should be submitted to the President for approval by August 15, 1973.

Henry A. Kissinger

49.   **Memorandum From Charles Cooper, Robert D. Hormats, and Richard H. Solomon of the National Security Council Staff to the President's Assistant for National Security Affairs (Kissinger)[1]**

Washington, August 16, 1973.

SUBJECT

Problems in the China Trade

We are increasingly concerned about several problems in our economic relations with the People's Republic of China which could cause substantial difficulties if they get out of hand. The two discussed in this memorandum are coming to a head, and you should be aware of them in case you may need to take action to resolve them.

The National Council for U.S.–China Trade

The National Council for U.S.–China Trade was set up, largely through the efforts of the Department of Commerce, to act as a facilitating organization in the promotion of U.S.–PRC trade. Through informational and liaison activities, it was to have served as a nongovernmental bridge between the American business community and the PRC in the same pattern of the private organizations that facilitate cultural and scientific exchanges. In practice, the Trade Council has gotten off to a very slow start because of a combination of staffing problems, the overshadowing influence of Commerce in various activities relating to the China trade, and the partisan, big-business and export orientation of the Council's board.

We recently have picked up some negative comments about the Council from the PRC Liaison Office staff, who are disappointed with both the slow growth of the organization and its big-business orientation. The Chinese also may be giving encouragement to some of their local "friends" to set up a rival organization formed largely of small importers of Chinese products—who can help the PRC in its effort to bring its trade with the U.S. into better balance. The present danger is of a polarization between the Council and a rival group which would weaken USG influence over the development of trade and enable the Chinese to play one group against another. We are encouraging the Council to broaden its membership to include small traders, and to

---

[1] Source: National Archives, Nixon Presidential Materials, NSC Files, Box 527, Country Files, Far East, People's Republic of China, Vol. 8, July 10–Dec 31, 1973. Confidential. Sent for information. Kissinger received the memorandum on August 22, and wrote at the top of the first page, "Make sure we reduce delegation to Canton."

separate itself at an appropriate distance from the USG to give itself the independence necessary to gain wider support.

In this regard, a Council group scheduled to go to the PRC in early October had informally asked Secretary of Commerce Dent to join them. Dent declined, but suggested Deputy Assistant Secretary for East-West Trade Steven Lazarus to join the tour. The Council has now had second thoughts about Lazarus' inclusion in the delegation, given his position in the USG and their desire to establish an independent position. We also feel that it would be unwise for Lazarus to visit the PRC with the Council group at this time. We trust that Commerce will accept the Council's reversal of its invitation for his participation, but there may be some complaint.

USG Involvement in the Canton Fair

We are also concerned about excessive USG presence at the fall session of the Canton Fair. As a recent cable from our Peking Liaison Office (Tab A)[2] indicates, present plans are for seven (7) USG officers (2 from the Liaison Office, 4 from the Hong Kong Consulate, and 1 man from Commerce) to staff at various times an office which the government would sponsor at the month-long Fair. In addition, the Trade Council is planning to establish an advisory facility to be of assistance to U.S. businessmen attending the Fair. While there is a legitimate role to be played by commercial specialists of the USG in assisting American businessmen, we may be—as the USLO cable suggests—"overloading" the Chinese by requesting that seven men participate at this stage of our commercial relations with the PRC. In addition, the USG presence will tend to overshadow the National Council, which is supposed to be playing the advisory role. Thus, we think it wise to discourage a highly-visible USG presence at the Canton Fair this fall. We are now attempting to cope with this issue through the China desk at State, which will suggest to USLO and the Hong Kong Consulate that they cut back on their representation.

---

[2] Attached but not printed is telegram 789 from Beijing, August 15, containing additional information about the Canton Trade Fair.

50.   Note From the Government of the United States to the Government of the People's Republic of China[1]

Washington, August 22, 1973.

The U.S. side wishes to inform the Chinese side that the United Nations Commission on the Unification and Rehabilitation of Korea (UNCURK) will include in its yearly report a call for the dissolution of the organization without prejudice to its past activities. As indicated in recent messages presented to the PRC Liaison Office, the U.S. side will support this position during the 28th Session of the UN General Assembly.

The U.S. side also wishes to reiterate its position that it will use its influence to insure that any debate on the Korean issue in this year's General Assembly not exacerbate tensions, but contribute to an orderly evolution of the Korean situation. On the basis of such circumstances, the U.S. side is prepared to discuss after the 28th Session of the General Assembly ways in which the question of the UN Command might be resolved. Efforts of the Chinese side in behalf of this objective will be welcomed.

---

[1] Source: National Archives, Nixon Presidential Materials, NSC Files, Kissinger Office Files, Box 95, Country Files, Far East, China Exchanges, July 10–Oct 31, 1973 [2 of 2]. No classification marking. According to a handwritten comment on the note, Solomon presented the note to Chi Ch'ao-chu and Chien Ta-yung on August 22. Kissinger wrote "OK" on an earlier draft of the note and, on August 21, Scowcroft sent the revised version to Kennedy for delivery by Solomon. (Ibid.)

---

51.   Memorandum From John A. Froebe, Jr., of the National Security Council Staff to the President's Assistant for National Security Affairs (Kissinger)[1]

Washington, August 25, 1973.

SUBJECT

Chinese Representation in the International Financial Institutions (IFI's)

---

[1] Source: National Archives, Nixon Presidential Materials, NSC Files, Box 527, Country Files, Far East, People's Republic of China, Vol. 8, July 10–Dec 31, 1973. Secret. Sent for action.

At Tab A[2] is a State cable, concurred in by Treasury, directing the 36 action posts to seek the support of the host governments in the event that the ROC position in the IFI's (the World Bank and International Monetary Fund) is challenged at the annual meeting of these organizations planned for September 24–28 in Nairobi. The cable was sent without either NSC clearance or that of the seventh floor of State—which we had asked to clear the cable with us. We have put a hold on any implementation of the cable instruction.

I agree with the State position that it continues to be in our interest to support the ROC's continued participation in the IFI's—both because of its importance to the ROC's diplomatic position and to its international financial position, and because of our desire to avoid injecting political issues into the operations of the IMF/IBRD.

As State notes, however, we have no indication that the PRC either wants to join the Bank or Fund or that it wants to have the ROC expelled. A preliminary sounding with selected posts a month ago turned up no evidence of any such PRC inclination. Speculatively, it would seem unlikely that the PRC is interested in making such a challenge at this juncture:

—Peking is unlikely to want to assume the financial obligations of membership in the Bank and Fund, which include divulging their reserves, undertaking to make their currencies convertible into other currencies, and providing gold to the IMF.

—Even short of wanting to seek membership for itself, it is less than likely to want to have the ROC expelled at this juncture: this would risk another contretemps with us (in addition to that which may possibly occur at the U.N. General Assembly on the Korean question), and would run counter to its current campaign for a peaceful reconciliation with Taiwan.

The possibility remains that another state such as Algeria might make a challenge on Peking's behalf, but independent of PRC guidance. On balance, however, this eventuality also seems improbable. As last year, the great majority of Bank and Fund members, so far as we know, strongly want to avoid having to face the issue. State's strategy approach is essentially the same as that used at the Bank and Fund annual meeting last September: if the ROC position is challenged, another member (Saudi Arabia has already indicated its willingness to do so) would propose that the question be referred to the Bank and Fund's Executive Directors for consideration after the annual meetings. Our role would be strictly supportive of initiatives taken by others. I have no problem with this basic approach. State argues that this is the least

---

[2] Attached but not printed is a revised draft of telegram 166065, August 21, which was sent to 36 posts.

contentious method for handling a challenge which also would seem effective in parrying the challenge. The Bank and Fund's management support this approach.

I believe that this is a preferred approach. The alternatives either would probably not be effective—as with a ruling from the Chair that attempted to refer the matter for study—or would probably be more contentious—as a proposal that the matter be shelved until the PRC had indicated its willingness to accept the obligations of membership.

State's recommended representations in support of this strategy

The State cable would instruct the 36 posts to take more definitive soundings, reiterate U.S. support for continued ROC participation in the IFI's, and seek the host governments' support for our strategy in the event of a challenge. Peace representations would also be aimed at acquainting the considerable number of new Bank/Fund governors from these countries with our strategy.

In my view, State's proposed representations carry too high profile: both in the number of posts involved and in the tenor of the substance of the proposed representations the State approach would risk stimulating that which it is designed to avoid. I recommend that the number of posts making representations be reduced to 21 (particularly in view of the weighted system of voting used in the Bank and Fund), and that the substance of the approach be pitched in a somewhat lower key. I have amended the State cable at Tab A to reflect both of these objections.

Recommendation:

That you approve the State cable at Tab A as amended.[3]

---

[3] Kissinger initialed the Approve option. The cable was sent as revised as a telegram, and posts were instructed to disregard telegram 166065. (Memorandum from Davis to Pickering, September 1; National Archives, Nixon Presidential Materials, NSC Files, Box 527, Country Files, Far East, People's Republic of China, Vol. 8, July 10–Dec 31, 1973)

---

52.   Editorial Note

On September 26, 1973, newly appointed Secretary of State Henry Kissinger met with People's Republic of China Representative to the United Nations Huang Hua. Kissinger analyzed the U.S.–PRC relationship in the United Nations and declared, "the only issue that I see that could give us some difficulty is Korea. We conveyed our thoughts to you some months ago. We think we should show restraint in having a confrontation because we are moving in the direction which the Prime Minister and I discussed."

Kissinger also noted, "We have agreed to the dissolution of UNCURK. If we could shelve the issue of the United Nations Command for one year at least. The problem now is that the armistice depends on the existence of the UN Command. That will give us an opportunity to look and work with you on this and to develop alternative legal arrangements." Huang Hua suggested, "If you could persuade South Korea to give up its position of perpetuating a division of Korea in contradiction of agreements between the two sides, I think this will help with rapprochement and relaxation in that area." In particular, Huang Hua suggested that South Korean President Park Chung Hee abandon his proposal to have both Koreas admitted into the United Nations. Kissinger, however, refused to commit himself on this question. The memorandum of conversation is in National Archives, Nixon Presidential Materials, NSC Files, Kissinger Office Files, Box 95, Country Files, Far East, China Exchanges, July 10–Oct. 31, 1973.

On September 29, Kissinger met with Ambassador Huang Zhen, Chief of the People's Republic of China Liaison Office, to follow up on discussions they had in July at the Western White House in San Clemente, California, on the Soviet threat to China (see Document 41). Kissinger deferred serious discussion on this topic until his visit to China scheduled for late October: "I also wish to go further into that problem which I discussed with you in San Clemente, the one which grew out of the June meetings (with Brezhnev). I want to discuss developments in that respect since June. I propose that any meeting on this particular issue be carried out in a restricted group, as we have done in the past." The Secretary of State also declared, "If there are any questions regarding developments in Southeast Asia we will be glad to discuss them, but we are not asking you to do anything in this regard now. We will also be prepared to discuss developments in South Asia, the area of Iran, Pakistan, and Turkey, the problems in this area that we discussed with the Premier before. And of course, there is Taiwan, Japan, as well as any other problems the Premier would like to discuss." The memorandum of conversation is in National Archives, Nixon Presidential Materials, NSC Files, Kissinger Office Files, Box 95, Country Files, Far East, China Exchanges, July 10–Oct 31, 1973.

On October 25, the Central Intelligence Agency disseminated National Intelligence Estimate 11/13/6–73, on "Possible Changes in the Sino-Soviet Relationship," which concluded that improvement in the relationship was unlikely in the next couple of years, but that war was also improbable. In the longer run, it predicted, "movement beyond limited accommodations toward a genuine and durable rapprochement . . . seems highly unlikely, even through 1980." (National Intelligence

Council, *Tracking the Dragon,* pages 615–630) One month earlier, National Intelligence Estimate 11–13–73, "The Sino-Soviet Relationship: Military Aspects," dated September 20, predicted that war between the Soviet Union and China was unlikely. (Ibid., from accompanying compact disk with additional documents)

---

53.   Notes on a Conversation Between Secretary of State Kissinger and the Ambassador to the Republic of China (McConaughy)[1]

Washington, October 3, 1973, noon.

(At some point HAK said he would not bring up Taiwan when he goes to Peking. Would focus on Soviets, Indochina and other topics.)

W [Walter]—greetings, congratulations on job. Grateful for fact of meeting, because it will be important for U.S.–ROC relations.

K—Give special regards to CCK and others. There is no people I regard more highly than those of Taiwan. I regret that the Chinese on Taiwan have suffered some blows, and my heart bled that we had to take the actions we did. If we had not, the U.S. would have been torn apart. We had to move on this in 1971 (in order to de-fuse the Vietnam issue so that we could proceed toward a Vietnam settlement at our own pace).

We are not turning our backs on Taiwan, and this attitude has not and will not change.

However we are moving inexorably toward full recognition of Peking, which is bound to come by 1980 at the latest. There may be some initial moves earlier, perhaps in 1975. But we will not press Taiwan to the wall. Our movements will include guaranteed enforceable

---

[1] Source: Department of State, Papers of William H. Gleysteen: Lot 89 D 436, Box 8132, PRC Related Papers 1973. Eyes Only. The meeting took place in Kissinger's office. Arthur Hummel, Acting Assistant Secretary of State for East Asian and Pacific Affairs, prepared these notes based on McConaughy's account of the meeting. Kissinger initially refused to meet with McConaughy or to authorize that Nixon meet with him. (Memorandum from Froebe to Kissinger, August 22; National Archives, Nixon Presidential Materials, NSC Files, Box 527, Country Files, Far East, People's Republic of China, Vol. 8, July 10–Dec 31, 1973) Hummel, with the support of Eagleburger and Pickering, convinced Kissinger to reconsider by suggesting that a refusal to meet with McConaughy might weaken the position of Jiang Jingguo and lead Taiwan to pursue a more independent foreign policy. (Memorandum from Pickering to Kissinger, September 30; ibid., RG 59, EAP ROC Files: Lot 76 D 441, PER 17–Amb. McConaughy, 1973)

provisions for ensuring continued separate status for Taiwan if that is what Taiwan wants.

W—This of course assumes no provocative acts by Taiwan, such as an announcement of separate status.

K—That is true; there should be no provocations, but in a de facto way they can go their separate way. If we move, we will build in assurances so that Taiwan will not automatically fall into mainland hands. For instance we might arrange so that the US-Taiwan defense treaty does not lapse, or if it does lapse that there could be automatic restoration of the treaty under certain circumstances.

(He then criticized Japan's devious game toward Taiwan, in counting on us to preserve, and getting a free ride without helping to bear the burden. The Japanese suggested in 1972 (Walter thinks Tanaka at Kuilima) that Japan could represent US interests in Peking in return for US representation of Japan on Taiwan.)

W—Hope there will not be a determined economic squeeze by Peking on Taiwan.

K—I discount this, and doubt the PRC will go all out to stifle Taiwan trade. If these is such a move, to make Taiwan non-viable, the Japanese might take steps, and we would also.

W—Reminded Kissinger of Pres Nixon's statements of Walter's mission in repeated statements of 1969–72—that is, hand-holding the GRC, and reassuring them. I assume these instructions still stand.

K—Yes indeed. I am well aware of those statements and I am sure the President still wants them to be operative. Now I want you to know that of course we will maintain an Amb in Taipei, and we *will* replace you after you leave. There have been rumors here and on Taiwan that we would not, but they are not true. I understand you are rather disposed to retire.

W—Yes, but I am not pushing. I've been there a long time and I'm past normal retirement age. I would like to leave in the reasonable future.

K—No time yet to focus on Ambs. Realize long time for you. I will soon focus.

W—Maybe next Spring would be good for me. Give time for leisurely departure, but of course could be earlier if you want.

54.   Telegram From the Liaison Office in China to the Department of State[1]

Beijing, October 16, 1973.

1216. Subj: Jackson Bill and PRC.

1. While I realize that overriding concern with Jackson Bill limiting President's authority to grant MFN treatment is centered on Soviet Union and its restrictions on Jewish emigration, I would like to call attention to fact that, if passed in present form, bill will apply equally to PRC and will be a major obstacle to developing U.S.–PRC trade relations. I am particularly concerned that members of Congress may not be fully aware of importance Peking attaches to MFN, both as a prerequisite for expanding its exports to the U.S. and thereby improving balance of trade and politically as a significant indicator of further progress in normalization of relations.

2. Recent discussion between Hong Kong ConGen officers and Senator Jackson's staff assistant, Richard N. Perle, (as reported to us by visiting FSO John J. Taylor) suggests ignorance in some congressional quarters of consequences for Sino-U.S. relations if free emigration imposed as condition for MFN. In describing Senator Jackson's views on this subject, Mr. Perle assumed that China would not be concerned over failure to receive MFN status. When the problems were pointed out to Mr. Perle, he had no response except to offer the hope that somehow the issue would not be raised. He made clear that the proposed legislation was aimed solely at the USSR.

3. In addition to difficulties posed for Sino-U.S. trade, Jackson Bill will also raise political problem of a public finding that PRC practices emigration policies making it subject to provisions of the bill. Given Chinese sensitivities on question of refugees and emigration this cannot help but have negative impact on our developing relations.

4. I realize fully that question of MFN for the PRC inevitably bound up with that of Soviet Union. Nevertheless, I think it important—and possibly useful in Soviet context as well—that Congress be made aware of significance which PRC attaches to this question and possible adverse impact Jackson Bill could have on U.S.–PRC commercial and political relations. Perhaps some additional educational efforts with the Congress might be useful.

Bruce

---

[1] Source: National Archives, Nixon Presidential Materials, NSC Files, Kissinger Office Files, Box 93, Country Files, Far East, China Trade and Exchanges, July 5, 1973–Feb. 28, 1974. Confidential; Nodis; Cherokee. No time of transmission appears on the telegram; however a stamped notation indicates it was received at 9:04 p.m.

55.   Memorandum of Conversation[1]

Beijing, November 10, 1973, 9:25–10:00 p.m.

PARTICIPANTS

Prime Minister Chou En-lai
Yeh Chien-ying, Chairman of the Military Affairs Committee
Vice Prime Minister Chiao Kuan-hua
Tang Wang-shen, Interpreter
Shen Jo-yen, Interpreter

Henry A. Kissinger, Secretary of State
Winston Lord, Director of Planning and Coordination, State Department

(As the group was walking toward the meeting room, Marshal Yeh indicated to the Secretary that he now had heavier burdens as Secretary of State. The Secretary replied that it was more complicated, but the direction of policy was the same. There had been major personnel changes.)

The Secretary: I thought, Mr. Prime Minister, we might have a brief talk on a particular problem that came up during the visit of General Secretary Brezhnev to the United States.[2] It rose in the following manner, and I'll give you the circumstances because they may be of some interest to you. During that week, during the visit, Mr. Brezhnev attempted to see the President alone without me (laughter). He went through extremely complicated maneuvers to accomplish this (laughter). For example, in California, he stayed in the house of the President and he pretended to go to bed, and then he thought I would leave. When he thought I had left, he got up and asked to see the President, who himself had gone to bed (laughter). I mention it only because it was not an accidental conversation. After all the maneuvers the President insisted that I be present. So it was myself, the President, Mr. Brezhnev and an interpreter.

And he (Brezhnev) said he wanted to have a conversation which only he and the President would know about and no one else. This led him into a long diagnosis of what he called the "China problem" which

---

[1] Source: National Archives, RG 59, Policy Planning Staff (S/P), Director's Files (Winston Lord) 1969–1977, Entry 5027, Box 380, Lord China Files. Top Secret; Sensitive; Exclusively Eyes Only. The meeting took place in the Great Hall of the People in Beijing. All ellipses are in the original. Kissinger visited China November 10–14 to provide reassurance about the prospect for improved U.S.–PRC relations despite the stresses produced by the Cambodian war, Watergate, and U.S.-Soviet détente. Winston Lord produced briefing papers for Kissinger's trip, which are ibid., Nixon Presidential Materials, NSC Files, Kissinger Office Files, Box 99, Country Files, Far East.

[2] Leonid Brezhnev visited the United States June 16–25.

was extremely violent and reported many examples of how the Russians were treated in China. That is of no consequence. But there were two major points he was making in this conversation. First, that the Soviet Union would resist by force any military arrangement between the United States and China, and he asked whether there existed a military arrangement. We didn't feel he had a right to ask that question. I know there doesn't exist one, but we do not feel that he had the right to ask that question. So we said the Chinese have never raised any military arrangement with us, which is correct. He then demanded an assurance that there would never by any military arrangements in the future, and he repeated the thought again that he would use force if anything like this happened.

The second point he made was independent of the United States and China. It had to do only with China. He said that the growth of the Chinese nuclear capability was unacceptable to the Soviet Union, and he proposed an exchange of information about what we knew about their nuclear program. We told them that we don't engage in an exchange of intelligence information. Since then . . . let me do this in sequence. This happened late one afternoon; it lasted a very long time, but I'm just giving the essence. Late that night Gromyko asked to see me, and asked me what I thought of what Brezhnev had earlier said to the President, even though Brezhnev had given his word that no one would know except Brezhnev and the President what he said. He said that Brezhnev had said to the President only two things and that I would know about them. I said it was an unheard of proposition, and I'd never heard this kind of talk between countries who were not allies.

He then said he wanted it understood that they might consider Chinese political relationships, and not only military relations, a provocation.

Prime Minister Chou: Chinese military relations or relations with other countries?

The Secretary: And I said like your friendship treaty with India? He then evaded the answer, and I told him that this was an inadmissible line of discussion and that we would not pursue it.

Since then, the Soviet Union has tried on three or four occasions to exchange information on China with us by putting it in the context of a discussion on strategic nuclear limitations. The way they do it is to say they should be entitled to have equality with the United States, and, in addition to this equality, enough weapons to destroy China. And those weapons must increase each year because of the Chinese situation.

I tell you this, Mr. Prime Minister, not out of altruism, but because I believe the destruction of China by the Soviet Union, or even a massive attack on China by the Soviet Union, would have unforeseeable consequences for the entire international situation. (The interpreter indicated that there was not total understanding of this point.) I don't tell this out of abstract altruism because I believe it is in our interest to prevent such an attack. You know as well as I do, Mr. Prime Minister, the consequences on Japan, Europe, South Asia, and the Middle East if such an attack even had the appearance of success.

Before these conversations, I believed the Soviets had a generalized hostility toward China, but I did not believe they had a specific plan. You may have had another idea. I do not now exclude the possibility of some specific ideas.

Now, as a result of these conversations, I ordered some studies in our government that only four or five people know about, of what we know about what such a threat could be, and what from our knowledge could be done to prevent it, and of what help we could be in ways that are not obvious, because I don't think a formal relationship is desirable for either of us. These would be of a technical nature. I don't have those papers with me here now, but I have them in my guest house. We have some ideas on how to lessen the vulnerability of your forces and how to increase the warning time, and I repeat that it has to be done in such a way that it is very secret and not obvious.[3]

If the Prime Minister is interested, I can have Commander Howe, or in some respects I could mention the details in a small group—either to the Prime Minister or someone he designates. This is not something that involves reciprocity or any formal relationship, but advice based on our experience and some regularized intelligence information. (The interpreter questions the meaning of "regularized.") "Regularized intelligence information" means the regularized information from us to you, not the other way.

Apart from that, I thought it might be of some importance to you to know the state of mind of Brezhnev as stated to us. As far as we are concerned, we don't believe we can permit this, though it is a very difficult problem how to work out in practice.

Prime Minister Chou: During your recent short visit,[4] it was probably not raised again.

The Secretary: No, he raised it again. He raised the question of exchanging military information again.

---

[3] In an October 22 memorandum to Kissinger, Fred Iklé, Director of the Arms Control and Disarmament Agency, suggested offering intelligence to China about the Soviet threat. Solomon sent Iklé's memorandum to Kissinger under a November 1 covering memorandum. (National Archives, RG 59, Policy Planning Staff (S/P), Director's Files (Winston Lord) 1969–1977, Entry 5027, Box 370, Secretary Kissinger's Visit to Peking, October 1973, S/PC, Mr. Lord, Vol. II)

[4] Kissinger visited Moscow October 20–22, mainly to discuss the Middle East war.

Prime Minister Chou: They have satellites that can survey China every day.

The Secretary: I know.

Prime Minister Chou: And they still want it?

The Secretary: Our belief is their photography is not as good as ours. But I think what they want is an indication from us that they would use as a symbol of cooperation rather than using it. They want us to accept the desirability of destroying China's nuclear capability or limiting it rather than the information itself. But the exchange of information is not a big problem, as that obviously we won't do, and they probably have what they need.

Prime Minister Chou: Even though the Middle East was so tense, they still discuss such an issue?

The Secretary: When I was there it was during the ceasefire discussion.

Prime Minister Chou: It was before our alert. You went originally for the ceasefire.

The Secretary: Yes.

Prime Minister Chou: They invited you?

The Secretary: At that time there was no question of military pressure on us. The military pressure started four days later, and since then, they have not raised it.

Prime Minister Chou: It was only mentioned during the visit.

The Secretary: During my visit and not since then.

Prime Minister Chou: I believe they would suggest such matters to Japan, too.

The Secretary: It is conceivable. In any event, even if they don't, if they started on this course, it is in my judgment not clear what Japan will do. We have not heard that they have proposed anything like this to Japan.

Prime Minister Chou: They always wanted to get Japan brought closer to them and away from us. They know they can't sever relations completely between you and Japan, but at least they want to get Japan closer to them than to you.

The Secretary: Yes.

Prime Minister Chou: We have also said to Japan that if they want to exploit Siberia, it is better to be done with you than alone. I believe Prime Minister Tanaka will tell you that when he meets you.

The Secretary: That is our view, too.

Prime Minister Chou: I told them that if they do, it is better to do it with the United States. We said we do not fear their exploiting Siberian resources. The only thing is that we are afraid that they might be taken in.

Have you found some difficulties within the Soviet leadership at present, among the three or four of them?

The Secretary: No, because we always deal with Brezhnev.

Prime Minister Chou: Yes, he monopolizes the scene.

The Secretary: At first we always dealt with Kosygin or Podgorny and Brezhnev. Gromyko is a functionary and not a leader.

Prime Minister Chou: Suslov doesn't take part in the negotiations.

The Secretary: Only once when the President was in Moscow. We have no special information on that. Our people think he's more ideological and less bureaucratic than the others. He's ideological and less bureaucratic than the others, but I don't know how we would know that.

Prime Minister Chou: He knows historical theory, but he follows the other line of thinking. He explains other peoples' theories. The Soviet party history has been changed three times, and all three times under his guidance.

The Secretary: That I didn't know. I knew it had changed three times; I didn't know he did it.

Prime Minister Chou: He is the one who finalized the draft, so he is that kind of author who follows the others.

The Secretary: There is no outstanding intellectual leader in the Soviet Union.

Prime Minister Chou: No, they don't have any. It is impossible to have any, because they are so oppressive.

Thank you for anyway for your information and for your notification. Anyway, Ambassador Huang Chen has passed on what you have told him, and we have taken note of that. At present, though they are quite busy on day-to-day policies and other matters, they have to curse us everyday in the newspapers anyway. There are some people here in our party who read and study the materials, but we don't have the time to go through them all.

So should we begin with a plenary session tomorrow?

The Secretary: Yes.

Prime Minister Chou: Would you like a plenary session or begin with five or six people as I just said now?

The Secretary: What do you think?

Prime Minister Chou: I think about four or five.

The Secretary: All right. We'll make it four or five. I think that's better.

Prime Minister Chou: Because you have travelled through so many countries.

The Secretary: If on the other matter, the Marshal or someone else wants the studies, they can get in touch with Mr. Lord, and Commander Howe can give those conclusions.

Prime Minister Chou: All right. You're leaving on the 14th, is that so?

The Secretary: Yes, in the morning.

Prime Minister Chou: The more you move eastward, the more time you lose.

The Secretary: That is true, but at the end you finally gain it all back.

---

56. Memorandum of Conversation[1]

Beijing, November 11, 1973, 3:15–7:00 p.m.

PARTICIPANTS

Prime Minister Chou En-lai
Foreign Minister Chi Peng-fei
Vice Foreign Minister Chiao Kuan-hua
Assistant Minister of Foreign Affairs Wang Hai-jung
Two Other Chinese Officials
Tang Wang-shen, Interpreter
Shen Jo-yen, Interpreter
Chinese note-taker

Henry A. Kissinger, Secretary of State
Ambassador David Bruce, Chief U.S. Liaison Office
Ambassador Robert Ingersoll, U.S. Embassy Tokyo
Ambassador Robert McCloskey, State Department Press Spokesman
Winston Lord, Director of Planning and Coordination, Department of State
John Holdridge, Deputy Chief U.S. Liaison Office

(After the press took pictures and there was light banter, the journalists and photographers left the room. There was then preliminary conversation in informal plenary session, from 3:15–3:25 p.m., highlights of which follow.)

Prime Minister Chou: Dr. Kissinger suggested that we separate into two groups to speed up the work. I also agree.

---

[1] Source: National Archives, Nixon Presidential Materials, NSC Files, Kissinger Office Files, Box 100, Country Files, Far East, Secretary Kissinger's Conversations in Peking, November 1973. Top Secret; Sensitive; Exclusively Eyes Only. The meeting was held in the Great Hall of the People.

Secretary Kissinger: I thought, Mr. Prime Minister, that we might have one group dealing with the essential political-international problems and the other group on some of the technical issues.

Prime Minister Chou: I agree to the two groups. Perhaps we can divide ourselves now. Who will be in the other?

Secretary Kissinger: Hummel will be in charge of the technical side and with me will be Ambassador Bruce, Ingersoll, McCloskey, Holdridge and Lord. We may change later.

Prime Minister Chou: Who will be with the other group?

Secretary Kissinger: Hummel, Armstrong, Jenkins and Solomon.

Prime Minister Chou: Mr. Solomon—is this Solomon the same one as the Indians?

Secretary Kissinger: I thought they had Moynihan.

Prime Minister Chou: It is a different case; and one of them is Solomon. Is he the same Solomon as the bible?

Secretary Kissinger: I have seen no evidence of that. He is very shy so he may not show it.

Prime Minister Chou: I thought he was interested in Confucius. If you are interested, I am also. I also have the interest to discuss it with you because we began our revolutionary activities by struggling to overthrow the school of Confucius during the reform movement.

They will go to the other hall. We will stay here. Shall we separate now? (The groups for the technical meeting left the room.)[2]

You must be familiar with this hall by now.

Secretary Kissinger: Yes. What is the name of this hall?

Prime Minister Chou: Just a reception hall. It does not have the name of any province.

Secretary Kissinger: You met here with the President.

Prime Minister Chou: The first time when we met with the President, it was in this hall, and Mr. Ziegler was making the announcement to the press outside.

Secretary Kissinger: Yes, about the (Mao) meeting. They were speculating about the great difficulties because the meeting started late.

Prime Minister Chou: But, of course, after the news got out, there were other ideas. Perhaps that is why there was a similar practice in Moscow.

Secretary Kissinger: The first meeting?

---

[2] Memoranda of conversation of the counterpart technical discussions are in National Archives, Nixon Presidential Materials, NSC Files, Kissinger Office Files, Box 87, Country Files, Far East, PRC Counterpart Talks, 1971–1973.

Prime Minister Chou: But that time your name did not appear, but I could determine that you must have been there.

Secretary Kissinger: You were right. That was the first evening of my arrival. He does everything openly, but it takes me a week to find out all of the implications of what he has said.

Prime Minister Chou: Ambassador Ingersoll, do you smoke?

Ambassador Ingersoll: No, my wife takes care of that. I have never done well with smoking.

Prime Minister Chou: First of all, we would like to express our welcome to our old friend who is now concurrently Secretary of State, and because of this dual capacity, we suppose we should express a dual welcome to you. But if you see Mr. Rogers, please also convey our regards to him.

Secretary Kissinger: I shall do that. Mr. Prime Minister, my colleagues and I always appreciate the opportunity to come here. I think that our two peoples and our two governments have established a very unique relationship which is founded on principle and in which we understand each other's over-all approach in an unusual and complete manner. We have agreed that we were brought together by mutual necessity but since then we have built on this foundation, on a basis of candor and honesty, and a long range view. There is no leader with whom we speak as comprehensively as with the Prime Minister. It is due to the fact that there are not many leaders in the world who can think in so complicated a fashion.

Prime Minister Chou: You have overestimated me, and I think the credit should go to Chairman Mao. And as his comrade in arms, I have not learned enough. I agree to what you said just now, that we have built on the basis of our initial relations, based on a principled manner and in a candid and honest way taking the long view. And in view of such amelioration of attitudes we can discuss anything.

Secretary Kissinger: I don't know how the Prime Minister would propose we should proceed in our discussion.

Prime Minister Chou: Yesterday we said that we would like to hear you first, and if you want to begin with an over-all picture or main issues, it is up to you.

Secretary Kissinger: Mr. Prime Minister, why don't I begin with a general review of the situation as we see it.

(There was then a brief, humorous discussion of the stenotype machine of Mrs. Hill. During this discussion there was reference by the Prime Minister to future visits by Secretary Kissinger to China. He assumed two trips a year.)

Secretary Kissinger: Mr. Prime Minister, I will not go into the bilateral relations. That will be discussed by the other group. If they have any difficulties, I may take the liberty of raising them with you. There is only one issue which is on my list and sometime while I am here we should settle it. We understand your point of view. It has to do with the Marine detachment, but we can reserve that for another occasion. It goes without saying that we will abide by your wishes, and our only concern is the impact in other countries where it has been our custom.

The primary thing I would say about our bilateral relations, leaving aside that one issue, is that we believe they are going well, and secondly, they have both a substantive and a symbolic aspect. The substantive issues will be discussed in the other group. The symbolic aspect is that our relationship continues to grow closer and beyond the technical side. We are prepared on our side to consider all means by which we can emphasize this symbolic aspect which we believe is very important.

Turning now to our political relationships—we recognize that the greatest difficulties we have had in our relationship have concerned the question of Taiwan. I would like to summarize again the understanding which we believe exists. We will conform strictly to the Shanghai Communiqué which affirms there is only one China and this is respected on both sides of the Formosa Straits.

Prime Minister Chou: That was your famous sentence.

Secretary Kissinger: Secondly, we will not . . .

Prime Minister Chou: But in the communiqué we talked about the Taiwan Straits.

Secretary Kissinger: That is correct. The second point is that we will not support any independence movement on Taiwan.

Prime Minister Chou: And this morning before going to bed I read an intelligence report that we received saying you were supporting the Taiwan independence movement. I did not quite believe it.

Secretary Kissinger: That cannot be correct, but if you should have information that any of our people are doing this I would appreciate it if you would inform us. It would be totally unauthorized. I don't believe it is correct.

Prime Minister Chou: If the information seems to be reliable, we would pass it on; but if in the first instance it is not to be credited, we then would not notify you. I did not even think of telling the Chairman about that piece of information. It would only be a waste of time.

Secretary Kissinger: Mr. Prime Minister, our firm policy is to oppose a two China policy. We have talked about this on my previous visits and we will strictly carry this out.

Prime Minister Chou: And we also heard some news from the United States that Taiwan wanted to add two consulates—to have two Consulates General in the United States.

Secretary Kissinger: I was going to get into this. I am familiar with one consulate they are planning to set up for the time that we may move in the direction of a full exchange of diplomatic relations between Peking and Washington, and it is intended as a point of contact in the United States for the contingency of the evolution of our policy. It is not intended as an expansion of their representation but as a contingency plan for their position they recognize as coming in the future. I do not know about a second one. I know about a Consulate General in New York. The basic direction which we established in July 1971 is one on which you can count on, and we will not engage in little maneuvers within that context, much less outside it.

Prime Minister Chou: Perhaps the Chaing Kai-shek side put that forward.

Secretary Kissinger: That may be, but it is a reflection of the reduction of their position in the United States, not an attempt to increase it.

We have also understood that we would not support any attempt by third countries to move into Taiwan.

Prime Minister Chou: And this has something to do with both our sides.

Secretary Kissinger: Fourthly, the United States will support any peaceful resolution of the problem.

And finally, we would discourage any military moves from Taiwan against the Mainland. In the context of the Shanghai Communiqué and our understandings we have kept you informed about the nature of our military establishments on Taiwan. We are in the process of carrying out the military movements which I informed you of in February—the withdrawal of the transportation squadrons from Taiwan.

In the same spirit, I would like to inform you of our plans for next year. During 1974 we shall remove the two squadrons of Phantom planes that are now on Taiwan—one squadron in each half of the year. One-half in the first half and the second squadron in the second half. We will remove the U–2 planes from Taiwan. And we will remove the nuclear weapons which are in Taiwan. This will reduce our presence on Taiwan to communications and logistics. We will keep you informed of the further reductions which will take place after that.

It is also our intention, which we have mentioned to you and which the President reconfirmed to you, to complete the full normalization of the relations between China and the United States during this term of office, before the middle of 1976. We are prepared at any point to intensify the existing relationship or to establish full diplomatic relations, but we have the difficulty of how to handle the relationship with Taiwan in the interim period. But we will be prepared to listen to any proposal that you might have in this connection and make every attempt to meet it. If at any point the Chinese thought the formulation of the Shanghai Communiqué or an adaptation would provide some-way to have diplomatic relations we would be prepared to proceed on that basis.

In the meantime, we need to be prepared to expand the status of the Liaison Offices so that they become more and more similar to full diplomatic recognition. I think it is obvious that your Ambassador in Washington today enjoys a more direct access to our top officials than any other Ambassador in Washington, certainly, more than the representative of Taiwan. We would be prepared to establish trade offices and other institutional links that you might consider appropriate. I wanted to emphasize that the course which we have established will be strictly maintained. Now perhaps I should turn to other matters, Mr. Prime Minister, unless you wish to discuss these issues further.

Prime Minister Chou: I will dwell on them later. I will dwell on the other aspects of this issue later. There is only one question I would like to ask. We hear you intend to assist Taiwan in building an airplane assembly factory, and we would like to know what form it would take—rented, leased, a gift, sold on credit or . . .

Secretary Kissinger: You asked me that . . .

Prime Minister Chou: Of course, there is no question the material would come from you, the United States.

Secretary Kissinger: You asked me that the last time, and in fact we have the details with us and I will answer you. I will answer you tomorrow. I will do it at the beginning of our discussion tomorrow. I don't have them here with me. I may say now, Mr. Prime Minister, it is for an airplane of short range. It cannot reach the Mainland. It is a defensive airplane, and a means of avoiding our having to sell longer range airplanes to Taiwan and to separate its military procurement to a greater degree from direct American sales. We have, as you know, Mr. Prime Minister, a rather delicate process of disengagement to conduct—in which the Chinese side has shown great patience and wisdom if I may say—but we understand the outcome that our current policy will have.

Now turning to other international problems. Let me speak first of our relations with the Soviet Union. There are many detailed issues which I am prepared to discuss, having to do with specific negotiations. I think the basic point to understand, Mr. Prime Minister, is that I believe analytically that the Soviet Union and we are pursuing almost identical policies toward each other and it remains to be seen whose judgment is better. The Soviet Union is pursuing a policy of relaxation of tensions with the West for a variety of reasons. One of the reasons undoubtedly is the Soviet conviction that if they can create the appearance of détente, the unity of the West will disintegrate and the defense of the West will weaken.

I have no quarrel with many of the comments that we have received from the Chinese side privately, and many of the analyses from the Chinese side that we have seen publicly, about the problem of the direction of Soviet policy. I stated our position vis-à-vis the Soviet Union in a speech before a conference and in my press conference a few weeks ago.[3] I don't know whether the Prime Minister has seen those. I stated then we would resist any aggressive tendencies directed outward. I said we would not permit détente to be used to undermine or weaken our relationships with our friends. And thirdly, that we would resist any attempts by the Soviet Union to use international trouble spots to expand its positions.

While these are our principles, we have a complex tactical problem about how to apply them. One of the problems is that while many of our commentators in America are very heroic in intervening in domestic affairs of other countries they are very unwilling to face the consequences of what these policies would involve. We believe that it is important for us to demonstrate that we have made a major effort to preserve the peace in order to be in a position to resist when aggressive action occurs. When aggressive action occurs, we will act decisively, and if necessary brutally, but we require the prior demonstration that we have been provoked. And I think we have proved this in our handling of the Middle East crisis.

I have read with great care your Vice Minister's criticisms of the Treaty for the Prevention of Nuclear War, and, of course, I have had the benefit of direct communications with the Prime Minister.[4] I do not quarrel with the specific points made by either the Prime Minister or the Vice Minister in terms of Soviet intentions. And it does not affect . . .

Prime Minister Chou: Why are there so many differing opinions inside your country concerning your President's action in the Middle East?

Secretary Kissinger: In the Middle East?

Prime Minister Chou: That is, your alert. We are in favor of it.

Secretary Kissinger: I have always believed, Mr. Prime Minister, that the people who understand our foreign policy best are in Peking.

Prime Minister Chou: Thank you for your just and fair words. Put that in the record.

Secretary Kissinger: This record never leaves my office. There are several reasons for this. Actually we have not had many domestic difficulties about this alert. It was relatively minor. In fact, after I testified

---

[3] See footnote 4, Document 42.
[4] See Documents 36, 38, and 42.

before the Senate Foreign Relations Committee, a group which does not generally support the Administration, Senator Symington, who almost always is critical of the Administration, went on TV and fully supported the alert; and so did Senator Fulbright.

Prime Minister Chou: I read about that.

Secretary Kissinger: This alert happened in the week in which public excitement about the Watergate problem was very high and some of the critics of the Administration merged those two issues. You have in America now in any event, Mr. Prime Minister, a combination of various forces that produce a rather contradictory pattern in the public discussion of foreign policy—not in the conduct of it. You have a combination of the intellectuals, who dislike the President for other reasons, with the old professional anti-communists of the right, so that, for the first time, some of these right wing groups are being given intellectual respectability. Basically, the alert had very wide public support and there was a public poll which showed that by about two to one the American people favored it.

But the reason, Mr. Prime Minister, we can maintain support for our foreign policy is partly because of its record and partly because of our using this strategy of forcing the Soviet Union into a posture of provocation. Sometimes our judgment may be wrong, but our strategy is clear. We have explained that treaty to you. Our judgment was that it was better to deprive it of the significance that the Soviet Union wanted to give it and to remove it as an issue from a public debate and from international quorums, than to have an endless debate in which public opinion would suffer more damage than it did from the treaty as in fact it was written.

I must point out, Mr. Prime Minister, that this session is a culture shock to my colleagues on the right, except for Ambassador Bruce, who have not been acquainted in the past with our method of talking with one another. In traditional diplomacy, we express ourselves more carefully.

But the primary thing we have accomplished in the Treaty is to link all its obligations but also third countries and to link conventional war to nuclear war in such a way that it is impossible to resort to conventional war without (sic) negating any obligations with respect to nuclear war and finally to make it impossible to resort to any war without prior consultation. And therefore, we have been given for the first time a legal basis to resist in areas where we have no formal obligation.

Therefore, on the night that we went on alert we received a message, as I told you, from General Secretary Brezhnev in which he demanded that we join a Soviet-American expeditionary force to the Middle East and, failing that they would then move unilaterally. They were demanding an immediate reply. We first of all did not reply but went on alert and replied only after we had been on alert for several hours. And then we told the Soviet Union that a unilateral Soviet move would violate Article 2 of the Treaty for the Prevention of Nuclear War and would be resisted accordingly.

Prime Minister Chou: We were clear about that. But the Soviet Union can evade that and engage in expansionism in other forms.

Secretary Kissinger: There is no question that legal obligations prevent Soviet expansionism. Our problem is how to get into a position to resist, and the strategy we are following is to try to create as many legal obstacles as possible; and, failing that, to use those legal obstacles as American obligations, especially in those areas where we have no formal obligation and therefore would have difficulties domestically.

The Prime Minister might note that I said publicly, in explaining the treaty, that operations such as in Czechoslovakia, or massive movement of arms across the frontier, would be in violation of that treaty and would be so treated by the United States.

Prime Minister Chou: Did you note that your alert also arose dissatisfaction on the part of your Western Alliance? They said you had not told them beforehand.

Secretary Kissinger: Mr. Prime Minister, I was going to talk about our Western Alliance. Our Western allies are distressed when we engage in activities as we did and are dissatisfied when we go on alert and dissatisfied when we conduct a disagreeable policy and dissatisfied when we conduct a half policy. It seems to be our destiny that they are doomed to be dissatisfied. I will give my explanations later.

Prime Minister Chou: Are they also dissatisfied with your journey to the Arab countries? Of course, the Soviet Union would be dissatisfied.

Secretary Kissinger: As a matter of fact, Mr. Prime Minister . . .

Prime Minister Chou: We appreciate that.

Secretary Kissinger: One has to analyze what is meant by dissatisfaction. If you want to play for high stakes with very little risk, then you are likely to be in a continued state of dissatisfaction. The secret dreams of our Western Allies in the Middle East is to restore their position of 1940 without any risk or effort on their part and therefore, to the extent that we are more active, there is a vague feeling of jealousy and uneasiness.

I think, Mr. Prime Minister, the nature of the European so-called dissatisfaction has to be understood. You have met many of the European leaders and you will have your own judgment as to their vision and ability to see matters comprehensively. But each of them faces the problem that for domestic reasons he has to say one thing while deep down he understands that what we are doing is essentially correct. Therefore, they very often, particularly after the event is already over, take a public position which is at variance of their understanding of the real situation.

On the question of the alert, we received the letter from Brezhnev threatening unilateral action at 10:00 at night, which is 3:00 in Europe. He demanded an immediate reply. The letter was supported by intelligence, which I believe we gave to your Ambassador, that the Soviet Union had alerted seven of eight of its airborne divisions.[5] I think I gave your Ambassador that. Under those circumstances we had no time to consult.

Secondly, speaking very frankly with you, Mr. Prime Minister, there is no point in consulting if there is only one thing you can do. If the European countries had not agreed with us, we still would have had to go on alert. Therefore, we had to proceed unilaterally, and I must say that in situations where we believe that the over-all equilibrium will be disturbed we will continue to behave in this manner if there is no time.

With respect also to the occasional criticism of our Soviet policy by our European allies, this has to be weighed against their equally strong criticism in the previous period. I think it is healthier for them to be worried about how far we might go and to have them in a position where they will try to make greater efforts in their own defense, than to have them pursue the policies which occurred while Ambassador Bruce was in London when they were constantly pushing us to be less intransigent to the Soviet Union and were constantly approaching us with ideas on how to bring about détente. If there is to be détente, we had rather manage it than have the Europeans do so.

But, if the Prime Minister wishes, I will be prepared to have a longer session on our relations with the Western Europeans. Despite the surface phenomena, I believe our relations are going along in a good direction. I am also prepared during this visit to go over with the Prime Minister the specific negotiations now going on with the Soviet Union, but I don't want to take all the time this afternoon.

Let me make a few comments now about the Middle East and about Southeast Asia, and perhaps we can leave all the other topics for later discussion.

Prime Minister Chou: All right.

Secretary Kissinger: You will remember that I saw your Ambassador the night the Middle East war started, and I explained to him what our basic strategy would be. I told him that for this period we were not in-

---

[5] On October 25, Kissinger informed Huang Chen of the Soviet alert. (Memorandum of conversation, October 25, 4:45–5:25 p.m.; National Archives, RG 59, Central Files 1970–73, POL 27 ARAB–ISR)

terested in the merits of the dispute between the Arabs and Israelis, but we were primarily interested in preventing a situation in which the Soviet Union would achieve its predominance in the Middle East. We believed that a Soviet victory in the Middle East, like 1971 in the Indian subcontinent, would have disastrous consequences not only there but elsewhere, and would encourage adventurism on a global scale.

You will see many tactical moves over the next month, and while I am here, I think we should have an opportunity to have a full discussion of the Middle East so you will understand specifically what we will do; but for this purpose, you should understand our basic strategy is to convince the Arabs that they can get weapons from the Soviet Union but a political settlement only from the United States. And therefore, we will always resist proposals that come to us from the Arabs through the Soviet Union. We are not asking for Chinese support on the specifics of the negotiations because the Chinese position is well known. We do think, however, that this basic strategy is in the common interest of both of our countries. We have no interest in a predominant position in the Middle East. That is not achievable, nor is it desirable. We are interested in keeping any other country from having a predominant position.

In this negotiation which we are now beginning, one of the big problems is that the Arab leaders are very active as individuals but are somehow given to excessive romanticism and to great impatience. We have, Mr. Prime Minister, a complex domestic situation with respect to the Arab/Israeli dispute. It cannot be an accident that the United States should become so heavily committed to a nation of two and one-half million at a distance of 6,000 miles which has no strategic or economic importance to the United States. These factors cannot be changed from one day to the next, any more than some of the factors in our relationship can be changed from one day to the next.

Prime Minister Chou: But perhaps Dr. Kissinger being the Secretary of State would be in a better position to change this situation. Perhaps . . .

Secretary Kissinger: Quite true.

Prime Minister Chou: Perhaps you would have more effect in remedying this situation.

Secretary Kissinger: Quite correct, but it has to be carefully organized. It would be a great mistake to fight the battle prematurely before we are organized and on minor issues. And I can tell the Prime Minister that we are as determined to bring about a just settlement in the Middle East as we were two years ago to improve our relationship with the People's Republic of China. But we are dealing with it.

Prime Minister Chou: But it will be considerably more difficult to obtain that.

Secretary Kissinger: It will be very difficult.

Prime Minister Chou: Madame Golda Meir styles herself a socialist.

Secretary Kissinger: My secret dream is to involve Madame Meir in negotiations with President Thieu.

Prime Minister Chou: They will have to go to London where they will meet their socialist friends.

Secretary Kissinger: She is in London now.

Prime Minister Chou: That is what I was saying. There are all kinds of socialists now.

Secretary Kissinger: It will be very difficult. It will be difficult with Israel and it will be difficult with the Arabs.

Prime Minister Chou: The passing of a United Nations resolution we were reading in your *Newsweek* magazine.

Secretary Kissinger: That is the international edition. I have not seen it. In the domestic issue there was a different cover.

Prime Minister Chou: You can also see from your expressions that it was extremely difficult.

Secretary Kissinger: If Mrs. Meir only gets ninety-eight percent of what she asks for she considers herself betrayed.

Prime Minister Chou: With regard to the resolution about Israel passed in the United Nations in 1947, the historical roots would go back to the Balfour Declaration. At that time you had heavy domestic pressure. Also there are Soviet intentions. Do you agree with that?

Secretary Kissinger: I agree that in 1947, when Israel was formed, the Soviet supported it because it wanted to create difficulties in the Middle East. No question about that. Nevertheless, while the United States is now supporting a peace settlement which will bring about an Israeli withdrawal from occupied territory, we are for the existence of Israel. We will defend the existence of Israel.

Prime Minister Chou: Does Mrs. Meir understand that if she continues in such an absurd manner that that will increase the possibilities of Soviet troops entering into the Middle East?

Secretary Kissinger: The Israelis are going through a traumatic experience at this moment because they had assumed they could remain militarily supreme for a long time. Even though they won the battles in this war, they have lost their supremacy. So they need a little time to adjust to a totally new reality for them. I don't know whether the Prime Minister agrees the most important aspect of the ceasefire that was achieved last week when I was in Cairo was not the specific terms—they are important—but that it was negotiated between Egypt and the United States without the Soviet Union.

Prime Minister Chou: I had thought of toasting you on that last night, but I was afraid the correspondents would hear us.

Secretary Kissinger: Yes.

Prime Minister Chou: We also talked to the Egyptians.

Secretary Kissinger: I was going to say, to the extent . . .

Prime Minister Chou: They said you would not do it because you are of Jewish descent. We said you would also look at the problem from the point of view that everything divides into two. There are also good Jewish persons and Karl Marx, whom we believe in, was also Jewish. Perhaps what we said had some effect on him.

Secretary Kissinger: It is very possible. To the extent, Mr. Prime Minister, that you can continue to do this, because there will be difficult periods in which we will not be able to move as fast as they want, but they can be sure we will move in the direction we have discussed here and that we have told them, and to the extent that you feel you could talk to them, it would be very helpful to our common approach.

I think I have already talked too long. On Southeast Asia there are two problems.

Prime Minister Chou: Have you finished with your Middle East issue?

Secretary Kissinger: On the Middle East, I thought we should have another discussion of the detailed tactics in the future. Let me make one point. These negotiations will start soon—we think in December—and there is no possibility of excluding the Soviet Union from the formal discussion. We have discussed with the Egyptians and with the Jordanians that the formal meetings should be conducted as the Paris Peace Conference on Vietnam, which is to say with only a repetition of formal positions as Ambassador Bruce knows only too well. The real negotiations will take place separately between the Egyptian Foreign Minister, who has been especially designated for this task, and myself and the Israelis. But separately.

Prime Minister Chou: We noticed that. Would that have an adverse effect on Syria?

Secretary Kissinger: I was going to say to the Prime Minister that we invited the Deputy Foreign Minister to visit me in Washington. And we have now sent a message to the Syrian Government through the Shah, and also through King Faisal who is paying for their reconstruction, that we would be prepared to talk to them at a higher level, and I am planning to visit Damascus in early December. They have indicated that they wanted to see me.

Prime Minister Chou: What about the knot in Iraq?

Secretary Kissinger: We have to prevent Iraq from dominating Syria.

Prime Minister Chou: But to put it another way, the Soviet Union is trying to dominate Iraq.

Secretary Kissinger: The Soviet Union is trying to dominate Iraq and have one front in the Mediterranean and another in the Persian Gulf. That is why our strategy is—first of all I wanted to say Mr. Prime Minister, we are pursuing in that region from Iran to the Mediterranean, the policy that we discussed with Chairman Mao when I was here last time. Our present policy is to keep as much pressure on the Government of Iraq as we can through Iran and other sources so that it is absorbed as much as possible in its domestic difficulties rather than with others. And as you know, they have a very significant problem with the Kurdish population. They were quiet during the Arab-Israeli war because it was not desirable to have all Arabs concentrate on the problems of the Kurds. But we will now make an attempt to establish the same relationship with Syria that we have established with Egypt, and to negotiate with Syria the Syria-Israeli settlement the same as the Egyptian settlement.

Prime Minister Chou: Anyhow the Soviet Union will not let loose of Iraq.

Secretary Kissinger: No. Unless Iraq throws them out as Egypt did.

Prime Minister Chou: That will take a period of time.

Secretary Kissinger: That is why we have to . . .

Prime Minister Chou: You perhaps will also know that even the Shah of Iran could not help from sort of dealing with the Soviet Union in that he also had to agree to consider the Soviet proposal of a collective security system. Of course, we knew that it was only a tactic to put the Soviet Union off, but he could not help saying that.

Secretary Kissinger: He misunderstood its significance also.

Prime Minister Chou: But this Shah does not seem very confused.

Secretary Kissinger: No. He is very good. One of the outstanding leaders.

Prime Minister Chou: He is in his middle age.

Secretary Kissinger: He is 54.

Prime Minister Chou: A little older than you.

Secretary Kissinger: A little. He understands the situation very well, and he will not make mistakes in practice. His was the only country that was bordering the Soviet Union that did not permit the overflight of Soviet planes during this crisis, and when one of his ministers permitted eight planes to fly over he fired him. It took great courage.

Until Iraq becomes disinvolved from the Soviet Union, we have to keep them isolated and from gaining success through its actions with the Soviet Union. We will see what can be achieved in the discussions with the Syrians in December. We have talked to Jordan and that is not a problem for us, and we have also established a preliminary contact with the Palestinians. Our basic strategy is to set up a formal conference which will have some UN blessing and some Soviet participation, and a series of bilateral negotiations in which we will attempt to be the intermediary together with whatever help we can get, but without the help of the Soviet Union.

Prime Minister Chou: Have the Palestinians agreed to participate?

Secretary Kissinger: In the conference? Yes. We will do it in two stages, Mr. Prime Minister. The initial phase of the conference will deal with disengagement of military forces and that does not involve the Palestinians. And since the Palestinians present a major problem for the Jordanians and Israel, we thought it best ... and since some success should be achieved rapidly, we thought in the first conference there should be only Syria, Egypt, Israel and Jordan dealing with military disengagement. And when the frontiers issue arises, the Palestinians should participate; and they have agreed and so has the King of Jordan. None of this is generally known, Mr. Prime Minister, and I have not discussed this, obviously, with the Soviets at all. But Egypt has agreed to this procedure. And I think it will work.

Prime Minister Chou: Because in the 1947 resolution the issue of Palestine was not solved. For instance, they have their military forces in Syria and other areas. Is it not possible for the Palestinians to participate in the military aspects also?

Secretary Kissinger: They will participate in the military aspects of disengagement after the first phase of the disengagement of forces that are now in contact. The immediate problem is to get some movement. If the negotiation immediately gets bogged down in procedural details, we will be back to 1967 in which the new line develops a sanctity of its own and the Israelis on the West Bank ... the probabilities for a new outbreak will be overwhelming. We thought we should get a negotiation in the first instance where we are not talking about forces now in contact with each other, that involves only those countries that have forces involved in contact.

Prime Minister Chou: I understand.

Secretary Kissinger: We expect that this first phase will be a matter of a few months. But in the meantime we will continue to talk to the Palestinians. We think it is important that this phase of talks, in which we are involved separately, be kept secret as long as possible because not every country has an interest in having it succeed.

Maybe I should say a word about Southeast Asia. In Southeast Asia we have two problems. One is the problem of maintaining the ceasefire in Vietnam. And the second is the problem of Cambodia. We believe that the resumption of large military operations in Vietnam would be extremely undesirable and have the potentiality of major involvement by our two countries. We would like to normalize our relations.

As far as Cambodia is concerned, I leave it up to the Prime Minister whether he wishes to have a more extended discussion. I simply want to say we are not, in principle, opposed to Sihanouk. In many of his private statements and public statements, he seems to be under the misapprehension that the United States Government is, in principle, opposed to him. That is absolutely incorrect. If he could return to Cambodia in a position of real independence for himself, we would be very interested in him as a leader. We are not interested in him if he is a captive of one particular faction that is simply using him for a very brief period of time in order to gain international recognition.

Prime Minister Chou: Have you taken note of the recent actions of the Soviet Union?

Secretary Kissinger: Yes. With respect to Sihanouk?

Prime Minister Chou: Perhaps Ambassador Bruce is more familiar.

Secretary Kissinger: I am familiar with it. I have taken note of it. Our interest in Cambodia, insofar as we have interest, is to keep it out of great power confrontation, and we are interested in a truly independent, neutral Cambodia. We want no position for the United States in Cambodia. And we are not committed to any particular group of individuals in Cambodia. I leave it up to the Prime Minister whether this is a subject that he wants to pursue at a later meeting.

Prime Minister Chou: We will have to consider this for a while before we can raise our opinions. I would like to ask now why it is that the two South Vietnamese sides have shown no progress in their Paris meetings on the political aspects.

Secretary Kissinger: I think the same qualities that make the Vietnamese a heroic people make them politically an extremely uncompromising people; and they sometimes combine, at least the ones I know, the worst aspects of Confucianism and the French Lycée. For example, when I negotiated this additional communiqué in June,[6] which will be my last one—I will never again negotiate with them—we had everything settled, when both parties conceived a new theory of international law: the order of obligations in which they appear in paragraphs determines the order in which they have to be performed. Each side attempted to push the obligations of the others into the beginning of the document and its own obligations to the end so its opponent would have to perform first. We spent nearly a week on the problem,

---

[6] Two joint communiqués of June 13 issued by the United States and the Democratic Republic of Vietnam are printed in Department of State *Bulletin,* July 9, 1973, pp. 50–53.

although no treaty could ever be written if this became an accepted practice.

Prime Minister Chou: The protocol you mean?

Secretary Kissinger: Yes. The protocol in June. Eventually, the objective situation in Vietnam will change for both sides, and then there will be real negotiating possibilities.

Prime Minister Chou: If we go into Cambodia, we will have to link it to the whole of Indochina, and if we are going to discuss it, we can do that later.

Secretary Kissinger: It is up to you, Mr. Prime Minister, and I will be prepared to do it. I will be prepared to discuss the whole of Indochina.

Prime Minister Chou: Of course, compared to the overall international situation, this is but a very small corner now, although it had troubled you for more than four and one-half years since your President came into office.

Secretary Kissinger: That is correct.

Prime Minister Chou: But from the point of view of the overall international strategy, you have taken too much time on that small issue.

Secretary Kissinger: That is true, too.

Prime Minister Chou: And you also said you no longer wished to continue Vietnam negotiations.

Secretary Kissinger: There was one moment, Mr. Prime Minister—the Vietnamese specialize in creating deadlock on irrelevant issues. There was a dispute over who should sign the document, the protocol. We made a proposal, the South Vietnamese made a proposal, and the North Vietnamese made a proposal. We then offered a compromise which accepted the North Vietnamese position, whereupon the South Vietnamese rejected it and moved to our original position, and the North Vietnamese moved to the original position of the South Vietnamese. At that point we had the North Vietnamese position, and the North Vietnamese had the South Vietnamese position. After three days of negotiations.

Prime Minister Chou: But you cannot blame them for this because it was the precedent established by your esteemed Secretary of State John Dulles. Because we have said that we were taken in and we have said this many times to our Vietnamese friends. You know that President Ho Chi Minh was a very eloquent man and he was a very open man too, and in his discussions with our Chairman, he did not agree to say that we had been taken in at that time. We continue to say we should have made greater efforts at the Geneva Conference. We should say that on the first Geneva Conference we should take some of the moral responsibility. Because, if at that time if we had refused to sign unless Dulles signed, he would have signed. But even though he would have signed, SEATO would have been established.

Secretary Kissinger: The lack of signature was not the determining factor.

Prime Minister Chou: No it was not, but it established a precedent. We have to admit our mistakes on that. It can be said to be a twist of history.

Now with one agreeing and one dissenting how are you going to get the Nobel Prize? I wonder who suggested that it go to two persons together.

Secretary Kissinger: It was domestic politics in Norway. Le Duc Tho has written me a very warm letter. It is like two war veterans exchanging ideas. It reminded me of our conversations at the last session of our peace talks.

Prime Minister Chou: Do you think we could take a rest for a few minutes?

(There was then a break from 5:30 to 5:45 p.m.)

Prime Minister Chou: So the two sides, Israel and Egypt, are going to sign at 9:00, Peking time.

Secretary Kissinger: I don't know the exact time. I know they will sign today.

Prime Minister Chou: That would be 4:00 their time.

Secretary Kissinger: That seems reasonable. They were supposed to meet at 2:00, and I guess it would take until 4:00.

Prime Minister Chou: First, the Soviet Union issued a news report and then they cancelled it.

Secretary Kissinger: They have never acknowledged the agreement, have they? They have not reported it in the press.

Prime Minister Chou: We heard that earlier that Tass had issued a news report saying that there were two different texts of the agreement issued—one in the United States and the other in Egypt.

Secretary Kissinger: That is not true.

Prime Minister Chou: Later on they cancelled that news item and reissued another one according to the Egyptian text.

Secretary Kissinger: Which is exactly the same as the other text.

Prime Minister Chou: It did not go into that in such detail.

Secretary Kissinger: There is only one text. My letter was approved by both the Egyptian Foreign Minister and the Israeli Cabinet before I sent it.

Prime Minister Chou: It was also the same as that you gave to Kurt Waldheim.

Secretary Kissinger: Exactly.

Prime Minister Chou: Is it five or six points?

Secretary Kissinger: Six.

Prime Minister Chou: At the beginning there were reports there were only five.

Secretary Kissinger: That was wrong too. I think we gave your Ambassador a letter 24 hours before it was published.

Prime Minister Chou: So shall we continue? Is there anything else you would like to say?

Secretary Kissinger: I think there are other topics we have discussed in the past, such as South Asia and Iran, that we can keep for another occasion. I wanted to cover the basic issues today.

Prime Minister Chou: In my view, South Asia is always an important aspect. What do you think of the developments there?

Secretary Kissinger: India is making a major effort to improve its relations with us, and we assume also with you.

Prime Minister Chou: Why do they have to insist on detaining those 195 prisoners of war?

Secretary Kissinger: That is the problem—the problem is that I think they want to keep them until Pakistan recognizes Bangladesh and until Bangladesh gives up the claim to try them. Now as part of this negotiation which brought about the settlement, we obtained from India an assurance that those 195 would not be turned over to Bangladesh. We would make it a matter of American Government policy if they broke this agreement.

Prime Minister Chou: There is the need to exert a certain pressure on them in this aspect because it is too unreasonable. Because in Pakistan they have already passed a resolution in their national assembly agreeing to the recognition of Bangladesh, giving the Prime Minister the authority to recognize Bangladesh at the proper time.

Secretary Kissinger: We are supporting Pakistan on the return of the 195. We have made this clear to India.

Prime Minister Chou: We also discussed this issue with Mr. Whitlam when he came this time.

Secretary Kissinger: That is an issue in which he may be willing to support you. Whitlam, I would suspect, would support you on this.

Prime Minister Chou: At the beginning, he expressed his opinion, being more favorable to Bangladesh, and that he did not understand our position. But later, after we explained our position, he did not say anything more. He said he had not read Maxwell's book, and I gave him a copy.[7]

Secretary Kissinger: I think the Prime Minister has increased the sales of that book.

---

[7] Neville Maxwell, *India's China War;* see footnote 11, Document 8.

Prime Minister Chou: Indeed. And we believe that that book was written in a very fair manner because we had never known him before, and we did not provide him any documents. He reached those conclusions entirely on Indian documents. Perhaps it did draw on my letter. I think he did quote my letter to Nehru, but I don't think he quoted the letter that I wrote—after we had returned the prisoners of war and ammunition—to India and to all other heads of State and heads of government concerned. We sent a letter to the five intermediary states and to all the heads of government. Of course, you would now have a copy of that. He is now commencing to write a book on the Sino-Soviet dispute.

Secretary Kissinger: We have seen articles on that in the London *Times*.

Prime Minister Chou: He said he is coming again.

Secretary Kissinger: With respect to India, our policy is to see what we can do that they will have greater freedom of action from the Soviet Union but basically we are moving very slowly. We are settling some economic issues with them now—the rupee debt and matters of this kind.

Prime Minister Chou: We believe the rupee debt should be settled rather generously. How many rupees do you have on your hands for food purchases?

Secretary Kissinger: I don't have the exact figure, but it was settled at I think about 15 percent. It depends on how you calculate it. You can calculate it without interest—it would be about 60 percent—without interest it would be less. The rupees were blocked in India; we could not get them out of India; we have nothing to spend them on in India; and, therefore, what we adopted was what we thought a rather realistic program.

Prime Minister Chou: In your settlement, would you have the portion that was to be returned converted into hard currency?

Secretary Kissinger: No. But we have established fixed categories on which it can be spent in India which was not the case before.

Prime Minister Chou: Can you invest with those rupees in India?

Secretary Kissinger: No. It is mostly for American governmental expenditures in India; for our Embassy and matters like this, and buildings.

Prime Minister Chou: But that should be a very small sum.

Secretary Kissinger: And buildings and things of this kind.

Prime Minister Chou: Would you buy commodities out of India with that sum?

Secretary Kissinger: I don't think so. I will get the details and let you know tomorrow.

Prime Minister Chou: I believe I have already told you of how they broke the Sino-Indian border negotiations in order to obtain that rupee settlement for buying grains from the United States. Do you remember my telling you that?

Secretary Kissinger: You told me that after these negotiations broke down, that they received a great deal of help. You think they broke them in order to get the help?

Prime Minister Chou: Exactly. Because when I met with the foreign press in India, I told them no issue had been solved, and therefore I had nothing to say to them, the correspondents. But, of course, other correspondents also put questions to me. But a correspondent from your country asked me whether I knew or not that the Indian Minister of Food was in your country waiting to sign. I thanked him for telling me this news, and I understood. And the day after the talks broke down and I went to Kathmandu, Nepal for a visit, I read in the papers that the deal had been signed. And it was decided that by that agreement that India would be buying American food grains with rupees—I think the sum of about 15 million tons; of course, not in one year, that was not the manner of buying grains, but it was going to be done over a period of five years or six years. But the actual deal perhaps exceeded that amount. I think there was something to do with that. They would not break it. Otherwise, they could have signed something (with us) that was very abstract, and in principle, and not go into details. Nehru could have done that but at that time he refused to make any concessions. Because at the end of those talks, I summarized a few points in his words to be taken as the basis for an agreement in principle to be later further discussed in detail, and he still refused to sign. But today you find that the rupees finally can be used in India and only a restricted number.

Secretary Kissinger: It was always the case that the rupee could only be used in India. I think the basic problem was what we called the counterpart fund; these accumulated funds which theoretically give one enormous power in a country where one has them. It is really not the purpose for which they were set up. They were set up so they could be spent there for development projects for the government concerned.

The second problem is that as foreign aid develops more and more countries owe us money; then if, for any reason, we shut off aid we shut off repayment of their debts, so that we are in the position of giving them aid so they can repay debts to us. This whole problem we are now examining, since it has consequences that were never intended.

Prime Minister Chou: I think your President said at one time that all the debts together accounted for nearly $10 billion.

Secretary Kissinger: Yes.

Prime Minister Chou: So perhaps you are preparing for the day when finding it difficult to pursue them, you will just wipe them off as with the stroke of one's beard.

Secretary Kissinger: No, but we have to do something creative with them because whether they are wiped off or not does not depend on us so completely anymore.

Prime Minister Chou: Correct. Of course, you would know that the Soviet Union whenever it leases something determines what it must be paid back in—for instance, in jute. You would know that, of course.

Secretary Kissinger: Yes, and also in the Middle East.

Prime Minister Chou: You will know that recently that Egypt has had to pay in hard currencies for the ammunition that it obtained from the Soviet Union. Because the Soviet Union told Egypt since you have so many friends who are rich in oil resources, you should pay us in money and not in goods.

And then we saw that you suddenly put a bill to your Congress concerning aid to Israel amounting to $2 billion. Of course, we understand that if you had not done that public opinion in the United States would not have been able to understand.

Secretary Kissinger: We did this as a pressure on the Soviet Union.

Prime Minister Chou: But they wanted money. They did not care for anything else. They, of course, would not pass a bill saying they would provide military arms immediately to Egypt.

Secretary Kissinger: But they were providing a great deal of arms during the war.

Prime Minister Chou: Of course, but for a price. Boumedienne went to the Soviet Union and held sixteen hours of discussion with the Soviets for the same purpose. They wanted to be paid. They gave him some things, but there were also other things they did not give him. One cannot fight well if one relies on such—if that is on what one must rely to fight with.

Have you paid attention to the prospects of the developments in Afghanistan?

Secretary Kissinger: Yes. We have looked at that situation since the coup, and, of course, Prince Daud is well known as having some pro-Soviet orientation; and many of the younger officers with him have no political experience and were trained in the Soviet Union. You are familiar with the fact there was a Soviet military mission there in the last few weeks that inspected the border with Pakistan. We talked to the Shah of Iran, and we also told the Soviet Union that if the Afghans spilled across their border that this would be considered an international development which we would take very seriously. We are concerned with the Pushtunistan agitation.

Prime Minister Chou: They also engage themselves in Baluchistan agitation. The final intention of the Soviet Union is to get it all in the Soviet hand. They have a map. We don't know whether President Bhutto showed it to you.

Secretary Kissinger: Yes. He showed me the map. It allegedly is an Afghanistan map because it has a very small slice of Soviet territory.

Prime Minister Chou: A piece of Pakistan, a piece of Iran, and a small piece of the Soviet Union.

Secretary Kissinger: The Shah of Iran is very concerned. He is building up his defenses at a considerable rate, and we are giving him more modern equipment. We have talked to Bhutto and so far our help has been primarily in the economic field, and we are now thinking of helping him build a port which is a project which he is extremely interested in. We have not yet fully solved the problems of weapons for Pakistan. We are trying to do it through Iran. And we are also . . .

Prime Minister Chou: I believe Prime Minister Bhutto wants to obtain weapons directly from you.

Secretary Kissinger: Yes. It is a very difficult problem for us because of Congress. We have given him a little, but it is really not very meaningful.

Prime Minister Chou: Can Iran give them some?

Secretary Kissinger: Yes. That is what we are working on now. We had our Ambassador from Iran visit Pakistan to see what arrangements could be worked out.

Prime Minister Chou: So India has such a great influence on your domestic public opinion.

Secretary Kissinger: India has a considerable influence on our domestic public opinion, not so much on the public at large which does not like it, but on the intellectuals which have had a romantic idea about India as a nonviolent country. We are also working with the Shah, as I told you earlier, on the problem of Iraq and the Gulf States. And we have this week, as you may have noted, sent one of our aircraft carriers and an escort into the Persian Gulf in order to demonstrate our presence. There have been Soviet ships there, but we have not had American ships there.

Prime Minister Chou: Anyway, those places are getting tense. You are spending such a huge amount in military expenditures in assisting other countries, could you not appropriate a portion of that—a portion of your expenditures to military assistance to other countries—could you not give a portion of that to Pakistan?

Secretary Kissinger: We are not spending that much, unfortunately. The budget is being decreased by Congress every year. Secondly, a specific prohibition was passed against direct military aid to either India or Pakistan. India does not need it because they are getting it from the Soviets. We have to look for indirect ways of doing it. I have talked to Prime Minister Bhutto about it, and I will look into it again when I get back to the United States. We agree with the necessity. Our problem is to find the legal means of doing it.

Prime Minister Chou: Another question is that of Korea. We have reached a compromise, but we believe the speed has to be slowed down—that is, the time when the draft resolution should be put to the First Committee, and the Chairman of the General Assembly, will be postponed. Because it was originally scheduled to have the discussion in the First Committee on the Korean issue on the 14th or 15th and you had already left Washington when you presented it with our Korean friends, and then we had to tell our delegation at the United Nations. Our delegation was very enthusiastic about this, as was your Ambassador.

Secretary Kissinger: He is by nature enthusiastic.

Prime Minister Chou: Perhaps something like Ambassador Huang Hua.

Secretary Kissinger: I did not have that impression from Ambassador Huang Hua.

Prime Minister Chou: But they very quickly agreed.

Secretary Kissinger: We were under the impression you were in a hurry. We are in no particular hurry.

Prime Minister Chou: Because you had not returned and we had not met you, and they even went into the details of drawing up the wording. Perhaps even before you authorized your Ambassador.

Secretary Kissinger: No. I approved the wording. It was sent to me as a cable, and I approved it.

Prime Minister Chou: Because we knew that you were very busy and preoccupied with the Middle East at that time, and we did not think there was the need to be so hasty because we also have to consult with other sponsor countries which Korea had mobilized, and we thought also that you would have to discuss with your sponsor countries. In the course of such consultation, it would be bound to leak. For instance, you will discuss it with Japan. You told Japan.

Secretary Kissinger: "Might possibly leak" is one of the kindest sentences I have heard. I was told that you were in a hurry. We had no particular reason to hurry. We were for it, and I approved the schedule, and I would have accepted any schedule you gave us. I am still prepared to accept it.

Prime Minister Chou: Yes, I think the main thing is we should give them some time because our Korean friends need to discuss and persuade some other sponsor countries. We think it would be very bad if we two decided after discussing it and tried to impose it on others.

Secretary Kissinger: I agree.

Prime Minister Chou: So I would kindly ask you to convey this to Ambassador Scali, and he could go into further consultations with Ambassador Huang Hua, that is to say that originally the issue was to be put to the First Committee on the 14th and what we mean is we don't think it need be done in such a hurry—that the date . . .

Secretary Kissinger: The compromise was to be on the 14th on the Korean issue?

Prime Minister Chou: No, it was originally scheduled that the issue would be put to the Committee on the 14th and then all sides would have their say and then go on to the resolutions. But we would propose that it would be better to postpone the discussion of the issue to a later date—later than the 14th. We think it would be beneficial if you could notify your Ambassador at the United Nations, and he and our Ambassador could discuss it and see if they approved. If they thought it was suitable to postpone it then it could be done.

Secretary Kissinger: I don't know about your Ambassador, but if you and I agreed that it should be postponed, ours will postpone it.

Prime Minister Chou: But you know there is also the question of Korea. We agree with your assessment that our Ambassador seems to be in a hurry and I don't know why he became all of a sudden so enthusiastic over this. Because originally when our Vice Minister was at the United Nations we agreed he should first consult the nonaligned countries and Korea, and we should not enter this consideration in such haste.

There now has appeared another issue—another aspect—of the issue and that is you are now in China. Because you know that on our side the Soviet Union and its followers are included in the sponsor countries and they would have something to say about this, and would try to create trouble on the basis of the fact that you were visiting China now and might create some confusion in other countries.

Secretary Kissinger: We have no reason to bring it to a decision this week. I don't know what the parliamentary situation is—how much trouble it would be to postpone it. The Vice Minister knows about the technical details. If it is possible to postpone it, I have no objection. I am assuming the same compromise is still agreed to, and you are just talking about a delay, not about changing the agreement.

Prime Minister Chou: No change of the compromise.

Secretary Kissinger: How much of a delay—two weeks?

Prime Minister Chou: We can ask them to discuss that.

Secretary Kissinger: All right.

Prime Minister Chou: Because in that interim period we can also discuss it more thoroughly with the nonaligned countries. The Soviet group will definitely try to create trouble on this issue and they will stand on the so-called left. They constantly forget that the United Nations troops were sent into Korea when they were absent from the United Nations Security Council. And Ambassador Bruce . . .

Secretary Kissinger: We will instruct Ambassador Scali as soon as we return to our Guest House to get in immediate touch with your Ambassador that they should both work out a delay for a period.

Prime Minister Chou: If necessary.

Secretary Kissinger: How do they determine what is necessary?

Prime Minister Chou: They can discuss it among themselves.

Secretary Kissinger: Our Ambassador is a little excitable. And unless I tell him the definition of necessity. Let me put it this way—to make it easier I am prepared to go ahead, then he should go ahead. We will leave it up to your Ambassador and hope that my judgment of him is correct—that he is not excitable.

Prime Minister Chou: Well, he is usually not so very easily excited but this time he has been over-enthusiastic.

Secretary Kissinger: That is more than I ever manage to achieve with him. Maybe I should have Scali work on Chinese problems.

Prime Minister Chou: I don't think this has anything to do with Ambassador Scali this time; perhaps because our two sides have reached agreement, he thought he would express his zeal in carrying out the order. He forgot the other sponsor countries, especially since he neglected the fact that there was the Soviet group among those sponsor countries.

Secretary Kissinger: Ambassador Scali will be instructed so there is no misunderstanding as of Monday morning New York time.[8] Should they get together? I will instruct him to meet whenever Huang Hua wants. I don't know where Scali is this weekend. We will send a message when we reach the Guest House and that will take three to four hours. If Scali is in New York, he should have it by the end of the day Sunday New York time.

Prime Minister Chou: I think it can wait until Monday morning.

Secretary Kissinger: You can assume that at the opening of business Monday, New York time, Ambassador Scali will be instructed. Who gets in touch with whom? We leave it to him. I will tell Scali if he has not heard from Ambassador Huang Hua in the morning he should call him. I shall instruct him first that the compromise remains in effect, but if Ambassador Huang Hua would like a delay, then Scali should cooperate with him to get a delay for the time period that Ambassador Huang Hua recommends. And that Scali should work with

---

[8] November 12.

the sponsors on our side to bring the delay about if it is desired. You can count on that being done.

Prime Minister Chou: Thank you. We don't want to give the Soviet Union an opportunity.

Secretary Kissinger: I agree, and if there is no necessity, there is no hurry.

Prime Minister Chou: Correct. You are going to Japan. What are your views on Japan?

Secretary Kissinger: My views on Japan are that what we discussed last February are still true—that Japan is at a crucial point and necessity will drive it to decide between a more traditional nationalism and maintaining its present orientation. And it has many temptations. It is very much affected by the Middle East oil situation.

Prime Minister Chou: I believe about 80 percent of its oil comes from the Middle East.

Ambassador Ingersoll: Eighty-five percent I would say; that is only about 40 percent from the Arab countries and 45 percent from Iran.

Prime Minister Chou: Yes.

Secretary Kissinger: It has temptations from the Soviet Union. It has temptations by its own economic strengths. And it is concerned that it will be left alone in any arrangement that we make with the Europeans. This is one reason why we may try to find a formula to associate Japan with our efforts in Europe. The intention is not to link it militarily with Europe but primarily psychologically, to prevent a total sense of isolation.

Prime Minister Chou: And have you expressed support or are you waiting to see the outcome of events with regard to your joint exploration of Siberia?

Secretary Kissinger: One problem is that no one knows exactly how much natural gas there is. There is some dispute between what the Soviets have told us and what some experts have said.

We have just authorized a loan which will be a joint American/Japanese exploration in Siberia to get a precise determination of what is involved. We have agreed in principle to make it a joint project with the Japanese. And we believe, for political reasons, it would be undesirable to have the Japanese so completely dependent on Soviet political decisions. And the Soviet Union will probably be more reluctant to tackle both the United States and Japan simultaneously than Japan alone. We have a problem in our Congress whether we can get any support for these long-term investments in the Soviet Union. And that will not be decided until the early part of next year.

Prime Minister Chou: Their salesmen don't seem to be very effective.

Secretary Kissinger: Soviet salesmen?

Prime Minister Chou: That is the impression we received both from West Germany, Japan and from you. Is the data and the material of the salesmen credible?

Secretary Kissinger: There are some questions in our mind about the reliability of these figures. The second question we have is to what degree we want to commit massive American investments in the Soviet Union. Our strategy up to now, quite candidly, has been to do enough to give the promise of future investments but not so much as to make a strategic difference in their situation.

Prime Minister Chou: That is a very complicated strategy.

Secretary Kissinger: That is true.

Prime Minister Chou: Ambassador Ingersoll will be, of course, very familiar with the lesson that General Secretary Brezhnev taught Prime Minister Tanaka. He brought out his map and began his lectures.

Secretary Kissinger: He has only one lecture. And I have heard it ten times.

Prime Minister Chou: He came at the same time when Brezhnev went to visit Bonn.

Secretary Kissinger: It is dangerous to underestimate German shortsightedness. My apologies to the Vice Minister.

Prime Minister Chou: Perhaps you say that out of your unhappiness with the present Brandt Government.

Secretary Kissinger: That too, but it is a historical phenomenon. The Germans have had only one leader of stature—that was Adenauer.

Prime Minister Chou: Yes, because he had been active.

Secretary Kissinger: Who, Adenauer?

Prime Minister Chou: Adenauer.

Secretary Kissinger: He knew the importance of it, but he never let himself be deflected. While Brandt, if he persists in his present policy, will have given the Soviet Union veto over German policy.

Prime Minister Chou: There is such a danger. And the opposition party did not carry out the elections very well either.

Secretary Kissinger: No. They had very incompetent leadership. You met their best man but he is not very energetic, Schroeder. He is their best man.

Prime Minister Chou: He is not so very active. Why not? Because of temperament or because of his position in the party?

Secretary Kissinger: Schroeder, he is not the new leader. I have not met the new leader. Schroeder was ill for a while, and he also does not have and is not good in appealing to public opinion. And he was not very strong nor able to take over the party himself.

Strauss was with Ambassador Bruce in Germany for many years. Strauss is extremely intelligent and a very forceful personality, but he is a South German phenomenon so he has not much support in the north. His self-discipline leaves something to be desired. I think I told the Prime Minister once about what Adenauer said to me about Strauss.

Prime Minister Chou: At that time you did not mention a specific name. I thought it might be him.

Secretary Kissinger: It was Strauss.

Prime Minister Chou: Yes, you can see the clarity of Adenauer's mind because he must have spoken to you when he was over 80.

Secretary Kissinger: Yes. A month before his death, 88. He was a man of very clear views. He understood the danger for Germany if it maneuvered too much.

Prime Minister Chou: It is time for a short break, and you are going to the ballet. We will have more time tomorrow. Perhaps this evening, if we have something more to discuss, I might pay a call on you.

Secretary Kissinger: It would be very nice.

---

57. Memorandum of Conversation[1]

Beijing, November 12, 1973, 3:00–5:30 p.m.

PARTICIPANTS

Prime Minister Chou En-lai
Foreign Minister Chi Peng-fei
Vice Foreign Minister Chiao Kuan-hua
Assistant Minister of Foreign Affairs Wang Hai-jung
Two Chinese Foreign Ministry Officials
Tang Wang-shen, Interpreter
Shen Jo-yen, Interpreter
One Chinese Notetaker

Henry A. Kissinger, Secretary of State
Ambassador David Bruce, Chief, U.S. Liaison Office
Ambassador Robert Ingersoll, U.S. Embassy Tokyo
Winston Lord, Director of Planning and Coordination, Department of State
Alfred Jenkins, U.S. Liaison Office

---

[1] Source: National Archives, Nixon Presidential Materials, NSC Files, Kissinger Office Files, Box 100, Country Files, Far East, Secretary Kissinger's Conversations in Peking, November 1973. Top Secret; Sensitive; Exclusively Eyes Only. The meeting took place in Guest House Villa #3.

Secretary Kissinger: I have the answer for you, Mr. Prime Minister, on the production of planes in Taiwan.[2] It is not a production of airplanes but an assembly for which we supply the parts. And it is for short-range fighter aircraft which will not increase the total number of airplanes on Taiwan. When we stop supplying the parts, they will no longer be able to produce them. So in practice it is different than giving them the airplanes. They have no independent capability for producing the airplane being developed. And that is true of all other co-production arrangements. It is an F5E, and there are to be 100 for a period between 1973–1978.

Prime Minister Chou: In this way Chiang Ching-kuo will be reassured.

Secretary Kissinger: Our impression is that he (Chiang Kai-shek) is not active today.

Prime Minister Chou: It is impossible for him to be, and it is difficult for him to live for another five years. But I am not asking him to die. He can live as long as he wishes. If he wishes he can live to be 100. What I meant was in that way Chiang Ching-kuo will be reassured because he could rule the country until 1978.

Secretary Kissinger: We have no plans on this plane, on this project, beyond 1978.

Prime Minister Chou: You say it is a short distance one. Actually, the radius can stretch as far as 180 kilometers. That is the fighting radius.

Secretary Kissinger: And come back? One way, it is possible, but not to come back.

Prime Minister Chou: If he has a refueling tank, he will be able to come back.

Secretary Kissinger: F5E?

Prime Minister Chou: Yes. It does not matter even if the plane is bigger. I just wanted to make clear whether it is an assembly plant.

Secretary Kissinger: It is an assembly plant, not a production. We supply the parts. They do not produce the parts. So they have no independent capability.

Prime Minister Chou: Is Japan able to produce planes like this or greater?

Secretary Kissinger: Japan has not produced any planes like this, but it certainly has the capability. I have to check but—do you know, Ambassador Ingersoll, if we have some co-production?

Ambassador Ingersoll: Not on the F5s; on the F4s.

---

[2] See Document 56.

Secretary Kissinger: They are producing F4s. F4s have radius to reach effectively. The F5 is not a bombing plane. The F4 can be used effectively for bombing.

Prime Minister Chou: Actually, the F5E is also capable of bombing. The only difference is, it is lighter. The F4, which is the Phantom type, can carry greater weight.

Secretary Kissinger: Yes. The F4 can carry greater weight.

Prime Minister Chou: But the distance is the same for both.

Secretary Kissinger: I don't believe this. I really don't have the characteristics in mind. We have always considered it, strategically thinking, that the F5 is purely a fighter plane, with no bombing capability. We use it for tactical support.

The F4 is something we call deep interdiction which goes further behind the line and has a strategic impact, but I don't know the exact characteristics. In our own strategic planning for Vietnam, for example, the F5 was always considered to be used for support of ground troops at the front line with bombs, and the F4 for the interdiction of communications because it has a heavy bomb load, and I thought it had a longer range. I will have to check on that. I will have the answer tomorrow.

Ambassador Ingersoll: The F4 is refuelable.

Prime Minister Chou: It does not matter. It would be pretty good if it could be delayed for another five years, because in that way they can envisage it for another five years. In that case, your recent word will be able to be realized in this way: It will not give rise to the ambitions of a third country. I see it in this way. It does not matter whether it is 100 planes or 200 planes.

And there is, of course, another point. It could be allowed to attack the Mainland, but if they insist on attacking the Mainland, we welcome them. Let them have a try.

Secretary Kissinger: You have our assurance they will not be allowed to attack the Mainland. If they do, they will lose American support completely.

Prime Minister Chou: If they ever try to do that, they will do it unilaterally.

Secretary Kissinger: There will be no attack nor an American-sponsored attack in the future or any attacks that our President can control.

Prime Minister Chou: What you told me yesterday has already been reported to the Chairman. There was one point that I did not explain very much because I did not entirely understand. Yesterday you mentioned that there was a possibility of finding, that you would like to find, a way with regard to our bilateral relations to find some wording similar to the Shanghai Communiqué or slightly altered that would be able to promote the development of our relations. I did not have the opportunity to issue a communiqué or some other form?

Secretary Kissinger: I wanted to ask the Prime Minister whether he thought it appropriate to issue a communiqué at the end of my visit and if so we will be prepared to do this. My comment was in reference to the establishment of formal diplomatic relations. We cannot go faster than the schedule which I gave you if it is on the Japan formula. However, if we could find a formula which is more flexible, as long as we understand that we will end up there, we are prepared to establish diplomatic relations sooner.[3]

Prime Minister Chou: Yesterday you mentioned that you also reaffirmed that you would not support the idea of two Chinas. Under this condition, what kind of flexible formula have you in mind? It is also a difficult problem to us. Perhaps you have worked out a good idea.

Secretary Kissinger: No, I have not actually yet worked out a good idea. If the Prime Minister would like, I might submit one to him later today after I have had an opportunity to meet with my colleagues. I have in mind something like the Shanghai Communiqué which would make clear that the establishment of diplomatic relations does not mean giving up the principle that there is only one China.

Prime Minister Chou: She (the interpreter) had made a good guess of what you meant. When we were with the Chairman I dared not explain the statement, but she dared to make an explanation of the statement.

Secretary Kissinger: As I understand it, Mr. Prime Minister, your problem in having diplomatic relations while we have relations with Taiwan is that it might give rise to a two-China policy which we have agreed not to support. What we should search for is a formula for consideration that makes clear that that principle is not being abandoned; that there is only one China by either side.

Prime Minister Chou: She (the interpreter) has guessed very correctly what you think.

Secretary Kissinger: Yes.

---

[3] On October 11, Lord prepared a briefing memorandum for Kissinger in anticipation of his November visit to Beijing. Although Lord believed a significant gesture was necessary in order to further improve relations with China, he recommended against a formal security commitment to defend China against the Soviet Union. Instead, he argued that the United States should commit itself to a specific target date for normalization during Nixon's second term. (National Archives, Nixon Presidential Materials, NSC Files, Kissinger Office Files, Box 100, Country Files, Far East, Kissinger Trip to Peking—Papers, November 1973)

Prime Minister Chou: So the elder people are not as good as the younger people.

Secretary Kissinger: She had a long talk with Mr. Lord on the airplane.

Mr. Lord: We had our own counterpart talks.

Interpreter: Another matter was discussed on the plane.

Prime Minister Chou: There is another matter that is mentioned concerning the Consulate General. Perhaps you have not made an investigation concerning this point. As far as we know, there are twelve in all at the moment. Originally there were ten. Recently they have added two.

Secretary Kissinger: I know of one in New York.

Mr. Jenkins: There is one in Atlanta.

Secretary Kissinger: This one must be in honor of Mr. Jenkins.

I have not paid attention to the one in New York. And our interpretation, which we made to ourselves, is the one which I gave you yesterday: that the Taiwan authorities are preparing for the day that we will move toward the sole recognition of Peking; a day which we know is inevitable. At that time, they want to have a representation in America that permits them to continue exchanges with us, and I believe for that reason they have chosen the Consulate General in New York, since it would be inappropriate to have it in Washington. That was our own interpretation.

And our own internal interpretation of it also was that this was envisaged as a possible contact point with the People's Republic of China whenever discussions would take place.

Interpreter: You mentioned yesterday a point of contact with Chiang Kai-shek.

Secretary Kissinger: A contact point to the United States after we have moved, say from no later than the middle of 1976, and secondly, a possible point at which the Taiwan authorities would negotiate with the People's Republic of China. This is not based on knowledge but on our interpretation of their motives. This second interpretation may be wrong.

Prime Minister Chou: That is just an idea.

Secretary Kissinger: It is our own analysis of the problem.

Prime Minister Chou: Is there anything you would like to tell me first.

Secretary Kissinger: I have some information now on the rupee negotiations situation which you were interested in. Our difficulty was that we could not spend all the rupees we had accumulated. And, therefore, what we did was to settle for 35 percent of the total amount of rupees in these blocked accounts that could be spent only in India, but even that will take us twenty years to spend. The real difficulty was that we permitted such huge debts to accumulate without analyzing what we could ever do with them. There was also a speed-up in dollar debts that they owed us, but of a much smaller amount. That was the basic reasoning of that.

Prime Minister Chou: So the phenomenon in India . . . you do not have the similar phenomenon in other countries.

Secretary Kissinger: Not to quite the same extent. We had it in Japan, but it is being settled. We do have another phenomenon in other countries where aid loans that were given over a period of years become repayable and where, in effect, we give more aid so that they can repay the loans; and when we don't give aid they don't repay the loans so they get aid anyway. For example, we helped Pakistan, which holds a substantial amount of our money, by rescheduling its debt after the 1971 war which was a way really of giving it additional money.

Two other small items. I understand that Ambassador Huang Hua has already met a representative from our Mission, and as I understand from our telegram, they have had a satisfactory meeting. If that is not correct, we will change it. We will give appropriate instructions. I think they have achieved an adequate understanding.

Prime Minister Chou: Thank you, and we have heard about this point.

Secretary Kissinger: Your information is the same.

Prime Minister Chou: The same.

Secretary Kissinger: We will proceed. We have instructed our Mission that we follow Ambassador Huang's recommendation so you have the initiative as to timing.

The only other item I have is that I understand that in these talks on the private blocked assets, there is only one item that is still unsettled which has to do with your proposal that blocked assets belonging to third country banks be excluded from the settlement. That is one item that is impossible for us to accept because we could never get Congressional approval for the agreement if that item were excluded.

Prime Minister Chou: It seems the third countries have already given us the money. What shall we do? Give them back the money?

Secretary Kissinger: Our people believe that they can sue those banks and get the money.

Prime Minister Chou: Take for instance, Belgium.

Secretary Kissinger: Yes, I know. That is the primary problem.

Prime Minister Chou: The figure is not very big but they were very . . . once they established diplomatic relations with us, they gave us the money.

Secretary Kissinger: But illegally from our point of view.

Prime Minister Chou: For us, it is legal.

Secretary Kissinger: The difficulty for us is it would reduce the pro rata payments from 40 percent to 25 percent which we do not believe Congress would accept.

Prime Minister Chou: Do you mean that by excluding the money given to us already by the third country banks there is only 25 percent left?

Secretary Kissinger: Then I think it would be about 22 percent in blocked assets as against private claims. While with that money it would be about 40 percent. And our experience has been that the Congress would not approve a settlement that was as low as 22 percent.

Prime Minister Chou: But to us the figure is very small. Up to now I still find it difficult to understand the proportion of the taxes levied between those countries which you have given most favored nation treatment and those which you have not. To me, that is if we are not given most favored nation treatment your taxes are different.

Secretary Kissinger: We are in principle prepared to grant you most favored nation treatment. However, we have not been able to do this in the past when there were outstanding claims. If this settlement were made, we would in principle be prepared to grant most favored nation status to the PRC. The difficulty that now arises with most favored nation has nothing to do with China, but people who are adding amendments which are aimed at the Soviet Union which may apply to the PRC even though the people may be favorable to the PRC. Like Senator Jackson. I will have to have a meeting with Senator Jackson as soon as I return to remove those obstacles. I know he has no intention of directing his measures against the PRC. His measures are against the Soviet Union. Insofar as the administration is concerned, we are prepared to grant most favored nation status to the PRC, and we are prepared to grant them the same economic status as the Soviet Union.

Prime Minister Chou: Whereas just now you talked politics with me, as to the point you mentioned, I fully understand it. Because what I want to know is financially speaking does the most favored nation treatment mean the reduction of taxes?

Secretary Kissinger: From the United States? There are not any export taxes. We don't have any export taxes.

Prime Minister Chou: It is limited to import taxes?

Secretary Kissinger: Yes.

Prime Minister Chou: What is the difference between the taxes levied on those countries which enjoy the most favored nation treatment and those who do not enjoy that treatment?

Secretary Kissinger: I will have to check, but it is substantial and it varies; but in several categories it is very substantial. I will have the answer for you tomorrow.

Prime Minister Chou: You give most favored nation treatment to Japan.

Secretary Kissinger: Yes. We give it to about 100 nations.

Prime Minister Chou: They belong to different categories.

Secretary Kissinger: The socialist states were excluded after the Korean War. This is really the origin of the discrimination.

Prime Minister Chou: And Yugoslavia?

Secretary Kissinger: Yes. We have given it to Yugoslavia and to Poland.

Prime Minister Chou: And Romania?

Secretary Kissinger: No, but we will give it to Romania. Romania has had to wait because in the past in order to get most favored nation status we have had to submit a separate bill to the Congress for each country. We have now submitted a bill to the Congress which gives the Executive Branch the discretion to grant most favored nation status to any country and that bill is still before Congress. We would prefer to be able to do it on a general basis, but, if necessary, we still have the possibility of introducing action for individual countries.

Prime Minister Chou: But as far as the bill for giving most favored nation treatment to the Soviets, it has been postponed.

Secretary Kissinger: No, Prime Minister, this is not a bill to give most favored nation . . .

Prime Minister Chou: It is demanded by your government.

Secretary Kissinger: It is not a bill to give most favored nation status to the Soviet Union but a bill to give the Executive Branch the discretion to give it to almost anybody and therefore the Soviet Union. I can explain to the Prime Minister the complexity which led us to the postponement of that bill. The reason is that in the Senate we expect an amendment sponsored by Senator Jackson which would not only not enable us to give most favored nation status to the Soviet Union but would also limit the possibility of credits, and is so written that it would also apply to China. Jackson has not thought of this. It refers to emigration. Jackson is thinking of the Jewish problem. We have to find a refinement of this bill. In order to do this we have to get a maximum difference between the House and the Senate so when these two bills become reconciled there is an area of negotiation. Therefore, we first asked the House to eliminate most favored nation completely. When they did not do this, we asked them to postpone consideration of the bill for two reasons. One, to have some control of Soviet behavior on the Middle East, and secondly in order to enable us to discuss with the Senators and Congressmen the fact that we have written a bill which they are aiming at the Soviet Union but which applies to too many other countries and therefore defeats its own purpose. But it will definitely come to a vote no later than the first part of February.

Prime Minister Chou: We will make a study of this question. There is only one item left, and there is no other question as to the blocked assets.

Secretary Kissinger: Yes. One item. That is the only item. I think the other questions can be settled. You raised the third question. We can settle two of them.

Prime Minister Chou: I like to make several clarifications on some international questions. As we have discussed the situation in the Middle East, it is complex. Yesterday you mentioned the two steps to be taken and the first step is to carry out the disengagement of military forces, and the agreement has already been signed between Egypt and Israel.

Secretary Kissinger: No, Mr. Prime Minister. There are three steps in that sense. The first is stabilizing the ceasefire. Then peace negotiations begin. These peace negotiations will have two steps. A first step is what we call disengagement of forces, but whose real purpose is to move the Israeli forces back some distance, and a second step which settles the final border.

Prime Minister Chou: And there is also the question of carrying out the observed ceasefire on the part of Syria. They will also sign it?

Secretary Kissinger: Yes. Syria has already agreed to the ceasefire. But we believe that Syria should become an integral part of the negotiations and our impression is that it is prepared to be.

Prime Minister Chou: Then, when it comes to the discussion of disengagement of military forces will there be a conference held for discussing this question or will it be discussed separately?

Secretary Kissinger: No, it will be the first phase of the peace conference. But, as I explained to the Vice Minister this morning,[4] and I believe to you yesterday, my judgment is that the formal peace conference will not be much more productive than the formal Vietnam Conference. And it is probable that the real negotiations will take place separately outside the formal framework. As I explained to the Vice Minister this morning, the problem is that at the formal conference, the Soviet Union will probably attempt to regain some of the territory it has lost by taking rather extreme positions. Therefore, it may be necessary for us on occasion to create a stalemate in order to demonstrate that this is not the road to a settlement.

Prime Minister Chou: Will Britain and France take part in the conference?

---

[4] Kissinger is most likely referring to a discussion he had with Vice Foreign Minister Qiao Guanhua during a car ride.

Secretary Kissinger: It is not finally settled yet. I would doubt it because Israel will not participate if Britain and France participate. But Britain and France may move to a position closer to the Soviet position. So it is not such an asset to have them there.

Prime Minister Chou: But in their public opinion they have expressed their desire to take part in the conference.

Secretary Kissinger: There is always, as I told you yesterday, a difference in what they say publicly and what they say privately. Not always, but very often.

Prime Minister Chou: In order to meet their demands at home?

Secretary Kissinger: Yes. We will not exclude them if they want to participate and if the others want them. We have no reason to exclude them. But frankly, I cannot imagine a settlement occurring in a public forum of this composition. With so many different groups represented as it is.

Prime Minister Chou: It seems that among the Arab states they have also quite a few extremist positions.

Secretary Kissinger: Yes. Iraq and, to some extent, Algeria.

Prime Minister Chou: Libya.

Secretary Kissinger: Libya, Southern Yemen. Libya was not exceptionally heroic during the war, but its courage has increased as the ceasefire has been prolonged.

Prime Minister Chou: Libya has not severed relations with you?

Secretary Kissinger: No. They have only made impossible the life of the people who are there. They are very anti-Soviet.

Prime Minister Chou: He is also a friend of Chaing Kai-shek.

Secretary Kissinger: Really? This I did not know.

Prime Minister Chou: A very peculiar phenomenon. But we don't look into that matter. There are so many queer things in the world. Is that the companies in the United States which have investments in oil sources in Libya?

Secretary Kissinger: There are many European countries that also have investments there, and most of the Libyan oil goes to Europe, not to the United States. Only 12 percent of our oil comes from the Middle East. Most of that comes from Saudi Arabia.

Ambassador Ingersoll: And Iran.

Secretary Kissinger: Six percent. We get another 6 percent from Iran.

Prime Minister Chou: So the total proportion would be nearly 20 percent?

Secretary Kissinger: Yes. Eighteen percent.

Prime Minister Chou: What do you think of King Faisal?

Secretary Kissinger: A complex phenomenon.

Prime Minister Chou: He is also an old friend of mine and I came to know him very well at the Bandung Conference.

Secretary Kissinger: A very complex man. Of a previous period. Very principled, but in a very traditional framework. He is in a very complex situation because he is encircled on the one hand by Iraq on the north and South Yemen on the south. So he is very vulnerable to the radical states. On the other hand, emotionally, he is a good friend of the United States. My impression is that he is attempting to find a way to escape from the policy he adopted in the war. I think he will find a way in the next month or two. I am talking about the oil policy, escape from the oil policy.

Prime Minister Chou: The Japanese oil is from Iran and Kuwait.

Ambassador Ingersoll: They get about 85 percent of their oil from the Middle East as such. About 40–45 percent from Iran and the balance from Iraq and others. Five percent from Indonesia, Borneo and Eastern Europe.

Secretary Kissinger: We have started a major program to reduce, and to eventually eliminate, our dependency on oil from abroad. We believe that we can successfully conclude this within this decade.

Prime Minister Chou: That would be a very grand plan, and you will have to economize in the United States with oil.

Secretary Kissinger: We are doing this. You may have seen the President's speech.[5] There may be an interim period where we have to economize on the use of oil. We are trying to liquify coal, for which we have the scientific way to do this, but we must make it economically feasible. We will use oil shale and rely on Alaskan oil and oil from Canada. With this combination, we believe we can be self-sufficient by the early 1980s.

Prime Minister Chou: The production cost is very high for liquified coal.

Secretary Kissinger: Yes, but we expect to reduce that cost very substantially during this decade. We know the scientific principle. It is primarily a production problem. On engineering problems we are very good.

Prime Minister Chou: Is it true that most of the oil from Venezuela goes to your country?

Secretary Kissinger: Yes, a substantial part.

Ambassador Ingersoll: I was going to say that the increase in the price of oil in the Middle East is making it economical to use this liquified coal and the shale. It is an incentive for us to work harder at it.

---

[5] On November 7, President Nixon addressed the Nation concerning policies to deal with energy shortages. (*Public Papers: Nixon, 1973,* pp. 916–926)

Prime Minister Chou: What is Japan going to do?

Ambassador Ingersoll: They wish they knew. They have been trying to diversify for a long time, but they have not many other sources for oil than the Middle East.

Secretary Kissinger: We may be prepared to share with Japan in some common research and development on alternative resources, and also on some joint ventures on nuclear energy.

Prime Minister Chou: But at the beginning, perhaps the cost is also very high.

Secretary Kissinger: Of what? Of nuclear energy, yes. At the beginning, but we have that under study. I think the installations are very expensive, but if the cost of the nuclear fuel can be reduced, of which there is a good possibility, then it becomes much more economical.

Prime Minister Chou: It would be better if there are any by-products.

Secretary Kissinger: Unfortunately, most of the by-products are most useful for nuclear weapons.

Prime Minister Chou: That is also a subject for debate between the two big powers. Do you really believe that the Soviet Union will reduce her quantity of nuclear weapons?

Secretary Kissinger: The first problem is to stabilize the number of nuclear weapons because they are still increasing the number. And, of course, they have the theory that they need nuclear weapons for more than one threat. So we believe in the strategic arms limitation talks. We first have to place a ceiling on the total number of weapons, and then bring about a gradual reduction.

In the first phase of the agreement, the Soviet performance has been, to put it kindly, ambiguous. They are supposed to destroy one category of weapons as replacement for submarine-based weapons called SS7s. They are old. And they have destroyed a few of those, but they appear to have replaced them with mobile missiles which are technically not banned by the agreement but which are certainly not in the spirit of the agreement. If this continues, we will have to take countermeasures, and then the agreement will be meaningless. We will put missiles into airplanes which is also not banned by the agreement.

Prime Minister Chou: About the Korean question. At first, I intended to discuss it at some other occasion, but now I think we had better discuss it. What is your idea of the next step to be taken? I am not referring to the step taken this year. I am referring to the step that will be taken in the future. There is an Armistice Committee at the demarcation line, and this Committee meets often. What do you think will be a way out for that?

Secretary Kissinger: Our problem with respect to the United Nations is that its disappearance would also remove the legal basis for the armistice.

Prime Minister Chou: That is why I was asking. What form would it take in order to settle the question of the Armistice Committee? If you have not anything in your mind, we had better not discuss it today.

Secretary Kissinger: I do not have a concrete proposal, but we are prepared to discuss it over the next year on the schedule we have discussed.

Prime Minister Chou: But there is an advantage here that the Soviet Union has not had a hand in the Korean question.

Secretary Kissinger: I cannot judge on the North Korean side.

Prime Minister Chou: You can or cannot?

Secretary Kissinger: We do not have a judgment.

Prime Minister Chou: But it is possible that there would be minor troubles, but one cannot find a legal basis for that because the Soviet Union is not a participant to the armistice agreement. Because there were only four parties which signed the armistice agreement, but it was fortunate that the Soviet Union was not a participant in that. So over the last twenty years nothing—no troubles had occurred with regard to the armistice agreement. Although Dulles refused to settle this question, peace has been maintained over more than twenty years. This has given Korea an opportunity to move towards peaceful communication. Of course, this is something that will call for a long period of time before it can be settled.

Anyway, a way must be found out how to settle this. We should pay attention to this question.

Secretary Kissinger: We will work with you during the next year to find a solution to the question of the legal basis of the armistice, and we will do that. We will make a major effort before the next General Assembly to come to an agreement with you on that issue. Should we discuss this with Ambassador Huang Chen? Of course, Ambassador Bruce will also be instructed on this.

Prime Minister Chou: But we think that the members of the four nations with the Advisory Committee are very comfortable. They were just stationed there, without asking to withdraw from Korea, whereas the Canadians have been withdrawn from Vietnam and they stayed there for quite a long period of time. The International Committee has been there for a long time with nothing to do. That is why members often came to Peking. Who pays the expenses for those? The Vice Minister also took part in the negotiations then.

I would like to ask you a question. It has been proven that expansionism in the world is doomed to failure. But the Soviet Union wants to follow in the steps of their predecessors, and they want to overtake them and they are stretching their hands everywhere. Do you think this can be stopped?

Secretary Kissinger: I think it is a difficult problem of this period.

Prime Minister Chou: It is also a crucial issue.

Secretary Kissinger: It is the most crucial issue. I told the Vice Minister in the car today that I had no illusions, for example, that in the Middle East, if it were not for the Soviet Union, you and we would have quite different views. But we have a first objective to prevent the domination by the Soviet Union. I believe if the countries that are potential victims of expansionism cooperate in a formal way, but they have to understand the main lines of each other's policy. I believe that major military expansionism can be stopped. That is our policy—to resist if the Soviet Union engages in a major military movement. But I think it can be stopped.

Prime Minister Chou: Do you mean that it is not easy to stop political expansionism?

Secretary Kissinger: The political expansionism is more difficult to stop.

Prime Minister Chou: For instance, the so-called friendship treaty between the Soviet Union and India.

Secretary Kissinger: I think the political expansionism can also be stopped if one pursues an intelligent policy and if the countries against which it is directed keep in mind the principal requirement. I think if you, we and Western Europe understand each other, and if we behave intelligently in other parts of the world, we can contain Soviet expansionism. I don't believe that Soviet policy is very intelligent. It is very brutal, but not very intelligent.

Prime Minister Chou: But sometimes they have put on many masks.

Secretary Kissinger: Yes, but sooner or later the brutality comes forward.

Prime Minister Chou: But so far as the Soviet Union itself is concerned this is perhaps their main aspect.

Secretary Kissinger: Brutality?

Prime Minister Chou: But as for their opponents, things will be complicated. For instance, it will not be so easy for the Western European countries to share their common view.

Secretary Kissinger: Of the three major components that I mentioned, the West Europeans are the weakest link in terms of their understanding. But on the other hand, they are also the most difficult area for the Soviet Union to attack. So they are trying to undermine them by such measures as the European Security Conference and other negotiations. And what the Prime Minister has to understand is that if in these efforts we keep slightly to the left of the West Europeans, this is a means to prevent them from going further because then they will be afraid we will make a separate arrangement with the Soviet Union and that will worry them sufficiently so that they start thinking about their own defense.

Prime Minister Chou: You also mentioned this point the day before yesterday and also yesterday. But as for this point, the people would not be able to comprehend it.

Secretary Kissinger: I admit to you, Mr. Prime Minister, that this is the great danger in the present course. If at the same time we do two things, if we insist that the discussions are very detailed so that they cannot have many symbolic successes, and if secondly, we resist brutally whenever there is the slightest military threat, that danger can be reduced if not eliminated. I forgot, of course, to mention Japan which is a very crucial one.

Prime Minister Chou: Although it is crucial, the reaction would not be as quick as the European countries.

Secretary Kissinger: No. If they are not submitted to too many temptations by having too many pressures put on them from too many sides, I think they can be kept on their present course. I think you and we have acted wisely in this direction.

Prime Minister Chou: Because it is easier than dealing with the Western European countries.

Secretary Kissinger: Yes. They are a tougher people. And then, of course, we have to build this southern axis through the Near East.

Prime Minister Chou: It seems you will have to make a very great effort towards this end. It is not easy to do that.

Secretary Kissinger: No, but we are prepared to do more with Turkey as soon as its governmental crisis is overcome.

Prime Minister Chou: So the crisis is not yet over?

Secretary Kissinger: They still don't have a firm government. And they did not behave very strongly during the Middle East crisis. They permitted Soviet airplanes to fly over their territory.

Prime Minister Chou: It is said so. Is that bridge across the strait built by you?

Secretary Kissinger: It is now open—over the Bosporous—it was opened on October 3. I don't know whether it was built by us. I don't know.

Prime Minister Chou: I learned of it from the television.

Secretary Kissinger: Did it say so?

Prime Minister Chou: It did not say so, but perhaps with your help.

Secretary Kissinger: I don't know. I would not be surprised. I don't have the same attention for detail as you, Mr. Prime Minister. But I would suspect so. We will find out overnight.[6]

Prime Minister Chou: Of the four fleets owned by the Soviet Union, three are in the Mediterranean.

Secretary Kissinger: Yes and a part of the Atlantic Fleet came in during the crisis. They had over one hundred ships in the Mediterranean at the height of the crisis. At one point they had over 103. They are now withdrawing them.

Prime Minister Chou: It is difficult for them to move about because they are separated from each other. Not linked together.

Secretary Kissinger: The Russian fleet is the only fleet in modern history that has ever surrendered. It surrendered to the Japanese in 1903.

Prime Minister Chou: The war started in 1904.

Secretary Kissinger: But they surrendered in 1903 because they had to come around from St. Petersburg. They first sank some British fighting vessels, thinking the Japanese had come into the English Channel to stop them. They came all the way around the world.

Prime Minister Chou: From the Cape of Good Hope.

Secretary Kissinger: What today is Vietnam, and steamed straight into a Japanese trap. The Japanese were waiting there.

Prime Minister Chou: You know that the Japanese made a film for the feats he performed in the war. In the film they slandered Lenin. Upon seeing the film, the Soviets were quite indifferent. They also praised the Russian admiral that surrendered. And the Soviets seemed very pleased.

Secretary Kissinger: He was the one who attacked us.

Prime Minister Chou: Togo also appeared in that film. In that film they slandered Lenin, saying he bought ammunition in Europe in order to carry out the uprising of 1905 to tie down the Russian Emperor. It was also said in the film that Lenin helped the Japanese to get information. In that way the Japanese Navy gave money to Lenin to buy ammunition. Out of that Lenin staged the uprisings of 1905 in Moscow.

Secretary Kissinger: It was not staged by Lenin to begin with.

Prime Minister Chou: But Lenin had something to do with it.

Secretary Kissinger: Yes. He took part, but he was not the principal.

---

[6] The United States was "not involved in financing, engineering or constructing the bridge across the Bosporus." (Telegram 223192 to Beijing, November 12; National Archives, Nixon Presidential Materials, NSC Files, Kissinger Office Files, Box 100, Country Files, Far East, Kissinger Trip to Peking—Papers, November 1973)

Prime Minister Chou: It was just a slander by the Japanese, but the present Soviet authorities should stay apathetic about it and should have accepted it. Actually it was sheer slander. And the Soviets should have accepted it as something very queer.

Secretary Kissinger: The impression of our Navy people is that the Soviet Navy lacks a great deal of experience, from observing their maneuvering and their reaction to our action.

Prime Minister Chou: You have the experience of the Carribean Sea.

Secretary Kissinger: And many other experiences.

Prime Minister Chou: They deliberately carried out many demonstrated actions here in the Far East. Their Far Eastern fleet deliberately carried out many actions here in order to tie down your Seventh Fleet. And they also deliberately passed through the S. Straits to the middle section of the Pacific to Midway Island and Guam to make military operations there. After your fleet went there, they also left the place.

Secretary Kissinger: Our impression is that they could not stand up to our fleet on the open sea.

Prime Minister Chou: And sometimes their planes will circle around that area. But your Ambassador is familiar with this fact.

Secretary Kissinger: I know the time they went through these straits. But we never make our fleet movement depend on what they do.

Prime Minister Chou: But sometimes you will have to make some reactions and to make some movements.

Secretary Kissinger: We did it when they tried to build a submarine base in Cuba. Then we took strong action in 1970. We put a destroyer in the mouth of that harbor and we publicly reaffirmed what President Kennedy had said about the Cuban crisis, and then they pulled out their submarine support.

Prime Minister Chou: So much for their opponents. That is, they posed a threat to Western Europe countries and just now you added Japan. And now their focus of contention is in the Middle East. Just what you mentioned just now, the period for the contention will be very short but will last for a period of time. I hope that in this case you would not spend such a long time as four and a half years as you settled the Vietnam question.

Secretary Kissinger: No. It is a different problem. In Vietnam we were directly involved.

Prime Minister Chou: The direct involvement, of course, is one of the reasons, but that was left over. It was left over by your predecessor. But you yourself had made some mistakes. Perhaps you would not agree to what I say. I would not say it very straightforwardly because we understand this possibility. It is inevitable that human beings will make mistakes.

Secretary Kissinger: We may have. I think if the North Vietnamese had proposed the settlement that we achieved in the end in the first year we would have accepted it at any point. Our difficulty was that the North Vietnamese always asked us to overthrow a friendly government and that we could not do. That was the one thing I have always told you, Mr. Prime Minister, that it was a point of honor with us.

Prime Minister Chou: This question again is left over historically. The responsibility should not remain entirely on your present Administration.

Secretary Kissinger: This problem is easier from one point of view and more difficult from another. It is easier because no one is asking us to destroy a friendly government. But now all parties accept the existence of Israel which is essential for us too.

Prime Minister Chou: I think that it would not be so quick that all parties would recognize the existence of Israel.

Secretary Kissinger: All parties to which I have talked accept the existence of Israel.

Prime Minister Chou: But the party with which you have discussions, the number is not so big. You think so. It is not so easy. While the fighting was going on, there was an ill wind of break in diplomatic relations with Israel on the part of African countries. This was part of a just voice on the part of the Africans, and you cannot say they are not correct. Because you cannot expect everyone to be like us who have combined principles with realities. We objected to the establishment of Israel to start with. Now the population of Israel has reached 2.5 million and as far as we know perhaps reached 3 million—can you drive them to the sea? No. So when your press people ask me about it, I answer them, "of course not." I ask them how can there be any strength in things like that in the world. That is why one is bound to find some way to settle this question. Would that be a reason to have the Palestinians driven out? This question should also be settled.

Secretary Kissinger: I agree this question should be handled.

Prime Minister Chou: It would not be fair if this question would not be settled at the same time. Only when these two questions are settled can there be any co-existence, and a peace to be spoken of. Otherwise, there would be no co-existence. This is why that we agree to your having direct dealings with the Arab States. This is just a first step. But I think, although the first step has been taken, the journey will be even longer than the journey you traveled when you first came to China to prepare for the visit of President Nixon. Because it only took half a year for your President to come for a visit to China.

Secretary Kissinger: I think it will take more than a half a year but not half a year to show progress. We can show progress in less than half a year.

Prime Minister Chou: There might be some progress, but it is not so easy to settle the question because it is very complex.

Secretary Kissinger: The most difficult is Jerusalem. We can settle the Palestinian question. We had some discussion with Sadat and even with the Palestinians. The question is not easy, but the issue regarding Jerusalem is very hard.

Prime Minister Chou: Is it that there is some blind faith in the fact? It seems that the problem of Jerusalem is even harder than the question of Taiwan.

Secretary Kissinger: The question of Taiwan, I think—the nature of its solution is obvious. It is only a question of timing.

Prime Minister Chou: Jerusalem.

Secretary Kissinger: Jerusalem. The nature is not obvious, because both sides consider it a holy city.

Prime Minister Chou: Would it not be better if this city would be shared by both sides?

Secretary Kissinger: That is my solution, but I can find no one to agree with me. I once proposed this to the Israelis. And once I thought I had agreement from the Israelis to give up the three mosques on the hill looking toward Israel, but it turned out the Israelis would not agree to give up one hill and one street because they said it was a holy place.

Prime Minister Chou: That is a kind of superstition. Well, we will not dwell upon this in detail, but anyway, I think the Middle East is not an easy thing to settle.

Secretary Kissinger: I know. It has frontiers, Palestinians, Jerusalem. They all have to be settled simultaneously, except Jerusalem.

Prime Minister Chou: I hope you won't spend another three years and a half in order to settle this question.

Secretary Kissinger: That is why I think there should be an initial withdrawal of Israeli forces in order to give the Arabs some hope and courage.

Prime Minister Chou: Besides you have also to meet with your domestic difficulties. And only you as the Secretary of State will show the responsibility to settle these questions. Just now we discussed the question of the Soviet expansionism in the world. Actually, there is consensus between the expansion and the old expansionism. Some of your press people asked me if it is possible for you to go back to isolationism. I told them it was absolutely impossible, but they did not believe me. I think the times are different. Although people might talk about it as a congress, the real politics would not be like that.

Secretary Kissinger: I agree that it is objectively impossible, but I do not agree that it is subjectively inconceivable.

Prime Minister Chou: Although some people might think of it that way, actually they would not be able to realize it. If they should become a president themselves they would have to pursue your present policies.

Secretary Kissinger: The danger is that someone may attempt to pursue an isolationism policy and thereby permit expansion of other countries and by the time he realizes what the dangers are he may have paid a very heavy price. I think the probability is that the policy we are now pursuing—in these main outlines, not necessarily in its tactics which are complex—will be pursued in the future.

Prime Minister Chou: It would not do for you not to contract it. What I say is the policy you are pursuing now is not an isolation policy, but you have contracted yourself a bit, retracted yourself a bit on certain questions in order to concentrate on settling the main questions. Your government had overstretched itself.

Secretary Kissinger: I agree.

Prime Minister Chou: You spent a lot of money and a lot of energy but the question had not been solved. If you would ask us as revolutionaries, of course, we would say we agree with your spreading yourself out. From a point of view of a revolutionary, we would be in favor of your spreading yourself out to be loose and vulnerable. But since now we have come together yourself and we are discussing some realistic and practical questions, we must talk about politics.

Secretary Kissinger: It was partly inexperience and partly the weakness of every other country.

Prime Minister Chou: There are so many countries—would you take care of them all? Did you ever expect that there would be a student movement in Bangkok? Does the CIA learn about it beforehand?

Secretary Kissinger: If Dulles had been more polite in 1954 he could have learned a lot.

Prime Minister Chou: It was impossible for him to do so because the developments of things are sometimes independent of human will.

Let's do some preparation because Chairman Mao has invited you to go there. Mr. Lord can come too.

Secretary Kissinger: Can I take Ambassador Bruce, as well?

Prime Minister Chou: I thought you would bring Mr. Lord along because of your habits. I did not ask.

Secretary Kissinger: If it is difficult . . .

Prime Minister Chou: We will ask. (Miss Wang goes out to inquire.) Perhaps we should call the attention to Mr. Jenkins that, according to news from sources of Chaing Kai-shek the guided missile ship *Oklahoma City* . . . Do you have such a guided missile cruiser?

Secretary Kissinger: All cruisers are named after states.

Ambassador Ingersoll: It is the flagship of the Seventh Fleet.

Prime Minister Chou: At 1:37 this afternoon, the cruiser had approached an island near the Taiwan Straits. It passed through the Taiwan Straits. It was only about 25 kilometers from our territory.

Secretary Kissinger: Mr. Prime Minister, there is no defense against stupidity. I cannot watch every cruiser in the American Navy. I tell you the truth, Mr. Prime Minister, I ordered every airplane to stop flying near your territory. I would have thought that when one ordered airplanes not to fly that they would have thought the cruisers should not go either.

Prime Minister Chou: It is nothing very particular. Only they are nearing our territorial waters. I did not pay much attention to that.

Secretary Kissinger: It should not happen at anytime this close, and it should not happen while I am in China under any circumstances.

Prime Minister Chou: They have intruded into our territory by mistake. Just tell them and ask them to leave.

Secretary Kissinger: I will take care of it tonight. Wherever they are I will move them away. If they can tell the difference between left and right, they will move away.[7]

(The Chinese side then confirmed that Ambassador Bruce was also invited to see the Chairman.)

---

[7] On November 12, the USS *Oklahoma City* passed through the Taiwan Straits on a routine cruise from Yokosuka to Hong Kong. (Telegram 223189 to Beijing, November 12; ibid.)

58.   Memorandum of Conversation[1]

Beijing, November 12, 1973, 5:40–8:25 p.m.

PARTICIPANTS

Chairman Mao Tse-tung
Prime Minister Chou En-lai
Foreign Minister Chi Peng-fei
Assistant Minister of Foreign Affairs Wang Hai-jung
Tang Wang-shen, Interpreter
Shen Jo-yen, Interpreter

Henry A. Kissinger, Secretary of State
Ambassador David Bruce, Chief U.S. Liaison Office
Winston Lord, Director of Planning and Coordination, Department of State

(There was informal conversation as Chairman Mao greeted the Secretary, Ambassador Bruce, and Mr. Lord in turn while the photographers took pictures. The Chairman said that he had not seen the Secretary in a long time and that he now had a higher position. The Secretary responded that the Chairman looked well, and the Chairman commented that he was fair. To Ambassador Bruce, the Chairman commented that he was advancing in age like him, but younger. Ambassador Bruce responded that he was not much younger. To Mr. Lord, the Chairman noted that he was very young.)

Chairman Mao: What did you discuss?

Prime Minister Chou: Expansionism.

The Secretary: That's correct.

Chairman Mao: Who's doing the expanding, him (indicating the Secretary)?

Prime Minister Chou: He started it, but others have caught up.

The Secretary: The Foreign Minister criticizes us from time to time for the sake of equilibrium, but I think he knows the real source.

Chairman Mao: But that expansionism is a pitiful one. You should not be afraid of them.

The Secretary: We are not afraid of them, Mr. Chairman. Every once in a while we have to take some strong measures as we did two weeks ago.

Chairman Mao: Those were not bad, those measures.

---

[1] Source: National Archives, Nixon Presidential Materials, NSC Files, Kissinger Office Files, Box 100, Country Files, Far East, Secretary Kissinger's Conversations in Peking, November 1973. Top Secret; Sensitive; Exclusively Eyes Only. The meeting took place at Chairman Mao's residence.

At that time, we were not yet able to persuade Egyptian Vice President Shafei. He came here and said that they had no confidence in you. He said you were partial to Israel. I said not necessarily. I said that those of Jewish descent are not a monolithic bloc; for example, we cooperated with Engels and not with other Jewish capitalists.

The Secretary: The problem in the Middle East is to prevent it now from being dominated by the Soviet Union.

Chairman Mao: They can't possibly dominate the Middle East, because, although their ambition is great, their capacities are meager. Take, for instance, Cuba. You intimidated them, and they left.

The Secretary: And since then we've done that a second time, although we did not announce it.

Chairman Mao: Recently?

The Secretary: Recently. They moved several submarines, and we moved several ships, and they left.

Chairman Mao: I'm very suspicious that this country wants to have some relations with us. At the beginning it was done through delegations sent by Castro. At that time, the head of the Delegation was Rodriguez. He led a delegation of six Latin American compatriots to China to try to make peace with us on behalf of the Soviet Union. The second time they tried to make peace through Ceaucescu of Romania, and they tried to persuade us not to continue the struggle in the ideological field.

The Secretary: I remember he was here.

Chairman Mao/Prime Minister Chou: That was long ago.

Prime Minister Chou: The first time he came to China. (Said in English.)

Chairman Mao: And the second time Kosygin came himself, and that was in 1960. I declared to him that we were going to wage a struggle against him for ten thousand years (laughter).

Interpreter: The Chairman was saying ten thousand years of struggle.

Chairman Mao: I also declared to him that neither of us two were socialists, and that we had been labeled by you (Soviet Union) as being dogmatists and that this is anti-Marxist. So I said let us also give you a title, and that is "revisionism." (Laughter) And, therefore, neither of us is Marxist. And this time I made a concession to Kosygin. I said that I originally said this struggle was going to go on for ten thousand years. On the merit of his coming to see me in person, I will cut it down by one thousand years (laughter). And you must see how generous I am. Once I make a concession, it is for one thousand years. (Chou and Mao confer.)

And then there was another time, also Romania, and a Mr. Bordeoloski came also to speak on behalf of the Soviet Union.[2] This time I again made a concession of a thousand years (laughter). You see, my time limit is becoming shorter and shorter.

And the fifth time the Romanian President Ceaucescu came again—that was two years ago—and he again raised the issue, and I said "this time no matter what you say, I can make no more concessions" (laughter).

The Secretary: We must adopt Chinese tactics.

Chairman Mao: There is now some difference between you and us. I do not speak with such ease now because I've lost two teeth. And there is a difference between your and our activities, that is, we just hit back at everything that comes. And we seized upon the fact that the agreement reached between Prime Minister Kosygin and us has never really been implemented, that is, the September 11, 1969, agreement at the Peking Airport.[3]

The Secretary: I explained to the Prime Minister, going in the car or elsewhere, that our tactics are more complex and maybe less heroic, but our strategy is the same. We have no doubt who is the principal threat in the world today.

Chairman Mao: What you do is a Chinese kind of shadow boxing (laughter). We do a kind of shadow boxing which is more energetic.

Prime Minister Chou: And direct in its blows.

The Secretary: That is true, but where there is a real challenge, we react as you do.

Chairman Mao: I believe in that. And that is why your recent trip to the Arab world was a good one.

The Secretary: The Chairman is learning English.

Chairman Mao: Why is it in your country, you are always so obsessed with that nonsensical Watergate issue?[4] (There is much laughter on the Chinese side as the interpreter tries to explain that she couldn't really translate the Chairman's wording for "nonsensical" which really

---

[2] Not further identified.

[3] The two sides agreed to settle the Sino-Soviet border dispute through peaceful negotiations and to maintain the status quo of the border until the dispute was settled.

[4] When Scowcroft sent the President a summary report of Kissinger's meeting with Mao, the President highlighted the sentence, "He [Mao] was scathing of opposition to you because of Watergate which he considered to be a meager, nonsensical incident blown out of proportion." Next to the highlight, Nixon left a note for Haig: "Al note!" (Memorandum from Scowcroft to Nixon, November 12; National Archives, Nixon Presidential Materials, NSC Files, Kissinger Office Files, Box 96, Country Files, Far East, China Exchanges, November 1, 1973–March 31, 1974)

meant "to let out air." Prime Minister Chou asks Mr. Lord if he knew the meaning of the Chinese word, "pee." Mr. Lord said "no" and the Prime Minister said that he could ask his wife. The Chinese side explained that it was an adjective used to qualify the incident.) The incident itself is very meager, yet now such chaos is being kicked up because of it. Anyway, we are not happy about it.

The Secretary: But not in the conduct of foreign policy, Mr. Chairman, which will continue on its present course, or in our capacity to take actions in crises as we've shown.

Chairman Mao: Yes. And even in the domestic aspects, I don't think there's such an overwhelming issue for you and the President.

The Secretary: No. For me there is no issue at all because I am not connected with it at all. The President, too, will master it.

Chairman Mao: What I mean by domestic aspects is your inflation, rising of prices, increase in unemployment, because it seems that the number of unemployed has been cut down by an amount and the U.S. dollar is relatively stable. So there doesn't seem to be any major issue. Why should the Watergate affair become all exploded in such a manner?

The Secretary: There are many complex factors, including the fact that there are many old style politicians who dislike the President because he pursues unorthodox policy. And too many intellectuals have become nihilistic and want to destroy everything.

Chairman Mao: For instance, James Reston and Joseph Alsop are all now triggered against President Nixon. I can't understand that.

The Secretary: I can understand James Reston because he follows others, and he is always a reflection of the fashionable view. Joseph Alsop—I think—that was a brief aberration, and he will return to his original position very soon.

Chairman Mao: Do you think they are writing articles, for instance, in trying to taste public opinion?

The Secretary: They all like to think that they are running the country. And they play President alternately every other day and take turns at it (laughter). If we had paid attention to them, Mr. Chairman, I'd never have been here on my first trip (laughter). Everything important has been done against their opposition.

Chairman Mao: Yes. People say that Americans can keep no secrets.

The Secretary: That's true.

Chairman Mao: I think Americans can very well keep secrets.

The Secretary: That's basically true, Mr. Chairman, but you may be sure that as long as we keep the information in the White House, you can be sure that nothing has ever come out of our discussions.

Chairman Mao: Take the Cuban incident, for instance. Take, for instance, your visit to China. And another situation would be your recent dealing with the Soviet Union. In all these cases, secrets were kept quite well.

The Secretary: That's true. Things we can keep in my office, we can keep quite well. But there are no secrets with the Soviet Union. We always tell you everything we are doing with the Soviet Union. There is nothing we are doing with the Soviet Union that you don't know. You can count on that for the future.

The Soviet Union likes to create the impression that they and we have a master plan to run the world, but that is to trap other countries. It's not true. We are not that foolish.

Chairman Mao: You are always saying with respect to the Soviet Union something we are ourselves are also saying. And your views seem approximately the same as ours, that is, there is the possibility that the Soviet Union wants to attack China.

The Secretary: Well, Mr. Chairman, I used to think of it as a theoretical possibility. Now I think it is more a realistic possibility, and I've said it, especially to your Prime Minister and also your Ambassador. I think they above all want to destroy your nuclear capability.

Chairman Mao: But our nuclear capability is no bigger than a fly of this size (laughter).

The Secretary: But they are worried about what it will be ten years from now.

Chairman Mao: I'd say thirty years hence or fifty years hence. And it is impossible for a country to rise up in a short period.

The Secretary: Well, as I have said on many occasions, and as I said to the Chairman last time, we believe that if this eventuality were to happen, it would have very serious consequences for everybody. And we are determined to oppose it as our own decision without any arrangement with China.

Chairman Mao: Their ambitions are contradictory with their capacity.

The Secretary: That may be true.

Chairman Mao: Beginning from their Pacific Ocean, there is the United States, there is Japan, there is China, there is South Asia, and westward there is the Middle East, and there is Europe, and the Soviet forces that are deployed along the lines through Siberia way up to the Kurile Islands only account for one-fourth of their forces.

Prime Minister Chou: East of the Urals.

The Secretary: A little closer to one-half. Two-fifths maybe.

Chairman Mao: Excluding the Middle East, that is. The Middle East would be counted on the other side.

The Secretary: I see.

Chairman Mao: But that includes Kazakistan, the Uzbek Republic, Urquiz and other small republics. Also, some other minority nationality troops stationed in the East.

The Secretary: We know where every Soviet division is. And we have occasionally discussed some of this with you. But I agree with the Chairman . . .

Chairman Mao: (Before translation) They have to deal with so many adversaries. They have to deal with the Pacific. They have to deal with Japan. They have to deal with China. They have to deal with South Asia which also consists of quite a number of countries. And they only have a million troops here—not enough even for the defense of themselves and still less for attack forces. But they can't attack unless you let them in first, and you first give them the Middle East and Europe so they are able to deploy troops eastward. And that would take over a million troops.

The Secretary: That will not happen. I agree with the Chairman that if Europe and Japan and the U.S. hold together—and we are doing in the Middle East what the Chairman discussed with me last time—then the danger of an attack on China will be very low.

Chairman Mao: We are also holding down a portion of their troops which is favorable to you in Europe and the Middle East. For instance, they have troops stationed in Outer Mongolia, and that had not happened as late as Khrushchev's time. At that time they had still not stationed troops in Outer Mongolia, because the Chienpao Island incident occurred after Khrushchev. It occurred in Brezhnev's time.

The Secretary: It was 1969. That is why it is important that Western Europe and China and the U.S. pursue a coordinated course in this period.

Chairman Mao: Yes.

The Secretary: Because in that case, nobody will be attacked.

Chairman Mao: Japan's attitudes is also good.

The Secretary: That's very important, yes.

Chairman Mao: And the attitudes of major European countries are not bad either.

The Secretary: Their attitude is better than their courage. (Prime Minister Chou explains something in Chinese to Chairman Mao.)

Chairman Mao: The main trouble now is those small Nordic countries. (The interpreters then corrected.) No, mainly the Benelux countries.

The Secretary: The Benelux countries and the Scandinavian countries, and there's some ambiguity in the evolution of the German position.

Chairman Mao: In my opinion, Germany is still a part of the West and will not follow the Soviet Union, while Norway is quite fearful of the Soviet Union. Sweden is a bit wavering. Finland is slightly tended to be closer to the Soviet Union.

The Secretary: Because of its geographic position, not because of its conviction.

Chairman Mao: That's correct. And they were very courageous during that war.

The Secretary: Very.

Chairman Mao: They are the country of one thousand legs.

The Secretary: That's true.

Chairman Mao: The Soviet Union first carved out a part of their country and then gave it back, and that country is not one to be easily offended. Because they are hemmed in too close to the Soviet/Finnish border.

Prime Minister Chou: Why were they cut off?

The Secretary: They did take part. They were in the Karelian Isthmus.

Chairman Mao: And even during the time of Hitler's occupation of Poland, Stalin still did not dare attack some of the countries that used to exist along the Baltic Sea.

The Secretary: But he took them shortly afterwards.

Chairman Mao: That was because Hitler attacked Poland, and the Soviet Union seized the opportunity to act in such a manner. They tried an agreement of cooperation. The Soviet Union was able to resist that opportunity to seize these three countries.

Perhaps these three representatives have embassies in your country.

The Secretary: And they still do, Mr. Chairman.

Chairman Mao: And the Soviet Union did not ask you first to abolish those embassies before they established diplomatic relations with you.

The Secretary: That is correct.

Chairman Mao: In 1933.

The Secretary: In 1933, those countries still existed, and we established diplomatic relations in 1933.

Prime Minister Chou: It's not so convenient for them to go to the United Nations.

The Secretary: They are not in the United Nations.

Prime Minister Chou: They probably have some nationals residing in your country.

The Secretary: Yes. I frankly . . . they have ambassadors and are accredited, but I don't know what they do.

Ambassador Bruce: They don't do anything. One of them appears. I think it is Estonia, once a year, and gives an annual day reception (laughter).

The Secretary: You're quite right. It has not affected our diplomatic relations with the Soviet Union.

Chairman Mao: Let's discuss the issue of Taiwan. The question of the U.S. relations with us should be separate from that of our relations with Taiwan.

The Secretary: In principle . . .

Chairman Mao: So long as you sever the diplomatic relations with Taiwan, then it is possible for our two countries to solve the issue of diplomatic relations. That is to say like we did with Japan. As for the question of our relations with Taiwan, that is quite complex. I do not believe in a peaceful transition. (To the Foreign Minister) Do you believe in it?

The Secretary: Do I? He asked the Foreign Minister.

Chairman Mao: I'm asking him (the Foreign Minister). (Prime Minister Chou said something that was not translated.)

They are a bunch of counterrevolutionaries. How could they cooperate with us? I say that we can do without Taiwan for the time being, and let it come after one hundred years. Do not take matters on this world so rapidly. Why is there need to be in such great haste? It is only such an island with a population of a dozen or more million.

Prime Minister Chou: They now have 16 million.

Chairman Mao: As for your relations with us, I think they need not take a hundred years.

The Secretary: I would count on that. I think they should come much faster.

Chairman Mao: But that is to be decided by you. We will not rush you. If you feel the need, we can do it. If you feel it cannot be done now, then we can postpone it to a later date.

The Secretary: From our point of view we want diplomatic relations with the Peoples Republic. Our difficulty is that we cannot immediately sever relations with Taiwan, for various reasons, all of them having to do with our domestic situation. I told the Prime Minister that we hope that by 1976, during 1976, to complete the process.[5] So the question is whether we can find some formula that enables us to have diplomatic relations, and the utility of it would be symbolic strengthening of our ties, because, on a technical level, the Liaison Offices perform very usefully.

Chairman Mao: That can do.

---

[5] See Document 57.

The Secretary: What can do?

Chairman Mao: (Before translation) It can do to continue as now, because now you still need Taiwan.

The Secretary: It isn't a question of needing it; it is a question of practical possibilities.

Chairman Mao: That's the same (laughter). We are in no hurry about Hong Kong either (laughter). We don't even touch Macao. If we wanted to touch Macao, it would only take a slight touch. Because that was a stronghold established by Portugal back during the Ming Dynasty (laughter). Khrushchev has cursed us, saying why is it you don't want even Hong Kong and Macao. And I've said to Japan that we not only agree to your demand for the four northern islands, but also in history the Soviet Union has carved out one and a half million square kilometers from China.

The Secretary: As I see the problem of diplomatic relations, Mr. Chairman, it's this. On the question of Taiwan, I believe we have a very clear understanding to which we will stick. So the problem we have is . . . also, the Liaison Offices are doing useful work at this time. So the only question is whether at some point either or both of us thinks it is useful to demonstrate symbolically that our relationship is now normal in every respect. In that case, we should find a formula to make it possible, but it is not a necessity.

Chairman Mao: We have established diplomatic relations with the Soviet Union and also with India, but they are not so very good. And they are not even as good as our relations with you, which are better than our relations with them. So this issue is not an important one. The issue of the overall international situation is an important one.

The Secretary: I agree with the Chairman completely and on that we must understand each other, and I believe we substantially understand each other.

Chairman Mao: Our Chief of our Liaison Office was talking to you about grand principles and referred to George Washington's opposing Britain.

The Secretary: Yes, he made a great speech to me a few weeks ago. I'd heard it before from the Prime Minister.

Chairman Mao: That set of language can be cut down. And we are now facing a contradiction. On the one hand, we have supported various Arab countries against Israeli Zionism. On the other hand, we have to welcome the U.S. putting the Soviet Union on the spot, and making it so that the Soviet Union cannot control the Middle East. Our Ambassador Huang Chen mentioned this support of the Arab world, but he didn't understand the importance of U.S. resistance to the Soviet Union.

The Secretary: Well, I took him by surprise, and he repeated the formal position from the United Nations (laughter). And I understand that publicly you have to take certain positions, and it is not against our common position that you do so. But the reality is that we will move matters toward a settlement in the Middle East, but we also want to demonstrate that it was not done by Soviet pressures.

So, whenever the Soviets press we must resist apart from the merits of the dispute. Then when we have defeated them, we may even move in the same direction. We are not against Arab aspirations; we are against their being achieved with Soviet pressure.

Chairman Mao: Exactly.

The Secretary: And that is our strategy right now.

Chairman Mao: And now there is a crucial issue, that is the question of Iraq, Baghdad. We don't know if it is possible for you to do some work in that area. As for us, the possibilities are not so very great.

Prime Minister Chou: It is relatively difficult to do that. It is possible to have contacts with them, but it takes a period of time for them to change their orientation. It is possible they would change their orientation after they have suffered from them. They've already suffered once, that is with regard to the coup.

The Secretary: You can do good work in Iran, and Iran is active in Iraq. And we have encouraged the Shah to establish good relations with you. Our strategy with Iraq is first to try to win Syria away from it, and then to reduce its influence in sheikdoms along the Persian Gulf. And then when it sees it can achieve nothing by leaning to the Soviet Union, then we will move toward them. But first they have to learn that they gain nothing from their present course.

Chairman Mao: And this country it contains no banks or coasts of the Arab gulf, that is the Persian Gulf. Recently, your naval ships have gone in that part of the world. I said that was good.

The Secretary: They are still there, and we will keep them there a little longer.

Chairman Mao: That is one carrier.

The Secretary: A carrier and escort ships.

Chairman Mao: And the Soviet Union often passes through the Japanese straits, for example, the Tsrumi Straits eastward to the vicinity of the Midway Islands. And they go in and out of the Japanese Islands. Sometimes they test their missiles in the Pacific Ocean, too.

The Secretary: Yes.

Chairman Mao: In my opinion, their aim is to tie down a portion of your strength in the Pacific Ocean to avoid your sending a large number of troops westwards.

The Secretary: First, we don't mind their testing missiles in the Pacific, because this makes it very easy to find out what their characteristics are. As for the fleet, our difficulty about operating in the Indian

Ocean and the Arab Sea has been that we have not had a base in that area. But we have now developed an island called Diego Garcia as a base, and we have also discussed with Pakistan the possibility of building a port. And we are establishing very close relationships with the Shah of Iran. And I believe you will see we will be stationing more ships in the Indian Ocean from now on.

Chairman Mao: Why is it that Iran is favoring the Soviet Union's Asian collective security system?

The Secretary: First, of the leaders in that area that I know, the one who understands the Soviet danger best is the Shah of Iran. And he's buying very large numbers now of military equipment from us in order to defend himself against the Soviet Union and also to be able to protect Pakistan. So if we sat here, Mr. Chairman, he would agree completely with your analysis of the situation. But he has a tactical problem, and he wanted to say that he was for peace in general. I think he made a mistake, but he is not really for an Asian security system.

Prime Minister Chou: He will be arriving in China during the first three months of next year. (The Prime Minister and the Foreign Minister discuss the date.) It's going to be postponed. It is not going to be so early.

The Secretary: He is very much interested in good relations with China, and we have recommended it very strongly. And he sees your attitude and our attitude about Pakistan and Afganistan.

Chairman Mao: It seems to me that the comparatively weaker place in the contemporary international situation would still be Iraq.

The Secretary: Iraq right now is the most difficult place in that area.

Prime Minister Chou: (Laughing) Quadaffi went to Iraq to stir up something there.

Chairman Mao: What have they done now?

Prime Minister Chou: He has gone and returned. He went there to persuade them not to accept a ceasefire.

The Secretary: Quadaffi is not the most stable intellect that leads countries right now.

Chairman Mao: He is a man I do not understand. There's another, that is South Yemen. The President of South Yemen approached me. He said he wanted to sever diplomatic relations with the Soviet Union. He asked me my opinion. I was not taken in by him and said he must be prudent. Now they are tying themselves very closely to the Soviet Union.

The Secretary: Very closely tied to the Soviet Union. And they are stirring things up all over the Gulf.

Chairman Mao: Do you have diplomatic relations with them?

The Secretary: We have technically diplomatic relations with them but no useful influence. But we give assistance to Muscat and Oman and North Yemen in order to contain them. (The interpreter and Prime Minister Chou explain the location of Muscat and Oman to the Chairman.)

Chairman Mao: Let's discuss something about Japan. This time you are going to Japan to stay a few more days there.

The Secretary: The Chairman always scolds me about Japan. I'm taking the Chairman very seriously, and this time I'm staying two and a half days. And he's quite right. It is very important that Japan does not feel isolated and left alone. And we should not give them too many temptations to maneuver.

Chairman Mao: That is not to force them over to the Soviet side.

The Secretary: And not force them into too many choices, for example, between us.

Chairman Mao: That would not come about.

The Secretary: Not from our side either (not translated).

Chairman Mao: Their first priority is to have good relations with the United States. We only come second.

The Secretary: We have no objection to good relations between Japan and China. We want to prevent them from moving too close to the Soviet Union.

Prime Minister Chou: And they should not be taken in.

The Secretary: That's why if they do something in the Soviet Union, we sometimes join them, so they are not all alone in facing the Soviet Union.

Chairman Mao: And we also encourage them to do things together with the United States to avoid their being taken in.

Prime Minister Chou: Recently, Tanaka and others paid a visit to the United States. Was that on the West Coast or in Hawaii?

The Secretary: No, he went to Washington before they went to the Soviet Union during the summer. Our relations now are better than they were when I was here last time. They are no longer so nervous (laughter).

Chairman Mao: They are afraid of you and you should try to lessen their fear. The Soviet Union is doing its utmost to go all out to win them over, but Japan is not so trustful of them.

The Secretary: No, they had a very bad historical experience, and that is very fortunate for all of us. And the Russian temperament doesn't harmonize very well with the Japanese.

Prime Minister Chou: During Tanaka's visit to the Soviet Union, the Russians acted very stupidly.

Chairman Mao: They didn't have any discussions the first two days.

Prime Minister Chou: They lectured them.

Chairman Mao: They only made proposals about the resources of the Soviet Union.

The Secretary: Yes, they did that to us, too. It creates the impression they are trying to buy us. But the proposal is that we have to invest there for ten years, and only after everything is built, then they'll start paying us back (laughter). We have not yet agreed and there is no prospect of an early agreement to any of their big projects.

Chairman Mao: And that includes most favored nation treatment. Now it is put on the shelf. I thought it was good upon hearing that news. I think it is best to put it on the shelf for a longer period of time.

The Secretary: But we would like to have MFN for China (laughter).

Chairman Mao: Not necessarily. So long as the Soviet Union doesn't get it, that would be enough (laughter).

The Secretary: The prospects of that legislation are not very promising.

Chairman Mao/Prime Minister Chou: Is that so?

The Secretary: It won't be taken up again until February. That's in the House. And then it must be taken up in the Senate. But all in all, it seems it will be finally passed if not next year, the year after. The big problem, Mr. Chairman, is not the MFN clause, because the Soviet Union doesn't have goods to sell us. The obstacle to Soviet trade is not our duties, but the low quality of Soviet products.

Chairman Mao: But they can give you energy which you need.

The Secretary: Mr. Chairman, that is not exactly accurate. Even if they were able to produce the natural gas they have claimed, and there is still some dispute about that, it would only amount to about five percent of our needs. And it would take ten years to deliver. And within that ten-year period, we will have developed domestic alternatives, including natural gas in America. That makes it much less necessary, in fact probably unnecessary, to import natural gas in quantities.

Chairman Mao: That would be good.

The Secretary: The problem is credits more than MFN. And those we have controlled very rigidly. We haven't given any credits.

Chairman Mao: I'm lacking in knowledge and cannot understand this problem. I cannot understand this. Probably what you said is correct. At present, the Soviet Union seems in need of such great amounts as $8 billion in credits.

The Secretary: Yes, and we've given them up to now $330 million. They want $8 billion dollars just for natural gas.

Chairman Mao: Your President issued the Nixon Doctrine at Guam, I believe, and we see that you are gradually resisting his policy in putting out the flames of war in Southeast Asia. In this manner, you will be able to achieve a greater initiative.

The Secretary: That is correct.

Chairman Mao: What you issued was a new Atlantic Charter. (There was some discussion of the translation of this word and the difference between "Charter" and "Constitution.") But they mean the same thing. I would think we will realize the basic objective of that proposal within the first half of that year. Most of the Charter is already drafted in the military sphere; we've almost completed a draft, and in the political sphere, we've almost completed drafting it. The economic one requires more work.

Chairman Mao: In the economic field, there are some contradictions.

The Secretary: Yes. That's true, but they have to be overcome too, because of the great need, and I think we can work them out. Our press always concentrates on disagreements. Those diplomats who are willing to talk publicly are usually least reliable, and their reports are always published. But basically, we are making good progress.

Chairman Mao: That is why I believe it will be greatly difficult for the Soviet Union to seize Europe and put it on its side. They have such ambition but great difficulty.

The Secretary: I think it is very difficult for them to seize militarily, and if they attempt it, they will certainly have to fight us. (Chairman Mao talks to Prime Minister Chou.)

The greatest danger with the Soviet Union is where they either move land armies quickly, as in Czechoslovakia, or make a sudden air attack in areas where they think we will not do anything.

Chairman Mao: Take, for instance, the manner of their actions in Czechoslovakia. It is completely unseemly. For instance, they engaged in intriguing against Czechoslovakia; they sent civilian aircraft and used troops in the civilian aircraft.

The Secretary: To control the Prague Airport.

Chairman Mao: Later they sent troops there. Others thought they carried civilian passengers in that aircraft, but they sent troops. In that manner, they were able to control the Prague Airport. They sent troops there and reduced Czechoslovakia to inertia.

The Secretary: That's true. That's exactly how it happened.

Chairman Mao: And, therefore, in my opinion, with regard to the Soviet Union, it has a great ambition—and that is, it wishes to seize in its hands the two continents of Europe and Asia, and North Africa and elsewhere, but they will have trouble doing that.

The Secretary: As long as countries that are threatened stay united. (Chairman Mao toasts everyone with his tea.)

Chairman Mao: They made use of the opportunities when both of your feet were stuck in the quagmire of Southeast Asia. And in this, your President can't take all the blame for that. The Johnson Administration was responsible for that.

The Secretary: Where did they take advantage of their opportunity?

Chairman Mao: That is to enter Czechoslovakia.

Prime Minister Chou: And also India.

Chairman Mao: And I don't pay so much attention to these minor things. That is, they have so-called nonaggression pacts with Egypt, Iraq and India, like the Treaty of Friendship with India. I don't believe that settles things. Therefore, we would not agree to any such treaties when they propose them to us.

The Secretary: Yes. I have noticed that.

Chairman Mao: And there are some people here who are commenting that you had lost an opportunity to take action when you did not do so when Egypt chased out Soviet military personnel. The commentary goes that at that time you should have assisted Egypt a bit. Upon hearing that I thought further. I thought that because at that time both your feet were in the whole of Southeast Asia, and you had not yet climbed out.

The Secretary: You are quite right, Mr. Chairman. There were two problems. We had our election. And, secondly, we were still in Vietnam, and we couldn't tackle both at once.

Chairman Mao: That is so. You are now freer than before.

The Secretary: Much more.

Chairman Mao: And the philosopher of your motherland, Hegel, has said—I don't know whether it is the correct English translation—"freedom means the knowledge of necessity."

The Secretary: Yes.

Chairman Mao: Do you pay attention or not to one of the subjects of Hegel's philosophy, that is, the unity of opposites?

The Secretary: Very much. I was much influenced by Hegel in my philosophic thinking.

Chairman Mao: Both Hegel and Feuerbach, who came a little later after him. They were both great thinkers. And Marxism came partially from them. They were predecessors of Marx. If it were not for Hegel and Feuerbach, there would not be Marxism.

The Secretary: Yes. Marx reversed the tendency of Hegel, but he adopted the basic theory.

Chairman Mao: What kind of doctor are you? Are you a doctor of philosophy?

The Secretary: Yes (laughter).

Chairman Mao: Yes, well, then won't you give me a lecture?

The Secretary: I think the Chairman knows much more philosophy than I. And he has written profoundly about philosophy. I used to shock my colleagues, Mr. Chairman, by assigning essays from your collected works, in my courses in the 1960s at Harvard.

Chairman Mao: I, myself, am not satisfied with myself. The main thing is that I don't understand foreign languages and, therefore, I am unable to read books of Germans or Englishmen or Americans.

The Secretary: I can't read German in its original form. I must translate into English, because it is too complicated in its original form. This is quite true. Some of the points of Hegel—quite seriously—I understand better in English than German, even though German is my mother language.

Prime Minister Chou: Because of the intricate structure of the German grammar, it sometimes gets misinterpreted if one doesn't understand the grammar correctly. Therefore, it's not easy to understand the German language and especially the reasoning of various works.

Chairman Mao: (To Prime Minister Chou) Don't you know some German?

Prime Minister Chou: I learned in my youth; now I've forgotten it.

The Secretary: German sentences are long, and the grammar is involved. Therefore, it's easier to understand English than German. One of the characteristics of the German language . . .

Prime Minister Chou: Yesterday, a few of those who know German were joking together that German sentences are so long in length that they are quite a few pages, and one does not understand the sentences until you find the final verb, and the verb is at the very end. That, of course, is exaggerated. One sentence does not take several pages.

Chairman Mao: Did you meet Kuo Mo-juo who understands German? Now we are discussing Hegel, and I give you an opinion.

The Secretary: I don't know the gentleman that the Chairman was mentioning.

Chairman Mao: He is a man who worships Confucius, but he is now a member of our Central Committee.

Let's go back to Hegel. In Hegel's history of philosophy, he mentioned Confucius who he showed great disrespect. He showed more respect for Laotze, but he showed the greatest respect for the philosophy of Indian Buddhism.

The Secretary: I don't quite agree with him (the Chairman) on that last point. That's a very passive philosophy.

Chairman Mao: And I also believe that that was not a correct way of saying. And this is not only true of Hegel.

The Secretary: There is a sentimental love affair between Western intellectuals and India based on a complete misreading of the Indian philosophy of life. Indian philosophy was never meant to have a practical application.

Chairman Mao: It's just a bunch of empty words.

The Secretary: For Gandhi, nonviolence wasn't a philosophic principle, but because he thought the British were too moralistic and sentimental to use violence against. They are nonsentimental people. For Gandhi it was a revolutionary tactic, not an ethical principle.

Chairman Mao: And he himself would spin his own wool and drink goat's milk.

The Secretary: But it was essentially a tactical device for him.

Chairman Mao: And the influence of Gandhi's doctrine on the Indian people was to induce them into nonresistance.

The Secretary: Partly, but also given the character and diversity of the English people, it was only a way to conduct the struggle against the British. So I think Gandhi deserves credit of having won independence against the British.

Chairman Mao: India did not win independence. If it did not attach itself to Britain, it attaches itself to the Soviet Union. And more than one-half of their economy depends on you. Did you not mention during your briefings that India owes ten billion dollars in debt to the U.S., or was that all debts?

The Secretary: That was all debts together. It's not $10 billion but closer to $6 billion. I will have to check. I thought it was $10 billion to everybody, of which India owed 60 percent. But you may be right. I have to check. (To Lord: can you check, Win?)[6]

Prime Minister Chou: That includes the rupees debt.

The Secretary: Including the rupee debt, that is correct. Yes. And one can mention the dollar debt, too.

Chairman Mao: I recall your President told us the various debts at the World Bank were $10 billion.

The Secretary: Yes. When one includes the unilateral debts and the rupee debts and the bilateral debts, then it is $10 billion and probably a little more even.

Chairman Mao: That is also something you've imparted to me. In the past, I had not known that. And if you come to China again, besides talking politics, talk a bit of philosophy to me.

The Secretary: I would like that very much, Mr. Chairman. That was my first love, the study of philosophy.

---

[6] No follow up by Lord on India's external debt was found.

Chairman Mao: Perhaps it is more difficult to do now as Secretary of State.

The Secretary: Yes.

Chairman Mao: And they say you are a galloping horse whose hooves never stop (laughter).

The Secretary: He (Prime Minister Chou) called me a "cyclone" (laughter).

Chairman Mao: There is a cyclone around the world.

The Secretary: Your Vice Foreign Minister told me your views, Mr. Chairman, about the Arab world when he talked to me in October, and I paid great attention to them.

Chairman Mao: That is the matter of my discussions with the Vice President of Egypt which was somehow gotten hold of by Lord Chiao (laughter).

The Secretary: He didn't tell me who he had talked to.

Chairman Mao: It was Shafei. Did you see him?

The Secretary: I saw Sadat and two or three others.

Chairman Mao: At that time I was trying to persuade him to get closer to you, because I noted that after you announced your position as Secretary of State and you'd only been that a few days, you met the Arab Foreign Ministers and later on invited them to lunch. Only the Foreign Ministers of Iraq Syria, Libya, and South Yemen declined. I think even Egypt accepted.

The Secretary: That is correct.

Chairman Mao: That is why I was following behind you (laughter). I was very happy that you entertained those Arab Foreign Ministers.

The Secretary: Yes. It was my first official function.

Chairman Mao: And your predecessor, the previous Secretary, I think did not do so.

The Secretary: He was interested, but I don't think he ever had them as a group.

Chairman Mao: And these Arab countries, which spread up from the Atlantic to the Persian Gulf, account for more than a hundred million people.

Prime Minister Chou: The population is now one hundred and fifty million.

Chairman Mao: And they are composed of 19 countries.

The Secretary: And we are making a major effort to improve our relations with them and take this very seriously.

Chairman Mao: And the difficulties are also great because these countries are both united and engaged in internal struggles. It is not so easy to deal with.

The Secretary: Libya quarrels with all its neighbors. (Prime Minister Chou leaves the room.)

Chairman Mao: Perhaps he's that kind of cock that loves fighting. That's the way Khrushchev cursed us. He said we were a cock that liked fighting.

The Secretary: He did not have a very successful visit here in 1959.

Chairman Mao: We fell out by 1959. We began to fall out in 1958 when they wanted to control China's seacoast and also China's naval ports. And during my discussions with them, with their Ambassador, I almost slammed the table, and I gave him hell (laughter). And he reported that to Moscow and Khrushchev came. At that time, he put forth the notion of a joint fleet, that is, for the Soviet Union and China to form a joint naval fleet. That was the suggestion he raised. And at that time, he was quite arrogant because he had seen General Eisenhower who was then President, and he attained the so-called "spirit of Camp David." And he boasted to me in Peking that he got to know the President and the two English words concerning President Eisenhower were that he was "my friend." (To Ambassador Bruce: You knew that?)

Ambassador Bruce: No, I never knew that.

Chairman Mao: And also a piece of news. Since then, he never came again. But he had been to Vladivostok and he went there from China.

Prime Minister Chou: There he made an anti-China speech.

Chairman Mao: None of the present leaders of the Soviet Union have been as far eastward as Vladivostok. Kosygin himself has said he is not quite clear about matters in Siberia. (The Chinese check the time.)

Prime Minister Chou: It's been two and one-half hours.

Chairman Mao: And there's another issue I would like to discuss with you. It seems today we have talked too long. Over two and one-half hours. We have taken up time originally set aside for other activities. (*Note:* He meant Ambassador Bruce's reception.) The question I would like to discuss is that I am quite suspicious that if the Democratic Party comes into office, they will adopt the policy of isolationism.

The Secretary: That is a very serious question, Mr. Chairman. I think there may be trends now among the intellectuals and some Democrats in the direction of isolationism. On the other hand, objective realities would force them to understand that there is no alternative to our present policy. Now, what damage would be done until they learned this, and whether they would continue with the same tactical complexity, this I don't know. But I think they would pursue the present course. (The last sentence is not translated.)

Chairman Mao: Then you seem to be in the same category as myself. We seem to be both more or less suspicious.

The Secretary: I'm suspicious, and I have some questions about some leaders. But I believe the overwhelming necessity of the situation will force us to return to the policy we are now pursuing.

But this, Mr. Chairman, is why I believe we should use this period, when all of us are still in office and understand the situation, to so solidify it that no alternative will be possible anymore.

Chairman Mao: And this is mainly manifested in that one point—that is the advocacy of troop withdrawals from Europe.

The Secretary: Yes.

Chairman Mao: This will be a great assistance to the Soviet Union.

The Secretary: We will not carry it out in our Administration. It occurs in two things, the troop withdrawals from Europe and maybe less of a willingness to be very brutal very quickly in case there is a challenge.

Chairman Mao: What you mean by "brutality" is probably going to war.

The Secretary: If necessary, but . . .

Chairman Mao: I am not happy you are putting up a diplomatic front to me.

The Secretary: If necessary, but our experience has been that, if they know we are going to war, they draw back. Up to now, they've always been afraid of us.

Chairman Mao: Because I also think it would be better not to go to war. I'm not in favor of that either, though I'm well known as a warmonger (laughter). If you and the Soviet Union fight a war, I would also think that would not be very good. If you are going to fight, it would be better to use conventional weapons, and leave nuclear weapons in the stockpile, and not touch them.

The Secretary: We will not start a war in any event.

Chairman Mao: That's good. I heard you put forward the opinion before that you want to gain time.

The Secretary: We want to gain time, but we also want to be in a position that, if the Soviet Union attacks any major areas we discussed, we can resist. And it's in those circumstances we have to be prepared.

Chairman Mao: That's entirely correct. As for the Soviet Union, they bully the weak, and are afraid of the tough. (Laughter as he points to Miss Wang and Miss Tang.) And you shouldn't try to bully either Miss Wang or Miss Tang because they are comparatively soft.

The Secretary: Mr. Chairman, in my experience they are not very soft. They also don't carry out the Chairman's advice (laughter).

Chairman Mao: She (Miss Tang) is American, while she (Miss Wang) is a Soviet spy (laughter).

(The Chairman then got up unassisted and escorted the Americans to the outer lobby. He said goodbye to the Secretary, Ambassador Bruce, and Mr. Lord in turn, and asked photographers to take pictures. As he shook hands with the Secretary, he said "and please send my personal greetings to President Richard Nixon." The Secretary said he would do that. Ambassador Bruce and Mr. Lord indicated that it was a great honor to see Chairman Mao. The Chairman mentioned to Mr. Lord that he had met him before, and Mr. Lord acknowledged this.)

---

59.   Memorandum of Conversation[1]

Beijing, November 13, 1973, 4:30–7:15 p.m.

PARTICIPANTS

Prime Minister Chou En-lai
Foreign Minister Chi Peng-fei
Assistant Minister of Foreign Affairs Wang Hai-jung
Lin Ping, Director, Foreign Ministry
Tsien Ta-yung, PRC Liaison Office, Washington
One other Chinese official
Tang Wang-shen, Interpreter
Yang Yu-yung, Interpreter
Chinese notetaker

Secretary of State Henry A. Kissinger
Ambassador David Bruce, Chief, U.S. Liaison Office
Ambassador Robert Ingersoll, U.S. Embassy Tokyo
Winston Lord, Director of Planning and Coordination, Department of State
Acting Assistant Secretary Arthur Hummel, East Asian and Pacific Affairs

(Prime Minister Chou En-lai mentioned previous Chinese Nationalist Foreign Minister Wellington Koo.)

Ambassador Bruce: I heard him make a great number of speeches. He is a brilliant speaker.

Prime Minister Chou: And he speaks very good English. Only the young people are able to catch up with him speaking English and like T. F. Tsiang who only speaks English, he speaks Chinese. He is also from Shanghai.

---

[1] Source: National Archives, Nixon Presidential Materials, NSC Files, Kissinger Office Files, Box 100, Country Files, Far East, Secretary Kissinger's Conversations in Peking, November 1973. Top Secret; Sensitive; Exclusively Eyes Only. The meeting took place at Guest House Villa #3. All brackets are in the original.

I received your text of the Communiqué last night and your guidance on working out that text.[2] So we received it at one o'clock in early morning, and then we have to make suggestions and some changes. We still want to preserve and keep your good points. Now, I have also gotten myself involved.

Secretary Kissinger: Is that the text of yours?

Prime Minister Chou: Ours is even shorter than yours. About the same length. I have kept back points. We are having it typed. After we have finished typing it, we will have one person from each side . . .

Secretary Kissinger: As long as your representative isn't the Vice Minister.

Prime Minister Chou: Obviously if you agree to our views, it will be all right. We have tried our best to take in your main points.

Secretary Kissinger: I think we will have no difficulty. Maybe on our side it should be Mr. Hummel and Mr. Lord.

I have some answers to some of the questions you asked yesterday. First, about the *Oklahoma City*.[3] I would like to be able to say . . .

Prime Minister Chou: The *City* is already in Hong Kong.

Secretary Kissinger: That's right. I wanted to say that for once I wish you were wrong in pointing these things out to us, but you were right and there is no answer except stupidity. Before coming here we had prohibited airplanes coming anywhere close to China, but we forgot to specify ships. So I can only apologize. It was bad taste. It was legal but stupid.

Prime Minister Chou: The Taiwan authorities are getting great publicity about it.

Secretary Kissinger (to Lord): Can we find out how they knew about it?

Prime Minister Chou: We learned about this news from the Taiwan authorities because only when they talked about these facts did we know about it. We learn about activities of vessels or planes in Taiwan space because they have islands that are quite close. They use these as instances. They derive merits from it because they make publicity of the fact that ships have come close to them.

Secretary Kissinger: I can only say it was stupidity. The capacity for stupidity seems to be infinite. I can't think of what new stupidity people are thinking up.

---

[2] See footnote 7, Document 60.

[3] On November 12, Zhou remarked that the USS *Oklahoma City* had entered the Taiwan Straits during Kissinger's visit. See Document 57 and footnote 7 thereto.

Prime Minister Chou: You are right. And so the vessels that deliberately sailed close to Taiwan were also Soviet ships. That shows they did it deliberately.

Secretary Kissinger: Yes. In this particular case, we knew nothing about it. It seems inconceivable to us that anyone would do it deliberately. Ships would also be prohibited when planes were.

Prime Minister Chou: But for some occasions you cannot prohibit it beforehand. You can only settle after it comes up. So there is also a matter of mutual trust in such a case. Now, Doctor, you have had a very deep discussion with our Chairman. So in the future I believe our mutual understanding will be deep.

Secretary Kissinger: We do too, and we consider the meeting with the Chairman to be extremely important.

Prime Minister Chou: And my discussion with you the day before yesterday—that is, your discussion with me prepared the way for your talks with the Chairman. Since we have touched these points, I don't think it is necessary to dwell upon these issues.

Now, today, what we have to do is make clarification on some issues and settle some issues. The first point is concerning the Soviet Union. You said that a big question concerning that is about the prevention of nuclear war, and you hoped there would be no endless debate about it.

Interpreter: You thought it better to complete the treaty than have endless debate on the issue.

Secretary Kissinger: Yes.

Prime Minister Chou: I think you are right in saying so because on the whole it is right not to have an endless debate on this issue. But there is one point on the legal basis of that issue—I think that treaty was not yet agreed by the Congress. And the second point is that if any strong evidence should come up there should be some prior consultation.

Secretary Kissinger: Between you and us or between us and the Soviet Union?

Prime Minister Chou: I was referring to between the Soviet Union and the U.S. because it was part of your agreement. But the whole world should be made clear about the principles including your allies. Otherwise, they will think the two big powers will discuss other subjects behind their back. That's why there is a wave in the world. That's what made it necessary for us to make a comprehensive assessment at the United Nations. You had contacts with us beforehand, and I am sure you also contacted your allies before.

Secretary Kissinger: It may amuse the Prime Minister to give you their state of mind, that some of our allies helped us draft the agreement and they saw it before some of our own people. Some were critical of their own draft. You can ask Prime Minister Heath when he visits you.

Prime Minister Chou: But you can still remember our position?

Secretary Kissinger: Your position was understood.

Prime Minister Chou: So we had to make criticism because we think it is necessary for Third World countries to have such an understanding on this issue. But you had given your consent to the treaty signed by Latin American countries, the Treaty on a Nuclear Free Zone. You were the first to show your consent. But still you haven't withdrawn your military bases there in Cuba so Cuba had to file a protest in order to free their hands. In order to satisfy the demands of countries like Mexico, we signed that Treaty but we made a separate statement. We hope that the Soviet Union would sign the treaty. Or would they prefer to stay isolated to the end?

Secretary Kissinger: So far the Soviet Union has not.

Prime Minister Chou: What is the reason? Is it because of Cuba?

Secretary Kissinger: Partly because of Cuba; or maybe they have other expectations in Latin America.

Prime Minister Chou: There is a new issue cropping up in Latin America, that is concerning Chile. Could you exercise some influence on Chile? They shouldn't go in for slaughtering that way. It was terrible.

Secretary Kissinger: We have exercised considerable influence, and we believe after the first phase when they seized power there have been no executions with which we are familiar going on now. I will look into the matter again when we return and I will inform you. To the best of my recollection when we left there were no executions taking place, but I will check on it.

(To Lord) Get Kubisch to check on this.[4]

Secretary Kissinger: After the first week—I am talking now up to the time I had left Washington.

Prime Minister Chou: But as you know, our emissary has been staying on.

Secretary Kissinger: Yes, and we appreciate it.

Prime Minister Chou: And just because our emissary is still there, that's how we have been able to learn about many facts. Mr. Lin Ping

---

[4] Jack Kubisch was Assistant Secretary of State for Inter-American Affairs. Lord prepared a November 20 memorandum for Kissinger on the number of executions in Chile. (National Archives, Nixon Presidential Materials, NSC Files, Kissinger Office Files, Box 96, Country Files, Far East, China Exchanges, November 1, 1973–March 31, 1974) Kissinger wrote that this information "should be watered down," but accepted Lord's recommendation that it be shared verbally with Han Xu. (Ibid.)

is our Ambassador in Chile, because their government is much too complicated. Even without the support on the part of the CIA, they perhaps work on the same (perhaps their own virtue).

Secretary Kissinger: No, I wish the Prime Minister were right. I wish the CIA was as competent as the Prime Minister believes.

Prime Minister Chou: But you wouldn't be able to control it.

Secretary Kissinger: Not be able to control the CIA?

Prime Minister Chou: What I meant is did they have a hand in the coup?

Secretary Kissinger: They would not have a hand in the coup, but it is true they could not control the situation.

Prime Minister Chou: They could only control one thing. Remember when your chargé d'affaires in Laos during the recent coup ran to the airport and told the official of the coup.

Secretary Kissinger: That's true. In Laos, we attempted to restrain the situation. In Chile, it was the incompetence of the Allende government. We would not give assistance, would not make their task easier, but we did not have anything to do with the actual coup.

Prime Minister Chou: But that government itself was much too complicated. Allende himself admitted that if one wanted to seize political power in the true sense of the word . . . but on the other hand their subordinates made great publicity. And those Communists in that country who were close to the Soviet Union wanted the Soviet Union to supply them with weapons. Whereas those Che Guevarists in Cuba that took up arms found themselves divorced from the masses by doing quite similarly those activities which they carried out in their Cuban guerrilla forces. They thought that once they had weapons in hand, they could kill some people and burn down some houses. Their putschist group was active in Chile and other countries. Have you ever read the diary written by Che Guevara?

Secretary Kissinger: Yes.

Prime Minister Chou: He had very great influence among the young people in Latin America. And in the American countries on the whole there are two patriots. You can imagine what they are.

Secretary Kissinger: Guevara?

Prime Minister Chou: Another one.

Secretary Kissinger: I don't know, but they are different. Guevara was an adventurist. Chairman Mao is a student of the Revolution.

(There is further discussion of Che Guevara.)

Prime Minister Chou: We went to the Soviet Union to celebrate October Revolution in 1964 because, at that time, we still placed some hope in Brezhnev, and he also shared our view. Che Guevara also told me he was also opposed to that view of calling a conference to support the Soviet Union against China. He said when I got back he would anyway oppose it. And after he got back, he came again with the other five delegations to China. He expressed opposition to that conference but he actually took part in that conference. So when he came and met with me—just by himself—he only spoke one thing to me: I don't like to stay on in Cuba. And after he got back, he went to the United Nations to make a statement. Perhaps you have heard that statement. As a result, you know where he went. He went to the eastern part of Bolivia and there was guerrilla warfare going on there. He went there together with other armed Latin Americans.

Secretary Kissinger: It was not easy for them to meld into the population there.

Prime Minister Chou: It was very difficult for them. And then Che Guevara went there and he intended to carry out guerrilla warfare. The result was that after he got there, he gave me a letter by the Ambassador in Cuba, and he asked us to help him in building the largest kind of broadcasting station which should be able to broadcast to the whole world. I said to myself, was that man mad to think of having large broadcasting station to go along with such a small guerrilla force? Because he signed his letter only with the notation Che. It turned out the letter was really written by him.

(Prime Minister Chou then described Che's activities in Latin America and the Congo, and Chairman Mao's connotations on these activities.)

Secretary Kissinger: He was silly. He had no objective or political hope in either place, either in the Congo or in Bolivia. You cannot arrive merely posing as a specialist in guerrilla warfare.

Prime Minister Chou: And besides it was really absurd to think the peasants in Bolivia were all spies. He suspected this person and that person. How could he expect to live on? So there are some sections of people in Chile that are doing things his way. And in 1971, the year before last, his influence was also found in Sri Lanka, where there were Guevarists and Trotskyites.

Secretary Kissinger: This I didn't know.

Prime Minister Chou: It was reknowned. And in Chile you can find both. And the Soviet Union was not only making use of Che Guevara, they were also making use of Trotskyites.

Secretary Kissinger: It is an amazing turn of history.

Prime Minister Chou: It is a kind of irony.

Secretary Kissinger: Yes.

Prime Minister Chou: But we think it was indeed true that in Chile the government did engage in massacres in the capital, Santiago. Hundreds of bodies were thrown out of the stadium.

Secretary Kissinger: We don't believe it was this many, but what I will do . . . Mr. Prime Minister, I will look into it, as in Iraq, and I will send you our own honest assessment of the situation when I return. I know there were executions. I think there were less than 100s. I think they have now stopped. I will check and let you know. We will use our influence in that direction.

Prime Minister Chou: But I should think that massacres will give rise to revolution on the part of the people. It is also inevitable that it will be so but how long it will last, we don't know. There is also reason why the public opinion in the world has shown sympathy for the Latin American countries. It has also enabled the Soviet Union to gain publicity about it. Their Foreign Minister was saying at the United Nations that a trade union official in Chile was about to be hanged, and he wanted the Vice Foreign Minister to say something about it, and he refused. I think that was instigated.

Secretary Kissinger: That was a case where the Soviet Union appealed to us. We looked into it and there was nothing to it.

Prime Minister Chou: Later that man was not killed.

Secretary Kissinger: Yes.

Prime Minister Chou: And as for their economic performance, we often told them to prepare for nationalization, and they didn't. So as a result of that their production was going down and they made too many promises to the people which could not be honored. That was the way some of the people . . .

Secretary Kissinger: There was no organization. There was no discipline. This, plus total incompetence, led to the collapse of the Allende government. There were great divisions among the factions. These were the basic reasons for the downfall. The Prime Minister correctly described many of the elements. They did everything in fits of enthusiasm without preparation.

Prime Minister Chou: But there is also a good point in that event in Chile. For the past nearly 200 years there, there was the American tradition of not having any military coup in their country. So it would be good.

Secretary Kissinger: It was good that there was a military coup?

Prime Minister Chou: It was good because it could show a bad thing could be turned into good account. That is our way of seeing this thing. We told them about this, but they didn't believe us. That kind of phenomenon was caused by themselves. We give only limited support to Latin American countries' revolutions. We are still learning.

Secretary Kissinger: I hope you don't learn too fast.

Prime Minister Chou: You don't have to be afraid of that. It takes time to have the people rise up.

Secretary Kissinger: I am in favor of very careful long studies by our Chinese friends.

Prime Minister Chou: I only wrote one letter to President Allende, asking him not to do too many things in hurry. It only concerned economic problems that they should make preparation beforehand. They shouldn't do everything at one go; they should take steps. They should not promise too many things to people; otherwise, they would not be able to honor these things. Because we believe the life of the people can only be improved on the basis of production. Whenever one speaks of Socialism, also think of welfare. And my letter to President Allende was carried in the newspaper, but it was useless because the word of a foreigner meant nothing.

Secretary Kissinger: He also was not master in his own house. He was not a free agent. He could not do what he wanted.

Prime Minister Chou: Latin America is a complicated area and Latin America is quite different from Asia. So there is the expansionist aspect to the Soviet policy which Chairman Mao mentioned yesterday. There was nothing very terrible about it. On the other hand, there is nothing really to be afraid of, either their deceptive tricks or their expansionism, because they will be exposed. It is possible for a time they might succeed in creating some trouble, because in nearly everything they have tried to create some trouble.

We will expose them in the United Nations. Miss Thomas, the correspondent, asked if I would go to the UN. Vice Minister Chiao will probably represent us. I myself have no interest in going there because I am advanced in age and quite useless now.

Secretary Kissinger: It is not obvious to others.

Prime Minister Chou: There is a Chinese saying which goes "Know yourself." And I should be able to know myself. And since after tonight's banquet we will still have another discussion, so I will leave the Soviet discussion until then.

Secretary Kissinger: Could I say one thing before we discuss the treaty on prevention of nuclear war, so we understand each other. I understand the necessity of your formal position, Mr. Prime Minister, and we do not object to occasional comments such as were made by the Vice Minister. As long as you and we understand to what use we will put this treaty.

First, it was our judgment that an endless debate in which we refused to discuss the prevention of nuclear war would cost us more than it was worth. But to us the principal utility of the treaty is that it makes it impossible for the Soviet Union to launch a conventional attack against others without violating the treaty to prevent nuclear war. We have integrally linked the prevention of a conventional attack and of a nuclear attack which had never been done before. And with this link it makes it impossible for the Soviet Union to engage in a military operation against any country if they have not had a prior consultation with us without violating Article 4.

Now many countries have objected to the consultation clause but let us be realistic. If we want to encourage the Soviet Union to attack anyone, we don't need Article 4 of the treaty to do it. They will be very eager to do it. If we use this treaty, it will be to prevent Soviet aggression, not to encourage it. And it gives us an opportunity to have a legal basis for resistance in other areas where we have no other legal basis.

And as the President has pointed out to you, Mr. Prime Minister, we are undertaking never to use Article 4 against China without prior consultation with China.

I am not asking you to change your public position. I just want to make certain we understand the real position. We intend to use this in support of the objectives that Chairman Mao and I discussed yesterday.

Prime Minister Chou: But there is still one thing. Despite this treaty, do you think it is possible for you to prevent local aggression? That is, to stop a kind of local war.

Secretary Kissinger: Quite frankly, no. It depends on the local situation. But it will make it easier for us to resist in those areas where we do not have a formal treaty.

Prime Minister Chou: That is true.

Secretary Kissinger: For example, Mr. Prime Minister, during this alert we invoked this treaty. We said that if they sent troops to Egypt, that would be in violation of Article II of the Agreement on Prevention of Nuclear War. We showed our reply to leading Senators, and nobody objected to it.

Prime Minister Chou: And this, of course, proves the effectiveness of the relationship between the Soviet Union and your country on this point. And it also provides you with an opportunity to speak to the Congress to increase your defense budget, not decrease it, during the period of the crisis. But you could do the same without the Treaty. That was during the period of President Kennedy. At that time, of course, President Kennedy was not as courageous as President Nixon and perhaps he couldn't sleep well.

Secretary Kissinger: Kennedy's nerves were not always good.

Prime Minister Chou: And it was exactly at that time that Khrushchev was about to collapse. And Nehru was getting very cocky. He wanted to put us on the spot, and we tried to keep down his cockiness. Khrushchev supported him. So actually in history, both sides failed. Of course, I think without a treaty, things will be just the same as with the treaty. It is in a certain sense a factor.

Secretary Kissinger: We don't need the treaty to increase the defense budget. We take action on our own. In the Caribbean, it is easier to take action alone than in countries further away. And the domestic situation was simpler in 1962 than in 1973.

Prime Minister Chou: Let me say it this way. If Arab space should ever be occupied by the Soviet Union, the whole strategic situation will be greatly changed, and I think your colleagues will understand. The West European countries, in that they fail to support you, they said you did not consult them beforehand. They then put the blame on you.

Secretary Kissinger: We don't consult you beforehand, and you didn't blame us.

Prime Minister Chou: If I do not tell this to Heath, perhaps Chairman Mao will do so, saying that we do not blame you.

Secretary Kissinger: I would appreciate it if you both would do so. It would be a very good experience for him.

Prime Minister Chou: He has done many good things, so you have to praise him first before you blame him.

Secretary Kissinger: Heath is the best of the European leaders, but he does not understand the importance of NATO as well as you, Mr. Prime Minister.

Prime Minister Chou: [Laughter] There is a Chinese saying. If you stand in the midst of the mountains, you wouldn't be able to see the whole picture; if you look at the mountain from a distance away, you will be able to see it more clearly.

Secretary Kissinger: His talks here will be very helpful.

Prime Minister Chou: And I think it is necessary to talk to all those leaders who come from European countries. But you should not imagine that local wars will not arise.

Secretary Kissinger: I think it is very possible that they will occur. I have no illusions. I do not believe documents stop wars, although I may sometimes say so.

Prime Minister Chou: You can say this in a crisis, but you don't say entirely to Congress in this way. But we are in different circumstances. We tend to speak in a more straightforward way than you do.

Secretary Kissinger: I think it is important that we understand each other. But I think it is quite helpful to have different points of view expressed. We should also ask our colleagues to understand that if we always agreed with each other publicly, it would make both of us too vulnerable.

Prime Minister Chou: That is true.

Now, about bilateral issues. Two points. One is about a fact that you mentioned earlier. Should we use wording of the Shanghai Communiqué to move the issue a little bit forward; and, of course, we have worked hard on one sentence in the text, and you will examine it to see if it is useful or not.

Another point is that your press people expressed a desire for their representatives to be stationed here. There will be no difficulty on our part because there are so many correspondents here. And there will be no doubt that we would welcome the U.S. ones because we have correspondents from many major countries.

Secretary Kissinger: On a permanent basis?

Prime Minister Chou: Yes.

Secretary Kissinger: Shall we put that in the Communiqué? I was hoping to make an arrangement where you would take some newsmen and not give them an exit visa. [Laughter all around]

Prime Minister Chou: No, not in the Communiqué. But if we do it that way, they would go to Japan. But the difficulty lies in the fact that if we have our correspondents going to Washington, they will have to meet with situations where they meet with Chiang Kai-shek correspondents, at clubs and because there are so many press conferences. It took us a great deal of effort to keep Chiang Kai-shek correspondents away from United Nations and our Ambassadors presented many protests to the UN representatives. Now this issue has been settled in quite a forceful manner.

In the past three years, the number of correspondents coming to Peking is extremely big; not stationed here, that is, on a temporary basis. And the number of correspondents from Japan is the biggest. So I think we will have to work out a way to settle this issue. Our part is easy, but how to settle the Washington issue is up to you. Correspondents coming on a temporary basis would be no problem. This question journalists discuss because it concerns public opinion.

What do you think about this question?

Secretary Kissinger: I don't have a good idea of how to exclude the Taiwan correspondents from press conferences and press groups since they are out of our control. We would, of course, be prepared to have your correspondents in Washington or any other place you want. That doesn't solve your problem.

Prime Minister Chou: But the Japanese, they do not recognize the legal status of Taiwan correspondents there in Japan. Sometimes the Taiwan correspondents were present, but on formal occasions they were excluded.

Secretary Kissinger: I have given a great deal of thought to our conversation and to the comments the Chairman made on Taiwan, and as with all the things in my experience the Chairman says there were many layers of meaning.

Prime Minister Chou: That is true.

Secretary Kissinger: At least that was my impression. It was not a simple statement. And, therefore, I thought I should study his remarks for a brief time after I return and submit to you possible ideas. It would take account of your position but also some of the things he said in terms of your patience, etc. Because my first impression was that the Chairman's remarks opened many possibilities which we would like to explore with you. Within a month we would make some tentative suggestions as to how this might develop. And maybe this evening we could exchange some preliminary thoughts on it.

Prime Minister Chou: Good.

Secretary Kissinger: And it is in this context the press question can be handled more easily.

Prime Minister Chou: The second question is about trade. About question of the assets, it was through a kindness on your part the idea that this question should be settled from a political viewpoint, and that is your President's opinion. You gave us that document in March after your visit here in February.

And the second document which was given to us through the Paris channel was somewhat different from the first one, a slight difference.

Secretary Kissinger: Too many lawyers got into it. [Laughter]

Prime Minister Chou: And you said yesterday that out of the three questions, it is not necessary to discuss two of them. There is only one left to be discussed.

Secretary Kissinger: This is my impression. I mean, the other two I thought could be solved. I am not underestimating Mr. Hummel's ability to make things complicated. [Laughter]

Prime Minister Chou: And you said you wouldn't be able to recognize our title; it would not be able to be used in the memorandum.

Mr. Hummel: The use of the term "designated nationals."

Secretary Kissinger: That is a different issue than the one I discussed with the Prime Minister. I raised with you the issue of third countries accounts.

Prime Minister Chou: The other two issues can be solved.

Secretary Kissinger: That's my conviction.

Prime Minister Chou: What I mean is, since it is not necessary to discuss the question you accept the term "nationals of the People's Republic of China."

Mr. Hummel: [Gives explanation] The legal people have very strong views. Maybe we can get them to change their minds.

Secretary Kissinger: I am bringing in a new legal man in the State Department. I frankly have no opinion on this question. It is purely a legal question. We cannot do it in side letters? Outside this framework?

Prime Minister Chou: But the point here is we have our own term of describing and you have your term. And your term was adopted during the period you were hostile to our country, and if we adopt it, it would mean we think you are right in doing so. And you said several times since you have not recognized China. That is why you blocked our assets. This is also a legal question. Why should you not accept our term?

Secretary Kissinger: I have to be honest with you. I had not heard of this issue until two days ago. It seems to be one of those trivial things in a negotiation that gets settled politically.

Prime Minister Chou: With something that gets your concern.

Secretary Kissinger: I am personally not well enough acquainted to make a decision here. When I return, I will talk to our lawyers.

Prime Minister Chou: Try not to get too many technicians involved.

Secretary Kissinger: And I will talk to Mr. Hummel, and I will see if I can come up with some solution that meets your terms.

Prime Minister Chou: I agree. And the second point is what are we going to do with those bond indebtedness issued in the days when we still have not established diplomatic relations. Even if we had established diplomatic relations with you . . . How do you intend to settle the question of the bond indebtedness?

Secretary Kissinger: The U.S. Government will not legally support any claims connected with those bonds.

[Secretary Kissinger to Mr. Hummel: There is no need for the Chinese side to take a position.]

And we can possibly give you a letter expressing the practice in this matter and our intention.

Prime Minister Chou: You know it is said by your side that on the one hand the U.S. Government cannot support any claims about these bonds, but you say a judiciary man would have the right to ask for these claims.

Mr. Hummel: We have no right to block their claims. There could be attempts through the Bondsmen Protective Association. We hope it will be suitable to the PRC if we do not, as a government, approve or allow these claims, but we cannot prevent our citizens from making claims to the courts for this purpose.

Prime Minister Chou: To make such dealings, whom would they approach: since the bonds were issued by former governments, Chiang Kai-shek or the Ching Government which was non-existent?

Secretary Kissinger: Our judgment is that our courts would not support private claims for the reasons which the Prime Minister gave.

Prime Minister Chou: If they can approach and make representation with those former Chinese governments, to whom would they approach?

Secretary Kissinger: This is an important question. Since we don't recognize the People's Republic, how they can sue the People's Republic is not clear. So they would have to sue Taiwan as the successor government.

Prime Minister Chou: There is also that question. If you gave money to Chiang Kai-shek, that is all right. If you gave loans, are we supposed to return the money? That is the question.

Secretary Kissinger: We are not now giving military aid to Taiwan. We do give Export-Import Bank loans, which are for commercial purposes.

Prime Minister Chou: Well, what are you going to do with the second question? Are you going to consult with your colleagues when you get back?

Secretary Kissinger: Of course, you could agree with Mr. Hummel's point of view. There is a severe morale problem at this end of the table. I think both our negotiators are trying to prove how tough they are.

I don't think the problem will get any easier. If you would like, if we can't settle it here, I will study it immediately when I return. I will make a proposal which in my judgment will be the honest maximum of what we can do. The significance of this agreement is not the amount of money, which is ridiculous. We should prove that we can settle this so we can go on to more substantial things. Therefore, it should be done in a generous spirit so a year from now we won't even remember what it was.

Within two weeks of my return, we will tell you in our best judgment if and to what extent we can modify our position.

Prime Minister Chou: The third point is concerning the sum of money which amounts to $17 million.

Secretary Kissinger: Yes.

Prime Minister Chou: This issue concerns 15 banks. One is Belgium, England, Switzerland, West Germany, Netherlands, Canada. Six.

Starting from 1954 after we have established diplomatic relations with these countries, we issued special orders to return money blocked by the U.S. As early as the 1950s some of them have started to give back money to us. Of course, the main portion of the money was given to us during 1972. The Banque Belge gave back a sum of $10 million. This is the major portion. Was it that things should turn out this way? In the initial years after Liberation, it was our custom and our practice to deposit U.S. dollars in the banks, and in some cases we deposited money in the French banks in China. The bank I referred to now was a case in point. The Charter Bank of Britain also had their branch in Shanghai.

At that time we not only deposited our money in foreign banks in China but also in foreign banks abroad because we used U.S. dollars in our transactions. Besides, it was a practice of those banks in their international relations they have to register money that was deposited in their banks in New York. Then, after the outbreak of the Korean War, after we sent Chinese volunteers, you blocked deposits in your own banks. (Further discussion of these events.) So perhaps you sent a notification to French banks about blocked Chinese deposits only in dollars. If we had deposited the money in francs, there would have been no problem. We acted in a clumsy way.

Secretary Kissinger: This would not have arisen. We think we need enough to justify our position to our Congress.

Prime Minister Chou: I just wanted to give you the origin.

Because at that time we were inexperienced. Later we changed our way of doing things. We started to deposit our money in other terms. (Further discussion.)

Secretary Kissinger: So I think our legal position . . .

Prime Minister Chou: The amount of money involved is very small.

Secretary Kissinger: $17 million.

Prime Minister Chou: Now we have already got much of this back. Starting from the 1950s we got money back. We have made a study of this question. (Further discussion.) I think there are two ways of doing this. We will return the money to you or to these banks. After you get back, study the legal questions of this matter because we don't like these issues to be discussed with your Congress. It will be all right to give your . . .

Secretary Kissinger: Let me understand, Mr. Prime Minister. You are prepared to give us the money either through the banks or directly?

Prime Minister Chou: I am quite reluctant to give money back through the banks. They had the kindness to give it back to us, and it would not be right to ask them to give it to you.

Secretary Kissinger: You would give it to us. We have to find some way of accomplishing it. If the sum is available to pay off the private claims, and you avoid having to pay back through private banks, then it will not become an issue in the Congress. The terms of the settlement will have to be taken to Congress, but we do not have to discuss separately the sum of $17 million. The value of the $17 million is that it brings the total up to 40%. That is acceptable to Congress, 20% is not. We do not have to discuss how the 40% is arrived at.

Prime Minister Chou: The MFN issue is like this. If you must take up this matter do not discuss it with the Congress at the same time you discuss MFN with the Soviet Union. We are not in a hurry. We are not willing to have the two issues discussed together.

Secretary Kissinger: We will deal with it separately. We will not deal with it along with MFN status for the Soviet Union. What we are asking for is the right to ask for MFN for everybody, not individual countries. And this will not help the Soviet Union to gain most favored nation status. The utility of this agreement is that it makes it easier. It helps the general climate. We discuss MFN with the PRC separately and in a different context than the Soviet Union.

We would present this to the Congress on its own merits without reference to MFN. And then we can discuss later the timing of MFN status.

Prime Minister Chou: Anyway, we don't like to have this question together with the Soviet Union. We would rather have this issue settled not in a hurry.

Secretary Kissinger: We will not discuss MFN for you with our Congress, Mr. Prime Minister, until you personally tell us you want us to do it.

Prime Minister Chou: You have to have a document with the Congress first.

Secretary Kissinger: There are two ways. If we follow present procedure, we have to introduce a bill for each country. If we follow the procedure Congress is now discussing, the Administration will get general authorization to grant MFN to any country it decides is eligible under that bill. We have made no particular claim for the PRC. The only reason the Soviet Union has come up is that there have been so many amendments added. Once that authority is granted, then it is up to us to grant MFN. If it is not granted, then it is up to us to introduce separate bills for each country. That possibility still exists.

Prime Minister Chou: You know when you mentioned postponement of this question of the bill, was it the Soviet bill or . . .

Secretary Kissinger: The bill in general.

Prime Minister Chou: And the general bill would be adopted first?

Secretary Kissinger: It is possible that the bill will never be adopted. In that case, we still have the right to request MFN for individual countries. It is possible that the bill will be adopted with certain restrictions. It would then apply to you even though they are directed against the Soviet Union. For example, about emigration controls. We, therefore, cannot—in any event, we have to make no argument about the People's Republic in gaining progress on the general bill.

Prime Minister Chou: If the general bill is adopted, it is not necessary to adopt a separate bill about our MFN?

Secretary Kissinger: That is correct.

Prime Minister Chou: Then if the general bill is not adopted, then a separate bill would have to be adopted?

Secretary Kissinger: Yes, that is correct.

Prime Minister Chou: And let's come back to the question of money. We think it will be suitable only if we give back the money to you, but it will be difficult for our position to give back the money through the banks because the banks have already given it back to us. If we do it that way, it would mean we recognize the blocking of the funds, and we don't want to settle the question in this way. We can discuss it later.

Secretary Kissinger: I am also certain that you can return the money directly to us. I think it would be absurd to have you return it through the banks so they might sue you or each other.

Prime Minister Chou: Yes. Because we would like to settle this issue from the standpoint of political issues.

Secretary Kissinger: I understand, Mr. Prime Minister, and that we should certainly be able to accommodate. Let us go back and consult with our legal people. There is no sense prolonging this. We will make one proposal and that will be the maximum we can make. I will do that within two weeks.

Prime Minister Chou: And on our side we are not in a hurry. We have a very great inferior balance in our trade. We would like to increase our exports to your country.

Secretary Kissinger: The major use of this agreement is to show major progress in our relationship. There is no economic need for it.

Prime Minister Chou: Yes, many politics will be involved.

Secretary Kissinger: I have two or three minor items, but we can do it later.

Prime Minister Chou: Please.

Secretary Kissinger: You asked about the F–5s.[5] You have extremely good information about the radius but not with a full bomb load. It's radius is only about 100 nautical miles.

Prime Minister Chou: What do you mean by full bomb load?

Secretary Kissinger: If it carries all the bombs. For ground support it is about a third of the regular bomb load. It can go 600 miles, but then it can carry only two bombs. It cannot carry both fuel tanks and a full bomb load. So it is not basically an offensive weapon.

Prime Minister Chou: What about the Bosporus Bridge? It was not built by the United States.[6]

Secretary Kissinger: I have one humanitarian problem which does not directly concern the PRC. There are a number of American journalists who have disappeared in Cambodia.

---

[5] See Document 57.

[6] See footnote 6, Document 57.

Prime Minister Chou: How many?

Secretary Kissinger: I have the total number here. I have all the details. Some are Japanese journalists. Eighteen journalists. I have taken the liberty of bringing material. All the information we have was given to me by a committee of American journalists who asked me if there were any way on a purely humanitarian basis if this could be given to Prince Sihanouk, or on any other basis, we would be very grateful. It is not a formal governmental request. It is a personal request.

Similarly, we are constantly being harassed about MIAs in China. We believe you, that you have given us a full account—but the families ask us if we have asked you the question. If you could at some point give us a statement, we could say that we have asked you. This does not in any way suggest that we have any question about your response. In fact, if we could say at a press conference that we have asked you and you have assured us that there are no missing in action, that would be sufficient.

Prime Minister Chou: We have been carrying on an investigation concerning MIAs, and up to now we haven't found any in that area referred to—neither bodies left or information. There are several areas concerned—three areas. One is along the coast, another is quite near the land and still another is far at sea. You refer to the area which you would like us to search. So far we have found no bodies or information. The investigation is still going on. If we should be able to get more information, we will tell you. That is for when you hold a press conference.

Secretary Kissinger: May we say that you have made searches in the areas that we gave you, that you have found no bodies or information, but that the investigation is continuing and if any new information turns up, you will let us know?

Prime Minister Chou: The areas that you have defined are not very big. We have asked them to enlarge the areas for investigation.

Secretary Kissinger: We appreciate this very much, and we will answer in the press conference exactly as you have indicated.

May I suggest that the best way to handle the communiqué is after dinner? Or should they meet while we meet?

Prime Minister Chou: Let's do it this way. After dinnertime, we will ask some persons from each side to discuss this matter while we discuss other matters, and after they discuss we can.

Secretary Kissinger: Could we have an English text? [Laughter all around.]

Oh, and then there are the Marines.

Prime Minister Chou: How about discussing the question of the Marines after dinner?

Secretary Kissinger: That is a good idea.

60.   Memorandum of Conversation[1]

Beijing, November 13–14, 1973, 10 p.m.–12:30 a.m.

PARTICIPANTS

    Chou En-lai, Premier of the State Council
    T'ang Wen-sheng (Interpreter)
    Mrs. Yang Yu-yung (Interpreter)
    Stenographer

    Secretary of State Henry A. Kissinger
    Ambassador David Bruce
    Commander Jonathan T. Howe, NSC Staff
    Mrs. Wilma G. Hall, Notetaker

SUBJECT

    Marines, Southeast Asia

Prime Minister Chou: There are a few other matters we should discuss. First, on the matter of the Marines.[2] Do you have them everywhere in the world?

Secretary Kissinger: In every Embassy in every part of the world. I don't know why it is—it is tradition. The concern our people have is if we remove them in one place, it will set up competition in another place. Then we have to find civilian guards and that's more complex.

Prime Minister Chou: And in countries that used to be Socialist, do they wear uniforms?

Secretary Kissinger: They wear military uniforms, yes, although we don't insist on their wearing uniforms.

Prime Minister Chou: On the other hand, do they send their military personnel with arms to your country?

Secretary Kissinger: No. What you have said is absolutely logical. What we have said is traditional. Logically you are absolutely right and if you insist, we would withdraw them without any hard feelings.

Prime Minister Chou: For instance, during Ambassador Bruce's experience in Britain, Germany and France, did they not ask for any reciprocity?

---

[1] Source: National Archives, Nixon Presidential Materials, NSC Files, Kissinger Office Files, Box 96, Country Files, Far East, China Exchanges, November 1, 1973–March 31, 1974. Top Secret; Sensitive; Exclusively Eyes Only. The meeting took place at the Great Hall of the People. All brackets are in the original.

[2] The Chinese Government expressed displeasure with the use of U.S. Marines to guard the U.S. Liaison Office in Beijing. Telegram 1297 from Beijing, November 1, suggested that their uniformed appearance offended Chinese observers. (Ibid., NSC Files, Box 527, Country Files, Far East, People's Republic of China, Vol. 8, July 10–Dec 31, 1973)

Ambassador Bruce: In that sense, no.

Secretary Kissinger: But not as guards.

Ambassador Bruce: But our Marines do not wear uniforms. They did. [Ambassador Bruce gives explanation] I think the real difficulty, as I understand it, is that our 6 Marines make a recognizable unit. They are the elite of our military in their own opinion. They are the oldest service with a history that extends back some 198 years. With 400 people at the Soviet Embassy, some must be guards. But I don't know who the guards are.

The other embassies have their guards too. They are probably KGB. They are not Soviet Marines or at least they are not recognizable to us as such.

Prime Minister Chou: The Soviet Embassy is probably less concerned with security than intelligence or KGB activities.

Ambassador Bruce: I think they probably are KGB guards. You are right.

Prime Minister Chou: And they don't admit that they are such if you bring up the subject.

Secretary Kissinger: That's the problem.

Prime Minister Chou: This is the first time I knew of the military being established in diplomatic missions throughout the world. 198 years being established throughout the world. Then when you establish diplomatic relations with a new country, you must notify them of this.

Secretary Kissinger: Yes. Our position has always been that the Embassy is extraterritorial and that we can put anyone in there we want as guards.

Prime Minister Chou: Does that mean that they do not openly make public that they are Marines in other countries?

Secretary Kissinger: In every other country I am familiar with, they wear their uniforms. Because of the concern you have expressed, they are not worn in China. But the guards in embassies all over the world I am familiar with have always been Marines.

Prime Minister Chou: They might not necessarily all be in military uniforms.

Secretary Kissinger: They wore their uniforms here on duty until July 4th.

Prime Minister Chou: They are internal? They don't stand outside the gate?

Ambassador Bruce: We have a PLA at the gate. They wear their uniform only inside the building.

Prime Minister Chou: So that is something new to me.

Ambassador Bruce: One of their difficulties is they live in an apartment and they put up a poster saying anyone that wants to join the Marine Corps will have a perfectly wonderful life. [Laughter all around] They got no recruits. [Laughter all around]

Prime Minister Chou: Then do all other countries agree to your tradition?

Secretary Kissinger: I know of no exception. Uganda threw out our Marines two days before everyone left.

Prime Minister Chou: I read about that in the papers.

Secretary Kissinger: But I don't believe there is any other exception. It is an easily solved issue anyway.

Prime Minister Chou: Yes, it can be easily solved. First of all, they would not contact others, that is, persons other than those of the Liaison Office, in the name of the Marines.

Ambassador Bruce: I have got to confess that these Marines are a gay lot of people. There are six of them in one room. [Ambassador Bruce tells about their dances and the fact that their female neighbors appreciated it.] [Laughter all around]

[Secretary Kissinger aside to Cmdr. Howe: Can't you square this away with Zumwalt? We are not running a rest camp. They have just got to be brought under control.]

Prime Minister Chou: There is some good from the study of historical matters and traditions but on the other hand, the customs of a sovereign country must be respected. We must try to find some and settle between the two. For instance, we are not accustomed to such matters. In other countries we have internal security but not the PLA.

Secretary Kissinger: I would hate to think what would happen in Washington if members of the People's Liberation Army showed up to protect their office. So I have to say with regard to logic, you are absolutely right.

Ambassador Bruce: [Tells about the fact that when the Marines couldn't wear their uniforms, they had to buy civilian clothes and DOD wouldn't pay for civilian clothes so they had a morale problem.]

Secretary Kissinger: We shouldn't spend our time on this. If you agree to let them stay and you tell us what you want us to do, we will see what is possible. If those six can't live without a dance floor, then we will get six who can. So if you would tell us exactly what you want us to do, then we can handle them. We will tell them what they can do.

Prime Minister Chou: The first thing we believe is that it would be best if they do not wear military uniforms. We do not care if they switch out of civilian clothes in their bedroom. But when they come out, we do not wish to see them in uniforms. As for their weapons, they will need them only for internal security purposes. I hope they will not carry them on the streets or outside the Liaison Office. We do not care if they are not Marines. We would show no preference as to whatever persons you would like to pick. Indeed, we do think it would be quite sensational if the People's Liberation Army would appear in Washington. [Laughter all around]

Secretary Kissinger: It might even take some attention away from Watergate.

Prime Minister Chou: It might also be interesting to put some of our Red Guards in Washington. Perhaps your long-haired youth would pay visits to them. We think that at the early stage of having established Liaison Offices (our goal) is to work in a harmonious way and not create trouble for each other.

Southeast Asia

Secretary Kissinger: I have one point I just wanted to mention. I think a major offensive in Vietnam would be against everyone's interest, especially if it were done with weapons provided massively from outside. We are certainly using our influence with our friends to maintain restraint.

Prime Minister Chou: With regard to this issue, recently we have received two documents from Vietnam and we have not yet released them. One reason is your presence in Peking. They have made clear in those documents that the provocations are not from them but from Thieu. They have no intention of launching a major offensive now. I have discussed this matter with Le Duan, Pham Van Dong, General Giap and also . . .[3]

Secretary Kissinger: He is my new colleague, although I know Le Duc Tho better.

Prime Minister Chou: And they have all assured me they have no desire to launch a major offensive now. They are sending certain materials southward but that is only for building a road. Some of our people have been south of the 17th parallel in Quang Tri Province and they have seen there that it has been leveled by bombing. They have had to begin from scratch. We accredited our Ambassador to them and he stayed there to present his credentials. They lived in tents. And they are mainly concentrating on building up their production. We not long ago sent a ship with feed grains. They (GVN) attacked it saying that it was filled with military equipment. Actually it was food grains.

Secretary Kissinger: We have no objection to civilian equipment but when it is transported in tanks, we get worried. We are not talking about China.

---

[3] The name did not sound like Nguyen Duy Trinh but it probably was. [Footnote in the original.]

Prime Minister Chou: We heard that Thieu mentioned 500 tanks and 500 guns from major sides. I asked our friends about this and they said it could not possibly be true. From here I can hear our Cambodian friends complain that they are not receiving enough military support from North Vietnam.

Secretary Kissinger: That has other reasons.

Prime Minister Chou: But according to our account, it is extremely meager. You can hear Sihanouk on this issue.

T'ang Wen-sheng: You left the material you wanted to give the Premier about correspondents in Cambodia on the conference table in the Guest House.[4]

Secretary Kissinger: I intended that.

T'ang Wen-sheng: Mr. Lord said that and the Premier picked it up.

Prime Minister Chou: From what we know, they have no such intentions.

Secretary Kissinger: We are prepared to help the North in rehabilitation. However much military equipment there is in the North, it is a fair amount. If the North does not get a major amount of military equipment from outside, then it can't start a major attack.

Prime Minister Chou: That is true. But to our knowledge small frictions have never ceased.

Secretary Kissinger: That is true and that is inevitable.

Prime Minister Chou: Thieu has concentrated all the people in villages. So the population has become very concentrated in small areas without enough land. There is a lack of food. I think it would be impossible for you to provide them the amount of food grains. The population there has always worked for peace so they could return and till the land. And that is where the contradiction arises. And that is where the friction often comes from because the National Liberation Forces want to make it possible for the people to go back to their homelands and till their lands. Thieu is fearful of this and it often results in minor conflicts.

Secretary Kissinger: Minor conflicts are inevitable and we would not involve ourselves in them. If it was a problem like 1972, it would present a problem for us and we would engage ourselves.

Prime Minister Chou: There have been several major conflicts. Like in 1968, 1970, and then February 1971, Route 9 in Laos. There were two

---

[4] Material on journalists missing in Cambodia was included in a checklist from Kissinger's trip. (National Archives, Nixon Presidential Materials, NSC Files, Kissinger Office Files, Box 100, Country Files, Far East, Kissinger Trip to Peking—Papers, November 1973)

offensives in 1968. One was Tet and one was that summer. Then in February 1971 there was Route 9 in Laos. And then in 1972, it was on a larger scale south of the 17th parallel and into the four areas.

[Secretary Kissinger to Cmdr. Howe: What's the name of that place that was besieged?]

[Commander Howe: An Loc.]

Secretary Kissinger: The South Vietnamese had the most incompetent General in military history in charge of that. In four months of fighting, there were four divisions against one brigade, yet he could not move 10 miles to relieve them.

Prime Minister Chou: You mean the General in charge of An Loc?

Secretary Kissinger: The General in charge south of An Loc.

Prime Minister Chou: He wasn't able to contact them?

Secretary Kissinger: He never made it, no. But he drew beautiful maps with arrows.

Prime Minister Chou: In my opinion, I do not believe there will be major fighting in Vietnam because their views are different from those they held before the ceasefire.

Secretary Kissinger: That would be a serious matter.

Prime Minister Chou: Because you mentioned an evolution we had discussed.

Secretary Kissinger: Yes, but that requires some time.

Prime Minister Chou: It will take several years.

Secretary Kissinger: Yes.

Prime Minister Chou: And exactly what the outcome will be will depend on themselves and also on the political settlement. We think it would be good if there was a political settlement.

Secretary Kissinger: We agree.

Prime Minister Chou: There does not seem to be any major fighting in Cambodia. We think it would be best for you to let go of that area.

Secretary Kissinger: If there is no major fighting, we will not interfere.

Prime Minister Chou: You have no treaty obligations to Lon Nol as you have with Thieu and the military dictatorship in Bangkok has undergone changes but they won't be of very major portions. It would be relatively better if that area could be one of peace and neutrality.

Secretary Kissinger: I will speak frankly. Our major problem with Cambodia is that the opponents of President Nixon want to use it as an example of the bankruptcy of his whole policy. So if there is a very rapid collapse, it will be reflected in our other policies. That frankly is our only concern.

Prime Minister Chou: Why is it that Senator Mansfield is in favor of letting loose and allowing Sihanouk to return?

Secretary Kissinger: Senator Mansfield is first of all an isolationist in the classical tradition. He is a true isolationist from the Middle West. Secondly, he has a sentimental attachment to Prince Sihanouk which is not related to reality and not reciprocated in any way. Because I think the Prince is a very shrewd calculator.

[Secretary Kissinger to Cmdr. Howe: See if they want to have a leadership meeting about my trip next week. Ask Scowcroft tonight.]

Prime Minister Chou: And because we also know of it. It is futile to do as he has. Because he also knows you will not meet him, he spoke very loudly at the Non-Aligned Nations Conference. He abused not only you but me.

Secretary Kissinger: We are not opposed to Prince Sihanouk's return.

Prime Minister Chou: But they do not wish to do it that way. The only thing I wish to bring to your attention is that the Soviet Union wants to have a hand in that pie.

Secretary Kissinger: Not with our cooperation.

Prime Minister Chou: They might try to do it with the French. Thank you for bringing his mother here.[5] It was a humanitarian effort.

Secretary Kissinger: That was only the right thing to do.

Prime Minister Chou: And when you were very enthusiastically discussing this matter with Lon Nol, your chargé d'affaires discussed it with Lon Nol and the Commission and said that to enable the Queen to come to China, you might be able to provide the plane and medical personnel. But the French doctors who had been treating her for so long were so emotionally disturbed that they were on the verge of tears. Your chargé understood the situation and let the French do it.

Secretary Kissinger: We finally got our chargé under control. It was the first constructive thing he had been able to do in a year. So he is very grateful to you for giving him this opportunity.

Prime Minister Chou: Because the French were thinking, after having taken care of her for one whole year, you were just brushing them aside.

What do you now think of the situation in Bangkok?

---

[5] On October 26, the Department of State informed the Embassy in Saigon that Queen Kossamak Nearireak would be flown from Phnom Penh to Beijing, where her son, Prince Sihanouk, was currently residing. (Telegram 211294; National Archives, RG 59, Central Foreign Policy Files)

Secretary Kissinger: Thailand will move to a more neutralist position slowly and carefully. I don't know whether the Prime Minister is aware that the Indians are very interested in Thailand.

Prime Minister Chou: And the Soviet Union.

Secretary Kissinger: Yes, but they want to offer a friendship treaty, the same as they have with the Soviet Union. The Indians have told us they would do it and the Thais have asked our opinion.

Prime Minister Chou: Are you familiar with the new Prime Minister?

Secretary Kissinger: I frankly have never heard of him. I frankly think he will be a transitional figure.

Prime Minister Chou: The King probably trusts him.

Secretary Kissinger: Yes.

Prime Minister Chou: Their Vice Premier and the son of the Premier went together to Taiwan to try to get help from Chiang Kai-shek.

Secretary Kissinger: I know Thanom very well. He is not anti-Chinese.

Prime Minister Chou: Slightly, but this only meant that he would not engage in trade with China.

Secretary Kissinger: The Thais are afraid of China in general because of their population.

Prime Minister Chou: It is the conservative nature of those Chinese. And when the Australian Prime Minister came, he discussed with me the Southeast Asian countries and their establishing relations with China.[6] We discussed if it would be possible to establish relations with Singapore. I wonder if a communiqué or public declaration that none of those Singapore citizens would maintain dual citizenship might set him at ease.

Secretary Kissinger: Would you like me to discuss this with Lee Kuan Yew? I think he takes me more seriously than he does Whitlam.

Prime Minister Chou: That is, we would be willing to establish relations in a pattern which would set other countries at ease because a large percentage of the Singapore population is Chinese.

Secretary Kissinger: I will talk to him.

Prime Minister Chou: And Singapore being a free port, we think it would be better for them to maintain a neutral problem. The Soviet Union is casting a covetous eye on them.

---

[6] Gough Whitlam visited the People's Republic of China from October 31 to November 4.

Secretary Kissinger: Lee Kuan Yew is primarily worried about the organization of Communist groups.

Prime Minister Chou: To my knowledge there is none there. There are perhaps some leftists but to my knowledge there are no Communist parties in Singapore.

Secretary Kissinger: But he is not against the People's Republic. He is afraid you will engage in subversive activities there.

Prime Minister Chou: We are not going to subvert them. We haven't even subverted Hongkong. Why would we go there. Why give up Hongkong at our door step to go so far. Hongkong has 4 million while Singapore has slightly over one and a half million.

Secretary Kissinger: I will send a letter to Lee Kuan Yew.

Prime Minister Chou: He has not been so bad to us. There is a branch of the bank of China there.

Secretary Kissinger: He is not against you. I know him very well. He is one of the few leaders with whom it is worth talking. Aside from his having power, he has a great understanding of England.

Prime Minister Chou: He is a very eloquent speaker. I believe he was trained by McDonald.

Secretary Kissinger: He was at the London School of Economics.

Prime Minister Chou: Because McDonald had been Governor General of Singapore.

Secretary Kissinger: He always comes to Harvard once every two years.

Prime Minister Chou: You mean the son of Ramsey McDonald?

Secretary Kissinger: Lee Kuan Yew comes to Harvard and shocks my liberal colleagues by calling them fools. They are not used to Socialists calling them that.

[*Note:* At 12:30 a.m. on November 14, the meeting adjourned for about 30 minutes and then resumed with additional participants to discuss the communiqué.][7]

---

[7] Chou and Kissinger met until 2:20 a.m. to finalize the communiqué. (National Archives, Nixon Presidential Materials, NSC Files, Kissinger Office Files, Box 100, Country Files, Far East, Secretary Kissinger's Conversations in Peking, November 1973) The final text of the Joint Communiqué is printed in Department of State *Bulletin,* December 10, 1973, pp. 716–717.

61.   Memorandum of Conversation[1]

Beijing, November 14, 1973, 7:35–8:25 a.m.

PARTICIPANTS

Prime Minister Chou En-lai
T'ang Wen-sheng, Interpreter
Secretary of State, Henry A. Kissinger
Commander Jonathan T. Howe, NSC Staff
Mrs. Bonnie Andrews, Notetaker

SUBJECT

Japan, Congress, Pakistan

Prime Minister Chou: I wish to discuss with you our assessment of Japan. You mentioned two probable alternatives. There is a third alternative because they are under your nuclear umbrella and they have a very clear conception. And when you arrive on Japanese soil you will see that without the American umbrella, you will see what state they would be in. Then they would be under a different nuclear umbrella. I think that is a tendency that both of us should try to deviate. And the more farsighted statesmen of Japan must see the danger.

Of course, we don't think it would be possible for you to tell them all of your own plans with regard to your nuclear umbrella over Japan. You have a defense treaty with them and you can't tell them all the details but we feel you can come very close to them. Because at the present they cannot leave your nuclear umbrella or your energy resources. And to them their needs are not confined to energy but to all resources of their economy. Their main shortcoming is that some of their statesmen tend to be shortsighted, but I believe that in the turmoil of the world persons of great stature will gradually emerge. You have also included them in the economic aspect of the new Atlantic Charter.[2] That will reassure them. They will meet with new difficulties and they have various odd notions.

Secretary Kissinger: They specialize in that.

Prime Minister Chou: You cannot ask too much out of consideration of their foundations. If the foundations are comparatively shallow,

---

[1] Source: National Archives, Nixon Presidential Materials, NSC Files, Kissinger Office Files, Box 100, Country Files, Far East, Secretary Kissinger's Conversations in Peking, November 1973. Top Secret; Sensitive; Exclusively Eyes Only. The meeting was held at the Guest House. All brackets are in the original.

[2] On April 23, Kissinger called for "a new Atlantic Charter," which would include both Western Europe and Japan, to facilitate economic and security cooperation within the Western Alliance. The text of Kissinger's speech appeared in *The New York Times*, April 24, 1973, p. 14.

then you must have imagination and also when you have such hodge-podge public opinion. They are perhaps not second to us. (To you.)

Secretary Kissinger: Their public opinion is even more complex than ours and their government has even less freedom of action. In foreign affairs our government has greater possibility for action.

Prime Minister Chou: Although Congressional action has limited your President to war only 60 days, it would be temporary.

Secretary Kissinger: Yes. And in practice, it will not make much difference, because what will they do if we go into a war?

Prime Minister Chou: But you would have to report that to them.

Secretary Kissinger: Yes, but you can't hide a war.

Prime Minister Chou: Some of your measures do not seem too scientific.

Secretary Kissinger: Once we are in a war, they cannot stop us.

They could have always stopped us in Vietnam by withholding appropriations. But while they made unbelievable amounts of noise, they voted the appropriations each year.

Prime Minister Chou: That is the result of your constitutional system because various members wanted to make their views known to their constituents.

Secretary Kissinger: You saw Senator Magnuson.[3]

Prime Minister Chou: And this time the second visit of Senator Mansfield has been postponed. When there is a good time you might reconsider and tell us the result. We will also determine when the appropriate time would be. We don't think it would be good to have it put off indefinitely.

Secretary Kissinger: I agree. We don't have any objections to Mansfield.

Prime Minister Chou: And Senator Jackson.

Secretary Kissinger: Jackson will be quite an experience. I meant, it would be helpful.

Prime Minister Chou: He is a Republican?

Secretary Kissinger: No, he is a Democrat. If I may make a suggestion as a friend about Senator Jackson. He is a friend of mine. You will find that he agrees with you completely about the Soviet Union but he has enemies in America who are more pro-Soviet but who are not against you. So, he should be handled in a way that when he comes back from here he doesn't take such an extreme position that he alienates men like Senator Fulbright whom we need and who is his enemy.

---

[3] See footnote 3, Document 41 and footnote 7, Document 43.

Prime Minister Chou: [Laughs questioningly] Oh?

Secretary Kissinger: It is a complex situation, but I think he should come.

Prime Minister Chou: Another issue would be that of South Asia which the Chairman mentioned to you the other night. And that is that we will be in great favor of your assisting Pakistan and building a naval port in Pakistan. Of course, that would take time but it would be a significant step. And as you told us, and as Prime Minister Bhutto and other Pakistani friends have mentioned, you are also considering how to assist them in military ways. We cannot help them much because our arms are lightweight. We have small arms but not heavy arms. You have heavy arms. The Soviet Union is always wanting to break through that knot. In South Asia it would be through India/Pakistan. And in the Middle East—it would be Iraq. And we can see that at present their greatest ambitions are there and to link the chain.

Secretary Kissinger: We have a tough time with our Congress on Pakistan—and their attitude is ridiculous. You should talk to Senator Mansfield when he comes.

Prime Minister Chou: They are probably favorable toward India.

Secretary Kissinger: Yes.

Prime Minister Chou: Perhaps it is the national character of the Americans to be taken in by those who seem kind and mild.

Secretary Kissinger: Yes.

Prime Minister Chou: But the world is not so simple.

Secretary Kissinger: On Senator Mansfield. If he comes, I might perhaps offer another thought. And we know it is difficult for him not to see Prince Sihanouk but it could help us if he does not receive too much ammunition from the Chinese side on Cambodia.

Prime Minister Chou: We understand. Perhaps he is partial on certain matters.

Secretary Kissinger: Right, he is singleminded.

Prime Minister Chou: But as a man, he is quite honorable.

Secretary Kissinger: Yes, he is a fine and decent man.

Prime Minister Chou: And when he feels that your President is correct or when you are able to convince him, he is not obstinate. Perhaps you now, as Secretary of State, can play that role. Because you will now meet with Congress.

Secretary Kissinger: Yes and now I am doing that systematically. And as the Prime Minister may have noted, many Congressmen have made favorable comments supporting our foreign policy since I became Secretary of State. And when I return, I will meet with four Congressional Committees and with the leaders.

Prime Minister Chou: We wish you success and also success to the President.

Secretary Kissinger: Thank you and thank you for the reception we have received as always.

Prime Minister Chou: It is what you deserve. And once the course has been set, as in 1971, we will persevere in the course.

Secretary Kissinger: So will we.

Prime Minister Chou: That is why we use the term farsightedness to describe your meeting with the Chairman.

Secretary Kissinger: We maneuver more than you but we will get in the same direction.

Prime Minister Chou: That is dialectic but we understand. Perhaps you need to maneuver. We want to be more straightforward.

Secretary Kissinger: We don't complain. On the release time on the communiqué, would 10:00 Japan time in the evening be convenient?

Prime Minister Chou: It is most convenient.

Secretary Kissinger: We will adjourn then.

Prime Minister Chou: Please convey our regards to your President and his wife.

The meeting adjourned at 8:25 a.m. As the Prime Minister was leaving, the following exchange took place:

Prime Minister Chou: Give my regards to Prime Minister Tanaka and Foreign Minister Ohira.

Secretary Kissinger: Can I?

Prime Minister Chou: Yes, of course. That is why I mentioned it.

Secretary Kissinger: I will do so.

---

62.   Memorandum From the President's Assistant for National Security Affairs (Kissinger) to President Nixon[1]

Washington, November 19, 1973.

SUBJECT

My Visit to China

---

[1] Source: National Archives, Nixon Presidential Materials, NSC Files, Kissinger Office Files, Box 96, Country Files, Far East, China Exchanges, November 1, 1973–March 31, 1974. Top Secret; Sensitive; Exclusively Eyes Only.

Overview

The four-day visit to the People's Republic of China was a positive success on all planes. The two and three-quarter hour session with Chairman Mao (the fact that it was the longest session with a foreign official in recent years is of itself very significant); fourteen hours of private meetings and several more of informal conversation with Prime Minister Chou; additional talks with Vice Minister Chiao Kuan-hua on sightseeing tours; and six hours of counterpart meetings on technical bilateral issues added up to the following:

—*Confirmation and deepening of the close identity between you and the Chinese leaders' strategic perspectives on the international situation.* As I pointed out after my February 1973 trip,[2] we have become tacit allies. We share essentially the same views about the Soviet strategy (though the Chinese are firmly convinced of Soviet hegemonial ambitions while we still hold out the possibility that our combination of firmness and negotiation can steer Moscow on a constructive course); the necessity of a strong American world role and defense capability; and the strategic importance of Europe, Japan, the Middle East, and the Near East–South Asia axis.

—*A positive joint communiqué that expands our existing bilateral relationship and establishes the framework for further forward movement.*[3] The key element in the document—indeed the most significant development of the visit—is the breakthrough proposed by Chou on Taiwan that requires only that the "principle" of one China be respected as we normalize relations. We now have to explore how to give concrete expression to this concept which could provide an opening for maintaining a substantial bilateral tie with Taiwan as and when we establish diplomatic relations with the PRC.

—*Clear statements by Mao and Chou of support for your firm diplomacy and their strong hope that you will surmount domestic difficulties.* They were scathing in their criticism both of the neoisolationists in the United States and those whom they consider are exaggerating and exploiting Watergate to attack you.

—*Recognition by the Chinese of your position that a military flareup in Indochina will have adverse effects on our mutual interests.* Chou strongly suggested that they have throttled way down their assistance to North Vietnam and Cambodia. He stated that there would be no major offensive in South Vietnam in the near term. On Cambodia, the Chinese seemed content to let the parties further exhaust themselves on the battlefield to get into a negotiating mood; he did not pick up my offer to listen to their (or Sihanouk's) ideas on a settlement.

---

[2] See Documents 17 and 18.

[3] See footnote 7, Document 60.

—A continuing warm reception for our party, including truly major coverage of our activities in the Chinese press.

Progress with Some Caveats

These elements constitute substantial forward progress. The driving force on the Chinese side remains their preoccupation with the Soviet Union which infuses their discussion of every major international issue. Their crucial calculation is the steadiness and strength of America as a counterweight.[4] In this regard your strong handling of the Middle East, particularly the alert,—Chou called you more courageous than President Kennedy as a leader—was an ideal prelude to my visit.[5] It served the same purpose that your policy during the 1971 Indian subcontinent [crisis] did in the period between my first trip and your summit conversations.

Your strong policies, the Chinese concerns about encirclement, our developing mutual trust and reliability the past few years, our profound exchanges at the highest levels have all combined to move us forward at a steady pace. In addition, the two major obstacles to improvement in relations have been eased: last January's Vietnam settlement all but removed Indochina as an impediment, though Cambodia is a lingering problem; and the Chinese continue to show patience on Taiwan and may have supplied us with a breakthrough on this trip with their one China principle formula in the communiqué.

We cannot by any means be complacent about our relationship, however. The following caveats are in order:

—*The Sino-Soviet Split.* We have been in probably the ideal situation with regard to the two communist giants: they both want and need to deal with us because they cannot deal with one another. We are walking a delicate tightrope of public détente with Moscow and tacit alliance with Peking. This will continue to require the most careful handling. The meticulous care and feeding of the Chinese on our Soviet policy has paid off, but Peking sees our détente pursuit as at least objectively threatening its security, whatever our motives. And even if we don't make mistakes, events beyond our control could turn one or the other against us or propel them toward each other.

---

[4] Nixon underlined this sentence and in the margin next to it wrote, "K—the key."

[5] On a memorandum summarizing two of Kissinger's meetings with Zhou Enlai, Nixon underlined and put an exclamation mark next to the following statement about Zhou's reaction to the U.S. nuclear alert during the 1973 Mideast crisis: "He again praised your alert, saying that you were more courageous than Kennedy." (Memorandum from Scowcroft to Nixon, November 13; National Archives, Nixon Presidential Materials, NSC Files, Kissinger Office Files, Box 96, Country Files, Far East, China Exchanges, November 1, 1973–March 31, 1974) The memorandum of conversation containing Zhou's original statement is printed as Document 59.

—*The U.S. Domestic Scene.* Our domestic situation clearly troubles the Chinese. For the short term they are worried about the attacks on you and hope you will overcome them. More fundamentally, they are wary of our domestic and Congressional mood which they see potentially leading to American disengagement from the world. Once they become convinced that we cannot or will not act as a major force on a global scale, we will lose our principal value to them. In this case, Taiwan and other bilateral pursuits notwithstanding, they would be likely to explore other alternatives.

—*The Chinese Leadership Succession.* Mao and Chou both looked well and demonstrated their usual mental prowess (Mao more than ever). But they are old, and there appears in any event to be some domestic challenge to them, though probably mostly on domestic issues.[6] We just don't know much about their politics—nor does any other outside country. We have no idea who will succeed the present leadership or what their foreign policy tendencies will be. The one element we can be certain of is that they will not be as far-sighted or as sophisticated as Mao and Chou, who may well be the most impressive twosome in history. A worrisome aspect is the fact that on all our trips we have dealt with a restricted circle of Chou and his lieutenants. We have had virtually no contact with other elements of the political leadership, such as the Shanghai radicals. Since a reasonable case can be made for accommodation with Moscow or some other option than their present course, we have no assurance that the PRC will continue its policy toward us when Mao and Chou depart. This puts a premium on solidifying our relationship while the current leadership is directing their policy.

The Joint Communiqué

As I have already reported, the communiqué we issued is a positive document and contains a possible breakthrough on the fundamental question of Taiwan.

The Shanghai Communiqué established a framework and principles for our relationship. Since your trip we have given these concrete expressions. This communiqué further accelerates momentum in these areas:

—It expands the principle of opposing *hegemony* from the Asia-Pacific region to "any other part of the world." This reflects our parallel strategic interests and sends some clear, though sufficiently muted signals to Moscow.

---

[6] Solomon followed domestic politics in the People's Republic of China at the NSC. He sent an August 31 memorandum to Kissinger on the 10th Party Congress, which highlighted domestic political challenges to Zhou Enlai. (National Archives, Nixon Presidential Materials, NSC Files, Box 527, Country Files, Far East, People's Republic of China, Vol. 8, July 10–Dec 31, 1973)

—We have extended the process of *consultation* "to maintain frequent contact at authoritative levels" and "to engage in concrete consultations". In addition to suggesting closer collaboration in general, it balances off somewhat our consultation procedures with the Russians under the Agreement to Prevent Nuclear War.

—We have agreed to expand "the scope of the functions of the *Liaison Offices*". This will result in larger missions performing wider tasks. They are becoming embassies in all but name.

—We will work for the further development of *trade*. This has already reached the level of some $900 million in exports to the PRC (and less than $100 million Chinese exports to us). We made major progress on the principal technical issues which should expand trade further.

—We have arranged "a number of new *exchanges* for the coming year." This program is important both substantively in promoting mutual knowledge and awareness, and symbolically in highlighting the progress of our relations.

In addition, Chou tabled language that provides the framework for the central bilateral problem in the coming period, *Taiwan*: ". . . normalization of relations between China and the United States can be realized only on the basis of confirming the principle of one China." This suggests that we might be able to continue a substantial relationship with Taiwan when we establish diplomatic relations with Peking so long as we maintain the "principle" of one China.[7] They may be willing to settle for considerable autonomy for Taiwan and continuing U.S. ties so long as the nominal juridical framework reflects the one China approach. Our task now is to come up with some formulas that can begin to move toward this goal. They are clearly ready to hear from us; I said that we would get back to them within a few weeks.

Thus once again the Chinese have demonstrated their patience and shrewdness with respect to this delicate issue. Just as the Shanghai Communiqué formula allowed us to launch our bilateral relationship so may this one allow us to proceed eventually to diplomatic relations while continuing close ties (as yet undefined) with Taiwan.

More generally, this communiqué follows the pattern of previous ones by fleshing out the framework already established and shaping a fresh framework for the next stage.

The Meeting with Mao

I have already sent you the highlights of this extraordinary session. The Chairman looked much healthier and thinner than last February when in turn he looked much better than during your trip. (It is

---

[7] In the margin next to this and the previous sentences, Nixon wrote: "K—very significant."

now clear in retrospect that he was quite ill when you saw him.) He moved and walked unaided and used his hands continuously and expressively as he talked in his slow, low, gravelly tones.

Mentally he was extremely impressive, improving his previous performances. He led the conversation, covered all major international issues with subtlety and incisiveness and an unerring knack at striking the essential chords in a seemingly casual way. By the time he was finished he had sketched their strategic vision comprehensively and laid down the essential elements of their policies region by region. He went from issue to issue in an ostensibly random, but always purposeful, manner. And all of this was done without a single note of his own or prompting by Chou, who once again was clearly deferential in his presence.

The Chairman obviously enjoyed himself. Throughout he employed his earthy phrasing and bawdy humor to illustrate a point or color a tone; the females present laughed easily, almost coquettishly and were again at ease in his presence. After the conversation had gone beyond one and three quarters hours, several on the Chinese side looked at their watches and made tentative moves to close out the meeting, but Mao prolonged the talk and toward the end engaged in exchanges on philosophy.

Indeed one of the striking aspects of the visit was the fact that this time Mao presented the bulk of the Chinese positions while Chou generally stuck to details and asking questions and making comments on our positions. Before, Chou had taken his cue from Mao but made extensive substantive presentations of his own.

The Chairman was vigorously *supportive of you* as I have reported. He praised your strong policies, singling out the recent alert and Middle East policy generally. He found your actions much firmer and steadier than the Cuban missile crisis scenario.

He discussed the Watergate events in bawdy fashion, calling it no more than a breaking of wind (the interpreter had amusing difficulty).[8] He considered the incident meagre, yet much chaos was being made of it and "we are not happy about it." He pointed out that other domestic policies, especially economic, were going well. I assured him you would surmount your current troubles and explained the domestic political tides.

Mao was also concerned in general about *trends in America* toward disengagement. He asked me if we would revert to isolationism if the Democrats took office. I said that many (not all) of them would want to move in that direction but objective reality would prevent them at some point; the problem was how much damage would already have

---

[8] Nixon underlined most of this sentence.

taken place before they checked this trend. On the whole I thought that future Administrations would have to pursue the same general course, though perhaps in less complex fashion than your tactics. I emphasized that in any event these concerns pointed up the need to solidify U.S.-Chinese relations now so there would be no alternative for successors.

The world wide preoccupation with the *Soviet Union* once again dominated his conversation. Almost every subject was linked to this theme. He painted the global Soviet threat and recounted how he had contemptuously rejected their offers, direct and through emissaries, for improved relations. I rehearsed our own, less direct policy with Moscow. The Chinese still remain somewhat suspicious of our approach, especially of the objective dangers of false détente; the Chairman compared our policy to shadow-boxing in contrast to their more straightforward opposition. I also acknowledged that the Soviet threat to China seemed to have increased since my last visit. I repeated our opposition to these pressures and the dangers we saw in a Soviet attack. He made clear that they didn't want a war but were prepared if necessary.

Indeed, Mao seemed basically optimistic about containing the Soviet Union, citing his familiar *axis of potential or tacit allies* in China, Japan, the United States, Europe and the Near East–South Asia axis. He again stressed the importance of our working closely with these countries—maintaining close ties with Japan; keeping our military presence in Europe; and countering Soviet influence in the Middle East (as we were now doing), Pakistan, Iran, India, the Persian Gulf and the Indian Ocean. I outlined our efforts to support these various countries; offset Soviet influence; maintain a strong national defense; keep forces in Europe; anchor Japan securely, etc.

We discussed several specific countries. He was very worried about Soviet influence in the radical Arab states, especially Iraq. He applauded your efforts to increase our influence in the region. He criticized their Chief of their Liaison Office in Washington for his recent lecture to me on the Middle East which rehearsed their standard pro-Arab line. The Chairman made clear that Ambassador Huang should have comprehended the more important U.S.-Soviet strategic aspect of the regional conflict.[9]

Mao was both patient and somewhat inscrutable on *Taiwan* and *diplomatic relations*. He said that the Taiwan issue "is not an important one; the issue of the overall international situation (i.e., the Soviet Union) is an important one." The PRC would not rush us on this question or that of diplomatic relations, he stated. After all, their relations

---

[9] Nixon highlighted the last two sentences of this paragraph, and wrote and underscored, "Note."

with us were better than those with countries like the USSR and India, with whom they have diplomatic ties; the Liaison Offices "could do." But Mao also made some elusive references (including on maintaining ties with the Soviet Baltic states) that suggested flexibility to allow us to move more rapidly. I followed up for clarification with Chou, and we emerged with the language in the Communiqué.

Mao strongly suggested that they would not use force against Taiwan, pointing to their restraint on Macao and Hong Kong. He didn't believe in peaceful transition with the counter-revolutionaries, but Peking could wait 600 years to absorb the small island. In any event the question of relations with us should be separated from this issue and shouldn't take so long.

I will shortly send you the full transcript of this remarkable conversation.

Meetings with Chou

I have already given you the highlights of my conversation with Chou.[10] They were stimulating, and he was impressive as always, but his role was considerably more subordinate to Mao's this trip. As I have indicated in earlier reports, our first meeting was taken up largely by my presentation of our position on major international issues, with Chou commenting and probing. The second session was largely a holding action of questions from him while they prepared for my meeting with the Chairman. And the meetings on the final day largely consisted of his elaborations of Mao's basic lines; sensitive exchanges about the strategic international scene; discussion of bilateral matters, including trade; and negotiation of the communiqué.

Following are the major points that emerged from these sessions:

—He strongly praised your *Middle East* policy and our growing dialogue with the Arabs. He indicated he had been helpful with Egypt. He suggested we talk directly to Syria; was suspicious of Iraq; urged inclusion of the Palestinians in the negotiations; and shared our positive view of the Shah. On the alert he compared you favorably with President Kennedy and suggested the incident gave us a chance to increase our defense budget.

—On *Vietnam*, Chou said that the North Vietnamese leaders have assured him they have no desire of launching a major offensive. He claimed the material moving south was for rebuilding roads and building up production. From what the Chinese know, Hanoi has no intention of launching a major attack. He alluded to the gradual political evolution that I

---

[10] Memoranda from Scowcroft to Nixon containing highlights of Kissinger's meetings with Zhou are in National Archives, Nixon Presidential Materials, NSC Files, Kissinger Office Files, Box 96, Country Files, Far East, China Exchanges, November 1, 1973–March 31, 1974.

had told him on previous visits we could live with. I underlined the dangers of a North Vietnamese offensive.

—Chou declared that their friends in *Cambodia* were complaining about lack of military support from Hanoi which according to him is "extremely meagre." He didn't foresee major fighting in Cambodia; favored a political settlement; and thought the area should be peaceful and neutral. He also indicated opposition to Sihanouk's return and a Soviet desire to have their "hand in the pie."

—Chou pointed to vigorous efforts by Moscow to the *south of China*. He urged support of Pakistan and approved our building a port there. I reaffirmed our policies and said that we were also trying gradually to improve relations with New Delhi to counter Soviet influence there.

—Discussion on *Korea* was restricted to the ongoing discussions in the United Nations. The Chinese had just given us a satisfactory compromise solution in New York and needed time to line up their allies. I agreed that we would work closely with them on timing so long as they stuck by their substantive position.

—He thought we should come closer to *Japan* on defense matters (i.e., the nuclear umbrella) and indicated he agreed that it was preferable for us to join the Japanese in Siberian development than to leave them alone.[11] I emphasized the importance of keeping the Japanese tied to us and not subjected to too many pressures.

—Chou criticized Allende's rashness in Chile and Che Guevara's adventurism. In response to my comments, he in effect said that the PRC would not cause trouble in *Latin America*.

—I went over our *Soviet* strategy in some detail, including our rationale for the agreement which you had used during the Middle East alert. He continually sounded their by now familiar preoccupations.

—Chou strongly supported NATO and our troop presence in *Europe*. He said he would continue to educate European leaders, beginning with Heath who will visit Peking soon.

—I reaffirmed our intentions on *Taiwan* in political terms and outlined our plans concerning our military presence.

—At his own initiative, Chou said he would not attend the *United Nations* session next fall.

—I described to Chou, as I did later to Mao, our *domestic mood* and its impact on foreign policy.

---

[11] Nixon underlined the phrase, "that it was preferable for us to join the Japanese in Siberian development than to leave them alone," and, in the margin next to it, wrote and underscored, "note."

Bilateral Technical Issues

Counterpart negotiations conducted on our side by Acting Assistant Secretary Hummel focused on trade and exchange matters.[12]

We presented to the Chinese our view of the importance to the evolution of normal *economic relations* of concluding the private claims/blocked assets problem— agreed to in principle during my visit last February. In the only harsh aspect of all our discussions (apparently reflecting the acerbic personality of negotiator Lin Ping, formerly Ambassador to Chile during the Allende period and now Director of the Foreign Ministry's Bureau of American and Oceanic Affairs) the Chinese side attacked our proposed technical language defining the source of their blocked assets as being an unwarranted reference to the former "hostile" attitude of the U.S. toward the PRC. More substantively, they demanded that we exclude from the settlement $17 million blocked in third-country banks, some of which has been repaid indirectly to the PRC despite our warnings to the banks of the illegality of such action. Our side indicated that these positions were unacceptable, primarily because exclusion of the third-country blocked assets from a settlement would reduce the sum of the total available for repaying our domestic claimants to a level unacceptable to the Congress, but as well because of the disastrous precedent for our international banking relations of such actions.

In my final session with the Premier, we made some progress on this matter. I reiterated the desirability of resolving the claims/assets problem, but the unacceptability of the Chinese position on the third-country bank question. We concluded by agreeing to further exchanges on the technical issues in the coming weeks in an effort to reach a final resolution of this matter in about a month.

The Chinese were relaxed about the *most favored nation* issue. Chou probed about the relationship between the present Congressional obstruction of this aspect of the trade bill because of the Soviet internal scene and extension of MFN to Peking. They do not mind delay. Their only concern is to keep the Soviet and Chinese aspects separate in Congressional and public discussion.

Scientific, cultural, and public affairs *exchanges* were discussed, with agreement reached on twenty specific programs which will be implemented in 1974. Included in this total is a visit to the U.S. by a delegation of Chinese mayors, and acceptance by the PRC of our proposal that a group of American state governors tour China. As well, the PRC proposed another Congressional delegation visit in the summer of next

---

[12] Memoranda of conversation of the counterpart negotiations are in National Archives, Nixon Presidential Materials, NSC Files, Kissinger Office Files, Box 87, Country Files, Far East, PRC Counterpart Talks, 1971–73.

year by a bipartisan group of fifteen. We will be presenting suggestions to you shortly on which Representatives and Senators might most usefully be included in this group. (We suggest this trip *not* be mentioned to members of Congress at this time, as it will generate a flood of requests, making it difficult to organize purposefully a group which will most effectively support your programs.)

We also proposed *longer-term cooperative programs* with the PRC in the areas of agricultural research, earth resources surveying, and language study. They indicated only that they would consider these ideas.

We also requested agreement from the Chinese side to our making a public statement regarding American servicemen *missing in action* in the vicinity of the PRC as a result of the Indochina hostilities or our past military activities in the Taiwan area. Premier Chou indicated to me that his officials were making a detailed search for information regarding a number of MIAs. He also agreed to our publicly stating that we have discussed the problem of MIAs, that the PRC has been conducting searches, that no new information has been turned up, that they are continuing to investigate, and that they will provide us any new information which comes up. We can release this statement at an early press conference. This should clear the air on a lingering problem of concern to MIA families and their Congressmen.[13]

I raised with Premier Chou the issue of permanent U.S. *press representation* in Peking.[14] He replied that they saw no problem with our newsmen in their capital; but there is concern with possible awkward confrontations in Washington between PRC newsmen and reporters of Taiwan's official Central News Agency. We will look into ways that this latter problem might be handled and then present further proposals to the Chinese.

Finally, we managed to resolve a potentially difficult issue concerning the U.S. Marine security contingent in our Liaison Office. The Chinese have complained of some of the social activities of the guard, which they feel calls public attention to their presence as a foreign military unit on PRC territory. Their sensitivity seems derived from the historical experience of foreign troops on Chinese soil during the last century which were part of the treaty post system of forced foreign access to the country. Lower level officials had almost demanded that we remove the Marines from China, but in my talks with Premier Chou it was agreed that the guard can remain based on our assurances to keep them low profile. We may replace some of the more exuberant of the

---

[13] Nixon highlighted the last two sentences of this paragraph and in the margin wrote, "follow up."

[14] Nixon highlighted the first sentence of this paragraph and in the margin wrote, "K—don't press this—It is not in *our* interest in view of press attitudes."

young men who have proved restive in the austere Peking environment with older, seasoned troops.

The Atmosphere

Our reception in Peking was as cordial as it has been on my last several trips. While the government still does not bring out welcoming crowds, in private contacts they are with few exceptions affable and responsive—yet never intimate. The Premier sent five officials to Pakistan to escort us to Peking—three of whom were on my first secret visit—and held a welcoming banquet on the first night that included, in all, almost 200 people on the Chinese and American sides. I gave a return banquet for the same guests the final night of our visit. Both events took place in the Great Hall of the People and, as during your trip, featured a Chinese military ensemble playing American and Chinese tunes.

Press play of our negotiating sessions was extensive in the PRC's electronic media and newspapers. My meeting with Chairman Mao was given banner-headline treatment, including the Chairman's wish that I convey his greetings to you. Other sessions were also reported on the front page of the *Peoples' Daily*.

I did little sight-seeing this trip, although a morning's visit to the Temple of Heaven and a walk through the streets attracted a lively and curious crowd. One morning we visited an agricultural commune on Peking's southern outskirts. While this was evidently a model facility and reasonably liveable, it nonetheless gave a clear sense of the limited capitalization of China's farms, the minimal economic amenities of the people, and their enduring burden of physical labor. The second evening we were given a performance of a revolutionary ballet, "The White Haired Girl." This propaganda pot boiler gives depressing evidence of the intellectual impoverishment of contemporary life in the PRC. One sees little evidence in the media or intellectual life of the brilliance and far-sightedness of China's top leaders with whom we deal nor of China's rich culture.

While a comfortably familiar pattern has now evolved in our periodic trips to Peking, and while we now have regularized contacts with the highest leaders in the PRC which—on the basis of past exchanges of view—facilitates the development of parallel policies in our international relations, we continue to have dealings with a highly restricted element of the leadership. While we have no indications from our talks of tensions and differences of policy orientation among various leaders, signs of conflict and debate persist in the press. Thus, in a situation where we can expect the passing of Mao and Chou in the next few years, there are grounds for concern about the depth and continuity of our relationship.

63.   Minutes of Secretary of State Kissinger's Staff Meeting[1]

Washington, November 19, 1973, 12:05 p.m.

[Omitted here are comments unrelated to China.]

[Secretary Kissinger:] Now—about China.

The newspapers report that we came to China in order to establish diplomatic relations, and that we did not achieve that objective. That is total nonsense. The last thing we could afford at this moment is diplomatic relations with China. It is not that we are short of domestic debates at this moment in this country. So that the absolutely last thing we attempted to do in China is to settle the relationship between Taiwan, Peking and the United States.

First of all, the diplomatic relations with China are a surface phenomenon. Between the liaison offices and these periodic exchanges, our relations with the Chinese are fuller than with most governments in the world with which we do have diplomatic relations. I can think of nothing that we are missing in our relations with the Chinese as a result of not having formal diplomatic relations. So that at no stage in the discussion did the issue of formal diplomatic relations come up.

The purpose of the discussion was, first, to exchange—well, as far as we are concerned, we have dealt only with three men; with Mao, Chou and Chai Cheng-wen (?).[2] No senior American has ever dealt with any authoritative person other than those three.

It is therefore essential that we meet with them periodically for the sort of conceptual review that the Chinese appreciate, and in which we have found their assurances in the past absolutely reliable—that what they say at these meetings they will do over a six-month period or a year's period, we have found one could absolutely rely upon.

So the purpose was to review the international situation in the light of events since our last meeting. Secondly, to maintain the momentum in our relationships, both symbolically and substantively.

I would urge any of you who are interested to compare the Shanghai Communiqué with the communiqué that was published last week. Now, for a variety of reasons we were not eager to get too much press attention to the differences between the Shanghai Communiqué and

---

[1] Source: National Archives, RG 59, Transcripts of Secretary of State Kissinger's Staff Meetings, 1973–1977, Entry 5177, Box 1, Secretary's Staff Meetings. Secret. Kissinger chaired the meeting, which was attended by all the principal officers of the Department or their designated alternates.

[2] The notetaker was unsure of the third name that Kissinger mentioned. Kissinger was likely referring to Qiao Guanhua.

this communiqué, because we did not want to get involved or we didn't want to shake up Moscow more than has already been the case in recent weeks. I think if you take the key paragraphs of the Shanghai Communiqué and the key paragraphs of this communiqué, you will see a qualitative advance in almost every essential category.

The common objectives in the Shanghai Communiqué were confined to the Northeast Pacific. In this communiqué, they were extended to a global basis. In the Shanghai Communiqué we talked in a general way about consultations. In this one we talked about authoritative exchanges and concrete consultations. And there was a major change in the Chinese position with respect to diplomatic recognition, which in the past they have made dependent on a whole series of very concrete conditions, and which in this communiqué they made dependent only on the acceptance of one China.

So essentially we went further than I actually thought we would go on this trip. And we went to the absolute maximum of where we could go, given the international situation and given our domestic situation.

[Omitted here are comments unrelated to China.]

With respect to China, that policy is essentially on a good track. But we have established it with two aged leaders, and we have absolutely no clue as to what anyone else in China thinks about it, except that the necessities of their position would tend to drive them in the direction that they are now pursuing, although whether successors will have the tactical skill is not so clear.

[Omitted here are comments unrelated to China.]

---

64.   Memorandum of Conversation[1]

Washington, November 19, 1973, 5 p.m.

SUBJECT

Ambassador Shen's Call on the Secretary

---

[1] Source: Department of State, Papers of William H. Gleysteen: Lot 89 D 436, Box 8132, PRC Related Papers 1973. Secret; Exdis. Drafted by Sullivan and cleared by Hummel. The meeting took place in the office of the Secretary of State.

PARTICIPANTS

The Secretary
Ambassador James C. H. Shen, Republic of China
Minister Henry Chen, Republic of China Embassy
Roger W. Sullivan, Director, Republic of China Affairs, EA/ROC

Ambassador Shen began the meeting by noting the Secretary had spent more time in Peking than in any other country. The Secretary commented that he had spent three days in Peking but that this had always been planned. The other stops were added. He reminded Shen that he had intended to visit Peking in August but that the timing of the trip kept slipping.

Ambassador Shen asked how the visit had gone. The Secretary responded that the Communiqué said everything there was to say, and that there was no substantial change from previous visits. Our statement on Taiwan repeated the section in the Shanghai Communiqué. The Peking statement on Taiwan was somewhat different but, the Secretary said, he had not had a chance to explore what it meant since it was put in on the last day. When Shen asked why the PRC had added that sentence at the last moment, the Secretary said he did not know and asked Shen what he thought. Shen said that he could not say since he was not there, but wondered about the significance of the difference between the PRC statement in this communiqué and the earlier longer and more detailed statement in the Shanghai Communiqué. The Secretary noted that the statement "normalization of relations can be accomplished on the basis of confirming the principle of one China" did not say that we had to withdraw our military forces or break diplomatic relations with the ROC.

The Secretary then asked again what Shen thought; "You have a Chinese mind, what does it mean to you?" Ambassador Shen responded that they want the U.S. to do something to confirm that there is one China. The Secretary then said that he had not discussed the statement with the Chinese, adding only that Premier Chou En-lai had said it was a new point. The Secretary emphasized that it was not an agreed point but a PRC statement and reiterated that he would have to study it.

Ambassador Shen asked why the U.S. statement in this Communiqué had not repeated the Shanghai Communiqué expression of interest in a peaceful settlement. The Secretary assured him this had no significance. The U.S. is absolutely firm on the defense commitment, the Secretary continued, and we have made that abundantly clear.

Referring to the Secretary's banquet toast, Ambassador Shen noted that the Secretary had assured the Chinese that U.S.–PRC friendship would be a constant factor in U.S. foreign policy. Shen wondered why the Secretary had given this assurance and whether Chou had made a similar pledge. The Secretary said that Chou had given substantially the same assurances and commented that surely Ambassador Shen would not have expected him to say that there would be a change in our policy. In response to Shen's question about stability on the mainland and possible PRC concern that U.S. China policy could change under a new administration, the Secretary said that there was some concern about what future administrations might do. As for the stability of the PRC, "What can you say when the leaders are 75 and 79." He added that he had no idea who would be the next PRC head of State.

Shen then asked what would happen next in U.S.–PRC relations. The Secretary assured him that nothing dramatic is going to happen and that the U.S. has no immediate intention and no plan to do anything. Shen commented to the Secretary that in an earlier conversation he had said that there would be no change until 1974 and asked if the timetable had been changed. The Secretary reminded Shen that 1974 is only a month away, but reiterated that there was no timetable. His reference to 1974 was just a general statement. The newspapers have picked up the idea of diplomatic relations, the Secretary continued, but the idea that we are compulsively seeking diplomatic relations is "nonsense." "What difference does it make?" he asked, "We have as much exchange as we need."

Ambassador Shen then asked if the Secretary had seen the ROC Ministry of Foreign Affairs statement on his trip. The Secretary said he had and that he found it fairly mild. Shen commented that the ROC could make it stronger if it was what we wished. He then asked what expanding the functions of the Liaison Office would include. The Secretary noted that we had no trade or commercial attachés there now and that expanding the functions would include things like that. In response to Shen's question, he added that we were not thinking in terms of military attachés. Shen then asked if the reference in the Communiqué to frequent high-level contact meant that there would be high-level visits from Peking to the U.S. The Secretary pointed out that Shen had drafted enough communiqués to know that not everything in them means something concrete. He added, however, that he did not intend to go to Peking as frequently as he had up until now.

Asked where this leaves us, the Secretary replied that this leaves us where we were before. The PRC's major concern is the USSR not Taiwan. Taiwan was barely discussed. When asked to confirm that the U.S. was moving in the direction of diplomatic relations, the Secretary said "by little steps at a time." Shen then asked how many more steps there were to take. The Secretary responded that we have no plan and that he did not see it coming in 1974. He repeated that the PRC has more pressing problems which preoccupy them more than Taiwan. He noted that he had seen Mao Tse-tung three times. During the second meeting there had been no mention of Taiwan. In his last meeting it was mentioned, but with no sense of urgency. Commenting on the Secretary's statement that it was the Soviet Union that preoccupied the Chinese, Shen asked if he was also concerned about the Soviet Union. The Secretary replied that he was not as concerned as the PRC is and observed that they never dug air raid shelters when we were confronting them.

The Secretary again asked Shen what the Communiqué meant to him. Shen said that they want the U.S. to do something to confirm the principle of one China and then in time they would take care of Taiwan either unilaterally or with U.S. acquiescence. The Secretary dismissed this as "impossible."

Ambassador Shen then observed that the ROC would like some reassurance from the U.S. He said that he had nothing specific in mind but asked if the Secretary would consider some expression or gesture of support. The Secretary said that after dealing in the same year with the Arabs and Israelis and three kinds of Vietnamese, he had no new ideas to suggest. Emphasizing the need for reassurances, Ambassador Shen commented that before the Secretary went to Peking, there were some people in Taipei who thought that he would establish diplomatic relations. When the Secretary observed that Taipei should be relieved that he did not, Shen noted that the Secretary had said that he intended to complete the process. The Secretary replied that this would not occur rapidly or in the next few weeks or months. He repeated that he did not have the same compulsion as the press. Before leaving for Peking he said he told the press he had no intention of establishing diplomatic relations on this trip. Shen commented that he could understand that the Secretary could not put a time limit on this U.S. position and emphasized that his own government had every intention of remaining friends and allies of the U.S. In reply, the Secretary reiterated that we have no plans to establish diplomatic relations with the PRC and that we will not give up the defense commitment.

Once the U.S. recognizes the PRC as the sole legitimate government of China, Shen asked, how could the U.S. maintain a defense treaty with part of a country? The Secretary replied that there may be many variations to this interesting question but reminded Shen that it is the PRC which feels the need to move toward diplomatic relations. We are not spending sleepless nights on this issue. Asked if he thought the PRC was spending sleepless nights on this issue, the Secretary replied, "Probably not;" they are pretty cold-blooded and do only enough to satisfy their domestic requirements.

Shen asked for the Secretary's advice on what the ROC should do. The Secretary responded that the ROC has pursued a wise policy, showing great restraint and wisdom. Painful as it may be, the ROC should continue this policy. He said he had no other suggestions.

Turning again to the PRC statement in the Communiqué on confirming the principle of one China, Shen asked the Secretary what his "Chinese advisers" thought it meant. The Secretary replied that his Chinese advisers did not know a damned thing. The statement may mean we can keep diplomatic relations with the ROC as long as we acknowledge that there is but one China, he said. On the other hand it may mean nothing. The Secretary added, however, that in his experience such PRC statements usually mean something. They are very subtle. Asked if he thought the Chinese considered him subtle, the Secretary commented that by Chinese standards they probably think he is of average intelligence which is a great compliment. The Secretary went on to say he wanted to explore what the Chinese meant by confirming the principle of one China. This will take time, he continued, and even when we find out what they want, we won't necessarily do it.

The Secretary ended the conversation by noting that after meetings such as he had in Peking, often nothing happens for a while. He noted in this connection that Ambassador Huang Chen had just returned home.

---

65.   **Memorandum From Richard H. Solomon of the National Security Council Staff to Secretary of State Kissinger**[1]

Washington, December 31, 1973.

SUBJECT

The Current State of U.S.–PRC Relations: Parallelism in International Affairs; Shaky Bilateral Ties

A number of [*less than 1 line not declassified*] reports, and concurrent developments at our Peking Liaison Office, lead me to summarize the current state of U.S.–PRC relations. Basically, while your discussions with the top Chinese leadership over the past two and one-half

---

[1] Source: National Archives, Nixon Presidential Materials, NSC Files, Box 527, Country Files, Far East. People's Republic of China, Vol. 8, July 10, 1973–Dec 31, 1973. Secret; Sensitive. Sent for action. Scowcroft sent this memorandum to Kissinger at the Western White House in San Clemente. At the top of the memorandum, Kissinger wrote, "Excellent paper." A handwritten note on the memorandum reads, "Comments are HAK's."

years have developed a certain conceptual consensus which now imparts a parallelism to our respective foreign policies, our bilateral ties are developing at best slowly and have uncertain stability for the future. Events of the past six months suggest that strong political and bureaucratic forces within China are limiting the institutionalization of a durable relationship between the U.S. and the PRC. Available evidence suggests Chairman Mao and Premier Chou have found it difficult to get their views on U.S.–PRC normalization accepted both ideologically and operationally by the Chinese bureaucracy, thus raising for the U.S. the question of the survivability of our relations with Peking after Mao and Chou have passed from the scene.

In conclusion, this analysis suggests a number of actions you may wish to take in order to strengthen the development of stronger bilateral ties with the Chinese.

Official PRC Fears of U.S.-Soviet "Collusion"

A [*less than 1 line not declassified*] report[2] confirms your speculation of last summer that the results of the Brezhnev Summit in June (coupled with Congressional action on the Cambodia bombing question) led to a cooling of Peking's attitude toward us. [*4 lines not declassified*]

[*less than 1 line not declassified*] assessed the implications of the just-concluded Brezhnev Summit in Washington in an official [*less than 1 line not declassified*] analysis. He concluded that the U.S. had stepped up its collusion with the Soviets, heightening pressure on the world's revolutionary forces. [*1 line not declassified*] Previous [*less than 1 line not declassified*] reporting on this document also indicates that Mao at the same time criticized [*less than 1 line not declassified*] for bogging down the development of China's new contacts with the U.S. in a sea of daily trivia which could sour the relationship. Mao added that if his officials did not keep in mind the major issues which required accommodation with the U.S., then excessive attention to the minor issues would lead to internal squabbling within the Chinese government.

[*2½ lines not declassified*] Then, in September 1973—after the Tenth Party Congress—an official [*less than 1 line not declassified*] document was circulated which formally criticized [*less than 1 line not declassified*] analysis and reaffirmed the correctness of Mao's "revolutionary line in foreign policy," which was admitted to be a matter of "struggle between the two lines" [of revolution versus "revisionism"][3] within the Party. [*3½ lines not declassified*]

---

[2] Attached but not printed.

[3] Brackets are in the original.

The one difficult conclusion that must be drawn [*less than 1 line not declassified*] is that even officials closely identified with Chou—and who presumably are privy to your exchanges with both the Chairman and the Premier—have doubts about the direction of our policy and the wisdom for the PRC of Mao's pro-U.S. policy. One can only speculate about the questions which may exist in the minds of those officials further removed from the Chairman and Premier. The argument which we by implication attribute to the late Lin Piao—that China can better preserve her security by mitigating its conflict with the Soviets than by balancing the Russian threat with a closer relationship with the U.S.—may have more appeal than we are aware, and is likely to have continuing attraction for those who do not share Mao's pathological hatred of the Soviets.

The "Sea of Trivia" Which Continues to Impede U.S.–PRC Bilateral Ties

The above information comes at a time when we have a worrisome record for 1973 of petty difficulties in developing smooth working relations with PRC officials via our Peking Liaison Office, together with indications that the Chinese are not prepared to deepen their exchange contacts or other dealings with the U.S. in a way that would begin to build durable ties between the two countries.

In a recent cable (Tab B)[4] Ambassador Bruce has written of his "deep concern" with "recent picayune incidents such as refusal to issue temporary duty visas for USLO replacements, obviously exaggerated complaints over the Marine Guard, long delays in answering requests for appointments with officials, and various indications of a marked lack of reciprocity here for our sensitive treatment of PRCLO representatives in the United States." To this evaluation must now be added concern about the implications of the recent PRC demand that we withdraw from USLO one of our most effective young FSOs who was involved not long ago in a fatal traffic accident in which he was not evidently at fault.

In terms of substantive issues, concern should also be expressed about the way the Chinese bureaucracy handled the claims/blocked assets problem. While there was some basis for suspicion of our proposals regarding the mechanics of a settlement of this issue, the ad hominem and uncompromising way in which the ascerbic Lin P'ing (Director of the American Division of the Foreign Ministry) presented the PRC position in the counterpart talks during your November trip to Peking gives little confidence that the Chinese bureaucracy is enthusiastic about promoting U.S.–PRC normalization.[5] Mao and Chou apparently have good reason to be concerned about the Foreign Ministry souring our developing relationship.

---

[4] Attached but not printed is telegram 1695 from Beijing, December 29.

[5] See footnote 12, Document 62.

In terms of the exchange program, one can only add that available evidence indicates great reluctance on the part of the PRC to develop meaningful, longer term scientific and cultural contacts. They have shown little interest in having additional American cultural groups such as the Philadelphia Orchestra come to China to develop a positive public mood about our new relationship. They have been equally unresponsive to our proposals that they send their scientists or scholars to the U.S. for periods of substantive research. Indeed, one recent [*less than 1 line not declassified*] report indicates that a plan to send Chinese physicists to American laboratories to do work on basic nuclear science has been scrapped in favor of closer cooperation with European researchers.

There appear to be two reasons for the reluctant and at times self-righteous posture the Chinese have taken in our bilateral dealings—both related to the continuing unsettled state of PRC domestic politics: One is a long tradition of the bureaucrats and Party cadre to be cautious about appearing too enthusiastic in support of "rightist" policies. The political struggles of the past two decades have taught them that "the line" always swings back to "the left"; and when it does those who were active supporters of a less revolutionary stand become vulnerable to political attack. The current indications of on-going political factionalism in the wake of the Cultural Revolution and the Lin Piao affair—even though apparently directed against "the left"—suggest that the political atmosphere within the Chinese bureaucracy would engender caution about actively supporting the policies of aged leaders which eventually may be vulnerable to radical criticism. The second reason is that the current debate in the PRC about Confucius has a strong element of criticism of the intellectual community. U.S.–PRC exchanges involve, above all, China's intellectuals; and it seems likely that exchanges will have to remain at a tenuous level for a considerable period of time, until (if at all) the Chinese sort out a positive role for their scientists and academics that will permit this "bourgeois" element of their society to have greater contact with the "outside."

The one area of our bilateral relations where progress has outpaced expectations is trade. Even here, however, we have received reports of frustration on the part on Chou En-lai about conservative and unimaginative economic policies on the part of the bureaucracy which have hindered the growth of China's export potential. This situation led the Premier last fall to sack his Minister of Foreign Trade and replace him with a man presumably more responsive to official guidance.

What Is To Be Done?

This analysis has been based on the assumption—now strengthened by the [*less than 1 line not declassified*] report at Tab A[6]—that

---

[6] Attached but not printed.

Chairman Mao and Premier Chou continue to encounter difficulties in bringing their bureaucracy fully behind the process of U.S.–PRC normalization. What, if anything, can we do about such a situation? While obviously we are in a position of largely having to follow the lead of the Chairman and the Premier, there are a number of initiatives we could take which might help them to confront bureaucratic foot-dragging in their own house and identify a larger slice of their top leadership with the policy of U.S.–PRC normalization than has been the case thus far:

—State is now considering a démarche to the Chinese Liaison Office at the Assistant Secretary level raising our concern about the overall trend of developments regarding our Liaison Office in Peking. I suggest that this would be most effective if done in parallel with a personal message from you to the Premier, transmitted via Ambassador Bruce, which indicated in general terms your concern about recent trends and their implication for both the workings of the Liaison Office and more generally for the prospect of normalized dealings between the U.S. and PRC which will stand the test of time.

—The PRC is planning to send a trade delegation to the U.S. this spring. You might personally invite an important high political official—either Vice Premier Li Hsien-nien, or Minister of Foreign Trade Li Ch'iang—to head up this delegation.

—During your next trip to China you should seek opportunities to meet with a broader range of PRC officials than has been the case in the past. This might include a trip to several key provincial cities where you could meet with key regional leaders.

Recommendations:

1. That we prepare a draft message from you to Premier Chou expressing your personal concern about prospects for insitutionalizing normalized U.S.–PRC relations (to be coordinated with any State démarche to PRCLO about recent developments regarding the functioning of USLO).

2. That we take steps to explore the possibility of inviting a high-level PRC official to head the trade delegation which will visit the U.S. this coming spring.[6]

3. That we include in planning for your next trip to the PRC events which would hold the possibility of meeting with a broader range of Chinese officials, perhaps including a tour of several key provincial cities.[7]

---

[7] Kissinger initialed the Approve option under recommendations 1 and 2.

[8] Kissinger checked Disapprove option and wrote, "Let's wait." Beneath the recommendation, Kissinger ordered, "There is to be no State démarche without my clearance."

66.   Memorandum of Conversation[1]

Washington, January 23, 1974, 6:15–6:45 p.m.

PARTICIPANTS

> The Secretary of State
> Winston Lord
>   Director of Planning and Coordination Staff
> Arthur Hummel
>   Acting Assistant Secretary for East Asian and Pacific Affairs
> Han Hsu
>   Acting Chief, PRC Liaison Ofice
> Chi Chao Chu
>   PRC Liaison Office

Dr. Kissinger: Are we ever going to see your Ambassador again? (laughter)

Ambassador Han: He is enjoying the Spring Festival in China now.

The Secretary: I thought we might have a brief meeting to go over two problems. One is this issue on the Paracel Islands, and the other is my trip to the Middle East. Let me talk about the unpleasant one first. I bet you think I'm going to talk about the Middle East now, but I'll fool you.

There are only two points I wanted to make with respect to the Paracel Islands issue.[2] The South Vietnamese government is making a number of representations to international organizations, to SEATO as well as to the United Nations. We wanted to let you know we do not associate ourselves with those representations. We are concerned, however, about the prisoners, and we noted that your government has indicated that the prisoners will be released at an appropriate time. We wanted to urge that this appropriate time be very soon, especially as there is an American included in that group. And that would certainly defuse the situation as far as the United States is concerned. That's really all I wanted to say about that issue.

(To Mr. Hummel) Or is there more, Art?

Mr. Hummel: For domestic political reasons we would like to say that we have been in touch about this American.

---

[1] Source: National Archives, Nixon Presidential Materials, NSC Files, Kissinger Office Files, Box 96, Country Files, Far East, China Exchanges, November 1, 1973–March 31, 1974. Secret; Sensitive; Nodis. The meeting was held at Kissinger's office in the Department of State.

[2] Chinese forces captured Gerald Emil Kosh, an employee of the Department of Defense, during a battle between South Vietnam and China over competing claims to the Paracel Islands.

The Secretary: We will say it only in response to questions. (Mr. Lord mentioned to the Secretary that there was some question as to the exact status of the American.)

Ambassador Han: I would like to say a few words about this matter. First, we call these islands Hsi Sha because that is our territory. We make clear in our statements that we are a socialist country; we never invade other's territory, but we don't let others invade our territory.

The Secretary: That's not true of every Socialist country.

Ambassador Han: We have always said that we will not attack if we are not attacked, but if we are attacked by others, we will counterattack. So what we say is clear.

As for when the prisoners will be released, our statement said that at an appropriate time they will be released. It was the Foreign Ministry statement.

But as a personal observation, I would just like to express surprise that there should be an American citizen at that particular area at that particular time. We don't know the actual circumstances—whether he was there or not or whether he was captured or not.

The Secretary: He was not there on any permanent basis; he was there at the request of the South Vietnamese on some temporary, technical mission, precisely because we thought it was a quiet period. He was only going to stay a day or so, very briefly; then he found himself caught. There are no Americans permanently or even temporarily on these islands. This was an unfortunate incident.

Ambassador Han: As for whether he was taken prisoner or not, we are not aware of it.

The Secretary: Could you attempt to confirm this for us?

Ambassador Han: We will see what is the circumstance.

The Secretary: We would appreciate it very much. The U.S. has taken no position in supporting the South Vietnamese claims to these islands. I wanted to make this clear, also.

Now, a few words about my trip to the Middle East, or did you want to pursue this other subject?

Ambassador Han: With regard to Mr. Hummel's suggestion whether to publicize this to the media would this be quickly, right away?

The Secretary: We can wait. What do you want? You report to Peking. Not having said anything up to now, we can survive another 24 hours. We can take the heat. We will give it until Friday morning,[3] but the more quickly you can let us know, the better. Eventually, we will have to say that we have talked to you.

---

[3] January 25.

Ambassador Han: After we have reported to the government, we will see what the reply is.

Mr. Hummel: All we have in mind is to say that we have talked, not to make the other points that the Secretary raised.

The Secretary: We will wait until Friday. We can give you until Friday a.m. to see whether you get an answer. We have been accused of so many things, we can be accused of neglecting an American interest for a day.

Shall we talk about the Middle East for a few minutes?

Ambassador Han: Please.

The Secretary: There is really not all that much to say because I think we are pursuing the policy the Prime Minister has urged upon me, which is to reduce Soviet influence in the Middle East. I have the impression that it is reasonably successful. You know from our public discussions the nature of the agreements. But I thought you may be interested to know that the Egyptians are very dissatisfied with their relationship with the Soviet Union, and they are very interested in improving their relationship with the Peoples Republic. And I have strongly recommended that they do this. They would like you to establish a MIG–21 factory in Egypt. They will pay you for it; it's up to you. I thought you should know their interest in improving relations with the Peoples Republic.

In Syria, we are just at the beginning of the process, but it is basically what I described with the Prime Minister, to keep them separate from Iraq.

I think it was your Prime Minister who urged me to become active in the Middle East. I don't know whether he thinks we have become too active now (laughter).

Ambassador Han: We do not know about the content of your discussions with the Prime Minister in Peking, but I do know of the talk that Vice Minister Chiao had with yourself and Ambassador Hummel in New York.

The Secretary: It was in the same spirit; the Prime Minister went into greater detail.

Are you ever going to get a vacation?

Ambassador Han: Starting today, there are three days of the Spring Festival.

The Secretary: We are retaliating. We are bringing Ambassador Bruce home for a few weeks. It's not a question of reciprocity; I just want his advice, including European problems. I may send him to Europe as a matter of fact for a few weeks.

Ambassador Han: I remember you mentioned this the last time.

Is that all?

The Secretary: Yes.

Ambassador Han: Thank you for receiving us.

67.   Memorandum From Richard H. Solomon of the National Security Council Staff to Secretary of State Kissinger[1]

Washington, January 25, 1974.

SUBJECT

Confucius and the State Governors' China Trip: Is Peking Debating Foreign Policy?

PRC Liaison Office personnel called on me yesterday to report no progress in our efforts to set a date for the state governors' visit. Several weeks ago Jim Falk of the Domestic Council and I initiated efforts through the National Governors' Conference to form a delegation, based on the agreement in principle of November that a group could visit the PRC by June of this year. We subsequently presented the Liaison Office a list of the likely members of the delegation, and indicated that mid-May would be the most convenient time for the governors. We also gave the Chinese a draft press release patterned on the previous Congressional releases, and requested their comments. During yesterday's call, the PRC officials said that they had been instructed by Peking to inform us that the draft press release was inappropriate, both because it implied too much of an official exchange—rather than people-to-people contact—and because no time for the visit has as yet been set. In short, we were told that the PRC is not prepared at this time to move ahead with semi-official exchanges.[2] (For this reason I have not initiated any planning activity for the next Congressional visit, also agreed to in principle during your last trip to Peking.)

This development is but one of a range of indicators that our bilateral relations with Peking are immobilized: Other facilitated cultural and scientific exchanges are in abeyance; USLO has had turn-downs of eight applications for visas for U.S. officials—including Ambassador Ingersoll;[3] and the Chinese appear to be delaying a response to your latest proposal for settlement of the claims/blocked assets problem. What is going on in Peking?

---

[1] Source: National Archives, Nixon Presidential Materials, NSC Files, Box 528, Country Files, Far East, People's Republic of China, Vol. 9, Jan 1, 1974–. Secret; Sensitive. Sent for information. Kissinger initialed this memorandum at the time, and later quoted it in his memoir, *Years of Upheaval*, p. 680. All brackets are in the original.

[2] In telegram 17433 to Beijing, January 25, the Department reported on the visit that Chi Ch'ao-Chu and Hsu Hsin-Hsi of the PRC Liaison Office paid to Solomon. (National Archives, RG 59, Central Foreign Policy Files, 1974)

[3] On January 12, the Liaison Office informed the Chinese Foreign Ministry that since it had received no response to its request for a visa, Assistant Secretary Ingersoll was regretfully canceling the Beijing stop of his tour of East Asia. (Telegram 67 from Beijing, January 12; ibid.)

Have the Chinese Been Debating Foreign Policy?

Press material is now coming available which suggests that foreign policy has been actively debated by the leadership in Peking—thus leading to a stand-down of our bilateral contacts with the PRC. A *Red Flag* article of November which has just been translated suggests—in the Aesopian language of the on-going polemic on Confucius—that the military in China have questioned the policy of rapprochement with the U.S. The most significant passage states that the Chou figure in the historical debate criticized his opponents,

> "for advocating the policy of 'making friends with neighboring countries [i.e., the Soviets] and attacking the distant ones' [the U.S.] in order to preserve their own hereditary prerogatives, and went further in putting forward the policy of 'making friends with distant countries and attacking the neighboring ones.' San Sui's [Chou's] line won the approval of King Chao [Mao]," and he was accordingly appointed as a guest minister in charge of military affairs.
> "However, although San Sui [Chou] had become Prime Minister, he was actually perched on the top of the crater of a volcano that could erupt at any time. In the Chu state the power of the old aristocrats [the regional military commanders?] was still rather powerful."

Subsequent to the publication of this article, China's regional military commanders were shuffled around, suggesting that Chou's "volcano" did not explode under him.[4]

More recently, a January *Red Flag* article entitled "Confucius in Moscow" implies by historical analogy that leaders within China are cooperating with the Soviets to attack Mao/Chou policies. The article even asserts that the "Soviet social imperialists" are supporting Confucius together with the "Kuomintang reactionaries on Taiwan." (Perhaps Peking has already received word of the Soviet approach to the Nationalists via the Chinese professor they invited to Moscow in December, although the timing of the article's publication would not be strong evidence in this direction.)[5] The article concludes that, "The farce in Moscow of worshipping Confucius has merely drawn a calm response [in Peking]," and asserts that the Soviets will get nowhere in their effort to find supporters in China. The recent expulsion from Peking of five Soviet diplomats on charges of spying seems to add

---

[4] A briefing memorandum from David Mark of INR to the Acting Secretary of State, January 2, reported that the Chinese Government had abruptly shifted command in eight of China's eleven military regions, thus culminating "a long effort to reassert central and civilian authority." (Ibid., Nixon Presidential Materials, NSC Files, Kissinger Office Files, Box 87, Country Files, Far East, China—Reports Sensitive)

[5] On December 31, 1973, Jiang Jingguo informed McConaughy that the Soviet Union had approached a ROC citizen about the future of Taiwanese-Soviet relations. (Memorandum from Smyser to Kissinger, January 10; ibid., Box 524, Country Files, Far East, China, Vol. XII, Oct 25, 1973–)

weight to the interpretation that the dominant leadership in Peking is concerned about Soviet game-playing within China—or at least wants to make a visible point that the Russians are still the primary enemy.

By all evidence, Premier Chou appears to be in the dominant position in Peking, although the continuing signs of debate in the press suggest that he is having to defend his policies against on-going criticism. Given these recent indications that foreign policy has been at issue, our present interpretation is that the lack of PRC responsiveness to us on bilateral issues reflects the Premier's desire not to give his challengers the added ammunition that would come with a more visible relationship. If the present signs of Chou consolidating his position persist, however, one would anticipate some further movement in U.S.–PRC relations, such as a favorable decision on the claims settlement and more receptivity to exchanges and official travel. My present guess is that the current state of immobilism will persist well into the first half of 1974, at least until a National People's Congress has been convened to give further institutional legitimacy to the Premier's policies and supporters.

---

68.   **Notes on a Conversation Between Secretary of State Kissinger and *Time* Incorporated Editors and Correspondents**[1]

Washington, February 5, 1974.

[Omitted here are Kissinger's statements about wiretaps, Secretary Schlesinger, and the Soviet Union.]

China in dealing with us has been meticulous but there has been no advance. When I was there in November I committed a fantastic faux pas when I started talking about Confucious with the Chinese.[2]

---

[1] Source: Department of State, RG 59, Lot 89 D 436, Papers of William H. Gleysteen, Box 8132, PRC Related Papers, Jan–Mar 1974. No classification marking. Drafted by George Vest, Special Assistant to the Secretary of State for Press Relations.

[2] In the third volume of his memoirs, Kissinger says that this exchange occurred during a dinner in the Great Hall of the People. (Henry Kissinger, *Years of Renewal*, pp. 160–161) No record of the dinnertime conversation was found. For the unsuccessful effort by the NSC staff to verify this anecdote, see Solomon to Scowcroft, March 6, 1974; National Archives, Nixon Presidential Materials, NSC Files, Box 528, Country Files, Far East, People's Republic of China, Vol. 9, Jan 1, 1974–. Confucianism also became a topic of conversation during a couple of Kissinger's more formal November 1973 meetings, although neither fits the description here. See Documents 56 and 57.

They got excited and it led to a ½ hr argument with Chou taking the lead, arguing it had nothing to do with their world. We can now see this still is an issue.

There is enormous instability in China. Their Ambassador has been called back for months, now. Still, Mao is associated with our steps toward normalizing and Chou is the primary actor.

Whenever I read over what Mao has said to me I realize his enormous intellectual discipline. Even his jokes have meaning. He told me a joke, I missed the point and responded with one of my own. He repeated his joke, and I told another. Then for the third time he repeated his joke, to make sure I did not miss the meaning. He and Chou are integrally linked to an improved US-China relationship. It has its benefits. Thus Kosh was released on the Tuesday after we said on Friday that we expected him to be released.[3]

The internal problems of China are eating at the leadership. Their obsession with the Soviets is greater now than in any of my previous visits. All foreigners are in trouble. An Algerian dance group got into bureaucratic difficulty and cancelled out. Only a Canadian symphony carried through their visit. Our LO is confined to contacts with officials. A diplomat invited a Chinese official to lunch and was told he was unavailable that day or any other day.

---

[3] See footnote 2, Document 66.

---

69.   Memorandum From Richard H. Solomon of the National Security Council Staff to Secretary of State Kissinger[1]

Washington, February 5, 1974.

SUBJECT

Chinese Now Move to Public Phase of the "Confucius/Lin Purge:" Problems of the American Press Response

On February 2 the *People's Daily* published an editorial signalling the opening phase of a mass campaign, keyed to the anti-Confucius/

---

[1] Source: National Archives, Nixon Presidential Materials, NSC Files, Kissinger Office Files, Box 96, Country Files, Far East, China Exchanges, November 1, 1973–March 31, 1974. Confidential. Urgent; Sent for action.

Lin Piao polemic of the past six months, which apparently will move to purge the remaining sources of opposition to the Mao/Chou "mainstream" leadership as it attempts to re-establish the predominant role of the Chinese Communist Party. The editorial makes explicit that Chairman Mao himself is behind the new phase of the campaign, that it is directed against "ringleaders of various opportunist lines" who have been intriguing "in dark corners behind people's backs," and that it is necessary to "arouse the masses" in order to "carry the struggle to criticize Lin Piao and Confucius through to the end."

The editorial stresses that the new phase of the campaign will be "a test for every leading comrade" as part of the process of "destroying the roots of Lin Piao's revisionist line." It thus seems clear that high leaders are likely to fall during this new phase of mass criticism. Given developments of recent months (the reshuffle of the regional military commanders, and subtle attacks aimed at Chiang Ch'ing—such as the criticism of Beethoven and Schubert), it seems most likely that the targets will be some combination of military leaders and ideological "leftists"—the groups which seemed to be forming an alliance of convenience last summer to defend themselves against the Mao/Chou mainstream in advance of the Tenth Party Congress. The exact pace of this new phase of mass attack, and specific identification of the victims, however, is not yet evident. It is becoming clear, however, that the Chinese are "battening down the hatches" for a period of rough political weather, and are becoming increasingly sensitive to foreign observation and comment as they go through a semi-public purge.

In this context, it is clear that the publication of the January 30 *People's Daily* attack on Antonioni[2] (which the PRC Liaison Office widely distributed to journalists in Washington and New York) was an act of "guidance" to the U.S. about how to interpret the present criticism campaign. To recapitulate my reading of this piece, it seems to make three points: those in China who want to "restore the past" of the Cultural Revolution are in trouble; Chairman Mao's foreign policy of opposition to the Soviets and friendship for the U.S. is still operative; and Americans who now highlight China's current difficulties will only be working to the benefit of the Russians and against U.S.–PRC friendship.

It should be noted, however, that press reports out of Hong Kong are misinterpreting the current thrust of China's internal political movement. The most recent and disturbing article, front paged on

---

[2] The *People's Daily* criticized Michelangelo Antonioni, the Italian filmmaker who had made the movie *China*. At approximately the same time, the newspaper also attacked "bourgeois" composers like Beethoven and Schubert. (Memorandum from Solomon to Kissinger, February 4; ibid., Box 528, Country Files, Far East, People's Republic of China, Vol. 9, Jan 1 1974–)

today's *New York Times* interprets the *People's Daily* editorial of February 2 as signalling a return to the Cultural Revolution, i.e., a resurgence of China's "left" and hostility to all foreign influence. Given the gratuitous manner in which the PRC has called attention to recent developments (by mailing copies of the Antonioni attack to our press) it seems likely that we will see numerous stories begin to circulate in coming days playing up the line that U.S.–PRC relations are in real trouble in the face of a radical resurgence in China.

In these circumstances, we have basically two options: to let our press speculate about domestic PRC developments and their implication for the U.S. without official guidance; or to "deep background" the media on the view that current developments in China are not directed against U.S.–PRC normalization. My own view is that the best approach would be for you to "deep background" the press on where we stand with the Chinese, and at the same time enjoin the bureaucracy from speculating in public about developments within the PRC. Such a backgrounding session might make the following points:

—We see no indication that Mao or Chou are in trouble; indeed, the recent reshuffling of the regional military commanders and the rehabilitation of Teng Hsiao-p'ing suggest that the Chairman and Premier are strengthening the return to regularized, civilian leadership.

—We see no indication of a shift in China's foreign policy line away from the trend of U.S.–PRC normalization. As the PRC sorts out its internal affairs, however, it may be that the Chinese will want to temporarily downplay contact with foreigners.

—We must respect the right of the Chinese to deal with their own internal affairs without speculation by officials of foreign countries.

Recommendation:[3]

That you "deep background" appropriate members of the press on developments in the PRC.

---

[3] Although Kissinger initialed this memorandum, indicating that he had seen it, he marked neither the Approve nor Disapprove options. On March 13, Kissinger gave "deep background" comments during a luncheon at the *Washington Post* building. On the subject of China, he said, "What about Ambassador Bruce? He asked some time ago if he could come back for consultation. While here I got his judgment on Europe. His presence here had nothing to do with China. The Chinese have been going to great efforts to signal to us that their own policy initiative to the U.S. is unchanged. It is true that they don't seem at the moment to have the time to cultivate our relationship as they did last year." (Memorandum of conversation; ibid., Box 1028, MemCons-HAK & Presidential, March 1–May 8, 1974)

70.   Memorandum From W. R. Smyser of the National Security Council Staff to Secretary of State Kissinger[1]

Washington, February 6, 1974.

SUBJECT

Backgrounder on Chinese Internal Developments

I concur with Dick Solomon's recommendation (Tab A)[2] that you brief selected journalists on a "deep background" basis about current developments in China.

But I want to add two obvious words of caution, in case they have not already occurred to you:

—I think there will be a great temptation in the next few months for members of the press to attack our China effort as "another element of détente that has not worked out as promised." Chinese hardening on travel and Chinese domestic turmoil will provide ammunition adequate for this though not as good as the ammunition that the Russians have provided.

—Some people could argue that your backgrounder represents an effort to stave off that kind of attack.

I think this means that, if you give the backgrounder, it must be done on a highly selective basis, perhaps even on an individual basis with journalists who have come to see you on some other topic.

Let me add that this underlines the need for you to keep an independent China expertise here if you choose to let Solomon go. Hong Kong has already shown that it does not understand the issue either in Chinese or American terms. USLO in Peking will do no better, I fear. The Department and much of our press will be swept away by their analysis, and without independent capacity we will not be able to counter them from here.

---

[1] Source: National Archives, Nixon Presidential Materials, NSC Files, Box 528, Country Files, Far East, People's Republic of China, Vol. 9, Jan. 1, 1974–. Secret; Sensitive; Eyes Only. Urgent; sent for information.

[2] Tab A is a copy of Solomon's February 5 memorandum, Document 69.

71.   **Letter From the Acting Assistant Secretary for East Asian and Pacific Affairs (Hummel) to the Acting Chief of the Liaison Office in China (Jenkins)[1]**

Washington, February 14, 1974.

Dear Al:

This is a genuinely informal letter designed to let you know some of our thoughts, and some items of pending business that we are working on. I don't expect you to take any particular action on any of the items discussed herein.

As things are working out here, the center of gravity in U.S.–PRC relations seems to have followed Henry into the State Department. Win Lord and I have wound up jointly doing the staff work for most of our important business with your clients. The Secretary, of course, retains very close control of all the important aspects of the relationship. However, his necessary preoccupation with a host of other matters—for instance the Middle East and now the Energy Conference—makes it difficult to get his attention on day-to-day problems. Brent Scowcroft and Dick Solomon of course still play active roles in PRC affairs.

Here follow some status reports.

(1) Before Ambassador Bruce's arrival, Henry on two occasions told Han Hsu that he would be asking Ambassador Bruce to give attention on a temporary basis to some of our European problems. On one of these occasions, Henry jokingly said he was "retaliating" for the prolonged absence of Ambassador Huang Chen.[2] You will have seen State 28116 regarding the announcement that Ambassador Bruce will be occupied for about a month with Western Europe.[3] He has already been intimately involved with the Secretary in the difficult and fascinating proceedings of the Energy Conference.

(2) There was considerable confusion about Deputy Secretary Rush's possible trip to Peking. As early as January 7, Henry mentioned

---

[1] Source: Department of State, Papers of William H. Gleysteen: Lot 89 D 436, Box 8132, PRC Related Papers, Jan–Mar 1974. Secret; Eyes Only; Official–Informal. In an attached note to "Bob" (probably Ingersoll), Hummel refered to this letter as an attempt to start "a normal dialogue with that abnormal post."

[2] See Document 66.

[3] Telegram 28116 to Taipei, February 13. (National Archives, RG 59, Central Foreign Policy Files)

to Han Hsu that Ken Rush might be planning such a trip.[4] Han's reaction was noncommittal. Your telegram of February 12 was most welcome because it helped to focus attention on the problem.[5] To put it bluntly, it was up to Ken Rush to talk this out with Henry, and the result, as you will have seen, is a belated request for a visa. None of us are optimistic about the result.

(3) We all regret the delay in responding to your sensible suggestions about talking to the Chinese about future space requirements. We got all tangled up (the current cliche is "wrapped around the axle") with various options for Henry of how and whether to mention possible longer-term requirements. Henry put the whole problem on the back burner for discussion with Ambassador Bruce and the result is as you have seen in our telegram. I wish we had been able to get this simple answer to you earlier. Our retraction of the first authorization to start discussing immediate needs resulted from a "hold everything until I return from the Middle East" reaction by Henry to a proposed telegram on long-term requirements.

(4) We have been toying with the idea of trying to have a frank—American-style rather than Chinese-style—dialogue between myself and Han Hsu concerning some of the procedural problems that we have had with the PRC. The object would be two-fold: (a) to talk frankly about some of the things that bother us (rejection of TDY assignments, long delays in issuance of visas for consultation, your difficulty in getting appointments in Peking, and the somewhat twisted use of the principle of reciprocity), and (b) most important, a sincere and heartfelt appeal for better understanding on both sides so that our relations can progress smoothly to a higher stage, without misunderstandings caused by the real differences between our social systems.

I invented this idea in the first place a coule of months ago. However, I am now not sure that point (b) above will come through in a sufficiently positive way to the authorities in Peking. It seems quite possible that Lin P'ing and others might distort the whole approach so that instead of constituting a positive and sincere appeal, it would appear merely as a list of accusations and complaints. I would welcome any thoughts that you have.

(5) We have heard in New York that Ambassador Huang Hua may be returning to Peking for what he says is a routine consultation of about six weeks. Such a trip makes sense at this time of year and I don't

---

[4] As reported in a memorandum of conversation, January 7. (Ibid., Nixon Presidential Materials, NSC Files, Kissinger Office Files, Box 96, Country Files, Far East, China Exchanges, November 1, 1973–March 31, 1974)

[5] Hummel is likely referring to telegram 240 from Beijing, February 11. (Ibid., RG 59, Central Foreign Policy Files)

want to read too much into it. However, the thought has crossed my mind that from Peking's point of view the UNGA session last year may not have been satisfactory, and their UN tactics may be up for criticism, internally. We should be alert to any signs that Vice Minister Chiao or Ambassador Huang Hua are in trouble, possibly for compromising on Korea or for failing to get a majority on Cambodia.

(6) By the time you get this, you will have seen a White House announcement of Ambassador Unger's nomination to succeed Walter McConaughy in Taipei.[6] We planned to have only a routine announcement but we have run into a peculiar angle. When McConaughy was nominated in 1966, the announcement, and also his letters of credence, called him "Ambassador to China". This time, we think it is only accurate to call Ambassador Unger "Ambassador to the Republic of China". This difference may be noticed, but on balance we feel that it is better to use the more accurate and less ambiguous phraseology.

(7) Henry has approved a scenario for further military withdrawals from Taiwan, which we are slowly and painfully working out with the different agencies in Washington. This will involve telling the ROC everything that we plan during the coming year, on the theory that only by exposing a whole package can we reassure the ROC that this is all we have in mind. We will soon be authorizing Ambassador McConaughy to discuss withdrawal of U–2's, the schedule of withdrawal of the two USAF squadrons, [1½ lines not declassified]. We will try to send you a copy of the instruction when it goes to Taipei.

You may be interested to know that Han Hsu, in conversation with Henry and Win and me recently, said that he had not received any word of any of the conversations that Henry held in Peking in November. We also know from comments by PRCLO officials that they have no information about my counterpart talks in Peking, except for the list of agreed exchanges. I found this rather surprising, but Henry observed privately in his inimitable style: "they must be following *my* practice."

I have shown this letter to Ambassador Bruce, and will show it to Winston Lord.

I have felt for some time that we should do a better job of keeping you and John informed on an interim basis, before instructions are finally released through our sometimes cumbersome processes. I would welcome a freer flow of Eyes Only letters between us.

Best regards to everyone,

Sincerely,

Arthur W. Hummel, Jr.[7]

---

[6] Unger was nominated on March 14, 1974.

[7] Printed from a copy that bears Hummel's typed signature.

72.   Telegram From the Liaison Office in China to the Department of State[1]

Beijing, February 19, 1974, 0345Z.

284. Subject: PRC Cancellation of DepSec's Visit. Ref: State 032525.[2]

1. USLO was most disappointed to learn that we will not have opportunity to meet with Deputy Secretary in Peking, but Chinese decision that present time "not convenient" came as no surprise. Since planning for visit first began in December the ideological campaign to criticize Lin Piao and Confucius has moved into a new stage involving mass participation on a scale unseen since the Cultural Revolution. Although the campaign thus far has remained under firm control, the debates over central versus regional control, party versus military and the course of China's educational and cultural development have produced internal tensions which would make high visibility visit by a senior American official difficult at this time. We continue to feel that Chou remains in control of the situation, but a slightly lower profile on his part may be considered prudent for the time being.

2. While the ideological debate has thus far not significantly affected foreign policy, current ultra-nationalist themes in field of culture and attacks on Western influences have already delayed decisions on cultural exchanges with U.S. and other countries and produced much greater caution on part of decision makers. Criticism of Western music and Antonioni film are probably more relevant to internal political struggles than foreign policy, but Chou and MFA probably see Deputy Secretary's visit as a complicating factor best avoided in China's present atmosphere.

3. While we feel the above mentioned domestic political concerns are overriding factors in PRC decision on Deputy Secretary's visit, we would also not exclude possibility that there may be growing impatience in Peking over pace of development of Sino-U.S. relations. Signals such as appointment of new U.S. Ambassador to Taiwan and indication that we foresee no qualitative change in our relationship with ROC in the near future probably make it more difficult for the architects of the policy of Washington–Peking détente to advocate a high level visit in the absence of likelihood there will emerge concrete evidence of further progress.

---

[1] Source: National Archives, RG 59, Central Foreign Policy Files. Secret; Priority; Exdis.

[2] In telegram 32525 to Beijing, February 18, the Department reported that Han Xu had told Hummel that the dates for Rush's visit were not convenient, but the Chinese would welcome a future visit by Rush at an appropriate time. (Ibid.)

4. Nevertheless, Han Hsu's statement that PRC would "welcome" visit by Deputy Secretary "at appropriate time" is encouraging sign that fundamentals of PRC policy toward U.S. have not changed. Needless to say, we second Han Hsu's welcome for a visit at the earliest feasible time.

Jenkins

---

73. Memorandum From the President's Assistant for National Secretary Affairs (Kissinger) to President Nixon[1]

Washington, March 11, 1974.

SUBJECT

Withdrawal of US Forces on Taiwan

State and Defense have studied the question of when to withdraw the most significant part of our forces from Taiwan—[*less than 1 line not declassified*] our two F–4 squadrons [*1 line not declassified*].[2] Removal of these forces will reduce our presence on the island to about 2800 men who could all be termed logistics, support, and communications personnel. I originally believed all these moves could be accomplished by the end of 1974—without liability to the GRC.

However, removing the second F–4 squadron by the end of this year would create serious problems for GRC Prime Minister Chiang Ching-Kuo. Even if suitable replacement aircraft (F–5Es) were diverted to the GRC (from *both* Korea and Vietnam), his Air Force could not assimilate them due to training problems, and in the interim his air defense capability would be substantially degraded. The spirit if not the letter of our Enhance Plus agreement with the GRC[3] would be called

---

[1] Source: National Archives, Nixon Presidential Materials, NSC Institutional Files (H-Files), Box H–245, National Security Decision Memoranda, NSDM 248. Top Secret; Sensitive. Sent for action. Kennedy, Smyser, and Solomon sent this memorandum to Kissinger on March 7, with the recommendation that he sign and send it to the President. (Ibid.) A stamped notation at the top of the page indicates the President did see it.

[2] On December 5, 1973, Hummel sent Kissinger a memorandum on the withdrawal of U.S. forces on Taiwan. (Ibid.) William P. Clements, the Deputy Secretary of Defense, sent Kissinger a February 20, 1974, memorandum, on the withdrawal of U.S. F–4 squadrons from Taiwan. (Washington National Records Center, OSD Files: FRC 330–78–0010, Box 3, China Nats, 320.2, 1974)

[3] The Republic of China had assisted the United States in implementing the "Enhance Plus" program (an effort by the United States to expand and improve the armed forces of

into question, and this could be interpreted in Taipei as forcing on them an agreement made in Peking. The impact of the diversions would also fall heavily on the GVN.

To avoid these problems, State and Defense—with my approval—recommend that you delay withdrawal of the second F–4 squadron for five months, until the end of May 1975. The delay of five months will allow the GRC to train its F–5E pilots and crews while still under a USAF umbrella. Prime Minister Chiang would presumably be able to accommodate this schedule, and we would have more time for diversions, allowing us to depend on planes now earmarked for Korea rather than Vietnam.

Otherwise, the NSDM at Tab A allows us to withdraw other units on Taiwan by the end of this year, and directs CIA and Defense to review US communications and intelligence activities on Taiwan as a basis for making decisions about further personnel reductions on the island.

Recommendation

That you authorize me to sign the NSDM at Tab A,[4] delaying the withdrawal of the second F–4 squadron by five months to May 1975 but withdrawing most of our other units and personnel by the end of 1974; and ordering studies of further reduction in communications and intelligence personnel.[5]

---

the Republic of Vietnam) by providing 48 F–5E aircraft from its active inventory for use in South Vietnam. (Memorandum from Laird to Nixon, January 13; ibid., FRC 330–78–0001, Box 65, China Nats, 091.3, 1973)

[4] See Document 74.

[5] Nixon initialed the Approve option.

---

74.   National Security Decision Memorandum 248[1]

Washington, March 14, 1974.

TO

The Secretary of Defense
The Director of Central Intelligence
The Deputy Secretary of State

---

[1] Source: National Archives, Nixon Presidential Materials, NSC Files, NSC Institutional Files (H-Files), Box H–245, National Security Decision Memoranda, NSDM 248. Top Secret; Sensitive. A copy was sent to the Chairman of the JCS.

SUBJECT

Changes in U.S. Force Levels on Taiwan

Having reviewed the studies and recommendations developed in response to NSSM 171,[2] the President directs the following changes in deployments and status of US forces based on Taiwan:

—withdraw one of the two F–4 squadrons by July 31, 1974, using Peace Basket F–5As to meet the related US obligation to replace 20 of the 48 F–5As borrowed from ROC under Enhance Plus;

—withdraw the second F–4 squadron by May 30, 1975, complying with the related US obligation to provide F–5Es as replacements for 28 of the Enhance Plus F–5As by using diversions of ROK earmarked F–5Es as temporary replacements until ROC co-produced F–5Es are available;

—withdraw our [1½ lines not declassified] on alert status on Taiwan;

—place Tainan Air Base on a caretaker basis, [less than 1 line not declassified] and reduce support personnel as appropriate;

—submit for Presidential review plans to reduce MAAG size, staffing, or structure in consonance with the F–5E program, and;

—submit for Presidential review any change in staffing or structure of Taiwan Defense Command.

To permit determination of force level changes in the intelligence and regional communications activities, the President directs that:

—The Secretary of Defense, in coordination with other agencies as appropriate, review US communications activities on Taiwan in terms of need and recommend changes in mission, manning and organization deemed necessary for greater efficiency and effectiveness.

—The Director of Central Intelligence review and assess the value of all US intelligence activities [1 line not declassified] and recommend changes in mission, requirements, manning and organization considered appropriate to improve efficiency and effectiveness.

These reviews with recommendations are to be submitted by April 15, 1974.

Henry A. Kissinger

---

[2] See footnote 2, Document 48.

75.   Memorandum of Conversation[1]

Washington, March 20, 1974, 4:05–4:25 p.m.

PARTICIPANTS

Han Hsu, Acting Chief, PRC Liaison Office
Chi Chao-chu, Interpreter
Secretary of State Henry A. Kissinger
Winston Lord, Director, Policy Planning Staff, Department of State
Arthur W. Hummel, Jr., Deputy Assistant Secretary for East Asian Affairs
  Department of State

Secretary Kissinger: It's been a long time since I have seen you. Are we ever going to see your Ambassador?

Ambassador Han: I think so.

Secretary Kissinger: I thought we should meet briefly before I go to the Soviet Union so that your Prime Minister will have some idea of what we are doing and to give you some of my views.

First, on my trip to the Soviet Union—I think it will not be a happy trip because we are not in complete agreement about my activities in the Middle East. I keep telling them I am merely following your Vice-Minister's advice. Seriously, they are very much interested in joint activities with us in the Middle East, but we are not. Thus, this will be a difficult subject. We may agree to something on paper that looks like joint action, but it will not be substantive. We have no concrete ideas on this subject. In fact, I will pursue the strategy that I have outlined to you.

Secondly, we will discuss strategic arms limitation. The negotiations have not been making very much progress, and we may discuss some limited subject like multiple warheads. I have no idea of what progress will be achieved, but I don't expect much. We will inform you after my return.

They want to discuss force reductions in Europe. No substantive agreement on this is likely. There may be token progress but nothing of strategic significance. Even that may not be achieved on this visit.

Then on bilateral subjects with the Soviets, we may come to agreement on cooperation on an artificial heart and maybe on another space mission—matters of a technical kind.

At any rate, there will be no great surprises.

---

[1] Source: National Archives, Nixon Presidential Materials, NSC Files, Kissinger Office Files, Box 96, Country Files, Far East, China Exchanges, January 1, 1973–March 31, 1974. Top Secret; Nodis. This meeting was held in the Secretary's office.

What the Soviets want from us is overtly cooperative relations in the Middle East. They have also asked us for a complete ban on nuclear testing which we would then ask others to observe. We will reject this.

These are the major issues with the Soviets. Do you have any questions?

Ambassador Han: No.

Secretary Kissinger: Then on the Middle East, in effect we are pursuing the strategy I discussed with your Prime Minister, to engage the U.S. more directly in order to restrict Soviet influence. We also wish to break up the ties between Iraq and Syria. We are making some progress in that matter. We hope we may get a disengagement agreement with Syria by the end of April. We have Israeli representatives coming here, the Syrians will come later, and then I may go back for another Middle East trip. You can see that your Vice-Minister has started me on a course of very extensive activities. Will he be coming to the special session of the General Assembly?

Ambassador Han: We have no news now.

Secretary Kissinger: On the subject of Europe, your Prime Minister should know that there is less here than meets the eye. We must frankly state our views but that does not change the basic structure of our relations.

On our bilateral relations with you, I want the Prime Minister to know that we are prepared to proceed along the implications of the last communiqué we signed in Peking.[2] We would be prepared to discuss that here, or if later this year. I should make my annual visit to Peking to pursue the subject then.

But I would like your government to know that what I have discussed with your Prime Minister is unchanged with respect to basic orientation,[3] and we have understood the changes he made in the draft last year to which he specially called our attention.[4]

One matter that I had mentioned to him in Peking was certain withdrawals we would carry out with regard to Taiwan this year,

---

[2] See footnote 7, Document 60.

[3] On February 16, Solomon sent Kissinger a memorandum that detected "a number of public and private signals which seem to constitute a low-key warning to us about future problems in the development of U.S.–PRC relations." Solomon suggested "you may wish to consider some form of personal message to Premier Chou giving him whatever reassurances you can about our commitment to follow through on normalization, despite the President's domestic difficulties." (National Archives, Nixon Presidential Materials, NSC Files, Kissinger Office Files, Box 96, Country Files, Far East, China Exchanges, November 1, 1973–March 31, 1974)

[4] Kissinger reported to Nixon on his discussions with Zhou on the communiqué; see Document 62.

F–4s, Phantoms. There is going to be a delay of a few months in the withdrawal of the second squadron. It will be withdrawn by May of 1975 for technical reasons. We are just delaying somewhat the schedule that I gave the Prime Minister by a few months. But they will definitely both be withdrawn and the first one is coming out by the end of June, on schedule.

Also, you might tell our friends in Peking that we are working on the Korean matter in the spirit of the discussions we had last year.

Ambassador Han: Those are the major items I have. Some of these things were mentioned in the discussions with the Prime Minister. We were not there and do not know about this. We will report what you have said.

Secretary Kissinger: One other subject. India has come to us with a desire to improve relations with the United States in order not to be so tied to the Soviet Union. We may be starting discussions with them to see how this may be brought about. We will keep you informed of any developments. We are likely to have some technical discussions with them on economic relations and other things. No military matters obviously. But our strategy is to attempt to wean them away from the Soviet Union.

You have not been back to Peking since you arrived in Washington?

Ambassador Han: No.

Secretary Kissinger: I have been there more often than you have. I am getting practically to be an Arab. When the Foreign Minister greets me at the airport next time, I may embrace him.

I remember with great pleasure my conversations with Chairman Mao and Prime Minister Chou. We are proceeding in the spirit of those discussions. Please communicate my best wishes to our friends in Peking.

Ambassador Han: Thank you. I will do that.

Secretary Kissinger: Are you properly treated here?

Ambassador Han: Yes, all right.

Secretary Kissinger: (Pointing across the room) What do you think of this piece of art?

Ambassador Han: (Laughing). I don't understand it.

Secretary Kissinger: That's why I have it here.

Ambassador Han: I have seen it in several of the published photographs taken in your office.

Secretary Kissinger: (Pointing to art object on shelf) Perhaps you have noticed that. That was given to me as a gift by your government when I visited in November.

Ambassador Han: We will make a full report of what you have said. I know you are very busy.

76.   Memorandum of Conversation[1]

Washington, April 12, 1974, 2:30 p.m.

PARTICIPANTS

> Leonard Unger, United States Ambassador to the Republic of China
> Maj Gen Brent Scowcroft, USAF, Deputy Assistant to the President for National Security Affairs
> Richard H. Solomon, Senior Staff Member, NSC
> John A. Froebe, Jr., Staff Member, NSC

SUBJECT

> Reaction to Ambassador Unger's Appointment, Future Moves in U.S.–PRC Relations, Present Problems with Taipei, ROC–Soviet Contacts, Use of Backchannel

Reaction to Ambassador Unger's Appointment[2]

Ambassador Unger: I am going to a land neighboring that which I just came from—Thailand. I appreciate the opportunity to get from you whatever background and guidance that I haven't gotten elsewhere.

General Scowcroft: You certainly must have most of it by now. I'm delighted to see you. Your name is famous.

Ambassador Unger: It has become famous in Taipei but I don't take that as flattery. I know they are pleased. It gets them out of the jitters.

General Scowcroft: It has helped in that respect. But it has caused concern farther north.

Ambassador Unger: How seriously does Peking take that?

General Scowcroft: With slight disappointment at what they hoped would be a continuing decline in our relations with Taiwan.

Ambassador Unger: But they know that our relations with the ROC will continue. They might even see some benefit in having someone of prestige there, since he would be better able to work constructively with Taipei.

General Scowcroft: On the other hand, they probably face some domestic pressure on the Taiwan question. Although Chou and Mao can look at this question philosophically, they have problems with their own domestic constituencies.

---

[1] Source: National Archives, Nixon Presidential Materials, NSC Files, Box 524, Country Files, Far East, China, Vol. XII, Oct 25, 1973–. Secret; Sensitive. The meeting took place in the White House. According to an attached April 19 memorandum by Froebe, Scowcroft approved this memorandum of conversation.

[2] Leonard Unger was appointed Ambassador to the Republic of China on March 14 and presented his credentials on May 25.

Ambassador Unger: In the past month the PRC has seemed to be reconsidering their approach to the Taiwan issue.

General Scowcroft: The leadership in Peking can't appear to be caving in to the imperialists. Dick Solomon, as our tea-leaf reader, might have something to add on this subject.

Mr. Solomon: Your appointment to Taipei probably has impacted on their current domestic leadership problem. The evidence is seen in the different way they handled this year the celebration of the February 28, 1947 uprising on Taiwan. Last year they talked of "peaceful" liberation. This year they pulled back somewhat from that formulation. We believe that there is a policy dispute in Peking over the Taiwan question. We also have other signals that they are concerned.

General Scowcroft: We have been walking this tightrope on our China policy. We are firm that we will maintain our commitment to the ROC. At the same time, we will continue to normalize relations with Peking.

Advance Notice to Ambassador Unger on New Moves with Peking

Ambassador Unger: In Taipei I would like to have maximum information for myself. I would also like to have maximum advance consultation on new moves toward Peking. I realize that this may not always be possible. But some advance consultation might help ameliorate any ROC tendencies to make trouble.

General Scowcroft: We will do whatever we can.

Ambassador Unger: I know how some Washington decisions are made, and that advance consultation is not always possible. But I believe that in this case whenever advance consultation is possible it would help keep the ROC from becoming embittered and would help keep them on the reservation.

General Scowcroft: We wll make every effort to keep you informed. We would also appreciate your evaluation of their reactions.

Ambassador Unger: Yes. I consider this a standard part of my task out there.

General Scowcroft: It would help us walk this narrow line.

Present Problems in U.S.–ROC Relations

Ambassador Unger: On the program side, there does not seem to be a great deal going on. Our big package was what Ambassador Mc-Conaughy put before the ROC just before he left.[3] I feel that we will get through this all right.

---

[3] Unger is referring to the changes to the U.S. force levels on Taiwan; see Document 74.

General Scowcroft: I agree—but they will probably try to extract a price.

Ambassador Unger: But if the price is not too steep, I would hope that we could accommodate them wherever possible.

Similarly, on the economic side if the present well-being can be maintained, this will reduce the political complications. We have, for example, the recent Exim Bank delays in processing loans for the ROC.

General Scowcroft (to Mr. Froebe): Is the Exim Bank still holding up the loans?

Mr. Froebe: I will have to check on that, sir.

General Scowcroft: I believe Exim is beginning to move again on these loans.

Japan–PRC Civil Air Agreement

Mr. Solomon: Another current issue of interest to us is the Japan–PRC Air Agreement.

Ambassador Unger: I believe we should continue to stay out of that arrangement.

General Scowcroft (to Mr. Froebe): Where does this stand at the present time?

Mr. Froebe: The negotiations now seem to be in their last week or two. A Japanese team is now in Peking winding up the negotiations. Prime Minister Tanaka seems determined to push through to a quick conclusion, both because he wants to show continued progress in normalizing relations with Peking and because he wants to clear this away as a source of dispute within his own Liberal Democratic Party. His objectives also relate to the major political test he faces in next June's Upper House elections.

General Scowcroft: How far apart are the two at this point?

Mr. Froebe: The crunch issues are still the two involving Japan's air links with Taiwan—China Airlines' continued use of that name and retention of ground facilities at Japan's civil airfields. The PRC has shown some flexibility on these issues, but at this point the Tanaka Government seems disposed to move to close the gap on these issues and to confront the ROC with a fait accompli. The ROC at the same time is attempting to face the Tanaka Government down. According to a ticker report today, the ROC Foreign Minister issued a five-point statement taking a fairly hard line and threatening unspecified consequences, although his language was sufficiently ambiguous to allow Taipei a face-saving way out.

Mr. Solomon: Interestingly, Finance Minister Fukuda within the past few weeks has come out publicly in support of Tanaka's approach on the Civil Air Agreement.

Mr. Froebe: I may not have seen that report, but almost all other reporting has indicated that Fukuda has scrupulously maintained a neutral position on this question, presumably in order not to alienate the support of some right-wing groups in the LDP such as the Seirankai.

Mr. Solomon: The airline name issue involved in this question is quite important in traditional Confucian terms—the rectification of names.

Giving GRC Better Idea of Future Course of U.S.–PRC Relations

Ambassador Unger: The GRC probably would like me to speak to the question of the future pace of our normalization of relations with Peking. I am hoping to talk with the Secretary before leaving and to get his guidance on this score.

General Scowcroft: Yes—although I'm not sure how specific he would be willing to be on this subject.

Ambassador Unger: I don't believe that I have to break new ground. We are still hewing to the basic decision that we took at the time of the Shanghai Communiqué. As long as there are no sharp departures, I believe that my existence in Taipei will be reasonably calm.

General Scowcroft: We here will try to keep calm and quiet—although we can't commit ourselves in advance.

Ambassador Unger: Are there any particular questions that I should watch?

General Scowcroft: I don't believe so. I think you understand very well what we are about. We have a basic strategy, the tactics of which must be adapted according to the circumstances of the particular moment.

ROC–Soviet Contacts

Mr. Solomon: I would suggest that Soviet interest in Taiwan might be worth keeping an eye on. We have learned through a special channel which might not have come to your notice that the ROC Embassy Minister Counselor for Political Affairs recently expressed interest in contacting Federenko (former Soviet Ambassador to the UN) through an academic intermediary here. I don't think this business was developed to the point of a meeting, however. In addition, the Soviets last December invited a ROC national who resides in the U.S. to Moscow, where they indicated their interest in further contacts with Taiwan.[4] You may also be aware that the Soviets seem to be playing games in South Korea as well.

Ambassador Unger: I know that Ambassador McConaughy's judgment is that it would be exceedingly unlikely that Premier Chiang

---

[4] See footnote 5, Document 67.

Ching-kuo would authorize any probes with the Soviet Union. Nevertheless, I agree that we must watch this aspect of the question.

Use of Backchannel

Just on procedures—I have not asked for a meeting with the President because I didn't feel this was necessary at this point.

General Scowcroft: At this point, probably not. But it might be useful in the future. You are enough of a celebrity to make this inadvisable at present.

Ambassador Unger: But if I feel it might be necessary in the future, I will come in to you to that effect.

General Scowcroft: When are you leaving?

Ambassador Unger: April 28. I will be in the Department through next week. Following that, I plan to spend a couple of days in San Francisco to see people at the Asia Foundation and other institutions there. In Hawaii I intend to see Admiral Gayler. That will get me to Taipei no later than May 4 or 5.

General Scowcroft: Any time that you want to use a backchannel feel free to do so. If for example you want to sound us out on something informally, this will enable you to do so without getting the wide circulation that usual State channels would involve.

Ambassador Unger: Very good. As you know, I have some experience with this from Bangkok.

General Scowcroft: You could also use a backchannel if you want to get to the Secretary on something that you did not want to have such wide distribution.

(After closing amenities, Ambassador Unger took his leave of General Scowcroft.)

---

77.   **Memorandum From Richard H. Solomon of the National Security Council Staff to Secretary of State Kissinger**[1]

Washington, April 12, 1974.

SUBJECT

The PRC and Termination of the U.N. Command in Korea

---

[1] Source: National Archives, Nixon Presidential Materials, NSC Files, Kissinger Office Files, Box 96, Country Files, Far East, China Exchanges, April 1–August 8, 1974. Top Secret; Sensitive. Sent for action.

You will recall that last summer, in preparing our position on the Korean issue for the fall session of the U.N. General Assembly, you indicated to PRC officials that we would be willing to reconsider the future of the U.N. Command (UNC) if UNCURK were dissolved in a non-contentious manner. On June 19, 1973 you handed a note to Ambassador Huang Chen[2] which contained the following paragraph:

Following the 28th session to the U.N. General Assembly, the United States will be prepared to discuss ways in which the question of the U.N. Command might be resolved, with the understanding that any adjustment of security arrangements will not result in a diminution of the security situation on the Korean Peninsula.

The PRC in fact played an important role in managing the Korean issue at the General Assembly session in November in such a manner that UNCURK died a quiet death. Thus, the Chinese undoubtedly expect some indication from us of our intentions regarding the future of UNC. Indeed, as noted below, both the North Koreans and the Chinese have already staked out initial positions on the UNC in public statements issued late last month.

The USG position on the future of the U.N. Command is embodied in NSDM 251, which you signed on March 29.[3] It directs that we seek ROK concurrence to a substitute arrangement in place of the UNC which would contain the following elements:

—Substitution of U.S. and ROK military commanders for the Commander-in-Chief United Nations Command as our side's signatory to the 1953 Korean Armistice Agreement. The ROK and North Korean representatives should then become the principal members of the Military Armistice Commission.

—Tacit acceptance by the other side of a continued U.S. force presence in South Korea for at least the short term, in return for a Shanghai-type communiqué committing ourselves to reduce and ultimately withdraw U.S. forces as the security situation on the Peninsula is stabilized.

—A non-aggression pact between the two Koreas.

—U.N. Security Council endorsement of the agreed-upon package of substitute security arrangements.

—Avoidance of other changes in the Armistice Agreement.

Once the ROK has agreed to these points (or we have negotiated a mutually acceptable alternative arrangement based on them), we

---

[2] See Document 37.

[3] Material on NSDM 251 is in National Archives, Nixon Presidential Materials, NSC Files, NSC Institutional Files (H-Files), Box H–246, National Security Decision Memoranda, NSDM 251.

would pursue a two-track negotiating strategy based on Seoul carrying the burden of contacts with Pyongyang, while the U.S. attempts to backstop the ROK and place constraints on Pyongyang through consultations with Peking.

Ambassador Habib presented our negotiating proposal to Foreign Minister Kim Dong Jo on April 9. He expects agreement with Seoul on a package proposal which could be presented to Pyongyang and Peking "within a few weeks." While you thus may not want to indicate to Teng and Ch'iao in great detail the contents of our proposal pending agreement with the ROK, it seems important that you give them a clear signal that we are moving on this issue. In addition, you may wish to give them a general feel of what we have in mind regarding an alternative arrangement to the UNC. A series of talking points on this subject written from the above perspective are included at the end of this memo.[4]

While Peking was decidedly helpful to us last fall in handling the Korean issue at the U.N., the unsettled state of China's domestic political scene and the more strident tone of her recent foreign policy statements have injected some uncertainty into our estimate of what role Peking may be willing or able to play on the UNC issue over the coming months. On March 27 the *People's Daily* indirectly expressed support for a proposal put forward by North Korean Foreign Minister Ho Tam two days earlier calling for a peace treaty to be negotiated directly between North Korea and the United States. The PRC editorial *directly* supported the following position:

The U.S. government should remove the beret of "UN Forces" from the U.S. troops stationed in South Korea, pull out lock, stock, and barrel together with all their arms and equipment, stop its military assistance to the Pak Chong-hui clique of South Korea, and cease instigating this clique to make savage provocations against the northern half of the republic.

Our guess is that Peking will respond in generally favorable terms to our alternate arrangement for abolition of the UNC if it can be presented to Pyongyang as a transitional arrangement which would hold out some possibility for the eventual realization of North Korea's maximum goal of a complete U.S. withdrawal from Korea.

The North Koreans have sought to press the idea of a peace treaty negotiated between Pyongyang and Washington by appealing directly to our Congress for support. Pyongyang's observer mission to the U.N. made attempts in early April to get our U.N. mission to transmit an official proposal from their Supreme People's Assembly to the Congress. USUN turned aside the North Korean appeal for assistance in

---

[4] Attached but not printed.

transmitting the proposal. You should indicate to the Chinese that North Korea's attempts to deal with the U.S. directly will not be welcomed until there is a reciprocal willingness on the part of Peking to have contact with Seoul, and that Pyongyang's efforts to sow distrust between the U.S. and ROK will not create a climate conducive to the negotiation of new security arrangements between North and South Korea.

Pyongyang will probably attempt to have the Korean issue debated in the General Assembly again this year in order to apply pressure on the UNC issue. You should emphasize to the Chinese our belief that it will be most effective if North and South work out their differences in direct, confidential talks rather than polarizing the situation by public debate in an international forum. Thus, we believe it is most useful to progress on this issue if Seoul and Pyongyang can reach agreement on an alternative to the UNC in private talks. Their agreed position can then be endorsed by the U.N. Security Council.

---

78.   Memorandum of Conversation[1]

New York City, April 14, 1974, 8:05–11:00 p.m.

PARTICIPANTS

Teng Hsiao-p'ing, Vice Premier of the PRC
Ch'iao Kuan-hua, Vice Foreign Minister of the PRC
Ambassador Huang Hua, PRC Permanent Representative to the UNGA
Chang Han-chih (F) (Acted as Interpreter)
Lo Hsu (F) (Acted as Notetaker)
Kuo Chia-ting (Acted as Notetaker)

Henry A. Kissinger, Secretary of State
Joseph P. Sisco, Under Secretary of State
Brent Scowcroft, Major General, National Security Council

---

[1] Source: National Archives, Nixon Presidential Materials, NSC Files, Kissinger Office Files, Box 96, Country Files, Far East, China Exchanges, April 1–August 8, 1974. Top Secret; Sensitive; Exclusively Eyes Only. The meeting took place at the Secretary's suite at the Waldorf Astoria Hotel. On April 12, Kissinger received a memorandum from Solomon discussing the political background of Deng Xiaoping's trip. Solomon suggested that his trip was part of a campaign to make China the leader of the "have not" nations. In addition, Deng was "to take the temperature of the Sino-U.S. relationship while in New York." (Ibid.) The same day, Lord and Hummel also sent Kissinger a memorandum in anticipation of his meeting with Deng. (Ibid.) All brackets are in the original.

Winston Lord, Director, Policy Planning Staff, Department of State
Arthur W. Hummel, Jr., Deputy Assistant Secretary (EA) Department of State
Charles W. Freeman, Jr. (EA/PRCM), Department of State (Acted as Notetaker)

SUBJECT

Secretary's Dinner for the Vice Premier of the Peoples Republic of China

(The Chinese party arrived at 8:05 and were escorted to suite 35A by Mr. Freeman. When the party was seated, the conversation began.)

Secretary Kissinger: It is a very great pleasure to meet you, Mr. Vice Premier. I understand that the Vice Foreign Minister has taken up the same step recently as I . . .[2]

(At this point the press was admitted to take photographs and the conversation was broken off briefly.)

Vice Premier Teng: This is a very large group of press we have here.

Secretary Kissinger: They are asking me to shake hands. (Shakes hands with the Vice Premier and the Vice Foreign Minister.) They want us all three to shake hands at once. Your photographers are much better disciplined than ours, I'm afraid.

Vice Premier Teng: We shouldn't listen to their orders.

Secretary Kissinger: But we have to listen to their orders. Otherwise they will print the worst picture that they take.

(The press was escorted out of the room.)

How long will you be staying in the U.S.?

Vice Premier Teng: We will be leaving the day after tomorrow.

Secretary Kissinger: Will the Vice Foreign Minister be going with you?

Vice Premier Teng: We will be traveling together.

Secretary Kissinger: How will you be going? By way of the Pacific or by way of Europe?

Vice Premier Teng: We will be going through Europe. Do you mind if I smoke?

Secretary Kissinger: Please go ahead. I have never taken to smoking myself, I'm afraid.

Vice Premier Teng: You've missed something. You ought to try it.

Secretary Kissinger: I concentrate on other vices. How is your back coming along, Ambassador Huang?

Ambassador Huang: So-so.

Secretary Kissinger: Have you used the doctor that I arranged for you?

---

[2] Qiao, like Kissinger, had recently gotten married.

Ambassador Huang: I am keeping him on standby.

Secretary Kissinger: He's afraid if he uses our doctor he will install a microphone in his back.

Vice Premier Teng: I believe of all who are present here tonight your earliest acquaintance was Ambassador Huang.

Secretary Kissinger: Yes. He met me at the Peking Airport in 1971. He may have forgotten this but he gave me some very valuable lessons on how to negotiate. When we meet with the Russians to discuss a communiqué, they suggest that each side put forward its maximum position and that we then try to discuss a way of bridging the difference. But Ambassador Huang suggested that we write our real positions down at the outset, and that in this way we could more easily reach agreement. And it was as he said it would be.

Vice Premier Teng: You've had quite a few years of experience in dealing with the Soviet Union.

Secretary Kissinger: Yes. Quite a few years. It is always very fatiguing and always the same. On the first day the atmosphere is very pleasant. On the second day there is an explosion. On the last day, two hours before the departure, when they see that we will not abandon our position, they become accommodating and pleasant. It is always the same.

Vice Foreign Minister Ch'iao: (In English) Dialectics!

Secretary Kissinger: Well, I don't want to get into that with the Vice Foreign Minister. You still owe me a poem.

Vice Foreign Minister Ch'iao: That's right.

Vice Premier Teng: I also have quite a bit of experience with the Soviet Union.

Secretary Kissinger: Oh, in what years?

Vice Premier Teng: Well, I have been to the Soviet Union seven times.

Secretary Kissinger: Then you have been there once more than I have. Tell me, are they always so very difficult? Do they yell at their allies as well as at others?

Vice Premier Teng: In my experience we could never reach agreement.

Secretary Kissinger: We can reach agreement but only very slowly. Their idea of arms control is that we should start from the base which we have now, but they should have five years in which to do what they want.

(At this point Mrs. Kissinger entered the room and was introduced to the guests.)

We've just been talking about negotiations with the Soviet Union. The Vice Premier has been to the Soviet Union on seven occasions. His experience has been that the Soviets never agree to anything. We have reached some agreements with them.

Vice Premier Teng: You are more advanced than I am.

Secretary Kissinger: But I know that, now that I have explained all this, the next time I am in Peking the Vice Foreign Minister will yell at me just to see what the result is.

Vice Premier Teng: You must have had quite a few quarrels with him by now.

Secretary Kissinger: Negotiations with him are always hard but reasonable. And we can reach agreement. For example, on the Shanghai Communiqué, we spent many, many nights going over the details of the language together.

Vice Premier Teng: Each side should speak its mind. That is what is most important.

Secretary Kissinger: But in those negotiations I had had so much mao tai that I was negotiating in Chinese.

Vice Premier Teng: Then you have that in common with the Vice Foreign Minister. He also likes to drink mao tai.

Vice Foreign Minister Ch'iao: If you had drunk a lot, it was not my fault.

Secretary Kissinger: But you were not defeated in those negotiations.

(Pause)

You know, I have had some complaints from Mr. Gromyko about your speech the other day.[3]

Vice Premier Teng: Was he very dissatisfied?

Secretary Kissinger: He felt he was being attacked and he wanted me to answer on both our behalfs.

Vice Foreign Minister Ch'iao: (In English) Very clever tactics!

Secretary Kissinger: But even if you listen very carefully to what I am going to say tomorrow, you will not hear much criticism.

Vice Premier Teng: I got acquainted with Mr. Gromyko in 1957 for the first time.

Secretary Kissinger: Has he changed much since then? What is your opinion?

Vice Premier Teng: He is not one of the people who decide policy in the Soviet Union.

Secretary Kissinger: That's right. In my experience he has been used as a straight man for Brezhnev. He never expressed an opinion

---

[3] A translation of Deng's UN speech, in which he condemned both superpowers, is excerpted in *The New York Times*, April 12, 1974, p. 12.

himself on the negotiations except on technical matters. Lately he has become somewhat more assertive because he is now on the Politburo.

Vice Premier Teng: Brezhnev was also not one who decided policy before 1964.

Secretary Kissinger: Correct. And he was not supposed to understand foreign policy at that time. After what he did to Khruchshev he has been very, very careful about going away on vacation.

(The party went into the dining room and was seated.)

Whenever you need any advice, you just ask Mr. Sisco.

Ambassador Huang: Mr. Sisco is an expert on the Middle East.

Secretary Kissinger: I'm sure that you know all my associates here tonight. Sisco handles political affairs for us. He is the number three man in the Department of State. And, of course, you know General Scowcroft of the National Security Council. Commander Howe, you remember, worked for him. I wanted him here because he handles all matters connected with my work at the White House. And Mr. Sisco is my alibi on the Middle East.

Vice Foreign Minister Ch'iao: You mean if you achieve success, it belongs to you but if you fail, the failure is Sisco's!

Secretary Kissinger: But the one who is really responsible for what has happened in the Middle East is the Vice Foreign Minister. Last year we talked about the Middle East question, and I have followed the outlines of that conversation since in what we have done.

Vice Foreign Minister Ch'iao: Last time I met you, we talked according to what Chairman Mao had said to the Egyptian Vice President. You have two hands. You should use both. Give one to Israel and one to the other side.

Secretary Kissinger: We have been following the policy we discussed then.

Vice Premier Teng: That is true. Both hands should be used.

Secretary Kissinger: Exactly!

Vice Premier Teng: In your view is there any hope for disengagement now between Syria and Israel?

Secretary Kissinger: I hope that in the next three weeks we will make considerable progress on this. As you know, I talked yesterday with the Chief of the Syrian Military Intelligence and today I talked to the Israeli Ambassador. In about two weeks, I will go to the Middle East and try to do for the Syrians and the Israelis what I did with Israel and Egypt. And for your information, the Syrian has told me that after disengagement has been achieved, they will turn towards Iraq and work to reduce the Soviet Union's presence in Iraq. You remember that I discussed this with Chairman Mao and Premier Chou as a long-term strategy.

Vice Premier Teng: Exactly so! President Asad of Syria has visited Moscow lately. What influence do you think that will produce on the situation?

Secretary Kissinger: The Soviet Union has been very eager to play a major role in the negotiations, and they have been conducting themselves with the delicacy for which they are well known. For example, when I was in Moscow, Brezhnev yelled at me for three hours, saying that they must take part in the negotiations. The difficulty is that the Arabs and Israelis do not want the Soviets in the negotiations. While I was in Moscow I sent Asad a telegram asking what he wanted. He replied he wanted the same handling as we had given in the case of the Egyptians. I believe he went to Moscow to balance off the visit of his representative to Washington. But we have no impression of any change in the Syrian position. In fact, Gromyko suggested that I should meet him in Damascus, but when I asked the Syrian in Washington what he thought about this, he said he was not in favor of it. Everything now depends on whether we can succeed in getting the Israelis to agree to withdraw from part of the Golan Heights. (*Note:* The Chinese interpreter omitted the words "part of" in the Chinese.)

Secretary Kissinger: This is mao tai. Mr. Vice Premier, we welcome you to New York. It is a very great pleasure to see you here.

Mr. Sisco: This is the first time I've had it.

Secretary Kissinger: If you were like the Vice Foreign Minister you would drink it bottoms-up every time.

Mr. Lord: I believe that with mao tai we could solve the energy crisis!

Vice Premier Teng: But could we also solve the raw materials crisis?

Secretary Kissinger: I think if we drink enough mao tai we can solve anything.

Vice Premier Teng: Then, when I go back to China, we must take steps to increase our production of it.

Secretary Kissinger: You know, when the President came back from China he wanted to show his daughter how potent mao tai was. So he took out a bottle and poured it into a saucer and lit it, but the glass bowl broke and the mao tai ran over the table and the table began to burn! So you nearly burned down the White House!

Actually, in about two weeks I'll be in the Middle East again.

Vice Foreign Minister Ch'iao: Do you think that the change in the Israeli Cabinet will affect your mission?

Secretary Kissinger: It will make it more difficult. I have relied most in the past on Madame Meir and Defense Minister Dayan. Both now will be replaced. Nevertheless, I believe we will succeed. It is, of course, an extremely difficult negotiation because the Israelis are very difficult to deal with. But if the Syrian disengagement succeeds, then we can go back to the Egyptians and seek a peace agreement. The Egyptians are very determined to separate themselves from Moscow as much as possible. Do you have much contact with the Egyptians? Have you seen them recently?

Vice Premier Teng: We've not seen them in recent months. It seems as though your success to date is mainly the result of your method of using both hands. Will it be the same with Syria?

Secretary Kissinger: Syria does not have quite as strong a leadership, so it is different. It will be more difficult but we hope for success.

Ambassador Huang: What is the attitude of the Syrian Defense Minister, Mr. Mustafa Talas?

Secretary Kissinger: I do not believe I have met him. I know the Foreign Minister and the President, of course, and the Chief of Intelligence. It is possible that the Defense Minister would be more pro-Soviet. All Syrian military equipment comes from the Soviet Union. But, they have to pay for it! Our strategy is that after settling the Syrian problem, we will go back to the Egyptians for a peace agreement. And then, after that, we will go back to Syria.

Vice Foreign Minister Ch'iao: The key point is that we hope you will give more word to the Israelis so that they will be persuaded to withdraw from the Golan Heights.

Secretary Kissinger: We have to do this in stages. What we want to do now is to withdraw from part of Golan. This way we can get them to do it. If we ask too much at this point, this would lead to a stalemate, and the Soviets would come back in. We do not support the Israeli position on staying on the Golan Heights.

Vice Premier Teng: This is a very important point.

Secretary Kissinger: We have not supported it.

Vice Premier Teng: Otherwise, there would be no progress and then the Soviets would certainly come back in.

Secretary Kissinger: If we are successful in these disengagement talks, we can hope to reduce Soviet influence in Syria, as we did in Egypt. And, we intend to do more with Egypt.

Vice Premier Teng: If the Soviet Union succeeds in Syria, then the Soviets will have three places in the Middle East on which they can rely: Syria, Iraq and Southern Yemen.

Secretary Kissinger: We are trying to prevent this from happening in Syria. And, we are already working on Southern Yemen. We think the Egyptians will help us in this.

Vice Premier Teng: Chairman Mao touched on this point in his discussions with you. Our attitude is that, on the one hand we support the Arabs, but, on the other hand, we work with you to fix the bear in the north together with you.

Secretary Kissinger: That is exactly our position. If we can get into a position in which we can disagree on the Middle East, that would show there had been progress. Afterwards, that is after there has been a settlement, of course, we can expect to have some disagreements.

(The Chinese interpreter had some difficulty with this sentence and there was a brief discussion in Chinese over how to interpret it.)

Secretary Kissinger: I have not seen Ambassador Huang Chen since he returned, but I plan to see him next week.

Vice Premier Teng: There has been no change in the relationship we have so far. (*Note:* The Vice Premier's original statement did not contain the words "so far." These two words were added by the Chinese interpreter.)

Secretary Kissinger: We continue to attach the utmost importance to good and friendly relations between the United States and the Peoples Republic of China. We intend to pursue the course of normalization of our relations, as I have said in my talks with Chairman Mao and Premier Chou.[4]

Vice Premier Teng: This policy, and the principles on which it is based, are personally supported by Chairman Mao. I believe that from your two long talks with Chairman Mao you ought to have this understanding. The last time you met him you talked for three hours, I believe.

Secretary Kissinger: We went into great detail in those discussions, so I never pay any attention to the newspaper accounts of our relationship. In our experience, the Chinese word always counts.

(The Secretary toasted the Vice Foreign Minister.)

Vice Premier Teng: Now that you have drunk all this mao tai, your speech tomorrow is bound to be excellent.

Secretary Kissinger: It will be moving! I shall probably attack the superpowers! I am glad that the Vice Premier has confirmed what the Vice Foreign Minister has already said to Ambassador Bruce in Peking. Our relationship has not changed.

Vice Premier Teng: I have read the record of your talk with Chairman Mao Tse-tung. It was very explicit. You had a discussion of the relationships between the United States and China from a strategic

---

[4] When Kissinger later recounted this conversation to Nixon over the telephone, he said, "I have the feeling Chou is on the way out. They didn't mention him once during the evening. And every time I brought him up they changed the conversation to Mao." (National Archives, Nixon Presidential Materials, Kissinger Telcons, Box 25, 2 March–April 1974)

point of view. The only difficulty is on where the Soviet strategic focus is. On this point, we have some differences, but these differences do not matter, for practice will show where the true focal point is.

Secretary Kissinger: Exactly. Wherever the first focal point is, the next focal point is obvious. If the focal point is in Europe, then the next is on China. If the focal point is China, then the next one is Europe. If the focal point is on the Middle East, then the next is also obvious.

Vice Premier Teng: In the East we have talked to the Japanese—our Japanese friends—about this. They do not seem to realize this point. They seem to think that the Soviet intentions in the East do not include them. For example, in our discussion of the Tyumen project—the exploitation of oil fields in Siberia—the Japanese said they would have to reconsider their position so as not to offend the Chinese. But they did not really think that their interests would be affected by this development.

Secretary Kissinger: The Japanese do not yet think in strategic terms. They think in commercial terms.

Well, I am particularly glad tonight to see my old friends from China. Speaking from our side, we can confirm every detail of our discussions with Chairman Mao and with Premier Chou, and we can confirm the direction on which our policy is set. We have had some debate with our European allies to make them realize the facts and to be realistic. But this does not influence our long-term strategy. It does not influence our desire to construct a strong Europe. But you, as old friends, understand this. The French have been taking a rather short-term viewpoint. You have talked to them recently, I believe. But this cannot influence the realities of the United States and the Soviet position vis-à-vis Europe. This is nothing but a quarrel within the family.

Vice Premier Teng: Just so. There are minor quarrels, but the unity remains.

Secretary Kissinger: Well said!

Vice Premier Teng: But if you were to show more consideration for the Europeans, would there not be a better result?

Secretary Kissinger: Depends to whom. They are very much divided.

Vice Foreign Minister Ch'iao: What we mean—we are not much qualified to speak on the European question—what I mean is, mostly consideration for France. Speaking frankly, we know that you have some opinions against the French. But must it be so open? That's the first point. The second is that we wonder whether you could show more consideration to the French. They have a very strong sense of self-respect and national pride.

Secretary Kissinger: The problem is that we started out working with France because we have believed the French were in many ways most supportive of Europe and they were the best on this point. So with regard to every move we made in the Middle East we went to the French and got their approval. Then we discovered they were opposing us on every point—every detail—behind our backs. In our last conversation the Vice Foreign Minister said that we have a coordinated strategy. But the French have no strategy, only tactics. So in the Middle East they have been working to undermine us. This is of no advantage to anyone, not even to the French. So we decided that it would be useful to make it public—to bring it out in the open where the issues could be clarified.

Vice Premier Teng: That is good—if it does not continue in the open.

Vice Foreign Minister Ch'iao: I tell you quite frankly that when I read your talk to the wives of the Congressmen I was very alarmed.

Secretary Kissinger: You know, I have never persuaded anyone of what really happened on that occasion. It is the perfect example of what happens in an unplanned ceremony. I arrived at my office and found that I was scheduled to talk to the Congressional wives, so I screamed at my colleagues and objected. But it was on the schedule, so I went to see them. I thought that no three of them could ever agree on what I said and that I would be safe. About two-thirds through the talk I joked that I was glad to see no press there. It was then that I found that there were press there. Everyone thinks this was very carefully planned. But you are right. I do not intend to repeat that particular speech.

(The Secretary rose to give a toast.)

Mr. Vice Premier, Mr. Vice Foreign Minister, Friends:

This is an informal occasion and not one for formal speechmaking. But as I look back on my experience in government, I continue to believe that the most important mission I have engaged in was my first trip to Peking. The normalization of relations between the United States and the Peoples Republic of China is the most important event of our Administration, and it is a major factor in the protection of world peace. Many things have happened in this country and in the world since that first trip, but each time we meet we confirm our commitment to each other. The United States remains committed to all the undertakings and all the strategies which we have discussed. We believe that the progress and independence of the Peoples Republic of China is a fundamental factor in world peace. We appreciate the constructive and frank nature of all our discussions. I would like to express the joy of all my colleagues in welcoming another friend from the Peoples Republic of China.

Now I ask you to drink with me to the health of Chairman Mao, to the health of Premier Chou, to the health of our honored guests here tonight, and to the friendship between the American and Chinese peoples!

(The party was seated.)

(Pause)

I am always at a disadvantage with the Vice Foreign Minister. The Vice Foreign Minister has studied philosophy. And he has studied Hegel, but I have only studied as far as Kant. I am sure that it's all right with the Vice Foreign Minister if I criticize France, but not Germany. He would not let me get away with that!

Vice Premier Teng: Why is there still such a big noise being made about Watergate?

Secretary Kissinger: That is a series of almost incomprehensible events, and the clamor about it is composed of many people who for various reasons oppose the President.

Vice Premier Teng: Chairman Mao told you that we are not happy about this. Such an event in no way affects any part of our relations.

Secretary Kissinger: I assure you we have carried out our foreign policy without regard to the Watergate incident, and we will continue to carry it out regardless of Watergate.

Vice Premier Teng: We do not care much about such an issue.

Secretary Kissinger: In our foreign policy we continue to have very wide support from the American public. When I first met the Prime Minister I spoke of China as the land of mystery. Now the U.S. must seem a very mysterious country.

Vice Premier Teng: Such an issue is really incomprehensible to us.

Secretary Kissinger: It has its roots in the fact that some mistakes were made, but also, when you change many policies, you make many, many enemies.

(The Vice Premier rose.)

Vice Premier Teng: I should like to propose a toast.

First, I should like to thank the Doctor for giving us a dinner with such a warm welcome. Since the President's visit and Dr. Kissinger's visits to China, and since the signing of the Shanghai Communiqué, relations between our two countries can be said to be fine. Of course, our hope is that basing our relations on the Shanghai Communiqué we can continue to develop our relations. I should like to propose a toast to Dr. Kissinger and to the friendship of the American and Chinese peoples.

(Everyone was seated.)

Secretary Kissinger: Of course, we always read a great deal in the Hong Kong papers about Chinese domestic developments.

Vice Premier Teng: There is much news in the newspapers, of course. But it is not reliable at all, as you just said. I touched on this point in my speech the other day at the U.N.

Secretary Kissinger: We do not pay much attention to newspaper reports.

Vice Premier Teng: Doctor, are you familiar with Confucius?

Secretary Kissinger: Well, generally, but not in detail.

Vice Premier Teng: Confucius, in short, was an expert in keeping up the rites, and very conservative. His ideology has been binding the Chinese for over two thousand years. These ideas have a deep influence on the ideology of the people. If we wish to emancipate the people's ideology from old thinking, we must remove Confucius. This is a move to emancipate the people's thinking.

Secretary Kissinger: Our newspapers have said that this is directed against individuals, living individuals, and not against ancient individuals.

Vice Premier Teng: There is some ground in what they say. When you criticize a conservative ideology, then, naturally, it will affect some working staffs—some people who represent the conservative ideology being attacked.

Secretary Kissinger: I have been observing your foreign policy for a long time, and I conclude that it has always been consistent. We, of course, do not comment on your internal policies and your internal situation.

Vice Premier Teng: Those comments in the newspapers are not reliable.

Secretary Kissinger: Of that, I am sure.

(Pause.)

Mr. Gromyko asked me about the situation in China, and I told him we see no change in your foreign policy.

(Pause)

You know, one reason I never take Sisco to China is that I never fail in China, so I don't need him. But I did take one of his associates, Mr. Atherton, last time.

(Pause)

Vice Foreign Minister Ch'iao: [in Chinese to Mr. Freeman] How is your reading of the 24 Dynastic histories coming along?

Mr. Freeman: [in Chinese] I haven't yet finished them. We all have little time for reading now.

Vice Foreign Minister Ch'iao: [in Chinese] Well, nobody could read those books through to the end.

Secretary Kissinger: What is this—a private negotiation going on?

Mr. Freeman: The Vice Foreign Minister asked me whether I had been reading the 24 Dynastic histories, and I was about to tell him that you leave us no time for that kind of reading.

Secretary Kissinger: Yes, they have no time for any reading, not even reading of my instructions. Where are the books kept?

Mr. Freeman: They are in the Department of State library, displayed prominently in the handsome case in which they were stored when the Government of the Peoples Republic of China presented them to us.

Secretary Kissinger: I must go down and see them. Perhaps I will do it this week.

Well, shall we go out to the sitting room and have some coffee and tea?

(The party adjourned to the sitting room.)

The last time I was in this room was when the Arab-Israeli war started. Sisco woke me up at 6:00 a.m. He said, if you can get on the telephone you can perhaps stop it. I thought anyone with this kind of judgment deserved to be promoted.

Vice Foreign Minister Ch'iao: The last time we met here also, didn't we?

Secretary Kissinger: I have this for when I come up to the U.N. Mr. Lord is still working on my speech for tomorrow, but I tell you if I say anything significant at all that will be a mistake.

Vice Foreign Minister Ch'iao: Not because of the mao tai!

Secretary Kissinger: I thought with your permission, Mr. Vice Premier, we might review a few problems. We have already talked about the Middle East, and now I would summarize our discussion as follows: We agree with your assessment that the three Soviet strong points in the Middle East are Syria, Iraq and South Yemen. We are bringing about substantial changes in Egyptian foreign policy. For your information we have reason to believe that the Egyptians will abrogate their treaty with the Soviet Union this year. This is, of course, very confidential. But I have never read a leak in a Chinese newspaper! We will start soon to give some economic assistance to Egypt. We are thinking in terms tentatively of about $250 million and the World Bank at the beginning may add another $200 million. And we are organizing support in Europe for Egypt as well. We are working with Chancellor Brandt on this. Next week, as you know, he will visit Egypt. We are also approaching the British and the Dutch.

The Egyptians may need some help if the Soviet Union cuts off its military assistance. We plan to give some assistance through Saudi Arabia and Kuwait. We hope Yugoslavia will be willing to give the Egyptians some spare parts. I do not know whether China—they would like to build MIGs themselves. It is up to you, but I think they would be responsive to discussion of this point. They are working with us on the South Yemen problem. Syria will work on the Iraq problem, and so will Iran, which is also active in Oman. We think we can reduce Soviet influence in the area systematically.

The Soviets are extremely anxious about our efforts. I may agree with them to some face-saving thing, which would not, however, affect the substance. For example, I may agree to meet Gromyko in Geneva before I go to the Middle East. I will not tell him anything and, in fact, I will not be able to tell him anything because I will not yet have gone to the Middle East. I will do this to prevent them from agitating their supporters in Syria.

I also had a very good talk with Boumediene last week. He was very impressed with his visit to China. This did not surprise me at all. I believe he will also help us in Syria.

That is about where we stand on the Middle East at the moment. I will be going to the Middle East in about two weeks, depending on the situation in Israel. I will probably also go to Iran and to Kuwait and to one or two of the little sheikhdoms in the Persian Gulf. We will probably deepen our bilateral cooperation with Iran. This is all in line with what I have discussed with Chairman Mao and Premier Chou.

Vice Foreign Minister Ch'iao: Where do we stand on the Pakistani tanks? Has the Shah agreed to supply them?

Secretary Kissinger (to Sisco): What is the status of that?

Mr. Sisco: The Shah is looking at it very systematically.

Secretary Kissinger: We are trying to do what we can to modernize their tank inventory.

Vice Foreign Minister Ch'iao: But hasn't Iran helped India recently more than it has helped Pakistan?

(Mr. Lord mentioned to Secretary Kissinger Iran's efforts to ease India's problem on oil prices.)

Secretary Kissinger: It has provided some economic, but not military aid. This has to do with oil and the energy situation. The Shah is a very tough-minded individual.

Vice Foreign Minister Ch'iao: Is there any new situation in Iraq?

Secretary Kissinger: We are leaving them to sit there. We are keeping them occupied so they can't intervene in Syria. We told President Boumediene that at the right moment we were prepared to make a move toward Iraq but it is a little premature at the moment. After Syria is a little closer to us we can approach Iraq.

Vice Premier Teng: When the Vice President of Egypt visited China, we touched on this question of giving some assistance but we never got into details. They did not raise it directly with us.

Secretary Kissinger: Because they are not ready yet.

Vice Foreign Minister Ch'iao: But, they raised the question of light weapons.

Vice Premier Teng: In this respect, our power is very limited.

Secretary Kissinger: We recognize that. Should the Egyptians talk to you? Or do you want to stay out of it?

Vice Premier Teng: We adopted a positive attitude when we talked to them.

Secretary Kissinger: Wouldn't it be better to talk directly with the Egyptians than through us?

Vice Premier Teng: We've kept very good relations with the Egyptians, so that would be easy.

Secretary Kissinger: That is very useful! Very good!

Vice Foreign Minister Ch'iao: Isn't there some way in which you can provide more military help to Pakistan?

Secretary Kissinger: On the military side, we have a domestic problem—the problem of Congressional opposition. But, we are encouraging Iran and attempting to ease Iran's problems in helping them.

Vice Premier Teng: Why has Iran rendered more help to India than to Pakistan?

Secretary Kissinger: That is inconceivable! Is it possible?

Mr. Sisco: No.

Secretary Kissinger: I will look into it.

Mr. Sisco: The Iranians have tried to ease the Indian situation with regard to oil—to calm them down.

Secretary Kissinger: In all my discussions with the Shah he has always considered India a major threat to his security.

Vice Premier Teng: The reality probably is so.

Secretary Kissinger: Yes. But now there is so much money in the Moslem countries we will see what we can do to get Pakistan military aid.

Vice Foreign Minister Ch'iao: Let me be frank with you. Our Pakistani friends feel that the indirect assistance (since you have problems giving them direct assistance) comes too slowly.

Secretary Kissinger: They are right. There are so many legal restrictions which we face. But, we are doing everything which we can.

Vice Premier Teng: I feel that you could do much more.

Secretary Kissinger: If you have some concrete suggestions on how to accomplish that, we would be happy to consider them.

Vice Premier Teng: I have no concrete suggestions. But, we understand that our Pakistani friends are a little anxious.

Secretary Kissinger: You are right. This is the case of a curious and complex situation in our own country.

Vice Foreign Minister Ch'iao: I might mention another problem. In the last few days since we left Peking, the tripartite talks between India, Pakistan and Bangladesh have reached agreement. I wonder how you feel about this. We think this is a good thing. The issue of the Pakistani prisoners has finally been settled.

Secretary Kissinger: We think Bangladesh is not an Indian satellite. When relations are normal between India and Bangladesh, contradictions between them will emerge. I have also always believed that India will live to regret what it did in 1971. Do you plan to establish relations with Bangladesh now?

Vice Premier Teng: There is no obstacle to that now.

Secretary Kissinger: We are trying to move India further away from the Soviets.

Vice Premier Teng: There have always been good relations between the peoples of Bangladesh and China.

Secretary Kissinger: Yes.

Vice Foreign Minister Ch'iao: I have a question. How do you view the current situation between the Soviet Union and India? Are relations looser or has there been no change?

Secretary Kissinger: I think there has not yet been a significant change, but India is trying to loosen its relations with the Soviet Union. It is trying hard to get closer to us. It is my impression that their policies are not so closely coordinated with the Soviet Union as they were before. So, the situation is not like before in that respect.

Vice Premier Teng: How was your trip to Moscow?

Secretary Kissinger: That was the next question I wanted to discuss. You know that the President will be going to Moscow in June. We discussed arrangements for the visit and the agreements we might reach during it. The trip followed the pattern I have described to you. That is, there was a very good first day and the last half day was very good. But, the day and a half in the middle was not so good at all. It is very curious. I have been to the Soviet Union six times. I have always had the experience of being yelled at, but I have never made any concessions after having been yelled at; so I conclude that Mr. Brezhnev does it for the Politburo and not for any concrete purpose.

Vice Premier Teng: Why did they suddenly hold a long session of the Politburo?

Secretary Kissinger: Let me review what is being planned for the Summit. There will not be any major agreements this year, in my opinion. But, we plan agreement in the following areas: First, on medical research, primarily in the area of heart disease. I think this will not change the course of history. Another agreement which we plan is in the area of space flight. As you know, we have planned a joint space flight for 1975. Now we are planning one for 1977. The second agreement I wanted to mention is on the exchange of long-term economic information. This is called a long-term economic agreement, but it does not involve any quantities. Just an exchange of statistics.

They have proposed to us also that we agree to stop all underground testing and appeal to all other countries to stop. We totally rejected a joint appeal to any other country. We may agree, however, to limit underground tests but not to ban them. We think this will not affect the Peoples Republic of China, since you do not test much underground anyway.

Vice Premier Teng: Even if you signed an agreement with the Soviet Union that would not affect us.

Secretary Kissinger: Whatever we do with them will be bilateral, and there will be no appeal to the Peoples Republic of China.

Vice Foreign Minister Ch'iao: (In English) You have done it right.

Secretary Kissinger: The level of permitted underground tests which we fix will be set above 100 kilotons. Frankly, we have set a limit above what we want to test. Since we hadn't planned to test anything above that limit anyway, there will be no effect on us. This is not a major move. That leaves the Strategic Arms Limitation Talks. Oh, one other agreement which they have proposed to us is not to build—you see under our Strategic Arms Limitation Agreement, each side can build two defensive sites. They have suggested that we not build the second. At the moment each side has one.

In the field of Strategic Arms Limitations, I personally do not expect any agreement. The position of the two sides is too far apart. In effect, what the Soviet Union has proposed to us is that they give us a limit but not have one immediately for themselves. The limit they have picked for us is what we already have in our arsenal. Their limit, which they propose for themselves, is what they will have in five years. On the basis of this proposal, no agreement is possible. There would have to be a radical change in positions for an agreement to take place. I think that is unlikely. So this is why I have been speaking as I have to the press about this question.

Incidentally, you may have read in the American newspapers that we are behind the Soviet Union in strategic weapons. This is nonsense. In the number of warheads, that is, the number of warheads in our strategic forces alone, not including our Air Forces in Europe and Korea and elsewhere, the U.S. superiority to the Soviet Union is approximately four and a half to one. Simply counting the warheads on missiles we are ahead three and a half to one. If you add the B–52s, then we are four and a half to one. If you add aircraft carriers, tactical fighters and our Air Forces, we are ahead five and a half to one. Also, our missiles are much more accurate than theirs. But you read so much nonsense in the American press. Even I sometimes get scared when I read these reports! So far the Soviet Union does not have any multiple warheads on its missiles. They are testing them, but they do not have them. I will give you some figures sometime on this in a smaller group. I can't have Hummel find it out!

Vice Premier Teng: I also feel in this respect it is hardly possible that you could reach agreement.

Secretary Kissinger: I may be wrong, but I see no sign that an agreement will be concluded. We may be able to achieve an optical agreement. The issue of inspection is very hard. We have made an interim agreement. Frankly, the number of launchers is not so very important. Each launcher has many weapons on it. For example, each missile on our submarines has 10 warheads that can be independently targeted with very great accuracy. So you can't make judgments on the basis of the numbers alone any more. Therefore, an agreement is quite difficult. The Soviets have still not started to test multiple warheads on their submarine-launched missiles. On land, they are testing three types. We think that by year-end they may complete the testing of one of these. But, then they must produce it. They have not done so yet.

Vice Premier Teng: As far as we are concerned in our relations with the Soviet Union, that is, on the eastern part of our border, there has been no change. It is still the same. There seems to be no change in deployments.

Secretary Kissinger: I think there has been a slight change, but I am not sure. I thought they had added three divisions recently, but I will check.

Maj Gen Scowcroft: Yes. That's right.

Secretary Kissinger: Three divisions are not significant.

Vice Premier Teng: Basically, they have not changed.

Secretary Kissinger: That is our impression as well.

Vice Premier Teng: There are one million Soviet troops deployed on our very, very long border, and they are scattered all over the place. They use this simply to scare people with weak nerves! I believe that, when you discussed this with Chairman Mao, he said even one million was not enough for defensive purposes and for an offensive purpose they must increase them by another million.

Secretary Kissinger: It depends on what they want. If they want to take all of China, that is right. It depends on what their objective is.

Vice Premier Teng: If they occupy some places on the border, what is the significance of that? They would simply get bogged down.

Secretary Kissinger: I have no estimate that they have any such intent, but it could be that, at some point, they would try to destroy your nuclear capacity. I'm not saying that they definitely plan it, but I say that that would be conceivable.

Vice Premier Teng: Chairman Mao has said that our nuclear power is only that much (holding up narrow gap between thumb and fore-finger). But, we thank you very much for telling us all this.

Secretary Kissinger: Are there any outstanding problems in our bilateral relations which we should discuss?

Vice Premier Teng: Ask the Vice Foreign Minister if there are any outstanding problems.

Vice Foreign Minister Ch'iao: There is nothing significant. The departure and the return of the heads of our respective liaison offices is a normal occurrence.

Secretary Kissinger: Chairman Mao told me that he would call Ambassador Huang Chen back to Peking for consultations. We were not surprised.

Vice Foreign Minister Ch'iao: When I met Ambassador Bruce before leaving Peking I told him that this coming and going by him was something normal and it had no significance.

Secretary Kissinger: No, it was not significant. I wanted his advice on some European matters. And, we announced it that way.

Vice Foreign Minister Ch'iao: I said to Ambassador Bruce once, wondering about his involvement with Europe—he said—I liked his answer—that just because he knew the grandfathers of the European leaders, this was no reason to put him in charge of European affairs. But I am sure this was not a criticism of you.

Secretary Kissinger: Ambassador Bruce is a good friend of mine.

Vice Foreign Minister Ch'iao: I asked Ambassador Bruce if this was true and he said yes.

As for our bilateral exchange program—in cultural exchange, that is in our people-to-people cultural exchanges, there have been some slight delays, but just for normal reasons.

Vice Premier Teng: Anyway, we are going along the track of the Shanghai communiqué.

Secretary Kissinger: So are we.

Vice Premier Teng: Do you think of any issue on bilateral affairs which we should discuss?

Secretary Kissinger: (To Hummel) Is there anything else? . . . (To Teng) On Korea, we are now talking with the South Koreans about the removal of the UN Command. We think you and we should stay related to the armistice in order to influence our friends in this situation. (*Note:* The Chinese interpreter rendered the sentence simply as "we should influence our friends in this situation." She did not mention the armistice agreement in this context.) We are also prepared in principle to make a statement on the withdrawal of our forces along the lines of the Shanghai communiqué statement. But, we cannot withdraw immediately. After we have worked out the details with South Korea, we will let you know informally. We appreciate your acts with respect to the UN Command last year very, very much, and particularly appreciate the meticulous way in which you carried out our understanding. Our Ambassador to the UN is a little excitable—Scali—but Ambassador Huang will understand. He had several heart attacks along the way. He has very great respect for Ambassador Huang.

I want you to know I have been thinking about the phrase in the last communiqué which we issued in Peking. We can discuss the meaning of this through Ambassador Huang Chen, or later in the year, if I take my annual trip to Peking.

Vice Premier Teng: (The Vice Premier indicated inconclusively that this topic could be discussed with Ambassador Huang Chen.) What is to be done on the Taiwan question?

Secretary Kissinger: We are continuing to reduce our presence there as I told you. We are thinking of methods of how we can give effect to the principle of one China as expressed in the last communiqué. We have not worked out all our thinking yet, but we are willing to listen to any ideas you have. You drafted the phrase.

Vice Foreign Minister Ch'iao: I think on this question, I understand the essence of the question. I participated in the drafting of the communiqué and in the drafting of this language. The essential meaning is as Chairman Mao told you. The normalization of our relations can only be on the basis of the Japanese pattern. No other pattern is possible. So, I might also mention that, with regard to the present relations between our two countries, my view is that our relationship should go forward. It should not go backward. I talked frankly on this with Ambassador Bruce. We had a friendly talk on this.

Secretary Kissinger: I am aware of what you said to him. We keep this very much in mind.

Vice Premier Teng: With regard to this question, there are two points. The first point is that we hope we can solve this question relatively quickly. (Note: Chinese interpreter rendered this in English as "as quickly as possible.") But, the second point is that we are not in a hurry on this question. These points have also been mentioned to you by Chairman Mao.

I suppose we have discussed everything that we have to discuss tonight. We have taken up a great deal of your time. You must be tired. Tomorrow, you must speak at the UN.

Secretary Kissinger: I must make sure to say nothing at all. I think I am on the verge of achieving success in this—with the dedicated assistance of my associates. Please give my regards and those of the President to our friends in China and especially give my respects to Chairman Mao and the Prime Minister.

(The dinner ended at approximately 11:00 p.m. The Secretary escorted his Chinese guests to the elevator.)[5]

---

[5] Afterward, Kissinger told Nixon, "I had a good talk with the Chinese last night. You know the highest-ranking official ever was here. They fully reaffirmed our policy and he went on and on about your visit. And he strongly reaffirmed the course that was outlined." (Ibid.)

---

79. Memorandum From the President's Assistant for National Security Affairs (Kissinger) to President Nixon[1]

Washington, April 24, 1974.

SUBJECT

Nuclear Sales to the PRC

The Under Secretaries Committee (USC) has reported to you that several U.S. companies are seeking authorization to negotiate the sale of nuclear power reactors and uranium fuel to the PRC (Tab B).[2] No Communist country has purchased Western power reactors, and as far as the PRC is concerned, the necessary intergovernmental agreements regulating the sale and transfer of nuclear equipment and fuel are not in place.

The USC's study has concluded that the export of light water reactors and slightly enriched uranium fuel would be consistent with our policy of facilitating the development of trade with the PRC, would have no adverse strategic implications, and would not be contrary to our obligations under the NPT.

---

[1] Source: Ford Library, NSC Institutional Files (H-Files), Box H–53, NSDM 261, Nuclear Sales to the PRC. Secret. Sent for action. A stamped notation on the memorandum indicates Nixon saw it. According to an attached, undated draft of this memorandum, Scowcroft and McFarlane revised it on March 26. McFarlane further revised the recommendation section on April 24. Solomon and David Elliot sent this memorandum to Kissinger under a March 22 covering memorandum summarizing it.

[2] Attached but not printed. On October 31, 1973, the Chairman of the Under Secretaries Committee requested that an interagency working group, under the leadership of the Department of State, study the question of nuclear sales to the People's Republic of China. Deputy Secretary of State Rush, Chairman of this group, submitted the report to the President on February 14, 1974. (Memorandum from Rush to Nixon, February 14; ibid.)

In order that these exports might proceed, the USC recommends that we should indicate to the Chinese our willingness to conclude a standard bilateral intergovernmental agreement for nuclear transfers. This agreement would provide for the application of safeguards, as we require for all nuclear exports to any country.

Future requests for nuclear exports to Communist countries would continue to be considered on a case-by-case basis.

I recommend that you approve the USC's recommendations, including the imposition of U.S. safeguards, until such time that the PRC takes its seat in the International Atomic Energy Agency (IAEA) and becomes subject to its safeguards. (If the PRC, subsequently, were to withdraw from the IAEA, the U.S. safeguards would again become operative.) The Joint Congressional Committee on Atomic Energy would be informed if the PRC indicates interest in negotiating the bilateral intergovernmental agreement.

Recommendation

That you approve our offering to conclude with the PRC an intergovernmental atomic energy agreement with standard safeguard provisions, thereby establishing the necessary conditions for possible sale of U.S. nuclear power reactors and fuel. Subject to your approval, I will sign the necessary implementing directive at Tab A.[3]

---

[3] The draft NSDM is attached but not printed. Nixon initialed the Approve option. The attached correspondence profile indicates that he made this decision on May 1. For the signed NSDM, see Document 83.

---

80.   Telegram From the Liaison Office in China to the Department of State[1]

Beijing, May 24, 1974, 0435Z.

870. Subject: Present U.S.–PRC Relationship.

1. After having been here a year I would like to make some personal comments on the Sino-American relationship, derived almost entirely from my own untutored reflections on the subject.

---

[1] Source: National Archives, Nixon Presidential Materials, NSC Files, Kissinger Office Files, Box 96, Country Files, Far East, China Exchanges, April 1–August 8, 1974. Secret; Immediate; Nodis.

2. First and foremost in domestic and foreign speculation is the power position of Chou En-Lai. I cannot believe he has in any degree whatever forfeited his unique standing with Chairman Mao; only an ingrate would repudiate a loyalty, extending over half a century, that has so largely contributed to the present prestige of the PRC chief and his cult, not to mention the spectacular manner in which the Prime Minister has handled the complex internal and external policies of this country.

Moreover, from every credible source there is testimony to the deep affection entertained by the Chairman for his gifted colleague. They are undoubtedly two old men in a hurry, anxious to secure, if such be possible, an orderly succession to the regime they have invented and administered.

3. Chou has always played second fiddle to Mao. No one has ever accused him of ambition to supplant his master. Why then are rumors so prevalent about the decline of his influence?

4. I think they are chiefly inspired by enemies who, afraid to attack the deified Chairman, would like to fish in troubled waters in case of Mao's decease, if Chou, the twin bastion of present stability, survived him. If Chou were to predecease Mao, the resultant shape of the succession might be simpler to fashion.

The real question is whether any individual could soon replace this duumvirate except by an improbable military coup. The more likely immediate solution might be administration by a collectively faithful for an unspecified time to the doctrines so amply propagandized by the Chairman.

5. I do not decry the notion that there are also young men in a hurry, to whom the memories of the early vicissitudes of the CCP, and the stirring exploits of the Long March are like notes of scarce-heard bugles. But the discrediting or even the overthrow of Chou seems to me beyond compass, even if they plot to precipitate chaos.

6. Therefore, I am inclined to think the two, or even one, if the other dies, will persevere in trying to establish the governmental apparatus on a base so firm it cannot easily be dismantled.

The relief of Chou from his ceremonial functions is a natural development, particularly in view of his age, and the exhausting life—some say an average workday of 18 hours—he has led for decades. I read nothing significant of a schism between him and the Chairman in this change of pattern. Of course, if the Prime Minister becomes physically incapacitated to carry on his reduced burdens that is another matter.

7. Given a continuance of moderately good health for Chou what should we expect in the next few months to mark the Chinese-American relationship? Has there indeed been a "cooling off", a disappointment amongst Chinese leaders of their expectations of its fruitfulness for their country? The answer to this is, in my opinion, a

modified "Yes". Some of the veiled attacks against Chou are launched by those who for doctrinaire reasons oppose his opening windows to the West, as well as by those who clandestinely disapprove the extent of the rift with the USSR. These considerations animate his opponents who dare not attack the sacrosanct Chairman.

8. What foundation is there for the disappointment to which I have referred? Primarily, I think it is ascribable (1) to latent fears that our détente with the USSR will lead us into actions and agreements inimical to the national interests of the PRC. (2) To a suspicion that we will not within the next couple of years proceed to a full diplomatic recognition of the PRC, and a withdrawal of our Embassy from Taiwan. (3) To impatience with our alleged lack of interest in a decisive solution of the problem of Cambodia, where their own diplomacy has recently taken a sharp turn toward more support for the Khmer Rouge, and a downgrading of Sihanouk, though they will keep him in the picture. (4) To fear of the repercussions on U.S. policy vis-à-vis China because of our concern with crises elsewhere, and our domestic political tribulations.

9. I think it would be futile to elaborate on these four points, but they should be borne in mind. Chinese officials sometimes talk to foreigners other than Americans in this strain.

During the past two months I have had conversations individually with more than forty Ambassadors stationed in Peking; their refrain, regardless of their political sympathies, has been much as I have stated. I do not take this as necessarily representing the authoritative view of Chinese policy-makers, for these diplomats have little access to them, but I believe it does fairly accurately mirror current PRC attitudes toward us.

Bruce

81.   Memorandum of Conversation[1]

Washington, June 24, 1974, 8:10–9:15 p.m.

PARTICIPANTS

Huang Chen, Chief of the Liaison Office of the People's Republic of China
Tsien Ta-yung, Political Counselor
Chi Ch'ao-chu, Interpreter

Henry A. Kissinger, Secretary of State
Arthur W. Hummel, Deputy Assistant Secretary for East Asian and Pacific
     Affairs, Department of State
Winston Lord, Director, Policy Planning Department of State
Richard H. Solomon, Senior Staff Member, National Security Council

SUBJECT

Tour d'Horizon Discussion on the Eve of the Secretary's Departure for Europe
and Moscow

Ambassador Huang: You are going tomorrow?

Secretary Kissinger: Yes, I depart tomorrow morning. Did my colleagues tell you what we have planned to cover in this session?

Mr. Lord: This is to preview the Soviet trip, our improving relations with the NATO allies—we haven't discussed the specific topics.

Secretary Kissinger: Right. I just wanted to tell you that I can see no agreement of major significance coming from this trip [to the Soviet Union]. I don't want to make you unhappy; we could make a special effort to speed up our negotiations.

Ambassador Huang: In saying that, I recall your discussions with Vice Premier Teng Hsiao-p'ing in New York.[2]

Secretary Kissinger: No agreement is now foreseeable on strategic armaments—nothing major.

Ambassador Huang: Secretary Schlesinger also said that in general terms in a speech on the 18th.

Secretary Kissinger: There would be some negotiating progress, but I do not expect the conclusion of an agreement on this trip. If there will be some progress, it will be in limiting the number of missiles on which the Soviets can put MIRVs.

---

[1] Source: National Archives, Nixon Presidential Materials, NSC Files, Kissinger Office Files, Box 96, Country Files, Far East, China Exchanges, April 1–August 8, 1974. Secret; Sensitive. The meeting took place in the Secretary's office at the Department of State. All brackets are in the original. In a June 24 memorandum, Lord informed Kissinger, "I genuinely believe that a failure to touch base with the Chinese before you leave for Moscow could cause very serious damage to our relations with Peking." Kissinger acceded to Lord's request and agreed to this meeting with Huang. (Ibid.)

[2] See Document 78.

In addition, we will discuss limits on underground testing. That also is a totally unresolved issue. The issue concerns what level to put the threshold [of underground nuclear explosions]. As far as an underground quota is concerned—the number of tests—we will not accept a quota. We will not accept a threshold higher than 200 kilotons. The Soviets want a much higher threshold.

We will not write into an agreement any recommendation for universality [of limits on underground testing].

The third category concerns [ABMs]. You know that in the ABM agreement each side can build a second site in addition to the one they have already constructed. We will probably agree that both sides agree to forego the second site, although they can move [the ABM installation] from one site to the other.

We also may begin negotiations on environmental warfare through climatic changes.

As for the rest, all the other subjects we will discuss are technical in nature: energy, exchanges of information, research and development. There will be no agreement on U.S. financial investment in the Soviet Union. (To Winston Lord:) Send Ambassador Huang a list tomorrow. (To Ambassador Huang:) We will send you a list of each issue with a one paragraph explanation.[3]

So this is what we expect from the summit. The Soviets will press us on Middle Eastern problems. Our position is that the countries of the region should solve these problems themselves.

Ambassador Huang: I want to inform you of one thing. Mr. Ilichev, head of the Soviet delegation to the Sino-Soviet border negotiations, will return to Peking for discussions tomorrow. This gentleman has been away for almost a year. He is returning at his own initiative on the eve of President Nixon's visit [to Moscow]. This is being done just for you to see. We do not expect anything to come of his return. We do not think he is bringing any new position.

Secretary Kissinger: Subtlety is not their strong point. When I was in Syria the Russians asked what time I would be leaving. The Syrians said I would depart at 12:00. The Soviets then announced their arrival for 1:00. My departure was then delayed, and they had to delay their departure several times.

Ambassador Huang: Another issue: As I mentioned to you at the Mayflower Hotel, we informed Senator Jackson that our invitation to him was at your suggestion . . .

---

[3] Not found.

Secretary Kissinger: Your invitation hasn't changed his behavior toward me at all.

I understand that regarding the Middle East my colleagues have already briefed you. Our strategy is to continue on our present course. We may have to let the Geneva Conference reconvene, but not before September. We will continue to deal with each issue bilaterally, as we have done thus far.

I appreciate your kind invitation for my wife and I to join you for dinner. If you will permit it, I will set a date when I return, sometime in the second half of July. But I accept now with great pleasure. The only reason I don't want to set a date now is that my schedule is not yet settled.

Ambassador Huang: I know you are very busy.

I was just joking with my colleagues, noting that at the time your press was attacking you, expressing their lack of confidence in you, I cast a vote for you [through my invitation].

Secretary Kissinger: I appreciate that. You know I have a rule that I never accept embassy invitations. This rule does not apply to Liaison Offices, however.

Ambassador Huang: Haven't you accepted any embassy invitations?

Secretary Kissinger: Not invitations for receptions or dinners in my honor. However, I have gone several times to receptions if a Foreign Minister was in town. Once I accepted an invitation from the Indian Embassy, but that was in honor of Senator Mansfield.

Ambassador Huang: I also invited your wife, the dinner is in her honor as well. And you should bring your colleagues and friends.

Secretary Kissinger: She has many more friends than me—can you accommodate six hundred guests?

Ambassador Huang: At the reception at the Mayflower there were more than six hundred.

There is also one issue regarding Senator Mansfield. I should tell you about his visit to China, inasmuch as you expressed your concern about it at the Mayflower. At the Mayflower you said it would be best if he could go to China before the Congressional delegation. Subsequently Peking decided that Senator Mansfield's visit should be postponed until after September—we have aleady informed him of this. We will welcome him a second time. This time he can stay longer, and travel to many more places. But during July and August we will be very busy. Senator Jackson will be going soon. We have given Senator Jackson priority as he has not been to China before. In addition, the Senator and Mrs. Mansfield dislike hot weather, and that is the hottest time of the year. So we suggest that he come after September.

In addition, I told him frankly that if he goes at the present time it is likely to give rise to speculation about Cambodian peace negotiations. He knows our position: we support the Cambodian people in continuing their struggle. We don't want to involve ourselves in peace negotiations. The present time is not convenient, but he can come after September.

Secretary Kissinger: Do you think the Cambodian situation will be solved by September?

Ambassador Huang: I cannot predict anything. You know our position.

Secretary Kissinger: At my press conference today I was asked when I would take another trip to China. I replied that I have been going about once a year. I would be glad to go for an exchange of views sometime in the second half of this year.

Ambassador Huang: We will welcome you.

Secretary Kissinger: For me it would be best if I could go after October 1.

Ambassador Huang: At your convenience. We will welcome you.

Secretary Kissinger: Should we propose a time? Or would you like to?

Ambassador Huang: At your convenience. Let us know a time that would be convenient to you.

Secretary Kissinger: When I am back from this current trip I will propose a time—perhaps in mid-October.

Ambassador Huang: There is time. When you come back just tell us your tentative dates and I will report them to Peking.

Secretary Kissinger: When you have considered our proposal regarding the UN Command in Korea, inform Mr. Hummel in my absence.[4]

Ambassador Huang: We haven't received any word yet.

Secretary Kissinger: My theory is that if you have something to tell us, you will tell us. My colleagues are afraid you are too shy. They keep sending me notes to remind me to ask you about various issues.

---

[4] On June 13, Lord gave Han Xu a paper expressing U.S. willingness to consider abolition of the UN Command in Korea. In place of the UN structure, the United States suggested that the U.S. and ROK military commanders substitute for the Commander in Chief of the United Nations Command, that the two Koreas enter into a nonaggression pact, and that the People's Republic of China and North Korea accept the continued presence of American forces in Korea as an interim measure. (Memorandum of conversation and attached proposal, June 13, 5:40–6:10 p.m.; National Archives, Nixon Presidential Materials, NSC Files, Kissinger Office Files, Box 96, Country Files, Far East, China Exchanges, April 1–August 8, 1974)

Ambassador Huang: I'm sure I will tell you [when we have a reply].

Secretary Kissinger: When I'm back from Moscow, I will see you after the first few days. I will travel in Europe after leaving the Soviet Union, to reassure our allies and also to see the World Cup soccer matches. I will be back on July 9—I will be away almost as long as your absence. You are not going to leave Washington suddenly?

Ambassador Huang: I cannot tell. I just obey orders.

Secretary Kissinger: Our press speculates a good deal about a loss of interest on our part in our relations with China. This is not true. We maintain our interest in the policies which we have discussed with your leaders.

Ambassador Huang: You know our *People's Daily* published your talk at the Mayflower Hotel.

Secretary Kissinger: I noticed that. I was very pleased.

Ambassador Huang: (to Tsien Ta-yung:) Is there anything else?

Mr. Tsien (in Chinese to Ambassador Huang:) He did very well in the Middle East.

Mr. Chi: The Ambassador just asked if we have any notes to hand to you, as your colleagues just did. Mr. Tsien said that in the Middle East you did very well in your shuttle diplomacy. You were warmly received. We approve of this.

The Ambassador mentioned to your colleagues before we came in a cartoon he had seen in the *Washington Post* around June 17th. It shows a pyramid with President Nixon and President Sadat running up one side, and Brezhnev going down the other side. There is an American flag at the top. There is only one problem with the cartoon. Dr. Kissinger should be just ahead of President Nixon.

Secretary Kissinger: We were encouraged by some good Chinese advice.

Ambassador Huang: You are very busy. You will be leaving about eight tomorrow morning?

Secretary Kissinger: I am sorry to have kept you waiting. I had to testify before a Congressional committee.

Ambassador Huang: Mrs. Kissinger is not well? Please give her my regards.

(The meeting then concluded.)

82.   Memorandum of Conversation[1]

Washington, July 15, 1974, 11:45 a.m.–12:20 p.m.

PARTICIPANTS

>Huang Chen, Chief of the Liaison Office of the People's Republic of China
>Tsien Ta-yung, Political Counselor
>Chi Ch'ao-chu, Interpreter

>Henry A. Kissinger, Secretary of State
>Robert S. Ingersoll, Deputy Secretary of State
>Winston Lord, Director, Policy Planning, Department of State
>Richard H. Solomon, Senior Staff Member, National Security Council

SUBJECT

>The Secretary's Meeting with PRC Liaison Office Chief Huang Chen After the Moscow Summit

As the Chinese were escorted into the Secretary's office, the Secretary commented on Ambassador Huang's summer suit.

Ambassador Huang: It's summer!

Secretary Kissinger: Fortunately, we now have a house with a swimming pool so we can endure the summer weather.

Ambassador Huang: I'm also fortunate in that my house also has a pool.

Secretary Kissinger: One of my colleagues said the other day (after the Wu Shu performance) that, one, we should avoid a quarrel with the Chinese, and, two, if we ever do get into a fight with them never engage in hand-to-hand combat.[2]

Ambassador Huang: Yes, I saw that remark quoted in the papers.

Secretary Kissinger: The little girl in the Wu Shu troupe was just adorable. Everyone was good.

I think you know that I sent a message to Prime Minister Chou through Ambassador Bruce saying that I hope he gets well soon.

---

[1] Source: National Archives, Nixon Presidential Materials, NSC Files, Kissinger Office Files, Box 96, Country Files, Far East, China Exchanges, April 1–August 8, 1974. Secret; Sensitive. The meeting was held in the Secretary's office at the Department of State. All brackets are in the original. On July 9, Lord prepared briefing materials for this meeting. (Ibid.)

[2] The 48-person Wu Shu Martial Arts and Acrobatic Troupe visited the United States on a four-city tour as part of the cultural exchange program between the People's Republic of China and the United States. The members performed at the Kennedy Center from July 10 through 14. On July 12, they visited the White House for a meeting with the President.

Ambassador Huang: The Premier has received your letter of concern. He has asked me to express to you his thanks. He is now convalescing in the hospital. When the Premier met Senator Jackson[3] he told the Senator that he had been invited to China at the recommendation of the President and Secretary of State. The Premier sent his personal greetings to you and the President [via Senator Jackson].

Secretary Kissinger: I think it was a good move [that you invited the Senator to China].

Ambassador Huang: It was on your recommendation.

Secretary Kissinger: Even though the Senator is critical of me, I think it is a good thing to have had him in China.

Ambassador Huang: As far as I know, you are a good friend of the Senator's.

Secretary Kissinger: I am on good personal terms with him. I will see him later this week. He is running for President [which is why he is critical of me in public]. One good way to get your name into the paper is to raise my name.

Ambassador Huang: Has the Senator decided to run for President?

Secretary Kissinger: Not formally. But seriously, he is a friend of mine. On general policy direction I agree with him. Sometimes his tactics are rather crude, however. He lacks a certain measure of subtlety. In terms of objectives I agree with him. I don't disagree with his orientation to the Soviets. I just approach them in a more complicated way—but to achieve the same objectives. On that issue we're in complete agreement. His tactics are more those of frontal attack; mine are more complicated.

In Moscow, Gromyko said that they had finally discovered my policy to be more complicated than they had at first thought. Now they will have to consider how to deal with this situation. I don't think they have solved this one.

Ambassador Huang: You have dealt with them for some time, so you understand them.

Secretary Kissinger: I know them well.

I wanted to talk to you about the Summit meeting, and one or two other matters:

At the Summit there couldn't have been any surprises for you, at least in the published documents.

Ambassador Huang: You told us your estimate [of the projected results] when we met before you left.[4]

---

[3] Senator Jackson's visit to China, July 1–6, is reported in telegrams 1126, 1128, and 1131, all from Beijing, July 5. (National Archives, RG 59, Central Foreign Policy Files)

[4] See Document 81.

Secretary Kissinger: Yes; it came out exactly as I told you. I'll be glad to comment on any aspect of the situation—but it went just as I told you.

One thing that did come up was their attempt on a number of occasions to involve us in documents or agreements which had an escape clause regarding China. They made one proposal to us which was for a treaty of friendship and cooperation to go to each other's assistance if either was attacked by a third party. This we will certainly refuse. You are the only other government we have mentioned this to—except for Britain.

Ambassador Huang: Was it a treaty of "cooperation," or "mutual assistance?"

Secretary Kissinger: The former. The key issue was to come to the aid of the other if one was attacked by a third party. They gave us no text, however. The way it came up was that Brezhnev mentioned it to the President when I wasn't there—he didn't dare raise it while I was present. Then Brezhnev afterwards mentioned it to me; he said he had discussed it with the President. I said I could not see such a situation arising. I made a joke. I told them about the Treaty of Björkö. The Czar and the German Emperor signed a treaty between themselves, but it lasted only for one day. We will not negotiate [with the Soviets] on this subject.

Ambassador Huang: We really don't have any worries on this. [Mr. Chi incorrectly translates the Ambassador's phrase as "worries." It is more accurately rendered as "we don't care about this."]

Secretary Kissinger: If Japan attacks you, then both we and the Soviet Union will help you. [Laughter]

I mentioned this to you so that they won't raise mischief with it. But we will not negotiate on this issue.

Ambassador Huang: For us it's not a question of worrying. We don't care about such things. [Mr. Chi comments on his inaccurate translation.]

Secretary Kissinger: This is a question of mentality, and that is significant. On many levels [such a treaty] is a stupid thing to offer. If we signed such an agreement, none of our European allies would trust us—this is not just a question of China. So it is significant from that point of view. But at any rate, we won't proceed with it.

As for the rest, now that the SALT discussions are in a longer time frame, we plan to begin discussions in Geneva about September 1. Then sometime in October I may go to Moscow again. But the only reason I might go would be to discuss SALT. But the timing depends on the Geneva discussions. It also depends on how long your delegate to the United Nations [Vice Foreign Minister Ch'iao Kuan-hua] is in New York. I don't dare leave the U.S. while your delegate is at the UN.

Ambassador Huang: You are old friends. There is no need to worry. [Laughter]

Secretary Kissinger: This is our present plan. There are also some basic figures I want to give you, so that you can give them to Peking.

Ambassador Huang: I remember that you discussed these figures with Vice Premier Teng in New York.

Secretary Kissinger: [The strategic balance is] four and a half to one, four to one in our favor.

Ambassador Huang: I remember your comments to the Vice Premier: 3.5 to 1 in strategic forces; if you add the B–52s it's 4.5; if you add your carriers it's 5.5.

Secretary Kissinger: When the Trident submarine system comes in, it will shift the balance even further in our direction. The Soviets have not yet deployed one single multiple warhead. They are still testing this system. One type has been a complete failure. Another type is nearly completed, but it is only like our early model. They have a perfect record on their [MIRVs for] big missiles: all failures.

(Ambassador Huang interjects: They are trying to surpass you.) There is no possibility of that. After ten years, after 1978, when the Trident, the B–1 bomber are produced, the curves will separate even farther.

Ambassador Huang: The Russians still have the mentality of wanting to surpass you.

Secretary Kissinger: But their technology is not as good as ours.

Ambassador Huang: Of late we have been reading press reports by the former Chief of the Joint Chiefs, and by Mr. Nitze, criticizing you.

Secretary Kissinger: Zumwalt. When I read them I get scared myself! We don't have the practice in our country of sending our military leaders off to the provinces. [Laughter] This is just nonsense. Every time we get in a difficult situation [Mr. Chi translates this as "crisis situation"] we put our navy forward and dare them to take us on. But each time they do not dare to do so.

Ambassador Huang: That is a good thing.

Secretary Kissinger: These [press] statements are really nonsense. They count the number of ships, but don't count the relative fire power on them. So I would pay no attention to them. We certainly didn't act as if we were scared last year in the Middle East crisis. [Ambassador Huang interjects: I understand.] We will continue to act exactly the same way.

About the return of Ambassador Bruce: He is a good friend of mine. I like to get his advice on the general international situation. His return is not related to U.S.–PRC relations.

Ambassador Huang: This is quite a normal situation—for a vacation, for discussions. I just told Mr. Lord that our Deputy Chief, Han Hsu, is going back in a few days. [Secretary Kissinger interjects: You haven't been back in awhile.] But as you said, Ambassador Bruce can come back twice. I haven't been back once this year.

Secretary Kissinger: You were giving me a complex. Each time I saw you [last year] you would tell me you were going back. [Laughter]

Other Matters: Last time I mentioned Korea. In Indochina, we want to keep the situation as quiet as possible. In Laos, with the Premier sick we want to keep things peaceful, we hope we can avoid instability.

Ambassador Huang: Regarding Korea, we have received no reply as yet.[5] Concerning Laos, we also were happy about the establishment of the coalition government. We hope it can continue. I also understand that Prince Souvanna is ill, but I hear from the Laotian Ambassador here that he is improving. I was a friend of the Ambassador in Paris. His [Souvanna's] illness came on suddenly. He [the Laotian Ambassador] is coming to my residence soon. [At this point Ambassador Huang makes a move to depart.]

Mr. Chi [to the Secretary]: The Ambassador looks forward to meeting you at his residence [when he holds his party for you].

Secretary Kissinger: We will give you another date—after August 1—as the first date was inconvenient.

Ambassador Huang: Mrs. Kissinger should bring her friends.

[On this note, the meeting concluded.]

---

[5] Huang is referring to a proposal received from the U.S. Government on June 13. See footnote 4, Document 81.

83.   National Security Decision Memorandum 261[1]

Washington, July 22, 1974.

TO

The Secretary of Treasury
The Secretary of Defense
The Secretary of Commerce
The Chairman, Atomic Energy Commission
The Director of Central Intelligence
The Deputy Secretary of State
The Director, Arms Control and Disarmament Agency
The Assistant to the President for International Economic Policy

SUBJECT

Nuclear Sales to the PRC

The President has reviewed the report of the Under Secretaries Committee of February 14, 1974 on Nuclear Sales to the People's Republic of China (PRC).[2] He has approved the recommendations that:

—The PRC should be informed that we are prepared to negotiate an Agreement for Cooperation Concerning Civil Uses of Atomic Energy which would authorize the export of U.S. light-water reactors and slightly enriched uranium. The Agreement would call for the application of bilateral safeguard rights which would be suspended in favor of those administered by the International Atomic Energy Agency (IAEA) if the PRC joins that organization. (The U.S. safeguards would again take effect should the PRC withdraw or IAEA safeguards cease to be effective.)[3]

—The Joint Committee on Atomic Energy and other interested Congressional committees should be informed of our offer to the PRC at such time as the Chinese express interest in negotiating an Agreement for Cooperation.

—Following Congressional notifications, interested U.S. companies should be authorized to proceed with discussions with the PRC

---

[1] Source: Ford Library, NSC Institutional Files (H-Files), Box H–53, NSDM 261, Nuclear Sales to the PRC. Secret. Copies were sent to the Chairman of the Joint Chiefs of Staff and to the Counsellor to the President for Economic Policy. Nixon approved this NSDM on May 1; see footnote 3, Document 79.

[2] See Document 79 and footnote 2 thereto.

[3] In a memorandum of March 22, Solomon and David Elliot advised Kissinger, "we have strong doubts that Peking will, in fact, be interested in signing a bilateral agreement with us which includes safeguard measures—at least at present." Kissinger wrote on the last page of their memorandum, "After Pres. approval [of the NSDM] let me consider how to inform Chinese." (Ford Library, NSC Institutional Files (H-Files), Box H–53, NSDM 261, Nuclear Sales to the PRC)

on the possible sale of light-water reactors and slightly enriched uranium fuel.

—Nuclear exports to Communist countries by the U.S. or other COCOM countries should continue to be treated on a case-by-case basis, and U.S. or IAEA safeguard standards and procedures for equipment or materials transferred or produced therefrom shall be applied to all recipient countries.

Henry A. Kissinger

---

84.   Paper Prepared in the Central Intelligence Agency[1]

Washington, July 1974.

[Omitted here are the title page, the table of contents, and two quotes from Mao about the future.]

CHINA IN 1980–85 AND IN THE YEAR 2000

Principal Judgments

Neither in the period 1980–85 nor even by the year 2000 will China be a superpower in the class of the US or the USSR. But, barring Soviet attack, China will have become a great power, probably the greatest in East Asia.[2]

The most menacing contingency for China is that of a Soviet military attack. Soviet leaders may be seriously tempted, but the chances

---

[1] Source: Central Intelligence Agency, OPI 10, Job 80–M01048A, Box 2, Communist China, 280174–151174. Secret. A note on the first page of the paper indicates that it was prepared from contributions by the Office of Political Research, the Office of Economic Research, the Office of Strategic Research, and the Central Reference Service of the Directorate of Intelligence, and by the Office of Weapons Intelligence and the Office of Scientific Intelligence of the Directorate of Science and Technology. The Office of Current Intelligence of the Directorate of Intelligence, the Defense Intelligence Agency, and the Bureau of Intelligence and Research of the Department of State were consulted.

[2] On August 12, Colby wrote in a letter to Kissinger, "Earlier this year President Nixon asked us for a speculative study of the prospects for the People's Republic of China, looking ahead for 10, 15, and even 25 years. Specifically, he wished to know whether ideology would continue to be important, whether the Chinese could make genuine economic advances, whether China would be a major military power, what kind of leadership it would have, and what kind of policies these leaders would be likely to pursue." (Ibid.) On August 19, Kissinger responded in a letter, "The study is a solid, thoughtful piece of work of which your people can be justly proud and I have sent it to the President for his background reading." (Ibid.)

of either a Soviet invasion or a Soviet nuclear strike in the decade ahead (through 1985) seem to us to be not very high, perhaps no more than one in five. Furthermore, a Soviet attack will probably be increasingly discouraged, in the period 1985–2000, by the growth of Chinese strategic power.

Another threat to Chinese development will be instability in the top leadership. Peking is already in another period of purges and uncertainty, and a still more serious situation will probably follow the anticipated departure of both Mao and Chou in the next few years, as divergent groups compete for position. After a period—possibly prolonged—of post-Mao or post-Chou instability, the intense nationalism of the leaders of all groups will probably enable a "collective" Party leadership, even as it changes composition, to pursue a coherent and constructive set of policies—although with continuing periodic "course corrections" to left or right.

Chinese Communist ideology seems certain to continue to play a critical role in shaping China's programs of political, economic, and social development. While some of the most distinctive elements in "Maoism" are likely to be softened in the interests of modernization, Chinese ideology will continue to be more puritanical and combative than that of almost all other Communist states.

Economic prospects depend chiefly on China's degree of success in controlling population growth and stimulating greater food production. More likely than not, China will be making progress in these respects by 1980–85, and will have doubled industrial production by 1985. While everything could go wrong economically in the event of weather disasters or a military defeat, the food/population problem should be eased by the year 2000, and by that time the industrial base to support economic development should be about four times the present size. Nevertheless, in economic strength, China will still trail far behind the US and the USSR, and, probably, will still not have caught up with Japan and Western Europe.

By 1980–85, the Chinese strategic weapons force will probably include some hardened silos for ICBMs capable of reaching both the European USSR and the continental US, but the emphasis is likely to be on a combination of land-based semi-mobile systems (totaling no more than a few hundred missiles), plus, perhaps, a handful of ballistic missile submarines.[3] As of the year 2000, even if the US and USSR have

---

[3] NIE 13–8–74, June 13, stated that the PRC nuclear weapons program had slowed since 1971, and predicted that by 1980 China would be able to strike the continental United States with a few nuclear weapons. (National Intelligence Council, *Tracking the Dragon*, pp. 633–674)

increased the gap in strategic capabilities between themselves and China, the latter's strategic nuclear forces—backed up by immense conventional defense capabilities—will constitute a formidable deterrent.

Throughout this century, Peking's foreign policy will probably continue to be shaped in large part by hatred and fear of the USSR. In the short term, China's effort will be concentrated on avoiding a war with the USSR and reducing the Soviet military presence on the border. To this end, the Chinese may make the necessary compromises to get a border settlement, without changing their view that the USSR is their main enemy.

A broader—though still limited—accommodation between the two powers will remain a possibility, especially in the longer run: movement in that direction could be induced by mutual Chinese and Soviet interest in lessening the temper of controversy. Such movement could have considerable significance for US strategic and other interests, even though such a Sino-Soviet détente would almost certainly stop far short of anything resembling the Sino-Soviet alliance of 1949–53. The Chinese will in any event continue to compete fiercely with the USSR, worldwide, probably making even more trouble for the Soviets around the world than they do now.

Throughout this century, China will attempt to use US influence to deter the USSR from attacking China and to offset Soviet efforts to encircle or contain China. The Chinese will try to avoid direct military confrontations with the US, and are likely to support some US positions which cut across Soviet policies. In pursuing these courses, the Chinese leaders will almost certainly not become pro-American, or seriously interested in an alliance with the US. The chances will indeed be greater that the Chinese leaders will become more assertive, initiating challenges to US interests in various countries and situations. The degree of their assertiveness will depend in large part upon the Chinese leaders' assessment of the overall value of the Sino-American relationship in countering the USSR. In any event, Taiwan will be high on Peking's list of priorities and will remain a painful issue between China and the US; with the passage of time the Taiwan problem will— if still unresolved by negotiations—increasingly tempt Peking's leaders to resort to military force.

Maoist revolutionary impulses will probably sustain Chinese activism toward various developing countries through 1980–85. China's ability to exercise its power will remain greatest in East Asia—that is, in the peripheral arc of Japan and Southeast Asia. Peking's main line in Southeast Asia will probably be a combination of conventional diplomacy and subversive support of insurgency, the short-range goal being to encourage the development of a chain of benevolently neutral neighbors. With respect to Japan, Chinese leaders will almost certainly seek to encourage those forces and factors working for a "soft" Japan, rather than a hostile or nuclear-armed Japan. As of the year 2000, the Chinese will probably be the dominant power in East Asia and will be able to compete with both the US and the USSR for influence in the Middle East, Africa, and Latin America.

As for China's form of leadership, there are real possibilities of either a military dictatorship, coming after a period of high instability, or a neo-Maoist dictatorship riding in on a resurgence of fundamentalist "Maoism." The more likely leadership, however, is a "collective" dominated by Party careerists. On this view, the Party Chairman will not have Mao's degree of authority, but—somewhat like Brezhnev's present situation—will be obliged to rule by consensus. From what we know of the candidates for the leadership in both 1980–85 and 2000, these leaders will be hard, dedicated men, determined to make their China strong and influential, but ready to deal with the West when they consider this to China's interest.

[Omitted here are the introductory notes, the body of the study, and an annex on possible future leaders.]

---

85.   **Editorial Note**

On July 18, 1974, NSC Staff member W. Richard Smyser submitted to the President's Assistant for National Security Affairs, Henry Kissinger, a memorandum with the title, "Where Do We Stand in Asia?" In regard to China, Smyser wrote, "Solving the two-China problem between Peking and Washington looked easier when all the governments were strong. Now détente is under fire at home; Chou En-Lai is sick in Peking; even CCK [Chiang Ching-kuo] is starting to have problems with his military. Before we work out a normalization formula, the politicking may get a lot nastier than we had hoped. We cannot count on either the PRC or the ROC to remain on course with us in the difficult and complex process of normalization, or to be able to tolerate all the upcoming tactical uncertainties. Fortunately, the Russians will probably be too inept to pick up the pieces. Also, many Asian governments are now moving toward Peking, so the shock waves of our normalization may not be too severe. But our initial objective of normalizing relations without substantial adverse impact at home or in Asia will be difficult and perhaps impossible to reach." Kissinger wrote and underscored, "Good job" on Smyser's memorandum. (National Archives, Nixon Presidential Materials, NSC Files, Box 1338, Unfiled Materials, 1974)

On August 9, after Richard Nixon's resignation, Gerald Ford became President of the United States. Later that day, he met with Huang Chen, Chief of the PRC Liaison Office, and affirmed his desire to continue Nixon's policy of improving relations between their two countries. (Memorandum of conversation, August 9, 5:25–5:40 p.m.; Ford Library, National Security Adviser Memcons, Box 4, July–September 1974) The next day, Kissinger sent Ambassador Bruce a letter to be delivered to Chairman Mao from President Ford indicating that the new administration would continue the policies expressed in the Shanghai Communiqué. (Backchannel message from the White House to Bruce, August 9; ibid., Kissinger–Scowcroft West Wing Office Files, 1969–1977, China, unnumbered items [1]) Bruce reported in backchannel telegram 66 to Kissinger, August 10, that he delivered the letter to Qiao Guanhua, who had been entrusted by Zhou to receive it. (National Archives, Nixon Presidential Materials, NSC Files, Kissinger Office Files, Box 96, Country Files, Far East, China Exchanges, April 1–August 8, 1974)

86.   Memorandum of Conversation[1]

Washington, September 25, 1974, 2:50–3:20 p.m.

PARTICIPANTS

>   Ambassador George Bush, Chief-Designate of the United States Liaison Office in Peking
>   Lt. General Brent Scowcroft, Deputy Assistant to the President for National Security Affairs
>   Mr. Richard H. Solomon, Senior Staff Member, NSC

SUBJECT

>   Ambassador George Bush's Courtesy Call and Briefing Before Assignment in Peking

The conversation began with Ambassador Bush expressing his personal concern about the state of health of former President Nixon. He made some observations about the lack of balance in the U.S. media—and indeed in public attitudes in general—about the entire Watergate

---

[1] Source: Ford Library, National Security Adviser, Presidential Country Files, East Asia, Box 13, PRC (1), 8/9/74–9/30/74. Top Secret; Sensitive. The meeting took place in the White House. All brackets are in the original. Scowcroft's talking points for this meeting are ibid.

affair and Mr. Nixon's resignation. He noted the positive contributions Mr. Nixon had made during his tenure, and commented on the fact that his (Bush's) ability to represent the U.S. in China was one of these positive contributions. At the same time, there was no question that Mr. Nixon had his dark side, and this had dragged him down into the mud; but Ambassador Bush could not accept the lack of balance in the way that the press and certain individuals responded to the Nixon situation.

Mr. Solomon commented that, curious as it seemed, the Chinese showed such a degree of balance. Ironically, their capacity to evaluate historical figures in a balanced way was revealed in the way they talked about Stalin, as Mr. Bush would see when he was in China. [At this point in the conversation General Scowcroft was interrupted to take a telephone call from Mr. Nixon. When he returned he remarked that the former President sounded rather weak, and noted that it was the personal dimension of what had happened to Mr. Nixon that was particularly upsetting.]

At this point Mr. Bush directed the conversation to his forthcoming assignment in the PRC.

General Scowcroft: When you first get there you may feel a bit of frustration which I hope you are mentally prepared for. You will find yourself rather isolated. However, you will find it a most fascinating, a marvelous experience. You will see some real action while you are there. I don't know when, but we are in the middle of a period of transition, although we don't know exactly how it will develop.

Our official contacts with the Chinese have been very narrow—you are going up to New York next week with the Secretary—you'll see Vice Foreign Minister Ch'iao Kuan-hua. But we don't have much dealing with the next generation in the leadership. Anything that you can do in this regard in the way of developing contacts will be helpful, although of course you can't do anything that they don't want you to do.

Ambassador Bush: When I was up at the U.N. we brought them out to my family home; they toasted my mother. Ambassador Huang Hua was asking all kinds of questions: Why did they have a toll bridge? Why is our industry so concentrated? We didn't push them into a relationship, but we found them responsive. Of course they don't want to see a brash American running around Peking.

General Scowcroft: Those people understand subtlety. But don't hesitate to write us of your impressions, your feel of the situation in Peking.

Ambassador Bush: You normally get the routine cables which are sent through State channels?

General Scowcroft: Yes—although you probably know that you have a private channel to us here, to the Secretary and the President, which should be used for sensitive material.[2]

Ambassador Bush: If I don't plow any new ground?

General Scowcroft: You should use both channels. You can make general reports via the State channel, and then send sensitive or specific elements via the White House channel. Basically, the communications use the same circuits, they just use a different encryption system. The CIA man out there holds the key. But anything you don't want to get into the bureaucracy you should send via the White House channel.

Ambassador Bush: Lord, Habib, and Hummel mentioned that much of the China business is done here in Washington. I hope you will keep me informed. I don't want to be out there like Adlai Stevenson [who was never told about the Bay of Pigs operation by President Kennedy when he was our Ambassador to the U.N.].

General Scowcroft: When we have any meetings with the Chinese here we'll certainly inform you. This will not be a problem.

Ambassador Bush: Is Art Hummel aware of this channel?

General Scowcroft: I think he must know one exists, although he doesn't normally read that material. But you know you have John Holdridge out there as your deputy. He is outstanding; he spent four years on the NSC.

Ambassador Bush: He came up to the U.N. several times. He briefed us on developments with Al Jenkins.

Mr. Solomon: He has been here through the entire development of our relations with Peking, and knows all the material.

General Scowcroft: I'm glad that you are reading into the past record. It is fascinating.

Ambassador Bush: It's very useful. It also will be helpful to be at the dinner in New York next week.[3]

How do you feel about our relationship—not just about the future but its current state.

General Scowcroft: We are on track—well, I'd say that we are in a period where things are a little bit stagnant. There are no major problems, the relationship is just not active. I feel they are having their own preoccupations, sorting things out internally. They are ambivalent

---

[2] Scowcroft is referring to the Voyager channel, which circumvented the State Department by sending messages to the White House. James Lilley discusses this channel in *China Hands*, pp. 173–175.

[3] A dinner with Qiao Guanhua and Kissinger was scheduled for October 2. See Document 87.

about Taiwan, partly because of anticipations that we have built into the relationship. But there is not the closeness of contact that we had a year ago.

Ambassador Bush: Contact on trips [by Secretary Kissinger] or at USLO?

General Scowcroft: It applies to either case.

Ambassador Bush: Does USLO feel there has been a pullback?

General Scowcroft: I'd say it's more a matter of no movement. For example, last year we tried to get something going on Cambodia. We tried to wrap things up a year ago, but the effort passed without getting anywhere and has faded.

Ambassador Bush: When I had a recent discussion with Huang Chen I remarked that as [Republican] party leader perhaps I could have discussions in Peking on that wavelength. I told Huang I would be glad to give him my views on our political situation. I thought that might be a useful way to draw them out on their own political situation. When I was up at the U.N. Huang Hua said that now I should be called "Chairman Bush." I said there was a helluva difference between that and the position of Chairman Mao. Huang Chen replied that they would be interested in political discussions both here and in Peking.

General Scowcroft: I'm sure they are intensely interested in our political situation. Understanding theirs is often rather difficult to do. If you compare the letters their leadership sent to President Nixon and President Ford you get some interesting nuances.[4]

Mr. Solomon: They have shown a remarkable degree of loyalty and personal warmth to Mr. Nixon.[5] The way they communicate their political situation to us is indeed subtle. During Secretary Kissinger's July, 1971 trip to Peking Chou En-lai made a comment about the gifts which had been brought to Chairman Mao, Lin Piao, and himself on behalf of the President. He replied, "You may say that Chairman Mao

---

[4] The Chinese note to Ford congratulated him on becoming President and declared, "We are glad to note your indication that you will continue to adhere to the principles of the Shanghai Communiqué, and we would like to avail ourselves of this opportunity to reiterate that, as in the past, we shall act according to the spirit and principles of the Shanghai Communiqué which we jointly released during President Nixon's visit to China." (Ford Library, National Security Adviser, Kissinger/Scowcroft West Wing Office Files, China Exchanges, Box 4, unnumbered [2])

[5] Zhou Enlai's message to Nixon stated, "Both Chairman Mao and I have happy memories of your 1972 visit to China, during which we held frank and beneficial talks and issued the Shanghai Communiqué. The unlocking of the doors to friendly contacts between the Chinese and American peoples and the promotion of the relations between our two countries towards normalization are the common desire of our two peoples. The efforts which you have made in this connection will not be forgotten." (National Archives, Nixon Presidential Materials, NSC Files, Kissinger Office Files, Box 96, Country Files, Far East, China Exchanges, April 1–August 8, 1974)

and I accept the gifts with pleasure." This was the first subtle indication that we had of Lin Piao being in trouble.

General Scowcroft: They are fascinating people, very nice—no, civilized. At the same time they can be quite vicious in their politics. This will be a great experience for you.

Ambassador Bush: This assignment will give me a chance to start reading again.

General Scowcroft: Yes, you have been doing things at a different pace during the past several years. If there is anything that we can do for you just whip me off a cable. Anything that you send through the White House channel will be as private as talking here.

Ambassador Bush: I will. There is one point: Henry and General Haig said that I might want to beef up my staff, increase it somewhat. Do you know anything that might be behind this—new facilities? Or is there something currently being planned on this?

General Scowcroft: Well, first there is a matter of pressure we get from other departments, particularly Agriculture and Commerce. When the Liaison Office was set up we sent in what was assumed to be an initial cadre to get the facility in operation. We haven't changed things much since then—except Jenkins, we haven't replaced him yet I don't think.

Mr. Solomon: The communiqué published at the end of the Secretary's November visit last year contained the sentence about "expanding the scope of the functions of the Liaison Offices."[6] Exactly what this means has never been clearly spelled out. It was intended to convey a sense of accelerating the development of our relations. In fact, the Chinese have expanded their staff here in Washington substantially in the past year. They now have over 70 people. With that 400 room hotel they are living in they have plenty of room for expansion. On our side, however, we are faced with constraints posed by the lack of residential housing units in Peking. We had some people living in a hotel there for more than a year.

Ambassador Bush: I gather there was some talk being given to finding a larger plot of ground in Peking, or to renting additional space.

General Scowcroft: Well, this is the kind of issue you will be grappling with directly soon. We wish you the best of luck.

After a final exchange of pleasantries, which included Ambassador Bush recalling some of the courtesies the Chinese had shown his family when they visited his house in the outskirts of New York City, the session concluded.

---

[6] See footnote 7, Document 60.

87.   Memorandum of Conversation[1]

New York City, October 2, 1974, 8:15–11:35 p.m.

PARTICIPANTS

Ch'iao Kuan-hua, Vice Foreign Minister of the PRC
Huang Hua, PRC Permanent Representative to the United Nations
Chi Tsung-chih, Deputy Director, West European Department, PRC Ministry of
    Foreign Affairs
Chang Han-chih, Deputy Director, Asian Department, PRC Ministry of Foreign
    Affairs (Interpreter)
Kuo Chia-ting, Second Secretary at the PRC Mission to the U.N. (Notetaker)

Henry A. Kissinger, Secretary of State
Philip Habib, Assistant Secretary of State for East Asian and Pacific Affairs
George Bush, Chief-Designate of the United States Liaison Office in Peking
Winston Lord, Director, Policy Planning, Department of State
Arthur W. Hummel, Jr., Deputy Assistant Secretary of State for East Asian and
    Pacific Affairs
Richard H. Solomon, Senior Staff Member, National Security Council

SUBJECT

Secretary's Dinner for the Vice Foreign Minister of the People's Republic of
China

(The evening began at 8:15 as the Chinese were escorted into the Secretary's living room for informal discussion and drinks before dinner.)

Vice Foreign Minister Ch'iao: We are late.

Ambassador Huang: The car came on 57th Street and the traffic was bad.

(At this point photographers entered the room to take pictures.)

Secretary Kissinger: My Chinese is getting better. We can't smile; we are mad at each other. (Laughter)

I must say the Vice Foreign Minister fired full cannons today [in his General Assembly speech], no empty cannons.[2]

Vice Foreign Minister Ch'iao: I suppose what I said you had already anticipated?

---

[1] Source: Ford Library, Kissinger–Scowcroft West Wing Office Files, 1974–1977, China Exchanges, Box 4, unnumbered (4). Top Secret; Sensitive; Exclusively Eyes Only. The meeting took place in the Secretary's suite at the Waldorf Towers. All brackets are in the original. Hummel, Lord, and Solomon sent Kissinger a briefing memorandum for this meeting on September 27. (Ibid.)

[2] On October 3, The New York Times reported on Qiao Guanhua's speech at the United Nations in which he attacked détente and criticized both superpowers. ("China, in U.N., Hails Arabs' Oil Weapon," p. 1)

Secretary Kissinger: No. You are establishing a degree of equivalence between us [the U.S. and the Soviet Union].

Vice Foreign Minister Ch'iao: No, this is wrong. If you study the speech more carefully . . .

Secretary Kissinger: We'll have to study it more carefully.

Vice Foreign Minister Ch'iao: It [the characterization of the U.S. and the Soviets in the speech] was like that in the past. I feel this speech was more unequal than in the past.

Secretary Kissinger: I want the Vice Foreign Minister to understand that we appreciate equal treatment, but not on all occasions. (Laughter)

Vice Foreign Minister Ch'iao: We both speak with touches of philosophy, so our speeches are not easy to understand.

Secretary Kissinger: I don't say there was full equivalence, but more so than in the past. But this is a compliment to you. Of all the General Assembly speeches, I read only yours.

Vice Foreign Minister Ch'iao: I also can tell you that yours was studied most carefully—although I was not here when you delivered it.

Secretary Kissinger: Mine did not touch on China.

Vice Foreign Minister Ch'iao: I know. That was also the case in the past. As for myself, I have to give you some criticisms. If I don't, then I'm not on good grounds for criticizing our neighbor [the Soviet Union].

Secretary Kissinger: I just want you to know that we won't feel neglected if you don't. (Laughter)

Vice Foreign Minister Ch'iao: The day before yesterday I met Ambassador Malik. He said he would come to hear my speech. I replied, "You can't run away." So today he just threw a copy [of the speech] down on the table.

Secretary Kissinger: I was worried that I didn't go to his reception, as I went to yours. However, Malik solved my problem as he came to yours.

Vice Foreign Minister Ch'iao: Yes. I recall that last night the three of us sat in a triangle, in a circle. You can draw the circle in many ways.

Secretary Kissinger: But it still comes out the same. We keep it constant; it comes out the same.

Vice Foreign Minister Ch'iao: Well, but frankly, since we met last April there have been many changes.

Secretary Kissinger: Before we get to these, there is one aesthetic point I wanted to raise. You said we overthrew the government in Cyprus. We did not. We did not oppose Makarios. It would serve no political purpose for us [to have overthrown him]. The only problem is that his talents are greater than the island he runs. But that's a vice of most Greek politicians. Basically this is just for your information—it is not an important point. This was not an event which we desired. Once it happened, our basic desire was to keep the Soviet Union out, not to permit them to undermine the situation. I liked your description of their policy [in the G.A. speech] very much.

Vice Foreign Minister Ch'iao: Speaking of the Cyprus events, I have one question. You surely knew something of the situation before the event. Why didn't you take steps to prevent it? In our view it was a stupid event.

Secretary Kissinger: Yes. If I get you to come and visit Washington I could explain our system of govenrment. (Laughter) There are many intelligence reports which float around, but if no one brings them to me I assume they do not exist. I can assume that a subordinate will leak to the press one I *do* see. What they don't leak are the ones I do not see.

When the coup occurred I was in Moscow. My people did not take these intelligence reports seriously as such reports had been very numerous in the past. Every three months there was a rumor of a possible coup. An intelligence officer even told Makarios about these rumors, but he didn't believe them. He was away on a weekend holiday. If I had known about the report, I would have stopped it [the coup]. Once the coup occurred, I assumed that Turkey would intervene, as there was no government in Cyprus and Greece was unstable. Our press is violently anti-Greece. They were criticizing us [for our attitude on Greece]. The reason I didn't criticize Sampson was that we assumed we could get rid of him in any 36-hour period. But we knew that the Soviets had told the Turks to invade. We didn't want them [the Soviets] to have any other excuse to involve themselves in the situation. But the "Second World" in Europe, and the American press, kept egging on the Turks.

So it is an unfortunate situation, but it will come out all right. The Soviets can't do anything for either party. We will move to a settlement in a few weeks once the Greeks calm down.

Actually our problem is in calming down the Greek population in the U.S. We already have the basis for an agreement with the Greeks and the Turks, but if Congress cuts off aid, then they will remove our basis for a settlement. So if you have any influence with the Congress please use it. (Laughter) Fortunately there are more Chinese here than Greeks. They have better discipline.

Vice Foreign Minister Ch'iao: Well, it really was a bad situation at the beginning, after things first happened. As for the situation later, we can't criticize you.

Secretary Kissinger: I agree, the beginning was bad. But later it became better. The worst thing that the Chinese can say about a person is that he is stupid. (Laughter)

Vice Foreign Minister Ch'iao: Since you have contacts with the two sides, what do you think about the question of the withdrawal of Turkish troops? Will they make a demonstration of good will?

Secretary Kissinger: As I know that you don't leak to the press (Ch'iao: On that you can rely.) I will tell you. It is really contingent on our Congress. While I am on my Middle Eastern trip I will go to Ankara. While I am in Ankara the Turks will make a gesture of good will—like withdrawing five to seven thousand troops, or withdrawing from some territory. Then we will ask Clerides and Denktash to agree to principles for a political dialogue, for political talks. These principles essentially have been agreed to already. The Greek government will then express approval that political talks are starting. Then, nothing will happen until after November 10, which is the date of the Greek elections. They don't want anything to happen before then. After the election, we will put the issue in a larger framework, one which will solve such questions as territorial rights in the Aegean Sea, etc. This is all agreed to, but our Congress may upset these plans. If these maniacs will only leave the situation alone! I'm convinced that eighty percent of the madmen in the world live in the Eastern Mediterranean. So I can't be sure [of the outcome of the situation].

(At this point in the conversation, at 8:40 p.m., the living room conversation broke up and the group resumed the discussion at the dinner table.)

Secretary Kissinger: We have a number of new friends here tonight. Ambassador Habib is our new Assistant Secretary for East Asia. Of course you know George Bush. (Ch'iao: Our old friend.) He may not be used to the frankness with which we discuss issues. (Laughter) I always tell our Chinese friends the outlines of our policies. There have been no disappointments thus far. It is so rare to meet officials who understand what we are doing.

Incidentally, I joked with the Mongolian Foreign Minister that I would visit his country. He took me seriously and extended me an invitation. Should I pay his country a visit? (Laughter) Seriously, there are no U.S. interests in Outer Mongolia, other than creating a sense of insecurity in other capitals. I don't have to pursue this. I want your frank opinion.

Vice Foreign Minister Ch'iao: Considering this question, our position has been the same since the Yalta Conference. I've always told this to the Doctor. Maybe I am wrong, but you talked with Premier Chou about this.

Secretary Kissinger: Yes, but I don't know how you would view American efforts to establish relations with Outer Mongolia. I know your historical view and what it represents.

Well, I can defer a decision until a later occasion. The only reason to go is to show activity in this area. But if you object—to a visit by me—I won't go. Diplomatic relations, that we'll do. (To Ambassador Habib:) Where do we stand on this?

Ambassador Habib: We have had no response.

Mr. Solomon: I believe their northern neighbor objects to Mongolia establishing relations with us.

Vice Foreign Minister Ch'iao: There are two aspects to the situation there. We maintain diplomatic relations [with the Mongolian People's Republic], so there is no question of law. But this is really just a puppet state. It is in a situation of being occupied. So in such circumstances you will have to decide [whether or not to visit].

Secretary Kissinger: No, I can tell you now that it won't be done.

You spoke of changes regarding Cyprus. Are there any others— our two countries?

Vice Foreign Minister Ch'iao: Not just our two countries. Primarily I was referring to the world besides our two countries. As for changes in your country, I believe we have explained our view. This is your domestic affair, and it won't affect relations between our two countries.

Secretary Kissinger: Exactly. We will pursue the policies that we have agreed to. During the course of the evening I want to discuss some specific issues with the Vice Foreign Minister. As for the specific understandings, we will completely uphold them.

What changes do you see in the world since April?

Vice Foreign Minister Ch'iao: (Pauses to reflect on a reply.) Superficially, Cyprus was the most drastic change. But our analysis is that two areas are in upheaval: the Balkans and the South Asian subcontinent.

Secretary Kissinger: Cyprus makes much noise, but no strategic difference—unless we are prevented by domestic developments from conducting our foreign policy. The situation will probably come out with the Turks in a slightly stronger position.

In the Balkans, do you mean pressure on Yugoslavia? (Ch'iao: Yes.) You know that I will visit Yugoslavia in November. We told you about my visit to the Soviet Union. From there I will go to India, Pakistan, Romania, and Yugoslavia. So how serious do you think the pressures are on Yugoslavia?

Vice Foreign Minister Ch'iao: You know, that friend of ours is an opportunist. If you don't create some counter pressures they will take advantage of the situation. The situation is not as calm as it looks.

Secretary Kissinger: I agree. Especially after Tito dies. But the Soviets would not consider a move against Yugoslavia on the order of what they did to Hungary or Czechoslovakia. We would not treat such a development in the same category as Hungary or Czechoslovakia. We would take such a development with great seriousness. In fact, I plan to discuss this situation when I visit [Peking].

Vice Foreign Minister Ch'iao: I don't know how you view the situation in South Asia. Of course, we have discussed this many times.

Secretary Kissinger: I separate the strategic consideration from tactics. Our strategic analysis is the same as yours. For a "peace loving" people, the Indians create a great sense of insecurity. If they were not pacifists I would really worry about them. (Laughter) They are attempting to create a situation of great imbalance in strength with their neighbors.

They have repeatedly urged me to come for a visit. I have postponed one three times already. The general intention [of my visit] is to produce a greater degree of independence of Indian foreign policy in relation to the Soviets—and to create some discouragement on the part of the Soviets regarding their investment in India.

Practically, what will come out of the visit? We will set up a scientific and economic commission, but there will be no American financial commitment—other than that already in the budget. But Congress won't approve it, and we won't fight for it. (Laughter)

Ambassador Huang: Did you promise to give a certain amount of wheat to India?

Secretary Kissinger: We haven't made any promises yet. The amount we are now considering is substantially below the figures you read in the newspapers. (Mr. Lord: A half million tons.) But we haven't committed this yet. They have asked for three million tons. That is less than we are giving to Egypt. We are giving the Egyptians 600,000 tons, Syria 200,000–250,000. I just want you to understand our relative priorities in relation to the populations involved. In Pakistan, we hope to have the most constructive talks possible. I hope to pursue the line which we discussed in Peking. Don't believe the statements you read by our Cabinet members. This particular one made two statements, and his second one was worse than the first. In the first he called the Shah "a nut." Then he said he had been quoted out of context, and that only in some circumstances did he consider the Shah to be "a nut." (Laughter)

On oil, we have good relations [with the Shah]. Our negotiations will have a positive outcome.

What is your assessment of South Asia?

Vice Foreign Minister Ch'iao: We have discussed this many times. Our views are similar to yours, although perhaps we view the situation as more serious [than you do].

Secretary Kissinger: Will there be a military outcome?

Vice Foreign Minister Ch'iao: Our feeling is that our friend [the Soviet Union] is more shrewd in his actions than you are. Their activities are more covered up. They make better use of domestic contradictions in various countries. Perhaps you don't pay attention to such things closely enough.

Secretary Kissinger: Perhaps because I know their leaders I don't rate them too highly. My judgment is that they usually prevail with brutality, not cleverness. But this is an interesting point. How do they use domestic contradictions?

Vice Foreign Minister Ch'iao: In one respect they use contradictions between the various countries in the region, especially Pakistan, Afghanistan, and Iran. Don't you feel the question of Baluchistan, promoted by Afghanistan, has gone further than before.

Secretary Kissinger: Not Pushtunistan? I thought . . .

Vice Foreign Minister Ch'iao: Openly the Afghanistanis are talking about Pushtunistan, but they also make use of Baluchistan.

Secretary Kissinger: I'll look into this situation. I'll talk to the Shah when I see him. He has a Baluchi area on his border.

Vice Foreign Minister Ch'iao: Generally I agree with you [about the Soviets]. They are doing some stupid things. Eventually they will have to resort to brutality, but before they reach this point they take advantage of the situations.

Secretary Kissinger: Is it true that the three Soviet border negotiators have all had nervous breakdowns?

Vice Foreign Minister Ch'iao: That's probably just a story. Didn't you see that our comrade Ilichev, after he returned to Moscow, went to Cyprus?

Secretary Kissinger: He went to Greece also.

I'm tempted to accept the Soviet proposal on a conference on Cyprus just because it is comprehensive. We won't, but you described their situation very accurately.

Chang Han-chih: Yes, the phrase [in Ch'iao's U.N. speech] was they were acting like "ants on a hot pot."

Secretary Kissinger: When Gromyko came [to Washington] he raised the idea of a joint guarantee for Cyprus. I said let's try this on Poland first.

Vice Foreign Minister Ch'iao: Very good idea.

Secretary Kissinger: I hope for your emotional stability that you don't follow the European Security Conference. There is the issue of peaceful change of frontiers—this is the German problem. We support the German formulation. When Gromyko was in Washington he told us he had said the Germans told him that they would support any position we two could agree upon. I said I would think about it for a few days. I then checked with the Germans. They said they had told the Soviets no such thing.

Gromyko then called me from New York. He said he had a compromise formula which he told me he had checked with the Germans. I then checked with the Germans and they said Gromyko had discussed a different proposal with them.

This is stupid. These little tricks don't bring changes about. A clause in a treaty won't change things.

Vice Foreign Minister Ch'iao: Didn't you agree that the last stage of the European Security Conference would be a summit conference?

Secretary Kissinger: We haven't agreed to this. We don't want our European allies to agree and then have us being the only ones who don't agree. So we follow the opinion of Europe. We don't care for such a summit. The idea of 39 heads of state in one room is more than my constitution can bear. They'll all have to talk.

My opinion is that there will be one. (Ch'iao: This year?) No, in March or April next year. That is a guess—certainly not before.

Now they are debating "Basket Three." That will take six weeks just to state the issues, not even to get into negotiations.

We are not in a hurry. We just don't want the European Security Conference to do any damage. We are passive. We don't want it to do very much.

Vice Foreign Minister Ch'iao: South Asia?

Secretary Kissinger: As I said last year [in Peking], we support Pakistan's territorial integrity. We are arranging to have 300 Pak tanks rebuilt in Iran. We will contribute to the expenses, and the Shah will pay for the remainder. On my visit we will try to arrange for the training of Pak military men on Iranian weapons so that they can be used interchangeably. (To Ambassador Bush:) You are learning more about international politics this evening than you ever did at the U.N. (To Ch'iao:) Senator Fulbright thinks you don't give enough emphasis to the U.N. My staff, when they read a statement in my U.N. speech on torture, said I should apply this criterion to the way I treat my staff. (Mr. Lord: So far there has been no change. [Laughter]) Given our bureaucracy it was a miracle this didn't appear in the final text.

We understand completely your views on Pakistan. Strategically we agree, but practically we have some difficulties which I have described to you. We are thinking of ways to overcome them after November. It is an absurd situation: India, a big country, can import arms in great quantity. But if you supply arms to Pakistan then you are "threatening peace."

Vice Foreign Minister Ch'iao: We have discussed the Subcontinent many times. I don't want to appear to attach too much importance to the situation there. But it is important to you. I discussed this with Senator Jackson. He wanted to talk about Diego Garcia. I told him that considering the present situation in South Asia, we understand your position on Diego Garcia. But suppose the Soviets one day realize their ambition of gaining a direct passage into the Indian Ocean. Then Diego Garcia will be of no use.

Secretary Kissinger: There is one point. We think of South Asia as closer to China than to the U.S.

Vice Foreign Minister Ch'iao: Yes, but there is another side to the question. We don't have anything in the Indian Ocean, no fleet. You know that Pakistan for a long time was in an antagonistic position against us. But we lived through that. Some day the Soviets may control all of South Asia . . .

Secretary Kissinger: We would oppose that. I don't say we would approve of such a situation.

Vice Foreign Minister Ch'iao: Even if this happened, we don't think this is the focal point of Soviet strategy. There has been no change in this, they have not shifted [the focal point of their efforts] to South Asia. They can only have one key point. If too many areas are called "key areas," then there will be no key area.

Secretary Kissinger: You see, my education stopped with Kant. So you are ahead of me! (Laughter)

Anyone's strategic situation will be affected by the Soviet situation. If the situation in one area becomes favorable to the Soviets, it can affect anyone's strategic situation, even though the focal point may be in Europe.

Vice Foreign Minister Ch'iao: Specific situations may have changed, but the world situation has remained the same.

Secretary Kissinger: But my point is that if any one country falls to Soviet hegemony it will affect the overall situation.

I agree that Europe is a major strategic concern of the Soviets, but there is nothing in Europe that can't wait for a few years.

Vice Foreign Minister Ch'iao: And what about the East? Isn't it the same?

Secretary Kissinger: My judgment is that in the East there is greater time urgency for the Soviets.

Vice Foreign Minister Ch'iao: I really don't agree.

Secretary Kissinger: I'd be delighted—I'm just giving you my assessment. I don't insist on it. It is my genuine belief. But the problem is the same either way. If the Soviets have a strategic success in the East, it will affect the West. If they have a strategic success in the West, it will affect the East. So the situation is the same [for both of us].

Vice Foreign Minister Ch'iao: True. Whatever happens in different areas of the world it will affect other areas. But the focal point is still important.

Secretary Kissinger: Well, we will see in two or three years.

Vice Foreign Minister Ch'iao: Maybe we won't be able to tell in just two or three years.

Secretary Kissinger: Is this glass for mao-t'ai? (The Chinese: It is too big!) We want to torture the Vice Foreign Minister. Because we didn't have a Cultural Revolution our bureaucracy has to make decisions by committee. Winston Lord has formed a mao-t'ai committee. (Laughter)

Mr. Vice Foreign Minister, when you come to Washington we have a superb serving person at Blair House. He has an exquisite sense of timing. He clatters plates just as the toast is being given, especially when an American official is giving the toast. (Laughter)

Ambassador Huang: I had a similar experience in Ghana.

Secretary Kissinger: You were Ambassador to Ghana? (Huang Hua: Yes.)

Mr. Foreign Minister, to your health, to our friendship.

Vice Foreign Minister Ch'iao: You have done outstanding work in the Middle East, but it is only the beginning.

Secretary Kissinger: I agree. The situation is getting more complicated now. I'm going there next week. The next step has to be made with Egypt, then with Palestine, and then with Syria.

Vice Foreign Minister Ch'iao: We had heard that if it is not possible for you to supply sophisticated weapons to Egypt, then you would give the Soviets a loophole.

Secretary Kissinger: I'll discuss this matter in a smaller group when I am in Peking.

Mr. Foreign Minister, these annual dinners are useful, and pleasant personal events.

Vice Foreign Minister Ch'iao: They are not really annual. This is our second one this year. I think you know that we will welcome you on your visit.

Secretary Kissinger: You mentioned international changes. Of course, we've had internal changes. It was no accident that three hours after taking the oath of office President Ford received the Chief of your Liaison Office. He reaffirmed the continuity of our policy.[3] Tonight I want to reaffirm that continuity. A few years ago we set ourselves certain objectives. Despite changes in the international situation, we will hold to these objectives, including the full normalization of relations.

We have kept in touch with you on major international events. We intend to continue to do this. I look forward to continuing such talks.

---

[3] See Document 85.

I would like to propose a toast: To the friendship of the Chinese and American peoples. To the health of Chairman Mao. To the health of the Premier. (All rise and toast.)

Vice Foreign Minister Ch'iao: Just now you talked about the world situation. As we described it in the Shanghai Communiqué, we are opposed to hegemony. Last time Doctor was in Peking we elaborated on this point: oppose hegemony. This is our basic principle.

Although domestically the U.S. has undergone many changes, you have told us such changes would not affect our relations. We believe that.

We talked about normalization of relations the last time Doctor was in Peking. You talked with Chairman Mao about this. He said that the Japan formula was the only way we could consider normalization. You asked the Premier at dinner what he [Chairman Mao] had meant by this.

Secretary Kissinger: I've learned that there is always more to what the Chairman says than appears at first glance.

Vice Foreign Minister Ch'iao: I remember you told the Premier there were "many layers" to what the Chairman says.

I would like to toast to the friendship of the peoples of China and the U.S., and to the continuation of this friendship. To President Ford. We wish to say he is already one of our friends. When he was in China he left a deep impression on us. So let us drink to the health of President Ford—I don't like to toast you as "Secretary of State." I prefer your title of "Doctor."

Secretary Kissinger: That is a more lasting title. (All rise and toast.)

Secretary Kissinger: (in German to Ch'iao:) You forgot to toast Ambassador Bush.

Vice Foreign Minister Ch'iao: Doctor just reminded me to toast Ambassador Bush. I forgot . . .

Secretary Kissinger: I just wanted you to remember him. He's one of our best men. A good friend—also a Presidential candidate.

Vice Foreign Minister Ch'iao: Ambassador Scali invited me to attend Ambassador Bush's farewell party on the 11th. Unfortunately I'll be leaving on the 8th. So I will take this opportunity provided by Doctor to welcome Ambassador Bush, to drink to the success of his mission. I am sure you will fulfill your mission. I hope you will like Peking. (All rise and toast Ambassador Bush.)

Secretary Kissinger: He could have had any post he wanted. He selected Peking.

Vice Foreign Minister Ch'iao: (to Ambassador Bush): How's your mother?

Ambassador Bush: She is fine. She wants to come to Peking at Christmas time to visit her little boy.

(At this point, 10:30 p.m., the dinner conversation broke up and the group retired to the Secretary's living room.)

Secretary Kissinger: Let's talk a few minutes about your last point. I want to explore this further. (At this point the serving personnel came in with coffee and liqueurs.) I'll wait until after they have finished serving.

Are they going to have passionate debates in the General Assembly? On Korea, is it possible that our two Ambassadors can work out something as they did last year? Your Ambassador [Huang Hua] is such a master. The Soviets asked me how it was worked out last year on Korea. They still don't understand how you did it.

I don't think you have given us a reply to our last proposal [on Korea].[4]

Vice Foreign Minister Ch'iao: I'll be very frank with you. You wanted us to convey your last proposal to the [North] Koreans. We did this. We didn't receive a further response. Finally this question was put on the U.N. agenda. So now we will have a debate with each side speaking on its own separate views.

Secretary Kissinger: I understand. Didn't we have a debate last year? (Huang Hua: In the First Committee.) The question is whether we can have some way of eliminating the United Nations Command without abrogating the Armistice. This is basically what we are after.

Vice Foreign Minister Ch'iao: Do you have any specific form in your mind?

Ambassador Habib: Our proposal is that the Armistice in its present form be maintained, with South Korea and the U.S. . . .

Secretary Kissinger: Yes, with the People's Republic, which is already a signatory, and North Korea on the other side.

Vice Foreign Minister Ch'iao: You understand that we keep on good relations with the Democratic People's Republic of Korea. On this issue we have to respect their views. Of course if you have more detailed views, more comprehensive views on this question, we will convey them to them.

Secretary Kissinger: Our problem is that we cannot accept abolition of the United Nations Command if there is no legal basis on both sides for the continuation of the Armistice. For your information, we

---

[4] See footnote 4, Document 81. On July 31, the Chinese Government rejected the U.S. proposal as an obstacle to peaceful Korean reunification. (National Archives, Nixon Presidential Materials, NSC Files, Kissinger Office Files, Box 96, Country Files, Far East, China Exchanges, April 1–August 8, 1974) In response, U.S. officials conveyed to the PRCLO a truncated version of the June 13 proposal: the UN Command could be abolished if North Korea and China accepted the U.S. and ROK commanders as "successors in command." (Memorandum from Hummel and Solomon to Kissinger, August 27; Department of State, Papers of William H. Gleysteen: Lot 89 D 436, PRC Related Papers, July–Sept. 1974)

have had several approaches from North Korea—from the Romanians, the Egyptians, even David Rockefeller, he is perhaps the largest power involved (laughter)—but we can't respond to their initiatives until the issue of the U.N. Command is resolved. In principle we are not opposed [to having contact with them]. You can convey this to them.

Vice Foreign Minister Ch'iao: Regarding all these details on the Korean question, we don't feel they are of great significance. As you know from your discussions with Chairman Mao, this is not a major issue if you look at it in terms of the overall world situation.

Secretary Kissinger: As I told the Chairman and the Premier, we are not committed to a permanent presence in Korea. This is not a principle of our foreign policy. But we also don't want the speed of our withdrawal to create a vacuum into which some other power might project itself.

Vice Foreign Minister Ch'iao: It seems as if Japan does not feel the behavior of [ROK President] Park is satisfactory.

Secretary Kissinger: I wouldn't pay too much attention to that.

Ambassador Habib: There has been no major change in their relationship.

Vice Foreign Minister Ch'iao: True. Japan's policy regarding Korea is formulated according to many considerations.

Secretary Kissinger: But any sudden change in Korea could stimulate Japanese nationalism. You have to watch that former student of mine, Nakasone.

Vice Foreign Minister Ch'iao: How is it that you have so many bad students?

Secretary Kissinger: Like Ecevit.

Vice Foreign Minister Ch'iao: History will lay [responsibility for] all this on your shoulders! (Laughter)

Secretary Kissinger: Should Scali be in touch with Ambassador Huang Hua? Will there be confrontations?

Vice Foreign Minister Ch'iao: There will be confrontations, but it can also be said that there will not be confrontations.

Secretary Kissinger: But we know the vote. We don't care about the speeches. Ambassador Huang can perhaps create diversions.

Ambassador Huang: The differences in this respect are too great. It is beyond my capability [to resolve them].

Secretary Kissinger: Perhaps you can consider this [matter further]. We attach some importance to this question.

Vice Foreign Minister Ch'iao: I don't think it will bring any complications if the resolution [favorable to North Korea] passes.

Secretary Kissinger: But if it does, it will create complications in Korea, in Japan, or elsewhere.

Vice Foreign Minister Ch'iao: I met Foreign Minister Kimura[5] [in New York]. We touched on this question, although we didn't go into any details. We'll wait a little while and see how the situation develops.

I want to repeat this—I wasn't using diplomatic language: We keep on good relations with the Democratic People's Republic of Korea. This is mainly their position. This is not just a matter of just what China wants.

Secretary Kissinger: We have our Korean friends too. But if we have a general understanding then we can influence the situation.

We have reports that you may be interested in contacts with South Korea.

Vice Foreign Minister Ch'iao: They may not be accurate.

Secretary Kissinger: Let us return to the topic in your toast.

On my visit to Peking I want to talk more concretely about this issue, and work out a timetable. We think late 1975 or early 1976 would be a relatively good time for the completion of this process. But we are prepared to discuss its precise nature beforehand.

We understand your basic position. Your basic position is that normalization should be on the Japanese model. But as you correctly pointed out, there are many layers of meaning. In particular, our conditions are not the same as Japan's. The history of our relations [with the Republic of China on Taiwan] are not the same, our internal situation is more complicated, and our legal requirements are complex. We want to move so that our public opinion does not have a bad feeling about our relations with China.

In general, given our concern with hegemony, it is important that we not be seen as throwing our friends away. I am now giving you our considerations, not a specific proposal.

As I interpret the Japanese formula, this would involve us having embassies in our respective capitals. There would be no embassy in Taipei. Ambassador Unger would then be unemployed. (Laughter) One point which Chairman Mao mentioned intrigued me. We understand that there would be no ambassador in Taipei, but he mentioned that there were ambassadors of the Baltic states in Washington and that this wasn't a situation of any importance.

Vice Foreign Minister Ch'iao: It is my understanding that Chairman Mao talked about this mainly as part of a discussion of political subjects. It was not closely related [to the discussion of normalization].

---

[5] Toshio Kimura was the Foreign Minister of Japan for part of 1974.

Secretary Kissinger: Not exactly, but it puzzled me. That's why I asked [about his remark].

Vice Foreign Minister Ch'iao: I remember that Chairman Mao discussed with you that whether or not we have formal diplomatic relations is not so important. We have diplomatic relations with India, but our relations with them are cold. With you, although we have no diplomatic relations, our contacts are warm. We can either solve this problem, or just leave it as it is. But concerning our relations, if you wish to solve this problem there is only one model, the Japanese model.

Secretary Kissinger: Let me ask two questions. First, you say that the quality of our relations does not depend on whether we have solved this problem. Whether we have liaison offices or embassies, our relations depend on other problems.

Vice Foreign Minister Ch'iao: I remember in your discussion with Chairman Mao this was also touched upon. The major basis of our relationship is that we seek common ground on international problems. Of course in our relations this problem [of Taiwan] lies between us. Diplomatic relations are affected by this situation, but it is not of too great significance. (Secretary Kissinger: We don't have . . .)

For example, you started your visits to Peking in 1971. In 1972 you came with President Nixon. Then in 1973 we made further progress, but we still have this issue [of Taiwan]. So our relations do develop to a certain extent, but then we do confront this question. As this problem does exist, when you think of a timetable, then there is the question of the Japanese model. So I believe that in April, Vice Premier Teng Hsiao-p'ing mentioned that there were two aspects to our position: We hope that our relations can be normalized; but we are not in a hurry.[6]

When Senator Fulbright visited China he asked this question: Can we have further development of our relations? As far as our relations are concerned, before normalization our relations will meet some obstacles. When I was discussing this issue with Senator Fulbright I gave an example. Each year I come to the United States, but I can only go to New York, not to Washington. (Secretary Kissinger: I'll lift the travel restriction on you. [Laughter]) He invited me to Washington. I said I can't come because Chiang Kai-shek has an Embassy there. (Secretary Kissinger: You know that President Ford would welcome a visit by you. You could just come from the airport directly to the White House and then back again if you wished.) Thank you, but I think President Ford will understand my problem.

Secretary Kissinger: Let me tell you our problem. We are in no hurry either. The question is whether our difficulties are ripe for overcoming.

---

[6] See Document 78.

We see several problems. First, what sort of office we will maintain in Taipei after normalization. One obvious possibility is a liaison office there, which has the additional advantage that for the first time in four years we would do something which Senator Jackson can't oppose.[7]

Vice Foreign Minister Ch'iao: This idea was his own. He did not talk with me about it, or with the Vice Premier. After he left China I read this [proposal of his] in the press. I was quite surprised.

Secretary Kissinger: Another possibility is a consulate. But we have a second problem which is more difficult. The defense relationship. We clearly cannot have a defense relationship with part of a country—at least we are not aware that you can. (Laughter)

Vice Foreign Minister Ch'iao: You can create this.

(A secretary enters the room and hands Secretary Kissinger a message.)

Secretary Kissinger: Please excuse me for five minutes. This is the second call I have had from the President tonight. He's about to go to bed. (The Secretary departs the room for about ten minutes.)

Vice Foreign Minister Ch'iao: (to Ambassador Bush): When are you going to Peking?

Ambassador Bush: On the 15th. My wife is now studying Chinese at the Foreign Service Institute. She talked to Huang Chen in Washington and used some of her Chinese. He laughed, and she thought it was a compliment. (Laughter) When will you be going?

Vice Foreign Minister Ch'iao: On the 8th.

Mr. Lord: Will you be going to Germany?

Vice Foreign Minister Ch'iao: Yes. I'll be there [in Peking] to greet Ambassador Bush. I will toast you (to Ambassador Bush).

Ambassador Bush: I have a weak stomach, and can't drink too much.

Vice Foreign Minister Ch'iao: Ambassador Bruce came to enjoy mao-t'ai—with beer.

(There was then some light discussion about the visit of the Fulbright delegation to China, including Senator Humphrey's late night swim in West Lake at Hangchow.)

Ambassador Bush: These Congressmen must be confusing to you. (Ch'iao: Not very much.) They come back and argue among themselves—they loved the warm hospitality, the food, and then they come back and argue about what they should have said.

---

[7] Following his trip to China, Jackson advocated raising the Liaison Office in Beijing to an Embassy and reducing the Embassy in Taipei to a Liaison Office. ("Closer China Ties Urged by Jackson," *The New York Times*, July 9, 1974, p. 11)

Vice Foreign Minister Ch'iao: We are happy to have the opportunity to meet American friends of different views.

(The Secretary re-enters the room.)

Ambassador Huang: Ambassador Bruce is now in the United States? I met General Haig at the President's United Nations reception.

Secretary Kissinger: Yes. We will have a strong NATO team. Two close personal friends [will represent us there].

The President sends his warm regards to the Chairman and to yourself [the Vice Foreign Minister]. He apologizes for interrupting me.

We had just reached the interesting legal question [before the telephone call interruption] of how to have a defense treaty with a portion of a country. This would be an interesting question for Ambassador Huang Hua to present to the U.N. It would call on all his subtlety. (Laughter)

Let me discuss our problem. We obviously can't—our problem is how to present a new relationship with you where we have not just abandoned people who we have had a relationship with, for whatever reason—to ensure a peaceful transition. This was emphasized by Chairman Mao and the Premier in our talks.

We have to keep in mind that what has distinguished our relationship from that which we have with the Soviets is that there is no organized opposition. There is no Senator Jackson on China policy. It is not in our interest with respect to the hegemonial question to make our relationship controversial. If it will, then it is best to defer [the issue of normalization] for a while. This distinguishes us from Japan.

So there are two issues of principle: the nature of the office we will maintain [in Taipei]; and the nature of the guarantee for a peaceful transition.

Vice Foreign Minister Ch'iao: On the question of a peaceful transition on Taiwan, maybe your understanding is different than mine. In our view these are two different problems: the Taiwan question and relations between our two countries, and then our relations with Taiwan. Our idea is to separate these two questions. As for our relations with Taiwan, as Chairman Mao said, the main idea is that we don't believe in the possibility of a peaceful transition. But in our relations with the United States, that is another question.

Talking about a peaceful transition, there are also two aspects. That is, at present our [U.S.–PRC] relations, now you recognize Taiwan . . .

Secretary Kissinger: That is why when our [domestic] transition came, the President received the Chief of your Liaison Office, while the Deputy Secretary of State received the Ambassador from Taiwan.

Vice Foreign Minister Ch'iao: I'm not finished. The transition in our relations can be smooth. But the possibility for a smooth transition in our relations with Taiwan is very small. I recall that this was the focal point in your discussion with Chairman Mao.

Secretary Kissinger: But I recall that he said the transition [in PRC relations with Taiwan] could take a hundred years—by then Bush will be Secretary of State. (Laughter)

Let me sum up your points: The transition in U.S.–PRC relations will go smoothly. As for the transformation of the form of government on Taiwan, this will be over a long period. It does not have to occur immediately, but it isn't likely to be smooth. Do I understand your position correctly. (Ch'iao: Yes.)

Then why don't we consider these problems further, and then discuss them in Peking.

There's one other question on which I wanted the Vice Foreign Minister's views, Cambodia. You agree that we should postpone debate for a year? (Ch'iao: We can't have our way.) I feel sorry for the Vice Foreign Minister surrounded by so many small, intractable countries. He can only have his way with the great powers. What would he do if a hundred Laotian elephants headed north? (Laughter)

The Ambassador (Huang Hua) should take a vacation, visit his family. He is so subtle that he cuts you but you don't know it until you have moved your limb. (Laughter)

Vice Foreign Minister Ch'iao: Let's think of this problem another way. Sooner or later the Lon Nol government will quit the stage. (There is some discussion of how to best translate the Chinese phrase to "quit the stage." The Secretary says there is no elegant way to translate the idea. Everyone laughs.) That is to say, the U.N. debate is something that neither of us can control. So if the GRUNK is admitted, Lon Nol will be expelled. Why not let it happen? It will pave the way for you in solving this problem.

Secretary Kissinger: Especially as there are not many royal governments in Peking nowadays.

What is your idea—this is not a proposal—in order to end the war in Cambodia, to convene an Asian conference, including the People's Republic, the United States, the Soviet Union, Japan, and Cambodia, to solve the problem.

Vice Foreign Minister Ch'iao: At the present moment I don't see what benefit such a conference would bring.

On this question, I'd go back and say that we have spent too much time settling small old problems which are a legacy of the past. As for yourself, you spent so much energy on Vietnam and finally a settlement was reached. Now there is Cambodia.

What I now say may turn out to be only empty words, but in my view the final result [of the present situation in Cambodia] is clear;

it is only a matter of time. You see you solved the Vietnam question, and now only Cambodia is there each year as an obstacle. So now this question is not worthwhile, but it doesn't matter very much. Events have their own laws.

Mr. Solomon, didn't Fulbright raise this question?

Mr. Solomon: No.

Ambassador Huang: You discussed Vietnam with him.

Vice Foreign Minister Ch'iao: I said [to Senator Fulbright] that your aid [to Vietnam] was a mountain, while ours was a small hill. I told Fulbright that on the whole we took a restrained attitude [toward the Vietnam situation].

Secretary Kissinger: Our attitude is that we are prepared to restrict our military aid to replacements.

We believe we should announce my trip to the People's Republic when I return from India—about November 8. I'll be in touch with the Ambassador.

Vice Foreign Minister Ch'iao: On these technical issues we don't have many problems. I'll consult with my government [regarding the timing of your trip].

Secretary Kissinger: Are there any questions I haven't raised?

Mr. Lord: Our European relations are better than they were in April.

Secretary Kissinger: You said last time that we were too harsh on the Europeans. Our relations are better.

Vice Foreign Minister Ch'iao: We have seen this. I think you remember that Chairman Mao also wished that you remain longer in Japan.

Secretary Kissinger: I never thought I'd hear him say that!

Vice Foreign Minister Ch'iao: So we are glad to see that, in comparison to April, you have improved your relations with Japan and with Europe. You had talks with Heath?

Secretary Kissinger: Yes. He was very impressed with his trip to China. I bought him a Chinese antique bowl as a present.

Vice Foreign Minister Ch'iao: Do you think he will lose [the upcoming elections]?

Secretary Kissinger: I'm afraid so. We have particularly strong relations with the Conservative leaders, although the Labor leaders are easy to get along with on a day-to-day basis.

Vice Foreign Minister Ch'iao: Many thanks for your hospitality this evening. I can only reciprocate in Peking.

(At this point, 11:35 p.m., the Chinese got up to depart. They were escorted to the elevator by the Secretary and the other American participants where final farewells were expressed.)

Move Toward Normalization of Relations, October 1974–July 1975

88. National Security Study Memorandum 212[1]

Washington, October 8, 1974.

TO

The Secretary of Defense
The Deputy Secretary of State
The Director of Central Intelligence

SUBJECT

U.S. Security Assistance to the Republic of China

The President has directed a study of U.S. policy on the transfer of American military equipment to the Republic of China over the next three to five years. The study should define relevant U.S. interests and objectives, and should be based upon the following assumptions:

—That the process of normalization in U.S.–PRC relations will continue.

—That there will be no radical change in the Sino-Soviet conflict.

—That the U.S. defense commitment to the Republic of China will continue.[2]

The issues to be examined in the study should include, but not necessarily be limited to, the following:

—The threat to the security of Taiwan over this period.

—The roles of U.S. and ROC forces in deterring and defending against a possible PRC attack on Taiwan and the Pescadores.

---

[1] Source: Ford Library, National Security Adviser, NSSMs and NSDMs, 1974–77, NSSMs File, Box 2, NSSM 212. Top Secret; Sensitive. A copy was sent to the Chairman of the JCS.

[2] Kennedy, Smyser, and Solomon promoted this study as a way "to gain control over the transfer of U.S. arms and military equipment to the Republic of China," but they disagreed on the assumptions that should underlie it. Kennedy and Smyser argued in favor of the three assumptions stated in the NSSM. Such a study, they contended, would be "bureaucratically preferable since it deals with a limited set of contingencies and is less likely to raise questions—public or private—about where we are going," and would also likely avoid a "massive requirements estimate." Solomon, in contrast, asserted that the study should address a broader range of possible scenarios. (Memorandum from Smyser and Solomon to Kissinger, September 24; ibid., NSC Institutional Files (H-Files), Box H–32, NSSM 212, U.S. Security Assistance to the Republic of China)

542

—In light of these roles, the principal deficiencies in ROC defensive capabilities.

—In light of these deficiencies, and taking into account the constraints posed by the continuing normalization of U.S.–PRC relations, the study should define and evaluate policy options for further transfers of U.S. military equipment to the ROC. The evaluation should include consideration of the ROC's economic and technological ability to support the acquisition and maintenance of new weapons systems, and should consider the possibility and feasibility of the ROC developing alternative sources of supply.

The study should be prepared by the NSC Interdepartmental Group for East Asia, which should be chaired by a representative of the Department of State. The study should be submitted to the Assistant to the President for National Security Affairs no later than November 1, 1974, for consideration by the Senior Review Group prior to consideration by the President.

Henry A. Kissinger

---

89.   **Paper Prepared in the Central Intelligence Agency**[1]

Washington, October 1974.

[Omitted here are the title page and table of contents.]

THE SHIFT TO HARSHNESS IN PEKING'S POLICY
TOWARD THE US

Principal Judgments

Since mid-1973 progress in normalizing Sino-US relations has slowed markedly. The Chinese in the past year have expressed dissatisfaction with the US, both privately and publicly; they have hinted to the US that it should commence formal diplomatic disengagement from Taiwan; and they have been less concerned about avoiding clashes of interest with the US.

The impetus for Peking's shift has come from Mao himself, supported—probably reluctantly—by Chou En-lai. The Chinese leaders

---

[1] Source: Central Intelligence Agency, OPI 10, Job 80–M01048A, Communist China, 280174–151174. Secret; Exdis; No Foreign Dissem/Controlled Dissem; No Dissem Abroad; Background Use Only. On October 26, William Colby sent this paper to Kissinger under a covering memorandum stating that a senior analyst in the Office of Political Research of the Directorate of Intelligence had prepared it. (Ibid.)

had anticipated a *phased American disengagement* from formal diplomatic ties with the Chinese Nationalists. Mao's personal disappointment with the pace of US moves in respect of Taiwan has been genuine and crucial to the change in Peking's policy.

Other apparent reasons for the shift have been:

—decreased fear of military attack by the USSR, permitting Peking to argue (unconvincingly) that the US needs China more than China needs the US;
—new perception of the Third World as the area from which Peking can obtain the most political help for those policies it directs against both superpowers; and
—Mao's wish to synchronize foreign policy with the sharp leftward movement in Chinese domestic policies, particularly the intensification of the anti-Confucian campaign.

The most striking features of the shift have been:

—assertions by Chinese officials that Peking has been "deceived" about American policy, and that American "words" were satisfactory, but actions were not with respect to severing ties with Taiwan;
—decreased concern about risking public clashes with the US, e.g., in the UN and in special international conferences;
—reaffirmation by Mao himself that China will continue to assist "liberation" movements (expressed most importantly in increased material aid to the Communist insurgents in Cambodia); and
—a political swing to the Third World, identifying China more closely than ever before with the less developed countries and supporting them in a policy of increasing prices on oil and other raw materials.

Peking can be expected to prod the US harder to speed its disengagement from Taiwan. Specifically, what Peking seems to desire most now is for Washington to upgrade the US liaison office in Peking to an embassy while downgrading the US embassy in Taipei to a liaison office or consulate-general (roughly following the Japanese example). Peking will probably suggest this during the forthcoming high-level Sino-American talks.

The USSR will remain the "main enemy" for Peking, even if the US rejects the anticipated Chinese proposal. This basic fact sets limits on the degree of pressure the Chinese are willing to exert on the US; a visibly high degree of pressure would give aid and comfort to the Soviets. On the other hand, so long as Chinese fear of a Soviet attack remains low, as it is now, the Chinese will probably try to carry on with three not entirely harmonious lines of action:

—to continue the Sino-American détente as a long-term deterrent to the Soviet threat, while insisting that US disengagement from Taiwan must be a part of such a détente;
—to continue to selectively support "liberation" movements, most importantly in Cambodia; and

—to exploit the Third World against both the USSR and the US (immediately, on the oil-pricing issue), if this can be done without alienating the US to the point that the US is no longer interested in a new relationship with Peking.

[Omitted here are the evidence and analysis for the principal judgments.]

---

90.   **Study Prepared by the Ad Hoc Interdepartmental Regional Group for East Asia and the Pacific**[1]

Washington, November 12, 1974.

U.S. Security Assistance to the Republic of China

[Omitted here are the title page and table of contents.]

THE SETTING

Introduction

The changed context of U.S. China policy requires a new look at the question of providing military equipment to the ROC. Political and psychological considerations will have to play an increasingly important role in Taiwan's security if we are to find the narrow ground on which the contradictory objectives of advancing normalization with the PRC while assuring the security of the ROC can be successfully pursued.

Assumptions:

The assumptions governing this study are:

1. U.S.–PRC normalization will continue;
2. There will be no radical change in the Sino-Soviet dispute;
3. The U.S. defense commitment to the ROC will continue;
4. Over the next three to five years, the political and psychological importance of the U.S. supply of weapons to the ROC will be greater than the objective military importance of the weapons themselves.

---

[1] Source: Ford Library, NSC Institutional Files (H-Files), Box H–32, NSSM 212, U.S. Security Assistance to the Republic of China. Top Secret; Sensitive. This study was prepared in response to NSSM 212, Document 88. Scowcroft received the study under a November 12 covering letter from Habib, who chaired this interdepartmental group. (Ibid.) On January 10, 1975, Jeanne Davis sent it to the Secretary of Defense, Deputy Secretary of State, and Director of Central Intelligence. The Chairman of the JCS also received a copy. (Washington National Records Center, OSD Files: FRC 330–78–0059, China (Nats), 1975, 091.3, 10 Jan 1975)

Interests and Objectives

The basic U.S. interest is a peaceful settlement of the Taiwan issue by the Chinese themselves. Progress toward a peaceful settlement will depend on many factors, but because of the great disparity between PRC and ROC capabilities some form of U.S. involvement in Taiwan's security will continue to be important to inhibit the possibility of force being used to resolve the issue.

The *U.S. objectives* governing the supply of arms to the ROC are to:

—avoid actions which the PRC would interpret as inconsistent with "normalization" or which the ROC might interpret as a weakening of our commitment in the Shanghai Communiqué to normalize relations with the PRC.

—maintain confidence on the part of ROC leaders and public that Taiwan is sufficiently secure to minimize the dangers of domestic instability or desperate acts that would hinder U.S.–PRC normalization, including a possible ROC attempt to involve other parties in its fate.

—avoid actions which might lead the PRC to conclude that we no longer have an important interest in the security of Taiwan.

Arms Supply and Taiwan's Security

Along with the deterrent effect of the U.S.–PRC relationship, the U.S. security treaty and the remaining U.S. force presence on Taiwan, ROC access to U.S. military equipment is a major element in Taiwan's sense of security. As our China policy evolves, the relative importance of these elements will change. Access to U.S. arms will become increasingly important to the ROC to the extent that other elements of Taiwan's security equation appear uncertain in its eyes. Specifically, the eventual withdrawal of all U.S. troops or changes in the nature of our security commitment would have that effect.

ROC willingness to rely less on military factors in assuring Taiwan's security has evolved to some extent as a result of the conditioning effects of our policy, but the evolution has been heavily dependent on the assumption of our continued commitment to Taiwan's defense. Somewhat grudgingly the ROC has come to appreciate the deterrent value of the PRC's preoccupation with the Soviet Union and the PRC's related interest in détente with the U.S. The ROC has thus shown increasing resignation to the inevitability of a growing PRC military superiority and has accepted reduction in U.S. force levels on Taiwan, MAP phase-out and FMS cuts, and non-supply of F–4s. Nevertheless, the view which will continue to permeate ROC society for the foreseeable future is that the PRC remains an unregenerate enemy and that the island's survival is dependent on possession of a credible military deterrent and a continued U.S. commitment to Taiwan's security.

A Political Approach to Arms Supply

Current circumstances necessitate an even more political approach to decisions on supply of arms to Taiwan. The nature and level of our arms supply will obviously affect normalization of our relations with the PRC, but it will also have a major impact on the ROC's tolerance of a changing political and security environment. To date the pattern of our arms supply, while posing no major problems with Peking, has contributed significantly to the flexibility with which the ROC has adjusted to rather drastic changes in its status. As our relations with the PRC evolve, however, the ROC may ask for more weapons to help compensate for the weakening of its political and security situation.

Dangers of Sharply Changed ROC Access

Significantly Higher Access—Although a higher level of supply, which satisfies most ROC weapon requests, could ease ROC adjustment to further changes in the ROC–U.S. relationship, the upward direction would disturb Peking. It could also convey the wrong impression to Taipei about our intent to pursue normalization (i.e., that we were no longer moving further in that direction) and could encourage an inflexible ROC approach to the politics of the Taiwan issue.

Greatly Reduced Access—Severely reduced access to U.S. equipment leading to an unmistakable deterioration of ROC military capabilities would risk the danger of setting off a train of developments on Taiwan seriously harmful to our (and possibly PRC) interests. This would be particularly true if it coincided with other changes in our China policy. Our performance would be interpreted on Taiwan as clear evidence that we were washing our hands of the Taiwan problem. The ROC political and military leaders would be the quickest to arrive at such a judgment, but the issue is of such fundamental importance that the rest of Taiwan's society, including Taiwanese oppositionists, would not be far behind in arriving at a similiar conclusion. The resultant erosion of confidence could lead to political dissension which would threaten the stability of the current leadership, to severe repression of popular unrest by a shaky government, or even to the ultimate disintegration of social order on Taiwan. A panic-stricken government's efforts to deal with a deteriorating situation could lead to desperate attempts to change Taiwan's juridical status or involve others in its fate. The readily perceived direct U.S. responsibility for this state of affairs would confront us with serious problems at home and abroad.

Effect of ROC Military Nuclear Program—Loss of confidence in the U.S. could lead the ROC to intensify efforts to acquire a military nuclear capability. To date these efforts have been effectively inhibited by our firm and explicit opposition and by an unwillingness to jeopardize Taiwan's rapidly growing civilian nuclear power program which is hostaged to the U.S. because no other country can legally supply reactors to the ROC. Nevertheless, the ROC has not abandoned its covert military nuclear energy research program and it probably possesses most of the technological know-how for the development of a nuclear device. It has a small safeguarded Canadian heavy water reactor (similar to that used by the Indians), but was blocked by us from acquiring a chemical separation facility necessary to extract plutonium.

The inhibitions which have kept the ROC in line could be swept aside by a ROC calculation that a nuclear capability was required as an effective substitute for the vanishing U.S. security commitment. However, it would still take the ROC considerable time to fabricate a nuclear device.

Peking's Viewpoint

We do not know with precision the extent to which at any given time our military relationship with the ROC is an obstacle to normalization of relations with the PRC. Peking keeps careful track of ROC millitary capabilities, but it does not appear to conduct this assessment in isolation from other political factors. U.S. arms supplies are only one variable in a more complicated equation in which other aspects of the relationship between Washington on the one hand and Taipei and Peking on the other, as well as the overall international situation in East Asia, are all factors.

Peking obviously does not desire that U.S. support for the ROC should be offered at a level that might cause the leadership in Taipei to conclude that it is essentially invulnerable to pressures. On the contrary, it would like to see an attenuation in the U.S. military relationship with the ROC sufficient to demoralize the ROC to the point where it would be receptive to political accommodation. Nevertheless, there have been indications from Peking that it does not wish our presence in Taiwan—of which arms supply is an aspect—to be withdrawn so fast that others would be tempted to intervene or that uncontrollable changes on the island become likely. In any event, our military involvement with the ROC will be monitored by a PRC suspicious about our ultimate intentions on Taiwan. Insensitivity in our handling of this issue could undermine the position of those within the PRC who advocate normalization or lead them to a change in attitude.

Particular PRC Sensitivities—Given these various and somewhat conflicting considerations, it seems reasonable to conclude that Peking would be bothered by an indefinite and formal U.S. military involvement with Taiwan. In this general context, the following U.S. actions would appear to be particularly bothersome to Peking:

—The introduction into Taipei's arms inventory of weapons which were *clearly offensive* in nature (e.g., strategic bombers, long-range missiles, or modern amphibious equipment);

—The creation in Taiwan of a *domestic capacity to produce*—or co-produce—sophisticated weapons (e.g., advanced aircraft or major missile production capabilities);
   —The provision on a high priority basis of the *most advanced weapons in the U.S. inventory* (e.g., F–15 aircraft, TV guided bombs, advanced ECM systems);
   —The rapid introduction of *large quantities* of weapons into Taipei's inventory (e.g., an Enhance Plus type of program).[2]

An additional factor relating to *delivery schedules* ought also be considered. Given the long lead time before various weapons systems which presently interest the ROC would be available for delivery, the actual arrival of such weapons on the island—even if agreement on delivery were made well in advance and even if Peking became aware of such an agreement—might occur in a somewhat changed international environment resulting from further progress in normalization of relations with Peking. At that time the PRC might react strongly to the introduction of the weapons on the island, even though the agreement with the ROC for the supply of the weapons had been reached under different circumstances.

Room for Maneuver Narrowing

We will continue to be confronted with ROC demands for weapons which are unacceptable given our policy toward the PRC, as well as displays of PRC displeasure over our having any military dealings with the ROC. To date both sides have not evidenced a serious expectation of complete satisfaction of their respective positions because they judge their overall interests require concessions to U.S. views on the Taiwan problem. As normalization proceeds, we will have less room for maneuver in dealing with the issue of arms supply to the ROC, especially as we complete substantial withdrawals of our forces from Taiwan and as the focus shifts to other elements of our security relationship with the ROC.

Third Country Sources

Under prevailing international circumstances there is little prospect of the ROC finding reliable third country sources of major weapons. It is doubtful, for example, that any of the few nations capable of producing advanced aircraft would risk endangering their relationship with the PRC by providing such a high profile weapon to the ROC. However, some weapons would be available to the ROC from third country sources which, within limits, could spare us problems with the PRC that might arise if we provided such weaponry. Israel and possibly Italy are prepared to supply surface-to-surface missiles to the ROC and Taipei apparently would not have much difficulty in

---

[2] See footnote 3, Document 73.

obtaining patrol crafts from European sources. Moreover, through packages comprised of various third country components the ROC could probably satisfy some of its electronic and naval requirements. Light arms would be readily available to the ROC on the international market, although at a cost to logistical efficiency. Nevertheless, third country channels will represent limited and unreliable sources of supply for the ROC and will not appreciably reduce our key role in maintaining a credible ROC military deterrent.

Technological and Economic Factors

The ROC has had no serious technological difficulties in handling the present levels and sophistication of U.S. equipment and would be technologically capable of absorbing any of the weaponry contemplated under the options presented later in this paper. Present projections indicate that Taiwan's economic resources would be sufficient to permit purchase of certain new weapon systems even in the event of drastically reduced FMS and Excess Defense Articles availabilities. Over the next five-year period, however, the capability of the ROC economy to support continued increases in defense spending at past rates will diminish. Moreover, the ROC would have to greatly reduce the size of its bloated army and would have to sacrifice much of its current economic infrastructure program if it were to try to greatly improve its current military capabilities vis-à-vis the PRC. (A discussion of ROC Economic Capabilities is presented in Annex A.[3])

II

PRC Military Threat to Taiwan

Although political factors will play an even greater role in determining our position on supply of military equipment to the ROC, the strictly military aspects of Taiwan's security and the ROC's preoccupation with these must be considered. The PRC military threat to the ROC as summarized below and discussed in Annex B assumes that there will be no change in the PRC–USSR confrontation; that the PRC will neither use nor threaten to use nuclear weapons in invading Taiwan; and that the U.S. will not intervene at least initially in the event of a PRC attack:

1) The Sino-Soviet border confrontation is a major constraint on Chinese military resources. This confrontation will continue to tie up more than 40% of the PRC ground and air forces and the strongest of its three naval fleets—the North Sea Fleet—for an indefinite period. Nevertheless, the remaining available PRC forces would be sufficient to overcome ROC defenses.

---

[3] Annexes A–C are attached but not printed.

2) The PRC Air Force could gain air supremacy over the Taiwan Strait in a period of perhaps two or three weeks although only by accepting extremely high losses to the more sophisticated but considerably smaller ROC Air Force. Such losses would gravely compromise Peking's air arm. This assessment assumes the completion of the ROC's co-production program of 100 F–5Es and the provision of adequate hardening and anti-aircraft artillery and missiles for key ROC air defense assets.[4]

3) The PRC, utilizing only units of its East Sea Fleet, would establish naval supremacy in the Taiwan Strait. If control of the air had been gained, this could be accomplished in short order, perhaps in a matter of days. Once such supremacy is established, PRC naval forces could isolate the off-shore islands and effectively blockade Taiwan's ports.

4) Either prior to or concurrent with the establishment of air and naval superiority, the PRC could assemble, load, dispatch, and assault beaches on Taiwan with an amphibious force of some 30,000 infantry troops with equipment plus an additional 75,000 lightly equipped troops by using some 500 small landing craft. (These landing craft, which are largely 60–90-foot LCN's and which are normally devoted to non-military uses, are all that the PRC is known to have, and thus would have to be mobilized country-wide.) These forces could probably maintain a beachhead for several days—long enough to be reinforced in strength, if air and naval superiority had been established.

5) In three to five years, the PRC's capability for a successful attack could be improved through acquisition of air-to-air missiles and additional more advanced aircraft.

III

ROC Force Composition

The ROC's inability to withstand a determined PRC attack on its own has necessarily required military contingency plans under the Mutual Defense Treaty for active participation of U.S. air and naval forces in Taiwan's defense in the event of such an attack. Such planning, however, assumes that the ROC would have to meet the first four to five days of a PRC attack with its own forces, giving us time to resort to

---

[4] On January 14, 1975, Davis distributed a memorandum that asked recipients of the study to insert a footnote that reads: "USAF and DIA believe that the initial PRC air assault against Taiwan would be carried out with sufficient forces to overwhelm the ROC AC&W system, thus negating the ROC advantages in equipment and training, reducing PRC losses, and insuring the early attainment of PRC superiority." (Ford Library, NSC Institutional Files (H-Files), Box H–32, NSSM 212, U.S. Security Assistance to the Republic of China)

diplomatic efforts to end the conflict and to assess the need and extent of U.S. involvement in the defense of Taiwan.

Given Taiwan's location, the nature of the PRC threat, and role ROC forces would have to play in the island's initial defense, the optimum structure of the ROC military force would be:

—an Air Force designed primarily for air-to-air capability against fighters, bombers and airlift forces, and for countering a PRC naval attack;

—a navy capable of withstanding attacks by PRC submarine forces and missile-equipped surface craft and of countering PRC amphibious forces in coordination with the ROC Air Force;

—a relatively small but mobile and well-equipped ROC Army, including surface-to-air missiles for air defense, backed by a trained reserve force.

ROC Deficiencies

Existing major ROC deficiencies in achieving such a military force are as follows:

Air Defense—The replacement of older aircraft with 100 F–5E aircraft under the current co-production program will provide the ROCAF with a strong air combat capability for the next few years. Completion of this program, however, will still leave the Air Force with over 100 older aircraft (F–104's and F–100's) which should be replaced in the early 1980's. In addition, the ROCAF will presumably continue to require at least some all-weather interceptors, a role now filled by 36 F–104G's. These also will need to be replaced within the next five to ten years. Depending on PRC capabilities, the ROC may require a follow-up aircraft such as the YF–16 or 17 for the 1980's.

ROCAF facilities on the ground remain vulnerable to PRC bombardment, and improvements are necessary. An aircraft shelter program, introduction of two battalions of the improved Hawk surface-to-air missile, one of which has already been approved by the USG, and acquisition of modern anti-aircraft artillery such as the Vulcan system would help correct these deficiencies. In addition, improved command and control equipment for the ROC air defense system, including improvements in the air operations center, are necessary.

Defense Against Naval/Amphibious Attack—The Navy is probably the weakest of the ROC services, and has the most immediate deficiencies. Not only is it greatly outnumbered by PRC naval forces, but its ships are inferior. Its most critical deficiency is the limited defense against the PRC's high speed patrol boats equipped with Styx anti-ship missiles. The Navy is also hampered by a limited anti-submarine warfare (ASW) capability. Finally, incompatible communications between the Navy and Air Force, and questionable Air Force capabilities against surface ships result in serious naval defense deficiencies.

Improved electronic countermeasures (ECM) equipment on ROC ships would reduce their vulnerability to attack by the PRC's Styx missiles, but the most effective counter would be for the ROC to obtain its own anti-ship missiles such as Harpoon. These would best be mounted on high-speed patrol boats; construction of five such craft under a co-production arrangement has already been approved by the USG. The ROC's deficiencies in ASW are of less immediate importance. These could be remedied with improved aircraft (16 S–2E ASW aircraft were recently approved for sale to the ROC), improved sonar and improved torpedoes for the ROC's destroyers. Finally, a compatible communications system for ROC ships and aircraft and improved anti-ship munitions for the ROCAF, perhaps laser guided bombs, would add considerably to the ROCAF's ability to participate in defense against an amphibious attack.

IV

OPTIONS

Introduction

The options presented below relate the question of supply of military equipment to the ROC to our overall China policy objectives. They range from handling the issue in a manner designed to minimize arms supply as an obstacle to U.S.–PRC normalization to one designed to maximize ROC confidence in the U.S. security commitment.

The options were developed on the assumption that over the next three to five years the political and psychological importance of U.S. supply of weapons to the ROC will be greater than the objective military importance of the weapons themselves. Both the ROC and PRC will view our handling of this issue as an indicator of the relative importance the U.S. attaches to each. Nevertheless, their reactions to what we do in this sphere may be asymmetric. As an example, the ROC would regard a significant restriction on its present access to weapons as a serious matter while the PRC response might not be equivalently favorable.

It is also worth reiterating that ROC arms access cannot be considered in isolation from the other elements of Taiwan's security: the deterrent effect of U.S.–PRC relationship, our defense commitment and the remaining U.S. force presence. Not only are these elements inextricably bound up, but their relative importance can—and will—shift markedly depending on events.

Option I, *Complete Cut-Off of Access to U.S. Equipment,* would completely terminate ROC access to U.S. arms, either immediately or gradually over the next three to five years. Option II, *Freezing ROC Access to Current Types and Levels,* would restrict ROC access to replacement of items already in its inventory (e.g., the F–5E program would be completed and could be extended to replace additional obsolescent aircraft on a one-for-one basis); no new weapons systems would be authorized.

Option III, *Limited ROC Access to New Weapons*, would at its lower range permit ROC access to some additional and new weapons which we would judge as unlikely to be provocative to the PRC (e.g., improved air-to-air missiles and possibly Harpoon missiles); at its upper range, we would permit access to new weapons which run a higher risk of provoking the PRC if we thought such weapons were necessary to shore up ROC confidence or to counter a growing PRC capability (e.g., Harpoon missile and ASROC). Option IV, *Substantial ROC Access to New Weapons*, would permit ROC access to a broad range of new weapons systems (e.g., large number of laser-guided bombs and YF–16 or 17 aircraft as follow-on to F–5E). Under all of these options, even Option I, we would not interfere with ROC purchases from third countries, unless under exceptional circumstances; in some cases we might encourage such ROC purchases.

We have considered these options in light of the following criteria:

1) the impact on our objective of reducing the military component of Taiwan's security;
2) the effect on U.S.–PRC normalization;
3) the effect on Taiwan's confidence and stability;
4) the deterrent effect against a PRC use of force to resolve the Taiwan issue;
5) the effect on chances of ROC–PRC political accommodation;
6) the ROC's economic and technological capabilities.

Option I. Complete Cut-Off of Access to US Equipment

This option would seek to eliminate or minimize to the greatest extent possible the issue of U.S. arms supply to Taiwan as an obstacle to normalization of relations with the PRC. At the lower range of the option, ROC access to U.S. arms would be terminated abruptly. At the upper range, ROC access would be phased out over the next three to five years. In either case, the cut-off would be complete: no additional equipment or spare parts would be authorized for sale to Taiwan.

Advantages:

—would promote normalization of U.S.–PRC relations;

—would impose least economic burden on the U.S. and ROC;

—upper range of option could ease PRC pressure for an abrupt arms supply cut-off, while offering ROC transitional period to adjust to new reality;

—could be used as bargaining chip in negotiations with Peking;

—although at the risk of chaos on Taiwan, would increase pressures on ROC to seek accommodation with the PRC.

Disadvantages:

—would cause deep erosion of ROC confidence, leading to possible disintegration of social order or desperate acts which could complicate rather than ease U.S.–PRC relations; our direct responsibility for such consequences would confront us with serious problems at home and abroad;

—could cause PRC to miscalculate our intentions with respect to Taiwan, tempting it to use, or more likely to threaten to use, force as Taiwan's defense capabilities rapidly deteriorate;

—would result in a severe decline in our influence with the ROC;

—so long as security treaty remained in effect, would necessitate earlier and more substantial U.S. role in meeting our defense commitment in event of PRC attack;

—might prompt accelerated ROC efforts to develop nuclear weapons;

—could cause serious concern in other Asian nations dependent on the U.S.;

—would endanger U.S. investment on Taiwan.

Option II. Freezing ROC Access to Current Types and Levels

This option would place new limitations on arms supply to the ROC in order to improve the climate for U.S.–PRC normalization. Over a three to five-year period it would involve an unmistakable deterioration of ROC military capabilities relative to the PRC. Under this option we would permit continued access to spare parts, replacement of equipment or items already in the ROC inventory and certain improved models made necessary by phase-out of weapons in the U.S. inventory (e.g., F–5Es, improved Hawk missiles). Under this option no new weapons systems would be authorized. An illustrative list of the kinds of equipment which could be provided under this option is at Annex C I.

Advantages:

—could for a time at least reduce arms supply as obstacle to normalization of U.S.–PRC relations;

—would for the next few years maintain a credible ROC military deterrence;

—would preserve some elements of our arms relationship with the ROC as a bargaining chip for later use with Peking;

—would reduce U.S. economic burden;

—could over time help convey to the ROC our interest in its seeking accommodation with the PRC.

Disadvantages:

—as departure from present practice would erode ROC confidence in U.S. support, possibly leading to instability on Taiwan or to ROC moves which could complicate our relations with the PRC;

—could over time tempt PRC to threaten the use of force since disparity in relative military power in the Taiwan Strait area would gradually increase;

—to extent ROC's self-defense capability is limited, would imply earlier and more extensive US role in the event of PRC attack;

—might prompt accelerated ROC efforts to develop nuclear weapons.

Option III. Limited ROC Access to New Weapons

This option is divided into a lower and upper range. Under the lower range the ROC would not be permitted to obtain "controversial" new equipment; under the upper range we would permit limited acquisition of such equipment. We would define "controversial" as any major, new weapon which would be seen by the PRC as providing the ROC clear technological superiority or altering the current relative military "balance". Since we cannot be confident in assessing Peking's views, we would also have to take into account the role in the U.S. inventory, and popular "image" of the weapon.

Under the lower range, we would permit the ROC to replace or modestly increase existing equipment (including F–5E aircraft), and would also permit it to obtain new equipment which is not "controversial" (e.g., anti-tank missiles, certain kinds of ECM equipment, improved command and control systems for air defense; the Harpoon missile to counter the rapidly growing PRC Styx missile boat threat would be a borderline case). We assume the ROC would turn where possible to third-country sources for "controversial" weaponry and we would not interfere. Our objective under this lower range of equipment supply would be to maintain a balance between accommodating PRC sensitivities and fulfilling ROC needs for psychological confidence in its security. An illustrative list of the kinds of equipment which could be provided under this lower range option is at Annex C II.

Under the upper range, we would permit the ROC to replace and modestly increase existing equipment, including a limited number of new equipment items the PRC might consider "controversial", but which would help to maintain ROC confidence in U.S. intentions and in its ability to deal with what it perceives to be serious and growing PRC capabilities. However, if there were alternative sources of such "controversial" equipment available to the ROC, we would not feel compelled to supply our equipment. The objective would be to give, within limits, greater emphasis to ROC psychological concerns over its security, while accepting some risk of PRC displeasure over our actions in the arms supply area. We would have to make a careful case-by-case examination of all ROC requests keeping in mind that the extent to which any weapons system is "controversial" might well change, either over time or because of other changes in the relationships between the U.S. and the two Chinese parties. Under this option we would provide the Harpoon missile or laser guided bombs. An illustrative list of the kinds of equipment which could be provided under this upper range option is at Annex C III.

Advantages:

—should be sufficiently reassuring to ROC (particularly at upper range) to prevent instability on Taiwan or acts of desperation; would cushion the impact of any further changes in the ROC's political environment;

—provides flexibility to deal with weapons supply in the context of evolving U.S. China policy and probable changes in other elements of Taiwan's security;

—would maintain credible, though gradually deteriorating, ROC military deterrent;

—would inhibit PRC temptation to use force;

—would provide the U.S. with a bargaining chip in later negotiations with the PRC.

Disadvantages:

—particularly at upper range could give rise to both PRC and ROC doubts about our interest in normalization and peacefully resolving the Taiwan problem;

—might involve modest risk to ROC (particularly at lower range) by acquiescing in a gradual deterioration of ROC defense capability relative to that of the PRC;

—provides the least precise practical guidelines for judging specific items of military equipment;

—at upper range would place strain on ROC economic capabilities;

—long lead times for many new weapons systems may lead to misunderstanding of U.S. intentions by PRC when weapons delivered.

Option IV—Substantial ROC Access to New Weapons

Under this option we would permit the ROC to attempt to maintain or enhance its military capabilities relative to those of the PRC. The ROC would be permitted to increase its inventory of weapons systems already held, and also obtain new weapons systems in significant numbers. The distinction between "controversial" or "non-controversial" equipment would be minimized, but not ignored, and we would continue to prevent the ROC from acquiring a serious offensive capability for use against the PRC. Our objective under this option would be to use arms supply as a means of enhancing ROC confidence in its security and of minimizing the effects of any other changes in our security relationship with the ROC. Under this option we would provide both Harpoon missiles and laser guided bombs and eventually YF–16 or 17 follow-on aircraft. An illustrative list of equipment which would be provided under this option is at Annex C IV.

Advantages:

—by maximizing ROC confidence, would entail least risk of ROC instability or acts of desperation and would cushion the impact of any further changes in its political environment;

—greater ROC capability might reduce need for more direct U.S. involvement in Taiwan security.

Disadvantages:

—would hinder normalization of U.S.–PRC relations and the wider U.S. objectives associated with it;

—would mislead ROC about U.S. interest in achieving a peaceful resolution of the Taiwan problem in keeping with Shanghai Communiqué;

—strain in U.S.–PRC relations would reduce the political deterrent against a PRC attack;

—would place maximum burden on the ROC economy, and would require substantial new U.S. financial assistance;

—PRC would be likely to view this course as an increased threat to it, and might augment its own forces in the area;

—long lead times involved would mean deliveries into late eighties of approvals within this period.[5]

[Omitted here are Annex A on ROC economic capabilities, Annex B on the PRC military threat, and Annex C of illustrative lists of equipment under various options.]

---

[5] A memorandum prepared by the NSC staff reported the various departmental views: State favored Option III in its lower range; Defense supported Option III in its upper range; CIA took no formal position but asserted that Options II or III, singly or in combination, were the most realistic means to maintain the U.S. relationships with the PRC and the ROC while preserving stability in Taiwan. The authors of the memorandum agreed with State that Option III in its lower range provided the best broad policy guidance. (Memorandum from Solomon, Granger, and Froebe to Kissinger, May 23, 1975; Ford Library, NSC Institutional Files (H-Files), Box H–32, NSSM 212, U.S. Security Assistance to the Republic of China)

91.   Backchannel Message From the Chief of the Liaison Office in China (Bush) to Secretary of State Kissinger[1]

Beijing, November 18, 1974, 0740Z.

91. Subject: China's Internal Scene on the Eve of Your Visit.

1. In hopes that it might be helpful to you, we have prepared the following assessment of China's internal scene on the eve of your visit, as it looks to us in Peking.

2. The ideological campaign which was just gathering steam at the time of your last visit now seems to be drawing to a close. Almost identical reports from three cities in China describe a recent Central Committee directive which quote no less than Chairman Mao as saying that eight years of the Cultural Revolution is enough. It appears that a National People's Congress could be convened at any time, a step which would mark further movement toward the creation of a leadership structure to take China into the anticipated succession period. Mao Tse-tung continues to remain outside Peking, however, and has now been gone at least four months, a fact which injects some uncertainty into any projection of PRC political developments. Mao's return to Peking could, as has happened in the past, signal entirely new directions in Chinese policy, although this does not appear likely.

3. What was accomplished by the recent political campaign? In our view, a variety of issues, all parts of which is perhaps Mao's last effort to shape China in his image, were at stake. They include the role of China's military and its relationship to the party, the degree of central control over China's massive regional and provincial bureaucracies, the Middle Kingdom's relationship with the barbarian states, most importantly the U.S. and the Soviet Union, and last but not least, a genuine effort to eradicate traditional, Confucian thought and behavior patterns among the Chinese people. While it is impossible to measure with anything like precision the regime's success in resolving these issues, we suspect the results have been mixed at best, and many questions have been compromised but not solved.

4. Perhaps the most important changes have taken place in the military field. Early in the campaign eight of China's eleven regional military commanders were wrenched loose from their long standing power bases in a massive shift the impact of which remains unclear. Whereas they previously had occupied both military and political positions, usually as provincial party first secretary, most have now

---

[1] Source: Ford Library, Kissinger–Scowcroft West Wing Office Files, 1974–1977, China Exchanges, Box 4, Unnumbered items (6). Top Secret; Sensitive; Exclusively Eyes Only; Immediate; Via Voyager Channel.

been stripped of their political functions. The apparent debate over military priorities and strategy also seems to have been resolved in favor of the Maoist position stressing convential over nuclear preparedness, and in addition emphasizing economic development over massive military budgets. In our judgment, however, these issues, while resolved for the present, will continue to be a major focus of debate as China moves into the uncertain period of succession.

That the issue of central versus local control remains unresolved was illustrated by series of authoritative articles in the November issue of *Red Flag*. Implicit in the articles was allegation that provincial and local authorities had substituted their authority for that of the party central, and once again the role of the revolutionary committees is in some doubt. The problem of creating a governmental structure in China which is responsive to Peking's authority, a problem as old as China, remains unsolved.

The debate over China's relationship with the West was expressed in the field of culture through the polemics over the Antonioni film and the attacks on Western music.[2] In the fields of commerce and technology, the debate has centered on self reliance as opposed to the import of foreign goods and advanced techniques. The problem in both cases is to what extent can China move into the modern world and widened contacts with the West without its people being overwhelmed by outside influences. We suspect that in the course of the debate a compromise position has been reached which, for the present at least, has satisfied Chinese leaders that they can move toward greater contact and exposure to the West while maintaining the essential principle of self reliance and a uniquely revolutionary-tinged Chinese culture.

Finally, the centerpiece of the present campaign, the attack on Confucius and the weight of traditional thought on the Chinese populace has, in our view, had the least impact of all. While it is impossible to document, it is our impression based on our exposure to the Chinese bureaucracy and the man on the street that little has changed in the Middle Kingdom. Materialism rather than revolutionary ideology remains the most important impetus in Chinese society, which also retains an innate conservatism.

In the process of attempting these changes and reaching a new consensus, however, new turmoil and uncertainty have been generated in China. The calls for struggle and "going against the tide" reopened old wounds of the Cultural Revolution and aroused the ambitions of those who rose to positions of power during that movement only to be relegated to obscurity when order had to be restored. New factional fighting and poster attacks reminiscent of the Cultural Revolution erupted

---

[2] See footnote 2, Document 69.

during the spring and summer, but were quickly curtailed by directives from the center. Apparently it was agreed that China could not afford another Cultural Revolution at this time. Although factional disputes and poster attacks continue, it is our estimate that these represent a minority fighting a forlorn campaign in an effort to reestablish the role of "mass representatives" created during the Cultural Revolution.

At the center, it appears that a minimum consensus has been reached on the basic issues confronting China. The overriding succession issue has both intensified the maneuvering for power and reinforced the impetus for unity. Teng Hsiao-ping now seems clearly to have moved into the Acting Premier's role. This plus the recent announcement of Chiao Kuan-hua's appointment as Foreign Minister indicate that some basic issues have been resolved probably including China's continuing relationship with the U.S. Our assumptions in this regard are strengthened by what we feel is markedly more relaxed atmosphere in our dealings with our Chinese hosts at all levels since the fall of this year. Your visit will, of course, provide a much clearer insight into the balance of forces in China.

To sum up, it seems to us that the direction of Chinese policy remains very much in the hands of the same establishment which first decided to permit the opening of the present U.S.–PRC relationship, even if the active cast of characters within this establishment has changed somewhat. Chinese actions, both internal and external, also remain essentially unchanged even if they are portrayed for purposes of gaining the widest possible support in more radical or "revolutionary" terms. Domestically, attention is focussed upon building up the national economy while maintaining a sufficient degree of political unity to take the country through a transition in leadership; in international affairs China is following an essentially defensive philosophy (despite the attacks on superpower hegemonism and support for the Third World) which does not commit the country to any initiative not immediately linked to China's own national interest.

92.   Memorandum of Conversation[1]

Beijing, November 26, 1974, 10:20–11:02 a.m.

PARTICIPANTS

> Teng Hsiao-p'ing, Vice Premier of the State Council, People's Republic of China
> Ch'iao Kuan-hua, Minister of Foreign Affairs
> Ambassador Huang Chen, Chief of the PRC Liaison Office, Washington
> Lin P'ing, Director, Department of American and Oceanic Affairs, Ministry of Foreign Affairs
> T'ang Wen-sheng, Deputy Director, Department of American and Oceanic Affairs, Ministry of Foreign Affairs
> Chu Ch'uan-hsien, Director, Protocol Department, Ministry of Foreign Affairs
> Tsien Ta-yung, Counselor, PRC Liaison Office, Washington
> Ting Yuan-hung, Director, United States Office, Department of American and Oceanic Affairs Ministry of Foreign Affairs
> Chao Chi-hua, Deputy Director, United States Office, Department of American and Oceanic Affairs, Ministry of Foreign Affairs
> Chang Han-chih, Translator
> Lien Cheng-pao, Notetaker

> Dr. Henry A. Kissinger, Secretary of State and Assistant to the Preident for National Security Affairs
> Donald Rumsfeld, Assistant to the President
> Ambassador George Bush, Chief of the United States Liaison Office, Peking
> Ambassador Robert Anderson, Special Assistant to the Secretary of State for Press Relations
> Winston Lord, Director, Policy Planning Staff, Department of State
> Philip C. Habib, Assistant Secretary of State for East Asian and Pacific Affairs
> William H. Gleysteen, Deputy Assistant Secretary of State for East Asian and Pacific Affairs
> John H. Holdridge, Deputy Chief, United States Liaison Office, Peking
> Oscar V. Armstrong, Director, People's Republic of China and Mongolian Affairs, Department of State
> Richard H. Solomon, Senior Staff Member, National Security Council
> Robert C. McFarlane, National Security Council
> Karlene Knieps, Notetaker

SUBJECT

> Introductory Tour d'Horizon: Japan; Bilateral Relations and Normalization

[*Note:* The discussions began with members of the American press party traveling with the Secretary in the room. Some of Vice Premier Teng's remarks seemed oriented to this press presence.]

---

[1] Source: Ford Library, National Security Advisor, Kissinger Reports, Box 2, November 25–29, 1974, Kissinger's Trip. Top Secret; Sensitive; Exclusively Eyes Only. The meeting took place in the Great Hall of the People. All brackets are in the original.

Vice Premier Teng: I would like to take this opportunity to once again express our welcome to the Doctor on his seventh visit to China. I might also say this is the third time we have had the opportunity to exchange views this year. And we hear that the Doctor has made a trip around the globe recently. So we are happy to have this opportunity to have an exchange of opinions again with the Doctor and all the other friends on your staff—to provide us with the opportunity to exchange views not only with old familiar friends, but with new friends like, for instance, Mr. Rumsfeld.

Secretary Kissinger: I want to thank you on behalf of my colleagues for the very warm reception we have received here. We have, as you said, had three exchanges this year with you and with the Foreign Minister, and we always progress in our relationship.

Vice Premier Teng: It probably would be good if one day we would be able to exchange views in Washington.

Secretary Kissinger: I hope we can do that very soon—

Vice Premier Teng: I think it is a common desire, and that is good.

Secretary Kissinger: —because your Foreign Minister always refuses my invitations.

Vice Premier Teng: It is difficult for him to come now. What will he do if he meets the Chiang Kai-shek Ambassador in Washington?

[*Note:* At this point in the conversation the press is ushered from the room.]

Secretary Kissinger: I thought he wanted to wait until the Ambassador's [Huang Chen's] residence was fully furnished. I think we can arrange a visit so that there is no danger of his meeting anybody there he wishes to avoid.

Vice Premier Teng: It might be difficult.

Secretary Kissinger: That we could arrange, and we are prepared on this visit to discuss the whole question of normalization.

Vice Premier Teng: That is good. We have just received news that Tanaka has resigned.[2]

Secretary Kissinger: Yes. I think I told your Foreign Minister last night that we knew he would resign this morning. Our indications are that there will now be a rush of consultations in which—. All the candidates are in favor of consultation because they think they will emerge as the Prime Minister. I think there will be an election around December 9. We think that Ohira is the most likely to succeed him, and if he doesn't make it then Shiina will probably become the successor.

---

[2] Japanese Prime Minister Kakuei Tanaka resigned November 26, 1974.

Vice Premier Teng: What about Fukuda?

Secretary Kissinger: We don't think Fukuda can make it now, and therefore if they want Fukuda they will first put in Shiina as a transitional figure.

Vice Premier Teng: But you should also know that Fukuda would be voted for by the Soviet Union too.

Secretary Kissinger: This I frankly would not know.

Vice Premier Teng: Their relationship is growing closer day-by-day.

Secretary Kissinger: Between Fukuda and Shiina, or between the Japanese and Soviets?

Vice Premier Teng: No, between Fukuda and the Soviet Union.

Secretary Kissinger: This I was not aware of.

Vice Premier Teng: Would you vote for Ohira?

Secretary Kissinger: I, personally? Ohira personally is a good friend of mine. And we would be very content with Ohira. And we are certainly not supporting Fukuda.

Vice Premier Teng: So we would have similiar opinions.

Secretary Kissinger: We have no difficulty at all with Ohira. He would support the policy we are familiar with.

Vice Premier Teng: That is so, and we also feel that one of the characteristics of Ohira is that what he says counts. And perhaps, in this respect, if he carries out a certain policy he might be even more firm than Tanaka.

Secretary Kissinger: Well, he is more experienced than Tanaka. In any event, we think that in all probability Ohira will be Prime Minister. And if for any reason he should not be, which we do not expect—but it isn't certain where it could line up. My student [Nakasone] has not yet declared himself. He has his uses. But if there should be some other Prime Minister, you should know that the U.S. believes that the Japanese foreign policy is continuing, and we will encourage them to maintain the course they have begun, particularly regarding China.

Vice Premier Teng: Even if Fukuda should be Prime Minister, we don't think it would be of any great consequence. Perhaps there might be some twists and turns because in the development of events there are always difficulties.

Secretary Kissinger: We think Japan would have to be very careless to come closer to the Soviet Union. It is a very dangerous course for Japan.

Vice Premier Teng: But no matter whoever comes to office, they still have a fundamental issue they cannot solve. This issue we discussed last night. The question of the Northern Territories [the four northern islands which Japan wants the Soviets to return].[3]

Secretary Kissinger: We will know in ten days, which is more than you can say of most international events. Perhaps after the Prime Minister is selected, if there is an unexpected development, we can exchange ideas.

Vice Premier Teng: So how do you think we should carry on our talks?

Secretary Kissinger: I think perhaps we can make a few observations now of a general nature, and then we might work in smaller groups. One set of views should concern our usual review of the international situation, and then discussion of continuing the process of normalizing relations. The second set of views covers more technical issues, which we should have discussed among our experts.

On the bilateral issues, if I could perhaps say one word before the experts get carried away with their enthusiasm: Such issues as the bilateral exchanges and cultural agreements are essentially a symbolic aspect of our foreign policy, of our political relations, and therefore we will deal with them in this context. Frankly I am indifferent as to whether there is a million dollars more or less in settling the question of blocked accounts, or whether one group more or less goes back and forth between the United States and China. We should use these as a symbol of our overall relationship. So when you want to settle them [the claims/asset problems] you let us know, and we will find a way of settling them.

We believe that, hopefully conditions are favorable to show some advance in our relationship. We think this is, would be, a fulfillment of the principles of the Shanghai Communiqué as well as some of the discussions we had when we made our first visits to China. We think it is desirable in terms of the overall international situation, so that there is no misunderstanding about the evolution of our relationship in the eyes of other countries.

So we are prepared. On the other hand, we won't press you, and you let us know at what speed you want to proceed on these technical bilateral issues. The advantage of discussing them while I am here is that the complexity of the issues tends to increase by the size of my staff, and on this basis you and I and the Foreign Minister can talk and we can cut through the complexities somewhat more rapidly.

---

[3] According to the memorandum of conversation of the November 25 meeting, 7:33–7:50 p.m., the islands dispute between Japan and the Soviet Union was not discussed during Deng's welcome of Kissinger. (Ford Library, National Security Advisor, Kissinger Reports, Box 2, November 25–29, 1974, Kissinger's Trip.) The subject was apparently discussed during the ensuing banquet hosted by Foreign Minister Qiao Guanhua.

To return to the more decisive issues I spoke about with the Foreign Minister in New York in October:[4] With respect to our general views on normalization, and this is one of the topics we can discuss with greater precision when we meet in smaller groups, I simply wanted to say that we are prepared to discuss seriously and in an attempt to meet the time limit we previously discussed in my past meetings with the Prime Minister [Chou En-lai].

The second category of problems is our usual detailed review of the international situation. The press always asks me before I come here whether I am coming to reassure the Chinese. They also always tell me that our relationship has deteriorated. But you cannot reassure serious people by words. What we have done, as you know and as all our friends who have been at these meetings [know], is to give you as detailed a description of our intentions and strategy as is possible—and I would say more detailed than with any other country. As you know—I think you may have learned that our word counts, and that you have not been surprised by any foreign policy moves we have made. I think that during the course of the last year things have evolved about as we discussed when I was here [in November, 1973]. And we are prepared to do this [review] again for the near future.

This would seem to me to be the most useful way we could spend our time, but we are open to any suggestions as to approaches that you would suggest.

Vice Premier Teng: That's all?

Secretary Kissinger: It is one of my shortest speeches. [Laughter] I also have a fifty minute version, as your Foreign Minister knows.

Vice Premier Teng: As for the way of holding the talks, we are in agreement that some questions can be discussed in smaller groups as you suggested. And in the Doctor's discussions with the Foreign Minister this October, you laid stress on both bilateral and especially international issues. And we welcome the words expressed by Dr. Kissinger in his toast yesterday[5] to the effect that you would foresee further progress on the issue of normalization along the lines of the Shanghai Communiqué. Outside there are many opinions in the world and a lot of talk saying that our relations have chilled and our speed has slowed down. But in the essence I believe that both sides hold that the progress of our relations has been normal.

But we should also say it is not correct to say that there is no ground whatsoever for such talk. For instance, the Doctor mentioned

---

[4] See Document 87.

[5] Kissinger's and Qiao's exchange of toasts on the evening of November 25 is printed in Department of State *Bulletin*, December 23, 1974, pp. 905–907.

yesterday and also in October in his discussions with the Foreign Minister that our cannon are sounding more frequently.

Secretary Kissinger: Yes, and also becoming more accurate.

Vice Premier Teng: And it is only natural that there should be some speculation and talk when you send an Ambassador to Taiwan,[6] and when they increase the number of their consulates in the United States.

Secretary Kissinger: Especially since you will never believe that some of our actions are the result of stupidity and not planning. I never knew about the consulates until it had been done.

Vice Premier Teng: As for our views on the question of normalization, I believe the Doctor and other American friends are familiar with these: that is, the Japan way. And in this aspect, you have expressed the desire that we on our side should put forward specific mode of how we should do it. But actually we have given our opinion long ago: that is, the Japan way. On our side we would also hope that you on your side can move forward a few steps.

Secretary Kissinger: Mr. [Vice] Prime Minister, the point in reflecting about what you said—you have given us a general idea, which is the Japan way. But it is always said the Japanese imitate us. Now you are forcing us to imitate the Japanese. This is a new style. But we can accept that basic principle. But we have a number of special circumstances which the Japanese do not have. And at various stages of our relationship we have found means, which were consistent with your principles, which also took into account our necessities. It is perhaps not proper to ask you to make a specific proposal on an issue that is of such profound principle to you.

I remember when we drafted our first communiqué, on my very first visit, when I did not have the pleasure of knowing the Foreign Minister—I was still being treated gently by the Chinese. But Ambassador Huang Hua, with whom I was drafting the communiqué, before we started working on the text said let us have a frank talk about what we must have, each of us, and when we do we can find the words. And it worked out that way.

And I think that within the framework of the Japanese model we should have a frank talk of some of our necessities consistent with your principles, and then see whether we can find some way to reach our goal. After this then we can put forward a specific proposal.

Vice Premier Teng: We perhaps can go into more detail in the smaller groups.

Secretary Kissinger: I agree.

Vice Premier Teng: But I must first fire a cannon.

---

[6] See footnote 2, Document 76.

Secretary Kissinger: At me?

Vice Premier Teng: Well, empty or full, as you like. That is, on this issue, as we see it, you owe us a debt. We don't have to discuss it now.

As for the bilateral issues, as we have said many times, and as Chairman Mao has said and also as Premier Chou En-lai has said in the past, we can sum up our views in two sentences: According to our wishes, we would like this matter to come more quickly; but secondly, we are not so much in a hurry. That is to say, if we are able to reach a point acceptable to both sides in a relatively quicker period of time, we would welcome this.

But Chairman Mao has also said in his talk with the Doctor that we pay special attention to international issues. And therefore we agree with the Doctor that it would be good to do as you proposed; that is, to exchange views on international and bilateral issues in smaller groups.

So we can nominate some people on both sides to discuss the more technical issues and bilateral matters.

Secretary Kissinger: On our side, Secretary Habib and Mr. Armstrong, and maybe one or two others, will be having our discussions. And Mr. Holdridge from the Liaison Office.

Vice Premier Teng: On our side we will have Director Lin P'ing and Mr. Tsien Ta-yung from our Liaison Office, and also a few others. Would you agree?

Secretary Kissinger: Yes.

Vice Premier Teng: See how easy it is to reach an agreement. [Laughter]

Secretary Kissinger: Our first agreement. We should make a special announcement.

Vice Premier Teng: So do you think that is about all for this section of our discussion?

Secretary Kissinger: We can now go into smaller groups.

Vice Premier Teng: And we can leave it to that group to decide themselves when they would like to meet and what they would like to discuss. Good.[7]

Secretary Kissinger: Good.

Vice Premier Teng: So would you want to rest?

[The meeting adjourned at 11:00 a.m.]

---

[7] A memorandum of conversation of these counterpart discussions, which took place on November 26, 2–3:15 p.m., is in Ford Library, National Security Advisor, Kissinger Reports, Box 2, November 25–29, 1974, Kissinger's Trip.

93.   Memorandum of Conversation[1]

Beijing, November 26, 1974, 11:15 a.m.–12:20 p.m.

PARTICIPANTS

Teng Hsiao-p'ing, Vice Premier of the State Council of the People's Republic of
China
Ch'iao Kuan-hua, Minister of Foreign Affairs
Amb. Huang Chen, Chief of PRC Liaison Office, Washington
Wang Hai-jung, Vice Minister of Foreign Affairs
Lin P'ing, Director, Department of American and Oceanic Affairs
T'ang Wen-sheng, Deputy Director, Department of American and Oceanic Affairs
Chang Han-chih, Deputy Director, Department of American and Oceanic Affairs
Chu Tsien Ta-yung, Counselor, PRCLO, Washington
Dr. Henry A. Kissinger, Secretary of State and Assistant to the President for
National Security Affairs
Amb. George Bush, Chief, U.S. Liaison Office
Donald Rumsfeld, Assistant to the President
Winston Lord, Director, Policy Planning Staff
Philip Habib, Assistant Secretary of State for East Asian and Pacific Affairs
Richard Solomon, National Security Council Senior Staff
Peter W. Rodman, National Security Council Staff
Karlene Knieps, Department of State (notetaker)

Teng: So how should we commence? I suggest we listen to the
Doctor first, because you have traveled to so many lands.

Kissinger: Perhaps we should have a general review of events since
we last met. I'm deciding whether to read the black [briefing] book,
which has 400 pages, or the green book, which has 200. [Laughter]

Teng: It is up to you.

Kissinger: Let me review the international situation as we see it,
as it has developed during the year.

I agree with the analysis of Chairman Mao that we should make
progress in normalization, but also that there is an international environment which brought us together in the first place and which determines in many respects our relationship.

In this respect, the factor in which we both have an interest, and
which has produced some common fronts, is your ally and northern
neighbor. In this respect, our assessment has not changed since last

[1] Source: Ford Library, National Security Advisor, Kissinger Reports on USSR,
China, and Middle East Discussions, Box 2, China Memcons and Reports, November
25–29, 1974, Kissinger's Trip (1). Secret; Nodis. The meeting took place in the Great Hall
of the People. All brackets are in the original.

year. We believe Soviet purposes are still essentially hegemonial. We don't think it is particularly fruitful to debate in which direction the primary thrust is going, because in whichever direction it goes, the ultimate consequences will be the same. And therefore, we believe the principal necessity is to keep in mind the overall objectives and the means to prevent them from being realized.

In this respect, we have to keep in mind—and I'm being very frank with you—a very complicated domestic situation. For the United States to take strong actions in crises, it is necessary to do so from a position of having demonstrated to our people that we have exhausted every avenue for peace. I think Chairman Mao, last year, said the United States plays complicated games, and China too plays complicated games, but more energetically. [Laughter]

Teng: I think he had discussed actually the difference between shadow-boxing and boxing in the Sha-lin style, which is more energetic.

Kissinger: Yes, shadow-boxing. But it was a profound observation. We have to do a lot of shadow-boxing to get into a position to take action when we are in a crisis. I say this only so you will distinguish between appearances and reality. We will not permit a strategic gain for Soviet power. We will attempt to reduce Soviet power where we can. We do not, however . . . At the same time we go through many stages which create either diplomatic obstacles to the extension of Soviet power or psychological and political obstacles against Soviet military action. We do not intend to create a condominium with the Soviet Union, because such a policy—by removing all obstacles to Soviet expansion—would eventually, with certainty, turn against us.

So events of this past year fitted this pattern. We have made a number of agreements with the Soviet Union on limiting arms competition to some extent, and certain technical cooperation on specific subjects. But this has enabled us, at the same time, to prevent any further extension of Soviet power. If we were in a position of open confrontation with the Soviet Union it would create the domestic situation I have described. And in addition, in each European country, the European left would be able to polarize the political spectrum by labeling us as the source of world tensions. Our present policy forces the Communist parties of Italy and France to support NATO, and [this is] despite their domestic battles on purely domestic issues.

We will have a separate session, I suppose, in which we can go into greater detail on the recent discussions in Vladivostok, than I can now in a general review. On that occasion I will give you the exact figures that were agreed upon. But you know now that the Soviet Union agreed upon equal numbers without counting our overseas based systems, which means in effect that we have a substantial advantage. And, in addition, we will have a very substantial advantage in warheads for the entire period of the agreement. I will explain this when I go through the figures with you.

So we believe the agreement in Vladivostok demonstrates the Soviet Union is not as strong as it sometimes pretends, or they would not have agreed to that—at least vis-à-vis us. Perhaps during our discussions we can set aside an hour for detailed discussion of the Soviet situation.

In other parts of the world, our relations with Western Europe have substantially improved since I was last here. Relations between France and the United States are much better, and the discussions of last year have resulted in greater cohesion of the Atlantic Alliance along the lines we pointed out [to you in previous discussions].

In the Middle East, since I was here last year we have brought about two agreements, between Egypt and Israel and between Syria and Israel. Let me explain our Middle East strategy to you: The Soviet Union attempts to produce a comprehensive solution rapidly. And every time I see your ally Gromyko he gives me a list of 10 principles, 20 main points, 40 points, 160 sub-sub paragraphs which he would like me to agree to. [Laughter] There is only one thing wrong with their proposals—the United States has to do all the work, and the Soviet Union will get all the advantages. That we are not prepared to do.

For us, quite candidly, the problem of Israel is an issue which has profound domestic consequences. If we do not behave carefully, we can produce a situation within the United States in which a very serious domestic problem is created in the Middle East which will affect our overall foreign policy. And this China should keep in mind as well. So we have to divide the problem into parts, each of which can be handled separately, and each of which can be managed domestically. And this is why we are proceeding step by step.

[Teng bends over and spits loudly into his spittoon.]

Our press, which has a great desire to see American setbacks, is always seeing stalemates. The fact of the matter is we are now proceeding by methods different from the spectacular methods of last year. We are now proceeding by the methods of the Vietnamese negotiations and our early contact with you, and we are confident we can produce another step within the next 3 or 4 months. But we would like to have it culminate a little closer to Mr. Brezhnev's visit to Egypt, so they'll have something to celebrate when he comes there. So those negotiations are going on quietly. And we are announcing today that the Israeli Foreign Minister is coming to Washington next week and you should assume this will be an integral part of our approach.

With respect to the Palestinians, this is an issue on which the last word has not yet been spoken. We would have preferred it if negotiations had taken place between King Hussein and Israel, and then subsequent negotiations between the Palestinians and Hussein.

T'ang: First between Hussein and Israel?

Kissinger: Yes, [negotiations] which could have restored the West Bank to Arab control, and then with the ultimate disposition settled between the Palestinians and Hussein.

Teng: You mean by returning the West Bank to the Arabs, returning it to Jordan?

Kissinger: Our idea, specifically, was—and it is a tragedy—we had achieved agreement that the West Bank, or a substantial part of the West Bank, with two-thirds of the population, would go technically to Jordan, but under U.N. supervision, so we would have been in a position to have discussions in the U.N. in another year or so as to the ultimate disposition. From this point of view, the Rabat decision was premature.

Now we need a period on this issue of some moderation and cooling off, to allow both sides to adjust to the new circumstances.

It is, in any event, important to keep the following in mind: The Arabs cannot win a war in the next 5 years. Historically they may be stronger, but in the short term they are certainly not the stronger. Therefore, any political progress has to come through the United States. There is no other way. The only interest we have in the political process is that it appear that our decisions are made at our own free will. If we are pressed [by the Arabs] we will resist long enough to demonstrate that pressure cannot possibly succeed. And if we are pressed by the Soviet Union, we will simply do nothing and we will tell the Soviet Union to produce progress.

I think President Asad, whom I like very much, visited you last year.

Teng: No, it was their Vice President, Shafei. Asad or Sadat?

Kissinger: Asad.

Ch'iao: He didn't come here. He went to North Korea.

Kissinger: Oh!

Ch'iao: He didn't come from the South.

Kissinger: I think you would like him. He gets many arms from the Soviet Union, but he is a realist. At any rate, I mention him only because even he has understood that under conditions of pressure the United States diplomacy will not operate. And he has now agreed to the extension of the United Nations forces in Syria, and we are going to ask Austria to introduce a resolution which he has worked out with us, and which, for your information, Israel has already accepted. So, we hope you will not veto it. [Laughter]

This isn't known yet. We have negotiated it for the last week with Syria. I don't think the Soviet Union knows about it yet. They made very many threatening statements about Syria in Vladivostok.

I mention it only to indicate that even good friends of the Soviet Union in the Arab world have to understand our policy.

Our policy is to produce progress that returns Arab territory to Arab control, but gradually at a pace that doesn't produce paralysis of our foreign policy because of the domestic reaction. And we will not do it under Soviet pressure at all.

Eventually, there will be a return to the Geneva Conference, but that will produce a certain stalemate.

In the area of Iran, I think things have gone approximately as we foresaw.

Teng: May I insert a question here?

Kissinger: Certainly.

Teng: Have you decided with the Soviet Union when the Geneva Conference will be convened?

Kissinger: No.

Teng: I think the Soviet Union thinks it should be quicker and they will be attending.

Kissinger: Yes, we spent 4 months preparing for it, and then it met one day, after which we closed it. [Laughter] The Soviet Union always urges us to hold it. Eventually, it will have to take place. I don't think it can possibly be before March.

As long as the Arabs think they are making progress outside the Conference, they will be in no hurry to get there. No one wants it except the Soviet Union. They have an Ambassador in Geneva, Vinogradov, who spends all his time waiting for a conference that doesn't take place. We occasionally send Ambassador Bunker once every two months to keep him company there doing nothing. But we have not agreed on a resumption date. The earliest I could foresee would be March—unless there is a total breakdown in the secret discussions now going on between Egypt and Israel and the other Arab countries and Israel through us. And I don't foresee such a breakdown.

On Iran, as I have said, things have developed in the direction of my discussions with Chairman Mao and the Prime Minister last year.

[Refreshments are brought in]

I was getting worried. No food was coming in for 20 minutes. [Laughter] I didn't see how I was going to live through it. [Laughter] [to Rumsfeld] See, I have gained 5 pounds here on every visit.

We can discuss that in great detail too. I mean about Iran, not about food. [Laughter]

In other parts of the world: I took a trip to India, as you know, As I explained to your Ambassador, my primary purpose was contributing giving India another opening except [besides] total reliance on the Soviet Union. Our assessment is India's intentions in Southeast Asia are hegemonial, and that they would like to reduce all neighboring countries to the status of Bhutan, and that we are not prepared to accept.

Ch'iao: May I insert something here? As I recall it, the Doctor made a speech to some scholarly association in which he said about the leading position of India on the sub-continent.

Kissinger: No, I said that India, as the strongest country on the subcontinent had a special obligation for restraint. And the intention was to point out the necessity for restraint. At any rate, we intend during the first half of next year to resume some cash arms sales to Pakistan which will restore some relationship. I will probably have to shoot half of Mr. Lord's staff before we can execute this.

But that is the direction in which we are moving. We have invited Prime Minister Bhutto to Washington, and within a few months after that we will do it.

Now, two events that have happened since last year that we did not discuss are the internationalization of the problem of energy, and the problem of food.

We are prepared in principle to discuss these issues with you, and to explain our views to you. They are areas in which we know you are sensitive to some statements that have been made by us. We are not indifferent to cannons that are fired at us with respect to these issues. And I think we should attempt to avoid unnecessary confrontations, because we have to solve the energy problem, not for ourselves, but because if it continues in its present form it will lead to the political disintegration of Western Europe. We can solve it for ourselves easily—relatively easily. And this cannot be a matter of indifference to the People's Republic. It has for us nothing to do with the Third World against the industrialized world, and we don't think it should be approached from a strictly theoretical point of view. But while I am here I am prepared to discuss it in greater detail.

So this is the general situation. I have spoken for 50 minutes, which is what doctors do. I would propose, as we continue our discussions—in addition to normalization, we could pick an area for discussion in greater detail—the Soviet Union, the Middle East.

There is another issue which I leave it up to the Chinese side whether it wishes to discuss, and that is the problem of Cambodia. We don't insist on discussing it. I have the impression that whenever it is raised it creates a degree of irritation on the Chinese side, which is uncharacteristic—and in addition to being uncharacteristic is out of proportion to the intrinsic importance of the subject being raised. From this I conclude the Chinese side considers us more than usually stupid on the issue of Cambodia. [Laughter] And that you must have the impression we are missing some point that should be perfectly obvious. So I thought, if you want to, we could give you our analysis.

Because in one respect we are really not in disagreement. We are not opposed to Sihanouk. We have no interest in Sihanouk returning to Cambodia as a figurehead for Hanoi. But we would have no objection to him if he could head a truly independent government. And if you want to, we could have an exchange of views on this subject—if you promise me not to get irritated.

Ch'iao: I don't think we have ever become irritated.

Kissinger: No, not personally. No, we understand your interest in Sihanouk and we are prepared to discuss it.

So this is the international scene as we see it, quickly. And then in our subsequent discussions we will go into more detail on each area.

[They confer]

Teng: Yes, it seems we don't have very much common language when it comes to the question of agriculture and energy. But we can exchange views.

Kissinger: I actually think we should have some common interests.

Teng: As for China itself, the food problem and energy problem do not exist for us, in that sense.

As for the Cambodian issues, I think you should be clear about our views, that is, both Samdech Norodom Sihanouk and the resistance forces within the country are neither puppets of Hanoi nor puppets of China as some people say. Figureheads.

Kissinger: We agree they aren't figureheads of China.

Teng: Nor of Hanoi.

Kissinger: That we are not sure of.

Teng: We can assure you. They are entirely figureheads for the independence of their own country and nation. Actually why does the United States have to get itself involved in this issue? Because from the beginning it was their own problem. Let them solve their own problem.

Kissinger: The United States is already involved in the issue. It can't make the decision whether to get involved.

Teng: Since you have the power to decide whether to get involved, you also have the power to decide not to be involved.

Kissinger: That may be partly true, but for the U.S. to simply abandon people with whom we have been working has a larger significance and it is not a habit we should acquire lightly.

Teng: It should also be true to say you have worked with Sihanouk for an even longer period of time.

Kissinger: We don't exclude Sihanouk. We think we should find a formula for a negotiation to get started, the outcome of which would, in all probability be Sihanouk.

Teng: On this issue you would know we support Samdech Norodom Sihanouk and the resistance forces within the country and we support their position. And to put it frankly, we think if the United States is to place its hopes on Lon Nol or on any force you think would replace Lon Nol, that is not reliable.

Kissinger: We think it is possible to produce a negotiation, at the end of which Sihanouk could quite possibly emerge as the controlling factor. We think it is in his own interest not to be totally dependent on one force. He should have many forces, factors to play with.

Teng: That is your idea.

Kissinger: It is our idea that it is possible to achieve a solution in Cambodia in which Sihanouk could emerge as the dominant force, yes.

Teng: As you wanted to discuss this specifically, we can.

Kissinger: All right.

Teng: But I think that is all for this morning.

Kissinger: That is probably right.

Teng: How should we proceed this afternoon?

Kissinger: It is up to you. We have not discussed normalization and we are prepared.

Teng: Perhaps we will invite you this afternoon to discuss what you didn't finish: bilateral relations and normalization. Because we will only have half an hour this afternoon. Tomorrow morning we can continue with our views.

Kissinger: That will be fine. That will be important.

Teng: 3:30 p.m. this afternoon.

Kissinger: At the Guest House?

Teng: Yes. It might be more convenient for you.

Kissinger: It is very courteous.

Teng: The same people?

Kissinger: The same numbers. I will probably add Mr. Gleysteen and drop somebody else.

Teng: That is your decision.

Kissinger: But the same numbers.

Teng: An agreement on quantity and not quality! [Laughter]

[The meeting ended]

94. Memorandum of Conversation[1]

Beijing, November 26, 1974, 3:45–5:00 p.m.

PARTICIPANTS

Teng Hsiao-p'ing, Vice Premier of the State Council, People's Republic of China
Ch'iao Kuan-hua, Minister of Foreign Affairs
Wang Hai-jung, PRC Vice Foreign Minister
Ambassador Huang Chen, Chief of the PRC Liaison Office, Washington
Lin P'ing, Director, Department of American and Oceanic Affairs, Ministry of
    Foreign Affairs
T'ang Wen-sheng, Deputy Director, Department of American and Oceanic
    Affairs, Ministry of Foreign Affairs
Tsien Ta-yung, Counselor, PRC Liaison Office, Washington
Ting Yuan-hung, Director, United States Office, Department of American and
    Oceanic Affairs, Ministry of Foreign Affairs
Chao Chi-hua, Deputy Director, United States Office, Department of American
    and Oceanic Affairs, Ministry of Foreign Affairs
Chang Han-chih, Translator
Notetaker

Henry A. Kissinger, Secretary of State and Assistant to the President for National
    Security Affairs
Donald Rumsfeld, Assistant to the President
Ambassador George Bush, Chief of the United States Liaison Office, Peking
Winston Lord, Director, Policy Planning Staff, Department of State
Philip C. Habib, Assistant Secretary of State for East Asian and Pacific Affairs
Peter Rodman, Staff Member, National Security Council
Richard H. Solomon, Senior Staff Member, National Security Council
Karlene Knieps, Notetaker

SUBJECT

Normalization

Secretary Kissinger: They outnumber us today.

Vice Premier Teng: Some more on our side are coming. I don't think you will ever outnumber us because we have 800 million.

Secretary Kissinger: My children and my wife very much appreciated the tour of the Forbidden City this morning. It was very nice.

Vice Premier Teng: Did they like it at all?

Secretary Kissinger: Very much.

Vice Premier Teng: How is the health of your wife? I hope it is better.

---

[1] Source: Ford Library, National Security Adviser, Kissinger Reports on USSR, China, and Middle East Discussions, Box 2, China Memcons and Reports, November 25–29, 1974, Kissinger's Trip. Top Secret; Sensitive. The meeting took place in the Great Hall of the People. All brackets are in the original.

Secretary Kissinger: It is much better.

Vice Premier Teng: If you need any medical help you just let us know.

Secretary Kissinger: You are very nice. She is going to watch acupuncture.

Vice Premier Teng: Well that medical technique of China is almost as old as the Great Wall of China. A few hundred years later than the Great Wall. It was created at the time of the Han Dynasty.

Secretary Kissinger: On one trip I brought a doctor along who was very skeptical of it and after he saw it he was very impressed.

Vice Premier Teng: It goes as far back as about two hundred years after Christ. During the time of the three kingdoms. It was during that time people were able to have an operation with acupuncture.

Secretary Kissinger: It is interesting to reflect how it could have been invented. Because as I understand it, to this day nobody understands the theory, why it works, just that it works.

Vice Premier Teng: I think mainly it was through practice.

Secretary Kissinger: Who got the first idea to stick a needle into somebody?

Vice Premier Teng: It was combined with the use of herb medicine.

Secretary Kissinger: Who would have thought if you stick a needle into somebody it would help him? No other civilization thought about that.

Vice Premier Teng: Shall we come back to our subject? We will listen to the Doctor. All right?

Secretary Kissinger: Let me discuss the subject of normalization. I understand that Mr. Habib has already had a talk on the bilateral relations.[2]

I am confident that our side can keep multiplying the complexities as long as your side can. It is something we are very good at.

Let me speak about the normalization problem.

When we met the first time, in our first two meetings [in 1971] we discussed completing the process during the second term of President Nixon.

We said that we would reduce our military forces on Taiwan, and we repeated that in the Shanghai Communiqué. We said we would not support any two Chinas solution, or a one China–one Taiwan solution, or any variation.

---

[2] A memorandum of conversation of this counterpart discussion, which took place on November 26, 2–3:15 p.m., is ibid.

And we would not encourage other countries to pursue such a policy.

We have substantially maintained these commitments.

We have reduced our forces on Taiwan from over 10,000 to about 3,200 today. We encouraged the Japanese movement towards the People's Republic. This is in fact why you can speak of a Japanese solution. We have given no encouragement to a two Chinas or one China–one Taiwan solution; quite the contrary.

Now the problem is how we can complete the process. I would like to divide it into a number of parts:

—There is the problem of the diplomatic status of Taiwan, and of course of the diplomatic relations between us.
—There is the problem of our military forces on Taiwan.
—And there is the problem of our defense commitment to Taiwan.

Our problem is different from the situation of Japan, or for that matter from the situation of any other country with which you have normalized relations, in two respects:

First, there is a formal defense relationship. Secondly, there is a rather substantial group in the United States that historically has been pro-Taiwan.

Together with your cooperation we have been able to neutralize the pro-Taiwan element in the United States by moving step-by-step in a very careful manner. But what we have to keep in mind for our common interest is to prevent Sino-American relations from becoming an extremely contentious issue in the United States.

It is not in your interest, or in that of the United States, to have emerge a Senator or Senatorial group which does to Sino-American relations what Senator Jackson has attempted to do to United States-Soviet relations.

I am speaking very frankly to you so that we understand each other exactly. After I have put my considerations before you, you will of course give me yours. Then we will see if we can solve the problem. I am here to remove obstacles, not to hide behind them.

We believe, as I have said, that while cannons have been fired—mostly in one direction—we have also had common fronts.

As the Premier said yesterday, they were mostly produced by the "polar bear."

We do not want to jeopardize that possibility [of developing common fronts with the PRC] given the dangers that may be ahead, and keeping in mind what Chairman Mao said to me last year of the two strands—normalization, and the international environment.

Now having said this, let me go back to the specific issues between us.

First, on the issue of the diplomatic status: We are prepared to solve this on substantially the Japan model; and with the one variation that it would be easiest for us if we could maintain a liaison office in Taiwan and an embassy in Peking. Except for that we would follow the Japan model.

With respect to the presence of [U.S.] troops on Taiwan, we are prepared to remove all our troops from Taiwan. We would like to agree with you on a schedule, a time-frame within which this will be accomplished—by which we would reduce the forces by half by the summer of 1976, and the remainder to be removed by the end of 1977.

Incidentally, what I am discussing is not something to which we want to agree—we can agree to it here, but it should not be announced until the end of 1975, the agreement we make. But we want to come to an understanding about it now, that this is what would happen.

Now that leaves the last problem, which is our defense relationship to Taiwan. And this is a problem to which, in all frankness, we have not come up with a good answer.

Our problem is this: on the face of it, it is of course absurd to say one has a defense arrangement with a part of a country one recognizes, that is, which belongs to that country.

Secondly, we obviously have no interest in maintaining a strategic base on Taiwan after we have established diplomatic relations with Peking and recognized Peking as the legal government of all China.

But as I told the Foreign Minister in New York, we need a formula that enables us to say that at least for some period of time there are assurances of peaceful reintegration which can be reviewed after some interval in order to avoid the difficulties which I have described.

If we can, this would mean that we would have accepted Peking as the [legal] government [of China]. We would have withdrawn our recognition from Taiwan, we would have broken diplomatic relations with Taiwan. We would have withdrawn our troops from Taiwan. All that would remain is that we would have some relation to peaceful reintegration.

Speaking here frankly and realistically, the political and psychological effect of breaking relations is that our defense relationship will be eroded by the act of recognition. But we need a transition period for our public opinion in which this process can be accomplished without an excessive domestic strain.

These are our basic considerations. If we agree on the principles, we can then see what formula can then be worked out.

Vice Premier Teng: Is that all?

Secretary Kissinger: This is the essence, yes.

Let me emphasize one point. To us the question of the defense commitment is primarily a question of the way it can be presented politically. It is not a question of maintaining it for an indefinite period of time.

Vice Premier Teng: Well, actually this law was formulated by yourselves. Is that so?

Secretary Kissinger: Which law?

Vice Premier Teng: You are the ones who make the law. That is, the law of that defense commitment you have with Taiwan. That was fixed by yourselves.

Secretary Kissinger: Of course. That is absolutely true.

Vice Premier Teng: Well, since you can formulate a law, naturally you can also do away with it.

Secretary Kissinger: That is also true. Our point is not that it could not be done. Our point is that for reasons I have explained to you, it is not expedient to do—well, the act of recognition in itself will change the nature of that arrangement because you cannot have a defense treaty with part of a country.

Vice Premier Teng: I have noticed the consideration which the Doctor has just mentioned. And I understand that all of these imaginations the Doctor has discussed with the Foreign Minister while he was in New York in October.

Secretary Kissinger: That is correct.

Vice Premier Teng: And I believe in principle the Foreign Minister gave you the answers on our side concerning the principal matters. In essence your imaginations—your considerations—cannot be considered as being in accord with the Japan model.

And we feel that in essence it is still a variation of one China and one Taiwan.

Secretary Kissinger: Why is that?

Vice Premier Teng: Well, this is primarily that you just reverse the position, change the position of the liaison office. The present situation is that we have established a liaison office in Peking—we have established our liaison office in Washington and you have established one in Peking. And you keep an embassy in Taiwan. This in itself indicates there has not been the necessary conditions for the normalization of relations.

In other words, if you change this order, that is, to have an embassy in Peking and a liaison office in Taiwan, it is not the way to correct the problem.

People will come to the conclusion that it is actually a variation of one China and one Taiwan. Therefore, we find it difficult to accept this formula.

And just now you touched upon the question of the defense treaty. That is, the defense treaty which you have with Chiang Kai-shek on Taiwan. Of course, if we are to achieve the normalization of relations between our two countries and abide by the course set in the Shanghai Communiqué, then the treaty you have with Taiwan must be done away with.

The reasons actually have been given by the Doctor yourself just now.

Secretary Kissinger: The defense treaty can have no international status after the normalization of relations.

Vice Premier Teng: But still it has a substantial meaning.

So it appears that time is not ripe yet to solve this question, because according to your formula, it would not be possible for us to accept this method of normalization. It still looks as if you need Taiwan.

Secretary Kissinger: No, we do not need Taiwan. That is not the issue. I think that it is important to understand. That would be a mistake in understanding the problem.

What we would like to achieve is the disassociation from Taiwan in steps, in the manner we have done until now. There is no doubt that the status of Taiwan has been undermined by the process which we have followed. And this process would be rapidly accelerated by the ideas which we have advanced.

Vice Premier Teng: And the other question is the way [method] to solve the Taiwan problem. As for solving the Taiwan question, suppose you have broken diplomatic relations with Taiwan. Then the Taiwan question should be left with us Chinese to solve among ourselves.

As to what means we will [use to] solve the Taiwan question, I believe Chairman Mao Tse-tung made it very clear in his talk.

Secretary Kissinger: Chairman Mao, if I understood him correctly, made two statements: One was that he believed that the question would ultimately have to be solved by force. But he also stated that China could wait for one hundred years to bring this about, if I understood him correctly.

Vice Premier Teng: That was true. He did say that.

Of course, the number of "one hundred years" is a symbolic one.

Secretary Kissinger: Of course, I understand this. I was going to say that in one hundred years I will not be Secretary of State. I have to say this occasionally to give some hope to my associates. I understood it was symbolic. I understand also that after normalization that any attributes of sovereignty in the relationship between Taiwan and the U.S. have to be eliminated.

Vice Premier Teng: Chairman Mao Tse-tung made it very clear that the solving of the Taiwan problem is an internal affair of China, and should be left to the Chinese to solve.

Just now Dr. Kissinger said that on the Taiwan issue you wish to have a peaceful reintegration.

Secretary Kissinger: That is correct.

Vice Premier Teng: And I believe you mentioned something like a wish of the U.S. in having some part in this guarantee relationship.

Secretary Kissinger: Let me explain what is our concern. We have not worked out a legal formula. We believe that it is—what I am saying is capable of misinterpretation. Let me explain our position exactly.

When I came here in 1971, it was clear that we were starting a process that would lead to the gradual erosion of the position of Taiwan.

You would certainly not have been admitted to the United Nations in 1971—eventually it would have happened, but not in 1971. It would have taken longer. And the normalization with Japan would not have been accomplished so soon. We fully cooperated in this, and we established principles that sooner or later have been implemented. And we did this in all seriousness.

You know we have made no effort with any country to keep them from establishing relations with you and breaking them with Taiwan.

The problem we have is the impact internationally of a sudden total reversal of an American position on other friendly countries, and even perhaps on countries that are not friendly to either of us.

Vice Premier Teng: But on the other hand, if we agree to your formula we will also be creating an impact internationally that we have agreed to the formula of one China–one Taiwan.

Secretary Kissinger: No, we will work to make it clear that it is not this type of situation. We will not now accept a solution which we have both rejected.

We have, it seems to me, two basic choices. There are two roads we can now follow: We can continue the present process, which is tolerable, and gradually withdraw our forces from Taiwan, which will continue in any event—whatever you decide here. We will increase our relationship with you as we have done in the past three years, and wait for the opportune time to complete the process with one decision.

Or, we can do a process in which we complete the political part of our relationship quickly and make it clear that we are solving the issues of sovereignty—of one China and one Taiwan—at once, and find a formula in which the symbolic thought of Chairman Mao is expressed. An effort of peaceful reintegration over a reasonable period of time.

We do not want a voice in the discussion on peaceful reintegration. That should be left to the Chinese. We do not want to participate in that process.

Chang Han-chih: I'm not clear about the first part of your statement.

Secretary Kissinger: The Vice Premier said that of course the one hundred years is symbolic. I understood the symbolic nature of Chairman Mao's statement about a hundred years. I understood it to mean that you are willing to give the peaceful process time to work—that while philosophically the resolution will probably come about by force, you are prepared to give the peaceful road a long opportunity.

We do not want to participate in the process of reintegration. And we have no difficulty affirming the principle of one China. So our issue is not one China, one Taiwan.

Foreign Minister Ch'iao: If I understand correctly, I see what you mean is that you are for one China, but the one China you want is a one China which is achieved through peaceful means.

Secretary Kissinger: Exactly. For at least a reasonable period of time. We want to avoid a situation where the United States signs a document which leads to a military solution shortly after normalization. But we do not want a commitment which maintains the separation. What we have in mind—we may not know the formula, but what we have in mind seems compatible with what Chairman Mao says in terms of the process.

Vice Premier Teng: We have just now checked on what Chairman Mao exactly said when he talked with Doctor, and we understand what he said is, "I don't think the normalization of relations between China and the United States will take one hundred years." So from this we understand that it does not mean that from what Chairman Mao says, that we do not wish to complete a process of the normalization as quickly as possible.

I think concerning the Taiwan question that at the same time it is also a question of the normalization of relations between China and the United States.

There are three principles to which we cannot give other consideration, which we cannot barter away. The first principle is that we insist—that we should insist on the Shanghai Communiqué. That is, we refuse any method which will lead to the solution of "two Chinas," or "one China, one Taiwan," or any variation of these two.

The idea of setting up an embassy here in Peking and a liaison office in Taiwan is a variation on "one China–one Taiwan," which we cannot accept.

The second principle is that the solution of the Taiwan question is an internal issue of the Chinese people, and it can only be left to the

Chinese people themselves to solve. As to what means we will use to finally solve the Taiwan question—whether peaceful methods or non-peaceful methods—it is a matter, an internal affair, which should be left to the Chinese people to decide.

The third point, which is also a principle to us, is that we do not admit that there can be another country which will take part in the solution of the Taiwan question, including the United States.

So it looks as if there is quite a distance between our two sides concerning this question. As I said just now, it appears that you still need Taiwan. If you still need Taiwan we can wait. We can wait until the time is more ripe for the solution of the question.

Secretary Kissinger: Let me comment on the three points. Then let me say one other thing.

Vice Premier Teng: We were checking with the records we have about what Chairman Mao said last year and we feel our understanding is correct. What Chairman Mao said last year is that we should separate the two things, that is, the relations between the United States and us and the relations between Taiwan and the United States. These two things should be separate.

Then the Chairman went on to say that if you break your diplomatic relations with Taiwan, then it will be possible to solve the issue of diplomatic relations. That is to say, like what we did with Japan. We understand that refers to the Japan model.

And then the Chairman went on to say that, as for the relation between Taiwan and us, we do not believe in peaceful transition.

Then the Chairman said we can do without Taiwan—we can wait for one hundred years to solve the problem. And the Chairman also said, "As for the relation between you and us, I do not think that will take one hundred years to solve."

I think from this conversation the meaning is clear.

Secretary Kissinger: I agree. This is exactly my recollection of the conversation. From this I also made certain deductions, produced by my brain which is somewhat slower than that of the Chinese. I have never had a Chinese contradict me on my statement (laughter).

I remember once Prime Minister Chou En-lai made the comment that I was intelligent, and I said by Chinese standards you mean I am of medium intelligence. He did not contradict me either (laughter).

But let me say what I deduce from this conversation; because my understanding is exactly the same as what the Vice Premier has said.

I deduce from it that the precondition for normalization of relations is breaking diplomatic relations with Taiwan. That we are prepared to do. And I believe we can find a mutually satisfactory formula for this.

The second conclusion I draw from the statement of the Chairman was he believes diplomatic relations could be established, and after that there might be a time interval until the real integration [of Taiwan into the PRC] is complete—in his perspective of history.

Now of the three principles you have mentioned, Mr. Vice Premier, the first is, in our judgment, no problem. We will work out a solution that leaves no doubt there is no "one China–one Taiwan." This is a soluble problem—much easier than many other problems we have solved before.

Vice Premier Teng: But it won't do if you establish a liaison office in Taiwan, or for that matter a consulate.

Secretary Kissinger: I still believe this is a problem to which we can find a solution. I see the Ambassador [Huang Chen] has a very proprietary interest in the concept of a liaison office. He is the head of the only liaison office in the world which is headed by a Chinese Ambassador.

Huang Chen: My understanding about the nature of a liaison office is according to the ideas which Chairman Mao gave—the nature of a liaison office.

Secretary Kissinger: I repeat, I believe we can find a solution to the first problem. Although we are not now in a detailed consultation. I believe we can find a solution to it.

The second question: We do not wish to participate in any way in the process of reintegration, or in the process of realization of reintegration.

The third problem is the one I have put to you: How we can avoid the impression that we have simply jettisoned people with whom we have been associated without giving—as in the passage you read to me, how we can have a period of time to give this process a chance to work.

Namely, that diplomatic relations can be established before the process of reintegration is completed—how this can be expressed in our agreement. This is the serious question.

It seems to me we have two roads we can take, and we are prepared to take either.

One road is that we, the United States, proceed unilaterally to reduce its standing on Taiwan, the way we have been doing. We will do this by withdrawing troops. And at the appropriate time before 1976 [reducing] the seniority of our diplomatic representation.

The other is that we begin a negotiation on the three points which we have discussed here. I do not believe our differences need be insurmountable.

Vice Premier Teng: I believe we can continue our discussion on this issue. I do not think we have too much time this afternoon for the question. It looks as if probably it is difficult for both sides to reach any agreement on this visit of yours.

We have another consideration about the relations between our two countries. That is, as I have said before, some people have been saying the relations between our two countries have been cooling down. The Chinese Government is therefore extending an invitation to you. That is to say, the Chinese Government wishes to extend a formal invitation to the Secretary of Defense of the United States, Mr. Schlesinger, to visit China. We think this would be a good answer to all these opinions which are going on in the world.

Secretary Kissinger: It will produce a Politburo meeting in the Kremlin.

Vice Premier Teng: We don't mind. Well, actually, it is our wish that they have a Politburo meeting there. But we really extend this invitation with all seriousness.

Secretary Kissinger: I appreciate this, and let me think about it. Let me say, however, one thing in principle. We believe from our side it is highly desirable to show that our relationship has not chilled and that we should continue to show not only that it has not chilled but that it is continuing to improve. And whatever the decision on this particular invitation, I am certain we can between us find methods of showing a substantial improvement in our relationship.

Vice Premier Teng: We will be waiting for your answer then—from your government.

Foreign Minister Ch'iao: We understand Mr. Bush is going to give a reception this afternoon.

Ambassador Bush: My wife has spent most of her time waiting, so don't worry about that.

Vice Premier Teng: We suggest 9:00 tomorrow morning [for the next meeting].

Secretary Kissinger: I suggest that at the beginning, for perhaps one-half hour, we have a very small group. On your side it is up to you. I will bring only three people, including me. You can have as many as you want.

Vice Premier Teng: We shall decide the number of our participants according to the percentage of our whole population (laughter).

Secretary Kissinger: In relation to ours! So you will have 12. It will not take very long.

95.   Memorandum of Conversation[1]

Beijing, November 27, 1974, 9:45–11:32 a.m.

PARTICIPANTS

Teng Hsiao-p'ing, Vice Premier of the State Council, People's Republic of China
Ch'iao Kuan-hua, Minister of Foreign Affairs
Amb. Huang Chen, Chief of the PRC Liaison Office, Washington, D.C.
Wang Hai-jung, Vice Minister of Foreign Affairs
T'ang Wen-sheng, Deputy Director, Department of American and Oceanic Affairs
Lien Cheng-pao (Notetaker)

Dr. Henry A. Kissinger, Secretary of State and Assistant to the President for National Security Affairs
Amb. George Bush, Chief of the U.S. Liaison Office, Peking
Winston Lord, Director, Policy Planning Staff
Bonnie Andrews, Secretary's Office (Notetaker)

SUBJECT

President's Visit; Nuclear War; SALT; Yugoslavia

Kissinger: When the Foreign Minister spoke at the United Nations,[2] his most violent attacks were not understood by most Americans.

Teng: You mean including the interpreters?

Kissinger: Oh no, they understood.

Teng: Oh yes. And before I forget, the Marshal [Yeh Chien-ying] asked yesterday evening that I send greetings to the Doctor and his wife.

Kissinger: I appreciate that very much; he is an old friend.

Teng: And he also asked me to say that because of his busy schedule, he will not be able to meet with you. I think he has met you several times.

Kissinger: I understand. He greeted me on my first visit.

Teng: Actually, on our side, he is the Minister of National Defense and Chief of the General Staff. And that is why he is very happy that our government has extended the invitation to your Secretary of Defense.

Kissinger: Yes. I wondered if that meant he would speak only to the Secretary of Defense and not to the Secretary of State.

---

[1] Source: Ford Library, National Security Adviser, Kissinger Reports on USSR, China, and Middle East Discussions, Box 2, China Memcons and Reports, November 25–29, 1974, Kissinger's Trip. Top Secret; Nodis. The meeting took place at Guest House 18. All brackets are in the original.

[2] Kissinger is likely referring to Qiao's October 2 speech at the United Nations; see footnote 2, Document 87.

Teng: I don't think it means that. It means that the U.S. Secretary of Defense is invited to Peking and in that event I don't think it would be very easy for people to say that our relations have become even more cold.

Kissinger: That's true. Let me make a few observations if I may. First, we agree on the desirability of demonstrating not only that our relations have not become colder, but in fact our relations are becoming warmer. We think that is in the interest of both of our countries. And we are prepared to do this not only symbolically, but substantively.

Now, in the security field, I had some discussions with the Prime Minister on my last evening here last time and I want you to know that those principles we still maintain.[3]

Now, about the invitation of the Secretary of Defense. This presents us with a problem. The Soviet leaders have repeatedly invited our Secretary of Defense to Moscow and have asked for a reciprocal exchange of visits between our Secretary of Defense and their Minister of Defense. And we have consistently refused. And then they proposed meetings of military commanders in Europe, and we have turned that down too. So if we begin using our Secretary of Defense for diplomatic travels, he will begin going to places that I don't believe are desirable.

But we have two possibilities. First, we would approve a visit by any other Cabinet member to Peking. And secondly, I believe also that we could consider an invitation to President Ford if that were considered desirable. So it is not a lack of interest in demonstrating a close relationship.

Teng: So, as the Doctor just now mentioned this, if President Ford desires a possibility to come to China, we would welcome him.

Kissinger: I suppose we could envisage it for the second half of next year. Or, what are your ideas?

Teng: Anytime would be all right for us.

Kissinger: We don't have to fix an exact date. When I was here the first time, we did not fix a date—only a certain time period.

Teng: It can be decided upon on a different time.

Kissinger: Let us agree then in 1975.

Teng: I think that is all right.

Kissinger: And I think that would be an important event.

Teng: So then we can later on go into specific dates, because we don't have to settle now.

---

[3] On November 13, 1973, Zhou and Kissinger discussed policies for dealing with the Soviet Union. See Document 59.

Kissinger: We don't have to settle now. What is your idea? Should we announce the invitation and acceptance at the end of my visit?

Teng: What would you think?

Kissinger: I think it's a good idea. We should have a communiqué at the end of my visit—which we would perhaps publish Saturday or Sunday[4]—in which we should announce this, yes.

Teng: So then we will consider the announcement and communiqué and discuss it with you later.

Kissinger: I think there is an advantage to relating it to my visit here. When it should be published—Saturday or Monday—we are open-minded. Or later even.

Teng: So we will leave it to the Foreign Minister to work out the wording of the announcement with you.

Kissinger: Must I work it out with him? We spent a week one time. He is a very tough negotiator. It will be a great pleasure.

Teng: You are both philosophers.

Ch'iao: But we two must quarrel each time we meet because we belong to two different schools of philosophy.

Kissinger: That is true. But they are related.

Ch'iao: Both linked and related.

Kissinger: Like our relationship.

Teng: But you don't have to go into such length at these meetings. Just have some more mao tai. [Laughter]

Kissinger: OK. The Foreign Minister and I will discuss what should be said in the communiqué.

Teng: It should be like a press communiqué.

Ch'iao: Brief; not long, taking two weeks.

Kissinger: Yes, one page. Not like the Shanghai Communiqué.

Teng: I don't think we have anything else very much now to say.

Kissinger: You mean in the communiqué. We could reaffirm a few general principles and then make the basic announcement.

Teng: I'll leave it to you to quarrel about.

Kissinger: We could do it in German!

Teng: They say that is a very difficult language to read.

Kissinger: Yes. In German you know a man is on the stairs. But it may take two pages to know if he is going up or down. [Laughter]

Teng: And about the invitation to the Secretary of Defense. We request that your government continue to consider the invitation.

---

[4] November 30 or December 1.

Kissinger: Maybe after the President visits we can arrange this. But we are prepared to do similar things in that area. If you are concerned about concrete things, we are prepared to do them.

Teng: Actually our invitation to your Secretary of Defense isn't mainly to discuss any specific issues. The meaning is in the invitation itself.

Kissinger: We understand.

Teng: As for the discussions of problems, it is probably still up to the Doctor and the President.

Kissinger: The last time we were here, we had to arrange a whole set of negotiations of extreme delicacy—that will not be necessary this time—between your Foreign Minister and ours. We will consider the invitation to our Secretary of Defense and if we can both determine the right moment to do it, we will certainly do it. We will be glad if there is any other Cabinet member you think would be desirable to have here. We can arrange it very quickly. But it is entirely up to you.

Teng: So this request is still for the consideration of your government.

Kissinger: Yes, and we will keep it between your Ambassador and me. That is on the assumption that he comes back soon.

Now, I wanted to tell you one other thing that I have already mentioned to your Ambassador for your information: When I was in Moscow in October, Brezhnev made a proposal for a new treaty to us and repeated it in more detail to President Ford in Vladivostok. And it is a rather novel and ingenious proposition. The proposal is as follows: The U.S. and Soviet Union should make a treaty with each other in which they will defend each other against any attack by any other country or they will defend each other's allies against nuclear attack from any other country.

[Meeting temporarily interrupted by Chinese girl opening outer door.]

Kissinger: I have people in the other room but they will join us for the later discussion.

Translator: They must be able to hear me because of my loud voice.

Kissinger: We asked for a practical explanation of how this would operate. The practical explanation is that in any use of nuclear weapons, regardless of who initiates it, in a war between the Soviet Union and another country or between the U.S. and another country, or between an ally of each, then the U.S. and Soviet Union would have to help each other, and if physical help is not possible, then they would have to observe benevolent neutrality.

We think it has two, well three, general purposes. The first is to undermine NATO, because it would specifically oblige us to cooperate with the Soviet Union against our allies if nuclear weapons were involved. Secondly, it would force those Arabs who are afraid of nuclear weapons being used by Israel into an alliance relationship with the Soviet Union. And third, I think, China. Those seemed to us the three purposes, together with the general impression of condominium.

We did not accept a serious discussion of this proposal. Nor will we.

Ch'iao: Actually your treaty on preventing nuclear war could be interpreted in this way also.

Kissinger: No, absolutely not.

Teng: Because your consultations know no bounds.

Kissinger: First of all, that treaty has never been invoked. We have used that treaty and intend to use it to get a legal basis for resistance in areas that are not covered by treaty obligations. The only time that treaty has been used was by the U.S. during the October alert.

Secondly, that treaty deliberately says that to prevent nuclear war, one has to avoid conventional war. And, therefore, by the reverse, to resort to conventional war involves the danger of retaliation by nuclear war. The new Soviet proposal separates nuclear war. It makes no distinction about who uses the weapons first, and it is directed at a kind of nuclear condominium.

In the October alert, we warned the Soviet Union that if they used force in the Middle East it would be in violation of Article 2 of the Treaty on Prevention of Nuclear War, which says that the use of conventional weapons implies the risk of nuclear weapons, and we used it as a warning to the Soviet Union.

But I agree with the Foreign Minister that the Soviet intention in their draft to us on the Treaty to Prevent Nuclear War was to achieve what they are now proposing in this new treaty.

Teng: Their goals and purposes have been constant all along.

Kissinger: And their diplomacy clumsy and obvious.

Teng: But their purpose is also very clear. And their goals are clear. And we think their purposes can only be these: First of all, to utilize the signing of such an agreement with you to develop their own nuclear weapons to standards either equivalent to yours or surpassing yours. And the reason they are expressing such interest in signing such an agreement naturally shows that they have tasted a sweet taste out of such agreements. If I recall things correctly, you signed your first treaty pertaining to nuclear matters in July 1963. At that time I was in Moscow carrying on negotiations between our two parties, and on the very day I was leaving you signed that treaty.

Kissinger: We were not informed about all your movements at the time. [Laughter]

Teng: And it must be said that at that time the level of Soviet weapons was lagging a considerable distance behind yours. But in the eleven years since, I must say they have been able to reach a level about the same as yours.

Kissinger: That is not exactly correct, and I will explain that to you. It is inevitable that a large industrial power will increase the numbers of its nuclear weapons. And it is the characteristic of nuclear weapons because of their destructiveness that beyond a certain point superiority is not as effective as in conventional weapons.

But in numbers, diversity, accuracy and flexibility, our nuclear weapons will be considerably superior to the Soviet Union for the whole period of the arrangement which we signed in Vladivostok. And I will explain that to you if you want, or some other time while I am here. That is true both in numbers and characteristics.

Ch'iao: I would like to add a few words if possible. We thank the Doctor for telling us of Soviet intentions, but as we have said many times, we do not attach such great importance to such treaties. We still have a treaty with the Soviet Union that has not been outdated yet and now they have now proposed to us a new treaty for mutual non-aggression. Of course, how we will deal with this new treaty will have to be seen. But on the whole, we do not attach such great importance to such matters. And the decisive fact is not any treaty but a policy, the principles and the lines.

Teng: But I haven't finished now. I have only mentioned the first goal of the Soviet Union. The second is, as Dr. Kissinger mentioned, to try to divide the U.S. from its allies, which you have discovered or perceived. But it seems that although you have revealed this point, they will never give up this goal, whether in the past, present or future. And the third purpose will be to maintain the monopolistic status of your two countries in the field of nuclear weapons.

And they will try to use this point not only to compare with your country but also intimidate countries with only a few nuclear weapons and thus reach their aim of hegemony.

So our overall view of such treaties is that we attach importance to their political significance, and as always our attitude toward such matters is that we believe they are not of much consequence, and we are not bound by any such treaty or agreement. And as the Doctor has repeated many times, your aim is not to bind others either.

Kissinger: In every meeting with the Soviet Union in discussing proposals directed against China such as nuclear testing and nuclear proliferation, we have always avoided formulations whose purpose is directed against third countries.

Teng: But even if they were so, even if they succeeded, what role would those treaties play? They would not be able to play much of a role. And if they signed such agreements, they would still be waving their baton, and if they don't sign they would still have nuclear weapons. As for our nuclear weapons, as Chairman Mao says, they are only so much [gesturing with fingers].

Kissinger: We have never discussed nuclear weapons with you from our side.

Teng: That is right.

Kissinger: We inform you of Soviet overtures not because you should pay attention but because if they should ever tell you, you will know what is happening. And also we have an understanding with you not to do anything with the Soviet Union without informing you. And so we inform you of things with them whether you attach significance to them or not. And we are not asking you to do anything about it.

There is one other matter that came up in Vladivostok that I wanted to mention to you. The Soviet proposed to us to have consultations on Japanese-Chinese relations and to prevent them from becoming too close. We have refused this, and we have told the Japanese in a general way about this, and have told the Japanese about our refusal.

Teng: So from this too we can see the aims of the Soviet Union. You know, their Foreign Minister, Mr. Gromyko, has a characteristic of which we were told by Khrushchev in 1957 when Chairman Mao went to Moscow. Khrushchev introduced Gromyko to us, and he told us that Gromyko had a lot of things in his pocket. And Khrushchev told us that this fellow Gromyko could produce this formula today, and tomorrow, and he has so many things he can produce that that is his major trait—that was Khrushchev's introduction to Gromyko. And it seems that Brezhnev has learned that trait from Gromyko and has a lot of things in his pocket too.

As for our dealings with the Soviet Union, we do not rely on our nuclear weapons. And we don't have very much skill other than digging tunnels and having rifles. As for your signing such agreements, we do not attach such great significance to them. Maybe we won't even comment.

Kissinger: That is entirely up to you. The agreements we sign have nothing to do with China except the one on preventing nuclear war which to us gives us legal possibilities. But the agreement, or the tentative one in Vladivostok, we consider very favorable in the overall strategic balance. It is up to you if you comment or not. It has nothing to do with the People's Republic of China.

Teng: I would like to raise a question. We have heard the Doctor say that the recent meeting and the recent signing of such an agreement was a great breakthrough. Was it really so? To be more specific—

how reliable can it be—how reliable are the prospects for ten years of détente and a cease of competition in the military field?

Kissinger: First of all, you have to understand that we have to fight on many fronts. And our domestic strategy is to isolate our left, if that is a proper thing to say in the People's Republic.

Teng: We like those on the right!

Kissinger: The ones on the right have no choice but to be with us anyway. The ones on the right are no problem with us.

Teng: Isn't Mr. Heath of Great Britain a well-known man on the right?

Kissinger: Oh, yes.

Teng: And wasn't Mr. Adenauer of your former father-land a well-known man of the right? And in France, De Gaulle, Pompidou and Giscard, Tanaka, and Ohira are famous men on the right. We like this kind, comparatively speaking.

Kissinger: We send our leftists to Peking.

Bush: I don't think I understand that.

Kissinger: The Ambassador is a left-wing Republican. No, he is here because he has our total confidence.

But it is important in the U.S. to isolate and paralyze those who would undermine our defense program and who generally conduct what I consider a stupid policy. And we can do this by pursuing policies which adopt this rhetoric.

And to answer your question, I do not believe that this guarantees ten years of détente—not for one minute. But I do believe that if détente breaks down, or when it does, we will be better able to mobilize our public opinion having made every effort to preserve peace rather than being accused of having provoked them.

Teng: On our side we don't believe it is possible to reach détente— still less maintain ten years of détente. And we don't think there is any agreement that can bind the hands of Russia.

Kissinger: No, but there is no way they can violate this agreement without our knowing it. I don't think it was a very intelligent agreement for them. They have two choices: they can either respect the agreement, in which case we preserve a certain strategic advantage, or they can violate the agreement, in which case we have the psychological and political possibility of massive breakout ourselves, which we would not have otherwise for domestic reasons.

Teng: As we see it, it is still necessary to have vigilance.

Kissinger: There is no doubt about that for us.

Teng: That would be good.

Kissinger: I once studied the foreign policy of Metternich, and he said the trick to dealing with Napoleon was to seem to be a fool without being one. There is no question—in terms of our domestic situation, it is, strangely enough easier to get Congress to give funds for limits in agreements than to get funds for the same amounts without an agreement. [To Bush:] Do you think so, George?

Bush: Yes, I do.

Teng: There is something else I would like to ask about your SALT agreement. Does it mean strategic arms? Does it apply only to nuclear arms?

Kissinger: Yes, and only those with an intercontinental range.

Teng: That means that only those strategic weapons are included, not others.

Kissinger: According to the definitions of the agreement.

Teng: But outside of that agreement, what is meant by strategic weapons? For example, conventional weapons have been considered strategic?

Kissinger: No.

Teng: Then we differ a bit here. Because here is the question of whether a future war would be a nuclear war.

Kissinger: What do you think?

Teng: We don't think so necessarily.

Kissinger: I agree. But I would like to say, as I said to the Chairman and Prime Minister, we would consider any sign of expansion of the Soviet sphere—either to the West or East, whether countries were covered by treaty or not, as a threat to our long-term security. It has nothing to do with our affection for the countries covered but strategic reality. Secondly, we don't care if that expansion comes with conventional or nuclear weapons.

Teng: You know there is a story, after Khrushchev came to Peking. He came to Peking in 1954, and he gave us this reasoning: During that visit, aside from boasting of his corn planting, he also boasted about the uselessness of naval vessels. He said that in the missile era naval vessels were nothing other than moving targets and they would be finished off at once. And the Soviet Union actually ceased to build their Navy for two or three years. But they very quickly rectified that. And since then, while energetically developing their nuclear weapons, they are at the same time continuing to build their conventional weapons and their navy also.

Kissinger: That is true, but we don't think that they have a strong navy.

Teng: But they have increased their numbers.

Kissinger: They have increased their numbers, but according to our observations—we may be wrong—in each Middle East crisis their navy maneuvered with very great clumsiness and we judge they would be a very easy target. We thought their panicky behavior in each crisis suggested that this is true.

Teng: But no matter what, in the past the Soviet Union had no naval forces in the Mediterranean or Indian Oceans and their activities were confined very close to their Pacific shores. But now they go everywhere, even Latin America. During the subcontinent crisis their vessels moved with greater speed than yours.

Kissinger: They are after ours.

Ch'iao: But anyway, that time your naval vessels moved too slowly.

Kissinger: Be that as it may, but in conventional land strength, we do not underestimate the Soviet Union. They are very strong in conventional land strength. In naval strength they are absolutely no match for us. We have hysterical admirals who, when they want money, say that no matter what country we are in war against, including Switzerland, that we are going to lose. But in reality, the only way the Soviet Union could hurt our fleet in the Mediterranean is with their land-based aircraft. And if they did that, that would be a general nuclear war. But if it is a naval battle, our carriers can strike theirs with so much greater distance and force, that there is absolutely no possibility for them to survive.

Teng: But from our discussions with some Europeans, they seem much more worried than you—not just on naval forces but on the whole question of conventional forces.

Kissinger: On the question of conventional forces, everyone has reason to worry. On the question of naval forces, I believe we are far superior.

Teng: But the Soviet Union develops itself with greater speed. If the Soviet Union launches a war, it might not be a nuclear war; it might quite possibly be a conventional war. Under this condition, conventional weapons should not be neglected.

Kissinger: I completely agree. That is a problem the western countries do have, not in naval forces but ground conventional forces. But you will notice that we have increased the number of our divisions recently. But it is a problem. There is no question.

Teng: But your increase is proportionately much smaller than the Soviet Union.

Kissinger: That is true. But I think it would be extremely dangerous for the Soviet Union. First of all, in Europe, the Soviet Union could not achieve a decisive victory without a very large battle and in those circumstances we would use nuclear weapons.

Teng: But under those conditions, where the Soviet Union has the same destructive strength as you, would it be easy for you to make up your minds?

Kissinger: The Soviet Union does not have the same destructive force as we.

Teng: Not even enough strength for a first strike?

Kissinger: No. Let me explain the composition of the forces to you because there is so much nonsense written in the U.S. by people with specific purposes in mind that there is a very misleading impression created.

We have 1,054 land-based missiles, 656 sea-based, on submarines. 435 B–52 bombers, 300 F–111 bombers which are never counted for some reason. This is just in the strategic forces. In addition, we have over 500 airplanes in Europe and over 700 airplanes on aircraft carriers. Starting in 1979 we are going to get at least 240 new missiles on submarines—the so-called Trident submarine.

Teng: Aren't you violating the treaty?

Kissinger: No. I will explain the treaty in a minute. And at least 250 new bombers, the B–1. But the number 240 and 250 are only planning numbers. Once we begin producing, we can produce as many as we want.

Now of those missiles, the only ones that will eventually become vulnerable to attack are the 1,000 land-based ones. This cannot happen before 1982. I'll explain to you why in a minute. And before that can happen we will be producing the Trident missile which will be in serial production by 1979. And we don't have to put it on a submarine; we can put it on land if we want to.

So the Soviet Union would have to be insane to attack 1,000 missiles when we would have 1,500 and more left over even if they destroy all the land-based missiles—which they also couldn't do.

Teng: So for either side to use nuclear weapons against the other, it is a matter for great care by both sides.

Kissinger: That is without question. I was answering the question about the Soviet Union being able to make a first strike. My argument is that that is impossible.

Let's look at the reverse. The U.S. has about 30% in land-based missiles, the rest either at sea or on airplanes. I would also like to tell you, we are planning to put long-range missiles into our airplanes—something the Soviet Union cannot do because they don't have airplanes large enough to do that. The Soviet Union has 85% of its force in land-based missiles. And its sea-based missiles, up to now, are very poor. And it has only 120 airplanes that can reach the U.S., and we don't think they are very well trained. In fact, under the agreement they have to reduce their numbers. They can compose their forces any way they want—but the level we have agreed on is 2,400 for both sides. It is below their level and above ours—if you don't count overseas weapons. So they will have to reduce their forces. We think they will get rid of their airplanes, but we don't know.

Teng: But they will not violate the agreement when they improve qualitatively.

Kissinger: Yes, but neither will we.

Teng: So you still have your race then.

Kissinger: But we have planned our forces for the 1980's and they have planned their forces for the '70's. By the early 1980's, both land-based forces will be vulnerable. And 85% of theirs are land-based while only 35% of ours are land-based. Secondly, they are making all their improvements in the most vulnerable forces, namely in the land-based forces. We are making ours in the sea-based and air-based forces—which are not vulnerable, or much less vulnerable. For example, on their submarines, they have not begun to test a multiple warhead—which means they could not possibly get it before 1980 into production. Which means, in turn, we will be, in accuracy and technical procedures, 10 to 15 years ahead of them.

Teng: We are in favor of your maintaining a superiority against the Soviet Union in such aspects.

Kissinger: And I repeat that if we launched a first strike against them we could use overseas forces which are added to the strategic forces that I gave you.

Teng: I thought what we were exploring today was the position of nuclear and conventional weapons.

Kissinger: I just wanted to answer the Foreign Minister's statement that they could first attack us. But it is true that it is more difficult to use nuclear weapons today than 15 years ago. This is without question true.

Ch'iao: What I was saying was this: At present if the Soviet Union should launch an attack with conventional weapons on not necessarily a large scale, on a medium scale, for you to use nuclear weapons under those circumstances would be a difficult thing to make up your minds about.

Kissinger: It is more difficult now than 10 to 15 years ago. It depends on where the attack takes place.

Ch'iao: As we discussed in New York, if there are changes in Yugoslavia—they need not make a direct attack, but if they incite pro-Soviet elements to bring in the Soviet armed forces—what would you do?

Kissinger: Yugoslavia? I went to Yugoslavia after our talk and talked to Marshal Tito and his colleagues about exactly this problem. For one thing, we will begin selling military equipment to Yugoslavia next year. We are now studying what to do in such a case. We will not let it happen unchallenged. It will not be like Czechoslovakia or Hungary. We have not yet decided on the precise measures. But we believe that if the Soviet army is permitted to move outside its sphere, it will create appetites that might not stop. This is why we reacted so violently when they mobilized their airborne divisions during the Middle East crisis. Because it was our judgment that once permitted to operate far from their territory in foreign wars, not in internal quarrels, there would be no end to their appetites.

Teng: In our opinion, not only the Middle East is explosive but also the Balkan Peninsula. And this is an old strategy of the Czar.

Kissinger: For your information, if there is a European Security Conference in the spring, which is, as you know, something we have never wanted, if the President attends, he plans to stop in Bucharest and Belgrade to help make clear the American interest in the independence of these two countries. But we have not announced this, obviously.

Teng: We have no reason to be in disagreement.

Kissinger: It was no accident that on my recent trip I stopped in Afghanistan, Yugoslavia and Romania, and made speeches in each about an independent foreign policy.

Teng: So we have been exploring some strategic issues today.

Kissinger: Yes.

Teng: Do you have anything else you want to discuss in this group?

Kissinger: No.

Teng: So, maybe after a short rest, do you want to bring in the others?

Kissinger: Yes.

[The meeting recessed at 11:32 a.m. and then reconvened in a larger group at 11:40.]

96.   Memorandum of Conversation[1]

Beijing, November 27, 1974, 11:40 a.m.–12:20 p.m.

PARTICIPANTS

Teng Hsiao-p'ing, Vice Premier of the State Council, People's Republic of China
Ch'iao Kuan-hua, Minister of Foreign Affairs
Ambassador Huang Chen, Chief of the PRC Liaison Office, Washington
Wang Hai-jung, Vice Minister of Foreign Affairs
T'ang Wen-sheng, Deputy Director, Department of American and Oceanic
    Affairs, Ministry of Foreign Affairs
Tsien Ta-yung, Counselor, PRC Liaison Office, Washington
Ting Yuan-hung, Director, United States Office, Department of American and
    Oceanic Affairs, Ministry of Foreign Affairs
Chang Han-chih, Translator
Lien Cheng-pao, Notetaker

Dr. Henry A. Kissinger, Secretary of State and Assistant to the President for
    National Security Affairs
Ambassador George Bush, Chief of the United States Liaison Office, Peking
Ambassador Robert Anderson, Special Assistant to the Secretary of State for
    Press Relations
Winston Lord, Director, Policy Planning Staff, Department of State
Philip C. Habib, Assistant Secretary of State for East Asian and Pacific Affairs
William H. Gleysteen, Deputy Assistant Secretary of State for East Asian and
    Pacific Affairs
Richard H. Solomon, Senior Staff Member, National Security Council
Bonnie Andrews, Notetaker

SUBJECT

Sino-Soviet Relations; Europe

Vice Premier Teng: This evening I invite you to a Peking meal.

Secretary Kissinger: Thank you.

Vice Premier Teng: Mr. Bush has had it [this type of meal].

Ambassador Bush: In Peking and in Canton!

Vice Premier Teng: But Peking—there are two best meals here. One is Peking Duck, and the other is the Hot Pot.

Secretary Kissinger: I have never had a Peking Hot Pot before. I look forward to it very much. Thank you very much. Did you say in a restaurant?

Vice Premier Teng: Yes, it is tasteless anywhere else.

---

[1] Source: Ford Library, National Security Adviser, Kissinger Reports on USSR, China, and Middle East Discussions, Box 2, China Memcons and Reports, November 25–29, 1974, Kissinger's Trip. Top Secret; Sensitive; Exclusively Eyes Only. The meeting took place at Government Guest House 18. All brackets are in the original.

Secretary Kissinger: I have never had a meal in a restaurant here.

Vice Premier Teng: Then tonight we invite you to a restaurant.

Secretary Kissinger: You know I remember receiving a call after one of my trips here. A singer wanted to perform in a night club [in Peking]. I told her there were none. She couldn't belive it. Now I turn these calls over to the Ambassador [Huang Chen]. He convinces them there is no China. [Laughter]

Vice Premier Teng: Shall we continue? We would like to thank the Doctor for telling us about your global trips—or, to use a Chinese phrase, about your "travels to various lands."

I would like to give a brief summary of our understanding of some issues. I should think the first matter that the Doctor would be concerned about is the Soviet Union and Sino-Soviet relations.

Secretary Kissinger: I will adopt your method and say it is up to you. [Laughter]

Vice Premier Teng: You know that the differences between the Soviet Union and China are profound. And you know that after Brezhnev left Vladivostok, he flew to Ulan Bator to attend the anniversary of the People's Republic of Mongolia, and he made a speech. I read the press reports—the part relating to Sino-Soviet relations, and he was boasting a little about the agreements you reached in Vladivostok.

Secretary Kissinger: I explained those to you.

Vice Premier Teng: He still repeated the old words about China and the Soviet Union. The most important [of these] was that he said between China and the Soviet Union there does not exist any border dispute. And by "disputed area" he wasn't even speaking of the larger part—the one and one-half million kilometers. He only mentioned the smaller, spotted area along the border. So the content of the so-called "non-aggression" treaty, non-use-of-force, doesn't even include the essence of the border dispute.

Secretary Kissinger: Our analysis is the same. I noticed he praised the Foreign Minister. This I approve of highly.

Vice Premier Teng: Which one?

Secretary Kissinger: His, and ours! [Laughter]

Vice Premier Teng: That means that the very issue the two sides are negotiating about doesn't exist at all. That means also that the provisional agreement reached by the Prime Ministers, reached between our two countries in 1969, is gone with the wind. It also means that the words they mouth about improvements in relations are all empty. Of course, they pay lip service to "improving relations." And over the years the postures they have struck have many aspects, varied forms, including mediation by the Cubans and the Romanians. I recall that Chairman Mao discussed this with you. And you will also recall that

Chairman Mao made the concessions of 2,000 years and said that no further concession would be made.

Secretary Kissinger: We will explain that to our Ambassador. It will give him courage. (The Secretary quietly explains the story to Ambassador Bush.)

Vice Premier Teng: So we can see from that that the recent talk about the publicization of the telegram we sent to the Soviet Union on its National Day is not quite in accord with facts.

Secretary Kissinger: Did you publish it, or did they?

Vice Premier Teng: We did not. But they deleted a bit [from the Chinese text] when they did. Actually, we put congratulations in the cable, we put in just the content of the agreement reached between the two Premiers in 1969, we just mentioned the essence of the agreement between the two Premiers: that we should maintain the status quo on the border; prevent armed conflict and avoid clashes on the border; and it has what they put forward about an agreement on non-aggression and non-use-of-force.

Secretary Kissinger: This is new?

Vice Premier Teng: It is not new. It was also part of the understanding of 1969.

Secretary Kissinger: But if they should succeed—it will be the first such non-aggression treaty among allies.

Vice Premier Teng: Their proposals were put forward under the circumstances that the treaty still exists, our treaty of mutual assistance still exists. So it seems that the Soviet policy of hostility against China has not changed. And, of course, this doesn't exclude more tricks, such as asking this person or that person to come and mediate, but it doesn't change the essence [of China's dispute with the Soviets]. The methods that they continue to use are military threat and subversion. And they will continue their tricks such as the Asian Collective Security system. That also was something mentioned [by Brezhnev] in Ulan Bator.

Secretary Kissinger: Apparently, he discussed that with Bhutto, but he rejected it. Brezhnev also discussed it with the Shah in Moscow.

Vice Premier Teng: It was the same old theme. Others expressed a certain degree of favor for it, but—

Secretary Kissinger: The Shah will not go along with it.

Vice Premier Teng: That is also our opinion. Even India hasn't dared to openly accept it. Actually the Asian Collective Security system, although in name is directed against China, it is really aimed at dividing and controlling the countries of the area. This is the same [tactic] as the European Security Conference. It is to help Soviet forces [gain access] into the Indian Ocean and Pacific.

Secretary Kissinger: I think by now the Soviets—the European Security Conference is ridiculous. It can no longer achieve anything significant.

Vice Premier Teng: And the Chairman asked Mr. Heath when he was in China if he thought the European Security Conference would be a success. He replied that rather than ask if it would be successful one should ask "when will it be finished?" What is your assessment of the conference? Will it be a success, or will it be concluded?

Secretary Kissinger: It cannot be a success. Our view is that it should be concluded. We feel that if it goes on it will create the impression of success, which is not warranted. This should be avoided. There will be no substantive agreement of any kind. They are discussing principles—one of the issues they are now debating is about the peaceful change of frontiers. The Soviets want to say that frontiers are inviolable. The Germans want to say that frontiers can be changed only by peaceful means.

The other issue is that the Soviets say that all principles should be equally applied. The Germans want to say that all [principles] have equal validity. I have tried to explain the difference [between these two formulations] to the President, but I do not understand it myself. This is the sort of thing they are discussing at the Security Conference right now.

Vice Premier Teng: It is very confusing to me.

Secretary Kissinger: The instructions to the members of our delegation are to stay out of such things. For this, one must have a German or Soviet mind.

Vice Premier Teng: One can probably only write this now in German.

Secretary Kissinger: That is right. But there is no possible conclusion now that can be called a success. You cannot change history by sentences in a treaty! However, I think it will be finished in the early part of next year.

Vice Premier Teng: As for the Soviet threat, as we have said many times, we don't pay much attention. We don't think those one million troops can be of much consequence. The Soviet military strength in the East is not just directed against China. It is also directed against Japan and your Seventh Fleet, your air and naval forces. And if they are going to attack China, as the Chairman has discussed [with you], it will be impossible to take over China with just one million troops. They will have to increase their troops by one million, and even that would not be sufficient because if they are going to make up their minds to fight with China, they will have to make up their minds to fight for 20 years. The Chinese have no great virtue, but they do have [the virtue of] patience.

Secretary Kissinger: They have a few other virtues.

Vice Premier Teng: They also have "millet plus rifles"—and tunnels.

Secretary Kissinger: I have never seen the tunnels.

Vice Premier Teng: Hasn't Ambassador Bush done this for you? He is shirking his responsibilities.

Ambassador Bush: Not yet. I am delighted to know that I can see them.

Vice Premier Teng: The next time you can write a report to the Doctor about the tunnels.

Secretary Kissinger: Don't encourage him.[2] Between him and the Ambassador in India [Patrick Moynihan] I have nothing to do but read cables—although the Ambassador in India publishes his in the newspapers.

Vice Premier Teng: So that is the order of relations between the Soviet Union and China. As for the strategic emphasis of the Soviet Union, we see it as "a feint toward the East to attack in the West"—to attack in Europe. It doesn't matter if we have different views, we can see what happens.

Secretary Kissinger: I think the strategic situation is the same. If they attack in the East it will be a threat to the West, and if they attack in the West it will be a threat to the East. The danger is the same either way. We don't need to decide this abstractly.

Vice Premier Teng: But this strategic assessment has its practical side, especially with the Western European countries. We have exchanged views on this many times.

Secretary Kissinger: I don't believe Europe could be indifferent to an attack in the East. I don't believe you could be indifferent to an attack in the West.

Vice Premier Teng: We agree to this view. An attack in any quarter is of significance to other areas too. But to establish a strategic point of view and preparations will be of significant importance, especially to your allies in Europe. Because without [these preparations], they will suffer. When we say the emphasis is in the West, it does not mean we will ignore our own defenses.

Secretary Kissinger: We agree, and we will add to our preparations too. Unfortunately, as you know, some of the leaders in Europe are not

---

[2] At a meeting with Ford and Scowcroft on November 11, Kissinger said, "We will have to slow George Bush down. We need to keep things quiet there—he is saying we have been neglecting the Chinese." (Memorandum of conversation, November 11; ibid., Memoranda of Conversation, Box 7, October–December 1974)

the most heroic right now. You have met them and can form your own opinions. But we will do our best.

I might add something about the oil problem: The U.S. has two options. Economically, we can deal with the problem on our own better than in cooperation with others. But the reason I have made several specific suggestions and proposals is because I believe if Europe continues to suffer a balance of payments drain, they will lose so much confidence that they will not be able to resist Soviet pressures. And if they take money from countries like Libya and Algeria, this will continue the process of their political demoralization. So you should understand that the proposals I have made, and our policies, have nothing to do with economic considerations, because economically we would be better off making bilateral agreements with the Saudis, and we could leave Europe alone. We do this because we feel the defense of the West will be weakened if these countries are demoralized by their economic condition.

Vice Premier Teng: So, I think we spent quite a lot of time this morning. We must have something to eat, otherwise our stomachs will make revolution. Shall we meet again at 3:30 p.m. in the Great Hall of the People? In the Original Hall. All right?

Secretary Kissinger: I don't know what the Original Hall is, but I am sure someone will take us there.

Vice Premier Teng: It is the Sinkiang Room.

Secretary Kissinger: Thank you.

[The meeting adjourned at 12:20 p.m.]

---

97.   Memorandum of Conversation[1]

Beijing, November 27, 1974, 3:36–5:45 p.m.

PARTICIPANTS

    Teng Hsiao-p'ing, Vice Premier of the State Council, People's Republic of China
    Ch'iao Kuan-hua, Minister of Foreign Affairs
    Ambassador Huang Chen, Chief of the PRC Liaison Office, Washington

---

[1] Source: Ford Library, National Security Adviser, Kissinger Reports on USSR; China, and Middle East Discussion, Box 2, China Memcons and Reports; November 25–29, 1974, Kissinger's Trip. Top Secret; Sensitive; Exclusively Eyes Only. The meeting took place in the Great Hall of the People. All brackets are in the original.

Wang Hai-jung, Vice Minister of Foreign Affairs
Lin Ping, Director, Department of American and Oceanic Affairs, Ministry of
    Foreign Affairs
T'ang Wen-sheng, Deputy Director, Department of American and Oceanic
    Affairs, Ministry of Foreign Affairs
Tsien Ta-yung, Counselor, PRC Liaison Office, Washington
Ting Yuan-hung, Director, United States Office, Department of American and
    Oceanic Affairs, Ministry of Foreign Affairs
Chao Chi-hua, Deputy Director, United States Office, Department of American
    and Oceanic Affairs, Ministry of Foreign Affairs
Chang Han-chih, Translator
Lien Cheng-pao, Notetaker

Dr. Henry A. Kissinger, Secretary of State and Assistant to the President for
    National Security Affairs
Donald Rumsfeld, Assistant to the President
Ambassador George Bush, Chief of the United States Liaison Office, Peking
Winston Lord, Director, Policy Planning Staff, Department of State
William H. Gleysteen, Deputy Assistant Secretary of State for East Asian Affairs
John H. Holdridge, Deputy Chief, United States Liaison Office, Peking
Richard H. Solomon, Senior Staff Member, National Security Council
Peter W. Rodman, National Security Council
Lora Simkus, National Security Council

SUBJECTS

Europe; Japan; Middle East; South Asia; Cambodia; Energy and Food;
Normalization

Vice Premier Teng: I hope you're not too tired.

Secretary Kissinger: No, I'm in good shape.

I see the Vice Premier has a list here, which he hasn't completed [discussing] yet. [Laughter]

Europe

Vice Premier Teng: We touched upon the question of Europe this morning.[2]

Secretary Kissinger: Yes.

Vice Premier Teng: Actually we believe it is essentially the same with Europe as with Japan. We have often expressed the view that it is our wish that the U.S. keep its good relations with Europe and Japan.

Secretary Kissinger: In fact the Chairman scolded me last year for not having good enough relations with Europe. [Laughter]

Vice Premier Teng: This opinion of ours is based on consideration of the whole [global] strategy. Because now the Soviet Union is determined to seek hegemony in the world, if they wish to launch a world war and don't get Europe first, they won't succeed in achieving hegemony in

---

[2] See Documents 95 and 96.

other parts of the world, because Europe is so important politically, economically and militarily. And now that Europe is facing the threat from the polar bear, if they don't unite and try to strengthen themselves, then only one or two countries in Europe will not be able to deal with this threat [in isolation]. We feel with respect to the United States that when the United States deals with the polar bear, it is also necessary for the United States to have strong allies in Europe and Japan. With these allies by your side you will have more assurances in dealing with the polar bear.

Secretary Kissinger: We agree with you.

Vice Premier Teng: So it is always our hope that relations between the United States and Europe and Japan will be in a position of partnership based on equality. It is only on the basis of equality that you can establish real partnership.

Secretary Kissinger: I agree with you. I always say that the People's Republic is our best partner in NATO. [Laughter] If you want to arrange seminars here for visiting European Ministers, I can mention a few who would benefit by it. [Laughter] You had a very good effect on the Danish Prime Minister, although his nerves may not be up to your considerations.

Vice Premier Teng: We had very good talks.

Secretary Kissinger: Very good, very good.

Vice Premier Teng: Actually, the Prime Minister of Denmark really fears war very much.

Secretary Kissinger: Anyone who plans to attack Denmark doesn't have to prepare for a 20-year war or build so many underground tunnels. [Laughter] But seriously, we know your talks with the European Ministers are very helpful and we appreciate them.

Vice Premier Teng: But we also fire some cannons. With respect to our attitude toward Europe, we also say that if Europe wishes to establish relations with the United States on the basis of real equality, they should unite and strengthen themselves. This is in your interest too.

Secretary Kissinger: We agree. The only thing we object to—and you should also—is if they try to unite on the basis of hostility toward the United States, because this defeats the strategy we are discussing.

Vice Premier Teng: It is not possible that Western Europe will separate itself from the United States.

Secretary Kissinger: That is our conviction.

Vice Premier Teng: From our contacts with people from Western Europe, we have this impression—including the Prime Minister of Denmark.

Secretary Kissinger: You will see. Last year we had a period of turmoil, leading to a higher degree of order. [Laughter]

Vice Premier Teng: I suppose you will start talking philosophy again. [Laughter]

Secretary Kissinger: The President will meet with the German Chancellor on December 5th, and with the French President in the middle of December—the 14th, 15th, and 16th. And I think you will see those meetings will be very successful.

Vice Premier Teng: The Doctor mentioned that the United States fears that the Left in Europe might get into power.

Secretary Kissinger: We have in France and Italy Communist Parties that are substantially influenced from Moscow.

Vice Premier Teng: That is true.

Secretary Kissinger: They are now performing a strategy—which is very intelligent—of appearing very moderate and responsible. On the other hand, I think it has been one of the successes of our foreign policy that they have had to show their responsibility by supporting NATO—at least the Italians.

Vice Premier Teng: But that is not reliable.

Secretary Kissinger: Absolutely unreliable. Absolutely unreliable. When you analyze our foreign policy you have to understand we have to do certain things and say certain things designed to paralyze not only our Left but the European Left as well. But we are opposed to, and we shall resist, the inclusion of the Left in European governments. We shall do so in Portugal because we don't want that to be the model for other countries. And we shall do so in Italy. And of course in France.

Vice Premier Teng: In our view it is by no means easy [for them] to get into power.

Secretary Kissinger: That is right.

Vice Premier Teng: Even if they do get into power, and they wish to appear on stage and give some performances, it may not be a bad thing.

Secretary Kissinger: I disagree with you.

Vice Premier Teng: For example, in Algeria: The people in Algeria have had a very good experience with the so-called Communist Party of France. After the Second World War in France, with De Gaulle as head of the Government, there was a coalition in which the French Communist Party took part. Some Ministers were from the Communist Party. One of the Ministers who was Communist was the Minister of the Air Force. It is exactly this Communist Minister of the Air Force who sent planes to bomb guerrillas in Algeria. And from then, the Algerians had good [sufficient] experience with the Communists in France.

Secretary Kissinger: You should have no misunderstanding: If the Communists come to power in France or Italy, it will have serious consequences first in Germany. It will strengthen the Left wing of the Social Democratic Party, which is very much influenced by East Germany.

Vice Premier Teng: We don't like this Left. It is not our liking that they should come into power. What we mean is, suppose they do come into power and given some performances, they will be teachers by negative example.

Secretary Kissinger: If they come into power, we will have to face it. But it will have very serious consequences; it will create a period of extreme confusion. It will have a serious effect on NATO. As long as President Ford is President and I am Secretary of State, we shall resist it.

Vice Premier Teng: That is right. It is true that, should they come into power, it will produce this effect, but even if it happens, it will not be so formidable. We don't really disagree.

Secretary Kissinger: No, you are saying that if it happens, we should not be discouraged, and it will not be a final setback. I agree.

Vice Premier Teng: This is what I wish to say about Europe.

Secretary Kissinger: One thing more: You know about the discussions on Mutual Force Reductions that are going on, and I know the Chinese views with respect to those.

Foreign Minister Ch'iao: In Vienna.

Secretary Kissinger: In Vienna. And I know the Chinese view with respect to them. It is probably true that troops that disappear from one area will not disappear from the world. We face here the irony that the best way for the United States to keep very substantial forces in Europe is to agree to a very small reduction with the Soviet Union, because this reduces pressure from the internal Left. I see no possibility of very rapid progress, and there is no possibility whatever for very substantial reductions. Right now the negotiations are stalemated, and it is not impossible—but this is based only on a psychological assessment—that before Brezhnev comes to the United States next year they may make some small reduction. There is no indication [of this at the present time]; it is my psychological assessment based on the way they work. But we are talking about only something like 20–25,000 people, nothing substantial. This is just my instinct; it is not based on any discussion [with the Soviets]. So through 1976 I do not see any substantial change in the military dispositions.

Vice Premier Teng: We have not read much of the comments from Western Europe about your Vladivostok agreements with the Russians. But from what we have read, it seems Western Europe is a little worried that the agreements you reached in Vladivostok might lead to a reduction of American troops in Western Europe.

Secretary Kissinger: I haven't seen these accounts, but they are ridiculous. We discussed this this morning: as nuclear war becomes more complex, we have to increase conventional forces, not weaken them. There is no understanding about reduction of American forces in Europe. We paid no price for this agreement in Vladivostok, of any kind, in any area.

Vice Premier Teng: Of course this is a question to be discussed among NATO themselves, and between you and your Western European allies.

Secretary Kissinger: I am going to Europe for the NATO meetings on December 12th, and our allies will understand, at least by that time, that the Vladivostok meeting was a sign of Soviet weakness and was not purchased at the expense of concessions in any other areas.

Vice Premier Teng: Next, I wish to say a few words about the Middle East.

Japan

Secretary Kissinger: You are finished with Japan? The same principles as Europe.

Vice Premier Teng: I believe we have touched on the things we wish to say about Japan. And we have on many occasions expressed our views concerning relations between the United States and Japan. We have made our position clear.

Secretary Kissinger: Yes, and we discussed this this morning, and with the Foreign Minister on a few occasions.

I haven't seen any new reports about a new government [to replace the Tanaka cabinet].

Vice Premier Teng: We can say it in one sentence, which is what we say to Japanese friends: That first, they should keep good relations with you, the United States; and second, with us. The Chairman said you should stay longer there. [Laughter]

Secretary Kissinger: That is right. He scolded me, and said I should spend as much time in Japan as in China. Actually, after the President's [recently concluded] visit to Japan, our relations are much steadier. And this is very important for Japan. And as I have said, we will do nothing to interfere with Japan's improvement of relations with the People's Republic of China. We have encouraged them to work with the People's Republic.

Vice Premier Teng: We understand that.

Middle East

Vice Premier Teng: About the Middle East. It is the most sensitive area in the world now.

We have the impression, starting from early this year, that you have improved relations with Egypt. This is so?

Secretary Kissinger: This is so.

Vice Premier Teng: Then why is the Soviet Union going back to Egypt?

Secretary Kissinger: I don't think the Soviet Union is going back to Egypt. I think Egypt has to show, for domestic reasons, and for inter-Arab reasons, that it also has relations with the Soviet Union. But the Soviet Union stopped military aid and has reduced its economic aid.

Vice Premier Teng: It is said you promised to give Egypt something but didn't keep your promise. Is this true?

Secretary Kissinger: I don't know what you are referring to specifically. We promised Egypt $250 million in economic aid which Congress has not yet approved. But we expect Congress will approve it, hopefully by the end of the year.

Vice Premier Teng: Anyway, our views—as Chairman Mao said to you personally—are that you must use both of your hands. Of course, it is not possible for you to stop aiding Israel. But once you aid Israel, you should use both your hands [and assist the Arabs].

Secretary Kissinger: I completely agree. In addition to the $250 million [in economic aid], we have arranged another $250 million from the World Bank; so it is $500 million. And in addition we have arranged for 500,000 tons of grain, and we may give them more.

Vice Premier Teng: What about military aid? Weapons.

Secretary Kissinger: I think we had better have a small meeting again tomorrow. There were one or two things I neglected to mention.

Vice Premier Teng: Chairman Mao has made very clear our policy on the Middle East question. In the first place, we support the Arabs and the Palestinians in their just struggle; and secondly, we feel that a heavy blow should be dealt to the polar bear in this area. [Teng laughs.] We have this feeling recently—it may not be very accurate—that in the Arab world the Soviet Union has somehow gotten the upper hand on you.

Secretary Kissinger: I don't believe this will be true in three months. I think by February it will be apparent that further progress is being made as a result of American initiatives, and we will then see a repetition of last year's situation.

Vice Premier Teng: In the Middle East, the basic contradiction is Israel and the whole Arab world and Palestine. That is the basic contradiction in that area. And it is known to all that you are giving Israel an enormous amount of military aid as well as economic aid. As for the Arab world, since you are giving Israel so much aid, in order to resist Israel the Arab people will look to other people for aid, because if you don't give them some aid, others will. They aren't able to make what they need. And the Soviet Union will say, "We have things for you." And by giving them what they need, the Soviet Union gains politically, and by selling arms to the Arab world they gain economic benefits. And you get yourself bogged down in the Middle East.

Secretary Kissinger: But the Soviet Union faces the contradiction that they can give military aid but they can't promote political progress. And in country after country, once they give arms, they get into difficulty. We are studying the question of giving arms to selected Arab countries now.

Foreign Minister Ch'iao: I have a question. Is it possible to encourage the European countries to give some arms to the Arabs?

Secretary Kissinger: Let's have a discussion of this tomorrow in a small meeting. We are aware of the problem, and we share your analysis. If you look at the Arab countries concretely—in Egypt I think it will be apparent in the next three months that there is no significant change. In Syria, it is my judgment Syria would be prepared to move away from the Soviet Union if Israel were prepared to make any concessions at all in the negotiation.

Vice Premier Teng: The key point is whether you are using only one of your hands or both.

Secretary Kissinger: We are using both our hands, but in a way to minimize our domestic problem. And in Iraq, it is our impression—as you may have noticed, there is some pressure in Iraq from Iran, and this has led to certain strains between the Soviet Union and Iraq. So much will depend on . . .

First of all, we agree with your basic principle, that we must have an even-handed policy. And I have to confess that because of the Presidential transition in the summer, we lost two months, two to three months. In June, July, and August we could not begin to operate as effectively as we might. After the Syrian disengagement we had to pause because of our domestic situation at that time. We are regaining this ground, although for various reasons we are now using spectacular methods.

Vice Premier Teng: I have also noticed your comment on the Rabat Conference.

Secretary Kissinger: Public comment? Here?

Vice Premier Teng: The comment you made here.

Secretary Kissinger: Oh yes, I remember.

Vice Premier Teng: I am afraid if you adopt an antagonistic attitude toward the Rabat Conference, it will not be conducive to your relations with the Arabs.

Secretary Kissinger: We will not adopt an antagonistic attitude. It is a question of timing.

Vice Premier Teng: The Arab question is not a question that can be solved in a few months. It will have to go on for a long period.

Secretary Kissinger: Therefore it is important to pick the right time. But you should remember the following principle, no matter how many cannons have to be fired: The United States will not yield to pressure in the Middle East, especially Soviet pressure. No diplomatic progress can be made without the United States. Therefore, everyone who wants progress in the Middle East will sooner or later have to come to the United States, no matter what they say in the interval. Thirdly, the United States is determined to bring about diplomatic progress, and it will succeed. The problem is how to do it so that we can handle our domestic situation in the meantime. But you will see on this matter that President Ford is determined.

We will keep you informed of our methods. But there will be ups and downs, especially when 15 Arabs get together in one room—because they can't always make a distinction between epic poetry and foreign policy.

I must tell the Vice Premier something about the Arab mentality. After one consultation with the Israelis, we wrote a letter to all the Arab Foreign Ministers, and one said to me, "We know you are not telling the truth." I said, "How?" "Because we compared letters. You told each of us the same thing. So we know it is not the truth." [Laughter]

Vice Premier Teng: But in our view, it is not right to underestimate the strength of our Arab people.

Secretary Kissinger: We don't underestimate it. We have one particular problem. If we propose grandiose schemes, we will be enmeshed in an endless domestic debate. We have to move a step at a time. As long as we move a step at a time, a solution is inevitable.

I have great respect for the Arabs, and have many friends there.

Vice Premier Teng: We believe the Arab people may not be able to win the war in a few months, but they are able to fight.

Secretary Kissinger: That is true. That is the change in the situation. No, we believe it is essential for Israel to make peace.

Vice Premier Teng: Our view is whether soldiers can fight or not depends on the principle for which they are fighting, whether they are fighting for the people. Here I will tell you a story. For the Chinese, it was a long-standing concept that the people of Kiangsi Province couldn't fight. But Ching Kang Shan Mountain was situated in Kiangsi Province. And at that time in the Red Army, led by Chairman Mao Tse-tung, it turned out that most of the cadre were people from Kiangsi Province. I believe among our American friends here there are some who are very familiar with Chinese history and know it was a concept for many years that Kiangsi people couldn't fight. And it turned out that when the people in Kiangsi knew what they were fighting for, they turned out to be the best fighters. And in America, people had the impression that people in Indochina couldn't fight. But it turned out that the people in Indochina fixed you up very hard. And the Cambodians—but they can fight too.

Secretary Kissinger: The only ones who have yet to prove it are the Laotians. [Laughter]

Vice Premier Teng: You have a point in that. What I mean is you should never underestimate the strength of the Arabs.

Secretary Kissinger: We don't. We have the practical problem of making progress—which we believe is necessary—in a way that makes further progress possible. And to do it fast enough so the Soviet Union doesn't reenter the area. We believe we can solve both of these problems.

Vice Premier Teng: Actually the position of the United States in the Middle East, the weakest point of the U.S. is that you support Israel against the Arab world, which has a population of 120 million, and on this point the Soviet Union is in a better position than you.

Secretary Kissinger: Except that impotence never gives you a good position. Israel is both our weakest point and our strongest point. Because when all is said and done, no one else can make them move. Because the Arabs can't force them, and the Soviets can't do it. And anyone who wants progress will have to come to us. And this even includes the Palestinians.

Vice Premier Teng: With the Russians, their habit is wherever there is a little hole, a little room, they will get in.

Secretary Kissinger: It is extremely dangerous for the Russians to start a war in the Middle East. They will rapidly face the same dilemma they faced in October 1973.

Vice Premier Teng: So much about the Middle East.

South Asia

Vice Premier Teng: The Doctor mentioned India and the question of the Subcontinent yesterday. On this issue I believe we have exchanged views on many occasions in the past and we don't have anything new to add. Recently you visited India, and after your visit you improved your relations with India, and we believe that this was a good move. Because if there is only the Soviet Union there [they will be the only ones with influence], it is better to have you in India than the Soviets alone.

Secretary Kissinger: That was the intention of the trip. And it also will make it easier to do things in Pakistan without being accused of an anti-Indian motivation. [Teng spits loudly into his spittoon beside his chair.] And as you know, we have invited Prime Minister Bhutto to Washington, and after that, there will be some concrete progress.

Vice Premier Teng: I think you said it would be possible for you to sell weapons to Pakistan. But will Pakistan be able to pay?

Secretary Kissinger: Yes.

Vice Premier Teng: That would be good.

As for India, you mentioned earlier that India was hegemonistic.

Secretary Kissinger: It is my assessment. One of my colleagues said he was not only in favor of giving arms to Pakistan, but arms and nuclear weapons to Pakistan and Bangladesh. [Ambassador Huang laughingly leans across the table and wags his pencil at Mr. Lord.] Mr. Lord [laughter], head of our Policy Planning Staff.

Vice Premier Teng: There is something very peculiar about Indian policy. For example, that little kingdom of Sikkim. They had pretty good control of Sikkim. Why did they have to annex it?

Secretary Kissinger: It is a good thing India is pacifist. I hate to think [of what they would do] if they weren't. [Laughter]

Vice Premier Teng: Sikkim was entirely under the military control of India.

Secretary Kissinger: I haven't understood Sikkim. It is incomprehensible.

Vice Premier Teng: After the military annexation, their military position was in no way strengthened.

Secretary Kissinger: They had troops there already.

Vice Premier Teng: And they haven't increased their troops there. We published a statement about it. We just spoke up for the sake of justice.

Secretary Kissinger: Is it true that you have set up loudspeakers to broadcast to the Indian troops on the border? It makes them very tense. [Laughter]

Vice Premier Teng: We have done nothing new along the borders, and frankly we don't fear that India will attack our borders. We don't think they have the capability of attacking our borders. There was some very queer talk, some said that the reason why the Chinese Government issued that statement about Sikkim was that the Chinese were afraid after Sikkim that India would complete the encirclement of China. Well, in the first place, we never feel things like isolation or encirclement can ever matter very much with us. And particularly with India, it is not possible that India can do any encirclement of China. The most they can do is enter Chinese territory as far as the autonomous Republic of Tibet, Lhasa. And Lhasa can be of no strategic importance to India. The particular characteristic of Lhasa is it has no air—because the altitude is more than 3,000 meters. During the Long March we did cross the region of Tibet.

Secretary Kissinger: Really.

Vice Premier Teng: Not the Lhasa area, but the southern part. Our experience was that when we wanted to take one step futher, we couldn't.

Secretary Kissinger: It is a very dangerous area for drinking mao tai. [Laughter]

Vice Premier Teng: Frankly, if Indian troops were able to reach Lhasa, we wouldn't be able to supply them enough air. [Laughter]

Secretary Kissinger: I don't think their intention is with respect to Tibet; their immediate intention is in Nepal.

Vice Premier Teng: That is correct. They have recently been exercising pressure on Nepal, refusing to supply them with oil. It is the dream of Nehru, inherited by his daughter, to have the whole South Asian subcontinent in their pocket.

Secretary Kissinger: And to have buffer zones around their border.

Vice Premier Teng: It is not necessary.

Secretary Kissinger: It is like British policy in the 19th Century. They always wanted Tibet demilitarized.

Vice Premier Teng: I believe even the British at that time didn't make a good estimate of whether there was enough air. [Laughter]

Secretary Kissinger: I think an Indian attack on China would be a very serious matter that couldn't be explained in terms of local conditions, but only in terms of a broader objective.

Vice Premier Teng: There is no use in attacking Tibet, for the Indians. The most they can do is that the Indians give their troops to fight for a broader objective.

Ms. T'ang [helping with translation]: Provide manpower for a broader objective.

Secretary Kissinger: Very serious. There is no purely Indian objective that could be served.

Vice Premier Teng: We're not worried about that.

Secretary Kissinger: We're just analyzing the situation.

Cambodia

Vice Premier Teng: And next, according to the Doctor's order, is the question of Cambodia. On the question of Cambodia I also made myself clear, and I have nothing to add.

Secretary Kissinger: Your Ambassador [Huang Hua] fired a whole bunch of cannons [on Cambodia] yesterday, at the United Nations. [Laughter]

Foreign Minister Ch'iao: That's the routine work of our Ambassador. [Laughter]

Secretary Kissinger: But this time he hit a few fortified positions. [Laughter]

Vice Premier Teng: That proves these cannons are not so formidable—but cannons will have to be fired.

Secretary Kissinger: We understand.

Vice Premier Teng: It can't be imagined that we will stop supporting the struggle of the Cambodian people.

Secretary Kissinger: Can I give you our analysis? The United States has nothing to gain in Cambodia. Having withdrawn from Vietnam, we can have no interest in a long-term presence in Cambodia. On the other hand, as a question of principle, we do not simply abandon people with whom we have worked. But this is not the key issue right now. The key issue right now is, according to our conception, the best solution of the Indochinese peninsula is one in which easy country can realize its national aspirations. And therefore we believe that solutions in which each of the states in the area can maintain its national independence, without being dominated by one, is quite frankly—though you're a better judge—in your long-term interest. If Indochina was dominated from one center, an aggressive force, in the context of some of the schemes for Asian collective security, could cause you problems.

Therefore we prefer a national solution for Cambodia. We believe Sihanouk offers perhaps the best possibility for a national solution. We believe that for Sihanouk to act effectively he must be in charge of a balance of forces in Cambodia, similar to Souvanna in Laos. Souvanna Phouma.

Foreign Minister Ch'iao: The situation is not the same.

Secretary Kissinger: It's of a different nature. I'm just being professorial; I'm not saying it can be achieved. If Sihanouk comes back as the head of the insurgent forces, he will not last long. He will just be a figurehead. And in our analysis the insurgent forces are under Hanoi's influence. So, curiously, we think it's in Sihanouk's interest to govern with some element of—not Lon Nol—but some other forces in Phnom Penh that he can use as a balance to help him preserve his position.

To be concrete, we would be prepared to cooperate in a peace conference whose practical result would be the return of Sihanouk, the transformation of the existing structure in Phnom Penh, and the participation of the resistance forces. And then Sihanouk could have a more balanced structure to govern.

Vice Premier Teng: I'm afraid that your information is not accurate. For example, there is talk that the Cambodian war is being fought by the Vietnamese. The accurate information which I can give you is that there is not a single Vietnamese soldier fighting in Cambodia.

Secretary Kissinger: That I believe, but the supplies come from Vietnam.

Vice Premier Teng: That's why I say your information is not accurate. You have to watch out, because the information supplied to you by Lon Nol is not accurate. And then you mentioned that the United States can't abandon those it has worked with. But, come to think of it, your relation with Lon Nol is only for four years.

Secretary Kissinger: I've told you we would be prepared to see a change in the structure in Phnom Penh as part of the solution. [Teng again spits into his spittoon.]

Vice Premier Teng: On this issue, Samdech Norodom Sihanouk has made many statements, and we support his statements.

Secretary Kissinger: With great passion.

Vice Premier Teng: That's true, and you don't lack passion either.

Secretary Kissinger: We have no emotional investment. And we don't oppose Sihanouk. He'll drive many people crazy before his political life is finished. [Laughter]

Vice Premier Teng: How is that possible? Who will be driven mad?

Secretary Kissinger: He's rather changeable, if you look at his history. But he's the biggest national figure in Cambodia, and as I said, we're not opposed to him.

Vice Premier Teng: Regardless of his changes, he's a nationalist.

Secretary Kissinger: We agree, and we consider him the leader of the nationalist forces. Perhaps after the UN vote there could be a further exchange of views.

Vice Premier Teng: Well, so much about Cambodia then.

Energy and Food

Vice Premier Teng: Next, the Doctor has mentioned on a number of occasions the questions of energy and food. On these two questions both sides are clear about the viewpoints of the other. We have heard a lot of talk and opinions from the Western world and Japan that the recent economic recession and inflation crisis are due to the recent rise of oil prices. Our view is that this is not the case. Before the rise of oil prices, there already existed a serious problem of inflation. And before the rise of oil prices, many of the products' prices had already gone up many times. Grain, for example, and many industrial products. With the rise of prices of many products, the losses suffered by the oil-producing countries were very great. And the time since the rise of oil prices is only about one year, starting from the Middle East war in October last year. Actually, the present situation is that the price of oil is falling down.

We agree with the view expressed by many Third World or oil-producing countries. They oppose the talk about the cause of inflation being the rise of oil prices. We agree this sort of talk has no grounds. As for the rising of oil prices itself, it was only after it went up that we knew of that. We didn't encourage the rise in oil prices and didn't participate in planning it. But on the question of the Arab countries finding oil as a weapon for their struggle, we support that. Of course it's also the fact that at the present moment, following the rise of oil prices, the inflation and economic difficulties in consuming countries were also intensified. That's also true.

There are solutions for this question. One method is the method of confrontation and the other is the method of dialogue. And we noticed the method you've adopted is the method of confrontation. [Secretary Kissinger smiles.] Don't you agree?

Secretary Kissinger: It is contrary to every principle of mine. [Laughter] It is energetic shadow boxing. [Laughter]

Vice Premier Teng: I've read articles in your press regarding this question and I believe these reflect the views of the American government.

Secretary Kissinger: No, the views of the American government are reflected in my speech in Chicago. For example, many articles reflect criticism of the Shah. I am totally opposed to criticism of the Shah, because he is the crucial element of the strategy we've discussed.

Vice Premier Teng: I was not referring to that part of the press opinion that is against the Shah. They sum up only three methods: The first is psychological warfare; the second is the secret activity—

Ms. Tang: In *Newsweek* magazine.

Secretary Kissinger: *Newsweek* is my favorite fiction magazine.

Vice Premier Teng: The third is military intervention.

Secretary Kissinger: That's all nonsense. [Laughter]

Vice Premier Teng: Anyway, we feel the method of waving a big baton and the method of confrontation may not be conducive to a solution, but will only sharpen the contradiction betwen the consumers and the producers. So when we talk to our friends coming from Europe, we tell them we are in favor of dialogue.

Secretary Kissinger: Are you finished?

Vice Premier Teng: Yes.

Secretary Kissinger: Let me make two observations. First, concerning the Chinese attitude favoring the use of the oil weapon, I recognize the People's Republic stands for certain principles and these have to be followed. But at some point a contradiction develops between all-out support for this and the necessity of achieving a common front against the threats to international security. It is up to the People's Republic to decide where this point is reached. But if objectively Europe and Japan are reduced to a sense of impotence, this is something to which one cannot be indifferent from the point of view of international security. But this is a question for the People's Republic, and I will leave it.

Let me turn to U.S. relations with the producers. *Newsweek* is not distinguished for its support of the Administration, and it is the last magazine we would tell what our strategy is. Of the three methods they mention, military intervention on the question of oil prices is out of the question. In the case of a total embargo, that would be another matter, but on the question of oil prices, it is out of the question. Psychological warfare against the Arabs is something I'd like to see. I can't imagine what it would be like. Anyway, we have no capability for it.

Our policy is quite different.

Vice Premier Teng: Well, if we give another term to psychological warfare, it would be "threats."

Secretary Kissinger: We're not making any threats.

We agree there should be dialogue. But I think for leaders who were on the Long March, they will not believe that conversation in the abstract will solve problems. Before the consumers talk to the producers, we think it is important for the consumers to know what they want and to adopt a comparable position. So we're attempting to organize the consumers precisely so they can have a dialogue in which they can speak with something like a common voice.

We believe it is also important that Japan and Europe should not be left in positions where they feel their future is in the hands of forces totally outside their control.

But our basic approach to the producers will be conciliatory. And we will agree to the French proposal provided there is prior consultation among the consumers.

Vice Premier Teng: I don't believe we can give you good suggestions on this question.

Secretary Kissinger: But we want you to understand our position. There will not be American military moves on the question of oil prices—or military threats.

Vice Premier Teng: For us, China cannot be considered one of the producing countries, because the oil we produce is very little and we produce just enough for our own consumption. And we can't be considered an oil-consuming country. And even if we speak on this issue, I don't think the oil producers will listen to us.

Secretary Kissinger: We don't ask you to speak; we want you to understand. There may be an occasion when visitors come here, but we're not asking you.

Vice Premier Teng: Whenever visitors ask us, we give the same answer. We want the method of dialogue.

Secretary Kissinger: That is our approach.

Vice Premier Teng: As for food, we don't have anything to say.

Secretary Kissinger: I don't think this is an issue between us.

Vice Premier Teng: The basic question is to encourage countries to go into production to produce enough grain for themselves.

Secretary Kissinger: That is right.

Vice Premier Teng: For countries not to produce enough and to look to the United States is not the right solution.

Secretary Kissinger: That is exactly right. And the debate that went on at the Rome Food Conference—whether the United States should give a million tons more or less—is irrelevant to the problem. The deficit can be closed only if the countries with a deficit produce more food. The United States alone can't close the deficit. But we are prepared to help with technical assistance and matters of this kind.

Normalization

Vice Premier Teng: Last time we talked a lot about normalization of relations, and I have only a few words to add to that. On this issue, the Doctor gave us some concrete formulas. And yesterday I summed up three points as matters of principle that we would not agree to:

The first principle is that we will not accept any form of two Chinas or one-China–one-Taiwan, or one-and-a-half-Chinas, or any formula like that. It can only be the Japan model.

The second principle is that after the United States abolishes the defense treaty it signed with Chiang Kai-shek, the Taiwan problem should be left to the Chinese people themselves to solve; it is an internal matter for China, in which no one has the right to interfere.

The third principle is that in the course of the solution of the Taiwan question by the Chinese themselves, there should be no other country which should be allowed to interfere in the solution of the problem. Any kind of reviewing or guarantee or any kind of involvement in the process we will not accept.

And if the United States feels the time is not yet ripe for the solution of this problem and you still need Taiwan, we can wait. A so-called transitional period is too complicated. So we can wait until the time is ripe and then solve the problem in one gulp, like with Japan.

On this issue, the Doctor also mentioned that you have some domestic difficulties, the so-called Taiwan lobby or pro-Taiwan elements. Actually, as far as we know, the Taiwan lobby is much stronger in Japan than in the United States. But still, as I said before, if you have domestic difficulties, we can wait.

The second question is the method by which we are going to liberate Taiwan, and also includes the time of the solution.

I just wish to sum up the comments I made yesterday.

I wish to say the reason why the problem can't be solved as we visualize it should be solved is that on your side you have difficulties. It's not that we don't want to solve it.

Secretary Kissinger: I understand that.

Vice Premier Teng: This is all I want to say. I believe we've touched upon all the problems.

The Doctor took 18 days to tour 18 countries. I just took two hours to tour the circle [of global problems on the agenda for discussion]. [Laughter]

Secretary Kissinger: But you talked more sense. [Laughter]

Ms. T'ang: This shows the advanced technology of the Chinese!

Secretary Kissinger: Let me think about your last remarks, and I'll answer while I'm here in a general way. [Teng spits again into his spittoon.]

Vice Premier Teng: I don't think we can finish our talks on this issue this time.

Secretary Kissinger: I don't think so either.

Vice Premier Teng: So, shall we stop here? And you'll have a little rest, and I'll invite you to taste the well-known Peking mutton [at a restaurant for dinner].

Secretary Kissinger: I'm looking forward to it. I've never had it. Let me do a draft of what we discussed this morning, and then I'll bring it to dinner. It will give the Foreign Minister a whole night to tear it to pieces. Or do you have one [draft of your own]?

Foreign Minister Ch'iao: I'm entirely with your suggestion, but only don't give me such a draft that it upsets my appetite for the mutton. [Laughter]

Secretary Kissinger: No more than ten pages. [Laughter] And you won't know whether we're going up or down until the last sentence. [Laughter] It's a brief statement, in the spirit of our discussions.

Vice Premier Teng: You don't want meetings tomorrow? Some rest, or some work to do?

Secretary Kissinger: We'll decide tonight.

Foreign Minister Ch'iao: In the morning, or tonight?

Secretary Kissinger: We can do it tomorrow morning.

Vice Premier Teng: You wanted another small group meeting. Should we do it in the morning or afternoon?

Secretary Kissinger: It really makes no difference.

Vice Premier Teng: Shall we say 4:00 in the afternoon? [It is agreed.] So I hope you can sleep more in the morning.

Secretary Kissinger: I will see you at dinner.

Foreign Minister Ch'iao: I'll come fetch the communiqué.

98.   Memorandum of Conversation[1]

Beijing, November 28, 1974, 4:00–6:15 p.m.

PARTICIPANTS

Chinese
Teng Hsiao-ping, Vice Premier[2]

American
The Secretary
Mr. Rumsfeld, Assistant to the President
Ambassador Bush, Chief of the Liaison Office
Mr. Philip Habib, Assistant Secretary for East Asian Affairs
Mr. Winston Lord, Director, Policy Planning Staff
Miss Christine Vick, Secretary's office (notetaker)

Teng: Have you have a good rest this morning?

Kissinger: It was kind of the Foreign Minister to go with us to the Temple. Our Ambassador told me what is going on in China. Then I showed Mr. Rumsfeld the Forbidden City and the German Ambassador who is an old friend, called on me to tell me what is going on in China too.

Teng: What do the Germans think is going on in China?

Kissinger: Frankly, he wanted to hear from me what is going on.

Teng: You can tell him we are digging tunnels here.

Kissinger: And storing grain.

Teng: Right. Three sentences—dig tunnels deep, store grain everywhere, and never seek hegemony. These are the three things we are to note.

Kissinger: As Chairman Mao said last year.

Teng: This, I think, will be our final session here. We will hear you first.

Kissinger: The last word will be the Foreign Minister's tonight and I will have no possibility to reply. I wanted to cover a few odds and ends of yesterday's discussion. First, with respect to our relations with the Arab countries, we have not been inactive, as I told you yesterday, we have 250 million for Egypt and in addition we have given them 150 million for other kinds of various assistance, primarily in the agricultural field and we have asked the World Bank to give them

---

[1] Source: Ford Library, National Security Adviser, Kissinger Reports on USSR, China, and Middle East Discussions, Box 2, China Memcons and Reports, November 25–29, 1974, Kissinger's Trip. No classification marking. The meeting took place in the Great Hall of the People.

[2] None of the participants on the Chinese side was listed except for Deng Xiaoping.

250 million. So altogether they have received about 650 million. And we have given even Syria 100,000 tons of agricultural products. In the military field, which the Vice Premier correctly mentioned, it is true that the Soviet Union has cut off Egypt and there has not yet been any replacement. We have a massive domestic problem about giving military aid to Arab countries. What we are doing, on a very confidential basis, is we have a rather substantial military assistance program to Saudi Arabia beyond the needs of Saudi Arabia. Secondly, after the next step in the Egyptian/Israeli disengagement agreement, we plan to permit the acquisition of military equipment by Egypt, and Saudi Arabia has already set aside 500 million for that purpose. Again for your information, the Israelis will run out of credits in March and we will link new credits to Israel for the right to sell arms to Egypt. In the meantime we are encouraging the Federal Republic to also sell arms to Egypt and France needs no encouragement as long as cash is involved. We would also encourage Britain to develop helicopter production in Egypt. I wanted you to know these things on a very confidential basis.

As for the negotiations—given the Soviet pressure on the radical Arab countries, we believe it is best to conduct the new negotiations rather quietly and then to surface them suddenly. We are discussing with the Israelis a withdrawal of something like 75 kilometers toward the East and about 150 kilometers toward the South, which would return the oil fields to Egypt and would withdraw Israeli forces beyond the passes in the Sinai.

To be quite frank, the schedule we have is to have progress in this direction before the visit of Brezhnev to Cairo, but have disclosure only afterward to discourage enthusiasm. But the Egyptians will know that it is substantially achieved before Brezhnev gets there. But if they move too far toward the Soviet Union, they will jeopardize it. So, after that we will turn to Syria.

This is our strategy, but it will be pursued without great visible signs until it is practically completed and then I might follow Brezhnev to the Middle East until it is finished. I wanted you to know this.

A word about Iran. I had some long talks with the Shah about our relationship and about Afghanistan and Pakistan. I urged the Shah to establish closer relations with the People's Republic. In my judgment he is very prepared to do this.

Interpreter: Closer relations between the United States and the People's Republic?

Kissinger: I talked to him about the U.S. relations with the People's Republic, but because he takes the lead from us, I told him we would favor closer Iranian relations with the People's Republic.

My understanding is that he is very prepared to establish much closer relations with the People's Republic and our impression is that his trip to the Soviet Union was not very reassuring to him.

My understanding is that he would be very glad to visit the People's Republic but since the Empress has been here he would appreciate a visit by a senior Chinese official first so that he would have a good excuse to come here. I say this to you for your information.

I think his basic attitude with regard to Afghanistan and Pakistan and India is one which is consistent with what we discussed yesterday.

Also, you should know that we are establishing—well there are two other things. First, that we are establishing co-production with Iran in various advanced military fields which will put Iran in a position to be more immediately helpful in surrounding areas. Secondly, with respect to Iraq. Our information is that the Turkish offensive against the Turks[3] is going very badly, partly because a great deal of Russian equipment has been supplied recently to the Turks.

Teng: You mean by the United States.

Kissinger: Yes, through Iran. Our information is that the Iraqi Army is quite demoralized and very unhappy with its Soviet ally. This is again, for your information. And our information, which you also probably know, is that Bhutto's feeling is that he has substantially defeated the Baluchistan problem.

Those were the major foreign policy issues which I wanted to discuss. I have one or two other items which I wanted to raise with you, if I may.

One is we are always under great pressure by the families of individuals who were Missing in Action during the Vietnamese War. We greatly appreciate the information that was given us in the last trip with respect to some American servicemen—that were lost over China. It would be a great help to us and very much appreciated if any additional information that comes available be passed to our Liaison Office. Secondly—

Teng: We don't presently have any further news. If we do we will pass it.

Kissinger: Well, we can say that you have no further news and if you have you will pass it.

Teng: All right.

Kissinger: Secondly, our Liaison Office will submit any question we have and we would be grateful for a report on these specific

---

[3] Kissinger is most likely referring to the Kurds rather than to the Turks.

questions about individuals that come to our attention that may have been missing.

Teng: I don't think they have received anything yet.

Kissinger: No, but we have been given some additional queries and we will raise it in the next day or so.

Teng: All right.

Kissinger: And finally, we would be very grateful if the remains of any of those who crashed over China or died in China could be returned to the United States, if they can still be found.

Teng: If they cannot be found then it will be very difficult.

Kissinger: We have made many unreasonable demands, but we have never asked for the return of unfound remains.

Finally, in connection with the Missing In Action—this is not your direct responsibility or under your responsibility at all, but we have found great difficulty in getting any answers from North Vietnam, as is called for by the Paris Agreement and any influence or advice you could give to Hanoi we would greatly appreciate.

Teng: I thought you had direct channels with the North Vietnamese.

Kissinger: We have direct channels but our persuasiveness does not seem to be adequate. Sometime when we have time I will tell you about North Vietnamese negotiating methods. But we will save it for a social occasion. They are unique in diplomatic history. But in this connection, I would like to say one thing. The North Vietnamese have been in total violation of the Paris Agreement in building up forces in the South. We hope that there will not be a major offensive because that would produce serious consequences. We will certainly prevent any offensive on the part of the South Vietnamese.

Teng: From what we have heard, it is the United States and Nguyen Van Thieu who are not abiding by the Agreement.

Kissinger: I think your information is not accurate. President Thieu has recently offered negotiations which implement all the provisions and we are only replacing the equipment that has been lost and therefore it is easy for North Viet Nam to control the rate of loss and our deliveries.

Teng: We feel that this issue is one to be discussed only between you and the Democratic Republic of Vietnam and the People's Revolutionary Government of South Viet Nam. As to the piece of information when we discussed Cambodia. I remember saying to you that if you listen to the information from Lon Nol it won't be accurate. As for the information provided by Thieu, we think it is also unreliable. We think the fundamental question is this. It is good that you have withdrawn your armed forces, but you have not really disengaged. Your feet are still bogged down there and probably all these specific issues all stem from the fact that the fundamental issue has not been completely resolved. I should think that that is true about the entire Indo-Chinese issues too.

Kissinger: I finally want to say one thing about normalization. Secretary Habib has informed me of his conversations here.[4] On the claims/assets agreement, I understand the principal Chinese concern and I will, when I return, see whether our lawyers can come up with a definition compatible with Chinese principles.

My impression is that the other aspects are soluble and I will try to find a way of solving that aspect.

Interpreter: That . . .

Kissinger: That particular one.

Teng: I hear that he has placed great emphasis on matters of United States law.

Kissinger: That is what I will look into when I return.

Teng: How can U.S. laws govern China? That is not logical.

Kissinger: Mr. Rumsfeld was a Congressman, he can explain that. I can't.

Teng: How you explain the matter is your business, but our explanation is that U.S. law doesn't govern China.

Kissinger: But there are some Congressmen who think that China is a suburb of Chicago.

Teng: I think that you have touched precisely on the essence of the matter. Perhaps the negotiator on your side reflects that mentality.

Rumsfeld: I could explain it but it would take a great deal of Mao Tai.

Teng: It is not important anyway.

Kissinger: I understand your problem. I owe you an answer and I will try to find a solution. I will talk to the lawyers, for me I could not care. But about the issue here, for me, this is primarily a political and symbolic matter. So I don't want an acrimonious negotiation. I will see whether we can find a formulation we can submit to you.

Teng: This is an issue of which one hundred years lack of a solution will not be of great consequence.

Kissinger: We will certainly accept the principle that American law does not apply to China.

Teng: I think this is a point that must be confirmed.

---

[4] See footnote 7, Document 92. A record of another counterpart discussion on the morning of November 28 is in Ford Library, National Security Adviser, Kissinger Report on USSR, China, and Middle East Discussions, Box 2, China Memcons and Reports, November 25–29, 1974, Kissinger's Trip.

Kissinger: That is the easiest problem we have between us. On other things—like exchanges, Congressional visits and so forth. I would like to suggest the desirability of changing the pattern a little bit, so that every year is not like the last year. And not expose our relationship to unnecessary speculation in the U.S. to see if any special progress has been made. So if our experts could find some slight variation in the pattern, it could be quite helpful.

In practice with the Congressional visits—there is one Subcommittee that votes the State Department budget, that has a great interest in coming here. I say this for your consideration.

Teng: We can think that over.

Kissinger: You will be visited in the next few weeks by Senator Mansfield.

Teng: We expressed our welcome to him long ago.

Kissinger: And we have supported it and we appreciate your inviting him. It will be helpful. Senator Mansfield is the majority Leader of the Senate and a former professor of political science at the University of Montana. On foreign policy problems, he is here in his capacity as former professor of political science at the University of Montana.

Teng: We would welcome him in any capacity. And we will see to it that he is taken to a dinner of Hot Pot.

Kissinger: We really favor a very friendly reception for him. But you should remember that what I said to you about foreign policy reflects the views of President Ford and of the United States government.

Teng: And we have understood with regard to the views of various Senators and Congressmen, and their various views do not all represent the government's view, but their own. We won't sign any agreements with them.

Kissinger: This was especially fortunate with regard to the visit of Senator Magnuson.[5] Mao tai left a lasting impression on him.

Teng: (Laughter)

Kissinger: Now perhaps a word about normalization. We have paid serious attention to what the Vice Premier said yesterday and we shall study it very carefully. We believe that the three principles mentioned by the Vice Premier are not insurmountable obstacles. And we have one problem, which the Foreign Minister summed up well in one of our earlier meetings, which is that we do not ask to be a guaranteeing power but we do prefer the solution of the reintegration to be peaceful. We shall think about specific proposals with respect to the three points and we shall submit them to you for your consideration.

---

[5] See footnote 3, Document 41 and footnote 7, Document 43.

In the meantime, we shall undertake a substantial reduction of our remaining military forces in Taiwan. We will give the precise figures to your Liaison Office in Washington before the end of the year.

And we shall also, over the next eighteen months, bring about a reduction in the size and in the status, or at least seniority, of our diplomatic representation. This is independent of whatever we agree on the other three points. These are unilateral steps. These are the major points that I wished to discuss. We will have to discuss something about the Communiqué.

FMinister: You will remember that I have promised to think up a few simple sentences to bring to your attention. But simple sentences are not easy to conceive and it is much more difficult to write a brief rather than a long Communiqué.

Kissinger: Bernard Shaw said I didn't have time to write a short letter, so I wrote a long one.

Teng: I think that is a question to be discussed between you and the Foreign Minister.

FMinister: I will inform you when we are ready to discuss. I think it is not possible to solve it here at the table.

Kissinger: Do you mind if two of my associates join us now? We are not going to discuss the Communiqué.

Teng: It is up to you.

Kissinger: One point that Ambassador Bush raised that I was going to raise. We were considering whether it would be desirable to increase the Liaison Office by a few spaces. We would transfer some of our functions from Hong Kong to Peking. That would be most appreciated.

Teng: A few spaces.

Kissinger: To handle functions here in Peking.

Teng: You would like to add to the present building.

Kissinger: The first thing is to add to the number of personnel, which in turn would mean we would have to add some additional space.

Teng: We will study that. We have noted what the Dr. has told us and we don't have very much else to say. So let's begin from the final issue that the Dr. mentioned, that is the question of Normalization. The Dr. has mentioned again the question of the time table and I remember that I said last time, what is the need to complicate the matter in such a way. Wouldn't it be better to do it more briskly and to solve the matter briskly. So the pace is not a very important matter. Whether you cut down your forces by a little bit or increase them by a bit, or when you do it; whether you raise them by a bit—that isn't very important. And since you have already sent your Ambassador there, whether or not it is necessary to lower the seniority is not a very important issue either.

So, if the solution is not to be brisk, what is the reason to drag the Taiwan issue like the question of the Vietnam and Cambodia issues into such an untidy mess. What is the need to drag along such untidiness, because that is not necessary to solve these issues.

And with the question of the three principles that we mentioned in our three previous meetings. There cannot be any other consideration about these principles. And we have also said that if you need Taiwan now, we can wait. This in no way means that we do not want to solve this issue as early as possible between the United States and China. It does not mean from a moral and political point of view that we have no right to demand or ask an early solution.

As I mentioned in our earlier discussion on this issue, it is you who are not deflecting to us. Because it is U.S. troops who are occupying Taiwan. Just now the Dr. mentioned certain reductions or certain actions which would be unilateral measures on the part of the United States. What bilateral measures can be called for?

Kissinger: There aren't any called for.

Teng: There is a Chinese saying that it is for the one who has tied the knot to unfasten it. And to sum it up, since you believe the time has not yet come to solve the issue, then we can wait. We can wait until you have thought this out clearly and then it can be solved briskly. It can be written off at once. We can wait say for a few years. We won't even have to ask you to hurry up. But if it is to be solved, it must be on the basis of the three principles.

Kissinger: I understand this and I believe it can be solved in connection with these three principles. I appreciate the opportunity to do some more thinking about it and I recognize that there is great wisdom, generosity and self restraint on the Chinese side in taking the position which the Vice Premier has outlined here. Because this is something basic in our previous conversations and observations that we owe to you.

If I may say one thing in this connection with the three principles. The principles are accepted. In all of them, the only practical problem we have is how to implement it. The phrase that Chairman Mao quoted that Normalization can be achieved before reintegration is completed . . . how to express that in practical terms.

Teng: As for the establishment of diplomatic relations, I think we have expressed it clearly in severing diplomatic relations, withdrawal of troops and abolishment of the treaty. And as for how and when the Chinese settle these issues between themselves, that is our own affair and belongs to Chinese internal affairs.

And we cannot undertake any commitments or make any promises in internal affairs like when and how we will do or establish things that pertain to internal affairs.

Kissinger: But theoretically, you could make a general statement of your unilateral intentions. Not to us, but just as a general statement.

Teng: What are we to say in it. Anyway, we think this is something that we are bound to discuss again.

Kissinger: Yes, that is the only remaining issue. The other problems are soluble and let me think about the last question.

Teng: As for the other specific issues, we don't have anything more we think needs to be said. We believe in our discussions these few days, we have had a wide range of views in the international situation. I would like to take this opportunity to make clear our basic concept of this whole question. As Chairman Mao has said repeatedly to visiting guests, the present world is not tranquil.

And the Foreign Minister also mentioned that there is great disorder under heaven. And yesterday, that was just what I was coming to—then the Dr. mentioned the talk between Chairman Mao and the Danish Foreign Minister.

Kissinger: I agree with Chairman Mao.

Teng: That there is the existence of the danger of a war. No matter how this war might be brought about and if the peoples and countries of the world are not prepared against this, they will suffer. Last time we discussed the Soviet strategy. Of course, we have different opinions on that. But our general view and impression is that the Soviet Union is making a feint in the East to attack the West. We think this is more in conformity with reality. It is not a purely theoretical matter. Chairman Mao has actually discussed this before with the Dr. He did not put it in such words in that talk, but it can be summarized to this phrase: "The polar bear is after you."

Kissinger: And it is about equal distance whether he comes East or West, to the United States, I mean.

Teng: That's geographically. As for us, to be honest, our character is to fear neither heaven or earth and we fear neither isolation or embargo. As for nuclear weapons, they are not of any use. Since to speak of nuclear weapons is of others attacking us with nuclear weapons and in this sense, we fear nothing. And Chairman Mao has even mentioned to the Danish Foreign Minister, to this effect, if a war should truly come, would it necessarily be a bad thing?

Kissinger: This is what shook him a little bit.

Teng: And we Chinese believe that if a war should come, it might not be so formidable; it might not necessarily be so bad. There is the possibility that bad things can turn into good things. He also told the Danish Foreign Minister there is no use to be afraid. If it is to come, what can you do to prevent it. Anyway, we are going to make preparations. As for preparations, they are just what we have said before.

Tunnels, millet and rifles. Do you know when we began to put forth that slogan, millet, _____[6] rifles?

Kissinger: In the sixties.

Teng: No during the Anti-Japanese War. When we were still in the S_____, in essence, we _____ rifles the only shortcoming was that in S_____, they didn't grow millet. Once we got to _____,[7] the main staple found was millet. That is why the main staple is millet and rifles. You can say we met millet by accident.

Another matter is that which the Dr. has repeatedly mentioned, the question of firing cannons. It seems the Dr. is very concerned about cannon fire.

Kissinger: I dig tunnels very deeply.

Teng: I am in favor of that. Cannons must be fired. And the Dr. has mentioned that the frequency and accuracy of the cannon fire has been raised and since the accuracy has been raised, it is quite clear that cannon fire cannot afford to cease. We think there might be a necessity to study the matter of whether or not the cannon fire is reasonable. And, therefore, I think it might be of some use to raise this point to your attention. That is, that in many issues now, the United States is in the forefront. The Dr. has mentioned many times here the energy question and the food issue. The United States is always in the forefront. You mention the fact that it is Western Europe and Japan and other countries that are most affected by the crises, but they are not in the forefront.

Kissinger: They are also not in the forefront of military defense.

Teng: Of course, it isn't in all issues that the United States is in the forefront, but in the recent period of time, you have been in the forefront on many important issues. On the contrary, the Soviet Union has been hiding behind. For instance in Cyprus and the Middle East, you have also been in the forefront. And no matter how you look at the issue in the Middle East, for the U.S. to foster Israeli expansionism, which is what it is, in essence against 120 million Arab people—from the political point of view, you are bound to be in a weaker position. Of course, the Dr. has repeatedly explained that this is because of domestic issues. No matter out of what reason, so long as the Arab countries are not able to regain their lost territory, the principal issue remains unsolved. Tactics will not be able to settle the problem, the Communiqué will not be able to solve the issue. There is already some similarity between this

---

[6] Omission is in the original. The missing word is probably "tunnels."

[7] Omissions in the original. Deng may be discussing his experience at Yenan, in Shensi. The Chinese Communist Party reached Shensi at the conclusion of the Long March and it regrouped there before fighting the Japanese.

and the Indochina issue and the Korean issue too. I don't think that the Dr. will take these views to be ill-intentioned.

Kissinger: No. Mr. Vice Premier, I have summed up our views on many of these issues. The Vice Premier was finished, I understood?

Teng: Yes.

Kissinger: I have summed up the U.S. view on many of these issues. If I could perhaps say one or two words. First of all, I agree with the Chairman, who, I believe, is a very great man. In any event, that it is important to be prepared for war and it is our policy to prepare for all eventualities and not to rely on the words of others or their assurances for peace. And in this analysis and in the manner of the quotation you just mentioned to me, we agree with his analysis of the overall situation.

Whether the attack comes in the East or the West is a subsidiary issue in this respect because wherever it comes it is ultimately intended for us and in this analysis I agree. If it comes first in the West, it still will affect the East and if it comes first in the East, it will still affect the West. And in either case it will affect us, but this is not a difference between us. The practical consequences for us—we have to do the same things in either case.

With respect to the United States being in the forefront. That is imposed on us by the particular necessity of the various analyses you have made. The Vice Premier has correctly pointed out that neither Europe or Japan is in the forefront of the energy problem, even though they are the primary victims. They are also not in the forefront of the defense problem, even though they are the primary victims according to your own analysis. For a variety of reasons it would be interesting to discuss sometime, neither of these societies are in a position to take a leading role for their own survival without strong American support. This is a historical reality. And if they were to separate from the United States, they would very soon become impotent and what one could call synthesized(?) or Finlandized. And therefore, they are not capable of being a second world under the present circumstances by themselves. It would be much more convenient for us if they could be. And in any event, we believe in what the Vice Premier said earlier—an equal partnership. And therefore, on the energy problem—I wanted to report our view that neither Europe or Japan can play a strategic role in which you and I agree—if at the same time they are demoralized by economic pressures which are beyond their capacity to solve. This is why we are in the forefront.

On the Middle East, I have explained to you our tactics which are complicated. I agree with you that unless there is a fundamental solution, a tactical solution is not going to be permanent. So, on this we are agreed, and I have explained to you what our strategy will be and their strategy will lead inexorably to a radical solution. The Vice Premier knows himself, from his own experience in political and military warfare that if one accumulates enough minor changes, sooner or later a fundamental change becomes _____.[8]

As for Cyprus and the Middle East and the Soviet role, the Soviet Union will not be able to create anything. It can only make noise. We would prefer not to be in the forefront on these issues, and in Cyprus we tried to push Britain into the forefront and that produced its own complications. As to firing cannons, we recognize the necessity and we have our tunnels and you will consider that you should not hit your own fortifications.

Teng: They haven't.

Kissinger: I am not saying they have, so we rely on you for this.

Teng: You can study our cannons.

Kissinger: We generally do not do any counterbatting fire. But more fundamentally, I think we have had a very useful, very beneficial exchange and in what I consider a friendly spirit of many subjects of common interest. We have always known that we stood for different principles and neither of us have asked the other or will ask the other to transcend the difference.

Teng: That's right.

Kissinger: But both of us have been able to work jointly on these matters which we have understood represent common views. And I believe that this has been fortified by our exchange and I would like to thank the Vice Premier for the warm reception we have had here, the frankness of the exchange; the constructiveness of the dialogue and I believe it has been a very positive contribution to the relations between the United States and the People's Republic of China.

Teng: Do you think that will be all for our talks.

Kissinger: Except for . . .

Teng: And we should like to take this opportunity to thank the Dr. again for his seventh visit.

Kissinger: . . . for our encounter after the banquet tonight.

Teng: But that has nothing to do with me.

Kissinger: If I may ask a question about releasing whatever we agree on tonight. Our President is giving a press conference tomorrow night at 8:00 Washington time, which is 9:00 Saturday your time. So if we could release it Saturday morning your time, it would enable him to answer questions not only on his trip but on my trip too.

---

[8] Omission is in the original.

Teng: You can solve that.

Kissinger: You are very optimistic. It usually take three nights to settle things with the Foreign Minister.

Teng: (Laughter) Well, that means that the press release will come out next February.

Kissinger: You tell me when you are ready.

---

99.   Memorandum of Conversation[1]

Beijing, November 28, 1974, 9:45–11:15 p.m.

PARTICIPANTS

Ch'iao Kuan-hua, Minister of Foreign Affairs
Wang Hai-jung, Vice Minister of Foreign Affairs
Lin Ping, Director, Department of American and Oceanic Affairs, Ministry of Foreign Affairs
T'ang Wen-sheng, Deputy Director, Department of American and Oceanic Affairs, Ministry of Foreign Affairs
Notetaker

Dr. Henry A. Kissinger, Secretary of State and Assistant to the President for National Security Affairs
Donald Rumsfeld, Assistant to the President
Amb. George Bush, Chief, USLO Peking
Winston Lord, Director, Policy Planning Staff
Philip C. Habib, Assistant Secretary for East Asian and Pacific Affairs
Lora D. Simkus, Notetaker

SUBJECT

Drafting of Communiqué of Visit

Kissinger: You are outnumbered tonight.

Ch'iao Kuan-hua: But we have 800 million.

Kissinger: But if they are not here, you are outnumbered.

Ch'iao Kuan-hua: This morning I told you about our basic thinking. And our thinking is to try our best to avoid superfluous words and to inquire and to put main things in the most prominent place. Of course, our assessment of these talks is they have been very beneficial.

---

[1] Source: Ford Library, National Security Adviser, Kissinger Reports, Box 2, November 25–29, 1974, Kissinger's Trip. Top Secret; Nodis. The meeting took place in the Meeting Room of Guest House Villa 18. All brackets are in the original.

This wide range of exchange of views has been very good. That is one thing. And, of course, the important substantial part of what you will want to say is that both sides have decided that your President will visit China.

Kissinger: This is what we did in July, 1971.

Ch'iao Kuan-hua: So we made up a few words. It took me a whole day to compose three sentences! It shows that our effectiveness is very low. But because this morning you insisted I make a try, I could only do so.

So the three items we will be thinking of putting into the announcement would be three main thoughts:

The Secretary of State visited certain places from when to when— the two sides had pleasant talks. The formal wording is:

"Dr. Henry A. Kissinger, U.S. Secretary of State and Assistant to the President for National Security Affairs, visited the People's Republic of China from November 25 through November 29, 1974. The Chinese and U.S. sides held friendly and useful talks. Knowing of the expressed desire of President Gerald R. Ford to visit China, the Government of the People's Republic of China has extended an invitation to President Ford to visit China in 1975. President Ford has accepted this invitation with pleasure."

Kissinger: At any rate . . . well, for one thing, I don't know whether President Ford had expressed a desire that you could know of to visit the People's Republic of China.

Ch'iao Kuan-hua: Through you.

Kissinger: I think, frankly, we should use a frankly different formulation from the 1971 communiqué.[2] This quite candidly is my view on the subject. I have two suggestions. I have no great . . . One is—and I have to do it in light of our opinion—to say only that in two previous visits we accomplished two pages on the talks and to deal with these four days with six or seven words is going to be noticed. I think we should at least say, "and reaffirmed the principles of the previous communiqués" or something like this. Now, as far as the invitation is concerned . . . this point can be made with an additional sentence. It does not require a paragraph. With respect to the invitation, I think it would be best to relate it to the statement in our communiqué last year of the desirability of frequent exchanges at authoritative levels. And say, "in the light of the decisions in the year 1973 of the desirability of

---

[2] President Nixon read the 1971 communiqué during his televised "Remarks to the Nation Announcing Acceptance of an Invitation To Visit the People's Republic of China." The text is in *Public Papers: Nixon 1971*, pp. 819–820.

frequency of exchanges, the Government has extended an invitation to President Ford." Those are may two suggestions except to express protest for my associates whose names are not being mentioned. But that is a question of internal policy.

Ch'iao Kuan-hua: There is no question the names have been published in the Chinese press numerous times.

Kissinger: I am sure Rumsfeld's wife has read it in the *People's Daily*.

Those are my two suggestions.

Ch'iao Kuan-hua: Now on the first point, our idea is that since during this visit of yours, both of us have made two speeches respectively, so I think we have said quite a lot. So we don't think it necessary to keep on repeating the same words. Of course, you told me about your thinking this morning. Nevertheless, we would still be willing to see the sentence you would be willing to produce. That is one thing. And the second point which I think all the friends here on your side know is that the actual sequence of events was our side first invited your Secretary of Defense, Mr. Schlesinger, and your side suggested President Ford.

Kissinger: Were you very surprised?

Ch'iao Kuan-hua: Were you surprised?

Kissinger: I was surprised by the invitation to Schlesinger, but I understand its significance. [Laughter]

Ch'iao Kuan-hua: And on our side, of course, we believe that your proposal of President Ford's visit is very important, too, but to be frank, perhaps we weren't so surprised as you to the previous invitation to the Secretary of Defense.

Kissinger: Since you made it, you should not be surprised.

Ch'iao Kuan-hua: My surprise did not equal your surprise. [Laughter] But I must remind you that the invitation stands—it is a standing one.

Kissinger: I know. That is understood.

Ch'iao Kuan-hua: Actually, the 1973 statement was a redirection of the Shanghai Communiqué about the authoritative levels.

Kissinger: [To Mr. Lord] Have we got the Shanghai Communiqué here? [Mr. Lord produces a copy.]

Ch'iao Kuan-hua: Because in . . .

Kissinger: We can refer to the Shanghai Communiqué, too. The 1973 communiqué—the Shanghai Communiqué—says they will stay in contact. "The two sides agreed that they will stay in contact through various channels, including the sending of a senior U.S. representative to Peking from time to time." In the [November] 1973 communiqué we said, "The two sides agreed that in present circumstances it is of particular importance to maintain frequent contact at authoritative levels in order to exchange views." It is a better formulation.

Ch'iao Kuan-hua: But I should think the basic thinking is consistent.

Kissinger: Oh, yes, it is consistent.

Ch'iao Kuan-hua: But the sequence of events was we first invite your Secretary of Defense and then you proposed inviting your President. Do you have any wording?

Kissinger: We could say the Chinese invited the Secretary of Defense to the United States. [Laughter]

Ch'iao Kuan-hua: I agree. My idea was we don't on this issue—we would not need to quote any communiqué, because you are authoritative, too. Isn't that true?

Kissinger: You knew you would get me at my weak point. I want to thank you on behalf of my father for mentioning me first here tonight. [Laughter]

We could use a more neutral formulation. For example, I don't have the exact . . . Let me give you the idea.

Ch'iao Kuan-hua: So maybe for your convenience, we could have a short break and you could discuss it and then you could give us your wording.

Kissinger: Why don't we have 15 minutes? Will you be in this building? Will you stay here?

Ch'iao Kuan-hua: You can drive us off—out of this room. [Laughter]

Kissinger: There are more of us.

Ch'iao Kuan-hua: [Turns back as he leaves room] Including both of your points?

Kissinger: Yes. It will be about two pages, but only four sentences. I will draft it in German. [Laughter]

Ch'iao Kuan-hua: If so, are you going to change Soochow to Hang-chow? [Laughter]

[There was a break between 10:02 p.m. and 10:21 p.m., during which the new draft communiqué was typed.]

Kissinger: We have . . . Why don't I give it to you? We have added one sentence and changed one a little bit. We picked up the adjectives you had used and mentioned the atmosphere because it was mentioned in every previous communiqué and should be noted.

Ch'iao Kuan-hua: So my initial reaction beginning from the end . . . shall we work from the end upwards?

Kissinger: I think you accept the first sentence.

Ch'iao Kuan-hua: Our feeling is that the phrase "to deepen contacts at authoritative levels" would, quite on the contrary, lower the importance of President Ford's visit, because I recall when I was in New York and we toasted each of you, we specifically mentioned President Ford, and when you met with the Premier at the hospital, he asked you to give his regards; and in this evening's toast, we also mentioned President Ford.

Kissinger: We can take that out. We don't need that sentence. You are saying something extremely offensive—you know that. You have said I am an authoritative level and by mentioning the President at my level, we are lowering it. Old friends can speak frankly.

Ch'iao Kuan-hua: It is a good thing knowing each other for a long time.

Kissinger: Let's take it out.

Ch'iao Kuan-hua: And as for the formation of the rest of the sentence, we would also suggest some changes. That is . . .

Kissinger: We can take the word "President Ford" out. [Laughter]

Ch'iao Kuan-hua: That is what you said.

Kissinger: [Referring to Rumsfeld] He is not used to this method of negotiation.

Ch'iao Kuan-hua: We think it might be better to say the two sides agree that President Ford would visit the People's Republic of China in 1975." In Chinese, it wouldn't seem useful to mention it more.

Kissinger: What adjective would be useful?

Ch'iao Kuan-hua: Because to us the visit of such a person of high rank as the President to the People's Republic of China would be a very important event, and to characterize it as being of use or not of use is not the question.

Kissinger: I would say this. In English, to say President Ford would visit the People's Republic of China in 1975 is too stark. Can we say "to deepen contacts—and leave out authoritative—President Ford will visit the People's Republic of China in 1975."

Ch'iao Kuan-hua: It also would give the impression that the purpose of the President's visit would be merely for the sake of deepening contacts.

Kissinger: It is a good point.

Ch'iao Kuan-hua: My school of thinking is it would be better to say less than to say too much.

Kissinger: I understand your point. I just don't want to make you overconfident. [Laughter]

Let me provisionally accept it. Let's see what else we have got.

Ch'iao Kuan-hua: So, let's go up a sentence. So my view of the Shanghai Communiqué and subsequent joint statements is that between parent and child. So, in both your toast and mine, we only mentioned the Shanghai Communiqué. That is a well-known document in the world.

Kissinger: You want to drop the word "subsequent?"

Ch'iao Kuan-hua: So perhaps for the sake of brevity we could just mention the Shanghai Communiqué.

Kissinger: I would like to see an artist at work. Now that you knocked out the end of the sentence, are you going to take out the beginning? [Laughter]

All right. Shall we go up one more? All right, we will take it out. We have agreed on the word "Announcement" though? [Laughter]

Ch'iao Kuan-hua: We are working from the bottom up. [Laughter]

Kissinger: This is nothing . . . the Shanghai Communiqué was negotiated in Chinese. I never saw the English text.

Ch'iao Kuan-hua: But later on, they were all published in both.

Kissinger: I have to say something to you that impressed us very much. We trusted you to produce the Shanghai Communiqué. Wherever you had a choice, you picked the Chinese word that we used on the draft that gave us a slight advantage.

We accept that sentence.

Ch'iao Kuan-hua: The term "wide-ranging" . . .

Kissinger: That was last year; in a conversation with Chairman Mao this word was used.

Ch'iao Kuan-hua: We can consider characterizing the talks as frank, wide-ranging and beneficial. As for the atmosphere, I don't think it was used in any other communiqué. That was in the press release.

Kissinger: It was . . . Here it is with the Chairman.

Ch'iao Kuan-hua: But that was just the news.

Kissinger: And in 1973, we said "in an unconstrained atmosphere." The danger of eliminating it makes, in reality . . . We know what occurred. It is because the two previous communiqués had this reference.

Ch'iao Kuan-hua: Perhaps I could explain it a bit. Because the meeting with the Chairman would be one meeting in itself. So the atmosphere characterized the atmosphere of that meeting. This here would characterize the whole set of talks.

Kissinger: You don't think they were friendly? [Laughter]

Ch'iao Kuan-hua: Would that indicate that all of the words used to characterize the talks did not happen? So, frankly, my views are that the question of whether or what the atmosphere was like—actually, the characterizing of atmospheres in communiqués is a foreign influence and we don't think it is very necessary. So our thinking is to conduct it in a more straightforward way. Atmospheric things are not substantial.

Kissinger: Could we say "in a straightforward atmosphere?" In 1973, I want to point out, we said all these talks were conducted in an unconstrained atmosphere. Frankly, I don't think what we say about atmosphere . . . For example, I don't think *The New York Times* would say the talks in Peking were conducted in a friendly atmosphere. It is simply that the China watchers will notice there was an unconstrained atmosphere in 1973, then there was a friendly atmosphere, and now nothing. That is the only point.

Ch'iao Kuan-hua: But "frank" also is an atmosphere. Only friends can talk very frankly.

Kissinger: In that case, let's drop "frank." [Laughter]

Ch'iao Kuan-hua: But if we are ready to talk about atmosphere, it might be more accurate to characterize these talks as being frank and unconstrained.

Kissinger: Why don't we say frank, unconstrained, wide-ranging and mutually beneficial? [Laughter]

Ch'iao Kuan-hua: And add "constructive."

Kissinger: Let's leave out the word "atmosphere."

Ch'iao Kuan-hua: Shall we conclude an agreement that we will never talk about atmosphere in the future? [Laughter]

Kissinger: I think that would be tremendous news all over the world.

Ch'iao Kuan-hua: I would like now to solicit your opinion as to whether we should cut off the head of the announcement?

Kissinger: You mean the word "Announcement?" [Laughter]

Ch'iao Kuan-hua: No, the first sentence.

Kissinger: My father wouldn't stand for that. [Laughter] I will leave the heading to you.

Ch'iao Kuan-hua: It doesn't really matter.

Kissinger: We don't really need a heading.

Ch'iao Kuan-hua: We can cut off the head; that is the "announcement." We will not be cutting the head—we will refrain from discussing the questions of outer space.

Kissinger: You just don't call it anything?

Ch'iao Kuan-hua: Call it a News Release or a Press Release?

Kissinger: There are three options: To say nothing and just put it out—it speaks for itself—or, call it a Communiqué, or call it an Announcement. If we give the heading in English, "Communiqué" or "Joint Statement" is better.

Ch'iao Kuan-hua: "Communiqué" would also be accepted.

Kissinger: We will call it "Communiqué." Are we then agreed on the heading?

Ch'iao Kuan-hua: So let's read it again.

Kissinger: "Dr. Henry A. Kissinger, the U.S. Secretary of State and Assistant to the President for National Security Affairs, visited the People's Republic of China from November 25 through November 29, 1974. The Chinese and U.S. sides held frank, wide-ranging and mutually beneficial talks. They reaffirmed their unchanged commitments to the principles of the Shanghai Communiqué. The two sides agreed that President Gerald R. Ford would visit the People's Republic of China in 1975."

Ch'iao Kuan-hua: Actually, you don't need in the final sentence: "The two sides have agreed."

Kissinger: If we played chess with each other, it would be an interesting game. Because I can predict your moves. It looks better in English to have it in. However, it is improbable that we would come here without an invitation and technically extremely difficult.

Ch'iao Kuan-hua: But you, yourself, come here for the seventh time. Everytime the announcement of your visit is "Both sides have agreed . . ."

Kissinger: But I am only an authoritative level. We don't consider it appropriate for our President to travel without an invitation.

Ch'iao Kuan-hua: But it actually would be an agreement between the two sides where they consulted with each other and agreed upon the following. Of course, we had also thought it possible to say, "The two sides agreed through consultation."

Kissinger: Oh, unanimously! [Laughter] We went through this in July 1971. It is a little bit embarrassing for me to sort of say I make President Ford come to China, which is the implication, and therefore we would like some implication of decision by him. That is why we wanted the word "accepted."

Ch'iao Kuan-hua: Then what about "The two governments agreed . . ." or "the Government of the People's Republic of China and the Government of the United States agreed," to avoid the impression that you were the one who decided the matter. It doesn't stand very logically as it is now: "The two sides agreed . . ." Of course, when the President comes, it will be on invitation. That is normal procedure. This is just an agreement now.

Kissinger: Okay, we will accept it. It doesn't make any difference.

Ch'iao Kuan-hua: What is the meaning of the agreement? It is that the two sides consulted each other. One side made a proposal, the other side accepted it and that is an agreement. In the winter of 1971—November—the announcement issued then was "The Government of the People's Republic of China and the Government of the United

States agreed that the visit of President Nixon would begin on the date of February _____."[3]

Kissinger: Okay. We will drop the last sentence.

Ch'iao Kuan-hua: Would you want to change "the two sides" to "the two governments?" We don't have any definite opinion on that. If you want to avoid the possible misunderstanding that you just now mentioned, you could use "the two governments."

Kissinger: Okay. Let's say "the two governments agreed." Okay, you got it down to three sentences again. No, four. [Laughter]

Ch'iao Kuan-hua: So, it took you one hour to write three pages, and it took me a whole day to write three sentences. And now it took you an hour, and with your assistance, it has been increased to four sentences.

Kissinger: Now those of you present know why it took a week to do the Shanghai Communiqué. [Laughter]

Ch'iao Kuan-hua: All the new colleagues will understand. But I must also say here that I have to report this to our government first, before it can be finalized. You are very fair about our procedures.

Kissinger: Oh, yes. I am experienced.

Ch'iao Kuan-hua: And I will tell you if there are any suggested changes.

Kissinger: When will you do that?

Ch'iao Kuan-hua: Can I jump from this to the time of release? I don't think there will be any question about that.

Kissinger: It is now short enough that President Ford could read it at the beginning of his Press Conference which is 9:00 a.m. Saturday, Peking time.

Ch'iao Kuan-hua: Well, I will give our reply on whether there are any other changes as soon as possible. But anyway, in any case, it won't be when you are just entering your plane.

Kissinger: Tomorrow morning? Tomorrow evening? I have this practical problem. Given the differences in time now, it is still the working day in Washington. Whatever happens tomorrow, all day tomorrow is night in America. Moreover, I don't have communications in Soochow; I won't until I get to the plane in Shanghai. I tell you what I will do. I will send this to Washington. If I can get any changes tomorrow morning—they will not be major, I am sure—they can work with this and then we can change it. We will not consider it official until we have heard from your government.

Ch'iao Kuan-hua: And we will try to give a reply as soon as possible. If possible, tomorrow morning.

---

[3] Omission is in the original.

Kissinger: Yes. It is not a decisive matter because we have 34 hours. I have communications on my plane so as soon as I reach Shanghai, we can make any corrections needed, and we can make preliminary arrangements on the basis of this text. I have worked with you before. Your suggestions will be mine. If you could get Mr. Lord's name in it, his mother would appreciate it. [Laughter]

Do you wish us to type it and give you the correct version? Can you wait five minutes?

Ch'iao Kuan-hua: Yes.

[The new draft Communiqué was typed][4]

Kissinger: Can we make an agreement that when President Ford is here we will not negotiate an agreement? We will do it ahead of time.

Ch'iao Kuan-hua: Of course! Otherwise, the visit would be prolonged.

Kissinger: Very long. Actually, the last time, we had two-thirds done before we came here. Three-fourths, even. All right, you let us know.

Ch'iao Kuan-hua: [As he was leaving the meeting room] Dr. Kissinger, you will visit before the President?

Kissinger: I think probably I will have to come here two months before he visits. Mr. Foreign Minister, again, thank you for your cooperation.

[The meeting concluded at 11:15 p.m.]

---

[4] For text of the joint communiqué issued on November 29, see *Public Papers: Ford, 1974*, p. 662.

100.   Letter From President Ford to Republic of China Premier Jiang Jingguo[1]

Washington, January 8, 1975.

Dear Mr. Premier:

Thank you very much for the kind sentiments expressed in your letter of September 20. I particularly appreciate your thoughtful comments on our current relationship.[2]

As you observed, the depth and breadth of our ties is indeed impressive. We have both shown a determination to overcome problems. We can take mutual pride in our present relationship. I would like to express appreciation for the cooperative spirit displayed by your government through the years.

I also wish to mention my continuing admiration for the remarkable achievements of your government and your people. These are due in large part, I am convinced, to the extraordinary leadership of your distinguished father and yourself. During my visit to Taiwan in 1953, I was able to see many of the challenges which have confronted you. I therefore find your subsequent accomplishments all the more impressive. I am particularly gratified by the productive use your government has made of economic assistance provided by my government in earlier years. We continue to cite your achievements as an outstanding example of what a determined people can accomplish if given help when they most need it.

Upon assuming office, I stressed the continuity of American policies throughout the world. I also reaffirmed our worldwide commitments, including our commitment to the security of the Republic of

---

[1] Source: Ford Library, National Security Adviser, Presidential Correspondence with Foreign Leaders, 1974–77, Box 1, China, Republic of. No classification marking. A typed note on the letter indicates that it was "dispatched" on January 9. On January 6, Kissinger sent the President a draft of this letter under a covering memorandum that stated, "I believe a specific reaffirmation of the Mutual Defense Treaty would not now be wise as the overall direction of our China policy is to seek to sustain Taiwan's security by political rather than legalistic means. We have not specifically affirmed the treaty over the last six months, and we will want to move away from it over the long run as the process of normalizing our relations with the People's Republic of China progresses." (Ibid.)

[2] Jiang's post-inauguration letter to Ford, delivered by Ambassador Shen on October 9, praised Ford's willingness to uphold U.S. commitments, discussed the importance of the 1954 Mutual Defense Treaty, and affirmed the value of the relationship between his country and the United States for the well-being of East Asia. (Ibid.) Smyser and Solomon agreed with the Department of State that a response to Jiang should be delayed until after Kissinger's trip to Beijing, when they could better formulate a reply appropriate with the overall context of the administration's China policy. (Memorandum from Smyser and Solomon to Kissinger, December 12; ibid.)

China.[3] I can assure you that we do not forget our friends. We will continue to value our cordial and constructive relationship.

Our policies throughout the world are designed to construct a framework for peace that will allow mankind's intellectual and physical resources to be devoted increasingly to meeting our common challenges. We realize that this will not be an easy task and that firmness as well as conciliation will be required. I am sure that we can count on your cooperation in achieving this difficult goal desired by both of our peoples.

Sincerely,

Gerald R. Ford

---

[3] A Department of State draft reply to Jiang suggested that "we appreciate your needs and interests, including your concern for Taiwan's security." (Ibid.) Kissinger, on the advice of Smyser and Solomon, strengthened this language to express a stronger American commitment to Taiwan's security. In his covering memorandum to Ford, Kissinger argued, "This would not violate the spirit of our efforts to normalize relations with the PRC. It would also help to sustain the confidence of the Republic of China, which we need to do."

---

101. Memorandum From Richard H. Solomon and W. Richard Smyser of the National Security Council Staff to Secretary of State Kissinger[1]

Washington, January 15, 1975.

SUBJECT

Calls by ROC Ambassador Shen

We have received reports that ROC Ambassador Shen is demoralized over our turndown of a successor.[2] In this context, we also need to decide about Shen's expressed desire to pay calls on Vice President Rockefeller and General Scowcroft.

---

[1] Source: Ford Library, National Security Adviser, Presidential Country Files, Box 4, East Asia, ROC. Secret; Sensitive; Eyes Only. Sent for action.

[2] Shen's request and the U.S. Government's planned refusal of this request is described in telegram 2686 to Taipei, January 7. (National Archives, RG 59, Central Foreign Policy Files)

[*3½ lines not declassified*] it is becoming known to embassy employees that Ambassador James Shen is demoralized about the State Department's turndown of his recent proposal that he be replaced by a new man. The ROC [*less than 1 line not declassified*] officer was aware of the details of Shen's démarche to Deputy Secretary Ingersoll and its outcome. He also seemed aware that Chow Shu-kai was the man likely to be Shen's replacement. The [*less than 1 line not declassified*] officer commented [*less than 1 line not declassified*] that Shen now believes President Ford's trip to Peking later this year will result in some major development unfavorable to ROC interests.

This exchange [*less than 1 line not declassified*] indicates that the news of the Department's turndown of a replacement for Shen is beginning to circulate rather widely. It seems likely that before long this development will become public, or at least will come to Peking's awareness through private contacts.

ROC reaction to the turndown also indicates that substantial demoralization is taking place within the Nationalist bureaucracy. The same ROC [*less than 1 line not declassified*] officer noted in late December that you had not been willing to receive Ambassador Shen after your November trip to Peking—as you had after previous trips to the PRC—and that you had not made a public reaffirmation of the U.S.–ROC defense relationship.[3] The Nationalist official indicated that he thought this was an indicator of a major shift in our relations away from Taipei toward Peking.

In this context, we need to consider how we should deal with Ambassador Shen's request to meet with Vice President Rockefeller and with a dormant but standing commitment for Brent Scowcroft to meet with Shen.

Shen's request to see the Vice President was included in his congratulatory letter (Tab A) to Mr. Rockefeller.[4] We recommend that the Vice President decline because such a meeting could create needless problems with the PRC and could give Shen a false impression of our intent on access. The Vice President could reply that he does not meet with Ambassadors.

---

[3] Kissinger cancelled a meeting with Shen scheduled for December 3, 1974. Shen instead met with Ingersoll and Habib. (Telegram 266817 to CINCPAC Honolulu, December 7; ibid.) The briefing memorandum for this meeting noted that Shen had last called on Kissinger on November 29, 1973. (Memorandum from Hummel to Kissinger on November 27; ibid., Subject Files of the Office of ROC Affairs, E5412, Box 15, Lot 76 D 441, POL 17[d]-Amb. Shen's calls on State, W.H. Officials, 1974)

[4] Dated December 20, 1974, attached but not printed.

Our commitment to have Brent Scowcroft meet with Shen arose when we declined Shen's request to meet with the President before the President's trip to the Far East. Jack Froebe told Shen at that time, under instructions, that the President could not meet with him but that Brent Scowcroft would be pleased to do so after the President's return. It was not made clear whether we were to call Shen or he was to call us, but we are on the record as suggesting a Scowcroft/Shen meeting. Such a meeting, in the present context, might represent a convenient way to boost ROC morale slightly after the several blows Shen has received recently. It would also enable Brent to reinforce the message that the President gave Premier Chiang Ching-kuo in his recent letter.[5]

Recommendations:

a. That we inform Vice President Rockefeller's office that we recommend against a meeting with Shen.

b. That General Scowcroft invite Shen in for a brief call, citing our earlier statement that we would do so after the President's trip.[6]

---

[5] Document 100.

[6] Kissinger initialed the Approve option under both recommendations.

---

102. Letter From President Ford to People's Republic of China Premier Zhou Enlai[1]

Washington, January 23, 1975.

Dear Mr. Premier:

Please accept my congratulations on your appointment by the Fourth Session of the National People's Congress as Premier of the People's Republic of China.

I look forward to meeting with you later this year to discuss matters of common concern and interest. While, as you noted in your report to the Congress, fundamental differences remain between our two

---

[1] Source: Ford Library, National Security Adviser, Presidential Correspondence with Foreign Leaders, 1974–77, Box 4, People's Republic of China, Premier Chou En-lai. No classification marking. Solomon hand-delivered the letter to the PRCLO on January 23. On January 20, Solomon sent a draft to Kissinger with a recommendation that he send it to the President. (Ibid.) Kissinger sent it to the President on January 23 under an undated covering memorandum with the recommendation that Ford sign it.

countries, I remain hopeful that through common efforts we can overcome these differences and advance the cause of normalizing Sino-
American relations and thus fulfill the joint commitment expressed in
the Shanghai Communiqué of 1972.[2]

Sincerely,

Gerald R. Ford

---

[2] Kissinger, in his undated covering memorandum, wrote, "Your reply is intended
to convey the implication that it will take joint efforts to overcome these differences if
we are to make further progress in normalizing Sino-American relations. I believe this
is the most effective posture for you to adopt in advance of your trip to Peking later this
year."

---

103.   Memorandum From the President's Assistant for National Security Affairs (Kissinger) to President Ford[1]

Washington, January 27, 1975.

SUBJECT

China's National People's Congress Formalizes the Continuity of the PRC's
Recent Policies: But Where is Mao?

Following is an analysis of the results of Peking's recent National
People's Congress which I thought you might find of interest.

Peking's long-delayed National People's Congress was held secretly between January 13 and 17. Prior to the session the Chinese
Communist Party convened a three day Central Committee Plenum
which gave formal approval to the list of Congress delegates and the
basic documentation, and elevated Vice Premier Teng Hsiao-p'ing to
membership in the Politburo's Standing Committee and to a Party Vice
Chairmanship. Premier Chou En-lai delivered a political report in person to the Congress in which he confirmed continuity of Peking's foreign and domestic policies of the past several years. As well, senior

---

[1] Source: Ford Library, National Security Advisor, Presidential Country Files for
East Asian and Pacific Affairs, Box 13, People's Republic of China. Secret. Sent for information. All brackets are in the original. Ford initialed the memorandum. On January
21, Solomon sent Kissinger a draft of this memorandum. (Ibid.)

leaders we have been dealing with since 1971 have, without exception, been reaffirmed in high state positions. Civilian control over the military has been strengthened, and the organization influence of the left wing of the Communist Party has been further attenuated. The one curious note in these proceedings has been the absence of Chairman Mao as a direct participant. His policies, however, are strongly represented in the Congress documents.

Continuity in Key Personnel

The Congress reappointed Chou En-lai as Premier of the State Council. One senses that Chou is now resuming a more active political role after a period of illness. He not only delivered the political report to the Congress but also left his hospital to participate in the funeral of a long-time associate a few days before the leadership meetings began. How much of his old work load Chou will reshoulder remains to be seen. My own guess is that he will continue to delegate much of the day-to-day business to Teng Hsiao-p'ing and other deputies, and increasingly play the role of a Mao—arbiter of key political decisions and above the play of administration and bureaucratic politics.

Yeh Chien-ying was formalized as Minister of Defense, thus confirming Teng Hsiao-p'ing's hint to me during my November trip that such a development was in the offing. The elderly Yeh represents continuity for Mao's national defense policy, although his appointment probably is a reflection of continuing problems with the military, from which the Party was unable to draw a younger candidate. The Congress explicitly named Mao as Commander-in-Chief of China's armed forces, thus reasserting Party control over the military.

Ch'iao Kuan-hua was formalized as Foreign Minister. He was not, however, made a Vice Premier (as was his long-term predecessor Chen Yi). This suggests Ch'iao's domestic political base remains rather narrow, or that he is somewhat controversial. Mao, for example, has contemptuously referred to the Foreign Minister on several occasions as "Lord Ch'iao"; and Teng Hsiao-p'ing needled him in front of the Fulbright Congressional delegation by referring to himself [Teng] as a "rural bumpkin" and then characterizing Ch'iao as a "foreign bumpkin."

PRC Liaison Office Chief Huang Chen, who was a delegate to the Third National People's Congress in 1964, was—for unknown reasons—*not* a delegate to the present session. Huang left Peking for Washington while the Congress was in session, although he did presumably participate in the Central Committee Plenum which preceded it.

Attenuation of the Political "Left"

The list of Ministerial posts confirmed by the Congress indicates that the left wing of the Chinese Communist Party, which we have hypothesized has been on the political defensive during the past three years (despite their polemicizing in the press), was further attenuated in its organizational influence at the Congress. Mao's wife Chiang Ch'ing, the young Shanghai leader Wang Hung-wen, and the propagandist Yao Wen-yuan, are noticeable in their absence from posts in the state administration. None of the three were even made members of the permanent presidium of the NPC; and it is difficult to identify newly appointed state officials who represent the Party's left wing.

Conversely, there are a number of appointments which clearly go against the influence of the left. The Minister of Education, for example, is a professional bureaucrat who was criticized and removed from office during the Cultural Revolution for supporting a "bourgeois" educational line. The left has attempted to repoliticize the Chinese educational system since the summer of 1973, but these efforts have apparently failed. The Secretary-General of the Congress, in addition, is a man who was under attack from the left in 1974 for having allowed the performance of a play in 1973 which was a veiled ridicule of Chiang Ch'ing.

In policy terms, however, there are several areas where compromises with the left appear to have been made. The Revolutionary Committees of the Cultural Revolution era—through which the left and military exercised administrative power—are given permanent status, although they are clearly placed under Party and state control. Similarly, the new state constitution affirms the legitimacy of mass debates via big character posters, which the left used during the Cultural Revolution to attack Party "revisionists." As well, Chou En-lai—known for being a balancer of political factions—made several verbal bows in the direction of policies supported by Mao's wife, but these seem unlikely to have a major influence on the otherwise moderate program approved by the Congress.

Implications for the Succession

We have assumed for some time that the 63 year old Shanghai leader Chang Ch'un-ch'iao—who hosted President Nixon in that city in 1972—is a good bet as one of the more likely leaders for a successor to Party and state leadership after Mao and Chou leave the scene. Chang appears to have eclipsed his younger protégé Wang Hung-wen at the Congress by reading the delegates a report on the new state constitution. (Wang delivered the report on the Party Constitution at the 10th Party Congress in 1973.) Chang appears to be situated in both the Party and state systems as a key "organization man," positioned to be able to build a national political following over the long run. At the same time, the overall list of ministerial appointments indicates that the generation of leaders in their 50s and 60s has yet to take the reins of national leadership. The Congress returned administration of the state apparatus to men in their 70s who were removed from power during the Cultural Revolution. China remains a gerontocracy.

The new state constitution does *not* provide for a chief of state. Thus the post which Mao held concurrently with his position as Party chairman until 1959, has been abolished. This is a victory for Mao in that Lin Piao had tried to gain the post of state chairman in 1970. Mao objected to there even being such a post at that time as a way of undercutting Lin's efforts to consolidate his power. The fact that the new constitution is consistent with Mao's view of 1970 can be seen as evidence of the Chairman's continuing influence, as well as the leading role of the Party over the state bureaucracy.

Continuity of Foreign and National Defense Policies

The Congress documents express support for "Chairman Mao's revolutionary line in foreign affairs" and assert that "we [Chinese] should ally ourselves with all the forces that can be allied with." As well, the key Congress documents reaffirm Mao's national defense policy when they express support for his "principle" of "dig tunnels deep, store grain everywhere, and never seek hegemony."

At the same time, the Congress communiqué calls on China to ally with the Third World and to support the Second World in their struggle against "superpower control, threats, and bullying." The document also asserts that "the contention for world hegemony between the two superpowers, the United States and the Soviet Union, is becoming more and more intense. The factors for both revolution and war are increasing. The peoples of all countries must get prepared against a world war."

Chou En-lai's political report makes it clear that the *Soviet Union* remains China's primary security problem, and that Peking has not relented in its political feud with Moscow, which he predicted will continue "for a long time." The Premier asserts in his speech that the "Soviet leading clique has betrayed Marxism-Leninism" and indicates that Peking's intransigent stand on the border negotiations has not changed: "We [Chinese] wish to advise the Soviet leadership to sit down and negotiate honestly, do something to solve a bit of the [border] problem and stop playing deceitful tricks."

Chou makes a brief and low-key statement on *Sino-American relations* that seems intended to convey to us the message that Peking looks to the U.S. to "earnestly" follow through on the terms of the Shanghai Communiqué:

There exist fundamental differences between China and the United States. Owing to the joint efforts of both sides the relations between the two countries have improved to some extent in the last three years, and contacts between the two peoples have developed. The relations between the two countries will continue to improve so long as the principles of the Sino-American Shanghai Communiqué are carried out in earnest.

Regarding *Taiwan*, the Premier's report asserts in familiar terms, "We are determined to liberate Taiwan! Fellow countrymen in Taiwan and people of the whole country, unite and work together to achieve the noble aim of liberating Taiwan and unifying the Motherland!"

Economic Policy: How to Control a "Rightist" Line?

The Congress approved an economic policy line which allows for contract labor, private plots, and the continuity of the commune system as it was in the early 1960s. This is the same set of policies which was criticized heavily during the Cultural Revolution, and for which men like Teng Hsiao-p'ing were removed from power. This indicates that PRC leaders remain concerned about their economic base, and will attempt to make a big push in economic production in the coming year. Premier Chou indicated in his speech that the PRC leadership sees the coming decade as "crucial" for consolidating a viable economic system.

The "rightist" economic line approved by the Congress is very likely the subject of controversy within the leadership, however. Chou En-lai's political report revealed, for example, that China's recent policy of importing foreign technology has drawn criticism from the "left" as representing "servility to things foreign." He indicates all the same that imports will continue, but stresses the goal of developing an independent economy. Chang Ch'un-ch'iao's report on the constitution contains the one overtly threatening political note of the Congress when he warns that "in some [economic] enterprises the form is that of socialist ownership, but the reality is that their leadership is not in the hands of Marxists and the masses of workers. The bourgeoisie will seize hold of many fronts if the proletariat does not occupy them." Chang seems to hint at political pressures on economic managers to counteract the otherwise rightist economic line.

Where Was Mao?

Mao Tse-tung was conspicuous by his absence from both the Central Committee Plenum and Congress. Ill health does not seem to be the issue, inasmuch as the Chairman received Maltese leader Dom Mintoff on January 9, and West German leader Strauss on January 16. Both meetings appear to have taken place in South China, where Mao has been for more than six months.

It is difficult to conclude from the Congress documents that Mao's political influence has diminished. The new state constitution reaffirms that "Mao Tse-tung thought" is one of the "theoretical bases guiding the thinking of our nation"; and the speeches of Premier Chou and Chang Ch'un-ch'iao make repeated references to the "principles" and policies of "our great leader Chairman Mao." Indeed, except for agricultural policy, the decisions of the Congress—designating the Chairman as commander of the PRC's armed forces, accepting Mao's personal proposal that the constitution contain a provision ensuring the freedom of workers to strike, and abiding by Mao's view that there should be no state chairman—are unquestionably Maoist positions.

We would just note that in past periods of diminished power and conflict over policy Mao has "retreated" to the provinces and has absented himself from formal leadership conclaves. We do not know if Mao's current aloofness represents such a situation. There is tenuous evidence in the Chinese press that the Chairman wants to carry the struggle against political dissenters and military renegades through to the end. It is possible that while Mao accepts the consolidation of the bureaucratic organs of state power, as was accomplished by the National People's Congress, at the same time he wishes to avoid personal identification with this development as he has more disruptive political objectives in mind—such as purging remaining dissidents from the military. We do not know if this is the case, yet the questions raised by Mao's absence from the Party Plenum and Congress will be worth watching in the months ahead.

---

104. Memorandum of Conversation[1]

Washington, February 8, 1975, 10:30–10:45 a.m.

PARTICIPANTS

PRC
Amb. Han Hsu, Deputy Chief of Liaison Office
Mr. Chi Ch'ao-chu, PRC Liaison Office
Mrs. Shen Jo-yun, First Secretary of Liaison Office

United States
Henry A. Kissinger, Secretary of State
Philip Habib, Assistant Secretary of East Asian and Pacific Affairs
Winston Lord, Director, Policy Planning Staff

Secretary Kissinger: I wanted to talk to you for a couple of minutes. I understand that Messrs. Habib and Lord have already talked to you about my trip. About the Gromyko visit, I don't know whether you know American football, but the Soviets act as if they were playing American football and they know only one play and are always

---

[1] Source: Ford Library, National Security Adviser, Kissinger–Scowcroft West Wing Offices Files, 1969–1977, Box 5, China, unnumbered items, 2/5/75–2/28/75. Secret; Nodis. The meeting took place in the Secretary's office.

running it. Their play is for Gromyko to see me so that they can pretend that they are part of the process. I am seeing him at the end of my discussions so it is clear that they are not part of it. We will have a meaningless conversation on the Middle East with him. They have told us that they want to raise other issues. We will not raise other issues. We will let you know when we return what we discussed.

In addition to visiting the people already announced, I plan to see the Shah in Switzerland on this trip. This is really all I need to add about the trip to what my colleagues told you.

Ambassador Han: As Vice Premier Teng told you in Peking, on the Middle East question we support the Palestinian Arabs at the same time that we support the way you are dealing with the Russians.[2]

Secretary Kissinger: There will be no results on this trip. We are planning for results in March, not now. We are trying to create the objective conditions on this trip for results in March.

Now I would like to say a word to you about Cambodia. We hear many Chinese views through the French Ambassador [in Peking],[3] but we are not always sure that the French Ambassador's emotions are in tune with his reason. I want to make clear that we are prepared for an outcome of a government which will be headed by Prince Sihanouk, as I already indicated in November, with the idea that some elements of the existing structure in Phnom Penh, but not Lon Nol, might be integrated into the government of Prince Sihanouk. If Prince Sihanouk wanted to hear from us rather than the French Ambassador, we would be glad to authorize a member of our Embassy to explain our position to Prince Sihanouk or to a person designated by Prince Sihanouk.

So this is the message I wanted to send to your Foreign Minister. I am sure you are fully authorized to answer it immediately (laughter).

Ambassador Han: As I have said to Mr. Habib, the Chinese position on this matter is that we wish that the United States not interfere in Cambodian internal affairs and that the Cambodian people should be left to solve their problems by themselves. The Chinese position is to give complete support to the just struggle of the Cambodian people and not to interfere in the internal affairs of Cambodia. Just recently Prince Sihanouk and GRUNK reiterated their determination to continue the struggle and not engage in peaceful negotiations, and we support their position.

Secretary Kissinger: I would appreciate your passing this message to your Foreign Minister, and you can communicate the answer to Habib, or to me after I return.

---

[2] See Documents 93 and 97.

[3] Brackets in the original.

Ambassador Han: I will report this. I don't know if there is anything new, though.

Secretary Kissinger: I am not surprised by your answer but I would appreciate your reporting this for the record, and since this is an official communication I am assuming that your government will give us an answer.

---

105. Memorandum From the President's Assistant for National Security Affairs (Kissinger) to President Ford[1]

Washington, March 3, 1975.

SUBJECT

Chou En-lai's Message of Appreciation to You

On February 21, I called in Ambassador Huang Chen, Chief of the Liaison Office of the People's Republic of China, for a brief review of the results of my recent trip to the Middle East and the discussion with Soviet Foreign Minister Gromyko in Geneva.[2]

During the meeting Ambassador Huang asked me to transmit to you a letter of appreciation from Premier Chou En-lai in response to your letter to Chou of January 23 congratulating him on his reappointment as Premier of the State Council by the Fourth National People's Congress.[3]

Chou's letter, at Tab A, conveys a friendly if somewhat reserved air.[4] It expresses welcome in anticipation of your visit to Peking later this year, and expresses the hope that there will be continuous improvement in U.S.–PRC relations on the basis of earnest implementation of the principles of the Shanghai Communiqué.

---

[1] Source: Ford Library, National Security Adviser, Presidential Correspondence with Foreign Leaders, 1974–77, Box 4, People's Republic of China, Premier Chou En-lai. Confidential. Sent for information. Ford initialed this memorandum. On February 24, Solomon sent a draft of the memorandum to Kissinger with a recommendation that he sign and pass it on to the President. (Ibid.)

[2] A memorandum of conversation of this meeting, which lasted from 6:45 until 7:05 p.m., is ibid., Kissinger–Scowcroft West Wing Office Files, 1969–1977, Box 5, China, unnumbered items, 2/5/75–2/28/75.

[3] Document 102.

[4] Tab A, dated February 19, is attached but not printed.

I received a similarly worded note of appreciation from Foreign Minister Ch'iao Kuan-hua, who also expressed interest in the discussions which will be held later in the year.

We will, of course, be taking a hard look at the various political issues which might be put on the agenda of your discussions in Peking some months in advance of the China summit meeting, perhaps in a trip which I might make to the PRC shortly after the anticipated Brezhnev visit.

---

106. Memorandum From W. Richard Smyser and Richard H. Solomon of the National Security Council Staff to Secretary of State Kissinger[1]

Washington, April 11, 1975.

SUBJECT

Again, on the Leadership of the Chiang Kai-shek Funeral Delegation

We understand that Chief Justice Burger is unable to accept the responsibility of heading up the delegation to Chiang Kai-shek's funeral. We feel very strongly that we will be making a mistake of the most serious proportions if Secretary Butz heads up the delegation. We now have ample indication in reporting from Taipei that if the Secretary of Agriculture were the leading figure it would generate a major outcry from Americans friendly to the ROC and engender great bitterness in Taiwan.[2]

Let us emphasize the following arguments (which lead us to the conclusion that the Vice President remains the best choice to head up the delegation):

—Having repeatedly reassured Peking on the direction of our China policy (most recently in the President's speech of last evening),[3]

---

[1] Source: Ford Library, National Security Adviser, Presidential Country Files for East Asian and Pacific Affairs, Box 4, People's Republic of China. Confidential. Sent for Action. Scowcroft initialed this memorandum.

[2] As reported in telegram 1864 from Taiwan, April 10, the Embassy received many complaints from Chinese and Americans in Taipei over the "insulting" selection of Secretary Butz to represent the United States (National Archives, RG 59, Central Foreign Policy Files)

[3] In Ford's April 10 address to Congress on U.S. foreign policy, he declared, "we are firmly fixed on the course set forth in the Shanghai communiqué," and noted that he would visit China later in the year in order "to accelerate the improvement in our relations." (*Public Papers: Ford, 1975*, vol. I, pp. 469–470)

if the PRC domestic political situation will turn against us on the symbolic matter of the Vice President attending the funeral, an argument can be made that our relationship with Peking is so fragile that it is no relationship at all. PRC leaders are in the political big-leagues, and they should be able to put their priorities in proper perspective. Moreover, they are more likely to respect us if we behave with dignity and a sense of self-confidence in difficult times; and to humiliate an old ally by sending an obviously insulting funeral delegation will not engender respect in Peking. It will be seen as a sign of weakness.

—The outcry we will get from Americans friendly to the ROC, and the press, if Secretary Butz heads the delegation, will significantly complicate our domestic political problems later this year if we wish to fully normalize relations with Peking. As Barry Goldwater's letter to the Secretary indicates, our decision on this issue could mobilize the ROC's supporters in a serious way.[4]

—We will engender great bitterness in Taiwan if Butz heads the delegation, which also will make it much more difficult to elicit compliance from ROC officials if we wish to alter our status with them later this year. We have clear indications that Taipei is already disturbed about the aloof quality of the official condolence messages that have been sent to them on behalf of the President.

Recommendation:

For these reasons, we (including Win Lord), strongly urge you to choose one of the following options—which are in decreasing order of desirability:

(1) Have the Vice President head the delegation.[5]
(2) Reclame on the Chief Justice.
(3) Have Secretary Morton head the delegation.

---

[4] Goldwater's letter was not found. Communications questioning the selection of Butz from Senator Strom Thurmond, Representative John Myers, Senator Jesse Helms, Senator Hiram Fong, and the Reverend Billy Graham are in Ford Library, National Security Adviser, Presidential Country Files for East Asian and Pacific Affairs, Box 4, People's Republic of China.

[5] None of these options is marked, but the decision was to send the Vice President. Habib met with Han Xu to inform him in advance of the public announcement about Rockefeller's attendance at Jiang Jieshi's funeral: "I explained that this action, which had no international political meaning, was purely in response to our internal requirements and regular custom. I emphasized that our policy continued to be governed by the Shanghai Communiqué and Peking could be confident the Vice President would make no international political comments in Taipei." (Memorandum from Habib to Kissinger, April 12; ibid., NSC Staff for East Asia and Pacific Affairs, Convenience Files, Box 39, Solomon Subject Files)

107. Briefing Memorandum From the Assistant Secretary of State for East Asian and Pacific Affairs (Habib) to Secretary of State Kissinger[1]

Washington, April 22, 1975.

Vice President Rockefeller's Attendance at Chiang's Funeral

The attendance of the Vice President at Chiang's funeral served our China interests well. His presence reassured Taiwan that America continues to act responsibly and with dignity in dealings with it. Instead of a brooding and distrustful ROC complicating the already difficult Taiwan problem, by sending the VP we gained credit which can be useful in moving the ROC in desired directions. This has been achieved without a public sound from Peking on the subject.

The VP carried out your suggestions without deviation. He did not discuss China issues with the press and his public remarks while on Taiwan were confined to arrival and departure statements which you earlier reviewed. The VP resisted suggestions by Senator Fong to incorporate greater warmth and a personal note in his arrival statement references to President Chiang. In his substantive meeting with the Premier, he read from his talking points and avoided mention of commitments. A report of this meeting is attached.[2]

---

[1] Source: National Archives, RG 59, E5412 Lot Files 77 D 255, Subject Files of the Office of ROC Affairs, 1951–75, Box 16, Letters, Memos, Etc., Pres. Chiang. Secret. Burton Levin, Director of the Office of ROC Affairs, drafted this memorandum on April 18.

[2] This report, White House telegram 50708, April 17, is not attached, but a copy is in Ford Library, National Security Adviser, Presidential Country Files for East Asian and Pacific Affairs, Box 4, People's Republic of China.

108.   **Memorandum From the Assistant Secretary of State for East
Asian and Pacific Affairs (Habib), the Deputy Assistant
Secretary of State for East Asian and Pacific Affairs
(Gleysteen), the Director of the Policy Planning Staff (Lord),
and Richard H. Solomon of the National Security Council
Staff to Secretary of State Kissinger[1]**

Washington, May 8, 1975.

SUBJECT

Your Tour d'Horizon with Huang Chen on Friday, May 9, 1975, at 5:00 p.m.

You requested this meeting with PRC Liaison Office Chief Huang
Chen for a general review of international developments. The Chinese
interpreter for this session is likely to be Miss Shen Jo-yun. Mr. Chi has
returned to Peking. We mention this in part because Miss Shen's English is not up to Mr. Chi's standard, and hence some of the more elliptical ways of discussing the delicate issues which will be covered in
this session may not get through to her. In addition, we have always
wondered about Miss Shen's particularly close association with Mao's
wife, Chiang Ch'ing. She (Shen) has not presented herself as open and
flexible on political issues, or as sympathetic to the American connection, as Mr. Chi.

The following memorandum has been put together with two purposes in mind. Primarily it is to brief you for your meeting with Huang.
However, we also use the tabbed sections on the various topics for
discussion to review developments since your November, 1974 visit
to Peking, inasmuch as you indicated an interest in covering a wide
range of topics with Huang. We are concerned about the length of the
memo, but feel it is the best way to bring you up to date for your tour
d'horizon.

The Objectives of the Meeting

This will be your first major substantive discussion with a PRC official since your last trip to Peking in November, 1974. In the interim,
developments in Indochina and elsewhere have radically transformed
the political context within which both we and the Chinese are operating. (We review changes in this context in some detail below.) We see
four primary purposes to be served by the meeting:

---

[1] Source: Ford Library, National Security Adviser, Kissinger–Scowcroft West Wing
Office Files, 1969–1977, Box 5, China, unnumbered items (12), 5/8/75–5/9/75. Secret;
Sensitive. Sent for action. Solomon initialed for Habib, Gleysteen, and Lord. A handwritten notation indicates that a copy was sent to Scowcroft. The memorandum is on
National Security Council stationery.

—*Global:* To project firmness and purposefulness regarding the Administration's foreign policy; a sense of determination to persist in efforts to influence world events in order to attain the primary goals of our foreign policy—despite the developments in Indochina and our domestic political mood. In this regard, you should outline the state of play and our objectives in various key areas, including: the Soviet factor in world affairs; the President's trip to Europe and our relations with NATO and Japan; prospects for the Middle East and Persian Gulf, etc.

—*Asia:* To caution the Chinese about the threat to our shared interests if recent developments in Indochina heighten tensions in other parts of Asia. You should, in particular, indicate concern about possible developments in Korea in the wake of Kim Il-song's visit to Peking. At the same time, you should mention the problems we both now face in stabilizing the region so that the Soviets are impeded in their efforts to seek greater access to Southeast and Northeast Asia. In effect, you should imply possible linkage between Chinese cooperation on third-country issues and further progress in our bilateral relations.

—*Bilateral:* To further position ourselves for the dialogue in coming months on normalization. Bilateral relations should not comprise a major element in this particular discussion. However, you should obliquely indicate to Huang that the domestic political forces which have been mobilized in the wake of the collapse of the American position in Indochina will not be helpful to the evolution of U.S.–PRC relations. At the same time, you should state that we continue to adhere to the normalization process, and perhaps make some low-key reference to the question of the timing of the President's visit to Peking. You may also wish to indicate an interest in sustaining a visible political relationship over the coming months, as by raising the question of the timing of a Congressional visit to the PRC in the next four months (as was agreed to in principle last November), or by responding to Huang's request that his wife have an opportunity to call on the First Lady.

You should assume that the Chinese are somewhat confused, and perhaps actively disturbed, by apparently contradictory statements on China policy made recently by the President, yourself, and Secretary Schlesinger—particularly Mr. Ford's statement in his press conference of May 6 that he intends to "reaffirm our commitments to Taiwan."[2] You should not initiate a defensive comment on these apparently contradictory statements, but wait to see whether Huang raises any questions about them. If he does not, at the end of the session you might

---

[2] A transcript of this press conference is printed in *Public Papers: Ford, 1975,* vol. I, pp. 641–652.

conclude by stating that our commitment to normalization is unchanged, and that particular attention should be paid to the President's speech to the Congress of April 10, and your press conference of April 29, as authoritative expressions of our constant position.[3]

—*Chinese views:* To seek to draw Huang Chen out on PRC perceptions of recent developments and their immediate intentions in the Asian region and elsewhere. In preparing for this discussion he will have received some new substantive guidance from Peking. Conceivably you will be able to gain some insight from him regarding Chinese perspectives on recent developments—rather than just conducting the kind of monologue that has characterized most of your sessions with Huang.

The Altered Political Context

The rapid erosion of the American presence in Indochina and other developments (e.g., southern NATO and the Middle East) has substantially altered the political climate within which we and the PRC will operate over the coming year. For the U.S. the collapse of friendly governments in Saigon and Phnom Penh has initiated a period of retesting our relationships with other governments in Asia. Inevitably the prospect is one of some further reduction of our ability to project American influence in the region.

Recent developments have also substantially complicated the political context which will affect the normalization process. Domestic critics of normalization will assert the need to hold to all existing security relationships to prevent the further erosion of trust in our intentions and the credibility of our commitments. Friendly foreign governments which still look to the U.S. for security assistance will interpret our actions over the coming months as indicators of how we are reordering our priorities and coping with Congressional constraints on foreign policy.

As far as Peking's reaction to recent devents is concerned, we have received multiple indications from diplomatic and CAS reporting that the Chinese hope for a sustained, if consolidated, American role in Asia and the world—principally in countering the Soviets. As Foreign Minister Ch'iao Kuan-hua (perhaps posturing somewhat for his audience) told a group of British journalists in late April, "The Communist victory in Vietnam has unloaded a burden off the back of the United States, and now they can maybe play a more positive role in the Pacific. Certainly, the Soviets will expand anywhere they are able."

---

[3] See footnote 3, Document 106. The text of Kissinger's April 29 press conference is printed in Department of State *Bulletin,* May 19, 1975, pp. 625–633.

For Peking, the stunningly rapid insurgent victories in Vietnam and Cambodia have generated substantial new forces which will require the PRC to play a more active role in the Asian region. The Chinese already face increasingly difficult policy choices between their ideological pretentions, the interests of neighboring allies, the PRC's own national objectives, and the maneuverings of the Soviets. As was most vividly revealed in Kim Il-song's visit to Peking, China's ideological and geographical neighbors are pressing (in the face of an uncertain American presence in the region) to pursue their own interests in ways which cut across Peking's foreign policy objectives. Both Pyongyang and Hanoi have shown considerable skill in influencing Peking through a combination of dealings with the Soviets and cultivation of China's would-be "third world" constituency.

The Chinese are undoubtedly more concerned than ever now about the Russians finding openings in areas on their immediate periphery. This might come about through diplomatic maneuvering, as Hanoi, Bangkok, and other states in the region seek greater security and political flexibility through balanced big-power pressures. It might also come about as a result of the development of new areas of instability—as seems most likely in Korea. By all evidence, Peking continues to see its interests served by further developing its relationship with the U.S. and does not desire to push the American presence totally out of Asia. The Chinese do, however, seem to look toward further consolidation of our military presence, limited perhaps to Japan, Okinawa, and Guam.

Our problem, in this regard, is how to develop a positive working relationship with the Chinese on regional issues of mutual concern (as should be the case, in particular, in Korea). We are increasingly faced with a situation where the Chinese expect our help in areas of high concern to them where their ability to act is limited (as in their repeated requests for aid to Pakistan, their diplomatic support for your negotiating efforts in the Middle East, and—most generally—their encouragement of our efforts to counter the Soviets) while they remain aloof and generally uncooperative in areas central to their security (as in Indochina and Korea).

While one can explain away this situation in terms of the complicated game Peking must play in maneuvering between the interests of its small peripheral neighbors and Soviet pressures, it nonetheless creates a situation where people increasingly ask, "What are we getting out of our relationship with the PRC?" In short, the Chinese must understand (as perhaps they do) that the domestic political consensus which thus far has supported normalization is changing—and with it the prospects for developing the kind of a relationship which would enhance the security of both the PRC and the U.S.

Specific Areas for Discussion

At the following tabs are brief summaries of recent developments in the specific areas we believe you should cover in the discussion. The summaries are followed by suggestive talking points. We present the various topics roughly in the order we think they should be raised.[4] As noted above, we believe bilateral issues should be downplayed, and left for the end of the discussion, although some low-key clarification of the President's May 6 press conference remarks on Taiwan is in order.

---

[4] Attached but not printed are briefing papers and talking points prepared by the NSC Staff on Indochina, Korea, the Soviet Union, Europe, the Middle East, South Asia, and U.S.–PRC bilateral relations.

---

109.   Memorandum of Conversation[1]

Washington, May 9, 1975, 5:35–6:40 p.m.

PARTICIPANTS

Huang Chen, Chief of the PRC Liaison Office in Washington
Tsien Ta-yung, Political Counselor
Shen Jo-yun, Interpreter
Yang Yu-yung, Notetaker

Henry A. Kissinger, Secretary of State
Philip C. Habib, Assistant Secretary of State for East Asian and Pacific Affairs
Winston Lord, Director, Policy Planning Staff, Department of State
Richard H. Solomon, Senior Staff Member, National Security Council

SUBJECT

Tour d'Horizon with Huang Chen

Secretary Kissinger: Mr. Ambassador, I haven't seen you for a long time.

Ambassador Huang: You must be very busy.

Secretary Kissinger: We have had an active period.

---

[1] Source: Ford Library, National Security Adviser, Kissinger–Scowcroft West Wing Offices Files, 1969–1977, Box 5, China, unnumbered items (12), 5/8/75–5/9/75. Secret; Sensitive. This meeting took place in the Department of State. All brackets are in the original.

I thought it would be useful if we had a review of the international situation, and Indochina.

We've had Prime Minister Lee Kuan-yew here the last two days. Now I know so many Chinese proverbs that you had better be careful.

Would you like to start?

Ambassador Huang: I would like to hear Mr. Secretary's views.

Secretary Kissinger: I know you are a great believer in counter-attack.

Ambassador Huang: Soldiers are used to all kinds of attacks.

Secretary Kissinger: I will make a few observations. I read an editorial in the *People's Daily*; there was one comment I didn't fully agree with. It said that the United States is in a period of strategic passivity. The chief victim in the editorial was not the U.S., so I am not complaining. There are many points in the assessment with which I agree, especially regarding your northern neighbor, who was the chief target of the attack.

My main point is that we are not in a period of strategic passivity, and we will not remain passive. We now need a brief period of reassessment, but in many respects we are in a psychologically stronger period as we don't have to debate Vietnam every week.

So, my main point is that we have absolutely no intention of remaining passive. There is absolutely no change in our assessment of the dangers of hegemony as they are expressed in the Shanghai Communiqué. That will be the guideline of our policy.

With regard to specifics: Our relationship—we maintain fully the principles and objectives of the Shanghai Communiqué. Occasional statements which may not be fully in accord with these objectives are purely due to inadvertence.

Secondly, with regard to our general approach, we will maintain close relations with Japan, and with some of our friends in Southeast Asia. We believe that we now will see an evolution of the Soviet's Asian Security System, which we do not favor. It is up to other countries to consider their views about hegemonies within their region. On the whole we don't favor it. But we will cooperate in preventing it where there is a reasonable chance of preventing it—but we won't do other people's work for them.

With respect to Korea, I want to make clear that under no circumstances will we tolerate a military attack on Korea, and a military attack on Korea will involve the certainty of American involvement. We will support peaceful evolution on the Korean Peninsula. We are prepared to discuss measures which would bring about the dissolution of the United Nations Command. And we will work to create conditions for coexistence on the Peninsula. But we are not prepared to accept another attack on the American presence.

In the Middle East, I see two main dangers: one, the danger of Soviet domination; the other is the danger of diplomatic stagnation. The one is related to the other. We will not accept a diplomatic stalemate. You should not be deluded by our public debate at this moment. We are organizing ourselves to have a confrontation with special pressure groups, and will insist on territorial concessions by Israel.

We have not decided whether to adopt a step-by-step approach, or to work towards an interim solution. In any event, we will maneuver so as to make it clear that a solution will have been achieved substantially through American efforts.

We will discuss—we may discuss some of these issues with the Soviet Union, but always from a position of prior agreement with the Arabs and Israel, so that the Soviets will be in a position to ratify, not to create, terms.

Your government might like to know that on the opening day of the Suez Canal a U.S. ship will be the only warship to traverse the canal—it probably will be an aircraft carrier.

So, after we have met with President Sadat and Prime Minister Rabin, you can expect significant American initiatives in the Middle East.

With respect to NATO, to Europe: As you know the President is going to NATO in order to strengthen our relations with the allies. There will be no American withdrawals from anywhere—except Thailand—during this Administration, but especially from Europe—except for Taiwan. I am not talking about total withdrawals—

Miss Shen: What did you mean about "total withdrawals?" Did you mean Taiwan?

Secretary Kissinger: No—we will proceed as we have told you, and we will keep you informed as we proceed. This is just a general discussion.

Ambassador Huang: The sounds of "Taiwan" and "Thailand" are rather similar and are confusing to us.

Secretary Kissinger: That also happens with our public statements. (Laughter)

In Europe we have two objectives: To strengthen the defense; and to strengthen the left—as we discussed—no, to *prevent* the shift to left-wing parties.

Miss Shen: I got that.

Secretary Kissinger: I will meet with Gromyko in Geneva on the 19th and 20th. The purpose will be three-fold; there will be three major items: the European Security Conference, in which our basic strategy is to remain two steps behind our allies; the Strategic Arms Limitation Talks, in which we are trying to get agreement this year; and the Middle East. We will have nothing to tell him [about the Middle East situation] until after we talk to Israel and the Arabs.

There will be no other initiatives discussed [with Gromyko].

Now we expect the Brezhnev summit at the end of September or the first week in October, but the basic outline of our policy [regarding the Soviets] is as I have discussed it many times in China. Our assessment of the Soviet Union has not changed. The major point I want to make to the Ambassador and to your leadership is that we are determined to try to emerge from this period to rally all the forces opposed to hegemony.

So one problem we will have is that—I have noticed that with respect to India your relations have cooled, as have ours.

With respect to Iran, our relations are close and will become closer.

One problem we have, as I have said before, is that we think that when we pursue parallel objectives, we should avoid peripheral confrontations. The President has asked me to tell your leadership that he is determined to pursue the course that we have discussed in the past.

Your Foreign Minister told a group of foreigners that he thought we could emerge stronger from this period. We believe this also.

So these are the main things. We would like to hear the current views of your leaders on the President's visit to Peking, [your views] as to timing, agenda, and preparations.

Ambassador Huang: Are you through?

Secretary Kissinger: Yes.

Ambassador Huang: As for you last point, we will welcome him [the President]. This point was covered in your discussions in Peking with the Vice Premier. As for us, any time will be convenient.

Secretary Kissinger: At some point, we would appreciate some concrete suggestions from you regarding timing, topics to be discussed, and what you expect to emerge [from the visit].

Ambassador Huang: Is there any plan from your side that I can report to Peking?

Secretary Kissinger: As to date, or to substance?

Ambassador Huang: The points you just covered. Have you envisaged anything regarding your President's visit to China?

Secretary Kissinger: Originally we thought about the period mid-November through the first week in December. And our thought, in terms of preparation was that we would work out a communiqué substantially in advance of the visit, to avoid complexities during the visit.

We would be delighted to welcome the Foreign Minister to Washington for that purpose.

Ambassador Huang: As for your plan, I will mention this to Peking. As for the Foreign Minister visiting Washington, it is inconceivable that he can come. We have stated the reasons why several times. Before you left Peking you said that you would visit again for that purpose.

Secretary Kissinger: We can arrange it that way also.

Ambassador Huang: It would be better if you come to Peking.

Secretary Kissinger: What is the view from Peking?

Ambassador Huang: Just now you have covered quite a few issues; we have learned of your views. I would like simply to put things this way: We have been consistent in our principled stand on various international issues. These principled positions are clearly stated in the Shanghai Communiqué, and in Dr. Kissinger's many conversations with Chairman Mao.

Just now Mr. Secretary has covered the Indochina question. We think it was a gross mistake for the U.S. to have its feet mired in the quagmire of Indochina. We have urged you to disengage yourself, and not to dilly dally. Now the U.S. has disengaged, and shaken off this burden. It should learn correct lessons from this experience.

Secretary Kissinger: Everyone should learn lessons from this.

Ambassador Huang: You should learn correct lessons from this.

As for the Korean question, our consistent position, all along we have consistently and resolutely supported the Korean people in their struggle for the independent and peaceful reunification of their country, for termination of the United Nations Command, and for the withdrawal of all foreign forces from the Korean Peninsula.

Secretary Kissinger: We are not asking you to change that position, but military action on the Peninsula would have grave consequences.

Ambassador Huang: And our position is consistent. As far as we know, the South Korean side, the Pak Chung-hee clique, has made provocations against the North, made attacks against them. And Chairman Kim Il-song has repeatedly stated his intention to carry on the struggle for the independent and peaceful reunification of Korea.

Secretary Kissinger: Just so he doesn't define "peaceful" too generously. We will not permit South Korean attacks against the North.

Ambassador Huang: And Chairman Kim Il-song has repeatedly stated his position on the independent and peaceful reunification of his country. We wouldn't necessarily accept your definition of peace. Kim Il-song's proposals were warmly received by all the people in Korea, and the Pak Chung-hee clique has disrupted them. The fact that the South Korean side has repeatedly made provocations and attacks is inseparable from their consideration that they have the support of the U.S. side.

Secretary Kissinger: We will do our utmost to prevent that [any actions by the South against the North]; but when war starts on the Korean Peninsula, it will be clear on which side of the line the troops are, and when that is known, we will take actions accordingly.

But we will take seriously what you have said.

Ambassador Huang [somewhat agitatedly]: I did not intend to come over here to have a conversation on Korea, but as you raised it, I intended to clarify our position.

Secretary Kissinger: I understand. We should understand your position. We are not objecting to your government's position in general; we are not asking you to change it.

Miss Shen: Ambassador Huang just said to me that we are not in a position to discuss these questions on behalf of the Koreans.

Ambassador Huang: Just now you have touched on relations between our two countries . . .

Secretary Kissinger: China and the United States?

Ambassador Huang: Yes. Our leaders have discussed [this issue] clearly during your visits to China, in the Shanghai Communiqué, and in your talks with Chairman Mao. Our relations can only develop if the principles of the Shanghai Communiqué are carried out in earnest.

Just now you touched on the European Security Conference, the SALT talks, and your visit with Gromyko. I have nothing to say about these points. But we appreciate the statement of a senior U.S. official not too long ago that [it was] in the spirit of Camp David, the spirit of Glasboro, and détente that the Soviet Union has expanded its power.

Secretary Kissinger: Who said that?

Ambassador Huang: You should know that!

Just now Mr. Secretary mentioned your relations with your allies and with Japan. We think this is very good. We think a powerful Europe and Japan are good. But I would like to ask how you intend to strengthen your relations with Europe and Japan?

Secretary Kissinger: I would like to say something about senior officials: There are only two who make policy, the President and myself. There are many who talk on the fringes. But I happen to agree with this assessment [of the official Ambassador Huang said he was quoting].

Ambassador Huang: You have only *two* senior officials in your government?

Secretary Kissinger: No, only two who make policy regarding the Soviets.

Now, how will we strengthen these relationships: First, we will sustain our policy of encouraging the Japanese to strengthen their ties with the People's Republic. We will work closely with them in developing common policies on such issues as energy and food, and give them a sense of involvement in our policy making.

With Europe, we will assure them that we will not withdraw any forces during the remainder of this Administration. We will try to settle some arguments still existing between us and our European friends.

Again, for the information of your government, the French President will come to Brussels to have dinner with his colleagues. Afterwards he will meet with the President. This will be the first time a French President has participated in a NATO event.

We also want you to know that after my meeting with Gromyko, I will go to Berlin, Bonn, then Turkey, where we will have a meeting of the CENTO organization—Pakistan, Iran, and Turkey—and if the President goes to the European Security Conference, he will also stop in Berlin. This is for your private information. He also plans to stop in Warsaw, Belgrade, and Bucharest on the way back from the European Security Conference.

Ambassador Huang: Just now you are having a meeting with the foreign ministers of the Organization of American States. How are your relations with these countries?

Secretary Kissinger: Actually they are very good. This has been a positive meeting. Recent events—contrary to what the press is saying—their relations with us are important, they are improving.

Ambassador Huang: Africa. The other day I attended a reception given by the Ambassador of Senegal. I met your Assistant Secretary, Mr. Davis. He said that that afternoon you had received all the Ambassadors from Africa. How are your relations with these countries?

Secretary Kissinger: We will strengthen our relations; we will become more active. Mr. Davis is now in West Africa. In Angola, we hope that the group backed by the Soviets will not become dominant.

Ambassador Huang: I wouldn't like to take up too much more of your time. You must have much preparing to do.

Secretary Kissinger: Yes. My schedule is that I will see Gromyko in Geneva on the 19th and 20th. Then I will be in Berlin on the 21st. I go to Ankara on the 22nd and 23rd. I come home on the 23rd, meet three days with the President, and then go to Europe for two days before the President for a meeting with the Energy Agency and the OECD. Then, I will go to Brussels to meet the President.

Ambassador Huang [as he rises to depart]: You are very busy.

Secretary Kissinger: Mr. Ambassador, I am glad you came over and that we had this exchange of views.

(At this point the conversation concluded and the Ambassador and his party were escorted from the Secretary's office to the elevator.)

110.   Editorial Note

On the morning of May 12, 1975, United States officials in Washington learned that the Khmer Rouge government of Cambodia had captured an American merchant ship, the *Mayaguez*. Because the United States did not have diplomatic relations with Cambodia, Deputy Secretary of State Robert Ingersoll transmitted a message to the Cambodian Government through Huang Zhen, Chief of the People's Republic of China Liaison Office. Ingersoll declared that the seizure of the ship was "an act of international piracy" and stated, "the Government of the United States demands the immediate release of the vessel and of the full crew. If that release does not immediately take place, the authorities in Phnom Penh will be responsible for the consequences." (Ford Library, National Security Adviser, Kissinger–Scowcroft West Wing Office Files, 1969–1977, Box 5, China, unnumbered items (13), 5/11–5/30/75)

According to telegram 110673 to Beijing, May 13, Huang refused to relay Ingersoll's message and replied, "This is your matter. It has nothing to do with us." The Department informed the Liaison Office that "Huang Chen will of course report to his govt in Peking, and we assume Chinese will inform Cambodians of our approach and their reaction." (Ibid.) The Department also asked that the Liaison Office deliver the same message to both the Chinese Foreign Ministry and the Cambodian Embassy in Beijing, an action accomplished on May 13. (Ibid.)

The same day, Deputy Premier Deng Xiaoping, while on a visit to Paris, received a question from a journalist about how his government would respond if the United States intervened to recover the *Mayaguez*. Deng laughed and said, "If they intervene, there is nothing we can do." (AP report from May 13; ibid.) The next day, the Chinese Foreign Ministry informed the Liaison Office, "it is not in a position to pass the U.S. message on to the Royal Government of the National Union of Cambodia and hereby returns the May 13 note of the U.S. side." (Telegram 925 from Beijing, May 14; ibid.)

On May 16, the Liaison Office reported that the *People's Daily* had quoted a Chinese official, Li Xiannian, as saying that the *Mayaguez* had been in Cambodian territorial waters at the time of its seizure. (Telegram 950 from Beijing, May 16; ibid.) In response, U.S. officials in Washington communicated to the Chinese Government their displeasure with anti-U.S. statements during the *Mayaguez* crisis. Richard Solomon informed Kissinger, "Per your instructions, Win Lord, Bill Gleysteen, and I met with Han Hsu of the PRC Liaison Office Friday afternoon to convey the points you authorized about the unhelpful impact of their public statements regarding the *Mayaguez* on our relationship." ("Welcome Home" Book Submission, May 23; ibid, National Security Adviser, NSC Staff for East Asian and Pacific Affairs, Convenience File, Box 40, Solomon Chronological File)

---

111. Backchannel Message From the Chief of the Liaison Office in China (Bush) to President Ford[1]

Beijing, May 23, 1975, 0758Z.

91. Brent, please pass the following to the President. I hope it will be shared only with SecState and not be passed to NSC Staff or Department. It is pure politics, but I feel strongly about it.

"Dear Mr. President:

After talking to Rog Morton when he was out here about domestic politics, I have a better feel for what is happening at home. It is his impression and mine that there is little focus in the U.S. on the political aspects of your trip to China.

The Taiwan issue is on the back burner right now as it relates to domestic politics. I am very concerned that as your trip to China approaches this will change dramatically. Your own personal interests dictate that serious thought be given to what is possible from a purely political standpoint.

Answers to the Taiwan question that may have been possible before the collapse in Cambodia and Viet Nam may no longer be any answers at all. I would strongly suggest the following:

(A) An in-depth poll be taken to measure public opinion on various solutions to the Taiwan question (the last poll, I believe, was by Gallup late last year). The poll should probe into opinion of conservatives and liberals and should sound out attitudes towards various solutions. Obviously this polling should be done in great confidence and commissioned by outside sources.

(B) An in-depth research job be done on what the conservatives in the U.S. have said and are likely to say on this issue. A similar study

---

[1] Source: Ford Library, National Security Adviser, Kissinger–Scowcroft West Wing Office Files, 1969–1977, Box 5, China, unnumbered items (13), 5/11–5/30/75. Secret; Via Voyager Channel. Sent through Scowcroft.

should be undertaken on what the leading Democrats have been saying. N.B.: It seems to me that your political problems arising from this issue are quite different pre-GOP convention compared to post-GOP convention.

(C) Thought be given as to how to keep this issue from building into a major weapon for your opponents be they Republican or Democrat. Some will try to paint a China visit without a final solution to Taiwan as a diplomatic failure, an inability to solve the tough problems. Others, particularly the right wing, will soon start criticizing the visit itself and will be on guard to immediately criticize any concessions as a sell-out of Taiwan.

In this communication I am not attempting to go into the foreign policy merits of China options. I firmly believe, however, that your coming to Peking this year, whatever the concrete results, is the right thing to do. What is done at this stage to assess the politics of the visit should be separate from the foreign policy machinery and not in any way inhibit the thinking and planning which undoubtedly is going forward at the State Department and NSC. I an suggesting that a trusted confidant who would not be involved with this planning be encouraged to think out the domestic political implications of your China visit.

I have already discussed with the State Department my concern that work need be done fairly soon to minimize expectations. Many journalists are saying, 'the President can't possibly go to China without solving the Taiwan problem.' It is to your advantage to have this talk dampened, so that expectations be realistic not euphoric and that a visit that does not solve the big Taiwan problem will not, post facto, be considered a diplomatic failure.

Pardon my intrusion on your busy schedule, but, based on my own political past, I worry that this issue can build into a political nightmare unless a lot of pure political thought gets into it soon.

Barbara and I are happy out here. We feel we are most fortunate to be in this fascinating job in this fascinating land.

Warmest regards to Betty.

Sincerely, George"

**112.   Memorandum From the Assistant Secretary of State for East
Asian and Pacific Affairs (Habib), the Deputy Assistant
Secretary of State for East Asian and Pacific Affairs
(Gleysteen), the Director of the Policy Planning Staff (Lord),
and Richard H. Solomon of the National Security Council
Staff to Secretary of State Kissinger[1]**

Washington, July 3, 1975.

SUBJECT

> U.S.–PRC Relations and Approaches to the President's Peking Trip: Tasks for the
> Rest of 1975

Our China policy at present straddles two very contradictory
trends: In one direction we are postured toward the objective established by the Shanghai Communiqué. The President, in his April 10
speech to the Congress, reaffirmed his interest in visiting Peking later
this year in order to "accelerate" the normalization of relations.[2] In your
May 9 session with Huang Chen you raised questions about the timing and agenda of the Presidential trip, and expressed interest in
Peking's views on these issues.[3] Thus, publicly and privately we have
sustained the expectation both for Chinese leaders and our own public that there is still momentum in the normalization process.

In the other direction, however, there are domestic and international political forces enhanced by events in Indochina, and sustained
by developments elsewhere abroad, which raise new obstacles to
change in our relationship with the Republic of China on Taiwan. Senator Goldwater's public challenge to the Administration at the time of
the Chiang Kai-shek funeral[4] is but the most visible indicator of a range
of pressures on the President to avoid or delay the modification of our
legal and security relations with Taiwan which are at the heart of "normalization" with Peking. As a reflection of these pressures, the President has now publicly (if inadvertently) reaffirmed our commitments
to Taipei, and you have stated both privately (to the Japanese Foreign

---

[1] Source: Ford Library, National Security Adviser, NSC Staff for East Asia and Pacific Affairs, Convenience File, Solomon Chron File, Box 40, July 1–3, 1975. Top Secret;
Sensitive; Completely Outside the System. Sent for action. The memorandum is on National Security Council stationery. All brackets are in the original.

[2] See footnote 3, Document 106.

[3] See Document 109.

[4] Goldwater's challenge was, "If they want to change our relationships with Taipei,
as I told the President and I told Kissinger, they've got a helluva fight on their hands."
As quoted in Lou Cannon, "Goldwater Warns President Against Abandoning Taiwan,"
The Washington Post, April 15, 1975, p. A2.

Minister) and publicly (in *U.S. News and World Report*) that the President's trip to Peking will not necessarily lead to full normalization.

Underlying these contradictory trends, of course, is the continuing importance to the U.S. of normalization with the PRC for the longer term restructuring of great power political and military relationships. This objective is now in conflict, however, with the immediate need to reassure key allies (and warn possible adversaries) in the wake of our Indochina setbacks. It is further complicated by the domestic political factors the President must consider as he faces re-election in 1976.

This memorandum seeks to give you a sense of several very different ways we might proceed in our relationship with Peking during the remainder of this year. We assume that the actual decisions the President will make on China policy this fall will be shaped by a combination of international developments during the next several months (particularly those associated with Middle Eastern diplomacy and Soviet-American relations) and his own judgment about the impact of possible further moves with Peking on both his foreign policy and domestic political future.

In order to give you a range of approaches to our dealings with the PRC during the remainder of 1975, we explore in the following sections of this paper the problems and issues associated with three ways of handling the Peking summit:

—An indefinite postponement.
—A "sustaining" visit.
—Full normalization.

• In addition, we review the issues which must be addressed if you wish to at least explore with Chinese leaders the terms for a comprehensive normalization agreement.
• We summarize the tasks which remain for this year in our dealing with the PRC irrespective of the type of summit you and the President wish to organize.
• We suggest some problem areas and themes relating to our official dialogue with the Chinese, and their relationship to your forthcoming discussions in Peking.
• In an appendix (Tab A) we review the PRC's current orientation toward the normalization process.[5]

Our own judgment is *not* that there should be "normalization at any price," but that long-term American foreign policy interests will be served by a consolidation of our present, if limited, relationship with Peking, and that we can *avoid* future problems with the PRC at a relatively low price as well as posture ourselves in Asia favorably for the

---

[5] Tab A, "Peking's Current Posture Towards Normalization," is attached but not printed.

future if an acceptable normalization deal can be worked out now. We believe that at minimum there are important reasons for making a serious attempt to explore with senior PRC leaders the terms for a comprehensive agreement on full normalization, even though the President will ultimately have to decide how far he can go. The Chinese—in the wake of Indochina developments—appear to be more anxious than ever to have a visible relationship with the U.S. for security reasons. Thus, they probably are as likely as they may ever be to accommodate our political needs; and while Mao and Chou still live there is the authority in Peking to strike a deal and implement it. The exact degree of Chinese flexibility on the most sensitive issue of Taiwan's future security, however, will only be known through direct negotiations.

At the same time, senior PRC leaders in recent days have publicly indicated that they will accept a Presidential visit which does *not* lead to full normalization. This gives us greater flexibility in planning for the President's trip, although there remain risks (primarily in China's domestic political process) in trying to sustain our relationship with Peking at its present level for several more years. Thus, we believe that if you can get substantial assurances from the Chinese on the Taiwan security question, and if other political and economic elements of a package agreement on normalization are positive, that our interests will be served by consummating a deal in association with the President's trip.

Three Approaches to the Peking Summit: Indefinite Postponement;
  a Sustaining Visit; or Full Normalization

We assume, without a review of all the arguments, that it is still a basic American foreign policy commitment to work toward the full normalization of U.S.–PRC relations, and to complete the process in as short a period of time as is politically feasible. The questions which remain are the precise terms for a normalization agreement, and the timing of their realization.

We also assume (as you indicated to Huang Chen on May 9) that whatever type of a Presidential trip you wish to organize will be preceded by an advance visit by yourself to negotiate the political issues. This advance could be scheduled either before or after the Brezhnev summit, although we feel there are political advantages to such a trip beforehand. A visit to Peking sometime after your July meeting with Gromyko (in August, or the second half of September) would presumably build additional heat on the Soviets in advance of the Brezhnev visit; and while the Chinese might be inclined to be less forthcoming on terms for normalization as a price for being played so obviously against the Russians, they would be concerned that a stalling of the U.S.–PRC relationship would incline us toward a closer relationship with Moscow.

From another perspective, Chinese uncertainty about the exact outcome of the Soviet summit (as will be the case prior to Brezhnev's visit to Washington) could provide a better context for your discussions in Peking than a post-summit situation where we might appear to PRC leaders to have moved toward greater "collusion" with Moscow. All the same, however, it can be argued that even substantial movement in Soviet-American relations will just motivate Peking to want to "keep up" with us rather than back away (as appeared to be the case last November after the Vladivostok summit meeting).

Our summary judgment of these considerations is that an advance visit to Peking by yourself before the Brezhnev summit would be most useful and timely. If you were to go to Peking in October or early November there would be the additional disadvantages of having minimal lead time before the President's visit to permit technical planning and preparations related to possible political developments. Such a late advance might force a delay in the President's trip until December or the early winter of 1976.

Indefinite Postponement of the Peking Summit

Inasmuch as we now have a fairly clear sense of the likely elements of a normalization agreement, you and the President may decide that the time is not ripe to consummate a fully normalized relationship with Peking, and that as a consequence the PRC summit should be postponed indefinitely. Such a determination presumably would be crystallized by the discussions you will hold during your advance trip, although if you do not wish to formalize the Chinese or American negotiation positions you might work out a postponement indirectly through contacts with the PRC Liaison Office.

The impact of an indefinite postponement of the Presidential trip would be substantial on both the future of the U.S.–PRC relationship and on our other international dealings. A major source of pressure on the Soviet Union would be called into question (although this might be of lessened short-term importance in the wake of a successful Brezhnev summit), and there would be a general sense abroad that the U.S.–PRC relationship was stalling out. Indeed, we assume that a decision on our part to postpone the President's trip to Peking would effectively freeze any substantial movement in the relationship until after the elections in the fall of 1976, presumably well into 1977.

In such circumstances, while the leaders in Peking that we have been dealing with will—by all currently available evidence—seek to sustain the relationship in its present form, we would be gambling that a number of developments would not occur which could close off the prospects of attaining a stable, fully normalized relationship with the PRC: Mao and/or Chou are quite likely to die in the next two or three years. As a result there could well be a diffusion of the policy consensus and leadership coalition which now gives Peking's politics a coherence unknown for two decades.[6] Pressures which we have seen reflected in PRC media for a moderated policy toward the Soviet Union—a line which seems to emanate from the military—might find expression in a succession struggle. And the possibility of a change of Administration in Washington after 1976 could confront Peking with a new cast of characters they might well view without sympathy, and with whom they would have to build a dialogue de novo.

In short, delay risks the intervention of political forces which could substantially complicate efforts to normalize—a consideration which of course has to be weighed against the factors on the other side of the equation which should continue to make it in the national interests of both the PRC and U.S. to complete the process which you and President Nixon, Chairman Mao and Premier Chou initiated in 1970.

Based on the above considerations, we frankly assume that indefinite postponement of the Presidential trip is a non-option. The political rationale which led to the onset of the normalization process still holds true; and despite some cooling of the atmospherics in our dealings with the Chinese, the importance of a stable U.S.–PRC relationship for the larger structure of the Administration's foreign policy would make the virtual termination of the political dialogue with Peking and the elimination of even the optical aspects of our relationship more costly than, for example, a cosmetic Presidential trip. Furthermore, the Chinese are now signalling to us—in Teng Hsiao-p'ing's remarks to a group of American newspaper editors in early June, and in other official guidance which reaches us via CAS reporting—that they want the Presidential visit to be held whether or not it leads to full normalization.

---

[6] There is increasing uncertainty, however, about the physical health and political standing of both Mao and Chou. Indications persist that the Chairman's relations with other senior leaders, particularly in the military, are somewhat strained; however, since his return to Peking in mid-April after a ten month absence, Mao has resumed an overtly active role in political affairs, as by receiving foreign visitors. At the same time, the Chairman's health (as always) appears to be deteriorating. Chou's health and role are also uncertain factors.

We find it very difficult to draw any firm conclusions about the impact of the current leadership situation on our bilateral relations with Peking, although we do have a general sense of Mao and Chou fading from the scene. Day-to-day affairs are ever-more firmly grasped by a "successor" group led by Vice Premier Teng Hsiao-p'ing and Chang Ch'un-ch'iao (on the Party side). We see no evidence, however, which would indicate that Mao and Chou will not continue to influence major foreign policy decisions, or that their foreign policy line of the past five years is being modified. [Footnote is in the original.]

A "Sustaining" Summit

If you and the President were to decide that Peking's terms for normalization are politically unacceptable, but that you wish to sustain a visible relationship with the Chinese, we believe that Peking would see its own interests served by an optical summit meeting which did not produce a major breakthrough to establishment of diplomatic relations. As senior Chinese leaders have repeatedly told you, while they wish to move on the Taiwan question, they are prepared to wait if the U.S. "needs Taiwan." The world press carried Teng Hsiao-p'ing's comment on June 3 that President Ford will be welcome in China even if there are no agreements on any major questions between the two countries [i.e., Taiwan].

We do not even totally rule out the interpretation that PRC leaders may *not* want to move on normalization at this time, either because they know our price is unacceptable to them in terms of their domestic politics or because they do not wish to induce further political changes in their region in the wake of Indochina developments which would give the Soviets additional openings that China might have to counter with limited assets. At least one can say that the present state of U.S.–PRC relations, and the American "holding" position on Taiwan, represent an acceptable minimum position in terms of PRC interests at this time.

We see two problems, however, with a cosmetic summit meeting designed just to sustain our relationship with Peking at its present level—each related to problems of constructing a meaningful agenda. There will be problems in formulating a significant outcome short of full normalization which would clearly justify a second Presidential visit to Peking. A trip merely to "exchange views on issues of common concern" could be criticized in the press as unworthy of the occupation of so much of Mr. Ford's time and an unnecessary commitment of Presidential prestige to a second visit to the Chinese capital. It would encourage cynicism about the U.S.–PRC relationship.

What agreements might we reach with Peking short of full normalization which would justify to our public a second Presidential trip? Thus far the Chinese have been unwilling to move with us on certain economic and exchange issues (solution of the claims/assets problem, or a more active cultural exchange relationship) in the absence of progress on the key political issue of Taiwan. The Chinese would have to re-evaluate this posture and be willing to show more flexibility in solving secondary issues than they have done to date. Thus, we might seek a final resolution of the claims/assets problem. Maritime or air transport agreements, or a governmental trade agreement, might be worked out "in principle" (although considerable time will be needed to negotiate the details of such arrangements). Or certain visible cultural programs might be worked out, such as exchange of students or permanent press representation. In return, we might "give" Peking virtually full withdrawal of our military presence from the island (except for a residual intelligence and liaison cadre of a few hundred men), or a reduction of the level of our diplomatic representation.[7]

Based on Peking's position up to now, however, we have limited expectation that the Chinese will agree to further increments of the above sort without some fairly specific commitments to progress on the Taiwan issue. The problem the President faces, of course, is that any commitment he might make on the political issues really requires implementation in conjunction with his trip to Peking or its immediate aftermath. It will be difficult, for domestic political reasons, to reveal or institute substantial changes in our relationship with Taiwan during the 1976 campaign season; and the President presumably would not want to offer (and the Chinese would probably not accept) a political deal which is contingent upon his re-election—or left to the discretion of his successor.

A related agenda problem is reaction on the PRC side to a second summit meeting that does not solve the Taiwan question. Even though we believe senior PRC leaders wish to have a Presidential visit which may not produce a breakthrough, they may be faced with growing domestic pressures for some visible benefit to China from the Washington connection. A case can be made from a Chinese perspective that Peking has made all the compromises thus far while receiving little in return. Not only has Taiwan not been "liberated," but the U.S. has a new senior Ambassador there and the ROC has two additional consulates in the U.S. Trade is substantially in America's favor, is weakening China's "self-reliance," and is inducing PRC scientists to "worship foreign things." The cultural exchange program is exposing Chinese intellectuals to disturbing foreign ideas; while the American journalists and intellectuals who visit the PRC return to the U.S. to publicly criticize what they see in China, especially domestic political problems.

While the above sort of argument can be overdrawn, there is good evidence from CAS reporting that our bilateral contacts with the PRC have generated the above sorts of criticism, especially from China's political left. The argument that China increases her security against the Soviets by dealing with the U.S. is a very sophisticated rationalization accepted by a limited few. Indeed, China's military seems to be

---

[7] See a more extensive check-list of possible areas for agreements which would sustain or broaden the relationship at Tab B. [Footnote is in the original. Tab B, a "Checklist of Possible Areas for Bilateral Agreements Which Would Strengthen U.S.–PRC Relations," is attached but not printed.]

a continuing source of pressure for a less hostile attitude toward the Russians (although we have no direct evidence of their opposition to dealings with the U.S.).

Given these considerations, the strategy of a "sustaining" agenda should be to include developments which will enable PRC leaders to hold the commitment of the "left" and military to our present relationship. Unilateral security actions we might take (such as further troop reductions from Taiwan), or proposals in such areas as technology transfer or military cooperation which would enhance PRC defenses, will be helpful in minimizing resistance to the relationship from the Chinese military. Unfortunately some of the things we need in order to cope with conservative American opinion, such as future sales of military equipment to Taiwan, will probably antagonize the PLA. Similarly, the kinds of cultural and scientific exchanges which will hold the interest of our intellectuals and journalists in the China relationship are exactly the programs which are seen as threatening by China's political radicals. Such contradictory factors will have to be balanced out in almost any trip agenda, but particularly in one which seeks to sustain the U.S.–PRC relationship in its present, semi-consummated condition.

A Normalization Summit

We believe that despite certain signs of a hardening in Peking's foreign policy orientation (such as increasing unwillingness to be cooperative with us on certain third country issues, their pressuring Japan on terms for a peace treaty, and somewhat more visible support for certain Maoist insurgent movements abroad) that the Chinese continue to see U.S.–PRC normalization as in their own interest. Developments in Indochina have sharpened PRC concerns about the Soviets having new political openings on their periphery; and we interpret the heightened visibility of Chinese support for North Korea and the new government in Cambodia as an effort to preempt Soviet access by presenting themselves to these and other countries in the region as a more reliable political ally than the Soviet Union. CAS reporting in recent weeks has revealed active concern among Chinese officials that President Ford might cancel his trip to Peking. Evaluated solely from the perspective of Peking's mood, the current context may be as favorable as we may have for some time (in terms of the motivation of the Chinese leadership, and the state of the PRC political system) for a move to full normalization.

If there is one crucial point of concern in Peking about their dealings with us, it is uncertainty about how far we will go with Moscow, and new doubts about how actively we can and will work to counter the Soviet presence in their region. While the Chinese will not be in a position to pressure us on our dealings with Moscow as they are now attempting to do with the Japanese, there is no question that developments in Soviet-American relations in the coming months will be a major factor affecting the mood of the Peking summit.

The Chinese cannot demand that we give up "détente" as a price for normalization with them; but to the degree that we appear to be casting our dealings with the PRC solely in terms of our Soviet policy, we will heighten their fears about being exposed on security and political issues by their relationship with us. As Chou En-lai indicated to you as early as February, 1973, there are high-level concerns in Peking that we are dealing with them merely to get at the Soviets "by standing on China's shoulders."[8]

The implication of the above line of reasoning for the President's trip is that our approach to resolving the Taiwan question and finding terms for a fully normalized relationship—along with the outcome of the Brezhnev summit—will be an important test for the Chinese of how seriously we take our relationship with them. If we are correct in the assumption that the Chinese see normalization as much in their interest as ever, the effort to negotiate an agreement on your next advance trip should expose their maximum degree of flexibility, especially on the issue of Taiwan's security. Even if you are unable to achieve terms acceptable to the President, you will at least have put on the record for discussion at some future time as accommodating a position as the Chinese are likely to find acceptable. Moreover, we will be able to say to our own people (as well as to the Chinese) that we made a determined effort to reach agreement, and that we expect peaceful assurances on the Taiwan question before any future normalization deal can be made. In sum, we believe a serious effort should be made now to determine if agreement is possible.

Where do we now stand on the specific issues which must be addressed in negotiating a package normalization deal? Without reviewing in detail all the elements of such an agreement (which are discussed in the October, 1974 analysis, at Tab C),[9] following are the major points which remain at issue:

—*Recognizing the PRC as the "sole legal government"* of China, exchanging ambassadors, and upgrading our liaison offices to embassies. These developments will require working out arrangements to the following associated problems:

• Agreeing with Peking on some verbal formula by which we go beyond the Shanghai Communiqué statement that the U.S. "does not

---

[8] See Document 8.

[9] Tab C, "The Operational Issues Associated With a Normalization Agreement," is attached but not printed.

challenge" the assertion of "all Chinese on either side of the Taiwan Strait" that Taiwan is part of China to *a more direct formulation implying or expressing support for the principle of the unity of China.* This could be an indirect approach stressing continuity with past American policy by reaffirming our commitment that Taiwan be returned to Chinese control as was expressed in the Cairo and Potsdam declarations, or it could draw on the precedents of other recent recognition formulas in which various states have "taken note of," "acknowledged," "recognized" or expressed "understanding and respect for" Peking's assertion that Taiwan is an inalienable part of China. (Our specific position on this issue might be linked in negotiations to the degree of Peking's assurances on the future security of the island.)

• We will have to develop an understanding with Peking about *a residual (official or semi-official) presence on the island* to replace the withdrawal of our embassy. Peking has now rejected the notion of such a presence being called a "liaison office" or a consulate. We will presumably have to find some new verbal formulation (possibilities range from a broad formulation such as a "U.S. Representative's Office" or "Sino-American relations society" to a more narrowly conceived "trade office") and institutional arrangements which will make it possible for seconded State Department and other governmental personnel to handle our contacts with the authorities on Taiwan.

Undoubtedly Peking would prefer that our remnant presence in Taipei be formally unofficial—on the Japanese pattern. Such an arrangement, however, will be undesirable with regard to its impact on Taiwan and here at home. Furthermore, a preliminary analysis of such a non-governmental arrangement indicates there would be significant problems related to USG funding, the handling of consular matters, and management of a military sales program, if our Taipei embassy operation were to be taken over by a private American association. In addition, unless we maintain a government consulate in Taipei (by whatever name), the need for Congressional legislation to enable us to fund and conduct USG business through a private association would open up the Administration to the complicating political effects of legislators on the Hill shaping the process of institutionalizing a normalized China policy. These aspects of the situation are being thought through in a separate analysis which will give you options on how to retain a USG presence in Taipei.[10]

• We will have to negotiate with Peking an understanding that *the U.S. will maintain its present economic and social ties to the island,* including the ability to sustain investment in the island's economy and

---

[10] This analysis was not found.

physical access to Taiwan via air and sea communications. (In this regard, the playing out of the negotiations between Peking and Tokyo in 1973 on Japan's air service with the PRC, in which the Japanese acceded to the Chinese demand that they cease treating the Republic of China's flag airlines as a national airline, has set a difficult precedent for Taipei, and for us.)

—*The future security of Taiwan* remains the core issue to be negotiated. The Chinese may ask us for an explicit, public declaration that we are abrogating the U.S.–ROC Mutual Defense Treaty. They also will probably want a constricting limit—and perhaps a rapid cut-off—in sales of American arms to the island. (Their counter concern will be that too-rapid a removal of the entire American security relationship with Taiwan might stimulate the ROC to turn elsewhere for weapons and political support. CAS reporting indicates that PRC officials see such a possibility enhanced now that Chiang Kai-shek has passed from the scene.) Chinese leaders also have not encouraged us to believe that they might make a public commitment of some sort expressing the intention to "liberate" the island by peaceful means only. Not only has Teng Hsiao-p'ing repeatedly emphasized to you privately that the PRC will permit no foreign interference in the process of Taiwan's eventual reincorporation into the mainland, but in his June 2 interview with American editors he implied that force might have to be used, "as in removing dust from a floor with the aid of a broom" (a Mao quote). While past public and private statements to you by Chou En-lai suggest some hope for a Chinese statement of peaceful intentions regarding Taiwan, we are not overly optimistic that an acceptable unilateral formulation will be forthcoming.

State Department lawyers, in contrast, have urged that you seek from Peking a joint statement expressing a mutual commitment not to use force in settling the Taiwan question. Such a statement, they say, would at least enable us to plausibly claim that the U.S. retained a legal basis for assisting Taiwan in its defense if it were ever attacked from the mainland. We have no expectation, however, that Peking would agree to such a joint statement; indeed, the Chinese would very likely see a proposal for such an arrangement as a provocation or an unacceptable demand designed to stall negotiations. Other proposals for dealing with the security question (which we have not explored as they seem impractical) include an agreement between the U.S. and PRC to treat Taiwan and the Strait as a demilitarized zone, or to encourage Peking and Taipei to negotiate a mutual renunciation-of-force agreement.

Your own approach to this problem, since you first raised the idea during your October, 1971 trip to Peking, has been to seek from Peking a unilateral and general statement of intention—presumably to be included in a normalization communiqué—expressing the willingness to strive for a peaceful settlement of the Taiwan question. Last fall you had us draft parallel, unilateral American statements (which could be either included "back-to-back" with a Chinese statement in a communiqué, issued separately in a press conference, or embodied in a Congressional resolution) expressing a residual interest in Taiwan's security, the desire that the island's future be resolved peacefully, and perhaps linking the maintenance of our fully normal relationship with Peking to the assumption that force will not be used against Taiwan.

Teng Hsiao-p'ing hinted to you on the last day of your November, 1974 talks that he assumes he will be discussing some arrangement of this type with you at a later date.[11] Exactly how far Peking will go in this direction will not be known in the absence of direct negotiations. *We believe you should negotiate for a unilateral statement by Peking expressing the idea that the PRC does not contemplate the use of force in resolving the Taiwan question.* We assume that we will have to accept language which qualifies the circumstances under which Peking would exercise restraint (see suggestive alternative formulations which were drafted for your November, 1974 trip, at Tab D).[12] We also assume we will parallel Peking's statement with a unilateral statement of our own, as is noted above.

A less favorable alternative would be a statement by Peking which merely expresses the "hope for" and a willingness to strive for a peaceful settlement of the Taiwan issue. A further fall-back would be a statement from the PRC side expressing a willingness to exercise patience and restraint in seeking settlement of the island's future (see alternative formulations at Tab D).

We assume that the exact content of the parallel, unilateral statements which we and Peking might make about the future security of Taiwan will be linked in the negotiating process to agreement on a residual program of sales of American military equipment to the island (i.e., the more forthcoming a statement from the Chinese, the more limited our sales program might be). As noted above, the PRC will probably see its own interests served by having a gradual trail-off in U.S. arms sales; but you may wish to relate an understanding with Peking about the level and duration of such sales to the specific language of restraint that the PRC is willing to agree to, as part of a package agreement on normalization.

(An additional aspect of the modification of our security relationship with Taiwan will be further withdrawals of our residual military

---

[11] See Document 98.

[12] Tab D, "Conceptual Approaches to Formulating U.S. and PRC Statements on the Security of Taiwan," is attached but not printed.

(and intelligence) presence on the island. While this will not be an issue you would *negotiate* with Peking, it will constitute one element of your discussions with PRC leaders. As such, further troop withdrawals directly relate to the consummation of a normalization agreement. You have been sent, via NSC channels, two options papers on reduction schedules for our remaining troop and signal intelligence presence on the island, and a residual program of military sales.)[13]

—Thus far in your approach to a normalization agreement, you have not linked third-country issues to consummation of the process—except for the matter of troop withdrawals from Taiwan being related to "reduction of tensions in the area." For reasons that we detail on pages 25 and 26 below, you may want to consider relating increased PRC cooperation on issues like Korea to the evolution of a fully normal bilateral relationship.[14]

If the above issues are the key bilateral questions to be resolved through negotiation, it must be said that at this point in the evolution of your discussions with PRC leaders *the room for maneuver on a normalization agreement does not seem great.* If there is to be full normalization, we will have to recognize Peking as the sole legal government of China, and imply or express in some verbal formulation acceptance of the view that Taiwan is part of China. We will maintain some type of "private-but-governmental" office in Taipei staffed by seconded State Department personnel, and—on the Japanese pattern—we will maintain our trade and social contact with the island. At the time of normalization we will indicate tacitly or explicitly that the U.S.–ROC Mutual Defense Treaty is no longer operative, but that the end of this formal relationship will be compensated for by a Chinese statement of peaceful intent, by our own unilateral expression of concern (perhaps expressed in a Congressional resolution) for the future security of Taiwan and the expectation that its differences with the mainland will be resolved peacefully, and by a residual program of American arms sales to the island.

[If Peking proves unwilling to agree to *any* package of arrangements relating to the future security of Taiwan (including such elements as parallel public statements, a residual American arms supply

---

[13] On May 23, the NSC staff sent Kissinger a memorandum on U.S. force reductions and future U.S. military assistance for Taiwan. (Memorandum from Solomon, Granger, and Froebe to Kissinger, May 23; Ford Library, NSC Institutional Files (H–Files), Box H–32, NSSM 212) [*text not declassified*] The Department of Defense also produced a study of options for changing U.S. force levels on Taiwan. (Memorandum from Deputy Secretary of Defense William P. Clements to Scowcroft, November 20, 1974; Washington National Records Center, OASD/ISA Files: FRC 330–77–0063, Box 3, China, Rep. of, 1974, 0001–320.2)

[14] Reference is to the paragraphs at the end of the paper immediately preceding the Recommendation.

arrangement, and a paced withdrawal of our remaining military presence) it seems likely that the President would find it impossible to reach a normalization agreement. Indeed, we would recommend against a deal on such a basis.]

We will have to answer those who criticize a normalization agreement on the grounds that we denied the people of Taiwan the option of self-determination with the argument that self-determination has never been an element at issue in America's China policy, and that those Taiwanese intellectuals who have advocated independence (primarily as residents of the U.S. or Japan) have been unable to evoke a substantial response from the people or authorities on the island.

For those who would criticize normalization on the grounds of our having sold out an old ally, we will have to respond that even our recently deceased "old ally" maintained that Taiwan was part of China, and that our national interests require recognizing—belatedly in comparison with the rest of the world—the enduring reality of Peking's control over the preponderance of Chinese territory. We will point to those aspects of the Asian political and military balance which are likely to stay Peking's hand from a direct military effort to gain control over the island, and mention our continuing economic ties and program of military sales as a way of helping to preserve for Taiwan the reality of its present status. And we will presumably have a sufficiently direct statement of peaceful intent from Peking to reaffirm our own concern that the people of the island be able to work out in a peaceful manner the nature of their future relations with the mainland.

And for some, there will be the question of what, if anything, the U.S. has gained from Peking in return for normalizing on the PRC's terms. This is a question that can only be answered in terms of the strategic value to us of a non-confrontation posture with the PRC, the impetus it has given the diplomacy of "détente" with the Soviets, and the long-term benefits to the U.S. of having eliminated one front of the Cold War battle lines of the 1950s and '60s. (One additional reason for seeking greater PRC cooperation on third-country issues, of course, is to be able to justify normalization on broader international grounds than just gaining leverage over the Soviets.)

Tasks for the Remainder of 1975

In view of the above discussion and analysis, the following tasks remain for 1975 if you are to at least explore with PRC leaders the possibilities for further steps toward a fully normalized relationship:

—*Preparing a negotiating package.* If you will give us guidance on your preferred approaches to further negotiations with the Chinese on the question of normalization, we will prepare a negotiating package for use during your advance trip to Peking later in the year. In addition to the bilateral questions which must be considered in such a package, there is the related issue of how you might wish to coordinate negotiations with the PRC with the evolution of our contacts with the Soviets during the year—specifically whether you want to schedule an advance trip to Peking before or after the Brezhnev summit. As well, there is the question of whether you want to begin to link [lack of] PRC cooperation on third-country issues (such as Korea) and perhaps international questions (food, energy, etc.) to further steps in our bilateral relations.

—*Planning further force withdrawals from Taiwan.* On February 8, Mr. Habib informed PRCLO that by mid-1975 we will have drawn down our military manpower level on Taiwan to about 2,800 men, put Taiwan airbase on caretaker status by mid-year and Ching Chuan Kang airbase on caretaker status by the end of the year. The PRC was also told that they would be informed later about an even lower manpower level to be reached by the end of 1975.[15]

Two major inter-agency studies relating to the U.S. military manpower presence on Taiwan and our military sales program have just been completed and sent to you and the President for decision via NSC channels. The NSSM 212 response provides you options on general policy guidelines for future sales of military equipment to—and U.S. force levels in—the ROC.[16] The second study is an Intelligence Community staff analysis of our signal intelligence presence on Taiwan (which is oriented largely toward the PRC). This study presents options for further reduction of the approximately 715 military SIGINT personnel who will remain on the island after July 1975.[17]

—*Preparing our public.* Thus far our relations with Peking have evolved with the government shaping public opinion through various official initiatives. You or the President have acted; the public has responded—with a substantial degree of support. We are now at a point in the evolution of U.S.–PRC relations, however, where difficult decisions are less likely to evoke a generally favorable public response. If there is progress toward a fully normalized relationship, certain issues (particularly those related to Taiwan) are likely to provoke a negative reaction from some members of Congress, the media, and private citizens. And if there is no progress, there are likely to be questions about why not. "Why has the relationship stalled" may become an issue in the 1976 campaign.

The PRC in recent months has initiated more active efforts to shape opinion on the normalization question. These include the encouragement and covert funding of the "U.S.–China People's Friendship

---

[15] Telegram 29717 to Beijing, February 10, summarized this meeting. (Ford Library, National Security Adviser, Presidential Country Files, East Asia, Box 14, People's Republic of China, DOS telegrams from SECSTATE–NODIS (5))

[16] See Document 90.

[17] Not printed. See footnote 13 above.

Association" to tout PRC political views, cultivation of the Chinese-American community through the cultural exchange program and trips to the PRC, and various efforts to stimulate sympathetic Congressmen and the American press on the normalization issue. The Nationalist Chinese, for opposite reasons, have similarly sought to project their views on the growing U.S.–PRC connection in the Congress and the media. In the early months of this year Taipei's diplomats embarked on an active effort to convince important opinion groups in the U.S. that normalization has proceeded as far as necessary to serve American interests, particularly by calling on the support of influential Americans like Senator Goldwater. Since the Gimo's passing ROC public relations efforts have flagged, but we can anticipate more activity as the President's trip to Peking approaches.

The question we now face is how to try to shape with greater purpose from the Administration's perspective public attitudes on the remaining issues associated with U.S.–PRC normalization.

There is a basic problem to such an effort. Until you have made your advance trip to Peking and sounded out PRC leaders on the prospects for an agreement, it is obviously in our interest to prevent the build-up of a positive mood of anticipation about the Ford trip.[18] This would only constrain your room for maneuver in negotiations with Peking, and might also mobilize groups hostile to further progress. At present we should project an attitude of "we would like to see further progress, but we have significant problems which have to be resolved—and which will require PRC accommodation—before further progress can be made."

Depending on the results of your advance trip, our public relations effort could go in several directions: If you see a strong possibility of full normalization associated with the President's trip, you will have to build support for the terms of an agreement with the Congress (which may have to assist by passing a supporting resolution, or enabling legislation as we move to a "private" relationship with Taiwan) and prepare public opinion for anticipated developments. If your advance trip implies limited prospect for further progress, or perhaps a postponing of the President's trip, we will be faced with the task of ex-

---

[18] Teng Hsiao-p'ing's comments of June 2 to the American newspaper editors has already helped to deflate expectations that there must be a major outcome from the trip. We believe Teng made his remarks precisely because PRC leaders are concerned that the President might back out of the trip. They are well aware of pressures on him which make it difficult to bring about further change in the relationship. (This interpretation is supported by collateral CAS reporting.) We are also receiving indications of recent date that Chinese officials at PRCLO and in Hong Kong are sustaining Teng's relaxed attitude about the need for progress on Taiwan, and their desire for a Presidential visit under any circumstances. [Footnote is in the original.]

plaining to the Congress and public why the relationship has "stabilized" at its present level.

At this point we will not go any further into the public relations aspects of our dealings with Peking other than to flag the issue as one which will have to be considered in greater detail as the year progresses.

—*Preparing Taiwan for normalization.* Should the results of your advance trip imply strong prospects for a normalization agreement, there will also be the need to begin more active measures to prepare the authorities on Taiwan for the further evolution of our relations with both Taipei and Peking. There is obviously some danger in giving ROC authorities the kind of advance notification which might enable them to work against further progress with the PRC. At the same time, there are dangers in being totally passive about preparing the leadership in Taipei for moves on our part which will affect their basic interests (although they clearly anticipate that sooner or later we will recognize Peking and break with them).

The recent passing of Chiang Kai-shek has removed one major constraining, and stabilizing, factor which has held Taiwan to a "one China" course for more than a quarter-century. There is *no* evidence as yet that the elder Chiang's death has destabilized the situation on the island, or is inclining the Nationalists in some other direction. But as Peking, Taipei, and Washington adjust their policies to the new political and international context in the months ahead, we should be sensitive to new possibilities in the Taiwan factor, and seek to actively influence the evolution of the island's policies consonant with America's larger interests. (We are now preparing a separate paper for you on the Taiwan situation.)

—*Preparing Japan.* While the Japanese, at some level of perception, assume we will eventually normalize with Peking, there still lingers the hope (particularly in the business community, and among Foreign Ministry officials) that the U.S. will sustain its present "two China" position. Our enduring relations with Taiwan give the Japanese a sense that their interests on the island are protected; and the measured pace of our diplomacy with Peking has given Tokyo greater freedom of action in dealings with the Chinese. Should we recognize Peking this fall, for example, the Japanese would feel under greater pressure to conclude a peace and friendship treaty with the PRC on Peking's "anti-hegemony" terms.

For these reasons, as well as to avoid recriminations on the basis that the U.S. never learned the lessons of the first "Nixon shocks," we should make an effort to at least inform the Japanese in good time of any further developments in our relations with the PRC.

—*Preparing the PRC*. While your advance trip to Peking will be the primary vehicle for developing the basis for further developments in U.S.–PRC relations, you may also want to take certain unilateral steps in advance of the President's trip to generate an appropriate mood in Peking. These might include symbolic measures (such as having the President, or yourself, give a major speech on China in the fall, or having Mr. Ford receive at the White House the major PRC trade and scientific delegations which will visit Washington in September), or certain unilateral actions such as communicating to Peking further U.S. troop reductions from Taiwan, or perhaps an initiative in the economic area.

Some Final Thoughts on a Negotiating Posture

By way of conclusion, let us suggest several problem areas relating to the pace and orientation of our negotiations with Peking on the normalization issue which could significantly affect the future evolution of U.S.–PRC relations:

—*To Move or Not to Move to Full Normalization?* As noted in the above analysis, the short-run costs of moving to establish diplomatic relations with Peking are substantial for the President, particularly in the wake of developments in Indochina and in the context of the approaching 1976 election campaign. All the same, we remain convinced that there are strong reasons for attempting to negotiate a normalization agreement within the coming five months which would help to stabilize a non-confrontation relationship with PRC. Without reviewing all of the arguments about the long-term value to us of such a development, we would like to emphasize three arguments for such an effort:

First, by following through on the diplomatic momentum we have established since 1971 *we would complete normalization at our own initiative* and on the basis of a relatively cooperative relationship with Peking. If we let this momentum lapse, however, our relations with the PRC could deteriorate as internal pressures in Peking about being strung along by the Americans intensify. This could then mean that Peking would revert to pressure tactics to get us out of Taiwan and recognize the PRC as the sole legal government of China. Obviously in such a situation "normalization" would be much more costly for an Administration to carry out, for we would be doing it in a reactive way. Recall that in 1969 the Administration was concerned about the PRC playing on our domestic politics. This could become a problem again.

Secondly, the other side of the first argument is that if the Mao/Chou initiative toward the U.S. appears to have been successful from China's perspective, we will have maximized the possibilities of the Chairman sustaining an anti-Soviet foreign policy line within China—with all its obvious benefits for our own foreign policy.

Thirdly, there remains the complex of international factors which make normalization basic to stabilizing the structure of the Administration's foreign policy: maintaining one of our primary levers over the Soviet Union; preventing American isolation on the China issue in multilateral forums (such as the U.N.) and in our bilateral diplomacy; and maximizing the possibility of sustaining if not enhancing parallel foreign policy moves with Peking in a number of third-country areas (Europe, the Middle East and Subcontinent, Japan, and—hopefully— regarding Korea and Southeast Asia).

—*What Negotiating Themes to Emphasize?* In reviewing the evolution of our negotiations with Peking on the normalization issue, we are concerned about the manner in which the Chinese have attempted to box us in on the themes of the "Japanese model" and Teng Hsiao-p'ing's "three principles." This is obviously a good tactic from Peking's perspective; but at the same time we believe the Chinese have given us an opening on a more flexible general theme which could be used to structure the final phase of negotiations. In the November, 1973 Communiqué,[19] Premier Chou En-lai explicitly gave you an apparently more flexible "condition" for full normalization—on the basis of "confirming the principle of one China." We never really responded to Chou's opening. *It seems notable that the Premier repeated this formulation as the only condition which Chairman Mao had set for normalization* in the unpublished version of his speech to National People's Congress delegates in January of this year.[20] It is possible that the Premier (and perhaps the Chairman), in using this phrase both publicly and privately, are indicating the basis upon which they would attempt to sell a compromise normalization agreement to their own cadre. In preparing for your next round of talks in Peking, you could structure your discussion of the normalization issue around this theme and avoid being boxed in on the question of whether or not our terms strictly meet the "Japanese model" or Teng's "three principles"—although obviously at this point in the discussions we will have to take these aspects of Peking's private negotiating position into account.

Similarly, we may find it in our interest to press the Chinese to make good on Mao's comment to you about not needing direct control of Taiwan for "a hundred years." While this statement may very well have been intended by the Chairman only as a symbolic formulation, it is one of the few points on which we can seek to box in the Chinese with the sacred words of their own leader. Similarly, past public and private statements by Premier Chou about a willingness to strive for a peaceful settlement of the Taiwan situation should be cited as

---

[19] See footnote 7, Document 60.
[20] See Document 103.

precedents for a forthcoming unilateral statement by the Chinese on the issue of the island's security.

—*Who's Afraid of the Big Bad Bear?* While the Soviet factor has obviously been central to the evolution of our relations with Peking over the past five years, we are disturbed by signs that the Chinese feel they are being manipulated by us with the Soviet threat. There were a number of statements in 1974 by Vice Premier Teng and Foreign Minister Ch'iao to the effect that they were not certain they were getting the straight story on the Russians from the U.S.; and beginning as far back as the winter of 1973 Mao and Chou shifted from a posture of emphasizing the Soviet threat to China to the view that the Russians had *only* a million men on their border (which was not enough for defense, much less an attack) and that Moscow was "feinting toward the East while intending to attack in the West." This led to some rather unproductive exchanges with the Foreign Minister over whether China or the U.S. was the party more threatened by the Soviet Union. Obviously the Chinese have attempted to create the impression that our leverage over them because of what we presume to be their fear of the Russians was not as great as we might wish it to be.

Whatever the realities of the Russian threat to China, there are several difficult psychological dimensions to the way we might play the Soviet issue. To the degree that we appear to be emphasizing the Russian threat to "scare" Peking, we make the Chinese feel they are being manipulated, and thus erode whatever credibility we have built up with them. Moreover, in an ironic way we may be increasing the pressure on Mao to be more flexible in China's dealing with Moscow. We know that in the wake of the 1973 U.S.–Soviet agreement on preventing nuclear war that Chang Wen-chin, one of your interlocutors in drafting the Shanghai Communique, and now PRC Ambassador to Canada, wrote a paper in the Foreign Ministry calling into question the value of China's relationship with the U.S. in the context of our increasingly active dealings with the Soviets. The suspicion that we are manipulating them with the Soviet threat must also increase the inclination of "pragmatic" politicians like Teng Hsiao-p'ing (and perhaps even the Premier) to give greater flexibility to China's foreign policy by a limited accommodation with the Russians (and to concurrently reduce our own maneuverability).

How to be straightforward with Peking about our assessment of Soviet capabilities and intentions while not appearing manipulative in our use of this factor is a difficult problem in negotiating tactics.

Furthermore, to the degree that the Chinese assume that our dealings with them are largely a function of our efforts to gain leverage over the Russians, the more they will probably assume that we will accommodate them on bilateral issues in order to sustain our position vis-à-vis Moscow. We believe such a situation would create substantial problems for the evolution of U.S.–PRC relations. Not only would it engender cynicism in Peking about their dealing with us, but it would increasingly tempt the Chinese to pose us with difficult choices about whether to accommodate their interests on particular bilateral issues or risk visibly damaging the Sino-American relationship—and by extrapolation, our leverage over Moscow. And to the degree that decisions on our part begin to convince our press, the Congress, and academic community that we are being "soft" on the Chinese, we will erode support for our China policy among important vocal elites whose patience with PRC game-playing is already wearing thin. (It was precisely for this reason, among others, that we urged a firm position on the Taiwan "liberation" song issue.[21])

In short, for tactical reasons if nothing else, we should approach Peking with a greater sense of concern about the evolution of our *bilateral* relationship. If we do not appear to take the Chinese seriously on their own grounds, we are unlikely to build a relationship with the PRC that will gain sustained support in Peking and the U.S.

—*Link U.S.–PRC Normalization to Cooperation on Third Country Issues.* While the Shanghai Communiqué linked our military withdrawal from Taiwan to the reduction of tensions in Indochina, in general our relationship with Peking has evolved without much effort to directly relate further progress on bilateral issues to cooperation in international affairs. This is as it should have been, inasmuch as to press Peking for visible cooperation with us in areas where China's own security interests would have been compromised (as in Indochina) very likely would have overburdened the fragile beginnings of normalization. Moreover, a review of Peking's behavior on Vietnam and Cambodia over the past four years indicates that while the Chinese have not been positively cooperative, neither were they actively obstructionist in a situation where the trend of events was clearly in the direction of their allies, where our own ability to act was increasingly constrained by domestic factors, and where to actively resist the trend would have exposed them to serious political pressures from the Russians, who would have tried to embarrass them with their "third world" claque. Moreover, Peking was helpful to us on an issue like Korea as late as the fall of 1973—but pulled back from such "collusion" precisely when Moscow undercut their position at the UNGA on the basis of their cooperation with the U.S.

---

[21] On March 20, Habib informed Han Xu that the United States "cannot allow the tour [of a PRC performing arts troupe] as long as the song about [liberating] Taiwan remains in the program." (Memorandum of conversation, March 20; Ford Library, National Security Adviser, West Wing Office Files, 1974–1977, Box 5, China Exchanges, unnumbered, 3/13/75–3/27/75) As a result, the tour was cancelled. See "U.S. Bars Chinese Troupe," *The Washington Post*, March 28, 1975, p. A1.

At the same time, more recent PRC behavior on a range of international issues—Korea and the U.N. Command, Indochina, the food and energy conferences—has been such as to give us little prospect that after normalization we might expect to work positively with Peking in coping with a range of third country questions. There is now some grumbling both within the USG and in public to the effect that we are really getting very little out of our relationship with Peking.

There are major limitations on the leverage we might develop with the Chinese which might induce them to be cooperative on a range of international issues (Korea being a prime example); but at the same time you may wish to consider laying the groundwork for some linkage between further steps toward full normalization and more cooperation on third country questions. Just as important leadership groups in this country will ask what we are getting from Peking in bilateral affairs in return for our concessions on Taiwan, there will also be questioning about "normalization" if we cannot point to some degree of Chinese cooperation on international problems.

Recommendation:

That you convene a meeting with us at an early date to discuss the issues explored in this paper, and to give us instructions on how we should proceed in preparing for your advance trip to Peking.

---

113.   Memorandum of Conversation[1]

Washington, July 6, 1975.

PARTICIPANTS

>The Secretary, Henry A. Kissinger
>Assistant Secretary Habib
>Mr. Winston Lord
>Deputy Assistant Secretary Gleysteen
>Mr. Richard Solomon, NSC
>Jerry Bremer, Notetaker

SUBJECT

>China

---

[1] Source: Ford Library, National Security Adviser, Kissinger–Scowcroft West Wing Office Files, 1969–1977, Box 5, China, unnumbered items (16), 7/6/75–7/23/75. Secret; Sensitive.

The Secretary: I don't really have that much to say. I have read your paper and I just won't do it that way.[2] It's exactly the same paper you presented me last year.

Lord: No, it isn't. The question is: On your advance trip do you make some serious effort to find their security requirements?

The Secretary: For political reasons it's just impossible for the U.S. to go for normalization before '76. If there's any one thing that will trigger a conservative reaction to Ford, that's it.

Lord: We recognize that and felt that if the terms were decent enough perhaps it's less of a political problem.

The Secretary: I've got a problem with Panama and China. I don't even agree with your intellectual thesis—that this is the right time to force it.

Lord: The last time they didn't want to discuss it.

The Secretary: Even if they did, what they said to the Professor was for domestic consumption. You can't hold a government to what they say for domestic consumption.[3]

Lord: Presumably we would make our own statement.

The Secretary: What is our legal basis for defending part of one country?

Gleysteen: There is none.

The Secretary: If that's the case, we can't afford to have it in a campaign.

Solomon: They have clearly indicated in seven or eight places recently their desire to be flexible. They're afraid Ford will cancel his trip.

The Secretary: The trip is clear. They are anxious for it but I see no flexibility on Taiwan.

Lord: We recognize there is not much room for maneuverability. The only issue is whether you try to see the terms.

Habib: It's difficult to avoid discussing during your trip.

The Secretary: But suppose they give us generous terms? What do I do then? Pocket it and say, "We'll have no deal for two years." Anyway can they go beyond what they've told this guy?

---

[2] See Document 112.

[3] Professor C.P. Li, after meeting with Chinese officials, informed Bush that President Ford was welcome in Beijing regardless of progress on Taiwan. Li had also asked whether, as a step toward normalization, the United States would be satisfied with a PRC statement "for domestic consumption" that would declare the PRC's intention to use only peaceful means to reunite with Taiwan. (Telegram 155344 from Beijing, July 1; National Archives, RG 59, Central Foreign Policy Files)

Gleysteen: No, the question is what kind of relationship would they permit.

The Secretary: We can consider that when we have to sell this to Congress. What do we say then, by the way? Are we going to continue to send arms?

Gleysteen: You have to be able to say yes.

The Secretary: But do we have a legal basis?

Gleysteen: There is no legal barrier if the host government tolerates it. That's the most crucial aspect.

Habib: They would have on a sales basis. No credit.

The Secretary: But then it is essentially within their power to stop it at any point.

Lord: We have always had this dilemma from the time we started this relationship. You have to make it clear in your unilateral statement.

The Secretary: I'm wondering where we'll be if we go down this road. I'll try to raise it with the President but I know the answer. Those guys over there won't even take on Panama right now.

Lord: The paper argues the importance of doing this from our international position, and also argues that there is a need for some serious discussion when you go there in August.

The Secretary: Who said I was going in August? I am certainly not going in August.

Lord: If they give you a bad deal in return, your position would be strengthened. But if it generates an offer then I agree we have a bind.

The Secretary: What if they go to the limit?

Gleysteen: I think the chances are not very high they'd go that far. I think the terms in the pre-visit will be very tough.

The Secretary: I think we're better off saying we don't think we're quite ready. We've told them what we need.

Lord: I think we can be more concrete and say that we cannot do it without satisfaction on security.

Habib: I don't think they'll give you their last position when you are there. Won't they hold that out for the President?

Lord: No.

The Secretary: It is not their way of negotiating.

Solomon: They might make the Presidential trip conditional on something.

The Secretary: No. How would they react if he visited other countries in Asia do you think—like the Philippines and Indonesia?

Habib: If he did in on the way back, it would be no problem at all. I think that's a good idea.

The Secretary: Then it's not a special trip to China. What about Malaysia?

Habib: I think the essential ones are the Philippines and Indonesia.

The Secretary: How about Australia?

Habib: It depends on what's happening there.

The Secretary: Can they do Australia and not New Zealand?

Habib: It's difficult. The New Zealanders wouldn't understand.

The Secretary: They are the worst bores in the world.

Habib: That's because we never have any problems with them. All they ever talk about is cheese and butter.

The Secretary: And mutton. What do I want from them this evening?

Lord: Do you want to discuss your trip?

The Secretary: They have to make a proposal to us.

Lord: Since the last time you've seen them, they are more nervous.

The Secretary: I noticed that whatever you said to them about Schlesinger didn't get through. They told a group of Iranians that they thought Rumsfeld's and Hartmann's influence was rising over mine. That's just stupid. Rumsfeld I can see, but Hartmann I don't understand at all.[4]

Solomon: They're fed by third countries.

The Secretary: Hartmann is slipping in the White House and certainly has no relation to me.

Lord: It should be up to them to suggest something on your trip. (Secretary is interrupted for a phone call.)

Habib: On the visit, you did put some suggested times for the President's trip and they answered that any time was all right. I suppose you could mention a specific time now.

The Secretary: Why can't they raise the visit?

Habib: I think they probably think that they've already replied to you.

Solomon: If you really want to raise their anxieties, don't mention it at all. Otherwise, you could just mention your trip which will make them only slightly less nervous.

Lord: Or ask if they've had any further word from Peking.

Habib: His answer will be—"It's up to you."

The Secretary: I won't go next time unless they understand that I am to see Mao. I will not go through that BS again with our press.

---

[4] Robert T. Hartmann was a Counsellor to President Ford and supervised the writing of the President's speeches.

Lord: I agree that we should not explore normalization unless we're prepared to go through with it.

The Secretary: My experience with the Chinese is to tell them exactly what our position is. Be frank with them.

Lord: Our concern is that the relationship is apt to unravel if nothing happens in the next two years.

The Secretary: I don't know. In my view, the relationship is based on their fear of the Russians.

Gleysteen: It is, but our people interpret it differently.

Habib: Another problem is your relationship to the process itself and to the understandings they've developed with you. You're the only one left. And that has meaning to them.

Gleysteen: One point that is not made in the paper is that the period of six months to a year now is a good one in Taiwan where the people are braced for a change.

The Secretary: If we could find a step toward normalization, I'd be receptive to it. But what kind of steps are there?

Lord: Things like lowering Taiwan to a Chargé level and lowering our arms supplies.

Gleysteen: You could get into some domestic problems with that.

The Secretary: Perhaps you could strengthen the unity point and find some formula to do that.

Solomon: That is always the strongest card with them. That's the core of normalization. I think they could be playing Teng as the front man.

The Secretary: If that's what they want, then we can do something along those lines.

Habib: I think you want to start this afternoon anyway with a review of what you're going to say to Gromyko and then go on the trip.

Solomon: There's only one argument for doing something and that is that if their situation dissipates so badly there, that they were to turn to the Soviets. Doing something might enable Chou and Mao to hold their domestic constituency for our relationship.

The Secretary: Well, I'm willing to find some step short of normalization.

114.   Memorandum of Conversation[1]

Washington, July 7, 1975, 5:35–6:15 p.m.

PARTICIPANTS

Huang Chen, Chief of the PRC Liaison Office in Washington
Tsien Ta-yung, Political Counselor
Shen Jo-yun, Interpreter
Yang Yu-yung, Notetaker

Henry A. Kissinger, Secretary of State
Philip C. Habib, Assistant Secretary of State for East Asian and Pacific Affairs
Winston Lord, Director, Policy Planning Staff, Department of State
Richard H. Solomon, Senior Staff Member, National Security Council

SUBJECT

Discussion of the Secretary's Forthcoming Trip to Europe; the President's China Trip

Ambassador Huang: You will be leaving again!

Secretary Kissinger: Yes, Wednesday morning—for Paris, Geneva, Bonn, and London.

We are going to announce tomorrow that I will see the Israeli Prime Minister while I am in Bonn. So it will be a very hectic trip.

What is the news from our friends in Peking?

Ambassador Huang: (pointing to the staff present): Some of you read our newspapers in Peking, or our broadcasts. (To the Secretary) Your colleagues must know [what the news is].

Secretary Kissinger: You have no secrets? You must be following our practice. (Laughter)

Ambassador Huang: What needs to be broadcast will be broadcast; what needs to be published will be published.

Secretary Kissinger: So you have nothing to add?

Ambassador Huang: According to Dr. Kissinger's usual arrangement, I will be pleased to listen to your views.

Secretary Kissinger: I know that as a good general the Ambassador doesn't commit his reserves too early.

---

[1] Source: Ford Library, National Security Adviser, NSC Staff for East Asia and Pacific Affairs, Convenience Files, Box 39, Solomon Subject Files, PRCLO (3). Secret; Sensitive. The meeting took place at the Department of State. All brackets are in the original. On July 3, Habib, Lord, and Solomon submitted a memorandum to Kissinger containing suggested talking points. (Ibid.)

There were no especially urgent matters to discuss. It is just that as we have not met for several months I thought it would be useful to have a general review.

We have read a number of statements by your leaders to our journalists and others. We have paid attention to these.

As you know, I am going to see Foreign Minister Gromyko on Thursday evening, and Friday. He will want to discuss with us the Middle East, the Strategic Arms Limitation Talks, and the European Security Conference to a limited extent.

On the Middle East: As I told you last time, our effort is to gain some control over events and reduce the possibilities of some other power increasing its influence in the region. Since we last met, we have restored some momentum to our diplomacy. Therefore, I won't have very much to discuss with Gromyko in the way of concrete steps that the U.S. will be prepared to take with the Soviet Union [regarding the Middle East].

We still want to leave open the possibility of agreement between Israel and Egypt, and therefore we are not prepared to assemble the Geneva conference until that possibility is exhausted. So, for the time being, we will still pursue a separate course in the Middle East.

On the Strategic Arms Limitation Talks, the Soviet Union owes us an answer, and I find it hard to predict if there will be some movement. But as I stated publicly, we will not have a summit meeting in Washington if there is no agreement on Strategic Arms Limitation.

Then, the European Security Conference will meet at the end of July. I was never a great enthusiast for it. At this moment we think it will produce mediocre results.

Beyond that, as I have said, whether Brezhnev comes or not depends on where we make significant progress—and there are no areas where this might happen other than those you know about.

In other parts of the world, our relations with our European friends are better than they have been in many years. If there is a European Security Conference, the President will probably stop in Bonn on the way—and he will also visit Warsaw, Belgrade, and Bucharest [on the way back] to make it clear that we do not accept a dividing line—a sphere of influence—that ends in the middle of the continent.

On other areas, in India, we notice not without interest Madame Gandhi's recent actions.[2] I do not think I will be attacked in the U.S. for being hard on her, as I was several years ago.

---

[2] On June 26, Indira Gandhi declared a state of emergency and had many of her political opponents imprisoned.

In Indochina, we are not playing any particular role at this moment. We hope that other countries won't use it for military bases— but we are not active in any way.

We have noted that your government has restored relations with the Philippines and with Thailand. We believe that this is commensurate with present realities.

I am sure you are familiar with the proposal we made with respect to Korea in the United Nations.[3] (Mr. Lord hands the Secretary a piece of paper, which he pauses to read.)

With respect to Japan, we are pursuing compatible policies. You know that Prime Minister Miki is coming here in August; and the Emperor will come in October. But we won't discourage Japan from pursuing its friendly relations with China.

These are the major areas I wanted to cover. You know our friendly relations with Pakistan, our desire to help them. So these are the major trends in our foreign policy right now.

Ambassador Huang: I would like to put this question to Mr. Secretary: We know that you started your reassessment of your Middle East policy for a long time. Has anything come out of it? We know that Mr. President, and the Secretary, met with Mr. Sadat [in Europe in June]. We have also learned from the press today that the cabinet of Israel will wait a week before deciding [on their position regarding the negotiations with Egypt]. And Mr. Secretary has just now told us he will also meet Mr. Rabin in Bonn.

Another question, which is related to the first, is what prospect do you see for your step-by-step diplomacy?

Secretary Kissinger: Well, we will never formally announce the conclusion of the step-by-step approach, as it is too much fun answering press questions. But as you no doubt are aware, being located here in Washington, this [Middle East diplomacy] is partly a domestic question. You know that we have moved to a much more impartial position [between Israel and the Arabs] than several years ago; and we are urging very strongly progress on all parties concerned, especially Israel. But I think that the chances of making some further step forward have improved in recent weeks.

---

[3] According to Kissinger's talking points, the United States sent a letter to the UN Security Council on June 27 announcing U.S. willingness to see the UN Command for Korea dissolved on January 1, 1976, if the Governments of the PRC and North Korea agreed to uphold the armistice by accepting the United States and the Republic of Korea as the "successors in command." (Memorandum from Habib, Lord, and Solomon to Kissinger, July 3; Ford Library, National Security Adviser, NSC Staff for East Asia and Pacific Affairs, Convenience Files, Solomon Subject Files, Box 39, PRCLO (3), May–July 1975)

Ambassador Huang: Chairman Mao once said that it is important to follow a policy of two hands in the Middle East, to be even-handed.

Secretary Kissinger: I remember his comment very clearly. This is our policy, with our reassessment, to pursue an even-handed policy more actively.

Ambassador Huang: What prospects do you then see for the step-by-step approach?

Secretary Kissinger: I think it has improved. In fact, I am receiving the Israeli ambassador later this evening. He will give me his government's formal position—we have not yet received the content of their position.

Ambassador Huang: We have learned from the press that the U.S. side is thinking that if a step-by-step approach does not produce results then you will go in for an overall settlement in the framework of the Geneva Conference.

Secretary Kissinger: Yes, but we would have to put forward our own plan. So we would prefer to hold off for a while as Sadat has invested so much in another step. We will work with him, and later we will work in the Geneva framework.

On our bilateral affairs, have you heard any reflections on the possible Presidential visit to China?

Ambassador Huang: I already discussed this problem the last time we met. Our attitude has been very clear all along. That is—Mr. Secretary also mentioned that our leaders had a discussion with American friends visiting China, with the newspaper editors. Vice Premier Teng Hsiao-p'ing said that if President Ford would like to visit China we will welcome him. The Vice Premier said that if he comes to discuss matters it is all right; or if he prefers not to discuss matters that is all right too. If their minds meet in discussions that is fine; but if there is no meeting of minds, that is also fine. So on the question of the visit of the President, Vice Premier Teng said that this matter is up to the President to decide.

Secretary Kissinger: So let me ask you frankly if we should consider this statement of the Vice Premier's as official? You have already answered my question. (Huang interjects: Doubtlessly [the Teng statement is official]; without question.)

One possibility is whether there can be intermediate points between a full meeting of the minds and no progress at all.

Ambassador Huang: Perhaps Doctor remembers what Chairman Mao told [Edgar] Snow before President Nixon visited China. Chairman Mao made several statements to the same effect [as the recent Teng statement]. So it is my personal opinion that we will not bring any difficulties on our guests.

Secretary Kissinger: So, I will discuss this conversation with the President. When I return [from the forthcoming European trip] we will further discuss this question more concretely.

Our idea would be that about six to eight weeks before the President goes, I would go to work out preliminary arrangements and understandings. But we will make a concrete proposal to you.

Ambassador Huang: We will wait until you come back, and then have a further discussion. When will you return?

Secretary Kissinger: This will be a quick trip. I leave on Wednesday and will be back Saturday night.

Ambassador Huang: Are there any other points?

Secretary Kissinger: We appreciate the Congressional visits that will be taking place. We will try to prepare them—but then you have handled so many different delegations, and after Senator Magnuson you are prepared for anything. (Laughter)

Ambassador Huang: There will be two Congressional visits in August.

Secretary Kissinger (to Mr. Solomon): Are you going with one of the groups, Dick?

Mr. Solomon: I'll see how busy I am then with other things.

Ambassador Huang: So we will see you when you get back.

[At this point the discussion ended and Mr. Solomon escorted the Chinese party to the door.]

---

115.   Memorandum of Conversation[1]

Washington, July 22, 1975, 6:45–8:00 p.m.

PARTICIPANTS

    Senator Jacob K. Javits
    Senator James B. Pearson
    Senator Claiborne Pell
    Senator Charles H. Percy
    Senator Adlai E. Stevenson, III

---

[1] Source: Ford Library, National Security Adviser, Kissinger–Scowcroft West Wing Office Files, 1969–1977, Box 5, China, unnumbered items (16), 7/6/75–7/23/75. Confidential; Sensitive. The meeting took place in the Madison–Monroe Room at the Department of State. All brackets are in the original.

Representative John B. Anderson
Representative Paul Findley
Representative Paul N. McCloskey, Jr.
Representative John Slack

Henry A. Kissinger, Secretary of State
Philip C. Habib, Assistant Secretary of State for East Asian and Pacific Affairs
Robert J. McCloskey, Assistant Secretary of State for Congressional Relations
Winston Lord, Director, Policy Planning, Department of State
Oscar V. Armstrong, Director, People's Republic of China and Mongolia Affairs,
    Department of State
Richard H. Solomon, Senior Staff Member, National Security Council

SUBJECT

Secretary Kissinger's Briefing of Congressional Delegates Before Their Visit to
the People's Republic of China

Secretary Kissinger: I appreciate your coming. Let me give you our impressions of our relations with China, and then I will be glad to answer your questions. None of you have been there before?

Let me give you my experience. When I first met the Chinese I found them the most fascinating, intelligent and charming people I had known. To some extent this is true, but I can add to it now that they are the most self-centered, the most cold-blooded, analytical people I have encountered. I'd say that nothing in my experience matches it. Whether it's talking with a counter girl at the Shanghai Airport, or with Chou En-lai, everything seems to have one grand design. Nothing is accidental. Dealing with them is like one endless negotiation. I don't know if this is true when a Congressional delegation travels but it has been my experience. They make the totally planned appear spontaneous.

Even their sight-seeing is a totally planned activity. For example they will take you out to the Ming Tombs or the Great Wall. You can set your clock on the schedule they follow, but when you are there no one is looking at their watches; there is no sense of pressure. I asked their protocol chief Han Hsu how they did it. He replied: (1) they don't give a detailed schedule to the guests, and (2) they estimate what their guests will do and then segment the activity into eight minute segments. If the guests do more in any given segment then they just take out some of the later segments; if they do less, they just add on some segments. I am not sure what this says about their view of the attention span of foreigners. All this is done without using walkie-talkies.

When I have reviewed the records of my talks in China, in retrospect you can see how it fits into one grand scheme. The first time that President Nixon met Chairman Mao I thought—with my characteristic humility—that it was a "B" conversation; there was nothing spectacular. Mao just seemed to ramble from one subject to another. Two weeks later I reread the record of the conversation. Mao's comments were like the overture to a Wagner opera. Every theme discussed during the week [of the Nixon visit] had its predicate in the Mao conversation. Every other statesman in the world would say, "I have fifteen points I want to make," and then he would read them. Mao just rambled along. He didn't say, "Remember this point." They are not like the Soviets: "Here are ten points" and a baseball bat. Someday I expect to be in an elevator in the Soviet Union and to push a button and I will over load the whole system.

On the negative side, they [the Chinese] basically don't give a damn about what you think. They truly consider themselves the Middle Kingdom. They have such a feeling of arrogant self-sufficiency.

Those things that they see as essential to their survival they study with meticulous attention. They give the most cold-blooded, amoral attention to the geopolitical factors of containing the Soviet Union. Mao and Chou En-lai have been through the revolution from the beginning, on the Great March. They are men of principle, of great conviction. They combine the ideological level with a cold-blooded pragmatism. Teng might not impress you this way, but if you were to meet Chou, you would see this combination of principle and cold-bloodedness. Their basic reason for moving to us has nothing to do with Formosa. It has everything to do with their fear of the Soviet Union. They don't want to appear to want us, rather they will warn everyone about the Soviet threat. Their basic interest in the U.S. is in maintaining a world balance of power. If they lose this view, they will lose interest in us. I believe the Turkish aid situation has had an impact on them. Everytime I have seen Mao he talks about a tier of states to the south of the Soviet Union. This will affect their perception of our ability to effect our own survival.

Everytime I see Mao he gives a magnificent explanation of the geopolitical situation and talks of the need to take actions to control the Soviet Union—Chou En-lai also. You don't see the bureaucratic factor in Chou.

Formosa: Of course we have discussed it, but it is not central. If they make a list of topics they put it last. They are not eager, partly because they don't want to create complications for us. It is not the central issue in our relationship. As the Shanghai Communiqué says, we have to move toward a new relationship; but whether it is this year or next, or later, it is not critical.

There is one school of thought that says you have to move while Mao and Chou are alive. I don't fully agree with this view as they haven't offered us a better deal. The mistake of many visitors is that they try to solve the Taiwan problem. It is not excessively helpful for people to try to solve it now. The Chinese have said that the President will be welcome regardless of the Taiwan problem. If you raise this question they may be compelled to take some action.

Their overriding concern is with the Soviets having new openings in Indochina. Indochina was a moral defeat for the U.S., but a geopolitical defeat for the Chinese. They now have on their southern border a country of 45 million trying to create an empire of 90 million—if you include the Laotians and the Cambodians. This may spill over into Thailand. The Chinese look at international affairs in terms of power relationships—as De Gaulle did. If they [the North Vietnamese] succeed, China will be in the unenviable position of having a major military power on every border. They know that the Vietnamese historically distrust China. Hanoi leans on the Soviets because of this. The Chinese are the only foreign power active in Cambodia—the only country in Indochina trying to insulate Cambodia against the Vietnamese. They are anxious to keep us in Asia.

They are not interested in—unlike my academic friends—cultural exchanges and trade. They want us to be strong in Asia, strong in the world. They are our best NATO allies. Every European leader [who visits China] gets a lecture on maintaining NATO. Everytime I go there I get scolded for not maintaining good relations with our allies.

They have certain parallel interests with us. They want us to have strong relations with Europe, want to have good relations between the United States and Japan. But we shouldn't delude ourselves. In five years if they become strong they could just cold-bloodedly push us away. Someday they may treat us like the Soviet Union, like an enemy. But for the foreseeable future, their fear of the Soviet Union is the basis of their assessments.

They are endlessly fascinating.

Representative McCloskey: If they want us to maintain NATO, do they not want us in Korea?

Secretary Kissinger: On the one hand they don't want us involved. They have certain obligations to North Korea, as they did in Indochina. They will tell you that they want our troops out. But they would be very disturbed if Japan struck out on an independent and militaristic path—which would happen if we withdrew from Korea. They will restrain North Korea from making an attack, but will support them in the UN.

Senator Javits: Mr. Secretary, I wonder if you could tell us what their aspirations are for their country; and what is their attitude toward Japan.

Secretary Kissinger: I only know Chinese in their 60s and 70s. I don't know younger people there. It sounds ridiculous to say that I only know Mao, Chou, Ch'iao Kuan-hua and Teng Hsiao-p'ing. Very few Americans have conversations with these people outside of their senior officials. Mao, Chou, and Teng have enormous pride in their accomplishments. They remember the Long March. I remember Marshal

Yeh Chien-ying—their acting Defense Minister, now their Defense Minister—on my first trip. He made some comments that sounded spontaneous. He said, "When I joined Mao, I never thought I was doing anything for the present generation. When I joined the revolution, I thought I was joining a teacher, yet here we are and here you are." He saw Mao just as a teacher, not a military man. They want economic advancement, but also an egalitarian society. Mao has a conception that if you have Communism you create a bureaucracy, a new Mandarin class. Mao believes in permanent revolution, that every ten years you have to do away with it all. He is right.

On my first trip to China Chou En-lai talked to me about their Cultural Revolution. I said, "This is your domestic problem." He said, "No, no, you have to understand." They want permanent revolution; this is a major issue of principle to them. If you appeal to their principles they are happy. Not the Soviets. They are happy only when they are chiseling you. My experience is that the Chinese give you an honest position and then stick to it. When we were drafting the Shanghai Communiqué, the Chinese included several sentences we felt were inappropriate to a document that the President would sign. I said to Chou En-lai that if you take out these sentences, I'll give you several of ours that are objectionable to your side. Chou said, "Keep your sentences, I don't want them. You tell me why you find our sentences offensive. If you can convince me, I will take them out." So we talked about them and they later took out those sentences. But the Chinese are very thrifty. A short time later they used these same sentences in a speech that Ch'iao Kuan-hua gave at the United Nations.

Those who knew China before are impressed that visible poverty has been eliminated; it is not like India. There is no squalor, plenty of food. And they have done it without foreign help.

Japan: They are ambivalent. The first time I came they were very hostile toward Japan. Now they want a positive relationship with the Japanese, and they never attack our relations with Japan. In one of my meetings with Mao he asked if I had been in Japan. I said I had been there for a day and a half. Mao said that that was not enough, that I should not offend the Japanese. But they are afraid of a nationalistic Japan. In five years, they might try to move Japan away from us, but not now. They could raise hell by forcing Japan to chose between China and the U.S.

Senator Percy: What are they up to in Vietnam and Cambodia?

Secretary Kissinger: The Chinese are now saying that the Soviets have military bases in Indochina. This is not their governmental people but some of their people in Hong Kong. According to our information that is not correct. I don't believe Hanoi won the war to become a Soviet stooge. They are just playing them both off (the Chinese and the Soviets). The Chinese are trying to gain a foothold in Cambodia. Hanoi sustains the heritage of Ho Chi Minh. His vision of a united Indochina. The Vietnamese hope to gain control of Cambodia. Le Duc Tho told us this in Paris. So at present there is greater Soviet influence than Chinese in Hanoi, but Hanoi isn't a Soviet stooge.

The Chinese nightmare is of a Soviet security system coming down to surround them. They see India as a Soviet stooge, an extension of the Soviet Union. They have contempt for them. They think India started the border war. This is the view expressed by Neville Maxwell in his book on the border war.[2] In Indochina the Chinese are supporting the Cambodians; they warn the Thai against the North Vietnamese. I have the impression that the Chinese did not urge the Thai to get rid of the United States. This was also the position they took with the Filipinos.

Senator Pearson: Are they likely to have a succession crisis?

Secretary Kissinger: We don't have any idea of what will happen after Mao and Chou die. Anyone who tells you that he does is full of nonsense. For example, Chou En-lai's situation: We don't know whether he is in the hospital; whether he is hiding in the hospital during a purge; or whether he is there masterminding the purge. Mao is slipping. With Chou it is very hard to know. He came out of the National People's Congress in a dominant position. There is evidence that his health is failing. Mao a year and a half ago was intellectually in good shape. Teng Hsiao-p'ing now is the dominant figure. But we don't know what will happen when that age-group goes.

Mr. Solomon: We believe Chang Ch'un-ch'iao may be an important figure in the succession. Teng Hsiao-p'ing has some major political liabilities.

Secretary Kissinger: It's like the guessing when Stalin was alive. No one picked Khrushchev. The military could be influential in a succession struggle.

Senator Pell: What are their objectives regarding nuclear weaponry?

Secretary Kissinger: They say that they have no intention of using nuclear weapons first. They also say they will not accept any limitations on nuclear weapons short of their total destruction. Since this won't happen, they are proceeding with their nuclear weapons program. They are building a submarine and ICBMs.

Mr. Habib: They are having problems with their ICBM program.

Secretary Kissinger: The Soviets are in range of a number of their rockets. It is a minor number; less than a hundred. But it is growing.

---

[2] Neville Maxwell, *India's China War* (London, Cape, 1970).

We used to estimate that by 1978 the Soviets would not be able to strike China without suffering unacceptable damage.

Mr. Lord: They are very sensitive to the U.S. nuclear balance with the Soviets.

Secretary Kissinger: They like Schlesinger's tough statements about maintaining our strength.

I would like to meet with you when you get back. They will take seriously what you have to say. I hope you will take full notes. They are likely to drop things into the conversation that they assume will get back to us. They assume that we will see a full report on your conversations.

Senator Stevenson: Whom do you think we'll see? Do you have any suggestions about topics we might raise?

Secretary Kissinger: I think you will find the Foreign Minister—Ch'iao Kuan-hua—more rewarding than Teng.

Anything that your conscience would enable you to say about the United States maintaining a global role in Asia and Europe they will welcome. They don't want us to collapse in the Middle East or to collaborate with the Soviet Union. You could emphasize that we will not collapse; that it's not just that we support Israel but that we will also compete with the Soviets for the moderate Arabs. Their major concern is that the Soviets will inherit the Middle East.

You might convey a sense of continuity in our foreign policy, that if the Democrats win there will be no change in our foreign policy.

Taiwan: It would be helpful for you to push suggestions. They have already rejected a number of them, like our leaving a Liaison Office in Taipei. This is not a question of finding some gimmick. There is one point: If we had some assurance that they would not use force then we could make progress. If they won't, we will have difficulty in turning over 15 million—especially in the year when we lost Indochina. This issue is more important than what we call our office in Taipei.

They told us that the Jackson formula—switching our Liaison Office and Embassy—was unacceptable before we raised it as a proposition. Our representation in Taiwan will not be a problem. Our problem is the future relationship of Taiwan with the mainland. This is the basic problem. If you raise this, this point would be helpful. Stress the desire for a peaceful settlement of this issue, that there be no use of force. Especially in a bipartisan group this might help them move in that direction.

Senator Percy: Han Hsu told me that they want more normal relations with the Soviet Union and are willing to be reasonable, but the Soviets are hostile toward them. Where's the truth?

Senator Javits: Huang Hua says just the opposite.

Secretary Kissinger: All of them say that the Soviets are hostile to China. Some of the issues could be easily settled. But what bothers the

Chinese is the withdrawal of the Soviet technicians in 1960 which paralyzed the Chinese economy. Secondly, they see the Soviets as basically expansionist. If they could concentrate enough force they could go after China. Mao, and to some extent Chou, are psychopathic on this point. I think the next generation may be less hostile to the Soviets; somewhat more accommodating. From the Soviet point of view, there are over 800 million highly disciplined Chinese. There will be ups and downs, but a 3,000 mile border is a geopolitical fact. They will continue to be competitive powers.

Do any of my colleagues want to add anything? Win.

Mr. Lord: They are now stressing that the Soviet threat is directed at Europe. This is partly for tactical effect, but they do see the CSCE conference as weakening Europe.

Secretary Kissinger: The Chinese are against popular front governments in Europe. Phil, did you want to add anything?

Mr. Habib: Regarding Korea, you might reinforce the thought that North Korea should not engage in any adventurism against the South.

Senator Percy: Do you think they will be troubled by the fact that we were recently in the Soviet Union? I took pains to be as open with them about our recent trip as possible. Han Hsu seemed to have been fully briefed on it.

Mr. Solomon: I don't think you will find them upset about this. They seem to have great confidence that they will outshine the Soviets. Virtually every group I have talked to who has been to both Russia and China has found the Chinese much more sophisticated and appealing.

Representative Findley: Have they expressed any interest in getting MFN?

Secretary Kissinger: Some newsmen asked the Chinese what they thought of the Jackson–Vanik amendment. The Chinese responded that they will be glad to export 30 million Chinese to the United States any time we are interested. They are not pushing us on this.

I look forward to seeing you when you get back.

116.   Memorandum From Richard H. Solomon of the National Security Council Staff to Secretary of State Kissinger[1]

Washington, July 31, 1975.

SUBJECT

"Mood-Setters" in Our Relations With the Chinese

There are a number of opportunities which will present themselves early in the fall for the President to identify himself publicly with the People's Republic of China. You may wish to have him take advantage of one or a number of the following occasions both to signal to Peking his orientation to the current state of U.S.–PRC relations and to set the mood for our own public in advance of his trip to China.

—The Chinese will be sending their official trade delegation (the China Council for the Promotion of International Trade) to the U.S. in September. The President has received a request from the organizers of the Washington leg of their trip that he receive this group for a few minutes if his schedule permits. You may wish to have Mr. Ford meet with this group as an expression of his personal interest in our growing trade with the PRC.

—The Chinese are also sending to the U.S. their official scientific organization which promotes exchanges with other countries, the All-China Scientific and Technical Association. This group will also be in Washington in September. The President might meet with this group as an expression of his support for our scientific exchanges with the PRC.

—The President has received an invitation from the National Committee on U.S.–China Relations, the group that handles our cultural exchanges with the PRC, to give an address to their membership during their annual meeting in late October. As you may have completed your advance trip to Peking by this time, you might want the President to make some form of public statement to this group as a way of setting the public mood in advance of his trip to Peking. Alternatively, the President could just send the National Committee a statement of support, or you might address the group. (Based on our recent discussion, however, you may wish to adopt a lower "China profile" than would be implied by a speech by the President or yourself.)

---

[1] Source: Ford Library, National Security Adviser, Kissinger–Scowcroft West Wing Office Files, 1969–1977, Box 5, China, unnumbered items (17), 8/4/75–8/31/75. No classification marking. Sent for action. Lord forwarded this memorandum to Kissinger on August 22 under a covering memorandum that advised the Secretary to approve "the following recommendations by number: 1 or 2, 4 and 6, but I would not move on any of them until we hear from the Chinese concerning dates for the two visits." (Ibid.)

—You will recall that last October Huang Chen requested that his wife have an opportunity to call on the First Lady. No such meeting was held, however. The Chinese raised the issue again early in the spring. Again no action was taken because of the conjunction of the request with developments in Indochina. You may wish to consider having the First Lady receive Madame Huang within the new few months (particularly if the First Lady will accompany the President on his trip to Peking).

If you will provide guidance, we will handle the staffing of these requests as you indicate.

Recommendations:[2]

1. That the President receive the delegation from the China Council for the Promotion of International Trade:

2. That the President receive the delegation from the All-China Scientific and Technical Association:

3. That the President accept the invitation of the National Committee on U.S.–China Relations to address their annual meeting (in late October):

Alternatives:

4. That the President send the annual meeting a message (which we will prepare):

5. That you address the National Committee's annual meeting:

6. That the First Lady receive Madame Huang Chen at some convenient time in advance of the President's trip to Peking:[3]

---

[2] The recommendations were numbered by hand, presumably by Lord. Kissinger initialed the Approve option under recommendations 1, 2, 4, and 6 and the Disapprove option under recommendation 3. He did not initial either option under recommendation 5.

[3] A note beneath Kissinger's initials indicates that he made this marking on September 3.

The Summit in Beijing, August–December 1975

117. **Briefing Memorandum From the Assistant Secretary of State for East Asian and Pacific Affairs (Habib), the Deputy Assistant Secretary of State for East Asian and Pacific Affairs (Gleysteen), the Director of the Policy Planning Staff (Lord), and Richard H. Solomon of the National Security Council Staff to Secretary of State Kissinger[1]**

Washington, August 4, 1975.

Partial Steps Toward Normalization of U.S./PRC Relations in Conjunction with the President's Trip to Peking

1. As you asked in our meeting of July 7,[2] we have examined whether there are further steps short of full normalization which we might take in conjunction with the President's trip this fall to sustain the momentum in U.S./PRC relations. Bearing in mind the need not to stir up excessively those who are opposed to a changeover in relations, we have looked at moves which would:

—indicate to people in the United States, PRC, and elsewhere that we are continuing to move toward full normalization of relations.
—signal the Soviets that our relationship with the PRC remains sound.
—ease doubts among PRC elements who may question wisdom of Peking's acquiescing in normalization delays.
—discourage Taiwan from assuming there had been a setback or that it could exploit the lack of dramatic movement in our relations with Peking.

2. We find that the concept of an interim step has some merit as an alternative for reaching full normalization this year (or as a fallback in the event such an attempt were authorized and proved unsuccessful). There is, we think, some possibility of devising adequately balanced U.S. and PRC measures which would not involve major concessions on our part or invite serious domestic criticism. Even though the Chinese might be hard to budge, they might see the advantage of small, matched concessions to provide an aura of success at the summit.

---

[1] Source: Ford Library, National Security Adviser, Kissinger–Scowcroft West Wing Office Files, 1969–1977, Box 5, China, unnumbered items (17), 8/4/75–8/31/75. Secret; Nodis.

[2] The meeting was on July 6; see Document 113.

3. Nevertheless, the boundaries for an interim step are quite narrow. Peking continues to set three political preconditions to full normalization: breaking diplomatic relations with Taipei and recognition of Peking "as the sole legal government of China;" full withdrawal of the American military presence from Taiwan and abrogation of our defense treaty with the ROC; and U.S. recognition of Taiwan as part of China.

4. For the purpose of this paper, we assume that domestic and international constraints will prevent us from fully and explicitly accepting any of these conditions at this time. However, we could touch on these various conditions by unilateral statements going beyond those we made in the Shanghai Communiqué. We would not, of course, wish to go so far as to make a major unilateral concession in the absence of agreement on other elements of a final normalization package. Without the elements of reassurance that would hopefully be included in full normalization arrangements, we would also have to be especially careful not to panic Taiwan and its supporters in this country.

5. A second category of steps—which hopefully might be combined with any political statements—would involve agreement with the Chinese on practical issues such as claims, exchanges, trade, or governmental relations (branch liaison offices, etc.). Agreement along these lines, which would require some shift in PRC positions, would convey a sense of strengthened ties and continuing momentum toward normalization.

Political Half Steps

6. *One China Formulations.* As a sign of political movement we could make a unilateral statement in the communiqué taking us beyond our Shanghai Communiqué position of not challenging the view that "all Chinese on either side of the Taiwan Strait maintain there is but one China and that Taiwan is part of China." Short of a direct affirmation, which would seem premature in this context, the most far-reaching formulation would be a fairly clear though indirect acknowledgment that "Taiwan is part of China." (See Tab 1).[3] Such an important concession on our part, even if accompanied by progress on practical issues, would entail rather serious risks. In the absence of some offsetting statement about our concern for Taiwan's security, it would intensify anxieties on Taiwan, possibly to the danger point, and it would almost surely come under attack in this country from both self-determinationists and more conservative supporters of the ROC. We

---

[3] Tab 1, attached but not printed, contains draft language for "formulation indirectly acknowledging Taiwan as part of China."

would face political criticism, and conceivably legal problems, from the contradiction of continued diplomatic recognition of the ROC, while having acknowledged in an official communiqué with the PRC that Taiwan was part of China.

7. A considerably more attractive possibility would play on the PRC's November 1973 Communiqué statement that "the normalization of relations between China and the United States can be realized only on the basis of confirming the principle of one China."[4] Given Chou's initiative on this point, it should have some appeal for Peking. This variant could, moreover, be phrased to maintain linkage to the "peaceful settlement of the Taiwan question by the Chinese themselves." (See Tab 2).[5] The impact on Taiwan should be constructive because the formulation would constitute a useful conditioning step toward the future without setting up shock waves. Proponents of normalization might criticize it as a rather empty, teasing step, but such complaints could be countered by coupling it with some other measures of a practical nature in a package suggesting distinct, if not dramatic, progress.

8. *Full Normalization.* In the summit communiqué, we could either unilaterally or jointly speak in terms of further progress toward *full* normalization of relations, a phrase which we have not so far used in formal declarations. The nuance would raise the communiqué's temperature several degrees, especially if coupled with the "one China" formulation discussed above. It would not be welcome in Taiwan but would hardly come as a great surprise. In this country it might stimulate unhelpful counter moves trying to box us in regarding the unstated but inevitable corollary prospect of a break in U.S./ROC diplomatic relations. However, we believe these risks are manageable.

9. *Military Withdrawals.* An interim step could also include further unilateral reference to U.S. military withdrawals from Taiwan. There is a range of statements we could make short of announcing a complete withdrawal. The most extreme would be a statement that, assuming continued reductions in tensions in the area, we intended substantially to complete withdrawals of our military forces from Taiwan by some specific date. This would attenuate the basic linkage in the Shanghai Communiqué between complete withdrawals and the prospect of a peaceful settlement of the Taiwan problem. A more immediate disadvantage would be great anxiety in Taiwan and unhelpful questioning here. If the reaction in Taiwan appeared to threaten the

---

[4] See footnote 7, Document 60.

[5] Tab 2, attached but not printed, contains an "alternative formulation regarding the 'principle of one China.'"

island's "stable" adjustment to our evolving relations with Peking, the statement might even misfire with the PRC which, in any event, does not seem to doubt our good faith on troop withdrawals. Thus we question whether this card should be played without some compensating PRC movement on the issue of peaceful settlement.

10. Most of the difficulties—and, to be sure, some of the drama—would be eliminated if the communiqué merely referred approvingly to the substantial withdrawals that have taken place on Taiwan and noted the prospect for additional cuts if tensions continued to ease.

11. Given our present schedule we should be in position by November/December to justify an additional withdrawal statement which would of course be unilateral, even though you might wish to inform the Chinese at the time of your trip of our contemplated drawdowns. (Last November you told Teng Hsiao-ping that we would reduce our forces in Taiwan even in the absence of a normalization agreement, and when we informed the PRC early this year of certain reductions in Taiwan you indicated there would be further drawdowns this year and that we would keep Peking informed.[6] The benefit of these moves vis-à-vis Peking might be increased if we also told the Chinese privately before the summit that we intended to consolidate the Taiwan Defense Command and MAAG and/or to reduce the rank of the commanding officers. However, we have not yet decided on this step which would be quite unsettling in Taiwan.)

12. *Diplomatic Representation.* The only diplomatic measure we could adopt short of a break in U.S./ROC relations would be lowering the level of our representation from an ambassador to chargé, or reducing the size of the embassy. (You told the Chinese in November 1974 that we would reduce the seniority of our diplomatic representation before 1976 even in the absence of full normalization.[7] However, replacement of Unger with a junior ambassador might be counterproductive in view of the fuss Peking made over our replacement of McConaughy.) Either of these steps, especially, if announced in a communiqué, would be welcomed by Peking but we think they would be ill-advised. More than any of the other measures discussed above, they would be seen on Taiwan as impending notice of radical change. Some of the same destabilizing tendencies which would come into play with a full break in U.S./ROC relations would be stimulated with plenty of time to cause us serious trouble and without our being in position to make the kind of reassuring gestures that might be possible in the context of full normalization.

---

[6] See Documents 94, 98, and Document 109.

[7] See Document 98.

13. In sum, after considering the balance of advantage and disadvantage, the political measures which seem promising would be the play on Chou En-lai's November 1973 statement on "confirming the unity of China" (para 7 above), a reference to "full normalization" (para 8), and possibly a rounded reference to continuing progress in the withdrawal of U.S. forces from Taiwan (para 10). Even without some matching advance from the Chinese side, we might find one or possibly more of these initiatives in our interest as a means of getting the right message to various audiences, not simply the PRC. Obviously it would be far better if our statements were part of a carefully balanced package, including some bilateral agreements with the PRC. Such a package might consist, for example, of one or more U.S. political statements, a claims agreement, exchange of defense liaison officers or a hot line, and some qualitative improvement in the exchange program. (Even if not in a publicly useable form it would be helpful if you were able to obtain PRC agreement to adopt a less antagonistic tone toward us on international issues.) The Chinese might resist such an extensive "interim step," but we should have enough choice to ensure that the measures were adequately balanced in terms of US interests.

Bilateral Issues Where Progress Might Be Made

14. Irrespective of any progress in resolving the political issues which remain between us and Peking in conjunction with the President's trip, you should seek agreement on a number of outstanding bilateral issues in the areas of claims, exchanges, trade, and governmental relations. Agreements of this kind would strengthen our ties with the PRC, sustain abroad a sense of continuing momentum in our relationship, and help justify to domestic audiences a second Presidential trip to Peking. The alternative to such agreements is conclusion of a modest set of understandings in already-familiar exchange areas which would do little more than indicate to the world that U.S./PRC relations were coasting at their present level.

15. Following are a number of possible areas for agreement which would strengthen our bilateral relationship with the PRC. Some would constitute a step forward in ongoing matters; others would break new ground. We must emphasize that to date the Chinese have indicated an unwillingness, for example, to solve the claims/assets problem before our relationship is fully normalized. They may not shift their position, either because doing so would limit their future leverage on the outstanding normalization issues, and/or because there probably exist domestic PRC political constraints on concessions in these areas in the absence of progress toward full normalization. Nevertheless, if the Chinese share our desire to demonstrate continuing momentum in our relationship, they may be more receptive to one or more of these steps than they have been in the past.

16. *Claims Settlement.* A settlement, despite the existing agreement in principle in March 1973,[8] would have a sizable symbolic value: the issue has received considerable public attention, and it would be the first formal U.S./PRC intergovernmental agreement. More concretely, a settlement would remove a major impediment to further progress in economic/commercial relations, such as banking, trade exhibits and air and sea links.

17. Settlement has been prevented by the Chinese unwillingness to compromise on several issues. However, in the counterpart talks during your November 1974 visit, it became clear that the Chinese did not want a settlement then and were using the few remaining problems as a pretext for stalling.[9] We believe that whenever the Chinese decide that a settlement is desirable, those problems can be resolved relatively easily. If they are receptive, an agreement could be signed during the Presidential trip.

18. *Branch Liaison Offices.* An agreement to establish branch liaison offices, e.g., in San Francisco and Canton, would have considerable symbolic value. However, the Chinese would derive far more benefit; they could take full advantage of our open society, while our branch would be of limited value to us. This situation might change if our branch were involved in implementing an agreement on the re-uniting of families (see separate item).

19. *Defense Liaison Officers.* We could suggest an exchange of "defense liaison officers." In addition to publicly expanding the scope of our two Liaison Offices, the move might be welcomed by the Chinese because of its impact on the Soviets. We would need to carefully consider such an exchange in terms of our relations with Moscow, and Taipei would be displeased. In a more practical vein, foreign military attachés in Peking have minimal contact with the Chinese military, and our Liaison Office is so crowded that Chinese cooperation in providing more office space would probably be necessary.

20. *Hot Line.* We could propose that a "hot line" be established between Washington and Peking and that an announcement be included in the communiqué. You have tentatively floated this idea before with the PRC without any interest on their part. But it remains the only feasible step in the arms control area.

---

[8] In a memorandum to Kissinger, March 9, 1973, Theodore Eliot reported that the PRC "has agreed to settle U.S. private claims through an assignment of blocked Chinese assets to the U.S. Government for use in compensating American claimants." (National Archives, Nixon Presidential Materials, NSC Files, Box 527, Country Files, Far East, People's Republic of China, Vol. 7, May, 1973–Jul 9, 1973)

[9] See footnote 4, Document 98.

21. *Exchanges.* We have already been requested by the two committees involved in our exchange program to support their efforts to improve the quality of the exchanges and to achieve a better balance between the benefits to the PRC and the interests of American participants. In addition to seeking this general improvement, we could again propose several specific steps which would visibly demonstrate forward movement. The possibilities include:

—Exchange of students for language study.
—Longer term joint research efforts, preferably intergovernmental, in such fields as agriculture or environment.
—Permanent press representation in Peking and Washington.

22. *Reuniting Families.* The Canadians have an agreement with the PRC designed to make it easier for Chinese in the PRC to join their close relatives in Canada. In this country there are probably thousands of Chinese-Americans who want to bring their close relatives in China to the United States, and many members of Congress receive requests for assistance. Moreover, the 1974 Trade Act makes the extension of MFN partially contingent on the other country's willingness to permit the reuniting of families. We seriously doubt that the PRC, in the absence of full diplomatic relations, would be prepared to negotiate an agreement, and they will not want to appear to be yielding to the Trade Act provisions on emigration policies. Nevertheless, since an intergovernmental agreement on this subject would have a substantial positive impact in this country, we could make a low-key effort to determine the PRC attitude.

23. *Trade Agreement and MFN.* We have indicated to the PRC that once the claims issue is settled, we would be prepared to discuss extension of the Most Favored Nation treatment to PRC exports to the United States. However, the 1975 Trade Act provides that MFN can be extended only through a bilateral trade agreement under which we would receive some comparable benefits. Moreover, the "emigration" provisions of the Act (the Jackson–Vanik amendment and an article about reuniting families) will be unacceptable to the PRC. Proposing preliminary discussions of a trade agreement, including MFN, therefore seems pointless. However, we could suggest a more limited agreement, e.g., on trade exhibits, trademarks, and arbitration of business disputes.

24. *Embassy Sites.* Our Liaison Office in Peking is now so crowded that little expansion of staff is possible. The PRC Liaison Office here has plenty of room, and we do not know if they would move when embassies are established. In any event, we could tell the Chinese that in anticipation of the time when our two Liaison Offices are changed to embassies, we would like to start discussions on permanent sites for our respective missions. A statement to this effect could be included in a communiqué, along the following lines: "The two sides, looking for-

ward to the further normalization of relations, have agreed to initiate discussions regarding more permanent facilities for their respective missions in each other's capital." Such a statement would obviously have significant symbolic impact.

25. *Jamming of VOA.* The Chinese continue to jam the Chinese-language broadcasts of VOA. As far as we know, these are the only foreign broadcasts which are jammed (even those from the Soviet Union are not jammed). We could express our puzzlement and our hope that the jamming could be ended. If they agreed, we would not press for any mention of jamming in the communiqué, but we could make the change public by other means.

26. We will continue to work on formulas and other ideas but wanted you to have our thoughts so far.

---

118.   Memorandum of Conversation[1]

Washington, August 12, 1975, 3:45 p.m.

SUBJECT

1) President Ford's Trip to Europe and the Miki Visit to Washington
2) The President's and the Secretary's Trips to China

PARTICIPANTS

U.S. Side:
The Secretary
Assistant Secretary Philip C. Habib
Director Winston Lord
Deputy Assistant Secretary William Gleysteen

PRC Side:
Ambassador Huang Chen
Chien Ta-yung
Shen Jo-yun
Yang Hsu-ching

Ambassador Huang: You must be very busy Mr. Secretary.

Secretary: Yes. I wanted to have dinner with you tonight at Marquis Childs' but unfortunately I have to work on a speech instead,

---

[1] Source: Ford Library, National Security Adviser, NSC Staff for East Asia and Pacific Affairs, Convenience Files, 1969–1977, Box 39, Richard Solomon Subject Files, 1974–76. Secret; Nodis. Drafted by Gleysteen.

my speech in Birmingham.[2] Perhaps it could be arranged on another occasion. We could have dinner at the house of another mutual friend.

Ambassador: Good. Let's do that.

Secretary: It's been too long since we last saw each other. I thought we should have a brief review of events. We have, as you know, just come back from the Helsinki meetings and Eastern Europe.

Ambassador: Are you going away soon on another round of shuttle diplomacy in the Middle East?

Secretary: It's not settled yet, but chances are now better than 50–50. The chances are that I will go the middle of next week.

Let me say a few things about our recent trip. The President's trip was obviously not designed to strengthen Soviet control over Eastern Europe. We deliberately visited those countries in Eastern Europe that have shown the most independence. In Romania we found deep concern and hostility toward the Soviets. I am sure you are familiar with the situation in Yugoslavia. As we announced during our trip, we will start selling some military equipment to Yugoslavia.

Ambassador: Is it decided already?

Secretary: Yes. It has been decided.

Let me first say something about the formal conference at Helsinki. I think it is a great mistake to overstate the significance of the conference. We do not see it as having ratified any frontiers. No new legal status was accorded to frontiers beyond the status they had from previous agreements. The Declaration dealt only with the methods of change, not the sanctity of borders.

In the bilateral meetings with Soviet leaders, Brezhnev seemed to us to have been in better health in other places we have met him than he was in Helsinki. He seemed to have a little trouble concentrating. We talked primarily about the problems of strategic arms limitation, but we haven't come to any final conclusions; we are not even sure they are possible.

On other issues, I made clear that we would not participate in the Soviet scheme for an Asian collective security system. (The Secretary turned to Lord and asked if he had sent to the Chinese his Helsinki press statement which ruled out U.S. participation in such an exercise. Lord replied that he had.) Of course, if China should favor our participation, we might reconsider our position.

---

[2] Marquis Childs was a prominent journalist. On August 14, Kissinger spoke before the Southern Commodity Producers Conference at Birmingham, Alabama. Kissinger's address is printed in Department of State *Bulletin*, September 15, 1975, pp. 389–396.

Ambassador: I received a copy of your statement. We think that the Soviets will have a very hard time peddling their collective security system.

Secretary: I agree. We will oppose it. We also told Brezhnev privately about our position. Those were the only significant issues in our bilateral discussions with the Soviet leaders. The President also had an extremely good meeting with the British Prime Minister, the President of France, and the German Chancellor concerning ways of strengthening cooperation. The meeting was extremely constructive and may be followed by another one in the fall dealing with the economic situation.

Ambassador: I understand from the press that less than a week after the Helsinki conference, the Soviets violated Norwegian airspace. This would seem to confirm our view that the conference represents no change in basic Soviet strategy. They will continue to feint toward the East and move toward the West.

Secretary: Maybe they will feint toward the West and move toward the East, but for us the problem is the same. Although I am not aware of the Norwegian overflight, I won't contest that it actually occurred. I agree there has not been any fundamental change in Soviet policy.

Ambassador: We do not think that the CSCE will change things, especially the Soviet strategy of feinting to the East but moving to the West.

Secretary: It won't change our determination to prevent an attack in either direction.

I would also like to tell you about our meetings with Prime Minister Miki of Japan. We told the Japanese we supported their attempt to improve relations with you. Miki asked me privately about the antihegemony clause in the treaty negotiations. I told him we couldn't object to what we put in our own communiqué with you.

The Japanese expressed great concern over the Korean situation. We agreed with them on the extreme importance of maintaining peace in the Korean peninsula. We also told the Japanese that we were opposed to the Soviets' Asian collective security scheme or any other moves which seemed directed at the People's Republic of China.

At some point, not necessarily now, we would be interested in your Government's assessment of the Indochina situation, especially the relations of Cambodia and Viet-Nam.[3] We would like your real assessment.

Ambassador: I think our leaders have already discussed this with some of your recent visitors.

---

[3] There had been reports of fighting between Vietnam and Cambodia. ("Vietnamese Forces Reported in Clash With Cambodians," *The New York Times*, June 14, 1975, p. 1)

Secretary: I haven't seen any such reports. You must get your reports faster than we do.

Ambassador: The situation in Cambodia is good.

Secretary: Except for all the people who had to leave Phnom Penh.[4] Seriously, although I would not have recommended or endorsed the measures adopted by the Government in Phnom Penh, we are genuinely interested in Cambodian independence.

Ambassador: Cambodian conditions are really very good.

Chien: We don't discuss such relationships or even make suggestions.

Ambassador: We are opposed to expansionism in Southeast Asia.

Secretary: Expansionism? I agree.

Do you have any views or comments on my review?

Ambassador: Nothing in particular.

Secretary: I also wish to discuss the possibility of the President's visit to China. We are thinking of the beginning of December, give or take a day or so. Specifically, the President might arrive on November 29th or 30th. For my trip, I would plan to go to China five or six weeks earlier than the President, around the 16th of October or so. And if these plans are convenient, we could first announce my visit, perhaps in mid-September, and then when I leave China we could announce the President's trip.

Ambassador: We will report.

Secretary: Please confirm to my colleagues or me, if this is convenient.

Ambassador: We will report and tell your colleagues. Did you say your own trip would be around the 16th?

Secretary: Yes, the 15th or 16th.

Ambassador: For how long?

Secretary: Maybe three or four days. I think we should agree on the communiqué while I am there. It would be too precarious to leave it until the President's trip. The President is also thinking of a stay of about four days. Of course, we are open to suggestions.

Ambassador: We would follow the old practice of making a joint announcement of the President's trip at the end of your trip. Is that correct?

Secretary: Exactly.

---

[4] Reports had reached the United States about the forced evacuation of Phnom Penh, slave labor, and mass starvation. ("Fleeing Cambodians Tell of Khmer Rouge Killings," *The Washington Post*, July 21, 1975, p. A1)

I should tell you that the President is also thinking of visiting a few other countries, not on the way to Peking but on the way home. He certainly would not visit India because of the situation there, but he probably will go to the Philippines, Australia, and possibly Indonesia.

Ambassador: Will he go to Singapore? I saw something in the press about his visiting Singapore.

Secretary: Certainly not. We cannot go to Singapore without going to Malaysia. We have no scheme to visit Singapore or Malaysia.

Ambassador: How definite is Indonesia?

Secretary: There is a good chance of stopping in Indonesia. We haven't discussed these plans with any of the countries involved. In my own case, I have to get to a NATO meeting by the 11th of December. I know you wouldn't want me to miss it.

Ambassador: Yes. You should help strengthen NATO. How about the situation in Turkey and Greece? What is happening on the southern flank of NATO?

Secretary: I have told many friends that China would be watching the southern flank even though it was far away, because I remember my conversation with Chairman Mao. What is happening is a total stupidity. I think we can get it reversed by mid-September when Congress returns.

Ambassador: Good.

Secretary: By then, there is also hope for an interim agreement in the Middle East.

Ambassador: Will you spend about ten days in the Middle East?

Secretary: A week to ten days.

Ambassador: I see that there are two Israeli delegations here.

Secretary: Yes. They are here right now to help us draft.

Ambassador: I understand one delegation is here about aid.

Secretary: Yes. We have held up aid matters. However, it has also been understood that we would give aid after the agreement was reached. The technical studies just happen to coincide with the arrival of the aid delegation.

Who is going to head your delegation to the UN General Assembly?

Ambassador: Even I do not yet know.

119.   Memorandum of Conversation[1]

New York City, September 28, 1975, 8:10–11:55 p.m.

PARTICIPANTS

Ch'iao Kuan-hua, Foreign Minister of the People's Republic of China
Huang Hua, PRC Permanent Representative to the United Nations
Chang Han-chih, Deputy Director, Asian Affairs Department, Ministry of Foreign Affairs
Lo Hsu, Deputy Director, African Affairs Department, Ministry of Foreign Affairs
Shih Yen-hua, Ministry of Foreign Affairs, Interpreter [Notetaker]
Kuo Chia-ting, Second Secretary, PRC United Nations Mission, Notetaker [Interpreter]

Henry A. Kissinger, Secretary of State and Assistant to the President for National Security Affairs
Patrick Moynihan, U.S. Ambassador to the United Nations
Philip C. Habib, Assistant Secretary of State for East Asian and Pacific Affairs
Winston Lord, Director, Policy Planning Staff, Department of State
William H. Gleysteen, Jr., Deputy Assistant Secretary of State for East Asian and Pacific Affairs
Richard H. Solomon, Senior Staff Member, National Security Council

SUBJECT

The Soviet Union; CSCE; Europe; Japan; Angola; Indochina; the President's China Trip; the Global Strategic Situation; Korea

[Foreign Minister Ch'iao and his party were escorted into the Secretary's suite. After initial greetings, representatives of the press were brought in for a few minutes to photograph the Secretary and Foreign Minister.]

Foreign Minister Ch'iao: It has been almost ten months since we last met.

Secretary Kissinger: Your Ambassador [Huang Hua] has since learned the he has less of an [English] accent than I do.

You have met all of my friends here. Ambassador Moynihan—he is extremely competent. The other day the Albanian Ambassador attacked the U.S. Moynihan responded by attacking the Soviet Union. Malik did not know what hit him.

Ambassador Moynihan: What I said was that the Albanian Ambassador had missed an opportunity to attack that superpower which styles itself as Socialist.

---

[1] Source: Ford Library, National Security Adviser, Kissinger Reports on USSR, China, and Middle East Discussions, Box 2, China Memcons and Reports, September 28, 1975, Kissinger's Meeting with PRC Officials. Top Secret; Sensitive; Eyes Only. The dinner meeting took place in the Secretary of State's suite on the 35th floor of the Waldorf Towers. All brackets are in the original.

Secretary Kissinger: I have read the Foreign Minister's speech.[2] This time you fired some real cannons.

Foreign Minister Ch'iao: Half real; half empty.

Secretary Kissinger: The empty ones were fired at the British.

I told the Soviet Ambassador that we are gaining on them. Of course, he was so wounded by what you said [about the Soviet Union] that he didn't notice [Ch'iao's attacks on the U.S.]. But I told him that in every category we are gaining on him.

Foreign Minister Ch'iao: So much about my speech. I would like to listen to your views, as I have not seen you in a while. I would like to listen to your views on the international situation as a whole.

Secretary Kissinger: We have kept you informed through Ambassador Huang Chen.

Foreign Minister Ch'iao: We appreciate that. Every time there has been some development you have informed us. But what is your view of the international situation as a whole?

Secretary Kissinger: The basic situation—with respect to the Soviet Union—let me begin there. The basic tendencies which we have commented on before are continuing, or somewhat increasing. We believe they are divided evenly between East and West.

According to our perception, the [Soviets'] physical strength and the capabilities for pressure are the same in either direction. The danger is about even.

Our assessment is that they [the Soviets] are probably in a period of transition from one leadership to another.

Foreign Minister Ch'iao: But what is the tendency?

Secretary Kissinger: Well—[pause] I think the tendency—

[Mrs. Kissinger enters the room and is introduced to the Foreign Minister and the other Chinese guests. She departs after a few words with the Secretary on her plans for the evening.]

Secretary Kissinger (continuing): What is the tendency of their policy? It is very hard to tell in a succession situation, as those with the highest inclination to grasp power have the highest motivation to mask their intentions. Assuming that Kirilenko[3]—[the Chinese discuss among themselves to clarify the Soviet leader mentioned by the Secretary].

---

[2] Qiao delivered a speech on September 26 to the UN General Assembly. President Ford received and initialed a copy of it while at Camp David. (White House telegram 51893 to the President at Camp David, September 28; ibid., Presidential Country Files for East Asian and Pacific Affairs, 1974–1977, Box 13, People's Republic of China)

[3] Andrei P. Kirilenko was a member of the Politburo and the Soviet Communist Party Central Committee.

We would expect them to continue on their present course, but with some less flexibility. But since he [Kirilenko] is likely to be even more dependent on vested bureaucratic interests than Brezhnev, the military element is likely to have a relatively larger influence. This [first] successor group is likely to be succeeded in three or four years by a younger group which will almost certainly try to establish the supremacy of the Party.

This is our assessment. I do not know whether it agrees with yours?

Foreign Minister Ch'iao: Well, on some points we do not share your views. We differ in that a change in the leadership in the Soviet Union—if a new leadership comes which is not the same as the old one, we are sure that its tendency will not change. As for the flexibility of that leadership, I have no information to indicate that Kirilenko will be less flexible than Brezhnev. We know him well, and have no such impression.

Secretary Kissinger: Will he be more flexible?

Foreign Minister Ch'iao: Such is the case with the Soviet Union that when a man is in power he sings a different tune when he is in power than a man who is not in power. So we do not think that the new man will be much different.

In 1964 when Khrushchev fell from power we knew this man Brezhnev well. When he took office we thought some change in their policy might be possible, as we had had previous contact with Brezhnev. But Brezhnev continued his expansionist policy even more viciously and actively.

Secretary Kissinger: So you think they will continue [on their present course]?

Foreign Minister Ch'iao: Basically. There is a false impression held by some of our Western friends because Brezhnev talks peace and co-existence. But their military talks strength. These are two tendencies in one situation.

Secretary Kissinger: Are we one of those friends?

Foreign Minister Ch'iao (with a somewhat surprised look on his face): At least I think this idea is widespread in Europe.

Last year I met Chancellor Schmidt [and raised this topic with him]. He thought that Brezhnev was more flexible, and if it was a question of others coming to power it was better to keep Brezhnev.

Secretary Kissinger: You will see Schmidt in November?

Foreign Minister Ch'iao: Late October.

Secretary Kissinger: My view of the basic tendency of Soviet policy is that there is no basic disagreement within their leadership. But as in this country [the U.S.], ambitious people will express different attitudes. But this is not a reflection of basic differences in philosophy.

Foreign Minister Ch'iao: Of course you have made a very detailed study of this. Since there are [now] economic difficulties in the world, all the Soviet leaders have made the same assessment of the West. They do not speak out [directly], but their scholars have. These scholars expressed differences in tactics, although their major assessments [of the situation in the West] are the same.

This is one subject. We can leave it aside and continue our studies [of Soviet intentions].

Secretary Kissinger: Let me say one thing. Our assessment of Soviet tendencies does not differ from yours, but our strategic problem is different than yours.

Your strategic problem is to call the attention to the dangers of this tendency. Our strategic problem is to be in a position to resist these tendencies when they occur. To do this we have to demonstrate for our domestic situation that no other alternative is available.

Therefore we must use language [descriptive] of our relations [with the USSR] which you do not like. But this is the only way for the United States to pursue a really strong policy. If you observe our actual policies in the Middle East, Portugal, Angola, or other areas, when the Soviet Union tries to expand we resist—even in the face of domestic or foreign criticism.

There is a prize fight on television every Tuesday night. You cannot stand flat-footed in the middle of the ring waiting for people to hit you. But not everyone who moves is running away.

Shall we have dinner?

[The party moved from the sitting room and seated themselves at the dining table.]

Secretary Kissinger: This is a brief visit for you, Mr. Foreign Minister. Are you going back [to China] next week?

Foreign Minister Ch'iao: Yes.

Secretary Kissinger: How is the Prime Minister's health?

Foreign Minister Ch'iao: He is still in the hospital, but he is better now.

Secretary Kissinger: I still think of him with respect and affection.

Foreign Minister Ch'iao: Thank you.

Well, you said just now that in my speech to the UN General Assembly I fired some real cannons. I feel that after a period of time you will come to understand [my reasons for firing these cannons].

One other point on which I do not agree with you: the Soviet Union, geographically speaking, is in the middle. But proceeding from the realities of the situation, as I have often told you on many occasions, the focal point of the Soviet Union is in the West, not the East.

Secretary Kissinger: Frankly, I can develop an equally plausible interpretation for either course. I am not saying the focal point *is* in the East. I am saying that I do not know. But whether the focal point is in the West or the East, if they attack one, then the other will be the next victim. So it does not matter.

Foreign Minister Ch'iao: Well, this is a point of major importance, which affects how you look at the present situation and events of the future.

Secretary Kissinger: If the focal point is in the West, what should we be doing differently? How should we act [if the Soviets are primarily focusing on the West] as opposed to their focusing on the East? I am openminded—

Foreign Minister Ch'iao: Quite differently. Well, let me give you an historical analogy on this. If in 1938 the Western politicians had had a clear idea that the focal point of Germany was in Europe, things might have turned out quite differently.

Secretary Kissinger: But if in 1939 the Soviet Union had understood whether the focal point was in the East or the West, the situation would also have been quite different. But I am openminded.

Foreign Minister Ch'iao: To return to philosophy, you are a Kantian agnostic.

Secretary Kissinger: You have this basic advantage over me. You progressed to Hegel.

The Soviet Union believes that they can undermine the will to resist of the West politically—

Foreign Minister Ch'iao: Of course they wish to achieve this.

Secretary Kissinger: —but in the East, they must undermine it militarily. That is my view, but it is based on agnosticism.

Our policy is based on the proposition that a strategic gain on either [the U.S. or China] is a disaster for the other. Therefore we seek to prevent either.

Foreign Minister Ch'iao: You are right on this point. But you must have a very clear judgment about what is the focal point, as this has a bearing on many policies.

Secretary Kissinger: But if it is in the West, what should we be doing differently?

Foreign Minister Ch'iao (pauses in reflection): Your—

Secretary Kissinger (Ambassador Huang Hua): You are my advisor this evening!

Chang Han-chih (whispers in Chinese to Ch'iao): Helsinki.

Foreign Minister Ch'iao: Of course, your moves have both internal and external considerations. We have our differences. We notice your moves in the West and Eastern worlds. But some of your moves are not necessary.

Secretary Kissinger: But we are speaking now as friends. I know you want to strengthen Western Europe. We want to also. I would not consider this criticism.

Foreign Minister Ch'iao: I would not like to mention highly controversial points, even among ourselves. But I should mention the Helsinki Conference. We do not see why it was necessary for you to take such a step. Why didn't you delay? I do not know why you permit them to take such a form which is of need to the Soviet Union.

We do not exactly know your idea. Perhaps it was that Brezhnev is relatively good among the Soviet leaders and you thought you wanted to stabilize his position among these leaders. This is my own idea [of what the Secretary had in mind].

I will be very candid. There is a contradiction [in your position]: On the one hand you said that the Helsinki agreement has no binding force. On the other hand, [your agreement with the Soviets] took the form of a conference. This is contradictory.

Secretary Kissinger: Our motives had nothing to do with Brezhnev personally.

I once had the intention of writing a book on Bismarck. I find him more interesting than Metternich, with whom I am usually identified. Bismark was more modern. He once wrote that a sentimental policy knows no reciprocity.

The European Security Conference cannot be analyzed in the context of just this year. You have to understand it in terms of its history. It was around for more than ten years as an idea. We negotiated on it for three years. We used it as a safety valve these past three years for other problems.

My instructions to our delegation were that they should remain one step behind the other European governments. We did not take the lead—although we did not block the conference either.

Foreign Minister Ch'iao: This is what you told me last year. But at that time you had not decided whether to convene it as a summit meeting or a conference of foreign ministers.

Secretary Kissinger: That is correct. The foreign ministers' meeting was preempted as a result of Giscard's meeting with Schmidt in December [during which they agreed to hold the Conference at the summit level].

But I submit that you overestimate the European Security Conference.

Foreign Minister Ch'iao: No. That is not the case.

Secretary Kissinger: What is its significance?

Foreign Minister Ch'iao: The American press has almost compared the European Security Conference to another Munich.

Secretary Kissinger: The American press is in a mood of nihilism, complete unreality.

Mr. Foreign Minister, the same people who called the European Security Conference another Munich would organize a real Munich at the first crisis. The most destructive thing we can do is to pay attention to our press in its presently destructive mood.

There is one certain prediction: The only way to pursue a strong foreign policy is to do as we are now doing with the Soviet Union. If we are only rhetorically strong, the *Washington Post* and *New York Times* would be saying that we missed an opportunity for progress. Any third secretary in the Soviet Embassy could dangle hints of progress before the press, and we would be spending all of our time explaining why we are unresponsive. Just read our press of the 1960s! I would much rather have the *New York Times* to my right than on my left.

Foreign Minister Ch'iao: About our assessment of the Helsinki conference, there is one point I would like to clarify: We do not attach much importance to that conference. There has not been even one editorial in our papers, only some commentaries.

Secretary Kissinger: I do not know if I like that. Indifference is a worse punishment than criticism.

Foreign Minister Ch'iao: In our recent speeches we made criticism of the Helsinki conference. The Soviet Union has lauded it to the skies. But in terms of the international situation, this will all soon evaporate.

Secretary Kissinger: I agree. It [the conference] had to be brought to a conclusion, as its continuation gave it a greater significance than it deserved. It was not worth a battle over the question of [whether to hold] a summit. If the Soviet Union gained [from the conference], it was internally not internationally.

Foreign Minister Ch'iao: Whether this conference was convened or not, how long it was held, or the form it took—a summit meeting or foreign ministers' conference—these things cannot affect the international situation.

Secretary Kissinger: I do not think the results of the conference affected either. Borders—there are no unrecognized borders in Europe. They were all recognized before the conference.

Foreign Minister Ch'iao: But there are some difficulties in it. Politically, they [the Soviets] can make some propaganda—not legally—that the borders are now more settled.

Secretary Kissinger: But the borders of the Balkans were fixed in 1946; the borders between Poland and the Federal Republic were established at Yalta. There are no unrecognized frontiers. What fixes the borders now is the presence of 25,000 Soviet tanks between the Oder and the Elbe. Until that situation changes there will be no [political] changes.

Foreign Minister Ch'iao: But at least this conference gives people the idea that the Soviets can station troops in Europe.

Secretary Kissinger: I doubt that we gave the Soviets anything in this agreement. We are trying to weaken Soviet influence [in central Europe] by [Presidential] visits and by our developing military relations with the Yugoslavs. But change requires a political process in Europe.

At the conference, the attitudes of Yugoslavia and Romania, and less so Poland, were most interesting.

At any rate, I do not exclude the possibility that we make mistakes—although I seldom will admit it. But our strategy is to weaken the Soviet Union.

Foreign Minister Ch'iao: I know you have taken some steps toward the Soviet Union—tactical measures.

Secretary Kissinger: At present no other strategy is possible—unless you have some other idea?

Foreign Minister Ch'iao (after a pause): Your former Secretary of State Stimson had a policy of "non-recognition."

Secretary Kissinger: We tried that with you for twenty years. It was not one of our most successful policies. (Laughter)

Foreign Minister Ch'iao: But in the end you gained the initiative. You did not recognize the Japanese occupation of northeast China as legal. In this you gained the initiative, so at the end of World War II as you did not recognize the Japanese occupation, the initiative was in American hands.

Secretary Kissinger: But the Soviets haven't—

Foreign Minister Ch'iao: Hasn't the United States accorded more or less recognition to what the Soviets are doing in Eastern Europe?

Secretary Kissinger: This is a different situation from northeast China, as technically there are independent governments there [in Eastern Europe]. But our strategy is to weaken the Soviet presence in Eastern Europe; to make it more costly for them to hold on.

Foreign Minister Ch'iao: But that is only one example. I agree that it is not an exact analogy.

Secretary Kissinger: We do not believe that the European Security Conference changed that situation in favor of the Soviet Union.

Foreign Minister Ch'iao: Perhaps this is the case with you, but quite many other countries think that the problems in Europe have been settled.

Secretary Kissinger: Which [countries]?

Foreign Minister Ch'iao: Just read their General Assembly speeches! You will see their groundless optimism, their great expectations about détente.

Secretary Kissinger: My impression—we have taken your advice about strengthening our relations with Europe. My meetings with my colleagues from Britain, Germany, and France, and others, indicate that they have no illusions.

Foreign Minister Ch'iao: You are right. Our European friends also told us the same thing. Our friends in Britain, Germany, France, and Italy said that they would first of all strive for détente, and secondly heighten their vigilance. Some of our friends told us that they would seek to strengthen their defenses.

Secretary Kissinger: I would not necessarily rely on the Italians. The others, more so.

Foreign Minister Ch'iao: Theoretically speaking, this is a two-sided policy. In actuality, what do they stress? Do they strive for détente, or to prepare for war?

Secretary Kissinger: The basic problem in every European country is the complexity of their domestic situations. Strong Communist Parties directed by the Soviet Union seek to use their influence to pressure the Socialists—except in Germany.

Foreign Minister Ch'iao: Therefore, the illusion of détente can only help the revisionist parties gain in influence.

Secretary Kissinger: Unless a series of crises create a situation where what you call the revisionist parties can claim that only they can create peace.

Foreign Minister Ch'iao: But now there is such a tendency.

Secretary Kissinger: It existed all the time.

Foreign Minister Ch'iao: But the atmosphere of détente has helped them.

Secretary Kissinger: That is a matter of judgment. I believe the previous atmosphere was of more help of them [than the present one]. But I understand the argument [you are making]. I do not believe it is a trivial one.

You remember that I suggested that you invite Senator Jackson to China as he represents a tendency which, if strengthened, would make a really strong policy impossible.

Foreign Minister Ch'iao: I understand that.

Secretary Kissinger: I agree with your concern about Europe. The European political structure was so affected by two wars that their leadership has lost confidence.

Take the Italian situation. This has nothing to do with détente. There is a complete collapse of will on the part of the leadership of the Christian Democrats and a misperception on the part of the Church of the real danger. Italy does not have a foreign policy.

Foreign Minister Ch'iao: How do you look at Portugal?

Secretary Kissinger: I don't want to be scolded by the Chinese representative at the United Nations again, so I will be careful. (Laughter)

One superpower has been active, so we are not far behind. Basically we thought that this was an internal Portuguese situation. And because of our internal situation we did very little.

We are now working with our European friends to keep groups supported by Moscow from gaining the upper hand. These has been a tactical improvement—a great tactical improvement—in the situation. The problem now is whether our European friends will celebrate a victory or realize that these Moscow-supported groups have to be systematically reduced in influence.

Foreign Minister Ch'iao: This struggle will be a long-term one. No matter what you tell your European friends, we tell our European friends not to overestimate the strength of the Communist Parties. We think we know them better than you do. We once told Western European friends to give a free hand to the so-called Communist Parties. Let them take power and expose themselves in power. They said that they couldn't think of such a thing.

Secretary Kissinger: I do not think you really do either. Do you mean [let them take power] in Portugal, or elsewhere?

Foreign Minister Ch'iao: Portugal. In that case, the Communist Party of Portugal cannot control the Portuguese army.

Secretary Kissinger: We do not overestimate the strength of the Communist Party of Portugal. We have to let things mature to a certain point. First, we did not have the domestic capability; and secondly we had to bring Western Europe to understand what the situation was. Thirdly, we had to make certain that Soares was not Kerenski.[4]

Anyway, the situation in Portugal is at an early stage and can go in either direction.

Foreign Minister Ch'iao: Well, I think that if our European friends, backed by our American friends, take tactful action, the Soviets cannot gain the upper hand.

---

[4] Aleksandr F. Kerensky became the leader of Russia following the revolution that overthrew the Czarist government in 1917. He was himself overthrown in the Bolshevik revolution later that year. Mario Soares, as the leader of the Portuguese Socialist Party, became prominent following a violent change of government in 1974.

I do not know if you remember, but you told me that ultimately the Soviet Union will have to use its army to gain influence.

Secretary Kissinger: What I said was that the Soviets cannot expand [their influence] without using military power to make their point. They have not won a political victory yet.

Foreign Minister Ch'iao: There is a good example to illustrate your point. If it were not necessary for the Soviets to rely on military force then it would not be necessary for them to put so many troops in Central Europe.

Secretary Kissinger: Yes, it is striking that thirty years after they put in troops [in the various Central European countries], the governments have no legitimacy. They have to govern with traditional nationalism.

Foreign Minister Ch'iao: In our view, if the Soviet Union takes adventuristic action it will lose Eastern Europe.

Secretary Kissinger: I agree, where do you think they will take action? Western Europe? This is why I have my doubts about their real focal point being Western Europe.

Foreign Minister Ch'iao (after a short pause): Well, the situation is very difficult. There are contradictions in everything.

We have stated our views to you on many occasions. Western Europe is the focal point—Chairman Mao told you—if the Soviet Union cannot gain hegemony over Western Europe, it cannot control the world. In our view, and your view, Eastern Europe is a liability of the Soviet Union, but they see it as an asset.

Secretary Kissinger: I agree that the Soviet Union's long-range objective is to turn Western Europe into a kind of Finland. The question is how it will really do that. I am speaking now as a professor, not as Secretary of State. Either they can do it by a direct move against Europe, or they can do it by moves which will demonstrate to Western Europe that they are [an] irresistible [force].

The question is whether they might make some move in the Middle East, or in the Far East [to demonstrate their power to Western Europe]. But I am speaking now as a professor; I am not making any predictions. From where I sit, as Secretary of State, we have to be prepared for any possibility.

Foreign Minister Ch'iao: Yes, you are right, but you have to have priorities on the basis of the urgency of the problem. I agree that the best way the Soviet Union can do this is to defeat Western European countries one by one, and turn the area into a Finland.

Secretary Kissinger: Yes, that is their strategy.

Foreign Minister Ch'iao: That is the first part of their strategy, because the Soviets realize that unless they do this they cannot realize the rest of their objectives.

There is an old Chinese expression said more than 2,000 years ago by a military strategist named Sun Tzu—Mr. Solomon will know this—that the best way to bring your opponents to their knees is not to use soldiers [but a political stratagem]. The Soviets want to do this, but in our opinion it is difficult to do.

Now the Soviet Union is waiting for an opportune time. Eventually it will see that its strategy will not work, and then it will have to use military means. Of course, now conditions are not right [for a resort to military force].

When I talked about the European Security Conference, I did not mean that it was important. I just meant that some words spoken in some quarters were not beneficial to Europe or to the U.S. This has caused some confusion in Europe.

Secretary Kissinger: Any confusion in Europe is not a result of the European Security Conference; it is a result of the domestic situation, particularly in Italy, and to some extent in Great Britain. It has to be dealt with at that level.

Foreign Minister Ch'iao: Let me add one point. After the European Security Conference, due to exaggerated and groundless propaganda, this has heightened the tendency of certain European friends to be negative [passive], especially these Christian Democratic parties.

Secretary Kissinger: The European Social Democrats are vulnerable to the Communist Parties. In Italy especially; not in Germany.

Foreign Minister Ch'iao: Not long ago I talked with Strauss. He said to me—this is no secret—the Soviet Union intends to bring up Willy Brandt again.

Secretary Kissinger: Perhaps that is correct.

Foreign Minister Ch'iao: As he told me, they had grounds to expect this. I don't know, as I don't know Schmidt very well.

Secretary Kissinger: Brandt wants to bring up Brandt again!

Foreign Minister Ch'iao: Schmidt is not in good health.

Secretary Kissinger: Schmidt is a good man, although he is not in good health. He has a thyroid condition, and some other [physical] problems, but he is very strong [as a leader]. Schmidt made a great mistake—we are old friends; we were introduced in 1955 as we were both considered promising young men—when I was made Secretary of State he was made Finance Minister. I thought I had finally gotten ahead of him. He now has retaliated and I can never outmatch him because of our Constitution [which prevents a foreign born citizen from being President]. So now I am a revolutionary. (Laughter)

He made a basic mistake. When he was made Chancellor, he did not also have himself made head of his party.

Foreign Minister Ch'iao: The Soviet strategy is to foster the Christian Democrats in Western Europe and then to encourage the Communist Parties to merge with them.

Secretary Kissinger: Yes. This is why the Italian Christian Democrats are no barrier [to the expansion of Soviet influence] as they cooperate with the Communist Party. But as long as Schmidt is Chancellor in the Federal Republic, this cannot happen [in Germany].

Foreign Minister Ch'iao: Let me tell you a joke I read recently. The German Christian Democratic leader Kohl visited Moscow at the same time that Strauss was visiting Peking to attend the West German [industrial] exhibition. Our press issued an announcement about Strauss' visit to China, and so the Soviet Union refused to receive Kohl for three days.

Secretary Kissinger: The Soviet Union is very stupid. They should know that it is Strauss' nature to visit all sorts of industrial exhibitions.

When I visited the Soviet Union last year, when I was in the Crimea, Brezhnev complained bitterly about Schmidt and Genscher. I said, "Of course you didn't have to send two spies." They replied, "First, East Germany sent the spies; and secondly, we did not order Brandt to hire them."

Foreign Minister Ch'iao: I heard that later Brezhnev apologized to Brandt. I do not know if this is true or not.

Secretary Kissinger: But Brandt did it to himself.

Anything we can do to strengthen Schmidt will be helpful. He is coming to Washington soon.

You mentioned earlier the Soviet speculation about the economic situation in the West. You might like to know that we are planning a meeting soon between the President, Giscard, Schmidt, and the Japanese to coordinate economic policy and deal with this situation.

Foreign Minister Ch'iao: May I ask a question? How do you evaluate the Miki government? Because last year in Soochow we [Ch'iao and the Secretary] talked about the situation in Japan. We had not thought such changes [as have occurred since] were possible. We said we would keep you informed. I can tell you that before Miki took power we thought he was a friend of China.

Secretary Kissinger: I know he is a friend of China. He is a thoughtful man, but he heads a weak government. He does not have very great confidence. They are very timid. We do not think [the Miki government] will last more than two years. But I agree that his policy towards China is one of friendliness.

Foreign Minister Ch'iao: Not completely so.

Secretary Kissinger: Because of the hegemony clause?

Foreign Minister Ch'iao: Exactly! Do you agree?

Secretary Kissinger: I told their Foreign Minister that you [Ch'iao] were right when you said I had something to do with drafting this [clause in the Shanghai Communiqué dealing with hegemony].

Foreign Minister Ch'iao: I told them to criticize either me or you.

Secretary Kissinger: They fear that you will apply the hegemony clause to us.

Foreign Minister Ch'iao: Yesterday I talked with the Japanese Foreign Minister about this situation and made an explanation. I told them on this point that, first, it was discussed and agreed upon by the U.S. and China; secondly, I indicated that the anti-hegemony clause is not aimed at undermining relations between Japan and the United States. He understands this. The main trouble is pressure on them by the Soviet Union.

Secretary Kissinger: You must know that we told him [Miyazawa] that we cannot oppose something that we ourselves signed.

Foreign Minister Ch'iao: Yes. I also told the Japanese Foreign Minister that China and the United States had reached agreement on this clause, and that also we had reached agreement with some small Southeast Asian countries—Thailand, the Philippines, and Malaysia. The Soviet Union did not protest then, only in the case of Japan.

Secretary Kissinger: Do you think they will sign [a peace and friendship treaty with the anti-hegemony clause]?

Foreign Minister Ch'iao: I don't know. I do not understand their internal problems.

Secretary Kissinger (rising with his glass): Mr. Foreign Minister, friends, it is a pleasure to welcome you to the United States. If I am not mistaken, this is your seventh visit to the U.S. It proves that you cannot let me be ahead in anything, even in the number of visits. (Laughter)

We have noted in general that you have this tendency not to let us get ahead of you. Next year we will be having our 200th anniversary. You sent us your archaeological exhibition to show us that 200 years is but a brief period in Chinese history.

Mr. Foreign Minister, your country and ours have a rather strange relationship. Many things we don't agree upon. Occasionally we make that public. And yet, we talk more frankly to each other, and in more depth, than with almost any other nation. This is because of certain objective factors, and certain necessities which have brought us together and which we assess in the same way. Among these [areas of agreement] I must include the phrases in the Shanghai Communiqué concerning hegemony, which we just discussed.

As I said in my speech to the UN General Assembly, we attach great importance to our relations with the People's Republic of China. We are prepared to cooperate in those basic perceptions we share.

We value these visits and our conversations; therefore, we welcome you.

So now let me propose a toast: to the health and long life of Chairman Mao and Premier Chou En-lai; to the health of Mr. Foreign Minister, and friends, to the friendship of the Chinese and American peoples. Kan-pei. (All rise and toast.)

(There was some discussion back and forth between the Chinese and American sides to clarify exactly how many times Foreign Minister Ch'iao had been to the United States. It was finally agreed that the number was seven, including two visits he had made to the U.S. in 1950.)

Foreign Minister Ch'iao: I would also like to say a few words.

Respected Mr. Secretary—or rather, respected Dr. Kissinger. We once reached an agreement that I would call you Mister Doctor, and that you would call me Mr. X. Today you have already breached our agreement. But this is not important, this is just a superficial phenomenon.

What is important is that each time we meet we discuss important questions. We are quite candid. Sometimes we have heated discussions, but this is not important. If we talked only superficially, that would be senseless.

As for relations between our two countries, they are stated clearly in the Shanghai Communiqué. I believe that our two countries, China and the United States, have a determination to continue on the path charted by the Shanghai Communiqué.

When I was young, I read a sentence—I do not know where, perhaps it was by a Marxist—"The situation is stronger than man. A man may think this way or that way, but the situation is stronger than man."

I believe that in the present changing world, we have many common grounds—although you belong to the Kantian school, and I belong to the Hegelian school. They lived at the same time, under similar circumstances.

Now I would like to propose a toast: To Mr. President Ford; to our friend Mr. Secretary of State; to our new friend Mr. Moynihan; and to our old friends, Mr. Habib, Mr. Gleysteen, Mr. Solomon, and to Mr. Lord—who is half Chinese, because he has a Chinese wife. (All rise and toast.)

Secretary Kissinger: May I raise a few relatively brief problems here. Then we can talk about the President's visit, and my visit.

First, Angola, I want to discuss this with you. First, what is the problem of Angola? Geographically the railways connecting Zaire and Zambia with the sea go through Angola. Therefore the future of Angola has considerable impact on countries beyond Angola.

The United States has been next to nothing in Angola for many years. Starting in the early part of this year, the Soviet Union greatly increased its arms deliveries in Angola, indirectly via the Congo Brazzaville and directly or through its friends in Portugal. Its sympathizers in the Portuguese army allowed soldiers to retire from the army and join the military in Neto. So the Neto forces, which were the weakest several months ago, now are the strongest—not by revolutionary activity, but by outside influence.

We agree with your view [expressed] in the General Assembly that the three revolutionary movements should combine. But if things are left as they are, Neto will defeat the others and there will be nothing left to combine. If nothing is done, Zaire and Zambia will learn that forces supported by the Soviet Union can prevail, and therefore they will shift toward the Soviet Union. So we are trying—so starting in August, not before, we began to try to establish a balance between the forces of Roberto, Savimbi, and Neto; to establish a balance, together with Kaunda and Mobutu.

I am surprised that China has said it would do nothing. As long as the Soviet Union is active in Africa, this is important to China. If we are concerned with hegemony, why let the Soviet Union stretch its hands into an area as far as this from the Soviet Union? We do not want anything for ourselves.

Foreign Minister Ch'iao: Our viewpoint perhaps is not alike.

We believe that by doing so, the Soviet Union will eventually fail even though it may gain some military advantages for a time.

Of course, what I said to the General Assembly is the policy of the Chinese Government. This policy is principled, and also may have some effect on our African friends.

I have discussed this question with some of our European friends. I told them that China will not object to their adopting measures to prevent the Soviet Union from taking advantage of Neto. It is clear now that the civil war in Angola was provoked by the Soviet Union. As they provoked it, they cannot prevent others from taking actions. Since the Soviet Union provoked the war, it has no moral justification for preventing others from taking action against its actions.

If you have made a detailed study of our speech, you will see we know where the blame lies.

Secretary Kissinger: But forget about the speech. What do we do now?

Foreign Minister Ch'iao: Some of our friends want to enlist the help of South Africa. This is short-sighted.

Secretary Kissinger: We have received the same proposal. We also refused. We worked with Tanzania and Zambia. This has to be done by the blacks there.

Foreign Minister Ch'iao: I suggest we give this further study.

Secretary Kissinger: We *have* studied the situation. Do you want to exchange ideas on it?

Foreign Minister Ch'iao: We have a rather strict position on national liberation movements. Chairman Mao, you remember, told you that regarding the Middle East it was necessary to use dual tactics, to use both hands.

Secretary Kissinger: That is just what we are trying to do.

Foreign Minister Ch'iao: But the case of Angola is different. So far we haven't given up hope that this problem can be solved between the African countries and the three liberation movements. Do you believe this cannot work?

Secretary Kissinger: No, I believe—I will be precise. Roberto and Savimbi have to be stronger. I get daily reports of Soviet military shipments to Luanda. It is mathematically certain that Neto will prevail unless Roberto and Savimbi are strengthened—or else when the Portuguese leave, Neto will take over. So unless Roberto and Savimbi are strengthened, then there can be no agreement between the three liberation movements and the African governments.

Foreign Minister Ch'iao: Can you do any work with the Portuguese government?

Secretary Kissinger: We are, but it does not help with the arms that the Soviets have already put in.

Foreign Minister Ch'iao: How large are the Soviet deliveries?

Secretary Kissinger: Armored cars, they have about 30. That is a lot for Africa. 122 millimeter artillery. In Coxito they used the 122 millimeter artillery to great effect. The troops which had been trained on the Chinese model ran away. They need heavier weapons and training. Particularly Savimbi.

I understand that Chinese arms are held up somewhere. It is important that Roberto and Savimbi control the large part of Angola before independence. Otherwise Neto will declare independence and go to the UN.

Our people think this is a soluble problem it we act quickly. I repeat, we favor an outcome negotiated between the three liberation movements. But in a few weeks the outcome will be decided.

Foreign Minister Ch'iao: Good. I have taken note of your views.

Secretary Kissinger: If you want to be more specific, have your Ambassador in Washington get in touch with us. We can give you more precise assessments of the weapons they have and the weapons they need.

This is a clear situation of interference from abroad. We are prepared to help Roberto and Savimbi with weapons. Indeed, we are helping already to some extent.

Now Habib will have another heart attack. This is against all the principles of his bureau.

Mr. Habib: We are just peace-loving.

(The party rises from the dinner table and returns to the Secretary's sitting room.)

Secretary Kissinger: I will arrive in China on the 19th. I will stay a day in Japan [before coming to China].

Foreign Minister Ch'iao: Will you bring your wife?

Secretary Kissinger: Yes. I also was thinking of bringing Mr. Lynn, the head of our Office of Management and Budget. I thought it would be useful for him to know something about China.

Foreign Minister Ch'iao: Well, we will consider this.

So you will arrive on the 19th. In the morning or in the afternoon?

Secretary Kissinger: About 3:00 p.m. in the afternoon.

Foreign Minister Ch'iao: How many days will you stay?

Secretary Kissinger: Maybe until the 23rd.

Before I get to this, let me briefly discuss Southeast Asia.

We, of course, no longer have a principal interest in Southeast Asia. In so far as we have, it is in preventing the hegemonial aspirations of others. In time we will have no reason not to establish relations with Vietnam.

Foreign Minister Ch'iao: Of course, regarding this question we know your domestic situation. We believe that the U.S. should not mind what happened in the past.

Secretary Kissinger: We don't. The question is that your friends in Vietnam do not have an excessively low opinion of themselves. Therefore, we want to let reality begin to sink in for a while. Then we can establish relations which will more accurately reflect the real world. This has nothing to do with the past.

Foreign Minister Ch'iao: Well perhaps. One thing that we told you is that you are too emotional in your actions.

Secretary Kissinger: We are trying to be practical.

Foreign Minister Ch'iao: Of course, it would not have been necessary for me to discuss this, but the *Mayaguez* was totally unnecessary.[5] But this is not important.

Secretary Kissinger: This gets me to the real point I wanted to discuss.

---

[5] See Document 110.

We see no reason not to begin discussions with Cambodia. If Prince Sihanouk or other members of the Cambodian delegation want to begin discussions, we are prepared.

Foreign Minister Ch'iao: I will be very honest with you. Prince Sihanouk and other members of the delegation feel that the U.S. harmed them so much that it is not easy for them to take the initiative.

In the interest of the overall situation, we hope you will have proper relations with Cambodia. Take the initiative with the Cambodians. I give you this advice as a friend and not on behalf of Prince Sihanouk, or the other Cambodian officials. Of course, I cannot reply on their behalf. But it is my estimate that they will give you proper courtesy.

Please go on with Southeast Asia.

Secretary Kissinger: Our only interest is in the independence of the various countries [in the region].

Foreign Minister Ch'iao: This is the same with us.

Secretary Kissinger: That is why we thought that the improvement of your relations with Thailand was a positive thing. We spoke in this sense to the Thai Foreign Minister last spring.

Foreign Minister Ch'iao: Chatchai. He has gone home already.

Secretary Kissinger: But he will come back.

So our policy is to support countries [in Southeast Asia] against foreign aggression.

Foreign Minister Ch'iao: Of course, bygones are bygones. But we hope you will learn lessons from the past and support the independence of these countries. This will make some real friends for the United States.

(The Foreign Minister rose and indicated he wished to take a break. The Secretary escorted him towards the washroom. After a few minutes the Foreign Minister returned and the conversation resumed.)

Secretary Kissinger: A great deal depends on Cambodia—on the exuberance of their language in the General Assembly—whether we can make any overtures to them this session.

Foreign Minister Ch'iao: Since they have come [to New York], and as the U.S. is a major power in the world, they should be received with a proper reception.

Secretary Kissinger: There are two questions here. First, they will receive a proper reception. But on the [second] issue of initiating discussions, it will be necessary for them to moderate their language.

Foreign Minister Ch'iao: This is their affair. The Cambodians—I think their language is strong, although their actual language is another thing.

Secretary Kissinger: I think there is a relationship between language and reality.

Foreign Minister Ch'iao: As I told you just now, I don't want to provoke a dispute—as there doesn't exist such a thing in our relationship—but the *Mayaguez* incident hurt their feelings. It will take them some time to forget.

Secretary Kissinger: Well, it is up to them. They can't do much for us. Hostile speeches won't be printed on the front page of the *New York Times*. As far as we are concerned, our only interest is in the independence of the countries of Southeast Asia. I wanted you to know this.

Foreign Minister Ch'iao: I'll very sincerely—I very sincerely hope you have learned your lessons from Indochina. It is up to you if you have learned your lessons. It is your affair whether you want to consider this [meeting with the Cambodians] or not.

In our view, the general situation in Southeast Asia is good. I don't know how you view the situation?

Secretary Kissinger: I think we are seeing the beginning of a process of evolution. As far as the United States is concerned, we have good relations with all of the countries [of the region] except for Indochina. I would not preclude the possibility of Vietnam having certain hegemonial aspirations with regard to Laos and Cambodia.

Foreign Minister Ch'iao: It is possible, as a result of the influence of outside forces. But we doubt that it can succeed.

Secretary Kissinger: With respect to Laos, it is easier to succeed than with Cambodia.

Foreign Minister Ch'iao: If such is the case, there has only been a short period of time.

Secretary Kissinger: Our estimate is that there are now 2,000 Soviet technicians in Laos.

Foreign Minister Ch'iao: What is the significance of 2,000 even 3,000 Soviet technicians? The main question is if they can achieve popularity there.

Secretary Kissinger: I think the main question is influence from Hanoi.

Foreign Minister Ch'iao: Perhaps. Anyway, the history of the 30 years after the war in Asia is that an outside country cannot dominate any country for long. The Soviet Union for ten years wanted to dominate China. They sent a large number of experts to us to try to dominate us.

Secretary Kissinger: The question is whether China is stronger than Laos. (Laughter)

Foreign Minister Ch'iao: This is only a matter of degree, not kind.

Secretary Kissinger: This is not our primary problem. I just wanted you to know our attitude.

Shall we talk abut the President's visit for a few minutes? We don't need to discuss practical problems. I can do this when I come to Peking next month. The issue is what we are trying to achieve. What in your mind is the purpose of the visit [of the President]?

Foreign Minister Ch'iao: We, when you were in China last time, when U.S. Senators or Congressmen visited China, we also discussed that it would be useful to exchange visits, to keep in contact. The visit of your President is a major event. In general we hope there will be some step forward on the basis of the Shanghai Communiqué.

Secretary Kissinger: It seems to me, as you said in your toast, the Shanghai Communiqué serves as a useful basis of our relationship, and we remain committed to it. We will carry out its provisions in all aspects.

Foreign Minister Ch'iao: That is good.

Secretary Kissinger: That is our policy.

Strategically, in light of our discussions, we [the U.S. and China] have pursued somewhat parallel policies despite profound ideological differences as we have common concerns.

Therefore, what we should look for—to us politically, domestically, this is not now a major event, but from a foreign policy point of view there should be some symbolic advance. This should not be a visit of two enemies who are using each other, but rather of two countries who are cooperating on certain questions.

Foreign Minister Ch'iao: There is no question about it. We have our common ground, as is stated in the Shanghai Communiqué.

Secretary Kissinger: But when you said we should have some advance [in our relationship], what did you have in mind?

Foreign Minister Ch'iao (laughs nervously): I was just speaking abstractly. As Vice Premier Teng Hsiao-p'ing told many U.S. friends, it is useful for the two sides to have discussions. We can see if there is a step forward on the basis of the Shanghai Communiqué. But it doesn't matter if there is none.

Secretary Kissinger: Do you have any idea about what kind of document might be published as a result of the President's trip?

Foreign Minister Ch'iao: On this question my mind is a blank.

Secretary Kissinger: Anyway, we will change it [the document] on the last night. You know, I cannot remember anything of the last night of our discussions [during President Nixon's visit to China], of any of the issues discussed.

Foreign Minister Ch'iao: I admire you. Immediately after our talks you held a press conference, and did so at great ease.

Secretary Kissinger: I remembered the document in great detail—every version we had drafted.

Let me speak of advances, on the problem of Taiwan, and then other problems.

On Taiwan: We cannot complete the process on this visit. It is domestically impossible on this visit, and I have told you this. But perhaps we can think of some formula that can take us short of [completion of] the process.

Foreign Minister Ch'iao: That depends on you. I can do nothing. The famous version of the Shanghai Communiqué was proposed by you.

Secretary Kissinger: Except for the two sections [where the U.S. and Chinese sides expressed their differing points of view]. That was proposed by you.

Foreign Minister Ch'iao: This is not a departure from diplomacy. This is a reflection of realities. The world is such that we have contradictions between us, but we also have common ground. So the Shanghai Communiqué is a new creation, a reflection of realities.

Secretary Kissinger: But should we have a communiqué, or just an announcement about the President's visit?

Foreign Minister Ch'iao: I cannot tell you at this moment. As I told you, my mind is a blank.

Secretary Kissinger: That in itself is an historic event.

Foreign Minister Ch'iao: We can discuss many problems in Peking.

Secretary Kissinger: My idea is not to take too many chances during the visit of the President. We should work out the outlines of a communiqué.

Foreign Minister Ch'iao: I agree.

Secretary Kissinger: Our idea is that in all categories of the Shanghai Communiqué on which we can come to some agreement, we be prepared to show some progress.

Foreign Minister Ch'iao: It would be good if we can achieve that. We understand that you have problems. We have no problems.

Secretary Kissinger: But you understand that we cannot complete the process regarding Taiwan, but we can have some progress [in other areas]?!

Foreign Minister Ch'iao (obviously seeking to reorient the discussion): As friends, as this is not the first time that we have met, how do you view the world situation? Can we have peaceful coexistence; or will war break out?

Secretary Kissinger: As a friend?

Foreign Minister Ch'iao: I am not the Foreign Minister, and you are not the Secretary of State!

Secretary Kissinger: It is possible for war to break out. As an historian it [the prospects for war] is more likely than not. As Secretary of State, I have to act as if war will not break out, or do my best to prevent it.

Foreign Minister Ch'iao: I do not think we disagree on this point. In your speech—in my speech to the General Assembly, my purpose was to raise the problem of the danger of war. Yours was to speak about the materialization of détente. But to speak of the materialization of détente, it may backfire.

Secretary Kissinger: But as a friend, when you speak of the focal point [of Soviet pressure being] in the West, this is part analysis and part tactics.

You are afraid—no, you are concerned that we will use détente to push the Soviet Union toward the East.

My view—that—maybe you are right. If the Soviet Union attacks in the West, we have no psychological problems, and of course we will resist. If the Soviet Union attacks in the East, the same psychological preconditions do not yet exist. And yet—if we are reasonable, the same strategic necessity exists [for U.S. resistance to a Soviet attack in either the East or the West].

Therefore, for us—a problem for us is to create enough of a relationship to China to make this [attempt to resist Soviet pressures] psychologically meaningful. This [discussion] is so you understand my thinking. From our point of view this is one purpose of the President's visit.

Foreign Minister Ch'iao: I do not agree with you on the point that our analysis of the focal point of the Soviet Union in the West is a tactic.

Secretary Kissinger: Partly, partly—

Foreign Minister Ch'iao: —and that China fears the West will use détente to push the Soviets to the East.

Secretary Kissinger: That does not matter. We have to be prepared in the West [for either eventuality].

Foreign Minister Ch'iao: I would like to remind you what Prime Minister Chou En-lai told you—

Secretary Kissinger: No, your position has been consistent.

Foreign Minister Ch'iao: Of course, when we talk you have your subjective views, and you have thought these out of our subjective views.

Secretary Kissinger: Mr. Foreign Minister, I do not exclude the fact that you may be right. We have to act as if you are right.

Shall we spend five minutes on Korea?

Foreign Minister Ch'iao: Okay—such a wide range [of topics]!

Secretary Kissinger: I think we have publicly stated our positions [on Korea]. They do not seem to be easily reconciled. But we are prepared to improve our relations with North Korea, but not if the price is isolating South Korea. I hope a way can be found during the UN debate not to drive this contradiction to its ultimate limit. Your Ambassador is a procedural genius. (Laughter)

Foreign Minister Ch'iao: This is not a big problem.

I think that after the events in Indochina, you exaggerated the situation in Korea. This problem is a very small one.

Our position is that your troops should withdraw at an early date. But you say this will not do. The overall situation of the world hinges on the situation in Korea?

Secretary Kissinger: You won't agree with me, but I do not think it is in your interests to see another precipitate withdrawal of American power. This would have a significant influence on Japan.

Foreign Minister Ch'iao: Things are quite complicated there, but this question has to be settled. I would advise you to have direct talks with the Korean side. But you have problems.

Secretary Kissinger: No, at the right time we are prepared to talk with sides that we have not talked to before. (Laughter)

One problem is that if the UN Command is abolished, we have to find some way to sustain the Armistice arrangement. Secondly, if we talk to North Korea at some point, it must include South Korea at some point.

Incidentally, your ally [North Korea] did not appreciate my proposal of holding talks with you. So they complained and rejected our proposal.

Foreign Minister Ch'iao: Never mind. Things in the world are so complicated. But some day there will be a solution.

Secretary Kissinger (with emphasis): But not in an American election year. It will not come in the fourth year!

Foreign Minister Ch'iao: Everyone will be pleased if this question can be resolved this year. But it will not be terrible if it is not settled this year.

Secretary Kissinger: But then we need to have *something* to talk about next year! (Laughter)

Foreign Minister Ch'iao (in English): If we didn't, Moynihan would be unemployed! (Laughter)

Secretary Kissinger: I can't imagine the titanic struggle when Moynihan and Huang Hua clash at the UN. I will tell Moynihan not to be the aggressor.

I am advised that some television people are outside. It is not necessary for you to say something to them. We didn't put them there. I think it is ABC.

Foreign Minister Ch'iao: I will meet them, but I won't talk.

(The Chinese arose to depart. There was some light chatter and exchanges of farewells as the American side escorted the Chinese party down the hall to the elevator.)

120.   Memorandum of Conversation[1]

Washington, October 17, 1975, 9:30–10:47 a.m.

PARTICIPANTS

President Ford
Dr. Henry A. Kissinger, Secretary of State and Assistant to the President for
National Security Affairs
Lt. General Brent Scowcroft, Deputy Assistant to the President for National
Security Affairs

SUBJECTS

China; Middle East; Sadat Visit

[Omitted here is discussion unrelated to China.]

Kissinger: On my China trip [October 19–23],[2] I would propose negotiating the communiqué of your trip so you don't have to do it. The Shanghai one had three parts: unilateral statements, an anti-hegemony statement, and a bilateral section—including statements on Taiwan. That language was ingenious.

What can come from your visit? There can't be complete normalization, although Nixon promised we would do it by 1976. But we can strengthen the anti-hegemony statement. On Taiwan, we have two options: One is to let the PRC state its position including peaceful change, we state our desire for normalization, and we note their view and our desire to work for a solution on the principle of one China. My staff likes this—I don't. They will reject it and then we will need a fallback. If they do, there will be pressure for full normalization because they will have approved peaceful change. The second option is to restate the Shanghai Communiqué but instead of saying "the U.S. does not challenge this position," we would affirm the one-China idea. That is unilateral and can be withdrawn. It would reduce our ability to recognize an independent Taiwan, but we could do that only in the context of a massive confrontation with the PRC anyway.

The President: Which formulation is better here politically?

Kissinger: I think mine is.

Scowcroft: I think there is no question about it.

Kissinger: The first option is the unanimous position of my advisors, but I don't support it. Once you accept it, we will be under pres-

---

[1] Source: Ford Library, National Security Adviser Memcons, Box 16, July–October 1975. Secret; Sensitive. The meeting took place in the Oval Office.

[2] Brackets are in the original.

sure to move because they have accepted peaceful change. We'll have all the liberals on us.

The President: What would the Japanese say if the Chinese tried to take over Taiwan?

Kissinger: They want us to protect Taiwan while they trade with Taiwan. The present situation where we protect Taiwan is best for everyone.

The President: What will we be doing for 4½ days in China?

Kissinger: They move at a leisurely pace. They will want to hear at length from you about the world situation—there is no substitute for that. They will expect a long session on the Soviet Union, Europe, Asia. If you get there Monday, they will give a dinner Monday night; on the following events there will be one cultural show, a reciprocal dinner, and then one evening free.

The President: How about Chou's health?

Kissinger: He may be on his last legs. You will meet with Mao. Soochow is nice; Hangchow is also. They will certainly want you to go to Shanghai.

The President: The first trip of Nixon was a tremendous extravaganza. There was massive television coverage. I think it would be good to do something different. What is there which is dramatic? See if you can find something different.

Kissinger: Why don't I suggest to them that you would like something Nixon didn't do? Sian is the first capital and there is excavating there.

The President: That might attract the television.

[Omitted here is discussion of the Middle East.]

121.   Memorandum of Conversation[1]

Beijing, October 20, 1975, 10:00–11:40 a.m.

PARTICIPANTS

China
Teng Hsiao-ping, Vice Premier of the State Council
Ch'iao Kuan-hua, Foreign Minister
Huang Chen, Chief, PRCLO, Washington, D. C.
Wang Hai-jung, Vice Foreign Minister
Lin P'ing, Director of American Oceanic Affairs, Foreign Ministry
T'ang Wen-sheng, Deputy Director of American Oceanic Affairs (translator)
Ting Yuan-hung, Director for U.S. Affairs, American and Oceanic Affairs, Foreign
    Ministry
Chao Chi-hua, Deputy Director for U.S. Affairs, American and Oceanic Affairs,
    Foreign Ministry
Shih Yen-hua, Translator
plus two notetakers

United States
Secretary of State Henry A. Kissinger
Ambassador George H. Bush, Chief, United States Liaison Office, Peking
Mr. Helmut Sonnenfeldt, Counselor of the Department
Mr. Philip C. Habib, Assistant Secretary of State, Bureau of East Asian and
    Pacific Affairs
Mr. Winston Lord, Director, Policy Planning Staff
Mr. William Gleysteen, Jr., Deputy Assistant Secretary of State, Bureau of East
    Asian and Pacific Affairs
Miss Karlene G. Knieps, Notetaker

Teng: Anyway, we welcome you on your eighth visit to Peking.[2]

Kissinger: This room is very familiar to me—I have been here quite often.

Teng: It is almost a year, eleven months actually, since your last visit. It should be said that there have been quite a few changes in the world in these eleven months and therefore there is a need to exchange views on these changed circumstances.

Kissinger: It is always useful for us to exchange views.

Teng: It doesn't matter even if we quarrel a bit.

Kissinger: It gives the press something to write about.

Teng: Yes, and I believe they are immediately going to report that sentence.

---

[1] Source: Ford Library, National Security Adviser, Kissinger Reports on USSR, China, and Middle East Discussions, 1974–76, Box 2, China Memcons and Reports, October 19–23, 1975, Kissinger's Trip. Secret; Sensitive. The meeting took place in the Great Hall of the People.

[2] Deng welcomed the U.S. party and briefly chatted with Kissinger the previous evening. (Memorandum of conversation, October 19; ibid.)

Kissinger: We should ask the Foreign Minister to fire the empty cannon; then they would have even more to report.

Teng: They are all men of letters and they have very deft hands.

Now, since the press have left, the Doctor is free to express his views.

Kissinger: Now we can say what we really think of each other.

Teng: Yes.

Kissinger: How does the Vice Premier propose that we proceed?

Teng: What is your idea?

Kissinger: We have a number of topics to discuss. As the Foreign Minister said yesterday, we have to prepare for the President's trip, and we should discuss that from the point of view of substance and procedure. With respect to substance, we would like to discuss both the public and the private aspect. That is, the sort of speeches that will be made and the sort of communiqué that will emerge. With respect to procedures, it is just a matter of where the President will go and what your proposals are. The second (topic) is a review of the world situation. The third is our bilateral topics.

And we would like with respect to the first topic to agree on an outline of a communiqué on this trip so that we avoid any possible misunderstandings during the President's trip.

Teng: As for the question of the communiqué, I believe you said last night that you have prepared a draft you would like to show to us. We can ask that you and our Foreign Minister first discuss the particular details (of a draft communiqué).

As to the places the President would like to visit, since he has been here before, we would like to defer to his preferences. I believe that is easy.

As for what we will say to each other after he comes, we can say whatever we want to say to each other. For instance, I have said before this to visiting American friends that it will be all right if we have discussions; also all right if we do not. It will be all right if our minds meet, or if they do not. We will welcome him.

Kissinger: There are two aspects to our discussions—the public and the private. The private discussions should be a very frank review of the world situation and our bilateral relations. (In the case of the public discussions,) it would serve the interests of neither side if it would appear that we were quarreling. I think we should reserve that for the UN and not for a Presidential visit.

Teng: There is still time for further discussions on that . . . for further concrete discussions. I suppose you mean the communiqué?

Kissinger: Quite frankly—and we can discuss it more privately on some occasion—I have in mind partly the communiqué and partly what our newspapers will be writing. What binds us together is our common concern about hegemonial aspirations. It is our hope that the visit will be properly understood by our public.

Teng: I believe we will touch upon such matters during our discussions here.

Kissinger: At the end of this meeting perhaps we could leave five or ten minutes and I will give our communiqué draft to the Foreign Minister and I will explain what we are trying to do so that you can adjust it in the direction that is appropriate for you.

Teng: Alright.

Kissinger: The present plan, if this is agreeable to you, would be for the President to arrive here Monday, December 1 in the afternoon. And then to leave the following Saturday afternoon. That would be the 6th.

Teng: There is nothing inconvenient about the time with us.

Kissinger: And he will not visit any other countries in Asia while he is on this trip. (Earlier) I indicated to the Chief of your Liaison Office, who, I understand speaks perfect English now, that we might visit Indonesia but we have found that the press of preparing the budget and the State of the Union Address and other matters require the President's return immediately via Hawaii.

For your information, we plan that the Vice President visit Asia in February or March instead of the President.

Would it be convenient for you if, assuming we agree on major things here, that we send a technical advance party here the first week of November for about a week? My paper here says the advance people would number 65 people, but that cannot be true. We will reduce the numbers, but at any rate we will need an advance party and we will agree on the numbers. That is ridiculous—65 people.

Teng: It is not a great matter. It will be alright if you send 100.

Kissinger: The first time that I came here Prime Minister Chou En Lai asked me how many people would come with the President. I had no idea and I said maybe 50. I didn't realize that there were more than 50 security people alone. Eventually about 500 came, if I remember correctly.

We will, then, send the technical advance people the first week of November?

Teng: That is agreed upon.

Kissinger: Alright. And we will be in touch with the Liaison Office about the precise times and numbers.

Teng: Fine.

Kissinger: And we recommend that the television networks work out their own arrangements with you rather than through us, if that is agreeable to you.

Teng: I think that is alright.

Kissinger: They will also get in touch with the Liaison Office.

Shall we assume that the total numbers will be comparable to the Nixon visit on our side, including press?

Teng: I think that would be possible. A little bit more or less would not be of consequence to us.

Kissinger: There is no need to arrange separate meetings for the Secretary of State on this trip. All right. Shall we discuss other matters now?

Teng: Please.

Kissinger: Maybe a brief review of the international situation and the issues that we face?

Teng: Fine.

Kissinger: We have never had any illusions about our differences. And in any event the Foreign Minister is always there to remind us of them. But we also believe that we were brought together by certain strategic necessities. And therefore to us our relationship is not that of two enemies using each other but of two countries having a similar problem and working on it cooperatively. The strategic necessity which we both face is that of the Soviet threat. I think it is important to understand that here we face three problems: one, the overall strategy; second, the tactics that we have to pursue; and third, our relationship as it relates to the overall international situation.

As far as our strategic assessment is concerned we believe that the Soviet Union is gaining in strength and that at some point it may be tempted to translate that strength into political adventures. We think it is gaining in strength, not as a result of détente policies, but as a result of the development of technology and the general state of the economy. Since the Soviet Union is both a European and an Asian country, it is important to prevent it from achieving hegemony in either place. And since we are the principal element of defense against the Soviet Union, we have to be strong in both places. As I have said to your Foreign Minister, I do not know which theory is correct—whether they are feinting in the East to attack in the West or feinting in the West to attack in the East. I do not think it makes any difference, because if they attack in the West and succeed, the East will eventually face a much more massive force; and if they attack in the East, then the West will eventually face a much more massive force. So, as far as the United States is concerned, the problem is not significantly different. Our strategy is to attempt to maintain the world equilibrium to prevent attacks in either the West or the East.

This leads to the second question: the tactics to be pursued in carrying out the strategy. And here, there is obviously a difference between us, although some of it arises from the difference in our geographic situation and our domestic situation. You believe in taking a public posture of great intransigence, though you do not necessarily act, for a variety of reasons, in every part of the world. We believe in taking a more flexible posture publicly, but we resist in any part of the world towards where the Soviet Union stretches out its hands. Therefore, in the Middle East, in Angola, in Portugal and in other places we have been quite active in order to prevent Soviet expansion, even when we had to do it alone and even when we were criticized for doing it.

In order to pursue this policy after the domestic upheavals we have had in America as a result of Vietnam and Watergate, it is absolutely essential for us that we are in a public posture at home that we are being provoked rather than causing the tension. You have to understand that those in America who talk most toughly are most likely to produce a paralysis of action in the various places around the world where we are now acting. The very people who are attacking us, now and then, for détente—I am speaking of Americans, I will speak of foreigners later—are also telling us what is wrong in the Middle East is that we are not settling it cooperatively with the Soviet Union—which has been our whole policy to avoid. You have seen enough of our people here so that you can form your own judgment. But if we had, for example, done what Mr. Vance and his crew recommended; namely, to renounce the first use of nuclear weapons, then the effect on our relative power rationale would lead to the Finlandization of Western Europe. But it cannot be, and we do not believe it can be in the interests of any country to allow the Soviet Union to believe we would accept a major strategic change—whether it is in the East or the West—concerning the use of nuclear weapons. It is in our interest to make the Soviet Union believe that we will not acquiesce in an overturning of the equilibrium no matter what weapons are involved. I cite this as an example of our position.

These are tactics for the conduct of our strategy. You need have no concern that we are conducting détente with illusions; we are conducting it as the best method for resisting Soviet expansionism. And we are not prepared to pay any significant price for it. Our being in this position enables us to maintain high military budgets year after year and to act as a brake on our allies.

Let me in this connection talk about some of our allies. With respect to Western Europe we think there are contradictory trends. On the one hand, our relations with the principal Western European countries have greatly improved. We have very many leadership meetings now at the highest levels, including the President and the Foreign Minister, where we have intimate exchanges.

On the other hand, we believe that in many European countries there is a tendency to base foreign policy on illusions. In many of them there is the temptation to substitute goodwill for strength. And in some of them parties controlled by Moscow are strong enough to influence foreign policy, as in Italy and to some extent France.

We greatly welcome the many visits of European leaders to the People's Republic of China, and we appreciate your willingness to give them your perception of the international environment. We think, therefore, that the visit of the German Chancellor here next week can be of great significance. Our assessment is that within the Social Democratic Party he is by far the most realistic. And he is much less of a vague and sentimental mind than his predecessor. So, he would greatly benefit from your perceptions. It would strengthen him domestically and I think it would benefit the whole European situation, since he also has great influence with Giscard.

But, as I pointed out, in Europe we have the problem of perhaps especially optimistic assessments of foreign policy and we are also concerned with a leftist trend—anti-defense rather than ideological— which invites a weak defense posture. We have had difficulties on the southern flank in the Mediterranean. Some of them caused by our own domestic situation, with which our Ambassador is no doubt fully familiar. No country can afford a weakening, extending over years, of its central authority without paying some price for it over the next years. But we are in the process of rectifying this, and if you separate the debate from the votes, you will see we have lately been winning on the votes in Congress, which is a reflection of public opinion.

We have improved the situation in Portugal and we hope that within the next four–six months we can solve or make major progress on the Turkish/Greek/Cyprus problem.

You are familiar with the situation in the Middle East. We believe that the Soviet Union has suffered a major setback, President Sadat is coming to Washington next week to continue the development of a common strategy. But here again it is an area where it is important for us to understand the relationship between strategy and tactics. We recognize that the best way to prevent hegemonistic desires in the Middle East is to bring about a permanent settlement. But we also realize that one cannot bring about a permanent settlement by rhetoric or by putting forward plans. Permanent settlement has a local component; it has an international component; and it has an American domestic component. Our problem is to synchronize these three aspects. We cannot master the local component unless we demonstrate the Soviet Union cannot bring about a conclusion. So that whenever the Soviet Union interferes, we have to go through a period of demonstrating its impotence. We also have to teach the Soviet clients in the Middle East that the only road to a settlement leads through Washington.

The second necessity we have is to get our domestic opinion used to a more even-handed policy between the Arabs and Israelis—as

Chairman Mao suggested when I saw him two years ago. Every previous comprehensive American effort has failed because of the inability to mobilize our domestic support. We now believe the objective conditions exist for a comprehensive settlement for the first time under American leadership. And we intend to move in that direction immediately after our elections.

In the meantime we will take interim steps to alleviate the situation. And in any event, no one else has any realistic alternatives. But it is our fixed policy to move towards a comprehensive settlement. The major danger now is Arab disunity exploited by the Soviet Union. And whatever influence other countries may have, especially on Syria, would be of great importance.

There are other issues: Japan, Southeast Asia, South Asia, and Korea. But we have several days to discuss them. I want to say one thing about Korea where we clearly have different views. We are not opposed to reunification and we are not opposed to a dialogue, but we are opposed to having separate talks with North Korea to the exclusion of South Korea. I would also like to say that it is possible that by forcing the pace of events too far, geopolitical realities could be created that are not always to the benefit of those who force the pace.

Let me say a word about our bilateral relations. On normalization, we have made clear our continuing commitment to the principles of the Shanghai Communiqué, and we will suggest to you some formulations in the communiqué which suggest some progress in that direction. We think it is important to show some vitality and forward movement in our bilateral relationship. We do not do this because we particularly care about the level of trade between the United States and China, and we believe also that China, having survived 2,000 years of its history without extensive contact with the United States, may manage to stagger on for many more years without extensive exchange between our various cultural troupes. We can even survive your favorite songs without revolution. But to us that is not the issue. To us the issue is how to be in the best position to resist hegemonial aspirations in the West as well as in the East. And if that is the case, it is important that we show some movement in our relationship. It is difficult to gain public support for what may have to be done if China is not an important element in American consciousness, and it cannot be unless there is some improvement in our bilateral relationship. This is entirely up to you. We have nothing very material to gain from it. But if there is an inequality in American public consciousness between relations with China and the Soviet Union, it is because nothing very substantial is happening in our relationship.

While I am here, Mr. Habib is prepared to meet with anybody you designate to discuss this relationship, if you are interested. It is up to you.

To sum up, we consider our relations with the People's Republic of China, as I have now said on two public occasions, a very significant element in our overall policy. It is that, because of our assessment of the world situation. It is that, because we believe it is important to maintain the overall situation against aspirations to hegemony. We are not doing it in order to be able to divide up the world in two with the Soviet Union—an opportunity which has often been offered to us, and which we have always rejected because we would become the ultimate victim of such a procedure. We told you about the treaty that Brezhnev offered to the President in Vladivostok.

So we are bound to have our differences in ideology and in specific countries, but I also believe we have some important common interests and it is those common interests which have brought me here eight times, I believe, for more extensive visits than to any other country. There are many other points we will want to discuss. I am sure you want to discuss Japan. And I have already discussed Angola with your Foreign Minister, where we would find it helpful if Tanzania would release some of your arms that they are blocking. But we can discuss that during the course of my visit here. You will have noticed that as a former professor, I spoke exactly fifty minutes.

Teng: Are you finished?

Kissinger: I have another fifty minutes at least, but I want to give you an opportunity first.

Teng: So, shall we first invite you to finish your speech and then we will give our opinion? You can go on to the next fifty minutes.

Kissinger: No. I have substantially stated my overall views. There is one additional point I wish to make. You must not judge the mood of the United States by the atmosphere in Washington. And you must not judge the attitudes of America by the mood of the most unrepresentative Congress we have ever had. This last Congress was elected in the immediate aftermath of the resignation of President Nixon when those who had been for him were very demoralized. I have been traveling through the country systematically and I am certain that we will get wide support for the policy that I have described to you. Your Liaison Office may not see that (mood) in Washington. It is no reflection on your Liaison Office—it is simply a reflection on Washington. This is all I have to say now and I will make more comments after I have heard from you.

Teng: I have listened carefully to the views and points regarding the international situation that the Doctor has given. There is a question I would like to ask. How much grain are you selling to the Soviet Union this year?

Kissinger: (Laughter) Let me explain the grain policy. I was going to mention it later. In the past the Soviet Union has bought grain in emergencies from the United States. Given the organization of our economy, we have no technical way of preventing this. So in 1972 they bought 20 million tons of grain. In subsequent years they bought very little. That means when they bought grain they have had an extremely disruptive effect on our economy. Also, we have had the problem of how to use their need for grain in order to bring about policies that are compatible with our interest, and how to do this in an economy that has no technical means of preventing the sale and to prevent pressures on us from our own agricultural interests. I want to explain our thinking to you so that you can understand it. So what we did this year is the following: they have a very bad harvest. We sold them about 9.8 million tons of grain. We then brought about a stoppage of further sales by pressure on the private companies, which caused us enormous domestic difficulties. We used this period of stoppage to force the Soviet Union to ship a substantial part of the grain in American ships, at about double the world rate, and giving us an opportunity to control the rate of delivery. We then insisted on a long-term grain agreement which will probably be signed today or tomorrow.

Teng: The annual amount?

Kissinger: About 6 million tons for five years.

Teng: The total is 6 million?

Kissinger: Annually 6 million tons. But the important point is that it forces them to buy when they don't need it, and it places a ceiling on what we have to sell when they are in an emergency.

Teng: Do you think that this massive buying of grain not only from the United States but also other quarters is only to fill their stomachs but also for strategic reserves?

Kissinger: We believe that they have had a catastrophic crop this year. It is about 160 million tons, below the normal of about 225. At Helsinki Brezhnev asked to buy 15 million tons from us on top of the 9.8 million he had already bought, but we are only going to sell him about 5 million more this year. All our information is that they will have to slaughter cattle this year to reduce their livestock because they are short of feed grains to feed them.

Teng: May I ask another question? That is, how are the negotiations about sales of American modern equipment and technology to the Soviet Union coming along?

Kissinger: What modern equipment and technology?

Teng: I believe you have constant communication with them on this.

Kissinger: They have constant interest in modern equipment and technology. We are not selling a great deal at this moment. Nothing of any significance.

Teng: We have noticed that France has been engaging in negotiations with them for long-term agreements involving about 2.5 million Francs.

Kissinger: While we have talked more than we have done in economic credits, the Europeans have done more than they have said. They have given altogether—between the Federal Republic and France—about $7.5 billion in credit. We have given them about 500 million over years.

Teng: $7 billion?

Kissinger: Yes. We have used the prospect of technology to moderate their foreign policy conduct and we are trying to employ a strategy of keeping the Soviets dependent by not selling plans but parts to them. It is the folly of the European countries that they are selling plans. Unfortunately the small amount of U.S. credits has had the effect of throwing the business into the hands of the Europeans who have no strategy at all. For us it is not a business proposition. We are doing it for a strategic proposition.

Teng: We have seen from publications that the amount of such dealings between the United States and the Soviet Union seems to have exceeded that of the European and other countries.

Kissinger: That is totally incorrect. The amount of dealings we can control; that is, governmental credits, have been less than $500 million. There may be another three or four hundred million of private credits. In any event, the things we can control we do in such a manner that they can always be shut off and that they do not have rapid completion dates.

Teng: May I ask another question? What is the Doctor's assessment of the consequences of the Helsinki Conference?

Kissinger: I do not believe . . . It is one point where I do not agree, where our assessments are totally different. We sometimes disagree on tactics. I do not agree the Helsinki Conference was a significant event. In America it has had no impact whatever and insofar as it is known in America, it is as a device to ask the Soviet Union to ease their control over Eastern Europe and over their own people.

In Western Europe if one looks at (specific) countries, it may have had some minor negative impact in a minority of countries. In France, Britain, and the Federal Republic it has had no impact. In Eastern Europe it is the countries like Yugoslavia, Romania and Poland which most want to be independent of the Soviet Union which have been the most active supporters of the Helsinki Conference. I do not think we should proclaim Soviet victories that do not exist. Our role in the European Security Conference, as I told you last year, was essentially passive. We do not believe it has had a major impact.

Teng: But we have noticed that those who have been most enthusiastic in proclaiming the so-called victories of the European Security Conference are first of all the Soviet Union and secondly the United States.

Kissinger: No. First of all the Soviet Union and secondly our domestic opponents in the United States. The United States Government has not claimed any great achievements for the European Security Conference. The Soviet Union has . . . must claim success since it pursued this policy for fifteen years.

Our indications are that the Soviet Union may feel—whatever they say publicly—that they have miscalculated with respect to the European Security Conference. All they got from the West were general statements about matters that had already been settled in the past while we have obtained means of very specific pressures on matters of practical issues.

There were no unsettled frontiers in Europe. The Balkan frontiers were settled in 1946–47 in the peace conferences in Paris. The Eastern frontier of Poland was settled at Yalta. The Western frontier of Poland was recognized by both German states. There are no frontiers in Europe that are not recognized. Not all of our politicians know this but this is legally a fact.

Teng: So shall we call it a morning and continue this afternoon?

Kissinger: Alright.

Teng: And we can give our opinions.

Kissinger: Shall I give the communiqué to the Foreign Minister?

Teng: Alright. Perhaps you could explain it here.

Kissinger: May I explain a few points? In the spirit of what I said earlier we expressed the most positive things which can be said which you may want to moderate. But leaving aside the rhetorical aspects of any communiqué there are three categories in our relationship which attract attention: one is what we say about hegemony; second is what we say about normalization; and the third is what we say about our bilateral relations. With respect to hegemony, what we say may help ease public opinion problems of some other countries, especially if we don't put it in the preamble. What we have attempted to do with respect to both hegemony and normalization is to go some steps beyond the Shanghai Communiqué.

Teng: One moment please. (Teng leaves the room.) You can continue. Please wait. Excuse us for a moment.

(Teng returns to the room.)

Kissinger: We did the same with the bilateral things. Since we don't know your thinking we put in everything that could conceivably be put down but to us the primary significance is symbolic. One or two things on the bilateral things I would like to explain in a more restricted meeting as I explained to the Foreign Minister yesterday in the car. More restricted on our side. I do not care who participates on your side.

[Secretary hands Communiqué to the Foreign Minister. Attached.][3]

Kissinger: Is two copies enough for you?

Teng: I think that is enough.

Kissinger: The last time I gave the Foreign Minister a three page Communiqué, he came back with three lines.

(Laughter)

Teng: If what you want to discuss in a restricted group is what you mentioned to the Foreign Minister in the car, if it is of that nature, then as Chairman Mao has made our position very clear to you in his discussions before, especially in the visit of 1973, it is our view that perhaps such restrictive talks will not be necessary.

Kissinger: It is up to you.

Teng: As for the Communiqué draft we will look it over and then we can further consult each other. I heard you have an idea you would like to . . . that you want to go to the Palace Museum this afternoon with your wife. Perhaps we should begin later. At 4:00 p.m.

Kissinger: Good.

Teng: So we shall agree upon meeting at 4:00 p.m. this afternoon. In this same room. Because this is very close to the Palace Museum.

Kissinger: That's fine.

Meeting ended at 11:40 a.m.

---

[3] The draft communiqué is attached but not printed. Brackets are in the original.

122. Memorandum of Conversation[1]

Beijing, October 20, 1975, 4:15–6:35 p.m.

PARTICIPANTS

Teng Hsiao-p'ing, Vice Premier of the State Council, People's Republic of China
Ch'iao Kuan-hua, Minister of Foreign Affairs
Wang Hai-jung, Vice Minister of Foreign Affairs
Huang Chen, Chief of the PRC Liaison Office, Washington
Lin P'ing, Director, Department of American and Oceanic Affairs, Ministry of Foreign Affairs
T'ang Wen-sheng, Deputy Director, Department of American and Oceanic Affairs, Ministry of Foreign Affairs
Tsien Ta-yung, Political Counselor, PRC Liaison Office, Washington
Ting Yuan-hung, Director, United States Office, Department of American and Oceanic Affairs, Ministry of Foreign Affairs
Chao Chi-hua, Deputy Director, United States Office, Department of American and Oceanic Affairs, Ministry of Foreign Affairs
Shih Yen-hua (Interpreter)

Henry A. Kissinger, Secretary of State and Assistant to the President for National Security Affairs
Philip C. Habib, Assistant Secretary of State for East Asian and Pacific Affairs
George Bush, Chief of the United States Liaison Office, Peking
Winston Lord, Director, Policy Planning Staff, Department of State
William H. Gleysteen, Deputy Assistant Secretary of State for East Asian and Pacific Affairs
Oscar V. Armstrong, Director, People's Republic of China and Mongolian Affairs, Department of State
Richard H. Solomon, Senior Staff Member, National Security Council

SUBJECT

Global Strategy for Dealing with the Soviet Union; the Historical Lessons of the 1930s

Vice Premier Teng: You visited the Forbidden City?!

Secretary Kissinger: I love to visit there. During my last trip I escaped my keepers and visited there by myself.

I appreciate all the arrangements you have made.

Vice Premier Teng: It seems to me that of all emperors and kings [in the world], the Chinese emperors did not know how to enjoy life.

Secretary Kissinger: Didn't know how to enjoy life?

Vice Premier Teng: In terms of food and clothing, yes; but in terms of the quality of their residences they did not know how to enjoy life.

---

[1] Source: Ford Library, National Security Adviser, Kissinger Reports on USSR, China, and Middle East Discussions, 1974–76, Box 2, China Memcons and Reports, October 19–23, 1975, Kissinger's Trip. Top Secret; Sensitive. The meeting took place in the Great Hall of the People. All brackets are in the original.

One other thing is that the Chinese emperors changed their clothes every day—new clothes every day! Do you think they would be very comfortable wearing new clothes every day? And at every meal the emperor would have 99 courses. Actually they could only take whatever was close to them.

Secretary Kissinger: It doesn't sound like trouble or hardship to me. If you give me one corner [of the Forbidden City] I would be comforable.

Vice Premier Teng: That was built by the Empress Dowager.

And the other feature of the Chinese emperors was that whatever [food] they thought of they would try to get immediately. The Imperial cooks would only give them food that was most obtainable. They didn't give them any other dishes, otherwise the emperor would kill the cooks!

Secretary Kissinger: Why was that?

Vice Premier Teng: Because the cooks could only get the things that were available in that season. If the emperor liked a dish and asked for it but could not get it, he would kill the cook.

Secretary Kissinger: That is what my staff does in the State Department. They try to limit my choices.

Vice Premier Teng: Let's turn to the subjects we are going to discuss. I will first explain our views.

Our relations were started in February, 1972. That was during President Nixon's visit to China. And before that Doctor made visits to Peking to prepare for President Nixon's visit to China. And we have stated on more than one occasion that we appreciate the first remarks by former President Nixon to Chairman Mao. When he met the Chairman he said, "I have come to China out of our national interest." We also appreciate that President Nixon took this courageous step. And we also understand the sincerity of President Nixon when he said that he had come to China out of the national interest of the United States. We believe this is not diplomatic talk.

And thereafter, the Doctor made several visits to China, and Chairman Mao told President Nixon, as well as the Doctor, that we have common points which were reflected in the Shanghai Communiqué. Our common aim is to fix the polar bear, deal with the polar bear.

I believe the Doctor also remembers that when in talking about the Middle East, Chairman Mao also advised the United States to use two hands. You should not only use one hand to help Israel, but also the other hand to help the Arab countries, especially Egypt. In the talk, Chairman Mao emphasized that China supported the Arab countries. And this position of China is different from that of the United States. But we can also see a common ground—that is we can both fix the polar bear.

Chairman Mao stressed on many occasions that between us there are certain problems of bilateral relations, but what is more important are the international problems. On international issues, we think we should look at the international problems from a political point of view. Only in this way can we have a common view, can we have coordination in some respects. And exactly on this point we appreciate the statesmanship of President Nixon. We have never attached any importance to what you call the Watergate event. By political problems I mean how we should deal with the Soviet Union. This is a question of strategy—a question of global strategy.

And this morning I listened attentively to the Doctor's remarks,[2] and according to what you said this morning the United States has a clear world view with regard to strategy, and now you are only thinking of tactics. As I understand it, tactics are guided by strategy and serve strategy. The tactics manifest in various fields may conform to the strategy and may also deviate from strategy.

The Doctor seems to believe that the Chinese are intransigent in tactics, and I know what you are referring to. You put stress on flexibility. If we are to make an assessment of ourselves, we can say that we have never been intransigent. We think that flexibility must conform to strategic needs. Too much flexibility leads people to wonder what the strategy really is.

This morning the Doctor first talked about strategy towards the Soviet Union. There exist differences between us in this respect. We believe the focus of the Soviet strategy is in the West, in Europe—in the Middle East, the Mediterranean, and the Persian Gulf—all the places linked to Europe.

Although the Soviet Union has stationed one million troops along the 7,200 kilometer border [between Russian an China] the Soviet strategy remains toward the West. The Soviet strategy is to make a feint toward the East while attacking in the West.

In this regard, the U.S. has stressed to us on many occasions the danger of a Soviet attack against China. I believe that the Doctor still remembers that Chairman Mao had a deep talk with you in this regard. He concluded that the polar bear is out to fix the United States.

We have heard, on not less than one occasion, that the Doctor has said that whether the Soviet Union was making a feint in the East while attacking the West, or making a feint in the West while attacking in the East, this makes not much difference.

We hold different views. How to assess Soviet strategy? This is not a matter of rhetoric but a matter of substance. This assessment is the

---

starting point of the tactics formulated to deal with international matters.

We say that the focus of the Soviet strategy is in the West and it is out to fix the United States. Even the one million Soviet troops stationed in the East are directed against the U.S. Seventh Fleet first of all and not merely against China. First we say that the Soviet troops are directed against the Seventh Fleet, and then Japan, and then China. Also we say that the Soviet focus is in the West.

We are also making solid preparations. But one should by no means be under the false impression that when China proposes this theory that China wants to direct the Soviet Union Westward so that the Soviet Union will not go to the East.

I heard that during your first trip to China, prior to President Nixon's visit, Premier Chou talked to you. I was not present, but he said China's strategy was to get prepared to deal with aggression from all sides. At that time we did not have the Shanghai Communiqué yet. Well, although I have read the verbal record of your talk, I do not remember what the original words were; but anyway, the Premier told you that even if the Soviet Union siezes the land north of the Yellow River, and Japan grabs the northeast, the United States the east, and India grabs Tibet, we are not afraid. That was what we thought at that time.

After the Shanghai Communiqué, we made no reference to these words. We have always believed that we should rely on our independent strength to deal with the Soviet Union, and we have never cherished any illusions about this. We have told this to the Doctor as well as to visiting American friends. We do not depend on nuclear weapons; even less on nuclear protection [by other countries]. We depend on two things: First is the perseverance of the 800 million Chinese people. If the Soviet Union wants to attack China it must be prepared to fight for at least two decades. We mainly depend on millet plus rifles. Of course, this millet plus rifles is different from what we had during Yenan times. We pursue a policy of self-reliance in our economic construction and also in our strategic problems.

As I said just now, we are not directing the evil of the Soviet Union Westward, but we are concerned about the West because if the Soviet Union is to make trouble its focal point is in the West. Naturally we are concerned about it. It is precisely proceeding from this assessment that we are interested in a unified and strong Europe—including the improvement of relations between Europe and the United States.

It is also precisely proceeded from this strategic assessment that we advised you to use both of your hands in dealing with Arabs and Israelis.

It is also precisely out of this strategic assessment that we expressed that we did not understand the attitude of the United States in the case when the Soviet Union and India dismembered Pakistan.

These are political problems as well as strategic problems, and these include tactics under the guidance of these problems, these strategic problems—for instance, when we advised you to use both of your hands [in the Middle East] this was tactics.

It was also precisely out of this strategic assessment that we have often told you, as well as Japan, that Japan should put a first priority on relations between Japan and the United States and then between Japan and China. This not only concerns the West but also the East.

On this point, we have advised our American friends on many occasions that the United States should formulate its own focus of strategy. We have often said the United States was keeping ten fleas under its ten fingers and that the United States should not let itself bog down in the quagmire of Indochina.

And out of this strategic consideration, when the United States was building its military base in Diego Garcia on the Indian Ocean China did not criticize this.

On these questions and a number of other issues we proceed from political and strategic considerations to deal with international problems as well as our bilateral relations. We have made our assessment of Soviet strategy after careful study of the international situation. In our talks with the Europeans, they have constantly raised the [following] question: "If there is trouble in Europe, what will be the attitude of the United States?" I will be very candid with the Doctor, the Europeans are very apprehensive on this point.

Secretary Kissinger: But *our* question is what will be the attitude of the *Europeans*?

Vice Premier Teng: Perhaps this has something to do with your relations with the Europeans. The Doctor may recall that in 1973 Chairman Mao asked you whether it was possible for the new isolationism to emerge in the United States.[3] You answered in the affirmative, negative term. You said no.

Secretary Kissinger: I just now said to Mr. Lord that I knew I was tricky, but I am not *that* tricky—to answer "affirmatively no." (Laughter)

Vice Premier Teng: But from that you can assess what Chairman Mao is thinking, what we are thinking about. This observation of the situation dates back as early as the first nuclear arms talks between the United States and the Soviet Union. Those talks took place in 1963. That

---

[3] See Document 58.

treaty was prepared by three countries, and it left a deep impression on me at that time. I made my last visit to the Soviet Union as head of the delegation of the Chinese Communist Party to negotiate with the Russians, and it [the non-proliferation treaty] was made public on the day when we left [Moscow].

At that time our talks with the Soviet Union were completely bankrupt, and we were certain that a most important part of the treaty was directed against China. I don't doubt that at that time the attitude of the United States and the British was to restrain the Soviet Union from nuclear development. Of course this is a strategic problem and, in terms of tactics, after more than nine years—nearly ten years—in this period things have changed. They show that the aim—the purpose—of these tactics has failed to be achieved.

In 1972, when you reached the second [SALT] agreement, the Soviet Union drastically quickened their pace in the development of nuclear arms. Their pace was quicker than the United States. When the third agreement [on prevention of nuclear war] was reached between your countries, it [the strategic balance] had reached equilibrium. In November last year when we met [after the Vladivostok meeting], the Doctor informed us that the number of Soviet missiles had not yet reached the ceiling, and this morning you told us that the number of Soviet missiles had exceeded the ceiling—leaving aside the quality.

This is our observation from one angle. And in the race between the Soviet Union and the United States, the United States has not gained. In terms of conventional weapons, the Soviet Union has far exceeded you and Europe.

It is almost eleven months since we met last year. During this period we have again made our observations. And through our observations we have got the impression that the Helsinki Conference is an indication—and not only the Helsinki Conference, but things before the Helsinki Conference—that it is worthwhile to recall history.

Secretary Kissinger: What things?

Vice Premier Teng: Well, problems of various descriptions [mentioned] earlier.

By recalling history, I mean the period prior to the Second World War—the period 1936 to 1939, which is particularly worthwhile to recall. The Doctor studies history and I think is more knowledgable than I.

As I understand, the Doctor once said that in actuality the Soviet Union has gone beyond the Rhineland. This shows that the Doctor has made a study of it. After the Germans entered into the Rhineland you may recall what was the attitude of the British and French, and what was the policy pursued by Chamberlain and Daladier. They pursued a policy of appeasement towards Hitler, and shortly after that the Munich agreement was concluded.

In pursuing such policies the purpose of Chamberlain and Daladier was obvious. They wanted to direct the peril Eastward, and their first aim was to appease Hitler so that he would not take rash actions. Their second aim was to direct the peril toward the East. The stark historical realities have brought out the failure of the policies carried out by Chamberlain and Daladier. Their policies have gone to the opposite of their wishes. They neither got international peace and stability nor achieved their purpose of directing the peril of Hitler to the East. Instead, the spearhead of Hitler was directed to the West—Czechoslovakia and Poland. These countries were in the West, and they [the Germans] did not attack the Soviet Union first.

If I remember correctly from what I read in newspapers, when Chamberlain visited Germany he carried an umbrella. But it neither shaded him from the moon or the sun—no, the rain or the sun. At that time France boasted that they had the Maginot line. But Germany did not attack the Maginot line. They attacked from Belgium and attacked France, and France collapsed and Chamberlain gave up all resistance. He mobilized all the ships to move from Dunkirk—that is, he wanted to slip away.

So in fact this appeasement policy led to an earlier break out of the Second World War. In our contacts with quite a number of Europeans they often raise the lessons of Munich. According to our observations, we may say that the danger of such historical tragedy is increasing.

The Doctor asked just now what were other things apart from the Helsinki Conference. I raised three questions to you this morning. This shows there were other things apart from the Helsinki Conference.

In terms of strategy, Soviet weapons have far exceeded those of the West. Also you have reached the equilibrium of weapons. In terms of total military strength, the Soviet Union has a greater military strength than the United States and the European countries put together. But the Soviet Union has two big weaknesses: One, they lack food grains; the second is that their industrial equipment and technology is backward. In the long run although the Soviet Union has a greater military strength, these two weaknesses have put the Soviet Union in a weak position. It is limited in its strength so that when a war breaks out the Soviet Union cannot hold out long.

Therefore, we do not understand why the United States and the West have used their strong points to make up for the Soviet weakness. If the United States and Europe have taken advantage of the weaknesses of the Soviet Union you might have been in a stronger negotiating position.

As for our views on the Helsinki Conference, I think you know our views, which differ from yours. We call it the European *Insecurity* Conference and you call it the European *Security* Conference. The Munich agreement pulled the wool over the eyes of Chamberlain, Daladier, and some European people. And in the case when you supply them, make up for the weak points of the Soviet Union, you help the Soviet Union to overcome its weaknesses. You can say you pulled the wool over the eyes of the West and demoralized the Western people and let them slacken their pace. We have a Chinese saying: A donkey is made to push the mill stone because when you make the donkey to push around the mill stone you have to blindfold it.

This is a political or we may say a strategic problem in the present situation which people are most concerned with. And we are now speaking our views on these problems very candidly.

As for the Russians, they now feel you cannot restrain them. They are not reliable and cannot be restrained. And, of course, in the West—including the United States—there are two schools of public opinion. A greater part of the public opinion has clearly seen this. A considerable, greater part of the public opinion has seen this. We understand that the Americans, Europeans, and including the Japanese, do not want a war because they have gone through two World Wars. This we can understand. They fear a war.

We always feel that to rely on the European Security Conference, or anything else in an attempt to appease the Russians, will fail. These things will be counter productive. For example, the Europeans fear war day and night. They hope to obtain peace for a certain period of time at any price. Exactly because of that, we should not blindfold them by the evolution of détente. We should remind them of the possibility of attack from the polar bear. So every time Chairman Mao meets foreign guests he advises them to get prepared. Without preparation they would suffer. The most effective way to deal with the possible attack from the Russians is not what you call agreements or treaties, [not] what is written on paper, but actual preparations.

As for China, we have told you on many occasions, and I will [again] tell you frankly, that China fears nothing under heaven or on earth. China will not ask favors from anyone. We depend on the digging of tunnels. We rely on millet plus rifles to deal with all problems internationally and locally, including the problems in the East.

There is an argument in the world to the effect that China is afraid of an attack by the Russians. As a friend, I will be candid and tell you that this assessment is wrong.

Today we are only talking about strategic problems. The Doctor was a former professor. I have taken my 50 minutes to talk and I have gone beyond 50 minutes. That was because I am only a soldier. It is not easy to confine oneself within 50 minutes. I once taught in a school. I gave a lecture for 50 minutes, but I have never been a professor. I have taken too much of your time.

Secretary Kissinger: No, it was interesting and important.

Can we take a five minute break, and maybe I will make a few observations?

Vice Premier Teng: Yes.

(There was a short break at this point.)

Secretary Kissinger: Do you want me to make some observations now, or how do you propose to proceed?

Vice Premier Teng: Yes. Please go ahead.

Secretary Kissinger: I listened with great interest to the Vice Premier's presentation and I would like to make a few observations.

First, I have noticed the frequent reference to President Nixon. I have worked very closely with President Nixon. And I think it is correct to say that we jointly designed the policy to which you referred approvingly. It is also the case that I am still in touch with him every two or three weeks at some length, so I know his views very precisely. I can safely say that the policy we are pursuing today is the policy that President Nixon would pursue if it had not been for Watergate. The policy toward the Soviet Union that is being pursued today was designed by President Nixon and myself and is the same that is being pursued today. There is no difference between President Nixon's policy toward the Soviet Union and President Ford's. If anything, President Ford is a nuance tougher toward the Soviet Union. And I say this as the one man in public life who has maintained contact with President Nixon and never criticized him and has stated publicly that he has made a great contribution in matters of foreign policy.

Leaving this aside, I must say I listened to the Vice Premier's presentation with some sadness. I had thought, obviously incorrectly, that some of the public statements which I had heard were said for public effect. But this is obviously not the case. Now what I regret is that I can understand two countries, operating from the same perception, can operate using different tactics—and can understand each other's tactics. That causes me no difficulty. But if there is not a common strategic perception, then one wonders what exactly the basis of our policy is. If you seriously think that we are trying to push the Soviet Union to attack in the East, then we are in grave danger of frittering away all our efforts—with yourself and everyone else.

The Vice Premier was kind enough to point out the lessons of history between 1936 and 1939. He pointed out that those in the West who tried to push the aggressor towards the East became the first victims of the attack; and that is true. But it is also true that those in the East who sought to escape their dilemma by pushing their aggressor toward the West eventually became the objects of the aggressor anyway.

And when we say that the West and the East have essentially the same strategic problem, we don't say this because we have an interest in participating in the defense of the East. Anyone who knows the American domestic situation must know that this cannot be our overwhelming ambition. We say it because strategically wherever the attack occurs it will affect the other. And you act on these assumptions too.

And we are saying this not to do you any favors, because you are not all that helpful to us in other parts of the world. We are doing this out of our own national interest.

In 1971, in January of 1971, before we had been in China, during the crisis in India, when India had dismembered Pakistan, I talked to your Ambassador in New York on a Friday evening. He told me that China always fights as long as it has one rifle. I then told him we would move an aircraft carrier into the Bay of Bengal. On Sunday morning, when we were on the way to the Azores to meet President Pompidou, we received a message that your Ambassador in New York wanted to see us; and we sent General Haig to see him. We thought then that you might be taking some military action. And we decided that even though we had no diplomatic relations—President Nixon and I decided—that if you moved, and if the Soviet Union brought pressure on you, we would resist and assist you, even though you had not asked us to. We did that out of our conviction of the national interest.

And we have said recently again to the Prime Minister of Pakistan—because he asked us about this—we said that we would not be indifferent if the Soviet Union brought pressure on China because of the Indian situation. He must have told you this. And again, you have not asked us to do this, nor did we do this as a favor to China.

So, since I have been in Washington we have gone to a confrontation with the Soviet Union three times: Once over a nuclear submarine base in Cuba; once over the Syrian invasion of Jordan; once over the question of the alert in the Middle East in 1973 and—no, four times—once on the question of access routes to Berlin. We did all of these things on our own, without knowing what any other country, much less China, would do.

The Vice Premier referred to the spirit of Munich. I have studied that period and I lived through it, as a victim, so I know it rather well. The Munich policy was conducted by governments who denied that there was a danger, and who attempted to avoid their problems by denying that they existed. The current United States policy, as we have attempted to tell you, has no illusions about the danger, but it attempts to find the most effective means of resistance given the realities we face. A country that spends $110 billion a year for defense cannot be said to be pursing the spirit of Munich. But the reality we face is a certain attitude that has developed in the United States and an attitude that exists also in Europe even much more.

I know some of the Europeans who you talk about. Some are personally good friends of mine. But there is no European of any standing that has any question about what the United States will do. In any threat, we will be there. Our concern is whether the *Europeans* will be there. It is the United States that organizes the defense of the North Atlantic and that brings about the only cohesion that exists. It was not the United States that advocated the European Security Conference. It was, rather, to ease some of the pressures on the European governments that we reluctantly agreed to it in 1971.

Now the Vice Premier is quite correct, this is a problem that greatly concerns us, whether the policy that is being pursued may lead to confusion. This is a serious concern. But the Vice Premier should also consider that the policy we are pursuing is the best means we have to rally resistance. If we pursued some other approach, the left wing parties in Europe might split the United States from Europe with the argument that the United States is a threat to the peace of the world.

If you follow the present investigations that are going on in America, you will see that it was the present Administration, including myself, that has used methods to prevent the Soviet Union from stretching out its hands—even if these are not your preferred methods.

And if we were slow in our disengagement from Indochina—and this was not a situation that we created—it was precisely to prevent the mood of neoisolationism from developing that Chairman Mao talked of. We do not rely on the European Security Conference. And we do not rely on détente. Nor is everyone in the United States who talks against détente a reliable opponent of the Soviet Union, because without a strategic grasp of the situation much of it [anti-détente talk] is simply politics. To talk tough is easy—to act with strength and maintain support for a strong policy over a period of time in a democracy is a difficult problem.

If the Soviet Union should stretch out its hands, we will be brutal in our response, no matter where it occurs—and we won't ask people whether they share our assessment when we resist. But to be able to do this we have to prepare our public by our own methods, and by methods that will enable us to sustain this policy over many years, and not go like Dulles from a period of intransigence to a period of excessive conciliation.

The Administration in the '50's started out not willing to shake hands with Communists [translated as, "with China"] and wound up almost giving away Berlin—had it not been for Khrushchev's clumsiness.

Our strategy is exactly as we discussed it with Chairman Mao three years ago. It has not changed, and it has the strategic advantage. But we have to be the best judge of the means appropriate to our situation. And we will not stand still for a strategic advance by the Soviet Union.

And we do not separate the fronts into East and West. If the Soviet Union feels strong enough to attack in either the West or the East, the policy will already have failed. The Soviet Union must not be in a position where it feels strong enough to attack at all.

Now I would like to correct a few other misapprehensions which the Vice Premier voiced, and then I will make one other observation.

One thing has to do with relative military strength. It is perfectly true that the Soviet Union has gained in relative strength in the last decade. This is not the result of the agreements that have been signed. This is the result of changes in technology, and the erroneous decision of the Administration that was in office in the 60's when the Soviet Union was building up its strategic forces. If you analyze the result of the [SALT] agreement of 1972, since 1972 the strategic strength of the United States has increased considerably relative to that of the Soviet Union. It is also true that after some point in the field of strategic weapons, it is difficult to translate military superiority into a political advantage.

With respect to the second agreement, the Vladivostok agreement, you must have translated what I said incorrectly from the German. There has been no change in the Soviet strength since Vladivostok. Since the Soviet Union does not dismantle their obsolete units, they have 2,700 units and they have had those for five years. After Vladivostok they would have to get rid of 200. Since we *do* get rid of our obsolete units we have somewhat less than 2,400. But numbers are not so important anyway, as each [U.S.] unit can carry more warheads. We have gone ahead by a ratio of 6 or 7 to 1. Moreover, since the Soviets like big things which take room, they have about 85 to 90 percent of their forces on land, where they are vulnerable because the accuracy of our forces is improved. Less than 20 percent of our forces are on land, and they are less vulnerable. So it is not true that in the strategic balance we are behind, even though there are many newspaper articles in America written for political purposes that assert this.

In 1960 President Kennedy was elected by speaking of the missile gap, even though the Soviet Union had only 30 missiles, each of which took ten hours to get ready to fire and we had 1,200 airplanes. Ever since then it has been the secret dream of every American presidential candidate to run on a missile gap campaign, so we are in danger of this issue erupting every four years.

In 1970 when we confronted the Soviets on the submarine base in Cuba, in 1970 in Jordan, in 1970 in Berlin, and in 1973 in the Middle

East, they always yielded within 36 hours when we made a military move. Their military calculations are not as optimistic as some of our European friends fear—such as Denmark.

On the question of food grains: We have moved at the slowest pace that is politically possible for us, and have even held up our grain sales —even while Canada, Australia, Argentina, and Western Europe have cleared out their bins in selling to the Soviets. The long term program we are now negotiating precisely prevents them from storing large quantities because it puts a ceiling on what they can buy in one year on the American market.

So our policy is quite clear, and in pursuing it we have not asked anything from China. We have kept you informed by our many discussions, but I don't recall that we have ever asked for anything from the People's Republic of China. Of course, China pursues its own policies, and we respect your independence. I hope you will make the positions which you made clear to us clear to every European visitor who comes here. We do not object to your public posture. We think it is essentially correct, and indeed it is even helpful. We *do* object when you direct it against us, when you accuse us of betraying our allies and endangering the security of the world by deliberately promoting war and standing on the side lines, when in fact we are doing actual things to prevent a war and preserve the world equilibrium.

And you should also consider that if the United States public finds too much discouragement around the world, and if everywhere we move we find the opposition of every country, then precisely this mood of isolationism which concerns so many other countries will develop.

We attach great significance to our relationship with the People's Republic of China because we believe you conduct a serious policy and because we believe your word counts. And we believe that the world is one entity from a strategic point of view and a political point of view.

We are prepared to coordinate actions along the lines of my conversations with Chairman Mao two years ago. But the world situation is extremely complex, and the domestic situations around the world are also extremely complex. It is important that you have a correct perception of our objectives. If you think we are engaged in petty tactical maneuvers then that would be a pity for both of us. You do not ask for favors, and we do not ask for favors. The basis of a correct policy is an accurate perception of the national interest and respect by each side for the perception of the national interest of the other.

This is why we think a visit by the President here would be useful, and that is the purpose of our policy. We don't need theater, and we don't need you to divert Soviet energies—that would be a total misconception and it might lead to the same catastrophe as in the 1930s.

After all we resisted Soviet expansion when we were allies, and we will resist it for our own reasons as you resist it for your own reasons.

I repeat, we attach great significance to our relations. We are prepared to coordinate. We think you are serious, and we are equally serious. On that basis I think we can have a useful relationship.

As I have not used up 50 minutes, I will use the remainder tomorrow.

Vice Premier Teng: Yes. It is quite late—shall we go on tomorrow afternoon?

Secretary Kissinger: Yes.

Vice Premier Teng: As to the time, we can discuss it later.

Secretary Kissinger: We are not going anywhere.

Vice Premier Teng: Right.

Secretary Kissinger: Good.

---

123.   Memorandum of Conversation[1]

Beijing, October 21, 1975, 5:07–6:08 p.m.

PARTICIPANTS

Teng Hsiao-p'ing, Vice Premier of the State Council, People's Republic of China
Ch'iao Kuan-hua, Minister of Foreign Affairs
Amb. Huang Chen, Chief of PRCLO, Washington
Wang Hai-jung, Vice Minister of Foreign Affairs
Lin P'ing, Director of American & Oceanic Affairs, MFA
T'ang Wen-sheng, Deputy Director of American & Oceanic Affairs, MFA, (Interpreter)
Chien Ta-yung, Counselor, PRCLO, Washington
Ting Yüan-hung, Director for U.S. Affairs, American & Oceanic Affairs, MFA
Chao Chi-hua, Deputy Director for U.S. Affairs, American & Oceanic Affairs, MFA
Mrs. Shih Yen-hua, MFA, (Interpreter) (plus two notetakers)

Dr. Henry A. Kissinger, Secretary of State and Assistant to the President for National Security Affairs
Amb. George H. W. Bush, Chief of USLO, Peking
Helmut Sonnenfeldt, Counselor of the Department
Winston Lord, Director, Policy Planning Staff

---

[1] Source: Ford Library, National Security Adviser, Kissinger Reports on USSR, China, and Middle East Discussions, Box 2, China Memcons and Reports, October 19–23, 1975, Kissinger's Trip. Top Secret; Nodis. The meeting took place in the Great Hall of the People. All brackets are in the original.

Amb. Philip C. Habib, Assistant Secretary for East Asian and Pacific Affairs
William H. Gleysteen, Jr., Deputy Assistant Secretary for East Asian and Pacific
    Affairs
Peter W. Rodman, NSC Staff
Miss Anne Boddicker, White House (notetaker)

SUBJECT

Southern Flank of Europe

[The press takes photos while the group is seated.]

Kissinger: Not all of us have recovered from the luncheon yet.

Teng: Yes, it seemed very arduous.

As you know, you cannot have a hot pot except in a very relaxed atmosphere because that will take a half hour.

Kissinger: I have not walked so much since I was in the infantry during the war. [Laughter] To me this is a Great March. [Laughter].

Teng: Yes, and when I was on the Long March I walked half the 25,000 li on foot; the other half was on the back of some kind of animal, a horse or such. At that time the highest luxury was to have one horse for each man.

Kissinger: I can imagine.

[The press leaves.]

Teng: So today we still have a bit of time left. Although it isn't very great, we still have the opportunity to have an exchange of views. Yesterday we had the opportunity to exchange opinions with you on questions pertaining to the international situation, policy and strategic. We think the exchange of views was frank, and we feel that such an exchange is beneficial for mutual understanding and also to the further development of possible cooperation between our two sides.

Kissinger: I agree.

Teng: So as for the questions pertaining to strategy, we don't have anything new to say on our side. And if you have nothing new to say on your side, then we can perhaps stop right here on that issue and turn to something else. But if you wish to tell us anything on that or any other position, you can tell us that.

Kissinger: I agree we have covered the issue of strategy and stated the various approaches. I have listed the possible topics yesterday and it is up to the Vice Premier what he thinks is most suitable.

Teng: And you have travelled the world several times in the past year and we are willing to listen to whatever you would like to say to us or whatever you think necessary to tell us, or whatever you find interesting to have an exchange of views on. If you are interested, you might begin with the southern flank of Europe.

Kissinger: All right. Mr. Habib would like me to try to convince you to vote with us on the Korean question, but I don't think I can do that in one hour. [Laughter] He has approached everyone except the Pope on that. [Laughter]

Well, on the southern flank of Europe, we have Portugal, Spain, Italy, Greece and Turkey. Each presenting a different situation.

In the case of Portugal, we find a situation where as a result of forty years of authoritarian rule, the democratic forces are not well organized, and where the political structure is very weak. The military have adopted some of the philosophy of African liberation movements, which they fought for 25 years. And the Communist Party of Cunhal, who spent his exile in Czechoslovakia—which is a curious place as a choice of exile—is very much under the influence of the Soviet Union. [Teng leans down beneath the table and spits into the spittoon beside his chair.]

In this vacuum, the Communist Party that I described achieved disproportionate influence, and for a while it seemed on the verge of dominating the situation. I think this trend has been arrested. And we are working with our West European friends to strengthen the forces that are opposed to Cunhal. Some of these forces unfortunately are better at rhetoric than at organization. But we think that the situation has improved, and we will continue to improve it.

Teng: We heard recent news that some of the military officers formerly under . . .

Chiao: . . . Gonçalves.[2]

Teng: . . . are prepared to stage a coup.

Kissinger: Yes. We had a report this morning they refused to turn over their weapons.

Teng: The news goes that they are preparing to do something on the 11th of November which is the date of the independence of Angola. News so specific as this can't be reliable.

Kissinger: No, I don't believe this. We have the report that there is one military unit that refuses to turn over its weapons. And there is no question Gonçalves is on the side of the Soviet Union. But we hope . . . We have been in touch with a number of other military leaders and we would certainly not approve such a coup and we will certainly oppose it.

Teng: But it is in our view that Portugal will see many reversals.

Kissinger: I agree.

Teng: And many trials of strength.

---

[2] Vasco dos Santos Gonçalves was Prime Minister of Portugal from July 18, 1974, to September 19, 1975.

We are not in a position to do anything else in that part of the world. There is one thing that we have done. They have approached us many times for the establishment of diplomatic relations, which we have not agreed to. Our point of departure is very simple: That is, we do not want to do anything that would be helpful to any Soviet forces gaining the upper hand.

Kissinger: I think that is a very wise policy. We support Antunes and Soares. [Teng leans down and spits again.] Antunes was in Washington a few weeks ago and we are cooperating with him.[3] But I agree with you that there will be many trials of strength. And the difficulty of our West European friends is they relax after a temporary success.

When we come back here in December, we will see the situation more clearly. But we are determined to resist a Soviet takeover there, even if it leads to armed conflict. It will not go easily. I mean, if they are planning a coup it will not be easy for them.

Now in Spain, the situation is more complicated. We have on the one hand a regime on its last legs, because Franco is very old.[4] But on the other hand we do not want to repeat the situation of Portugal in Spain.

We have been approached on a number of occasions by the Spanish Communist Party, but we consider it is controlled from Moscow. What is your assessment?

Teng: There are contradictions between the Spanish Communist Party and the Soviet Union. Among the revisionist Communist parties in Europe it can be said that the contradictions between the Spanish Communist Party and the Dutch Communist Party and the Soviet Union are comparatively deeper.

Kissinger: We have been negotiating a continuation of our base agreement with Spain, as you know. We will probably conclude this agreement within the next six weeks. We do this because we do not believe a shrinkage of American security interests in the Mediterranean is in the security interest of the world. [Teng spits again] Together with this, we are planning to set up a number of committees in the cultural and economic fields so that in the case of a new situation we have organic contacts with many levels of Spanish life.

Ch'iao: You mean after the regime is handed over to [Juan] Carlos?[5]

---

[3] Mario Soares was the leader of the Portuguese Socialist Party. Ernesto Antunes was the Portuguese Minister of Foreign Affairs during 1975 and again in 1975–1976.

[4] Generalissimo Francisco Franco had been the Spanish Head of Government since 1938 and the Head of State since 1939.

[5] Juan Carlos became the designated successor to Franco in 1969, and was proclaimed King of Spain on November 22, 1975.

Kissinger: Yes. We are setting up committees now in connection with the base agreement so that when Franco leaves we will not have to start, as we did in Portugal, looking around for contacts. We will have this infrastructure.

Teng: It is our impression that the influence of the Spanish revisionist party is not so deep as that of the Portuguese in the armed forces. I don't know whether your understanding would be the same.

Kissinger: One reason we need this base agreement is to stay in contact with the Spanish military. Our assessment is at the higher levels there is very little impact of what you call this revisionist party. At the lower levels, we have had some reports they are doing some recruiting.

Teng: The lowest levels do not play such a great role.

Kissinger: We have heard at the level of Captains. But at the commanding levels their influence can't be compared with the Portuguese situation.

Teng: But a captain is a very important man in African forces [laughter] but perhaps not so in Europe.

Kissinger: Not quite so in Europe. [Laughter]

Teng: What is your impression of the Spanish Prince?

Ch'iao: Carlos.

Kissinger: He is a nice man. Naive. He doesn't understand revolution and doesn't understand what he will face. He thinks he can do it with good will. But his intentions are good. He's a nice man. I don't think he is strong enough to manage events by himself.

Teng: We heard that Franco was going to hand over power to him.

Kissinger: We hear that every six months. But Mrs. Franco likes the palace too much to leave. [Laughter]

Teng: He must be in his 80's by now.

Kissinger: Yes, and not very active. In fact, he has a tendency to fall asleep while you are talking to him. [Laughter] I've been there with two Presidents, and he has fallen asleep both times. In fact, he had— when I was there with President Nixon—a hypnotic effect. I saw him falling asleep, so I fell asleep. So the only two people awake were President Nixon and the Spanish Foreign Minister. [Laughter]

No, it would be better if he handed over the power.

Teng: What do you think of Yugoslavia?

Kissinger: We are concerned about Yugoslavia. We are concerned that a number of things could happen after Tito's death. There could be a separatist movement from some of the provinces. There could be a split within the Yugoslav Communist Party. Both of these could be supported by the Soviet Union. And there could be Soviet military intervention.

Teng: During the recent visit of the Yugoslav Prime Minister Mr. Bijedic, we gained from what he said, although in different words, that they are also quite worried about such matters themselves.

Kissinger: In Montenegro—you know this—they discovered Soviet activities within the country.

Teng: Yes, but then they were able to find out about all these espionage activities and do something to end these activities.

Kissinger: Yes, but it shows the tendency of Soviet policy.

Teng: Indeed.

Kissinger: We are very interested in the independence and independent policy of Yugoslavia. And you have noticed that in the last year both the President and I have paid separate visits to Yugoslavia. And we are going to begin selling them military equipment within the next few weeks.

Teng: That will be very good. You must know that this nation is a very militant one. Although there are some contradictions among the various nationalities. And it seems to me that one of their relatively strong points is that they are comparatively clear-minded about the situation they face.

Kissinger: Yes. They will certainly fight if there is an invasion.

Teng: We have also posed this question to our European friends. That is, if there occurs a Soviet invasion of Yugoslavia, what will happen? And they felt that this was a difficult issue. And perhaps a similar question will confront you. Of course I do not ask you for an answer now. [They laugh.]

Kissinger: No, I can give you an answer. It is a difficult question. It is politically a difficult question and it's strategically a difficult question. We are now doing some military planning for this contingency. I can tell you this—you can keep secrets; I am not so convinced about all of my colleagues [laughter]—we have asked General Haig, in his capacity as American Commander, to do some planning.[6]

T'ang: About Yugoslavia?

Kissinger: Yes. [There is some commotion on the Chinese side.]

Teng: The Chairman will be prepared to meet you at 6:30. [The Secretary and Ambassador Bush exchange glances.] So, what . . . you are in a dilemma about your program [because of Ambassador Bush's reception for the Secretary scheduled for the International Club].

Kissinger: No. He [Bush] has a dilemma. I would be delighted.

---

[6] General Alexander M. Haig became Supreme Allied Commander Europe and Commander in Chief, U.S. European Command in December 1974.

T'ang: How many people would you be prepared to take with you?

Kissinger: The Ambassador, Mr. Lord . . .

Wang: Would your wife be going?

Kissinger: Has she been invited?

Wang: It is up to you.

Teng: We are willing to listen to your request or your opinion. It is up to you to suggest whom you would like to take on your side and whom you would like participating in the meeting and whom you would like to have shake hands.

Kissinger: Then I think . . . Can everyone here shake hands, and my wife? And then for the meeting Ambassador Bush, Mr. Lord, and Mr. Habib.

Teng: You mean all those seated here and your wife?

Kissinger: Yes, if you can find my wife. [Laughter] She's probably out shopping.

T'ang: We will try to find her.

Kissinger: If you can find her, it will save me a lot of money. [Laughter]

T'ang: So she is in the shops now?

[The Secretary discusses with Sonnenfeldt where she might be or whether she will have departed for the reception.]

Kissinger: Maybe we can still catch her.

[Wang Hai-jung goes out.]

Teng: So perhaps we can continue for about 15 minutes, and then perhaps you can make various preparations. [He spits into his spittoon.]

Kissinger: What I have said to you about military preparations with respect to Yugoslavia is known only to the top leaders of three European governments. Schmidt knows about it, of course. But it is a very complicated problem logistically. Because our best means of entering is through Italy and that is logistically very difficult. We can perhaps talk about this again when we come back in a few weeks.

Teng: Yes, and recently Italy has returned the B Zone of Trieste to Yugoslavia. We believe this is quite good.

Kissinger: Yes.

[Nancy T'ang gets up to leave. Mrs. Shih moves to the table.]

Shih: She is going to make some preparations. I will take her place.

Teng: So long as they have weapons in their hands, the Yugoslavs will fight.

Kissinger: We think so too. But as I said, we are starting in a few weeks to sell them some anti-tank weapons, and some other equipment.

Teng: We are thinking that in that area the main problem is conventional weapons and not nuclear weapons.

Kissinger: That is correct. Though any conflict that involves us and the Soviet Union is very complicated. It is bound to involve nuclear threats anyway. But the weapons we are selling to Yugoslavia are conventional weapons.

Teng: If the Soviet Union can control Yugoslavia, then the chessboard of Soviet strategy in Europe will become alive. The next will be Romania and Albania.

Kissinger: If the Soviet Union can get away with a military move on Yugoslavia, we will face a very grave situation. [Teng nods emphatically in agreement.] Which will require serious countermeasures.

Teng: For that not only involves military strategy; it will also have a very serious political influence. Its impact at least will spread to the whole of the southern flank.

Kissinger: I think that is correct. It will affect Italy and Germany, and France.

Teng: Also the Mediterranean. And the Middle East.

Kissinger: If this happens, whatever we do in Yugoslavia—which depends on the circumstances in which things develop—will lead to a very serious situation. We would not accept it. It will lead at least to serious countermeasures. It will not be like Czechoslovakia.

[Teng glances at his watch.]

What is your view on the Italian situation?

Teng: Well, one can hardly see the trend of the development of the situation in Italy. To us, it is all blank. We don't know how to look at the situation. Perhaps you know more clearly.

Kissinger: Perhaps the Foreign Minister should stop on the way back from the UN to call on the Pope. Gromyko was there a few weeks ago. [Laughter]

Teng: Really?

Kissinger: Actually you could be helpful in Italy, we think. At least with some of the Socialists. The Christian Democratic Party has very weak leadership. [They nod in agreement.] Their Prime Minister, Moro, also has a tendency to fall asleep when you meet him. [Laughter]

Teng: They change their Prime Ministers several times in a year. I don't know how many times since the War.

Kissinger: Yes, but it's always the same group. But the ruling group of the Christian Democratic Party is not very disciplined.

We totally oppose what is called in Italy the "historic compromise." We do not give visas to Italian Communists to come to the United States.

[Secretary Kissinger and Mr. Sonnenfeldt confer.]

Teng: In my view the so-called "historic compromise" cannot succeed.

Kissinger: Well, it can succeed, but it will lead to a disaster for the non-Communist parties.

I've just been handed a telegram that they have put a Communist into an Italian Parliamentary delegation that is coming to Washington, that we didn't select.

But that is a secondary issue. We will totally oppose it.

Teng: We think, with regard to the situation in Italy, where our two sides differ is that we don't attach so much importance to whether the Communist Party of Italy gets the power. It is not significant.

Kissinger: No, it is of importance because it will have an effect on France and even in the Federal Republic. And it is of significance to the support that America can give to NATO if there is a government there with a large Communist Party in the government.

Teng: [Laughs] Such a so-called "historic compromise" was once effected by the French. That was shortly after the War, when De Gaulle was in power. He let the Communist Party of France take part in the government, and Thorez was in power.[7]

Kissinger: But that was in a totally different situation. At that time they were declining, and not increasing.

Teng: The French Communist Party got several seats in the French Cabinet. One of them was the Minister of the Air Force, who was a Communist. [He laughs.] The decision to bomb Algeria was made by this man exactly. This we call their "performance on the stage."

Shall we end our talk here today? And prepare to meet the Chairman?

Kissinger: Can we leave from here?

Teng: Yes. We can take a short rest.

Kissinger: Okay.

Teng: But we will leave from here directly and meet you there.

[The meeting ended. The American party moved to another room to await Mrs. Kissinger, who arrived shortly, and then to depart for Changnanhai for the meeting with Chairman Mao Tsetung.]

---

[7] Maurice Thorez was the Deputy Premier of France from 1946 to 1947, a period during which the Communist Party cooperated with the Socialist Party to form a government.

124. Memorandum of Conversation[1]

Beijing, October 21, 1975, 6:25–8:05 p.m.

PARTICIPANTS

Chairman Mao Tse-tung
Teng Hsiao-p'ing, Vice Premier of the State Council of the People's Republic of
    China
Ch'iao Kuan-hua, Minister of Foreign Affairs
Amb. Huang Chen, Chief of the PRC Liaison Office, Washington
Wang Hai-jung, Vice Minister of Foreign Affairs
T'ang Wen-sheng, Deputy Director, Department of American and Oceanic Affairs
    and interpreter
Chang Han-chih, Deputy Director, Department of American and Oceanic Affairs

Dr. Henry A. Kissinger, Secretary of State and Assistant to the President for
    National Security Affairs
Ambassador George Bush, Chief of U.S. Liaison Office, Peking
Winston Lord, Director, Policy Planning Staff, Department of State

At 5:45 p.m. during a meeting with Vice Premier Teng Hsiao-ping, Secretary Kissinger was informed that Chairman Mao would like to see him at 6:30. He was asked to name those members of his party, including his wife, whom he would like to have greeted by the Chairman, as well as those two officials who would accompany him to the talks themselves. The meeting with Teng lasted another 15 minutes. Then Dr. Kissinger and his party rested until 6:15, when they went from the Great Hall of the People to the Chairman's residence.

Each of the following were introduced to the Chairman in turn and exchanged brief greetings while photographs and movies were taken: Secretary Kissinger, Mrs. Kissinger, Amb. Bush, Counselor Sonnenfeldt, Assistant Secretary Habib, Director Winston Lord, Mr. William Gleysteen, Mr. Peter Rodman (NSC), and Ms. Anne Boddicker (NSC). The Chairman stood and talked with considerable difficulty. When he saw Mrs. Kissinger, he sat down and asked for a note pad and wrote out the comment that she towered over Secretary Kissinger. He then got up again and greeted the rest of the party. Then the guests were escorted out of the room except for Secretary Kissinger, Ambassador Bush and Mr. Lord.

The participants sat in arm chairs in a semi-circle. Throughout the conversation the Chairman would either speak with great difficulty,

---

[1] Source: Ford Library, National Security Adviser, Kissinger Reports on USSR, China, and Middle East Discussions, Box 2, China Memcons and Reports, October 19–23, 1975, Kissinger's Trip. Secret; Sensitive. The meeting took place in Chairman Mao's residence.

with Miss Tang and Miss Wang repeating what he said for confirmation and then translating, or he would write out his remarks on a note pad held by his nurse. Throughout the conversation the Chairman gestured vigorously with his hands and fingers in order to underline his point.

Chairman Mao: You know I have various ailments all over me. I am going to heaven soon.

Secretary Kissinger: Not soon.

Chairman Mao: Soon. I've already received an invitation from God.

Secretary Kissinger: I hope you won't accept it for a long while.

Chairman Mao: I accept the orders of the Doctor.

Secretary Kissinger: Thank you. The President is looking forward very much to a visit to China and the opportunity to meet the Chairman.

Chairman Mao: He will be very welcome.

Secretary Kissinger: We attach very great significance to our relationship with the People's Republic.

Chairman Mao: There is some significance, not so very great. (Gesturing with his fingers) You are this (wide space between two fingers) and we are this (small space). Because you have the atom bombs, and we don't.

Secretary Kissinger: Yes, but the Chairman has often said that military power is not the only decisive factor.

Chairman Mao: As Vice Premier Teng Hsiao-ping has said, millet plus rifles.

Secretary Kissinger: And we have some common opponents.

Chairman Mao: Yes.

Secretary Kissinger: You said that in English and wrote it. Can I have it?

Chairman Mao: Yes. (He hands over the note he had written out.)

Secretary Kissinger: I see the Chairman is progressing in learning English.

Chairman Mao: No (holding two fingers close together). So you have quarreled with him (pointing toward Vice Premier Teng).

Secretary Kissinger: Only about the means for a common objective.

Chairman Mao: Yesterday, during your quarrel with the Vice Premier, you said the U.S. asked nothing of China and China asked nothing of the U.S. As I see it, this is partially right and partially wrong. The small issue is Taiwan, the big issue is the world. (He begins coughing and the nurse comes in to help him.) If neither side had anything to ask from the other, why would you be coming to Peking? If neither side had anything to ask, then why did you want to come to Peking, and why would we want to receive you and the President?

Secretary Kissinger: We come to Peking because we have a common opponent and because we think your perception of the world situation is the clearest of any country we deal with and with which we agree on some . . . many points.

Chairman Mao: That's not reliable. Those words are not reliable. Those words are not reliable because according to your priorities the first is the Soviet Union, the second is Europe and the third is Japan.

Secretary Kissinger: That is not correct.

Chairman Mao: It is in my view. (Counting with his fingers.) America, the Soviet Union, Europe, Japan, China. You see, five (holding up his five fingers).

Secretary Kissinger: That's not correct.

Chairman Mao: So then we quarrel.

Secretary Kissinger: We quarrel. The Soviet Union is a great danger for us, but not a high priority.

Chairman Mao: That's not correct. It is a superpower. There are only two superpowers in the world (counting on his fingers). We are backward (counting on his fingers). America, the Soviet Union, Europe, Japan, China. We come last. America, Soviet Union, Europe, Japan, China—look.

Secretary Kissinger: I know I almost never disagree with the Chairman, but he is not correct on this point—only because it is a matter of our priority.

Chairman Mao: (Tapping both his shoulders) We see that what you are doing is leaping to Moscow by way of our shoulders, and these shoulders are now useless. You see, we are the fifth. We are the small finger.

Secretary Kissinger: We have nothing to gain in Moscow.

Chairman Mao: But you can gain Taiwan in China.

Secretary Kissinger: We can gain Taiwan in China?

Chairman Mao: But you now have the Taiwan of China.

Secretary Kissinger: But we will settle that between us.

Chairman Mao: In a hundred years.

Secretary Kissinger: That's what the Chairman said the last time I was here.

Chairman Mao: Exactly.

Secretary Kissinger: It won't take a hundred years. Much less.

Chairman Mao: It's better for it to be in your hands. And if you were to send it back to me now, I would not want it, because it's not wantable. There are a huge bunch of counter-revolutionaries there. A hundred years hence we will want it (gesturing with his hand), and we are going to fight for it.

Secretary Kissinger: Not a hundred years.

Chairman Mao: (Gesturing with his hand, counting) It is hard to say. Five years, ten, twenty, a hundred years. It's hard to say. (Points toward the ceiling) And when I go to heaven to see God, I'll tell him it's better to have Taiwan under the care of the United States now.

Secretary Kissinger: He'll be very astonished to hear that from the Chairman.

Chairman Mao: No, because God blesses you, not us. God does not like us (waves his hands) because I am a militant warlord, also a communist. That's why he doesn't like me. (Pointing to the three Americans) He likes you and you and you.

Secretary Kissinger: I've never had the pleasure of meeting him, so I'm not sure.

Chairman Mao: I'm sure. I'm 82 years old now. (Points toward Secretary Kissinger) And how old are you? 50 maybe.

Secretary Kissinger: 51.

Chairman Mao: (Pointing toward Vice Premier Teng) He's 71. (Waving his hands) And after we're all dead, myself, him (Teng), Chou En-lai, and Yeh Chien-ying, you will still be alive. See? We old ones will not do. We are not going to make it out.

Secretary Kissinger: If I may say one thing about what the Chairman said earlier about our relative priorities.

Chairman Mao: All right.

Secretary Kissinger: Because the Soviet Union is a superpower it is inevitable that it has much priority, and we have to deal with it very frequently. But in terms of strategy we are trying to contain Soviet expansionism, and this is why in strategy China has priority for us. But we don't want to use China to jump to Moscow because that would be suicidal.

Chairman Mao: You've already jumped there, but you no longer need our shoulders.

Secretary Kissinger: We haven't jumped there. It's a tactical phase which the President will also affirm to you.

Chairman Mao: And please convey my regards to your President.

Secretary Kissinger: I will do this.

Chairman Mao: We welcome his visit.

Do you have any way to assist me in curing my present inability to speak clearly?

Secretary Kissinger: You make yourself very well understood even so.

Chairman Mao: This part (pointing to his brain) is working well, and I can eat and sleep. (Patting his knees) These parts are not good. They do not ache, but they are not firm when I walk. I also have some trouble with my lungs. And in one word, I am not well, and majorally (*sic*) unwell.

Secretary Kissinger: It's always a great joy to see the Chairman.

Chairman Mao: You know I'm a showcase exhibit for visitors.

Secretary Kissinger: I've read over our conversation two years ago, Mr. Chairman. I think it was one of the most profound expositions of international affairs, and we take it very seriously.

Chairman Mao: But there's still some things which we must wait to observe. Some of the assessments I made still have to be moved by the objective situation.

Secretary Kissinger: But I think the basic assessment the Chairman made at that time insofar as the situation has developed has proven correct, and we basically agree with it. We've had a difficult period because of the resignation of President Nixon, and we've had to do more maneuvering than we would have liked.

Chairman Mao: I think that can be done. Maneuvering is allowable.

Secretary Kissinger: It was essential, but we are putting that situation behind us.

Chairman Mao: Europe is too soft now.

Secretary Kissinger: We agree with the Chairman—Europe is too soft.

Chairman Mao: They are afraid of the Soviet Union.

Secretary Kissinger: They are afraid of the Soviet Union and their domestic situation.

Chairman Mao: Japan is seeking hegemony.

Secretary Kissinger: Japan is not yet ready to seek hegemony. That will require one more change in leadership. But potentially Japan has the potential for seeking hegemony.

Chairman Mao: Yes.

Secretary Kissinger: I think the next generation of leaders, my student Nakasone, he was a student of mine when I was a professor . . . That generation will be more ready to use the power of Japan.

Chairman Mao: Europe is too scattered, too loose.

Secretary Kissinger: Yes. We prefer Europe to be unified and stronger.

Chairman Mao: That is also our preference. But it is too loose and spread out, and it is difficult for it to achieve unity.

Secretary Kissinger: Also it does not have too many strong leaders.

Chairman Mao: Oh, yes.

Secretary Kissinger: But Schmidt, who comes here next week, is the strongest of the leaders in Europe today.

Chairman Mao: France is afraid of Germany (counting on his fingers). They are afraid of the reunification of West Germany and East Germany, which would result in a fist.

Secretary Kissinger: Yes, France prefers to keep Germany divided.

Chairman Mao: (Nodding yes) That's not good.

Secretary Kissinger: But they may unite on a nationalistic basis, East and West Germany.

Chairman Mao: Yes, we are in favor of reunification.

Secretary Kissinger: It depends under whom.

Chairman Mao: West Germany has a population of 50 million while East Germany has a population of 18 million.

Secretary Kissinger: West Germany is the strongest side materially.

Chairman Mao: But the reunification of Germany now would not be dangerous.

Secretary Kissinger: We favor the reunification of Germany, but right now it would be prevented militarily by the Soviet Union. But the U.S. supports the reunification of Germany.

Chairman Mao: We agree on that, you and we.

Secretary Kissinger: And we are not afraid of a unified Germany, but Soviet power in Europe must be weakened before it can happen.

Chairman Mao: Without a fight the Soviet Union cannot be weakened.

Secretary Kissinger: Yes, but it is important for us to pick the right moment for this, and during the period of Watergate we were in no position to do it. And that is why we had to maneuver.

Chairman Mao: And it seems it was not necessary to conduct the Watergate affair in that manner.

Secretary Kissinger: It was inexcusable. Inexcusable. (Miss Tang indicates puzzlement.) It was inexcusable to conduct it in that manner. It was a minor event that was played into a national and international tragedy by a group of very shortsighted people. President Nixon was a good President (Chairman Mao nods affirmatively) and I'm still in very frequent contact with him.

Chairman Mao: Please convey my regards to Mr. Nixon.

Secretary Kissinger: I'll call him when I return.

Chairman Mao: So please first of all send my regards to President Ford and secondly my regards to Mr. Nixon.

Secretary Kissinger: I'll do both of these with great pleasure.

Chairman Mao: You're too busy.

Secretary Kissinger: You think I travel too much?

Chairman Mao: I was saying that you are too busy, and it seems that it won't do if you're not so busy. You cannot keep from being so busy. When the wind and rain are coming, the swallows are busy.

Secretary Kissinger: That will take me several days to understand the full significance of that.

Chairman Mao: This world is not tranquil, and a storm—the wind and rain—are coming. And at the approach of the rain and wind the swallows are busy.

Miss Tang: He (the Chairman) asks me how one says "swallow" in English and what is "sparrow". Then I said it is a different kind of bird.

Secretary Kissinger: Yes, but I hope we have a little more effect on the storm than the swallows do on the wind and rain.

Chairman Mao: It is possible to postpone the arrival of the wind and rain, but it's difficult to obstruct the coming.

Secretary Kissinger: But it's important to be in the best position to deal with it when it does come, and that is not a trivial matter. We agree with you that the wind and rain are coming or may come, and we try to put ourselves in the best possible position, not to avoid it but to overcome it.

Chairman Mao: Dunkirk.

Secretary Kissinger: Not for us.

Chairman Mao: That is not reliable. You can see that that is not the case for you now.

Secretary Kissinger: That will not be the case for us in the future.

Chairman Mao: That is not reliable. A military correspondent for *The New York Times* put out a book in August.[2]

Secretary Kissinger: Who is he?

Miss Tang: (After consultations among the Chinese) We'll look it up and tell you.

Chairman Mao: Do you think that the 300,000 troops the U.S. has in Europe at the present time are able to resist a Soviet attack?

Secretary Kissinger: The weakness in Europe is not our troops but European troops. I think with nuclear weapons we can resist the attack.

Chairman Mao: That correspondent did not believe the U.S. would use nuclear weapons.

Secretary Kissinger: *The New York Times* has had a vested interest in American defeats the last ten years. If there's a substantial attack in Western Europe, we'll certainly use nuclear weapons. We have 7,000

---

[2] William Burr suggests that Mao was referring to Drew Middleton's book, *Can America Win the Next War?* (*The Kissinger Transcripts*, pp. 421–438)

weapons in Europe, and they are not there to be captured. That is in Europe. In the U.S. we have many more.

Chairman Mao: But there is a considerable portion of Americans who do not believe you'll use them. They do not believe Americans will be willing to die for Europe.

Secretary Kissinger: Mr. Chairman, we've come through a very difficult domestic period, partly caused by Indochina, partly caused by Watergate, in which many defeatist elements have been public. But if you watch what we've done the last five years, we always confront the Soviet Union and the Soviet Union always backs down. And I can assure you, as the President will reassure you, if the Soviet Union attacks Europe, we'll certainly use nuclear weapons. And the Soviet Union must never believe otherwise—it's too dangerous.

Chairman Mao: You have confidence, you believe in, nuclear weapons. You do not have confidence in your own army.

Secretary Kissinger: We have to face the reality that we will not have so large an army as the Soviet Union. That is a fact. And the most important fact is that no European country will build a large army. If they did, then there would not be a problem. And, therefore, we must build a strategy which is suited to that reality.

Chairman Mao: The Dunkirk strategy is not undesirable either.

Secretary Kissinger: Mr. Chairman, finally we have to have a minimum confidence in each other's statements. There will be no Dunkirk strategy, either in the West or in the East. And if there is an attack, once we have stopped the attack, after we have mobilized, we are certain to win a war against the Soviet Union.

Chairman Mao: (Gesturing with his fingers) We adopt the Dunkirk strategy, that is we will allow them to occupy Peking, Tientsin, Wuhan, and Shanghai, and in that way through such tactics we will become victorious and the enemy will be defeated. Both world wars, the first and the second, were conducted in that way and victory was obtained only later.

Secretary Kissinger: It is my belief that if there is a massive Soviet attack anywhere in the world, the U.S. will become involved very quickly. And it is also my conviction that the U.S. will never withdraw from Europe without a nuclear war.

Chairman Mao: There are two possibilities. One is your possibility, the other is that of *The New York Times*. That is also reflected in Senator Goldwater's speech of June 3 in the Senate.[3]

---

[3] Goldwater's speech is printed in the *Congressional Record*, vol. 121, pp. 16671–16674. For an account of the speech and the Senate debate of which it was a part, see Richard L. Madden, "Senators Differ on Arms Cutback as Debate Closes," *The New York Times*, June 4, 1975, pp. 1, 12.

Secretary Kissinger: What did he say?

Miss Tang: We will send you a copy. It was during the foreign policy debate in the Senate on June 3.

Secretary Kissinger: But what was the main point?

Chairman Mao: His disbelief in Europe.

Secretary Kissinger: You have to understand, Mr. Chairman, that it is the year before the election and much of what is said is said for domestic effect. *The New York Times* has had a certain position for 20 years and it has an unparalleled record for being wrong.

Chairman Mao: It is said that *The New York Times* is controlled by a Jewish family.

Secretary Kissinger: That is true.

Chairman Mao: And also the *Washington Post*.

Secretary Kissinger: The *Washington Post*—it is no longer true. (He then conferred with Ambassador Bush who pointed out that Mrs. Graham was Jewish, the daughter of Mr. Meyer.) You are right.

Chairman Mao: The proprietess is Jewish.

This Ambassador (looking toward Bush) is in a dire plight in Peking. Why don't you come and look me up?

Ambassador Bush: I am very honored to be here tonight. I think you are busy and don't have the time to see a plain Chief of the Liaison Office.

Chairman Mao: I am not busy, because I do not have to look over all the routine affairs. I only read the international news.

Secretary Kissinger: But the Chairman knows more about what is being written in America than I do. I didn't know about the book by *The New York Times* man or Senator Goldwater's speech.

Chairman Mao: You don't have the time. You are too busy.

(To Lord) Mr. Lord, you have now been promoted.

Mr. Lord: Yes, Mr. Chairman.

Chairman Mao: (To Bush and Lord) You have both been promoted.

Secretary Kissinger: He (Bush) not yet. He will be in 1980.

Chairman Mao: He can be President.

Secretary Kissinger: In 1980.

Chairman Mao: You don't know my temperament. I like people to curse me (raising his voice and hitting his chair with his hand). You must say that Chairman Mao is an old bureaucrat and in that case I will speed up and meet you. In such a case I will make haste to see you. If you don't curse me, I won't see you, and I will just sleep peacefully.

Secretary Kissinger: That is difficult for us to do, particularly to call you a bureaucrat.

Chairman Mao: I ratify that (slamming his chair with his hand). I will only be happy when all foreigners slam on tables and curse me.

Secretary Kissinger: We will think about it, but it will not come naturally to us. If we call the Chairman a bureaucrat, it will be a tactical maneuver separate from strategy.

Chairman Mao: But I am a bureaucrat. Moreover I am also a warlord. That was the title I was given by the Soviet Union and the title "bureaucrat" was given me by the Soviet Union.

Secretary Kissinger: But I haven't seen any Soviet visitors here lately.

Chairman Mao: They are cursing us every day. Every day.

Secretary Kissinger: But we don't share the Soviet assessment of China.

Chairman Mao: (Before Secretary Kissinger's sentence is translated) Therefore, I have accepted these two titles, "warlord" and "bureaucrat". No honor could be greater. And you have said that I am a warmonger and an aggressor.

Secretary Kissinger: I?

Chairman Mao: The United States in the UN. The UN passed a resolution which was sponsored by the U.S. in which it was declared that China committed aggression against Korea.

Secretary Kissinger: That was 25 years ago.

Chairman Mao: Yes. So it is not directly linked to you. That was during Truman's time.

Secretary Kissinger: Yes. That was a long time ago, and our perception has changed.

Chairman Mao: (Touching the top of his head) But the resolution has not yet been cancelled. I am still wearing this hat "aggressor". I equally consider that the greatest honor which no other honor could excel. It is good, very good.

Secretary Kissinger: But then we shouldn't change the UN resolution?

Chairman Mao: No, don't do that. We have never put forward that request. We prefer to wear this cap of honor. Chiang Kai-shek is saying that we have committed aggression against China. We have no way to deny that. We have indeed committed agression against China, and also in Korea. Will you please assist me on making that statement public, perhaps in one of your briefings? That is, the Soviet Union has conferred upon me the title of "warlord and bureaucrat", and the United States has conferred upon me "warmonger and aggressor".

Secretary Kissinger: I think I will let you make that public. I might not get the historically correct statement.

Chairman Mao: I have already made it public before you. I have also said this to many visiting foreigners, including Europeans. Don't you have freedom of speech?

Secretary Kissinger: Absolutely.

Chairman Mao: I also have freedom of speech, and the cannons I have fired exceed the cannons they have fired.

Secretary Kissinger: That I have noticed.

Miss Tang: You have noticed. . . .

Secretary Kissinger: The Chairman's cannons.

Chairman Mao: Please send my regards to your Secretary of Defense.

Secretary Kissinger: I will do that.

Chairman Mao: I am dissatisfied that he went to Japan without coming to Peking. We want to invite him here for the Soviets to see, but you are too miserly. The U.S. is so rich but on this you are too miserly.

Secretary Kissinger: We can discuss it when the President is here.

Chairman Mao: Bring him along. You can bring a civilian and a military member, with your President, both a civilian and a military man.

Secretary Kissinger: Me as the civilian and Schlesinger as the military?

Chairman Mao: Yes. But I won't interfere in your internal affairs. It is up to your side to decide whom you will send.

Secretary Kissinger: Well, he will not come with the President. Maybe later.

Chairman Mao: We would like to invite him to pay a visit to the northeast of our country, Mongolia and Sinkiang. He perhaps will not go, nor would you have the courage.

Secretary Kissinger: I would go.

Chairman Mao: (Looking toward Bush) He has been.

Secretary Kissinger: I would certainly go.

Chairman Mao: Good.

Secretary Kissinger: And we have tried to suggest to you that we are prepared to advise or help in some of these problems.

Chairman Mao: As for military aspects we should not discuss that now. Such matters should wait until the war breaks out before we consider them.

Secretary Kissinger: Yes, but you should know that we would be prepared then to consider them.

Chairman Mao: So, shall we call that the end?

Secretary Kissinger: Yes.

Secretary Kissinger, Ambassador Bush, and Mr. Lord then said goodbye to Chairman Mao. Secretary Kissinger confirmed with Vice Premier Teng that the Chinese would put out a public statement on the meeting and would send the text to the U.S. side immediately. (The Chinese statement is at Tab A.)[4] The Americans then said goodbye to the other Chinese officials and drove away in their cars.

---

[4] Dated October 21, attached but not printed.

---

125. Memorandum of Conversation[1]

Beijing, October 22, 1975, 3:40–4:45 p.m.

PARTICIPANTS

Teng Hsiao-p'ing, Vice Premier of the State Council, People's Republic of China
Ch'iao Kuan-hua, Minister of Foreign Affairs
Ambassador Huang Chen, Chief of PRCLO, Washington
Wang Hai-jung, Vice Minister of Foreign Affairs
Lin P'ing, Director of American & Oceanic Affairs, MFA
T'ang Wen-sheng, Deputy Director of American & Oceanic Affairs, MFA, (Interpreter)
Chien Ta-yung, Counselor, PRCLO, Washington
Ting Yüan-hung, Director for U.S. Affairs, American & Oceanic Affairs
Chao Chi-hua, Deputy Director for U.S. Affairs, American & Oceanic Affairs, MFA
Mrs. Shih Yen-hua, MFA (Interpreter) (plus two notetakers)

Dr. Henry A. Kissinger, Secretary of State and Assistant to the President for National Security Affairs
Ambassador George H. W. Bush, Chief of USLO, Peking
Winston Lord, Director, Policy Planning Staff
Ambassador Philip C. Habib, Assistant Secretary for East Asian and Pacific Affairs
Richard H. Solomon, NSC Staff

---

[1] Source: Ford Library, National Security Advisor, Kissinger Reports on USSR, China, and Middle East Discussions, Box 2, China Memcons and Reports, October 19–23, 1975, Kissinger's Trip. Secret; Nodis. The meeting took place in the Great Hall of the People. All brackets are in the original.

William H. Gleysteen, Jr., Deputy Assistant Secretary for East Asian and Pacific Affairs
Oscar V. Armstrong, Country Director, EA/PRCM
Robert L. Funseth, Director, Office of Press Relations
Peter W. Rodman, NSC Staff
Karlene Knieps, Sec. Kissinger's Office (Notetaker)

SUBJECTS

The President's Visit and Communiqué; Bilateral Relations; Indochina MIA; Korea; South Asia

Teng: So you visited the museum?

Kissinger: Yes. It was fascinating.

Teng: It is similar to this building, in relation to the Square. They were both built in the same year.

Kissinger: It is a tremendous achievement to put up two such structures in one year.

Teng: Not two—there were ten built, including the compound guest house.

Kissinger: It's an even greater achievement.

Teng: That was because we were commemorating the tenth anniversary.

Kissinger: Will you put out twenty structures on your twentieth anniversary? [Laughter]

Teng: That is past, and we have not added any more. That is sufficient.

Kissinger: There is only one thing I saw there I do not understand. There was a chariot that always pointed south. I do not understand what happened if you wanted to go north. [Laughter]

Teng: At that time the Emperor was situated in the northern part of China, where he had made his capital, and his attack was aimed at the nationalities in the southern part.

Kissinger: What if he wanted to go home again? [Laughter]

Teng: No. He must go through with his hegemonic aspirations to the end. Finally he won.

The President's Visit and Communiqué

I believe your discussions yesterday with Chairman Mao were very interesting.

Kissinger: And very important.

Teng: Yes, and it can be said that he has put forward all our basic points in an extremely concise manner.

Kissinger: I agree.

Teng: So what do you feel we have left to discuss?

Kissinger: Well, we have to discuss President Ford's visit.

Teng: Would you like to do that?

Kissinger: And your ideas as to the possible outcome. And your proposals as to how it will develop.

T'ang: The ideas or the outcome?

Kissinger: Both. What concretely will happen when he comes here.

Teng: We have said before that we think it would be all right if our minds meet or if they do not, or whether we discuss more or less. Either way will be all right. The importance we attach to this visit is to the visit itself. As for the protocol and other matters, I think there is no need for your President to be worried about such things.

Kissinger: It is difficult to explain to the American public that we are going to China for no other purpose than a visit. For example, what is your reaction to the Communiqué we gave you?

Teng: We will try to give you our draft later this evening. And after that you can have discussions with our Foreign Minister. As we have heard that you are of the opinion that the time may not be enough to complete the entire agreement on the Communiqué, we were thinking you could take back our draft for further study, and if, after reading our draft, you think it would be easy to reach a common view, then you can have discussions with our Foreign Minister this evening.

Kissinger: If I do not think we can agree, what will happen?

Teng: Further consultations!

Kissinger: I cannot make a judgment until I have read the Foreign Minister's draft.

Teng: Indeed. But there are some concrete issues in the matters in your draft that perhaps are not yet realistic, as can be seen from this morning's session between Director Lin P'ing and Director Habib.[2] Because, generally speaking, under circumstances where relations between states have not been normalized, it is not the normal practice to sign certain agreements between states, for example, commercial and navigation agreements, and on air traffic. We think it should be mainly the political aspect that should be able to manifest the significance of the visit. Of course, it should show that we are prepared to continue the move forward according to the principles of the Shanghai Communiqué; and of course, other matters such as trade, people-to-people exchanges, cultural exchanges, and things like that, can also be put into the Communiqué.

The important issue between us bilaterally is the Taiwan issue. And it seems to be that at present you are not yet prepared to put any

---

[2] The counterpart talks between Habib and Lin P'ing covered financial claims and "people to people" exchanges. Memoranda of conversation are ibid.

essentially new language into the Communiqué. Under these circumstances we think it is appropriate to reiterate the language of the Shanghai Communiqué.

Kissinger: We thought we had put some changes into the Communiqué.[3]

Teng: There is a bit. We have noticed that. We noticed one phrase: "We agreed with that view," something like that. [The Vice Premier leans down beside his chair and spits into his spittoon.]

Kissinger: But that is not a minor change. It picks up the principle of the November 1973 Communiqué.

Ch'iao: Of course, on the one hand it is slightly new; on the other side, it is not entirely. Because in the Shanghai Communiqué you have already stated that you did not challenge that view.

Kissinger: True. It is a nuance. It is related to our November 1973 Communiqué.

Teng: Anyway, when your President comes, we will be able to have a candid exchange of views, which might also be considered as a continuation of the exchange of views between the two sides during your visit this time.

Kissinger: The problem I think for both of us to consider is whether the points that have been made in today's various discussions about the balance in our international relationship, and whether we do certain things in order to gain favor somewhere or whether we do them for tactical reasons, that these problems can only be solved—or can be solved at one level more effectively—by showing some progress in Sino-American relations. We did not ask for it. We did not even ask for the visit, particularly. If we cannot show some progress, then given the way our media will report the visit, the only way to solve it is to show concrete progress in our relations.

Teng: As for the Presidential visit, it was the proposal put forward by the Doctor during your last visit to China last November. But we do not attach such great importance to who raised the visit. We anyway express our welcome.

Kissinger: I think it is very difficult to discuss this in the abstract. And relationships can progress anyway only with the concurrence of both sides. We have, therefore, to see what—we will have to look at your draft before we can make any conclusions.

---

[3] The U.S. draft communiqué, which Kissinger gave to Qiao Guanhua on October 20, stated, "The United States side, recognizing that all Chinese on either side of the Taiwan Strait maintain that there is but one China and that Taiwan is part of China, expressed its agreement with that view. In affirming the principle of one China, the United States reiterated its interest in a peaceful settlement of the Taiwan question by the Chinese themselves." See footnote 3, Document 121.

Bilateral Relations

Teng: Do you have any concrete ideas about any issues that you would like to have settled? Apart from those which I just now raised, which were unrealistic only because of the fact that relations between our two countries are not normalized?

Kissinger: We put what we thought were soluble into our draft of the Communiqué. But we do not insist on any one in particular. I do not have any beyond those I have mentioned. Those two or three are not important. And they do not all require formal agreement.

Our basic concern, Mr. Vice Premier, is not what is in those proposals, because the essence of our relationship does not depend on any of this. But the question we discussed yesterday[4]—the symbolism of whether China is our fifth priority, or a higher priority, which is what I would say—would be reflected, if we can find some concrete expression of it. I do not think China is our fifth priority, and I think we know our priorities better than anyone else knows them. If we want to give our public a stake in this relationship, then there has to be some concrete expression of it at some time. But we are willing to listen to any other proposals.

Teng: Of course there are certain issues like, for instance, the assets and private claims and so on, which might be where agreements might be reached. But according to my knowledge of this morning's session, each side was still at its original position. The words were not new at all. But this is not an issue we are concerned about; as we have said, it won't matter if it is not settled in one hundred years.

Kissinger: The claims issue too?

Teng: We were saying that it would be all right if it was not settled in one hundred years, but if you think it possible to reach an agreement and settle it during the President's visit, we would not oppose that. As for the Most-Favored-Nation treatment and so on, Chairman Mao has explained our view. He said we do not need such things. As long as you do not give it to that bastard. [Laughter] And there always exists the possibility that one hundred years might be cut down to one and a half months.

There also was the issue you raised in your previous visits about the search for American military men missing in China, due to the Vietnam war. There also have been some initial discoveries, but they are too few. Each side can just state this to each other. It is too small to be put into the Communiqué.

Kissinger: On the claims and assets . . . of course, we are primarily concerned with enabling the Foreign Minister to come to New

---

[4] See Document 124.

York via Anchorage in a Chinese aircraft, which will ease his discomfort when he arrives. [Laughter]

Teng: I believe a trial flight was made before I was planning to go for the Special Session.

Kissinger: And we had some legal complications.

But the sums themselves are trivial. We are not interested in the sums that are involved here. It is not a commercial problem with us. Mr. Habib put forward our latest thinking on the subject, this morning. Which represented some modification of our previous position.

Ch'iao: Too marginal to be perceived.

Teng: Our perception is that it is basically the same position. And as you just now mentioned, we do not think a few dollars more or less is of any importance, and we do not think it necessary to get involved in legal terms to express a settlement. If the terms and if these two points can be worked out, that would be a settlement. And if it is, as you have mentioned before, that without getting involved with legal terms one cannot settle such issues as Most-Favored-Nation and the legal status, we are willing to give them up.

Kissinger: Is it true . . . one of our newsmen told me he asked last year how you would react to a Jackson amendment in regard to Most-Favored-Nation and one of the Chinese said to him: "Anytime you want fifty million Chinese, we are ready."

That was a joke. It was told by a Chinese, not by us. [Laughter]

The basic obstacle to Most-Favored-Nation for the Chinese side is the claims problem. There is no other. There are no other obstacles.

Teng: I do not think it is necessary to get entangled in the legal matters of the Most-Favored-Nation status issue. We can just say that both of us agreed to settle it in one stroke.

Kissinger: To settle what?

Teng: To cancel the claims in one stroke. To just let it go with the wind.

Kissinger: Mr. Habib is afraid we will deprive him of his profession if we do that. [Laughter] If you can find some complicated way of expressing that same thought, he will probably be satisfied.

Teng: We can continue to study the problem. Anyway, we are not very interested or very concerned with the Most-Favored-Nation status issue. There is only one thing that is clear; it cannot be stated anywhere in any settlement that Chinese are required to observe American laws.

Kissinger: That is a very reasonable proposition, which is not self-evident to our Congress.

Teng: You can continue your study.

Indochina MIA

Kissinger: You said you had some information on missing in action. That would be of some interest to us if you could give us whatever you know.

T'ang: You mean now?

Kissinger: Whenever. Either now or later. It does not have to be expressed in a Communiqué.

Teng: There is no need to make a Communiqué for that.

Kissinger: No, but we would appreciate if there is any information that we could give to the families.

Teng: Yes, I think it perhaps would be most appropriate for us to give you the material and the information we have on these issues during your next visit.

Kissinger: All right. If you can use your influence on occasion with the Vietnamese, we would also appreciate that; but we do not have to know what you are doing. On the issue of the missing in action.

[Teng leans down again and spits into the spittoon.]

Teng: As I think I mentioned to you last time during your previous visit, we do not think our saying anything would be of any use, and it is our policy not to raise any such questions of such a nature.

Korea

Kissinger: About Korea . . . Let me get a few other housekeeping things done. The Foreign Minister and I will have to agree on a Communiqué for this visit.

Teng: You mean an announcement of the date of the President's visit?

Kissinger: I do not know whether there is any need to say anything about my trip here. The trip we are now concluding.

[The Chinese side confers.]

Teng: I think what is needed is just the announcement of the date of the President's visit. Everything else is already in the press.

Kissinger: Plus some things that did not happen. [Laughter] [To Funseth:] Where did you get Growald [Richard Growald of UPI]?

Funseth: He is from the White House.

Kissinger: [To Teng] I think we probably want to do that in Washington and not from here.

Teng: You mean to discuss it?

Kissinger: No, the announcement of the President's visit should be made from Washington.

T'ang: And discuss it later on?

Kissinger: No. We can agree on a text here. We can agree later on a time of the announcement.

T'ang: After your return?

Kissinger: Yes. We can agree on the text here, and then set the time of the announcement after we return to Washington. It makes no difference to you on the time of the announcement?

Teng: Anytime will be all right for us.

Ch'iao: Yes, we can decide on the text of the announcement here and you can just tell us when you want to have it announced after your return. Any time will be all right with us.

Kissinger: All right. That's how we'll do it.

Ch'iao: Good.

Kissinger: Now, on Korea: We have said that we are prepared to talk to North Korea, in any forum that includes South Korea.

Teng: I think the views of each side are very clear by now to the other. I think you have several sufficient channels leading to the Democratic People's Republic of Korea. They have an observer at the United Nations.

Kissinger: Who is extremely active. [Laughter] He thinks David Rockefeller runs the United States. [Laughter] So I hear from him periodically.

Teng: You have others.

Kissinger: We can communicate with them. We just want you to know our position.

Teng: I understand your position.

Kissinger: What is your understanding of how the legal position can be fixed in Korea if the UN Command is abolished?

Teng: You are asking . . . ?

Kissinger: As I read your Foreign Minister's speech at the UN, he said it is an easy problem, but he did not tell us how to solve it.[5] [Laughter]

Ch'iao: That is to say that an armistice and a cessation of hostilities—an armistice agreement—cannot go on forever. There is bound to come a day when it will be turned into a situation of peace. That can be said. Our view is that once the Armistice Agreement is replaced by a peace agreement, it will not be difficult to settle the issue in principle.

Kissinger: Yes, but if the UN Command is abolished and before there is a peace agreement, there will be no legal status at all.

Ch'iao: Our understanding of the position of our Korean friends is that these two things are connected, that is, that the Armistice Agreement will be replaced by a peace agreement.

---

[5] See footnote 2, Document 119.

Kissinger: Yes, but their position is also that the UN Command should be abolished.

Ch'iao: As for the concrete issue of dissolving the UN Command, I think it is something for you to discuss with Korea. And it seems that the time is not yet ripe for the solving of this issue.

Kissinger: I hope we will all not fire too many cannons in the debate that is now ahead of us. [Laughter]

Teng: It seems that it won't do if certain cannons are not fired. I think it is a saying with you, you also have a considerable number of cannons. [Laughter]

Kissinger: Yes, but we lack the eloquence of some of our critics. [Laughter] And Mr. Habib is very sensitive, because he was Ambassador in Korea. [Laughter]

South Asia

On South Asia, we are often asked by Pakistan about our attitudes. The Chief of the Pakistan Air Staff is coming to visit us the end of November, and we will begin selling some equipment to them then. And we have also warned the Soviet Union against military pressure against Pakistan by them or their friends.

Teng: That is good. We have given them a bit of what we have, but that is very backward. I think that what they need more is things that you can give them.

Kissinger: And we will begin it after the visit of the Air Marshal. We have already agreed to sell them some anti-tank weapons and I think some artillery.

Teng: How is your work going on with India?

Kissinger: They are very eager to improve their relations with us. Their Foreign Minister visited Washington a few weeks ago. Our basic assessment is that in the next five years they may bring pressure on both Bangladesh and Pakistan, and maybe attack them both. Our information is that they are seriously considering engineering a coup in Bangladesh or seriously considering engineering refugees to give them an excuse to bring pressure on Bangladesh.

Teng: I think we still have to wait to see the development of events.

Kissinger: They would be more active if they were not also pacifists. [Laughter]

Teng: Aren't they the origin of all peace? [Laughter] They have also been very eager to improve their relations with us.

Kissinger: Yes, they told us.

Teng: And want first of all to exchange Ambassadors. And during the recent visit of the Yugoslav Prime Minister Bijedic to China, he also brought us a message from India and we gave him a message back. It consisted of no other content than of asking Madame Gandhi to improve her relations and policies toward neighboring countries.

Kissinger: They have asked us to be helpful with you. But I assume they have many channels to you.

Teng: Yes, there are plenty of direct channels. On the evening of May Day 1971, when the Chairman met with their Chargé d'Affaires on Tien An Men, he had already said to him we do not think the present state of relations between our two countries can continue forever like this. That shows that the channels in Peking are not clogged up.

Kissinger: It is not a matter of primary concern to the United States.

Teng: Correct. But there is one point that seems to be worth noting. It seems the dissatisfaction among the people about Soviet control of India has considerably mounted.

Kissinger: Yes. I am assuming that the desire to improve relations with you and us reflects a public necessity. And we favor anything that lessens Soviet influence in India.

Teng: It is my personal impression that there will inevitably come the day when the Indians are going to rebel against the Soviet Union.

Kissinger: It seems to be the Soviet destiny whenever they have close relationships. [Laughter] The ability to maintain allies is not one of their specialities. [Teng nods agreement.]

Teng: So what else do we have to discuss? I think the main issue is still the Communiqué, which I will leave to our Foreign Minister to discuss with you at a later hour.

Kissinger: Yes.

Teng: As for the discussions we have had, especially the discussion you have had with Chairman Mao, we believe them to be of positive significance.

Kissinger: So do I.

Teng: We will be seeing each other very soon.

Kissinger: That's right. Very soon.

Teng: As for the announcement about your visit this time, perhaps we can save some of the words for the next visit, and use them for the next visit.

Kissinger: I agree. You save the words for the next visit. There is no need to say anything substantive.

Teng: So, do you think that will be about all for the talks?

Kissinger: Yes, I think so.

Teng: We will be seeing each other later on.

Kissinger: Yes, we will be seeing each other.

[The Secretary confers with Bush and Habib.]

All right.

Teng: We will see each other at half past seven.

Kissinger: Yes, half past seven.

[The Chinese side hands over an advance text of the Foreign Minister's banquet toast for that evening.]

Teng: Just words of gratefulness for your banquet this evening.

Kissinger: Thank you.

[The meeting adjourned.]

---

126. Memorandum of Conversation[1]

Beijing, October 23, 1975, 12:35–2:30 a.m.

PARTICIPANTS

> Ch'iao Kuan-hua, PRC Minister of Foreign Affairs
> Lin P'ing, Director, Department of American and Oceanic Affairs, Ministry of
>   Foreign Affairs
> T'ang Wen-sheng, Deputy Director, Department of American and Oceanic
>   Affairs, Ministry of Foreign Affairs
> Ting Yuan-hung, Director, United States Office, Department of American and
>   Oceanic Affairs, Ministry of Foreign Affairs
> Chao Chi-hua, Deputy Director, United States Office, Department of American
>   and Oceanic Affairs, Ministry of Foreign Affairs
> Shih Yen-hua (Interpreter)
>
> Henry A. Kissinger, Secretary of State and Assistant to the President for National
>   Security Affairs
> Philip C. Habib, Assistant Secretary of State for East Asian and Pacific Affairs
> Winston Lord, Director, Policy Planning Staff, Department of State
> William H. Gleysteen, Deputy Assistant Secretary of State for East Asian and
>   Pacific Affairs
> Richard H. Solomon, Senior Staff Member, National Security Council
> Karlene Knieps (Notetaker)

SUBJECT

> Discussion of the Draft Communiqué for the President's Visit

Secretary Kissinger: Mr. Foreign Minister, I thought I might give you our reaction to the PRC draft communiqué (attached at the end of

---

[1] Source: Ford Library, National Security Adviser, Kissinger Reports on USSR, China, and Middle East Discussions, Box 2, China Memcons and Reports, October 19–23, 1975, Kissinger's Trip. Top Secret; Sensitive. The meeting took place in Guest House #5. All brackets are in the original.

this memcon)[2] and in the very brief time left before our departure, you might think about it if you want to make a response.

Foreign Minister Ch'iao: I will first listen to your reaction and then I will tell you our reaction to your draft.

Secretary Kissinger: We received your draft near midnight. This does not permit serious consideration.

There is no point in discussing procedural matters that are now beyond repair. Let me therefore deal with substance.

The purpose of the communiqué is to explain to the world and to our people why the President of the United States visited China. We do not agree that just coming to China can be the purpose of a political move; there must be some [substantive] reason for it.

Now—going through your draft. I find it, quite frankly, difficult to find a reason [for the President's visit]. The draft follows the outline of the Shanghai Communiqué, but in almost every significant category it represents a step back from the Shanghai Communiqué. In no category is there a step forward.

In the Shanghai Communiqué, it was the first contact that the United States and the People's Republic had had in over 20 years. In rather abstracted ideas the two sides stated their diametrically opposite views at the beginning [of the document].

I would like to remind the Foreign Minister that at that time the Prime Minister was generous enough to take out of the Chinese section language that we considered particularly offensive—although these words later appeared in the Foreign Minister's public statements [at the United Nations]. However, it was your speech, it was not a document signed jointly with the United States.

In all frankness, the American people will ask why the President came here to sign a document which says, "The peoples of the third world countries have won a series of significant victories in their struggle against colonialism, imperialism and hegemonism." We are of that "imperialist" school I suppose. "The contention between the superpowers for world hegemony has become ever more intense." That seems inconsistent with us selling out to the Soviets. One of those two propositions cannot be correct. You can't do both a Munich and a world war simultaneously.

Above all, we cannot sign a document which accuses us of this, even if it is stated by just one party.

---

[2] The Chinese draft communiqué, given to U.S. officials on October 22, is attached but not printed.

Two paragraphs state some positive things, but they are better stated in the Shanghai Communiqué. They just repeat the Shanghai Communiqué in a shortened version.

Then, the Taiwan issue. We understand that the Chinese side repeats its Shanghai Communiqué position. It presents no problem, but the Foreign Minister knows very well that several sentences, several clauses, have been added which sharpen the Chinese position. These sentences will greatly complicate our efforts to move to full normalization—which we have said we would do.

And what your draft says regarding bilateral matters is insignificant.

So then, we have enormous difficulties with such a document. In fact, quite candidly, it presents an impossibility of explaining to our people what we were doing here. I hate to do this in so short a time before my departure, but we did not have the document so I had no opportunity. This document is completely unacceptable, even as a basis for discussion.

Let's leave aside the document. Let me make several general statements. We gave you a document, but we did not expect you to accept it in its [initial] form. We allowed three days for discussions. We were prepared to discuss it, change it, negotiate it. That opportunity did not present itself. But we made a very serious effort to show serious movement on issues of great concern to the Chinese side, such as the issue of hegemony, on world positions, as well as some other negotiations that you are conducting [with the Japanese]. And what we said about the principle of one China in the Taiwan section of our communiqué—stating it twice and affirmatively—was a serious attempt on our part to indicate movement on an issue that is leading to inevitable consequences over a measurable period of time.

So, that was our intention. Underlying this [present situation, however] may be a more profound understanding. That is, [you may think] we want to come here to use the shoulders of China to reach Moscow, or that we want something here.

Our assessment here, which has to be our policy, is to prevent Soviet expansionism. This we will do with or without China. It is also in China's interest to prevent Soviet expansionism for your own reasons. So we have parallel objectives here. We have refused all overtures from the Soviet Union that could have been used against the People's Republic, and I explained very frankly to Chairman Mao yesterday that we have a domestic situation which requires us to put more emphasis on tactics and maneuvers than we like.[3]

---

[3] See Document 124.

But we have dealt openly with you and you have always known what we did—especially regarding the Soviets, because we thought we had a parallel conception with you on world affairs. But if that is misunderstood, then we cannot be in a position of being supplicants, and of giving the impression that we need this relationship more than you do.

So I have spoken very frankly, because the foreign policy measure I have been most proud of has been our relations with China. We cannot accept either the position or the substance of this communiqué.

Therefore, I ask the Foreign Minister's opinion on where we go from here.

Foreign Minister Ch'iao: Okay, now I will give you my impressions. First, our reaction to your draft: As you had time to prepare [the draft U.S. document (attached at the end of this memcon)][4] when you handed it to us on the 20th, we studied it seriously. We also think that your document as a whole is unacceptable to us. The spirit of the Shanghai Communiqué is that neither side should conceal its views or policy. So, at the outset of the Shanghai Communiqué, each side stated its differences from the other so that the world knows both the differences and the common points.

But your draft has concealed the real views of our two sides on international affairs. This does not conform to reality. Since you have dealt with us for a long time you know that we speak facts. Our words count. The main defect in your draft is it is contrary to what you have said. Your draft has failed to include the views of our two sides on the international issues. In other words, the two sides have not stated the differences between us in your draft.

If one expects to go beyond the Shanghai Communiqué, it is necessary for the two sides to state their respective views. Because time is progressing, and the world is changing, and, of course, the views of the two sides may also change from the Shanghai Communiqué. This is the first point I would like to make.

(Ambassador Bush comes in. The Secretary says to him, "I asked you to come in to be a mediator. We have a little difference of opinion on the two sides." (Laughter))

Foreign Minister Ch'iao: A second point, on the Taiwan issue: The Taiwan section in your draft shows no substantial progress from the Shanghai Communiqué and what is more, there is a contradiction in logic.

Secretary Kissinger: I'll accept the first criticism, but for a Kantian the second is a little bit hard to take.

---

[4] Attached but not printed.

Foreign Minister Ch'iao: I will not go into details.

Secretary Kissinger: But you will give us a hint that we can think about.

Foreign Minister Ch'iao: As a matter of fact, there is nothing new in your draft on the Taiwan section apart from repeating the Shanghai Communiqué. The only change is in the word "does not challenge" to "agree." One phrase is active, the other one passive, but it doesn't change the meaning.

As for our draft, there are many ideas in our draft which go beyond the Shanghai Communiqué.

Secretary Kissinger: In the wrong direction.

Foreign Minister Ch'iao: In the correct direction. We speak facts. Yesterday you met with Chairman Mao. You said that we had a common opponent. With respect to our views on the third world, the position of the superpowers, we have stated our views on many occasions. We do not conceal our views.

These are our views on the current world situation. They also conform to the current realities more than the Shanghai Communiqué. According to the tradition of the Shanghai Communiqué, each side can state its views. The U.S. side can state anything [it wishes to state]. We have no objection. This is not rhetoric.

I do not agree with what Mr. Secretary said that almost every paragraph in the Chinese draft is a step backwards from the Shanghai Communiqué. We have reaffirmed all the principles agreed upon by our two sides in the Shanghai Communiqué, we have reaffirmed the Shanghai Communiqué and stressed opposition to world hegemony.

As for the Taiwan issue, we have put our views in a nutshell in two sentences and we have added two sentences. I think our position is also very clear to you. We are not being honest if we do not state our views like this.

As I said just now, there is nothing new in the Taiwan section except a repetition of the views of the Shanghai Communiqué.

As for our present bilateral relations, we also stated the present position in very brief words which also conform to present reality. In other words, what is said in this draft is more brief than what was said in the Shanghai Communiqué, and the substance is the same.

Secretary Kissinger: On bilateral relations?

Foreign Minister Ch'iao: Yes.

I would like to repeat that the Chinese draft was presented to you after full consideration in a short priod of time. We are not rash.

Mr. Secretary of State, you raised a fundamental question just now that the purpose of the communiqué is to explain why your President should visit China and I remember your saying that [his visit] was unconditional. I remember discussing this matter in another building in this compound [during your last visit to Peking]. I suggested a visit by your Secretary of Defense, and you replied with the suggestion of a visit by the President. We expressed welcome [to the President]. Thereafter, on many occasions we said it would be all right if they did not meet. Anyway, we express our welcome to your President's visit. Our Vice Premier has said that a visit by your President is itself a political move. In our opinion, a communiqué is not important. Who invented this communiqué form?

Secretary Kissinger: It must be a Chinese invention. They have long had diplomacy. (Laughter)

Foreign Minister Ch'iao: There is no such thing in Chinese history. If we have a communiqué we don't object. If there is no communiqué, that is not of much significance.

I have very frankly and very briefly presented our views. In such a short period of time it was impossible for us to discuss [our two draft communiqués] word-by-word as we did in 1972. So I suggest that you leave your draft with us, and take our draft with you and continue to consider our draft.

Secretary Kissinger: I can tell you now we can consider your draft for two more months and we will not change our position. We will not change our fundamental opinion. It is an impossibility for the President to agree to such a communiqué both for international and domestic reasons. It would be suicide for him to do it. Sometimes [a situation is created where] there are no decisions to make.

His opponents on the right would absolutely destroy him. This is a reality. Even from a foreign policy point of view, with respect to hegemony, what we would do is meet your point of view. This is not a Japanese situation. We want to go forward. We are prepared to find a formula which will help your Japanese problem, not complicate it.

Foreign Minister Ch'iao: Judging from your draft, you have confused the original ideas in the Shanghai Communiqué on hegemony. If this is what you mean by strengthening the statement on hegemony, we don't need it.

As for our relations with Japan, we know how to handle them. It is evident that they are bowing to pressure at home and abroad. The Japanese are making trouble. It does not matter to us. We are not in a hurry.

Secretary Kissinger: We do not consider our hegemony clause essential. We don't have any problem with yours as it is in the Shanghai Communiqué. It only raises the question of what is the necessity of saying it again. We have no objection to it. We can say it again.

Foreign Minister Ch'iao: In our opinion, in our draft we have reaffirmed all the principles in the Shanghai Communiqué, and we have stressed two points. One is our bilateral relations, the other is opposition to hegemony in world affairs, because they constitute the main common points between us.

Secretary Kissinger: We have no problem reaffirming the Shanghai Communiqué statement on hegemony; this is not a problem.

On Taiwan, our impression is that we made a step forward. That certainly was our intention.

Foreign Minister Ch'iao: On the Taiwan issue, yesterday Chairman Mao very thoroughly stated what our views are. You owe us a debt. This is your responsibility, not ours.

As we have discussed this problem many times, we are not constrained to tell you what our views are.

On the sentence on hegemony [in the U.S. draft], I have said that you have confused the conception. The section in your draft has different implications which we are opposed to, such as the words "whatever the source, whether in the East or the West." And I think our Vice Premier has discussed this with you.

Secretary Kissinger: Do you think that hegemony should be resisted only in the West? We do not consider this an important—

Foreign Minister Ch'iao: Look at our draft. "Each side is opposed to . . ." We stated that neither side should seek hegemony in any part of the world.

Secretary Kissinger: We can accept your language. We sincerely thought that you would find that interesting. We can drop that clause. The hegemony clause is not a problem. Our views are substantially the same.

Foreign Minister Ch'iao: In the first place this was raised by you.

Secretary Kissinger: This is quite true, but we thought that we were meeting your concerns. We are not gaining anything for ourselves. We don't need it. It makes no difference to us. We will drop that clause or go back to your clause.

What do you think should be done now?

Foreign Minister Ch'iao: We have stated our views very thoroughly. It is very good if we have [a communiqué]; we have no objection to having one. But if our two sides cannot agree, what will we do?

Secretary Kissinger: If we can't agree on the language, then there is no common position.

Foreign Minister Ch'iao: We have a common point on hegemony. You stressed this to the Chairman yesterday.

Secretary Kissinger: It does not seem to have been taken very seriously. But your communiqué is 98 percent disagreement, and only 2 percent agreement which is already in the other communiqué.

Foreign Minister Ch'iao: This is the reality, the problem of first priority at the moment. Why do the two sides have to come together? Why can't we speak it out?

Secretary Kissinger: We have no trouble with this. It is the five pages of disagreement you have to state before you can state one sentence of agreement.

Foreign Minister Ch'iao: There are only four pages.

Secretary Kissinger: We will do it on our typewriter. (Laughter)

Foreign Minister Ch'iao: Last year you said that our draft was too short. This year you say that our side's is too long.

Secretary Kissinger: But you have not included the U.S. position [which will expand the length considerably].

Foreign Minister Ch'iao: You are free to express your views. We won't object.

Secretary Kissinger (with irony): Thank you. I appreciate that very much, but my point is that the impression [created by the Chinese draft] is that the President of the United States travelled 8,000 miles to express 98 percent disagreement in order to express one sentence of agreement and this after his Secretary of State already spent considerable time discussing these issues in October.

Foreign Minister Ch'iao: The importance [of the document] should not be weighed by the number of words.

Secretary Kissinger: Mr. Foreign Minister, I am always astonished by how well informed you are. You saw what our press did on the first evening with your toast. What will they do with this document? It will damage our relationship! Therefore, both sides must consider the psychology of the other side.

Foreign Minister Ch'iao: We don't think it beneficial to cover up our differences. This will lead people astray. Indeed, as everyone knows, we really have great differences, but we have common points as well.

Secretary Kissinger: But it is simply a different situation when the President comes a second time, when there has been no return visit [to the United States] by a Chinese leader for understandable reasons, to restate these differences.

Foreign Minister Ch'iao: This is a reality. We have so many common points, and so many differences.

Secretary Kissinger: We have stated only one common point.

Foreign Minister Ch'iao: We are not discussing these documents in detail, but discussing the growth in exchanges and in friendship.

Secretary Kissinger: We can accept your point on social imperialism.

Foreign Minister Ch'iao: I would suggest that you consider our draft. It is not possible for us to have detailed discussions today.

Secretary Kissinger: We cannot accept this draft. I can't leave you in any doubt [about this point]. What modifications are possible we are willing to explore. There is no possibility of accepting this draft no matter how long we negotiate it.

Foreign Minister Ch'iao: We won't moderate it.

Secretary Kissinger: Basically are you saying either no communiqué or this?

Foreign Minister Ch'iao: In our draft we have basically stated our views, but you have not put in your views yet.

Secretary Kissinger: Let me understand you correctly. We can add our views. This is unchallenged. Are you saying that this communiqué with American views added, or no communiqué at all? Is this your position?

Foreign Minister Ch'iao: In substance. Our draft was drawn up after serious discussion.

Secretary Kissinger: So was ours.

Foreign Minister Ch'iao: I repeat what the Vice Premier said. I suggest you take back our draft and have a more serious consideration of it.

Secretary Kissinger: I want to understand your position. Are you saying either your draft or no communiqué or are you prepared to consider middle ground?

Foreign Minister Ch'iao: Basically this is our position. Of course, this is a document [prepared] by our two sides. We can discuss it, but we won't change its substance.

We are used to calling a spade a spade. Since 1972 there has been no basic change in our relations. This is reality. The communiqué should reflect this. As for concrete wording, we can discuss this.

Secretary Kissinger: How shall we proceed since the opportunity for direct exchanges is no longer practical?

Foreign Minister Ch'iao: What are your ideas?

Secretary Kissinger: I was not prepared to be this far apart on the last evening. I thought that as in October, 1971 we would have a basic document by now.

Foreign Minister Ch'iao: Shall we discuss this when you come again next time with the President?

Secretary Kissinger: I will have to discuss with the President what he wants to do.

Foreign Minister Ch'iao: There are two questions. One is the general pattern of the communiqué. There are two points here. The two sides can state their own views, and then their common points. The second question is concrete wording of the communiqué. We can discuss this later.

We cannot agree that we cannot state our differences. This is only to deceive people. This is no good. Our people won't accept it.

Secretary Kissinger: Neither will ours.

Foreign Minister Ch'iao: Actually what we need is to state the differences. This is objective reality. Of course, you have your problems and you cannot say we do not understand it fully.

For instance in the period before the Shanghai Communiqué [was signed] was your press so used to our words? They were not so used [to them]. So we say that you admit that the Shanghai Communiqué was a new example [of a diplomatic document].

Secretary Kissinger: I have stated many times in public in the United States that the way the Shanghai Communiqué was drafted was a tribute to the wisdom of the Chinese side, and a new way of negotiating. But that was a different occasion. It was the first contact at a top level between the U.S. and Chinese sides. That in itself was an historic event.

If we add as much as you have written [in your draft], this document will be six pages long.

I do not exclude stating some disagreement, but I think the balance between the two is not appropriate at this moment.

Foreign Minister Ch'iao: You are too much used to counting the words. Why not weigh the value of a document? As you have often said, you have often read many communiqués full of rhetoric. They are long, but people don't want to read them as they do not conform to reality.

Secretary Kissinger: Well—we will take into account your desire to state opposing views. We can send you what we think is an appropriate balance, maybe through Ambassador Bush, or your Ambassador. Then if we can agree in principle, we can work out the wording when we are here, as we did the last time.

Foreign Minister Ch'iao (with alacrity): Yes, we agree to your suggestion.

Secretary Kissinger: I think the Foreign Minister understands that what we will propose is a shortening of some key paragraphs. But he can give us his reaction later.

Foreign Minister Ch'iao: Three lines like mine? (Laughter)

Secretary Kissinger: Three lines.

Foreign Minister Ch'iao: Because you want to shorten the key paragraph.

Secretary Kissinger: Two–three lines each. Yes. I will do to you what you did to me last year.

Foreign Minister Ch'iao: Last year you complained we gave you too short a draft, so this year we gave you more.

Secretary Kissinger: You can be sure the statement about social imperialism will be in it.

Foreign Minister Ch'iao: I agree to your suggestion.

Secretary Kissinger: Let's . . . we will have Ambassador Bush give further drafts to you.

Foreign Minister Ch'iao: Okay.

Secretary Kissinger: And after that we can make a decision after we receive it.

Foreign Minister Ch'iao: This is not a big problem, the communiqué. The importance is the substance.

Secretary Kissinger: Given our [domestic] situation, if we have to spend the next two months defending ourselves on why we went to China, it will be of no help to you or the policy we are attempting to pursue and it will be totally counterproductive. And it will liberate all those [domestic political] forces that have been contained since 1971.

Foreign Minister Ch'iao: Merely because we have stated our views in this manner?

Secretary Kissinger: No, not because you have stated your views. It depends on the whole context, on the balance between the agreements and disagreements and overall tone. And I think the Foreign Minister, who is more subtle than I am, understands what I am talking about.

Foreign Minister Ch'iao: You are too polite. Okay. We accept your suggestion that you will give instructions to your Ambassador. Is there anything further you would like to say?

Secretary Kissinger: No. I assume in the meantime we will both consider each other's views. We will say to the press that we have had preliminary discussions about a communiqué but we will not discuss our disagreements or any substance.

Foreign Minister Ch'iao: It is not necessary to go into details. You can tell your press that we have had discussions about the communiqué but we will not tell them the substance.

Secretary Kissinger: That will be our position.

Foreign Minister Ch'iao: Your press is really a problem. What if we cannot reach an agreement on the communiqué? What if there is no communiqué at all? What will we tell them?

Secretary Kissinger: That is why it is impossible. Even if I agree with you, no one will remember all of the communiqués I have worked on since I became one of the key figures in our foreign policy. I remember only two. One of them is the Shanghai Communiqué.

Foreign Minister Ch'iao: And the other one?

Secretary Kissinger: I knew you were going to ask that! It was the visit of the Swiss President to the United States. (Laughter)

It is not possible, unfortunately, for us to have no communiqué. We face a practical problem, not to turn this into a crisis—because you are quite right, the essence of our relationship is not dependent on one sentence. We do not delude ourselves and neither do you. But for the essence—what to me—quite frankly, I consider the matters Habib discussed with your associate [Lin P'ing] of secondary importance. But for our public, unless there is some progress in tone we cannot rely on it to give impetus to the essence of the relationship, which is the hegemony problem.

Foreign Minister Ch'iao: Some questions cannot be settled at the moment.

Secretary Kissinger: I understand this. The fact of the matter is this: There are certain kinds of hegemonic moves which may now appear quite improbable, but if they ever arise it will require—it is necessary to prepare a more or less psychological framework. They [the hegemonic moves] may never arise. But apart from this purpose, the President's and my interest in these bilateral matters end. You notice I never raise them with you. But they will be used by our public to judge the degree of our relationship, and they give us the possibility to enlist support for political issues rather than economic and technical issues.

Foreign Minister Ch'iao: But there must be something practical. But if there is nothing practical in our bilateral relations, but only things of a symbolic nature, there is no reason for these things.

Secretary Kissinger: We agree, but we hope we will have things of both a symbolic as well as a practical significance.

Foreign Minister Ch'iao: That is a problem that confronts us both.

Secretary Kissinger: That is correct, and they is why I believe that with the talent available to both of us we should be able to produce something. I would be glad to assign Habib from tormenting me to doing something constructive. (Laughter)

Foreign Minister Ch'iao: What I mean is that if in our bilateral relations we could put in the draft something substantial, that would be good; but at the moment we do not have such things. No talent can create things like this, including Mr. Habib. They tried this morning.

Secretary Kissinger: The Chairman gave me this yesterday (the Secretary hands a small piece of paper to Ch'iao with the word "yes" written on it) and if you teach Lin P'ing to say this, you can make rapid progress. (Laughter)

Foreign Minister Ch'iao: This was given by the Chairman to you, so you should learn this.

Secretary Kissinger: I have learned. Maybe we can give it to him (Lin P'ing). I think we understand each other's necessities.

Foreign Minister Ch'iao: Okay. Is there anything left for us to discuss?

Secretary Kissinger: Did I see you show something to the Vice Premier—an announcement of the President's visit that you had in mind?

Foreign Minister Ch'iao: A very brief announcement. Only stating the date. (A copy is handed to Secretary Kissinger.)[5]

Secretary Kissinger: This is the style that I am used to. It has been a great tradition since you became Foreign Minister.

Foreign Minister Ch'iao: It has been the tradition since I started out.

Secretary Kissinger: What did we say when President Nixon's visit was announced? The same thing? Can we state our view on this matter separately?

Foreign Minister Ch'iao: It never hurts to listen to other views.

Secretary Kissinger: Can we have a Chinese and an American version?

Foreign Minister Ch'iao: Here is the Chinese version.

Secretary Kissinger: It is a good translation. (Laughter) If we have any views, which I doubt, we will let you know. And we will settle on this after we have had the next exchange—after Mr. Bush has talked to you next week. It is not an official visit unless we have one late night meeting.

Foreign Minister Ch'iao: It is better not to have a communiqué. We did the same last time when President Nixon was here.

Secretary Kissinger: I remember. Several nights. If we agree on the framework, we will probably have to do the final discussion when President Ford is here.

The meeting ended at 2:25 a.m.

---

[5] The undated announcement stating that President Ford would visit China December 1–6, is in the Ford Library, National Security Adviser, Kissinger Reports on USSR, China, and Middle East Discussions, Box 2, China Memcons and Reports, October 19–23, 1975, Kissinger's Trip.

127.   Memorandum From Secretary of State Kissinger to President Ford[1]

Washington, October 24, 1975.

SUBJECT

Possible Approaches to Your China Trip

As I have indicated in my reports to you,[2] I believe that our relationship with China has cooled. Certainly Peking wishes to sustain our relations: a pronounced souring or break would expose the Chinese even further to Moscow; we remain their only real option as a counterweight. Accordingly, the Chinese will maintain our connection at about present levels. But they will not be willing to show much progress in bilateral relations or cooperation on international issues; and they will stress our differences and keep up their ideological criticism of us in the public domain. They are ready, in short, to continue their recent phase of correctness, without warmth or much vitality.

This Chinese attitude has been the general pattern of recent months. In hindsight its origins can probably be traced back to the end of 1973 when several factors coincided: the initial impact of Watergate and the first instances of Congressional hobbling of Executive authority in foreign affairs; the beginning of the fading of the authority of Chou En-lai, the chief architect of the American opening; and our goofs in sending a high-level Ambassador to Taiwan and opening up two new Chinese Nationalist consulates in the U.S. shortly after my November trip to Peking and its positive communiqué, including a reasonable Chinese formulation on Taiwan.

Since then by far the key factor has been the Chinese perception of the erosion of our domestic foundation and loss of clout on the world scene. Furthermore, during my visit last year, I foreshadowed for the first time the unlikelihood of major progress on the Taiwan issue before 1977 unless China explicitly renounced the use of force. Since then détente has run into trouble, reducing our leverage with Peking—our best period in Chinese relations, 1971–3, was also our most active phase with the Soviet Union. We suffered a major setback in Indochina, which however ideologically pleasing to Peking, pointed up our domestic

---

[1] Source: Ford Library, National Security Adviser, Kissinger Reports on USSR, China, and Middle East Discussions, Box 2, China Memcons and Reports, October 19–23, 1975, Kissinger's Trip. Secret; Sensitive. There are no notations on the memorandum that indicate that Ford saw it.

[2] Ford received and initialed Kissinger's reports on his visit to China. (Memoranda from Scowcroft to Ford, October 19, 20, and 21; ibid.)

vulnerabilities and was a geopolitical reversal for the Chinese. In Europe the Chinese see the unravelling of the Southern flank of NATO and the lulling of the continent generally by what they call the "European Insecurity Conference." And the Congressional investigations and pre-election politicking have picked up steam. Finally, there has been intensive pre-succession jockeying in China itself, and their domestic politics has probably made them more musclebound in their decision-making, and perhaps includes criticism of policy toward America.

These cumulative factors over the past two years now add up to China's taking us less seriously as a world power that is capable of resisting a Soviet Union that continues to increase its military strength and expand its political influence. This changed attitude was clearly reflected in the scenario of my visit to China this time:

—Their Foreign Minister slammed us hard in the United Nations on the eve of my trip. They also needled us on the issues of Tibet and Puerto Rico.

—At the first night's banquet in Peking, their Foreign Minister publicly criticized our détente policy, knowing full well that this was bound to get major attention.

—The conversations with Vice Premier Teng were on the whole desultory, with their showing little interest in our perception of the world scene, except for the Soviet Union and Europe where they said we were following the policies of Munich and Dunkirk.

—Chairman Mao reinforced these themes in our conversation, clearly questioning our reliability as a serious power.

—For the first time they declined to hear some special briefings, perhaps partly because of their fear of leaks in the U.S., but also presumably to keep their distance.

—The contentious nature of both the content of their draft communiqué for your visit and their procedure was their most disdainful performance so far in our relationship. On substance they indicated that they want to highlight our differences and show little advance in our relations. And they waited until just a few hours before my departure before tabling their draft—when they had known for several weeks that we wanted to reach essential agreement on the outcome of your visit during my trip; their response was a complete rejection of our approach; and they did not give us any warning at all of the chasm during three days of talks during meetings, banquets, and sightseeing.

All of this is annoying, even somewhat disturbing. It is not a major crisis, however, and should be kept in perspective. They have no real strategic options at this time to continuing our relationship. They clearly are eager to have you visit China. The forces that brought us together remain basically at work. They still treat Moscow as the principal enemy and will maintain some restraint in their posture toward us. And for all our domestic problems, they know full well that we remain the strongest power in the world and are not to be trifled with.

The General Prospects

Against this background let me explore the outlook for your own trip and how I believe we should now proceed. You have my telegraphed account of our final evening in Peking and the exchanges we had on the unacceptable Chinese draft communiqué.[3] On the way to the airport Thursday[4] morning, the Foreign Minister indicated they would make an effort to meet our concerns when they get our new draft next week, though he reiterated they must have their three principles on Taiwan and the section on concrete bilateral relations would remain truncated. He said their first preference is no communiqué, and he doesn't understand why we think we need one. The political symbolism of your visit is the central factor in their view. He also suggested the promising possibility of a joint press statement in place of a communiqué. This could be a less contentious and more positive document describing the talks—instead of a formal document between two countries which would oblige them to state their principled views. I left it that we would be in touch with them early in the week through Ambassador Bush.

I made certain during my visit that you would receive a courteous and appropriate welcome. It is not in the Chinese interest to embarrass you in terms of hospitality or decorum. At the same time, it is now very clear, as we suspected all along, that there will be little drama and minimum results. We will not gain Chinese acceptance of a positive communiqué showing significant movement in our relations. No matter what course we pursue, we can expect domestic and international carping over the worth of a second Presidential visit to China that produces meager concrete results—notwithstanding the fact that we believe that your trip is justified by the symbolism of an ongoing relationship; the chance to exchange authoritative views on the international situation; the Soviet factor; the opportunity to size up the post-Mao, post-Chou leadership of the world's most populous nation; and whatever modest outcome we can achieve.

Options

We now have the following options:

(1) Push for the most positive communiqué we can get.

(2) Settle for a very brief, bland communiqué or none at all.

---

[3] Ford initialed the communiqué, which he received from Scowcroft. (Ibid.) The Chinese draft was given to U.S. officials on October 22; see Document 126 and footnote 2 thereto.

[4] October 23.

(3) Work toward a relatively brief but more upbeat joint press statement.

(4) Cancel your trip.

In considering our course of action we need to keep in mind the Chinese view of us; the Soviet reaction; our general international posture; and the American domestic reaction.

Let me briefly discuss each of the options in turn.

Positive Communiqué. This has been our objective. The weightier the results of the trip, of course, the more solid our bilateral relationship looks to the world, and the Soviet Union in particular, and the more justifiable your travels look to the domestic audience. We have emphasized that signs of a vital connection with Peking are required to maintain public support for our China policy and thus any help to Peking in case of Soviet pressures. On the other hand, it is now amply clear that the Chinese will continue to keep our relationship at the present level—alive enough to suit their geopolitical purposes but without significant progress so long as we are not able to complete normalization. More fundamentally, because of our domestic weaknesses they take us less seriously as a world power, and they see our relations with Moscow as being in trouble, which reduces our leverage. Either they do not understand our need to show continued momentum, or they find it impossible to move for ideological and domestic political reasons. And they insist on underlining our differences as well as areas of common agreement.

These factors mean that we cannot expect to work out a positive communiqué. We went for the maximum document in our draft, and the unacceptable Chinese response demonstrates their clashing view. With maximum effort we may be able to eliminate some of the negative aspects of their version and add a few positive elements. But the starting point is so bleak and the Chinese position so firm that the very best we could come out with is a carbon copy of the Shanghai Communiqué and that after major bargaining right down to the wire. Even this outcome would be criticized as a stalling out of our relations after three years, and the value of your journey would be questioned.

Brief Communiqué or None at All. This approach would recognize the impossibility of a positive outcome and forego the arduous task of battling with the Chinese over drafts to little avail. It would state neither agreements nor disagreements but simply use adjectives to describe the conversations. We would clearly indicate in advance of your visit that the emphasis will be on your private discussions with the new leadership in Peking and major movement was neither necessary nor to be expected at this stage of our relations. This would fit the Chinese mood. And it would look more honest to our various audiences, including the domestic one, than a lengthy replay of three years ago.

On the other hand, it would be very difficult to explain a second President's going all the way to China, holding several days of discussions, and then having nothing to announce in terms of mutual agreement. Foreign and domestic audiences would probably interpret this as signifying a stagnated relationship and question the purpose of your trip. The Soviets might take heart that we were going nowhere in our Chinese opening.

Joint Press Statement. As I said, Chiao floated this concept as allowing the Chinese to be more flexible in their presentations. The document would be informal and descriptive, rather than a formal taking of positions which would inevitably involve a more extensive cataloging of differences. Its overall character would be blander—but also more positive—than a communiqué. Another advantage would be that, unlike a communiqué, it would not be comparable to the Shanghai document and thus less susceptible to comparisons. It would thus be more extensive than a brief communiqué (or none at all) without many of the headaches of a lengthy communiqué.

The drawbacks would be the inevitable carping over lack of results. By definition there would be no specific agreements, only a narrative of the discussions with a positive sense of direction. It would probably be brief. Various audiences, including Moscow, would take it as a sign that our relationship with Peking was not progressing rapidly but they would not conclude that it was in bad shape.

Cancel the Trip. This is an option that should also be considered. Clearly little concrete can be expected to result from your journey. The sharper public rhetoric of the Chinese recently; their refusal to be visibly identified with us; the Middle Kingdom psychology of getting a second President to come to China even though he knew little would be achieved; and the disdainful way that they treated us and the communiqué process during my visit—all these suggest postponement of your trip should at least be considered. Your various audiences at home and abroad, including the Soviets might well consider your cancellation an act of strength. The Chinese might secretly respect such a move. You would explain that our relations with Peking are proceeding satisfactorily, but based on our exploratory contacts you decided that a summit meeting was not really required or justified at this juncture. You look forward to going when conditions were more ripe, and meanwhile we would sustain our relationship through established channels. It could be argued that this course would invite no more criticism of failure than a trip that seemed purely cosmetic, or even highlighted our divergences.

On the other hand, a cancellation of your trip—after all the firm expectations for a full year—would be a major event, no matter how low-keyed we tried to treat it. It would be seen probably as a major crisis in our relationship—either on general grounds or because of specific issues like détente or Taiwan. Coupled with the postponement of the Brezhnev summit, many would trumpet a general failure of our foreign policy, particularly in East-West relations. The Russians would certainly be pleased—though they might well be impressed with your sang-froid and would probably not attempt to exploit the event in strategic fashion. Finally it might well kill off the China opening. No matter how annoying some of the Chinese practices, they have made it amply clear that they look forward to your visit, and your cancellation would be a significant rebuff.

Conclusions

I look forward to discussing these issues with you. As of now, I lean strongly toward the following procedure:

—Reduce your China trip effectively to three-plus working days in Peking only. You would arrive on Monday afternoon, December 1 and leave Friday morning, December 5. It would be billed as a business-like exchange of views in the capital, with limited sightseeing and no visits to other cities.

—Work for a joint press statement which would eliminate most contentious language and be moderately upbeat.

—Proceed to the Philippines and Indonesia for a day each and return to the U.S. on Monday, December 8.

This course has the following advantages:

—It would indicate that our relationship with the PRC is being sustained and marginally advanced because of our mutual interests, though our respective differences prevent a major breakthrough.

—The stop in China could be seen as a working session with the new leader of a quarter of humanity without an extended sojourn, side trips or frills.

—The reduction of the China trip and the adding of two other countries would be an appropriate riposte to the general Chinese attitude and communiqué ploy. It would place them into a general Asian context rather than have the President travel all the way to Peking for meetings he knew would be marginal.

—We would strengthen our relations with the two key countries in Southeast Asia.

—Your trip (which would still only last one week), would become an Asian, rather than merely a Communist China, journey and would thus have a weightier and more balanced nature.

I recommend we proceed as follows. Ambassador Bush would present a draft of a joint press statement along the lines of Tab A.[5] (For reference the Chinese draft communiqué is at Tab B.)[6] He would be instructed to tell the Chinese the following:

(1) After reflecting on the exchanges during my trip and studying their communiqué, we decided that it would be impossible to work out an acceptable communiqué; in order to agree to some of their language spelling out our differences we would need a great deal of positive content elsewhere in the document—which they have made clear they are not prepared to accept. Therefore, per my conversation with the Foreign Minister on the way to the airport, we have decided that a joint press statement is the best outcome; being less formal, it would not require explicit and divisive taking of positions. Our draft picks up the positive aspects of their draft communiqué in verbatim fashion and expresses other sections (e.g. Taiwan) in as objective a manner as we can. Frankly we consider their positive elements inadequate, but we can live with them in a press statement that drops their contentious language.

(2) We believe it makes sense to make a working visit, keeping in mind the Chinese view that the trip itself is the significant political factor. Therefore you plan to arrive on Monday afternoon in Peking, leave Friday morning, and visit no other Chinese cities.

(3) You are reconsidering the possibility of visiting a couple of friendly Asian capitals after China; otherwise your travels would have an unbalanced coloration.

(4) We wish to announce the dates for the trip on Monday, November 3, so we need their response very quickly.

(5) Our advance team would proceed to Peking a week or so later.

---

[5] Tab A, attached but not printed, is the U.S. draft of the joint press statement as approved and revised by Kissinger. It was sent to the USLO in an undated backchannel message. (Ford Library, National Security Adviser, Kissinger–Scowcroft West Wing Office Files, 1969–1977, Box 5, China, unnumbered items (22), 10/25/75–10/31/75)

[6] Tab B is attached but not printed.

128.   Paper Prepared by the Director of the Policy Planning Staff (Lord)[1]

Washington, undated.

Analysis/Highlights of Secretary Kissinger's Meeting
with Chairman Mao, October 21, 1975

The Main Themes

This meeting was on the whole disturbing, signifying *a cooling of our relationship linked to the Chinese perception of the U.S. as a fading strategic power in the face of Soviet advance.* Though the session was cordial, it was considerably less so than previous encounters. In November 1973 the conversation was described by the Chinese as "friendly," "wide-ranging," and "far-sighted." This time the third adjective was omitted.[2] We both still have a "common opponent" but whereas before there was a feeling of working in parallel to counter this threat, this time the message was that the U.S. could not be counted upon to resist pressures and therefore China was going to have to go it alone.

To sum up the major theme in one sentence: The U.S. is "not reliable," Europe is "soft," Japan seeks "hegemony," and therefore China will dig tunnels, store millet and oppose the Soviet Union on its own, even as a naive and appeasing world curses the Chinese as "warlords" for sounding the alarm.

The Soviet Union therefore is still the enemy. *The U.S. is not so much hostile as it is ineffectual* (which perhaps is more insulting). For example, if Europe is attacked we would pull a Dunkirk and get out, rather than either seeing our heavily outnumbered troops get overwhelmed or resorting to nuclear weapons. If this is true in Europe, by extension it is true in Asia as well; China should not count on our defending it in a crunch; we need not discuss military matters as on previous occasions. In any event China is down the list of our priorities, and even our allies in Europe and Japan get less attention than the Soviet Union in our policies.

---

[1] Source: Ford Library, National Security Adviser, Trip Briefing Books and Cables for President Ford, Presidential Trips File, Box 19, 11/28–12/7/75, Far East, Briefing Book, Peking, Meeting with Chairman Mao, President's copy (3). Secret; Sensitive. A hand-written note at the top of the first page reads: "(Lord memo) HAK handed to President. 10/25/75." Kissinger gave this paper to Ford during a 9:30 a.m. meeting in the Oval Office. See Document 129.

[2] The Chinese press release, dated October 21, is attached but not printed.

In our relations with Moscow the theme of appeasement (Teng used the Munich analogy) *has overtaken* the one of *collusion.* Détente is dangerous not so much because it represents ganging up on China as it undermines the morale and defenses of the West through false illusions, thus increasing the pressures on the PRC. It is true that we "stood on the shoulders" of China to gain leverage on Moscow in the 1971–3 period, but that is "useless" now—presumably both because China won't let itself be used and because détente is in trouble. Thus our policy now is marked by maneuvering and Dr. Kissinger's very busy travels. We are flailing away in a rear guard action against the Soviet hegemonic tide which is sweeping toward war: we are "swallows" who are "busy" before "the wind and rain" come. We may be able to postpone the Soviet storm, but it is inescapably on its way.

The source of our troubles is domestic. "Not reliable" can refer to a failure of nerve, a general withdrawal from the fray, the release of classified documents, the incomprehensible (to the Chinese) destruction of a strong President over a minor incident. Our policies are increasingly hamstrung by a combination of the liberal appeasing establishment symbolized by *The New York Times,* and traditional conservative isolationists (and anti-PRC to boot) symbolized by Senator Goldwater.

This turbulent international situation is much more crucial than Taiwan. For now it is better to have the U.S. keep the island under control rather than having it go independent or toward Moscow or Tokyo. The Chinese can wait patiently until the time is ripe, but then they will have to use force. By implication, the U.S. should not ask for peaceful assurances, but it can take its time letting Taiwan go.

The future of China's policies is uncertain. Mao and his followers— Premier Chou, Marshal Yeh, and (noticeably) Vice Premier Teng—are all old and "will not do," "will not make it out." There is criticism, perhaps internal, of Mao as being a "warlord" (too anti-Russian?) and a "bureaucrat" (too much emphasis on production?).

Thus China will go it alone—"rifles and millet." Let all the world curse it as a "warlord" or "warmonger." That only makes Mao happy. The Chinese will prepare for "the wind and the rain." And if Moscow attacks, Peking will suck the Russians in, let them occupy the big cities à la Napoleon, and mobilize for a victorious counter-attack.

Some Specific Points

Mao is very sick. He looked it, despite his mental agility. He was unable to walk us to the door as on previous occasions. He had much more trouble standing. He was just about unable to speak at all, making most of his points on paper or in obscure grunts. He is "going to heaven" soon, and has an "invitation from God" (points he has made previously, however). And he described his various ailments all over him.

Mao is in charge of general international strategy. He was well briefed and he had clearly given Teng his script the day before. He hit all the major themes of their foreign policy. On the other hand, he is clearly incapable of detailed or sustained work; he himself said that he ignored "routine" affairs and suggested he confined himself to international matters.

Teng is the key official now. Mao referred to him several times in the conversation. He is certainly Chou's replacement, and perhaps Mao's. On the other hand Mao pointed to his age, grouped him with himself, Chou and Yeh, and suggested that they would all be soon irrelevant.

The U.S. (and Kissinger) are "not reliable." See the general themes above. We are "swallows" before the storm. We are "maneuvering" and "busy"—though both are allowable, they are apparently at best delaying actions. We are prone to "Dunkirks." We won't use nuclear weapons. We are no longer "far-sighted."

Our domestic structure is weak. Watergate was mishandled and magnified. Our media (*Times*) and our Congress (Goldwater) are sapping our strength.

China is relatively backward—both in strength and in our priorities. After America comes Russia, Europe, Japan and then China.

"Europe is too soft now." They are afraid of the Soviet Union. Europe is too "scattered," "loose," "spread out." East and West Germany should unite under West German domination (so as to pressure the Soviet Union).

"Japan is seeking hegemony."

U.S. policy toward the Soviet Union is confused and ineffectual. It is variously described as "Dunkirk" appeasement, frantic maneuvering, using China to get to Moscow, joining Moscow in hurling epithets at the PRC. At the same time Moscow remains a "common opponent" of both China and the U.S. and when war breaks out, then (but only then) we should consider joint cooperation.

In any event Schlesinger should come to China and visit the areas near the Soviet Union (so as to push us towards confrontation with Moscow). He is presumably welcome because he makes preparations and cries out rather than flying around like a "swallow."

"The small issue is Taiwan, the big issue is the world." They can wait 100 years, for Taiwan is "unwantable," indigestible ("full of counter-revolutionaries"). It's better for the U.S. to keep the island under control for the time being.

China will rely on itself. "Rifles and millet." The Dunkirk strategy if necessary. The Chairman likes to be cursed (unlike Americans who worry about their image?); only then does he pay attention to someone. Dr. Kissinger should go ahead and publicize Chinese aggression against China (Taiwan) and Korea. "I will only be happy when all foreigners slam on tables and curse me." China needs to know its enemies (including the U.S.?) so as to be vigilant: "If you don't curse me, I won't see you, and I will just sleep peacefully."

Concluding Caveat

Finally, *let us not pretend that we can fathom everything* the Chairman had to say. Some passages might have had layers that we are incapable of sensing; others might merely be literal; others might be haphazard, even meaningless.

The Chairman's basic message and principal themes were clear. They clearly formed the strategic framework for the Kissinger visit, indeed for the evolution in our relations in the past couple of years. But there were several cryptic passages that are unclear. The tendency is to dig for the subtleties, the deeper meanings behind the Chairman's laconic, earthy prose. In most instances the larger meaning is apparent. In others, however, there may be nothing particularly significant, or a somewhat senile man might have been wandering aimlessly for a moment. After all, he is a very frail 82. His words were either translated with great difficulty (and probably smoothed over and elaborated at times) by the three girls or written down. Chiao volunteered his own interpretation the next day, which is unprecedented, playing down the collusion theme and underlining the "common enemy" leverage.

To cite just one example of ambiguity: "Do you have any way to assist me in curing my present inability to speak clearly?" The odds are that this was basically small talk about his own health. It is very doubtful that he was seriously asking for medical assistance. But was the Chairman saying that his voice within China (or in the world) was not being heard, that his influence is being circumscribed, and that he wants U.S. help to strengthen his position through our policies? Does he want us to help him "speak clearly" in this larger sense?

There were several other obscure passages in the talk, e.g. the reference to the anti-Chinese Korean resolution, the cracks against Jewish influence in the American media, the invitation to Bush to pay a call on the Chairman. *These might have meant,* in turn, that the Chinese don't want to get involved in the Korean problem; that Jews are traditionally appeasers in history and are a major element in eroding American steadfastness; and that the U.S. should pay more attention to China.

Equally the passages may have had no deeper meaning whatsoever, despite the Chairman's well deserved reputation for the use of aphorism and symbolism and never wasting his words.

129.   Memorandum of Conversation[1]

Washington, October 25, 1975, 9:30 a.m.

PARTICIPANTS

President Gerald Ford
Dr. Henry A. Kissinger, Secretary of State and Assistant to the President for
    National Security Affairs
Lt. General Brent Scowcroft, Deputy Assistant to the President for National
    Security Affairs

[Omitted here is discussion of the loigistics and timetable for the President's proposed visit to East Asia, and of other matters unrelated to China.]

[The Secretary hands the President a summary/analysis of his conversation with Mao.][2]

President: How is Mao's health?

Kissinger: When you see him you think he is finished; he can hardly articulate. He speaks a few words of English but it is impossible to understand. The interpreter has to guess at the words until he nods—or he writes out the words. Mao's theme is our weakness. We are the "swallow before the storm." We are ineffectual. What we say is not reliable. He thinks we won't use nuclear weapons in Europe and would suffer another Dunkirk. He says we can no longer stand on Chinese shoulders to reach the Soviet Union. "China must be self-reliant." It is sort of admirable. These are the same people of the Long March.

I said we had a common opponent. He said he likes Schlesinger's view of the Soviet Union better than mine. They wanted Schlesinger to visit. That would drive the Soviet Union wild. But I said we could have military exchanges to see what we could do. He said, "No. After the war starts we will talk, not before the war." They want to do the same as Stalin did in World War II—be sure that a war starts in the West so both will be exhausted by the time China has to get in.

I guarantee you that if we do go into confrontation with the Soviet Union, they will attack us and the Soviet Union and draw the Third World around them. Good relations with the Soviet Union are the best for our Chinese relations—and vice versa. Our weakness is the problem—they see us in trouble with SALT and détente. That plays into their hands.

---

[1] Source: Ford Library, National Security Adviser, National Security Adviser Memcons, Box 16, July–October 1975. Secret; Nodis. The meeting took place in the Oval Office. All brackets are in the original, except those bracketed insertions describing the omission of material. According to the President's Daily Diary, Ford, Kissinger, and Scowcroft met from 9:35 until 11:05 a.m. (Ibid.)

[2] Document 128.

They can't understand the Congress—what the Congress did on Turkey, Hawk missiles, etc.

I think you can't take any guff from them, and you have to be cooler than Nixon in your toast.

[Discussion of schedule.]

Kissinger: I don't think you should not just go to China. People will say what did you go for? Then they will have you by the balls in terms of making it look worthwhile. The best thing you can do is something in contrast with Nixon: Don't stay long, don't go to another city. Any other city visit, even if it's different from where Nixon went, will look like a repeat to the American people.

When I saw the communiqué my first reaction was to cancel your trip. Bush's reaction was the same. But when we thought about it, we changed our minds. It would lose us all our leverage with the Soviet Union. It would upset the Japanese. It would give the Chinese a chance to invite all the Democratic candidates over to say you screwed up the Chinese policy.

President: How about adding India?

Kissinger: No. That's too big a shock. Manila and Djakarta is just a jab at them. India and Pakistan would add two days minimum. Manila/Djakarta bolsters our friends, and you'll get a big reception in Manila.

President: I agree. Manila will please the Conservatives. I think you are probably right. Let me think it over just a bit and I'll let you know.

[He hands the President the U.S. draft press statement on the China trip.][3]

President: It sounds all right. This sentence about peaceful settlement of Taiwan by the Chinese themselves—this is what we have said before, isn't it?

Kissinger: Yes. The conservatives will like it; the PRC won't like it much.

President: How is George Bush doing?

Kissinger: Magnificently. I am very, very impressed with him. I was not enthusiastic about his appointment, but he has grown into the job and I think he will one day be a considerable national leader. He is a big cut above Moynihan—who is turning into a disaster. To call Brazil a fascist dictatorship [because of its vote on the anti-Zionism resolution] . . .

President: When did he do that?

---

[3] See footnote 5, Document 127.

Kissinger: He is going wild about the Israeli issues. [*less than 1 line not declassified*]

President: I agree with you about George. He is a fine man.

Kissinger: [Reads parts from the analysis of the Mao conversation.]

President: What is going to happen when Mao dies?

Kissinger: There is no way anyone can know that. He is on the verge of becoming a vegetable, but he has the uncanny ability to go right to the heart of things. No small talk, in the sense that everything has meaning.

[Omitted here is discussion unrelated to China.]

130.   **Memorandum of Conversation**[1]

Washington, October 31, 1975.

PARTICIPANTS

President Gerald R. Ford
Henry A. Kissinger, Secretary of State
Brent Scowcroft, Assistant to the President for National Security Affairs

Kissinger: The Chinese turned down our statement but accepted the cut-down version of the trip. They stressed that you would be received with courtesy. They need us more than we need them. They may be doing this to prove their manhood; having done so they may give you a good trip. These are two options: cancel, or else go but get the word out that we don't expect anything of substance but that it is important to exchange views.

The President: I think we should do the latter.

Kissinger: Then I would tell the Chinese we find their communiqué unacceptable and since we submitted the last draft it is up to them to offer modifications. Ask them: Why does it serve their purpose to have the visit end on a statement advertising our differences? But say we are prepared to do without a statement. Then I think we

---

[1] Source: Ford Library, National Security Adviser, NSA Memcons, Box 16, July–October 1975. Secret; Nodis. The meeting took place in the Oval Office. According to the President's Daily Diary, it lasted from 9:18 to 10:10 a.m., with Scowcroft joining at 9:25. (Ibid.) All brackets are in the original, except the bracketed insertion describing the omission of material.

should get to Indonesia and the Philippines and announce it all next Tuesday. [Discussed the sequence of Jakarta–Manila.]

The President: Is there any diplomatic difference?

Kissinger: I don't know which way it would be easier to get out the crowds.

The President: Let's go to Jakarta first if there isn't any difference.

Kissinger: Okay. Let's notify all of them and say we want to announce it at noon here on Tuesday.[2] We will do a note to the Chinese: Since we have submitted something to them, could they submit their version of a press statement? Also could they tell us how to make our version acceptable. It is in the interest of both of us not to end on the point of our differences.

Actually the Chinese note was fairly conciliatory. Bush thinks it is best not to have a communiqué.

The President: I think to cancel it would be a disaster both internationally and with the left and right.

[Omitted here is discussion unrelated to China.]

---

[2] November 4.

---

131. Backchannel Message From the Chief of the Liaison Office in China (Bush) to Secretary of State Kissinger[1]

Beijing, November 6, 1975, 0855Z.

133. Subject: The President's Visit. The mood in our recent brief meetings with Foreign Minister Chiao Kuan-hua has been noticeably chilly. There has been no small talk and no relaxed opening sentences, only: "Let's proceed with the business at hand." On Tuesday,[2] Chiao delivered the PRC reply delaying the advance and the announcement and offered a seemingly gratuitous lecture on the need for airing differences. He rejected our communiqué draft out of hand, said again he would not care if there were no communiqué, and seemed to move

---

[1] Source: Ford Library, National Security Adviser, Kissinger–Scowcroft West Wing Office Files, 1969–1977, Box 5, China, unnumbered items (23), 11/1/75–11/6/75. Secret; Sensitive; Handle Via Voyager Channel. A stamped notation in the upper right hand corner of the first page indicates that the President saw this message.

[2] November 4.

away from the "we have time" theme to the hoary "you owe us a debt."[3] (His emphasis on this last point seemed curiously out of step with that of Chairman Mao on the Taiwan question.)

All this may merely be tactical posturing designed to strengthen the PRC negotiating position prior to the visit. However, I doubt this is the case, and it would be prudent in any case to assume that the Chinese will employ some fairly unpleasant language, both in public and in private, during the President's visit. Given the probable cost at home to the President for having to subject himself to this and the limited likelihood that there will be any forward movement on Sino-U.S. relations, I would incline toward postponing the visit if there were a genuinely legitimate reason to do so. (At this late date, of course, this seems highly unlikely and I do not advocate putting the visit off.)

The question at hand is how to best respond to tough Chinese statements on their view of the world scene, détente, and the Taiwan issue in a way that minimizes the dangers for the President without unduly disturbing our bilateral relationship. I would suggest the President come armed with a general exposition of U.S. support for the Shanghai Communiqué and hopes for the world—peace, freedom, equality, etc.—and our effort toward those goals which he could use both publicly and privately. This would not only have some propaganda value, it would also make it clear that the President formulates U.S. foreign policy based on his perception of right and the national interest and not in response to Chinese carping about our policies. Public Chinese criticism of détente could be handled as a portion of the banquet toast, perhaps by sharpening your theme that the United States has for many years taken and will continue to take firm action to oppose expansionism rather than rely on inflated rhetoric. If the Chinese raise the Taiwan issue along the lines of their draft communiqué, I believe the President would have to respond with a slightly embroidered exposition of our stand in the Shanghai Communiqué. If the Chinese escalate further by openly suggesting they may use military force to "liberate" Taiwan, it seems to me there is no alternative to the President's insisting that any settlement will have to be by peaceful means. The President can hardly afford to subject himself to public or private Chinese tirades on these critical issues without replying in some way, but we see no reason to spend our time merely responding to their statements. We should also be prepared to react if the Chinese decide to feed their line to the press through their underlings. (In this regard, you should know that shortly after the news of Schlesinger's

---

[3] The Chinese message was transmitted in backchannel message 129 from Beijing, November 4. (Ford Library, National Security Adviser, Kissinger–Scowcroft West Wing Office Files, 1969–1977, Box 5, China, unnumbered items (23), 11/1/75–11/6/75)

departure was carried by the wire services,[4] the MFA press man Ma Yu-chen gave a foreign correspondent here a lengthy pep talk of the PRC's great respect for Schlesinger and implied that he was the only person in the USG who fully understood the Soviet threat.)

Given the current Chinese frostiness, I think the President in both his private and public statements should strive to leave the Chinese leaders and the world audience with the unmistakable impression that Gerald Ford is a straight-talking man, contemptuous of overblown rhetoric, and a man who sets policy based on our own view of what is right and of our interests. All should know that the President is a good decent man, but one who can be tough as nails with the Soviets, the Chinese, or others when necessary. Needless to say, he (and other members of the party) should avoid effusive praise of the Chinese and their system or too many diplomatic niceties during banquet speeches which may be in answer to or followed by Chinese lectures on the poor state of the world and American impotence.

Warm regards

George Bush

---

[4] On November 2, Ford accepted Schlesinger's resignation as Secretary of Defense, Kissinger's as Assistant to the President for National Security Affairs, and Colby's as Director of Central Intelligence in a major realignment of his administration. They were replaced by Rumsfeld, Scowcroft, and Bush, respectively. Ford announced the changes on November 3; see *Public Papers: Ford, 1975*, vol. II, pp. 1791–1792.

---

132.   Memorandum From Secretary of State Kissinger to President Ford[1]

Washington, November 20, 1975.

SUBJECT

Your Trip to the People's Republic of China: A Scope Analysis for Your Discussions with Chinese Leaders

---

[1] Source: Ford Library, National Security Adviser, Trip Briefing Books and Cables for President Ford, Presidential Trips File, Box 20, 11/28–12/7/75, Far East, General. Top Secret; Nodis. This memorandum was attached to a November 22 covering memorandum from Scowcroft to the President, which noted, "It was prepared jointly by the NSC Staff and Department of State. It is meant to pull together the many aspects of U.S.–PRC relations that you will be reviewing in the other briefing materials we have sent."

As a basis for your preparations for your forthcoming trip to the People's Republic of China (PRC) we have prepared, in coordination with the NSC, the following analytical paper. It is intended to be a general scope analysis, and is designed to give you a comprehensive sense of the political context of your discussions with Chinese leaders. It reviews the manner in which our relations with the PRC have evolved over the past five years, and lays out in summary form the primary objectives of your meetings with Chairman Mao and Vice Premier Teng Hsiao-p'ing.

This scope analysis should also give you the kind of overview which will make more productive your reading of the other background materials being prepared for your trip by the Department, NSC, and CIA on international and bilateral issues.

The Political Context of Your Visit

Your trip to China comes at an important juncture. Our relations with the PRC are showing the first significant signs of strain since we initiated a direct dialogue with Chinese leaders during my secret trip to Peking in the summer of 1971. At the same time, both sides continue to see maintenance of the present relationship as in their respective interests. This situation will make your trip somewhat more difficult and less immediately productive than we had originally hoped. But it makes the visit all the more important if we are to sustain a relationship which has brought substantial strategic benefits to the foreign policy of the United States.

The U.S. Role in the World. There are several reasons for the current tension in our relationship with the Chinese. Probably the primary cause is a growing doubt in Peking that the United States is capable of playing the kind of major world role which will provide an effective counterweight to Moscow's efforts to project the Soviet presence abroad and to bring about a geo-political encirclement of China. In the wake of the Communist victories in Indochina this past spring, PRC media began to express in explicit terms a concern with the "strategic passivity" of the United States. Peking apparently believes that our domestic political situation is in such turmoil—as a result of the troubles of the last decade, the resignation of President Nixon, the increasingly assertive role of Congress in hobbling Executive Branch foreign policy actions, and the nihilistic mood of our press—that the United States is increasingly incapable of playing a coherent role in world affairs. To the degree that the Chinese downgrade our importance as a world power, or develop doubts about our ability to pursue our own interests abroad, they will question the significance of the relationship we have established over the past four years.

U.S.-Soviet Relations. A related factor prompting the Chinese to question the value of their relations with us is substantial concern about the effects on PRC interests of our détente policies for dealing with the Soviet Union. Chinese leaders seem to be reassessing—within limits— the impact on their interests of such developments as the Helsinki Conference, sales of American grain and technology to Russia, and our continuing efforts to pursue strategic arms limitation agreements with Moscow. Privately the Chinese fear that these developments will tend to isolate them politically and strengthen their major enemy. Publicly Peking is characterizing détente as outright appeasement of a growing Soviet threat to the security of the U.S. and Europe (and the PRC). Their media portray the West as repeating the mistakes of Chamberlain and Daladier in the 1930s in underestimating the menace of Hitler.

As much as the Chinese are concerned with détente, this issue itself cannot be the primary reason for Peking's current coolness, for the most active period of our relations with Moscow in 1972–73 was also the most positive period in the new U.S.–PRC relationship. While the Chinese did express to us privately in those years their concerns about some of our negotiations with the Russians—particularly the agreement on the prevention of nuclear war—Peking at least saw us capable of taking strong action against the Soviets, as we did in the Indian subcontinent in 1971 and Middle East alert of 1973. Thus the Chinese concern appears derived from the combination of increasing uncertainty about our world role and détente policies pursued from a position of apparent weakness rather than strength.

Of course it is self-serving for the Chinese to urge us toward more frontal opposition to the Soviets. Such a policy would clearly serve Peking's own interests, as it would strengthen Western counterpressures against the Russians and force Moscow to concentrate its military and political energies against the U.S. and Europe. Nevertheless the strongest incentive to the Chinese to cooperate with us comes from a combination of American forcefulness in international affairs, coupled with improving U.S. relations with Moscow. In this situation, the Chinese will at once have some assurance that the U.S. is capable of countering Soviet expansionist actions, and at the same time they will fear "falling behind" Moscow in developing constructive relations with us and being left isolated as the only critic of détente.

Your Approach to the Soviet Issue. Thus, much of your discussions with PRC leaders will undoubtedly focus on the central problem of the Soviet threat and our respective approaches to dealing with it. Our underlying position is that we will follow our national interests as we see them, and that neither Peking nor Moscow can presume to define those for us or lecture us on our policies. Your objective should be to forcefully assert your confidence in the overall approach you have adopted for coping with Moscow; to indicate that we have absolutely no illusions about Soviet intentions; but that our policies best serve American interests. You should say forthrightly that we will continue to seek agreements with Moscow which will lower tensions, reduce the dangers of war, and contribute to the evolution of a stable international equilibrium. You can emphasize that the American people are not deluded by détente (as our domestic debate clearly indicates), but that our efforts to encourage restrained behavior on the part of the Russians place us in the best position to mobilize the support of our people for resistance to Soviet expansionism. Only by demonstrating to our public that we have explored reasonable approaches with Moscow can we rally backing for firm actions when they are required.

You can state directly to Chinese leaders that we know they do not agree with our position, but emphasize that this is a disagreement over tactics rather than any difference in our fundamental assessment of the primary threat to the national security of either of our countries. You should recall that it was the problem of Soviet "hegemony" which first brought us together, that we continue to share a basic concern with this problem, and that because we basically agree about the source of expansionistic pressures in the world we can honestly disagree on a strategy for coping with it. While emphasizing that we will continue to pursue policies which we believe serve our own interests, the Administration will—as we have done since 1971—weigh the impact of our policies on China's interests, take no actions that are directed against the Chinese and actively consult with them.

Normalization. A third reason for some strain in our relations with Peking at this time appears to be reaction against the lack of movement toward full normalization of U.S.–PRC relations. As with their questions about détente, the concern of senior Chinese leaders regarding normalization is not simply a matter of disagreement with our current position on this issue; it is also our evident inability to act and implement policies which affect their interests.

From the very beginning of our relationship with Peking, the Chinese have clearly laid primary emphasis on strategic international considerations. These have always been the primary emphasis of our discussions in Peking. As recently as my conversation with Mao last month,[2] he said that the big issue is the international situation and the small issue is Taiwan. Nevertheless, they attach considerable significance to our position on Taiwan, and to whether we will move to recognize them as the sole legal government of China. This is a basic issue of principle for Peking, one with considerable domestic political weight, and which they view as an indicator of how seriously we take our relationship with them.

---

[2] See Document 124.

In addition, the Chinese had been led by President Nixon to expect that a major effort would be made before 1976 to resolve the Taiwan question and establish diplomatic relations. Since 1973 they have patiently worked to put us in a position where we would have to deal with this complex of issues on China's own terms (what Peking now likes to characterize as the "Japanese model" for normalization: breaking diplomatic relations with the Republic of China on Taiwan; withdrawal of all U.S. troops from the island; and abrogation of the U.S.–ROC defense treaty). Now there appears to be considerable uncertainty about our ability and willingness to follow through on the normalization question.

The Chinese leadership appears cross-pressured on Taiwan between a rational assessment of their strategic needs vis-à-vis the United States and the emotional weight of an issue of considerable domestic political impact. When your trip was set up in November of 1974, I had an inconclusive discussion with Vice Premier Teng Hsiao-p'ing on normalization.[3] It was clearly agreed that your trip would be without preconditions on Taiwan or any other issue. The Chinese may nevertheless have hoped a year ago that conditions would be such that you would be in a position to make some progress on this issue.

This past June, in the wake of the spring developments in Indochina, the Chinese appeared anxious that you might postpone your visit to the PRC out of concern that you would be pressured on normalization. They clearly wanted to preserve your visit. To pre-empt a decision to postpone it, Vice Premier Teng Hsiao-p'ing publicly told a group of visiting American newspaper editors on June 2 that you would be welcomed in Peking whether or not you had major business to transact.[4] Since that time, Chinese leaders have clearly and repeatedly stated—both privately and publicly—that they look forward to your visit even in the absence of progress toward full normalization (because of the desire to sustain a relationship with us for the larger security purposes it serves).

All the senior PRC leaders we have been dealing with—Chairman Mao, Vice Premier Teng, and Foreign Minister Ch'iao Kuan-hua—have repeatedly stated that they are prepared to be patient on the timing of normalization and resolution of the Taiwan question. During my most recent visit to Peking, Chairman Mao told me (perhaps with some measure of irony) that it is better for the present that the U.S. maintain control over Taiwan (presumably to keep the island from declaring itself an independent state, and to keep the Soviets out of the picture).

---

[3] See Document 93.
[4] See footnote 18, Document 112.

At the same time Teng and Ch'iao Kuan-hua recently have been right-eously telling us that the U.S. owes China a "debt" for their patience on this issue.[5] The stated position of the leadership in Peking on this question may well contrast with their real feelings on the issue.

There would seem to be a number of reasons for Peking's current attitude apart from any unhappiness with the lack of progress accord-ing to President Nixon's timetable. Chairman Mao, at 82, is nearing the end of his days as one of China's great political figures, and—despite his protestations of patience regarding Taiwan—no doubt would have liked to crown his career by fully unifying China. We also believe that the leadership in Peking is under some degree of pressure from their domestic political constituency for signs of progress on the Taiwan question. We cannot verify by intelligence means whether this is sim-ply a matter of lower-level Party officials feeling that China has not gained anything from the U.S. on an important issue for their country, or whether there are important divisions of opinion within the central leadership coalition. But it stands to reason that with questions being raised about the value to China of relations with the U.S. on security matters, and without movement on normalization, ambitious political figures in China may be pressing the Mao/Chou/Teng leadership to justify the wisdom of their opening to the United States.

Whether or not there are serious differences within the Chinese leadership over the value of their relationship with us, we think there must be quite strong opposition within China to making any further bilateral accommodations in the absence of agreement on full normal-ization of relations. This would help explain Peking's total lack of re-sponsiveness during my October visit to our suggestion that we take certain partial steps to improve our bilateral relations in such areas as a hot line or trade or cultural/scientific exchanges as a way of demon-strating some vitality in our relationship.

The Chinese Domestic Dimensions. The exact manner in which the play of forces within the Chinese leadership affects this situation, how-ever, is something we do not clearly understand. Chairman Mao, by all evidence, continues to set the major orientation in China's foreign policy; he is clearly the author of the current concern with our détente policies; and he also has been the primary articulator of policy on Tai-wan. We are confident that Premier Chou En-lai was close to Mao in both formulating and implementing the opening to the U.S. Chou, how-ever, now appears to be out of the picture as an active leader because of a serious illness. Vice Premier Teng Hsiao-p'ing has taken over Chou's role as the principal implementor of Peking's foreign policies.

---

[5] See Document 131.

We believe that Chairman Mao was responsible for the 1973 political rehabilitation of Teng Hsiao-p'ing (who was purged in 1967 during the Cultural Revolution), but we have other indications that Teng may be the object of a political challenge. Moreover, there have been signs that Mao himself has his differences with other leaders, particularly those in the military. The precise relationship between these domestic political factors and Peking's current foreign policy orientation, however, is not known. (The CIA analysis prepared for your visit will give you our best estimate of the interplay within the Chinese leadership and its impact on foreign policy.)[6]

Your Approach to the Normalization Issue. We do believe, however, that there is an element of tactics in Peking's current hardening in their dealings with us. The Chinese do not want us to become complacent about the relationship, and probably hope to extract from you some sense of how you might handle the normalization issue after 1976 (as well as to challenge your approach to dealing with the Soviets). They also probably seek to narrow our already limited range of options for handling the Taiwan question.

During the past year of our discussions on normalization, the Chinese have tried to turn issues we hope to resolve with them on a mutual basis into unilateral American requirements. They have brushed aside, for example, suggestions that we must find some mutually acceptable position on the question of a peaceful resolution of Taiwan's future. Teng Hsiao-p'ing's attitude has been that we owe China a "debt" for their patience on this issue; that China has no problems normalizing with the U.S. but we still "need" Taiwan; and that ultimately we must meet the PRC's terms. In addition, in the draft communiqué submitted by the Chinese side during my October visit to Peking, new language was added to the Shanghai Communiqué formulation on normalization which was both highly polemical in phrasing and also more restrictive of our options (such as the new position that our military forces must be withdrawn from "the Taiwan Strait area" as well as from the island, and the explicit condition that we must abrogate "the U.S.–Chiang 'joint defense treaty'.")

Thus a second major element of your discussions in Peking will be to convince the Chinese that we are not just stringing them along on Taiwan, and that we are prepared to seriously confront the question of normalization if a mutually acceptable way can be worked out, particularly of assuring that the future of Taiwan will be resolved by peaceful means. At the same time, the Chinese understand clearly that you are not prepared to resolve this matter during your forthcoming visit.

---

[6] Not found.

The Chinese Desire to Maintain the Relationship. Despite these areas of policy difference—as well as the evident ideological chasm between us, and our very different perspectives on specific international issues—we believe that the Chinese leadership still sees it in the interest of their country to maintain an official dialogue with the U.S. Frankly, during my October visit to the PRC and in its aftermath—when we exchanged messages with Peking on the question of a communiqué or press statement to be issued at the conclusion of your visit—the Chinese, by their insolent behavior and self-righteous lack of responsiveness in discussing international and bilateral issues, seemed to be daring us to postpone your visit. They appeared to have tried to put us on the psychological defensive, presumably in hopes of forcing us to re-evaluate some of our positions which they dislike, and creating a situation where we appeared to need a relationship with them more then they with us.

Their request of November 4 for a delay in announcing the date of your trip apparently was an effort to buy time in order to re-evaluate their position regarding the visit in the wake of your Cabinet changes.[7] The fact that they responded to us affirmatively on November 8—in a context where we had clearly indicated in a prior message the prospect of a postponement of your trip if they did not give us a favorable reply by that date—indicates that they had made a basic decision not to break off the official dialogue. Having thus exposed their position, there may now be a more healthy psychological balance in the relationship which will enable you to present your positions forcefully and to emphasize the need for mutual efforts in coping with international security questions of common concern and in completing the normalization process.

This does not mean, however, that they will not press you on Administration positions that disturb them. But it does mean that you can go to Peking confident that the Chinese see the need for a continuing relationship with the U.S. As Foreign Minister Ch'iao Kuan-hua said in a message of November 4—a statement otherwise filled with sarcastic comments about our relationship—"the Chinese side has always felt that the issuance of a joint communiqué of the nature of the Shanghai Communiqué, which shows the world that our two countries each maintains its principled position while sharing common points, would be helpful in dealing with international problems of common concern and moving towards normalization. The impact of the Shanghai Communiqué has clearly borne this out."[8]

---

[7] See Document 131.

[8] See footnote 3, Document 131.

THE EVOLVING PATTERN OF U.S.–PRC RELATIONS

The above analysis describes the immediate context of your visit to Peking. The following chronological review of the pattern of our dealings over the past several years should be helpful in giving you a sense of the importance and historical place of your discussions with PRC leaders.

The Opening: 1969–1971. During the decades of the 1950s and '60s—beginning with the Korean War and President Truman's "neutralization" of Taiwan with the Seventh Fleet, and running through the sterile ambassadorial-level talks at Geneva and Warsaw—the U.S. posture towards the PRC was one of "containment and isolation." For much of the period, we saw China as little more than an extension of Soviet power. For their part, the Chinese took the view that they would not even talk with the U.S. about establishing a normal relationship until we had returned Taiwan to their [control?].

Peking's position changed only when Sino-Soviet relations had deteriorated to the point where Peking felt its major security problem lay in Moscow, not in Washington. After the Soviet invasion of Czechoslovakia in the summer of 1968, and serious border clashes on the Sino-Soviet frontier in the spring and summer of 1969, the Chinese shifted their order of priorities. They decided to deal with us on strategic matters, while assuming that resolution of our bilateral differences would follow from cooperation on the more basic issue of a common concern with the Soviet threat and development of a positive "China mood" in the U.S.

In 1969 the Chinese leaders had strong incentives for re-establishing authoritative contact with the U.S. China was emerging from the self-imposed isolation of the Cultural Revolution period and was very apprehensive about its exposed position in the face of the Soviet threat. In June of that year Brezhnev had expressed his intention of creating an "Asian Collective Security System" that was demonstrably anti-Chinese in purpose. Japan had become the third major industrial state, and Chinese leaders were concerned that a power that had invaded their country in the 1930s might take the road of rearmament, or ally itself with a hostile power. In addition, India was an unfriendly state (with whom the Chinese had had a border war in 1962) and the Soviets had been trying to establish an active political relationship with New Delhi for almost a decade. In sum, six years ago the international environment confronting the PRC seemed increasingly threatening, yet fluid and capable of being influenced if China took the initiative.

In this context, the United States seemed the only country with the power to offset the Soviet Union. Despite two decades of confrontation, we presented to the Chinese leaders the least threat with regard to geography or recent behavior (having clearly indicated in the 1960s, for example, that we were not prepared to encourage military action by the Chiang Kai-shek government against the PRC). Despite two decades of mutual estrangement, there seemed to be a clean slate to write upon. It was obvious by 1969 that major adjustments in the U.S. posture in East Asia were going to occur and that these shifts would be of significance to China. President Nixon had indicated publicly in such statements as his "Guam Doctrine" press conference of July, 1969 that we were re-evaluating our entire position in Asia, from Vietnam to China, Japan, and Korea.[9] This situation was reinforced by the fact that only we could assist them in dealing with the Taiwan problem, and that over time our trade and technology could help China industrialize.

In turn, the United States had many reasons to open up an authoritative dialogue with Peking. This would give us more diplomatic flexibility in a multipolar world. It could give us much greater leverage with Moscow and induce it to establish a more constructive relationship with us. It could help reduce tensions and possible miscalculations in Asia. We also believed it could generate pressures on Hanoi which would move the North Vietnamese toward a reasonable settlement of the Indochina conflicts. And in a larger geo-political and historical framework, elimination of our military confrontation with China—a country embodying a quarter of mankind—at a time when the PRC was still strategically weak and vulnerable, would enable the United States to move away from one front of its two-front cold war of the 1950s and '60s. The hope was that we could, at our own initiative, eliminate the immediate causes of our differences with Peking and establish a relatively positive relationship with the PRC before the country acquired the strategic weaponry to directly threaten America's security.

Accordingly, the Administration purposefully pursued a series of carefully orchestrated moves beginning in early 1969 designed to forge an opening to China. After seeking to establish indirect contact with Peking by way of private messages routed through third parties, and on the basis of a series of unilateral public steps easing trade and travel restrictions, we established a reliable channel to the Chinese leadership through Pakistan in 1970–71. My secret trip to Peking in July 1971 paved the way for President Nixon's visit in February 1972.

The Early Advances: 1971–1973. This first phase in our constructive contacts with the PRC—which can be said to have been initiated with mutual suggestions at the Warsaw talks in January and February, 1970, that an authoritative dialogue in a secure environment would be of mutual benefit—concluded with issuance of the Shanghai Commu-

---

[9] Reference is to the Nixon Doctrine; see footnote 5, Document 18.

niqué in February of 1972. This document set the direction for the further normalization of relations.

President Nixon and I discovered in our early exchanges with the Chinese that we shared common views on many international issues and could develop parallel action where it served common interests. Both sides had a basic distrust of Soviet intentions, and neither of us saw Russian efforts to bring about a geo-political encirclement of the PRC as in our respective national interests. China was concerned about a weakened Europe, as was the United States; and we both opposed Soviet objectives in the Middle East and South Asia. Peking clearly appreciated, for example, our backing of Pakistan during the Indo-Pak war of 1971—a position we took despite considerable domestic criticism.

At the same time, we found the Chinese responsive to some of our arguments on issues where we had clear public differences. For example, after 1972 Peking shifted its antagonistic stance toward U.S.–Japan relations to one which recognizes that our close ties with Tokyo serve as a restraint on Japanese militarism. As well, the Chinese have been quietly supportive of our negotiating role in the Middle East, despite their public posture of opposition to Israel. At the same time, however, we have retained our differences on such issues as Korea and Cambodia—although even in these cases Peking's apparently hostile public stance appears to be derived from ideology and special circumstances, rather than a complete conflict of American and Chinese objectives. Neither of us wants hostilities on the Korean peninsula; both distrust a powerful Hanoi backed by Moscow.

It was in the larger context of our dialogue on international questions that the Chinese began to show signs of flexibility in their bilateral dealings with us in order to strengthen domestic support in the United States for U.S.–PRC normalization. The active growth of trade after President Nixon's visit to Peking, and the expansion of cultural and scientific exchanges, gave public visibility to this growing relationship.

Privately we reinforced the expectation in Peking that our relations would evolve step-by-step toward diplomatic recognition. We said that we would attempt to complete the normalization process by 1976, and assured them that we would not foster any "two Chinas" situation or a Taiwan independence movement. Moreover, we gave concrete expression to our desire to eliminate the remaining elements of our military confrontation of the cold-war era by unilaterally reducing our troop levels and offensive weaponry and aircraft on Taiwan—particularly after the end of U.S. involvement in the Vietnam war.

For their part, the Chinese have been farsighted enough not to press us unduly on normalization, knowing that had they begun our dialogue by presenting extreme demands the relationship probably would never get off the ground. At the same time, their objective undoubtedly was to draw us into a sufficiently positive relationship so that the difficult decisions affecting our ties with Taiwan would be weighed against the value of sustaining a positive relationship with the PRC—a relationship that would have strategic as well as bilateral advantages to the U.S.

With the end of America's direct role in the Vietnam war, the Chinese clearly indicated their desire to move to a more active relationship and to accelerate the normalization process. During my February, 1973 visit to Peking—just after the signing of the Paris Agreements— Chairman Mao received me for a long discussion of international developments.[10] The Chinese also agreed to open Liaison Offices in our respective capitals—thus reversing themselves on the long-held position that as long as the Republic of China (ROC) had an embassy in Washington they would not send their officials to our capital.

The Recent Slowdown: 1973–1975. It was in late 1973, however, that certain trends developed on both sides of the U.S.–PRC relationship which were to grow over the next two years into our present cooler dealings. On the American side, the bureaucratic goof of allowing the ROC to open two new consulates in the U.S. in late 1973, and the appointment in early 1974 of a senior FSO as a new ambassador to Taipei, must have raised doubts in Peking about the direction of our policy. Moreover, the evolution of the Watergate problem, coupled with the increasingly assertive role of the Congress in international affairs, gave the Chinese the impression of a weakened and chaotic America, unable to implement a coherent and forceful foreign policy. Peking reacted, for example, to the Congressional cut-off of the bombing in Cambodia (our primary source of influence over the insurgents, and a factor which we could control in coordination with the Chinese to affect the situation) by drawing back from certain helpful steps they had indicated they were prepared to take to stimulate a negotiated resolution of the conflict. Instead, they hardened their attitude toward us and heightened their support for the insurgents. Peking now had minimal incentive to track with us in Indochina because we had lost our major lever for influencing the situation.

The Chinese sense of an increasingly ineffectual United States deepened as the impact of Watergate spread in 1974, leading to the removal of President Nixon—the man who had initiated the opening with them, and a leader for whom they have continued to express admiration. Not only could they not clearly grasp the reasons for this serious weakening of Executive Branch authority, but they now saw us confronted by substantial difficulties in gaining Congressional ap-

---

[10] See Document 12.

proval for such policy moves which obviously served America's own interests as aid to Turkey and the interim agreement in the Middle East. The Chinese must now see the CIA hearings as a near complete breakdown of internal political discipline because of partisan rivalries.

Compounding this perception was Chinese concern that the agreements we were negotiating with the Russians—the 1973 agreement on limiting the dangers of nuclear war, the Vladivostok understanding of 1974, and the Helsinki Conference—represented an unwarranted trustworthiness in Washington of Soviet intentions and a naive belief in the value of agreements signed with the Russians. They may also have questioned whether we were concluding such accords from a position of weakness: a desire to create the appearance of stability rather than bear the continuing burden of an active defense, and to undercut domestic critics of détente with the argument that the relationship with Moscow was still yielding positive benefits.

At the least, the Chinese began to express concern to us privately in 1973 that we were merely using them against the Russians. As Premier Chou said to me during my February visit, "You want to reach out to the Soviet Union by standing on Chinese shoulders."[11] During the same trip Mao expressed concern that the Europeans were trying to push the Soviet threat eastward (toward China), and that if Russia attacked the PRC the United States would let the two countries fight it out for several years until—in Vietnam fashion—the Soviets had dissipated their strength before using American force to "poke your finger at the Soviet back."[12] While these statements reflected some measure of Chinese posturing for psychological effect, they did seem to reveal a growing concern in Peking about the impact on PRC interests of our approach to dealing with the Soviets.

Paralleling our own domestic difficulties after 1973 were increasing signs of tension in the Peking scene. In the summer of 1973, as PRC leaders prepared for their Tenth Party Congress, Premier Chou En-lai's position appeared to come under attack for rehabilitating formerly disgraced leaders such as Teng Hsiao-p'ing. The Chinese put our exchange program on ice in the second half of the year, apparently in a desire to sort out their own domestic situation before allowing in observant foreigners. There were reports that Chinese doctors and scientists who had visited the U.S. in 1972–73 were subject to criticism by radical elements in the leadership for being too "pro-American"; and the left wing of the Party appeared to appeal to Chinese military leaders for

---

[11] See Document 8.
[12] See Document 12.

support against the moderate Mao/Chou leadership, which was steadily depriving them of political influence.

At the turn of 1974, in a move to reduce the political influence of the army, Peking shuffled around the major military region commanders to new territorial bases in order to disorganize their local political machines.[13] During the rest of the year, however, there remained signs that the military continued to resist pressures from Mao for the removal of senior commanders considered disloyal to the Chairman's policies and person. Polemics in the PRC's internal media suggested that the military were challenging Mao's foreign policy orientation of dealing with the United States as a way of countering the Soviet threat. We believe that some voices in Peking may have asserted that China was "tilting" too far toward the United States, particularly at a time when our internal divisions made us appear to be a less effective counterweight to the Soviets. As a result—this argument may have gone—China should take steps to lower the level of tension with Moscow.

While the line never acquired official support, it does suggest one of the reasons why the Chairman and other Chinese leaders have become so overtly critical of our détente policies. Our actions may be exposing them to greater domestic criticism—this quite apart from the fact that it would obviously be to China's advantage to have us take on the Soviets frontally. Despite the signs of criticism of Mao's foreign policy orientation, however, the Chairman appears determined not to ease off pressures against what he sees as China's primary security problem, Soviet "hegemonism."

The signs of increasing political dissension in Peking in late 1973 coincided with the gradual diminution in the direct leadership role of Premier Chou En-lai—not only a major figure in the opening to the U.S., but also an urbane and far-sighted negotiator and moderating political influence within China. During my November 1973 visit to Peking, Chou adopted a rather passive role, while Mao—despite his age—discussed world events for over three hours and in great detail, clearly putting his stamp on policies which the Premier had articulated on my previous trip.

The Chinese apparently knew in late 1973 that Chou En-lai's health was failing, and consciously sought to reduce his load of responsibility. Peking sent Vice Premier Teng Hsiao-p'ing to New York for a special UN session in April 1974 in his first major foreign policy role since his rehabilitation a year earlier. During my first encounter with the Vice Premier, Chou's name was never mentioned. Throughout the rest of the year Teng assumed an ever-larger proportion of Chou's responsi-

---

[13] See footnote 4, Document 67.

bilities in foreign affairs, and when I visited Peking in November, I had only a brief and largely non-substantive discussion with the Premier. Teng became the principal interlocutor across the negotiating table.

The exact mixture of physical and political elements which account for the Premier's gradual withdrawal from a direct role in Chinese politics—and in our dealings with Peking—is difficult to estimate. We believe Chou has either heart trouble or stomach cancer, and may have had an operation this past September. Certainly the recent hardening in our dialogue with Peking is not merely an effect of Chou En-lai's withdrawal; yet there is no question but that the Premier imparted a degree of vision and finesse to our dialogue which is lacking in the style of his immediate successor, Teng Hsiao-p'ing. Teng does not display Chou's grasp of history or his deft handling of diplomatic discourse. His style is rather frontal and somewhat acerbic. Moreover, being a recent rehabilitee from the Cultural Revolution purges, Teng may feel the need to adopt a hard stance to limit his vulnerability to criticism from rivals unhappy with his remarkable return to political influence, and to retain the confidence which Chairman Mao appears to have vested in him in the past three years. In short, for both intellectual and political reasons, Teng does not appear to have the self-assurance to range very widely from his brief, or to take very innovative or controversial positions.

Apart from our sense of the respective positions of Chou and Teng, we believe that Chairman Mao continues to exercise the predominant influence in the formulation of China's foreign policy. This was borne out in my discussions with him last month. Distrust of the Soviet Union remains the cornerstone of his approach to dealing with the outside world. While the Chairman may be under some internal pressure for his policies, he gives no sign of wavering in his effort to construct a loose coalition of forces opposed to Soviet "hegemonism" as a way of countering Moscow's efforts to encircle China through détente with the West and promotion of an anti-PRC Asian Collective Security System.

If China's domestic political scene now produces greater caution, if not a certain immobilism and cooling of atmosphere, in their foreign policy stance, the Chinese perception of our own position may well reinforce such a tendency. While, as noted above, I believe the key factor accounting for this is the Chinese view that our domestic political foundation has eroded and that the U.S. is increasingly unable to project a coherent foreign policy, they also probably sense an increasing lack of responsiveness in our bilateral dealings. During my visit to Peking in November 1974, I foreshadowed for the first time the likelihood that there would be no major progress on the Taiwan issue before 1977 unless China explicitly renounced the use of force. I reinforced this view with the Chinese during the past summer, and explicitly told Foreign

Minister Ch'iao Kuan-hua in late September that we were not prepared to complete the normalization process at this time.[14]

The Chinese are well aware that our major setbacks in Indochina have increased the Administration's domestic and international political vulnerabilities, creating a context where any major change in our relationships with Taiwan which implied abandonment of yet another ally would be unacceptable at this time. Moreover, as our pre-election politicking gathers momentum—and with it criticism of détente and other foreign policies which Peking does not like—the Chinese may calculate that their most effective posture will be one of waiting to see how our politics and leading personalities evolve over the coming year.

These cumulative factors seem to account for the cooler attitude toward the U.S. which was reflected in the way the Chinese handled my visit in October. Prior to my arrival in Peking their Foreign Minister criticized our positions with unusual force in his speech at the United Nations,[15] and the Foreign Ministry highlighted our differences by creating problems in our bilateral dealings on issues of Tibet and Puerto Rico. During the banquet toasts on my first night in Peking, Ch'iao Kuan-hua publicly criticized our détente policy, knowing full well that this would generate considerable attention and speculation in the world press.[16]

My conversations with Vice Premier Teng were rather desultory, except for rather taunting questioning regarding our dealings with the Soviet Union and Europe which he indicated were reminiscent of the appeasement policies of Chamberlain and Daladier in the 1930s. Chairman Mao reinforced these themes in our conversation, and clearly questioned our reliability as a serious world power. He alleged that China was a lesser priority for us now. And against a backdrop of our ineffectual maneuvering, European weakness and disunity and Japanese ambivalence, he sounded a consistent theme of Chinese self-reliance. In their unforthcoming posture on trade issues and the exchange programs, and by their lack of interest in some special briefings, the Chinese indicated a desire to keep us at some distance. And finally, the contentious nature of both the content of their draft communiqué for your visit, and their insolent procedure of presenting it to me at the eleventh hour of my visit, represented their most disdainful performance with us since the opening of our relationship. On substance, the Chinese indicated a desire to highlight our differences on international questions while showing no interest in advancing our bilateral relations.

---

[14] See Document 119.

[15] See footnote 2, Document 119.

[16] See Department of State *Bulletin*, November 17, 1975, pp. 681–682.

This change in mood in our relationship is annoying, even somewhat disturbing. At the same time, we do not believe it represents a major crisis in the relationship, and should be kept in perspective. The Chinese have no real strategic alternative to maintaining at least the symbolic aspects of our relationship at this time. They clearly remain interested in your visit. The international forces which brought us together remain basically at work. They still treat the Soviet Union as their principal enemy, even while they appear to want to maintain somewhat greater restraint in their posture toward us. And for all our domestic problems, they know full well that we remain the strongest power in the world and are not to be trifled with.

THE OBJECTIVES OF YOUR TALKS IN PEKING

The above analysis represents our best estimate of Peking's perceptions of the U.S. and the Administration's various policies at this time. While we have confidence that the Chinese do not wish to break off a dialogue with the Administration, we have little expectation that Peking will make your visit much more than an occasion for symbolic contact and an opportunity to question Administration policies affecting them. On the other hand, it is not in their interest, given their concerns about the Soviet Union, to have your visit result in an apparent breakdown in the relationship. Moreover, we have been assured that you will be received courteously and with all appropriate protocol.

The Chinese Position. The results of my October trip to Peking indicate that the Chinese will not be very forthcoming on either international or bilateral issues in a way that will imply forward progress in our relationship. The draft communiqué which they tabled indicates that they are likely to highlight our differing approaches to dealing with the problem of "hegemony;" and we can expect no overt signs of cooperation on third country issues. They are most likely to try to sustain the relationship at its current level by limiting cultural and scientific exchanges to present levels; and they will continue to show no interest in movement on trade-related issues such as solution of the claims/assets problem. They will probably emphasize to you their continuing commitment to a policy of national "self-reliance." They are likely to state rather self-righteously that they will be "patient" on the Taiwan issue if we still "need" the island and that they are quite prepared to live with our relationship in its presently semi-normal condition.

Your Position. Thus, we believe the most realistic approach to your trip to Peking is that of a *sustaining visit,* an effort to maintain what has been a useful dialogue on world issues and a symbolic relationship of strategic value to both sides. A relationship such as this, because it lacks the substance of our ties to a country like Japan, requires periodic high-level exchanges on issues of common concern to maintain common perceptions and sustain its symbolic weight. Moreover, it will be very useful for you to get a direct sense of the way this leadership works and to size up those who are likely to succeed Chairman Mao and Premier Chou En-lai as the next generation of senior PRC officials.

In addition, your subsequent stops in Jakarta and Manila will put the Peking visit—and our overall relationship with the Chinese—in more balanced perspective as one element of American policy in the Pacific. Your speech at the East-West Center in Hawaii on December 7 can be used to articulate our overall objectives in the Pacific Basin: our desire to encourage the evolution of an equilibrium of forces in the Asian area; our intention to support change in the region through political means and not violence; our enduring commitment to sustain the security of our allies and support the sovereignty of all states in the region; and our desire to maintain mutually beneficial economic and political relations with all the countries of East Asia.[17]

In your discussions with Chairman Mao and Vice Premier Teng, I believe you should concentrate on the following themes:

—Confirm the Administration's position that we seek to build a vital relationship with the PRC on both international and bilateral matters so as to strengthen the basis for coordinated action on the security issues which have brought us together.

—Emphasize that the U.S. will continue to play a vigorous international role, and that we are not constrained on basic security issues despite the short-term effects of Congressional actions and our post-Vietnam/post-Watergate domestic mood. (You should not, however, appear defensive about our domestic situation.)

—Stress that our complex strategy of combining serious negotiations and basic firmness is the best U.S. approach toward the USSR. We are convinced that this strategy is the most effective way to constrain the Soviets and to achieve agreements which reduce the danger of war. Tactically, it also creates a public orientation in the United States which will enable us to rally public support for resistance to expansionist activities when they occur. You should review recent examples of American actions which indicate that we are both determined and capable of countering Moscow's outward pressures and that we are not "strategically passive." (You can cite such recent examples as Congressional support for your Middle East diplomacy, renewed aid to Turkey, our increased efforts in Portugal and Angola, and the results of the European Economic Summit meeting.)

—State your views regarding further steps toward full normalization of U.S.–PRC relations and the handling of the Taiwan question.

---

[17] For text of President Ford's speech, see *Public Papers: Ford, 1975*, vol. II, pp. 1950–1955.

Your objective is to assure the Chinese that we are not just stringing them along on normalization, but that *mutual* efforts will be required to resolved the Taiwan question.

—Briefly touch on bilateral relations in relaxed fashion. You can indicate your awareness of their position that they are not prepared at this time to take steps in our bilateral relations which would indicate at least partial forward movement. You should say that we are ready to accept this, but this will lead much of the world to believe our relationship is stagnating, which is not in the interests of either of us. You can reiterate that we do not view progress in our economic relations or exchange programs as ends in themselves, but rather as activities which will strengthen the support of our public for a normal relationship with the PRC and for actions that we may have to take which would affect the security of both our countries.

On the basis of the mood and substance of your exchanges on the first day or so of your visit, you will have to decide on an approach regarding a public document which might be issued at the conclusion of your visit.

Thus far, the Chinese have made it crystal clear that they are *not* prepared to negotiate a full-fledged communiqué which would have sufficient balance between our areas of disagreement and points of common interest on international issues, combined with signs of progress in our bilateral relations, to make such a document look like an advance in our relations. Indeed what they have in mind could well be interpreted as a setback in our relations, especially three years after the Shanghai Communiqué. We seriously doubt that this situation will change. Your choice is likely to be between no formal statement at all and a bland, descriptive press release which simply puts on the public record the fact that you visited the PRC and held "frank and useful" talks with Chinese leaders. We will have to make a judgment at the time about which approach is likely to be most useful (or least damaging) to our purposes.

While most of the substantive issues of common interest have been covered in my previous discussions in Peking, it is of course essential that the Chinese get a feel for your own approach to them. Ultimately, it will not be words that will modify Chinese positions on the issues which have induced some current strain in our relationship. They will decide how much vitality to inject into their dealings with us on the basis of the degree of pressure they feel under from Moscow, their estimate of our ability to act as a world power—especially against the Russians—and the measure of purpose they sense in Washington with regard to completion of the normalization process. Hopefully, your visit to Peking will not only sustain a useful relationship and deepen the official dialogue, but will also lay the basis for a more constructive evolution of our bilateral relations in the years to come.

133. Editorial Note

On November 21, 1975, at 9:30 a.m., President Gerald Ford met in the Oval Office with Secretary of State Henry Kissinger and Assistant to the President for National Security Affairs Brent Scowcroft. On the subject of Ford's upcoming visit to the People's Republic of China, Kissinger observed that the Chinese Government was becoming more conciliatory. "We have stared them down. What they respect is firmness." A few minutes later, Kissinger noted, "Without Congress, we would have the Soviet–Chinese triangle working again. I think we should tell the Chinese I am going to Moscow. The Soviet angle is what keeps the Chinese under control." Ford responded, "When we hung tough on the Peking visit, it obviously worked." (Memorandum of conversation; Ford Library, National Security Adviser, National Security Adviser Memcons, Box 16, November 1975–February 1976) Kissinger spoke on the telephone to Hugh Sidey of *Time* magazine on November 26 and told him that personal contact between U.S. and Chinese leaders was important, especially because Chinese "ambassadors have no authority." (Transcript of telephone conversation with Sidey, November 26, Department of State, Electronic Reading Room, Kissinger Telephone Transcripts)

On November 28, Ford, Kissinger, and Scowcroft met in the Oval Office. Ford said, "I think it [the trip to China] will be a good visit." Kissinger replied, "It is an important visit. Why have they insisted on your coming? These are unemotional people. Our kicking them around in October really paid off." (Memorandum of conversation, November 28, 9:30 a.m.; Ford Library, National Security Adviser, National Security Adviser Memcons, Box 16, November 1973–February 1976)

---

134. Memorandum of Conversation[1]

Beijing, December 2, 1975, 4:10–6:00 p.m.

PARTICIPANTS

Chairman Mao Tse Tung
Vice Premier Teng Hsiao-P'ing

---

[1] Source: Ford Library, National Security Adviser, Kissinger Reports on USSR, China, and Middle East Discussions, Box 2, China Memcons and Reports, December 1–5, 1975, President Ford's Visit to Peking. Secret; Nodis. The meeting took place at Mao's residence. Ford arrived in Beijing on December 1.

Vice Premier Li Hsien-Nien
Foreign Minister Chiao Kuan-hua
Ambassador Huang Chen, Chief of the PRC Liaison Office
Vice Foreign Minister Wang Jai-Hung
Chang Han-chih, Interpreter, Deputy Director, MFA
Tang Weng-shen, Interpreter, Deputy Director, MFA
Nurse/Interpreter

President Gerald R. Ford
Secretary of State Henry A. Kissinger
Ambassador George Bush, Chief of the United States Liaison Office
Mr. Brent Scowcroft, Assistant to the President
Mr. Winston Lord, Director, Policy Planning Staff, Department of State

(At approximately 3:00 p.m. the Chinese informed the United States party that Chairman Mao wished to see President Ford. The President, his wife and daughter, and other members of the United States party left the President's villa at 4:00 p.m. and drove to Chairman Mao's residence through a front gate of the Forbidden City complex. They were greeted at the entrance to the residence by Vice Premier Teng and the other Chinese officials and were escorted into the Chairman's den. The Chairman stood up to greet the American guests. While photographers took pictures, he shook hands and exchanged brief greetings with each of the following: President Ford, Mrs. Ford, Susan Ford, Secretary Kissinger, Ambassador Bush, Mr. Scowcroft, Under Secretary Sisco, Assistant Secretary Habib, Mr. Lord, and Mr. Solomon. After these greetings and pictures, the American guests left the room except for President Ford, Secretary Kissinger, Ambassador Bush, Mr. Scowcroft, and Mr. Lord. The Chinese officials present were those listed above. The group sat in a semi-circle on large arm chairs and the conversation began.)

Chairman Mao: So how are you?

President Ford: Fine. I hope you are too.

Chairman Mao: I am not well. I am sick.

President Ford: I think you look very well, Sir.

Chairman Mao: My appearance is not so bad. And how is Mr. Secretary of State?

Secretary Kissinger: I am very well. I am happy to be here.

Chairman Mao: And how are all the other American friends?

President Ford: They are all very healthy. We had a very good discussion this morning, Mr. Chairman.

Chairman Mao: So what did you discuss?

President Ford: We discussed the problems we have with the Soviet Union and the need to have parallel actions as we look at the overall circumstances internationally, the need for your country and mine to work in parallel to achieve what is good for both of us.

Chairman Mao: We do not have much ability. We can only fire such empty cannons.

President Ford: I do not believe that, Mr. Chairman.

Chairman Mao: With regard to cursing, we have some ability in that respect.

President Ford: We can too.

Chairman Mao: And you also? Then we shall reach an agreement.

President Ford: We can also use force against a country which causes much trouble.

Chairman Mao: That is not bad. Then we have reached another agreement.

President Ford: We were very specific this morning in discussing whom we were talking about.

Chairman Mao: It can be none other but the Socialist Imperialists.

President Ford: There was some strong language used this morning, Mr. Chairman.

Chairman Mao: (pointing to Teng) That is, you criticized him.

President Ford: We strongly criticized another country.

Chairman Mao: The one in the North.

President Ford: Yes.

Chairman Mao: Your Secretary of State has been interfering in my internal affairs.

President Ford: Tell me about it.

Chairman Mao: He does not allow me to go and meet God. He even tells me to disobey the order that God has given to me. God has sent me an invitation, yet he (Secretary Kissinger) says, don't go.

Secretary Kissinger: That would be too powerful a combination if he went there.

Chairman Mao: He is an atheist (Secretary Kissinger). He is opposed to God. And he is also undermining my relations with God. He is a very ferocious man and I have no other recourse than to obey his orders.

Secretary Kissinger: We are very glad.

Chairman Mao: Yes indeed. I have no other way out, no way at all. He gave an order (Secretary Kissinger).

President Ford: To God?

Chairman Mao: No, to me.

(Chairman Mao speaks with Ambassador Huang in Chinese.)

How are things going, Mr. Huang Chen? Are you still going back (to the United States)?

Ambassador Huang: I listen to the Chairman's instructions.

Chairman Mao: Mr. President, do you want him?

President Ford: We certainly want him back. Our relationship has been excellent. It is important that the Ambassador be back and that Mr. Bush be here in Peking.

Chairman Mao: (to Ambassador Bush) Are you staying?

Ambassador Bush: Just a few days.

Chairman Mao: You have been promoted.

President Ford: Yes, he has been. We are going to submit a name for a replacement within a month.

Chairman Mao: We are reluctant to let him go.

President Ford: He is an outstanding person and that is why I have asked him to come back to the United States. But we will replace him with an equally good man.

Chairman Mao: That would be good. And it seems to me that it will also be better for Huang Chen to go back to the United States.

Ambassador Huang: I will firmly carry out the Chairman's instructions. I do want to come back (to China) because I have been abroad too long. But I will do what the Chairman says.

Chairman Mao: You should stay there one or two years more.

Ambassador Huang: All right, I definitely will go back and firmly carry out the Chairman's instructions.

Chairman Mao: There are some young people who have some criticism about him (Ambassador Huang). And these two (Wang and Tang) also have some criticism of Lord Chiao. And these people are not to be trifled with. Otherwise, you will suffer at their hands—that is, a civil war. There are now many big character posters out. And you perhaps can go to Tsinghua University and Peking University to have a look at them.

President Ford: I would not understand the signs.

I hope your telling the Ambassador to stay two more years means that we are going to continue the good relations between our two countries, Mr. Chairman.

Chairman Mao: Yes. Yes, relations between our two countries should continue. It seems to me at present there is nothing very much between our two countries, your country and mine. Probably this year, next year, and the year after there will not be anything great happening between our two countries. Perhaps afterwards the situation might become a bit better.

President Ford: In the meantime, Mr. Chairman, I think we have to work in trying to achieve better coordination on the international scene, with emphasis on the challenges from some countries such as the Soviet Union.

Chairman Mao: Yes. Anyway we have no confidence in the Soviet Union. And Teng Hsiao-P'ing does not like the Soviet Union either.

President Ford: We have similar feelings as to their overall designs to expand on a worldwide basis—territorially, economically and otherwise. But we are going to meet the challenge.

Chairman Mao: Good. We are also going to meet their challenge.

President Ford: We expect on a bilateral basis, Mr. Chairman, to improve our relations after next year. We think that is the time real progress can be made on a bilateral basis.

Chairman Mao: You mean between us?

President Ford: Yes.

Chairman Mao: That would be good.

President Ford: In the meantime, Mr. Chairman, if your country and mine work to meet the challenge, in the East and West, from the Soviet Union, it will develop greater support in the United States toward continued progress for normalization between the United States and the People's Republic.

Chairman Mao: Good. Anyway, this is just talk. And how the Soviet Union will actually act is something we will still have to wait and see.

President Ford: Mr. Chairman, in the meantime we will have to convince the Soviet Union by what is done by the United States and the People's Republic—not words, but backed up by action. We will continue to keep the pressure on them. I hope the pressure from the East will be strong like our actions on our side.

Chairman Mao: Just firing of some empty cannon, cursing.

President Ford: We will do more than that, Mr. Chairman, as we have in the past. And the American people expect their President to be firm. We have, and we will in the future. More than words and more than empty cannons.

Chairman Mao: So you have solid cannons?

President Ford: Yes, and we will keep our powder dry unless they seek to challenge us, and then it will not be kept dry.

Chairman Mao: That is all right. That will not be bad. Yes, now you peacefully coexist.

President Ford: But that does not mean that we will not meet a challenge of any expansionist country. As a matter of fact we have met those challenges and will continue to do so.

Chairman Mao: That is good. Shall we reach an agreement?

President Ford: (nodding yes) And we can with an effort that achieves the same result. You put pressure from the East, and we will put on pressure from the West.

Chairman Mao: Yes. A gentlemen's agreement.

President Ford: That is the best way to achieve success against a person who is not a gentleman.

Chairman Mao: They are not gentlemen.

President Ford: Those are kinder words than we used this morning.

Chairman Mao: I thank Mr. President very much for having come to see me. And I hope that in the future our two countries can be friendly to each other.

President Ford: Mr. Chairman, that is the great hope of the American people and myself. I want it clearly understood that the historic steps taken over the last three years by your country and my country are fully supported by the American people. They recognize, as we do, that there must be strength to prevent actions by expansionist countries such as the Soviet Union. We will maintain our military capability and be prepared to use it. In our opinion this is the best way to maintain the world in a stable and better position.

Chairman Mao: Good. So we don't have any conflicts.

President Ford: That's correct. And if we do have conflicts, we can sit down and discuss them and understand them and hope to eliminate them.

Chairman Mao: Indeed. Yes, there are bound to be conflicts because our two countries, China and the United States, have different social systems and different ideologies.

President Ford: But that should not interfere with our capability for looking at the broad international scene and working in parallel and working firmly for results that are in the best interests of both countries and all the peoples.

Chairman Mao: (After a brief coughing spell.) For instance, we have not had discussions, conversations with the Soviet Union like the ones we have had with you. I went to Moscow twice and Khrushchev came three times to Peking. On none of these occasions did the talks go really well.

President Ford: Mr. Chairman, I have met with Mr. Brezhnev twice. Sometimes the talks went well, sometimes badly. I think this is an indication of our firmness because we do not agree to all that they propose, and we will not. We are going to be firm and have the military capability to be firm. They understand it, and I think it is in the best interests of your country and our country if we are firm, which we intend to be.

Chairman Mao: Good.

How are your relations with Japan now? Better than before?

President Ford: Yes they are. As you know Mr. Chairman, I visited Japan about a year ago. It was the first time a President in office visited there. About a month ago the Emperor and Empress came to the United States, the first time their Majesties came to our country. We feel relations with Japan are the best they have been at any time since World War II.

Chairman Mao: Japan also is threatened by the Soviet Union.

President Ford: I would agree and therefore, Mr. Chairman, I think it is important that China and Japan have better and better relations—just as Japan and U.S. relations are getting better, in fact the best they have been.

Chairman Mao: And for Japan, its relations with you come first and their relations with us are second.

President Ford: Are your relations with Japan very good?

Chairman Mao: They are not bad. Nor are they so good.

President Ford: You want them to be better, don't you?

Chairman Mao: Yes. They have a pro-Soviet faction that is opposed to talking about hegemony.

Secretary Kissinger: Or just afraid.

Chairman Mao: Yes, indeed.

President Ford: How are your relations with Western European countries, Mr. Chairman?

Chairman Mao: They are better, better than our relations with Japan.

President Ford: It's important that our relations with Western Europe as well as yours be good to meet the challenge of any Soviet expansion in Western Europe.

Chairman Mao: Yes. Yes, and on this we have a common point there with you. We have no conflict of interests in Europe.

President Ford: As a matter of fact, Mr. Chairman, some of us believe that China does more for Western European unity and the strengthening of NATO than some of those countries do for themselves.

Chairman Mao: They are too scattered.

President Ford: Some of them are not as strong and forthright as they should be.

Chairman Mao: As I see it, Sweden is not bad. West Germany is not bad. Yugoslavia is also good. Holland and Belgium are lagging a bit behind.

President Ford: That's correct. And the Soviet Union is seeking to exploit some weaknesses in Portugal and Italy. We must prevent it, and we are trying to do so.

Chairman Mao: Yes, and now Portugal seems to be more stable. It seems to be better.

President Ford: Yes, in the last forty-eight hours it has gotten very encouraging. The forces we support have moved with great strength and taken the action that is needed to stabilize the situation.

We agree with you that Yugoslavia is important and is strong in its resistance against the Soviet Union, but we are concerned about what might happen after Tito.

Chairman Mao: Yes, perhaps after Tito it will be Kardelj.[2]

Secretary Kissinger: But we are concerned about outside pressures and within the country. And we are working on this now. Various factions are working with outside groups.

Chairman Mao: Yes, it has so many provinces and it is made up of so many former states.

President Ford: I had a very interesting trip, Mr. Chairman, to Romania this summer, and I was impressed by the strength and independence of President Ceausescu.

Chairman Mao: Good.

President Ford: We are very concerned about the situation in Spain as well, Mr. Chairman. The King we do support. We hope he will be able to handle the elements that would undermine his regime. And we will work with him in trying to have the necessary control of the situation during this period of transition.

Chairman Mao: Yes. And anyway we think it would be good if the European Common Market accepted them. Why doesn't the EEC want Spain and Portugal?

President Ford: Mr. Chairman, we urged the NATO alliance to be more friendly to Spain even under Franco. And we hope with the new King that Spain will be more acceptable to the NATO alliance. In addition we feel that the EEC ought to be responsive to movement by the Spanish Government toward unity with Western Europe as a whole. We will work in both directions as much as we can.

Secretary Kissinger: They are not radical enough for the Europeans.

Chairman Mao: Is that so? Yes, in the past they had fought each other. Yes, and in the past you did not curse Franco.

President Ford: No. And we support the new King because the whole southern belly of Western Europe must remain strong— Portugal, Spain, Italy, Greece, Turkey, Yugoslavia. All that must be strengthened if we are to meet any expansionist efforts by the Soviet Union.

Chairman Mao: Good. Yes, and we think Greece should get better.

President Ford: Yes, they went through a difficult time, but the new government we feel is moving in the right direction and we

---

[2] Edvard Kardelj was a Slovene politician and the heir apparent to Yugoslav President Josip Broz Tito.

will help them. And we hope they will come back as a full partner in NATO.

Chairman Mao: That would be good.

President Ford: There is a radical element, of course, in Greece that would not be favorable from our point of view and would tend to weaken NATO and give encouragement to the Soviet Union.

Chairman Mao: Oh?

President Ford: As we move further east in the Mediterranean, Mr. Chairman, we think the Sinai Agreement has helped reduce the Soviet influence, but we recognize there cannot be any stagnation in advancing toward a broader peace. As soon as the next election in the U.S. has taken place we expect to move with vigor to try and achieve a broad, just and permanent peace in that area.

Chairman Mao: Permanent peace would be difficult to achieve.

President Ford: Yes they have not had it there for centuries. But the effort to achieve it, a successful effort, would eliminate a great deal of Soviet influence in that area of the world. If there is stagnation, that gives the Soviet Union the opportunity to stir up trouble. Therefore, we are convinced that there must be continual movement. And the Sinai Agreement has helped us develop good relations with Egypt. And if we move forward after the next election and help move others toward a broader peace, it will have a significant impact in keeping the Soviet Union's influence out of that part of the world.

Chairman Mao: I don't oppose that.

President Ford: As we move into the subcontinent, we expect to have influence there with our base in Diego Garcia. Of course, we continue to improve our relations with Pakistan. We have lifted our arms ban so that they can help themselves and develop sufficient military capability to convince India that it would not be a successful venture if the Indians should attempt any military operation.

Chairman Mao: That would be good.

President Ford: What is your appraisal, Mr. Chairman, of the situation in Bangladesh?

Chairman Mao: The situation there now is better, but it is not yet stable. And we are prepared to send an ambassador there. Perhaps he will take some time in getting there.

President Ford: Are you concerned that India will move in and take any military action against Bangladesh to take advantage of the current situation?

Chairman Mao: There is such a danger, and we must beware.

President Ford: India has been known, Mr. Chairman, to do some unwise things against other nations. I would hope that they would not do it here (Bangladesh).

Chairman Mao: Indeed. If they should take such action in that area we would oppose it.

President Ford: We are working with Pakistan and Iran to prevent any such action, and we would condemn any such action by India.

Chairman Mao: Yes. We have reached another agreement.

President Ford: I am sure you are as concerned as well as we about the Soviet Union in the Indian Ocean, and of course their efforts on the east side of Africa. These developments are vigorously opposed by us. I speak here of course about Angola where we are taking forthright actions to prevent the Soviet Union from getting a stronghold in that part of that great continent.

Chairman Mao: You don't seem to have any means. Nor do we.

President Ford: I think we both could do better, Mr. Chairman.

Chairman Mao: I am in favor of driving the Soviet Union out.

President Ford: If we both make a good effort, we can.

Chairman Mao: Through the Congo—Kinshasha, Zaire.

Vice Premier Teng: (Talks in Chinese to the Chairman) The complicating factor here is that of South Africa, the involvement of South Africa. This has offended the whole of black Africa. This complicates the whole matter.

Chairman Mao: South Africa does not have a very good reputation.

President Ford: But they are fighting to keep the Soviet Union from expanding, and we think that's admirable. We are putting substantial money through Zambia and Zaire. We believe that if there is broad action by ourselves, the People's Republic and others, we can prevent the Soviet Union from having a very important naval facility and controlling substantial resources in Angola. And we are violently opposed to the substantial participation of Cuba. They now have five to six thousand troops in Angola. We think that's not a healthy thing; and the Soviet Union.

Vice Premier Teng: You mean you admire South Africa?

President Ford: No. They have taken a strong stance against the Soviet Union. And they are doing that totally on their own, without any stimulation by the United States.

Vice Premier Teng: In Angola.

President Ford: South Africa is against the MPLA.

Chairman Mao: This is a question that needs study.

President Ford: Time is of the essence.

Chairman Mao: It seems to me that the MPLA will not be successful.

President Ford: We certainly hope not.

Secretary Kissinger: If the other two forces get enough discipline and we can give them equipment, then we can prevent them (the MPLA) from being successful. They (the FNLA and UNITA) need training from those who understand guerrilla war. We can get them the equipment if others give them the training.

Chairman Mao: We supported them in the past through Tanzania, but Tanzania has a hold on certain things that were supposed to go through. Perhaps now we should work through Zaire.

Vice Premier Teng: Perhaps it is better through Zaire.

Secretary Kissinger: Through Zaire. And the Chinese side could perhaps use its influence with Mozambique. It would have a moral significance in Africa if Mozambique did not support the Soviet group, the MPLA. (There is discussion among the Chinese.)

President Ford: But, you know, Mozambique supports the MPLA. It would probably be difficult.

Vice Premier Teng: Impossible.

Secretary Kissinger: I know. They may not understand what they are doing because they also look up to China very much.

Chairman Mao: We might make a try.

Secretary Kissinger: I don't think Mozambique understands the issue in Angola. They need advice and they listen to China more than to us.

Chairman Mao: We can make a try.

Vice Premier Teng: We can make a try but it might not necessarily be effective.

Secretary Kissinger: That's true.

Chairman Mao: Zaire is probably more reliable.

Secretary Kissinger: Zaire should be a base for active assistance. We can't get help from Mozambique, but maybe they will stay out of it. We can't get help from Mozambique, but maybe at least they will stay neutral.

Chairman Mao: We can make a try.

President Ford: I say again that time is of the essence because the other two forces need encouragement. They were doing well up until recently. There is a stalemate at the moment. It would be tragic if the MPLA should prevail after the efforts that have been made by us and by you and others.

Chairman Mao: That's hard to say.

So you think that's about all?

President Ford: I might say in reference to Angola, just before I left Washington I approved another $35 million to help the other two forces. This is a solid indication to meet the challenge of the Soviet Union and defeat the MPLA.

Chairman Mao: Good. (Chinese photographers enter room and take movies.)

President Ford: I wish to thank you, Mr. Chairman, for the opportunity to discuss the world situation and indicate our desire to expand our bilateral relations and work in parallel on many, many problems on the global scene.

Chairman Mao: Yes there are now some newspaper reports that describe relations between us two as being very bad. Perhaps you should let them in on the story a bit and maybe brief them.

Secretary Kissinger: On both sides. They hear some of it in Peking.

Chairman Mao: But that is not from us. Those foreigners give that briefing.

President Ford: We don't believe all we read in our papers, Mr. Chairman. (The photographers leave the room.) I think it is vitally important that both countries create the impression on a world-wide basis that our relations are good. When I return to the United States I will report that they are good, and I hope your people will do the same. It's not only important to have good relations, but to have the world believe that they are good.

Chairman Mao: We can go at it bit by bit.

President Ford: We will work on it, too.

Chairman Mao: So.

(The group stood up and the American guests shook hands and said good-bye with the Chairman as the photographers took pictures. The Chairman then indicated that he would escort the President to the outside room. With the help of the nurse, he walked with the President to the outer room where once again the American guests said good-bye to the Chairman as pictures were taken. President Ford thanked the Chairman and said that he thought that the talks were mutually beneficial. Secretary Kissinger said that he was glad that the Chairman obeyed his orders, i.e. not to go to heaven. President Ford said that he hoped to straighten the Secretary out so that the Chairman could go to heaven, but he and the Secretary added that they hoped that this would not be soon. Chairman Mao indicated that he could not go since he was under orders from the Secretary. Secretary Kissinger said that he would maintain those orders. The other Americans thanked the Chairman and said good-bye. The party was then escorted outside by Vice Premier Teng and the Chinese officials. The Americans entered their cars and drove away.

The Chinese later issued a press announcement of the meeting which is attached at Tab A.)[3]

---

[3] Dated December 2, attached but not printed.

135.   Memorandum of Conversation[1]

Beijing, December 2, 1975, 11 p.m.–midnight.

PARTICIPANTS

> Ch'iao Kuan-hua, PRC Foreign Minister
> Lin P'ing, Director, Department of American and Oceanic Affairs, Ministry of
>   Foreign Affairs
> T'ang Weng-sheng, Deputy Director, Department of American and Oceanic
>   Affairs, Ministry of Foreign Affairs
> Ting Yuan-hung, Director, United States Office, Department of American and
>   Oceanic Affairs, Ministry of Foreign Affairs
> Chao Chi-hua, Deputy Director, United States Office, Department of American
>   and Oceanic Affairs, Ministry of Foreign Affairs
> Shih Yen-hua (Interpreter)
> Lien Cheng-pao (Notetaker)
>
> Henry A. Kissinger, Secretary of State
> Brent Scowcroft, Assistant to the President for National Security Affairs
> Joseph P. Sisco, Under Secretary of State for Political Affairs
> Philip C. Habib, Assistant Secretary of State for East Asian and Pacific Affairs
> Winston Lord, Director, Policy Planning Staff, Department of State
> William H. Gleysteen, Deputy Assistant Secretary of State for East Asian and
>   Pacific Affairs
> Richard H. Solomon, Senior Staff Member, National Security Council

SUBJECT

> Discussion of a Possible Communiqué; American Press and Public Support for
> U.S.–PRC Relations

Secretary Kissinger (looking at Scowcroft): Scowcroft has me in a dilemma. Notice him moving in on me?!

Foreign Minister Ch'iao: What about the communiqué? I believe the two sides are clear about the messages exchanged in the past. And since President Ford raised this matter, I would like to listen to any new ideas you have.

Secretary Kissinger: I simply thought we should decide at an early stage whether we should have any concluding document. If we do not, we should tell our press there will not be one and thus avoid the impression of a crisis where there is not one. I thought some exchange of views on how the visit might conclude would be useful. We do not insist there be something, but I thought there should be some discussion about it.

---

[1] Source: Ford Library, National Security Adviser, Kissinger Reports on USSR, China, and Middle East Discussions, Box 2, China Memcons and Reports, December 1–5, 1975, Ford's Visit to Peking. Secret; Sensitive. The meeting took place at Guest House 18. All brackets are in the original.

It also occurred to me that as you have already used part of your draft communiqué [tabled at the October 22 meeting][2] in the [Vice Premier's] toast, perhaps we might be able to accept the remainder. (Laughter)

Mr. Lord: He'll use the second half in the toast at the return banquet.

Foreign Minister Ch'iao: We can lump the four toasts together. That would be a good document. (Laughter)

Secretary Kissinger: Any remainder will then appear in your next UN speech. (Laughter)

Foreign Minister Ch'iao: That is the principle [of physics] that the substance will not vanish.

Secretary Kissinger: What are your considerations now about the possibility of a concluding document? Should we have a statement? If so, what sort of a statement? Or should we simply indicate areas in which we will seek to work together? We have no draft for you; we thought we should have an exchange of views before we make any decision.

Foreign Minister Ch'iao: Our ideas remain what we told you in October and in the messages exchanged between our two sides later on. We still maintain our views. If there is any communiqué, it should be a step forward from the Shanghai Communiqué.

Secretary Kissinger: But what is your definition of a step forward? In that [idea] we agree.

Foreign Minister Ch'iao: For instance, each side should state its own views on the international situation.

Secretary Kissinger: That we did before. That is not a step forward.

Foreign Minister Ch'iao: Because the situation is changing— although our basic position remains the same, in the face of the changing situation we have new views. This is what we mean by a step forward from the Shanghai Communiqué.

About the points we have in common, I don't know whether we can add something to the Shanghai Communiqué. To put it in a simple way, I believe that the draft we handed to you on October 22 has in many ways made a step forward from the Shanghai Communiqué.

Secretary Kissinger: It depends on one's sense of direction. (Laughter)

I think the problem is—I don't think we should have a debate [now] because we have debated it before—we do not insist on a communiqué or on any public statement. In fact, we can see the advantages of having nothing.

---

[2] See Document 126 and footnote 2 thereto.

Seriously, the problem is that you look at forward movement in a somewhat dialectic sense, as the movement of history. Our public will look at forward movement in a more linear sense; and they will make a specific comparison with the Shanghai Communiqué. This is what makes it a difficult problem.

Foreign Minister Ch'iao: Well, from our point of view, you can say that a dialectical way of looking at things is that if we do not make a step forward, if a [new] document is not as good as the Shanghai Communiqué, then in fact it will dilute the significance of the Shanghai Communiqué. So that I think it might be more advisable to have no communiqué at all.

Secretary Kissinger: I think that may be true. Is it your idea that there should be no statement at all at the end? Or should we have a simple press statement?

Foreign Minister Ch'iao: As you mentioned just now, you also see the advantages of no communiqué; and I remember at our last talk in the other building [Guest House #5, on the night of October 22–23] I mentioned there might be some advantages in having no communiqué.[3] For instance, Chairman Mao told President Ford that you could brief your newsmen and without a communiqué you will not be constrained in that respect. If there is a communiqué which is very dry, devoid of content, you will be constrained.

Secretary Kissinger: I agree with that.

Foreign Minister Ch'iao: Apart from this, I think the understanding between us may be more profound than what our opponents will think. That is such a subtle way of indicating our relations that they cannot guess what they are.

Secretary Kissinger: In fact that is so complicated [an approach] that my associates cannot figure it out. You know what you said [in the Vice Premier's toast on Monday evening] was a repeat of the draft communiqué you handed us in October. But there are only five people [on our side] who understood that. I remember what Palmerston said of the Schleswig–Holstein agreement: of the three men who really understood it, one was dead, one was in an asylum, and he—the third—had forgotten what it meant. (Laughter)

Let me say something candidly about our press. I think you understand—whether you agree with it in all details or not—the basic thrust of our foreign policy. But our press got the impression on the last trip—I have not talked with them on this trip—that the Chinese side was attacking the U.S. position. And this explains many of the sto-

---

[3] See Document 126.

ries to which the Chairman referred about the impression of an increasing coolness in our relations.

Our situation is somewhat complex. I personally, intellectually, agree with your analysis of the situation. But as Secretary of State I must make sure to position our country in such a way that we have the greatest ability to respond to a crisis. Our biggest problem in America is that Watergate started an attack on central authority. We have to rebuild this central authority with care, and we must not fight battles where we cannot support our position. Therefore, speaking quite frankly, many of our opponents will use any issue to undermine the credibility of what we are doing—articles they may hear from the Chinese side and which are useful to them—and that would not be very helpful vis-à-vis the Soviet Union because these same people are attacking us for what we are doing in Angola, Portugal, Chile, and Iraq.

Therefore, if we want to create the impression of which we spoke this afternoon, one has to understand the impact on our press, even though I agree with your analysis with which—personally, I do not disagree with what the Vice Premier has said. But while we each seek the same solution, you have your method and we must have our method, because a careful analysis of our domestic situation will show you that we are pursuing the strongest anti-Soviet policy that is possible. But it is not entirely up to us to say our relations are good, because if we say if and then our press interprets your statements which have a different purpose in a certain way, if [our statements] will simply be taken as self-serving propaganda. We are promoting the strongest policy against the Soviet Union that we can before the elections.

Foreign Minister Ch'iao: It is a well-known fact that there exist fundamental differences between our two sides on key issues. Now we should not confuse these differences. The Shanghai Communiqué was written in this spirit. In recent years many American friends have come to China—whether they be Senators, Congressmen, or friends from the press, and people from all walks of life. We have told them the relations between China and the United States are basically good. We have not stated to the contrary. Instead the sources of the stories about the cooling off of the relations between our two countries do not originate from the Chinese side but from the United States side.

Secretary Kissinger: There are a variety of reasons and we have to analyse it so that we understand. It is true that, for example, opponents of the Administration or opponents of myself will say our relations are cooling in order to have a point of attack. And therefore after my last trip there were many articles in newspapers which were written for the purpose of discrediting the policy and for either preventing the trip or depriving it of significance. It is important for you to understand that these do not come from the Administration but from opponents of the Administration—and occasionally from fools within the Administration who were fighting personal battles by making up stories that are contrary to the national interest. Also—and I do not say this in a critical spirit—some of the analyses our newsmen heard when they were here last time gave the same impression. So these two things came together.

Foreign Minister Ch'iao: They have not heard them from our side.

Secretary Kissinger: They got the impression—it is newsmen. Part of the reason is that when you give your analysis of the Soviet situation—I, for example, do not consider it directed against the United States but directed against the Soviet Union—but some of our newsmen interpret it as an attack on our foreign policy, especially when they hear it in your country—not otherwise.

I tell you this—I do not at all object—this does not bother me at all, in fact I think it is healthy for you to say the things you do about the Soviet Union. It is healthy for you to talk to the Europeans as you do. It is in our common interest. The only point on which I don't agree is when you imply that we might withdraw from Europe in the face of a crisis. The fact is that we will be fighting in Europe long after the Europeans.

Foreign Minister Ch'iao: Perhaps this issue of substance can be discussed tomorrow.

Our policy of détente has been the same since 1971. It is not true that this is only in our recent statements. We have been stating our position on détente publicly and privately on many occasions. But it is also true that the argument we hear of a cooling off of relations between China and the United States has been in circulation only in a recent period. It is important to understand that it did not come from our government.

Secretary Kissinger: This is true, but it is also true that our newsmen have used the mood of their visits here as a peg to gauge our relationship. There were many stories last time that you were cold at the farewell banquet, for example. I did not feel this, and I have denied it. We have always been treated with extraordinary courtesy, so we have no complaints. But we would like the impression that our relations are good and getting better. Maybe—you joked at the beginning that maybe we should publish our four toasts, but there is some sense in this. If, for example, at the final dinner each of our sides said among other things what Chairman Mao said this afternoon—that our relations are basically good and we are improving them, then everybody would hear it and—

Foreign Minister Ch'iao: But Chairman Mao also said about the improvement of relations between our two countries, that they would be gradually improving.

Secretary Kissinger: A gradual process. We agree. I am looking to see what you have—

Foreign Minister Ch'iao: I believe that in our toast last night we also included a sentence that relations between our two countries are basically good.

Secretary Kissinger: Yes, the President and I noticed it, although I am not sure our press noticed it. They were distracted by the cannons.

Foreign Minister Ch'iao: We have to fire our cannons.

Secretary Kissinger: The problem is to get it across to our press in a way that overcomes their nihilistic tendencies.

(Chinese service personnel enter the room and place dishes of cookies and other sweets on the table.)

I was getting weak.

Foreign Minister Ch'iao: But you tendencies are that you will get bigger. You have put on a lot of weight.

Secretary Kissinger: You are actually responsible for it.

Then let us agree not to have a communiqué!?

Foreign Minister Ch'iao: We believe it might be more advisable if we cannot have a communiqué better than the Shanghai Communiqué.

Secretary Kissinger: Should there be no statement at all?

Foreign Minister Ch'iao: We have put what we think in all our toasts.

Secretary Kissinger: So then you recommend no statement at all?

Foreign Minister Ch'iao: If we cannot have a communiqué which is a step forward from the Shanghai Communiqué.

Secretary Kissinger: That is acceptable to our side. Mr. Lin [P'ing] and Mr. Lord are very relieved. They can get some sleep. (Laughter)

Foreign Minister Ch'iao: We are both also relieved of the heavy burden. Almost every time you come we have to have discussions about a communiqué; and actually I think it might be more advisable to encourage the new style we have adopted now. Either we have a communiqué which is more weighty than the Shanghai Communiqué or we do not have a communiqué at all.

Secretary Kissinger: I do not think it will be helpful to tell this to our press since we cannot get a new communiqué—(Laughter)

Foreign Minister Ch'iao: I hope that our conversation tonight will not be leaked.

Secretary Kissinger: What do you think we should tell the press— not about our conversation, but about our conclusion?

Foreign Minister Ch'iao: But what ideas do you have, because we do not quite know your press? You are more skilled in handling the press.

Secretary Kissinger: You can tell my skill with the press from the articles they write! (Laughter)

Foreign Minister Ch'iao: I remember that in Shanghai you told me you could talk to the press for as long as one and one half hours without really giving any substance. You proved you could do it in Shanghai.

I still remember that you asked me what we should tell to the press, and I told you [to say] whatever you would like.

Secretary Kissinger: I will think about . . . we will, starting tomorrow we should explain to the press that there will not be a communiqué or a statement. I will explain that we decided to concentrate on the substance of the talks rather than take time out to draft fine points. And we will say that we reaffirmed the main lines of our policy.

I will brief the press on Thursday night after the banquet. I will express our gratification at the visit and say that from our point of view our relations are basically good and gradually improving. That will be the theme of what I will say.

Foreign Minister Ch'iao: You may say that our relations are basically good and they *will be* gradually improving. Not in a progressive tense, because it conforms more to the reality [to put it in the future tense].

Secretary Kissinger: I don't even understand the difference. But it is acceptable to us. (Laughter)

Foreign Minister Ch'iao: Chairman Mao talked to you in a very frank way. He said there will not be major changes [in our relationship] either this year, next year, or the year after next. Your President also agreed with this.

Secretary Kissinger: I think he meant the year after next he thinks there can be.

Foreign Minister Ch'iao: Basically that is—

Secretary Kissinger: There is one problem related to your point about the press writing that our relations are cooling. It is that if nothing at all happens in our relations on the sorts of issues that Habib and Lin P'ing are discussing, it will be taken in America by the press and public as a sign of stagnation. This should reflect on—may have some impact if the things you fear in the world happen. But it is up to you to consider.

I could not care less if there are seven exchange programs, or two. Contrary to many of my compatriots, I believe China lived 2,000 years without cultural contact with America and can live another 2,000 years without contact with America. But this is up to you to consider; we don't have to settle it now, it is something to reflect about.

I was going to say that during most of those 2,000 years America did not even exist. In my limited knowledge of Chinese history— Maybe we could think about whether there is anything in this category that could be examined and if so we could take it up, perhaps follow-ing the visit. If it could be said to have come out of the visit it would be helpful, but only if it is considered helpful to both sides. We do not need it.

Foreign Minister Ch'iao: It is the same case with us. The problem is that we have to take a realistic approach to our bilateral relations. As a matter of fact, the biggest problem is that before the normaliza-tion of relations between our two countries the various programs for exchange between our two countries will have to be limited. I have told you this, Mr. Secretary, as well as many other American friends. Logically speaking, the argument about expanding exchanges before normalization is not tenable.

As the two sides are well aware, the issue of Taiwan is the key problem preventing normalization of relations. Once the relations be-tween our two countries are normalized, the situation will be quite dif-ferent. But we are ready to listen to your new ideas about the bilateral relations if you have any.

Secretary Kissinger: I think they have been discussed between Habib and Lin P'ing. And we are always prepared, when your oil pro-duction increases, we will be prepared if you want to discuss some purchases. But you will let us know. We discussed it with the Vice Pre-mier at dinner yesterday—or to sell some equipment of a special nature.

Foreign Minister Ch'iao: This is a question which we have to leave to the future.

Secretary Kissinger: It is up to you to decide.

Foreign Minister Ch'iao: I do not think there are any new prob-lems in our bilateral relations except the MIAs.

Secretary Kissinger: You told us you might give us some new in-formation on this visit.

Foreign Minister Ch'iao: Yes, we will do that.

Secretary Kissinger: Will the Vice Premier do that with the Presi-dent, or will you give it us us here? Or how do you want to do it?

Foreign Minister Ch'iao: Not at the moment. Either way we will do it. It is up to you. We prefer the Vice Premier telling your President.

Secretary Kissinger: I think that would be best. Shall we then dis-cuss philosophy? (Laughter)

Assistant Secretary Habib: For the rest of the evening.

Foreign Minister Ch'iao: Shall we call it an evening? We could go on to discuss the philosophical problems, but everybody would not be able to go to bed. Once I discussed philosophy with some European friends. We had a big fight and then at the end I gave it up. We should not discuss it any more.

Secretary Kissinger: We will see you then at 9:30 [a.m.] here?

Foreign Minister Ch'iao: You will have a good time when you talk to your press about this trip to China.

Secretary Kissinger: Explaining to them all the signs of progress in our relations. But I will tell you, if you let in one additional professor from the University of Michigan you will keep Solomon happy.

Nancy Tang: We recently had one here. His name was Whiting, I think.

Secretary Kissinger: If you let Allen Whiting in, don't let him leave!

136.   Memorandum of Conversation[1]

Beijing, December 3, 1975, 9:25–11:55 a.m.

PARTICIPANTS

Teng Hsiao-p'ing, Vice Premier of the People's Republic of China
Ch'iao Kuan-hua, PRC Foreign Minister
Wang Hai-jung, Vice Foreign Minister
Huang Chen, Chief of the PRC Liaison Office in Washington
Lin P'ing, Director, Department of American and Oceanic Affairs, Ministry of Foreign Affairs
T'ang Weng-sheng, Deputy Director, Department of American and Oceanic Affairs, Ministry of Foreign Affairs
Ting Yuan-hung, Director, United States Office, Department of American and Oceanic Affairs, Ministry of Foreign Affairs
Chao Chi-hua, Deputy Director, United States Office, Department of American and Oceanic Affairs, Ministry of Foreign Affairs
Tsien Ta-yung, Political Counselor, PRC Liaison Office in Washington
Shih Yen-hua (Interpreter)
Lien Cheng-pao (Notetaker)
Sui Chu-mei (Notetaker)

Gerald R. Ford, President of the United States of America
Henry A. Kissinger, Secretary of State
Brent Scowcroft, Assistant to the President for National Security Affairs
George Bush, Chief of the United States Liaison Office in Peking
Philip C. Habib, Assistant Secretary of State for East Asian and Pacific Affairs
Winston Lord, Director, Policy Planning Staff, Department of State

---

[1] Source: Ford Library, National Security Adviser, Kissinger Reports on USSR, China, and Middle East Discussions, Box 2, China Memcons and Reports, December 1–5, 1975, President Ford's Visit to Peking. Secret; Sensitive. The meeting took place in Guest House 18. All brackets are in the original.

William H. Gleysteen, Deputy Assistant Secretary of State for East Asian and
  Pacific Affairs
Richard H. Solomon, Senior Staff Member, National Security Council

SUBJECT

The Soviet Union; Europe; the Middle East; South Asia; Angola

[The press was escorted into the room.]

Vice Premier Teng: Did you have a good rest?

The President: Yes, I rested very well. We had a walk through the garden.

Vice Premier Teng: Yesterday Mr. President had a very successful conversation with Chairman Mao Tse-tung.

The President: Yes, I agree. It was a very significant conversation which covered a very wide range of matters involving the international scene of great importance, and bilateral topics.

I am looking forward to the visit this afternoon to the agricultural center.

Vice Premier Teng: You will see our tradition of learning from Tachai. I presume that during your last visit you did not have a chance to visit there.

The President: But we did visit several agricultural communes in Liaoning Province.

Vice Premier Teng: Tachai is a very important model in our agriculture. It involves the whole country. It was the poorest [agricultural region] in the past, and now the average food grain—there is now a surplus of about 500 kilos for every person. In addition to accumulation for the commune and brigade, they can deliver 250 kilos of food grain as commodity grain for the state.

[The press is escorted from the room.]

The President: It is very encouraging to us, Mr. Vice Premier, that our relations are good and that the talks have been very beneficial and cover a wide range of subjects. And I am looking forward to the additional talks we will have before we depart.

Vice Premier Teng: Yes, we can continue our talks of yesterday. Mr. President, what subject do you have in mind for today's talks?

The President: Mr. Vice Premier, I thought we could have you lead off the discussions this morning. I would be very glad to have your observations and comments on the matters we discussed yesterday.

Vice Premier Teng: I think in your conversation with Chairman Mao yesterday we almost covered all the international issues. And yesterday our two sides talked about the strategy and tactics against the Soviet Union. And during the meeting with Chairman Mao yesterday afternoon, Mr. President, you also discussed with the Chairman the strategy regarding the Soviet Union. We have noticed that it seems recently the Soviet Union has adopted a tougher position—a fiercer position. And I believe that Mr. Secretary made a statement with regard to the problems in Angola and a warning to the Soviet Union. We have also noticed that the Soviet Union has given a tit-for-tat response.

Flaunting the banner of supporting the national liberation forces of the oppressed peoples, the Soviet Union is using [this banner] as a cover for gaining access to strategic ports in many places. And, of course, this has something to do with [Soviet] domestic politics because in February the [25th] Party Congress will be held. And the agenda for that Party Congress has been adopted in which Brezhnev will make a political report. And Kosygin is going to make the report on the five-year economic plan.

It is worth it to pay attention to the response of the Soviet Union with regard to the problems of Angola. In effect, in plain language it is their belief that détente should not prevent the Soviet Union from seeking hegemony.

The President: Mr. Vice Premier, I agree we covered a great deal of territory in our discussions with the Chairman yesterday. And in our talks I went into the things that the United States has done and is doing in our efforts to meet the expansionist efforts of the Soviet Union. And I noticed as you did that Mr. Brezhnev and Mr. Kosygin are going to make two significant talks at their Party Congress. Would it be appropriate for me to ask if you are sending a delegation [to their Congress]? (Laughter)

Vice Premier Teng: I went to Moscow seven times. I know almost all of the old-age leaders in the Soviet Union—of course, except those of relatively young age. As the Chairman told you yesterday, there is not a single time in our dealings with the Soviet Union that our minds have met.

The President: That is encouraging. (Laughter)

Vice Premier Teng: In 1963 I led a Chinese delegation to Moscow, and that was our last delegation. But even then we didn't give up hope. When Khrushchev fell and Brezhnev took power [in 1964] the Premier went to the celebration of the October Revolution anniversary to see if there was any change there. When the Premier arrived in Moscow the first sentence he heard from the Soviet leaders was that the policies of the Khrushchev time would not change. So Premier Chou did not fulfill his original itinerary and came back earlier than planned. To speak frankly—and I hope that it will not offend you—in the dealings with the Soviet Union, perhaps we are a little more experienced than you.

The President: Let me say, Mr. Vice Premier, we have had some experience in dealing with them and we met and challenged them in a number of cases as I indicated yesterday, and we will continue to do so. But I think it would be helpful in this frank talk with you if you could indicate the various places and ways—whether in Southeast

Asia, the Middle East, or Africa—what your country is doing to meet this challenge so we can better understand how we can act in parallel.

Vice Premier Teng (with some visible tension in his face): We have done only two things: One is to make preparations for ourselves—to make solid down-to-earth preparations. Second, we fire some empty cannons. The empty cannons include encouragement to Japan to strengthen its relations with the United States, and our encouragement of European unity and for the European countries to strengthen their relations with the United States.

And I believe you also understand that we told the Europeans that at present the total military strength of the Soviet Union is stronger than that of the United States and Western Europe put together. In view of this assessment, we have told our friends from Western Europe that the United States is not strong enough to deal with the Soviet Union alone; and the strength of Europe and Japan together are still not enough put together with that of the United States to be adequate.

The President: The Western alliance is not an empty cannon, and we believe the NATO alliance is being strengthened and will continue to be so, even though we think several of the countries are less vigorous than they should be in expanding their military capability. I think it is beneficial that you speak frankly to some of our allies and thereby help to strengthen ties between some of the Western European countries. This is the same as far as Japan is concerned.

And we think it is important also that you urge Thailand to strengthen its relations with Japan; and we also feel that we can and will under the proper circumstances take action as far as Cambodia is concerned.

Vice Premier Teng: That is good. As far as we know, Cambodia will not refuse to have relations with the United States.

Secretary Kissinger: We have approached them in New York—after my conversation with the Foreign Minister [Ch'iao][2]—and we also sent them a message through Thailand.

Vice Premier Teng: Probably you have noticed that Cambodia has first of all established relatively good relations with Thailand.

You are always saying we are criticizing you, but I must say we think you have overdone it [in the *Mayaguez* affair] with regard to that small island. And according to our information, the Cambodian leaders did not know about the incident—it was the people on that small island themselves. And then the United States began the bombing after the Cambodian leaders agreed to return the boat.

---

[2] See Document 119.

Secretary Kissinger: We didn't know this until after our military operation had begun. (Laughter from the Chinese side.)

The President: It is accurate to say we made diplomatic efforts at the very outset, in order to find an answer without taking the military steps; and we were very disappointed those diplomatic efforts were not responded to. [Huang Chen laughs, and Foreign Minister Ch'iao points at him in mock blame.]

Vice Premier Teng: Well, you should know that at that time they [the Cambodian leaders] were scarcely able to take care of their own affairs. But the Cambodian leaders were very sensible.

Secretary Kissinger: But the Vietnamese have solved the problem anyway by taking over the island. (Laughter)

Vice Premier Teng: Anyway, you have slightly overdone it with that incident. Because you are such a big country and Cambodia is such a small country.

During Chancellor Schmidt's visit to China we had very good talks. And, of course, we had a number of differences. And also on the issue of détente and on the assessement of the Helsinki Conference. But we have a common point—that is we worry about the Soviet Union. They are most worried about the development of the Soviet navy, more than Soviet nuclear weapons. But they hold a very clear view—they are aware of the role that NATO can play. That means they are placing their hopes on the strength of the United States to some extent.

In our talks with leaders of other countries, including France, we have found that they hold similar views. And to speak frankly, and also I suppose you know it, leaders of Western European countries are worried whether the United States will fight for Europe. Of course, they haven't raised such worries with us directly; we just sense them.

The President: The countries in Western Europe have no need whatsoever to worry. They have been told explicitly that we have not only the capabilities but also the will to fight for the countries of Western Europe. Just as you have advised some of our allies to strengthen their ties with us, I would like to also say that we have told Japan and we have told Thailand to strengthen their ties with you. And we also feel that the Soviet influence in Laos is a disturbing phenomenon in Southeast Asia as far as we are concerned.

Vice Premier Teng: Yes, that is the case with Laos. But the Soviet Union can only exert that much influence.

As I have said to you just now, the Europeans have worries on two things: that the United States and the Soviet Union are talking too much about so-called détente; and they worry they may start deals over their heads. Second are the domestic problems, and I presume you know there are the so-called leftist forces. They worry about the strength of the left.

The President: That, of course, was one of the primary reasons for meeting at Rambouillet. The six countries—four from Western Europe, Japan, and ourselves—met primarily for the purpose of coordinating our economic plans because if our economic recoveries are not coordinated or are not moving ahead at a reasonable rate, there is the possibility that the leftist forces might increase their strength. But it is our overall view in the United States that economic recovery is moving ahead very well, and I believe at Rambouillet there was a consensus—many of the economic plans were coordinated.

Vice Premier Teng: The problem I have raised just now, perhaps I can also by way of suggestion say that if the United States has such relations with the Soviet Union that get the Western European countries worried, and if the European countries are under the impression that they are not in an important position, then the role they may play in détente with the Soviet Union may go inappropriately too far or they will do too much with their relations with the Soviet Union. And the United States is in an important position politically and economically— and these tactics you have mentioned will affect Western Europe and Japan. And this tactic will surely lead to creating a favorable situation for the Soviet Union. It is favorable for the Soviet Union to disintegrate the European countries one-by-one, to so-called "Finlandize" the countries of Western Europe one-by-one.

The President: Mr. Vice Premier, you should have no apprehension as to our attitude and feeling toward the Soviet Union. The Secretary of State is meeting regularly with Ministers of four Western European countries to coordinate our diplomatic and other matters so that we are working together and we are not, through détente with the Soviet Union, going to—

Secretary Kissinger (interrupting): We meet secretly once a month to coordinate plans for Portugal, Spain, Italy, and Yugoslavia—and we are even making joint plans, for your information, for common action regarding Yugoslavia. But we don't announce the meeting to spare the feelings of the others. We will meet again next week in Brussels.

Vice Premier Teng: We are of the view that the top priority is that the United States should pay more attention to Europe, because this problem is relatively difficult, because the European countries are many and their problems are different, and they are not all in agreement.

We have disagreement on the point that the focus of the Soviet Union's strategy is in Europe. That doesn't matter, but the fact is the Soviet Union is paying more attention to the Europeans. In case war breaks out in Europe, as Chairman Mao mentioned yesterday, several countries in Europe would fight—West Germany, Yugoslavia, Romania, and Sweden. And even when our Chairman talked with some friends from the West, he told them the unification of the two Germa-nies is nothing to be feared. Germany, I believe, is Doctor Kissinger's first homeland.

The President: Mr. Vice Premier, the relations between the United States and Western Europe are today better than they have been for a number of years. Take France for example: Our personal and bilateral relations are far better, and I certainly believe that in case of any mili-tary activity in Europe France would be strong. And I agree with you that Western Germany would be strong. And they know our military coordination today is better than ever.

We are developing and strengthening our anti-tank capability. In the new budget I approved earlier this year the United States is in-creasing the M–60 tank capability. This tank is capable of handling any Soviet tank available. And General Haig in NATO is working closely to improve the overall capability of Western Europe.

We have no objection to the reunification of Germany, and as a matter of fact consider it inevitable.

Secretary Kissinger: The only problem in Sweden is that the army is stronger than the government.

Vice Premier Teng: During Chancellor Schmidt's visit he said that they are making efforts to strengthen their tank and anti-tank weapons, and their surface-to-air missiles. But I told him to be careful as the So-viet Union might not try to break through the center. It might attempt the tactic of outflanking Europe. There are not only problems in the northern wing, but also in the southern wing, and these are more com-plicated and important. We have learned from you that recently the situation in Portugal has improved, but it is possible there might be re-versals and trials of strength again.

The President: We are working closely with various governments in West Europe, urging them to take strong action in Portugal; and we ourselves, as I indicated yesterday, are helping to strengthen the anti-Communist forces in Portugal. I recognize that the situation is not yet stable, but the progress has been significant in the past several weeks.

As I told you yesterday, the United States is working with the gov-ernment forces against the Communists in Italy and France. And we think these problems must be recognized by the governments them-selves; and they must be able to take action against the elements in their own countries. For example, when Mitterrand came to the United States, we had no contact with him under any circumstances.

Secretary Kissinger: When he came I saw him, not the President, and only in the presence of the French Ambassador so that he could make no propaganda. And we told him we would not deal with him unless he broke with the Marchais group.

Vice Premier Teng: And I believe you can do more solid work to help Yugoslavia. And, of course, in Yugoslavia they had domestic problems: the pro-Soviet forces are considerably strong. These are what we called in the past the International Communist Intelligence Agency. But this nation [Yugoslavia] can fight.

The President: We had a very successful visit to Yugoslavia. We strongly feel they should take the strongest action possible to meet the challenge of this element that you indicated; and we were impressed with the recognition on the part of Tito that the nation must be kept together and the need to prepare a proper succession when he leaves the scene. We were impressed with his recognition of both problems.

We have a long record of helping Yugoslavia be independent going back to the 1950s; and we feel strongly as you do that they not only did fight but also that they will fight. And we would welcome any actions on your part to encourage or help Yugoslavia.

Vice Premier Teng: We have a very good (pu-tso) relations with Yugoslavia now. Not long ago their Prime Minister came to China for a visit, and we had good talks. And they told us that they had done much work to eliminate pro-Soviet forces, including an open trial; and they told us that they would conduct not just one open trial but others.

The President: We are resuming the sale of military equipment to Yugoslavia.

Vice Premier Teng: Very good.

The President: And we are having our military work closely with Romania as well.

Vice Premier Teng: I believe we have relatively covered the problems of Europe. Perhaps we can proceed to the problems of the Middle East.

I believe Doctor, Mr. Secretary, you may recall that during your conversation with Chairman Mao he told you that our position on the Middle East is two-fold: The first point—and I'm afraid we will have disagreement on this point—we must support the Arab countries against Israeli Zionism. The Soviet Union is trying to fix, get the United States in that area.

Through the Doctor's recent shuttle diplomacy several problems were solved, but it is still far from settling this [entire] problem.

It seems to me that in matters with the Soviet Union, more and more countries have come to realize that the Soviet Union is not reliable. Those countries which have had long dealings with the Soviet Union have come to realize this. They are distrustful or disillusioned.

The President: That is the feeling in the case of Egypt. They have been disillusioned with relations with the Soviet Union, and because of Dr. Kissinger's successful efforts relations between Egypt and the United States are closer than they have been in many years. Egypt is an important country in the [Middle East] region, and I intend to develop relations with Egypt in an economic and military sense.

Vice Premier Teng: In the past, when Vice Premier Shafei came to visit China, Chairman Mao encouraged him to improve relations with the Soviet Union—

The President: The Soviet Union?

Secretary Kissinger: That would be an amazing development!

Miss Tang (corrects the interpreter): The United States.

Miss Shih: The United States. (Laughter)

Vice Premier Teng: At that time they were not quite willing to do that, and later Chairman Mao told Doctor to use both hands. One for helping Israel, and the other one to help Egypt.

The President: And Mr. Vice Premier, we are doing both, and also urging some of our Western European friends to help Egypt break its military dependence on the Soviet Union. We have made some progress.

Vice Premier Teng: And we must pay attention to changes in the Arab countries: Iraq and South Yemen. Somalia cannot be included. We don't have sufficient knowledge of Somalia. And as far as we know, Syria is not monolithic [in their support for the Soviets]. They are on their guard against the Soviet Union too.

The President: Let me make a comment, and then Secretary Kissinger—who knows more about the Middle East than just about any person—can speak. We have been disturbed about Somalia. There is some evidence that it may not be as big a problem as we thought; but Somalia, if it stays with the Soviet Union, could cause serious military problems in that area.

Secretary Kissinger: In the Middle East, Mr. Vice Premier, we look at the various countries. We have a good relationship with President Assad. He has a complicated domestic situation. Some of his advisers, including the Foreign Minister, are closer to the Soviet Union than he is. But they are very suspicious of the Soviet Union, and they are using it only for military equipment. They are not a satellite of the Soviet Union. In fact, I am quite confident that when we are prepared to move in Syria, we can do to the Soviet Union in Syria what we did to the Soviet Union in Egypt. But we cannot take decisive action in Syria—to speak here among friends—until after our elections. But we will take decisive action some time after that. So we must give Assad some face-saving formulas for the next ten months; that is why we supported his resolution in the UN.

But on the other hand, we must not get pushed too hard in the Security Council debate in January, because it is an empty victory to get a resolution for the Arabs if our domestic support [for this policy in the Middle East] is eroded. We don't want that kind of a situation to exist in the next ten months. So we will, of course, have a bland resolution. You might keep this in mind in the Security Council.

But our direction is clear, and President Assad understands it. He just sent a message to President Ford thanking him for our recent action in support of his position.

With respect to Iraq, we brought great pressure on them in combination with Iran and other countries while they were very pro-Soviet. Partly as a result of this pressure, and partly because the Soviet Union seems unable to gain political support without an army of occupation, Iraq is moving away somewhat from the Soviet Union. We have many unofficial contacts with them, and I expect our relations will improve over the next year.

With respect to South Yemen, we again have a combination of pressure from Oman and somewhat from Saudi Arabia. I met with their Foreign Minister at the UN and we agreed to open diplomatic relations. We are only waiting for Saudi Arabia to do it first, so that the wrong impression is not created.

Somalia: The Soviet Union has military bases, as you know. But we are working—and you can help perhaps also with the Organization of African Unity—and we will use the influence of Saudi Arabia. In Somalia, influence usually means money.

The Soviet Union has put much military equipment into Libya. This is the most dangerous [situation] right now. And we think that Egypt will look after that in some period of time.

We will have about ten months of a defensive policy, but after that we will move decisively. But we can oppose Soviet actions as they are afraid of war in the Middle East, and because they can't achieve anything in the Middle East without our cooperation. As the President said yesterday to the Chairman, he will not have a period of stagnation, and it will be evident we will be working with both our hands.

Vice Premier Teng: In the past, I talked to some of your American friends—I don't remember if I told [this to] Doctor: The greatest reality in the Middle East is that there are 3 million Israelis fighting against 120 million Arabs. In this regard, the position of the United States has some advantages, but also considerable disadvantages. The Soviet Union has a lot of openings they can squeeze into.

Secretary Kissinger: But they can't produce anything—they can only talk.

Vice Premier Teng: It is important to pay attention to the national sentiment [of the Arabs]. In this perhaps we are more sensitive than you. If Mr. Sadat had gone beyond a certain limit, he would have lost the sympathy of the Arab countries.

Secretary Kissinger: But looking at it historically, it is the United States who can realize the aspirations of the Arab states. As the President said to Chairman Mao yesterday, he will move to an overall solution as soon as conditions permit—in about a year. And nobody can do anything better in the interim.

Vice Premier Teng: If no solution is arrived at for the Palestinian problem, it is far from a total settlement of the Arab problem. And the Doctor is complaining that sometimes we criticize the United States; but we must fire cannons sometimes. If we do not, we will not be in a position to do work with the Arab states.

Secretary Kissinger: We understand, but the Foreign Minister gets carried away with his barrages. (Laughter)

Vice Premier Teng: This is not going too far.

Regarding Iraq, we are advising them to be on the alert against the Soviet Union. We told this to the Iraqi Vice Premier when he came to visit China last September. And we told the same to Chairman Robaya of South Yemen when he came to China.

Secretary Kissinger: We are willing to deal with them in good will when they are ready to deal with us.

Vice Premier Teng: This has to be done slowly because we know how they feel about you. But Iraq is ready to improve relations with Iran, and they have adopted some good measures already. But you must be aware of the fact that these countries have very strong national pride.

So much about the Middle East issues. Should we proceed to the issue of South Asia?

The President: Very much so; and I might make a comment: It seems to me that we want to encourage the independence of Laos and Cambodia. And at the same time we will work with Thailand to strengthen its relations with those countries.

Vice Premier Teng: So that is the issue of the Southeast Asian countries. With regard to the issue of South Asia, we have advised you on many occasions to aid Pakistan.

The President: We had significant discussions—and we made an announcement that we were lifting the arms embargo with regard to Pakistan. And the Pakistani Air Chief is coming to Washington very shortly to negotiate the equipment and delivery.

Vice Premier Teng: You shouldn't give the Pakistanis the impression that the United States attaches more importance to India than to Pakistan. They [the Paks] are very much worried about dismemberment.

The President: As I indicated before, we are moving to help Pakistan militarily. At the same time we are seeking to move India away from the Soviet Union. This is not easy, but it may pay dividends if it's possible to achieve. And we strongly warned India not to pressure Bangladesh.

[Vice Premier Teng and his side converse.]

Vice Premier Teng: After your [Secretary Kissinger's] second visit to China, Pakistan was dismembered. And Premier Chou En-lai told the Doctor—and it might be counted as criticism, but with good intention—that you took no effective action, because your tone was of advice and not the tone of warning.

When the Soviet Union took action with regard to India, it paid attention to the attitude of the United States because it knew China's capability was quite limited. We have good relations with Pakistan and also have rendered some help to Pakistan, but our equipment is backward. Only the United States can give them some good things either directly or indirectly.

Secretary Kissinger: First of all, at that time the President was not in office. I agreed with Chou En-lai's analysis and I did not consider it an unfair comment. But our situation was complicated by two factors: One, the Vietnam war and the domestic difficulties caused by it; and second, President Yahya Khan was not the greatest leader of which history informs us. He made great mistakes politically and militarily. So he made it very hard for us, but you will [also] remember the difficulties President Nixon and I had in America. But President Nixon and I had made the decision—for your information—that if you had moved and the Soviet Union had brought pressure on you, we would have given [China] military support—even though the Shanghai Communiqué was not yet issued. We understand why you didn't, but you should know our position, our seriousness of purpose.

Vice Premier Teng: These are historical views. On the other hand, the Soviet Union has not given up its plan for Baluchistan.[3]

The President: We had discussions with the Shah in Washington on that particular problem. We understand that situation, and are working both with Iran and Pakistan on it.

Vice Premier Teng: That's good.

On the question of Bangladesh, Chairman Mao already discussed this question with you yesterday. We have established diplomatic relations with Bangladesh, and will send our Ambassador there at a later date. The only consideration we should make is to seek an opportune time which is favorable to the present government of Bangladesh. And according to our information, Pakistan has the same consideration.

---

[3] Deng is referring to charges that the Soviet Union was seeking to create a Soviet-dominated greater Baluchistan, which would combine the Baluch tribes of Pakistan, Iran, and Afghanistan.

About India, recently Mrs. Gandhi has also assumed the post of the Minister of Defense. What implications do you think it has?

The President: I can't give you any categorical answer, but I think it is probably indicative of a more aggressive attitude. Of course, it may be indicative that she is fearful of a coup within India itself.

Secretary Kissinger: She may have seen what General Scowcroft did. (Laughter) He did it while I was in China. (Laughter)

Vice Premier Teng: We could well hope that she did it out of domestic considerations.

The President: I would like your estimation of Afghanistan and Pakistan. We note a growing tension between the two.

Vice Premier Teng: In Afghanistan there are two tendencies: One is that Afghanistan cannot but rely on the Soviet Union; and the other is Afghanistan is vigilant against the Soviet Union. In this respect, maybe Iraq can do work with Afghanistan. It seems to be difficult to improve the relations of Afghanistan and Pakistan for the time being. There is still a long way to go.

Secretary Kissinger: The major thing is to keep the Indians out of Pakistan.

Vice Premier Teng: As a matter of fact, the Soviet Union in collusion with India, is trying to influence Pakistan from two sides.

The President: Do you feel there is any threat of an Indian invasion of Nepal?

Vice Premier Teng: Nepal itself feels the threat, but at the moment there are no indications that India will make open military actions.

Secretary Kissinger (in an aside to the President): Pressure.

Vice Premier Teng: The key element is that the King of Nepal and the Nepalese government has—can control the situation there. As a land locked country, Nepal has all its communications through India. This is the greatest practical difficulty for Nepal. And I believe that you can do more things with Nepal. We are doing what we can with our capability. We have established good relations with Nepal—we have mutual confidence—but what we can do is quite limited. Perhaps things will get better when our railroad into Tibet is accomplished.

The President: I am sending a personal friend [as Ambassador] to Nepal, Mrs. Maytag.

Secretary Kissinger: This shows the significance we attach to Nepal.

Vice Premier Teng: It is necessary to help Nepal. The Nepalese are a nation that can fight. Nepal isn't Sikkim or Bhutan.

So much about the issue of South Asia. Now to Southeast Asia?

Just now Mr. President discussed the situation in Southeast Asia. As far as Southeast Asia as a whole is considered, we feel that the situation there is relatively good. Three Indochinese countries have different attitudes. The attitude of Cambodia is relatively good. Undoubtedly the Soviet Union will increase its influence in Vietnam and Laos. But we also believe that it is not such a simple thing for a nation which has fought three wars to forget its independence so lightly. But the possibility should not be ruled out that the Soviet Union will try by every means to get the bases in Camranh Bay which you so painstakingly established. (Laughter)

The President: You may have noticed that the Secretary of State in Detroit last week opened the door a crack as far as Vietnam is concerned.

Vice Premier Teng: Yes, we have noticed. It is beneficial to have dealings with the Soviet Union over a long period of time. And we also believe that someday India will eventually rebel against the Soviet Union. Because the deeper the Soviet involvement, the more problems they [the client state] will confront. We know very well the way the Soviet Union is doing things. The salient characteristic of the Soviet Union is that it is very stingy. Anything it supplies will have some political conditions attached.

Secretary Kissinger: On the other hand, gratitude is not a characteristic India is famous for. The combination of these two factors is likely to produce some tensions.

Vice Premier Teng: The Soviet Union at present is pushing its collective security system in Asia, and particularly in Southeast Asia. I believe it will not succeed; even Vietnam will not agree to it. As to the five countries in ASEAN, they are very clear about it.

The President: We are totally opposed to it.

Vice Premier Teng: Because it is primarily those countries which are concerned. Those which accepted it would become the victims of the so-called collective security in Asia. Even India does not dare to give open support to the Soviet proposal.

The President: In my visit to Indonesia and the Philippines, I will make this very clear. We are vigorously opposed to it.

Secretary Kissinger: But it warrants attention that India has a treaty with the Soviet Union, and India wants to establish treaties with these countries.

Vice Premier Teng: We have seen that India is making efforts to sell the so-called collective security system of Asia, but to no avail. Their Vice President has made a round of trips to Southeast Asian countries especially for this purpose.

We have established diplomatic relations with a majority of the ASEAN countries. Indonesia does not have good relations with us, but we are in no hurry.

The President: When I am in Indonesia, we will speak very forcefully to them concerning this effort.

Vice Premier Teng: It seems not to be easy for the time being. The diplomatic relations between our two countries were suspended in 1965. And that [situation] also involves several million Chinese descendants. As far as China is concerned, we are willing to improve relations with Indonesia, but we have patience.

Finally, we may discuss the issue of Angola. Actually this issue was already discussed in Mr. President's conversation with Chairman Mao. We hope that through the work of the two sides we can both bring about a better situation there. The relatively complex problem is the involvement of South Africa. And I believe you are aware of the feelings of the black Africans toward South Africa.

Secretary Kissinger: We are prepared to push South Africa out as soon as an alternative military force can be created.

The President: We hope your Ambassador in Zaire can keep us fully informed. It would be helpful.

Vice Premier Teng: We have a good relationship with Zaire, but what we can help them with is only some light weapons.

Secretary Kissinger: We can give them weapons. What they need is training in guerrilla warfare. If you can give them light weapons it would help, but the major thing is training. Our specialty is *not* guerrilla warfare. (Laughter)

Vice Premier Teng: In the past we trained the three organizations—including Neto.

Secretary Kissinger: Like NATO! (Laughter)

Vice Premier Teng: And we helped to train the soldiers of FNLA for some time.

Secretary Kissinger: They needed it most.

Vice Premier Teng: And in the past, we assisted all three organizations, and more so to Neto. And the organization which we helped earliest was MPLA. With respect to UNITA—Savimbi—we supplied them with weapons by way of Tanzania, but they were not delivered.

The President: Both UNITA and FNLA need help particularly.

Vice Premier Teng: We have no way of transferring weapons into their hands.

Secretary Kissinger: Zambia or Zaire?

Vice Premier Teng: Zambia does not support Neto and the MPLA. If we asked them to allow our weapons to pass through their territory they wouldn't allow it.

Secretary Kissinger: Really?

Vice Premier Teng: Yes. As I mentioned to you just now, the primary problem is the involvement of South Africa. In those countries which originally did not support the MPLA, there is now a change in attitude exactly because of the involvement of South Africa. Some independent countries have begun to support Neto. I think through Zaire. If you can get South Africa out of Angola as soon as possible, or find some other means to replace South Africa on the southern front, this would be good. We are in no position to help except in the north through Zaire.

The President: We had nothing to do with the South African involvement, and we will take action to get South Africa out, provided a balance can be maintained for their not being in. In addition, if you would like, we can talk to Zambia with regard to transshipment.

Vice Premier Teng: I am afraid it is very difficult. Yesterday I said we could try with Mozambique, but we don't expect great results.

Secretary Kissinger: I talked with their Foreign Minister in New York. They feel very close to China.

Vice Premier Teng: Yes, we have good relations with Mozambique, but on this particular issue it is another matter, because Mozambique takes a very strong position on Zimbabwe—Rhodesia—and South Africa. I believe the better way is for you to help through the southern front, and I believe you will find the way.

There is one point which is evident. Since Nyerere would not permit transshipment through Tanzania, how could Zambia account to Tanzania if it accepted transshipment of weapons?

Secretary Kissinger: Can we talk to Kaunda and see what he thinks? We have some influence with him.

Vice Premier Teng: Please understand this with regard to African countries—even the small ones: they are extremely sensitive on matters involving national pride. [Because of this] we have not raised the suggestion with them, despite all our assistance to them—as in Tanzania and Zambia in railway construction.

The President: You have been effective. Will you move in the north if we move in the south?

Vice Premier Teng: But you should give greater help in the north too. As far as I know, you have many ways to help. Also through third countries.

The President: We have and will.

Vice Premier Teng: Good.

Secretary Kissinger: We are working with France. They will send some equipment and training.

The President: I just approved before I left Washington $35 million more above what we have done before; and that [amount] is on its way as I understand it.

Vice Premier Teng: It is worth spending more money on that problem. Because that is a key position of strategic importance.

The President: Yes. They have an important port; and their natural resources are vital.

Vice Premier Teng: So should we call it a morning and continue our talks tomorrow? We spent two and a half hours making a round the world trip.

The President: It has been very beneficial and encouraging to work with you, Mr. Vice Premier, to be very frank, and to see how our interests are similar in many, many areas of the world.

Vice Premier Teng: We have said we have many things in common.

Secretary Kissinger: What should we say to the press?

Vice Premier Teng: We may say that we have continued significant discussions on a wide range of international issues.

Secretary Kissinger: All right.

Vice Premier Teng: We will see you tomorrow.

Secretary Kissinger: We will actually see you—does that mean you are withdrawing your invitation for tonight? (Laughter)

Vice Premier Teng: No, we will see you at the performance tonight!

---

137.   Memorandum of Conversation[1]

Beijing, December 4, 1975, 10:05–11:47 a.m.

PARTICIPANTS

PRC

Teng Hsiao-p'ing, Vice Premier of the State Council

Ch'iao Kuan-hua, Minister of Foreign Affairs

Amb. Huang Chen, Chief, PRCLO, Washington

Wang Hai-jung, Vice Minister of Foreign Affairs

Lin P'ing, Director of American & Oceanic Affairs, Ministry of Foreign Affairs

T'ang Weng-sheng, Deputy Director of American & Oceanic Affairs, Ministry of Foreign Affairs, (Interpreter)

Chien Ta-yung, Counselor, PRCLO, Washington

---

[1] Source: Ford Library, National Security Adviser, Kissinger Reports on USSR, China, and Middle East Discussions, Box 2, China Memcons and Reports, December 1–5, 1975, President Ford's Visit to Peking. Secret; Nodis. The meeting took place in the Great Hall of the People. All brackets are in the original.

Ting Yuan-hung, Director for U.S. Affairs, American & Oceanic Affairs
Department
Chao Chi-hua, Deputy Director for U.S. Affairs, American & Oceanic Affairs
Department
Mrs. Shih Yen-hua, Ministry of Foreign Affairs, (Interpreter)
(Plus two notetakers)

U.S.
President Ford
Dr. Henry A. Kissinger, Secretary of State
Lt. Gen. Brent Scowcroft, Assistant to the President for National Security Affairs
Joseph J. Sisco, Under Secretary of State for Political Affairs
Amb. George H. W. Bush, Chief of the USLO, Peking
Winston Lord, Director, Policy Planning Staff
Amb. Philip C. Habib, Assistant Secretary for East Asian and Pacific Affairs
William H. Gleysteen, Jr., Deputy Assistant Secretary for East Asian and Pacific
Affairs
Peter W. Rodman, NSC Staff
Bonnie Long, Sec. Kissinger's Office (Notetaker)

SUBJECT

Taiwan; bilateral relations; MIA; trade (oil and computers); Dalai Lama; Korea;
Chinese minorities; agriculture; Amb. Bush

[A press pool was admitted at the beginning]

Vice Premier Teng: Did you have a good rest?

The President: I certainly did. I have had three beneficial, friendly,
and I think, constructive days. I am looking forward to the final session and I think it will be as helpful as the ones before.

Vice Premier Teng: I am sure they will be, Sir, and we are also very
pleased that our two sides are now setting a new style this time. That
is, we do not think we are compelled to issue a communiqué. We think
the importance lies in the visit itself, and that our two sides have had
significant discussions. We don't think importance lies in such superficial things as a communiqué.

The President: I agree. Actions and agreements are much more important than the words, and the discussions far more significant than
a piece of paper.

Vice Premier Teng: But perhaps the ladies and gentlemen of the
press won't be so satisfied by that. [Laughter] And perhaps they will
also notice that I have begun smoking again. [Laughter]

The President: Mr. Vice Premier, the relations between the United
States and the People's Republic of China—this relationship has been
strengthened by the visit and the meeting with Chairman Mao and
yourself, the kind of meetings that can be meaningful in the months
and years ahead.

Vice Premier Teng: I agree with that.

The President: I have my pipe out too. [Laughter] But they all know
I do that.

Helen Thomas (UPI): We want a rebuttal some day.

The President: She always has the last word. [Laughter]

Helen Thomas: I want a translation of that. [Laughter]

[The press was then ushered out.]

Secretary Kissinger: That made my press briefing a lot easier.

The President: That performance at the gymnasium last night was one of the finest things I have ever seen.

Vice Premier Teng: It is more relaxing, and we did not want the time to be too tiring.

The President: I am envious of those young people who can do all those things.

Secretary Kissinger: General Scowcroft was so moved that even though he fell asleep, he applauded. [Laughter] [To Foreign Minister Ch'iao:] You saw him.

Vice Premier Teng: Mr. Scowcroft is a Lieutenant General and I, after having fought twenty years in a war, still don't have a rank. I am only an ordinary soldier. You are my superior! [Laughter]

President Ford: Mr. Vice Premier, the Battle of the Potomac sometimes gets a little rough.

Taiwan

Vice Premier Teng: So we now enter our third session and I think the final session for this visit. I believe in the talks we had yesterday, we have covered almost all the ground, and I think especially the deep going conversation you had with Chairman Mao shows we have touched upon all aspects.

And the Taiwan issue that both sides are concerned about actually was also discussed during your wide-ranging conversation with Chairman Mao. And we have understood Mr. President's point; that is, that during the time of the election it will not be possible to make any new moves.

As for our side, we have told the Doctor many times that we are very patient. And in our relations we have always put the international aspect first and the Taiwan issue second.

The President: Mr. Vice Premier, you are absolutely correct. We have covered the globe in detail, ourselves as well as the discussions with the Chairman, and we did touch on the question of Taiwan. We are very grateful that you are understanding of the domestic political situation in the United States.

But I think it is important for us—and for me, I should say—to speak quite frankly about the political commitment that I feel the United States has concerning Taiwan. Although we understand and have discussed the situation, I think it is beneficial that I reaffirm for the record of these meetings what in the first instance President Nixon said in 1972. There were five points that were made:

—Number one, that we support the principle of the unity of China.

—Number Two, we will not support any independence effort by the Taiwan Government.

—And that we would actively discourage any third force from seeking to take some expansionist activities concerning Taiwan.

—Of course, you do know that we have significantly reduced, as President Nixon said, the military forces that we have on Taiwan. As I recall the figure in 1972, there were roughly 10,000 American military personnel on the island. That has been reduced, so that at the present time we have roughly 2,800. And it is my intention within the next year that we will reduce that by 50%, down to a figure roughly of 1,400. I want you to know that we have no offensive weapon capabilities on Taiwan.

—So, with the total reduced figure from 10,000 to 1,400, and the fact that we have no offensive military capability, there is a clear indication that the commitments made by President Nixon are being carried out by myself.

And, we do understand and we are grateful for the patience that your government has had. On the other hand, we want to say after the election we will be in a position to move much more specifically toward the normalization of relations, along the model perhaps of the Japanese arrangement, but it will take some time, bearing in mind our domestic political situation.

Teng: We have taken note of Mr. President's well-intentioned words, that is, that under suitable conditions you will be prepared to solve the Taiwan issue according to the Japanese formula. And of course, when the normalization of relations is realized, we are sure that will be in accordance with the three principles we have stated many times: It will go along with the abolishing of the so-called U.S.–Chiang Kai-shek defense treaty, and the withdrawal of United States troops from Taiwan, and the severing of diplomatic relations with the Chiang Kai-shek government. Of course, we can also realize the Japanese formula which also includes the remaining of some people-to-people, nongovernmental trade relations with Taiwan, as Japan maintains at the present time.

Other issues pertaining to Taiwan will be settled in accordance with the principle that it is the internal problem of China.

And under these conditions we are not worried about any third country, particularly Russia, being able to do anything of consequence on Taiwan.

[Teng bends over next to his seat and spits into a spittoon under the table.]

The President: We would certainly anticipate that any solution would be by peaceful means as far as your government and Taiwan are concerned. We certainly have to look at it from the point of view that we can't just cast aside old friends. It would have to be a peaceful solution, which I understand is the understanding President Nixon made at that time. I would agree that we would perhaps retain trade relations, etc. which would continue.

But I might add that I would hope that in our own relations, Mr. Vice Premier, we could move in a broadening sense, as friends, in the direction of trade relations, and educational and cultural exchanges. They are very meaningful, as the Ambassador [Huang Chen] knows, in the support that comes from the American people for the forward movement of our overall relations.

Teng: Of course, I believe the Doctor will well remember the talks he had with Chairman Mao during his recent October visit in which the Chairman has very explicitly discussed our position. And with regard to the thing you mentioned just now, to put it frankly, we do not believe in peaceful transition. Because there is a huge bunch of counter-revolutionaries over there, and the question of what method we will take to solve our internal problem is something that we believe belongs to the internal affairs of China, to be decided by China herself. And in his conversation with the Doctor, Chairman Mao mentioned five years, ten years, 20 years, 100 years. While the Doctor continued stressing the point that "you had mentioned 100 years." [Laughter] So, I think that is about all for that question.

The President: You can argue that 100 years is a peaceful transition. [Laughter]

Teng: But I think it is clear that the Chairman's meaning was that even in 100 years a peaceful transition would be impossible. There is still time left.

The President: But I would reiterate, Mr. Vice Premier, how it is beneficial for us to expand the visits and exchanges from our country to yours and your country to ours. The good will that has been engendered by the many groups that come to the United States has been very helpful, and we hope that those who have come to the People's Republic likewise are helpful, whether they are educational, agricultural, scientific or otherwise. It is a step that strengthens the ties between our two countries.

Teng: I believe our two sides have already discussed the specific programs that we will be exchanging next year. And we believe that the strengthening of mutual exchanges is always for the good.

There is another issue that your side has mentioned many times. That is the question of missing in action.

The President: Very important.

Teng: We have conducted many searches once again, and we have found out about what has happened to seven of them. And we have the ashes of two. But the remains of the others have not been able to be obtained. As for the others, there have also been cases in which planes have been shot down, some into the sea, and the remains have not been able to be found.

So we can hand over the information to you. [He hands paper at Tab A to the President.][2]

The President: Mr. Vice Premier, this is very helpful. [Teng spits into his spittoon.] Of course, I have not had a chance to read it, but the fact that you have responded to something that is of deep concern to the American people will be greatly appreciated. And I would hope that if any other developments take place in the future, either a plane shot down or ashes or remains, and means of identification are found, that you would do the same in those cases as you have done in these. This will have a very beneficial impact on the reaction in the United States.

And I notice on the last page here that you do indicate that if we wanted we can take back the remains of two Americans, Kenneth Pugh and Jimmy Buckley. My quick reaction is we perhaps can do it through the Red Cross or some way; that probably would be the best way to handle it. But the news will be very well received in the United States.

Teng: We agree then, if you want it handed over from the Chinese Red Cross to the American Red Cross.

Secretary Kissinger: Maybe at the briefing today, without giving names, can I say that you have informed us of seven missing in action? But we want to notify their families, so we will not release the names.

Teng: All right. In the future, if similar events occur, I think it will be much easier to handle because we can deal with it directly.

Secretary Kissinger: Do you mean overflights? There are no such . . . [Laughter]

Teng: Do you think you envisage such overflights? [Laughter]

Secretary Kissinger: No.

Teng: So there will not be the question arising. [Laughter]

The President: I notice, Mr. Vice Premier, that the Cambodians have indicated that they hold no American prisoners and have no information. I think this attitude on their part is helpful in trying to make some progress on relations if we can, as far as they are concerned. If you have any influence on other friends in Indochina it might be helpful in that regard to indicate to them that any information would

---

[2] Not attached and not found.

be very beneficial in the improvement, in the movement towards relations.

Teng: I think you mean Vietnam. [Laughter]

The President: You are very perceptive!

Teng: And as I believe we discussed with Dr. Kissinger during his recent visit, we mentioned that you have many channels leading to Vietnam. [Laughter]

The President: We do thank you for this information. It will be very helpful.

Teng: As for the question of oil and equipment and so on, as Mr. President mentioned, we think this can be conducted through trade channels.

The President: Very good.

Teng: And under our present relations we believe it also conforms to reality that the volume of trade between our two countries has not been very stable. Of course this also includes our ability to pay for certain things. And I also believe that with the developing of our economy, the prospects will be better.

The President: I admire . . .

Teng: For instance, under the present situation, some things we are interested in perhaps you find it impossible to supply. Like for instance computers of a speed of 10 million times. We do not think such issues are of great consequence.

Secretary Kissinger: Our problem is we have refused certain computers to the Soviet Union. [Teng spits into his spittoon.] I think we could approve computers to the People's Republic of China that would be of considerable quality. As long as we can at the same time maintain our policy with the Soviet Union.

Teng: I think that such issues can be discussed through trade channels. And we do not think it matters if perhaps you at the present will find it difficult to proceed; it would not be of very great consequence.

The President: Mr. Vice Premier, in principle we would be very anxious to be helpful in the computer area, and I think we can be. And certainly those matters can be discussed by the trade people, but I think with the overall attitude that we have, progress can be made in that regard.

Teng: Fine.

Secretary Kissinger: Could I make a suggestion, Mr. Vice Premier?

Teng: Okay.

Secretary Kissinger: I know your normal procedure is to do it through trade channels. But this has the consequence that you may ask for a particular model that then comes to us for decision and we refuse it for a reason that may have to do with our Soviet relationship and not the Chinese relationship. If your Ambassador could tell us informally ahead of time what you have in mind, we may be able to find a model of good quality which meets your needs which you can be sure will be approved, and we could work with the companies. Because there are many varieties which could be effective to you. If we can just find a model with technical differences to preserve the principle with the Soviet Union, then we can give it to you, and we can certainly work that out.

Teng: To our understanding, what we term trade channels actually are controlled or influenced heavily by the governments.

Secretary Kissinger: Yes, but there are two ways it comes to our attention. One is if you go through the technical channel, and we do not know until you have already made a specific proposal. If you tell us informally, I can . . . For example, the other day I had dinner with the President of Burroughs Corporation, and he told me of your interest in some computers. He said there are many computers he could give you, various models, if he knew your needs. If we could have some preliminary talks with your Ambassador, or whoever you designate, I could talk to Burroughs Corporation or whoever you want to deal with, and then we could give an appropriate model and we would not be made to get into the position of having to accept or reject a specific model, once we know what you have in mind.

Teng: We can think over that suggestion. And the Chairman said that our Ambassador will be staying in your country for one or two more years. [Laughter]

Kissinger: It will be with the intention of approving it, not refusing it.

The President: The Secretary has suggested the better procedure for the handling of the matter, and I would like you to know, Mr. Vice Premier, that we are very anxious to be helpful in this area. If we follow the right procedure it makes it very possible that we can cooperate.

Teng: Fine. So we think that, first of all, we can study the issue and then further consider it. And we think that the solving of specific issues like this, or their all remaining unsolved, will not be of great effect to our general relations. [The Chinese all laugh.] There are also many small issues like this between us.

For instance, the question of the Dalai Lama having set up a small office in your country. And during my discussions with some of your visitors, I said that was like chicken feathers and onion skin. [Laughter] Do you have such an expression?

Ambassador Bush: We have an impolite one.

Teng: In Chinese it means something of very little weight. Feathers are very light.

The President: Let me assure you, Mr. Vice Premier, that we oppose and do not support any governmental action as far as Tibet is concerned.

Teng: Things might be easier if you refused them visas.

The President: No United States governmental action was taken. This was done privately, Mr. Vice Premier.

[Teng spits into his spittoon.]

Teng: It is not so important.

Kissinger: When they become Communists, then we have a legal basis to refuse them visas. [Laughter]

Teng: The present Palace of Culture of Various Nationalities, which I pointed out to you in the car and which your daughter visited, was built for the Dalai Lama. And in 1959, when the Dalai Lama came to Peking, he stayed there for one period. After he went back to Tibet he staged a rebellion and left, fled the country. At that time actually it was possible for us to have stopped his leaving the country. It was entirely within our capacity to stop him from leaving. But Chairman Mao said it is better to let him go. [The Chinese all laugh.]

You can see the difference in Tibet now. Recently a woman writer, Han Suyin, visited Tibet. She is of British citizenship, but very often visits the United States. And the standards of living in Tibet are much higher than before, and in comparison to other areas in China it can not be considered very low.

So that is all the bilateral issues we can think of.

The President: I think we have covered the bilateral and I think we have covered the international issues in great depth.

I may just add that we do not approve of the actions that the Indians are taking as far as Tibet is concerned.

Teng: We do not pay much attention to that because it is of no use. And to put it in more explicit terms, the Dalai Lama is now a burden on India. [The Chinese laugh.] If he should want to come back to Tibet, we might even welcome him back for a short visit. And perhaps he can see what changes have been wrought by the serfs that he had so cruelly ruled.

The President: I do not think you want to relieve India of any extra burdens that it has.

Teng: We do not want to. Let them carry it for 100 years! We will think about it after that. The Dalai Lama must be in his 30's, at the most 40. He was very young at that time. He might still live another 60 years, to 100. So let India carry that burden for another 60 years at least.

The President: We are very grateful, Mr. Vice Premier, for your warm welcome. We feel very strongly that the discussions both on bilateral, as well as international matters, have been very fruitful and significant. I think the opportunity to meet you personally and meet the Chairman will be very productive in the long run in our efforts to make possible affirmative action on a parallel basis. And on behalf of myself and my family and all of the delegation from the United States, we are very grateful for the frank and significant, fruitful discussions that we have had.

Teng: I agree with the words of the President, and I would like to take this opportunity to once again express our thanks to the President for the visit.

So, do you think we have come to the end of our discussion?

The President: The only apprehension that I have, Mr. Vice Premier, is that we have gotten along so well that we have not had to take as much time this morning as we anticipated. And our friends in the press might misconstrue that, and they often times do. [Laughter] So if there is anything that we could discuss, informally, or otherwise, it might be helpful. [Laughter]

Teng: Fine.

Kissinger: See, if the meeting runs longer than planned, it proves we quarreled. If it runs shorter than planned, it also proves we quarreled. [Laughter]

Teng: Yes, the press people do not seem to have any particular noses or ears. I wonder how they get so sensitive.

Kissinger: There were two British correspondents here, Mr. Vice Premier, who wrote articles that there was great tension in our first meeting here.

Teng: I sometimes think perhaps that is due to inspiration. [Laughter]

The President: Mr. Vice Premier, the Secretary has told me that the two Foreign Ministers did discuss Korea, and their discussions I think will not require that we discuss the situation, but I think it is important for them to have a dialogue on this issue.

Teng: As for the Korean issue, during the Doctor's previous visit we discussed that with him, and this time Foreign Minister Ch'iao has discussed it with him again. So I think that our position is very clear and both sides understand each other very well on this issue. We have noticed that there seems to be an idea that various parties, including ourselves, should participate in the discussion of this question. This is something that we cannot agree to. Because we no longer have any military forces in Korea. Only your side has. But we are in favor of your side having a dialogue with Korea. You also have your channels, for instance, in the United Nations; they have an observer there.

But we can say that we are not of the same impression that you seem to be under. We are not worried like you are about a military attack by the North against the South. But we hope that the American side will keep an eye on Park Chung Hee. Not now and neither in one or two years. The question is that you must keep an eye over him when he gets in a particularly difficult position.

The President: Mr. Vice Premier, we are encouraged when you say that the North has no intention and I can assure you that we will keep our eye on the South. We think it would be very ill-advised and very harmful for any military action in that area whatsoever. As a matter of fact, we would not tolerate it. [Teng spits into his spittoon.]

Teng: When Mr. Cyrus Vance led a delegation of world affairs organization people to China, we discussed this with him.

Kissinger: That is like the Dalai Lama. [Laughter] A government in exile. [Laughter]

Teng: They stressed that South Korea should be linked with Japan. They stressed the linkage that should be maintained between Japan and South Korea. Of course, if that is perceived from a purely geographical point of view, that might be of some sense. But if you are speaking from a political point of view, Japan and Korea are issues of two different natures. We are always reminding our friends that one must pay attention to the question of national feeling, national sentiment. And to be very frank, on this issue we find that your people, and including European friends, do not seem to have such acute and deep feeling about this issue as we have. Because we have passed through that period.

Take our situation, our state of affairs, pertaining to Taiwan. Some people are saying this is a two-China issue. And so we can feel very acutely the feelings that others have on other similar issues. And we feel that the question of the so-called two Koreas, two Vietnams, and two Germanies, are all issues of the same nature. And although the Soviet Union is now in control of East Germany, we believe that not only the West German people, but also the East German people have the same desire to reunify their country, and we feel certain that such an aspiration will eventually be realized.

There are a lot of people who have taken a lot of notice to our mention of 100 years. We think even if it takes 100 years, or even if it exceeds 100 years, this desire will finally be realized. Such a national urge cannot be resisted. Take for instance the question of the two Vietnams. One part of the nation has fought for reunification for 30 years. In Korea, the war did not go for so many years but shows a basic feeling there too.

President: With respect to the reunification of Germany, as I said the other day, we feel the reunification of Germany is inevitable. How soon I would not predict, but it would surprise me if it were 100 years, Mr. Vice Premier.

As for Korea, I think it might be helpful if the Secretary made an observation.

Kissinger: Only on the relationship between Japan and South Korea, Mr. Vice Premier. I think we both have an interest to prevent Japan from becoming militaristic. If there is turmoil in Korea and if South Korea is threatened, then there is a danger Japan will move in a more militaristic direction. On the other hand, we do not favor Japan having a more political and military role in Korea, and this is why we have attempted to move in the direction we have.

Teng: Japan's interest in South Korea is no lower than that of the United States.

Kissinger: It is greater.

Teng: There is some sense in those words. And there indeed exist forces in Japan that want to restore militarism. These are also forces that are most enthusiastic about South Korea and Taiwan.

Kissinger [to Ch'iao]: My student.

President: You mentioned Mr. Nakasone.

Teng: Your student is such a man.

Kissinger: I just said it to the Foreign Minister.

President: You mentioned earlier Mr. Cyrus Vance. He was a classmate of mine in Law School. I don't expect he will be back in government for some time. If ever.

It was mentioned to me several months ago when Mr. Paul Miller of AP came to see me following his visit to your country—and I understand he had talked with your people—about the possibility of setting up an AP bureau here. I would hope you would seriously consider that, Mr. Vice Premier. Mr. Vice Premier, they might be more constructive than the British correspondents.

Teng: But under the present state of affairs, it perhaps will be difficult for this to be. Perhaps it will be more appropriate for us to consider this after the elections, when there will have been a change in the situation.

President: I mention again, we are very grateful.

Teng: We still have some time left, though. Perhaps we can chat about Tibet. [Laughter] The features of Tibet today are completely different from what were before. In history, in Tibet, almost 40% of the population were lamas, that is, Buddhist priests, including very small children, who were also lamas. These lamas first of all could not till the land. Secondly, they did not reproduce the human race, because they were not allowed to marry. And they relied completely on the other 60% of the population, the serfs, to feed them. And their rule was very cruel. It was very cruel oppression of the people. They had very many varieties of torture.

They only produced a kind of barley, a different strain that perhaps you may not have found in any other place in the world. It is a kind of barley which has a very low yield. Now they are growing wheat. In the past it was thought impossible. But now they are having very high yields.

Kissinger: Are any Chinese settling there?

Ch'iao: You mean of the Han nationality?

Kissinger: Yes.

Teng: There are. After our army went in, some of them settled down there. And there are also people engaging in a lot of construction there. But the new generation of Tibetans has also produced a new generation of specialists, in new fields, and workers that they never had before because they did not have the industry. In the past they did not grow vegetables. Now they have successfully grown new varieties of vegetables in an area of such high altitude that was not thought possible before, and of such growth that the turnips they grow there are much larger than those grown in our area.

President: Do you have a Tachai project there? That was very impressive yesterday.

Teng: Yes. In Tibet, one of the characteristics of the agriculture in Tibet is that they have done a lot of work in water conservancy. Because that is an area in agriculture, and we found that though it is very high and lacking in air, it is closer to the sun and is therefore more bountiful, and it has more sunshine.

So, no matter what the Dalai Lama can boast about himself, he cannot affect the prospects of Tibet. They have begun to develop a bit of industry there too.

President: He should stay in India.

Teng: Yes, and we wish him a long life and a long stay there. [Laughter]

On the whole, our country is still very backward. But we pay attention to the policy towards the different nationalities, and no matter whether it is in the Tibetan area. The area where the Tibetans live is larger than Tibet itself. In Kueichow Province, and on the western borders, also in Sinkiang Province, there are many Tibetans. It is populated with Hans too. Where we have dozens of Khazaks and other peoples of minority nationalities, we have tried to provide a standard of living for people of minority nationalities that is slightly higher than the other ones.

Our country has a weakness in that it has too large a population. We have had to pay attention to birth control. And the increase in the population is lowering down a bit in some provinces. But in the minority nationality areas we have encouraged an increase in the population. Because in the places that they live in, they have large areas and few people.

President: In the three years since I was here in the first place, I have noticed on this trip tremendous progress. And I have seen a tremendous amount of new construction and new developments. [Teng spits into his spittoon.] So I think your initiatives have been quite successful. We of course compliment you and your people for the progress that has been made. It is very evident to someone who has been away for three years and comes back.

Teng: Still not very great. We still have a lot of work ahead of us. For instance, in agriculture we are only barely sufficient in food. And on the average we only have the per capita of output of food grain of only 335 kilograms. It can only be said that that is barely sufficient. We have only barely sufficient food and clothing.

So now the whole country is trying to learn from Tachai agriculture. This means that whole counties are trying to learn from the standards adopted in Sian county, where Tachai is. And if only one-third of the counties of the nation are able to do as well as they have done, that would make a great difference. And if, say, 200 million of our population would have been able to learn from Tachai and do as well as they do—on the average section they are doing 250 kilograms per person—then these 200 million people should be able to produce something around 50 million tons.

That is commercial grain that they now produce. That is excluding what they use for their own purposes. If they are able to increase a bit over that, that will be something around 60 or 70 million tons.

What we are concerned about in our country, first of all, is agriculture, because we have a population of 800 million and first of all they have to eat. And food and clothing and the things that we use mainly come from agriculture. So it seems that there is hope.

President: It is very obvious that you are doing far better than the Soviet Union in meeting the needs of your people for food as well as clothing, particularly food. That is a great achievement.

Teng: But there is still quite a lot to do. To achieve the standard, or just to get close to the standard of the West in various fields, will take years, at least 50 years. That is speaking of the overall situation. But if you cut it down to the income per capita, then it will take more than 50 years.

President: When I was here in 1972, in a meeting with the Foreign Minister, we talked bout the mechanization of agriculture in the United States, and he indicated that you were moving forward to further mechanize. And I noticed in the exhibition concerning agriculture there has been great progress in agricultural mechanization, irrigation and all of the modern methods of increasing the productivity of the soil. Overcoming the problems of floods on the one hand and drought on the other. A very impressive demonstration.

Teng: But mechanization alone will not be able to solve our problems. We also have to till the land scientifically and intensively. In this aspect we are different from your country, because in our country 7½ people share 1 hectare of cultivated land. You have wide and vast cultivated lands.

President: You should come and see our agricultural lands, Mr. Vice Premier.

Teng: Maybe I will have the chance in the future. It would be quite interesting.

But I do not think your methods in agriculture would be entirely applied to ours. In some typical places in the South, on one plot we would grow seven different crops.

President: Seven, one after the other? Or mixed?

Teng: Seven times in rotation. That is, before the first one is harvested, you sow in the second, between the rows.

President: We are trying to integrate, in some areas of the United States, fruit, and put in the rows between the trees another crop. And it is developing very successfully. We have been trying to diversify crops for the farmers so that he will not depend solely on fruit, and can have another crop that will bolster their income.

Teng: Your agriculture has been doing very well.

President: I can see the Vice Premier has a deep interest in and a deep knowledge of agriculture.

Teng: Once, during wartime, I was for a long time in the countryside, and therefore I have some feeling for the land. I am also familiar with it, to a certain extent.

President: Mr. Vice Premier, our Ambassador is leaving, as you know.[3] He is a very close colleague and close personal friend of mine, and has been for many years. When he comes back to the United States he will be very capable and effective and very helpful in explaining to the American people the relationship that we have and the importance of that relationship. I can assure you that his successor will be an equally capable and high-level individual and a person in whom I have the greatest personal confidence and trust as I have had with Ambassador Bush.

Teng: You have given him a post that is not considered to be very good. [Laughter]

Bush: You're talking like my wife, Mr. Vice Premier. [Laughter]

---

[3] Bush left Beijing on December 7.

Teng: But it won't matter so very much. If you deal with it correctly, it might not be of such great harm.

President: Mr. Vice Premier, it is a post of great importance in the United States, and I picked him because I know that he has great competence and great abilities. It will be a sacrifice for him because he has enjoyed very greatly his opportunity to be in your country. But for handling a very difficult job I wanted the best person that I could find.

Teng: So perhaps I was impolite in interfering in your internal affairs. [Laughter]

So do you think we can call it a day now? Thank you very much for coming.

President: And thank you for giving us the opportunity to be here.

[The meeting ended.]

Chinese Domestic Power Struggles, January 1976–January 1977

138. Editorial Note

On January 15, 1976, Brent Scowcroft, Assistant to the President for National Security Affairs, received an executive summary of a report entitled "US Policy Interests in the Asian-Pacific Area" by William R. Kintner, former Ambassador to Thailand. Kintner argued that the ideological bitterness of the Sino-Soviet conflict provided the United States with unique opportunities for creative diplomacy in the Asian-Pacific theater of the Cold War. He noted that this area was "lining up into two groups: pro-Soviet and pro-Chinese countries." At the same time, he warned, "The evolving American relationship with Peking is complicated by the basic outlook of Chinese foreign policy. Peking has pioneered a new conceptualization of today's international disorder. The Chinese strategy for achieving global ascendancy is based on mobilizing the Third World (most of the globe's population, resources and real estate) against both the capitalist-imperialist power, the U.S., and the social-revisionist power, the USSR. The Chinese identify themselves with the Third World, not as a superpower, and assert that the ultimate conflict is between 'rural' Asia, Africa and Latin America and 'urban' Europe and North America. The PRC is continuing to foster the 'hardest' revolutionary activity in many parts of the world."

Among Kintner's recommendations, he suggested "continuing liaison with the PRC and case-by-case cooperation." On the issue of Taiwan, he wrote, "Do not recognize the PRC and concurrently derecognize the ROC in a manner or time frame that could lead both our adversaries and our friends to further doubt our interest in and commitment to retaining active and cooperative security, political and economic relations with other Asian states." (Letter from Kintner to Scowcroft, with attached study, October 31, 1975; Ford Library, National Security Adviser, Presidential Country Files for East Asia and Pacific Affairs, Box 1, Ambassador Kintner's Study of U.S. Policy Interests in the Asian-Pacific Area)

Thomas J. Barnes of the National Security Council staff, who analyzed Kintner's study before passing the summary on to Scowcroft, wrote that it was the "first comprehensive review of our Asian posture" since the collapse in 1975 of U.S. efforts to preserve non-Communist regimes in Indochina. Yet he observed, "While many of its judgments are sound, it reflects much of the traditional hard-line Kintner approach about the Soviet Union, which features more prominently than actual Soviet presence and influence in Asia would dictate." (Memorandum from Barnes to Scowcroft, January 15, 1976; ibid.) Scowcroft initialed Barnes' memorandum.

139.   Memorandum of Conversation[1]

Washington, January 15, 1976.

SUBJECT

Ambassador Unger's Meeting with the Secretary

PARTICIPANTS

The Secretary
Ambassador Unger, Republic of China
Philip C. Habib, EA

Ambassador Unger asked the Secretary what guidance he had for him in the period ahead, now that the President's visit had taken place. The Secretary asked what the Ambassador thought would be the reaction in Taiwan to normalization carried out according to the Japanese model. The Ambassador said that as far as it went this might be satisfactory but it did not cover the security question. There ensued some discussion as to what kind of formula it might be possible to persuade Peking to issue unilaterally at the time of normalization and also what might be said on the U.S. side. Ambassador asked whether, assuming Peking continues to desire to maintain good relations with the United States, it would not be possible for us to make the satisfactory resolution of this problem a condition for our proceeding with normalization.

There followed some discussion of what might occur on Taiwan if normalization does not give the island reasonable assurance of a stable future. Ambassador Unger mentioned possible initiative by independentists for example to try to establish a Republic of Taiwan and he expressed concern about Peking's likely reaction to this. This led to some discussion of the possibilities of Peking taking military action against Taiwan and also of action short of military assault such as blockade. The Secretary several times referred to the reluctance if not the likely refusal of the U.S. Congress to intervene militarily to help Taiwan.

---

[1] Source: Department of State, Papers of William H. Gleysteen: Lot 89 D 436, Box 8132, PRC Related Papers 1976. Secret; Exdis. Drafted by Unger on January 16 and designated as a "rough draft." A copy was sent to Habib and notations indicate he and Gleysteen saw it. Unidentified handwritten notations read: "Gleysteen only" and "Lord should be aware of this & if your [illegible] Solomon." On January 12, Unger met with Scowcroft and informed him that the decision against rapid normalization of relations with the PRC had "defused consternation on Taiwan," and that Jiang Jingguo was a leader with whom the United States could successfully work. Unger also advised that the United States continue to withdraw troops from Taiwan in a measured manner. (Memorandum of conversation, January 12; Ford Library, National Security Adviser, Presidential Country Files for East Asian and Pacific Affairs, Box 5, People's Republic of China)

The Secretary then referred to the probable timing of normalization saying first that it might come sometime in 1977 but then adding that mid-1978 might be the first likely time. He anticipated that around a year from now the PRC may choose to make an important issue of Taiwan and would emphasize in any case that it regards Taiwan as an internal Chinese matter. In the year ahead the Secretary said that there is not much to do on this matter and it would be advisable to keep the issue quiet and to play it down. Ambassador Unger said that he took this to mean that he should in a continuing, steady fashion keep before the GROC that we continue to intend to carry through normalization of our relations with the PRC so that the conditioning process continues. This point however does not have to be vigorously played but can be handled in low key.

Ambassador Unger returned to the question of actual arrangements which will have to be made if normalization is to be carried out without serious destabilizing effects on Taiwan. In addition to the security question already discussed he mentioned a whole range of economic issues including most favored nation treatment, the continued supply of nuclear fuel etc. and Mr. Habib mentioned also the continued supply of military equipment. The Ambassador said that it not only would require our formulating our plans in the executive branch but certain matters might require consultation with the Congress and even some Congressional expression; he felt this would be important particularly with regard to the security question. He added that it may also be necessary in advance of any final decisions or announcements to have further consultations with Peking on some of these matters. The Secretary acknowledged these points and turned to Mr. Habib to inquire whether studies of these matters were underway and Mr. Habib confirmed that they were.

140.   Briefing Memorandum From the Assistant Secretary of State
for East Asian and Pacific Affairs (Habib) to Secretary of
State Kissinger[1]

Washington, January 16, 1976.

Implications of Chou En-lai's Death[2]

As I depart for Hawaii, I would leave you with EA's thoughts on
the policy implications of Chou En-lai's death. I understand that INR
is working on a more detailed analysis.

The broad consensus is that the succession to Chou has been carefully prepared, that Teng Hsiao-p'ing is the odds-on favorite to move
up to the premiership, and that PRC leaders will make determined efforts to project an image of continuity and stability in the wake of
Chou's death. We agree this is the most likely outlook for the immediate future.

If the scenario in fact develops in this fashion, we have little reason to reassess our current expectations and policy assumptions at this
time, particularly regarding PRC relations with the U.S. and the USSR.

But you should at least have in mind some of the imponderables
that could alter this perspective.

—Chou's death is qualitatively different in its impact on the Chinese political process from the passing of other party elders before him.
Even though the decision was probably made some time ago for Teng
to succeed Chou as premier, and the Chinese body politic has been con-
ditioned for this eventuality, the steps necessary to formalize this
process—e.g. the holding of a party plenum and the convening of a
National People's Congress—entail risks and uncertainties for Teng,
with Chou no longer around to work out the necessary compromises
with his unique prestige and skills.

—If Teng becomes premier, he probably will not remain as PLA
Chief of Staff. Chou is also the second Vice Chairman of the party and
the third member of the powerful Standing Committee of the Politburo
to die in less than a year. An effort to strike a new balance in the party
and the army at the same time that Teng is raised to the premiership
will be tricky. One question is what roles are given to Chang Chun-
ch'iao. Another major question is whether Wang Hung-wen (a most

---

[1] Source: Department of State, American Embassy (Beijing) Files: Lot 80 F 64, POL
2, General Reports and Statistics, Internal, Jan–Feb 1976. Confidential. Drafted by J.
Stapleton Roy and Oscar V. Armstrong (EA/PRCM).

[2] Zhou died on January 8.

unlikely successor to Mao) will remain as the titular number two to Mao in the party. All of these moves must be made in the context of the succession to Mao.

—Teng, with the evident backing of Mao and Chou, has been moving cautiously but steadily to tidy up the political mess left by the Cultural Revolution, to restore the party and government apparatus to a position of leadership, and to reduce the political role of the military. But this process is still incomplete. The recurrent domestic campaigns suggest that there remain many troublesome loose ends—that impasses and modi vivendi rather than solutions have been reached in many areas—even though the overall trend has clearly been in the direction of a return to rationality and viable development policies.

—Teng differs from Chou in temperament and style but he probably views China's external environment in much the same way Chou did. Events of the last few years demonstrate, however, that the Chou line has encountered recurrent difficulties in its implementation. Without Chou's authority, prestige, and special talents, Teng may find the going even tougher.

—To oversimplify, in the Mao–Chou team, Mao was the visionary with occasional manic tendencies while Chou was the pragmatist. While a pragmatist like Chou, Teng probably lacks Chou's ability to say "Yes, but . . ." to Mao or to implement Mao's ideas in the least disruptive way.

Even assuming that the succession to Chou proceeds smoothly, his death highlights the Mao succession problem, and at present there is no indication that the Chinese have sorted out this process, which is far more delicate and potentially disruptive.

141. Letter From President Ford to Republic of China Premier Jiang Jingguo[1]

Washington January 24, 1976.

Dear Mr. Premier:

Thank you for your letter of October 14.[2] I am always glad to have your views, and welcome the frankness with which you stated them.

In recognition of your concern over our China policy, I asked Assistant Secretary Habib to proceed to Taiwan from Peking to brief you on my recent visit to the People's Republic of China. I understand from Mr. Habib that his meeting with you was not only useful and constructive, but also reflected the trust and friendship which has characterized our relationship for these many years.[3]

As Mr. Habib made clear in the course of his presentation, in our search for better relations with Peking over the past several years, we have shown a prudent regard for the vital interests of your people. You may be assured that as we pursue our goal of normalizing relations with the People's Republic of China, we will continue to act in this same manner.

---

[1] Source: Ford Library, National Security Adviser, Presidential Correspondence with Foreign Leaders, 1974–77, Box 1, China, Republic of. No classification marking. The Department of State prepared and submitted to the NSC a draft of this letter. (Memorandum from Jay Taylor to Paul Theis, December 30, 1975; ibid.) The Department sent this letter by telegram to the Embassy in Taipei for delivery to the ROC Government, and pouched the signed copy. (Telegram 19617 to Taipei, January 27; ibid.)

[2] Jiang's attached letter of October 14, 1975, written in anticipation of Kissinger's October 19–23, 1975, visit to Beijing, warned, "If 'normalization' implies eventual diplomatic recognition, it will virtually mean negation of the existence of the Republic of China." Jiang also avowed that total diplomatic isolation of his country "would entail consequences surpassing in magnitude and gravity the debacle of Indochina."

[3] During their meeting on December 9, 1975, Habib briefed Jiang on Ford's talks in Beijing, and discussed the overall state of U.S.–ROC relations. (Telegram 7854 from Taipei, December 10; Ford Library, National Security Adviser, Presidential Country Files for East Asian and Pacific Affairs, Box 5, Republic of China, State Department Telegrams) On December 26, in a memorandum to Scowcroft recommending rejection of Ambassador Shen's request for an appointment with the President to discuss the PRC visit, Springsteen noted, "As part of the conditioning process toward the ROC and to avoid arousing the PRC, for the past two years we have restricted Shen's access to high level U.S. officials." (Ibid.)

I believe our shared recognition of the importance of a prudent and understanding approach to the issues before us represents the best means to ensure the prosperity and well-being of your people and the continuation of the close and valued ties of friendship and cooperation between us.

Sincerely,

Gerald R. Ford

---

142.   Minutes of a Senior Review Group Meeting[1]

Washington, February 27, 1976, 3:03–3:40 p.m.

SUBJECT

    U.S. Troops Withdrawal from Taiwan

PARTICIPANTS

    Chairman:
    Brent Scowcroft

    State: *CIA:*
    Robert Ingersoll   George Bush
    Robert Miller   James Lilley
    William Gleysteen   Theodore Shackley

    DOD: *NSC Staff:*
    William Clements   William G. Hyland
    Amos Jordan   Thomas Barnes
    Morton Abramowitz   Richard Solomon
                                      Col. Clint Granger
    JCS: Michael Hornblow
    Gen. George S. Brown
    Lt. Gen. William Smith

General Scowcroft: We are meeting to pick up the threads on the issue of troop reductions from Taiwan. The President wants a 50%

---

[1] Source: Ford Library, NSC Institutional Files (H-Files), Box H–67, NSDM 339. Top Secret. The meeting was held in the White House Situation Room. The minutes are labeled "Part I of II," and do not include the second part of the meeting, which began at 3:40 and addressed the topic of the U.S. equipment captured in Indochina. On February 4, Scowcroft approved a memorandum from several NSC staff members that recommended the convening of an SRG meeting to discuss U.S. troop reductions on Taiwan. (Memorandum from Barnes, Solomon, and Granger to Scowcroft, February 4; National Archives, Nixon Presidential Materials, NSC Files, NSC Institutional Files (H-Files), Box H–245, NSDM 248)

reduction over the course of the year for a year-end total of 1,400. Now how many people do we have there?

Gen. Brown: 2,277.

Mr. Gleysteen: 2,700 including civilians.

Mr. Jordan: Is that 50% figure based upon the 2700 total?

General Scowcroft: I am talking about a basic 50% reduction. We should make reasonable drawdowns and see where we come out. There have been two studies on this. Defense did a study a year ago [*less than 1 line not declassified*].[2] Bill, do you have an update for us?

Mr. Clements: A new paper was prepared this morning.

Mr. Abramowitz: We have provided the NSC staff with a summary of our suggested cuts.[3]

Mr. Clements: Our study excludes civilians. It is based upon a total of 2,200 military personnel and does not include intelligence personnel. The figure of 2,229 was used. We studied the alternatives of where the cuts should be to get to 50% and the implications of alternate locations. There are several alternatives. We chose alternative two with one small deletion. We would transfer the communications mission to Okinawa and Clark and continue in a minimum posture for the time being.

General Scowcroft: [*1 line not declassified*]

Mr. Clements: Yes. Before this meeting we were just talking about the recommendation about the F–4 depot maintenance and I am having second thoughts. We can have a savings of $10 million a year by leaving it there. We may come back to that one. Let's leave those 27 people alone unless there are some political reasons for pulling them out.

General Scowcroft: Those 27 are military personnel. Can't we civilianize them?

Mr. Clements: Yes we could.

Mr. Ingersoll: That's a small number.

General Scowcroft: Do we want to keep that?

---

[2] The Department of Defense study provided alternative plans to accomplish reductions of U.S. force levels on Taiwan. (Memorandum from Deputy Secretary of Defense William P. Clements to Scowcroft, November 20, 1974; Ford Library, NSC Institutional Files (H-Files), Box H–16, SRG Meeting, 2/27/76, Taiwan) This study was based on a memorandum from the Joint Chiefs of Staff to Secretary of Defense Schlesinger. (Memorandum from Vice Admiral Harry Train to Schlesinger, November 9, 1974, JCSM–442–74; Washington National Records Center, OASD/ISA Files: FRC 330–77–0063, Box 3, China, Rep. of, 1974, 0001–320.2) [*text not declassified*]; see footnote 13, Document 112.

[3] The summary of "50 percent reduction alternatives" is in the Ford Library, NSC Institutional Files (H-Files), Box H–67, NSDM 339. The JCS also provided a position paper for this meeting. (Memorandum from Train to Schlesinger, February 26, 1976, JCSM–62–76; Washington National Records Center, OASD/ISA Files: FRC 330–79–0049, Box 67, China [Nats], 320.2, 1976)

Mr. Clements: Yes, it is highly efficient. We could civilianize it if we wanted to.

General Scowcroft: Well we don't have to face that now.

Mr. Clements: We are continuing our planning to reduce our man-power down to 1105 and can plan on meeting with the Japanese and Filipinos about the transfer [*less than 1 line not declassified*]. There is no problem.

Mr. Abramowitz: There may be a problem with the Philippines. It may complicate our negotiations over the bases.

Mr. Ingersoll: I suggest that a study be made of the present needs before moving. [*2 lines not declassified*]

Mr. Bush: [*7 lines not declassified*]

Gen. Scowcroft: After normalization we would still need to retain a sophisticated [*less than 1 line not declassified*] capability.

Mr. Bush: [*1 line not declassified*]

Mr. Clements: We are in basic agreement with George.

General Scowcroft: Is the equipment moveable?

Mr. Lilley: Yes. We could move it out. The 80 people would be under civilian control. [*less than 1 line not declassified*]

Mr. Bush: [*1 line not declassified*]

Mr. Clements: 80 people?

Mr. Bush: [*less than 1 line not declassified*]

Mr. Clements: The only glitch between you and Lou is that he talks in terms of 125 people. That would mean a reduction of 350 people.

Mr. Ingersoll: This would increase our reliance on the ROC.

Mr. Shackley: [*1 line not declassified*]

Mr. Gleysteen: Would there be 3rd country involvement?

Mr. Shackley: [*less than 1 line not declassified*]

General Scowcroft: It would take two years?

Mr. Lilley: It would be finished between October 1976 and January 1977.

Mr. Abramowitz: If after normalization we could not keep the facility, [*less than 1 line not declassified*].

Mr. Jordan: We would have to look at the Philippines and Okinawa.

Mr. Bush: [*less than 1 line not declassified*]

Mr. Gleysteen: There have already been cuts [*less than 1 line not declassified*].

Mr. Shackley: [*less than 1 line not declassified*]

General Scowcroft: There would be a two year wait [*less than 1 line not declassified*].

Mr. Lilley: 18 months.

Mr. Clements: It would take 18 months after you got started.

Mr. Shackley: It is back to the drawing board.

Mr. Solomon: You should look at the present level of [*less than 1 line not declassified*] and see if it is all necessary, and then study the question of alternate sites.

Mr. Shackley: [*1 line not declassified*] We could not do it from anywhere else.

Mr. Lilley: There are other unique areas of [*less than 1 line not declassified*]. Moving would cause some degradation.

Mr. Clements: What is our objective, Brent?

General Scowcroft: Our objective is to have a 50% reduction of the total.

Mr. Clements: [*1 line not declassified*]

Mr. Shackley: We are looking at different time frames.

Mr. Bush: There are different assumptions on drawdowns by the end of the year.

Mr. Jordan: We can get down to 1000–1100 spaces but it might take a bit longer.

Mr. Solomon: I would like to ask what are the objections to resiting in terms of maintaining a stable base [*1 line not declassified*].

Mr. Lilley: [*2 lines not declassified*]

Mr. Shackley: [*1½ lines not declassified*]

General Scowcroft: [*1½ lines not declassified*]

Mr. Gleysteen: There is no great problem but it may not be a timely thing to do. We may have to balance things off. The original concept was to have a 50% reduction [*less than 1 line not declassified*]. With regard to [*less than 1 line not declassified*] you have to decide whether it would really be worth spending a great deal of money. You can hedge this by some resiting and some reduction of requirements. We should look at the stages leading up to a fallback position on the [*less than 1 line not declassified*] facility. Then the other factor is that it may not be possible to keep a [*less than 1 line not declassified*] facility on Taiwan after the normalization of relations with the PRC.

Mr. Ingersoll: Could the [*less than 1 line not declassified*] facility be used in other locations?

Mr. Lilley: [*1½ lines not declassified*]

General Scowcroft: [*1½ lines not declassified*]

Mr. Bush: [*1½ lines not declassified*]

Mr. Abramowitz: Part of the answer depends on us and under what the conditions would be for the normalization of relations with the PRC.

Mr. Shackley: [*1½ lines not declassified*]

Mr. Gleysteen: I agree. I don't think there would be any problem from the ROC side.

Mr. Lilley: But what if normalization does not take place. There might be problems in the Taiwan Straits and there is a discrepancy between PRC and ROC power. [1½ lines not declassified]

General Brown: We are proceeding backwards. We are considering a series of administrative steps which will box us into policy positions instead of the reverse. We should talk about the total. What does the US want to do on Taiwan?

General Scowcroft: We want to get our troops out. That basically is what we are working on.

General Brown: Yes but what functions do the troops perform. Are we trying to have our cake and eat it too?

General Scowcroft: That is not necessarily true. Some of the functions can go on. Maybe we will [less than 1 line not declassified]. All that we are talking about now is getting all our troops out.

General Smith: All the troops? That is the first time I have heard that.

General Scowcroft: Eventually we will have to.

Mr. Gleysteen: As we carry out these steps now we should be realistic about our assessments. It is doubtful that we could retain a facility of this kind.

Mr. Bush: [2½ lines not declassified]

Mr. Gleysteen: That is a real possibility.

Mr. Bush: [2 lines not declassified]

Mr. Jordan: If it becomes an ROC installation you would need a few hundred civilians. [less than 1 line not declassified] 200 civilians would be needed but these could be drawn down to 125. You could continue pulling down the number of American personnel and turn it over to the ROC.

Mr. Gleysteen: We must have some [less than 1 line not declassified] facility if we turn that over to the ROC.

Mr. Abramowitz: [4 lines not declassified]

General Scowcroft: You would then end up with a gap. How long would it take to fill it.

Mr. Lilley: Well, will we be able to keep [4½ lines not declassified].

Mr. Bush: [2 lines not declassified]

Mr. Clements: I agree and that would give time for the Filipinos, Thais and Okinawans to settle down. We could then look at the situation. If we made a precipitous decision today it might be the wrong one.

Mr. Ingersoll: The $22 million is a budgetary consideration.

Mr. Bush: [1 line not declassified]

General Scowcroft: [*less than 1 line not declassified*] Look at the figures for next year—the FY 1977 budget—and see what you can do.

Mr. Bush: [*1½ lines not declassified*]

General Scowcroft: (To Clements) You are looking into the relocation of the Communications Command and the other things?

Mr. Clements: Yes. I personally am optimistic about the Philippines.

General Brown: It is hard to say now. It depends on how the negotiations go.

Mr. Miller: [*1 line not declassified*]

Mr. Clements: I think Marcos will be more cooperative than a lot of other people.

Mr. Miller: It is hard to tell. After a few months we will be in a better position to judge.

Mr. Bush: (To Scowcroft) We will look the stuff over and get something to you in a week or so. If the figures look alright we could then get back together.

Mr. Clements: In the meantime we (DOD) can proceed with what we are trying to do.

General Brown: We can do civilianizing. We want the uniforms out. Those 27 men in the depot can be civilianized.

General Scowcroft: But I don't want a one-for-one substitution.

Mr. Clements: A net reduction of 1100 people is what we are talking about.

---

143.   Memorandum From the President's Assistant for National Security Affairs (Scowcroft) to President Ford[1]

Washington, March 12, 1976.

SUBJECT

Peking's Current Political Instability and Its Import for U.S.–PRC Relations

In view of recent surprising developments in the Peking political scene—the unexpected announcement that a relatively unknown

---

[1] Source: Ford Library, National Security Adviser, Presidential Country Files for East Asian and Pacific Affairs, Box 13, People's Republic of China. Secret. Sent for information. The correspondence profile indicates that Ford noted this memorandum on March 16. (Ibid.)

leader, Hua Kuo-feng (rather than Vice Premier Teng Hsiao-p'ing), has been appointed as acting Premier; the release in December of a long-detained Soviet helicopter crew; and the February visit to China of former President Nixon—I have had a member of the staff prepare for you an interpretive analysis.[2]

The study at Tab A[3] places the political turmoil now apparent in China in the context of tensions within the leadership of the People's Republic of China which have been evident in a general way since 1970. It also suggests some implications of these recent developments for the course of U.S.–PRC relations in the year ahead.

The study reaches the following major conclusions:

—*Teng Hsiao-p'ing*, groomed for the Premiership since 1973 by Mao and Chou but under continuing criticism from Party radicals, was blocked in gaining the Premiership in January because he had *alienated key military leaders who have become temporary allies of the Party's radical faction*.

—*The outcome of the current conflict in Peking is indeterminate*, but the most likely developments are either, (a) once the radicals have brought about Teng Hsiao-p'ing's demise they will draw back and work within the coalition leadership which Chou-En-lai built up over the past several years, or (b) the radicals will overplay their attack on Teng and other rehabilitated leaders, alienate their temporary allies, and produce a counterattack that will lead to their own fall. It seems doubtful that the Party's leftist faction can dominate the Peking political scene for a sustained period.

—*Mao Tse-tung's role in the current leadership dispute is ambiguous*, probably because the Chairman is not in full control of the situation. He has been aloof from various radical leaders in recent years, and thus far has not given overt support for their attack on Teng. He probably withdrew his backing from the Vice Premier when he was unable to command sufficient support from the Politburo for the Premiership, and he appears to have given at least tentative support to Hua Kuo-feng.

Mao, however, has his differences with the leftist faction and the military and may be playing a rather passive role in the current conflict. At this point we are unable to tell how much the Chairman is being used by the anti-Teng forces as opposed to siding with them. Mao's physical frailty, difficulty in speaking, and personal isolation (heightened by the death of his long-time associate Chou En-lai) increasingly

---

[2] Solomon sent the study to Scowcroft on March 8 with a covering memorandum for Scowcroft to sign and forward to the President. (Memorandum from Solomon to Scowcroft, March 8; ibid.)

[3] Attached but not printed.

weaken him as an active leadership force. His death in the next year or two could compound the present instability in the leadership.

—The release of the Soviet helicopter crew last December, and the recent visit to China of former President Nixon, are indicators of *political cross-currents on foreign policy issues.* The military and some others in Peking may be urging a less hostile orientation toward the Soviets and greater aloofness from the U.S. Mao, however, remains determined to keep the Russians at a distance and strengthen relations with a U.S. that will actively counterweight the Soviets abroad.

—There is very little the U.S. can do to influence the PRC as the current leadership feud plays itself out. We are passive observers of that situation, as were the Chinese as they watched the unfolding of Watergate. *We are most likely to hold the Chinese to their foreign policy course of dealing with us if we can reassert a more active foreign policy* that combines efforts to reach agreements that serve our interests with both Moscow and Peking, and at the same time demonstrate a willingness to stand up to Soviet pressures. *Completion of normalization of U.S.–PRC relations might make the relationship less vulnerable to criticism in China,* but such a move would invite contempt rather than respect if taken from a position of weakness in foreign affairs, and with an attitude of beseeching China to hold to its "American tilt."

---

144.   Memorandum of Conversation[1]

Washington, March 19, 1976, 10:10–10:25 a.m.

PARTICIPANTS

President Ford
Thomas S. Gates, Chief-Designate of U.S. Liaison Office in Peking
Dr. Henry A. Kissinger, Secretary of State
Brent Scowcroft, Assistant to the President for National Security Affairs

[A press session takes place first for the public announcement. Then the press leaves.]

The President: The Ambassador issue is complicated. I can only grant it for six months.

---

[1] Source: Ford Library, National Security Adviser, Kissinger–Scowcroft West Wing Office Files, 1969–1977, Box 6, China, unnumbered items (28), 3/9/76–4/27/76. Secret; Nodis. Ford's talking points for this meeting are ibid. All brackets are in the original.

Gates: That would be fine. I gather it was in part because you plan some movement and want to signal the Chinese.

Kissinger: They will interpret it that way.

Scowcroft: It will be a sign of the importance we ascribe to them.

The President: We do have to begin some movement, perhaps in 1977. But we do have to bite the bullet sometime after the election.

Kissinger: They are cold, pragmatic bastards. The President is right—we will have to move after the election. I would like to give Tom a letter either to Mao or Hua. Then we could have a verbatim report of what they say, to see if there are nuances of change. Nixon didn't record enough detail to be helpful.[2]

Gates: Hua may not have the confidence to make a policy statement.

Kissinger: Even if he reads it, it would be good. And I will give a lunch for you and invite the Chinese and put myself squarely behind you. I could also have Bush and Bruce there.

---

[2] Nixon had recently visited China. Telegram 325 from Beijing, February 26, transmitted a report on his trip. (National Archives, RG 59, Central Foreign Policy Files)

---

145. Letter From President Ford to Chinese Premier Hua Guofeng[1]

Washington, April 27, 1976.

Dear Mr. Premier:

I am pleased to introduce to you by way of this letter Ambassador Thomas S. Gates, Jr. the new Chief of our Liaison Office in the People's Republic. I have the highest confidence in Ambassador Gates, who has been a personal friend and political associate of mine since the period of the Second World War. I know he will effectively represent the views of my Administration, as did Ambassador David Bruce and Ambassador George Bush before him.

---

[1] Source: Ford Library, National Security Adviser, Presidential Correspondence with Foreign Leaders, 1974–77, Box 4, People's Republic of China, Premier Hua Kuofeng. No classification marking. Solomon drafted this letter and sent it on April 20 to Scowcroft. Scowcroft forwarded it to the President on April 26. (Ibid.) Hua received the letter on June 10, during his first meeting with Ambassador Gates. (Telegram 1054 from Beijing, June 11; ibid., Presidential Country Files for East Asian and Pacific Affairs, Box 15, People's Republic of China, State Department Telegrams)

Mr. Gates has rich personal experience in matters that are of concern to both our countries. As a former Secretary of the Navy and Secretary of Defense, he clearly understands the global security concerns we face. Moreover, he has long been an advocate of a policy of security through a strong American defense capability.

As I remarked during Ambassador Gates' swearing-in ceremony, while China and the United States have differences which neither side attempts to hide, we believe our common interests in resisting hegemony, and in enabling all peoples to follow their own unique paths of national development, provide a strong foundation for a durable and growing relationship. We must maintain an authoritative dialogue between our two leaderships in this turbulent and complex world, and grasp occasions for parallel or cooperative actions which will support our common objectives.

At the same time, we understand that the opportunities for such action will be enhanced as we are able to consolidate our bilateral relationship. I have indicated on a number of occasions since returning from your country last December that I remain determined to complete the normalization of our relations through joint efforts based on the Shanghai Communiqué. This not only will serve the interests of our two peoples, but also will contribute to building a more secure world order.

I hope you will share with Ambassador Gates your perspectives on both international developments and our bilateral relationship. He is prepared to sustain our side of this authoritative dialogue. At the same time, we welcome the return to Washington of Ambassador Huang Chen.

In closing, let me again offer you my good wishes in your new post. I hope you will also convey my personal regards to Chairman Mao.

Sincerely,

Gerald R. Ford

146.   Memorandum of Conversation[1]

Washington, May 29, 1976, 10:05–10:55 a.m.

SUBJECT

U.S.-PRC Relations, Policy towards the Soviet Union, Africa, NATO, Turkey–Greece Relations

PARTICIPANTS

People's Republic of China
Huang Chen, Chief, PRC Liaison Office
Tsien Ta-yung, Counselor, PRC Liaison Office
Shen Jo-yun, First Secretary, PRC Liaison Office

United States
The Secretary
Philip C. Habib, Assistant Secretary, EA
Oscar V. Armstrong, Director, EA/PRCM (Notetaker)

(The meeting, held at the Secretary's request, started at 10:05 a.m. and ended at 10:55 a.m. Miss Shen interpreted.)

The Secretary: I'm very glad to see you again.

Huang Chen: I'm also glad to meet with you again.

The Secretary: I've missed you.

Huang Chen: I also missed you.

The Secretary: We appreciate the friendly reception given to Ambassador Gates in Peking. I think you'll find him an excellent man. He's a good friend of mine and of the President.

Huang: I understand.

The Secretary: I haven't seen you for some time, and wanted to have this opportunity to review the world situation.

I spoke to former President Nixon after his return, and found his remarks very interesting. As you know, I always worked very closely with him and have great respect for him.

Huang: Did you read his report?

The Secretary: Yes, and I had several conversations with him. In China you always read our press, and you probably noticed that when the press was carrying various stories about Mr. Nixon's visit, I always said I would read his report. I believe he's the only senior American to have met your Premier; I don't think the recent Congressional delegation met him.

---

[1] Source: Ford Library, National Security Adviser, Kissinger–Scowcroft West Wing Office Files, 1969–1977, Box 6, China, unnumbered items (30), 5/24/76–6/25/76. Secret. Drafted by Armstrong on June 1 and approved in S on June 8. The meeting was held in Secretary Kissinger's office.

(Miss Shen initially translated this incorrectly, i.e. that the Congressional delegation had met with the Premier. There was a brief back-and-forth to clarify the matter.)

Huang: Vice Premier Chang Ch'un-ch'iao met with the Congressional delegation.

The Secretary: I speak with Mr. Nixon about every two weeks, so we are in close contact.

I have followed with great interest the various statements about the main line of your foreign policy. I remember, of course, that Chairman Mao said that foreign policy is determined by the basic interests of each country.

Huang: During President Ford's visit, as well as yours, Chairman Mao made a clear presentation on our position on international and strategic issues, as well as on relations between our two countries.

The Secretary: On our side, we will pursue the policy discussed with Chairman Mao.

You will have noticed that during the Presidential campaign some candidates try to take advantage of our China policy and to raise embarrassing issues. But we are sticking to the Shanghai Communiqué and all the discussions we have had with your government. And I think that even if the Democrats win, they will follow the same policy. That's my strong impression. Only one man wouldn't follow that policy, and he won't be elected. (Huang laughed.)[2]

Huang: So far as the Chinese side is concerned, we will always carry out the line and the policy formulated by Chairman Mao, not only for foreign policy but also domestic policy.

The Secretary: I understand. As far as we are concerned, we deal with Chinese foreign policy, not domestic policy.

I hope you will understand—you are a careful student of the American scene—that during this election period we phrase our statements very carefully; we don't want any upheavals here.

Huang: We understand this. Frankly speaking, we have heard that some Senators and Congressmen have made anti-Chinese statements. We attach no importance to them. We also heard that a Senator said that you had told him that the U.S. would not normalize relations after the elections.

---

[2] Kissinger is referring to Ronald Reagan's criticism of Ford's China policy. During a telephone conversation with Habib one day earlier, Kissinger expressed concern about public reports indicating that the United States would recognize Communist China after the election, and had warned against publicly discussing improvements in U.S.–PRC relations, which might "give Reagan ammunition to flog the President with." (Transcript of telephone conversation with Habib, May 28, 8:12 a.m.; Department of State, Electronic Reading Room, Kissinger Telephone Transcripts)

The Secretary: That report is not correct. I said that we have made no concrete agreement; you know why I said that. We discussed this question in Peking on many occasions; the President has discussed it, and I have discussed it, with your leaders. We will continue on the course we started.

Huang: I am very clear about this point, and about the discussions with Chairman Mao.

The Secretary: Some of the stories come from Taiwan. The stories will probably stop when the nomination process is completed, because the Democrats will not make it an issue. So for about two months we'll have a lot of noise. But you're used to that; you've heard a lot of noise before.

Huang: Yes.

The Secretary: I remember when Watergate started . . . People in America sometimes say that China is incomprehensible, but I sometimes think we are incomprehensible to the Chinese.

On other parts of the world, Mr. Ambassador . . . Incidentally, when I was in England I spoke to former Prime Minister Heath; he has warm memories of his visit to China last year.

Huang: You have been very busy. You were in England, before that there was the NATO meeting, and in London there was also CENTO.

The Secretary: We are going to organize, in the context of our discussions with Chairman Mao, barriers to Soviet expansionism. First of all, in Africa, we are not going to permit another Angola to develop. You must have noticed my repeated statements that if there is another Soviet-supported military adventure, we will do something. We are attempting to organize various of these countries to increase their capabilities. The Secretary of Defense will go to Zaire in July to discuss military assistance to that country. We are working closely with Zambia and other countries. I know that you are also quite active in Africa, and you will have noticed that we have raised no obstacles to your activities.

Huang: Frankly speaking, we think the United States should learn a lesson from Angola.

The Secretary: What lesson?

Huang: Well, the fact that the military situation in Angola developed to the point it did is inseparable from U.S. policy towards the Soviets. U.S. policy abetted the Soviet efforts.

The Secretary: We discussed our Angola policy in Peking. Congress stopped us from doing what was necessary. We would have defeated the Soviets in Angola if Congress had not stopped our assistance.

Huang: (Deliberately changing the subject) It is said that the ministerial meeting of NATO went well.

The Secretary: It was the best meeting in many years. It took decisions on the strengthening of defense and on close cooperation and coordination of policies against the Soviet Union on a worldwide basis. In this connection, I can tell you, so you can tell your government—it won't become public for about a week—that President Ford has invited the leaders of England, France, Germany, Italy and Japan to a meeting in Puerto Rico to develop a common strategy. The meeting will probably be June 27–28.

Huang: From reading press stories, I learned that the ministers attending the NATO meeting expressed concern about Soviet expansion, and that they stressed the need to resist Soviet military and political pressures. I also noticed that the European Governments and the European public are seeing that the Soviet threat is getting more serious. All this shows that the ministers' understanding of the situation is clearer.

The Secretary: At NATO, and also at CENTO, I said that we cannot accept the principle of coexistence in one part of the world and permit aggression in another part. That is our policy.

Huang: The Soviet Union will not change its policy of dividing and weakening Europe, with military strength as its backing and détente as the smokescreen.

The Secretary: That is one reason we are opposed to the inclusion of European Communist parties in government. That is bound to weaken the defense of Europe.

Huang: It seems that the West is getting very nervous about this possibility. But there are contradictions between the European Communists and the Soviets.

The Secretary: Maybe, to some extent. Perhaps the Italians, but not the French. But in any event, we favor the strength and unity of Western Europe, and will not let the Soviets succeed in their policy of dividing and weakening Europe.

Huang: That's very important.

The Secretary: At the same time, we shouldn't overestimate Soviet strength. It is strong in some categories, but it is not as strong as some newspaper stories suggest.

Huang: This point was also touched on in the conversations between the President and the Secretary and our leaders. The Soviets have wild ambitions but their capacity is not adequate to living up to those ambitions. On the other hand, it is important to keep up the guard. At a minimum, the Soviets will continue their policy of dividing and weakening. It is very important to strengthen unity and defense.

The Secretary: Defense should be strengthened, but we should not have an attitude of being afraid of the Soviets. They cannot feed their people. In Europe, I found many, including in Sweden, who feel that the Soviet army is overrated. They have many men, but their army is not as strong as the numbers suggest. But we do have to strengthen defenses; all the NATO countries—almost all—are doing it.

Huang: How are relations between Turkey and Greece? They are in the Southern flank.

The Secretary: What success the Soviets have had has not been due to mistakes by the West.

The Turkey–Greece situation is complicated by the domestic situation in the two countries, and also, frankly, by the domestic situation here, because of the Greek lobby. I've talked to the Foreign Ministers of both Turkey and Greece. It is a weird situation. In the Middle East, the problem is objectively difficult. But Turkey and Greece have practically agreed on a solution. However, because of Makarios in Cyprus and their domestic situations, they have not been able to carry out what has been practically agreed upon. When the two Foreign Ministers met in Oslo, they spent most of the time not on substance but on procedures for putting forward a solution so they would not be attacked at home. I think that during this year they will move to a solution.

Will your Foreign Minister be coming to the General Assembly, or is it too early to know?

Huang: I don't know yet—I think he will come.

The Secretary: I will be delighted to see him and review matters with him. But we'll have opportunities before then to discuss matters.

Huang: It is always good to exchange views.

The Secretary: Always.

Huang: We are also good friends.

The Secretary: True. I have known you many years and consider you a good friend.

Huang: I understand you will visit Latin America next week.

The Secretary: Yes, for an OAS meeting. Then at the end of the month I will go back to Europe for an OECD ministerial meeting. While in Europe, I will try to do something to bring majority rule to Rhodesia, by meeting with black African leaders and maybe South African leaders.

Huang: You are always very busy, always keep moving.

The Secretary: It is better to dominate events rather than to let events run away. It also keeps me out of the political campaign.

Huang: Every time I come, I always like to exchange views. Are there any other points you wish to bring up?

The Secretary: Whenever you wish to discuss matters, you will always be welcome. When I come back from my next trip, I will ask you if you wish to exchange views again.

Huang: I am always pleased to exchange views.

The Secretary: If anything comes up in our political campaign that raises some question, you should not draw conclusions without consulting us. We have conducted our policy for five years with great care, and will not let it fail because of two months of political campaigns.

Huang: I understand.

(Miss Shen wanted to clarify the term "OECD" and there was a brief discussion of its membership.)

The Secretary: Mr. Habib is getting promoted.

Huang: I know—congratulations. I understand Mr. Hummel is coming back.[3]

The Secretary: Yes, as Assistant Secretary.

Huang: He is also Chinese.

The Secretary: Yes. I think he was born in China.

(There followed a brief discussion of Ambassador Hummel's China background.)

---

[3] Arthur Hummel was then serving as Ambassador to Ethiopia.

---

147. Editorial Note

On June 1, 1976, Thomas Barnes, Richard Solomon, and Clinton Granger of the National Security Council staff wrote a memorandum to Secretary of State Henry Kissinger recalling that the previous August they had recommended an interagency review of U.S. interests and security objectives in Southeast Asia in anticipation of the forthcoming Philippine base negotiations. At that time, Kissinger had recommended the expansion of the review to cover the entire Asia–Pacific region. (Memorandum from Barnes, Solomon, and Granger to Scowcroft, June 1; Ford Library, NSC Institutional Files (H-Files), Box H–17, SRG Meeting, 6/4/76, U.S. Interests and Objectives in the Asia–Pacific Area, NSSM 235) Accordingly, National Security Study Memorandum 235, issued on January 15, 1976, had tasked the NSC Interdepartmental Group for East Asia to review and prepare a study on "U.S. Interests and Security Objectives in the Asia–Pacific Region," especially as those interests and objectives pertained to "the upcoming base negotiations with the Philippines." (Ibid., National Security Decision Memoranda and Study Memoranda, Box 2)

According to the June 1 memorandum, the NSC staff received the Interdepartmental Group's study responding to the NSSM in March 1976, and circulated the first section to the Central Intelligence Agency and the Departments of State and Defense, which accepted it without changes. In the pages focusing on the People's Republic of China, the report argued that the top Chinese priority was "limiting the USSR's presence and influence in Asia." China also sought to avoid instability and conflict near its borders, while "constraining Japan's political-security role in East Asia" by encouraging the U.S.-Japanese alliance. The report stated that China had successfully sought "to isolate Taiwan diplomatically," but had avoided "a threatening posture toward the island" and placing "public pressure on the U.S. position." The report noted that the Sino-Soviet rivalry "has helped deter Peking from playing any useful role in brokering compromise solutions to the Korean issue in the United Nations." Although China sought to discourage offensive military action by North Korea, it had also "become the major supplier of military equipment to Pyongyang." In Southeast Asia, Chinese policies were shaped by rivalries with the Soviet Union, Vietnam, and Japan. For this reason, it was willing to give countenance to continued U.S. political and military involvement in the region, and had "given its blessing to the concept of Southeast Asian neutrality—as espoused by ASEAN." China had participated in a number of island disputes, which, the report suggested, could become a source of international tension in the future. Ending on a cautionary note, this section of the report warned that changes in Chinese domestic politics could produce major changes in Chinese foreign policy. (Response to NSSM 235, Section I, Subsection on "The Policies, Intentions and Capabilities of the People's Republic of China," undated; ibid., NSC Institutional Files (H-Files), Box H–17, SRG Meeting, 6/4/76, U.S. Interests and Objectives in the Asia–Pacific Area, NSSM 235)

On June 4, the Senior Review Group held a meeting in the White House Situation Room from 3:10 to 4:08 p.m. to consider the NSSM 235 response. Few of the comments dealt with China. Philip Habib, Assistant Secretary of State for East Asian and Pacific Affairs, wondered whether "the China section could be beefed up." Much of the discussion revolved around the appropriate outcome of the NSSM response. Scowcroft said, "What we need is a memorandum ratifying this document, saying that it is a useful background document. I just don't like things like this to go into limbo." (Memorandum from Jeanne Davis to Scowcroft with attached SRG minutes, June 28; ibid., H–39, SRG Meeting, 6/4/76, U.S. Interests and Objectives in the Asia–Pacific Area, NSSM 235)

148.   Paper Prepared in the Central Intelligence Agency[1]

PR 76 10053   Washington, June 1976.

THE FOREIGN POLICIES OF CHINA'S SUCCESSOR LEADERSHIP

Executive Summary

Mao's successors will be confronted with the same foreign policy problem Mao has been facing for a long time—namely, a desire to project China's influence globally but a limited capability to compete with the superpowers in doing so, or even to defend itself against them. At present, it cannot compete even with the larger European powers in providing advanced-technology material aid to the lower developed countries (LDCs). China is essentially a regional, not a global, power; it is still confined to a secondary role in most international developments outside Asia. Moreover, in some respects it can even be regarded as a LDC, reaching out to acquire the products and advanced technological skills of the developed capitalist countries.

However, its political favor is sought by both large and small countries, mainly because it is big, already much stronger militarily than most other countries, and has the potential military capability to worry even the superpowers. It thus provides an alternative to exclusive political dependence on either superpower. Mao's successors undoubtedly will try to exploit this situation, and they will have two additional assets:

—the Soviets are likely to make a series of overtures for an improvement of relations, and
—the successors will not be bound by Mao's personal intransigence, and are likely to respond to some degree, especially in the border dispute.

Mao is *trying* to bind his successors irrevocably to his main foreign policies; actually, he has no guarantee of anything, apart from objective considerations that would bind anybody. Mao's death will provide the opportunity for the successors to reassess and change foreign policies, including that toward the USSR and the US. Whether major foreign policies will be changed probably will depend greatly on the nature of the successor leadership—that is, whether the relatively simple-minded ideologues or the relatively sophisticated moderates

---

[1] Source: Central Intelligence Agency, OPI 10, Job 79–M00467A, Box 9, Communist China, 010176–311276. Secret; Noforn. [*name not declassified*] of the Office of Political Research in the Directorate of Intelligence prepared this executive summary and the larger paper. On June 29, Lewis J. Lapham, Director of Political Research, sent the executive summary to Bush under a covering memorandum. (Ibid.) On July 6, Bush wrote on the covering memorandum, "Dave—read with interest! GB"

win out. On present evidence, the result probably will be less revolution and more realism.

The trend toward realism, already present, almost certainly will continue if moderates attain a majority in the post-Mao leadership. Those regarded as moderates—such as Party First Vice Chairman and Premier Hua Kuo-feng, the military leader Yeh Chien-ying, and Foreign Minister Chiao Kuan-hua—probably *will* come to dominate the successor leadership. Most of the ideologues—such as Wang Hung-wen, Chiang Ching (Mme. Mao), and Yao Wen-yuan—do not seem to have an independent power base, and when Mao dies, they will lose their only real source of sustenance. At least two of the ideologues—Chiang Ching and Yao Wen-yuan—are intensely disliked by government functionaries and probably within the party and army as well, and their chances of survival in the Politburo in particular seem slight.

On the other hand, if the post-Mao Politburo should be dominated by an alliance of ideologues and opportunistic military leaders, the result might be an orthodox revolutionary attitude toward the US. That is, there might be more intense opposition to a wider range of US policies. They probably would prefer a more equal balance of anti-US and anti-USSR policies (as the "ultra-Leftist" former Defense Minister Lin Piao had preferred).

In the post-Mao era, Chinese foreign policies will continue to revolve primarily around China's concerns regarding the USSR. The Russians will still be the "main enemy" to the moderates and still an enemy to the ideologues.

Even if Mao's successors choose to moderate their line toward Moscow, hatred and fear of the USSR almost certainly will continue to be the principal factor in their foreign relations. They probably will retain their anxiety about China's national security—namely, whether the Russians will use their overwhelming military superiority to undertake either a large-scale invasion or a disarming nuclear strike. Because China will not be a superpower, the realistic course for the successors would seem to be to continue to try to use American influence to deter the USSR from attacking China and to offset Soviet efforts to encircle China. Clearly, the successors will have nowhere else to go.

However, within a few years after Mao's death, his successors probably will conclude from a reassessment of the Sino-Soviet border dispute that the danger and material costs to China necessitate a reduction of overt hostility to the USSR. His successors will probably not see the same necessity to use the border dispute as part of an overall political polemic (the "paper war") against Moscow.

This shift in attitude—again, more likely to occur if moderates (realists) rather than ideologues were to attain a majority in the post-Mao leadership—would open the way for serious border talks. But a final settlement would prove difficult to attain, inasmuch as the Chinese side would have to make the principal concession—i.e., dropping Mao's demands for a withdrawal of Soviet troops from all disputed areas before the Chinese will enter seriously into negotiations.

Any reduction in the degree of Peking's hostility toward Moscow following Mao's death almost certainly will fall far short of the cordiality which existed in the early 1950s. Even after a possible border settlement, the Chinese almost certainly will continue to feel less secure with the USSR (the in-area and still-menacing threat) than with the US (the out-of-area and receding threat).

Thus the successors probably will continue to view the Sino-US rapprochement in strategic terms—i.e., they will view the US as the only effective counterweight to the USSR. This assessment will reinforce the successors' view of Taiwan as being a secondary issue in the Sino-US relationship, subordinated to the strategic Sino-Soviet-US triangle and the national security of China. The successors will have to be "patient" and willing to "wait" (Peking's usage) for further US disengagement from Taipei.

Aside from the strategic consideration, there are other reasons for a probable subordination of the Taiwan issue. Briefly, Peking is militarily and politically impotent vis-à-vis Taiwan. The military obstacle (mainly insufficient airlift and sealift capability) forces the successors, like it or not, to try to reincorporate Taiwan by political methods. And that is likely to be a long-term matter.

Taipei's present leadership, and the immediate successors to the ailing Chiang Ching-kuo, almost certainly will be unwilling to negotiate any form of Communist annexation. Nor are attempts at subversion likely to hasten matters greatly. Central control of the police and security organs (used vigorously to crush real or suspected subversives) as well as general stability on the island will decisively impede Peking's efforts at least until the 1980s.

If, however, the US were *explicitly* to retreat from the Washington–Taipei defense treaty (e.g., declaring it void after establishing full diplomatic relations with the PRC), political and economic stability on the island would be put to a severe test. In such an event, the Republic of China (ROC) undoubtedly would act to sustain as much of the relationship with the US as possible, and undoubtedly would take steps to try to insure a "business as usual" psychology on the island. Taipei would make such capital as it could from the likely continuation of US commitments to supply it with defense needs (spare parts and assistance in aircraft manufacture). And it would strive to maintain current levels of trade with as many foreign countries as possible—although some economic diversification away from the US might be imposed as a new policy.

In any case, however, Mao's successors probably will be impelled to withhold a decision to gear up for an invasion until well into the 1980s or even later. Even if Taipei develops a nuclear device in the early 1980s, Peking probably would not feel compelled to prepare for an invasion any sooner.

Japan is the key element in Peking's anti-Soviet strategy in the Far East, and Mao's successors probably will encourage Tokyo to strengthen its defense forces. However, they probably will not agree to cooperate in any joint defense arrangement with the Japanese. In the political field, there is a good chance that Chinese moderates will be willing to conclude a Sino-Japanese peace treaty on Tokyo's terms in order to further exacerbate Soviet-Japanese relations.

In Korea and Indochina, the Chinese will be more concerned with impeding the expansion of Soviet influence than with seeking to establish the traditional hegemony of previous centuries.

It is primarily as a result of their decision to compete with Moscow for the good will of Kim Il-sung that the Chinese are now burdened with the task of keeping Kim's emotional revolutionary and militaristic policies from escalating into a war on the peninsula. The Chinese prefer long-term stability on the peninsula—that is, a de facto situation of "two Koreas"; Kim does not. However, they have increased their support for Kim on political issues apparently as part of the price for maintaining clear advantage over the USSR in Pyongyang.

Mao's probable successors are no more likely than he has been to extend their competition with Moscow to the point of supporting large-scale (and dangerous) North Korean harassment of the South. However, a Politburo majority of ideologues might be more willing to do so than a majority of moderates in the post-Mao era. Danger of military instability will arise when the US has left Korea and/or President Pak dies, retires, or is overthrown. If, on the other hand, US forces were to remain in the South at least through the 1970s, the Chinese would be assisted in keeping Kim deterred from initiating military provocations.

Although the Chinese are winning the competition with the Russians for influence in the northeast, they are losing it in Indochina. They retain an advantage in Cambodia, but they cannot prevent Vietnam and Laos from leaning toward the USSR. The Russians will continue to have an advantage over the Chinese in the post-Mao period on the matter of helping the Vietnamese and the Pathet Lao in the task of economic reconstruction. The Chinese will have the added problem of trying to manage a friction-sustaining territorial dispute with the Vietnamese over islands in the South China Sea. Moderates probably will do a better job of avoiding firefights between Chinese and Vietnamese forces than will ideologues in the post-Mao era.

The Chinese provided unprecedented assurances to a non-Communist government when they told Thai leaders in the summer of 1975 that if Vietnam eventually attacked Thailand in force, China would assist Thailand militarily.

The competition with the USSR probably will continue to be the controlling factor in other Chinese foreign policies, such as

—trying to regain some of Peking's past influence in India,
—sustaining support for the US policy of keeping troops in Europe and strengthening NATO, and
—lining up on the same side as LDCs on most political and economic issues between them and the developed capitalist countries (and of course between them and the USSR).

And the competition with Hanoi probably will become the controlling factor in sustaining Chinese support for Maoist insurgents in Southeast Asia.

Mao's legacy of revolution probably will not affect Peking's foreign policies in the future as much as will the *material constraint* of China's non-superpower status. Aside from the major political war to be waged against the USSR, China's goals must continue to be modest.

[Omitted here is the body of the report.]

---

149. Memorandum of Conversation[1]

Washington, July 12, 1976, 5 p.m.

SUBJECT

China Policy, Firebee Drones for the ROC

PARTICIPANTS

The Secretary
Under Secretary Philip C. Habib
Lawrence S. Eagleburger—M
Arthur W. Hummel—EA
Winston Lord—S/P
William H. Gleysteen, Jr.—EA
Richard A. Ericson—PM
David G. Brown—EA/ROC (notetaker)

---

[1] Source: Ford Library, National Security Adviser, Kissinger–Scowcroft West Wing Office Files, 1974–1977, Box 6, China Exchanges, unnumbered items (31), 7/12/76–7/14/76. Top Secret. Drafted by Brown and approved in S on August 24. The meeting was held in Secretary Kissinger's office.

The Secretary: Look, what I'm trying to prevent is the mindless operation of the bureaucracy. How is Peking supposed to understand $5 million in extra money for the ROC? Just because there's some unused money available.

Habib: Now wait, they won't even notice. It will just disappear into the Transition Quarter monies. It's a small . . .

Secretary: It's four-fifths of what you get for Indonesia after I've been beating you over the head.

Habib: Indonesia wants grants not credits. We're trying to educate them that grants are out, only credits are possible. A cable has gone out to (Amb.) Newsom already.[2]

Secretary: Yes, if they're crazy enough to buy weapons rather than tractors. Are you telling me that the figure of 2200 (US military on Taiwan) is what was there?

Habib: No, the figure was 2700 or so when you went. It's . . .

Secretary: Can we make it?

Gleysteen: It will be hard, but we can . . .

Secretary: Are you saying that having told them 1400, we won't make it?

Gleysteen: We will do it, once we get the order issued. We can't operate on the basis of oral orders alone.

Secretary: What is so tricky about getting the order issued?

Gleysteen: The political sensitivity of the situation. Defense knows the order is coming. They're planning, but have not yet . . .

Secretary: I must have naive ideas that if the President tells the Chinese something, then it will be done.

Habib: We've been pushing to get it . . .

Gleysteen: It's clear it's not going to be issued until after the Convention.

Habib: We're not the ones who have violated the President's word.[3]

Gleysteen: [less than 1 line not declassified] may help us achieve it, if we force the pace of those withdrawals into this year. We can make it, if we get the order issued in August.

Secretary: This is dangerous. If I were Carter, I would say that I favored these reductions and that the administration's inaction on them showed its weakness and cynicism.

---

[2] Not further identified.

[3] On December 4, 1975, President Ford told Vice Premier Deng that the United States had about 2,800 military personnel on Taiwan and planned "within the next year" to "reduce that by 50%, down to a figure roughly of 1,400." See Document 137.

Gleysteen: Yes, we have been overly cautious recently.

Eagleburger: Why not rush to move out the 700?

Secretary: I just have difficulty understanding why the instructions of the President and the Secretary only produce palaver in the bureaucracy.

Lord: Mr. Secretary, this is true, but we talked to Brent . . .

Secretary: When was I told? I wouldn't tolerate Brent sitting on such an order. I wasn't aware . . .

Gleysteen: In April, or March, you signed off . . .

Secretary: I don't accept the position that bureaus negotiate with Brent. You could get away with that with Rogers, but not with me.

Lord: I thought you understood, that you had discussed it with Rumsfeld and Brent.

Secretary: It is insanity to hold this up. It should have been done gradually, a hundred a month, no one would have noticed.

Gleysteen: That is just the point we made with Brent.

Lord: If you were not aware of this, we were delinquent.

Secretary: I naively believed it had been carried out. As nothing was mentioned to me, I thought we were below 2200.

Lord: We are delinquent . . .

Habib: You were informed . . .

Secretary: And I'm only raising hell for the fun of it.

Habib: I reminded . . .

Secretary: You didn't mention it in a way that made any impression on me, you probably just said something about a . . . NSDM.[4] By waiting, we have made this into a problem.

Gleysteen: I agree.

Habib: We just said that . . .

Secretary: It is one of the few things we have to show to the Chinese—our good faith. We must be meticulous.

Lord: We will make the deadline, and we lucked out on the publicity from the Quemoy–Matsu withdrawals.[5]

Secretary: I'm going to fire someone who tells me he's working with Scowcroft. I told the Chinese in October that it would be done.

Habib: . . . and the President reaffirmed it, yes.

Eagleburger: Why does it need a NSDM?

---

[4] The eventual NSDM, NSDM 339, is printed as Document 156.

[5] The Quemay-Matsu withdrawal refers to the June 1976 withdrawal of U.S. military advisors from the islands of Quemay and Matsu. "U.S. to Quit Quemay and Matsu," *Washington Post*, June 24, 1976, p. A1.

Secretary: I don't know.

Gleysteen: I was very disturbed by involving others. I predicted it would involve delays.

Secretary: Since 1971, we've been making withdrawals. Have we had NSDM's each time?

Gleysteen: Well, yes, basically.

Secretary: Now, don't you assume that I will accept today the NSC procedures I established while I was over there.

Gleysteen: I'm not willing to go to Defense without . . .

Secretary: If you want my political judgment, I assume everything leaks, and you can bet this will leak out, too, after the Convention, when it's issued. Carter can have it both ways; he'll be for the withdrawals and criticize the President for lack of leadership.

Gleysteen: And also, today we got a cable from Taipei pointing out that Nessen's remarks were at variance with our press guidance on withdrawals.[5]

Secretary: What did he say?

Gleysteen: He mentioned there would be no more withdrawals.

Secretary: When?

Gleysteen: During the Quemoy withdrawal.

Secretary: Was it brought to his attention?

Habib: Yes.

Secretary: Well, you better start bringing things to my attention. Our China policy is operating on a thread now. The Chinese are not used to the assumption that we are irresponsible. If Nessen said it, they believe it. They may discount his remarks as election politics. But the issue is that we have always kept our word.

Habib: There have been ongoing reductions.

Gleysteen: They think it is continuous . . .

Habib: It has been ongoing.

[Omitted here is discussion unrelated to the withdrawal of U.S. personnel from Taiwan.]

---

[5] Telegram 4659 from Taipei, July 10. (National Archives, RG 59, Central Foreign Policy Files)

150.   Memorandum of Conversation[1]

Washington, July 14, 1976, 7:02–7:43 p.m.

PARTICIPANTS

Dr. Henry A. Kissinger, Secretary of State
Philip C. Habib, Under Secretary of State for Political Affairs
Winston Lord, Director, Policy Planning Staff
Arthur Hummel, Assistant Secretary of State for East Asian and Pacific Affairs
William H. Gleysteen, Jr., Deputy Assistant Secretary for East Asian and Pacific Affairs
Peter W. Rodman, NSC Staff

SUBJECT

China: Comments on Taiwan by Chang Chun-chiao and Ch'iao Kuan-hua

REFERENCES

Peking 1282, 1283, 1284; Peking 161 (Voyager Channel)[2]

Kissinger: They have made the same points that they made to us in November of 1974.[3] Whenever it was. After Vladivostok.

Lord: But they never have been pressed like this. On two successive days, by a Congressman carrying a letter from the President.[4] It's like Magnuson on Cambodia.[5]

Gleysteen: We all had misgivings about Barnett [Robert Barnett, Director of the Asian Society, accompanying Senator Scott].

---

[1] Source: Ford Library, National Security Adviser, Kissinger–Scowcroft West Wing Office Files, 1969–1977, Box 6, China, unnumbered items (31), 7/12/76–7/14/76. Secret; Nodis. The meeting was held in Secretary Kissinger's office. All brackets are in the original.

[2] Telegram 1282, July 13, described a meeting between Senator Scott and Zhang Chunqiao. (National Archives, RG 59, Central Foreign Policy Files) Telegram 1283, July 14, provided a verbatim transcript of the Scott–Zhang meeting. (Ibid.) Telegram 1284, July 14, contained a transcript of a conversation between Scott and Qiao. (Ibid.) Backchannel message 161 was not found.

[3] Kissinger was referring to his November 25–29 trip to China in 1974, during which Deng Xiaoping articulated three principles regarding Taiwan and the normalization of U.S.–PRC relations. See Document 97.

[4] Pennsylvania Senator Hugh Scott (R), visited China for two weeks in the summer of 1976. On July 13, he met with Zhang Chunqiao, who told Scott that Taiwan could only be liberated by force. Afterward, Scott told President Ford, "they kept repeating the Taiwan line. It was rather chilling." (Memorandum of conversation, July 28; Ford Library, National Security Adviser, Kissinger–Scowcroft West Wing Office Files, 1969–1977, Box 6, China, unnumbered items (32), 7/16/76–7/31/76)

[5] U.S. officials believed that Senator Magnuson angered Zhou Enlai in 1973 by advising him to be "patient" while the United States intensified its bombing of Cambodia. See Document 43 and footnote 7 thereto.

Lord: I took him aside after breakfast and told him not to raise the Taiwan issue. He mumbled as if he wouldn't.

Kissinger: They all have this idea in their heads that we are going to do this between the election and the inauguration.

Gleysteen: If you look at the succession of three conversations with Chang Chun-chiao—one with the New Zealand Ambassador, then with the Congressman Price group, and this. He is tough as nails. And he is becoming more prominent in dealing with foreigners.

Kissinger: Have we met him?

Lord: He was the host in Shanghai for Nixon in 1972.

Kissinger: What is your judgment, Art?

Hummel: I am afraid it is significant. This is the first time we have seen a direct reflection of the leftists.

Gleysteen: I think so.

Hummel: This could be the first reflection of a divergence of opinion.

Kissinger: In tone, it's the sharpest. In substance, it's the same thing Mao said to us. But Mao used to say also: "But we can wait 100 years."

Hummel: Ch'iao said the day before: "We are in no hurry."

Kissinger: The first thing to do is calm Gates down. Send him some analysis. Tell him our analysis is that the tone is tougher but in substance it was the same thing as the last time we raised it formally—which was in December of 1974. They can't but be annoyed that we raise it when they don't raise it.

I am not sure they want us out of Taiwan now. Suppose we leave, and they can't take it?

Lord: They have always lately been tougher in tone but said they were patient.

Gleysteen: If I were Chinese and read all these newspapers—the *Wall Street Journal* and *The New York Times*, and then see Scott coming out, all puffed up, it would be logical to take a tough line.[6]

Kissinger: It would be logical to make clear that these terms that are being talked about are unacceptable. They are just as inflexible now as with the Japanese on the anti-hegemony clause.

Gleysteen: They have been expecting the fall of the Miki Government.

---

[6] Telegram 1288 from Beijing, July 14, discussed "the jelling of American editorial opinion in the most prestigious and influential papers behind the need to normalize with the PRC while preserving a relationship with Taiwan." (Ford Library, National Security Adviser, Presidential Country Files for East Asia and Pacific Affairs, Box 15, People's Republic of China, State Department Telegrams)

Kissinger: And here they are expecting the fall of the Ford Government. So why should they screw around with a Senator who is leaving office?

Gleysteen: There is a disturbing aspect. This is a leftist talking. There is more anti-Taiwan talk. And there are these maneuvers in the Taiwan Strait.

Kissinger: That could be interpreted both ways. The maneuvers are threatening, but the statements could be a way of compensating for not doing anything. They are showing what they could do.

Habib: The substance is the same as before.

Kissinger: No, what bothers me is the increasing element of disdain. On Angola, he says: You didn't handle it beautifully.

Habib: When they read Miyazawa's statement about the "division of labor" between us and Japan on Taiwan—after he's been in Washington—it will look like we set it up. Could they have seen Miyazawa's statement by that time?[7]

Gleysteen: Yes.

Kissinger: The Olympic thing must look like we are setting up two Chinas.[8]

Lord: Next year, if we look like a strong power . . .

Kissinger: But the White House is making a little defeat into a big one [on the Olympics]. Gates is sending back-channels to the White House saying it is going to explode domestically—that Scott will come back saying they have toughened their terms. They will put something in the Republican Platform demanding a peaceful transition.

They are all counting on our accomplishments and adding to it anti-Communism. [Laughter]

Gleysteen: We have seen this tone since October, in Angola.

Kissinger: In October, we looked pretty good about Angola.

Hummel: There is increasing disdain about the value of the U.S. relationship.

---

[7] An account of Miyazawa's conversation with Senator Mansfield was transmitted in telegram 10553 from Tokyo, July 13, and telegram 10624 from Tokyo, July 14. (National Archives, RG 59, Central Foreign Policy Files)

[8] Canada, the host of the Olympics, prohibited Taiwanese athletes from competing under the name "Republic of China." As a result, the International Olympic Committee threatened to withdraw its support for the Montreal Olympics, while the United States threatened to pull its athletes out of the games. (Steve Cady, "U.S. Threatens to Quit Olympics Over Taiwan," *The New York Times,* July 3, 1976, p. 47)

Kissinger: I am worried about Gates. Could you give him our analysis?[9] A realistic analysis. We see increasing leftist trends. Give him the context—with the Miyazawa statement; the Olympic flap; why it must have looked like a gratuitous insult to them. But make them calm down. Basically they need the relationship more than we do.

Gleysteen: That is true. Once before, Chang said: "The only common interest we have is the fear of the Soviet Union." This time he said "We have many international interests."

Kissinger: Each time they tried to turn the discussion to them, he [Scott] wouldn't let them. [Laughter]

[The Secretary takes a call from Secretary Simon on the Olympic flap.][10]

Simon used to be a member of the Olympic Committee. He says this could have been solved if someone had gotten to the key people on both sides at an early stage. Now it is hopelessly screwed up. He says it was almost impossible to screw it up like this but they did it. There were 100 ways it could have been solved.

I would like a message sent to Gates. Send a back-channel to the White House saying it will have severe domestic repercussions. Can you do it? For tomorrow. Also get to Scott to keep his mouth shut.

Habib: Barnett will write articles on it. He will mine this for weeks.

Kissinger: He will say we screwed it up by not doing it when Chou En-lai was alive.

Hummel: Chang made a point of confidentiality. Maybe we can get to them.

---

[9] In telegram 177799 to Beijing, July 17, the Department sent an analysis of Zhang Chunqiao's meeting with Senator Scott. (Ford Library, National Security Adviser, Presidential Country Files for East Asian and Pacific Affairs, Box 14, People's Republic of China, State Department Telegrams)

[10] No transcript of this telephone conversation was found.

151. Memorandum From the President's Assistant for National Security Affairs (Scowcroft) to President Ford[1]

Washington, July 19, 1976.

SUBJECT

The Passing of Chu Te and China's Domestic Politics

The death of Chu Te, the 90-year old Chairman of the Standing Committee of the National Peoples Congress, has further reduced the ranks of the old guard. Chu Te, as the founder of the Peoples Liberation Army, was the only Chinese leader after the death of Chou En-lai whose historical role and prestige approached that of Mao. Although his formal role in the regime was only ceremonial, Chu probably represented an independent voice in the Politburo during critical decisions. Chu, for example, reportedly supported the moderate policies of Chou En-lai and Teng Hsiao-p'ing. Two poems by Chu, published in March, implicitly criticized the campaign against Teng and the resultant disunity in the Party.

The Central Leadership Organs

Chu's death brings to four the number of vacancies in the Politburo Standing Committee (out of a membership of nine) and probably enhances the strength of the two Shanghai leftist leaders in the Standing Committee, Chang Ch'ung-ch'iao and Wang Hung-wen. The only remaining moderate in the Standing Committee is the aging and ailing Defense Minister Yeh Chien-ying. Premier Hua Kuo-feng, who is now Senior Vice Chairman of the Party, is presumably a Standing Committee member, although he has not been identified as such.

It is unlikely that the regime will in the near future be able to fill the vacant positions in the Politburo and the Standing Committee or to name a replacement for Teng Hsiao-p'ing as PLA Chief of Staff. The empty slots in the central leadership indicate the continuing standoff between the contending factions. It is problematic whether the Standing Committee itself is still functioning or whether an ad hoc group within the Politburo may currently be the ultimate decision-making body.

The Left

In any event, the leftists, with Mao's support, appear to have the political initiative. They should obtain further leeway with the passing

---

[1] Source: Ford Library, National Security Adviser, Presidential Country Files for East Asian and Pacific Affairs, Box 14, People's Republic of China. Secret. Sent for information. Ford initialed the memorandum and there is a notation on the first page that reads: "The President has seen." Sent to Scowcroft under cover of a July 13 memorandum from Barnes that recommended that Scowcroft send it to the President. (Ibid.)

of Chu Te. In addition to the Standing Committee and Party head-quarters, leftist political strength resides in the central media, the students, the militia, the PLA political department, and the industrial heart of China—Shanghai.

There are still many constraints on the leftists, however. Most importantly, they seem to have little support among provincial leaders, military commanders, or the government bureaucracy. The leftists also would be unlikely to control a meeting of the Central Committee as presently composed.

Thus, the leftists, a disparate group apparently led by Chang Ch'ung-ch'iao, are probably anxious to exploit the advantage they currently enjoy at the center before Mao dies. They must move on two fronts—seeking where possible to weaken their opposition and at the same time broaden their own support. The July 1 joint editorial marking the Chinese Communist Party anniversary, while relatively constrained, indicated the regime's preoccupation with the domestic political struggle, and clearly suggested the need for the removal of at least a small group of Teng and Chou supporters.

The left is most probably concerned about gaining allies among the military. The role of people like Chien Hsia-lien, the Commander of the Peking Military Region, will be critical. The alignment of military commanders, however, remains the murkiest element of the obscure Peking domestic scene. Most military commanders are probably biding their time until the Chairman dies.

The role of Premier Hua Kuo-feng, and several others in the leadership who are apparently not factional partisans but essentially Mao loyalists, will also be vital to the course of the power struggle. Hua's control over the Public Security organs has obvious implications. In line with Mao's proclivities, Hua will presumably seek to protect the left. But, like Mao, the thrust of Hua's leadership may be to retain a dynamic balance between the left and the right. If so, Hua will probably not wish to see the left consolidate or expand its position at the Party center in the wake of the death of Chu Te.

The Prospect

The political structure in the PRC is probably more fragile today than it has ever been—including during the Cultural Revolution. Mao's presence remains the key, but it is now a lingering presence and the old Chairman presumably cannot assert a dynamic role. Yet, so long as he lives, he retains the aura of political authority and the leadership stalemate is likely to continue. Realignments that will determine the shape of the post-Mao regime, however, may already be taking shape.

152.   Memorandum of Conversation[1]

Washington, August 18, 1976, 5 p.m.

PARTICIPANTS

Ambassador Huang Chen, Chief, PRC Liaison Office
Mr. Chien Ta-yung, Counselor, PRC Liaison Office
Ms. Shen Jo-yun, Interpreter, PRC Liaison Office

Secretary Kissinger
Arthur W. Hummel, Jr., Assistant Secretary, EA
Winston Lord, Director, S/P
William H. Gleysteen, National Security Council

Kissinger: When I asked to see you I saw no particular urgency but thought we would benefit from an exchange of views.

Huang: I agree.

Kissinger: We have already expressed our sympathy for the earthquake and the self-reliant approach you have taken in dealing with it.

Huang: Thank you.

Kissinger: It is certainly an unusual attitude in this day.

Huang: The earthquake was very serious, but under the leadership of Chairman Mao and the Central Committee of our Party and with the support of the people, we have learned to overcome great hardships.

Kissinger: Perhaps it would be helpful if I were to review a few issues and bring you up to date on our thinking.

Huang: Since our last meeting I think you have visited Iran, Pakistan and Afghanistan.

Kissinger: Correct. I think you may remember my talk with Chairman Mao where I emphasized the great importance and stabilizing influence of Iran in terms of the Soviet Union. During this trip we discussed continuing military relations and also a considerable expansion of our technological and industrial relations. I visited Afghanistan because the brother of the President said Afghanistan wanted to be more independent of the Soviet Union and hoped for more visible support from the United States. If we can conquer our bureaucracy, we will commence certain projects over the next few months. One of these is a power

---

[1] Source: Ford Library, National Security Adviser, Kissinger–Scowcroft West Wing Office Files, 1969–1977, Box 6, China, unnumbered items (33), 8/1/76–8/28/76. Secret; Nodis. The meeting was held in Secretary Kissinger's office. The attached correspondence profile indicates that on August 30 Scowcroft discussed the memorandum with President Ford.

project and another is an engineering school. We need a cultural revolution in our bureaucracy. (Laughter) Seriously, you know the importance of Pakistan and Prime Minister Bhutto to us. We are also working with Pakistan to improve our various relationships but these are affected by the nuclear issue on which our Congress has inhibitions.

Huang: Dr. Kissinger must still remember Chairman Mao's comment about forming a horizontal curve. You have just visited three of the countries. This is fine.

Kissinger: My visit was very much in the spirit of my conversation with Chairman Mao.

Huang: During that talk Chairman Mao singled out Iraq as a point of particular interest. What is the current situation there?

Kissinger: Iraq is becoming somewhat more dubious about the value of its connection with the Soviets. When the head of our interests section returns to Iraq, he will talk to them on re-establishing relations. Throughout the Middle East the Soviets have proceeded with their usual method of threats such as cutting off aid. Where they do, it has always had a bad effect as we have seen in Syria.

We have also been somewhat active in Africa working particularly with Tanzania and Zambia as well as putting pressure on South Africa to bring about a settlement in Rhodesia and Namibia. A settlement is a possibility, and depending on the prospects I may go to Africa in the first half of September.

Huang: After Angola I have the impression that Soviet influence has been expanding in an even more pronounced way in Africa.

Kissinger: Correct, but we are trying to counteract it. That is why we are giving arms aid to Zaire and Kenya.

Huang: Some time ago Castro claimed, I think through the Swedes, that he would soon withdraw Cuban troops from Angola. By now we can see that this was nothing but a false profession.

Kissinger: Right. That is why we will not accept them (Angola) in the UN. Angola is occupied by Cuba and they cannot maintain themselves without Cuban arms.

Huang: In the long run we believe that foreign forces cannot control and plunder countries such as Angola.

Kissinger: In the long run you are correct though we wish to avoid a repetition of the Angolan situation in Rhodesia and Namibia where the Soviets may otherwise be tempted.

Huang: In the press we have seen some discussion of this possibility.

Kissinger: Yes, but we think we have a chance of defeating such Soviet moves if we succeed with our policies.

I also wish to discuss the matter of communist party participation in West European governments. We oppose such participation. I recognize that you are perhaps not an ideal target for our views, because we once opposed communist participation in the Chinese government. (Laugher) People say that the West European communist parties are independent of Moscow. I don't know if one can judge this to be the case when it is so much in their (communist parties) interest to pretend this. I am suspicious, for example, of the French Communist Party which has always been one of the most loyal Stalinist parties, when it voted over-whelmingly 120 to 0 for a posture of independence. I would have been far more impressed by a closer vote. But the 120 to 0 vote suggests the largest mass conversion in history. I remember the time when the East European communist parties were saying the same thing that we are now hearing from the West European communist parties. I have had a compilation made of these statements and will send one along to you if you like. (Lord to send copy.) In any event our principal concern is that the communist parties will come into power with positions and the kind of public support that will undermine West European defense and lead to the Finlandization of Europe. This is what we are trying to prevent. If you believe the statements you have made to us that the Soviets' basic objective is to make a feint toward the East while attacking the West, I think you must share our concern.

Huang: During our last conversation we also talked about this. Our views are still the same. We think you are too worried about this matter. We believe the West European parties are not simply tools of the Soviets. In saying this I should point out, nevertheless, that we don't have connections with the French and Italian communist parties.

Kissinger: I just wanted to explain our position.

Huang: As we see it the problem faced by Western Europe is the Soviet expansionist threat. The Soviets operate under the banner of détente.

Kissinger: I agree that expansion is the Soviet strategy. The question is how do we deal with it.

Huang: Foreign Minister Chiao recently said to Senator Scott that a policy of détente with the Soviet Union is less and less effective. In any event we do not think the West European communist parties can be viewed simply as a Soviet fifth column.

Kissinger: I must say your Foreign Minister was effective in some-how managing to get his own views across during his discussions with the Senator. Senator Scott has his own ideas and his own solutions. I read with interest the reports of his conversations with your leaders.[2]

---

[2] See Document 150 and footnotes 2 and 4 thereto.

Huang: What did you think of Senator Scott's report?

Kissinger: The Senator raised a number of topics too insistently and he advanced certain solutions we would not have proposed. He was so persistent that he seems to have prompted some of your people into firing off some cannons. I say this on the basis of our reports though I recognize it is possible the reports were not accurate.

Huang: I would like to say something about this (Taiwan). Recently people in the United States have made many official and non-official comments about Sino-U.S. relations.

Kissinger: Which have been official? I don't consider the Republican Party platform official.[3]

Huang: (interrupting) I wish to say something. I have something to say. The United States invaded Taiwan (the interpreter incorrectly translated this as "committed aggression against Taiwan") thus owing China a debt. The U.S. must fulfill the three conditions of breaking diplomatic relations with Taiwan, withdrawing its military forces from Taiwan, and abrogating its defense treaty with Taiwan. There can be no exception about any of these conditions, and there is no room for maneuver in carrying them out. The delay in normalizing relations is entirely the responsibility of the United States. The method and the time for liberating Taiwan is an internal affair of China and is not discussable. The Chinese position was clear to you even before you sought to re-open relations with us. Now Americans are saying that China's liberation of Taiwan will cripple the development of Sino-U.S. relations. They (Americans) are saying that Sino-U.S. relations will prosper only if the Chinese side takes into account U.S. concerns. This is a premeditated pretext. It is a flagrant threat against China, and we cannot accept it.

Kissinger: What is a threat?

Huang: Vice Premier Chang Chun-chiao and Foreign Minister Chiao told Senator Scott very clearly (what is a threat), I think I should stop here.

Kissinger: I should point out that the statement about taking U.S. views into account doesn't apply principally to the Taiwan issue but rather to our broader cooperation. Certainly I thought reciprocity was a basic Chinese policy.

Huang: I hope we can proceed on the basis of the Shanghai Communiqué as Vice Premier Chang pointed out to Senator Scott.

Kissinger: It is our firm purpose to do so. We will act on this basis, and not on the basis of what is written in this or that platform.

---

[3] The Republican Party platform of 1976 expressed support for "the freedom and independence of our friend and ally, the Republic of China, and its 16 million people."

(This was translated in a way suggesting the Chinese did not make the connection to the party platforms.)

Huang: You remember Chairman Mao told you in 1973 that we would have to liberate Taiwan and that we do not believe in peaceful liberation. Vice Premier Chang explained to Scott that the Shanghai Communiqué did not specify that the solution to the Taiwan problem would be peaceful or otherwise. May I remind you that I did not come (to see you) for this discussion but I had to say something (about the Taiwan issue).

Kissinger: I appreciate your comments. Basically Vice Premier Chang did not say anything new. Chairman Mao and others have made the same points to us before. We appreciate that this is your basic view. Quite frankly we would not have recommended that Senator Scott open this issue with you as he did. As we told you last year, these election months in the United States are not the time for working out an agreement on normalization of our relations. We must instead move not long after our elections. I assure you we will maintain our support for the Shanghai Communiqué and will work to complete normalization. Nobody is authorized to speak for us. When we do it, we will do it at this level. I recognize there is not unlimited time. On our side we are doing our utmost to curb unhelpful discussion. We feel private discussion is better than public discussion.

Huang: Is there anything else? Are you going elsewhere in the near future?

Kissinger: Maybe to Africa, depending on the progress of discussions. And I am playing with the idea of going to the Philippines in October to discuss our base negotiations.

Huang: The Philippines also had an unfortunate earthquake.

Kissinger: We have offered them assistance. May I raise one or two bilateral matters. I remember a conversation with your trade minister and the President also mentioned that in certain special trade matters such as the sale of computers, we wish to be helpful to you. But the trouble is that you deal at a very low level through commercial channels. If you approach Mr. Lord or Mr. Hummel we will do our best to make special arrangements to help you. We have problems such as our procedures for dealing with the Soviets, but if we know what you want, we may be able to make exceptions.

Huang: (Following a query to Chien) As Chien says, President Ford did raise this issue with us, and he also points out that we have already replied that we will deal with these matters through commercial channels.

Kissinger: Yes I understand, but this creates infinite problems. I suggest instead that you informally tell Mr. Lord so we can watch and try to be helpful. We know your attachment to private enterprise (laughter), and we are not saying that you should avoid commercial channels. We are simply suggesting that you supplement these by keeping us privately informed.

Huang: All right. I understand and will report your suggestion to Peking.

Kissinger: On Korea. It would of course be best if we could avoid a confrontation. I realize you don't have instructions on the matter, but I should note that there was an event in Korea today in which two Americans were beaten to death.[4] This is a serious matter which could have grave consequences if restraint is not shown.

Huang: I heard about it on the radio, but I don't have any details. As for solution of the Korean question, I think our respective views are well-known to each other. Although I am not informed about the latest incident I can say that we know the Koreans pretty well since they are friendly to us. The Korean people will put up a strong self-defense when they are provoked.

Kissinger: Two U.S. officers are dead and we know from very good pictures that no Koreans were killed. The U.S. officers couldn't have beaten themselves to death.

Huang: Why were the cameras ready?

Kissinger: That is a good question.

Huang: Having the cameras there makes it look as though you were prepared for the incident.

Kissinger: The reason for the cameras is that the observation post nearby the site of the incident takes photographs constantly. Our people were trying to cut down trees which obstructed their view.

Huang: I see.

Kissinger: When is the Foreign Minister coming to the United Nations for the General Assembly?

Huang: I have no news of it so far.

Kissinger: Will you invite him to come down to Washington? I know he will not accept my invitation but he may accept yours.

Huang: As long as the Chiang Kai-shek Embassy is here, he will not come.

Kissinger: We can offer him Camp David.

Huang: We would prefer to come in through the front gate.

Kissinger: I hope we can have our annual exchange.

Huang: Sure we can in New York!

---

[4] U.S. and South Korean soldiers were attacked while pruning a tree in the Demilitarized Zone separating North and South Korea.

Kissinger: Of course.

Huang: Are you going to Kansas City? We have watched quite a bit of television lately. Last night I watched until 12, although I gave up after the voting.

Kissinger: All the rest was quite unimportant.

Huang: I won't take any more of your time.

Kissinger: You have had many visitors. I think you will have many visitors in September, won't you?

Huang: To whom are you referring?

Kissinger: I think Senator Mansfield is going, and I understand that my former colleague Schlesinger will be inspecting your fortifications during September.

Huang: He will not be making an inspection; rather he has asked to get around the country, and we are trying to accommodate him. Moreover, Senator Mansfield will go to even more places.

Kissinger: I don't object.

Huang: You remember that we invited him (Schlesinger) in 1974. Don't be jealous. You have been to China nine times I believe. You even said you yourself wanted to go to Inner Mongolia.

Kissinger: But I didn't get there. I wanted to go see the musk ox of Mongolia.

Huang: There is only one left. The Mayor of San Francisco offered us a second one, and it was reported to the State Department. But, there has been no action. I understand that the musk ox in San Francisco is related to the one we have in China.[5]

Kissinger: Either we didn't like the musk ox's political attitude or we feared incest. (Laughter) But, we will look into it.

---

[5] At the time of his February 1972 visit to the People's Republic of China, President Nixon brought two musk oxen as gifts for his hosts.

153. Memorandum for the Record[1]

Washington, August 25, 1976.

SUBJECT

Ambassador Gates' Meeting with the Secretary, August 25, 1976

Ambassador Gates met with the Secretary for about 45 minutes. Also participating were Mr. Hummel, Mr. Lord and myself.

Meeting with Foreign Minister Chiao

After opening exchanges about Ambassador Gates' service in Peking and the effects of the earthquake, the Secretary asked Ambassador Gates if he planned to stay in the U.S. until the meeting with Foreign Minister Chiao. In discussion of the probable date of the meeting, Ambassador Gates noted that Federal Reserve Chairman Burns was scheduled to arrive in Peking after the Manila meeting, which concludes October 7 or 8, and that a New York meeting after October 1 might put him (Ambassador Gates) in a time squeeze. The Secretary confirmed that Ambassador Gates "might as well sit in" on the Chiao meeting.

Chiao's Role; Hua's Potential

The Secretary asked Ambassador Gates to assess Foreign Minister Chiao's role in the PRC. Ambassador Gates said it is hard to fathom, that Chiao had recently been strangely quiet and not very visible. Ambassador Gates added that Chiao seems to be rather "unaligned", at least publicly, and remains a bit of a mystery. After the earthquake, Ambassador Gates said, Premier Hua Kuo-feng was much more visible than others.

The Secretary asked if Hua were smart enough to take charge of the country. Ambassador Gates said he didn't have such an impression, indicating that he thought that Chang Chun-chiao is a more likely candidate. The Secretary asked if this was the man who "beat up Scott," and this led to discussion of Senator Scott's visit.[2]

The Scott Visit; Chinese Hard Line

The Secretary noted that Senator Scott was "asking for it" from Chang; when Ambassador Gates mentioned Robert Barnett's

---

[1] Source: Ford Library, National Security Adviser, Kissinger–Scowcroft West Wing Office Files, 1969–1977, Box 6, China, unnumbered items (34), 9/1/76–9/29/76. Secret; Nodis. Drafted by Harry E.T. Thayer (EA/PRCM) on September 1 and approved in S on September 23.

[2] See Documents 150 and 152.

unhelpful role, the Secretary characterized Mr. Barnett as a "horse's ass." Speaking of the Presidential letter that Senator Scott carried with him, the Secretary first suggested that it was a responsibility of the "bureau" to prevent such letters. Mr. Hummel or Mr. Lord said they didn't know about the letter before it was sent. The Secretary said that, in any event, Senator Scott had no real mission for the President. Ambassador Gates said that Senator Scott and Mr. Barnett had no judgment or discretion, recalling his talk with the Senator before the Chang meeting at which Ambassador Gates had tried to dissuade Senator Scott from raising contentious subjects. Ambassador Gates said that Mr. Barnett apparently had restimulated the Senator unhelpfully. Ambassador Gates asked if the Secretary had received his back-channel message on the Scott visit.[3] The Secretary said he had and complimented Ambassador Gates on his handling of the problem. The Secretary went on to comment that now Scott had turned the Chinese hard line back onto the Taiwanese. He added that the Scott visit had not had the impact in the U.S. that he, the Secretary, had anticipated.

Ambassador Gates said that he had at first thought that Chang had been needled by the Senator into the hard position. Ambassador Gates now felt that the Chinese before the meeting had intended to take the line and have it go public. The Secretary speculated that perhaps the Chinese had thought that both the Republican and Democratic Parties were trying to "pocket" peaceful liberation before the election and that they were determined to avoid having a bipartisan consensus in the U.S. on this.

U.S. Response to Chinese Hard Line

Ambassador Gates thought that the Administration should now act, telling the Chinese that they are freezing U.S. public opposition to normalization. The Secretary recalled that he had said this to the Chinese last week.[4] Ambassador Gates said that it is important for the Secretary to do it more strongly. The Secretary asked if the idea would be to stop the Chinese from holding the view that military liberation will be required or to stop the Chinese from talking about it. It was agreed that the point is to stop the Chinese from talking about it. Ambassador Gates mentioned the Republican platform, wondering how the Administration could back off it. The Secretary noted that the platform means a two-China solution, adding that it would have been better to have said that Taiwan is the legitimate government of all China. He said that he will just have to ignore the Republican platform. He had

---

[3] Presumably backchannel message 161 from Beijing, not found. See footnote 2, Document 150.

[4] See Document 152.

told the Chinese last week not to pay any attention to the platform, although maybe they did not get the message clearly.

Ambassador Gates said that the Chinese now had to bear the responsibility for damaging our ability to progress on normalization. The Secretary recalled that Chou En-lai knew that the Chinese had to do something themselves to contribute to progress. He recalled that the most forthcoming meetings with the Chinese had been in 1973, as was reflected in that year's communiqué(s). Chou himself had pointed this out. But later, as soon as Chou was out of the picture, the Chinese dropped any effort to settle the claims issue. He lamented that if Nixon had stayed in office everything would have been easier. Ambassador Gates reiterated that it would be useful if the Secretary would say something further to the Chinese. The Secretary said he could do so to the Foreign Minister. Ambassador Gates urged that this be done before the election instead of during a possible lame-duck period.

The Secretary asked how Ambassador Gates thought the Taiwan issue should be settled. The Ambassador said that the only idea he had been able to come up with was a Congressional resolution expressing the sense of Congress on a peaceful solution. The Secretary characterized this as "ingenious". He went on to say that the question would have to be resolved probably by two unilateral statements—one by the PRC and one by the U.S. Reverting to the Scott visit, the Secretary said that even if the PRC had a peaceful liberation formula now they would still hold it back from us until one minute before final settlement. The Chinese are "not nuts," and therefore would not reveal their formula to Senator Scott.

Referring to earlier discussion of the Republican platform, Ambassador Hummel said he agreed with Ambassador Gates about the difficulty of going back on the platform, but he had noticed that Jimmy Carter had repudiated his adherence to the Democratic platform. Mr. Lord, in response to the Secretary's question as to how Governor Carter had done this, said that the Governor had announced that he was not bound by everything in the Democratic platform. The Secretary commented that if the President had repudiated the platform, it would have given Governor Reagan ammunition to assault him. The platform, nevertheless, is "an outrage," the Secretary said. Ambassador Gates said we could truthfully tell the Chinese that they had helped write the Republican platform. The Secretary responded that the "yahoos" would have written the platform that way anyhow. He went on then to confirm that he would "do it with" Chiao Kuan-hua.

Schlesinger Visit (first mention)

The Secretary, now referring to the Schlesinger visit, said that the Chinese were "bloody-minded", and that it was an outrage to invite him, particularly to invite a man they know to have been fired by the

President. All the news coming out of the Schlesinger visit is going to be anti-Administration, he said. (This portion of the conversation concluded by a general exchange on the Chinese habit of inviting people who were out of office. Mr. Lord noted that in this sense Tanaka would now be a new hero, and the Secretary jokingly said that they might be inviting him next.)

USLO's Role

Ambassador Gates said that he had a "gripe" which he would like to raise with the Secretary. He said that the people in the Department ought to think up opportunities to facilitate more contact between USLO and the Chinese. He said that USLO also should be more involved with the Secretary's meetings here with the Chinese. The Secretary agreed. Ambassador Gates said that it would have been helpful to know in advance that the Secretary was going to be seeing Ambassador Huang Chen. The Secretary said: "I want them to know in the future." He went on to add: "We should get the transcript to Peking within 48 hours and you should know about the meeting ahead of time." The Secretary said he didn't mind Ambassador Gates' getting this information if he could protect it. He added: "I just don't want country directors writing letters about it." (Referring presumably to the Official Informal letter transmitting the CDC memo,[5] the letter which went by international mail.) Ambassador Gates reiterated that he should know ahead of time and should have an input in the preparations for the Secretary's meetings here with Huang Chen. The Secretary indicated agreement.

Events in China

The Secretary asked about the mood in Peking. Ambassador Gates said that a struggle is going on, so the leadership is talking for internal purposes. It is hard to understand what is going on and he thought that Wang Hai-jung, for example, was talking for the record, directed internally. He said that he thought the struggle was so intense that the leadership is marking time. The Secretary asked if Hua would last. Ambassador Gates said that Hua was the only visible figure following the earthquake and he might last if he doesn't get shot. Ambassador Gates said he didn't buy the coalition theory and thought that somebody, some individual, is going to emerge, either Hua or Chang. He said it is certain that the struggle is intense, and would be narrowing down

---

[5] CDC in this instance probably stands for Control Data Corporation, a U.S. company that manufactured a computer that the Chinese Government wanted to buy as part of a seismic oil exploration system. (Telegram 261496 to Beijing, October 21; Ford Library, National Security Adviser, Presidential Country Files for East Asian and Pacific Affairs, Box 14, People's Republic of China, State Department Telegrams)

both the players and ideological issues. He noted that the Chinese showed themselves to be really organized following the earthquake, mentioning effective security and effective cleanup of streets after the Peking residents moved out of their tents and back into their residences.

Schlesinger Visit (second mention)

Mr. Hummel recommended that the Secretary, when he meets former Defense Secretary Schlesinger, ask him to request the Chinese to have USLO participate in any Schlesinger meeting with Chinese high officials. The Secretary said that he would "recommend" this to Schlesinger. However, he added, he knew what Schlesinger's answer would be (implying a negative answer). Ambassador Gates asked the identity of Schlesinger's host for the trip, and he was told that it was the Chinese Friendship group. (We have since discovered this to be an error; the host organization is the Chinese People's Institute of Foreign Affairs.) The Secretary, referring again to Mr. Hummel's recommendation, confirmed that he would tell Schlesinger, but went on to note that the Government had changed since Ambassador Gates was in Washington and that people aren't working for the country any longer but rather for themselves. He repeated: "I'll request and let him turn it down." The Secretary added that he did not think that the Chinese should get away with inviting Schlesinger to Peking. Gates said (ironically) that Schlesinger was a "decent fellow", since Schlesinger had decided to postpone his trip until after the political conventions. The Secretary said he had not known that Schlesinger had been invited to go last spring. In any case, he said, Schlesinger overestimates his own influence.

Japan Problems

Ambassador Gates said that he was worried about the effect of the Japanese now talking about Taiwan. The Secretary said that Tanaka had told former President Nixon that the U.S. should take care of Taiwan and the Japanese would take care of China. He said that the new element is that the issue now has become involved in Japanese domestic politics. Referring to the Lockheed scandals, the Secretary said that what we've done to the LDP guarantees that the Japanese will be increasingly nationalistic. He said, "We're going to pay for this in Japan." Ambassador Gates referred to his recent talks with a leading business executive in Tokyo, who said the LDP is finished. The Secretary again made the point that the Japanese would be moving toward an intense nationalism and the U.S. had been responsible for it, the damage growing from Senator Church's political ambitions. The United States has done this to Japan, the Secretary repeated. In the case of the Netherlands we can survive, but "in Japan it is going to take some very ugly forms."

154.   Letter From President Ford to Chinese Premier Hua Guofeng[1]

Washington, September 9, 1976.

Dear Mr. Premier:

Please accept my personal condolences, and those of the Government and people of the United States, on the occasion of the passing of Chairman Mao Tse-tung.

Few men in any era achieve historic greatness. Chairman Mao was one of these men. His leadership has been a decisive element in the shaping of the Chinese nation for several decades, and his works have left a deep imprint upon our civilization. He was truly a major figure of our times.

I was privileged to meet Chairman Mao during my visit to Peking in December 1975. Our discussion furthered the development of U.S.-China relations along the lines that our two countries had earlier envisaged. Let me affirm now, as I did then, the determination of the United States to complete the normalization of our relations on the basis of the Shanghai Communiqué. This would be a fitting tribute to his vision, and of benefit to the peoples of our two countries.

Sincerely,

Gerald R. Ford

---

[1] Source: Ford Library, National Security Adviser, Kissinger–Scowcroft West Wing Office Files, 1969–1977, Box 6, China, unnumbered items (34), 9/1/76–9/29/76. No classification marking. Ford received this letter for his signature under a September 9 covering memorandum from Scowcroft. (Ibid., Presidential Country Files for East Asian and Pacific Affairs, Box 14, People's Republic of China)

155.   Memorandum From the President's Assistant for National Security Affairs (Scowcroft) to President Ford[1]

Washington, September 17, 1976.

SUBJECT

Troop Drawdowns in Taiwan

You will recall from our discussion on Saturday[2] that I said the impact of the proposed troop drawdown from Taiwan could be moderated in important measure by moving ahead promptly with the deployment of the [*less than 1 line not declassified*]. As explained below, most of the remainder has already been taken care of by natural attrition. I have also modified the proposed NSDM to narrow its focus to troop drawdowns only.

When you originally told the Chinese in Peking in December 1975 that we intended to cut in half our then-current force levels on Taiwan (from 2800 to 1400) by the end of 1976, we contemplated that the drawdowns would come from a broad spectrum of units.[3] Although no specific plans were ever approved, DOD was considering a number of highly visible moves, including complete closure of our two air bases and return of the facilities to the ROC.

[*1 paragraph (4½ lines) not declassified*]

It was against the above background that you originally approved the issuance of the Taiwan troop drawdown NSDM last spring. (Attached at Tab B is the original package which you approved last spring. The original NSDM is at Tab B of that package.)[4]

---

[1] Source: Ford Library, NSC Institutional Files (H-Files), Boxes H–67, NSDM 339, U.S. Force Reductions on Taiwan. Top Secret; Umbra; Sensitive. Sent for action. The attached NSC correspondence profile indicates that Ford approved the recommendations in this memorandum on September 20. Scowcroft received this memorandum under a September 15 covering memorandum from Gleysteen. (Ibid.)

[2] According to the President's Daily Diary, Ford met with Scowcroft on Saturday, September 11, from 9:35 to 10:15 a.m. Kissinger was also present. (Ibid., President's Daily Diary)

[3] On December 4, 1975, President Ford told Vice Premier Deng that the United States had about 2,800 military personnel on Taiwan and planned "within the next year" to "reduce that by 50%, down to a figure roughly of 1,400." See Document 137.

[4] Attached but not printed. In the spring of 1976, Ford approved a memorandum from Scowcroft that recommended the issuance of a NSDM that would have reduced Defense Department personnel to a level of 1,400 or less. (Memorandum from Scowcroft to Ford, April 23; Ford Library, NSC Institutional Files (H-Files), Box H–67, NSDM 339, U.S. Force Reductions on Taiwan) This NSDM was not issued, however, and was superseded by NSDM 339 (Document 156).

A number of events in the last few months, however, have changed the picture significantly, permitting the proposed drawdown to be made with minimum adverse fallout.

[*1 paragraph (8 lines) not declassified*]

Moreover, since the beginning of the year, the number of DOD personnel actually on Taiwan has fallen below authorized levels to around 2300. This means that to achieve the goal of 1400, the number of [*less than 1 line not declassified*] personnel required to be drawn down will be in the range of 200–400. None of the drastic steps contemplated earlier (e.g., turning over air bases to the ROC) will be necessary.

Finally, to reduce the potential negative impact even further, I have eliminated a number of provisions in the earlier version of the NSDM, cutting out those measures which can be postponed. I have eliminated:

—A requirement that DOD submit to the NSC plans to transfer out of Taiwan the U.S. Army Communications Command and the War Reserve Matériel storage facility during 1977.

—The prohibition against any deployment of new military units or War Reserve Matériel to Taiwan.

[*1 paragraph (2 lines) not declassified*]

In light of the above, I believe the problems posed by the troop drawdown NSDM are manageable.

Recommendation:

That you authorize me to release the verbal hold on the NSDM directing deployment [*less than 1 line not declassified*]

and that you authorize me to sign the revised NSDM at Tab A calling for an authorized level of DOD personnel on Taiwan by December 31, 1976 of no more than 1400.[5]

---

[5] Ford initialed the Approve option under both recommendations. See also footnote 1 above.

156. National Security Decision Memorandum 339[1]

Washington, September 20, 1976.

TO

The Secretary of State
The Secretary of Defense
The Director of Central Intelligence

SUBJECT

U.S. Force Reductions on Taiwan

The President has approved the following:

—A manpower reduction on Taiwan to a ceiling of not more than 1400 by December 31, 1976 of Defense Department personnel, military as well as civilian. (This ceiling does not apply to those assigned to the American Embassy and contractual personnel, including those associated with the remoting facility to be installed at Shu Lin Kou).

—Notification to Embassy Taipei in advance of specific drawdowns.

—An injunction against the total withdrawal during 1976 of any single unit or activity without prior NSC approval.

[8 lines not declassified]

Brent Scowcroft

---

[1] Source: Ford Library, NSC Institutional Files (H-Files), Box H–67 and Box–68, NSDM 339. Top Secret; Umbra; Sensitive. A copy was sent to the Chairman of the Joint Chiefs of Staff.

157.   Memorandum of Conversation[1]

New York City, October 8, 1976, 8:30–11:30 p.m.

PARTICIPANTS

Chiao Kuan-hua, PRC Foreign Minister
Ambassador Huang Hua, PRC Permanent Representative to the United Nations
Lai Ya-li, Deputy PRC Permanent Representative
Chi Chao-chu, Interpreter
Kuo Chia-ting, Notetaker

Secretary Kissinger
Brent Scowcroft, Assistant to the President for National Security Affairs
Ambassador Thomas Gates, American Ambassador to the PRC
Arthur Hummel, Assistant Secretary of State for East Asia
Winston Lord, Director, Policy Planning Staff
William Gleysteen, National Security Council (Notetaker)

Chiao: Is this your first time here at our Mission headquarters?

Kissinger: It is my first time in this room. I was downstairs once. I was trying to be helpful finding a place for you. Ambassador Huang did better himself without my help. Do you find it satisfactory?

Huang: It is very convenient for both work and living.

Kissinger: I agree. Mr. Chi won't have time to go back to his alma mater? Both of us studied chemistry there. I got extremely high grades in chemistry but it reflected memory, not understanding of the subject. Those who deplore my political views could perhaps have spared the world by keeping me in chemisty. I once asked Professor Kistiakowsky whether I should keep on in chemistry, and he answered that anyone who had to ask such a question shouldn't. (Laughter)

Chiao: If you had continued your studies in chemistry, it might have benefited your political activities more.

Kissinger: My accomplishments in chemistry were just the result of brute memory. I remember once in the laboratory doing an elaborate experiment where I got results which were precisely opposite from the ones I was supposed to get. Perhaps the professor who analyzed how I managed to do this went on to get a Nobel Prize. (Laughter)

Chiao: How is Mrs. Kissinger?

Kissinger: She is fine and asks after Mrs. Chiao.

Chiao: She didn't go with you to Africa did she?

---

[1] Source: Ford Library, National Security Adviser, Kissinger–Scowcroft West Wing Office Files, 1969–1977, Box 6, China, unnumbered items (35), 10/2/76–10/8/76. Secret; Nodis. The meeting was held at the PRC Mission to the United Nations.

Kissinger: Yes she did.

Chiao: (Turning to Gates) How long have you been here?

Gates: I have been here since last week, and I am returning to Peking next week.

Chiao: (To Lord) How is your wife?

Lord: Fine, thank you.

Chiao: (Turning back to the Secretary) We last met in December, I believe.

Kissinger: Yes, when I was with President Ford in Peking. Before we go on, I would like to extend my personal condolences on the death of Chairman Mao. He was a great man in the history of our era. All of us who knew him felt that it was a great event in our lives.

Chiao: Thank you very much. I would also like to thank many of your friends who went to our offices to extend condolences. General Scowcroft was among them here in Washington and Ambassador Gates, of course, did so in Peking.

Of the Americans who knew Chairman Mao, you are probably one of the ones who saw the most of him.

Kissinger: Yes, five times. The first meeting was with President Nixon in 1972; then I met him in February 1973 and November 1973 when I had my long talk with him; and then again last year in October and with the President in December.

Chiao: He had a great effect on the Chinese people.

Kissinger: Surely. I remember during our meeting in October 1975 that while he had great difficulty speaking, the content of his thought was profound.

Chiao: He had difficulty speaking, but his thoughts were clear.

You have seen from our public statements and documents that the Chinese Government is determined to carry on the policies of Chairman Mao.

Kissinger: I saw it in your speech.[2]

Chiao: Actually, since liberation, our policy has always been grasped and looked after by Chairman Mao. I noted that President Ford also mentioned that Chairman Mao looked after (was responsible for) the opening of our relationship.

---

[2] Supplementary briefing material for Kissinger described Qiao's UN speech. (Memoranda from Hummel and Lord to Kissinger, October 5 and 8; ibid.) Qiao delivered his UN speech on October 5. ("China, at UN, Spurns Attempts by Soviets To Resume Old Ties," *The New York Times*, October 6, 1976, p. 1)

Kissinger: I remember that during our negotiations Chinese leaders would go to Chairman Mao at crucial points and return with instructions.

Chiao: Chairman Mao always kept an eye on many matters, not only major strategic issues.

Kissinger: I remember during negotiation of the Shanghai Communiqué when Premier Chou went to see Chairman Mao and came back with some rather firm proposals which permitted us to proceed successfully.

Chiao: Yes, that was the first part of the Shanghai Communiqué. It was a good method because it did not hide anything.

Kissinger: It was an original method which suited the circumstances.

Chiao: Not covering up contradictions is the beginning of their solution. Then, the agreements which follow are genuine.

Kissinger: Yes, the points of agreement then have more meaning. Mr. Foreign Minister, how do you propose to proceed tonight?

Chiao: Let's proceed as usual. I would like to take the opportunity to hear your views. Why don't you start? You have been to so many places.

Kissinger: Because we are in your place tonight. (Laughter)

Chiao: We have two sayings. One is that when we are the host, we should let the guests begin, and the other is that when we are guests, we should defer to the host.

Kissinger: You can always use this so I have to start in any event. (Laughter) But I will be glad to start. First, perhaps I could make a general assessment of the relations between us. Then I might say something about the world situation, and finally, we might discuss some specific issues.

Chiao: Quite alright.

Kissinger: I might begin in the spirit of the Foreign Minister's comment that pointing out contradictions may help their solution. Speaking frankly and as someone with some sentimental involvement in the start of our relationship—I was the first senior U.S. official visitor to China, my impression, and that of my colleagues, is that there has been a certain deterioration in our relationship since the time of President Ford's visit. It is seen in the way we exchange views and hear Chinese views much more through Chinese statements to visitors than official representatives.

Chiao: What we say to non-official visitors is at one with what we say to you officially.

Kissinger: True. But it is often at greater length and higher levels. Moreover, these delegations will usually repeat what you say so that it practically constitutes a form of public pressure on us.

Chiao: Can it be so said?

Kissinger: Despite the fact that I am attacked directly or indirectly, I still feel that the opening to China is the most important thing I have done in my public life. If the Foreign Minister will permit me to use it as an example, his speech to the General Assembly is a reflection of the problem. Some of his speech was so subtle that only a few people understood who was being attacked. But I can assure him that they knew. Don't worry, your efforts weren't wasted. I will pass on your views to Mr. Sonnenfeldt the next time I see him. (Laughter) If my father ever sits next to you at dinner, you can be sure he will explain his views on the subject.

As I understand it, you said in your speech that when the U.S. negotiates with the Soviets, it is engaging in appeasement and pushing the Soviets toward China. But when the United States resists the Soviets, it is engaging in a rivalry of the superpowers against which all mankind should unite. Under those conditions we are playing under rules where we cannot possibly win. It reminds me that the British Foreign Minister has a game where only he knows the rules. He keeps a point score. Every day he tells me of the score. Every day I'm defeated and the only question is the extent of my defeat. (Laughter) Possibly we have different assessments of the Soviet Union, but I doubt that the difference is so large. It is a tactical difference. Fundamentally, if you criticize our negotiations with the Soviet Union as appeasement and describe our efforts to resist them as superpower rivalry, then what did your Prime Minister have in mind when he suggested to Schlesinger that we "pool our efforts"?

Chiao: Right.

Kissinger: What do you mean by right?

Chiao: I mean the reference to pooling our efforts is right.

Kissinger: We are ready to pool our efforts, but I don't see how we can proceed when you attack us for our policy, e.g. in Europe and Africa. When we conduct negotiations out of tactical considerations you attack us. If you do so, how, in your view, can we oppose the Soviets?

Chiao: Your comments are too general. We are never against negotiations with the Soviet Union. We are negotiating with them now. We are not opposed to negotiations. The problem is the basic position from which one negotiates. You will recall that Chairman Mao discussed with you the problem of the Helsinki Conference. After Helsinki the Soviets went on a large scale offensive in Angola and we believe this was caused by the weak attitude you adopted at Helsinki toward the Soviets. In the Middle East, as you know, we have supported dual tactics. You adopted dual tactics and we supported them. We did not attack.

Kissinger: You couldn't attack us because you suggested it.

Chiao: We did not suggest it, but we put it forward for your consideration.

Kissinger: But you have opposed us in Africa.

Chiao: We have had doubts.

Kissinger: What doubts?

Chiao: We have doubts that you will reach your objective.

Kissinger: We have two objectives in Africa. One is the liberation of black Africa. The other is to prevent Soviet intervention of a direct or indirect kind. We must try to separate the issue of liberation from Soviet intervention.

Chiao: We have always separated these issues. In Angola we supported liberation and after the Angolans won a victory the Soviets moved in.

Kissinger: What we want—and it is a complicated process—is to create a basis for resisting Soviet intervention while not obstructing liberation movements.

Chiao: Just not opposing liberation movements is not enough.

Kissinger: We are supporting them.

Chiao: I have doubts that you are. You are not thoroughgoing, speaking quite frankly.

Kissinger: You said so publicly in your speech!

Chiao: Not quite.

Kissinger: What would be thoroughgoing? Or what should we do differently?

Chiao: You should support the demands of the blacks.

Kissinger: We are supporting them.

Chiao: The procedures you are adopting in Zimbabwe won't achieve their aim.

Kissinger: There are two ways events could develop in Zimbabwe. One is straight armed struggle which would bring in outside forces and add to the credit of those outside forces. If this were to occur, we could not resist those outside forces because we could not go to the support of white regimes against blacks. So we are trying the second way to bring together the black forces of Mugabe, Muzorewa, and Nkomo in one black government that we can support to resist the intervention of outside forces. I consider Smith's position only the opening move.

Chiao: You can try, but we have our doubts.

Kissinger: Maybe there are grounds for doubt. But we had to get control over events so we would have some basis to resist outside forces. We are not asking you to do anything but we are asking that you not oppose us.

Huang: You should analyze carefully the attitudes of the five front line African countries. If you do not (satisfy them), they will be forced to accept Soviet assistance.

Kissinger: That is just what we are trying to do. And we need help in doing so. I think we have the support of at least four of the five front line governments.

Huang: At most four.

Kissinger: We can't have more than four because Angola will never support us. It would be like trying to get the support of Outer Mongolia.

Chiao: I don't want to go into details, but your efforts are only half measures. You may keep on trying, but you may find that the result is the opposite of what you expect. You may end up angering the blacks.

Kissinger: What, in your opinion, would be thorough going measures?

Chiao: That would be going into detail. All I want to stress is the importance of attitude. Is the key, in your opinion, the interim government?

Kissinger: We can only have an interim government if the blacks will support it.

Chiao: The situation may not develop that way.

Kissinger: What is the alternative?

Chiao: As for the specific method, I cannot say that you should do this or that. But fundamentally, you must stand on the side of the blacks.

Kissinger: There are two approaches among the blacks. The bulk of the blacks are not happy about fighting and would like to find a way to avoid it. But there is a minority which is ready to fight with Soviet help.

Chiao: I do not think it is fair to look on proponents of guerrilla warfare as supporters of the Soviet Union.

Kissinger: I don't say that they are—at this time. But if developments proceed toward control by these elements, it will go that way.

Chiao: We will have to see.

Kissinger: I'm hopeful that Mugabe, Muzorewa, and Nkomo are going to join forces.

Chiao: We will have to see. We have reservations.

Kissinger: I see you have no better strategy.

Chiao: It is your problem.

Kissinger: It is more than our problem. I remember in November 1973 when Premier Chou spoke to me regarding the need for global equilibrium to prevent Soviet expansionism.

Chiao: That is your summation of his views, is it not?

Kissinger: To be sure, Premier Chou made many other points. But if expanionist countries gain advantages, eventually other countries will suffer.

Chiao: Yes. We recognized this in the Shanghai Communiqué where we said that we would not seek hegemony ourselves and would oppose the efforts of any others seeking hegemony. This was a common point between us.

Kissinger: But we are having difficulty putting it into practice. Let us leave Africa and discuss another issue which you have raised repeatedly; namely, the accusation that we are following a Munich-like policy of appeasement or that we are pushing to deflect the Soviets to the East, and so on. I have explained it to you before but let me summarize it again. I do it for you once a year and quite obviously it has never made a lasting impact.

I see Soviet expansionism as a geo-political problem not limited to one region. There is no solution where we can allow a push in one place and preserve our interests in another. I see the following as the Soviets' strategic problem: they face powerful countries in the West; potentially powerful countries in the East, in the case of China and Japan; and confusion and weakness to their south and in the Middle East. The Soviets have an inefficient bureaucratic system; they cannot create real power. They don't conduct a brilliant foreign policy. They are rather good at amassing physical power but they don't know what to do with it. The Red Army seems effective only when used against Soviet allies, not enemies. Soviet forces have not achieved a diplomatic success for the Soviet Union.

Chiao: Didn't the Soviets win a diplomatic victory at Helsinki?

Kissinger: I don't agree.

Chiao: Why did President Ford make those remarks (about Eastern Europe) at San Francisco?

Kissinger: You don't think this was the result of Helsinki! (Laughter) Actually, it reflected panic. In this case, the President transcended his advisors. (Laughter)

Let me get back to strategy and how the Soviets can be contained. As for their strength, the latest plane that we got in Japan shows that they are really quite backward.[3] The plane is about 10 percent better than our planes of 14 years ago. If this achievement is the result of a high priority project in the Soviet Union, I hate to think of the outcome of their low priority projects. (Laughter)

---

[3] On September 6, Victor Belenko, a Soviet Air Force officer, defected to the West by flying his MiG–25 jet fighter to Japan.

As I look at the Soviet Union, they have certain opportunities for the next ten–fifteen years. After that, their circumstances will prevent expansionism. In the Middle East, whatever they touch turns into disaster. All sides in Lebanon are fighting with Soviet weapons and the Soviets don't know which end to touch. The Soviets may try to break out of the situation at some point, though not under the present leadership which is too bureaucratic and too old. But they may try to break out under Brezhnev's successors. But the consequences will be the same for us wherever they try to break out.

I believe, personally—if the elections turn out the wrong way, you won't see me again and may not care about my personal views. In any event, I believe that if the Soviets attack, it would be best if they attacked in the West. Because if they do attack in the West, our political possibilities for resistance are very great. My strategic nightmare is that they will attack in the East—I recognize this would not be consistent with the line in your speeches and papers. If the Soviets attack in the East and have an initial success, it would have a massive impact on Japan and even in Europe and would contribute to the hegemonial effect we want so much to avoid. My own conviction is that if the Soviets were to attack in the East, the United States would still have to oppose them whether asked to or not. We would be doing it because of our own interests and not as a favor. But the psychological and political conditions for U.S. action would hardly be ideal. Nor is it our view that we can buy off the Soviet Union with little concessions in the West to deflect them toward the East. I agree with what you say about the importance of a strong West.

Even though you may not agree with my political analysis, I want the Soviets to negotiate first with us, not Europe, because we are stronger politically. If some of the people you admire come to power in the U.S. and are able to destroy our diplomatic flexibility, the Soviets will be able to move to negotiations with Europe and threaten Europe by a process of selective negotiations. They have recently approached the Germans and the French and they will surely approach the British. All are searching for concessions they can make to the Russians as a way of dealing with their internal pressures. Since the beginning of our détente policy in 1971, the defense effort in Europe is larger than before because we have been able to paralyze these compromising elements in Europe who oppose defense efforts.

Chiao: What is the logic of that? You took the lead in détente so you can hardly blame the Europeans for moving in the same direction.

Kissinger: No. We insist that we proceed toward détente together with no one going out in front. You can see the objective results of our policy on defense efforts as they are reflected in the United States, Germany, and to some extent throughout NATO. You just need to look at statistics to see what I mean.

Chiao: It is important not to confuse negotiations and strength.

Kissinger: I agree completely.

Chiao: For example, early this year you used strong language about Angola, but then you went ahead with negotiations on SALT. If you behave this way why do you think the Soviets will heed your warnings?

Kissinger: I was almost alone in the U.S. over Angola. Let me explain what I was trying to do. I forced the U.S. to do something about Angola. By December 1, we were on the verge of assembling a force which, when deployed, would have exhausted the Cubans. Several countries were involved. On December 8, President Ford called in Ambassador Dobrynin and told him to stop arms shipment to Angola. A few days later, the Soviets did stop shipments. We were prepared to have a resolution in the January 12th meeting of the OAU. Then on December 19, Congress voted to cut off all money for Angola, and there was no prospect of our using force. On December 24, the Soviets resumed armed shipments. When the time came for me to go to Moscow in January, the only thing left for me to use was a bluff and I tried it. It didn't work. Since then I have made violent attacks on the Soviets. In Angola we were defeated by our own people. I know this is no consolation to you. But I wanted to explain.

Chiao: When did you go to Moscow?

Kissinger: At the end of January.

Chiao: Our view is that the Soviets, through Helsinki, see your weakness.

Kissinger: Really, Mr. Foreign Minister, I don't want to be impolite, but I don't agree. We are not weak. Rather, we are temporarily weak until after our elections. We have gone though a period of temporary weakness when the forces which overthrew Nixon have been dominant in this country. But that will end on November 2.

Frankly, we considered the Helsinki Conference a second-rate enterprise. We gave instructions to our delegation to stay one-half step behind the Europeans and to take no initiative. Maybe I'm lacking in imagination, but I really can't see what you think the Soviets gained from Helsinki. All they got was just words.

Chiao: I know your views. You mentioned them in the car to me last year. I considered them seriously.

Kissinger: And rejected them!

Chiao: No, but we don't agree with you.

Kissinger: What is the Soviet victory at Helsinki?

Chiao: I don't want to be impolite. The Soviets, through Helsinki, have come to feel that the West is anxious to reach agreement. This is a long-range problem and nothing very terrible but it is a fact that the Soviets have reached such a conclusion.

Kissinger: I think you know the Soviets. Gromyko's strength is to pursue something relentlessly. I find that Gromyko persists even when it makes no sense whatsoever.

Chiao: We understand Gromyko's practice. We will persist in resisting this practice of Gromyko. This is our policy in our talks with them.

Kissinger: The Soviets started agitating for Helsinki in 1963–64. At that time they tried to exclude the U.S. and to push for abolishment of the Warsaw Pact and NATO. Finally, we decided to go along in 1971, and the talks dragged out four years. The Soviets got nothing out of the Conference; only empty principles. If they had made a demand on Berlin, I would advocate total resistance. In practice, however, they got nothing. Their foreign policy is ineffective. Helsinki didn't in any way affect the legal situation in Europe.

Chiao: I don't think it can be put this way. At least the Soviets gained your agreement that their boundaries can't be changed.

Kissinger: By force.

Chiao: Why not use the policy of non-recognition?

Kissinger: Because European borders were already set long before Helsinki. The Baltic borders were set in 1946–47 and then other borders were accepted by both Germanies in the 1960's. How could the U.S. oppose things accepted so long ago?

Huang: Why did President Ford have to go to Helsinki to give overall recognition to the Soviet empire in Eastern Europe?

Kissinger: He didn't give such recognition. Maybe we are stupid and not as intelligent as you. I remember once Premier Chou told me that I was intelligent. I said that he meant by Chinese standards I was not very intelligent. He didn't protest—he just laughed. (Laughter) I grant it may be just an example of our mediocre comprehension that led us to Helsinki. But it was not we who agreed to go. It was the British, French and Germans who agreed to go. If we had stayed away, it would not have helped. Of course, we would have stayed away if the conference had involved basic principles. But it didn't. Apparently this is also the Soviet interpretation because they have never mentioned any principles. As for the countries of Eastern Europe that the President so helpfully mentioned the other night, (laughter) they were the ones who were eager for the conference. Did you know we have a new campaign slogan on liberating Eastern Europe? We discovered the other night that we have already carried out the Republican platform of 1952 without anyone noticing it. (Laughter)

Chiao: Perhaps we should drop this.

Kissinger: In our view, the Helsinki agreements were rather irrelevant documents. The issues were drawn out for four years. At any rate, whether we were right or wrong, the matter is irretrievable.

Chiao: Regarding the policy . . .

Kissinger: There is a question of perception and a question of execution with regard to overall policy toward the Soviet Union. As for our perception, I have tried to explain our view—though without apparent success. In execution of our policy, we may make mistakes. Even with people on our staff like Mr. Lord who has a Chinese wife, we occasionally make mistakes.

But back to the matter you mentioned to the recent unofficial visitor—the question of pooling efforts.

Chiao: Chairman Mao mentioned that the U.S., China, Europe, Japan, Pakistan, and Iran should unite to oppose the Soviet Union.

Kissinger: I agree, but your criticism of our policy affects our ability to do this.

Chiao: We have mentioned our concerns because in our view we cannot adopt a weak attitude toward the Soviet Union.

Kissinger: We don't adopt a weak attitude toward the Soviet Union.

Chiao: You have your own attitude. We have ours. The real question is when, under what conditions, and with what objectives one negotiates with the Russians.

Kissinger: I agree there are differences in our approach. Your tactic is one of firmness with relatively little flexibility. Ours is one of protracted negotiations which don't achieve anything. We don't ask you to adopt ours; and I admire yours. However, we must adapt to our own requirements. The end result should be the same—no Soviet expansionism.

Chiao: Tactics must obey strategy. If they are divorced there can be no talk of tactics.

As for your "nightmare", that is one way of putting it, but I don't agree either with your nightmare or your way of thinking.

Kissinger: If we are really serious about the danger of Soviet expansionism, we must be prepared to look in all directions.

Chiao: On this we don't disagree.

Kissinger: Let's talk concretely. How should we do it?

Chiao: On the one hand, I agree there is Soviet expansionism all over, but the point of emphasis is in the West.

Kissinger: I won't dispute that.

Chiao: But the point of emphasis is important because it affects strategy. Before the end of the war in Vietnam, we told you that your forces were too scattered. The Soviets took advantage of the situation to expand elsewhere. As for China, we have not neglected Soviet expansionism towards China. We have preparations, and, as Chairman

Mao has said, we are all on the defensive against the Russians. We don't want to attack the Soviet Union. The point of emphasis is important, however, and I can't agree with your statement about your nightmare. Our defense posture is not less than others.

Kissinger: If the Soviets expand militarily in Europe, the political problems of a military response would be much easier for the U.S. The political problems would be much more difficult if the attack were to come in Asia. If it were to come in Asia, we should respond anyway. But creating the proper political conditions to do so is what makes it a nightmare. I am not referring to your military preparations, and I am not suggesting that you lack resolve or vigilance. Clearly you do not.

Chiao: I noted something in your General Assembly speech[4] about relations between our two countries that I don't agree with. Roughly speaking you said that you will take account of the interests and concerns of China in the conduct of your relations and that China must exhibit a similar attitude toward the United States. Your remarks seem to me to exceed what was said in the Shanghai Communiqué.

Kissinger: In what way?

Chiao: In the case of Taiwan?

Kissinger: No.

Chiao: On Taiwan, you owe us a debt.

Kissinger: These are separate issues. First, there is the Taiwan issue and second, there is the question of the conduct of our relations on a global basis. As for Taiwan, the problem has complexities . . . And in my speech I did not mention normalization in the same context as the need for mutuality in our approach to global issues. In the global context, you must understand our needs just as we try to understand yours. Of course, you can if you wish attack me for something I did not intend to say . . . On normalization, it seems to me that after our elections we should take an extremely serious look, keeping in mind the things that you have been saying recently—you can rest assured that we have gotten the message. As for the conduct of our relations on a global basis and our common resistance to hegemony, there has been no progress, only a barrage of attacks on us through unofficial delegations to Peking and sometimes even foreign delegations. We are trying to understand your position. You must try to understand ours. But this is quite separate from the problem of normalization.

Chiao: The first section of your speech dealt with normalization. The latter part with this global question.

---

[4] "Toward a New Understanding of Community," Department of State *Bulletin*, October 25, 1976, pp. 497–498.

Kissinger: The first part was on normalization, the second was on expanding global cooperation.

I might interject that I believe that Senator Scott did enormous damage with his letter from the President and the impression he conveyed that he had been sent by the President to negotiate with you and to make specific proposals. Scott did not reflect the views of the Administration. In fact, before he left, I told him not to discuss the matter of normalization because it was not a suitable issue to talk about before our elections.

Chiao: We were not clear about what you told Senator Scott. Our attitude was one of sincerity since he raised questions with us.

Kissinger: You had no choice, and we did not object to what you said.

Chiao: What we said to Scott was the same as what we have said to you. To normalize relations you must break diplomatic relations with Taiwan, withdraw all U.S. military forces from Taiwan, and abrogate your Defense Treaty. This has been our position all along. We have always said that how we liberate Taiwan is our internal affair. We have never agreed to peaceful means.

Kissinger: Correct. The President was wrong in his reference to the Shanghai Communiqué. He was referring to what we said, not what you said. This was an inadvertent, incorrect statement which will not be repeated by any U.S. official. I think we can guarantee that.

Huang: But what about the misunderstanding that has been caused?

Kissinger: We will arrange to have a question next week which will allow us to clarify our position. We can do it on Monday or Tuesday. Monday is a holiday so perhaps we should do it on Tuesday. We will have a question regarding the legal status of the Shanghai Communiqué in this regard. We will do this if you like. Or you yourselves could do it.

Chiao: It is better for you to do it since it was in your public debate.

Kissinger: I agree.

Chiao: I saw it myself and the President was obviously incorrect.

Kissinger: The President compressed a paragraph of the Shanghai Communiqué a little too much. (Laughter)

Chiao: It really affected our legal interest.

Kissinger: After our 1974 discussions in Peking, I saw no possibility of progress on the Taiwan issue before our elections. I haven't raised the issue since that time because I did not want to engage in fruitless discussion. I understand what you have said and what Chairman Mao has said. We could not do what would be necessary before our elections. After our elections, we must study very carefully what we can do. However, in addition to Taiwan, we have our global relations and that is what I was addressing in my speech. Incidentally, I was confident my words would get your attention. (Laughter)

Chiao: Right. What Chairman Mao said . . .

Kissinger: Your suffering days may soon be over. I believe we share your general strategic outlook. In the last two years, we have tended to drift apart because of the consequences in this country following Nixon's overthrow. After our elections, we will see if we cannot once again get together for some frank exchanges which will permit carrying out the kind of global cooperation we have in mind.

Chiao: Global cooperation is the big matter; Taiwan is the small matter. As for the former, we have never covered up our diferences of view.

Kissinger: I never said you did! (Laughter) Our government must make decisions, and if everybody is told by you that our policy amounts to a Munich or a Dunkirk—even foreigners are told this—then a malaise will develop in our relations with you. Of course, we can each go ahead with our separate policies, but there will be no collaboration.

Chiao: As for coordinated actions between our countries, I have explained before that our social organization and ideologies are different. We use our method to oppose Soviet expanionism and you use yours. Only in this way can our policies be as one.

Kissinger: Yes, but our policies must be in harmony.

Chiao: Yes. We will tell you when we see things we think are wrong. These will be our views and you will have to decide what to do.

Kissinger: I think to improve the situation we should tell you about events in advance, not after the event on U.S. television. Then you can choose either method.

Chiao: What do you mean?

Kissinger: We will keep you informed in good time before we initiate actions. You might sometimes do the same with us and perhaps take this into account in your actions. Recently we feel we have had pressure from you rather than discussions and this has led to the deterioration which I mentioned quite frankly at the beginning of our talk tonight.

Chiao: We have not—as I have said several times—said anything differently to our American guests from what we have said to you.

Kissinger: I have made my point. If we told everybody else what we have told you it would add a new dimension to our relations.

Chiao: Things aren't really that way. People come to Peking and ask our views. Then we tell them. If we didn't it wouldn't be good. It is quite different from what you have said. Furthermore, you know we haven't told them everything.

Kissinger: Not quite!

Chiao: We can't obscure the major strategic outlines of our relations.

Kissinger: If you study my remarks tonight, you will understand the pattern of our mutual relations as it appears to us. However, I want to assure you that even if the election goes against us, I attach the greatest importance to progress in U.S.–PRC relations and I would do my best to work for progress.

Chiao: To be quite frank, in global affairs you act as though everything is up to you and the Soviets to decide. In your General Assembly speech you referred first to the Soviets then Europe, Japan, and only then to the PRC. We were like this in importance (holding up his little finger).

Kissinger: I mentioned Western Europe, Japan, and then the Western hemisphere first.

Chiao: My impression is . . .

Kissinger: Of course, we do attach great importance to these areas.

Chiao: We recognize this and it's quite proper. You recall Chairman Mao told you about the importance of U.S. relations with Japan. Furthermore, we approve of your relations with Western Europe.

Kissinger: As for the Soviet section of my speech, most people thought it was very harsh. In the case of China, the speech unfortunately had to reflect the fact that there is not much going on. Our relations with the Soviet Union are in a different category from our relations with you. The Soviet Union is an adversary with whom we co-exist. China is an ideological opponent but a country that in strategic terms we cooperate with globally. In my conception, I attach an importance to China comparable to that of Western Europe as a factor on the world scene. But in the case of our bilateral relations there is nothing going on, and I think this is a mistake.

Chiao: Whose fault is it?

Kissinger: Frankly, it depends on your viewpoint. If you say there can be no progress in this area until normalization, then the fault lies with us. But if you say that we need to progress in this area to create the basis for normalization, then we both have responsibility.

Chiao: That is probably not a fair statement. On bilateral relations the responsibility is on your side. On other questions, such as our criticism of you, we have done it frankly giving our thoughts from a strategic point of view as to the best way to deal with our opponent. Don't take them (the opponent) lightly.

Kissinger: Precisely. Why was my statement unfair?

Chiao: From the beginning the Taiwan problem has been your affair. You said you had to maintain diplomatic relations, keep troops on Taiwan, and maintain the treaty.

Huang: How about the Olympics?

Chiao: It is true there has been some deterioration in our relationship, but the source of it is you. Why did you take your position on the Olympics?

Kissinger: If you must know the truth, because of the Republican Convention.

Huang: And perhaps the Taiwan lobby?

Chiao: And then we have Governor Scranton's remarks about welcoming Taiwan into the UN.

Kissinger: What's that?

Chiao: (Reading from a transcript of the October 3 NBC *Meet the Press*)

"Mr. Hunt: Just one more question, Bill. You mentioned the idea of universality, that every sovereign government should be a member of UN. On that basis, why should not Taiwan be readmitted?
Scranton: In my judgment, I would be glad to have them."

Kissinger: Ridiculous, outrageous! Perhps you can't believe me when I say I didn't know about this until you told me just now.

Chiao: This reflects a trend.

Kissinger: Yes, in public opinion.

Chiao: Not only in your society but in your government too.

Kissinger: Governor Scranton is a friend of mine. He is a fine man. I have no idea why he said what he did.

Chiao: I smile bitterly.

Kissinger: You have several choices. You can say that it was all a plot and smile bitterly. Or you can believe what I have said sincerely about our being in the last stages of the post-Watergate confusion. The day after the election you will see discipline and cohesion beginning in the United States. I recommend that you think in terms of the latter.

Chiao: I don't want to attach too much importance to these things.

Kissinger: You should attach no importance to them.

Chiao: Perhaps a little?

Kissinger: No, really none. Governor Scranton hadn't thought through what he was saying. I must say, however, that in the kind of cooling atmosphere that has been created there is less vigilance in this country about such remarks. But don't worry. I promised Premier Chou in 1971 that we wouldn't support two Chinas. We won't go back on this statement.

Chiao: The language in the Shanghai Communiqué on this point was your creation.

Kissinger: Scranton should have said that we don't recognize the Government on Taiwan as the Government of Taiwan.

Chiao: Yes. The cooling of relations is not our responsibility.

Kissinger: You have some responsibility for what has happened. Some Chinese actions have had a negative impact on developments.

Chiao: I don't agree. Our criticism of you proceeds from our common objective. If it were not for the common objective there would be no need to say anything. Do you remember in 1971 Premier Chou told you that China was ready to deal with the enemy from all sides.

Kissinger: Yes, it was in the Fukien Room.

Huang: Chairman Mao told some Germans that we wanted Europe to be strong and united. The Germans said then the Soviets would turn to the East. Mao said we were ready for them.

Chiao: Up to now, we have supported a strong Western Europe and strong U.S. West European relations.

Kissinger: Let us both reflect on this conversation and see if we can begin a dialogue on a governmental level to analyze the situation.

Chiao: (Turning to Huang and speaking in Chinese) Is there anything else we should raise?

Huang: At the beginning, Secretary Kissinger mentioned Soviet problems in developing their power. Do you foresee a period of protracted peace?

Kissinger: No. Up to 20 years I think it will be very dangerous. We are heading into a period of increasing danger. If we get through it, then there may be an era of peace.

Chiao: As for the Soviet threat, the Soviets are internally soft but one should not underestimate their expanionist ambitions. When we say there is a danger of war increasing, it is because we have given it very serious thought. The question is how to deal with the USSR. They bully the soft but fear the tough.

Kissinger: Mr. Foreign Minister, we have talked with each other for almost five years. You can't believe we are soft. We have to devise a strategy which suits our own and our allies' domestic requirements. It must be sustainable for the longest period of time. We would have won in Angola had it not been for Watergate in the United States. Please give us credit. We have no illusions.

Chiao: We have discussed this many times. Your tactical concepts negate your strategic objective.

Kissinger: I don't agree. We have held the Western Alliance in better shape than it was four years ago.

Chiao: We have criticized Munich thinking because it corrodes.

Kissinger: But we don't have Munich-like thinking. Frankly, we find it insulting. At Munich the allies sacrificed others. We have not.

Chiao: There is not much change in the trend of appeasement.

Kissinger: Repeating twice something we find insulting doesn't make it true. (Laughter) The increase of our Defense budget, our actions in Portugal, Angola, the Middle East, and Africa and the sale of arms hardly amount to a Munich.

Chiao: We have not opposed your Middle Eastern and Iranian policies, but you created some trouble for yourselves in Pakistan.

Kissinger: What trouble?

Chiao: I have been reading some things about trouble.

Kissinger: Bhutto wouldn't agree with you. Why don't you ask him?

Chiao: We approve of U.S.–Pakistan relations. It is good that they are improving.

Kissinger: If we keep on repeating these arguments, we will only create a controversial frame of mind.

Chiao: We should concentrate on the common objectives. Chairman Mao said you have interests which you want to preserve; the Soviets have expansionist desires. The Chairman said this to you. Some here tonight may not know that these were his words.

Kissinger: You used them in your speech. I agree with you about the danger of war. Our defense budget has increased 25 percent in two years.

Chiao: There are material means, but weapons are made for man and man must have high morale.

Kissinger: Yes. But each side must decide for itself what is best for its morale.

Chiao: I agree.

I have brought along this volume of Chairman Mao's poems. It includes the two final poems he wrote. It is in both Chinese and English.

Kissinger: Thank you so much. I recently read a beautiful poem by Chairman Mao. I believe it was the last one he wrote.

Chiao: This is the complete, published edition of Chairman Mao's poems.

Kissinger: I'm very touched and deeply moved by Chairman Mao's poems and I thank you very much for your volume.

Chiao: I promised it to you and I'm glad I remembered to bring it.

(Chiao then escorted the Secretary downstairs to the door of the PRC mission and the two bade a warm farewell.)

158. **Memorandum From the President's Assistant for National Security Affairs (Scowcroft) to Secretary of State Kissinger, Secretary of Defense Rumsfeld, and Director of Central Intelligence Bush**[1]

Washington, November 3, 1976.

SUBJECT

U.S. Force Reductions on Taiwan

The recommendation of the Department of Defense that the draw down to 1400 DOD civilian and military personnel on Taiwan directed in NSDM 339 be achieved by March 31, 1977 vice December 31, 1976, is approved.[2] The "authorized level" of DOD personnel on Taiwan should be reduced as directed to 1400 by December 31, 1976; however, the number of individuals actually on Taiwan should be approximately 1950. Status reports on the drawdown should be provided at regular intervals.

Brent Scowcroft

---

[1] Source: Ford Library, NSC Institutional Files (H-Files), Boxes H–67 and H–68, NSDM 339. Top Secret; Umbra; Sensitive. A copy was sent to the Chairman of the Joint Chiefs of Staff. In a November 5 memorandum to the same recipients, Jeanne Davis removed the codeword classification. (Ibid.) William Gleysteen, in an October 21 memorandum to Scowcroft, recommended the course of action set forth in this memorandum. (Ibid.)

[2] The recommendation was in an October 22 memorandum from Deputy Secretary of Defense Robert Ellsworth to Scowcroft. (Ibid.) NSDM 339 is printed as Document 156.

---

159. **Editorial Note**

On November 11, 1976, the Central Intelligence Agency issued National Intelligence Estimate 13–76 entitled "PRC Defense Policy and Armed Forces." This estimate concluded that the People's Republic of China perceived the United States as weakened and as less of a direct military threat than the Soviet Union. It also noted the PRC's fear of a U.S.–USSR compromise that would leave the PRC to confront the Soviets alone. (National Intelligence Council, *Tracking the Dragon* from accompanying compact disc with additional documents)

On December 21, Secretary of State Henry Kissinger met with Chief of the PRC Liaison Office Huang Zhen from 4:35 to 5:40 p.m.

Huang remarked that it had been several months since he had met with Kissinger. In the interim the United States had held a presidential election, while in the People's Republic of China, "Our Party's Central Committee headed by Chairman Hua Kuo-feng has followed Chairman Mao's behest and smashed at one blow the 'Gang of Four' and the anti-Party clique." Huang queried Kissinger about Cyrus Vance, whom President-elect Jimmy Carter had designated to be Secretary of State in his upcoming administration. Kissinger said, "It's my conviction that the line as we discussed it with Chairman Mao and other Chinese leaders, especially Chairman Mao, about having common interests, especially in relations with the Soviet Union, must be a basic principle of American foreign policy. I will always support this policy and do my best to see to it that it is maintained, and I believe that Secretary Vance will also see matters in a similar light." (Memorandum of conversation; Ford Library, National Security Adviser, Kissinger–Scowcroft West Wing Office Files, 1969–1977, Box 6, China, unnumbered items (38), 12/3–12/29/76)

A few weeks later, on January 8, 1977, Kissinger hosted Huang and Vance in the Secretary's Dining Room at the Department of State. Huang declared that his country continued to insist upon three actions that the United States must take before there could be an improvement in relations with the People's Republic of China: "sever the diplomatic relationship with Taiwan, withdraw U.S. troops from Taiwan, and abrogate the Treaty." Huang complained about Carter's recent interview in *Time* magazine, in which "he openly called Taiwan 'China' and even in the same breath put Taiwan on a par with the People's Republic of China. And we think this kind of remark runs counter to the principles of the Shanghai Communiqué." Vance responded, "As far as President Carter is concerned, let me assure you that he stands firmly behind the implementation of the Shanghai Communiqué as the guiding principle which should govern our bilateral relations." A few minutes later, Vance noted, "Let me say that I fully accept the principle of one China." (Memorandum of conversation; ibid., unnumbered items (39), 1/6–1/14/77)

Index

References are to document numbers

ISBN 978-0-16-077110-1

9 780160 771101

90000